D0164609

MICROECONOMIC THEORY

BASIC PRINCIPLES AND EXTENSIONS

TENTH EDITION

Walter Nicholson

Amherst College

Christopher Snyder

Dartmouth College

SOUTH-WESTERN
CENGAGE Learning

Australia · Brazil · Canada · Mexico · Singapore · Spain · United Kingdom · United States

Microeconomic Theory
Basic Principles and Extensions
Tenth Edition

Walter Nicholson Christopher Snyder

VP/Editorial Director:
Jack W. Calhoun

Editor-in-Chief:
Alex von Rosenberg

Executive Editor:
Mike Roche

Sr. Developmental Editor:
Susan Smart

Sr. Content Project Manager:
Cliff Kallemeyn

Production Technology Analyst:
Adam Grafa

Executive Marketing Manager:
Brian Joyner

Sr. Marketing Manager:
John Carey

Art Director:
Michelle Kunkler

Sr. First Print Buyer:
Sandee Milewski

Printer:
West Group
Eagan, MN

COPYRIGHT © 2008, 2005
South-Western, a part of
Cengage Learning.

Printed in Canada

   2 3 4 5 10 09 08

Book only:
ISBN-13: 978-0-324-58507-0
ISBN-10: 0-324-58507-1

Package:
ISBN-13: 978-0-324-42162-0
ISBN-10: 0-324-42162-1

ALL RIGHTS RESERVED.

No part of this work covered by the copyright hereon may be reproduced or used in any form or by any means—graphic, electronic, or mechanical, including photocopying, recording, taping, Web distribution or information storage and retrieval systems, or in any other manner—without the written permission of the publisher.

For permission to use material from this text or product, submit a request online at www.cengage.com/permissions.

Library of Congress Control Number: 2007921464

For more information about our products, contact us at:

Cengage Learning
Customer & Sales Support
1-800-354-9706

Cengage Learning
5191 Natorp Boulevard
Mason, OH 45040
USA

MICROECONOMIC THEORY

BASIC PRINCIPLES AND EXTENSIONS

TENTH EDITION

To Beth, Sarah, David, Sophia, and Abby

To Maura

About the Authors

Walter Nicholson is the Ward H. Patton Professor of Economics at Amherst College. He received his B.A. in mathematics from Williams College and his Ph.D. in economics from MIT. Professor Nicholson's principal research interests are in the econometric analyses of labor market problems including unemployment, job training, and the impact of international trade. He is also the co-author (with Chris Snyder) of *Intermediate Microeconomics and Its Application, Tenth Edition* (South-Western, a part of Cengage Learning, 2007).

Professor Nicholson and his wife, Susan, live in Amherst, Massachusetts, and Naples, Florida. What was previously a very busy household, with four children everywhere, is now rather empty. But an ever-increasing number of grandchildren breathe some life into these places whenever they visit, which seems far too seldom.

Christopher M. Snyder is a Professor of Economics at Dartmouth College. He received his B.A. in economics and mathematics from Fordham University and his Ph.D. in economics from MIT. Before coming to Dartmouth in 2005, he taught at George Washington University for over a decade, and he has been a visiting professor at the University of Chicago and MIT. He is currently President of the Industrial Organization Society and Associate Editor of the *International Journal of Industrial Organization and Review of Industrial Organization*. His research covers various theoretical and empirical topics in industrial organization, contract theory, and law and economics.

Professor Snyder and his wife Maura Doyle (who also teaches economics at Dartmouth) live within walking distance of campus in Hanover, New Hampshire, with their three elementary-school-aged daughters.

Brief Contents

Contents

PART 3   PRODUCTION AND SUPPLY   293

CHAPTER 9
Production Functions   295

CHAPTER 10
Cost Functions   323

PART 7   MARKET FAILURE   625

Preface

The 10th edition of *Microeconomic Theory: Basic Principles and Extensions* represents both a continuation of a highly successful treatment of microeconomics at a relatively advanced level and a major change from the past. This change, of course, is that Chris Snyder has joined me as a co-author. His insights have improved all sections of the book, especially with respect to its coverage of game theory, industrial organization, and models of imperfect information. Hence in many ways this is a new book, although on matters of style and pedagogy it retains much of what has made it successful for more than 35 years. This basic approach is to focus on building intuition about economic models while providing students with the mathematical tools needed to go further in their studies. The text also seeks to facilitate that linkage by providing many numerical examples, advanced problems, and extended discussions of empirical implementation—all of which are intended to show students how microeconomic theory is used today. New developments have made the field more exciting than ever, and I hope this edition manages to capture that excitement.

NEW TO THE TENTH EDITION

The primary change to this edition has been the inclusion of three entirely new chapters written by Chris Snyder:

- an extended and more advanced treatment of basic game theory concepts (Chapter 8);
- a thoroughly reworked and expanded chapter on models used in industrial organization theory (Chapter 15); and
- a completely new chapter on asymmetric information that focuses on the principal–agent problem and modern contract theory (Chapter 18).

The importance of these additions to the overall quality of the text cannot be overstated. Because the topics covered in these new chapters constitute some of the most important growth areas in microeconomics, the book is now well positioned for many years into the future.

Several other chapters of the book have undergone major revisions for this edition.

- A significant amount of material has been added to the chapter on mathematical background (Chapter 2); new topics include:

  - an expanded coverage of integration,
  - basic models of dynamic optimization, and
  - a brief introduction to mathematical statistics.

- The material on uncertainty and risk aversion has been thoroughly revised and updated (Chapter 7).

- Much of the theory of the firm, especially of the firm's demands for inputs, has been expanded (Chapters 9–11).

- The chapter on general equilibrium modeling (Chapter 13) has been thoroughly reworked with the goal of providing students with more details about how computable general equilibrium models actually work.
- The chapter on capital and time (Chapter 17) has been significantly expanded to include more on optimal savings behavior and on resource allocation over time.

Numerous minor changes have also been made in the coverage and organization of the book to ensure that it continues to provide clear and up-to-date coverage of all of the topics examined.

Two modifications have been made to the text to enhance its linkage to more general economic literature. First, the problems have been categorized into two types: basic problems and analytical problems. Whereas the basic problems are intended to reinforce concepts from the text, the analytical problems are intended to allow the student to go further by showing them how to obtain results on their own. The number of such problems has been significantly expanded in this edition. Many of the analytical problems provide references so that students who wish to pursue the topic can read more.

A second modification of the text has been to expand and rewrite many of the end-of-chapter Extensions. The common goal of these revised Extensions is to provide students better linkage between the theoretical material in the text and that material's use in actual empirical applications. Therefore, many of the Extensions introduce the functional forms customarily used as well as some of the econometric issues faced by researchers when using available data. The Extensions are thus intended to show students the importance of joining microeconomic theory and econometric practice.

SUPPLEMENTS TO THE TEXT

The thoroughly revised ancillaries for this edition include the following.

- The *Solutions Manual and Test Bank* (by the text authors). The *Solutions Manual* contains comments and solutions to all problems and is available to all adopting instructors in both print and electronic versions. The *Solutions Manual and Test Bank* may be downloaded only by qualified instructors at the textbook support Web site (academic.cengage.com/economics/nicholson).
- PowerPoint Lecture Presentation Slides (by Linda Ghent, Eastern Illinois University). PowerPoint slides for each chapter of the text provide a thorough set of outlines for classroom use or for students as a study aid. Instructors and students may download these slides from the book's Web site (academic.cengage.com/economics/nicholson).

ONLINE RESOURCES

South-Western, a part of Cengage Learning provides students and instructors with a set of valuable online resources that are an effective complement to this text. Each new copy of the book comes with a registration card that provides access to Economic Applications and InfoTrac College Edition.

Economic Applications

The purchase of this new textbook includes complimentary access to South-Western's Economic Applications (EconApps) Web site. The EconApps Web site includes a suite of regularly updated Web features for economics students and instructors: EconDebate Online, EconNews Online, EconData Online, and EconLinks Online. These resources can help students deepen their understanding of economic concepts by analyzing current news stories, policy debates, and economic data. EconApps can also help instructors develop assignments, case studies, and examples based on real-world issues.

EconDebates Online provides current coverage of economics policy debates; it includes a primer on the issues, links to background information, and commentaries.

EconNews Online summarizes recent economics news stories and offers questions for further discussion.

EconData Online presents current and historical economic data with accompanying commentary, analysis, and exercises.

EconLinks Online offers a navigation partner for exploring economics on the Web via a list of key topic links.

Students buying a used book can purchase access to the EconApps site at academic.cengage .com/economics.

InfoTrac College Edition

The purchase of this new textbook also comes with four months of access to InfoTrac. This powerful and searchable online database provides access to full text articles from more than a thousand different publications ranging from the popular press to scholarly journals. Instructors can search topics and select readings for students, and students can search articles and readings for homework assignments and projects. The publications cover a variety of topics and include articles that range from current events to theoretical developments. InfoTrac College Edition offers instructors and students the ability to integrate scholarship and applications of economics into the learning process.

ACKNOWLEDGMENTS

In preparation for undertaking this revision, we received very helpful reviews from:

Tibor Besedes, Louisiana State University
Elaine P. Catilina, American University
Yi Deng, Southern Methodist University
Silke Forbes, University of California–San Diego
Joseph P. Hughes, Rutgers University
Qihong Liu, University of Oklahoma
Ragan Petrie, Georgia State University

We have usually tried to follow their good advice, but of course none of these individuals bears any responsibility for the final outcome.

This edition of the book is the first that was written with my co-author, Chris Snyder of Dartmouth College. I have been very pleased with the working relationship we have developed and with Chris's friendship. I hope many more editions will follow. I am also indebted to the team at South-Western and especially to Susan Smart for once again bringing her organizing and cajoling skills to this edition. During her temporary absence from the project, we were completely lost.

Copyediting this manuscript was, I know, a real chore. Those at Newgen-Austin did a great job of penetrating our messy manuscripts to obtain something that actually makes sense. The design of the text by Michelle Kunkler succeeded in achieving two seemingly irreconcilable goals—making the text both compact and easy to read. Cliff Kallemeyn did a fine job of keeping the production on track; I especially appreciated the way he coordinated the copyediting and page production processes.

As always, my Amherst College colleagues and students deserve some of the credit for this new edition. Frank Westhoff has been my most faithful user of this text over many years. This time (with his permission, I think) I actually lifted some of his work on general equilibrium to significantly improve that portion of the text.

To the list of former students—Mark Bruni, Eric Budish, Adrian Dillon, David Macoy, Tatyana Mamut, Katie Merrill, Jordan Milev, Doug Norton, and Jeff Rodman—whose efforts are still evident I can now add the name of Anoop Menon, who helped me solve problems when I ran out of patience with the algebra.

As always, special thanks again go to my wife Susan; after seeing twenty editions of my microeconomics texts come and go, she must surely hope that even this good thing must eventually come to an end. My children (Kate, David, Tory, and Paul) all seem to be living happy and productive lives despite a severe lack of microeconomic education. As the next generation (Beth, Sarah, David, Sophia, and Abby) grows older, perhaps they will seek enlightenment—at least to the extent of wondering what the books dedicated to them are all about.

Walter Nicholson
Amherst, Massachusetts
June 2007

It was a privilege to collaborate with Walter on this tenth edition. I used this textbook in the first course I ever taught, as a graduate instructor at MIT, and I have enjoyed using it in my microeconomics courses in the thirteen years since. I have always appreciated the text's ambitious coverage of the concepts and methods used by professional economists as well as its accessibility to students, which is enhanced by numerous elegant examples together with Walter's lucid prose. It was a challenge to maintain this high standard with my contribution—although this was made easier by Walter's suggestions, patience, and example, for which I am grateful.

I encourage teachers and students to e-mail me with any comments on the text (Christopher.M.Snyder@dartmouth.edu).

I would like to add my wholehearted thanks to those whom Walter acknowledged for contributing to the book. I also thank Gretchen Otto and her colleagues at Newgen–Austin as well as Matt Darnell for carefully copyediting my portion of the revision. I thank Dartmouth College for providing the resources and environment that greatly facilitated writing the book. I thank my colleagues in the economics department for helpful discussions and understanding.

Committing to such an extensive project is in some sense a family decision. I am indebted to my wife, Maura, for accommodating the many late nights that were required and for listening to my monotonous progress reports. I thank my daughters, Clare, Tess, and Meg, for their good behavior, which expedited the writing process.

Christopher Snyder
Hanover, New Hampshire
June 2007

Introduction

This part contains only two chapters. **Chapter 1** examines the general philosophy of how economists build models of economic behavior. **Chapter 2** then reviews some of the mathematical tools used in the construction of these models. The mathematical tools from Chapter 2 will be used throughout the remainder of this book.

Economic Models

The main goal of this book is to introduce you to the most important models that economists use to explain the behavior of consumers, firms, and markets. These models are central to the study of all areas of economics. Therefore, it is essential to understand both the need for such models and the basic framework used to develop them. The goal of this chapter is to begin this process by outlining some of the conceptual issues that determine the ways in which economists study practically every question that interests them.

THEORETICAL MODELS

A modern economy is a complicated entity. Thousands of firms engage in producing millions of different goods. Many millions of people work in all sorts of occupations and make decisions about which of these goods to buy. Let's use peanuts as an example. Peanuts must be harvested at the right time and shipped to processors who turn them into peanut butter, peanut oil, peanut brittle, and numerous other peanut delicacies. These processors, in turn, must make certain that their products arrive at thousands of retail outlets in the proper quantities to meet demand.

Because it would be impossible to describe the features of even these peanut markets in complete detail, economists have chosen to abstract from the complexities of the real world and develop rather simple models that capture the "essentials." Just as a road map is helpful even though it does not record every house or every store, economic models of, say, the market for peanuts are also useful even though they do not record every minute feature of the peanut economy. In this book we will study the most widely used economic models. We will see that, even though these models often make heroic abstractions from the complexities of the real world, they nonetheless capture essential features that are common to all economic activities.

The use of models is widespread in the physical and social sciences. In physics, the notion of a "perfect" vacuum or an "ideal" gas is an abstraction that permits scientists to study real-world phenomena in simplified settings. In chemistry, the idea of an atom or a molecule is actually a simplified model of the structure of matter. Architects use mock-up models to plan buildings. Television repairers refer to wiring diagrams to locate problems. Economists' models perform similar functions. They provide simplified portraits of the way individuals make decisions, the way firms behave, and the way in which these two groups interact to establish markets.

VERIFICATION OF ECONOMIC MODELS

Of course, not all models prove to be "good." For example, the earth-centered model of planetary motion devised by Ptolemy was eventually discarded because it proved incapable of accurately explaining how the planets move around the sun. An important purpose of scientific investigation is to sort out the "bad" models from the "good." Two general methods have been used for verifying economic models: (1) a direct approach, which seeks to establish the validity of the basic assumptions on which a model is based; and (2) an indirect approach, which attempts to confirm validity by showing that a simplified model correctly predicts real-world events. To illustrate the basic differences between the two approaches, let's briefly examine a model that we will use extensively in later chapters of this book—the model of a firm that seeks to maximize profits.

The profit-maximization model

The model of a firm seeking to maximize profits is obviously a simplification of reality. It ignores the personal motivations of the firm's managers and does not consider conflicts among them. It assumes that profits are the only relevant goal of the firm; other possible goals, such as obtaining power or prestige, are treated as unimportant. The model also assumes that the firm has sufficient information about its costs and the nature of the market to which it sells to discover its profit-maximizing options. Most real-world firms, of course, do not have this information readily available. Yet, such shortcomings in the model are not necessarily serious. No model can exactly describe reality. The real question is whether this simple model has any claim to being a good one.

Testing assumptions

One test of the model of a profit-maximizing firm investigates its basic assumption: Do firms really seek maximum profits? Some economists have examined this question by sending questionnaires to executives, asking them to specify the goals they pursue. The results of such studies have been varied. Businesspeople often mention goals other than profits or claim they only do "the best they can" to increase profits given their limited information. On the other hand, most respondents also mention a strong "interest" in profits and express the view that profit maximization is an appropriate goal. Testing the profit-maximizing model by testing its assumptions has therefore provided inconclusive results.

Testing predictions

Some economists, most notably Milton Friedman, deny that a model can be tested by inquiring into the "reality" of its assumptions.[1] They argue that all theoretical models are based on "unrealistic" assumptions; the very nature of theorizing demands that we make certain abstractions. These economists conclude that the only way to determine the validity of a model is to see whether it is capable of predicting and explaining real-world events. The ultimate test of an economic model comes when it is confronted with data from the economy itself.

Friedman provides an important illustration of that principle. He asks what kind of a theory one should use to explain the shots expert pool players will make. He argues that the laws of velocity, momentum, and angles from theoretical physics would be a suitable model. Pool players shoot shots *as if* they follow these laws. But most players asked whether they precisely understand the physical principles behind the game of pool will undoubtedly answer that they do not. Nonetheless, Friedman argues, the physical laws provide very accurate predictions and therefore should be accepted as appropriate theoretical models of how experts play pool.

A test of the profit-maximization model, then, would be provided by predicting the behavior of real-world firms by assuming that these firms behave *as if* they were maximizing profits. (See Example 1.1 later in this chapter.) If these predictions are reasonably in accord with reality, we may accept the profit-maximization hypothesis. However, we would reject

---

[1]See M. Friedman, *Essays in Positive Economics* (Chicago: University of Chicago Press, 1953), chap. 1. For an alternative view stressing the importance of using "realistic" assumptions, see H. A. Simon, "Rational Decision Making in Business Organizations," *American Economic Review* 69, no. 4 (September 1979): 493–513.

the model if real-world data seem inconsistent with it. Hence, the ultimate test of either theory is its ability to predict *real-world events*.

Importance of empirical analysis

The primary concern of this book is the construction of theoretical models. But the goal of such models is always to learn something about the real world. Although the inclusion of a lengthy set of applied examples would needlessly expand an already bulky book,[2] the Extensions included at the end of many chapters are intended to provide a transition between the theory presented here and the ways in which that theory is actually applied in empirical studies.

GENERAL FEATURES OF ECONOMIC MODELS

The number of economic models in current use is, of course, very large. Specific assumptions used and the degree of detail provided vary greatly depending on the problem being addressed. The models employed to explain the overall level of economic activity in the United States, for example, must be considerably more aggregated and complex than those that seek to interpret the pricing of Arizona strawberries. Despite this variety, however, practically all economic models incorporate three common elements: (1) the *ceteris paribus* (other things the same) assumption; (2) the supposition that economic decision makers seek to optimize something; and (3) a careful distinction between "positive" and "normative" questions. Because we will encounter these elements throughout this book, it may be helpful at the outset to briefly describe the philosophy behind each of them.

The ceteris paribus assumption

As in most sciences, models used in economics attempt to portray relatively simple relationships. A model of the market for wheat, for example, might seek to explain wheat prices with a small number of quantifiable variables, such as wages of farmworkers, rainfall, and consumer incomes. This parsimony in model specification permits the study of wheat pricing in a simplified setting in which it is possible to understand how the specific forces operate. Although any researcher will recognize that many "outside" forces (presence of wheat diseases, changes in the prices of fertilizers or of tractors, or shifts in consumer attitudes about eating bread) affect the price of wheat, these other forces are held constant in the construction of the model. It is important to recognize that economists are *not* assuming that other factors do not affect wheat prices; rather, such other variables are assumed to be unchanged during the period of study. In this way, the effect of only a few forces can be studied in a simplified setting. Such ceteris paribus (other things equal) assumptions are used in all economic modeling.

Use of the ceteris paribus assumption does pose some difficulties for the verification of economic models from real-world data. In other sciences, such problems may not be so severe because of the ability to conduct controlled experiments. For example, a physicist who wishes to test a model of the force of gravity probably would not do so by dropping objects from the Empire State Building. Experiments conducted in that way would be subject to too many extraneous forces (wind currents, particles in the air, variations in temperature, and so forth) to permit a precise test of the theory. Rather, the physicist would conduct experiments in a laboratory, using a partial vacuum in which most other forces could be controlled or eliminated. In this way, the theory could be verified in a simple setting, without considering all the other forces that affect falling bodies in the real world.

---

[2]For an intermediate-level text containing an extensive set of real-world applications, see W. Nicholson and C. Snyder, *Intermediate Microeconomics and Its Application*, 10th ed. (Mason, OH: Thomson/Southwestern, 2007).

With a few notable exceptions, economists have not been able to conduct controlled experiments to test their models. Instead, economists have been forced to rely on various statistical methods to control for other forces when testing their theories. Although these statistical methods are as valid in principle as the controlled experiment methods used by other scientists, in practice they raise a number of thorny issues. For that reason, the limitations and precise meaning of the ceteris paribus assumption in economics are subject to greater controversy than in the laboratory sciences.

Optimization assumptions

Many economic models start from the assumption that the economic actors being studied are rationally pursuing some goal. We briefly discussed such an assumption when investigating the notion of firms maximizing profits. Example 1.1 shows how that model can be used to make testable predictions. Other examples we will encounter in this book include consumers maximizing their own well-being (utility), firms minimizing costs, and government regulators attempting to maximize public welfare. Although, as we will show, all of these assumptions are unrealistic, all have won widespread acceptance as good starting places for developing economic models. There seem to be two reasons for this acceptance. First, the optimization assumptions are very useful for generating precise, solvable models, primarily because such models can draw on a variety of mathematical techniques suitable for optimization problems. Many of these techniques, together with the logic behind them, are reviewed in Chapter 2. A second reason for the popularity of optimization models concerns their apparent empirical validity. As some of our Extensions show, such models seem to be fairly good at explaining reality. In all, then, optimization models have come to occupy a prominent position in modern economic theory.

EXAMPLE 1.1 Profit Maximization

The profit-maximization hypothesis provides a good illustration of how optimization assumptions can be used to generate empirically testable propositions about economic behavior. Suppose that a firm can sell all the output that it wishes at a price of p per unit and that the total costs of production, C, depend on the amount produced, q. Then, profits are given by

$$\textbf{profits} = \pi = pq - C(q). \tag{1.1}$$

Maximization of profits consists of finding that value of q which maximizes the profit expression in Equation 1.1. This is a simple problem in calculus. Differentiation of Equation 1.1 and setting that derivative equal to 0 give the following first-order condition for a maximum:

$$\frac{d\pi}{dq} = p - C'(q) = 0 \quad or \quad p = C'(q). \tag{1.2}$$

In words, the profit-maximizing output level (q^*) is found by selecting that output level for which price is equal to marginal cost, $C'(q)$. This result should be familiar to you from your introductory economics course. Notice that in this derivation the price for the firm's output is treated as a constant because the firm is a price taker.

Equation 1.2 is only the first-order condition for a maximum. Taking account of the second-order condition can help us to derive a testable implication of this model. The second-order condition for a maximum is that at q^* it must be the case that

$$\frac{d^2\pi}{dq^2} = -C''(q) < 0 \quad or \quad C''(q^*) > 0. \tag{1.3}$$

That is, marginal cost must be increasing at q^* for this to be a true point of maximum profits.

Our model can now be used to "predict" how a firm will react to a change in price. To do so, we differentiate Equation 1.2 with respect to price (p), assuming that the firm continues to choose a profit-maximizing level of q:

$$\frac{d[p - C'(q^*) = 0]}{dp} = 1 - C''(q^*) \cdot \frac{dq^*}{dp} = 0. \qquad (1.4)$$

Rearranging terms a bit gives

$$\frac{dq^*}{dp} = \frac{1}{C''(q^*)} > 0. \qquad (1.5)$$

Here the final inequality again reflects the fact that marginal cost must be increasing if q^* is to be a true maximum. This then is one of the testable propositions of the profit-maximization hypothesis—if other things do not change, a price-taking firm should respond to an increase in price by increasing output. On the other hand, if firms respond to increases in price by reducing output, there must be something wrong with our model.

Although this is a very simple model, it reflects the way we will proceed throughout much of this book. Specifically, the fact that the primary implication of the model is derived by calculus, and consists of showing what sign a derivative should have, is the kind of result we will see many times.

QUERY: In general terms, how would the implications of this model be changed if the price a firm obtains for its output were a function of how much it sold? That is, how would the model work if the price-taking assumption were abandoned?

Positive-normative distinction

A final feature of most economic models is the attempt to differentiate carefully between "positive" and "normative" questions. So far we have been concerned primarily with *positive* economic theories. Such theories take the real world as an object to be studied, attempting to explain those economic phenomena that are observed. Positive economics seeks to determine how resources are *in fact* allocated in an economy. A somewhat different use of economic theory is *normative* analysis, taking a definite stance about what *should* be done. Under the heading of normative analysis, economists have a great deal to say about how resources *should* be allocated. For example, an economist engaged in positive analysis might investigate how prices are determined in the U.S. health-care economy. The economist also might want to measure the costs and benefits of devoting even more resources to health care. But when he or she specifically advocates that more resources *should* be allocated to health care, the analysis becomes normative.

Some economists believe that the only proper economic analysis is positive analysis. Drawing an analogy with the physical sciences, they argue that "scientific" economics should concern itself only with the description (and possibly prediction) of real-world economic events. To take moral positions and to plead for special interests are considered to be outside the competence of an economist acting as such. Other economists, however, believe strict application of the positive-normative distinction to economic matters is inappropriate. They believe that the study of economics necessarily involves the researchers' own views about ethics, morality, and fairness. According to these economists, searching for scientific "objectivity" in such circumstances is hopeless. Despite some ambiguity, this book adopts a mainly positivist tone, leaving normative concerns for you to decide for yourself.

DEVELOPMENT OF THE ECONOMIC THEORY OF VALUE

Because economic activity has been a central feature of all societies, it is surprising that these activities were not studied in any detail until recently. For the most part, economic phenomena were treated as a basic aspect of human behavior that was not sufficiently interesting to deserve specific attention. It is, of course, true that individuals have always studied economic activities with a view toward making some kind of personal gain. Roman traders were not above making profits on their transactions. But investigations into the basic nature of these activities did not begin in any depth until the eighteenth century.[3] Because this book is about economic theory as it stands today, rather than the history of economic thought, our discussion of the evolution of economic theory will be brief. Only one area of economic study will be examined in its historical setting: the *theory of value*.

Early economic thoughts on value

The theory of value, not surprisingly, concerns the determinants of the "value" of a commodity. This subject is at the center of modern microeconomic theory and is closely intertwined with the fundamental economic problem of allocating scarce resources to alternative uses. The logical place to start is with a definition of the word "value." Unfortunately, the meaning of this term has not been consistent throughout the development of the subject. Today we regard value as being synonymous with the price of a commodity.[4] Earlier philosopher-economists, however, made a distinction between the market price of a commodity and its value. The term "value" was then thought of as being, in some sense, synonymous with "importance," "essentiality," or (at times) "godliness." Because "price" and "value" were separate concepts, they could differ, and most early economic discussions centered on these divergences. For example, St. Thomas Aquinas believed value to be divinely determined. Since prices were set by humans, it was possible for the price of a commodity to differ from its value. A person accused of charging a price in excess of a good's value was guilty of charging an "unjust" price. For example, St. Thomas believed the "just" rate of interest to be zero. Any lender who demanded a payment for the use of money was charging an unjust price and could be—and sometimes was—prosecuted by church officials.

The founding of modern economics

During the latter part of the eighteenth century, philosophers began to take a more scientific approach to economic questions. The 1776 publication of *The Wealth of Nations* by Adam Smith (1723–1790) is generally considered the beginning of modern economics. In his vast, all-encompassing work, Smith laid the foundation for thinking about market forces in an ordered and systematic way. Still, Smith and his immediate successors, such as David Ricardo (1772–1823), continued to distinguish between value and price. To Smith, for example, the value of a commodity meant its "value in use," whereas the price represented its "value in exchange." The distinction between these two concepts was illustrated by the famous water-diamond paradox. Water, which obviously has great value in use, has little value in exchange (it has a low price); diamonds are of little practical use but have a great value in exchange. The paradox with which early economists struggled derives from the observation that some very useful items have low prices whereas certain nonessential items have high prices.

---

[3]For a detailed treatment of early economic thought, see the classic work by J. A. Schumpeter, *History of Economic Analysis* (New York: Oxford University Press, 1954), pt. II, chaps. 1–3.

[4]This is not completely true when "externalities" are involved and a distinction must be made between private and social value (see Chapter 19).

Labor theory of exchange value

Neither Smith nor Ricardo ever satisfactorily resolved the water-diamond paradox. The concept of value in use was left for philosophers to debate, while economists turned their attention to explaining the determinants of value in exchange (that is, to explaining relative prices). One obvious possible explanation is that exchange values of goods are determined by what it costs to produce them. Costs of production are primarily influenced by labor costs—at least this was so in the time of Smith and Ricardo—and therefore it was a short step to embrace a labor theory of value. For example, to paraphrase an example from Smith, if catching a deer takes twice the number of labor hours as catching a beaver, then one deer should exchange for two beavers. In other words, the price of a deer should be twice that of a beaver. Similarly, diamonds are relatively costly because their production requires substantial labor input.

To students with even a passing knowledge of what we now call the *law of supply and demand,* Smith's and Ricardo's explanation must seem incomplete. Didn't they recognize the effects of demand on price? The answer to this question is both yes and no. They did observe periods of rapidly rising and falling relative prices and attributed such changes to demand shifts. However, they regarded these changes as abnormalities that produced only a temporary divergence of market price from labor value. Because they had not really developed a theory of value in use, they were unwilling to assign demand any more than a transient role in determining relative prices. Rather, long-run exchange values were assumed to be determined solely by labor costs of production.

The marginalist revolution

Between 1850 and 1880, economists became increasingly aware that to construct an adequate alternative to the labor theory of value, they had to come to devise a theory of value in use. During the 1870s, several economists discovered that it is not the total usefulness of a commodity that helps to determine its exchange value, but rather the usefulness of the *last unit consumed.* For example, water is certainly very useful—it is necessary for all life. But, because water is relatively plentiful, consuming one more pint (ceteris paribus) has a relatively low value to people. These "marginalists" redefined the concept of value in use from an idea of overall usefulness to one of marginal, or incremental, usefulness—the usefulness of an *additional unit of a commodity.* The concept of the demand for an incremental unit of output was now contrasted to Smith's and Ricardo's analysis of production costs to derive a comprehensive picture of price determination.[5]

Marshallian supply-demand synthesis

The clearest statement of these marginal principles was presented by the English economist Alfred Marshall (1842–1924) in his *Principles of Economics,* published in 1890. Marshall showed that demand and supply *simultaneously* operate to determine price. As Marshall noted, just as you cannot tell which blade of a scissors does the cutting, so too you cannot say that either demand or supply alone determines price. That analysis is illustrated by the famous Marshallian cross shown in Figure 1.1. In the diagram the quantity of a good purchased per period is shown on the horizontal axis and its price appears on the vertical axis. The curve *DD* represents the quantity of the good demanded per period at each possible price. The curve is negatively sloped to reflect the marginalist principle that as quantity increases, people are

---

[5]Ricardo had earlier provided an important first step in marginal analysis in his discussion of rent. Ricardo theorized that as the production of corn increased, land of inferior quality would be used and this would cause the price of corn to rise. In his argument Ricardo implicitly recognized that it is the marginal cost—the cost of producing an additional unit—that is relevant to pricing. Notice that Ricardo implicitly held other inputs constant when discussing diminishing land productivity; that is, he employed one version of the ceteris paribus assumption.

FIGURE 1.1   The Marshallian Supply-Demand Cross

Marshall theorized that demand and supply interact to determine the equilibrium price (p^*) and the quantity (q^*) that will be traded in the market. He concluded that it is not possible to say that either demand or supply alone determines price or therefore that either costs or usefulness to buyers alone determines exchange value.

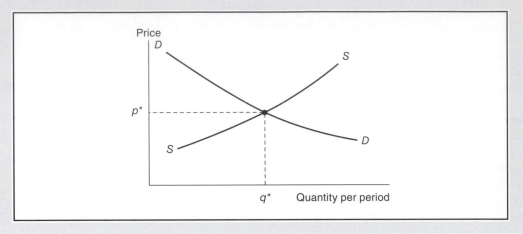

willing to pay less for the last unit purchased. It is the value of this last unit that sets the price for all units purchased. The curve SS shows how (marginal) production costs rise as more output is produced. This reflects the increasing cost of producing one more unit as total output expands. In other words, the upward slope of the SS curve reflects increasing marginal costs, just as the downward slope of the DD curve reflects decreasing marginal value. The two curves intersect at p^*, q^*. This is an *equilibrium* point—both buyers and sellers are content with the quantity being traded and the price at which it is traded. If one of the curves should shift, the equilibrium point would shift to a new location. Thus price and quantity are simultaneously determined by the joint operation of supply and demand.

Paradox resolved

Marshall's model resolves the water-diamond paradox. Prices reflect both the marginal evaluation that demanders place on goods and the marginal costs of producing the goods. Viewed in this way, there is no paradox. Water is low in price because it has both a low marginal value and a low marginal cost of production. On the other hand, diamonds are high in price because they have both a high marginal value (because people are willing to pay quite a bit for one more) and a high marginal cost of production. This basic model of supply and demand lies behind much of the analysis presented in this book.

General equilibrium models

Although the Marshallian model is an extremely useful and versatile tool, it is a *partial equilibrium model,* looking at only one market at a time. For some questions, this narrowing of perspective gives valuable insights and analytical simplicity. For other, broader questions, such a narrow viewpoint may prevent the discovery of important relationships among markets. To answer more general questions we must have a model of the whole economy that suitably mirrors the connections among various markets and economic agents. The French economist Leon Walras (1831–1910), building on a long Continental tradition in such analysis, created the basis for modern investigations into those broad questions. His method of representing the economy by a large number of simultaneous equations forms the basis for understanding the interrelationships implicit in *general equilibrium* analysis. Walras recognized that one cannot talk about a single market in isolation; what is needed is a model that permits the effects of a change in one market to be followed through other markets.

EXAMPLE 1.2 Supply-Demand Equilibrium

Although graphical presentations are adequate for some purposes, economists often use algebraic representations of their models to both clarify their arguments and make them more precise. As an elementary example, suppose we wished to study the market for peanuts and, on the basis of statistical analysis of historical data, concluded that the quantity of peanuts demanded each week (q, measured in bushels) depended on the price of peanuts (p, measured in dollars per bushel) according to the equation

$$\text{quantity demanded} = q_D = 1{,}000 - 100p. \tag{1.6}$$

Because this equation for q_D contains only the single independent variable p, we are implicitly holding constant all other factors that might affect the demand for peanuts. Equation 1.6 indicates that, if other things do not change, at a price of \$5 per bushel people will demand 500 bushels of peanuts, whereas at a price of \$4 per bushel they will demand 600 bushels. The negative coefficient for p in Equation 1.6 reflects the marginalist principle that a lower price will cause people to buy more peanuts.

To complete this simple model of pricing, suppose that the quantity of peanuts supplied also depends on price:

$$\text{quantity supplied} = q_S = -125 + 125p. \tag{1.7}$$

Here the positive coefficient of price also reflects the marginal principle that a higher price will call forth increased supply—primarily because (as we saw in Example 1.1) it permits firms to incur higher marginal costs of production without incurring losses on the additional units produced.

Equilibrium price determination. Equation 1.6 and 1.7 therefore reflect our model of price determination in the market for peanuts. An equilibrium price can be found by setting quantity demanded equal to quantity supplied:

$$q_D = q_S \tag{1.8}$$

or

$$1{,}000 - 100p = -125 + 125p \tag{1.9}$$

or

$$225p = 1{,}125, \tag{1.10}$$

so

$$p^* = 5. \tag{1.11}$$

At a price of \$5 per bushel, this market is in equilibrium: at this price people want to purchase 500 bushels, and that is exactly what peanut producers are willing to supply. This equilibrium is pictured graphically as the intersection of D and S in Figure 1.2.

A more general model. In order to illustrate how this supply-demand model might be used, let's adopt a more general notation. Suppose now that the demand and supply functions are given by

(continued)

EXAMPLE 1.2 CONTINUED

FIGURE 1.2 Changing Supply-Demand Equilibria

The initial supply-demand equilibrium is illustrated by the intersection of D and S ($p^* = 5$, $q^* = 500$). When demand shifts to $q_{D'} = 1,450 - 100p$ (denoted as D'), the equilibrium shifts to $p^* = 7$, $q^* = 750$.

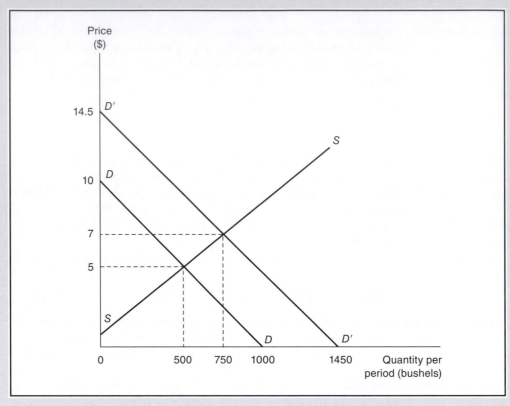

$$q_D = a + bp \quad \text{and} \quad q_S = c + dp \tag{1.12}$$

where a and c are constants that can be used to shift the demand and supply curves, respectively, and b (<0) and d (>0) represent demanders' and suppliers' reactions to price. Equilibrium in this market requires

$$q_D = q_S \quad \text{or}$$
$$a + bp = c + dp. \tag{1.13}$$

So, equilibrium price is given by[6]

$$p^* = \frac{a - c}{d - b}. \tag{1.14}$$

---

[6]Equation 1.14 is sometimes called the "reduced form" for the supply-demand structural model of Equations 1.12 and 1.13. It shows that the equilibrium value for the endogenous variable p ultimately depends only on the exogenous factors in the model (a and c) and on the behavioral parameters b and d. A similar equation can be calculated for equilibrium quantity.

Notice that, in our prior example, $a = 1{,}000$, $b = -100$, $c = -125$, and $d = 125$, so

$$p^* = \frac{1{,}000 + 125}{125 + 100} = \frac{1{,}125}{225} = 5. \tag{1.15}$$

With this more general formulation, however, we can pose questions about how the equilibrium price might change if either the demand or supply curve shifted. For example, differentiation of Equation 1.14 shows that

$$\frac{dp^*}{da} = \frac{1}{d - b} > 0,$$

$$\frac{dp^*}{dc} = \frac{-1}{d - b} < 0. \tag{1.16}$$

That is, an increase in demand (an increase in a) increases equilibrium price whereas an increase in supply (an increase in c) reduces price. This is exactly what a graphical analysis of supply and demand curves would show. For example, Figure 1.2 shows that when the constant term, a, in the demand equation increases to 1450, equilibrium price increases to $p^* = 7$ $[= (1{,}450 + 125)/225]$.

QUERY: How might you use Equation 1.16 to "predict" how each unit increase in the constant a affects p^*? Does this equation correctly predict the increase in p^* when the constant a increases from 1,000 to 1,450?

For example, suppose that the demand for peanuts were to increase. This would cause the price of peanuts to increase. Marshallian analysis would seek to understand the size of this increase by looking at conditions of supply and demand in the peanut market. General equilibrium analysis would look not only at that market but also at repercussions in other markets. A rise in the price of peanuts would increase costs for peanut butter makers, which would, in turn, affect the supply curve for peanut butter. Similarly, the rising price of peanuts might mean higher land prices for peanut farmers, which would affect the demand curves for all products that they buy. The demand curves for automobiles, furniture, and trips to Europe would all shift out, and that might create additional incomes for the providers of those products. Consequently, the effects of the initial increase in demand for peanuts eventually would spread throughout the economy. General equilibrium analysis attempts to develop models that permit us to examine such effects in a simplified setting. Several models of this type are described in Chapter 13.

Production possibility frontier

Here we briefly introduce some general equilibrium ideas by using another graph you should remember from introductory economics—the *production possibility frontier*. This graph shows the various amounts of two goods that an economy can produce using its available resources during some period (say, one week). Because the production possibility frontier shows two goods, rather than the single good in Marshall's model, it is used as a basic building block for general equilibrium models.

Figure 1.3 shows the production possibility frontier for two goods, food and clothing. The graph illustrates the supply of these goods by showing the combinations that can be produced with this economy's resources. For example, 10 pounds of food and 3 units of clothing could be produced, or 4 pounds of food and 12 units of clothing. Many other combinations of food and clothing could also be produced. The production possibility frontier shows all of them. Combinations of food and clothing outside the frontier cannot be produced because not enough resources are available. The production possibility frontier

FIGURE 1.3   Production Possibility Frontier

The production possibility frontier shows the different combinations of two goods that can be produced from a certain amount of scarce resources. It also shows the opportunity cost of producing more of one good as the amount of the other good that cannot then be produced. The opportunity cost at two different levels of clothing production can be seen by comparing points *A* and *B*.

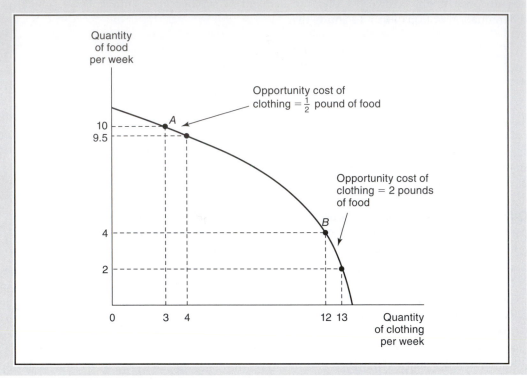

reminds us of the basic economic fact that resources are scarce—there are not enough resources available to produce all we might want of every good.

This scarcity means that we must choose how much of each good to produce. Figure 1.3 makes clear that each choice has its costs. For example, if this economy produces 10 pounds of food and 3 units of clothing at point *A*, producing 1 more unit of clothing would "cost" $\frac{1}{2}$ pound of food—increasing the output of clothing by 1 unit means the production of food would have to decrease by $\frac{1}{2}$ pound. So, the *opportunity cost* of 1 unit of clothing at point *A* is $\frac{1}{2}$ pound of food. On the other hand, if the economy initially produces 4 pounds of food and 12 units of clothing at point *B*, it would cost 2 pounds of food to produce 1 more unit of clothing. The opportunity cost of 1 more unit of clothing at point *B* has increased to 2 pounds of food. Because more units of clothing are produced at point *B* than at point *A*, both Ricardo's and Marshall's ideas of increasing incremental costs suggest that the opportunity cost of an additional unit of clothing will be higher at point *B* than at point *A*. This effect is shown by Figure 1.3.

The production possibility frontier provides two general equilibrium insights that are not clear in Marshall's supply and demand model of a single market. First, the graph shows that producing more of one good means producing less of another good because resources are scarce. Economists often (perhaps too often!) use the expression "there is no such thing as a free lunch" to explain that every economic action has opportunity costs. Second, the production possibility frontier shows that opportunity costs depend on how much of each good is produced. The frontier is like a supply curve for two goods: it shows the opportunity cost of producing more of one good as the decrease in the amount of the second good. The production possibility frontier is therefore a particularly useful tool for studying several markets at the same time.

EXAMPLE 1.3 The Production Possibility Frontier and Economic Inefficiency

General equilibrium models are good tools for evaluating the efficiency of various economic arrangements. As we will see in Chapter 13, such models have been used to assess a wide variety of policies such as trade agreements, tax structures, and environmental regulation. In this simple example, we explore the idea of efficiency in its most elementary form.

Suppose that an economy produces two goods, x and y, using labor as the only input. The production function for good x is $x = l_x^{0.5}$ (where l_x is the quantity of labor used in x production) and the production function for good y is $y = 2l_y^{0.5}$. Total labor available is constrained by $l_x + l_y \leq 200$. Construction of the production possibility frontier in this economy is extremely simple:

$$l_x + l_y = x^2 + 0.25y^2 \leq 200 \qquad (1.17)$$

if the economy is to be producing as much as possible (which, after all, is why it's called a "frontier"). Equation 1.17 shows that the frontier here has the shape of a quarter ellipse—its concavity derives from the diminishing returns exhibited by each production function.

Opportunity cost. Assuming this economy is on the frontier, the opportunity cost of good y in terms of good x can be derived by solving for y as

$$y^2 = 800 - 4x^2 \quad \text{or} \quad y = \sqrt{800 - 4x^2} = [800 - 4x^2]^{0.5} \qquad (1.18)$$

and then differentiating this expression:

$$\frac{dy}{dx} = 0.5[800 - 4x^2]^{-0.5}(-8x) = \frac{-4x}{y}. \qquad (1.19)$$

Suppose, for example, labor is equally allocated between the two goods. Then $x = 10, y = 20$, and $dy/dx = -4(10)/20 = -2$. With this allocation of labor, each unit increase in x output would require a reduction in y of 2 units. This can be verified by considering a slightly different allocation, $l_x = 101$ and $l_y = 99$. Now production is $x = 10.05$ and $y = 19.9$. Moving to this alternative allocation would have

$$\frac{\Delta y}{\Delta x} = \frac{(19.9 - 20)}{(10.05 - 10)} = \frac{-0.1}{0.05} = -2,$$

which is precisely what was derived from the calculus approach.

Concavity. Equation 1.19 clearly illustrates the concavity of the production possibility frontier. The slope of the frontier becomes steeper (more negative) as x output increases and y output falls. For example, if labor is allocated so that $l_x = 144$ and $l_y = 56$, then outputs are $x = 12$ and $y \approx 15$ and so $dy/dx = -4(12)/15 = -3.2$. With expanded x production, the opportunity cost of one more unit of x increases from 2 to 3.2 units of y.

Inefficiency. If an economy operates inside its production possibility frontier, it is operating inefficiently. Moving outward to the frontier could increase the output of both goods. In this book we will explore many reasons for such inefficiency. These usually derive from a failure of some market to perform correctly. For the purposes of this illustration, let's assume that the labor market in this economy does not work well and that 20 workers are permanently unemployed. Now the production possibility frontier becomes

$$x^2 + 0.25y^2 = 180, \qquad (1.20)$$

(continued)

EXAMPLE 1.3   CONTINUED

and the output combinations we described previously are no longer feasible. For example, if $x = 10$ then y output is now $y \approx 17.9$. The loss of about 2.1 units of y is a measure of the cost of the labor market inefficiency. Alternatively, if the labor supply of 180 were allocated evenly between the production of the two goods then we would have $x \approx 9.5$ and $y \approx 19$, and the inefficiency would show up in both goods' production—more of both goods could be produced if the labor market inefficiency were resolved.

QUERY: How would the inefficiency cost of labor market imperfections be measured solely in terms of x production in this model? How would it be measured solely in terms of y production? What would you need to know in order to assign a single number to the efficiency cost of the imperfection when labor is equally allocated to the two goods?

Welfare economics

In addition to their use in examining positive questions about how the economy operates, the tools used in general equilibrium analysis have also been applied to the study of normative questions about the welfare properties of various economic arrangements. Although such questions were a major focus of the great eighteenth- and nineteenth-century economists (Smith, Ricardo, Marx, Marshall, and so forth), perhaps the most significant advances in their study were made by the British economist Francis Y. Edgeworth (1848–1926) and the Italian economist Vilfredo Pareto (1848–1923) in the early years of the twentieth century. These economists helped to provide a precise definition for the concept of "economic efficiency" and to demonstrate the conditions under which markets will be able to achieve that goal. By clarifying the relationship between the allocation pricing of resources, they provided some support for the idea, first enunciated by Adam Smith, that properly functioning markets provide an "invisible hand" that helps allocate resources efficiently. Later sections of this book focus on some of these welfare issues.

MODERN DEVELOPMENTS

Research activity in economics expanded rapidly in the years following World War II. A major purpose of this book is to summarize much of this research. By illustrating how economists have tried to develop models to explain increasingly complex aspects of economic behavior, this book seeks to help you recognize some of the remaining unanswered questions.

The mathematical foundations of economic models

A major postwar development in microeconomic theory was the clarification and formalization of the basic assumptions that are made about individuals and firms. The first landmark in this development was the 1947 publication of Paul Samuelson's *Foundations of Economic Analysis*, in which the author (the first American Nobel Prize winner in economics) laid out a number of models of optimizing behavior.[7] Samuelson demonstrated the importance of basing behavioral models on well-specified mathematical postulates so that various optimization techniques from mathematics could be applied. The power of his approach made it inescapably clear that mathematics had become an integral part of modern economics. In Chapter 2 of this book we review some of the mathematical concepts most often used in microeconomics.

---

[7]Paul A. Samuelson, *Foundations of Economic Analysis* (Cambridge, MA: Harvard University Press, 1947).

New tools for studying markets

A second feature that has been incorporated into this book is the presentation of a number of new tools for explaining market equilibria. These include techniques for describing pricing in single markets, such as increasingly sophisticated models of monopolistic pricing or models of the strategic relationships among firms that use game theory. They also include general equilibrium tools for simultaneously exploring relationships among many markets. As we shall see, all of these new techniques help to provide a more complete and realistic picture of how markets operate.

The economics of uncertainty and information

A final major theoretical advance during the postwar period was the incorporation of uncertainty and imperfect information into economic models. Some of the basic assumptions used to study behavior in uncertain situations were originally developed in the 1940s in connection with the theory of games. Later developments showed how these ideas could be used to explain why individuals tend to be adverse to risk and how they might gather information in order to reduce the uncertainties they face. In this book, problems of uncertainty and information enter the analysis on many occasions.

Computers and empirical analysis

One final aspect of the postwar development of microeconomics should be mentioned—the increasing use of computers to analyze economic data and build economic models. As computers have become able to handle larger amounts of information and carry out complex mathematical manipulations, economists' ability to test their theories has dramatically improved. Whereas previous generations had to be content with rudimentary tabular or graphical analyses of real-world data, today's economists have available a wide variety of sophisticated techniques together with extensive microeconomic data with which to test their models. To examine these techniques and some of their limitations would be beyond the scope and purpose of this book. But, Extensions at the end of most chapters are intended to help you start reading about some of these applications.

SUMMARY

This chapter provided background on how economists approach the study of the allocation of resources. Much of the material discussed here should be familiar to you from introductory economics. In many respects, the study of economics represents acquiring increasingly sophisticated tools for addressing the same basic problems. The purpose of this book (and, indeed, of most upper-level books on economics) is to provide you with more of these tools. As a starting place, this chapter reminded you of the following points:

- Economics is the study of how scarce resources are allocated among alternative uses. Economists seek to develop simple models to help understand that process. Many of these models have a mathematical basis because the use of mathematics offers a precise shorthand for stating the models and exploring their consequences.

- The most commonly used economic model is the supply-demand model first thoroughly developed by

Alfred Marshall in the latter part of the nineteenth century. This model shows how observed prices can be taken to represent an equilibrium balancing of the production costs incurred by firms and the willingness of demanders to pay for those costs.

- Marshall's model of equilibrium is only "partial"—that is, it looks only at one market at a time. To look at many markets together requires an expanded set of general equilibrium tools.

- Testing the validity of an economic model is perhaps the most difficult task economists face. Occasionally, a model's validity can be appraised by asking whether it is based on "reasonable" assumptions. More often, however, models are judged by how well they can explain economic events in the real world.

SUGGESTIONS FOR FURTHER READING

On Methodology

Blaug, Mark, and John Pencavel. *The Methodology of Economics: Or How Economists Explain,* 2nd ed. Cambridge: Cambridge University Press, 1992.

A revised and expanded version of a classic study on economic methodology. Ties the discussion to more general issues in the philosophy of science.

Boland, Lawrence E. "A Critique of Friedman's Critics." *Journal of Economic Literature* (June 1979): 503–22.

Good summary of criticisms of positive approaches to economics and of the role of empirical verification of assumptions.

Friedman, Milton. "The Methodology of Positive Economics." In *Essays in Positive Economics,* pp. 3–43. Chicago: University of Chicago Press, 1953.

Basic statement of Friedman's positivist views.

Harrod, Roy F. "Scope and Method in Economics." *Economic Journal* 48 (1938): 383–412.

Classic statement of appropriate role for economic modeling.

Hausman, David M., and Michael S. McPherson. *Economic Analysis, Moral Philosophy, and Public Policy,* 2nd ed. Cambridge: Cambridge University Press, 2006.

The authors stress their belief that consideration of issues in moral philosophy can improve economic analysis.

McCloskey, Donald N. *If You're So Smart: The Narrative of Economic Expertise.* Chicago: University of Chicago Press, 1990.

Discussion of McCloskey's view that economic persuasion depends on rhetoric as much as on science. For an interchange on this topic, see also the articles in the Journal of Economic Literature, June 1995.

Sen, Amartya. *On Ethics and Economics.* Oxford: Blackwell Reprints, 1989.

The author seeks to bridge the gap between economics and ethical studies. This is a reprint of a classic study on this topic.

Primary Sources on the History of Economics

Edgeworth, F. Y. *Mathematical Psychics.* London: Kegan Paul, 1881.

Initial investigations of welfare economics, including rudimentary notions of economic efficiency and the contract curve.

Marshall, A. *Principles of Economics,* 8th ed. London: Macmillan & Co., 1920.

Complete summary of neoclassical view. A long-running, popular text. Detailed mathematical appendix.

Marx, K. *Capital.* New York: Modern Library, 1906.

Full development of labor theory of value. Discussion of "transformation problem" provides a (perhaps faulty) start for general equilibrium analysis. Presents fundamental criticisms of institution of private property.

Ricardo, D. *Principles of Political Economy and Taxation.* London: J. M. Dent & Sons, 1911.

Very analytical, tightly written work. Pioneer in developing careful analysis of policy questions, especially trade-related issues. Discusses first basic notions of marginalism.

Smith, A. *The Wealth of Nations.* New York: Modern Library, 1937.

First great economics classic. Very long and detailed, but Smith had the first word on practically every economic matter. This edition has helpful marginal notes.

Walras, L. *Elements of Pure Economics.* Translated by W. Jaffé. Homewood, IL: Richard D. Irwin, 1954.

Beginnings of general equilibrium theory. Rather difficult reading.

Secondary Sources on the History of Economics

Backhouse, Roger E. *The Ordinary Business of Life: The History of Economics from the Ancient World to the 21st Century.* Princeton, NJ: Princeton University Press, 2002.

An iconoclastic history. Quite good on the earliest economic ideas, but some blind spots on recent uses of mathematics and econometrics.

Blaug, Mark. *Economic Theory in Retrospect,* 5th ed. Cambridge: Cambridge University Press, 1997.

Very complete summary stressing analytical issues. Excellent "Readers' Guides" to the classics in each chapter.

Heilbroner, Robert L. *The Worldly Philosophers,* 7th ed. New York: Simon & Schuster, 1999.

Fascinating, easy-to-read biographies of leading economists. Chapters on Utopian Socialists and Thorstein Veblen highly recommended.

Keynes, John M. *Essays in Biography.* New York: W. W. Norton, 1963.

Essays on many famous persons (Lloyd George, Winston Churchill, Leon Trotsky) and on several economists (Malthus, Marshall, Edgeworth, F. P. Ramsey, and Jevons). Shows the true gift of Keynes as a writer.

Schumpeter, J. A. *History of Economic Analysis.* New York: Oxford University Press, 1954.

Encyclopedic treatment. Covers all the famous and many not-so-famous economists. Also briefly summarizes concurrent developments in other branches of the social sciences.

Mathematics for Microeconomics

Microeconomic models are constructed using a wide variety of mathematical techniques. In this chapter we provide a brief summary of some of the most important techniques that you will encounter in this book. A major portion of the chapter concerns mathematical procedures for finding the optimal value of some function. Because we will frequently adopt the assumption that an economic actor seeks to maximize or minimize some function, we will encounter these procedures (most of which are based on differential calculus) many times.

After our detailed discussion of the calculus of optimization, we turn to four topics that are covered more briefly. First, we look at a few special types of functions that arise in economic problems. Knowledge of properties of these functions can often be very helpful in solving economic problems. Next, we provide a brief summary of integral calculus. Although integration is used in this book far less frequently than is differentiation, we will nevertheless encounter several situations where we will want to employ integrals to measure areas that are important to economic theory or to add up outcomes that occur over time or across many individuals. One particular use of integration is to examine problems in which the objective is to maximize a stream of outcomes over time. Our third added topic focuses on techniques to be used for such problems in dynamic optimization. Finally, Chapter 2 concludes with a brief summary of mathematical statistics, which will be particularly useful in our study of economic behavior in uncertain situations.

MAXIMIZATION OF A FUNCTION OF ONE VARIABLE

Let's start our study of optimization with a simple example. Suppose that a manager of a firm desires to maximize[1] the profits received from selling a particular good. Suppose also that the profits (π) received depend only on the quantity (q) of the good sold. Mathematically,

$$\pi = f(q). \tag{2.1}$$

Figure 2.1 shows a possible relationship between π and q. Clearly, to achieve maximum profits, the manager should produce output q^*, which yields profits π^*. If a graph such as that of Figure 2.1 were available, this would seem to be a simple matter to be accomplished with a ruler.

Suppose, however, as is more likely, the manager does not have such an accurate picture of the market. He or she may then try varying q to see where a maximum profit is obtained. For example, by starting at q_1, profits from sales would be π_1. Next, the manager may try output q_2, observing that profits have increased to π_2. The commonsense idea that profits have increased in response to an increase in q can be stated formally as

$$\frac{\pi_2 - \pi_1}{q_2 - q_1} > 0 \quad \text{or} \quad \frac{\Delta \pi}{\Delta q} > 0, \tag{2.2}$$

---

[1]Here we will generally explore maximization problems. A virtually identical approach would be taken to study minimization problems because maximization of $f(x)$ is equivalent to minimizing $-f(x)$.

FIGURE 2.1   Hypothetical Relationship between Quantity Produced and Profits

If a manager wishes to produce the level of output that maximizes profits, then q^* should be produced. Notice that at q^*, $d\pi/dq = 0$.

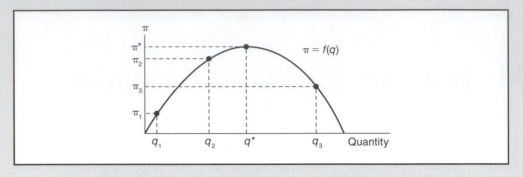

where the Δ notation is used to mean "the change in" π or q. As long as $\Delta\pi/\Delta q$ is positive, profits are increasing and the manager will continue to increase output. For increases in output to the right of q^*, however, $\Delta\pi/\Delta q$ will be negative, and the manager will realize that a mistake has been made.

Derivatives

As you probably know, the limit of $\Delta\pi/\Delta q$ for very small changes in q is called the *derivative* of the function, $\pi = f(q)$, and is denoted by $d\pi/dq$ or df/dq or $f'(q)$. More formally, the derivative of a function $\pi = f(q)$ at the point q_1 is defined as

$$\frac{d\pi}{dq} = \frac{df}{dq} = \lim_{h \to 0} \frac{f(q_1 + h) - f(q_1)}{h}. \tag{2.3}$$

Notice that the value of this ratio obviously depends on the point q_1 that is chosen.

Value of the derivative at a point

A notational convention should be mentioned: Sometimes one wishes to note explicitly the point at which the derivative is to be evaluated. For example, the evaluation of the derivative at the point $q = q_1$ could be denoted by

$$\left.\frac{d\pi}{dq}\right|_{q=q_1}. \tag{2.4}$$

At other times, one is interested in the value of $d\pi/dq$ for all possible values of q and no explicit mention of a particular point of evaluation is made.

In the example of Figure 2.1,

$$\left.\frac{d\pi}{dq}\right|_{q=q_1} > 0,$$

whereas

$$\left.\frac{d\pi}{dq}\right|_{q=q_3} < 0.$$

What is the value of $d\pi/dq$ at q^*? It would seem to be 0, because the value is positive for values of q less than q^* and negative for values of q greater than q^*. The derivative is the slope of the curve in question; this slope is positive to the left of q^* and negative to the right of q^*. At the point q^*, the slope of $f(q)$ is 0.

First-order condition for a maximum

This result is quite general. For a function of one variable to attain its maximum value at some point, the derivative at that point (if it exists) must be 0. Hence, if a manager could estimate the function $f(q)$ from some sort of real-world data, it would theoretically be possible to find the point where $df/dq = 0$. At this optimal point (say, q^*),

$$\left.\frac{df}{dq}\right|_{q=q^*} = 0. \tag{2.5}$$

Second-order conditions

An unsuspecting manager could be tricked, however, by a naive application of this first-derivative rule alone. For example, suppose that the profit function looks like that shown in either Figure 2.2a or 2.2b. If the profit function is that shown in Figure 2.2a, the manager, by producing where $d\pi/dq = 0$, will choose point q_a^*. This point in fact yields minimum, not maximum, profits for the manager. Similarly, if the profit function is that shown in Figure 2.2, the manager will choose point q_b^*, which, although it yields a profit greater than that for any output lower than q_b^*, is certainly inferior to any output greater than q_b^*. These situations illustrate the mathematical fact that $d\pi/dq = 0$ is a *necessary* condition for a maximum, but not a *sufficient* condition. To ensure that the chosen point is indeed a maximum point, a second condition must be imposed.

Intuitively, this additional condition is clear: The profit available by producing either a bit more or a bit less than q^* must be smaller than that available from q^*. If this is not true, the manager can do better than q^*. Mathematically, this means that $d\pi/dq$ must be greater

FIGURE 2.2 Two Profit Functions That Give Misleading Results If the First Derivative Rule Is Applied Uncritically

In (a), the application of the first derivative rule would result in point q_a^* being chosen. This point is in fact a point of minimum profits. Similarly, in (b), output level q_b^* would be recommended by the first derivative rule, but this point is inferior to all outputs greater than q_b^*. This demonstrates graphically that finding a point at which the derivative is equal to 0 is a necessary, but not a sufficient, condition for a function to attain its maximum value.

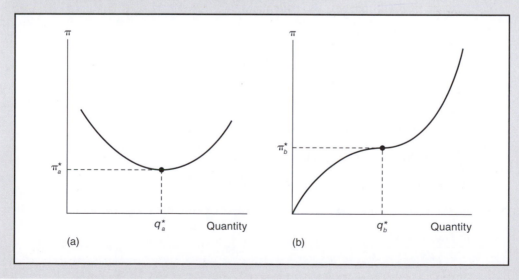

than 0 for $q < q^*$ and must be less than 0 for $q > q^*$. Therefore, at q^*, $d\pi/dq$ must be decreasing. Another way of saying this is that the derivative of $d\pi/dq$ must be negative at q^*.

Second derivatives

The derivative of a derivative is called a *second derivative* and is denoted by

$$\frac{d^2\pi}{dq^2} \quad \text{or} \quad \frac{d^2f}{dq^2} \quad \text{or} \quad f''(q).$$

The additional condition for q^* to represent a (local) maximum is therefore

$$\frac{d^2\pi}{dq^2}\bigg|_{q=q^*} = f''(q)\bigg|_{q=q^*} < 0, \tag{2.6}$$

where the notation is again a reminder that this second derivative is to be evaluated at q^*.

Hence, although Equation 2.5 ($d\pi/dq = 0$) is a necessary condition for a maximum, that equation must be combined with Equation 2.6 ($d^2\pi/dq^2 < 0$) to ensure that the point is a local maximum for the function. Equations 2.5 and 2.6 together are therefore sufficient conditions for such a maximum. Of course, it is possible that by a series of trials the manager may be able to decide on q^* by relying on market information rather than on mathematical reasoning (remember Friedman's pool-player analogy). In this book we shall be less interested in how the point is discovered than in its properties and how the point changes when conditions change. A mathematical development will be very helpful in answering these questions.

Rules for finding derivatives

Here are a few familiar rules for taking derivatives. We will use these at many places in this book.

1. If b is a constant, then

$$\frac{db}{dx} = 0.$$

2. If b is a constant, then

$$\frac{d[bf(x)]}{dx} = bf'(x).$$

3. If b is a constant, then

$$\frac{dx^b}{dx} = bx^{b-1}.$$

4. $\dfrac{d \ln x}{dx} = \dfrac{1}{x}$

   where ln signifies the logarithm to the base e ($= 2.71828$).

5. $\dfrac{da^x}{dx} = a^x \ln a$ for any constant a

   A particular case of this rule is $de^x/dx = e^x$.

Now suppose that $f(x)$ and $g(x)$ are two functions of x and that $f'(x)$ and $g'(x)$ exist. Then:

6. $\dfrac{d[f(x) + g(x)]}{dx} = f'(x) + g'(x).$

7. $\dfrac{d[f(x) \cdot g(x)]}{dx} = f(x)g'(x) + f'(x)g(x).$

8. $\dfrac{d[f(x)/g(x)]}{dx} = \dfrac{f'(x)g(x) - f(x)g'(x)}{[g(x)]^2},$

   provided that $g(x) \neq 0$.

Finally, if $y = f(x)$ and $x = g(z)$ and if both $f'(x)$ and $g'(z)$ exist, then

9. $\dfrac{dy}{dz} = \dfrac{dy}{dx} \cdot \dfrac{dx}{dz} = \dfrac{df}{dx} \cdot \dfrac{dg}{dz}.$

This result is called the *chain rule*. It provides a convenient way to study how one variable (z) affects another variable (y) solely through its influence on some intermediate variable (x). Some examples are

10. $\dfrac{de^{ax}}{dx} = \dfrac{de^{ax}}{d(ax)} \cdot \dfrac{d(ax)}{dx} = e^{ax} \cdot a = ae^{ax}.$

11. $\dfrac{d[\ln(ax)]}{dx} = \dfrac{d[\ln(ax)]}{d(ax)} \cdot \dfrac{d(ax)}{dx} = \dfrac{1}{ax} \cdot a = \dfrac{1}{x}.$

12. $\dfrac{d[\ln(x^2)]}{dx} = \dfrac{d[\ln(x^2)]}{d(x^2)} \cdot \dfrac{d(x^2)}{dx} = \dfrac{1}{x^2} \cdot 2x = \dfrac{2}{x}.$

FUNCTIONS OF SEVERAL VARIABLES

Economic problems seldom involve functions of only a single variable. Most goals of interest to economic agents depend on several variables, and trade-offs must be made among these variables. For example, the *utility* an individual receives from activities as a consumer depends on the amount of each good consumed. For a firm's *production function*, the amount produced depends on the quantity of labor, capital, and land devoted to production. In these circumstances, this dependence of one variable (y) on a series of other variables ($x_1, x_2, \ldots, x_n$) is denoted by

$$y = f(x_1, x_2, \ldots, x_n). \tag{2.7}$$

Partial derivatives

We are interested in the point at which y reaches a maximum and in the trade-offs that must be made to reach that point. It is again convenient to picture the agent as changing the variables at his or her disposal (the x's) in order to locate a maximum. Unfortunately, for a function of several variables, the idea of *the* derivative is not well-defined. Just as the steepness of ascent when climbing a mountain depends on which direction you go, so does the slope (or derivative) of the function depend on the direction in which it is taken. Usually, the only directional slopes of interest are those that are obtained by increasing one of the x's while holding all the other variables constant (the analogy for mountain climbing might be to measure slopes only in a north-south or east-west direction). These directional slopes are called *partial derivatives*. The partial derivative of y with respect to (that is, in the direction of) x_1 is denoted by

$$\frac{\partial y}{\partial x_1} \quad \textbf{or} \quad \frac{\partial f}{\partial x_1} \quad \textbf{or} \quad f_{x_1} \quad \textbf{or} \quad f_1.$$

It is understood that in calculating this derivative all of the other x's are held constant. Again it should be emphasized that the numerical value of this slope depends on the value of x_1 and on the (preassigned) values of $x_2, \ldots, x_n$.

EXAMPLE 2.1 Profit Maximization

Suppose that the relationship between profits (π) and quantity produced (q) is given by

$$\pi(q) = 1{,}000q - 5q^2. \tag{2.8}$$

A graph of this function would resemble the parabola shown in Figure 2.1. The value of q that maximizes profits can be found by differentiation:

$$\frac{d\pi}{dq} = 1{,}000 - 10q = 0, \tag{2.9}$$

so

$$q^* = 100. \tag{2.10}$$

At $q = 100$, Equation 2.8 shows that profits are 50,000—the largest value possible. If, for example, the firm opted to produce $q = 50$, profits would be 37,500. At $q = 200$, profits are precisely 0.

That $q = 100$ is a "global" maximum can be shown by noting that the second derivative of the profit function is -10 (see Equation 2.9). Hence, the rate of increase in profits is always decreasing—up to $q = 100$ this rate of increase is still positive, but beyond that point it becomes negative. In this example, $q = 100$ is the only local maximum value for the function π. With more complex functions, however, there may be several such maxima.

QUERY: Suppose that a firm's output (q) is determined by the amount of labor (l) it hires according to the function $q = 2\sqrt{l}$. Suppose also that the firm can hire all of the labor it wants at \$10 per unit and sells its output at \$50 per unit. Profits are therefore a function of l given by $\pi(l) = 100\sqrt{l} - 10l$. How much labor should this firm hire in order to maximize profits, and what will those profits be?

A somewhat more formal definition of the partial derivative is

$$\left.\frac{\partial f}{\partial x_1}\right|_{\bar{x}_2,\,\dots,\,\bar{x}_n} = \lim_{h \to 0} \frac{f(x_1 + h, \bar{x}_2, \dots, \bar{x}_n) - f(x_1, \bar{x}_2, \dots, \bar{x}_n)}{h}, \tag{2.11}$$

where the notation is intended to indicate that $x_2, \dots, x_n$ are all held constant at the preassigned values $\bar{x}_2, \dots, \bar{x}_n$ so the effect of changing x_1 only can be studied. Partial derivatives with respect to the other variables ($x_2, \dots, x_n$) would be calculated in a similar way.

Calculating partial derivatives

It is easy to calculate partial derivatives. The calculation proceeds as for the usual derivative by *treating $x_2, \dots, x_n$ as constants* (which indeed they are in the definition of a partial derivative). Consider the following examples.

1. If $y = f(x_1, x_2) = ax_1^2 + bx_1 x_2 + cx_2^2$, then

$$\frac{\partial f}{\partial x_1} = f_1 = 2ax_1 + bx_2$$

and

$$\frac{\partial f}{\partial x_2} = f_2 = bx_1 + 2cx_2.$$

Notice that $\partial f / \partial x_1$ is in general a function of both x_1 and x_2 and therefore its value will depend on the particular values assigned to these variables. It also depends on the parameters a, b, and c, which do not change as x_1 and x_2 change.

2.　If $y = f(x_1, x_2) = e^{ax_1 + bx_2}$, then

$$\frac{\partial f}{\partial x_1} = f_1 = ae^{ax_1 + bx_2}$$

and

$$\frac{\partial f}{\partial x_2} = f_2 = be^{ax_1 + bx_2}.$$

3.　If $y = f(x_1, x_2) = a \ln x_1 + b \ln x_2$, then

$$\frac{\partial f}{\partial x_1} = f_1 = \frac{a}{x_1}$$

and

$$\frac{\partial f}{\partial x_2} = f_2 = \frac{b}{x_2}.$$

Notice here that the treatment of x_2 as a constant in the derivation of $\partial f / \partial x_1$ causes the term $b \ln x_2$ to disappear upon differentiation because it does not change when x_1 changes. In this case, unlike our previous examples, the size of the effect of x_1 on y is independent of the value of x_2. In other cases, the effect of x_1 on y will depend on the level of x_2.

Partial derivatives and the ceteris paribus assumption

In Chapter 1, we described the way in which economists use the ceteris paribus assumption in their models to hold constant a variety of outside influences so the particular relationship being studied can be explored in a simplified setting. Partial derivatives are a precise mathematical way of representing this approach; that is, they show how changes in one variable affect some outcome when other influences are held constant—exactly what economists need for their models. For example, Marshall's demand curve shows the relationship between price (p) and quantity (q) demanded when other factors are held constant. Using partial derivatives, we could represent the slope of this curve by $\partial q / \partial p$ to indicate the ceteris paribus assumptions that are in effect. The fundamental law of demand—that price and quantity move in opposite directions when other factors do not change—is therefore reflected by the mathematical statement "$\partial q / \partial p < 0$." Again, the use of a partial derivative serves as a reminder of the ceteris paribus assumptions that surround the law of demand.

Partial derivatives and units of measurement

In mathematics relatively little attention is paid to how variables are measured. In fact, most often no explicit mention is made of the issue. But the variables used in economics usually refer to real-world magnitudes and therefore we must be concerned with how they are measured. Perhaps the most important consequence of choosing units of measurement is that the partial derivatives often used to summarize economic behavior will reflect these units. For example, if q represents the quantity of gasoline demanded by all U.S. consumers during a given year (measured in billions of gallons) and p represents the price in dollars per gallon, then $\partial q / \partial p$ will measure the change in demand (in billions of gallons per year) for a dollar per gallon change in price. The numerical size of this derivative depends on how q and p are measured. A decision to measure consumption in millions of gallons per year would multiply the size of the derivative by 1,000, whereas a decision to measure price in cents per gallon would reduce it by a factor of 100.

The dependence of the numerical size of partial derivatives on the chosen units of measurement poses problems for economists. Although many economic theories make predictions about the sign (direction) of partial derivatives, any predictions about the numerical magnitude of such derivatives would be contingent on how authors chose to measure their variables. Making comparisons among studies could prove practically impossible, especially given the wide variety of measuring systems in use around the world. For this reason, economists have chosen to adopt a different, unit-free way to measure quantitative impacts.

Elasticity—A general definition

Economists use elasticities to summarize virtually all of the quantitative impacts that are of interest to them. Because such measures focus on the proportional effect of a change in one variable on another, they are unit-free—the units "cancel out" when the elasticity is calculated. Suppose, for example, that y is a function of x and, possibly, other variables. Then the elasticity of y with respect to x (denoted as $e_{y,x}$) is defined as

$$e_{y,x} = \frac{\dfrac{\Delta y}{y}}{\dfrac{\Delta x}{x}} = \frac{\Delta y}{\Delta x} \cdot \frac{x}{y} = \frac{\partial y}{\partial x} \cdot \frac{x}{y}. \qquad (2.12)$$

Notice that, no matter how the variables y and x are measured, the units of measurement cancel out because they appear in both a numerator and a denominator. Notice also that, because y and x are positive in most economic situations, the elasticity $e_{y,x}$ and the partial derivative $\partial y / \partial x$ will have the same sign. Hence, theoretical predictions about the direction of certain derivatives will also apply to their related elasticities.

Specific applications of the elasticity concept will be encountered throughout this book. These include ones with which you should be familiar, such as the market price elasticity of demand or supply. But many new concepts that can be expressed most clearly in elasticity terms will also be introduced.

EXAMPLE 2.2 Elasticity and Functional Form

The definition in Equation 2.12 makes clear that elasticity should be evaluated at a specific point on a function. In general the value of this parameter would be expected to vary across different ranges of the function. This observation is most clearly shown in the case where y is a linear function of x of the form

$$y = a + bx + \textbf{other terms}.$$

In this case,

$$e_{y,x} = \frac{\partial y}{\partial x} \cdot \frac{x}{y} = b \cdot \frac{x}{y} = b \cdot \frac{x}{a + bx + \cdots}, \qquad (2.13)$$

which makes clear that $e_{y,x}$ is not constant. Hence, for linear functions it is especially important to note the point at which elasticity is to be computed.

If the functional relationship between y and x is of the exponential form

$$y = ax^b$$

then the elasticity is a constant, independent of where it is measured:

$$e_{y,x} = \frac{\partial y}{\partial x} \cdot \frac{x}{y} = abx^{b-1} \cdot \frac{x}{ax^b} = b.$$

A logarithmic transformation of this equation also provides a very convenient alternative definition of elasticity. Because

$$\ln y = \ln a + b \ln x,$$

we have

$$e_{y,x} = b = \frac{\partial \ln y}{\partial \ln x}. \tag{2.14}$$

Hence, elasticities can be calculated through "logarithmic differentiation." As we shall see, this is frequently the easiest way to proceed in making such calculations.

QUERY: Are there any functional forms in addition to the exponential that have a constant elasticity, at least over some range?

Second-order partial derivatives

The partial derivative of a partial derivative is directly analogous to the second derivative of a function of one variable and is called a *second-order partial derivative*. This may be written as

$$\frac{\partial(\partial f / \partial x_i)}{\partial x_j}$$

or more simply as

$$\frac{\partial^2 f}{\partial x_j \partial x_i} = f_{ij}. \tag{2.15}$$

For the examples above:

1. $\dfrac{\partial^2 f}{\partial x_1 \partial x_1} = f_{11} = 2a$

    $f_{12} = b$

    $f_{21} = b$

    $f_{22} = 2c.$

2. $f_{11} = a^2 e^{ax_1 + bx_2}$

    $f_{12} = abe^{ax_1 + bx_2}$

    $f_{21} = abe^{ax_1 + bx_2}$

    $f_{22} = b^2 e^{ax_1 + bx_2}$

3. $f_{11} = \dfrac{-a}{x_1^2}$

    $f_{12} = 0$

    $f_{21} = 0$

    $f_{22} = \dfrac{-b}{x_2^2}.$

Young's theorem

These examples illustrate the mathematical result that, under quite general conditions, the order in which partial differentiation is conducted to evaluate second-order partial derivatives does not matter. That is,

$$f_{ij} = f_{ji} \tag{2.16}$$

for any pair of variables x_i, x_j. This result is sometimes called "Young's theorem." For an intuitive explanation of the theorem, we can return to our mountain-climbing analogy. In this example, the theorem states that the gain in elevation a hiker experiences depends on the directions and distances traveled, but not on the order in which these occur. That is, the gain in altitude is independent of the actual path taken as long as the hiker proceeds from one set of map coordinates to another. He or she may, for example, go one mile north, then one mile east or proceed in the opposite order by first going one mile east, then one mile north. In either case, the gain in elevation is the same since in both cases the hiker is moving from one specific place to another. In later chapters we will make good use of this result because it provides a very convenient way of showing some of the predictions that economic models make about behavior.[2]

Uses of second-order partials

Second-order partial derivatives will play an important role in many of the economic theories that are developed throughout this book. Probably the most important examples relate to the "own" second-order partial, f_{ii}. This function shows how the marginal influence of x_i on y (i.e., $\partial y/\partial x_i$) changes as the value of x_i increases. A negative value for f_{ii} is the mathematical way of indicating the economic idea of diminishing marginal effectiveness. Similarly, the cross-partial f_{ij} indicates how the marginal effectiveness of x_i changes as x_j increases. The sign of this effect could be either positive or negative. Young's theorem indicates that, in general, such cross-effects are symmetric. More generally, the second-order partial derivatives of a function provide information about the curvature of the function. Later in this chapter we will see how such information plays an important role in determining whether various second-order conditions for a maximum are satisfied.

MAXIMIZATION OF FUNCTIONS OF SEVERAL VARIABLES

Using partial derivatives, we can now discuss how to find the maximum value for a function of several variables. To understand the mathematics used in solving this problem, an analogy to the one-variable case is helpful. In this one-variable case, we can picture an agent varying x by a small amount, dx, and observing the change in y, dy. This change is given by

$$dy = f'(x)\,dx. \tag{2.17}$$

The identity in Equation 2.17 records the fact that the change in y is equal to the change in x times the slope of the function. This formula is equivalent to the *point-slope* formula used for linear equations in basic algebra. As before, the necessary condition for a maximum is that $dy = 0$ for small changes in x around the optimal point. Otherwise, y could be increased by suitable changes in x. But because dx does not necessarily equal 0 in Equation 2.17, $dy = 0$ must imply that at the desired point, $f'(x) = 0$. This is another way of obtaining the first-order condition for a maximum that we already derived.

---

[2]Young's theorem implies that the matrix of the second-order partial derivatives of a function is symmetric. This symmetry offers a number of economic insights. For a brief introduction to the matrix concepts used in economics, see the Extensions to this chapter.

Using this analogy, let's look at the decisions made by an economic agent who must choose the levels of several variables. Suppose that this agent wishes to find a set of x's that will maximize the value of $y = f(x_1, x_2, \ldots, x_n)$. The agent might consider changing only one of the x's, say x_1, while holding all the others constant. The change in y (that is, dy) that would result from this change in x_1 is given by

$$dy = \frac{\partial f}{\partial x_1} dx_1 = f_1 dx_1.$$

This says that the change in y is equal to the change in x_1 times the slope measured in the x_1 direction. Using the mountain analogy again, the gain in altitude a climber heading north would achieve is given by the distance northward traveled times the slope of the mountain measured in a northward direction.

Total differential

If all the x's are varied by a small amount, the total effect on y will be the sum of effects such as that shown above. Therefore the total change in y is defined to be

$$\begin{aligned} dy &= \frac{\partial f}{\partial x_1} dx_1 + \frac{\partial f}{\partial x_2} dx_2 + \cdots + \frac{\partial f}{\partial x_n} dx_n \\ &= f_1 dx_1 + f_2 dx_2 + \cdots + f_n dx_n. \end{aligned} \qquad (2.18)$$

This expression is called the *total differential* of f and is directly analogous to the expression for the single-variable case given in Equation 2.17. The equation is intuitively sensible: The total change in y is the sum of changes brought about by varying each of the x's.[3]

First-order condition for a maximum

A necessary condition for a maximum (or a minimum) of the function $f(x_1, x_2, \ldots, x_n)$ is that $dy = 0$ for any combination of small changes in the x's. The only way this can happen is if, at the point being considered,

$$f_1 = f_2 = \cdots = f_n = 0. \qquad (2.19)$$

A point where Equations 2.19 hold is called a *critical point*. Equations 2.19 are the necessary conditions for a local maximum. To see this intuitively, note that if one of the partials (say, f_i) were greater (or less) than 0, then y could be increased by increasing (or decreasing) x_i. An economic agent then could find this maximal point by finding the spot where y does not respond to very small movements in any of the x's. This is an extremely important result for economic analysis. It says that any activity (that is, the x's) should be pushed to the point where its "marginal" contribution to the objective (that is, y) is 0. To stop short of that point would fail to maximize y.

---

[3]The total differential in Equation 2.18 can be used to derive the chain rule as it applies to functions of several variables. Suppose that $y = f(x_1, x_2)$ and that $x_1 = g(z)$ and $x_2 = h(z)$. If all of these functions are differentiable, then it is possible to calculate the effects of a change in z on y. The total differential of y is

$$dy = f_1 dx_1 + f_2 dx_2.$$

Dividing this equation by dz gives

$$\frac{dy}{dz} = f_1 \frac{dx_1}{dz} + f_2 \frac{dx_2}{dz} = f_1 \frac{dg}{dz} + f_2 \frac{dh}{dz}.$$

Hence, calculating the effect of z on y requires calculating how z affects both of the determinants of y (that is, x_1 and x_2). If y depends on more than two variables, an analogous result holds. This result acts as a reminder to be rather careful to include all possible effects when calculating derivatives of functions of several variables.

EXAMPLE 2.3 Finding a Maximum

Suppose that y is a function of x_1 and x_2 given by

$$y = -(x_1 - 1)^2 - (x_2 - 2)^2 + 10 \qquad (2.20)$$

or

$$y = -x_1^2 + 2x_1 - x_2^2 + 4x_2 + 5.$$

For example, y might represent an individual's health (measured on a scale of 0 to 10), and x_1 and x_2 might be daily dosages of two health-enhancing drugs. We wish to find values for x_1 and x_2 that make y as large as possible. Taking the partial derivatives of y with respect to x_1 and x_2 and applying the necessary conditions given by Equations 2.19 yields

$$\frac{\partial y}{\partial x_1} = -2x_1 + 2 = 0,$$

$$\frac{\partial y}{\partial x_2} = -2x_2 + 4 = 0 \qquad (2.21)$$

or

$$x_1^* = 1,$$
$$x_2^* = 2.$$

The function is therefore at a critical point when $x_1 = 1$, $x_2 = 2$. At that point, $y = 10$ is the best health status possible. A bit of experimentation provides convincing evidence that this is the greatest value y can have. For example, if $x_1 = x_2 = 0$, then $y = 5$, or if $x_1 = x_2 = 1$, then $y = 9$. Values of x_1 and x_2 larger than 1 and 2, respectively, reduce y because the negative quadratic terms in Equation 2.20 become large. Consequently, the point found by applying the necessary conditions is in fact a local (and global) maximum.[4]

QUERY: Suppose y took on a fixed value (say, 5). What would the relationship implied between x_1 and x_2 look like? How about for $y = 7$? Or $y = 10$? (These graphs are *contour lines* of the function and will be examined in more detail in several later chapters. See also Problem 2.1.)

Second-order conditions

Again, however, the conditions of Equations 2.19 are not sufficient to ensure a maximum. This can be illustrated by returning to an already overworked analogy: All hilltops are (more or less) flat, but not every flat place is a hilltop. A second-order condition similar to Equation 2.6 is needed to ensure that the point found by applying Equations 2.19 is a local maximum. Intuitively, for a local maximum, y should be decreasing for any small changes in the x's away from the critical point. As in the single-variable case, this necessarily involves looking at the second-order partial derivatives of the function f. These second-order partials must obey certain restrictions (analogous to the restriction that was derived in the single-variable case) if the critical point found by applying Equations 2.19 is to be a local maximum. Later in this chapter we will look at these restrictions.

---

[4]More formally, the point $x_1 = 1$, $x_2 = 2$ is a global maximum because the function described by Equation 2.20 is concave (see our discussion later in this chapter).

IMPLICIT FUNCTIONS

Although mathematical equations are often written with a "dependent" variable (y) as a function of one or more independent variables (x), this is not the only way to write such a relationship. As a trivial example, the equation

$$y = mx + b \qquad (2.22)$$

can also be written as

$$y - mx - b = 0 \qquad (2.23)$$

or, even more generally, as

$$f(x, y, m, b) = 0, \qquad (2.24)$$

where this functional notation indicates a relationship between x and y that also depends on the slope (m) and intercept (b) parameters of the function, which do not change. Functions written in these forms are sometimes called *implicit functions* because the relationships between the variables and parameters are implicitly present in the equation rather than being explicitly calculated as, say, y as a function of x and the parameters m and b.

Often it is a simple matter to translate from implicit functions to explicit ones. For example, the implicit function

$$x + 2y - 4 = 0 \qquad (2.25)$$

can easily be "solved" for x as

$$x = -2y + 4 \qquad (2.26)$$

or for y as

$$y = \frac{-x}{2} + 2. \qquad (2.27)$$

Derivatives from implicit functions

In many circumstances it is helpful to compute derivatives directly from implicit functions without solving for one of the variables directly. For example, the implicit function $f(x, y) = 0$ has a total differential of $0 = f_x dx + f_y dy$, so

$$\frac{dy}{dx} = -\frac{f_x}{f_y}. \qquad (2.28)$$

Hence, the implicit derivative dy/dx can be found as the negative of the ratio of the partial derivatives of the implicit function, providing $f_y \neq 0$.

EXAMPLE 2.4 A Production Possibility Frontier—Again

In Example 1.3 we examined a production possibility frontier for two goods of the form

$$x^2 + 0.25y^2 = 200 \qquad (2.29)$$

or, written implicitly,

$$f(x, y) = x^2 + 0.25y^2 - 200 = 0. \qquad (2.30)$$

Hence,

(continued)

EXAMPLE 2.4 CONTINUED

$$f_x = 2x,$$
$$f_y = 0.5y,$$

and, by Equation 2.28, the opportunity cost trade-off between x and y is

$$\frac{dy}{dx} = \frac{-f_x}{f_y} = \frac{-2x}{0.5y} = \frac{-4x}{y}, \tag{2.31}$$

which is precisely the result we obtained earlier, with considerably less work.

QUERY: Why does the trade-off between x and y here depend only on the ratio of x to y and not on the size of the labor force as reflected by the 200 constant?

Implicit function theorem

It may not always be possible to solve implicit functions of the form $g(x, y) = 0$ for unique explicit functions of the form $y = f(x)$. Mathematicians have analyzed the conditions under which a given implicit function can be solved explicitly with one variable being a function of other variables and various parameters. Although we will not investigate these conditions here, they involve requirements on the various partial derivatives of the function that are sufficient to ensure that there is indeed a unique relationship between the dependent and independent variables.[5] In many economic applications, these derivative conditions are precisely those required to ensure that the second-order conditions for a maximum (or a minimum) hold. Hence, in these cases, we will assert that the *implicit function theorem* holds and that it is therefore possible to solve explicitly for trade-offs among the variables involved.

THE ENVELOPE THEOREM

One major application of the implicit function theorem, which will be used many times in this book, is called the *envelope theorem*; it concerns how the optimal value for a particular function changes when a parameter of the function changes. Because many of the economic problems we will be studying concern the effects of changing a parameter (for example, the effects that changing the market price of a commodity will have on an individual's purchases), this is a type of calculation we will frequently make. The envelope theorem often provides a nice shortcut.

A specific example

Perhaps the easiest way to understand the envelope theorem is through an example. Suppose y is a function of a single variable (x) and a parameter (a) given by

$$y = -x^2 + ax. \tag{2.32}$$

For different values of the parameter a, this function represents a family of inverted parabolas. If a is assigned a specific value, Equation 2.32 is a function of x only, and the value of x that maximizes y can be calculated. For example, if $a = 1$, then $x^* = \frac{1}{2}$ and, for these values of x and a, $y = \frac{1}{4}$ (its maximal value). Similarly, if $a = 2$, then $x^* = 1$ and $y^* = 1$. Hence, an increase

---

[5]For a detailed discussion of the implicit function theorem in various contexts, see Carl P. Simon and Lawrence Blume, *Mathematics for Economists* (New York: W. W. Norton, 1994), chap. 15.

of 1 in the value of the parameter a has increased the maximum value of y by $\frac{3}{4}$. In Table 2.1, integral values of a between 0 and 6 are used to calculate the optimal values for x and the associated values of the objective, y. Notice that as a increases, the maximal value for y also increases. This is also illustrated in Figure 2.3, which shows that the relationship between a and y^* is quadratic. Now we wish to calculate explicitly how y^* changes as the parameter a changes.

TABLE 2.1 Optimal Values of y and x for Alternative Values of a in $y = -x^2 + ax$

Value of a	Value of x^*	Value of y^*
0	0	0
1	$\frac{1}{2}$	$\frac{1}{4}$
2	1	1
3	$\frac{3}{2}$	$\frac{9}{4}$
4	2	4
5	$\frac{5}{2}$	$\frac{25}{4}$
6	3	9

FIGURE 2.3 Illustration of the Envelope Theorem

The envelope theorem states that the slope of the relationship between y^* (the maximum value of y) and the parameter a can be found by calculating the slope of the auxiliary relationship found by substituting the respective optimal values for x into the objective function and calculating $\partial y / \partial a$.

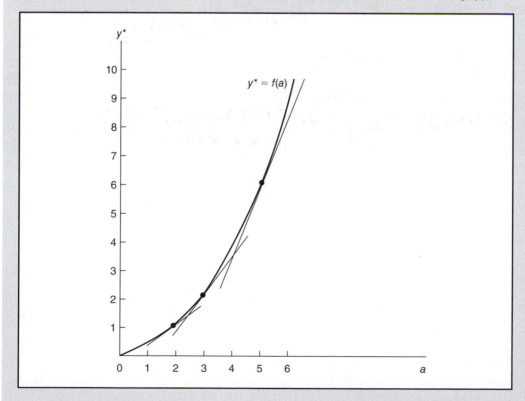

A direct, time-consuming approach

The envelope theorem states that there are two equivalent ways we can make this calculation. First, we can calculate the slope of the function in Figure 2.3 directly. To do so, we must solve Equation 2.32 for the optimal value of x for any value of a:

$$\frac{dy}{dx} = -2x + a = 0;$$

hence,

$$x^* = \frac{a}{2}.$$

Substituting this value of x^* in Equation 2.32 gives

$$y^* = -(x^*)^2 + a(x^*)$$

$$= -\left(\frac{a}{2}\right)^2 + a\left(\frac{a}{2}\right)$$

$$= -\frac{a^2}{4} + \frac{a^2}{2} = \frac{a^2}{4},$$

and this is precisely the relationship shown in Figure 2.3. From the previous equation, it is easy to see that

$$\frac{dy^*}{da} = \frac{2a}{4} = \frac{a}{2} \tag{2.33}$$

and, for example, at $a = 2$, $dy^*/da = 1$. That is, near $a = 2$ the marginal impact of increasing a is to increase y^* by the same amount. Near $a = 6$, any small increase in a will increase y^* by three times this change. Table 2.1 illustrates this result.

The envelope shortcut

Arriving at this conclusion was a bit complicated. We had to find the optimal value of x for each value of a and then substitute this value for x^* into the equation for y. In more general cases this may be quite burdensome since it requires repeatedly maximizing the objective function. The envelope theorem, providing an alternative approach, states that for small changes in a, dy^*/da can be computed by holding x constant *at its optimal value* and simply calculating $\partial y/\partial a$ from the objective function directly.

Proceeding in this way gives

$$\frac{\partial y}{\partial a} = x, \tag{2.34}$$

and at x^* we have

$$\frac{\partial y^*}{\partial a} = x^* = \frac{a}{2}. \tag{2.35}$$

This is precisely the result obtained earlier. The reason that the two approaches yield identical results is illustrated in Figure 2.3. The tangents shown in the figure report values of y for a *fixed* x^*. The tangents' slopes are $\partial y/\partial a$. Clearly, at y^* this slope gives the value we seek.

This result is quite general, and we will use it at several places in this book to simplify our analysis. To summarize, the envelope theorem states that the change in the optimal value of a function with respect to a parameter of that function can be found by partially differentiating the objective function while holding x constant at its optimal value. That is,

$$\frac{dy^*}{da} = \frac{\partial y}{\partial a}\{x = x^*(a)\}, \tag{2.36}$$

where the notation provides a reminder that $\partial y/\partial a$ must be computed at that value of x that is optimal for the specific value of the parameter a being examined.

Many-variable case

An analogous envelope theorem holds for the case where y is a function of several variables. Suppose that y depends on a set of x's $(x_1, ..., x_n)$ and on a particular parameter of interest, say, a:

$$y = f(x_1, ..., x_n, a). \tag{2.37}$$

Finding an optimal value for y would consist of solving n first-order equations of the form

$$\frac{\partial y}{\partial x_i} = 0 \quad (i = 1, ..., n), \tag{2.38}$$

and a solution to this process would yield optimal values for these x's $(x_1^*, x_2^*, ..., x_n^*)$ that would implicitly depend on the parameter a. Assuming the second-order conditions are met, the implicit function theorem would apply in this case and ensure that we could solve each x_i^* as a function of the parameter a:

$$x_1^* = x_1^*(a),$$
$$x_2^* = x_2^*(a),$$
$$\vdots \tag{2.39}$$
$$x_n^* = x_n^*(a).$$

Substituting these functions into our original objective (Equation 2.37) yields an expression in which the optimal value of y (say, y^*) depends on the parameter a both directly and indirectly through the effect of a on the x^*'s:

$$y^* = f[x_1^*(a), x_2^*(a), ..., x_n^*(a), a].$$

Totally differentiating this expression with respect to a yields

$$\frac{dy^*}{da} = \frac{\partial f}{\partial x_1} \cdot \frac{dx_1}{da} + \frac{\partial f}{\partial x_2} \cdot \frac{dx_2}{da} + \cdots + \frac{\partial f}{\partial x_n} \cdot \frac{dx_n}{da} + \frac{\partial f}{\partial a}. \tag{2.40}$$

But, because of the first-order conditions all of these terms except the last are equal to 0 if the x's are at their optimal values. Hence, again we have the envelope result:

$$\frac{dy^*}{da} = \frac{\partial f}{\partial a}, \tag{2.41}$$

where this derivative is to be evaluated at the optimal values for the x's.

EXAMPLE 2.5 The Envelope Theorem: Health Status Revisited

Earlier, in Example 2.3, we examined the maximum values for the health status function

$$y = -(x_1 - 1)^2 - (x_2 - 2)^2 + 10 \tag{2.42}$$

and found that

$$x_1^* = 1,$$
$$x_2^* = 2, \tag{2.43}$$

(*continued*)

EXAMPLE 2.5   CONTINUED

and

$$y^* = 10.$$

Suppose now we use the arbitrary parameter a instead of the constant 10 in Equation 2.42. Here a might represent a measure of the best possible health for a person, but this value would obviously vary from person to person. Hence,

$$y = f(x_1, x_2, a) = -(x_1 - 1)^2 - (x_2 - 2)^2 + a. \tag{2.44}$$

In this case the optimal values for x_1 and x_2 do not depend on a (they are always $x_1^* = 1$, $x_2^* = 2$), so at those optimal values we have

$$y^* = a \tag{2.45}$$

and

$$\frac{dy^*}{da} = 1. \tag{2.46}$$

People with "naturally better health" will have concomitantly higher values for y^*, providing they choose x_1 and x_2 optimally. But this is precisely what the envelope theorem indicates, because

$$\frac{dy^*}{da} = \frac{\partial f}{\partial a} = 1 \tag{2.47}$$

from Equation 2.44. Increasing the parameter a simply increases the optimal value for y^* by an identical amount (again, assuming the dosages of x_1 and x_2 are correctly chosen).

QUERY: Suppose we focused instead on the optimal dosage for x_1 in Equation 2.42—that is, suppose we used a general parameter, say b, instead of 1. Explain in words and using mathematics why $\partial y^* / \partial b$ would necessarily be 0 in this case.

CONSTRAINED MAXIMIZATION

So far we have focused our attention on finding the maximum value of a function without restricting the choices of the x's available. In most economic problems, however, not all values for the x's are feasible. In many situations, for example, it is required that all the x's be positive. This would be true for the problem faced by the manager choosing output to maximize profits; a negative output would have no meaning. In other instances the x's may be constrained by economic considerations. For example, in choosing the items to consume, an individual is not able to choose any quantities desired. Rather, choices are constrained by the amount of purchasing power available; that is, by this person's budget constraint. Such constraints may lower the maximum value for the function being maximized. Because we are not able to choose freely among all the x's, y may not be as large as it could be. The constraints would be "nonbinding" if we could obtain the same level of y with or without imposing the constraint.

Lagrangian multiplier method

One method for solving constrained maximization problems is the *Lagrangian multiplier method*, which involves a clever mathematical trick that also turns out to have a useful economic interpretation. The rationale of this method is quite simple, although no rigorous presentation will be attempted here.[6] In a prior section, the necessary conditions for a local maximum were discussed. We showed that at the optimal point all the partial derivatives of f must be 0. There are therefore n equations ($f_i = 0$ for $i = 1, \ldots, n$) in n unknowns (the x's). Generally, these equations can be solved for the optimal x's. When the x's are constrained, however, there is at least one additional equation (the constraint) but no additional variables. The set of equations therefore is overdetermined. The Lagrangian technique introduces an additional variable (the Lagrangian multiplier), which not only helps to solve the problem at hand (because there are now $n + 1$ equations in $n + 1$ unknowns), but also has an interpretation that is useful in a variety of economic circumstances.

The formal problem

More specifically, suppose that we wish to find the values of $x_1, x_2, \ldots, x_n$ that maximize

$$y = f(x_1, x_2, \ldots, x_n), \tag{2.48}$$

subject to a constraint that permits only certain values of the x's to be used. A general way of writing that constraint is

$$g(x_1, x_2, \ldots, x_n) = 0, \tag{2.49}$$

where the function[7] g represents the relationship that must hold among all the x's.

First-order conditions

The Lagrangian multiplier method starts with setting up the expression

$$\mathcal{L} = f(x_1, x_2, \ldots, x_n) + \lambda g(x_1, x_2, \ldots, x_n), \tag{2.50}$$

where λ is an additional variable called the Lagrangian multiplier. Later we will interpret this new variable. First, however, notice that when the constraint holds, $\mathcal{L}$ and f have the same value [because $g(x_1, x_2, \ldots, x_n) = 0$]. Consequently, if we restrict our attention only to values of the x's that satisfy the constraint, finding the constrained maximum value of f is equivalent to finding a critical value of $\mathcal{L}$. Let us proceed then to do so, treating λ also as a variable (in addition to the x's). From Equation 2.50, the conditions for a critical point are:

$$\frac{\partial \mathcal{L}}{\partial x_1} = f_1 + \lambda g_1 = 0,$$

$$\frac{\partial \mathcal{L}}{\partial x_2} = f_2 + \lambda g_2 = 0,$$

$$\vdots \tag{2.51}$$

$$\frac{\partial \mathcal{L}}{\partial x_n} = f_n + \lambda g_n = 0,$$

$$\frac{\partial \mathcal{L}}{\partial \lambda} = g(x_1, x_2, \ldots, x_n) = 0.$$

Equations 2.51 are then the conditions for a critical point for the function $\mathcal{L}$. Notice that there are $n + 1$ equations (one for each x and a final one for λ) in $n + 1$ unknowns. The equations can generally be solved for $x_1, x_2, \ldots, x_n$, and λ. Such a solution will have two

---

[6]For a detailed presentation, see A. K. Dixit, *Optimization in Economic Theory*, 2nd ed. (Oxford: Oxford University Press, 1990), chap. 2.

[7]As we pointed out earlier, any function of $x_1, x_2, \ldots, x_n$ can be written in this implicit way. For example, the constraint $x_1 + x_2 = 10$ could be written $10 - x_1 - x_2 = 0$. In later chapters, we will usually follow this procedure in dealing with constraints. Often the constraints we examine will be linear.

properties: (1) the x's will obey the constraint because the last equation in 2.51 imposes that condition; and (2) among all those values of x's that satisfy the constraint, those that also solve Equations 2.51 will make $\mathcal{L}$ (and hence f) as large as possible (assuming second-order conditions are met). The Lagrangian multiplier method therefore provides a way to find a solution to the constrained maximization problem we posed at the outset.[8]

The solution to Equations 2.51 will usually differ from that in the unconstrained case (see Equations 2.19). Rather than proceeding to the point where the marginal contribution of each x is 0, Equations 2.51 require us to stop short because of the constraint. Only if the constraint were ineffective (in which case, as we show below, λ would be 0) would the constrained and unconstrained equations (and their respective solutions) agree. These revised marginal conditions have economic interpretations in many different situations.

Interpretation of the Lagrangian multiplier

So far we have used the Lagrangian multiplier (λ) only as a mathematical "trick" to arrive at the solution we wanted. In fact, that variable also has an important economic interpretation, which will be central to our analysis at many points in this book. To develop this interpretation, rewrite the first n equations of 2.51 as

$$\frac{f_1}{-g_1} = \frac{f_2}{-g_2} = \cdots = \frac{f_n}{-g_n} = \lambda. \tag{2.52}$$

In other words, at the maximum point, the ratio of f_i to g_i is the same for every x_i. The numerators in Equations 2.52 are the marginal contributions of each x to the function f. They show the *marginal benefit* that one more unit of x_i will have for the function that is being maximized (that is, for f).

A complete interpretation of the denominators in Equations 2.52 is probably best left until we encounter these ratios in actual economic applications. There we will see that these usually have a "marginal cost" interpretation. That is, they reflect the added burden on the constraint of using slightly more x_i. As a simple illustration, suppose the constraint required that total spending on x_1 and x_2 be given by a fixed dollar amount, F. Hence, the constraint would be $p_1 x_1 + p_2 x_2 = F$ (where p_i is the per unit cost of x_i). Using our present terminology, this constraint would be written in implicit form as

$$g(x_1, x_2) = F - p_1 x_1 - p_2 x_2 = 0. \tag{2.53}$$

In this situation, then,

$$-g_i = p_i \tag{2.54}$$

and the derivative $-g_i$ does indeed reflect the per unit, marginal cost of using x_i. Practically all of the optimization problems we will encounter in later chapters have a similar interpretation for the denominators in Equations 2.52.

Lagrangian multiplier as a benefit-cost ratio

Now we can give Equations 2.52 an intuitive interpretation. They indicate that, at the optimal choices for the x's, the ratio of the marginal benefit of increasing x_i to the marginal cost of increasing x_i should be the same for every x. To see that this is an obvious condition

---

[8]Strictly speaking, these are the necessary conditions for an interior local maximum. In some economic problems, it is necessary to amend these conditions (in fairly obvious ways) to take account of the possibility that some of the x's may be on the boundary of the region of permissible x's. For example, if all of the x's are required to be nonnegative, it may be that the conditions of Equations 2.51 will not hold exactly, because these may require negative x's. We look at this situation later in this chapter.

for a maximum, suppose that it were not true: Suppose that the "benefit-cost ratio" were higher for x_1 than for x_2. In this case, slightly more x_1 should be used in order to achieve a maximum. Consider using more x_1 but giving up just enough x_2 to keep g (the constraint) constant. Hence, the marginal cost of the additional x_1 used would equal the cost saved by using less x_2. But because the benefit-cost ratio (the amount of benefit per unit of cost) is greater for x_1 than for x_2, the additional benefits from using more x_1 would exceed the loss in benefits from using less x_2. The use of more x_1 and appropriately less x_2 would then increase y because x_1 provides more "bang for your buck." Only if the marginal benefit–marginal cost ratios are equal for all the x's will there be a local maximum, one in which no small changes in the x's can increase the objective. Concrete applications of this basic principle are developed in many places in this book. The result is fundamental for the microeconomic theory of optimizing behavior.

The Lagrangian multiplier (λ) can also be interpreted in light of this discussion. λ is the common benefit-cost ratio for all the x's. That is,

$$\lambda = \frac{\text{marginal benefit of } x_i}{\text{marginal cost of } x_i} \tag{2.55}$$

for every x_i. If the constraint were relaxed slightly, it would not matter exactly which x is changed (indeed, all the x's could be altered), because, at the margin, each promises the same ratio of benefits to costs. The Lagrangian multiplier then provides a measure of how such an overall relaxation of the constraint would affect the value of y. In essence, λ assigns a "shadow price" to the constraint. A high λ indicates that y could be increased substantially by relaxing the constraint, because each x has a high benefit-cost ratio. A low value of λ, on the other hand, indicates that there is not much to be gained by relaxing the constraint. If the constraint is not binding at all, λ will have a value of 0, thereby indicating that the constraint is not restricting the value of y. In such a case, finding the maximum value of y subject to the constraint would be identical to finding an unconstrained maximum. The shadow price of the constraint is 0. This interpretation of λ can also be shown using the envelope theorem as described later in this chapter.[9]

Duality

This discussion shows that there is a clear relationship between the problem of maximizing a function subject to constraints and the problem of assigning values to constraints. This reflects what is called the mathematical principle of "duality": Any constrained maximization problem has an associated dual problem in constrained *minimization* that focuses attention on the constraints in the original (primal) problem. For example, to jump a bit ahead of our story, economists assume that individuals maximize their utility, subject to a budget constraint. This is the consumer's primal problem. The dual problem for the consumer is to minimize the expenditure needed to achieve a given level of utility. Or, a firm's primal problem may be to minimize the total cost of inputs used to produce a given level of output, whereas the dual problem is to maximize output for a given cost of inputs purchased. Many similar examples will be developed in later chapters. Each illustrates that there are always two ways to look at any constrained optimization problem. Sometimes taking a frontal attack by analyzing the primal problem can lead to greater insights. In other instances, the "back door" approach of examining the dual problem may be more instructive. Whichever route is taken, the results will generally, though not always, be identical, so the choice made will mainly be a matter of convenience.

---

[9]The discussion in the text concerns problems involving a single constraint. In general, one can handle m constraints ($m < n$) by simply introducing m new variables (Lagrangian multipliers) and proceeding in an analogous way to that discussed above.

EXAMPLE 2.6 Constrained Maximization: Health Status Yet Again

Let's return once more to our (perhaps tedious) health maximization problem. As before, the individual's goal is to maximize

$$y = -x_1^2 + 2x_1 - x_2^2 + 4x_2 + 5,$$

but now assume that choices of x_1 and x_2 are constrained by the fact that he or she can only tolerate one drug dose per day. That is,

$$x_1 + x_2 = 1 \tag{2.56}$$

or

$$1 - x_1 - x_2 = 0.$$

Notice that the original optimal point $(x_1 = 1, x_2 = 2)$ is no longer attainable because of the constraint on possible dosages: other values must be found. To do so, we first set up the Lagrangian expression:

$$\mathcal{L} = -x_1^2 + 2x_1 - x_2^2 + 4x_2 + 5 + \lambda(1 - x_1 - x_2). \tag{2.57}$$

Differentiation of $\mathcal{L}$ with respect to x_1, x_2, and λ yields the following necessary condition for a constrained maximum:

$$\frac{\partial \mathcal{L}}{\partial x_1} = -2x_1 + 2 - \lambda = 0,$$

$$\frac{\partial \mathcal{L}}{\partial x_2} = -2x_2 + 4 - \lambda = 0, \tag{2.58}$$

$$\frac{\partial \mathcal{L}}{\partial \lambda} = 1 - x_1 - x_2 = 0.$$

These equations must now be solved for the optimal values of x_1, x_2, and λ. Using the first and second equations gives

$$-2x_1 + 2 = \lambda = -2x_2 + 4$$

or

$$x_1 = x_2 - 1. \tag{2.59}$$

Substitution of this value for x_1 into the constraint yields the solution:

$$x_2 = 1, \\ x_1 = 0. \tag{2.60}$$

In words, if this person can tolerate only one dose of drugs, he or she should opt for taking only the second drug. By using either of the first two equations, it is easy to complete our solution by showing that

$$\lambda = 2. \tag{2.61}$$

This, then, is the solution to the constrained maximum problem. If $x_1 = 0$, $x_2 = 1$, then y takes on the value 8. Constraining the values of x_1 and x_2 to sum to 1 has reduced the maximum value of health status, y, from 10 to 8.

QUERY: Suppose this individual could tolerate two doses per day. Would you expect y to increase? Would increases in tolerance beyond three doses per day have any effect on y?

EXAMPLE 2.7 Optimal Fences and Constrained Maximization

Suppose a farmer had a certain length of fence, P, and wished to enclose the largest possible rectangular area. What shape area should the farmer choose? This is clearly a problem in constrained maximization. To solve it, let x be the length of one side of the rectangle and y be the length of the other side. The problem then is to choose x and y so as to maximize the area of the field (given by $A = x \cdot y$), subject to the constraint that the perimeter is fixed at $P = 2x + 2y$.

Setting up the Lagrangian expression gives

$$\mathcal{L} = x \cdot y + \lambda(P - 2x - 2y), \tag{2.62}$$

where λ is an unknown Lagrangian multiplier. The first-order conditions for a maximum are

$$\frac{\partial \mathcal{L}}{\partial x} = y - 2\lambda = 0,$$

$$\frac{\partial \mathcal{L}}{\partial y} = x - 2\lambda = 0, \tag{2.63}$$

$$\frac{\partial \mathcal{L}}{\partial \lambda} = P - 2x - 2y = 0.$$

The three equations in 2.63 must be solved simultaneously for x, y, and λ. The first two equations say that $y/2 = x/2 = \lambda$, showing that x must be equal to y (the field should be square). They also imply that x and y should be chosen so that the ratio of marginal benefits to marginal cost is the same for both variables. The benefit (in terms of area) of one more unit of x is given by y (area is increased by $1 \cdot y$), and the marginal cost (in terms of perimeter) is 2 (the available perimeter is reduced by 2 for each unit that the length of side x is increased). The maximum conditions state that this ratio should be equal for each of the variables.

Since we have shown that $x = y$, we can use the constraint to show that

$$x = y = \frac{P}{4}, \tag{2.64}$$

and, because $y = 2\lambda$,

$$\lambda = \frac{P}{8}. \tag{2.65}$$

Interpretation of the Lagrangian Multiplier. If the farmer were interested in knowing how much more field could be fenced by adding an extra yard of fence, the Lagrangian multiplier suggests that he or she could find out by dividing the present perimeter by 8. Some specific numbers might make this clear. Suppose that the field currently has a perimeter of 400 yards. If the farmer has planned "optimally," the field will be a square with 100 yards ($= P/4$) on a side. The enclosed area will be 10,000 square yards. Suppose now that the perimeter (that is, the available fence) were enlarged by one yard. Equation 2.65 would then "predict" that the total area would be increased by approximately 50 ($= P/8$) square yards. That this is indeed the case can be shown as follows: Because the perimeter is now 401 yards, each side of the square will be 401/4 yards. The total area of the field is therefore $(401/4)^2$, which, according to the author's calculator, works out to be 10,050.06 square yards. Hence, the "prediction" of a 50-square-yard increase that is provided by the Lagrangian multiplier proves to be remarkably close. As in all constrained maximization problems, here the Lagrangian multiplier provides useful information about the implicit value of the constraint.

(continued)

EXAMPLE 2.7   CONTINUED

Duality. The dual of this constrained maximization problem is that for a given area of a rectangular field, the farmer wishes to minimize the fence required to surround it. Mathematically, the problem is to minimize

$$P = 2x + 2y, \tag{2.66}$$

subject to the constraint

$$A = x \cdot y. \tag{2.67}$$

Setting up the Lagrangian expression

$$\mathscr{L}^D = 2x + 2y + \lambda^D(A - x \cdot y) \tag{2.68}$$

(where the D denotes the dual concept) yields the following first-order conditions for a minimum:

$$\frac{\partial \mathscr{L}^D}{\partial x} = 2 - \lambda^D \cdot y = 0,$$

$$\frac{\partial \mathscr{L}^D}{\partial y} = 2 - \lambda^D \cdot x = 0, \tag{2.69}$$

$$\frac{\partial \mathscr{L}^D}{\partial \lambda^D} = A - x \cdot y = 0.$$

Solving these equations as before yields the result

$$x = y = \sqrt{A}. \tag{2.70}$$

Again, the field should be square if the length of fence is to be minimized. The value of the Lagrangian multiplier in this problem is

$$\lambda^D = \frac{2}{y} = \frac{2}{x} = \frac{2}{\sqrt{A}}. \tag{2.71}$$

As before, this Lagrangian multiplier indicates the relationship between the objective (minimizing fence) and the constraint (needing to surround the field). If the field were 10,000 square yards, as we saw before, 400 yards of fence would be needed. Increasing the field by one square yard would require about .02 more yards of fence ($= 2/\sqrt{A} = 2/100$). The reader may wish to fire up his or her calculator to show this is indeed the case—a fence 100.005 yards on each side will exactly enclose 10,001 square yards. Here, as in most duality problems, the value of the Lagrangian in the dual is the reciprocal of the value for the Lagrangian in the primal problem. Both provide the same information, although in a somewhat different form.

QUERY: An implicit constraint here is that the farmer's field be rectangular. If this constraint were not imposed, what shape field would enclose maximal area? How would you prove that?

ENVELOPE THEOREM IN CONSTRAINED MAXIMIZATION PROBLEMS

The envelope theorem, which we discussed previously in connection with unconstrained maximization problems, also has important applications in constrained maximization problems. Here we will provide only a brief presentation of the theorem. In later chapters we will look at a number of applications.

Suppose we seek the maximum value of

$$y = f(x_1, \ldots, x_n; a),\tag{2.72}$$

subject to the constraint

$$g(x_1, \ldots, x_n; a) = 0,\tag{2.73}$$

where we have made explicit the dependence of the functions f and g on some parameter a. As we have shown, one way to solve this problem is to set up the Lagrangian expression

$$\mathcal{L} = f(x_1, \ldots, x_n; a) + \lambda g(x_1, \ldots, x_n; a)\tag{2.74}$$

and solve the first-order conditions (see Equations 2.51) for the optimal, constrained values $x_1^*, \ldots, x_n^*$. Alternatively, it can be shown that

$$\frac{dy^*}{da} = \frac{\partial \mathcal{L}}{\partial a}(x_1^*, \ldots, x_n^*; a).\tag{2.75}$$

That is, the change in the maximal value of y that results when the parameter a changes (and all of the x's are recalculated to new optimal values) can be found by partially differentiating the Lagrangian expression (Equation 2.74) and evaluating the resultant partial derivative at the optimal point.[10] Hence, the Lagrangian expression plays the same role in applying the envelope theorem to constrained problems as does the objective function alone in unconstrained problems. As a simple exercise, the reader may wish to show that this result holds for the problem of fencing a rectangular field described in Example 2.7.[11]

INEQUALITY CONSTRAINTS

In some economic problems the constraints need not hold exactly. For example, an individual's budget constraint requires that he or she spend no more than a certain amount per period, but it is at least possible to spend less than this amount. Inequality constraints also arise in the values permitted for some variables in economic problems. Usually, for example, economic variables must be nonnegative (though they can take on the value of zero). In this section we will show how the Lagrangian technique can be adapted to such circumstances. Although we will encounter only a few problems later in the text that require this mathematics, development here will illustrate a few general principles that are quite consistent with economic intuition.

A two-variable example

In order to avoid much cumbersome notation, we will explore inequality constraints only for the simple case involving two choice variables. The results derived are readily generalized. Suppose that we seek to maximize $y = f(x_1, x_2)$ subject to three inequality constraints:

---

[10]For a more complete discussion of the envelope theorem in constrained maximization problems, see Eugene Silberberg and Wing Suen, *The Structure of Economics: A Mathematical Analysis,* 3rd ed. (Boston: Irwin/McGraw-Hill, 2001), pp. 159–61.

[11]For the primal problem, the perimeter P is the parameter of principal interest. By solving for the optimal values of x and y and substituting into the expression for the area (A) of the field, it is easy to show that $dA/dP = P/8$. Differentiation of the Lagrangian expression (Equation 2.62) yields $\partial \mathcal{L}/\partial P = \lambda$ and, at the optimal values of x and y, $dA/dP = \partial \mathcal{L}/\partial P = \lambda = P/8$. The envelope theorem in this case then offers further proof that the Lagrangian multiplier can be used to assign an implicit value to the constraint.

1. $g(x_1, x_2) \geq 0$;
2. $x_1 \geq 0$;   and   **(2.76)**
3. $x_2 \geq 0$.

Hence, we are allowing for the possibility that the constraint we introduced before need not hold exactly (a person need not spend all of his or her income) and for the fact that both of the x's must be nonnegative (as in most economic problems).

Slack variables

One way to solve this optimization problem is to introduce three new variables (a, b, and c) that convert the inequality constraints in Equation 2.76 into equalities. To ensure that the inequalities continue to hold, we will square these new variables, ensuring that the resulting values are positive. Using this procedure, the inequality constraints become

1. $g(x_1, x_2) - a^2 = 0$;
2. $x_1 - b^2 = 0$;   and   **(2.77)**
3. $x_2 - c^2 = 0$.

Any solution that obeys these three equality constraints will also obey the inequality constraints. It will also turn out that the optimal values for a, b, and c will provide several insights into the nature of the solutions to a problem of this type.

Solution by the method of Lagrange

By converting the original problem involving inequalities into one involving equalities, we are now in a position to use Lagrangian methods to solve it. Because there are three constraints, we must introduce three Lagrangian multipliers: λ_1, λ_2, and λ_3. The full Lagrangian expression is

$$\mathcal{L} = f(x_1, x_2) + \lambda_1[g(x_1, x_2) - a^2] + \lambda_2(x_1 - b^2) + \lambda_3(x_2 - c^2). \quad \textbf{(2.78)}$$

We wish to find the values of x_1, x_2, a, b, c, λ_1, λ_2, and λ_3 that constitute a critical point for this expression. This will necessitate eight first-order conditions:

$$\frac{\partial \mathcal{L}}{\partial x_1} = f_1 + \lambda_1 g_1 + \lambda_2 = 0,$$

$$\frac{\partial \mathcal{L}}{\partial x_2} = f_2 + \lambda_1 g_2 + \lambda_3 = 0,$$

$$\frac{\partial \mathcal{L}}{\partial a} = -2a\lambda_1 = 0,$$

$$\frac{\partial \mathcal{L}}{\partial b} = -2b\lambda_2 = 0,$$

$$\frac{\partial \mathcal{L}}{\partial c} = -2c\lambda_3 = 0, \quad \textbf{(2.79)}$$

$$\frac{\partial \mathcal{L}}{\partial \lambda_1} = g(x_1, x_2) - a^2 = 0,$$

$$\frac{\partial \mathcal{L}}{\partial \lambda_2} = x_1 - b^2 = 0,$$

$$\frac{\partial \mathcal{L}}{\partial \lambda_3} = x_2 - c^2 = 0,$$

In many ways these conditions resemble those we derived earlier for the case of a single equality constraint (see Equation 2.51). For example, the final three conditions merely repeat the three revised constraints. This ensures that any solution will obey these conditions. The first two equations also resemble the optimal conditions developed earlier. If λ_2 and λ_3 were 0, the conditions would in fact be identical. But the presence of the additional Lagrangian multipliers in the expressions shows that the customary optimality conditions may not hold exactly here.

Complementary slackness

The three equations involving the variables a, b, and c provide the most important insights into the nature of solutions to problems involving inequality constraints. For example, the third line in Equation 2.79 implies that, in the optimal solution, either λ_1 or a must be 0.[12] In the second case $(a = 0)$, the constraint $g(x_1, x_2) = 0$ holds exactly and the calculated value of λ_1 indicates its relative importance to the objective function, f. On the other hand, if $a \neq 0$, then $\lambda_1 = 0$ and this shows that the availability of some slackness in the constraint implies that its value to the objective is 0. In the consumer context, this means that if a person does not spend all his or her income, even more income would do nothing to raise his or her well-being.

Similar complementary slackness relationships also hold for the choice variables x_1 and x_2. For example, the fourth line in Equation 2.79 requires that the optimal solution have either b or λ_2 be 0. If $\lambda_2 = 0$ then the optimal solution has $x_1 > 0$, and this choice variable meets the precise benefit-cost test that $f_1 + \lambda_1 g_1 = 0$. Alternatively, solutions where $b = 0$ have $x_1 = 0$, and also require that $\lambda_2 > 0$. So, such solutions do not involve any use of x_1 because that variable does not meet the benefit-cost test as shown by the first line of Equation 2.79, which implies that $f_1 + \lambda_1 g_1 < 0$. An identical result holds for the choice variable x_2.

These results, which are sometimes called *Kuhn-Tucker conditions* after their discoverers, show that the solutions to optimization problems involving inequality constraints will differ from similar problems involving equality constraints in rather simple ways. Hence, we cannot go far wrong by working primarily with constraints involving equalities and assuming that we can rely on intuition to state what would happen if the problems actually involved inequalities. That is the general approach we will take in this book.[13]

SECOND-ORDER CONDITIONS

So far our discussion of optimization has focused primarily on necessary (first-order) conditions for finding a maximum. That is indeed the practice we will follow throughout much of this book because, as we shall see, most economic problems involve functions for which the second-order conditions for a maximum are also satisfied. In this section we give a brief analysis of the connection between second-order conditions for a maximum and the related curvature conditions that functions must have to ensure that these hold. The economic explanations for these curvature conditions will be discussed throughout the text.

Functions of one variable

First consider the case in which the objective, y, is a function of only a single variable, x. That is,

$$y = f(x). \tag{2.80}$$

---

[12]We will not examine the degenerate case where both of these variables are 0.

[13]The situation can become much more complex when calculus cannot be relied upon to give a solution, perhaps because some of the functions in a problem are not differentiable. For a discussion, see Avinask K. Dixit, *Optimization in Economic Theory,* 2nd ed. (Oxford: Oxford University Press, 1990).

A necessary condition for this function to attain its maximum value at some point is that

$$\frac{dy}{dx} = f'(x) = 0 \tag{2.81}$$

at that point. To ensure that the point is indeed a maximum, we must have y decreasing for movements away from it. We already know (by Equation 2.81) that for small changes in x, the value of y does not change; what we need to check is whether y is increasing before that "plateau" is reached and declining thereafter. We have already derived an expression for the change in $y(dy)$, which is given by the total differential

$$dy = f'(x)\,dx. \tag{2.82}$$

What we now require is that dy be decreasing for small increases in the value of x. The differential of Equation 2.82 is given by

$$d(dy) = d^2y = \frac{d[f'(x)\,dx]}{dx} \cdot dx = f''(x)\,dx \cdot dx = f''(x)\,dx^2. \tag{2.83}$$

But

$$d^2y < 0$$

implies that

$$f''(x)\,dx^2 < 0, \tag{2.84}$$

and since dx^2 must be positive (because anything squared is positive), we have

$$f''(x) < 0 \tag{2.85}$$

as the required second-order condition. In words, this condition requires that the function f have a concave shape at the critical point (contrast Figures 2.1 and 2.2). Similar curvature conditions will be encountered throughout this section.

EXAMPLE 2.8 Profit Maximization Again

In Example 2.1 we considered the problem of finding the maximum of the function

$$\pi = 1{,}000q - 5q^2. \tag{2.86}$$

The first-order condition for a maximum requires

$$\frac{d\pi}{dq} = 1{,}000 - 10q = 0 \tag{2.87}$$

or

$$q^* = 100. \tag{2.88}$$

The second derivative of the function is given by

$$\frac{d^2\pi}{dq^2} = -10 < 0, \tag{2.89}$$

and hence the point $q^* = 100$ obeys the sufficient conditions for a local maximum.

QUERY: Here the second derivative is negative not only at the optimal point; it is always negative. What does that imply about the optimal point? How should the fact that the second derivative is a constant be interpreted?

Functions of two variables

As a second case, we consider y as a function of two independent variables:

$$y = f(x_1, x_2).$$ **(2.90)**

A necessary condition for such a function to attain its maximum value is that its partial derivatives, in both the x_1 and the x_2 directions, be 0. That is,

$$\frac{\partial y}{\partial x_1} = f_1 = 0,$$

$$\frac{\partial y}{\partial x_2} = f_2 = 0.$$ **(2.91)**

A point that satisfies these conditions will be a "flat" spot on the function (a point where $dy = 0$) and therefore will be a candidate for a maximum. To ensure that the point is a local maximum, y must diminish for movements in any direction away from the critical point: In pictorial terms there is only one way to leave a true mountaintop, and that is to go down.

An intuitive argument

Before describing the mathematical properties required of such a point, an intuitive approach may be helpful. If we consider only movements in the x_1 direction, the required condition is clear: The slope in the x_1 direction (that is, the partial derivative f_1) must be diminishing at the critical point. This is a direct application of our discussion of the single-variable case. It shows that, for a maximum, the second partial derivative in the x_1 direction must be negative. An identical argument holds for movements only in the x_2 direction. Hence, both own second partial derivatives (f_{11} and f_{22}) must be negative for a local maximum. In our mountain analogy, if attention is confined only to north-south or east-west movements, the slope of the mountain must be diminishing as we cross its summit—the slope must change from positive to negative.

The particular complexity that arises in the two-variable case involves movements through the optimal point that are not solely in the x_1 or x_2 directions (say, movements from northeast to southwest). In such cases, the second-order partial derivatives do not provide complete information about how the slope is changing near the critical point. Conditions must also be placed on the cross-partial derivative ($f_{12} = f_{21}$) to ensure that dy is decreasing for movements through the critical point in any direction. As we shall see, those conditions amount to requiring that the own second-order partial derivatives be sufficiently negative so as to counterbalance any possible "perverse" cross-partial derivatives that may exist. Intuitively, if the mountain falls away steeply enough in the north-south and east-west directions, relatively minor failures to do so in other directions can be compensated for.

A formal analysis

We now proceed to make these points more formally. What we wish to discover are the conditions that must be placed on the second partial derivatives of the function f to ensure that d^2y is negative for movements in any direction through the critical point. Recall first that the total differential of the function is given by

$$dy = f_1\, dx_1 + f_2\, dx_2.$$ **(2.92)**

The differential of that function is given by

$$d^2y = (f_{11}\, dx_1 + f_{12}\, dx_2)\, dx_1 + (f_{21}\, dx_1 + f_{22}\, dx_2)\, dx_2$$ **(2.93)**

or

$$d^2y = f_{11}\, dx_1^2 + f_{12}\, dx_2\, dx_1 + f_{21}\, dx_1\, dx_2 + f_{22}\, dx_2^2.$$ **(2.94)**

Because, by Young's theorem, $f_{12} = f_{21}$, we can arrange terms to get

$$d^2y = f_{11}\,dx_1^2 + 2f_{12}\,dx_1\,dx_2 + f_{22}\,dx_2^2. \qquad (2.95)$$

For Equation 2.95 to be unambiguously negative for any change in the x's (that is, for any choices of dx_1 and dx_2), it is obviously necessary that f_{11} and f_{22} be negative. If, for example, $dx_2 = 0$, then

$$d^2y = f_{11}\,dx_1^2 \qquad (2.96)$$

and $d^2y < 0$ implies

$$f_{11} < 0. \qquad (2.97)$$

An identical argument can be made for f_{22} by setting $dx_1 = 0$. If neither dx_1 nor dx_2 is 0, we then must consider the cross partial, f_{12}, in deciding whether or not d^2y is unambiguously negative. Relatively simple algebra can be used to show that the required condition is[14]

$$f_{11}f_{22} - f_{12}^2 > 0. \qquad (2.98)$$

Concave functions

Intuitively, what Equation 2.98 requires is that the own second partial derivatives (f_{11} and f_{22}) be sufficiently negative so that their product (which is positive) will outweigh any possible perverse effects from the cross-partial derivatives ($f_{12} = f_{21}$). Functions that obey such a condition are called *concave functions*. In three dimensions, such functions resemble inverted teacups (for an illustration, see Example 2.10). This image makes it clear that a flat spot on such a function is indeed a true maximum because the function always slopes downward from such a spot. More generally, concave functions have the property that they always lie below any plane that is tangent to them—the plane defined by the maximum value of the function is simply a special case of this property.

EXAMPLE 2.9 Second-Order Conditions: Health Status for the Last Time

In Example 2.3 we considered the health status function

$$y = f(x_1, x_2) = -x_1^2 + 2x_1 - x_2^2 + 4x_2 + 5. \qquad (2.99)$$

The first-order conditions for a maximum are

$$\begin{aligned} f_1 &= -2x_1 + 2 = 0, \\ f_2 &= -2x_2 + 4 = 0 \end{aligned} \qquad (2.100)$$

or

$$\begin{aligned} x_1^* &= 1, \\ x_2^* &= 2. \end{aligned} \qquad (2.101)$$

---

[14]The proof proceeds by adding and subtracting the term $(f_{12}\,dx_2)^2/f_{11}$ to Equation 2.95 and factoring. But this approach is only applicable to this special case. A more easily generalized approach that uses matrix algebra recognizes that Equation 2.95 is a "Quadratic Form" in dx_1 and dx_2, and that Equations 2.97 and 2.98 amount to requiring that the Hessian matrix

$$\begin{bmatrix} f_{11} & f_{12} \\ f_{21} & f_{22} \end{bmatrix}$$

be "negative definite." In particular, Equation 2.98 requires that the determinant of this Hessian be positive. For a discussion, see the Extensions to this chapter.

The second-order partial derivatives for Equation 2.99 are

$$f_{11} = -2,$$
$$f_{22} = -2,$$
$$f_{12} = 0. \tag{2.102}$$

These derivatives clearly obey Equations 2.97 and 2.98, so both necessary and sufficient conditions for a local maximum are satisfied.[15]

QUERY: Describe the concave shape of the health status function and indicate why it has only a single global maximum value.

Constrained maximization

As another illustration of second-order conditions, consider the problem of choosing x_1 and x_2 to maximize

$$y = f(x_1, x_2), \tag{2.103}$$

subject to the linear constraint

$$c - b_1 x_1 - b_2 x_2 = 0 \tag{2.104}$$

(where c, b_1, b_2 are constant parameters in the problem). This problem is of a type that will be frequently encountered in this book and is a special case of the constrained maximum problems that we examined earlier. There we showed that the first-order conditions for a maximum may be derived by setting up the Lagrangian expression

$$\mathcal{L} = f(x_1, x_2) + \lambda(c - b_1 x_1 - b_2 x_2). \tag{2.105}$$

Partial differentiation with respect to x_1, x_2, and λ yields the familiar results:

$$f_1 - \lambda b_1 = 0,$$
$$f_2 - \lambda b_2 = 0,$$
$$c - b_1 x_1 - b_2 x_2 = 0. \tag{2.106}$$

These equations can in general be solved for the optimal values of x_1, x_2, and λ. To ensure that the point derived in that way is a local maximum, we must again examine movements away from the critical points by using the "second" total differential:

$$d^2 y = f_{11} dx_1^2 + 2f_{12} dx_1 dx_2 + f_{22} dx_2^2. \tag{2.107}$$

In this case, however, not all possible small changes in the x's are permissible. Only those values of x_1 and x_2 that continue to satisfy the constraint can be considered valid alternatives to the critical point. To examine such changes, we must calculate the total differential of the constraint:

$$-b_1 dx_1 - b_2 dx_2 = 0 \tag{2.108}$$

or

$$dx_2 = -\frac{b_1}{b_2} dx_1. \tag{2.109}$$

[15]Notice that Equations 2.102 obey the sufficient conditions not only at the critical point but also for all possible choices of x_1 and x_2. That is, the function is concave. In more complex examples this need not be the case: The second-order conditions need be satisfied only at the critical point for a local maximum to occur.

This equation shows the relative changes in x_1 and x_2 that are allowable in considering movements from the critical point. To proceed further on this problem, we need to use the first-order conditions. The first two of these imply

$$\frac{f_1}{f_2} = \frac{b_1}{b_2},$$

(2.110)

and combining this result with Equation 2.109 yields

$$dx_2 = -\frac{f_1}{f_2} dx_1.$$

(2.111)

We now substitute this expression for dx_2 in Equation 2.107 to demonstrate the conditions that must hold for d^2y to be negative:

$$d^2y = f_{11} dx_1^2 + 2f_{12} dx_1 \left(-\frac{f_1}{f_2} dx_1 \right) + f_{22} \left(-\frac{f_1}{f_2} dx_1 \right)^2$$

$$= f_{11} dx_1^2 - 2f_{12} \frac{f_1}{f_2} dx_1^2 + f_{22} \frac{f_1^2}{f_2^2} dx_1^2.$$

(2.112)

Combining terms and putting each over a common denominator gives

$$d^2y = (f_{11} f_2^2 - 2f_{12} f_1 f_2 + f_{22} f_1^2) \frac{dx_1^2}{f_2^2}.$$

(2.113)

Consequently, for $d^2y < 0$, it must be the case that

$$f_{11} f_2^2 - 2f_{12} f_1 f_2 + f_{22} f_1^2 < 0.$$

(2.114)

Quasi-concave functions

Although Equation 2.114 appears to be little more than an inordinately complex mass of mathematical symbols, in fact the condition is an important one. It characterizes a set of functions termed *quasi-concave functions*. These functions have the property that the set of all points for which such a function takes on a value greater than any specific constant is a convex set (that is, any two points in the set can be joined by a line contained completely within the set). Many economic models are characterized by such functions and, as we will see in considerable detail in Chapter 3, in these cases the condition for quasi-concavity has a relatively simple economic interpretation. Problems 2.9 and 2.10 examine two specific quasi-concave functions that we will frequently encounter in this book. Example 2.10 shows the relationship between concave and quasi-concave functions.

EXAMPLE 2.10 Concave and Quasi-Concave Functions

The differences between concave and quasi-concave functions can be illustrated with the function[16]

$$y = f(x_1, x_2) = (x_1 \cdot x_2)^k,$$

(2.115)

where the x's take on only positive values, and the parameter k can take on a variety of positive values.

---

[16]This function is a special case of the Cobb-Douglas function. See also Problem 2.10 and the Extensions to this chapter for more details on this function.

No matter what value k takes, this function is quasi-concave. One way to show this is to look at the "level curves" of the function by setting y equal to a specific value, say c. In this case

$$y = c = (x_1 x_2)^k \quad \text{or} \quad x_1 x_2 = c^{1/k} = c'. \tag{2.116}$$

But this is just the equation of a standard rectangular hyperbola. Clearly the set of points for which y takes on values larger than c is convex because it is bounded by this hyperbola.

A more mathematical way to show quasi-concavity would apply Equation 2.114 to this function. Although the algebra of doing this is a bit messy, it may be worth the struggle. The various components of Equation 2.114 are:

$$\begin{aligned}
f_1 &= k x_1^{k-1} x_2^k, \\
f_2 &= k x_1^k x_2^{k-1}, \\
f_{11} &= k(k-1) x_1^{k-2} x_2^k, \\
f_{22} &= k(k-1) x_1^k x_2^{k-2}, \\
f_{12} &= k^2 x_1^{k-1} x_2^{k-1}.
\end{aligned} \tag{2.117}$$

So,

$$\begin{aligned}
f_{11} f_2^2 - 2 f_{12} f_1 f_2 + f_{22} f_1^2 &= k^3(k-1) x_1^{3k-2} x_2^{3k-2} - 2 k^4 x_1^{3k-2} x_2^{3k-2} \\
&\quad + k^3(k-1) x_1^{3k-2} x_2^{3k-2} \\
&= 2 k^3 x_1^{3k-2} x_2^{3k-2}(-1),
\end{aligned} \tag{2.118}$$

which is clearly negative, as is required for quasi-concavity.

Whether or not the function f is concave depends on the value of k. If $k < 0.5$ the function is indeed concave. An intuitive way to see this is to consider only points where $x_1 = x_2$. For these points,

$$y = (x_1^2)^k = x_1^{2k}, \tag{2.119}$$

which, for $k < 0.5$, is concave. Alternatively, for $k > 0.5$, this function is convex.

A more definitive proof makes use of the partial derivatives from Equation 2.117. In this case the condition for concavity can be expressed as

$$\begin{aligned}
f_{11} f_{22} - f_{12}^2 &= k^2(k-1)^2 x_1^{2k-2} x_2^{2k-2} - k^4 x_1^{2k-2} x_2^{2k-2} \\
&= x_1^{2k-2} x_2^{2k-2} [k^2(k-1)^2 - k^4] \\
&= x_1^{2k-1} x_2^{2k-1} [k^2(-2k+1)],
\end{aligned} \tag{2.120}$$

and this expression is positive (as is required for concavity) for

$$(-2k+1) > 0 \quad \text{or} \quad k < 0.5.$$

On the other hand, the function is convex for $k > 0.5$.

A graphic illustration. Figure 2.4 provides three-dimensional illustrations of three specific examples of this function: for $k = 0.2$, $k = 0.5$, and $k = 1$. Notice that in all three cases the level curves of the function have hyperbolic, convex shapes. That is, for any fixed value of y the functions are quite similar. This shows the quasi-concavity of the function. The primary differences among the functions are illustrated by the way in which the value of y increases as

(*continued*)

EXAMPLE 2.10   CONTINUED

both *x*'s increase together. In Figure 2.4a (when *k* = 0.2), the increase in *y* slows as the *x*'s increase. This gives the function a rounded, teacuplike shape that indicates its concavity. For *k* = 0.5, *y* appears to increase linearly with increases in both of the *x*'s. This is the borderline between concavity and convexity. Finally, when *k* = 1 (as in Figure 2.4c), simultaneous increases in the values of both of the *x*'s increase *y* very rapidly. The spine of the function looks convex to reflect such increasing returns.

FIGURE 2.4   Concave and Quasi-Concave Functions

In all three cases these functions are quasi-concave. For a fixed *y*, their level curves are convex. But only for *k* = 0.2 is the function strictly concave. The case *k* = 1.0 clearly shows nonconcavity because the function is not below its tangent plane.

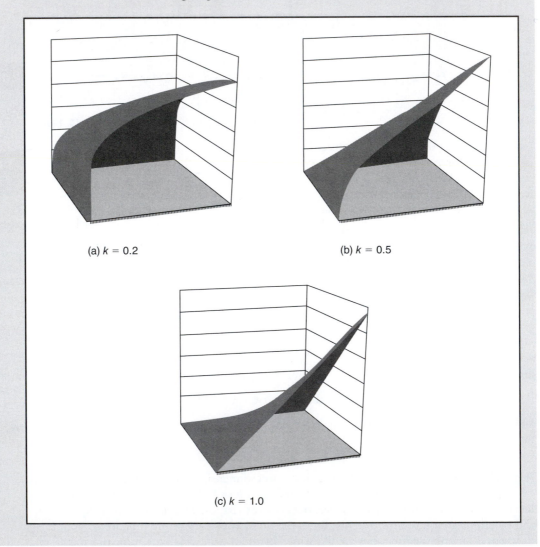

(a) *k* = 0.2

(b) *k* = 0.5

(c) *k* = 1.0

A careful look at Figure 2.4a suggests that any function that is concave will also be quasi-concave. You are asked to prove that this is indeed the case in Problem 2.8. This example shows that the converse of this statement is not true—quasi-concave functions need not necessarily be concave. Most functions we will encounter in this book will also illustrate this fact; most will be quasi-concave but not necessarily concave.

QUERY: Explain why the functions illustrated both in Figure 2.4a and 2.4c would have maximum values if the x's were subject to a linear constraint, but only the graph in Figure 2.4a would have an unconstrained maximum.

HOMOGENEOUS FUNCTIONS

Many of the functions that arise naturally out of economic theory have additional mathematical properties. One particularly important set of properties relates to how the functions behave when all (or most) of their arguments are increased proportionally. Such situations arise when we ask questions such as what would happen if all prices increased by 10 percent or how would a firm's output change if it doubled all of the inputs that it uses. Thinking about these questions leads naturally to the concept of homogeneous functions. Specifically, a function $f(x_1, x_2, \ldots, x_n)$ is said to be homogeneous of degree k if

$$f(tx_1, tx_2, \ldots, tx_n) = t^k f(x_1, x_2, \ldots, x_n). \tag{2.121}$$

The most important examples of homogeneous functions are those for which $k = 1$ or $k = 0$. In words, when a function is homogeneous of degree one, a doubling of all of its arguments doubles the value of the function itself. For functions that are homogeneous of degree 0, a doubling of all of its arguments leaves the value of the function unchanged. Functions may also be homogeneous for changes in only certain subsets of their arguments—that is, a doubling of some of the x's may double the value of the function if the other arguments of the function are held constant. Usually, however, homogeneity applies to changes in all of the arguments in a function.

Homogeneity and derivatives

If a function is homogeneous of degree k and can be differentiated, the partial derivatives of the function will be homogeneous of degree $k - 1$. A proof of this follows directly from the definition of homogeneity. For example, differentiating Equation 2.121 with respect to its first argument gives

$$\frac{\partial f(tx_1, \ldots, tx_n)}{\partial x_1} \cdot t = t^k \frac{\partial f(x_1, \ldots, x_n)}{\partial x_1}$$

or

$$f_1(tx_1, \ldots, tx_n) = t^{k-1} f_1(x_1, \ldots, x_n), \tag{2.122}$$

which shows that f_1 meets the definition for homogeneity of degree $k - 1$. Because marginal ideas are so prevalent in microeconomic theory, this property shows that some important properties of marginal effects can be inferred from the properties of the underlying function itself.

Euler's theorem

Another useful feature of homogeneous functions can be shown by differentiating the definition for homogeneity with respect to the proportionality factor, t. In this case, we differentiate the right side of Equation 2.121 first:

$$kt^{k-1}f_1(x_1,\ldots,x_n) = x_1 f_1(tx_1,\ldots,tx_n) + \cdots + x_n f_n(tx_1,\ldots,tx_n).$$

If we let $t = 1$, this equation becomes

$$kf(x_1,\ldots,x_n) = x_1 f_1(x_1,\ldots,x_n) + \cdots + x_n f_n(x_1,\ldots,x_n). \tag{2.123}$$

This equation is termed Euler's theorem (after the mathematician who also discovered the constant e) for homogeneous functions. It shows that, for a homogeneous function, there is a definite relationship between the values of the function and the values of its partial derivatives. Several important economic relationships among functions are based on this observation.

Homothetic functions

A homothetic function is one that is formed by taking a monotonic transformation of a homogeneous function.[17] Monotonic transformations, by definition, preserve the order of the relationship between the arguments of a function and the value of that function. If certain sets of x's yield larger values for f, they will also yield larger values for a monotonic transformation of f. Because monotonic transformations may take many forms, however, they would not be expected to preserve an exact mathematical relationship such as that embodied in homogeneous functions. Consider, for example, the function $f(x,y) = x \cdot y$. Clearly this function is homogeneous of degree 2—a doubling of its two arguments will multiply the value of the function by 4. But the monotonic transformation, F, that simply adds 1 to f [that is, $F(f) = f + 1 = xy + 1$] is not homogeneous at all. Hence, except in special cases, homothetic functions do not possess the homogeneity properties of their underlying functions. Homothetic functions do, however, preserve one nice feature of homogeneous functions. This property is that the implicit trade-offs among the variables in a function depend only on the ratios of those variables, not on their absolute values. Here we show this for the simple two-variable, implicit function $f(x,y) = 0$. It will be easier to demonstrate more general cases when we get to the economics of the matter later in this book.

Equation 2.28 showed that the implicit trade-off between x and y for a two-variable function is given by

$$\frac{dy}{dx} = -\frac{f_x}{f_y}.$$

If we assume f is homogeneous of degree k, its partial derivatives will be homogeneous of degree $k - 1$ and the implicit trade-off between x and y is

$$\frac{dy}{dx} = -\frac{t^{k-1}f_x(tx,ty)}{t^{k-1}f_y(tx,ty)} = -\frac{f_x(tx,ty)}{f_y(tx,ty)}. \tag{2.124}$$

Now let $t = 1/y$ and Equation 2.124 becomes

$$\frac{dy}{dx} = -\frac{f_x(x/y,1)}{f_y(x/y,1)}, \tag{2.125}$$

which shows that the trade-off depends only on the ratio of x to y. Now if we apply any monotonic transformation, F (with $F' > 0$), to the original homogeneous function f, we have

---

[17]Because a limiting case of a monotonic transformation is to leave the function unchanged, all homogeneous functions are also homothetic.

$$\frac{dy}{dx} = -\frac{F'f_x(x/y, 1)}{F'f_y(x/y, 1)} = -\frac{f_x(x/y, 1)}{f_y(x/y, 1)}, \tag{2.126}$$

and this shows both that the trade-off is unaffected by the monotonic transformation and that it remains a function only of the ratio of x to y. In Chapter 3 (and elsewhere) this property will make it very convenient to discuss some theoretical results with simple two-dimensional graphs, for which we need not consider the overall levels of key variables, but only their ratios.

EXAMPLE 2.11 Cardinal and Ordinal Properties

In applied economics it is sometimes important to know the exact numerical relationship among variables. For example, in the study of production, one might wish to know precisely how much extra output would be produced by hiring another worker. This is a question about the "cardinal" (i.e., numerical) properties of the production function. In other cases, one may only care about the order in which various points are ranked. In the theory of utility, for example, we assume that people can rank bundles of goods and will choose the bundle with the highest ranking, but that there are no unique numerical values assigned to these rankings. Mathematically, ordinal properties of functions are preserved by any monotonic transformation because, by definition, a monotonic transformation preserves order. Usually, however, cardinal properties are not preserved by arbitrary monotonic transformations.

These distinctions are illustrated by the functions we examined in Example 2.10. There we studied monotonic transformations of the function

$$f(x_1, x_2) = (x_1 x_2)^k \tag{2.127}$$

by considering various values of the parameter k. We showed that quasi-concavity (an ordinal property) was preserved for all values of k. Hence, when approaching problems that focus on maximizing or minimizing such a function subject to linear constraints we need not worry about precisely which transformation is used. On the other hand, the function in Equation 2.127 is concave (a cardinal property) only for a narrow range of values of k. Many monotonic transformations destroy the concavity of f.

The function in Equation 2.127 also can be used to illustrate the difference between homogeneous and homothetic functions. A proportional increase in the two arguments of f would yield

$$f(tx_1, tx_2) = t^{2k} x_1 x_2 = t^{2k} f(x_1, x_2). \tag{2.128}$$

Hence, the degree of homogeneity for this function depends on k—that is, the degree of homogeneity is not preserved independently of which monotonic transformation is used. Alternatively, the function in Equation 2.127 is homothetic because

$$\frac{dx_2}{dx_1} = -\frac{f_1}{f_2} = -\frac{k x_1^{k-1} x_2^k}{k x_1^k x_2^{k-1}} = -\frac{x_2}{x_1}. \tag{2.129}$$

That is, the trade-off between x_2 and x_1 depends only on the ratio of these two variables and is unaffected by the value of k. Hence, homotheticity is an ordinal property. As we shall see, this property is quite convenient when developing graphical arguments about economic propositions.

QUERY: How would the discussion in this example be changed if we considered monotonic transformations of the form $f(x_1, x_2, k) = x_1 x_2 + k$ for various values of k?

INTEGRATION

Integration is another of the tools of calculus that finds a number of applications in microeconomic theory. The technique is used both to calculate areas that measure various economic outcomes and, more generally, to provide a way of summing up outcomes that occur over time or across individuals. Our treatment of the topic here necessarily must be brief, so readers desiring a more complete background should consult the references at the end of this chapter.

Anti-derivatives

Formally, integration is the inverse of differentiation. When you are asked to calculate the integral of a function, $f(x)$, you are being asked to find a function that has $f(x)$ as its derivative. If we call this "anti-derivative" $F(x)$, this function is supposed to have the property that

$$\frac{dF(x)}{dx} = F'(x) = f(x). \qquad \textbf{(2.130)}$$

If such a function exists then we denote it as

$$F(x) = \int f(x)\,dx. \qquad \textbf{(2.131)}$$

The precise reason for this rather odd-looking notation will be described in detail later. First, let's look at a few examples. If $f(x) = x$ then

$$F(x) = \int f(x)\,dx = \int x\,dx = \frac{x^2}{2} + C, \qquad \textbf{(2.132)}$$

where C is an arbitrary "constant of integration" that disappears upon differentiation. The correctness of this result can be easily verified:

$$F'(x) = \frac{d(x^2/2 + C)}{dx} = x + 0 = x. \qquad \textbf{(2.133)}$$

Calculating anti-derivatives

Calculation of anti-derivatives can be extremely simple, or difficult, or agonizing, or impossible, depending on the particular $f(x)$ specified. Here we will look at three simple methods for making such calculations, but, as you might expect, these will not always work.

1. *Creative guesswork.* Probably the most common way of finding integrals (anti-derivatives) is to work backwards by asking "what function will yield $f(x)$ as its derivative?" Here are a few obvious examples:

$$
\begin{aligned}
F(x) &= \int x^2\,dx = \frac{x^3}{3} + C, \\
F(x) &= \int x^n\,dx = \frac{x^{n+1}}{n+1} + C, \\
F(x) &= \int (ax^2 + bx + c)\,dx = \frac{ax^3}{3} + \frac{bx^2}{2} + cx + C, \\
F(x) &= \int e^x\,dx = e^x + C, \\
F(x) &= \int a^x\,dx = \frac{a^x}{\ln a} + C, \\
F(x) &= \int \left(\frac{1}{x}\right) dx = \ln(|x|) + C, \\
F(x) &= \int (\ln x)\,dx = x\ln x - x + C.
\end{aligned}
\qquad \textbf{(2.134)}
$$

You should use differentiation to check that all of these obey the property that $F'(x) = f(x)$. Notice that in every case the integral includes a constant of integration because anti-derivatives are unique only up to an additive constant which would become zero upon differentiation. For many purposes, the results in Equation 2.134 (or trivial generalizations of them) will be sufficient for our purposes in this book. Nevertheless, here are two more methods that may work when intuition fails.

2. Change of variable. A clever redefinition of variables may sometimes make a function much easier to integrate. For example, it is not at all obvious what the integral of $2x/(1 + x^2)$ is. But, if we let $y = 1 + x^2$, then $dy = 2xdx$ and

$$\int \frac{2x}{1 + x^2} \, dx = \int \frac{1}{y} \, dy = \ln(|y|) = \ln(|1 + x^2|). \tag{2.135}$$

The key to this procedure is in breaking the original function into a term in y and a term in dy. It takes a lot of practice to see patterns for which this will work.

3. Integration by parts. A similar method for finding integrals makes use of the differential expression $duv = udv + vdu$ for any two functions u and v. Integration of this differential yields

$$\int duv = uv = \int u \, dv + \int v \, du \quad \text{or} \quad \int u \, dv = uv - \int v \, du. \tag{2.136}$$

Here the strategy is to define functions u and v in a way that the unknown integral on the left can be calculated by the difference between the two known expressions on the right. For example, it is by no means obvious what the integral of xe^x is. But we can define $u = x$ (so $du = dx$) and $dv = e^x dx$ (so $v = e^x$). Hence we now have

$$\int xe^x \, dx = \int u \, dv = uv - \int v \, du = xe^x - \int e^x \, dx = (x - 1)e^x + C. \tag{2.137}$$

Again, only practice can suggest useful patterns in the ways in which u and v can be defined.

Definite integrals

The integrals we have been discussing so far are "indefinite" integrals—they provide only a general function that is the anti-derivative of another function. A somewhat different, though related, approach uses integration to sum up the area under a graph of a function over some defined interval. Figure 2.5 illustrates this process. We wish to know the area under the function $f(x)$ from $x = a$ to $x = b$. One way to do this would be to partition the interval into narrow slivers of $x(\Delta x)$ and sum up the areas of the rectangles shown in the figure. That is:

$$\text{area under } f(x) \approx \sum_i f(x_i)\Delta x_i, \tag{2.138}$$

where the notation is intended to indicate that the height of each rectangle is approximated by the value of $f(x)$ for a value of x in the interval. Taking this process to the limit by shrinking the size of the Δx intervals yields an exact measure of the area we want and is denoted by:

$$\text{area under } f(x) = \int_{x=a}^{x=b} f(x) \, dx. \tag{2.139}$$

This then explains the origin of the oddly shaped integral sign—it is a stylized S, indicating "sum." As we shall see, integrating is a very general way of summing the values of a continuous function over some interval.

FIGURE 2.5   Definite Integrals Show the Areas under the Graph of a Function

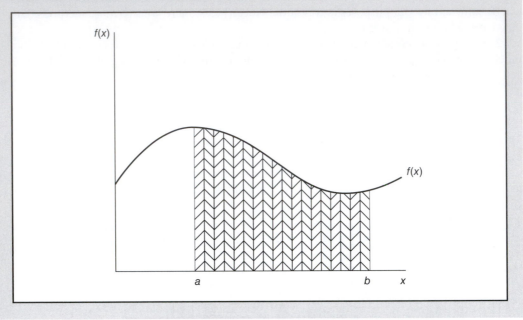

Definite integrals measure the area under a curve by summing rectangular areas as shown in the graph. The dimension of each rectangle is $f(x)dx$.

Fundamental theorem of calculus

Evaluating the integral in Equation 2.139 is very simple if we know the anti-derivative of $f(x)$, say, $F(x)$. In this case we have

$$\text{area under } f(x) = \int_{x=a}^{x=b} f(x)\, dx = F(b) - F(a). \tag{2.140}$$

That is, all we need do is calculate the anti-derivative of $f(x)$ and subtract the value of this function at the lower limit of integration from its value at the upper limit of integration. This result is sometimes termed the "fundamental theorem of calculus" because it directly ties together the two principal tools of calculus, derivatives and integrals. In Example 2.12, we show that this result is much more general than simply a way to measure areas. It can be used to illustrate one of the primary conceptual principles of economics—the distinction between "stocks" and "flows."

EXAMPLE 2.12 Stocks and Flows

The definite integral provides a useful way for summing up any function that is providing a continuous flow over time. For example, suppose that net population increase (births minus deaths) for a country can be approximated by the function $f(t) = 1{,}000e^{0.02t}$. Hence, the net population change is growing at the rate of 2 percent per year—it is 1,000 new people in year 0, 1,020 new people in the first year, 1,041 in the second year, and so forth. Suppose we wish to know how much in total the population will increase within 50 years. This might be a tedious calculation without calculus, but using the fundamental theorem of calculus provides an easy answer:

$$\text{increase in population} = \int_{t=0}^{t=50} f(t)\, dt = \int_{t=0}^{t=50} 1{,}000e^{0.02t}\, dt = F(t)\Big|_0^{50}$$

$$= \frac{1{,}000e^{0.02t}}{0.02}\bigg|_0^{50} = \frac{1{,}000e}{0.02} - 50{,}000 = 85{,}914 \qquad \textbf{(2.141)}$$

[where the notation $\big|_a^b$ indicates that the expression is to be evaluated as $F(b) - F(a)$]. Hence, the conclusion is that the population will grow by nearly 86,000 people over the next 50 years. Notice how the fundamental theorem of calculus ties together a "flow" concept, net population increase (which is measured as an amount *per year*), with a "stock" concept, total population (which is measured at a specific date and does not have a time dimension). Note also that the 86,000 calculation refers only to the total *increase* between year zero and year fifty. In order to know the actual total population at any date we would have to add the number of people in the population at year zero. That would be similar to choosing a constant of integration in this specific problem.

Now consider an application with more economic content. Suppose that total costs for a particular firm are given by $C(q) = 0.1q^2 + 500$ (where q represents output during some period). Here the term $0.1q^2$ represents variable costs (costs that vary with output) whereas the 500 figure represents fixed costs. Marginal costs for this production process can be found through differentiation—$MC = dC(q)/dq = 0.2q$—hence, marginal costs are increasing with q and fixed costs drop out upon differentiation. What are the total costs associated with producing, say, $q = 100$? One way to answer this question is to use the total cost function directly: $C(100) = 0.1(100)^2 + 500 = 1{,}500$. An alternative way would be to integrate marginal cost over the range 0 to 100 to get total variable cost:

$$\text{variable cost} = \int_{q=0}^{q=100} 0.2q\, dq = 0.1q^2\Big|_0^{100} = 1{,}000 - 0 = 1{,}000, \qquad \textbf{(2.142)}$$

to which we would have to add fixed costs of 500 (the constant of integration in this problem) to get total costs. Of course, this method of arriving at total cost is much more cumbersome than just using the equation for total cost directly. But the derivation does show that total variable cost between any two output levels can be found through integration as the area below the marginal cost curve—a conclusion that we will find useful in some graphical applications.

QUERY: How would you calculate the total variable cost associated with expanding output from 100 to 110? Explain why fixed costs do not enter into this calculation.

Differentiating a definite integral

Occasionally we will wish to differentiate a definite integral—usually in the context of seeking to maximize the value of this integral. Although performing such differentiations can sometimes be rather complex, there are a few rules that should make the process easier.

1. *Differentiation with respect to the variable of integration*. This is a trick question, but instructive nonetheless. A definite integral has a constant value; hence its derivative is zero. That is:

$$\frac{d\int_a^b f(x)\, dx}{dx} = 0. \qquad \textbf{(2.143)}$$

The summing process required for integration has already been accomplished once we write down a definite integral. It does not matter whether the variable of integration is x or t or anything else. The value of this integrated sum will not change when the variable x changes, no matter what x is (but see rule 3 below).

2. *Differentiation with respect to the upper bound of integration*. Changing the upper bound of integration will obviously change the value of a definite integral. In this case, we must make a distinction between the variable determining the upper bound of integration (say, x) and the variable of integration (say, t). The result then is a simple application of the fundamental theorem of calculus. For example:

$$\frac{d\int_a^x f(t)\,dt}{dx} = \frac{d[F(x) - F(a)]}{dx} = f(x) - 0 = f(x), \qquad \textbf{(2.144)}$$

where $F(x)$ is the antiderivative of $f(x)$. By referring back to Figure 2.5 we can see why this conclusion makes sense—we are asking how the value of the definite integral changes if x increases slightly. Obviously, the answer is that the value of the integral increases by the height of $f(x)$ (notice that this value will ultimately depend on the specified value of x).

If the upper bound of integration is a function of x, this result can be generalized using the chain rule:

$$\frac{d\int_a^{g(x)} f(t)\,dt}{d(x)} = \frac{d[F(g(x)) - F(a)]}{dx} = \frac{d[F(g(x))]}{dx} = f\frac{dg(x)}{dx} = fg'(x), \qquad \textbf{(2.145)}$$

where, again, the specific value for this derivative would depend on the value of x assumed.

Finally, notice that differentiation with respect to a lower bound of integration just changes the sign of this expression:

$$\frac{d\int_{g(x)}^b f(t)\,dt}{dx} = \frac{d[F(b) - F(g(x))]}{dx} = -\frac{dF(g(x))}{dx} = -fg'(x). \qquad \textbf{(2.146)}$$

3. *Differentiation with respect to another relevant variable*. In some cases we may wish to integrate an expression that is a function of several variables. In general, this can involve multiple integrals and differentiation can become quite complicated. But there is one simple case that should be mentioned. Suppose that we have a function of two variables, $f(x, y)$, and that we wish to integrate this function with respect to the variable x. The specific value for this integral will obviously depend on the value of y and we might even ask how that value changes when y changes. In this case, it is possible to "differentiate through the integral sign" to obtain a result. That is:

$$\frac{d\int_a^b f(x, y)\,dx}{dy} = \int_a^b f_y(x, y)\,dx. \qquad \textbf{(2.147)}$$

This expression shows that we can first partially differentiate $f(x, y)$ with respect to y before proceeding to compute the value of the definite integral. Of course, the resulting value may still depend on the specific value that is assigned to y, but often it will yield more economic insights than the original problem does. Some further examples of using definite integrals are found in Problem 2.8.

DYNAMIC OPTIMIZATION

Some optimization problems that arise in microeconomics involve multiple periods.[18] We are interested in finding the optimal time path for a variable or set of variables that succeeds in optimizing some goal. For example, an individual may wish to choose a path of lifetime

---

[18] Throughout this section we treat dynamic optimization problems as occurring over time. In other contexts, the same techniques can be used to solve optimization problems that occur across a continuum of firms or individuals when the optimal choices for one agent affect what is optimal for others.

consumptions that maximizes his or her utility. Or a firm may seek a path for input and output choices that maximizes the present value of all future profits. The particular feature of such problems that makes them difficult is that decisions made in one period affect outcomes in later periods. Hence, one must explicitly take account of this interrelationship in choosing optimal paths. If decisions in one period did not affect later periods, the problem would not have a "dynamic" structure—one could just proceed to optimize decisions in each period without regard for what comes next. Here, however, we wish to explicitly allow for dynamic considerations.

The optimal control problem

Mathematicians and economists have developed many techniques for solving problems in dynamic optimization. The references at the end of this chapter provide broad introductions to these methods. Here, however, we will be concerned with only one such method that has many similarities to the optimization techniques discussed earlier in this chapter—the optimal control problem. The framework of the problem is relatively simple. A decision maker wishes to find the optimal time path for some variable $x(t)$ over a specified time interval $[t_0, t_1]$. Changes in x are governed by a differential equation:

$$\frac{dx(t)}{dt} = g[x(t), c(t), t], \tag{2.148}$$

where the variable $c(t)$ is used to "control" the change in $x(t)$. In each period of time, the decision maker derives value from x and c according to the function $f[x(t), c(t), t]$ and his or her goal to optimize $\int_{t_0}^{t_1} f[x(t), c(t), t]\, dt$. Often this problem will also be subject to "endpoint" constraints on the variable x. These might be written as $x(t_0) = x_0$ and $x(t_1) = x_1$.

Notice how this problem is "dynamic." Any decision about how much to change x this period will affect not only the future value of x, it will also affect future values of the outcome function f. The problem then is how to keep $x(t)$ on its optimal path.

Economic intuition can help to solve this problem. Suppose that we just focused on the function f and chose x and c to maximize it at each instant of time. There are two difficulties with this "myopic" approach. First, we are not really free to "choose" x at any time. Rather, the value of x will be determined by its initial value x_0 and by its history of changes as given by Equation 2.148. A second problem with this myopic approach is that it disregards the dynamic nature of the problem by not asking how this period's decisions affect the future. We need some way to reflect the dynamics of this problem in a single period's decisions. Assigning the correct value (price) to x at each instant of time will do just that. Because this implicit price will have many similarities to the Lagrangian multipliers studied earlier in this chapter, we will call it $\lambda(t)$. The value of x is treated as a function of time because the importance of x can obviously change over time.

The maximum principle

Now let's look at the decision maker's problem at a single point in time. He or she must be concerned with both the current value of the objective function $f[x(t), c(t), t]$ and with the implied change in the value of $x(t)$. Because the current value of $x(t)$ is given by $\lambda(t)x(t)$, the instantaneous rate of change of this value is given by:

$$\frac{d[\lambda(t)x(t)]}{dt} = \lambda(t)\frac{dx(t)}{dt} + x(t)\frac{d\lambda(t)}{dt}, \tag{2.149}$$

and so at any time t a comprehensive measure of the value of concern[19] to the decision maker is

$$H = f[x(t),\, c(t),\, t] + \lambda(t)g[x(t), c(t), t] + x(t)\frac{d\lambda(t)}{dt}. \qquad (2.150)$$

This comprehensive value represents both the current benefits being received and the instantaneous change in the value of x. Now we can ask what conditions must hold for $x(t)$ and $c(t)$ to optimize this expression.[20] That is:

$$\frac{\partial H}{\partial c} = f_c + \lambda g_c = 0 \quad \text{or} \quad f_c = -\lambda g_c;$$

$$\frac{\partial H}{\partial x} = f_x + \lambda g_x + \frac{d\lambda(t)}{dt} = 0 \quad \text{or} \quad f_x + \lambda g_x = -\frac{\partial \lambda(t)}{\partial t}. \qquad (2.151)$$

These are then the two optimality conditions for this dynamic problem. They are usually referred to as the "maximum principle." This solution to the optimal control problem was first proposed by the Russian mathematician L. S. Pontryagin and his colleagues in the early 1960s.

Although the logic of the maximum principle can best be illustrated by the economic applications we will encounter later in this book, a brief summary of the intuition behind them may be helpful. The first condition asks about the optimal choice of c. It suggests that, at the margin, the gain from c in terms of the function f must be balanced by the losses from c in terms of the value of its ability to change x. That is, present gains must be weighed against future costs.

The second condition relates to the characteristics that an optimal time path of $x(t)$ should have. It implies that, at the margin, any net gains from more current x (either in terms of f or in terms of the accompanying value of changes in x) must be balanced by changes in the implied value of x itself. That is, the net current gain from more x must be weighed against the declining future value of x.

EXAMPLE 2.13 Allocating a Fixed Supply

As an extremely simple illustration of the maximum principle, assume that someone has inherited 1,000 bottles of wine from a rich uncle. He or she intends to drink these bottles over the next 20 years. How should this be done to maximize the utility from doing so?

Suppose that this person's utility function for wine is given by $u[c(t)] = \ln c(t)$. Hence the utility from wine drinking exhibits diminishing marginal utility ($u' > 0, u'' < 0$). This person's goal is to maximize

$$\int_0^{20} u[c(t)]\, dt = \int_0^{20} \ln c(t)\, dt. \qquad (2.152)$$

Let $x(t)$ represent the number of bottles of wine remaining at time t. This series is constrained by $x(0) = 1,000$ and $x(20) = 0$. The differential equation determining the evolution of $x(t)$ takes the simple form:[21]

---

[19]We denote this current value expression by H to suggest its similarity to the Hamiltonian expression used in formal dynamic optimization theory. Usually the Hamiltonian does not have the final term in Equation 2.150, however.

[20]Notice that the variable x is not really a choice variable here—its value is determined by history. Differentiation with respect to x can be regarded as implicitly asking the question: "If $x(t)$ were optimal, what characteristics would it have?"

[21]The simple form of this differential equation (where dx/dt depends only on the value of the control variable, c) means that this problem is identical to one explored using the "calculus of variations" approach to dynamic optimization. In such a case, one can substitute dx/dt into the function f and the first-order conditions for a maximum can be compressed into

$$\frac{dx(t)}{dt} = -c(t).$$
(2.153)

That is, each instant's consumption just reduces the stock of remaining bottles. The current value Hamiltonian expression for this problem is

$$H = \ln c(t) + \lambda[-c(t)] + x(t)\frac{d\lambda}{dt},$$
(2.154)

and the first-order conditions for a maximum are

$$\frac{\partial H}{\partial c} = \frac{1}{c} - \lambda = 0,$$

$$\frac{\partial H}{\partial x} = \frac{d\lambda}{dt} = 0.$$
(2.155)

The second of these conditions requires that λ (the implicit value of wine) be constant over time. This makes intuitive sense: because consuming a bottle of wine always reduces the available stock by one bottle, any solution where the value of wine differed over time would provide an incentive to change behavior by drinking more wine when it is cheap and less when it is expensive. Combining this second condition for a maximum with the first condition implies that $c(t)$ itself must be constant over time. If $c(t) = k$, the number of bottles remaining at any time will be $x(t) = 1,000 - kt$. If $k = 50$, the system will obey the end point constraints $x(0) = 1000$ and $x(20) = 0$. Of course, in this problem you could probably guess that the optimum plan would be to drink the wine at the rate of 50 bottles per year for 20 years because diminishing marginal utility suggests one does not want to drink excessively in any period. The maximum principle confirms this intuition.

More complicated utility.   Now let's take a more complicated utility function that may yield more interesting results. Suppose that the utility of consuming wine at any date, t, is given by

$$u[c(t)] = \begin{cases} [c(t)]^\gamma/\gamma & \text{if } \gamma \neq 0, \gamma < 1; \\ \ln c(t) & \text{if } \gamma = 0. \end{cases}$$
(2.156)

Assume also that the consumer discounts future consumption at the rate δ. Hence this person's goal is to maximize

$$\int_0^{20} u[c(t)] \, dt = \int_0^{20} e^{-\delta t} \frac{[c(t)]^\gamma}{\gamma} \, dt$$
(2.157)

subject to the following constraints:

$$\frac{dx(t)}{dt} = -c(t),$$

$$x(0) = 1,000,$$

$$x(20) = 0.$$
(2.158)

Setting up the current value Hamiltonian expression yields

$$H = e^{-\delta t} \frac{[c(t)]^\gamma}{\gamma} + \lambda(-c) + x(t)\frac{d\lambda(t)}{dt},$$
(2.159)

and the maximum principle requires that

(*continued*)

---

the single equation $f_x = df_{dx/dt}/dt$, which is termed the "Euler equation." In Chapter 17 we will encounter many Euler equations.

EXAMPLE 2.13 CONTINUED

$$\frac{\partial H}{\partial c} = e^{-\delta t}[c(t)]^{\gamma-1} - \lambda = 0 \quad \text{and}$$

$$\frac{\partial H}{\partial x} = 0 + 0 + \frac{d\lambda}{dt} = 0. \tag{2.160}$$

Hence, we can again conclude that the implicit value of the wine stock (λ) should be constant over time (call this constant k) and that

$$e^{-\delta t}[c(t)]^{\gamma-1} = k \quad \text{or} \quad c(t) = k^{1/(\gamma-1)} e^{\delta t/(\gamma-1)}. \tag{2.161}$$

So, optimal wine consumption should fall over time in order to compensate for the fact that future consumption is being discounted in the consumer's mind. If, for example, we let $\delta = 0.1$ and $\gamma = -1$ ("reasonable" values, as we will show in later chapters), then

$$c(t) = k^{-0.5} e^{-0.05t} \tag{2.162}$$

Now we must do a bit more work in choosing k to satisfy the endpoint constraints. We want

$$\int_0^{20} c(t)\, dt = \int_0^{20} k^{-0.5} e^{-0.05t}\, dt = -20 k^{-0.5} e^{-0.05t}\Big|_0^{20} \tag{2.163}$$

$$= -20 k^{-0.5}(e^{-1} - 1) = 12.64 k^{-0.5} = 1{,}000.$$

Finally, then, we have the optimal consumption plan as

$$c(t) \approx 79 e^{-0.05t}. \tag{2.164}$$

This consumption plan requires that wine consumption start out fairly high and decline at a continuous rate of 5 percent per year. Because consumption is continuously declining, we must use integration to calculate wine consumption in any particular year (x) as follows:

$$\text{consumption in year } x \approx \int_{x-1}^{x} c(t)\, dt = \int_{x-1}^{x} 79 e^{-0.05t}\, dt = -1{,}580 e^{-0.05t}\Big|_{x-1}^{x} \tag{2.165}$$

$$= 1{,}580(e^{-0.05(x-1)} - e^{-0.05x}).$$

If $x = 1$, consumption is about 77 bottles in this first year. Consumption then declines smoothly, ending with about 30 bottles being consumed in the 20th year.

QUERY: Our first illustration was just an example of the second in which $\delta = \gamma = 0$. Explain how alternative values of these parameters will affect the path of optimal wine consumption. Explain your results intuitively (for more on optimal consumption over time, see Chapter 17).

MATHEMATICAL STATISTICS

In recent years microeconomic theory has increasingly focused on issues raised by uncertainty and imperfect information. To understand much of this literature, it is important to have a good background in mathematical statistics. The purpose of this section is, therefore, to summarize a few of the statistical principles that we will encounter at various places in this book.

Random variables and probability density functions

A *random variable* describes (in numerical form) the outcomes from an experiment that is subject to chance. For example, we might flip a coin and observe whether it lands heads or tails. If we call this random variable x, we can denote the possible outcomes ("realizations") of the variable as:

$$x = \begin{cases} 1 & \text{if coin is heads,} \\ 0 & \text{if coin is tails.} \end{cases}$$

Notice that, prior to the flip of the coin, x can be either 1 or 0. Only after the uncertainty is resolved (that is, after the coin is flipped) do we know what the value of x is.[22]

Discrete and continuous random variables

The outcomes from a random experiment may be either a finite number of possibilities or a continuum of possibilities. For example, recording the number that comes up on a single die is a random variable with six outcomes. With two dice, we could either record the sum of the faces (in which case there are 12 outcomes, some of which are more likely than others) or we could record a two-digit number, one for the value of each die (in which case there would be 36 equally likely outcomes). These are examples of discrete random variables.

Alternatively, a continuous random variable may take on any value in a given range of real numbers. For example, we could view the outdoor temperature tomorrow as a continuous variable (assuming temperatures can be measured very finely) ranging from, say, $-50°C$ to $+50°C$. Of course, some of these temperatures would be very unlikely to occur, but in principle the precisely measured temperature could be anywhere between these two bounds. Similarly, we could view tomorrow's percentage change in the value of a particular stock index as taking on all values between -100% and, say, $+1,000\%$. Again, of course, percentage changes around 0% would be considerably more likely to occur than would be the extreme values.

Probability density functions

For any random variable, its *probability density function* (PDF) shows the probability that each specific outcome will occur. For a discrete random variable, defining such a function poses no particular difficulties. In the coin flip case, for example, the PDF [denoted by $f(x)$] would be given by

$$\begin{aligned} f(x = 1) &= 0.5, \\ f(x = 0) &= 0.5. \end{aligned} \tag{2.166}$$

For the roll of a single die, the PDF would be:

$$\begin{aligned} f(x = 1) &= 1/6, \\ f(x = 2) &= 1/6, \\ f(x = 3) &= 1/6, \\ f(x = 4) &= 1/6, \\ f(x = 5) &= 1/6, \\ f(x = 6) &= 1/6. \end{aligned} \tag{2.167}$$

---

[22]Sometimes random variables are denoted by $\tilde{x}$ to make a distinction between variables whose outcome is subject to random chance and (nonrandom) algebraic variables. This notational device can be useful for keeping track of what is random and what is not in a particular problem and we will use it in some cases. When there is no ambiguity, however, we will not employ this special notation.

Notice that in both of these cases the probabilities specified by the PDF sum to 1.0. This is because, by definition, one of the outcomes of the random experiment must occur. More generally, if we denote all of the outcomes for a discrete random variable by x_i for $i = 1, ..., n$, then we must have:

$$\sum_{i=1}^{n} f(x_i) = 1. \qquad (2.168)$$

For a continuous random variable we must be careful in defining the PDF concept. Because such a random variable takes on a continuum of values, if we were to assign any non-zero value as the probability for a specific outcome (i.e., a temperature of $+25.53470°C$), we could quickly have sums of probabilities that are infinitely large. Hence, for a continuous random variable we define the PDF $f(x)$ as a function with the property that the probability that x falls in a particular small interval dx is given by the area of $f(x)dx$. Using this convention, the property that the probabilities from a random experiment must sum to 1.0 is stated as follows:

$$\int_{-\infty}^{+\infty} f(x)\, dx = 1.0. \qquad (2.169)$$

A few important PDFs

Most any function will do as a probability density function provided that $f(x) \geq 0$ and the function sums (or integrates) to 1.0. The trick, of course, is to find functions that mirror random experiments that occur in the real world. Here we look at four such functions that we will find useful in various places in this book. Graphs for all four of these functions are shown in Figure 2.6.

1. *Binomial distribution*. This is the most basic discrete distribution. Usually x is assumed to take on only two values, 1 and 0. The PDF for the binomial is given by:

$$f(x = 1) = p,$$
$$f(x = 0) = 1 - p, \qquad (2.170)$$
$$\textbf{where} \quad 0 < p < 1.$$

The coin flip example is obviously a special case of the binomial where $p = 0.5$.

2. *Uniform distribution*. This is the simplest continuous PDF. It assumes that the possible values of the variable x occur in a defined interval and that each value is equally likely. That is:

$$f(x) = \frac{1}{b - a} \quad \text{for } a \leq x \leq b;$$
$$f(x) = 0 \qquad \text{for } x < a \text{ or } x > b. \qquad (2.171)$$

Notice that here the probabilities integrate to 1.0:

$$\int_{-\infty}^{+\infty} f(x)\, dx = \int_{a}^{b} \frac{1}{b-a}\, dx = \left.\frac{x}{b-a}\right|_{a}^{b} = \frac{b}{b-a} - \frac{a}{b-a} = \frac{b-a}{b-a} = 1.0. \qquad (2.172)$$

3. *Exponential distribution*. This is a continuous distribution for which the probabilities decline at a smooth exponential rate as x increases. Formally:

$$f(x) = \begin{cases} \lambda e^{-\lambda x} & \text{if } x > 0, \\ 0 & \text{if } x \leq 0, \end{cases} \qquad (2.173)$$

FIGURE 2.6   Four Common Probability Density Functions

Random variables that have these PDFs are widely used. Each graph indicates the expected value of the PDF shown.

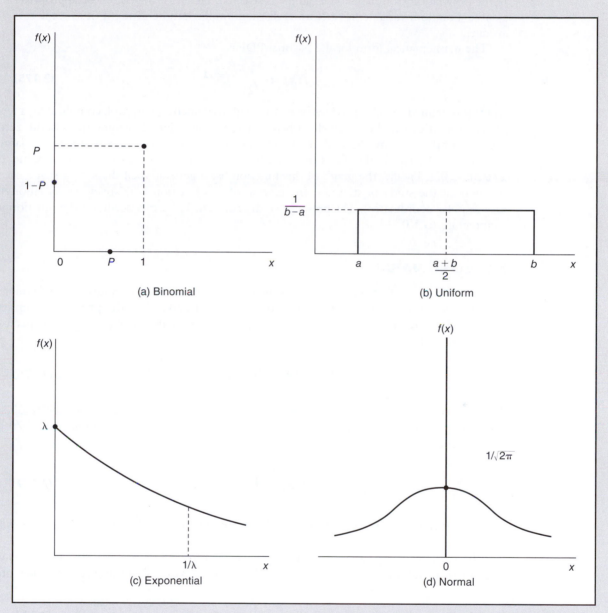

where λ is a positive constant. Again, it is easy to show that this function integrates to 1.0:

$$\int\limits_{-\infty}^{+\infty} f(x)\, dx = \int\limits_{0}^{\infty} \lambda e^{-\lambda x}\, dx = -e^{-\lambda x}\Big|_{0}^{\infty} = 0 - (-1) = 1.0. \qquad \textbf{(2.174)}$$

4. *Normal distribution*. The Normal (or Gaussian) distribution is the most important in mathematical statistics. It's importance stems largely from the *central limit theorem*, which states that the distribution of any sum of independent random variables will increasingly approximate the Normal distribution as the number of such variables increase. Because sample averages can be regarded as sums of independent random variables, this theorem says that any sample average will have a Normal distribution no matter what the distribution of the population from which the sample is selected. Hence, it may often be appropriate to assume a random variable has a Normal distribution if it can be thought of as some sort of average.

The mathematical form for the Normal PDF is

$$f(x) = \frac{1}{\sqrt{2\pi}} e^{-x^2/2},$$

(2.175)

and this is defined for all real values of x. Although the function may look complicated, a few of its properties can be easily described. First, the function is symmetric around zero (because of the x^2 term). Second, the function is asymptotic to zero as x becomes very large or very small. Third, the function reaches its maximal value at $x = 0$. This value is $1/\sqrt{2\pi} \approx 0.4$. Finally, the graph of this function has a general "bell shape"—a shape used throughout the study of statistics. Integration of this function is relatively tricky (though easy in polar coordinates). The presence of the constant $1/\sqrt{2\pi}$ is needed if the function is to integrate to 1.0.

Expected value

The *expected value* of a random variable is the numerical value that the random variable might be expected to have, on average.[23] It is the "center of gravity" of the probability density function. For a discrete random variable that takes on the values $x_1, x_2, ..., x_n$, the expected value is defined as

$$E(x) = \sum_{i=1}^{n} x_i f(x_i).$$

(2.176)

That is, each outcome is weighted by the probability that it will occur and the result is summed over all possible outcomes. For a continuous random variable, Equation 2.176 is readily generalized as

$$E(x) = \int_{-\infty}^{+\infty} x f(x) \, dx.$$

(2.177)

Again, in this integration, each value of x is weighted by the probability that this value will occur.

The concept of expected value can be generalized to include the expected value of any function of a random variable [say, $g(x)$]. In the continuous case, for example, we would write

$$E[g(x)] = \int_{-\infty}^{+\infty} g(x) f(x) \, dx.$$

(2.178)

---

[23]The expected value of a random variable is sometimes referred to as the *mean* of that variable. In the study of sampling this can sometimes lead to confusion between the expected value of a random variable and the separate concept of the sample arithmetic average.

As a special case, consider a linear function $y = ax + b$. Then

$$E(y) = E(ax + b) = \int_{-\infty}^{+\infty} (ax + b)f(x)\, dx$$

$$= a\int_{-\infty}^{+\infty} xf(x)\, dx + b\int_{-\infty}^{+\infty} f(x)\, dx = aE(x) + b. \qquad \textbf{(2.179)}$$

Sometimes expected values are phrased in terms of the *cumulative distribution function* (CDF) $F(x)$, defined as

$$F(x) = \int_{-\infty}^{x} f(t)\, dt. \qquad \textbf{(2.180)}$$

That is, $F(x)$ represents the probability that the random variable t is less than or equal to x. With this notation, the expected value of $g(x)$ is defined as

$$E[g(x)] = \int_{-\infty}^{+\infty} g(x)\, dF(x). \qquad \textbf{(2.181)}$$

Because of the fundamental theorem of calculus, Equation 2.181 and Equation 2.178 mean exactly the same thing.

EXAMPLE 2.14   Expected Values of a Few Random Variables

The expected values of each of the random variables with the simple PDFs introduced earlier are easy to calculate. All of these expected values are indicated on the graphs of the functions' PDFs in Figure 2.6.

1. Binomial. In this case:

$$E(x) = 1 \cdot f(x = 1) + 0 \cdot f(x = 0) = 1 \cdot p + 0 \cdot (1 - p) = p. \qquad \textbf{(2.182)}$$

For the coin flip case (where $p = 0.5$), this says that $E(x) = p = 0.5$—the expected value of this random variable is, as you might have guessed, one half.

2. Uniform. For this continuous random variable,

$$E(x) = \int_{a}^{b} \frac{x}{b - a}\, dx = \left. \frac{x^2}{2(b - a)} \right|_{a}^{b} = \frac{b^2}{2(b - a)} - \frac{a^2}{2(b - a)} = \frac{b + a}{2}. \qquad \textbf{(2.183)}$$

Again, as you might have guessed, the expected value of the uniform distribution is precisely halfway between a and b.

3. Exponential. For this case of declining probabilities:

$$E(x) = \int_{0}^{\infty} x\lambda e^{-\lambda x}\, dx = \left. -xe^{-\lambda x} - \frac{1}{\lambda}e^{-\lambda x} \right|_{0}^{\infty} = \frac{1}{\lambda}, \qquad \textbf{(2.184)}$$

where the integration follows from the integration by parts example shown earlier in this chapter (Equation 2.137). Notice here that the faster the probabilities decline, the lower is the expected value of x. For example, if $\lambda = 0.5$ then $E(x) = 2$, whereas if $\lambda = 0.05$ then $E(x) = 20$.

(continued)

EXAMPLE 2.14   CONTINUED

4. *Normal*. Because the Normal PDF is symmetric around zero, it seems clear that $E(x) = 0$. A formal proof uses a change of variable integration by letting $u = x^2/2$ $(du = x\,dx)$:

$$\int_{-\infty}^{+\infty} \frac{1}{\sqrt{2\pi}} x e^{-x^2/2}\, dx = \frac{1}{\sqrt{2\pi}} \int_{-\infty}^{+\infty} e^{-u}\, du = \frac{1}{\sqrt{2\pi}} \left[-e^{-x^2/2}\right]\Big|_{-\infty}^{+\infty} = \frac{1}{\sqrt{2\pi}}[0-0] = 0. \quad \textbf{(2.185)}$$

Of course, the expected value of a normally distributed random variable (or of any random variable) may be altered by a linear transformation, as shown in Equation 2.179.

QUERY: A linear transformation changes a random variable's expected value in a very predictable way—if $y = ax + b$, then $E(y) = aE(x) + b$. Hence, for this transformation [say, $h(x)$] we have $E[h(x)] = h[E(x)]$. Suppose instead that x were transformed by a concave function, say $g(x)$ with $g' > 0$ and $g'' < 0$. How would $E[g(x)]$ compare to $g[E(x)]$?

Note: This is an illustration of Jensen's inequality, a concept we will pursue in detail in Chapter 7. See also Problem 2.13.

Variance and standard deviation

The expected value of a random variable is a measure of central tendency. On the other hand, the *variance* of a random variable [denoted by σ_x^2 or $\text{Var}(x)$] is a measure of dispersion. Specifically, the variance is defined as the "expected squared deviation" of a random variable from its expected value. Formally:

$$\textbf{Var}(x) = \sigma_x^2 = E[(x - E(x))^2] = \int_{-\infty}^{+\infty} (x - E(x))^2 f(x)\, dx. \quad \textbf{(2.186)}$$

Somewhat imprecisely, the variance measures the "typical" squared deviation from the central value of a random variable. In making the calculation, deviations from the expected value are squared so that positive and negative deviations from the expected value will both contribute to this measure of dispersion. After the calculation is made, the squaring process can be reversed to yield a measure of dispersion that is in the original units in which the random variable was measured. This square root of the variance is called the "standard deviation" and is denoted as $\sigma_x\,(= \sqrt{\sigma_x^2})$. The wording of the term effectively conveys its meaning: σ_x is indeed the typical ("standard") deviation of a random variable from its expected value.

When a random variable is subject to a linear transformation, its variance and standard deviation will be changed in a fairly obvious way. If $y = ax + b$, then

$$\sigma_y^2 = \int_{-\infty}^{+\infty} [ax + b - E(ax + b)]^2 f(x)\, dx = \int_{-\infty}^{+\infty} a^2[x - E(x)]^2 f(x)\, dx = a^2 \sigma_x^2. \quad \textbf{(2.187)}$$

Hence, addition of a constant to a random variable does not change its variance, whereas multiplication by a constant multiplies the variance by the square of the constant. It is clear therefore that multiplying a variable by a constant multiplies its standard deviation by that constant: $\sigma_{ax} = a\sigma_x$.

EXAMPLE 2.15 Variances and Standard Deviations for Simple Random Variables

Knowing the variances and standard deviations of the four simple random variables we have been looking at can sometimes be quite useful in economic applications.

1. *Binomial*. The variance of the binomial can be calculated by applying the definition in its discrete analog:

$$\sigma_x^2 = \sum_{i=1}^n (x_i - E(x))^2 f(x_i) = (1 - p)^2 \cdot p + (0 - p)^2 (1 - p)$$
$$= (1 - p)(p - p^2 + p^2) = p(1 - p). \tag{2.188}$$

Hence, $\sigma_x = \sqrt{p(1 - p)}$. One implication of this result is that a binomial variable has the largest variance and standard deviation when $p = 0.5$, in which case $\sigma_x^2 = 0.25$ and $\sigma_x = 0.5$. Because of the relatively flat parabolic shape of $p(1 - p)$, modest deviations of p from 0.5 do not change this variance substantially.

2. *Uniform*. Calculating the variance of the uniform distribution yields a mildly interesting result:

$$\sigma_x^2 = \int_a^b \left(x - \frac{a + b}{2} \right)^2 \frac{1}{b - a}\, dx = \left(x - \frac{a + b}{2} \right)^3 \cdot \frac{1}{3(b - a)} \Big|_a^b$$
$$= \frac{1}{3(b - a)} \left[\frac{(b - a)^3}{8} - \frac{(a - b)^3}{8} \right] = \frac{(b - a)^2}{12}. \tag{2.189}$$

This is one of the few places where the number 12 has any use in mathematics other than in measuring quantities of oranges or doughnuts.

3. *Exponential*. Integrating the variance formula for the exponential is relatively laborious. Fortunately, the result is quite simple; for the exponential, it turns out that $\sigma_x^2 = 1/\lambda^2$ and $\sigma_x = 1/\lambda$. Hence, the mean and standard deviation are the same for the exponential distribution—it is a "one-parameter distribution."

4. *Normal*. In this case also, the integration can be burdensome. But again the result is simple: for the Normal distribution, $\sigma_x^2 = \sigma_x = 1$. Areas below the Normal curve can be readily calculated and tables of these are available in any statistics text. Two useful facts about the Normal PDF are:

$$\int_{-1}^{+1} f(x)\, dx \approx 0.68 \quad \text{and} \quad \int_{-2}^{+2} f(x)\, dx \approx 0.95. \tag{2.190}$$

That is, the probability is about two thirds that a Normal variable will be within ±1 standard deviation of the expected value and "most of the time" (i.e., with probability 0.95) it will be within ±2 standard deviations.

Standardizing the Normal. If the random variable x has a standard Normal PDF, it will have an expected value of 0 and a standard deviation of 1. However, a simple linear transformation can be used to give this random variable any desired expected value (μ) and standard deviation (σ). Consider the transformation $y = \sigma x + \mu$. Now

$$E(y) = \sigma E(x) + \mu = \mu \quad \text{and} \quad \text{Var}(y) = \sigma_y^2 = \sigma^2 \text{Var}(x) = \sigma^2. \tag{2.191}$$

Reversing this process can be used to "standardize" any Normally distributed random variable (y) with an arbitrary expected value (μ) and standard deviation (σ) (this is sometimes denoted

(*continued*)

EXAMPLE 2.15 CONTINUED

as $y \sim N(\mu, \sigma))$ by using $z = (y - \mu)/\sigma$. For example, SAT scores (y) are distributed Normally with an expected value of 500 points and a standard deviation of 100 points (that is, $y \sim N(500, 100)$). Hence, $z = (y - 500)/100$ has a standard Normal distribution with expected value 0 and standard deviation 1. Equation 2.190 shows that approximately 68 percent of all scores lie between 400 and 600 points and 95 percent of all scores lie between 300 and 700 points.

QUERY: Suppose that the random variable x is distributed uniformly along the interval $[0, 12]$. What are the mean and standard deviation of x? What fraction of the x distribution is within ± 1 standard deviation of the mean? What fraction of the distribution is within ± 2 standard deviations of the expected value? Explain why this differs from the fractions computed for the Normal distribution.

Covariance

Some economic problems involve two or more random variables. For example, an investor may consider allocating his or her wealth among several assets the returns on which are taken to be random. Although the concepts of expected value, variance, and so forth carry over more or less directly when looking at a single random variable in such cases, it is also necessary to consider the relationship between the variables to get a complete picture. The concept of covariance is used to quantify this relationship. Before providing a definition, however, we will need to develop some background.

Consider a case with two continuous random variables, x and y. The probability density function for these two variables, denoted by $f(x, y)$, has the property that the probability associated with a set of outcomes in a small area (with dimensions $dxdy$) is given by $f(x, y)dxdy$. To be a proper PDF, it must be the case that:

$$f(x, y) \geq 0 \quad \text{and} \quad \int_{-\infty}^{+\infty} \int_{-\infty}^{+\infty} f(x, y) \, dx \, dy = 1. \tag{2.192}$$

The single-variable measures we have already introduced can be developed in this two-variable context by "integrating out" the other variable. That is,

$$E(x) = \int_{-\infty}^{+\infty} \int_{-\infty}^{+\infty} xf(x, y) \, dy \, dx \quad \text{and}$$

$$\mathbf{Var}(x) = \int_{-\infty}^{+\infty} \int_{-\infty}^{+\infty} [x - E(x)]^2 f(x, y) \, dy \, dx. \tag{2.193}$$

In this way, the parameters describing the random variable x are measured over all possible outcomes for y after taking into account the likelihood of those various outcomes.

In this context, the *covariance* between x and y seeks to measure the direction of association between the variables. Specifically the covariance between x and y [denoted as $\text{Cov}(x, y)$] is defined as

$$\mathbf{Cov}(x, y) = \int_{-\infty}^{+\infty} \int_{-\infty}^{+\infty} [x - E(x)][y - E(y)]f(x, y) \, dx \, dy. \tag{2.194}$$

The covariance between two random variables may be positive, negative, or zero. If values of x that are greater than $E(x)$ tend to occur relatively frequently with values of y that are greater than $E(y)$ (and similarly, if low values of x tend to occur together with low values of y), then the covariance will be positive. In this case, values of x and y tend to move in the same direction. Alternatively, if high values of x tend to be associated with low values for y (and vice versa), the covariance will be negative.

Two random variables are defined to be *independent* if the probability of any particular value of, say, x is not affected by the particular value of y that might occur (and vice versa).[24] In mathematical terms, this means that the PDF must have the property that $f(x,y) = g(x)h(y)$—that is, the joint probability density function can be expressed as the product of two single-variable PDFs. If x and y are independent, their covariance will be zero:

$$\mathbf{Cov}(x,y) = \int_{-\infty}^{+\infty}\int_{-\infty}^{+\infty} [x - E(x)][y - E(y)]g(x)h(y)\,dx\,dy$$

$$= \int_{-\infty}^{+\infty} [x - E(x)]g(x)\,dx \cdot \int_{-\infty}^{+\infty} [y - E(y)]h(y)\,dy = 0 \cdot 0 = 0. \qquad \textbf{(2.195)}$$

The converse of this statement is not necessarily true, however. A zero covariance does not necessarily imply statistical independence.

Finally, the covariance concept is crucial for understanding the variance of sums or differences of random variables. Although the expected value of a sum of two random variables is (as one might guess) the sum of their expected values:

$$E(x + y) = \int_{-\infty}^{+\infty}\int_{-\infty}^{+\infty} (x + y)f(x,y)\,dx\,dy$$

$$= \int_{-\infty}^{+\infty} xf(x,y)\,dy\,dx + \int_{-\infty}^{+\infty} yf(x,y)\,dx\,dy = E(x) + E(y), \qquad \textbf{(2.196)}$$

the relationship for the variance of such a sum is more complicated. Using the definitions we have developed yields

$$\mathbf{Var}(x+y) = \int_{-\infty}^{+\infty}\int_{-\infty}^{+\infty} [x + y - E(x + y)]^2 f(x,y)\,dx\,dy$$

$$= \int_{-\infty}^{+\infty}\int_{-\infty}^{+\infty} [x - E(x) + y - E(y)]^2 f(x,y)\,dx\,dy$$

$$= \int_{-\infty}^{+\infty}\int_{-\infty}^{+\infty} [x - E(x)]^2 + [y - E(y)]^2 + 2[x - E(x)][y - E(y)]f(x,y)\,dx\,dy$$

$$= \mathbf{Var}(x) + \mathbf{Var}(y) + 2\,\mathbf{Cov}(x,y). \qquad \textbf{(2.197)}$$

Hence, if x and y are independent then $\text{Var}(x + y) = \text{Var}(x) + \text{Var}(y)$. The variance of the sum will be greater than the sum of the variances if the two random variables have a positive covariance and will be less than the sum of the variances if they have a negative covariance. Problems 2.13 and 2.14 provide further details on statistical issues that arise in microeconomic theory.

---

[24]A formal definition relies on the concept of conditional probability. The conditional probability of an event B given that A has occurred (written $P(B|A)$ is defined as $P(B|A) = P(A \text{ and } B)/P(A)$; B and A are defined to be independent if $P(B|A) = P(B)$. In this case, $P(A \text{ and } B) = P(A) \cdot P(B)$.

SUMMARY

Despite the formidable appearance of some parts of this chapter, this is not a book on mathematics. Rather, the intention here was to gather together a variety of tools that will be used to develop economic models throughout the remainder of the text. Material in this chapter will then be useful as a handy reference.

One way to summarize the mathematical tools introduced in this chapter is by stressing again the economic lessons that these tools illustrate:

- Using mathematics provides a convenient, shorthand way for economists to develop their models. Implications of various economic assumptions can be studied in a simplified setting through the use of such mathematical tools.

- The mathematical concept of the derivatives of a function is widely used in economic models because economists are often interested in how marginal changes in one variable affect another variable. Partial derivatives are especially useful for this purpose because they are defined to represent such marginal changes when all other factors are held constant.

- The mathematics of optimization is an important tool for the development of models that assume that economic agents rationally pursue some goal. In the unconstrained case, the first-order conditions state that any activity that contributes to the agent's goal should be expanded up to the point at which the marginal contribution of further expansion is zero. In mathematical terms, the first-order condition for an optimum requires that all partial derivatives be zero.

- Most economic optimization problems involve constraints on the choices agents can make. In this case the first-order conditions for a maximum suggest that each activity be operated at a level at which the ratio of the marginal benefit–of the activity to its marginal cost is the same for all activities actually used. This common marginal benefit–marginal cost ratio is also equal to the Lagrangian multiplier, which is often introduced to help solve constrained optimization problems. The Lagrangian multiplier can also be interpreted as the implicit value (or shadow price) of the constraint.

- The implicit function theorem is a useful mathematical device for illustrating the dependence of the choices that result from an optimization problem on the parameters of that problem (for example, market prices). The envelope theorem is useful for examining how these optimal choices change when the problem's parameters (prices) change.

- Some optimization problems may involve constraints that are inequalities rather than equalities. Solutions to these problems often illustrate "complementary slackness." That is, either the constraints hold with equality and their related Lagrangian multipliers are nonzero, or the constraints are strict inequalities and their related Lagrangian multipliers are zero. Again this illustrates how the Lagrangian multiplier implies something about the "importance" of constraints.

- The first-order conditions shown in this chapter are only the necessary conditions for a local maximum or minimum. One must also check second-order conditions that require that certain curvature conditions be met.

- Certain types of functions occur in many economic problems. Quasi-concave functions (those functions for which the level curves form convex sets) obey the second-order conditions of constrained maximum or minimum problems when the constraints are linear. Homothetic functions have the useful property that implicit trade-offs among the variables of the function depend only on the ratios of these variables.

- Integral calculus is often used in economics both as a way of describing areas below graphs and as a way of summing results over time. Techniques that involve various ways of differentiating integrals play an important role in the theory of optimizing behavior.

- Many economic problems are dynamic in that decisions at one date affect decisions and outcomes at later dates. The mathematics for solving such dynamic optimization problems is often a straightforward generalization of Lagrangian methods.

- Concepts from mathematical statistics are often used in studying the economics of uncertainty and information. The most fundamental concept is the notion of a random variable and its associated probability density function. Parameters of this distribution, such as its expected value or its variance, also play important roles in many economic models.

PROBLEMS

2.1

Suppose $U(x, y) = 4x^2 + 3y^2$.

    a. Calculate $\partial U/\partial x$, $\partial U/\partial y$.

    b. Evaluate these partial derivatives at $x = 1$, $y = 2$.

    c. Write the total differential for U.

    d. Calculate dy/dx for $dU = 0$—that is, what is the implied trade-off between x and y holding U constant?

    e. Show $U = 16$ when $x = 1$, $y = 2$.

    f. In what ratio must x and y change to hold U constant at 16 for movements away from $x = 1$, $y = 2$?

    g. More generally, what is the shape of the $U = 16$ contour line for this function? What is the slope of that line?

2.2

Suppose a firm's total revenues depend on the amount produced (q) according to the function

$$R = 70q - q^2.$$

Total costs also depend on q:

$$C = q^2 + 30q + 100.$$

    a. What level of output should the firm produce in order to maximize profits ($R - C$)? What will profits be?

    b. Show that the second-order conditions for a maximum are satisfied at the output level found in part (a).

    c. Does the solution calculated here obey the "marginal revenue equals marginal cost" rule? Explain.

2.3

Suppose that $f(x, y) = xy$. Find the maximum value for f if x and y are constrained to sum to 1. Solve this problem in two ways: by substitution and by using the Lagrangian multiplier method.

2.4

The dual problem to the one described in Problem 2.3 is

$$\textbf{minimize} \quad x + y$$
$$\textbf{subject to} \quad xy = 0.25.$$

Solve this problem using the Lagrangian technique. Then compare the value you get for the Lagrangian multiplier to the value you got in Problem 2.3. Explain the relationship between the two solutions.

2.5

The height of a ball that is thrown straight up with a certain force is a function of the time (t) from which it is released given by $f(t) = -0.5gt^2 + 40t$ (where g is a constant determined by gravity).

a. How does the value of t at which the height of the ball is at a maximum depend on the parameter g?

b. Use your answer to part (a) to describe how maximum height changes as the parameter g changes.

c. Use the envelope theorem to answer part (b) directly.

d. On the Earth $g = 32$, but this value varies somewhat around the globe. If two locations had gravitational constants that differed by 0.1, what would be the difference in the maximum height of a ball tossed in the two places?

2.6

A simple way to model the construction of an oil tanker is to start with a large rectangular sheet of steel that is x feet wide and $3x$ feet long. Now cut a smaller square that is t feet on a side out of each corner of the larger sheet and fold up and weld the sides of the steel sheet to make a traylike structure with no top.

a. Show that the volume of oil that can be held by this tray is given by

$$V = t(x - 2t)(3x - 2t) = 3tx^2 - 8t^2x + 4t^3.$$

b. How should t be chosen so as to maximize V for any given value of x?

c. Is there a value of x that maximizes the volume of oil that can be carried?

d. Suppose that a shipbuilder is constrained to use only 1,000,000 square feet of steel sheet to construct an oil tanker. This constraint can be represented by the equation $3x^2 - 4t^2 = 1,000,000$ (because the builder can return the cut-out squares for credit). How does the solution to this constrained maximum problem compare to the solutions described in parts (b) and (c)?

2.7

Consider the following constrained maximization problem:

$$\text{maximize} \quad y = x_1 + 5 \ln x_2$$
$$\text{subject to} \quad k - x_1 - x_2 = 0,$$

where k is a constant that can be assigned any specific value.

a. Show that if $k = 10$, this problem can be solved as one involving only equality constraints.

b. Show that solving this problem for $k = 4$ requires that $x_1 = -1$.

c. If the x's in this problem must be nonnegative, what is the optimal solution when $k = 4$?

d. What is the solution for this problem when $k = 20$? What do you conclude by comparing this solution to the solution for part (a)?

Note: This problem involves what is called a "quasi-linear function." Such functions provide important examples of some types of behavior in consumer theory—as we shall see.

2.8

Suppose that a firm has a marginal cost function given by $MC(q) = q + 1$.

a. What is this firm's total cost function? Explain why total costs are known only up to a constant of integration, which represents fixed costs.

b. As you may know from an earlier economics course, if a firm takes price (p) as given in its decisions then it will produce that output for which $p = MC(q)$. If the firm follows this profit-maximizing rule, how much will it produce when $p = 15$? Assuming that the firm is just breaking even at this price, what are fixed costs?

c. How much will profits for this firm increase if price increases to 20?

d. Show that, if we continue to assume profit maximization, then this firm's profits can be expressed solely as a function of the price it receives for its output.

e. Show that the increase in profits from $p = 15$ to $p = 20$ can be calculated in two ways: (i) directly from the equation derived in part (d); and (ii) by integrating the inverse marginal cost function $[MC^{-1}(p) = p - 1]$ from $p = 15$ to $p = 20$. Explain this result intuitively using the envelope theorem.

Analytical Problems

2.9 Concave and quasi-concave functions

Show that if $f(x_1, x_2)$ is a concave function then it is also a quasi-concave function. Do this by comparing Equation 2.114 (defining quasi-concavity) to Equation 2.98 (defining concavity). Can you give an intuitive reason for this result? Is the converse of the statement true? Are quasi-concave functions necessarily concave? If not, give a counterexample.

2.10 The Cobb-Douglas function

One of the most important functions we will encounter in this book is the Cobb-Douglas function:

$$y = (x_1)^\alpha (x_2)^\beta,$$

where α and β are positive constants that are each less than 1.

a. Show that this function is quasi-concave using a "brute force" method by applying Equation 2.114.

b. Show that the Cobb-Douglas function is quasi-concave by showing that any contour line of the form $y = c$ (where c is any positive constant) is convex and therefore that the set of points for which $y > c$ is a convex set.

c. Show that if $\alpha + \beta > 1$ then the Cobb-Douglas function is not concave (thereby illustrating again that not all quasi-concave functions are concave).

Note: The Cobb-Douglas function is discussed further in the Extensions to this chapter.

2.11 The power function

Another function we will encounter often in this book is the "power function":

$$y = x^\delta,$$

where $0 \le \delta \le 1$ (at times we will also examine this function for cases where δ can be negative, too, in which case we will use the form $y = x^\delta / \delta$ to ensure that the derivatives have the proper sign).

a. Show that this function is concave (and therefore also, by the result of Problem 2.9, quasi-concave). Notice that the $\delta = 1$ is a special case and that the function is "strictly" concave only for $\delta < 1$.

b. Show that the multivariate form of the power function

$$y = f(x_1, x_2) = (x_1)^\delta + (x_2)^\delta$$

is also concave (and quasi-concave). Explain why, in this case, the fact that $f_{12} = f_{21} = 0$ makes the determination of concavity especially simple.

c. One way to incorporate "scale" effects into the function described in part (b) is to use the monotonic transformation

$$g(x_1, x_2) = y^\gamma = [(x_1)^\delta + (x_2)^\delta]^\gamma,$$

where γ is a positive constant. Does this transformation preserve the concavity of the function? Is g quasi-concave?

2.12 Taylor approximations

Taylor's theorem shows that any function can be approximated in the vicinity of any convenient point by a series of terms involving the function and its derivatives. Here we look at some applications of the theorem for functions of one and two variables.

a. Any continuous and differentiable function of a single variable, $f(x)$, can be approximated near the point a by the formula

$$f(x) = f(a) + f'(a)(x - a) + 0.5f''(a)(x - a)^2 + \textbf{terms in } f''', f'''', \dots.$$

Using only the first three of these terms results in a *quadratic* Taylor approximation. Use this approximation together with the definition of concavity given in Equation 2.85 to show that any concave function must lie on or below the tangent to the function at point a.

b. The quadratic Taylor approximation for any function of two variables, $f(x, y)$, near the point (a, b) is given by

$$f(x, y) = f(a, b) + f_1(a, b)(x - a) + f_2(a, b)(y - b)$$
$$+ 0.5[f_{11}(a, b)(x - a)^2 + 2f_{12}(a, b)(x - a)(y - b) + f_{22}(y - b)^2].$$

Use this approximation to show that any concave function (as defined by Equation 2.98) must lie on or below its tangent plane at (a, b).

2.13 More on expected value

Because the expected value concept plays an important role in many economic theories, it may be useful to summarize a few more properties of this statistical measure. Throughout this problem, x is assumed to be a continuous random variable with probability density function $f(x)$.

a. (Jensen's inequality) Suppose that $g(x)$ is a concave function. Show that $E[g(x)] \leq g[E(x)]$. *Hint:* Construct the tangent to $g(x)$ at the point $E(x)$. This tangent will have the form $c + dx \geq g(x)$ for all values of x and $c + dE(x) = g[E(x)]$ where c and d are constants.

b. Use the procedure from part (a) to show that if $g(x)$ is a convex function then $E[g(x)] \geq g[E(x)]$.

c. Suppose x takes on only nonnegative values—that is, $0 \leq x \leq \infty$. Use integration by parts to show that

$$E(x) = \int_0^\infty [1 - F(x)] \, dx,$$

where $F(x)$ is the cumulative distribution function for x [that is, $F(x) = \int_0^x f(t) \, dt$].

d. (Markov's inequality) Show that if x takes on only positive values then the following inequality holds:

$$P(x \geq t) \leq \frac{E(x)}{t}.$$

Hint: $E(x) = \int_0^\infty xf(x) \, dx = \int_0^t xf(x) \, dx + \int_t^\infty xf(x) \, dx.$

e. Consider the probability density function $f(x) = 2x^{-3}$ for $x \geq 1$.

(1) Show that this is a proper PDF.

(2) Calculate $F(x)$ for this PDF.

(3) Use the results of part (c) to calculate $E(x)$ for this PDF.

(4) Show that Markov's inequality holds for this function.

f. The concept of conditional expected value is useful in some economic problems. We denote the expected value of x conditional on the occurrence of some event, A, as $E(x|A)$. To compute this value we need to know the PDF for x given that A has occurred [denoted by $f(x|A)$]. With this notation, $E(x|A) = \int_{-\infty}^{+\infty} x f(x|A)\,dx$. Perhaps the easiest way to understand these relationships is with an example. Let

$$f(x) = \frac{x^2}{3} \quad \text{for} \quad -1 \le x \le 2.$$

(1) Show that this is a proper PDF.

(2) Calculate $E(x)$.

(3) Calculate the probability that $-1 \le x \le 0$.

(4) Consider the event $0 \le x \le 2$, and call this event A. What is $f(x|A)$?

(5) Calculate $E(x|A)$.

(6) Explain your results intuitively.

2.14 More on variances and covariances

This problem presents a few useful mathematical facts about variances and covariances.

a. Show that $\mathrm{Var}(x) = E(x^2) - [E(x)]^2$.

b. Show that the result in part (a) can be generalized as $\mathrm{Cov}(x, y) = E(xy) - E(x)E(y)$. *Note:* If $\mathrm{Cov}(x, y) = 0$, then $E(xy) = E(x)E(y)$.

c. Show that $\mathrm{Var}(ax \pm by) = a^2\,\mathrm{Var}(x) + b^2\,\mathrm{Var}(y) \pm 2ab\,\mathrm{Cov}(x, y)$.

d. Assume that two independent random variables, x and y, are characterized by $E(x) = E(y)$ and $\mathrm{Var}(x) = \mathrm{Var}(y)$. Show that $E(0.5x + 0.5y) = E(x)$. Then use part (c) to show that $\mathrm{Var}(0.5x + 0.5y) = 0.5\,\mathrm{Var}(x)$. Describe why this fact provides the rationale for diversification of assets.

SUGGESTIONS FOR FURTHER READING

Dadkhan, Kamran. *Foundations of Mathematical and Computational Economics.* Mason, OH: Thomson/South-Western, 2007.

> This is a good introduction to many calculus techniques. The book shows how many mathematical questions can be approached using popular software programs such as Matlab or Excel.

Dixit, A. K. *Optimization in Economic Theory,* 2nd ed. New York: Oxford University Press, 1990.

> A complete and modern treatment of optimization techniques. Uses relatively advanced analytical methods.

Hoy, Michael, John Livernois, Chris McKenna, Ray Rees, and Thanasis Stengos. *Mathematics for Economists,* 2nd ed. Cambridge, MA: MIT Press, 2001.

> A complete introduction to most of the mathematics covered in microeconomics courses. The strength of the book is its presentation of many worked-out examples, most of which are based on microeconomic theory.

Mas-Colell, Andreu, Michael D. Whinston, and Jerry R. Green. *Microeconomic Theory.* New York: Oxford University Press, 1995.

> Encyclopedic treatment of mathematical microeconomics. Extensive mathematical appendices cover relatively high-level topics in analysis.

Samuelson, Paul A. *Foundations of Economic Analysis.* Cambridge, MA: Harvard University Press, 1947. Mathematical Appendix A.

> A basic reference. Mathematical Appendix A provides an advanced treatment of necessary and sufficient conditions for a maximum.

Silberberg, E., and W. Suen. *The Structure of Economics: A Mathematical Analysis,* 3rd ed. Boston: Irwin/McGraw-Hill, 2001.

> A mathematical microeconomics text that stresses the observable predictions of economic theory. The text makes extensive use of the envelope theorem.

Simon, Carl P., and Lawrence Blume. *Mathematics for Economists.* New York: W. W. Norton, 1994.

> A very useful text covering most areas of mathematics relevant to economists. Treatment is at a relatively high level. Two topics discussed better here than elsewhere are differential equations and basic point-set topology.

Sydsaeter, K., A. Strom, and P. Berck. *Economists' Mathematical Manual,* 3rd ed. Berlin: Springer-Verlag, 2000.

> An indispensable tool for mathematical review. Contains 32 chapters covering most of the mathematical tools that economists use.

Discussions are very brief, so this is not the place to encounter new concepts for the first time.

Taylor, Angus E., and W. Robert Mann. *Advanced Calculus,* 3rd ed. New York: John Wiley, 1983, pp. 183–95.

A comprehensive calculus text with a good discussion of the Lagrangian technique.

Thomas, George B., and Ross L. Finney. *Calculus and Analytic Geometry,* 8th ed. Reading, MA: Addison-Wesley, 1992.

Basic calculus text with excellent coverage of differentiation techniques.

EXTENSIONS

Second-Order Conditions and Matrix Algebra

The second-order conditions described in Chapter 2 can be written in very compact ways by using matrix algebra. In this extension, we look briefly at that notation. We return to this notation at a few other places in the extensions and problems for later chapters.

Matrix algebra background

The extensions presented here assume some general familiarity with matrix algebra. A succinct reminder of these principles might include:

1. An $n \times k$ *matrix*, **A**, is a rectangular array of terms of the form

$$A = \begin{bmatrix} a_{ij} \end{bmatrix} = \begin{bmatrix} a_{11} & a_{12} & \cdots & a_{1k} \\ a_{21} & a_{22} & \cdots & a_{2k} \\ \vdots & & & \\ a_{n1} & a_{n2} & \cdots & a_{nk} \end{bmatrix}.$$

   Here $i = 1, n$; $j = 1, k$. Matrices can be added, subtracted, or multiplied providing their dimensions are conformable.

2. If $n = k$, then **A** is a square matrix. A square matrix is symmetric if $a_{ij} = a_{ji}$. The *identity matrix*, $\mathbf{I}_n$, is an $n + n$ square matrix where $a_{ij} = 1$ if $i = j$ and $a_{ij} = 0$ if $i \neq j$.

3. The **determinant** of a square matrix (denoted by $|\mathbf{A}|$) is a scalar (i.e., a single term) found by suitably multiplying together all of the terms in the matrix. If **A** is 2×2,

$$|\mathbf{A}| = a_{11}a_{22} - a_{21}a_{12}.$$

   Example: If $A = \begin{bmatrix} 1 & 3 \\ 5 & 2 \end{bmatrix}$ then

$$|\mathbf{A}| = 2 - 15 = -13.$$

4. The *inverse* of an $n \times n$ square matrix, **A**, is another $n \times n$ matrix, A^{-1}, such that

$$\mathbf{A} \cdot \mathbf{A}^{-1} = \mathbf{I}_n.$$

   Not every square matrix has an inverse. A necessary and sufficient condition for the existence of $\mathbf{A}^{-1}$ is that $|\mathbf{A}| \neq 0$.

5. The *leading principal minors* of an $n \times n$ square matrix **A** are the series of determinants of the first p rows and columns of **A**, where $p = 1, n$. If

A is 2×2, then the first leading principal minor is a_{11} and the second is $a_{11}a_{22} - a_{21}a_{12}$.

6. An $n \times n$ square matrix, **A**, is *positive definite* if all of its leading principal minors are positive. The matrix is *negative definite* if its principal minors alternate in sign starting with a minus.[1]

7. A particularly useful symmetric matrix is the *Hessian matrix* formed by all of the second-order partial derivatives of a function. If f is a continuous and twice differentiable function of n variables, then its Hessian is given by

$$\mathbf{H}(f) = \begin{bmatrix} f_{11} & f_{12} & \cdots & f_{1n} \\ f_{21} & f_{22} & \cdots & f_{2n} \\ \vdots & & & \\ f_{n1} & f_{n2} & \cdots & f_{nn} \end{bmatrix}.$$

Using these notational ideas, we can now examine again some of the second-order conditions derived in Chapter 2.

E2.1 Concave and convex functions

A *concave function* is one that is always below (or on) any tangent to it. Alternatively, a *convex function* is always above (or on) any tangent. The concavity or convexity of any function is determined by its second derivative(s). For a function of a single variable, $f(x)$, the requirement is straightforward. Using the Taylor approximation at any point (x_0)

$$f(x_0 + dx) = f(x_0) + f'(x_0)dx + f''(x_0)\frac{dx^2}{2}$$
$$+ \textbf{higher-order terms}.$$

Assuming that the higher-order terms are 0, we have

$$f(x_0 + dx) \leq f(x_0) + f'(x_0)dx$$

if $f''(x_0) \leq 0$ and

$$f(x_0 + dx) \geq f(x_0) + f'(x_0)dx$$

if $f''(x_0) \geq 0$. Because the expressions on the right of these inequalities are in fact the equation of the tangent to the function at x_0, it is clear that the

---

[1] If some of the determinants in this definition are 0 then the matrix is said to be positive semidefinite or negative semidefinite.

function is (locally) concave if $f''(x_0) \leq 0$ and (locally) convex if $f''(x_0) \geq 0$.

Extending this intuitive idea to many dimensions is cumbersome in terms of functional notation, but relatively simple when matrix algebra is used. Concavity requires that the Hessian matrix be negative definite whereas convexity requires that this matrix be positive definite. As in the single variable case, these conditions amount to requiring that the function move consistently away from any tangent to it no matter what direction is taken.[2]

If $f(x_1, x_2)$ is a function of two variables, the Hessian is given by

$$H = \begin{bmatrix} f_{11} & f_{12} \\ f_{21} & f_{22} \end{bmatrix}.$$

This is negative definite if

$$f_{11} < 0 \quad \text{and} \quad f_{11}f_{22} - f_{21}f_{12} > 0,$$

which is precisely the condition described in Equation 2.98. Generalizations to functions of three or more variables follow the same matrix pattern.

Example 1

For the health status function in Chapter 2 (Equation 2.20), the Hessian is given by

$$H = \begin{bmatrix} -2 & 0 \\ 0 & -2 \end{bmatrix},$$

and the first and second leading principal minors are

$$H_1 = -2 < 0 \quad \text{and}$$
$$H_2 = (-2)(-2) - 0 = 4 > 0.$$

Hence, the function is concave.

Example 2

The Cobb-Douglas function $x^a y^b$ where $a, b \in (0,1)$ is used to illustrate utility functions and production functions in many places in this text. The first- and second-order derivatives of the function are

$$f_x = ax^{a-1}y^b,$$
$$f_y = bx^a y^{b-1},$$
$$f_{xx} = a(a-1)x^{a-2}y^b,$$
$$f_{yy} = b(b-1)x^a y^{b-2}.$$

Hence, the Hessian for this function is

$$H = \begin{bmatrix} a(a-1)x^{a-2}y^b & abx^{a-1}y^{b-1} \\ abx^{a-1}y^{b-1} & b(b-1)x^a y^{b-2} \end{bmatrix}.$$

The first leading principal minor of this Hessian is

$$H_1 = a(a-1)x^{a-2}y^b < 0$$

and so the function will be concave, providing

$$H_2 = a(a-1)(b)(b-1)x^{2a-2}y^{2b-2} - a^2 b^2 x^{2a-2}y^{2b-2}$$
$$= ab(1-a-b)x^{2a-2}y^{2b-2} > 0.$$

This condition clearly holds if $a + b < 1$. That is, in production function terminology, the function must exhibit diminishing returns to scale to be concave. Geometrically, the function must turn downward as both inputs are increased together.

E2.2 Maximization

As we saw in Chapter 2, the first-order conditions for an unconstrained maximum of a function of many variables requires finding a point at which the partial derivatives are zero. If the function is concave it will be below its tangent plane at this point and therefore the point will be a true maximum.[3] Because the health status function is concave, for example, the first-order conditions for a maximum are also sufficient.

E2.3 Constrained maxima

When the x's in a maximization or minimization problem are subject to constraints, these constraints have to be taken into account in stating second-order conditions. Again, matrix algebra provides a compact (if not very intuitive) way of denoting these conditions. The notation involves adding rows and columns of the Hessian matrix for the unconstrained problem and then checking the properties of this augmented matrix.

Specifically, we wish to maximize

$$f(x_1, \ldots, x_n)$$

subject to the constraint[4]

$$g(x_1, \ldots, x_n) = 0.$$

---

[2]A proof using the multivariable version of Taylor's approximation is provided in Simon and Blume (1994), chap. 21.

[3]This will be a "local" maximum if the function is concave only in a region, or "global" if the function is concave everywhere.

[4]Here we look only at the case of a single constraint. Generalization to many constraints is conceptually straightforward but notationally complex. For a concise statement see Sydsaeter, Strom, and Berck (2000), p. 93.

We saw in Chapter 2 that the first-order conditions for a maximum are of the form

$$f_i + \lambda g_i = 0,$$

where λ is the Lagrangian multiplier for this problem. Second-order conditions for a maximum are based on the augmented ("bordered") Hessian[5]

$$\mathbf{H_b} = \begin{bmatrix} 0 & g_1 & g_2 & \cdots & g_n \\ g_1 & f_{11} & f_{12} & & f_{1n} \\ g_2 & f_{21} & f_{22} & & f_{2n} \\ \vdots & & & & \\ g_n & f_{n1} & f_{n2} & \cdots & f_{nn} \end{bmatrix}.$$

For a maximum, $(-1)\mathbf{H_b}$ must be negative definite—that is, the leading principal minors of $\mathbf{H_b}$ must follow the pattern $- + - + -$ and so forth, starting with the second such minor.[6]

The second-order conditions for minimum require that $(-1)\mathbf{H_b}$ be positive definite—that is, all of the leading principal minors of $\mathbf{H_b}$ (except the first) should be negative.

Example

The Lagrangian for the constrained health status problem (Example 2.6) is

$$\mathcal{L} = -x_1^2 + 2x_1 - x_2^2 + 4x_2 + 5 + \lambda(1 - x_1 - x_2),$$

and the bordered Hessian for this problem is

$$\mathbf{H_b} = \begin{bmatrix} 0 & -1 & -1 \\ -1 & -2 & 0 \\ -1 & 0 & -2 \end{bmatrix}.$$

The second leading principal minor here is

$$\mathbf{H_{b2}} = \begin{bmatrix} 0 & -1 \\ -1 & -2 \end{bmatrix} = -1,$$

and the third is

$$\mathbf{H_{b3}} = \begin{bmatrix} 0 & -1 & -1 \\ -1 & -2 & 0 \\ -1 & 0 & -2 \end{bmatrix}$$
$$= 0 + 0 + 0 - (-2) - 0 - (-2) = 4,$$

so the leading principal minors of the $\mathbf{H_b}$ have the required pattern and the point

$$x_2 = 1, \quad x_1 = 0,$$

is a constrained maximum.

Example

In the optimal fence problem (Example 2.7), the bordered Hessian is

$$\mathbf{H_b} = \begin{bmatrix} 0 & -2 & -2 \\ -2 & 0 & 1 \\ -2 & 1 & 0 \end{bmatrix}$$

and

$$\mathbf{H_{b2}} = -4,$$
$$\mathbf{H_{b3}} = 8,$$

so again the leading principal minors have the sign pattern required for a maximum.

E2.4 Quasi-concavity

If the constraint g is linear, then the second-order conditions explored in Extension 2.3 can be related solely to the shape of the function to be optimized, f. In this case the constraint can be written as

$$g(x_1, \ldots, x_n) = c - b_1 x_1 - b_2 x_2 - \cdots - b_n x_n = 0,$$

and the first-order conditions for a maximum are

$$f_i = \lambda b_i, \quad i = 1, \ldots, n.$$

Using the conditions, it is clear that the bordered Hessian $\mathbf{H_b}$ and the matrix

$$\mathbf{H'} = \begin{bmatrix} 0 & f_1 & f_2 & \cdots & f_n \\ f_1 & f_{11} & f_{12} & & f_{1n} \\ f_2 & f_{21} & f_{22} & & f_{2n} \\ f_n & f_{n1} & f_{n2} & \cdots & f_{nn} \end{bmatrix}$$

have the same leading principal minors except for a (positive) constant of proportionality.[7] The conditions for a maximum of f subject to a linear constraint will be satisfied provided $\mathbf{H'}$ follows the same sign conventions as $\mathbf{H_b}$—that is, $(-1)\mathbf{H'}$ must be negative definite. A function f for which $\mathbf{H'}$ does follow this pattern is called *quasi-concave*. As we shall see, f has the property that the set of points x for which $f(x) \geq c$ (where c is any constant) is convex. For such a function, the necessary conditions for a maximum are also sufficient.

Example

For the fences problem, $f(x, y) = xy$ and $\mathbf{H'}$ is given by

---

[5]Notice that, if $g_{ij} = 0$ for all i and j, then $\mathbf{H_b}$ can be regarded as the simple Hessian associated with the Lagrangian expression given in Equation 2.50, which is a function of the $n + 1$ variables $\lambda, x_1, \ldots, x_n$.
[6]Notice that the first leading principal minor of $\mathbf{H_b}$ is 0.

[7]This can be shown by noting that multiplying a row (or a column) of a matrix by a constant multiplies the determinant by that constant.

$$\mathbf{H}' = \begin{bmatrix} 0 & y & x \\ y & 0 & 1 \\ x & 1 & 0 \end{bmatrix}.$$

So

$$\mathbf{H}'_2 = -y^2 < 0,$$

$$\mathbf{H}'_3 = 2xy > 0,$$

and the function is quasi-concave.[8]

Example

More generally, if f is a function of only two variables, then quasi-concavity requires that

$$\mathbf{H}'_2 = -(f_1)^2 < 0 \quad \text{and}$$

$$\mathbf{H}'_3 = -f_{11}f_2^2 - f_{22}f_1^2 + 2f_1f_2f_{12} > 0,$$

which is precisely the condition stated in Equation 2.114. Hence, we have a fairly simple way of determining quasi-concavity.

References

Simon, C. P., and L. Blume. *Mathematics for Economists.* New York: W.W. Norton, 1994.

Sydsaeter, R., A. Strom, and P. Berck. *Economists' Mathematical Manual*, 3rd ed. Berlin: Springer-Verlag, 2000.

---

[8]Since $f(x, y) = xy$ is a form of a Cobb-Douglas function that is not concave, this shows that not every quasi-concave function is concave. Notice that a monotonic function of f (such as $f^{1/3}$) would be concave, however.

PART 2

Choice and Demand

In **Part 2** we will investigate the economic theory of *choice*. One goal of this examination is to develop the notion of demand in a formal way so that it can be used in later sections of the text when we turn to the study of markets. A more general goal of this part is to illustrate the theory economists use to explain how individuals make choices in a wide variety of contexts.

Part 2 begins with a description of the way economists model individual preferences, which are usually referred to by the formal term *utility*. **Chapter 3** shows how economists are able to conceptualize utility in a mathematical way. This permits the development of "indifference curves," which show the various exchanges that individuals are willing to make voluntarily.

The utility concept is used in **Chapter 4** to illustrate the theory of choice. The fundamental hypothesis of the chapter is that people faced with limited incomes will make economic choices in such a way as to achieve as much utility as possible. Chapter 4 uses mathematical and intuitive analyses to indicate the insights that this hypothesis provides about economic behavior.

Chapters 5 and 6 use the model of utility maximization to investigate how individuals will respond to changes in their circumstances. **Chapter 5** is primarily concerned with responses to changes in the price of a commodity, an analysis that leads directly to the demand curve notion. **Chapter 6** applies this type of analysis to developing an understanding of demand relationships among different goods.

The final two chapters in this part look at individual behavior in uncertain situations. In **Chapter 7** we describe why people generally dislike risks and are willing to pay something to avoid taking them. **Chapter 8** then looks at uncertainties that arise when two or more people find themselves in a "game" in which they must make strategic choices. The equilibrium notions we develop in studying such games are widely used throughout economics.

Preferences and Utility

In this chapter we look at the way in which economists characterize individuals' preferences. We begin with a fairly abstract discussion of the "preference relation," but quickly turn to the economists' primary tool for studying individual choices—the utility function. We look at some general characteristics of that function and a few simple examples of specific utility functions we will encounter throughout this book.

AXIOMS OF RATIONAL CHOICE

One way to begin an analysis of individuals' choices is to state a basic set of postulates, or axioms, that characterize "rational" behavior. These begin with the concept of "preference": An individual who reports that "A is preferred to B" is taken to mean that all things considered, he or she feels better off under situation A than under situation B. The preference relation is assumed to have three basic properties as follows.

I. *Completeness.* If A and B are *any* two situations, the individual can always specify exactly one of the following three possibilities:

1. "A is preferred to B,"
2. "B is preferred to A," or
3. "A and B are equally attractive."

Consequently, people are assumed not to be paralyzed by indecision: They completely understand and can always make up their minds about the desirability of any two alternatives. The assumption also rules out the possibility that an individual can report both that A is preferred to B and that B is preferred to A.

II. *Transitivity.* If an individual reports that "A is preferred to B" and "B is preferred to C," then he or she must also report that "A is preferred to C."

This assumption states that the individual's choices are internally consistent. Such an assumption can be subjected to empirical study. Generally, such studies conclude that a person's choices are indeed transitive, but this conclusion must be modified in cases where the individual may not fully understand the consequences of the choices he or she is making. Because, for the most part, we will assume choices are fully informed (but see the discussion of uncertainty in Chapter 7 and elsewhere), the transitivity property seems to be an appropriate assumption to make about preferences.

III. *Continuity.* If an individual reports "A is preferred to B," then situations suitably "close to" A must also be preferred to B.

This rather technical assumption is required if we wish to analyze individuals' responses to relatively small changes in income and prices. The purpose of the assumption is to rule out certain kinds of discontinuous, knife-edge preferences that pose problems for a mathematical development of the theory of choice. Assuming continuity does not seem to risk missing types of economic behavior that are important in the real world.

UTILITY

Given the assumptions of completeness, transitivity, and continuity, it is possible to show formally that people are able to rank all possible situations from the least desirable to the most.[1] Following the terminology introduced by the nineteenth-century political theorist Jeremy Bentham, economists call this ranking *utility*.[2] We also will follow Bentham by saying that more desirable situations offer more utility than do less desirable ones. That is, if a person prefers situation A to situation B, we would say that the utility assigned to option A, denoted by $U(A)$, exceeds the utility assigned to B, $U(B)$.

Nonuniqueness of utility measures

We might even attach numbers to these utility rankings; however, these numbers will not be unique. Any set of numbers we arbitrarily assign that accurately reflects the original preference ordering will imply the same set of choices. It makes no difference whether we say that $U(A) = 5$ and $U(B) = 4$, or that $U(A) = 1,000,000$ and $U(B) = 0.5$. In both cases the numbers imply that A is preferred to B. In technical terms, our notion of utility is defined only up to an order-preserving ("monotonic") transformation.[3] Any set of numbers that accurately reflects a person's preference ordering will do. Consequently, it makes no sense to ask "how much more is A preferred than B?" since that question has no unique answer. Surveys that ask people to rank their "happiness" on a scale of 1 to 10 could just as well use a scale of 7 to 1,000,000. We can only hope that a person who reports he or she is a "6" on the scale one day and a "7" on the next day is indeed happier on the second day. Utility rankings are therefore like the ordinal rankings of restaurants or movies using one, two, three, or four stars. They simply record the relative desirability of commodity bundles.

This lack of uniqueness in the assignment of utility numbers also implies that it is not possible to compare utilities of different people. If one person reports that a steak dinner provides a utility of "5" and another reports that the same dinner offers a utility of "100," we cannot say which individual values the dinner more because they could be using very different scales. Similarly, we have no way of measuring whether a move from situation A to situation B provides more utility to one person or another. Nonetheless, as we will see, economists can say quite a bit about utility rankings by examining what people voluntarily choose to do.

The ceteris paribus assumption

Because *utility* refers to overall satisfaction, such a measure clearly is affected by a variety of factors. A person's utility is affected not only by his or her consumption of physical commodities, but also by psychological attitudes, peer group pressures, personal experiences, and the

---

[1]These properties and their connection to representation of preferences by a utility function are discussed in detail in Andreu Mas-Colell, Michael D. Whinston, and Jerry R. Green, *Microeconomic Theory* (New York: Oxford University Press, 1995).

[2]J. Bentham, *Introduction to the Principles of Morals and Legislation* (London: Hafner, 1848).

[3]We can denote this idea mathematically by saying that any numerical utility ranking (U) can be transformed into another set of numbers by the function F providing that $F(U)$ is order preserving. This can be ensured if $F'(U) > 0$. For example, the transformation $F(U) = U^2$ is order preserving as is the transformation $F(U) = \ln U$. At some places in the text and problems we will find it convenient to make such transformations in order to make a particular utility ranking easier to analyze.

general cultural environment. Although economists do have a general interest in examining such influences, a narrowing of focus is usually necessary. Consequently, a common practice is to devote attention exclusively to choices among quantifiable options (for example, the relative quantities of food and shelter bought, the number of hours worked per week, or the votes among specific taxing formulas) while holding constant the other things that affect behavior. This ceteris paribus (other things being equal) assumption is invoked in all economic analyses of utility-maximizing choices so as to make the analysis of choices manageable within a simplified setting.

Utility from consumption of goods

As an important example of the ceteris paribus assumption, consider an individual's problem of choosing, at a single point in time, among n consumption goods $x_1, x_2, \ldots, x_n$. We shall assume that the individual's ranking of these goods can be represented by a utility function of the form

$$\text{utility} = U(x_1, x_2, \ldots, x_n; \text{other things}), \tag{3.1}$$

where the x's refer to the quantities of the goods that might be chosen and the "other things" notation is used as a reminder that many aspects of individual welfare are being held constant in the analysis.

Quite often it is easier to write Equation 3.1 as

$$\text{utility} = U(x_1, x_2, \ldots, x_n) \tag{3.2}$$

or, if only two goods are being considered, as

$$\text{utility} = U(x, y), \tag{3.2'}$$

where it is clear that everything is being held constant (that is, outside the frame of analysis) except the goods actually referred to in the utility function. It would be tedious to remind you at each step what is being held constant in the analysis, but it should be remembered that some form of the ceteris paribus assumption will always be in effect.

Arguments of utility functions

The utility function notation is used to indicate how an individual ranks the particular arguments of the function being considered. In the most common case, the utility function (Equation 3.2) will be used to represent how an individual ranks certain bundles of goods that might be purchased at one point in time. On occasion we will use other arguments in the utility function, and it is best to clear up certain conventions at the outset. For example, it may be useful to talk about the utility an individual receives from real wealth (W). Therefore, we shall use the notation

$$\text{utility} = U(W). \tag{3.3}$$

Unless the individual is a rather peculiar, Scrooge-type person, wealth in its own right gives no direct utility. Rather, it is only when wealth is spent on consumption goods that any utility results. For this reason, Equation 3.3 will be taken to mean that the utility from wealth is in fact derived by spending that wealth in such a way as to yield as much utility as possible.

Two other arguments of utility functions will be used in later chapters. In Chapter 16 we will be concerned with the individual's labor-leisure choice and will therefore have to consider the presence of leisure in the utility function. A function of the form

$$\text{utility} = U(c, h) \tag{3.4}$$

will be used. Here, c represents consumption and h represents hours of nonwork time (that is, leisure) during a particular time period.

In Chapter 17 we will be interested in the individual's consumption decisions in different time periods. In that chapter we will use a utility function of the form

$$\text{utility} = U(c_1, c_2), \tag{3.5}$$

where c_1 is consumption in this period and c_2 is consumption in the next period. By changing the arguments of the utility function, therefore, we will be able to focus on specific aspects of an individual's choices in a variety of simplified settings.

In summary then, we start our examination of individual behavior with the following definition.

DEFINITION

Utility. Individuals' preferences are assumed to be represented by a utility function of the form

$$U(x_1, x_2, \ldots, x_n), \tag{3.6}$$

where $x_1, x_2, \ldots, x_n$ are the quantities of each of n goods that might be consumed in a period. This function is unique only up to an order-preserving transformation.

Economic goods

In this representation the variables are taken to be "goods"; that is, whatever economic quantities they represent, we assume that more of any particular x_i during some period is preferred to less. We assume this is true of every good, be it a simple consumption item such as a hot dog or a complex aggregate such as wealth or leisure. We have pictured this convention for a two-good utility function in Figure 3.1. There, all consumption bundles in the shaded area are

FIGURE 3.1   More of a Good Is Preferred to Less

The shaded area represents those combinations of x and y that are unambiguously preferred to the combination x^*, y^*. Ceteris paribus, individuals prefer more of any good rather than less. Combinations identified by "?" involve ambiguous changes in welfare because they contain more of one good and less of the other.

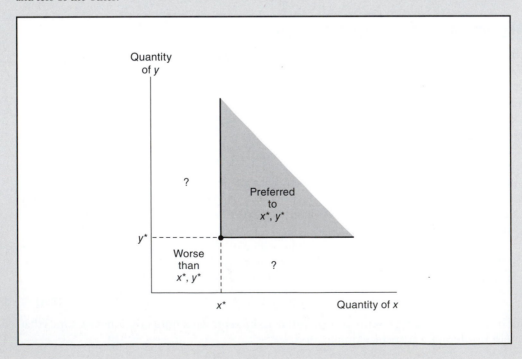

preferred to the bundle x^*, y^* because any bundle in the shaded area provides more of at least one of the goods. By our definition of "goods," then, bundles of goods in the shaded area are ranked higher than x^*, y^*. Similarly, bundles in the area marked "worse" are clearly inferior to x^*, y^*, since they contain less of at least one of the goods and no more of the other. Bundles in the two areas indicated by question marks are difficult to compare to x^*, y^* because they contain more of one of the goods and less of the other. Movements into these areas involve trade-offs between the two goods.

TRADES AND SUBSTITUTION

Most economic activity involves voluntary trading between individuals. When someone buys, say, a loaf of bread, he or she is voluntarily giving up one thing (money) for something else (bread) that is of greater value to that individual. To examine this kind of voluntary transaction, we need to develop a formal apparatus for illustrating trades in the utility function context.

Indifference curves and the marginal rate of substitution

To discuss such voluntary trades, we develop the idea of an *indifference curve*. In Figure 3.2, the curve U_1 represents all the alternative combinations of x and y for which an individual is equally well off (remember again that all other arguments of the utility function are being

FIGURE 3.2   A Single Indifference Curve

The curve U_1 represents those combinations of x and y from which the individual derives the same utility. The slope of this curve represents the rate at which the individual is willing to trade x for y while remaining equally well off. This slope (or, more properly, the negative of the slope) is termed the *marginal rate of substitution*. In the figure, the indifference curve is drawn on the assumption of a diminishing marginal rate of substitution.

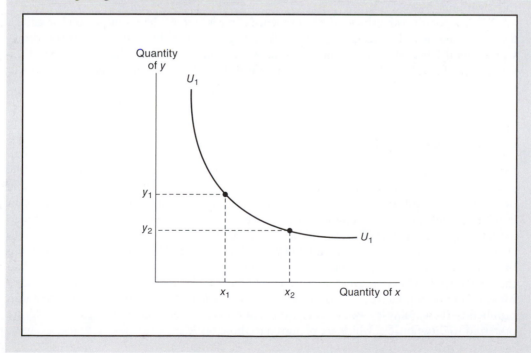

held constant). This person is equally happy consuming, for example, either the combination of goods x_1, y_1 or the combination x_2, y_2. This curve representing all the consumption bundles that the individual ranks equally is called an *indifference curve*.

DEFINITION

Indifference curve. An *indifference curve* (or, in many dimensions, an indifference surface) shows a set of consumption bundles about which the individual is indifferent. That is, the bundles all provide the same level of utility.

The slope of the indifference curve in Figure 3.2 is negative, showing that if the individual is forced to give up some y, he or she must be compensated by an additional amount of x to remain indifferent between the two bundles of goods. The curve is also drawn so that the slope increases as x increases (that is, the slope starts at negative infinity and increases toward zero). This is a graphical representation of the assumption that people become progressively less willing to trade away y to get more x. In mathematical terms, the absolute value of this slope diminishes as x increases. Hence, we have the following definition.

DEFINITION

Marginal rate of substitution. The negative of the slope of an indifference curve (U_1) at some point is termed the *marginal rate of substitution (MRS)* at that point. That is,

$$MRS = -\frac{dy}{dx}\Bigg|_{U=U_1},\tag{3.7}$$

where the notation indicates that the slope is to be calculated along the U_1 indifference curve.

The slope of U_1 and the *MRS* therefore tell us something about the trades this person will voluntarily make. At a point such as x_1, y_1, the person has quite a lot of y and is willing to trade away a significant amount to get one more x. The indifference curve at x_1, y_1 is therefore rather steep. This is a situation where the person has, say, many hamburgers (y) and little to drink with them (x). This person would gladly give up a few burgers (say, 5) to quench his or her thirst with one more drink.

At x_2, y_2, on the other hand, the indifference curve is flatter. Here, this person has quite a few drinks and is willing to give up relatively few burgers (say, 1) to get another soft drink. Consequently, the *MRS* diminishes between x_1, y_1 and x_2, y_2. The changing slope of U_1 shows how the particular consumption bundle available influences the trades this person will freely make.

Indifference curve map

In Figure 3.2 only one indifference curve was drawn. The x, y quadrant, however, is densely packed with such curves, each corresponding to a different level of utility. Because every bundle of goods can be ranked and yields some level of utility, each point in Figure 3.2 must have an indifference curve passing through it. Indifference curves are similar to contour lines on a map in that they represent lines of equal "altitude" of utility. In Figure 3.3 several indifference curves are shown to indicate that there are infinitely many in the plane. The level of utility represented by these curves increases as we move in a northeast direction; the utility of curve U_1 is less than that of U_2, which is less than that of U_3. This is because of the assumption made in Figure 3.1: More of a good is preferred to less. As was discussed earlier, there is no unique way to assign numbers to these utility levels. The curves only show that the combinations of goods on U_3 are preferred to those on U_2, which are preferred to those on U_1.

FIGURE 3.3   There Are Infinitely Many Indifference Curves in the *x–y* Plane

There is an indifference curve passing through each point in the *x–y* plane. Each of these curves records combinations of *x* and *y* from which the individual receives a certain level of satisfaction. Movements in a northeast direction represent movements to higher levels of satisfaction.

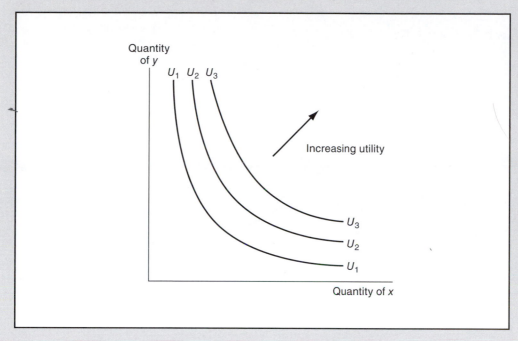

Indifference curves and transitivity

As an exercise in examining the relationship between consistent preferences and the representation of preferences by utility functions, consider the following question: Can any two of an individual's indifference curves intersect? Two such intersecting curves are shown in Figure 3.4. We wish to know if they violate our basic axioms of rationality. Using our map analogy, there would seem to be something wrong at point *E*, where "altitude" is equal to two different numbers, U_1 and U_2. But no point can be both 100 and 200 feet above sea level.

   To proceed formally, let us analyze the bundles of goods represented by points *A*, *B*, *C*, and *D*. By the assumption of nonsatiation (i.e., more of a good always increases utility), "*A* is preferred to *B*" and "*C* is preferred to *D*." But this person is equally satisfied with *B* and *C* (they lie on the same indifference curve), so the axiom of transitivity implies that *A* must be preferred to *D*. But that cannot be true, because *A* and *D* are on the same indifference curve and are by definition regarded as equally desirable. This contradiction shows that indifference curves cannot intersect. Therefore we should always draw indifference curve maps as they appear in Figure 3.3.

Convexity of indifference curves

An alternative way of stating the principle of a diminishing marginal rate of substitution uses the mathematical notion of a convex set. A set of points is said to be *convex* if any two points within the set can be joined by a straight line that is contained completely within the set. The assumption of a diminishing *MRS* is equivalent to the assumption that all combinations of *x* and *y*

FIGURE 3.4   Intersecting Indifference Curves Imply Inconsistent Preferences

Combinations *A* and *D* lie on the same indifference curve and therefore are equally desirable. But the axiom of transitivity can be used to show that *A* is preferred to *D*. Hence, intersecting indifference curves are not consistent with rational preferences.

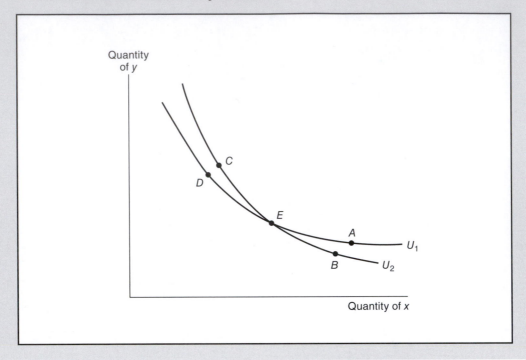

that are preferred or indifferent to a particular combination x^*, y^* form a convex set.[4] This is illustrated in Figure 3.5a, where all combinations preferred or indifferent to x^*, y^* are in the shaded area. Any two of these combinations—say, x_1, y_1 and x_2, y_2—can be joined by a straight line also contained in the shaded area. In Figure 3.5b this is not true. A line joining x_1, y_1 and x_2, y_2 passes outside the shaded area. Therefore, the indifference curve through x^*, y^* in Figure 3.5b does not obey the assumption of a diminishing *MRS*, because the set of points preferred or indifferent to x^*, y^* is not convex.

Convexity and balance in consumption

By using the notion of convexity, we can show that individuals prefer some balance in their consumption. Suppose that an individual is indifferent between the combinations x_1, y_1 and x_2, y_2. If the indifference curve is strictly convex, then the combination $(x_1 + x_2)/2, (y_1 + y_2)/2$ will be preferred to either of the initial combinations.[5] Intuitively, "well-balanced" bundles of commodities are preferred to bundles that are heavily weighted toward one commodity. This is illustrated in Figure 3.6. Because the indifference curve is assumed to be convex, all points on the straight line joining (x_1, y_1) and (x_2, y_2) are preferred to these initial points. This therefore will be true of the point $(x_1 + x_2)/2, (y_1 + y_2)/2$, which lies at the midpoint of such a line.

---

[4]This definition is equivalent to assuming that the utility function is quasi-concave. Such functions were discussed in Chapter 2, and we shall return to examine them in the next section. Sometimes the term *strict quasi-concavity* is used to rule out the possibility of indifference curves having linear segments. We generally will assume strict quasi-concavity, but in a few places we will illustrate the complications posed by linear portions of indifference curves.

[5]In the case in which the indifference curve has a linear segment, the individual will be indifferent among all three combinations.

FIGURE 3.5 The Notion of Convexity as an Alternative Definition of a Diminishing *MRS*

In (a) the indifference curve is *convex* (any line joining two points above U_1 is also above U_1). In (b) this is not the case, and the curve shown here does not everywhere have a diminishing *MRS*.

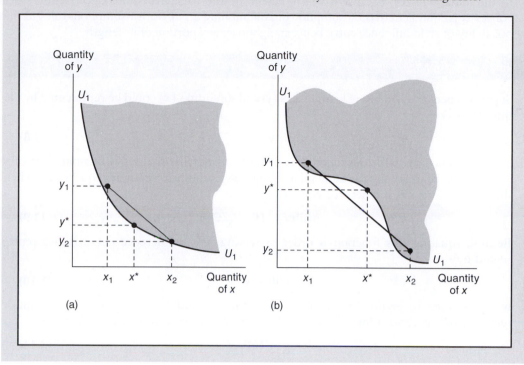

FIGURE 3.6 Balanced Bundles of Goods Are Preferred to Extreme Bundles

If indifference curves are convex (if they obey the assumption of a diminishing *MRS*), then the line joining any two points that are indifferent will contain points preferred to either of the initial combinations. Intuitively, balanced bundles are preferred to unbalanced ones.

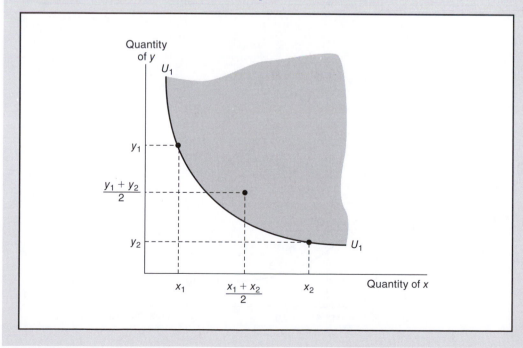

Indeed, any proportional combination of the two indifferent bundles of goods will be preferred to the initial bundles, because it will represent a more balanced combination. Thus, strict convexity is equivalent to the assumption of a diminishing *MRS*. Both assumptions rule out the possibility of an indifference curve being straight over any portion of its length.

EXAMPLE 3.1 Utility and the *MRS*

Suppose a person's ranking of hamburgers (y) and soft drinks (x) could be represented by the utility function

$$\text{utility} = \sqrt{x \cdot y}. \tag{3.8}$$

An indifference curve for this function is found by identifying that set of combinations of x and y for which utility has the same value. Suppose we arbitrarily set utility equal to 10. Then the equation for this indifference curve is

$$\text{utility} = 10 = \sqrt{x \cdot y}. \tag{3.9}$$

Because squaring this function is order preserving, the indifference curve is also represented by

$$100 = x \cdot y, \tag{3.10}$$

which is easier to graph. In Figure 3.7 we show this indifference curve; it is a familiar rectangular hyperbola. One way to calculate the *MRS* is to solve Equation 3.10 for y,

$$y = 100/x, \tag{3.11}$$

FIGURE 3.7   Indifference Curve for Utility $= \sqrt{x \cdot y}$

This indifference curve illustrates the function $10 = U = \sqrt{x \cdot y}$. At point A (5, 20), the *MRS* is 4, implying that this person is willing to trade $4y$ for an additional x. At point B (20, 5), however, the *MRS* is 0.25, implying a greatly reduced willingness to trade.

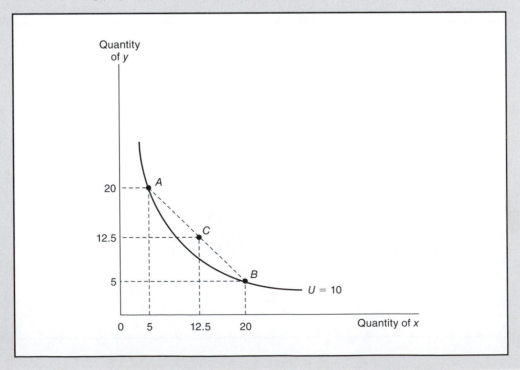

and then use the definition (Equation 3.7):

$$MRS = -dy/dx \text{ (along } U_1) = 100/x^2. \tag{3.12}$$

Clearly this MRS declines as x increases. At a point such as A on the indifference curve with a lot of hamburgers (say, $x = 5$, $y = 20$), the slope is steep so the MRS is high:

$$MRS \text{ at } (5, 20) = 100/x^2 = 100/25 = 4. \tag{3.13}$$

Here the person is willing to give up 4 hamburgers to get 1 more soft drink. On the other hand, at B where there are relatively few hamburgers (here $x = 20$, $y = 5$), the slope is flat and the MRS is low:

$$MRS \text{ at } (20, 5) = 100/x^2 = 100/400 = 0.25. \tag{3.14}$$

Now he or she will only give up one quarter of a hamburger for another soft drink. Notice also how convexity of the indifference curve U_1 is illustrated by this numerical example. Point C is midway between points A and B; at C this person has 12.5 hamburgers and 12.5 soft drinks. Here utility is given by

$$\text{utility} = \sqrt{x \cdot y} = \sqrt{(12.5)^2} = 12.5, \tag{3.15}$$

which clearly exceeds the utility along U_1 (which was assumed to be 10).

QUERY: From our derivation here, it appears that the MRS depends only on the quantity of x consumed. Why is this misleading? How does the quantity of y implicitly enter into Equations 3.13 and 3.14?

A MATHEMATICAL DERIVATION

A mathematical derivation provides additional insights about the shape of indifference curves and the nature of preferences. In this section we provide such a derivation for the case of a utility function involving only two goods. This will allow us to compare the mathematics to the two-dimensional indifference curve map. The case of many goods will be taken up at the end of the chapter, but it will turn out that this more complicated case really adds very little.

The *MRS* and marginal utility

If the utility a person receives from two goods is represented by $U(x, y)$, we can write the total differential of this function as

$$dU = \frac{\partial U}{\partial x} \cdot dx + \frac{\partial U}{\partial y} \cdot dy. \tag{3.16}$$

Along any particular indifference curve $dU = 0$, a simple manipulation of Equation 3.16 yields

$$MRS = -\frac{dy}{dx}\bigg|_{U=\text{constant}} = \frac{\partial U/\partial x}{\partial U/\partial y}. \tag{3.17}$$

In words, the MRS of x for y is equal to the ratio of the marginal utility of x (that is, $\partial U/\partial x$) to the marginal utility of y ($\partial U/\partial y$). This result makes intuitive sense. Suppose that a person's utility were actually measurable in, say, units called "utils." Assume also that this person consumes only two goods, food (x) and clothing (y), and that each extra unit of food provides 6 utils whereas each extra unit of clothing provides 2 utils. Then Equation 3.17 would mean that

$$MRS = \frac{dy}{dx}\bigg|_{U=\text{constant}} = \frac{6\,\textbf{utils}}{2\,\textbf{utils}} = 3,$$

so this person is willing to trade away 3 units of clothing to get 1 more unit of food. This trade would result in no net change in utility because the gains and losses would be precisely offsetting. Notice that the units in which utility is measured (what we have, for lack of a better word, called "utils") cancel out in making this calculation. Although marginal utility is obviously affected by the units in which utility is measured, the MRS is independent of that choice.[6]

The convexity of indifference curves

In Chapter 1 we described how the assumption of diminishing marginal utility was used by Marshall to solve the water-diamond paradox. Marshall theorized that it is the marginal valuation that an individual places on a good that determines its value: It is the amount that an individual is willing to pay for one more pint of water that determines the price of water. Because it might be thought that this marginal value declines as the quantity of water that is consumed increases, Marshall showed why water has a low exchange value. Intuitively, it seems that the assumption of a decreasing marginal utility of a good is related to the assumption of a decreasing MRS; both concepts seem to refer to the same commonsense idea of an individual becoming relatively satiated with a good as more of it is consumed. Unfortunately, the two concepts are quite different. (See Problem 3.3.) Technically, the assumption of a diminishing MRS is equivalent to requiring that the utility function be quasi-concave. This requirement is related in a rather complex way to the assumption that each good encounters diminishing marginal utility (that is, that f_{ii} is negative for each good).[7] But that is to be expected because the concept of diminishing marginal utility is not independent of how

---

[6]More formally, let $F(U)$ be any arbitrary order-preserving transformation of U (that is, $F'(U) > 0$). Then, for the transformed utility function,

$$MRS = \frac{\partial F/\partial x}{\partial F/\partial y} = \frac{F'(U)\partial U/\partial x}{F'(U)\partial U/\partial y}$$
$$= \frac{\partial U/\partial x}{\partial U/\partial y},$$

which is the MRS for the original function U. That the $F'(U)$ terms cancel out shows that the MRS is independent of how utility is measured.

[7]We have shown that if utility is given by $U = f(x, y)$, then

$$MRS = \frac{f_x}{f_y} = \frac{f_1}{f_2} = -\frac{dy}{dx}.$$

The assumption of a diminishing MRS means that $dMRS/dx < 0$, but

$$\frac{dMRS}{dx} = \frac{f_2(f_{11} + f_{12} \cdot dy/dx) - f_1(f_{21} + f_{22} \cdot dy/dx)}{f_2^2}.$$

Using the fact that $f_1/f_2 = -dy/dx$, we have

$$\frac{dMRS}{dx} = \frac{f_2[f_{11} - f_{12}(f_1/f_2)] - f_1[f_{21} - f_{22}(f_1/f_2)]}{f_2^2}.$$

Combining terms and recognizing that $f_{12} = f_{21}$ yields

$$\frac{dMRS}{dx} = \frac{f_2 f_{11} - 2f_1 f_{12} + (f_{22} f_1^2)/f_2}{f_2^2},$$

or, multiplying numerator and denominator by f_2,

$$\frac{dMRS}{dx} = \frac{f_2^2 f_{11} - 2f_1 f_2 f_{12} + f_1^2 f_{22}}{f_2^3}.$$

utility itself is measured, whereas the convexity of indifference curves is indeed independent of such measurement.

EXAMPLE 3.2 Showing Convexity of Indifference Curves

Calculation of the *MRS* for specific utility functions is frequently a good shortcut for showing convexity of indifference curves. In particular, the process can be much simpler than applying the definition of quasi-concavity, though it is more difficult to generalize to more than two goods. Here we look at how Equation 3.17 can be used for three different utility functions (for more practice, see Problem 3.1).

1. $U(x, y) = \sqrt{x \cdot y}$.

    This example just repeats the case illustrated in Example 3.1. One shortcut to applying Equation 3.17 that can simplify the algebra is to take the logarithm of this utility function. Because taking logs is order preserving, this will not alter the *MRS* to be calculated. So, let

    $$U^*(x, y) = \ln[U(x, y)] = 0.5 \ln x + 0.5 \ln y. \qquad (3.18)$$

    Applying Equation 3.17 yields

    $$MRS = \frac{\partial U^*/\partial x}{\partial U^*/\partial y} = \frac{0.5/x}{0.5/y} = \frac{y}{x}, \qquad (3.19)$$

    which seems to be a much simpler approach than we used previously.[8] Clearly this *MRS* is diminishing as x increases and y decreases. The indifference curves are therefore convex.

2. $U(x, y) = x + xy + y$.

    In this case there is no advantage to transforming this utility function. Applying Equation 3.17 yields

    $$MRS = \frac{\partial U/\partial x}{\partial U/\partial y} = \frac{1 + y}{1 + x}. \qquad (3.20)$$

    Again, this ratio clearly decreases as x increases and y decreases, so the indifference curves for this function are convex.

3. $U(x, y) = \sqrt{x^2 + y^2}$.

    For this example it is easier to use the transformation

    $$U^*(x, y) = [U(x, y)]^2 = x^2 + y^2. \qquad (3.21)$$

    Because this is the equation for a quarter-circle, we should begin to suspect that there

    (continued)

If we assume that $f_2 > 0$ (that marginal utility is positive), then the *MRS* will diminish as long as

$$f_2^2 f_{11} - 2f_1 f_2 f_{12} + f_1^2 f_{22} < 0.$$

Notice that diminishing marginal utility ($f_{11} < 0$ and $f_{22} < 0$) will not ensure this inequality. One must also be concerned with the f_{12} term. That is, one must know how decreases in y affect the marginal utility of x. In general it is not possible to predict the sign of that term.

    The condition required for a diminishing *MRS* is precisely that discussed in Chapter 2 to ensure that the function f is strictly quasi-concave. The condition shows that the necessary conditions for a maximum of f subject to a linear constraint are also sufficient. We will use this result in Chapter 4 and elsewhere.

[8]In Example 3.1 we looked at the $U = 10$ indifference curve. So, for that curve, $y = 100/x$ and the *MRS* in Equation 3.19 would be $MRS = 100/x^2$ as calculated before.

EXAMPLE 3.2   CONTINUED

might be some problems with the indifference curves for this utility function. These suspicions are confirmed by again applying the definition of the *MRS* to yield

$$MRS = \frac{\partial U^*/\partial x}{\partial U^*/\partial y} = \frac{2x}{2y} = \frac{x}{y}. \qquad (3.22)$$

For this function, it is clear that, as x increases and y decreases, the *MRS increases*! Hence the indifference curves are concave, not convex, and this is clearly not a quasi-concave function.

QUERY: Does a doubling of x and y change the *MRS* in each of these three examples? That is, does the *MRS* depend only on the ratio of x to y, not on the absolute scale of purchases? (See also Example 3.3.)

UTILITY FUNCTIONS FOR SPECIFIC PREFERENCES

Individuals' rankings of commodity bundles and the utility functions implied by these rankings are unobservable. All we can learn about people's preferences must come from the behavior we observe when they respond to changes in income, prices, and other factors. It is nevertheless useful to examine a few of the forms particular utility functions might take, because such an examination may offer insights into observed behavior and (more to the point) understanding the properties of such functions can be of some help in solving problems. Here we will examine four specific examples of utility functions for two goods. Indifference curve maps for these functions are illustrated in the four panels of Figure 3.8. As should be visually apparent, these cover quite a few possible shapes. Even greater variety is possible once we move to functions for three or more goods, and some of these possibilities are mentioned in later chapters.

Cobb-Douglas utility

Figure 3.8a shows the familiar shape of an indifference curve. One commonly used utility function that generates such curves has the form

$$\text{utility} = U(x, y) = x^{\alpha} y^{\beta}, \qquad (3.23)$$

where α and β are positive constants.

In Examples 3.1 and 3.2, we studied a particular case of this function for which $\alpha = \beta = 0.5$. The more general case presented in Equation 3.23 is termed a *Cobb-Douglas utility function*, after two researchers who used such a function for their detailed study of production relationships in the U.S. economy (see Chapter 7). In general, the relative sizes of α and β indicate the relative importance of the two goods to this individual. Since utility is unique only up to a monotonic transformation, it is often convenient to normalize these parameters so that $\alpha + \beta = 1$.

Perfect substitutes

The linear indifference curves in Figure 3.8b are generated by a utility function of the form

$$\text{utility} = U(x, y) = \alpha x + \beta y, \qquad (3.24)$$

FIGURE 3.8   Examples of Utility Functions

The four indifference curve maps illustrate alternative degrees of substitutability of x for y. The Cobb-Douglas and CES functions (drawn here for relatively low substitutability) fall between the extremes of perfect substitution (panel b) and no substitution (panel c).

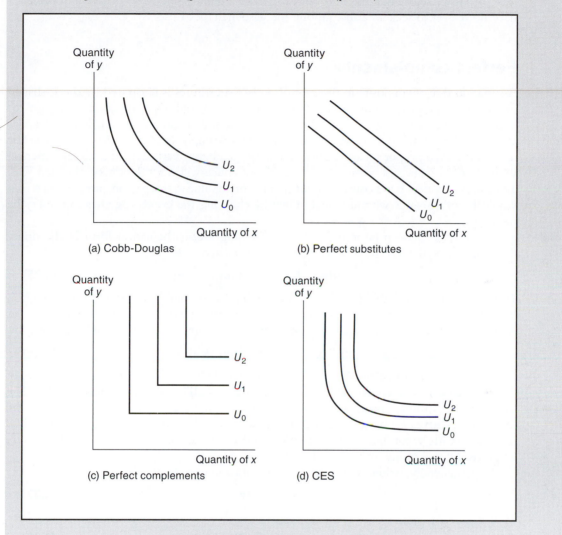

where, again, α and β are positive constants. That the indifference curves for this function are straight lines should be readily apparent: Any particular level curve can be calculated by setting $U(x, y)$ equal to a constant that, given the linear form of the function, clearly specifies a straight line. The linear nature of these indifference curves gave rise to the term *perfect substitutes* to describe the implied relationship between x and y. Because the *MRS* is constant (and equal to α/β) along the entire indifference curve, our previous notions of a diminishing *MRS* do not apply in this case. A person with these preferences would be willing to give up the same amount of y to get one more x no matter how much x was being consumed. Such a situation might describe the relationship between different brands of what is essentially the same product. For example, many people (including the author) do not care where they buy gasoline. A gallon of gas is a gallon of gas in spite of the best efforts of the Exxon and Shell advertising departments to convince me otherwise. Given this fact, I am always willing to give up 10 gallons of Exxon in exchange for 10 gallons of Shell because it does not matter to me which I use or where I got my last tankful. Indeed, as we will see in the next chapter, one implication of such a relationship is that I will buy all my gas from the least expensive seller. Because I do not experience a diminishing *MRS* of Exxon for Shell, I have no reason to seek a balance among the gasoline types I use.

Perfect complements

A situation directly opposite to the case of perfect substitutes is illustrated by the L-shaped indifference curves in Figure 3.8c. These preferences would apply to goods that "go to-gether"—coffee and cream, peanut butter and jelly, and cream cheese and lox are familiar examples. The indifference curves shown in Figure 3.8c imply that these pairs of goods will be used in the fixed proportional relationship represented by the vertices of the curves. A person who prefers 1 ounce of cream with 8 ounces of coffee will want 2 ounces of cream with 16 ounces of coffee. Extra coffee without cream is of no value to this person, just as extra cream would be of no value without coffee. Only by choosing the goods together can utility be increased.

These concepts can be formalized by examining the mathematical form of the utility function that generates these L-shaped indifference curves:

$$\textbf{utility} = U(x, y) = \min(\alpha x, \beta y). \qquad \textbf{(3.25)}$$

Here α and β are positive parameters, and the operator "min" means that utility is given by the smaller of the two terms in the parentheses. In the coffee-cream example, if we let ounces of coffee be represented by x and ounces of cream by y, utility would be given by

$$\textbf{utility} = U(x, y) = \min(x, 8y). \qquad \textbf{(3.26)}$$

Now 8 ounces of coffee and 1 ounce of cream provide 8 units of utility. But 16 ounces of coffee and 1 ounce of cream still provide only 8 units of utility because $\min(16, 8) = 8$. The extra coffee without cream is of no value, as shown by the horizontal section of the indifference curves for movement away from a vertex; utility does not increase when only x increases (with y constant). Only if coffee and cream are both doubled (to 16 and 2, respectively) will utility increase to 16.

More generally, neither of the two goods will be in excess only if

$$\alpha x = \beta y. \qquad \textbf{(3.27)}$$

Hence

$$y/x = \alpha/\beta, \qquad \textbf{(3.28)}$$

which shows the fixed proportional relationship between the two goods that must occur if choices are to be at the vertices of the indifference curves.

CES utility

The three specific utility functions illustrated so far are special cases of the more general constant elasticity of substitution function (CES), which takes the form

$$\textbf{utility} = U(x, y) = \frac{x^\delta}{\delta} + \frac{y^\delta}{\delta}, \qquad \textbf{(3.29)}$$

where $\delta \leq 1, \delta \neq 0$, and

$$\textbf{utility} = U(x, y) = \ln x + \ln y \qquad \textbf{(3.30)}$$

when $\delta = 0$. It is obvious that the case of perfect substitutes corresponds to the limiting case, $\delta = 1$, in Equation 3.29 and that the Cobb-Douglas[9] case corresponds to $\delta = 0$ in Equation 3.30. Less obvious is that the case of fixed proportions corresponds to $\delta = -\infty$ in Equation 3.29, but that result can also be shown using a limits argument.

The use of the term "elasticity of substitution" for this function derives from the notion that the possibilities illustrated in Figure 3.8 correspond to various values for the substitution parameter, σ, which for this function is given by $\sigma = 1/(1 - \delta)$. For perfect substitutes, then, $\sigma = \infty$, and the fixed proportions case has $\sigma = 0$.[10] Because the CES function allows us to explore all of these cases, and many cases in between, it will prove quite useful for illustrating the degree of substitutability present in various economic relationships.

The specific shape of the CES function illustrated in Figure 3.8a is for the case $\delta = -1$. That is,

$$\text{utility} = -x^{-1} - y^{-1} = -\frac{1}{x} - \frac{1}{y}. \tag{3.31}$$

For this situation, $\sigma = 1/(1 - \delta) = 1/2$ and, as the graph shows, these sharply curved indifference curves apparently fall between the Cobb-Douglas and fixed proportion cases. The negative signs in this utility function may seem strange, but the marginal utilities of both x and y are positive and diminishing, as would be expected. This explains why δ must appear in the denominators in Equation 3.29. In the particular case of Equation 3.31, utility increases from $-\infty$ (when $x = y = 0$) toward 0 as x and y increase. This is an odd utility scale, perhaps, but perfectly acceptable.

EXAMPLE 3.3 Homothetic Preferences

All of the utility functions described in Figure 3.8 are homothetic (see Chapter 2). That is, the marginal rate of substitution for these functions depends only on the *ratio* of the amounts of the two goods, not on the total quantities of the goods. This fact is obvious for the case of the perfect substitutes (when the MRS is the same at every point) and the case of perfect complements (where the MRS is infinite for $y/x > \alpha/\beta$, undefined when $y/x = \alpha/\beta$, and zero when $y/x < \alpha/\beta$). For the general Cobb-Douglas function, the MRS can be found as

$$MRS = \frac{\partial U/\partial x}{\partial U/\partial y} = \frac{\alpha x^{\alpha-1}y^\beta}{\beta x^\alpha y^{\beta-1}} = \frac{\alpha}{\beta} \cdot \frac{y}{x}, \tag{3.32}$$

which clearly depends only on the ratio y/x. Showing that the CES function is also homothetic is left as an exercise (see Problem 3.12).

The importance of homothetic functions is that one indifference curve is much like another. Slopes of the curves depend only on the ratio y/x, not on how far the curve is from the origin. Indifference curves for higher utility are simple copies of those for lower utility. Hence, we can study the behavior of an individual who has homothetic preferences by looking only at one indifference curve or at a few nearby curves without fearing that our results would change dramatically at very different levels of utility.

(continued)

---

[9]The CES function could easily be generalized to allow for differing weights to be attached to the two goods. Since the main use of the function is to examine substitution questions, we usually will not make that generalization. In some of the applications of the CES function, we will also omit the denominators of the function because these constitute only a scale factor when δ is positive. For negative values of δ, however, the denominator is needed to ensure that marginal utility is positive.

[10]The elasticity of substitution concept is discussed in more detail in connection with production functions in Chapter 9.

EXAMPLE 3.3   CONTINUED

QUERY: How might you define homothetic functions geometrically? What would the locus of all points with a particular *MRS* look like on an individual's indifference curve map?

EXAMPLE 3.4 Nonhomothetic Preferences

Although all of the indifference curve maps in Figure 3.8 exhibit homothetic preferences, this need not always be true. Consider the quasi-linear utility function

$$\text{utility} = U(x, y) = x + \ln y. \tag{3.33}$$

For this function, good y exhibits diminishing marginal utility, but good x does not. The *MRS* can be computed as

$$MRS = \frac{\partial U/\partial x}{\partial U/\partial y} = \frac{1}{1/y} = y. \tag{3.34}$$

The *MRS* diminishes as the chosen quantity of y decreases, but it is independent of the quantity of x consumed. Because x has a constant marginal utility, a person's willingness to give up y to get one more unit of x depends only on how much y he or she has. Contrary to the homothetic case, then, a doubling of both x and y doubles the *MRS* rather than leaving it unchanged.

QUERY: What does the indifference curve map for the utility function in Equation 3.33 look like? Why might this approximate a situation where y is a specific good and x represents everything else?

THE MANY-GOOD CASE

All of the concepts we have studied so far for the case of two goods can be generalized to situations where utility is a function of arbitrarily many goods. In this section, we will briefly explore those generalizations. Although this examination will not add much to what we have already shown, considering peoples' preferences for many goods can be quite important in applied economics, as we will see in later chapters.

The *MRS* with many goods

Suppose utility is a function of n goods given by

$$\text{utility} = U(x_1, x_2, \ldots, x_n). \tag{3.35}$$

The total differential of this expression is

$$dU = \frac{\partial U}{\partial x_1}\, dx_1 + \frac{\partial U}{\partial x_2}\, dx_2 + \cdots + \frac{\partial U}{\partial x_n}\, dx_n \tag{3.36}$$

and, as before, we can find the *MRS* between any two goods by setting $dU = 0$. In this derivation, we also hold constant quantities of all of the goods other than those two. Hence we have

$$dU = 0 = \frac{\partial U}{\partial x_i} dx_i + \frac{\partial U}{\partial x_j} dx_j; \tag{3.37}$$

after some algebraic manipulation, we get

$$MRS(x_i \text{ for } x_j) = -\frac{dx_j}{dx_i} = \frac{\partial U/\partial x_i}{\partial U/\partial x_j}, \tag{3.38}$$

which is precisely what we got in Equation 3.17. Whether this concept is as useful as it is in two dimensions is open to question, however. With only two goods, asking how a person would trade one for the other is an interesting question—a transaction we might actually observe. With many goods, however, it seems unlikely that a person would simply trade one good for another while holding all other goods constant. Rather, it seems more likely that an event (such as a price increase) that caused a person to want to reduce, say, the quantity of cornflakes (x_i) consumed would also cause him or her to change the quantities consumed of many other goods such as milk, sugar, Cheerios, spoons, and so forth. As we shall see in Chapter 6, this entire reallocation process can best be studied by looking at the entire utility function as represented in Equation 3.35. Still, the notion of making trade-offs between only two goods will prove useful as a way of conceptualizing the utility maximization process that we will take up next.

Multigood indifference surfaces

Generalizing the concept of indifference curves to multiple dimensions poses no major mathematical difficulties. We simply define an indifference surface as being the set of points in n dimensions that satisfy the equation

$$U(x_1, x_2, \ldots, x_n) = k, \tag{3.39}$$

where k is any preassigned constant. If the utility function is quasi-concave, the set of points for which $U \geq k$ will be convex; that is, all of the points on a line joining any two points on the $U = k$ indifference surface will also have $U \geq k$. It is this property that we will find most useful in later applications. Unfortunately, however, the mathematical conditions that ensure quasi-concavity in many dimensions are not especially intuitive (see the Extensions to Chapter 2), and visualizing many dimensions is virtually impossible. Hence, when intuition is required, we will usually revert to two-good examples.

SUMMARY

In this chapter we have described the way in which economists formalize individuals' preferences about the goods they choose. We drew several conclusions about such preferences that will play a central role in our analysis of the theory of choice in the following chapters:

- If individuals obey certain basic behavioral postulates in their preferences among goods, they will be able to rank all commodity bundles, and that ranking can be represented by a utility function. In making choices, individuals will behave as if they were maximizing this function.

- Utility functions for two goods can be illustrated by an indifference curve map. Each indifference curve contour

on this map shows all the commodity bundles that yield a given level of utility.

- The negative of the slope of an indifference curve is defined to be the marginal rate of substitution (MRS). This shows the rate at which an individual would willingly give up an amount of one good (y) if he or she were compensated by receiving one more unit of another good (x).

- The assumption that the MRS decreases as x is substituted for y in consumption is consistent with the notion that individuals prefer some balance in their consumption choices. If the MRS is always decreasing, individuals will have strictly convex indifference curves. That is, their utility function will be strictly quasi-concave.

- A few simple functional forms can capture important differences in individuals' preferences for two (or more) goods. Here we examined the Cobb-Douglas function, the linear function (perfect substitutes), the fixed proportions function (perfect complements), and the CES function (which includes the other three as special cases).

- It is a simple matter mathematically to generalize from two-good examples to many goods. And, as we shall see, studying peoples' choices among many goods can yield many insights. But the mathematics of many goods is not especially intuitive, so we will primarily rely on two-good cases to build such intuition.

PROBLEMS

3.1

Graph a typical indifference curve for the following utility functions and determine whether they have convex indifference curves (that is, whether the MRS declines as x increases).

    a. $U(x, y) = 3x + y$.

    b. $U(x, y) = \sqrt{x \cdot y}$.

    c. $U(x, y) = \sqrt{x} + y$.

    d. $U(x, y) = \sqrt{x^2 - y^2}$.

    e. $U(x, y) = \dfrac{xy}{x + y}$.

3.2

In footnote 7 we showed that, in order for a utility function for two goods to have a strictly diminishing MRS (that is, to be strictly quasi-concave), the following condition must hold:

$$f_2^2 f_{11} - 2f_1 f_2 f_{12} + f_1^2 f_{22} < 0.$$

Use this condition to check the convexity of the indifference curves for each of the utility functions in Problem 3.1. Describe any shortcuts you discover in this process.

3.3

Consider the following utility functions:

    a. $U(x, y) = xy$.

    b. $U(x, y) = x^2 y^2$.

    c. $U(x, y) = \ln x + \ln y$.

Show that each of these has a diminishing MRS but that they exhibit constant, increasing, and decreasing marginal utility, respectively. What do you conclude?

3.4

As we saw in Figure 3.5, one way to show convexity of indifference curves is to show that, for any two points (x_1, y_1) and (x_2, y_2) on an indifference curve that promises $U = k$, the utility associated with the point $\left(\frac{x_1 + x_2}{2}, \frac{y_1 + y_2}{2}\right)$ is at least as great as k. Use this approach to discuss the convexity of the indifference curves for the following three functions. Be sure to graph your results.

    a. $U(x, y) = \min(x, y)$.

    b. $U(x, y) = \max(x, y)$.

    c. $U(x, y) = x + y$.

3.5

The Phillie Phanatic always eats his ballpark franks in a special way; he uses a foot-long hot dog together with precisely half a bun, 1 ounce of mustard, and 2 ounces of pickle relish. His utility is a function only of these four items and any extra amount of a single item without the other constituents is worthless.

a. What form does PP's utility function for these four goods have?

b. How might we simplify matters by considering PP's utility to be a function of only one good? What is that good?

c. Suppose foot-long hot dogs cost $1.00 each, buns cost $0.50 each, mustard costs $0.05 per ounce, and pickle relish costs $0.15 per ounce. How much does the good defined in part (b) cost?

d. If the price of foot-long hot dogs increases by 50 percent (to $1.50 each), what is the percentage increase in the price of the good?

e. How would a 50 percent increase in the price of a bun affect the price of the good? Why is your answer different from part (d)?

f. If the government wanted to raise $1.00 by taxing the goods that PP buys, how should it spread this tax over the four goods so as to minimize the utility cost to PP?

3.6

Many advertising slogans seem to be asserting something about people's preferences. How would you capture the following slogans with a mathematical utility function?

a. Promise margarine is just as good as butter.

b. Things go better with Coke.

c. You can't eat just one Pringle's potato chip.

d. Krispy Kreme glazed doughnuts are just better than Dunkin'.

e. Miller Brewing advises us to drink (beer) "responsibly." [What would "irresponsible" drinking be?]

3.7

a. A consumer is willing to trade 3 units of x for 1 unit of y when she has 6 units of x and 5 units of y. She is also willing to trade in 6 units of x for 2 units of y when she has 12 units of x and 3 units of y. She is indifferent between bundle $(6, 5)$ and bundle $(12, 3)$. What is the utility function for goods x and y? *Hint*: What is the shape of the indifference curve?

b. A consumer is willing to trade 4 units of x for 1 unit of y when she is consuming bundle $(8, 1)$. She is also willing to trade in 1 unit of x for 2 units of y when she is consuming bundle $(4, 4)$. She is indifferent between these two bundles. Assuming that the utility function is Cobb-Douglas of the form $U(x, y) = x^\alpha y^\beta$, where α and β are positive constants, what is the utility function for this consumer?

c. Was there a redundancy of information in part (b)? If yes, how much is the minimum amount of information required in that question to derive the utility function?

3.8

Find utility functions given each of the following indifference curves [defined by $U(\cdot) = C$]:

a. $z = \dfrac{C^{1/\delta}}{x^{\alpha/\delta} y^{\beta/\delta}}.$

b. $y = 0.5\sqrt{x^2 - 4(x^2 - C)} - 0.5x.$

c. $z = \dfrac{\sqrt{y^4 - 4x(x^2 y - C)}}{2x} - \dfrac{y^2}{2x}.$

Analytical Problems

3.9 Initial endowments

Suppose that a person has initial amounts of the two goods that provide utility to him or her. These initial amounts are given by $\bar{x}$ and $\bar{y}$.

    a. Graph these initial amounts on this person's indifference curve map.

    b. If this person can trade x for y (or vice versa) with other people, what kinds of trades would he or she voluntarily make? What kinds would not be made? How do these trades relate to this person's MRS at the point $(\bar{x}, \bar{y})$?

    c. Suppose this person is relatively happy with the initial amounts in his or her possession and will only consider trades that increase utility by at least amount k. How would you illustrate this on the indifference curve map?

3.10 Cobb-Douglas utility

Example 3.3 shows that the MRS for the Cobb-Douglas function

$$U(x,y) = x^{\alpha} y^{\beta}$$

is given by

$$MRS = \frac{\alpha}{\beta}\left(\frac{y}{x}\right).$$

    a. Does this result depend on whether $\alpha + \beta = 1$? Does this sum have any relevance to the theory of choice?

    b. For commodity bundles for which $y = x$, how does the MRS depend on the values of α and β? Develop an intuitive explanation of why, if $\alpha > \beta$, $MRS > 1$. Illustrate your argument with a graph.

    c. Suppose an individual obtains utility only from amounts of x and y that exceed minimal subsistence levels given by x_0, y_0. In this case,

$$U(x,y) = (x - x_0)^{\alpha}(y - y_0)^{\beta}.$$

Is this function homothetic? (For a further discussion, see the Extensions to Chapter 4.)

3.11 Independent marginal utilities

Two goods have independent marginal utilities if

$$\frac{\partial^2 U}{\partial y \partial x} = \frac{\partial^2 U}{\partial x \partial y} = 0.$$

Show that if we assume diminishing marginal utility for each good, then any utility function with independent marginal utilities will have a diminishing MRS. Provide an example to show that the converse of this statement is not true.

3.12 CES utility

    a. Show that the CES function

$$\alpha\frac{x^{\delta}}{\delta} + \beta\frac{y^{\delta}}{\delta}$$

    is homothetic. How does the MRS depend on the ratio y/x?

    b. Show that your results from part (a) agree with our discussion of the cases $\delta = 1$ (perfect substitutes) and $\delta = 0$ (Cobb-Douglas).

    c. Show that the MRS is strictly diminishing for all values of $\delta < 1$.

    d. Show that if $x = y$, the MRS for this function depends only on the relative sizes of α and β.

e. Calculate the *MRS* for this function when $y/x = 0.9$ and $y/x = 1.1$ for the two cases $\delta = 0.5$ and $\delta = -1$. What do you conclude about the extent to which the *MRS* changes in the vicinity of $x = y$? How would you interpret this geometrically?

3.13 The quasi-linear function

Consider the function $U(x, y) = x + \ln y$. This is a function that is used relatively frequently in economic modeling as it has some useful properties.

a. Find the *MRS* of the function. Now, interpret the result.

b. Confirm that the function is quasi-concave.

c. Find the equation for an indifference curve for this function.

d. Compare the marginal utility of x and y. How do you interpret these functions? How might consumers choose between x and y as they try to increase their utility by, for example, consuming more when their income increases? (We will look at this "income effect" in detail in the Chapter 5 problems.)

e. Considering how the utility changes as the quantities of the two goods increase, describe some situations where this function might be useful.

3.14 Utility functions and preferences

Imagine two goods that, when consumed individually, give increasing utility with increasing amounts consumed (they are individually monotonic) but that, when consumed together, detract from the utility that the other one gives. (One could think of milk and orange juice, which are fine individually but which, when consumed together, yield considerable disutility.)

a. Propose a functional form for the utility function for the two goods just described.

b. Find the *MRS* between the two goods with your functional form.

c. Which (if any) of the general assumptions that we make regarding preferences and utility functions does your functional form violate?

SUGGESTIONS FOR FURTHER READING

Aleskerov, Fuad, and Bernard Monjardet. *Utility Maximization, Choice, and Preference*. Berlin: Springer-Verlag, 2002.

A complete study of preference theory. Covers a variety of threshold models and models of "context-dependent" decision making.

Jehle, G. R., and P. J. Reny. *Advanced Microeconomic Theory*, 2nd ed. Boston: Addison Wesley/Longman, 2001.

Chapter 2 has a good proof of the existence of utility functions when basic axioms of rationality hold.

Kreps, David M. *A Course in Microeconomic Theory*. Princeton, NJ: Princeton University Press, 1990.

Chapter 1 covers preference theory in some detail. Good discussion of quasi-concavity.

Kreps, David M. *Notes on the Theory of Choice*. London: Westview Press, 1988.

Good discussion of the foundations of preference theory. Most of the focus of the book is on utility in uncertain situations.

Mas-Colell, Andrea, Michael D. Whinston, and Jerry R. Green. *Microeconomic Theory*. New York: Oxford University Press, 1995.

Chapters 2 and 3 provide a detailed development of preference relations and their representation by utility functions.

Stigler, G. "The Development of Utility Theory." *Journal of Political Economy* 59, pts. 1–2 (August/October 1950): 307–27, 373–96.

A lucid and complete survey of the history of utility theory. Has many interesting insights and asides.

EXTENSIONS

Special Preferences

The utility function concept is a quite general one that can be adapted to a large number of special circumstances. Discovery of ingenious functional forms that reflect the essential aspects of some problem can provide a number of insights that would not be readily apparent with a more literary approach. Here we look at four aspects of preferences that economists have tried to model: (1) threshold effects; (2) quality; (3) habits and addiction; and (4) second-party preferences. In Chapters 7 and 17, we illustrate a number of additional ways of capturing aspects of preferences.

E3.1 Threshold effects

The model of utility that we developed in this chapter implies an individual will always prefer commodity bundle A to bundle B, provided $U(A) > U(B)$. There may be events that will cause people to shift quickly from consuming bundle A to consuming B. In many cases, however, such a lightning-quick response seems unlikely. People may in fact be "set in their ways" and may require a rather large change in circumstances to change what they do. For example, individuals may not have especially strong opinions about what precise brand of toothpaste they choose and may stick with what they know despite a proliferation of new (and perhaps better) brands. Similarly, people may stick with an old favorite TV show even though it has declined in quality. One way to capture such behavior is to assume individuals make decisions as if they faced thresholds of preference. In such a situation, commodity bundle A might be chosen over B only when

$$U(A) > U(B) + \varepsilon, \qquad \textbf{(i)}$$

where ε is the threshold that must be overcome. With this specification, then, indifference curves may be rather thick and even fuzzy, rather than the distinct contour lines shown in this chapter. Threshold models of this type are used extensively in marketing. The theory behind such models is presented in detail in Aleskerov and Monjardet (2002). There, the authors consider a number of ways of specifying the threshold so that it might depend on the characteristics of the bundles being considered or on other contextual variables.

Alternative fuels

Vedenov, Duffield, and Wetzstein (2006) use the threshold idea to examine the conditions under which individuals will shift from gasoline to other fuels

(primarily ethanol) for powering their cars. The authors point out that the main disadvantage of using gasoline in recent years has been the excessive price volatility of the product relative to other fuels. They conclude that switching to ethanol blends is efficient (especially during periods of increased gasoline price volatility), provided that the blends do not decrease fuel efficiency.

E3.2 Quality

Because many consumption items differ widely in quality, economists have an interest in incorporating such differences into models of choice. One approach is simply to regard items of different quality as totally separate goods that are relatively close substitutes. But this approach can be unwieldy because of the large number of goods involved. An alternative approach focuses on quality as a direct item of choice. Utility might in this case be reflected by

$$\text{utility} = U(q, Q), \qquad \textbf{(ii)}$$

where q is the quantity consumed and Q is the quality of that consumption. Although this approach permits some examination of quality-quantity trade-offs, it encounters difficulty when the quantity consumed of a commodity (e.g., wine) consists of a variety of qualities. Quality might then be defined as an average (see Theil,[1] 1952), but that approach may not be appropriate when the quality of new goods is changing rapidly (as in the case of personal computers, for example). A more general approach (originally suggested by Lancaster, 1971) focuses on a well-defined set of attributes of goods and assumes that those attributes provide utility. If a good q provides two such attributes, a_1 and a_2, then utility might be written as

$$\text{utility} = U[q, a_1(q), a_2(q)], \qquad \textbf{(iii)}$$

and utility improvements might arise either because this individual chooses a larger quantity of the good or because a given quantity yields a higher level of valuable attributes.

Personal computers

This is the practice followed by economists who study demand in such rapidly changing industries as personal

---

[1] Theil also suggests measuring quality by looking at correlations between changes in consumption and the income elasticities of various goods.

computers. In this case it would clearly be incorrect to focus only on the quantity of personal computers purchased each year, since new machines are much better than old ones (and, presumably, provide more utility). For example, Berndt, Griliches, and Rappaport (1995) find that personal computer quality has been rising about 30 percent per year over a relatively long period of time, primarily because of improved attributes such as faster processors or better hard drives. A person who spends, say, $2,000 for a personal computer today buys much more utility than did a similar consumer 5 years ago.

E3.3 Habits and addiction

Because consumption occurs over time, there is the possibility that decisions made in one period will affect utility in later periods. Habits are formed when individuals discover they enjoy using a commodity in one period and this increases their consumption in subsequent periods. An extreme case is addiction (be it to drugs, cigarettes, or Marx Brothers movies), where past consumption significantly increases the utility of present consumption. One way to portray these ideas mathematically is to assume that utility in period t depends on consumption in period t and the total of all prior consumption of the habit-forming good (say, X):

$$\text{utility} = U_t(x_t, y_t, s_t), \qquad \textbf{(iv)}$$

where

$$s_t = \sum_{i=1}^{\infty} x_{t-i}.$$

In empirical applications, however, data on all past levels of consumption usually do not exist. It is therefore common to model habits using only data on current consumption (x_t) and on consumption in the previous period ($x_t - 1$). A common way to proceed is to assume that utility is given by

$$\text{utility} = U_t(x_t^*, y_t), \qquad \textbf{(v)}$$

where x_t^* is some simple function of x_t and x_{t-1}, such as $x_t^* = x_t - x_{t-1}$ or $x_t^* = x_t / x_{t-1}$. Such functions imply that, ceteris paribus, the higher is x_{t-1}, the more x_t will be chosen in the current period.

Modeling habits

These approaches to modeling habits have been applied to a wide variety of topics. Stigler and Becker (1977) use such models to explain why people develop a "taste" for going to operas or playing golf. Becker, Grossman, and Murphy (1994) adapt the models to studying cigarette smoking and other addictive behavior. They show that reductions in smoking early in life can have very large effects on eventual cigarette consumption because of the dynamics in individuals' utility functions. Whether addictive behavior is "rational" has been extensively studied by economists. For example, Gruber and Koszegi (2001) show that smoking can be approached as a rational, though time-inconsistent,[2] choice.

E3.4 Second-party preferences

Individuals clearly care about the well-being of other individuals. Phenomena such as making charitable contributions or making bequests to children cannot be understood without recognizing the interdependence that exists among people. Second-party preferences can be incorporated into the utility function of person i, say, by

$$\text{utility} = U_i(x_i, y_i, U_j), \qquad \textbf{(vi)}$$

where U_j is the utility of someone else.

If $\partial U_i / \partial U_j > 0$ then this person will engage in altruistic behavior, whereas if $\partial U_i / \partial U_j < 0$ then he or she will demonstrate the malevolent behavior associated with envy. The usual case of $\partial U_i / \partial U_j = 0$ is then simply a middle ground between these alternative preference types. Gary Becker has been a pioneer in the study of these possibilities and has written on a variety of topics, including the general theory of social interactions (1976) and the importance of altruism in the theory of the family (1981).

Evolutionary biology and genetics

Biologists have suggested a particular form for the utility function in Equation iv, drawn from the theory of genetics. In this case

$$\text{utility} = U_i(x_i, y_i) + \sum_j r_j U_j, \qquad \textbf{(vii)}$$

where r_j measures closeness of the genetic relationship between person i and person j. For parents and children, for example, $r_j = 0.5$, whereas for cousins $r_j = 0.125$. Bergstrom (1996) describes a few of the conclusions about evolutionary behavior that biologists have drawn from this particular functional form.

---

[2]For more on time inconsistency, see Chapter 17.

References

Aleskerov, Fuad, and Bernard Monjardet. *Utility Maximization, Choice, and Preference*. Berlin: Springer-Verlag, 2002.

Becker, Gary S. *The Economic Approach to Human Behavior*. Chicago: University of Chicago Press, 1976.

———. *A Treatise on the Family*. Cambridge, MA: Harvard University Press, 1981.

Becker, Gary S., Michael Grossman, and Kevin M. Murphy. "An Empirical Analysis of Cigarette Addiction." *American Economic Review* (June 1994): 396–418.

Bergstrom, Theodore C. "Economics in a Family Way." *Journal of Economic Literature* (December 1996): 1903–34.

Berndt, Ernst R., Zvi Griliches, and Neal J. Rappaport. "Econometric Estimates of Price Indexes for Personal Computers in the 1990s." *Journal of Econometrics* (July 1995): 243–68.

Gruber, Jonathan, and Botond Koszegi. "Is Addiction 'Rational'? Theory and Evidence." *Quarterly Journal of Economics* (November 2001): 1261–1303.

Lancaster, Kelvin J. *Consumer Demand: A New Approach*. New York: Columbia University Press, 1971.

Stigler, George J., and Gary S. Becker. "De Gustibus Non Est Disputandum." *American Economic Review* (March 1977): 76–90.

Theil, Henri. "Qualities, Prices, and Budget Enquiries." *Review of Economic Studies* (April 1952): 129–47.

Vedenov, Dmitry V., James A. Duffield, and Michael E. Wetzstein. "Entry of Alternative Fuels in a Volatile U.S. Gasoline Market." *Journal of Agricultural and Resource Economics* (April 2006): 1–13.

Utility Maximization and Choice

In this chapter we examine the basic model of choice that economists use to explain individuals' behavior. That model assumes that individuals who are constrained by limited incomes will behave as if they are using their purchasing power in such a way as to achieve the highest utility possible. That is, individuals are assumed to behave as if they maximize utility subject to a budget constraint. Although the specific applications of this model are quite varied, as we will show, all of them are based on the same fundamental mathematical model, and all arrive at the same general conclusion: To maximize utility, individuals will choose bundles of commodities for which the rate of trade-off between any two goods (the *MRS*) is equal to the ratio of the goods' market prices. Market prices convey information about opportunity costs to individuals, and this information plays an important role in affecting the choices actually made.

Utility maximization and lightning calculations

Before starting a formal study of the theory of choice, it may be appropriate to dispose of two complaints noneconomists often make about the approach we will take. First is the charge that no real person can make the kinds of "lightning calculations" required for utility maximization. According to this complaint, when moving down a supermarket aisle, people just grab what is available with no real pattern or purpose to their actions. Economists are not persuaded by this complaint. They doubt that people behave randomly (everyone, after all, is bound by some sort of budget constraint), and they view the lightning calculation charge as misplaced. Recall, again, Friedman's pool player from Chapter 1. The pool player also cannot make the lightning calculations required to plan a shot according to the laws of physics, but those laws still predict the player's behavior. So too, as we shall see, the utility-maximization model predicts many aspects of behavior even though no one carries around a computer with his or her utility function programmed into it. To be precise, economists assume that people behave *as if* they made such calculations, so the complaint that the calculations cannot possibly be made is largely irrelevant.

Altruism and selfishness

A second complaint against our model of choice is that it appears to be extremely selfish; no one, according to this complaint, has such solely self-centered goals. Although economists are probably more ready to accept self-interest as a motivating force than are other, more Utopian thinkers (Adam Smith observed, "We are not ready to suspect any person of being deficient in selfishness"[1]), this charge is also misplaced. Nothing in the utility-maximization model prevents individuals from deriving satisfaction from philanthropy or generally "doing good." These activities also can be assumed to provide utility. Indeed, economists have used the utility-maximization model extensively to study such issues as donating time and money

---

[1]Adam Smith, *The Theory of Moral Sentiments* (1759; reprint, New Rochelle, NY: Arlington House, 1969), p. 446.

to charity, leaving bequests to children, or even giving blood. One need not take a position on whether such activities are selfish or selfless since economists doubt people would undertake them if they were against their own best interests, broadly conceived.

AN INITIAL SURVEY

The general results of our examination of utility maximization can be stated succinctly as follows.

OPTIMIZATION PRINCIPLE | **Utility maximization** To maximize utility, given a fixed amount of income to spend, an individual will buy those quantities of goods that exhaust his or her total income and for which the psychic rate of trade-off between any two goods (the *MRS*) is equal to the rate at which the goods can be traded one for the other in the marketplace.

That spending all one's income is required for utility maximization is obvious. Because extra goods provide extra utility (there is no satiation) and because there is no other use for income, to leave any unspent would be to fail to maximize utility. Throwing money away is not a utility-maximizing activity.

The condition specifying equality of trade-off rates requires a bit more explanation. Because the rate at which one good can be traded for another in the market is given by the ratio of their prices, this result can be restated to say that the individual will equate the *MRS* (of x for y) to the ratio of the price of x to the price of y (p_x/p_y). This equating of a personal trade-off rate to a market-determined trade-off rate is a result common to all individual utility-maximization problems (and to many other types of maximization problems). It will occur again and again throughout this text.

A numerical illustration

To see the intuitive reasoning behind this result, assume that it were not true that an individual had equated the *MRS* to the ratio of the prices of goods. Specifically, suppose that the individual's *MRS* is equal to 1 and that he or she is willing to trade 1 unit of x for 1 unit of y and remain equally well off. Assume also that the price of x is \$2 per unit and of y is \$1 per unit. It is easy to show that this person can be made better off. Suppose this person reduces x consumption by 1 unit and trades it in the market for 2 units of y. Only 1 extra unit of y was needed to keep this person as happy as before the trade—the second unit of y is a net addition to well-being. Therefore, the individual's spending could not have been allocated optimally in the first place. A similar method of reasoning can be used whenever the *MRS* and the price ratio p_x/p_y differ. The condition for maximum utility must be the equality of these two magnitudes.

THE TWO-GOOD CASE: A GRAPHICAL ANALYSIS

This discussion seems eminently reasonable, but it can hardly be called a proof. Rather, we must now show the result in a rigorous manner and, at the same time, illustrate several other important attributes of the maximization process. First we take a graphic analysis; then we take a more mathematical approach.

Budget constraint

Assume that the individual has I dollars to allocate between good x and good y. If p_x is the price of good x and p_y is the price of good y, then the individual is constrained by

FIGURE 4.1 The Individual's Budget Constraint for Two Goods

Those combinations of x and y that the individual can afford are shown in the shaded triangle. If, as we usually assume, the individual prefers more rather than less of every good, the outer boundary of this triangle is the relevant constraint where all of the available funds are spent either on x or on y. The slope of this straight-line boundary is given by $-p_x/p_y$.

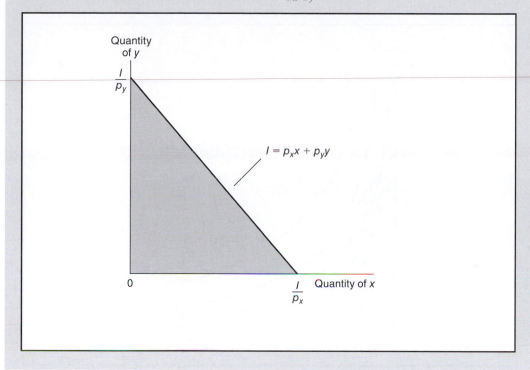

$$p_x x + p_y y \leq I. \tag{4.1}$$

That is, no more than I can be spent on the two goods in question. This budget constraint is shown graphically in Figure 4.1. This person can afford to choose only combinations of x and y in the shaded triangle of the figure. If all of I is spent on good x, it will buy I/p_x units of x. Similarly, if all is spent on y, it will buy I/p_y units of y. The slope of the constraint is easily seen to be $-p_x/p_y$. This slope shows how y can be traded for x in the market. If $p_x = 2$ and $p_y = 1$, then 2 units of y will trade for 1 unit of x.

First-order conditions for a maximum

This budget constraint can be imposed on this person's indifference curve map to show the utility-maximization process. Figure 4.2 illustrates this procedure. The individual would be irrational to choose a point such as A; he or she can get to a higher utility level just by spending more of his or her income. The assumption of nonsatiation implies that a person should spend all of his or her income in order to receive maximum utility. Similarly, by reallocating expenditures, the individual can do better than point B. Point D is out of the question because income is not large enough to purchase D. It is clear that the position of maximum utility is at point C, where the combination x^*, y^* is chosen. This is the only point on indifference curve U_2 that can be bought with I dollars; no higher utility level can be

FIGURE 4.2   A Graphical Demonstration of Utility Maximization

Point C represents the highest utility level that can be reached by the individual, given the budget constraint. The combination x^*, y^* is therefore the rational way for the individual to allocate purchasing power. Only for this combination of goods will two conditions hold: All available funds will be spent, and the individual's psychic rate of trade-off (MRS) will be equal to the rate at which the goods can be traded in the market (p_x/p_y).

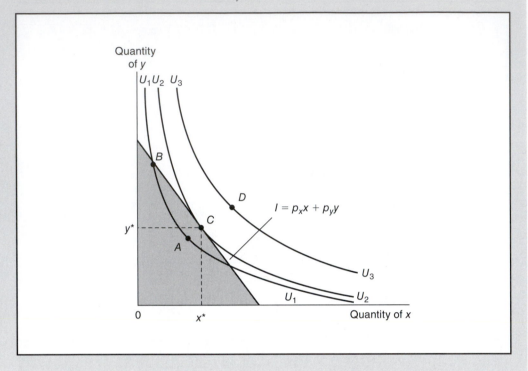

bought. C is a point of tangency between the budget constraint and the indifference curve. Therefore, at C we have

$$\textbf{slope of budget constraint} = \frac{-p_x}{p_y} = \textbf{slope of indifference curve}$$

$$= \frac{dy}{dx}\bigg|_{U=\text{constant}} \tag{4.2}$$

or

$$\frac{p_x}{p_y} = -\frac{dy}{dx}\bigg|_{U=\text{constant}} = MRS \text{ (of } x \text{ for } y\text{)}. \tag{4.3}$$

Our intuitive result is proved: for a utility maximum, all income should be spent and the MRS should equal the ratio of the prices of the goods. It is obvious from the diagram that if this condition is not fulfilled, the individual could be made better off by reallocating expenditures.

Second-order conditions for a maximum

The tangency rule is only a necessary condition for a maximum. To see that it is not a sufficient condition, consider the indifference curve map shown in Figure 4.3. Here, a point

FIGURE 4.3   Example of an Indifference Curve Map for Which the Tangency Condition Does Not Ensure a Maximum

If indifference curves do not obey the assumption of a diminishing MRS, not all points of tangency (points for which $MRS - p_x/p_y$) may truly be points of maximum utility. In this example, tangency point C is inferior to many other points that can also be purchased with the available funds. In order that the necessary conditions for a maximum (that is, the tangency conditions) also be sufficient, one usually assumes that the MRS is diminishing; that is, the utility function is strictly quasi-concave.

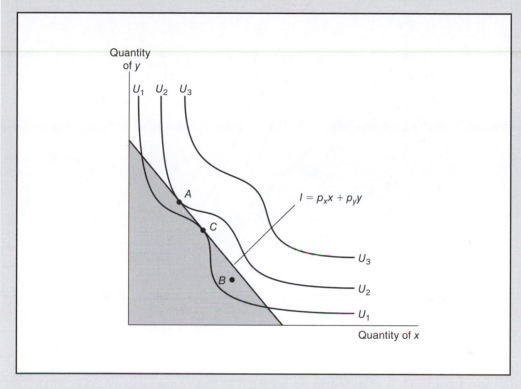

of tangency (C) is inferior to a point of nontangency (B). Indeed, the true maximum is at another point of tangency (A). The failure of the tangency condition to produce an unambiguous maximum can be attributed to the shape of the indifference curves in Figure 4.3. If the indifference curves are shaped like those in Figure 4.2, no such problem can arise. But we have already shown that "normally" shaped indifference curves result from the assumption of a diminishing MRS. Therefore, if the MRS is assumed to be diminishing, the condition of tangency is both a necessary and sufficient condition for a maximum.[2] Without this assumption, one would have to be careful in applying the tangency rule.

Corner solutions

The utility-maximization problem illustrated in Figure 4.2 resulted in an "interior" maximum, in which positive amounts of both goods were consumed. In some situations individuals' preferences may be such that they can obtain maximum utility by choosing to consume

---

[2]In mathematical terms, because the assumption of a diminishing MRS is equivalent to assuming quasi-concavity, the necessary conditions for a maximum subject to a linear constraint are also sufficient, as we showed in Chapter 2.

FIGURE 4.4   Corner Solution for Utility Maximization

With the preferences represented by this set of indifference curves, utility maximization occurs at E, where 0 amounts of good y are consumed. The first-order conditions for a maximum must be modified somewhat to accommodate this possibility.

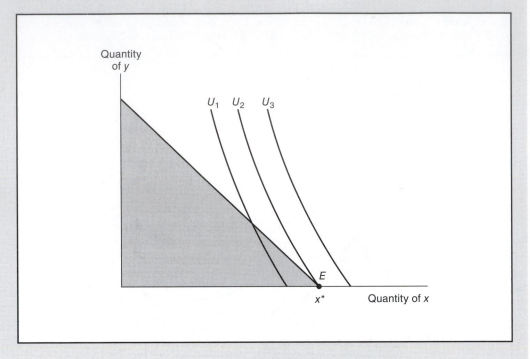

no amount of one of the goods. If someone does not like hamburgers very much, there is no reason to allocate any income to their purchase. This possibility is reflected in Figure 4.4. There, utility is maximized at E, where $x = x^*$ and $y = 0$, so any point on the budget constraint where positive amounts of y are consumed yields a lower utility than does point E. Notice that at E the budget constraint is not precisely tangent to the indifference curve U_2. Instead, at the optimal point the budget constraint is flatter than U_2, indicating that the rate at which x can be traded for y in the market is lower than the individual's psychic trade-off rate (the MRS). At prevailing market prices the individual is more than willing to trade away y to get extra x. Because it is impossible in this problem to consume negative amounts of y, however, the physical limit for this process is the X-axis, along which purchases of y are 0. Hence, as this discussion makes clear, it is necessary to amend the first-order conditions for a utility maximum a bit to allow for corner solutions of the type shown in Figure 4.4. Following our discussion of the general n-good case, we will use the mathematics from Chapter 2 to show how this can be accomplished.

THE n-GOOD CASE

The results derived graphically in the case of two goods carry over directly to the case of n goods. Again it can be shown that for an interior utility maximum, the MRS between any two goods must equal the ratio of the prices of these goods. To study this more general case, however, it is best to use some mathematics.

First-order conditions

With n goods, the individual's objective is to maximize utility from these n goods:

$$\text{utility} = U(x_1, x_2, \ldots, x_n), \tag{4.4}$$

subject to the budget constraint[3]

$$I = p_1 x_1 + p_2 x_2 + \cdots + p_n x_n \tag{4.5}$$

or

$$I - p_1 x_1 - p_2 x_2 - \cdots - p_n x_n = 0. \tag{4.6}$$

Following the techniques developed in Chapter 2 for maximizing a function subject to a constraint, we set up the Lagrangian expression

$$\mathcal{L} = U(x_1, x_2, \ldots, x_n) + \lambda(I - p_1 x_1 - p_2 x_2 - \cdots - p_n x_n). \tag{4.7}$$

Setting the partial derivatives of $\mathcal{L}$ (with respect to $x_1, x_2, \ldots, x_n$ and λ) equal to 0 yields $n + 1$ equations representing the necessary conditions for an interior maximum:

$$\frac{\partial \mathcal{L}}{\partial x_1} = \frac{\partial U}{\partial x_1} - \lambda p_1 = 0,$$

$$\frac{\partial \mathcal{L}}{\partial x_2} = \frac{\partial U}{\partial x_2} - \lambda p_2 = 0,$$

$$\vdots \tag{4.8}$$

$$\frac{\partial \mathcal{L}}{\partial x_n} = \frac{\partial U}{\partial x_n} - \lambda p_n = 0,$$

$$\frac{\partial \mathcal{L}}{\partial \lambda} = I - p_1 x_1 - p_2 x_2 - \cdots - p_n x_n = 0.$$

These $n + 1$ equations can, in principle, be solved for the optimal $x_1, x_2, \ldots, x_n$ and for λ (see Examples 4.1 and 4.2 to be convinced that such a solution is possible).

Equations 4.8 are necessary but not sufficient for a maximum. The second-order conditions that ensure a maximum are relatively complex and must be stated in matrix terms (see the Extensions to Chapter 2). However, the assumption of strict quasi-concavity (a diminishing *MRS* in the two-good case) is sufficient to ensure that any point obeying Equations 4.8 is in fact a true maximum.

Implications of first-order conditions

The first-order conditions represented by Equations 4.8 can be rewritten in a variety of interesting ways. For example, for any two goods, x_i and x_j, we have

$$\frac{\partial U / \partial x_i}{\partial U / \partial x_j} = \frac{p_i}{p_j}. \tag{4.9}$$

In Chapter 3 we showed that the ratio of the marginal utilities of two goods is equal to the marginal rate of substitution between them. Therefore, the conditions for an optimal allocation of income become

$$MRS(x_i \text{ for } x_j) = \frac{p_i}{p_j}. \tag{4.10}$$

This is exactly the result derived graphically earlier in this chapter; to maximize utility, the individual should equate the psychic rate of trade-off to the market trade-off rate.

---

[3]Again, the budget constraint has been written as an equality because, given the assumption of nonsatiation, it is clear that the individual will spend all available income.

Interpreting the Lagrangian multiplier

Another result can be derived by solving Equations 4.8 for λ:

$$\lambda = \frac{\partial U/\partial x_1}{p_1} = \frac{\partial U/\partial x_2}{p_2} = \cdots = \frac{\partial U/\partial x_n}{p_n} \qquad (4.11)$$

or

$$\lambda = \frac{MU_{x_1}}{p_1} = \frac{MU_{x_2}}{p_2} = \cdots = \frac{MU_{x_n}}{p_n}.$$

These equations state that, at the utility-maximizing point, each good purchased should yield the same marginal utility per dollar spent on that good. Each good therefore should have an identical (marginal) benefit-to-(marginal)-cost ratio. If this were not true, one good would promise more "marginal enjoyment per dollar" than some other good, and funds would not be optimally allocated.

Although the reader is again warned against talking very confidently about marginal utility, what Equation 4.11 says is that an extra dollar should yield the same "additional utility" no matter which good it is spent on. The common value for this extra utility is given by the Lagrangian multiplier for the consumer's budget constraint (that is, by λ). Consequently, λ can be regarded as the marginal utility of an extra dollar of consumption expenditure (the marginal utility of "income").

One final way to rewrite the necessary conditions for a maximum is

$$p_i = \frac{MU_{x_i}}{\lambda} \qquad (4.12)$$

for every good i that is bought. To interpret this equation, consider a situation where a person's marginal utility of income (λ) is constant over some range. Then variations in the price he or she must pay for good i (p_i) are directly proportional to the extra utility derived from that good. At the margin, therefore, the price of a good reflects an individual's willingness to pay for one more unit. This is a result of considerable importance in applied welfare economics because willingness to pay can be inferred from market reactions to prices. In Chapter 5 we will see how this insight can be used to evaluate the welfare effects of price changes and, in later chapters, we will use this idea to discuss a variety of questions about the efficiency of resource allocation.

Corner solutions

The first-order conditions of Equations 4.8 hold exactly only for interior maxima for which some positive amount of each good is purchased. As discussed in Chapter 2, when corner solutions (such as those illustrated in Figure 4.4) arise, the conditions must be modified slightly.[4] In this case, Equations 4.8 become

$$\frac{\partial \mathcal{L}}{\partial x_i} = \frac{\partial U}{\partial x_i} - \lambda p_i \leq 0 \quad (i = 1, \ldots, n) \qquad (4.13)$$

and, if

$$\frac{\partial \mathcal{L}}{\partial x_i} = \frac{\partial U}{\partial x_i} - \lambda p_i < 0, \qquad (4.14)$$

then

$$x_i = 0. \qquad (4.15)$$

---

[4]Formally, these conditions are called the "Kuhn-Tucker" conditions for nonlinear programming.

To interpret these conditions, we can rewrite Equation 4.14 as

$$p_i > \frac{\partial U / \partial x_i}{\lambda} = \frac{MU_{x_i}}{\lambda}.$$ **(4.16)**

Hence, the optimal conditions are as before, except that any good whose price (p_i) exceeds its marginal value to the consumer (MU_{x_i}/λ) will not be purchased ($x_i = 0$). Thus, the mathematical results conform to the commonsense idea that individuals will not purchase goods that they believe are not worth the money. Although corner solutions do not provide a major focus for our analysis in this book, the reader should keep in mind the possibilities for such solutions arising and the economic interpretation that can be attached to the optimal conditions in such cases.

EXAMPLE 4.1 Cobb-Douglas Demand Functions

As we showed in Chapter 3, the Cobb-Douglas utility function is given by

$$U(x, y) = x^\alpha y^\beta,$$ **(4.17)**

where, for convenience,[5] we assume $\alpha + \beta = 1$. We can now solve for the utility-maximizing values of x and y for any prices (p_x, p_y) and income (I). Setting up the Lagrangian expression

$$\mathcal{L} = x^\alpha y^\beta + \lambda(I - p_x x - p_y y)$$ **(4.18)**

yields the first-order conditions

$$\frac{\partial \mathcal{L}}{\partial x} = \alpha x^{\alpha-1} y^\beta - \lambda p_x = 0,$$

$$\frac{\partial \mathcal{L}}{\partial y} = \beta x^\alpha y^{\beta-1} - \lambda p_y = 0,$$ **(4.19)**

$$\frac{\partial \mathcal{L}}{\partial \lambda} = I - p_x x - p_y y = 0.$$

Taking the ratio of the first two terms shows that

$$\frac{\alpha y}{\beta x} = \frac{p_x}{p_y},$$ **(4.20)**

or

$$p_y y = \frac{\beta}{\alpha} p_x x = \frac{1-\alpha}{\alpha} p_x x,$$ **(4.21)**

where the final equation follows because $\alpha + \beta = 1$. Substitution of this first-order condition in Equation 4.21 into the budget constraint gives

$$I = p_x x + p_y y = p_x x + \frac{1-\alpha}{\alpha} p_x x = p_x x \left(1 + \frac{1-\alpha}{\alpha}\right) = \frac{1}{\alpha} p_x x;$$ **(4.22)**

solving for x yields

$$x^* = \frac{\alpha I}{p_x},$$ **(4.23)**

(*continued*)

---

[5]Notice that the exponents in the Cobb-Douglas utility function can always be normalized to sum to 1 because $U^{1/(\alpha+\beta)}$ is a monotonic transformation.

EXAMPLE 4.1   CONTINUED

and a similar set of manipulations would give

$$y^* = \frac{\beta I}{p_y}.$$

(4.24)

These results show that an individual whose utility function is given by Equation 4.17 will always choose to allocate α proportion of his or her income to buying good x (i.e., $p_x x/I = \alpha$) and β proportion to buying good y ($p_y y/I = \beta$). Although this feature of the Cobb-Douglas function often makes it very easy to work out simple problems, it does suggest that the function has limits in its ability to explain actual consumption behavior. Because the share of income devoted to particular goods often changes significantly in response to changing economic conditions, a more general functional form may provide insights not provided by the Cobb-Douglas function. We illustrate a few possibilities in Example 4.2, and the general topic of budget shares is taken up in more detail in the Extensions to this chapter.

Numerical example. First, however, let's look at a specific numerical example for the Cobb-Douglas case. Suppose that x sells for $1 and y sells for $4 and that total income is $8. Succinctly then, assume that $p_x = 1$, $p_y = 4$, $I = 8$. Suppose also that $\alpha = \beta = 0.5$ so that this individual splits his or her income equally between these two goods. Now the demand Equations 4.23 and 4.24 imply

$$x^* = \alpha I/p_x = 0.5 I/p_x = 0.5(8)/1 = 4,$$
$$y^* = \beta I/p_y = 0.5 I/p_y = 0.5(8)/4 = 1,$$

(4.25)

and, at these optimal choices,

$$\text{utility} = x^{0.5} y^{0.5} = (4)^{0.5}(1)^{0.5} = 2.$$

(4.26)

Notice also that we can compute the value for the Lagrangian multiplier associated with this income allocation by using Equation 4.19:

$$\lambda = \alpha x^{\alpha-1} y^\beta / p_x = 0.5(4)^{-0.5}(1)^{0.5}/1 = 0.25.$$

(4.27)

This value implies that each small change in income will increase utility by about one-fourth of that amount. Suppose, for example, that this person had 1 percent more income ($8.08). In this case he or she would choose $x = 4.04$ and $y = 1.01$, and utility would be $4.04^{0.5} \cdot 1.01^{0.5} = 2.02$. Hence, a $0.08 increase in income increases utility by 0.02, as predicted by the fact that $\lambda = 0.25$.

QUERY: Would a change in p_y affect the quantity of x demanded in Equation 4.23? Explain your answer mathematically. Also develop an intuitive explanation based on the notion that the share of income devoted to good y is given by the parameter of the utility function, β.

EXAMPLE 4.2 CES Demand

To illustrate cases in which budget shares are responsive to economic circumstances, let's look at three specific examples of the CES function.

Case 1: $\delta = 0.5$. In this case, utility is

$$U(x, y) = x^{0.5} + y^{0.5}.$$

(4.28)

Setting up the Lagrangian expression

$$\mathcal{L} = x^{0.5} + y^{0.5} + \lambda(I - p_x x - p_y y) \tag{4.29}$$

yields the following first-order conditions for a maximum:

$$\partial\mathcal{L}/\partial x = 0.5x^{-0.5} - \lambda p_x = 0,$$
$$\partial\mathcal{L}/\partial y = 0.5y^{-0.5} - \lambda p_y = 0, \tag{4.30}$$
$$\partial\mathcal{L}/\partial\lambda = I - p_x x - p_y y = 0.$$

Division of the first two of these shows that

$$(y/x)^{0.5} = p_x/p_y. \tag{4.31}$$

By substituting this into the budget constraint and doing some messy algebraic manipulation, we can derive the demand functions associated with this utility function:

$$x^* = I/p_x[1 + (p_x/p_y)], \tag{4.32}$$

$$y^* = I/p_y[1 + (p_y/p_x)]. \tag{4.33}$$

Price responsiveness. In these demand functions notice that the share of income spent on, say, good x—that is, $p_x x/I = 1/[1 + (p_x/p_y)]$—is not a constant; it depends on the price ratio p_x/p_y. The higher is the relative price of x, the smaller will be the share of income spent on that good. In other words, the demand for x is so responsive to its own price that a rise in the price reduces total spending on x. That the demand for x is very price responsive can also be illustrated by comparing the implied exponent on p_x in the demand function given by Equation 4.32 (-2) to that from Equation 4.23 (-1). In Chapter 5 we will discuss this observation more fully when we examine the elasticity concept in detail.

Case 2: $\delta = -1$. Alternatively, let's look at a demand function with less substitutability[6] than the Cobb-Douglas. If $\delta = -1$, the utility function is given by

$$U(x, y) = -x^{-1} - y^{-1}, \tag{4.34}$$

and it is easy to show that the first-order conditions for a maximum require

$$y/x = (p_x/p_y)^{0.5}. \tag{4.35}$$

Again, substitution of this condition into the budget constraint, together with some messy algebra, yields the demand functions

$$x^* = I/p_x[1 + (p_y/p_x)^{0.5}],$$
$$y^* = I/p_y[1 + (p_x/p_y)^{0.5}]. \tag{4.36}$$

That these demand functions are less price responsive can be seen in two ways. First, now the share of income spent on good x—that is, $p_x x/I = 1/[1 + (p_y/p_x)^{0.5}]$—responds positively to increases in p_x. As the price of x rises, this individual cuts back only modestly on good x, so total spending on that good rises. That the demand functions in Equations 4.36 are less price responsive than the Cobb-Douglas is also illustrated by the relatively small exponents of each good's own price (-0.5).

(continued)

---

[6]One way to measure substitutability is by the elasticity of substitution, which for the CES function is given by $\sigma = 1/(1 - \delta)$. Here $\delta = 0.5$ implies $\sigma = 2$, $\delta = 0$ (the Cobb-Douglas) implies $\sigma = 1$, and $\delta = -1$ implies $\sigma = 0.5$. See also the discussion of the CES function in connection with the theory of production in Chapter 9.

EXAMPLE 4.2   CONTINUED

Case 3: $\delta = -\infty$. This is the important case in which x and y must be consumed in fixed proportions. Suppose, for example, that each unit of y must be consumed together with exactly 4 units of x. The utility function that represents this situation is

$$U(x,y) = \min(x, 4y). \tag{4.37}$$

In this situation, a utility-maximizing person will choose only combinations of the two goods for which $x = 4y$; that is, utility maximization implies that this person will choose to be at a vertex of his or her L-shaped indifference curves. Substituting this condition into the budget constraint yields

$$I = p_x x + p_y y = p_x x + p_y \frac{x}{4} = (p_x + 0.25 p_y)x. \tag{4.38}$$

Hence

$$x^* = \frac{I}{p_x + 0.25 p_y}, \tag{4.39}$$

and similar substitutions yield

$$y^* = \frac{I}{4 p_x + p_y}. \tag{4.40}$$

In this case, the share of a person's budget devoted to, say, good x rises rapidly as the price of x increases because x and y must be consumed in fixed proportions. For example, if we use the values assumed in Example 4.1 ($p_x = 1, p_y = 4, I = 8$), Equations 4.39 and 4.40 would predict $x^* = 4$, $y^* = 1$, and, as before, half of the individual's income would be spent on each good. If we instead use $p_x = 2, p_y = 4$, and $I = 8$ then $x^* = 8/3, y^* = 2/3$, and this person spends two thirds $[p_x x / I = (2 \cdot 8/3)/8 = 2/3]$ of his or her income on good x. Trying a few other numbers suggests that the share of income devoted to good x approaches 1 as the price of x increases.[7]

QUERY: Do changes in income affect expenditure shares in any of the CES functions discussed here? How is the behavior of expenditure shares related to the homothetic nature of this function?

INDIRECT UTILITY FUNCTION

Examples 4.1 and 4.2 illustrate the principle that it is often possible to manipulate the first-order conditions for a constrained utility-maximization problem to solve for the optimal values of $x_1, x_2, \ldots, x_n$. These optimal values in general will depend on the prices of all the goods and on the individual's income. That is,

$$
\begin{aligned}
x_1^* &= x_1(p_1, p_2, \ldots, p_n, I), \\
x_2^* &= x_2(p_1, p_2, \ldots, p_n, I), \\
&\vdots \\
x_n^* &= x_n(p_1, p_2, \ldots, p_n, I).
\end{aligned}
\tag{4.41}
$$

In the next chapter we will analyze in more detail this set of *demand functions*, which show the dependence of the quantity of each x_i demanded on $p_1, p_2, \ldots, p_n$ and I. Here we use

---

[7]These relationships for the CES function are pursued in more detail in Problem 4.9 and in Extension E4.3.

the optimal values of the x's from Equations 4.42 to substitute in the original utility function to yield

$$\text{maximum utility} = U(x_1^*, x_2^*, \ldots, x_n^*) \qquad \textbf{(4.42)}$$

$$= V(p_1, p_2, \ldots, p_n, I). \qquad \textbf{(4.43)}$$

In words: because of the individual's desire to maximize utility given a budget constraint, the optimal level of utility obtainable will depend *indirectly* on the prices of the goods being bought and the individual's income. This dependence is reflected by the indirect utility function V. If either prices or income were to change, the level of utility that could be attained would also be affected. Sometimes, in both consumer theory and many other contexts, it is possible to use this indirect approach to study how changes in economic circumstances affect various kinds of outcomes, such as utility or (later in this book) firms' costs.

THE LUMP SUM PRINCIPLE

Many economic insights stem from the recognition that utility ultimately depends on the income of individuals and on the prices they face. One of the most important of these is the so-called lump sum principle that illustrates the superiority of taxes on a person's general purchasing power to taxes on specific goods. A related insight is that general income grants to low-income people will raise utility more than will a similar amount of money spent subsidizing specific goods. The intuition behind this result derives directly from the utility-maximization hypothesis; an income tax or subsidy leaves the individual free to decide how to allocate whatever final income he or she has. On the other hand, taxes or subsidies on specific goods both change a person's purchasing power and distort his or her choices because of the artificial prices incorporated in such schemes. Hence, general income taxes and subsidies are to be preferred if efficiency is an important criterion in social policy.

The lump sum principle as it applies to taxation is illustrated in Figure 4.5. Initially this person has an income of I and is choosing to consume the combination x^*, y^*. A tax on good x would raise its price, and the utility-maximizing choice would shift to combination x_1, y_1. Tax collections would be $t \cdot x_1$ (where t is the tax rate imposed on good x). Alternatively, an income tax that shifted the budget constraint inward to I' would also collect this same amount of revenue.[8] But the utility provided by the income tax (U_2) exceeds that provided by the tax on x alone (U_1). Hence, we have shown that the utility burden of the income tax is smaller. A similar argument can be used to illustrate the superiority of income grants to subsidies on specific goods.

EXAMPLE 4.3 Indirect Utility and the Lump Sum Principle

In this example we use the notion of an indirect utility function to illustrate the lump sum principle as it applies to taxation. First we have to derive indirect utility functions for two illustrative cases.

(continued)

---

[8]Because $I = (p_x + t)x_1 + p_y y_1$, we have $I' = I - tx_1 = p_x x_1 + p_y y_1$, which shows that the budget constraint with an equal-size income tax also passes through the point x_1, y_1.

EXAMPLE 4.3 CONTINUED

Case 1: Cobb-Douglas. In Example 4.1 we showed that, for the Cobb-Douglas utility function with $\alpha = \beta = 0.5$, optimal purchases are

$$x^* = \frac{I}{2p_x},$$
$$y^* = \frac{I}{2p_y}. \qquad (4.44)$$

So the indirect utility function in this case is

$$V(p_x, p_y, I) = U(x^*, y^*) = (x^*)^{0.5}(y^*)^{0.5} = \frac{I}{2p_x^{0.5} p_y^{0.5}}.$$

Notice that when $p_x = 1$, $p_y = 4$, and $I = 8$ we have $V = 8/(2 \cdot 1 \cdot 2) = 2$, which is the utility that we calculated before for this situation.

Case 2: Fixed proportions. In the third case of Example 4.2 we found that

$$x^* = \frac{I}{p_x + 0.25 p_y},$$
$$y^* = \frac{I}{4p_x + p_y}. \qquad (4.46)$$

So, in this case indirect utility is given by

$$V(p_x, p_y, I) = \min(x^*, 4y^*) = x^* = \frac{I}{p_x + 0.25 p_y}$$
$$= 4y^* = \frac{4}{4p_x + p_y} = \frac{I}{p_x + 0.25 p_y}; \qquad (4.47)$$

with $p_x = 1$, $p_y = 4$, and $I = 8$, indirect utility is given by $V = 4$, which is what we calculated before.

The lump sum principle. Consider first using the Cobb-Douglas case to illustrate the lump sum principle. Suppose that a tax of \$1 were imposed on good x. Equation 4.45 shows that indirect utility in this case would fall from 2 to 1.41 $[= 8/(2 \cdot 2^{0.5} \cdot 2)]$. Because this person chooses $x^* = 2$ with the tax, total tax collections will be \$2. An equal-revenue income tax would therefore reduce net income to \$6, and indirect utility would be 1.5 $[= 6/(2 \cdot 1 \cdot 2)]$. So the income tax is a clear improvement over the case where x alone is taxed. The tax on good x reduces utility for two reasons: it reduces a person's purchasing power and it biases his or her choices away from good x. With income taxation, only the first effect is felt and so the tax is more efficient.[9]

The fixed-proportions case supports this intuition. In that case, a \$1 tax on good x would reduce indirect utility from 4 to 8/3 $[= 8/(2 + 1)]$. In this case $x^* = 8/3$ and tax collections would be \$8/3. An income tax that collected \$8/3 would leave this consumer with \$16/3 in net income, and that income would yield an indirect utility of $V = 8/3$ $[= (16/3)/(1 + 1)]$. Hence after-tax utility is the same under both the excise and income taxes. The reason the lump sum result does not hold in this case is that with fixed-proportions utility, the excise tax does not distort choices because preferences are so rigid.

QUERY: Both of the indirect utility functions illustrated here show that a doubling of income and all prices would leave indirect utility unchanged. Explain why you would expect this to be a property of all indirect utility functions.

---

[9]This discussion assumes that there are no incentive effects of income taxation—probably not a very good assumption.

FIGURE 4.5   The Lump Sum Principle of Taxation

A tax on good x would shift the utility-maximizing choice from x^*, y^* to x_1, y_1. An income tax that collected the same amount would shift the budget constraint to I'. Utility would be higher (U_2) with the income tax than with the tax on x alone (U_1).

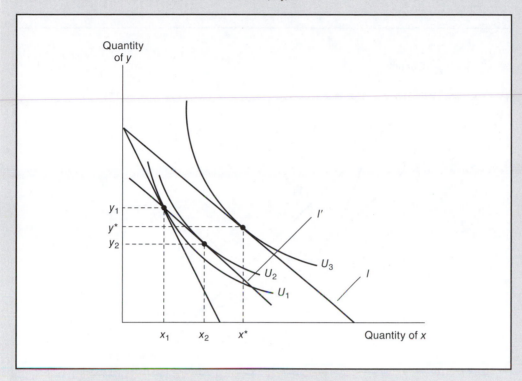

EXPENDITURE MINIMIZATION

In Chapter 2 we pointed out that many constrained maximum problems have associated "dual" constrained minimum problems. For the case of utility maximization, the associated dual minimization problem concerns allocating income in such a way as to achieve a given utility level with the minimal expenditure. This problem is clearly analogous to the primary utility-maximization problem, but the goals and constraints of the problems have been reversed. Figure 4.6 illustrates this dual expenditure-minimization problem. There, the individual must attain utility level U_2; this is now the constraint in the problem. Three possible expenditure amounts (E_1, E_2, and E_3) are shown as three "budget constraint" lines in the figure. Expenditure level E_1 is clearly too small to achieve U_2, hence it cannot solve the dual problem. With expenditures given by E_3, the individual can reach U_2 (at either of the two points B or C), but this is not the minimal expenditure level required. Rather, E_2 clearly provides just enough total expenditures to reach U_2 (at point A), and this is in fact the solution to the dual problem. By comparing Figures 4.2 and 4.6, it is obvious that both the primary utility-maximization approach and the dual expenditure-minimization approach yield the same solution (x^*, y^*); they are simply alternative ways of viewing the same process. Often the expenditure-minimization approach is more useful, however, because expenditures are directly observable, whereas utility is not.

FIGURE 4.6   The Dual Expenditure-Minimization Problem

The dual of the utility-maximization problem is to attain a given utility level (U_2) with minimal expenditures. An expenditure level of E_1 does not permit U_2 to be reached, whereas E_3 provides more spending power than is strictly necessary. With expenditure E_2, this person can just reach U_2 by consuming x^* and y^*.

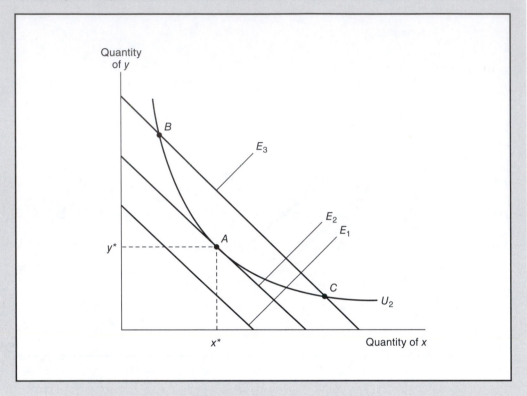

A mathematical statement

More formally, the individual's dual expenditure-minimization problem is to choose x_1, $x_2, ..., x_n$ so as to minimize

$$\text{total expenditures} = E = p_1 x_1 + p_2 x_2 + \cdots + p_n x_n, \qquad \textbf{(4.48)}$$

subject to the constraint

$$\text{utility} = \bar{U} = U(x_1, x_2, ..., x_n). \qquad \textbf{(4.49)}$$

The optimal amounts of $x_1, x_2, ..., x_n$ chosen in this problem will depend on the prices of the various goods ($p_1, p_2, ..., p_n$) and on the required utility level $\bar{U}_2$. If any of the prices were to change or if the individual had a different utility "target," then another commodity bundle would be optimal. This dependence can be summarized by an *expenditure function*.

DEFINITION   **Expenditure function.** The individual's expenditure function shows the minimal expenditures necessary to achieve a given utility level for a particular set of prices. That is,

$$\text{minimal expenditures} = E(p_1, p_2, ..., p_n, U). \qquad \textbf{(4.50)}$$

This definition shows that the expenditure function and the indirect utility function are inverse functions of one another (compare Equations 4.43 and 4.50). Both depend on market prices but involve different constraints (income or utility). In the next chapter we will see how this relationship is quite useful in allowing us to examine the theory of how individuals respond to price changes. First, however, let's look at two expenditure functions.

EXAMPLE 4.4 Two Expenditure Functions

There are two ways one might compute an expenditure function. The first, most straight-forward method would be to state the expenditure-minimization problem directly and apply the Lagrangian technique. Some of the problems at the end of this chapter ask you to do precisely that. Here, however, we will adopt a more streamlined procedure by taking advantage of the relationship between expenditure functions and indirect utility functions. Because these two functions are inverses of each other, calculation of one greatly facilitates the calculation of the other. We have already calculated indirect utility functions for two important cases in Example 4.3. Retrieving the related expenditure functions is simple algebra.

Case 1: Cobb-Douglas utility. Equation 4.45 shows that the indirect utility function in the two-good, Cobb-Douglas case is

$$V(p_x, p_y, I) = \frac{I}{2p_x^{0.5} p_y^{0.5}}. \qquad (4.51)$$

If we now interchange the role of utility (which we will now treat as a constant denoted by U) and income (which we will now term "expenditures," E, and treat as a function of the parameters of this problem), then we have the expenditure function

$$E(p_x, p_y, U) = 2p_x^{0.5} p_y^{0.5} U. \qquad (4.52)$$

Checking this against our former results, now we use a utility target of $U = 2$ with, again, $p_x = 1$ and $p_y = 4$. With these parameters, Equation 4.52 predicts that the required minimal expenditures are \$8 $(= 2 \cdot 1^{0.5} \cdot 4^{0.5} \cdot 2)$. Not surprisingly, both the primal utility-maximization problem and the dual expenditure-minimization problem are formally identical.

Case 2: Fixed proportions. For the fixed-proportions case, Equation 4.47 gave the indirect utility function as

$$V(p_x, p_y, I) = \frac{I}{p_x + 0.25p_y}. \qquad (4.53)$$

If we again switch the role of utility and expenditures, we quickly derive the expenditure function:

$$E(p_x, p_y, U) = (p_x + 0.25p_y) U. \qquad (4.54)$$

A check of the hypothetical values used in Example 4.3 $(p_x = 1, p_y = 4, U = 4)$ again shows that it would cost \$8 $[= (1 + 0.25 \cdot 4) \cdot 4]$ to reach the utility target of 4.

Compensating for a price change. These expenditure functions allow us to investigate how a person might be compensated for a price change. Specifically, suppose that the price of good y were to rise from \$4 to \$5. This would clearly reduce a person's utility, so we might ask what amount of monetary compensation would mitigate the harm. Because the expenditure function allows utility to be held constant, it provides a direct estimate of this amount. Specifically, in the Cobb-Douglas case, expenditures would have to be increased from \$8 to

(continued)

EXAMPLE 4.4   CONTINUED

$8.94 ($= 2 \cdot 1 \cdot 5^{0.5} \cdot 2$) in order to provide enough extra purchasing power to precisely compensate for this price rise. With fixed proportions, expenditures would have to be increased from $8 to $9 to compensate for the price increase. Hence, the compensations are about the same in these simple cases.

There is one important difference between the two examples, however. In the fixed-proportions case, the $1 of extra compensation simply permits this person to return to his or her prior consumption bundle ($x = 4, y = 1$). That is the only way to restore utility to $U = 4$ for this rigid person. In the Cobb-Douglas case, however, this person will not use the extra compensation to revert to his or her prior consumption bundle. Instead, utility maximization will require that the $8.94 be allocated so that $x = 4.47$ and $y = 0.894$. This will still provide a utility level of $U = 2$, but this person will economize on the now more expensive good y.

QUERY: How should a person be compensated for a price decline? What sort of compensation would be required if the price of good y fell from $4 to $3?

PROPERTIES OF EXPENDITURE FUNCTIONS

Because expenditure functions are widely used in applied economics, it is useful to understand a few of the properties shared by all such functions. Here we look at three such properties. All of these follow directly from the fact that expenditure functions are based on individual utility maximization.

1. *Homogeneity.* For both of the functions illustrated in Example 4.4, a doubling of all prices will precisely double the value of required expenditures. Technically, these expenditure functions are "homogeneous of degree one" in all prices.[10] This is a quite general property of expenditure functions. Because the individual's budget constraint is linear in prices, any proportional increase in both prices and purchasing power will permit the person to buy the same utility-maximizing commodity bundle that was chosen before the price rise. In Chapter 5 we will see that, for this reason, demand functions are homogenous of degree 0 in all prices and income.

2. *Expenditure functions are nondecreasing in prices.* This property can be succinctly summarized by the mathematical statement

$$\frac{\partial E}{\partial p_i} \geq 0 \quad \text{for every good } i. \tag{4.55}$$

This seems intuitively obvious. Because the expenditure function reports the minimum expenditure necessary to reach a given utility level, an increase in any price must increase this minimum. More formally, suppose p_1 takes on two values: p_1^a and p_1^b with $p_1^b > p_1^a$, where all other prices are unchanged between states a and b. Also, let x be the bundle of goods purchased in state a and y the bundle purchased in state b. By the definition of the expenditure function, both of these bundles of goods must

---

[10]As described in Chapter 2, the function $f(x_1, x_2, ..., x_n)$ is said to be homogeneous of degree k if $f(tx_1, tx_2, ..., tx_n) = t^k f(x_1, x_2, ..., x_n)$. In this case, $k = 1$.

yield the same target utility. Clearly bundle y costs more with state-b prices than it would with state-a prices. But we know that bundle x is the lowest-cost way to achieve the target utility level with state-a prices. Hence, expenditures on bundle y must be greater than or equal to those on bundle x. Similarly, a decline in a price must not increase expenditures.

3. *Expenditure functions are concave in prices.* In Chapter 2 we discussed concave functions as functions that always lie below tangents to them. Although the technical mathematical conditions that describe such functions are complicated, it is relatively simple to show how the concept applies to expenditure functions by considering the variation in a single price. Figure 4.7 shows an individual's expenditures as a function of the single price, p_1. At the initial price, p_1^*, this person's expenditures are given by $E(p_1^*, \ldots)$. Now consider prices higher or lower than p_1^*. If this person continued to buy the same bundle of goods, expenditures would increase or decrease linearly as this price changed. This would give rise to the pseudo expenditure function E^{pseudo} in the figure. This line shows a level of expenditures that would allow this person to buy the original bundle of goods despite the changing value of p_1. If, as seems more likely, this person adjusted his or her purchases as p_1 changed, we know (because of expenditure minimization) that actual expenditures would be less than these pseudo

FIGURE 4.7   Expenditure Functions Are Concave in Prices

At p_1^* this person spends $E(p_1^*, \ldots)$. If he or she continues to buy the same set of goods as p_1 changes, then expenditures would be given by E^{pseudo}. Because his or her consumption patterns will likely change as p_1 changes, actual expenditures will be less than this.

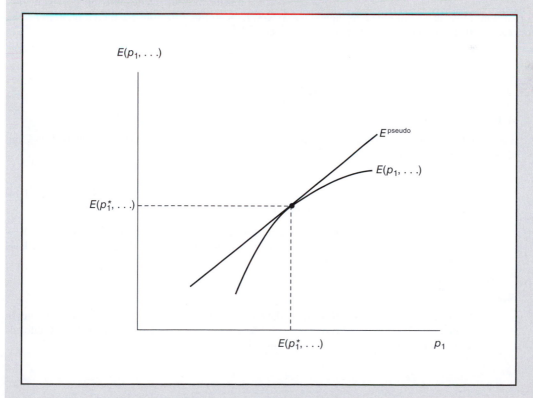

amounts. Hence, the actual expenditure function, E, will lie everywhere below E^{pseudo} and the function will be concave.[11] The concavity of the expenditure function is a useful property for a number of applications, especially those related to the construction of index numbers (see the Extensions to Chapter 5).

SUMMARY

In this chapter we explored the basic economic model of utility maximization subject to a budget constraint. Although we approached this problem in a variety of ways, all of these approaches lead to the same basic result.

- To reach a constrained maximum, an individual should spend all available income and should choose a commodity bundle such that the *MRS* between any two goods is equal to the ratio of those goods' market prices. This basic tangency will result in the individual equating the ratios of the marginal utility to market price for every good that is actually consumed. Such a result is common to most constrained optimization problems.

- The tangency conditions are only the first-order conditions for a unique constrained maximum, however. To ensure that these conditions are also sufficient, the individual's indifference curve map must exhibit a diminishing *MRS*. In formal terms, the utility function must be strictly quasi-concave.

- The tangency conditions must also be modified to allow for corner solutions in which the optimal level of con-

sumption of some goods is zero. In this case, the ratio of marginal utility to price for such a good will be below the common marginal benefit–marginal cost ratio for goods actually bought.

- A consequence of the assumption of constrained utility maximization is that the individual's optimal choices will depend implicitly on the parameters of his or her budget constraint. That is, the choices observed will be implicit functions of all prices and income. Utility will therefore also be an indirect function of these parameters.

- The dual to the constrained utility-maximization problem is to minimize the expenditure required to reach a given utility target. Although this dual approach yields the same optimal solution as the primal constrained maximum problem, it also yields additional insight into the theory of choice. Specifically, this approach leads to expenditure functions in which the spending required to reach a given utility target depends on goods' market prices. Expenditure functions are therefore, in principle, measurable.

PROBLEMS

4.1

Each day Paul, who is in third grade, eats lunch at school. He likes only Twinkies (t) and soda (s), and these provide him a utility of

$$\text{utility} = U(t, s) = \sqrt{ts}.$$

a. If Twinkies cost \$0.10 each and soda costs \$0.25 per cup, how should Paul spend the \$1 his mother gives him in order to maximize his utility?

b. If the school tries to discourage Twinkie consumption by raising the price to \$0.40, by how much will Paul's mother have to increase his lunch allowance to provide him with the same level of utility he received in part (a)?

4.2

a. A young connoisseur has \$600 to spend to build a small wine cellar. She enjoys two vintages in particular: a 2001 French Bordeaux (w_F) at \$40 per bottle and a less expensive 2005 California varietal wine (w_C) priced at \$8. If her utility is

---

[11]One result of concavity is that $f_{ii} = \partial^2 E / \partial p_i^2 \leq 0$. This is precisely what Figure 4.7 shows.

$$U(w_F, w_C) = w_F^{2/3} w_C^{1/3},$$

then how much of each wine should she purchase?

b. When she arrived at the wine store, our young oenologist discovered that the price of the French Bordeaux had fallen to $20 a bottle because of a decline in the value of the franc. If the price of the California wine remains stable at $8 per bottle, how much of each wine should our friend purchase to maximize utility under these altered conditions?

c. Explain why this wine fancier is better off in part (b) than in part (a). How would you put a monetary value on this utility increase?

4.3

a. On a given evening, J. P. enjoys the consumption of cigars (c) and brandy (b) according to the function

$$U(c, b) = 20c - c^2 + 18b - 3b^2.$$

How many cigars and glasses of brandy does he consume during an evening? (Cost is no object to J. P.)

b. Lately, however, J. P. has been advised by his doctors that he should limit the sum of glasses of brandy and cigars consumed to 5. How many glasses of brandy and cigars will he consume under these circumstances?

4.4

a. Mr. Odde Ball enjoys commodities x and y according to the utility function

$$U(x, y) = \sqrt{x^2 + y^2}.$$

Maximize Mr. Ball's utility if $p_x = \$3$, $p_y = \$4$, and he has $50 to spend. *Hint:* It may be easier here to maximize U^2 rather than U. Why won't this alter your results?

b. Graph Mr. Ball's indifference curve and its point of tangency with his budget constraint. What does the graph say about Mr. Ball's behavior? Have you found a true maximum?

4.5

Mr. A derives utility from martinis (m) in proportion to the number he drinks:

$$U(m) = m.$$

Mr. A is very particular about his martinis, however: He only enjoys them made in the exact proportion of two parts gin (g) to one part vermouth (v). Hence, we can rewrite Mr. A's utility function as

$$U(m) = U(g, v) = \min\left(\frac{g}{2}, v\right).$$

a. Graph Mr. A's indifference curve in terms of g and v for various levels of utility. Show that, regardless of the prices of the two ingredients, Mr. A will never alter the way he mixes martinis.

b. Calculate the demand functions for g and v.

c. Using the results from part (b), what is Mr. A's indirect utility function?

d. Calculate Mr. A's expenditure function; for each level of utility, show spending as a function of p_g and p_v. *Hint:* Because this problem involves a fixed-proportions utility function, you cannot solve for utility-maximizing decisions by using calculus.

4.6

Suppose that a fast-food junkie derives utility from three goods—soft drinks (x), hamburgers (y), and ice cream sundaes (z)—according to the Cobb-Douglas utility function

$$U(x, y, z) = x^{0.5} y^{0.5} (1 + z)^{0.5}.$$

Suppose also that the prices for these goods are given by $p_x = 0.25$, $p_y = 1$, and $p_z = 2$ and that this consumer's income is given by $I = 2$.

    a. Show that, for $z = 0$, maximization of utility results in the same optimal choices as in Example 4.1. Show also that any choice that results in $z > 0$ (even for a fractional z) reduces utility from this optimum.

    b. How do you explain the fact that $z = 0$ is optimal here?

    c. How high would this individual's income have to be in order for any z to be purchased?

4.7

The lump sum principle illustrated in Figure 4.5 applies to transfer policy as well as taxation. This problem examines this application of the principle.

    a. Use a graph similar to Figure 4.5 to show that an income grant to a person provides more utility than does a subsidy on good x that costs the same amount to the government.

    b. Use the Cobb-Douglas expenditure function presented in Equation 4.52 to calculate the extra purchasing power needed to raise this person's utility from $U = 2$ to $U = 3$.

    c. Use Equation 4.52 again to estimate the degree to which good x must be subsidized in order to raise this person's utility from $U = 2$ to $U = 3$. How much would this subsidy cost the government? How would this cost compare to the cost calculated in part (b)?

    d. Problem 4.10 asks you to compute an expenditure function for a more general Cobb-Douglas utility function than the one used in Example 4.4. Use that expenditure function to re-solve parts (b) and (c) here for the case $\alpha = 0.3$, a figure close to the fraction of income that low-income people spend on food.

    e. How would your calculations in this problem have changed if we had used the expenditure function for the fixed proportions case (Equation 4.54) instead?

4.8

Mr. Carr derives a lot of pleasure from driving under the wide blue skies. For the number of miles x that he drives, he receives utility $U(x) = 500x - x^2$. (Once he drives beyond a certain number of miles, weariness kicks in and the ride becomes less and less enjoyable.) Now, his car gives him a decent highway mileage of 25 miles to the gallon. But paying for gas, represented by y, induces disutility for Mr. Carr, shown by $U(y) = -1,000y$. Mr. Carr is willing to spend up to $25 for leisurely driving every week.

    a. Find the optimum number of miles driven by Mr. Carr every week, given that the price of gas is $2.50 per gallon.

    b. How does that value change when the price of gas rises to $5.00 per gallon?

    c. Now, further assume that there is a probability of 0.001 that Mr. Carr will get a flat tire every mile he drives. The disutility from a flat tire is given by $U(z) = -50,000z$ (where z is the number of flat tires incurred), and each flat tire costs $50 to replace. Find the distance driven that maximizes Mr. Carr's utility after taking into account the expected likelihood of flat tires (assume that the price of gas is $2.50 per gallon).

4.9

Suppose that we have a utility function involving two goods that is linear of the form $U(x, y) = ax + by$. Calculate the expenditure function for this utility function. *Hint:* The expenditure function will have kinks at various price ratios.

Analytical Problems

4.10 Cobb-Douglas utility

In Example 4.1 we looked at the Cobb-Douglas utility function $U(x, y) = x^\alpha y^{1-\alpha}$, where $0 \leq \alpha \leq 1$. This problem illustrates a few more attributes of that function.

   a. Calculate the indirect utility function for this Cobb-Douglas case.

   b. Calculate the expenditure function for this case.

   c. Show explicitly how the compensation required to offset the effect of a rise in the price of x is related to the size of the exponent α.

4.11 CES utility

The CES utility function we have used in this chapter is given by

$$U(x, y) = \frac{x^\delta}{\delta} + \frac{y^\delta}{\delta}.$$

   a. Show that the first-order conditions for a constrained utility maximum with this function require individuals to choose goods in the proportion

$$\frac{x}{y} = \left(\frac{p_x}{p_y}\right)^{1/(\delta-1)}.$$

   b. Show that the result in part (a) implies that individuals will allocate their funds equally between x and y for the Cobb-Douglas case ($\delta = 0$), as we have shown before in several problems.

   c. How does the ratio $p_x x / p_y y$ depend on the value of δ? Explain your results intuitively. (For further details on this function, see Extension E4.3.)

   d. Derive the indirect utility and expenditure functions for this case and check your results by describing the homogeneity properties of the functions you calculated.

4.12 Stone-Geary utility

Suppose individuals require a certain level of food (x) to remain alive. Let this amount be given by x_0. Once x_0 is purchased, individuals obtain utility from food and other goods (y) of the form

$$U(x, y) = (x - x_0)^\alpha y^\beta,$$

where $\alpha + \beta = 1$.

   a. Show that if $I > p_x x_0$ then the individual will maximize utility by spending $\alpha(I - p_x x_0) + p_x x_0$ on good x and $\beta(I - p_x x_0)$ on good y. Interpret this result.

   b. How do the ratios $p_x x / I$ and $p_y y / I$ change as income increases in this problem? (See also Extension E4.2 for more on this utility function.)

4.13 CES indirect utility and expenditure functions

In this problem, we will use a more standard form of the CES utility function to derive indirect utility and expenditure functions. Suppose utility is given by

$$U(x, y) = (x^\delta + y^\delta)^{1/\delta}$$

[in this function the elasticity of substitution $\sigma = 1/(1 - \delta)$].

   a. Show that the indirect utility function for the utility function just given is

$$V = I(p_x^r + p_y^r)^{-1/r},$$

where $r = \delta/(\delta - 1) = 1 - \sigma$.

b. Show that the function derived in part (a) is homogeneous of degree 0 in prices and income.

c. Show that this function is strictly increasing in income.

d. Show that this function is strictly decreasing in any price.

e. Show that the expenditure function for this case of CES utility is given by

$$E = V(p_x^r + p_y^r)^{1/r}.$$

f. Show that the function derived in part (e) is homogeneous of degree 1 in the goods' prices.

g. Show that this expenditure function is increasing in each of the prices.

h. Show that the function is concave in each price.

SUGGESTIONS FOR FURTHER READING

Barten, A. P., and Volker Böhm. "Consumer Theory." In K. J. Arrow and M. D. Intriligator, Eds., *Handbook of Mathematical Economics,* vol. II. Amsterdam: North-Holland, 1982.

Sections 10 and 11 have compact summaries of many of the concepts covered in this chapter.

Deaton, A., and J. Muelbauer. *Economics and Consumer Behavior.* Cambridge: Cambridge University Press, 1980.

Section 2.5 provides a nice geometric treatment of duality concepts.

Dixit, A. K. *Optimization in Economic Theory.* Oxford: Oxford University Press, 1990.

Chapter 2 provides several Lagrangian analyses focusing on the Cobb-Douglas utility function.

Hicks, J. R. *Value and Capital.* Oxford: Clarendon Press, 1946.

Chapter II and the Mathematical Appendix provide some early suggestions of the importance of the expenditure function.

Mas-Colell, A., M. D. Whinston, and J. R. Green. *Microeconomic Theory.* Oxford: Oxford University Press, 1995.

Chapter 3 contains a thorough analysis of utility and expenditure functions.

Samuelson, Paul A. *Foundations of Economic Analysis.* Cambridge, MA: Harvard University Press, 1947.

Chapter V and Appendix A provide a succinct analysis of the first-order conditions for a utility maximum. The appendix provides good coverage of second-order conditions.

Silberberg, E., and W. Suen. *The Structure of Economics: A Mathematical Analysis,* 3rd ed. Boston: Irwin/McGraw-Hill, 2001.

A useful, though fairly difficult, treatment of duality in consumer theory.

Theil, H. *Theory and Measurement of Consumer Demand.* Amsterdam: North-Holland, 1975.

Good summary of basic theory of demand together with implications for empirical estimation.

EXTENSIONS

Budget Shares

The nineteenth-century economist Ernst Engel was one of the first social scientists to intensively study people's actual spending patterns. He focused specifically on food consumption. His finding that the fraction of income spent on food declines as income increases has come to be known as Engel's law and has been confirmed in many studies. Engel's law is such an empirical regularity that some economists have suggested measuring poverty by the fraction of income spent on food. Two other interesting applications are: (1) the study by Hayashi (1995) showing that the share of income devoted to foods favored by the elderly is much higher in two-generation households than in one-generation households; and (2) findings by Behrman (1989) from less-developed countries showing that people's desires for a more varied diet as their incomes rise may in fact result in reducing the fraction of income spent on particular nutrients. In the remainder of this extension we look at some evidence on budget shares (denoted by $s_i = p_i x_i / I$) together with a bit more theory on the topic.

E4.1 The variability of budget shares

Table E4.1 shows some recent budget share data from the United States. Engel's law is clearly visible in the table: as income rises families spend a smaller proportion of their funds on food. Other important variations in the table include the declining share of income spent on health-care needs and the much larger share of income devoted to retirement plans by higher-income people. Interestingly, the shares of income devoted to shelter and transportation are relatively constant over the range of income shown in the table; apparently, high-income people buy bigger houses and cars.

The variable income shares in Table E4.1 illustrate why the Cobb-Douglas utility function is not useful for detailed empirical studies of household behavior. When utility is given by $U(x, y) = x^\alpha y^\beta$, the implied demand equations are $x = \alpha I / p_x$ and $y = \beta I / p_y$. Therefore,

$$s_x = p_x x / I = \alpha \quad \text{and}$$
$$s_y = p_y y / I = \beta, \tag{i}$$

and budget shares are constant for all observed income levels and relative prices. Because of this shortcoming, economists have investigated a number of other possible forms for the utility function that permit more flexibility.

E4.2 Linear expenditure system

A generalization of the Cobb-Douglas function that incorporates the idea that certain minimal amounts of each good must be bought by an individual (x_0, y_0) is the utility function

$$U(x, y) = (x - x_0)^\alpha (y - y_0)^\beta \tag{ii}$$

for $x \geq x_0$ and $y \geq y_0$, where again $\alpha + \beta = 1$.

Demand functions can be derived from this utility function in a way analogous to the Cobb-Douglas case by introducing the concept of supernumerary income (I^*), which represents the amount of purchasing power remaining after purchasing the minimum bundle

$$I^* = I - p_x x_0 - p_y y_0. \tag{iii}$$

Using this notation, the demand functions are

$$x = (p_x x_0 + \alpha I^*) / p_x,$$
$$y = (p_y y_0 + \beta I^*) / p_y. \tag{iv}$$

In this case, then, the individual spends a constant fraction of supernumerary income on each good once the minimum bundle has been purchased. Manipulation of Equation iv yields the share equations

$$s_x = \alpha + (\beta p_x x_0 - \alpha p_y y_0) / I,$$
$$s_y = \beta + (\alpha p_y y_0 - \beta p_x x_0) / I, \tag{v}$$

which show that this demand system is not homothetic. Inspection of Equation v shows the unsurprising result that the budget share of a good is positively related to the minimal amount of that good needed and negatively related to the minimal amount of the other good required. Because the notion of necessary purchases seems to accord well with real-world observation, this linear expenditure system (LES), which was first developed by Stone (1954), is widely used in empirical studies. The utility function in Equation ii is also called a Stone-Geary utility function.

Traditional purchases

One of the most interesting uses of the LES is to examine how its notion of necessary purchases changes as conditions change. For example, Oczkowski and

TABLE E4.1   Budget Shares of U.S. Households, 2004

	Annual Income		
	$10,000–$14,999	$40,000–$49,999	Over $70,000
Expenditure Item			
Food	15.3	14.3	11.8
Shelter	21.8	18.5	17.6
Utilities, fuel, and public services	10.2	7.7	5.4
Transportation	15.4	18.4	17.6
Health insurance	4.9	3.8	2.3
Other health-care expenses	4.4	2.9	2.4
Entertainment (including alcohol)	4.4	4.6	5.4
Tobacco	1.2	0.9	0.4
Education	2.5	1.1	2.6
Insurance and pensions	2.7	9.6	14.7
Other (apparel, personal care, other housing expenses, and misc.)	17.2	18.2	19.8

SOURCE: *Consumer Expenditure Report*, 2004, Bureau of Labor Statistics website: http://www.bls.gov.

Philip (1994) study how access to modern consumer goods may affect the share of income that individuals in transitional economies devote to traditional local items. They show that villagers of Papua, New Guinea, reduce such shares significantly as outside goods become increasingly accessible. Hence, such improvements as better roads for moving goods provide one of the primary routes by which traditional cultural practices are undermined.

E4.3 CES utility

In Chapter 3 we introduced the CES utility function

$$U(x,y) = \frac{x^\delta}{\delta} + \frac{y^\delta}{\delta} \qquad \textbf{(vi)}$$

for $\delta \leq 1$, $\delta \neq 0$. The primary use of this function is to illustrate alternative substitution possibilities (as reflected in the value of the parameter δ). Budget shares implied by this utility function provide a number of such insights. Manipulation of the first-order conditions for a constrained utility maximum with the CES function yields the share equations

$$s_x = 1/[1 + (p_y/p_x)^K], \qquad \textbf{(vii)}$$
$$s_y = 1/[1 + (p_x/p_y)^K],$$

where $K = \delta/(\delta - 1)$.

The homothetic nature of the CES function is shown by the fact that these share expressions depend only on the price ratio, p_x/p_y. Behavior of the shares in response to changes in relative prices depends on the value of the parameter K. For the Cobb-Douglas case, $\delta = 0$ and so $K = 0$ and $s_x = s_y = 1/2$. When $\delta > 0$, substitution possibilities are great and $K < 0$. In this case, Equation vii shows that s_x and p_x/p_y move in opposite directions. If p_x/p_y rises, the individual substitutes y for x to such an extent that s_x falls. Alternatively, if $\delta < 0$, then substitution possibilities are limited, $K > 0$, and s_x and p_x/p_y move in the same direction. In this case, an increase in p_x/p_y causes only minor substitution of y for x, and s_x actually rises because of the relatively higher price of good x.

North American free trade

CES demand functions are most often used in large-scale computer models of general equilibrium (see Chapter 13) that economists use to evaluate the impact of major economic changes. Because the CES model stresses that shares respond to changes in relative prices, it is particularly appropriate for looking at innovations such as changes in tax policy or in international trade restrictions, where changes in relative prices are quite likely. One important recent area of such research has been on the impact of the North American Free Trade Agreement for Canada, Mexico, and the United States. In general, these models find that all of the countries involved might be expected to gain from the agreement, but that Mexico's gains may be the greatest because it is experiencing the greatest change in relative prices. Kehoe and Kehoe (1995) present a number of computable equilibrium models that economists have used in these examinations.[1]

E4.4 The almost ideal demand system

An alternative way to study budget shares is to start from a specific expenditure function. This approach is especially convenient because the envelope theorem shows that budget shares can be derived directly from expenditure functions through logarithmic differentiation:

$$\frac{\partial \ln E(p_x, p_y, V)}{\partial \ln p_x} = \frac{1}{E(p_x, p_y, V)} \cdot \frac{\partial E}{\partial p_x} \cdot \frac{\partial p_x}{\partial \ln p_x}$$

$$= \frac{x p_x}{E} = s_x. \qquad \textbf{(viii)}$$

Deaton and Muellbauer (1980) make extensive use of this relationship to study the characteristics of a particular class of expenditure functions that they term an almost ideal demand system (AIDS). Their expenditure function takes the form

$$\ln E(p_x, p_y, V) = a_0 + a_1 \ln p_x + a_2 \ln p_y$$
$$+ 0.5 b_1 (\ln p_x)^2 + b_2 \ln p_x \ln p_y$$
$$+ 0.5 b_3 (\ln p_y)^2 + V c_0 p_x^{c_1} p_y^{c_2}. $$

$$\textbf{(ix)}$$

This form approximates any expenditure function. For the function to be homogeneous of degree 1 in the prices, the parameters of the function must obey the constraints $a_1 + a_2 = 1$, $b_1 + b_2 = 0$, $b_2 + b_3 = 0$, and $c_1 + c_2 = 0$. Using the results of Equation viii shows that, for this function,

$$s_x = a_1 + b_1 \ln p_x + b_2 \ln p_y + c_1 V c_0 p_x^{c_1} p_y^{c_2},$$
$$s_y = a_2 + b_2 \ln p_x + b_3 \ln p_y + c_2 V c_0 p_x^{c_1} p_y^{c_2}. \qquad \textbf{(x)}$$

Notice that, given the parameter restrictions, $s_x + s_y = 1$. Making use of the inverse relationship between indirect utility and expenditure functions and some additional algebraic manipulation will put these budget share equations into a simple form suitable for econometric estimation:

$$s_x = a_1 + b_1 \ln p_x + b_2 \ln p_y + c_1 (E/p),$$
$$s_y = a_2 + b_2 \ln p_x + b_3 \ln p_y + c_2 (E/p), \qquad \textbf{(xi)}$$

where p is an index of prices defined by

$$\ln p = a_0 + a_1 \ln p_x + a_2 \ln p_y + 0.5 b_1 (\ln p_x)^2$$
$$+ b_2 \ln p_x \ln p_y + 0.5 b_3 (\ln p_y)^2.$$

$$\textbf{(xii)}$$

In other words, the AIDS share equations state that budget shares are linear in the logarithms of prices and in total real expenditures. In practice, simpler price indices are often substituted for the rather complex index given by Equation xii, although there is some controversy about this practice (see the Extensions to Chapter 5).

British expenditure patterns

Deaton and Muellbauer apply this demand system to the study of British expenditure patterns between 1954 and 1974. They find that both food and housing have negative coefficients of real expenditures, implying that the share of income devoted to these items falls (at least in Britain) as people get richer. The authors also find significant relative price effects in many of their share equations, and prices have especially large effects in explaining the share of expenditures devoted to transportation and communication. In applying the AIDS model to real-world data, the authors also encounter a variety of econometric difficulties, the most important of which is that many of the equations do not appear to obey the restrictions necessary for homogeneity. Addressing such issues has been a major topic for further research on this demand system.

---

[1]The research on the North American Free Trade Agreement is discussed in more detail in the Extensions to Chapter 13

References

Behrman, Jere R. "Is Variety the Spice of Life? Implications for Caloric Intake." *Review of Economics and Statistics* (November 1989): 666–72.

Deaton, Angus, and John Muellbauer. "An Almost Ideal Demand System." *American Economic Review* (June 1980): 312–26.

Hyashi, Fumio. "Is the Japanese Extended Family Altruistically Linked? A Test Based on Engel Curves." *Journal of Political Economy* (June 1995): 661–74.

Kehoe, Patrick J., and Timothy J. Kehoe. *Modeling North American Economic Integration*. London: Kluwer Academic Publishers, 1995.

Oczkowski, E., and N. E. Philip. "Household Expenditure Patterns and Access to Consumer Goods in a Transitional Economy." *Journal of Economic Development* (June 1994): 165–83.

Stone, R. "Linear Expenditure Systems and Demand Analysis." *Economic Journal* (September 1954): 511–27.

Income and Substitution Effects

In this chapter we will use the utility-maximization model to study how the quantity of a good that an individual chooses is affected by a change in that good's price. This examination allows us to construct the individual's demand curve for the good. In the process we will provide a number of insights into the nature of this price response and into the kinds of assumptions that lie behind most analyses of demand.

DEMAND FUNCTIONS

As we pointed out in Chapter 4, in principle it will usually be possible to solve the necessary conditions of a utility maximum for the optimal levels of $x_1, x_2, \ldots, x_n$ (and λ, the Lagrangian multiplier) as functions of all prices and income. Mathematically, this can be expressed as n demand functions of the form

$$
\begin{aligned}
x_1^* &= x_1(p_1, p_2, \ldots, p_n, I), \\
x_2^* &= x_2(p_1, p_2, \ldots, p_n, I), \\
&\ \vdots \\
x_n^* &= x_n(p_1, p_2, \ldots, p_n, I).
\end{aligned}
\tag{5.1}
$$

If there are only two goods, x and y (the case we will usually be concerned with), this notation can be simplified a bit as

$$
\begin{aligned}
x^* &= x(p_x, p_y, I), \\
y^* &= y(p_x, p_y, I).
\end{aligned}
\tag{5.2}
$$

Once we know the form of these demand functions and the values of all prices and income, we can "predict" how much of each good this person will choose to buy. The notation stresses that prices and income are "exogenous" to this process; that is, these are parameters over which the individual has no control at this stage of the analysis. Changes in the parameters will, of course, shift the budget constraint and cause this person to make different choices. That question is the focus of this chapter and the next. Specifically, in this chapter we will be looking at the partial derivatives $\partial x / \partial I$ and $\partial x / \partial p_x$ for any arbitrary good x. Chapter 6 will carry the discussion further by looking at "cross-price" effects of the form $\partial x / \partial p_y$ for any arbitrary pair of goods x and y.

Homogeneity

A first property of demand functions requires little mathematics. If we were to double all prices and income (indeed, if we were to multiply them all by any positive constant), then the optimal quantities demanded would remain unchanged. Doubling all prices and income changes only the units by which we count, not the "real" quantity of goods demanded. This result can be seen in a number of ways, although perhaps the easiest is through a graphic approach. Referring back to Figures 4.1 and 4.2, it is clear that doubling p_x, p_y, and I does not affect the graph of the budget constraint. Hence, x^*, y^* will still be the combination that is chosen. Further, $p_x x + p_y y = I$ is the same constraint as $2p_x x + 2p_y y = 2I$. Somewhat more technically, we can write this result as saying that, for any good x_i,

$$x_i^* = x_i(p_1, p_2, ..., p_n, I) = x_i(tp_1, tp_2, ..., tp_n, tI) \tag{5.3}$$

for any $t > 0$. Functions that obey the property illustrated in Equation 5.3 are said to be homogeneous of degree 0.[1] Hence, we have shown that individual *demand functions are homogeneous of degree* 0 *in all prices and income.* Changing all prices and income in the same proportions will not affect the physical quantities of goods demanded. This result shows that (in theory) individuals' demands will not be affected by a "pure" inflation during which all prices and incomes rise proportionally. They will continue to demand the same bundle of goods. Of course, if an inflation were not pure (that is, if some prices rose more rapidly than others), this would not be the case.

EXAMPLE 5.1 Homogeneity

Homogeneity of demand is a direct result of the utility-maximization assumption. Demand functions derived from utility maximization will be homogeneous and, conversely, demand functions that are not homogeneous cannot reflect utility maximization (unless prices enter directly into the utility function itself, as they might for goods with snob appeal). If, for example, an individual's utility for food (x) and housing (y) is given by

$$\text{utility} = U(x, y) = x^{0.3}y^{0.7}, \tag{5.4}$$

then it is a simple matter (following the procedure used in Example 4.1) to derive the demand functions

$$x^* = \frac{0.3I}{p_x},$$
$$y^* = \frac{0.7I}{p_y}. \tag{5.5}$$

These functions obviously exhibit homogeneity, since a doubling of all prices and income would leave x^* and y^* unaffected.

If the individual's preferences for x and y were reflected instead by the CES function

$$U(x, y) = x^{0.5} + y^{0.5}, \tag{5.6}$$

then (as shown in Example 4.2) the demand functions are given by

$$x^* = \left(\frac{1}{1 + p_x/p_y}\right) \cdot \frac{I}{p_x},$$
$$y^* = \left(\frac{1}{1 + p_y/p_x}\right) \cdot \frac{I}{p_y}. \tag{5.7}$$

As before, both of these demand functions are homogeneous of degree 0; a doubling of p_x, p_y, and I would leave x^* and y^* unaffected.

---

[1]More generally, as we saw in Chapters 2 and 4, a function $f(x_1, x_2, ..., x_n)$ is said to be homogeneous of degree k if $f(tx_1, tx_2, ..., tx_n) = t^k f(x_1, x_2, ..., x_n)$ for any $t > 0$. The most common cases of homogeneous functions are $k = 0$ and $k = 1$. If f is homogeneous of degree 0, then doubling all of its arguments leaves f unchanged in value. If f is homogeneous of degree 1, then doubling all of its arguments will double the value of f.

QUERY: Do the demand functions derived in this example ensure that total spending on x and y will exhaust the individual's income for *any combination* of p_x, p_y, and I? Can you prove that this is the case?

CHANGES IN INCOME

As a person's purchasing power rises, it is natural to expect that the quantity of each good purchased will also increase. This situation is illustrated in Figure 5.1. As expenditures increase from I_1 to I_2 to I_3, the quantity of x demanded increases from x_1 to x_2 to x_3. Also, the quantity of y increases from y_1 to y_2 to y_3. Notice that the budget lines I_1, I_2, and I_3 are all parallel, reflecting that only income is changing, not the relative prices of x and y. Because the ratio p_x/p_y stays constant, the utility-maximizing conditions also require that the *MRS* stay constant as the individual moves to higher levels of satisfaction. The *MRS* is therefore the same at point (x_3, y_3) as at (x_1, y_1).

Normal and inferior goods

In Figure 5.1, both x and y increase as income increases—both $\partial x/\partial I$ and $\partial y/\partial I$ are positive. This might be considered the usual situation, and goods that have this property are called *normal goods* over the range of income change being observed.

FIGURE 5.1 Effect of an Increase in Income on the Quantities of x and y Chosen

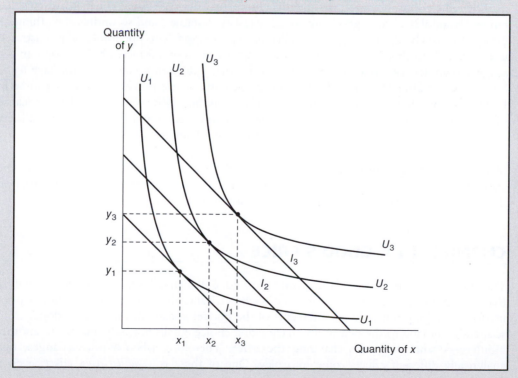

As income increases from I_1 to I_2 to I_3, the optimal (utility-maximizing) choices of x and y are shown by the successively higher points of tangency. Observe that the budget constraint shifts in a parallel way because its slope (given by $-p_x/p_y$) does not change.

FIGURE 5.2   An Indifference Curve Map Exhibiting Inferiority

In this diagram, good z is inferior because the quantity purchased actually declines as income increases. Here, y is a normal good (as it must be if there are only two goods available), and purchases of y increase as total expenditures increase.

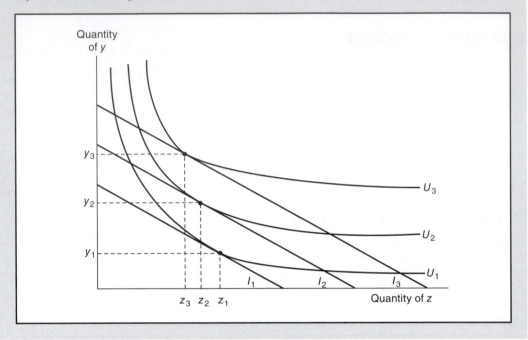

For some goods, however, the quantity chosen may decrease as income increases in some ranges. Examples of such goods are rotgut whiskey, potatoes, and secondhand clothing. A good z for which $\partial z/\partial I$ is negative is called an *inferior good*. This phenomenon is illustrated in Figure 5.2. In this diagram, the good z is inferior because, for increases in income in the range shown, less of z is actually chosen. Notice that indifference curves do not have to be "oddly" shaped in order to exhibit inferiority; the curves corresponding to goods y and z in Figure 5.2 continue to obey the assumption of a diminishing *MRS*. Good z is inferior because of the way it relates to the other goods available (good y here), not because of a peculiarity unique to it. Hence, we have developed the following definitions.

DEFINITION   **Inferior and normal goods.** A good x_i for which $\partial x_i/\partial I < 0$ over some range of income changes is an *inferior good* in that range. If $\partial x_i/\partial I \geq 0$ over some range of income variation then the good is a *normal* (or "noninferior") *good* in that range.

CHANGES IN A GOOD'S PRICE

The effect of a price change on the quantity of a good demanded is more complex to analyze than is the effect of a change in income. Geometrically, this is because changing a price involves changing not only the intercepts of the budget constraint but also its slope. Consequently, moving to the new utility-maximizing choice entails not only moving to another indifference curve but also changing the *MRS*. Therefore, when a price changes, two analytically different effects come into play. One of these is a *substitution effect*: even if the individual were to stay on the *same* indifference curve, consumption patterns would be allocated so as to equate the *MRS* to the new price ratio. A second effect, the *income effect*, arises because a price change necessarily changes an individual's "real" income. The individual cannot stay on the initial indifference curve and must move to a new one. We begin by analyzing these effects graphically. Then we will provide a mathematical development.

Graphical analysis of a fall in price

Income and substitution effects are illustrated in Figure 5.3. This individual is initially maximizing utility (subject to total expenditures, I) by consuming the combination x^*, y^*.

FIGURE 5.3   Demonstration of the Income and Substitution Effects of a Fall in the Price of x

When the price of x falls from p_x^1 to p_x^2, the utility-maximizing choice shifts from x^*, y^* to x^{**}, y^{**}. This movement can be broken down into two analytically different effects: first, the substitution effect, involving a movement along the initial indifference curve to point B, where the *MRS* is equal to the new price ratio; and second, the income effect, entailing a movement to a higher level of utility because real income has increased. In the diagram, both the substitution and income effects cause more x to be bought when its price declines. Notice that point I/p_y is the same as before the price change; this is because p_y has not changed. Point I/p_y therefore appears on both the old and new budget constraints.

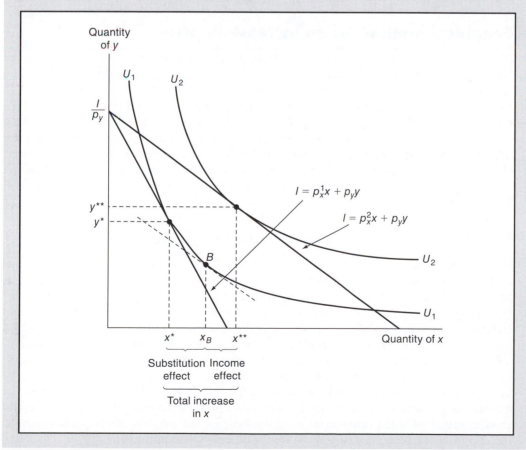

The initial budget constraint is $I = p_x^1 x + p_y y$. Now suppose that the price of x falls to p_x^2. The new budget constraint is given by the equation $I = p_x^2 x + p_y y$ in Figure 5.3.

It is clear that the new position of maximum utility is at x^{**}, y^{**}, where the new budget line is tangent to the indifference curve U_2. The movement to this new point can be viewed as being composed of two effects. First, the change in the slope of the budget constraint would have motivated a move to point B, even if choices had been confined to those on the original indifference curve U_1. The dashed line in Figure 5.3 has the same slope as the new budget constraint ($I = p_x^2 x + p_y y$) but is drawn to be tangent to U_1 because we are conceptually holding "real" income (that is, utility) constant. A relatively lower price for x causes a move from x^*, y^* to B if we do not allow this individual to be made better off as a result of the lower price. This movement is a graphic demonstration of the *substitution effect*. The further move from B to the optimal point x^{**}, y^{**} is analytically identical to the kind of change exhibited earlier for changes in income. Because the price of x has fallen, this person has a greater "real" income and can afford a utility level (U_2) that is greater than that which could previously be attained. If x is a normal good, more of it will be chosen in response to this increase in purchasing power. This observation explains the origin of the term *income effect* for the movement. Overall then, the result of the price decline is to cause more x to be demanded.

It is important to recognize that this person does not actually make a series of choices from x^*, y^* to B and then to x^{**}, y^{**}. We never observe point B; only the two optimal positions are reflected in observed behavior. However, the notion of income and substitution effects is analytically valuable because it shows that a price change affects the quantity of x that is demanded in two conceptually different ways. We will see how this separation offers major insights in the theory of demand.

Graphical analysis of an increase in price

If the price of good x were to increase, a similar analysis would be used. In Figure 5.4, the budget line has been shifted inward because of an increase in the price of x from p_x^1 to p_x^2. The movement from the initial point of utility maximization (x^*, y^*) to the new point (x^{**}, y^{**}) can be decomposed into two effects. First, even if this person could stay on the initial indifference curve (U_2), there would still be an incentive to substitute y for x and move along U_2 to point B. However, because purchasing power has been reduced by the rise in the price of x, he or she must move to a lower level of utility. This movement is again called the income effect. Notice in Figure 5.4 that both the income and substitution effects work in the same direction and cause the quantity of x demanded to be reduced in response to an increase in its price.

Effects of price changes for inferior goods

So far we have shown that substitution and income effects tend to reinforce one another. For a price decline, both cause more of the good to be demanded, whereas for a price increase, both cause less to be demanded. Although this analysis is accurate for the case of normal (noninferior) goods, the possibility of inferior goods complicates the story. In this case, income and substitution effects work in opposite directions, and the combined result of a price change is indeterminate. A fall in price, for example, will always cause an individual to tend to consume more of a good because of the substitution effect. But if the good is inferior, the increase in purchasing power caused by the price decline may cause less of the good to be bought. The result is therefore indeterminate: the substitution effect tends to increase the quantity of the inferior good bought, whereas the (perverse) income effect tends to reduce this quantity. Unlike the situation for normal goods, it is not possible here to predict even the direction of the effect of a change in p_x on the quantity of x consumed.

FIGURE 5.4   Demonstration of the Income and Substitution Effects of an Increase in the Price of x

When the price of x increases, the budget constraint shifts inward. The movement from the initial utility-maximizing point (x^*, y^*) to the new point (x^{**}, y^{**}) can be analyzed as two separate effects. The substitution effect would be depicted as a movement to point B on the initial indifference curve (U_2). The price increase, however, would create a loss of purchasing power and a consequent movement to a lower indifference curve. This is the income effect. In the diagram, both the income and substitution effects cause the quantity of x to fall as a result of the increase in its price. Again, the point I/p_y is not affected by the change in the price of x.

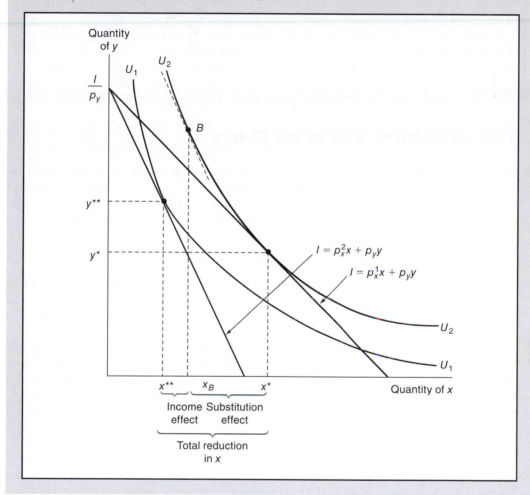

Giffen's paradox

If the income effect of a price change is strong enough, the change in price and the resulting change in the quantity demanded could actually move in the same direction. Legend has it that the English economist Robert Giffen observed this paradox in nineteenth-century Ireland: when the price of potatoes rose, people reportedly consumed more of them. This peculiar result can be explained by looking at the size of the income effect of a change in the price of potatoes. Potatoes were not only inferior goods, they also used up a large portion of the Irish people's income. An increase in the price of potatoes therefore reduced real income substantially. The Irish were forced to cut back on other luxury food consumption in order to buy more potatoes. Even though this rendering of events is historically implausible, the possibility of an increase in the quantity demanded in response to an increase in the price of a good has come to be known as *Giffen's paradox*.[2] Later we will provide a mathematical analysis of how Giffen's paradox can occur.

A summary

Hence, our graphical analysis leads to the following conclusions.

OPTIMIZATION PRINCIPLE

Substitution and income effects. The utility-maximization hypothesis suggests that, for normal goods, a fall in the price of a good leads to an increase in quantity purchased because: (1) the *substitution effect* causes more to be purchased as the individual moves *along* an indifference curve; and (2) the *income effect* causes more to be purchased because the price decline has increased purchasing power, thereby permitting movement to a *higher* indifference curve. When the price of a normal good rises, similar reasoning predicts a decline in the quantity purchased. For inferior goods, substitution and income effects work in opposite directions, and no definite predictions can be made.

THE INDIVIDUAL'S DEMAND CURVE

Economists frequently wish to graph demand functions. It will come as no surprise to you that these graphs are called "demand curves." Understanding how such widely used curves relate to underlying demand functions provides additional insights to even the most fundamental of economic arguments. To simplify the development, assume there are only two goods and that, as before, the demand function for good x is given by

$$x^* = x(p_x, p_y, I).$$

The demand curve derived from this function looks at the relationship between x and p_x while holding p_y, $\bar{I}$, and preferences constant. That is, it shows the relationship

$$x^* = x(p_x, \bar{p}_y, \bar{I}), \tag{5.8}$$

where the bars over p_y and I indicate that these determinants of demand are being held constant. This construction is shown in Figure 5.5. The graph shows utility-maximizing choices of x and y as this individual is presented with successively lower prices of good x (while holding p_y and I constant). We assume that the quantities of x chosen increase from x' to x'' to x''' as that good's price falls from p_x' to p_x'' to p_x'''. Such an assumption is in accord with our general conclusion that, except in the unusual case of Giffen's paradox, $\partial x/\partial p_x$ is negative.

In Figure 5.5b, information about the utility-maximizing choices of good x is transferred to a *demand curve* with p_x on the vertical axis and sharing the same horizontal axis as Figure 5.5a. The negative slope of the curve again reflects the assumption that $\partial x/\partial p_x$ is negative. Hence, we may define an individual demand curve as follows.

DEFINITION

Individual demand curve. An *individual demand curve* shows the relationship between the price of a good and the quantity of that good purchased by an individual, assuming that all other determinants of demand are held constant.

---

[2]A major problem with this explanation is that it disregards Marshall's observation that both supply and demand factors must be taken into account when analyzing price changes. If potato prices increased because of the potato blight in Ireland, then supply should have become smaller, so how could more potatoes possibly have been consumed? Also, since many Irish people were potato farmers, the potato price increase should have increased real income for them. For a detailed discussion of these and other fascinating bits of potato lore, see G. P. Dwyer and C. M. Lindsey, "Robert Giffen and the Irish Potato," *American Economic Review* (March 1984): 188–92.

FIGURE 5.5 Construction of an Individual's Demand Curve

In (a), the individual's utility-maximizing choices of x and y are shown for three different prices of x (p'_x, p''_x, and p'''_x). In (b), this relationship between p_x and x is used to construct the demand curve for x. The demand curve is drawn on the assumption that p_y, I, and preferences remain constant as p_x varies.

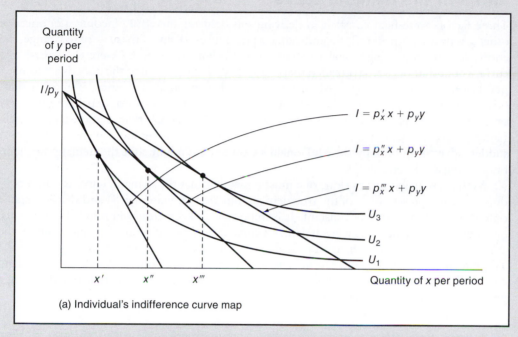

(a) Individual's indifference curve map

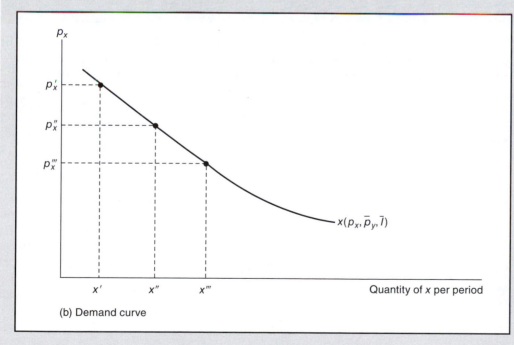

(b) Demand curve

The demand curve illustrated in Figure 5.5 stays in a fixed position only so long as all other determinants of demand remain unchanged. If one of these other factors were to change then the curve might shift to a new position, as we now describe.

Shifts in the demand curve

Three factors were held constant in deriving this demand curve: (1) income; (2) prices of other goods (say, p_y); and (3) the individual's preferences. If any of these were to change, the entire demand curve might shift to a new position. For example, if I were to increase, the curve would shift outward (provided that $\partial x / \partial I > 0$, that is, provided the good is a "normal" good over this income range). More x would be demanded at *each* price. If another price (say, p_y) were to change then the curve would shift inward or outward, depending precisely on how x and y are related. In the next chapter we will examine that relationship in detail. Finally, the curve would shift if the individual's preferences for good x were to change. A sudden advertising blitz by the McDonald's Corporation might shift the demand for hamburgers outward, for example.

As this discussion makes clear, one must remember that the demand curve is only a two-dimensional representation of the true demand function (Equation 5.8) and that it is stable only if other things do stay constant. It is important to keep clearly in mind the difference between a movement along a given demand curve caused by a change in p_x and a shift in the entire curve caused by a change in income, in one of the other prices, or in preferences. Traditionally, the term *an increase in demand* is reserved for an outward shift in the demand curve, whereas the term *an increase in the quantity demanded* refers to a movement along a given curve caused by a change in p_x.

EXAMPLE 5.2 Demand Functions and Demand Curves

To be able to graph a demand curve from a given demand function, we must assume that the preferences that generated the function remain stable and that we know the values of income and other relevant prices. In the first case studied in Example 5.1, we found that

$$x = \frac{0.3I}{p_x} \tag{5.9}$$

and

$$y = \frac{0.7I}{p_y}.$$

If preferences do not change and if this individual's income is $100, these functions become

$$x = \frac{30}{p_x},$$
$$y = \frac{70}{p_y}, \tag{5.10}$$

or

$$p_x x = 30,$$
$$p_y y = 70,$$

which makes clear that the demand curves for these two goods are simple hyperbolas. A rise in income would shift both of the demand curves outward. Notice also, in this case, that the demand curve for x is not shifted by changes in p_y and vice versa.

For the second case examined in Example 5.1, the analysis is more complex. For good x, we know that

$$x = \left(\frac{1}{1 + p_x/p_y}\right) \cdot \frac{I}{p_x}, \qquad \textbf{(5.11)}$$

so to graph this in the p_x–x plane we must know both I and p_y. If we again assume $I = 100$ and let $p_y = 1$, then Equation 5.11 becomes

$$x = \frac{100}{p_x^2 + p_x}, \qquad \textbf{(5.12)}$$

which, when graphed, would also show a general hyperbolic relationship between price and quantity consumed. In this case the curve would be relatively flatter because substitution effects are larger than in the Cobb-Douglas case. From Equation 5.11, we also know that

$$\frac{\partial x}{\partial I} = \left(\frac{1}{1 + p_x/p_y}\right) \cdot \frac{1}{p_x} > 0 \qquad \textbf{(5.13)}$$

and

$$\frac{\partial x}{\partial p_y} = \frac{I}{(p_x + p_y)^2} > 0,$$

so increases in I or p_y would shift the demand curve for good x outward.

QUERY: How would the demand functions in Equations 5.10 change if this person spent half of his or her income on each good? Show that these demand functions predict the same x consumption at the point $p_x = 1$, $p_y = 1$, $I = 100$ as does Equation 5.11. Use a numerical example to show that the CES demand function is more responsive to an increase in p_x than is the Cobb-Douglas demand function.

COMPENSATED DEMAND CURVES

In Figure 5.5, the level of utility this person gets varies along the demand curve. As p_x falls, he or she is made increasingly better-off, as shown by the increase in utility from U_1 to U_2 to U_3. The reason this happens is that the demand curve is drawn on the assumption that *nominal* income and other prices are held constant; hence, a decline in p_x makes this person better off by increasing his or her real purchasing power. Although this is the most common way to impose the ceteris paribus assumption in developing a demand curve, it is not the only way. An alternative approach holds *real* income (or utility) constant while examining reactions to changes in p_x. The derivation is illustrated in Figure 5.6, where we hold utility constant (at U_2) while successively reducing p_x. As p_x falls, the individual's nominal income is effectively reduced, thus preventing any increase in utility. In other words, the effects of the price change on purchasing power are "compensated" so as to constrain the individual to remain on U_2. Reactions to changing prices include only substitution effects. If we were instead to examine effects of increases in p_x, income compensation would be positive: This individual's income would have to be increased to permit him or her to stay on the U_2 indifference curve in response to the price rises. We can summarize these results as follows.

Compensated demand curve. A *compensated demand curve* shows the relationship between the price of a good and the quantity purchased on the assumption that other prices *and* utility are held constant. The curve (which is sometimes termed a "Hicksian" demand curve

DEFINITION

FIGURE 5.6   Construction of a Compensated Demand Curve

The curve x^c shows how the quantity of x demanded changes when p_x changes, holding p_y and *utility* constant. That is, the individual's income is "compensated" so as to keep utility constant. Hence, x^c reflects only substitution effects of changing prices.

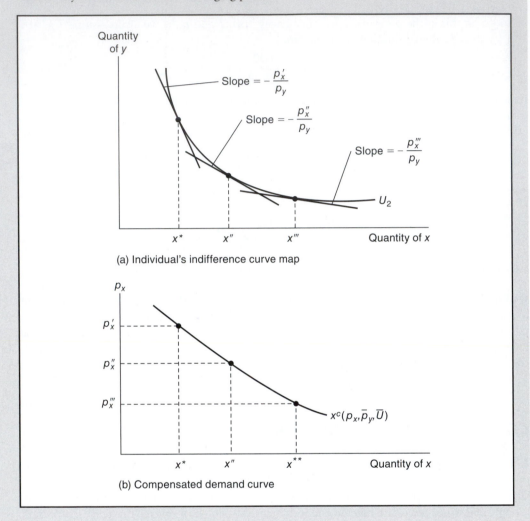

(a) Individual's indifference curve map

(b) Compensated demand curve

after the British economist John Hicks) therefore illustrates only substitution effects. Mathematically, the curve is a two-dimensional representation of the *compensated demand function*

$$x = x^c(p_x, p_y, U). \tag{5.14}$$

Relationship between compensated and uncompensated demand curves

This relationship between the two demand curve concepts is illustrated in Figure 5.7. At p_x'' the curves intersect, because at that price the individual's income is just sufficient to attain

FIGURE 5.7 Comparison of Compensated and Uncompensated Demand Curves

The compensated (x^c) and uncompensated (x) demand curves intersect at p_x'' because x'' is demanded under each concept. For prices above p_x'', the individual's income is increased with the compensated demand curve, so more x is demanded than with the uncompensated curve. For prices below p_x'', income is reduced for the compensated curve, so less x is demanded than with the uncompensated curve. The standard demand curve is flatter because it incorporates both substitution and income effects whereas the curve x^c reflects only substitution effects.

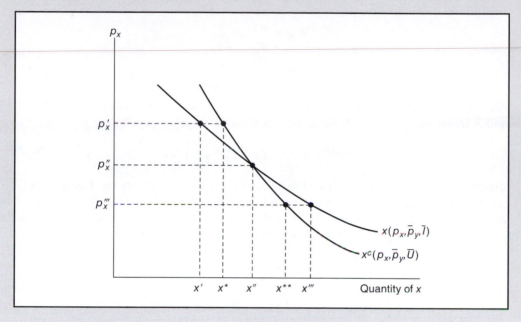

utility level U_2 (compare Figures 5.5 and Figure 5.6). Hence, x'' is demanded under either demand concept. For prices below p_x'', however, the individual suffers a compensating reduction in income on the curve x^c that prevents an increase in utility from the lower price. Hence, assuming x is a normal good, it follows that less x is demanded at p_x''' along x^c than along the uncompensated curve x. Alternatively, for a price above p_x'' (such as p_x'), income compensation is positive because the individual needs some help to remain on U_2. Hence, again assuming x is a normal good, at p_x' more x is demanded along x^c than along x. In general, then, for a normal good the compensated demand curve is somewhat less responsive to price changes than is the uncompensated curve. This is because the latter reflects both substitution and income effects of price changes, whereas the compensated curve reflects only substitution effects.

The choice between using compensated or uncompensated demand curves in economic analysis is largely a matter of convenience. In most empirical work, uncompensated curves (which are sometimes called "Marshallian demand curves") are used because the data on prices and nominal incomes needed to estimate them are readily available. In the Extensions to Chapter 12 we will describe some of these estimates and show how they might be employed for practical policy purposes. For some theoretical purposes, however, compensated demand curves are a more appropriate concept because the ability to hold utility constant offers some advantages. Our discussion of "consumer surplus" later in this chapter offers one illustration of these advantages.

EXAMPLE 5.3 Compensated Demand Functions

In Example 3.1 we assumed that the utility function for hamburgers (y) and soft drinks (x) was given by

$$\text{utility} = U(x,y) = x^{0.5}y^{0.5}, \tag{5.15}$$

and in Example 4.1 we showed that we can calculate the Marshallian demand functions for such utility functions as

$$x = \frac{\alpha I}{p_x} = \frac{I}{2p_x},$$
$$y = \frac{\beta I}{p_y} = \frac{I}{2p_y}. \tag{5.16}$$

Also, in Example 4.3 we calculated the indirect utility function by combining Equations 5.15 and 5.16 as

$$\text{utility} = V(I, p_x, p_y) = \frac{I}{2p_x^{0.5}p_y^{0.5}}. \tag{5.17}$$

To obtain the compensated demand functions for x and y, we simply use Equation 5.17 to solve for I and then substitute this expression involving V into Equations 5.16. This permits us to interchange income and utility so we may hold the latter constant, as is required for the compensated demand concept. Making these substitutions yields

$$x = \frac{Vp_y^{0.5}}{p_x^{0.5}},$$
$$y = \frac{Vp_x^{0.5}}{p_y^{0.5}}. \tag{5.18}$$

These are the compensated demand functions for x and y. Notice that now demand depends on utility (V) rather than on income. Holding utility constant, it is clear that increases in p_x reduce the demand for x, and this now reflects only the substitution effect (see also Example 5.4).

Although p_y did not enter into the uncompensated demand function for good x, it does enter into the compensated function: increases in p_y shift the compensated demand curve for x outward. The two demand concepts agree at the assumed initial point $p_x = 1$, $p_y = 4$, $I = 8$, and $V = 2$; Equations 5.16 predict $x = 4$, $y = 1$ at this point, as do Equations 5.18. For $p_x > 1$ or $p_x < 1$, the demands differ under the two concepts, however. If, say, $p_x = 4$, then the uncompensated functions (Equations 5.16) predict $x = 1$, $y = 1$, whereas the compensated functions (Equations 5.18) predict $x = 2$, $y = 2$. The reduction in x resulting from the rise in its price is smaller with the compensated demand function than it is with the uncompensated function because the former concept adjusts for the negative effect on purchasing power that comes about from the price rise.

This example makes clear the different ceteris paribus assumptions inherent in the two demand concepts. With uncompensated demand, expenditures are held constant at $I = 2$ and so the rise in p_x from 1 to 4 results in a loss of utility; in this case, utility falls from 2 to 1. In the compensated demand case, utility is held constant at $V = 2$. To keep utility constant, expenditures must rise to $E = 1(2) + 1(2) = 4$ in order to offset the effects of the price rise (see Equation 5.17).

QUERY: Are the compensated demand functions given in Equations 5.18 homogeneous of degree 0 in p_x and p_y if utility is held constant? Would you expect that to be true for all compensated demand functions?

A MATHEMATICAL DEVELOPMENT OF RESPONSE TO PRICE CHANGES

Up to this point we have largely relied on graphical devices to describe how individuals respond to price changes. Additional insights are provided by a more mathematical approach. Our basic goal is to examine the partial derivative $\partial x / \partial p_x$—that is, how a change in the price of a good affects its purchase, ceteris paribus. In the next chapter, we take up the question of how changes in the price of one commodity affect purchases of another commodity.

Direct approach

Our goal is to use the utility-maximization model to learn something about how the demand for good x changes when p_x changes; that is, we wish to calculate $\partial x / \partial p_x$. The direct approach to this problem makes use of the first-order conditions for utility maximization (Equations 4.8). Differentiation of these $n + 1$ equations yields a new system of $n + 1$ equations, which eventually can be solved for the derivative we seek.[3] Unfortunately, obtaining this solution is quite cumbersome and the steps required yield little in the way of economic insights. Hence, we will instead adopt an indirect approach that relies on the concept of duality. In the end, both approaches yield the same conclusion, but the indirect approach is much richer in terms of the economics it contains.

Indirect approach

To begin our indirect approach,[4] we will assume (as before) there are only two goods (x and y) and focus on the compensated demand function, $x^c(p_x, p_y, U)$, introduced in Equation 5.14. We now wish to illustrate the connection between this demand function and the ordinary demand function, $x(p_x, p_y, I)$. In Chapter 4 we introduced the expenditure function, which records the minimal expenditure necessary to attain a given utility level. If we denote this function by

$$\text{minimum expenditure} = E(p_x, p_y, U) \qquad (5.19)$$

then, by definition,

$$x^c(p_x, p_y, U) = x[p_x, p_y, E(p_x, p_y, U)]. \qquad (5.20)$$

This conclusion was already introduced in connection with Figure 5.7, which showed that the quantity demanded is identical for the compensated and uncompensated demand functions when income is exactly what is needed to attain the required utility level. Equation 5.20 is obtained by inserting that expenditure level into the demand function, $x(p_x, p_y, I)$. Now we can proceed by partially differentiating Equation 5.20 with respect to p_x and recognizing that this variable enters into the ordinary demand function in two places. Hence

$$\frac{\partial x^c}{\partial p_x} = \frac{\partial x}{\partial p_x} + \frac{\partial x}{\partial E} \cdot \frac{\partial E}{\partial p_x}, \qquad (5.21)$$

and rearranging terms yields

$$\frac{\partial x}{\partial p_x} = \frac{\partial x^c}{\partial p_x} - \frac{\partial x}{\partial E} \cdot \frac{\partial E}{\partial p_x}. \qquad (5.22)$$

---

[3]See, for example, Paul A. Samuelson, *Foundations of Economic Analysis* (Cambridge, MA: Harvard University Press, 1947), pp. 101–3.

[4]The following proof is adapted from Phillip J. Cook, "A 'One Line' Proof of the Slutsky Equation," *American Economic Review* 62 (March 1972): 139.

The substitution effect

Consequently, the derivative we seek has two terms. Interpretation of the first term is straightforward: It is the slope of the compensated demand curve. But that slope represents movement along a single indifference curve; it is, in fact, what we called the "substitution effect" earlier. The first term on the right of Equation 5.22 is a mathematical representation of that effect.

The income effect

The second term in Equation 5.22 reflects the way in which changes in p_x affect the demand for x through changes in necessary expenditure levels (that is, changes in purchasing power). This term therefore reflects the income effect. The negative sign in Equation 5.22 shows the direction of the effect. For example, an increase in p_x increases the expenditure level that would have been needed to keep utility constant (mathematically, $\partial E/\partial p_x > 0$). But because nominal income is held constant in Marshallian demand, these extra expenditures are not available. Hence x (and y) must be reduced to meet this shortfall. The extent of the reduction in x is given by $\partial x/\partial E$. On the other hand, if p_x falls, the expenditure level required to attain a given utility also falls. The decline in x that would normally accompany such a fall in expenditures is precisely the amount that must be added back through the income effect. Notice that in this case the income effect works to increase x.

The Slutsky equation

The relationships embodied in Equation 5.22 were first discovered by the Russian economist Eugen Slutsky in the late nineteenth century. A slight change in notation is required to state the result the way Slutsky did. First, we write the substitution effect as

$$\text{substitution effect} = \frac{\partial x^c}{\partial p_x} = \frac{\partial x}{\partial p_x}\bigg|_{U=\text{constant}} \tag{5.23}$$

to indicate movement along a single indifference curve. For the income effect, we have

$$\text{income effect} = -\frac{\partial x}{\partial E} \cdot \frac{\partial E}{\partial p_x} = -\frac{\partial x}{\partial I} \cdot \frac{\partial E}{\partial p_x}, \tag{5.24}$$

because changes in income or expenditures amount to the same thing in the function $x(p_x, p_y, I)$.

The second term in the income effect can be studied most directly by using the envelope theorem. Remember that expenditure functions represent a minimization problem in which the expenditure required to reach a minimum level of utility is minimized. The Lagrangian expression for this minimization is $\mathcal{L} = p_x x + p_y y + \lambda[\bar{U} - U(x, y)]$. Applying the envelope theorem to this problem yields

$$\frac{\partial E}{\partial p_x} = \frac{\partial \mathcal{L}}{\partial p_x} = x. \tag{5.25}$$

In words, the envelope theorem shows that partial differentiation of the expenditure function with respect to a good's price yields the demand function for that good. Because utility is held constant in the expenditure function, this demand function will be a compensated one. This result, and a similar one in the theory of the firm, is usually called *Shephard's lemma* after the economist who first studied this approach to demand theory in detail. The result is extremely useful in both theoretical and applied microeconomics; partial differentiation of maximized or minimized functions is often the easiest way to derive demand functions.[5] Notice also that the result makes intuitive sense. If we ask how much extra expenditure is necessary to compensate for a rise in the price of good x, a simple approximation would be given by the number of units of x currently being consumed.

By combining Equations 5.23–5.25, we can arrive at the following complete statement of the response to a price change.

Slutsky equation. The utility-maximization hypothesis shows that the substitution and income effects arising from a price change can be represented by

$$\frac{\partial x}{\partial p_x} = \text{substitution effect} + \text{income effect},\qquad(5.26)$$

or

$$\frac{\partial x}{\partial p_x} = \left.\frac{\partial x}{\partial p_x}\right|_{U=\text{constant}} - x\frac{\partial x}{\partial I}.\qquad(5.27)$$

OPTIMIZATION PRINCIPLE

The Slutsky equation allows a more definitive treatment of the direction and size of substitution and income effects than was possible with a graphic analysis. First, the substitution effect ($\partial x/\partial p_x|_{U=\text{constant}}$) is always negative as long as the MRS is diminishing. A fall (rise) in p_x reduces (increases) p_x/p_y, and utility maximization requires that the MRS fall (rise) too. But this can occur along an indifference curve only if x increases (or, in the case of a rise in p_x, if x decreases). Hence, insofar as the substitution effect is concerned, price and quantity always move in opposite directions. Equivalently, the slope of the compensated demand curve must be negative.[6] We will show this result in a somewhat different way in the final section of this chapter.

The sign of the income effect ($-x\,\partial x/\partial I$) depends on the sign of $\partial x/\partial I$. If x is a normal good, then $\partial x/\partial I$ is positive and the entire income effect, like the substitution effect, is negative. Thus, for normal goods, price and quantity always move in opposite directions. For example, a fall in p_x raises real income and, because x is a normal good, purchases of x rise. Similarly, a rise in p_x reduces real income and so purchases of x fall. Overall, then, as we described previously using a graphic analysis, substitution and income effects work in the same direction to yield a negatively sloped demand curve. In the case of an inferior good, $\partial x/\partial I < 0$ and the two terms in Equation 5.27 would have different signs. It is at least theoretically possible that, in this case, the second term could dominate the first, leading to Giffen's paradox ($\partial x/\partial p_x > 0$).

EXAMPLE 5.4 A Slutsky Decomposition

The decomposition of a price effect that was first discovered by Slutsky can be nicely illustrated with the Cobb-Douglas example studied previously. In Example 5.3, we found that the Marshallian demand function for good x was

$$x(p_x, p_y, I) = \frac{0.5I}{p_x}\qquad(5.28)$$

(continued)

---

[5]For instance, in Example 4.4, for expenditure we found a simple Cobb-Douglas utility function of the form $E(p_x, p_y, V) = 2Vp_x^{0.5}p_y^{0.5}$. Hence, from Shephard's lemma we know that $x = \partial E/\partial p_x = Vp_x^{-0.5}p_y^{0.5}$, which is the same result we obtained in Example 5.3.

[6]It is possible that substitution effects would be zero if indifference curves have an L-shape (implying that x and y are used in fixed proportions). Some examples are provided in the Chapter 5 problems.

EXAMPLE 5.4 CONTINUED

and that the Hicksian (compensated) demand function was

$$x^c(p_x, p_y, V) = \frac{V p_y^{0.5}}{p_x^{0.5}}.$$ (5.29)

The overall effect of a price change on the demand for good x can be found by differentiating the Marshallian demand function:

$$\frac{\partial x}{\partial p_x} = \frac{-0.5I}{p_x^2}.$$ (5.30)

Now we wish to show that this effect is the sum of the two effects that Slutsky identified. As before, the substitution effect is found by differentiating the compensated demand function:

$$\text{substitution effect} = \frac{\partial x^c}{\partial p_x} = \frac{-0.5 V p_y^{0.5}}{p_x^{1.5}}.$$ (5.31)

We can eliminate indirect utility, V, by substitution from Equation 5.17:

$$\text{substitution effect} = \frac{-0.5(0.5I p_x^{-0.5} p_y^{-0.5}) p_y^{0.5}}{p_x^{1.5}} = \frac{-0.25I}{p_x^2}.$$ (5.32)

Calculation of the income effect in this example is considerably easier. Applying the results from Equation 5.27, we have

$$\text{income effect} = -x \frac{\partial x}{\partial I} = -\left[\frac{0.5I}{p_x} \right] \cdot \frac{0.5}{p_x} = -\frac{0.25I}{p_x^2}.$$ (5.33)

A comparison of Equation 5.30 with Equations 5.32 and 5.33 shows that we have indeed decomposed the price derivative of this demand function into substitution and income components. Interestingly, the substitution and income effects are of precisely the same size. This, as we will see in later examples, is one of the reasons that the Cobb-Douglas is a very special case.

The well-worn numerical example we have been using also demonstrates this decomposition. When the price of x rises from \$1 to \$4, the (uncompensated) demand for x falls from $x = 4$ to $x = 1$ but the compensated demand for x falls only from $x = 4$ to $x = 2$. That decline of 50 percent is the substitution effect. The further 50 percent fall from $x = 2$ to $x = 1$ represents reactions to the decline in purchasing power incorporated in the Marshallian demand function. This income effect does not occur when the compensated demand notion is used.

QUERY: In this example, the individual spends half of his or her income on good x and half on good y. How would the relative sizes of the substitution and income effects be altered if the exponents of the Cobb-Douglas utility function were not equal?

DEMAND ELASTICITIES

So far in this chapter we have been examining how individuals respond to changes in prices and income by looking at the derivatives of the demand function. For many analytical questions this is a good way to proceed because calculus methods can be directly applied. However, as we pointed out in Chapter 2, focusing on derivatives has one major disadvantage for empirical work: the sizes of derivatives depend directly on how variables are measured.

That can make comparisons among goods or across countries and time periods very difficult. For this reason, most empirical work in microeconomics uses some form of elasticity measure. In this section we introduce the three most common types of demand elasticities and explore some of the mathematical relations among them. Again, for simplicity we will look at a situation where the individual chooses between only two goods, though these ideas can be easily generalized.

Marshallian demand elasticities

Most of the commonly used demand elasticities are derived from the Marshallian demand function $x(p_x, p_y, I)$. Specifically, the following definitions are used.

DEFINITION

1. *Price elasticity of demand* (e_{x, p_x}). This measures the proportionate change in quantity demanded in response to a proportionate change in a good's own price. Mathematically,

$$e_{x, p_x} = \frac{\Delta x / x}{\Delta p_x / p_x} = \frac{\Delta x}{\Delta p_x} \cdot \frac{p_x}{x} = \frac{\partial x}{\partial p_x} \cdot \frac{p_x}{x}. \qquad (5.34)$$

2. *Income elasticity of demand* ($e_{x, I}$). This measures the proportionate change in quantity demanded in response to a proportionate change in income. In mathematical terms,

$$e_{x, I} = \frac{\Delta x / x}{\Delta I / I} = \frac{\Delta x}{\Delta I} \cdot \frac{I}{x} = \frac{\partial x}{\partial I} \cdot \frac{I}{x}. \qquad (5.35)$$

3. *Cross-price elasticity of demand* (e_{x, p_y}). This measures the proportionate change in the quantity of x demanded in response to a proportionate change in the price of some other good (y):

$$e_{x, p_y} = \frac{\Delta x / x}{\Delta p_y / p_y} = \frac{\Delta x}{\Delta p_y} \cdot \frac{p_y}{x} = \frac{\partial x}{\partial p_y} \cdot \frac{p_y}{x}. \qquad (5.36)$$

Notice that all of these definitions use partial derivatives, which signifies that all other determinants of demand are to be held constant when examining the impact of a specific variable. In the remainder of this section we will explore the own-price elasticity definition in some detail. Examining the cross-price elasticity of demand is the primary topic of Chapter 6.

Price elasticity of demand

The (own-) price elasticity of demand is probably the most important elasticity concept in all of microeconomics. Not only does it provide a convenient way of summarizing how people respond to price changes for a wide variety of economic goods, but it is also a central concept in the theory of how firms react to the demand curves facing them. As you probably already learned in earlier economics courses, a distinction is usually made between cases of elastic demand (where price affects quantity significantly) and inelastic demand (where the effect of price is small). One mathematical complication in making these ideas precise is that the price elasticity of demand itself is negative[7] because, except in the unlikely case of Giffen's paradox, $\partial x / \partial p_x$ is negative. The dividing line between large and small responses is generally set

---

[7]Sometimes economists use the absolute value of the price elasticity of demand in their discussions. Although this is mathematically incorrect, such usage is quite common. For example, a study that finds that $e_{x, p_x} = -1.2$ may sometimes report the price elasticity of demand as "1.2." We will not do so here, however.

at -1. If $e_{x,p_x} = -1$, changes in x and p_x are of the same proportionate size. That is, a 1 percent increase in price leads to a fall of 1 percent in quantity demanded. In this case, demand is said to be "unit-elastic." Alternatively, if $e_{x,p_x} < -1$, then quantity changes are proportionately larger than price changes and we say that demand is "elastic." For example, if $e_{x,p_x} = -3$, each 1 percent rise in price leads to a fall of 3 percent in quantity demanded. Finally, if $e_{x,p_x} > -1$ then demand is inelastic and quantity changes are proportionately smaller than price changes. A value of $e_{x,p_x} = -0.3$, for example, means that a 1 percent increase in price leads to a fall in quantity demanded of 0.3 percent. In Chapter 12 we will see how aggregate data are used to estimate the typical individual's price elasticity of demand for a good and how such estimates are used in a variety of questions in applied microeconomics.

Price elasticity and total spending

The price elasticity of demand determines how a change in price, ceteris paribus, affects total spending on a good. The connection is most easily shown with calculus:

$$\frac{\partial(p_x \cdot x)}{\partial p_x} = p_x \cdot \frac{\partial x}{\partial p_x} + x = x(e_{x,p_x} + 1). \tag{5.37}$$

So, the sign of this derivative depends on whether e_{x,p_x} is larger or smaller than -1. If demand is inelastic ($0 > e_{x,p_x} > -1$), the derivative is positive and price and total spending move in the same direction. Intuitively, if price does not affect quantity demanded very much, then quantity stays relatively constant as price changes and total spending reflects mainly those price movements. This is the case, for example, with the demand for most agricultural products. Weather-induced changes in price for specific crops usually cause total spending on those crops to move in the same direction. On the other hand, if demand is elastic ($e_{x,p_x} < -1$), reactions to a price change are so large that the effect on total spending is reversed: a rise in price causes total spending to fall (because quantity falls a lot) and a fall in price causes total spending to rise (quantity increases significantly). For the unit-elastic case ($e_{x,p_x} = -1$), total spending is constant no matter how price changes.

Compensated price elasticities

Because some microeconomic analyses focus on the compensated demand function, it is also useful to define elasticities based on that concept. Such definitions follow directly from their Marshallian counterparts.

DEFINITION

Let the compensated demand function be given by $x^c(p_x, p_y, U)$. Then we have the following definitions.

1. *Compensated own-price elasticity of demand* (e_{x^c,p_x}). This elasticity measures the proportionate compensated change in quantity demanded in response to a proportionate change in a good's own price:

    $$e_{x^c,p_x} = \frac{\Delta x^c / x^c}{\Delta p_x / p_x} = \frac{\Delta x^c}{\Delta p_x} \cdot \frac{p_x}{x^c} = \frac{\partial x^c}{\partial p_x} \cdot \frac{p_x}{x^c}. \tag{5.38}$$

2. *Compensated cross-price elasticity of demand* (e_{x^c,p_y}). This measures the proportionate compensated change in quantity demanded in response to a proportionate change in the price of another good:

    $$e_{x^c,p_y} = \frac{\Delta x^c / x^c}{\Delta p_y / p_y} = \frac{\Delta x^c}{\Delta p_y} \cdot \frac{p_y}{x^c} = \frac{\partial x^c}{\partial p_y} \cdot \frac{p_y}{x^c}. \tag{5.39}$$

Whether these price elasticities differ much from their Marshallian counterparts depends on the importance of income effects in the overall demand for good x. The precise connection between the two can be shown by multiplying the Slutsky result from Equation 5.27 by the factor p_x/x:

$$\frac{p_x}{x} \cdot \frac{\partial x}{\partial p_x} = e_{x,p_x} = \frac{p_x}{x} \cdot \frac{\partial x^c}{\partial p_x} - \frac{p_x}{x} \cdot x \cdot \frac{\partial x}{\partial I} = e_{x^c,p_x} - s_x e_{x,I}, \tag{5.40}$$

where $s_x = p_x x / I$ is the share of total income devoted to the purchase of good x.

Equation 5.40 shows that compensated and uncompensated own-price elasticities of demand will be similar if either of two conditions hold: (1) The share of income devoted to good x (s_x) is small; or (2) the income elasticity of demand for good x ($e_{x,I}$) is small. Either of these conditions serves to reduce the importance of the income compensation employed in the construction of the compensated demand function. If good x is unimportant in a person's budget, then the amount of income compensation required to offset a price change will be small. Even if a good has a large budget share, if demand does not react strongly to changes in income then the results of either demand concept will be similar. Hence, there will be many circumstances where one can use the two price elasticity concepts more or less interchangeably. Put another way, there are many economic circumstances in which substitution effects constitute the most important component of price responses.

Relationships among demand elasticities

There are a number of relationships among the elasticity concepts that have been developed in this section. All of these are derived from the underlying model of utility maximization. Here we look at three such relationships that provide further insight on the nature of individual demand.

Homogeneity. The homogeneity of demand functions can also be expressed in elasticity terms. Because any proportional increase in all prices and income leaves quantity demanded unchanged, the net sum of all price elasticities together with the income elasticity for a particular good must sum to zero. A formal proof of this property relies on Euler's theorem (see Chapter 2). Applying that theorem to the demand function $x(p_x, p_y, I)$ and remembering that this function is homogeneous of degree 0 yields

$$0 = p_x \cdot \frac{\partial x}{\partial p_x} + p_y \cdot \frac{\partial x}{\partial p_y} + I \cdot \frac{\partial x}{\partial I}. \tag{5.41}$$

If we divide Equation 5.41 by x then we obtain

$$0 = e_{x,p_x} + e_{x,p_y} + e_{x,I}, \tag{5.42}$$

as intuition suggests. This result shows that the elasticities of demand for any good cannot follow a completely flexible pattern. They must exhibit a sort of internal consistency that reflects the basic utility-maximizing approach on which the theory of demand is based.

Engel aggregation. In the Extensions to Chapter 4 we discussed the empirical analysis of market shares and took special note of Engel's law that the share of income devoted to food declines as income increases. From an elasticity perspective, Engel's law is a statement of the empirical regularity that the income elasticity of demand for food is generally found to be considerably less than 1. Because of this, it must be the case that the income elasticity of all nonfood items must be greater than 1. If an individual experiences an increase in his or her income then we would expect food expenditures to increase by a smaller proportional amount, but the income must be spent somewhere. In the aggregate, these other expenditures must increase proportionally faster than income.

A formal statement of this property of income elasticities can be derived by differentiating the individual's budget constraint ($I = p_x x + p_y y$) with respect to income while treating the prices as constants:

$$1 = p_x \cdot \frac{\partial x}{\partial I} + p_y \cdot \frac{\partial y}{\partial I}. \tag{5.43}$$

A bit of algebraic manipulation of this expression yields

$$1 = p_x \cdot \frac{\partial x}{\partial I} \cdot \frac{xI}{xI} + p_y \cdot \frac{\partial y}{\partial I} \cdot \frac{yI}{yI} = s_x e_{x, I} + s_y e_{y, I}; \tag{5.44}$$

here, as before, s_i represents the share of income spent on good i. Equation 5.44 shows that the weighted average on income elasticities for all goods that a person buys must be 1. If we knew, say, that a person spent a fourth of his or her income on food and the income elasticity of demand for food were 0.5, then the income elasticity of demand for everything else must be approximately 1.17 [$= (1 - 0.25 \cdot 0.5)/0.75$]. Because food is an important "necessity," everything else is in some sense a "luxury."

Cournot aggregation. The eighteenth-century French economist Antoine Cournot provided one of the first mathematical analyses of price changes using calculus. His most important discovery was the concept of marginal revenue, a concept central to the profit-maximization hypothesis for firms. Cournot was also concerned with how the change in a single price might affect the demand for all goods. Our final relationship shows that there are indeed connections among all of the reactions to the change in a single price. We begin by differentiating the budget constraint again, this time with respect to p_x:

$$\frac{\partial I}{\partial p_x} = 0 = p_x \cdot \frac{\partial x}{\partial p_x} + x + p_y \cdot \frac{\partial y}{\partial p_x}.$$

Multiplication of this equation by p_x/I yields

$$0 = p_x \cdot \frac{\partial x}{\partial p_x} \cdot \frac{p_x}{I} \cdot \frac{x}{x} + x \cdot \frac{p_x}{I} + p_y \cdot \frac{\partial y}{\partial p_x} \cdot \frac{p_x}{I} \cdot \frac{y}{y}, \tag{5.45}$$

$$0 = s_x e_{x, p_x} + s_x + s_y e_{y, p_x},$$

so the final Cournot result is

$$s_x e_{x, p_x} + s_y e_{y, p_x} = -s_x. \tag{5.46}$$

This equation shows that the size of the cross-price effect of a change in the price of x on the quantity of y consumed is restricted because of the budget constraint. Direct, own-price effects cannot be totally overwhelmed by cross-price effects. This is the first of many connections among the demands for goods that we will study more intensively in the next chapter.

Generalizations. Although we have shown these aggregation results only for the case of two goods, they are actually easily generalized to the case of many goods. You are asked to do just that in Problem 5.11. A more difficult issue is whether these results should be expected to hold for typical economic data in which the demands of many people are combined. Often economists treat aggregate demand relationships as describing the behavior of a "typical person," and these relationships should in fact hold for such a person. But the situation may not be quite that simple, as we will show when discussing aggregation later in the book.

EXAMPLE 5.5 Demand Elasticities: The Importance of Substitution Effects

In this example we calculate the demand elasticities implied by three of the utility functions we have been using. Although the possibilities incorporated in these functions are too simple to reflect how economists actually study demand empirically, they do show how elasticities ultimately reflect people's preferences. One especially important lesson is to show why most of the variation in demand elasticities among goods probably arises because of differences in the size of substitution effects.

Case 1: Cobb-Douglas ($\sigma = 1$). $U(x, y) = x^\alpha y^\beta$, where $\alpha + \beta = 1$.
The demand functions derived from this utility function are

$$x(p_x, p_y, I) = \frac{\alpha I}{p_x},$$

$$y(p_x, p_y, I) = \frac{\beta I}{p_y} = \frac{(1-\alpha)I}{p_y}.$$

Application of the elasticity definitions shows that

$$e_{x, p_x} = \frac{\partial x}{\partial p_x} \cdot \frac{p_x}{x} = \frac{-\alpha I}{p_x^2} \cdot \frac{p_x}{\alpha I / p_x} = -1,$$

$$e_{x, p_y} = \frac{\partial x}{\partial p_y} \cdot \frac{p_y}{x} = 0 \cdot \frac{p_y}{x} = 0, \tag{5.47}$$

$$e_{x, I} = \frac{\partial x}{\partial I} \cdot \frac{I}{x} = \frac{\alpha}{p_x} \cdot \frac{I}{\alpha I / p_x} = 1.$$

The elasticities for good y take on analogous values. Hence, the elasticities associated with the Cobb-Douglas utility function are constant over all ranges of prices and income and take on especially simple values. That these obey the three relationships shown in the previous section can be easily demonstrated using the fact that here $s_x = \alpha$ and $s_y = \beta$.

Homogeneity: $e_{x, p_x} + e_{x, p_y} + e_{x, I} = -1 + 0 + 1 = 0.$
Engel aggregation: $s_x e_{x, I} + s_y e_{y, I} = \alpha \cdot 1 + \beta \cdot 1 = \alpha + \beta = 1.$
Cournot aggregation: $s_x e_{x, p_x} + s_y e_{y, p_x} = \alpha(-1) + \beta \cdot 0 = -\alpha = -s_x.$

We can also use the Slutsky equation in elasticity form (Equation 5.40) to derive the compensated price elasticity in this example:

$$e_{x^c, p_x} = e_{x, p_x} + s_x e_{x, I} = -1 + \alpha(1) = \alpha - 1 = -\beta. \tag{5.48}$$

Here, then, the compensated price elasticity for x depends on how important other goods (y) are in the utility function.

Case 2: CES ($\sigma = 2; \delta = 0.5$). $U(x, y) = x^{0.5} + y^{0.5}$.
In Example 4.2 we showed that the demand functions that can be derived from this utility function are

$$x(p_x, p_y, I) = \frac{I}{p_x(1 + p_x p_y^{-1})},$$

$$y(p_x, p_y, I) = \frac{I}{p_y(1 + p_x^{-1} p_y)}.$$

(continued)

EXAMPLE 5.5   CONTINUED

As you might imagine, calculating elasticities directly from these functions can take some time. Here we focus only on the own-price elasticity and make use of the result (from Problem 5.6) that the "share elasticity" of any good is given by

$$e_{s_x, p_x} = \frac{\partial s_x}{\partial p_x} \cdot \frac{p_x}{s_x} = 1 + e_{x, p_x}. \qquad (5.49)$$

In this case,

$$s_x = \frac{p_x x}{I} = \frac{1}{1 + p_x p_y^{-1}},$$

so the share elasticity is more easily calculated and is given by

$$e_{s_x, p_x} = \frac{\partial s_x}{\partial p_x} \cdot \frac{p_x}{s_x} = \frac{-p_y^{-1}}{(1 + p_x p_y^{-1})^2} \cdot \frac{p_x}{(1 + p_x p_y^{-1})^{-1}} = \frac{-p_x p_y^{-1}}{1 + p_x p_y^{-1}}. \qquad (5.50)$$

Because the units in which goods are measured are rather arbitrary in utility theory, we might as well define them so that initially $p_x = p_y$, in which case[8] we get

$$e_{x, p_x} = e_{s_x, p_x} - 1 = \frac{-1}{1 + 1} - 1 = -1.5. \qquad (5.51)$$

Hence, demand is more elastic in this case than in the Cobb-Douglas example. The reason for this is that the substitution effect is larger for this version of the CES utility function. This can be shown by again applying the Slutsky equation (and using the facts that $e_{x, I} = 1$ and $s_x = 0.5$):

$$e_{x^c, p_x} = e_{x, p_x} + s_x e_{x, I} = -1.5 + 0.5(1) = -1, \qquad (5.52)$$

which is twice the size of the substitution effect for the Cobb-Douglas.

Case 3. CES ($\sigma = 0.5; \delta = -1$): $U(x, y) = -x^{-1} - y^{-1}$.
    Referring back to Example 4.2, we can see that the share of good x implied by this utility function is given by

$$s_x = \frac{1}{1 + p_y^{0.5} p_x^{-0.5}},$$

so the share elasticity is given by

$$e_{s_x, p_x} = \frac{\partial s_x}{\partial p_x} \cdot \frac{p_x}{s_x} = \frac{0.5 p_y^{0.5} p_x^{-1.5}}{(1 + p_y^{0.5} p_x^{-0.5})^2} \cdot \frac{p_x}{(1 + p_y^{0.5} p_x^{-0.5})^{-1}} = \frac{0.5 p_y^{0.5} p_x^{-0.5}}{1 + p_y^{0.5} p_x^{-0.5}}. \qquad (5.53)$$

If we again adopt the simplification of equal prices, we can compute the own-price elasticity as

$$e_{x, p_x} = e_{s_x, p_x} - 1 = \frac{0.5}{2} - 1 = -0.75 \qquad (5.54)$$

and the compensated price elasticity as

$$e_{x^c, p_x} = e_{x, p_x} + s_x e_{x, I} = -0.75 + 0.5(1) = -0.25. \qquad (5.55)$$

So, for this version of the CES utility function, the own-price elasticity is smaller than in Case 1 and Case 2 because the substitution effect is smaller. Hence, the main variation among the cases is indeed caused by differences in the size of the substitution effect.

---

[8]Notice that this substitution must be made after differentiation because the definition of elasticity requires that we change only p_x while holding p_y constant.

If you never want to work out this kind of elasticity again, it may be helpful to make use of the quite general result that

$$e_{x^c, p_x} = -(1 - s_x)\sigma. \tag{5.56}$$

You may wish to check out that this formula works in these three examples (with $s_x = 0.5$ and $\sigma = 1, 2, 0.5$, respectively), and Problem 5.9 asks you to show that this result is generally true. Because all of these cases based on the CES utility function have a unitary income elasticity, the own-price elasticity can be computed from the compensated price elasticity by simply adding $-s_x$ to the figure computed in Equation 5.56.

QUERY: Why is it that the budget share for goods other than x $(1 - s_x)$ enters into the compensated own-price elasticities in this example?

CONSUMER SURPLUS

An important problem in applied welfare economics is to devise a monetary measure of the gains and losses that individuals experience when prices change. One use for such a measure is to place a dollar value on the welfare loss that people experience when a market is monopolized with prices exceeding marginal costs. Another application concerns measuring the welfare gains that people experience when technical progress reduces the prices they pay for goods. Related applications occur in environmental economics (measuring the welfare costs of incorrectly priced resources), law and economics (evaluating the welfare costs of excess protections taken in fear of lawsuits), and public economics (measuring the excess burden of a tax). In order to make such calculations, economists use empirical data from studies of market demand in combination with the theory that underlies that demand. In this section we will examine the primary tools used in that process.

Consumer welfare and the expenditure function

The expenditure function provides the first component for the study of the price/welfare connection. Suppose that we wished to measure the change in welfare that an individual experiences if the price of good x rises from p_x^0 to p_x^1. Initially this person requires expenditures of $E(p_x^0, p_y, U_0)$ to reach a utility of U_0. To achieve the same utility once the price of x rises, he or she would require spending of at least $E(p_x^1, p_y, U_0)$. In order to compensate for the price rise, therefore, this person would require a compensation (formally called a *compensating variation* or CV) of

$$\mathbf{CV} = E(p_x^1, p_y, U_0) - E(p_x^0, p_y, U_0). \tag{5.57}$$

This situation is shown graphically in the top panel of Figure 5.8. Initially, this person consumes the combination x_0, y_0 and obtains utility of U_0. When the price of x rises, he or she would be forced to move to combination x_2, y_2 and suffer a loss in utility. If he or she were compensated with extra purchasing power of amount CV, he or she could afford to remain on the U_0 indifference curve despite the price rise by choosing combination x_1, y_1. The distance CV, therefore, provides a monetary measure of how much this person needs in order to be compensated for the price rise.

Using the compensated demand curve to show CV

Unfortunately, individuals' utility functions and their associated indifference curve maps are not directly observable. But we can make some headway on empirical measurement by determining how the CV amount can be shown on the compensated demand curve in the

FIGURE 5.8 Showing Compensating Variation

If the price of x rises from p_x^0 to p_x^1, this person needs extra expenditures of CV to remain on the U_0 indifference curve. Integration shows that CV can also be represented by the shaded area below the compensated demand curve in panel (b).

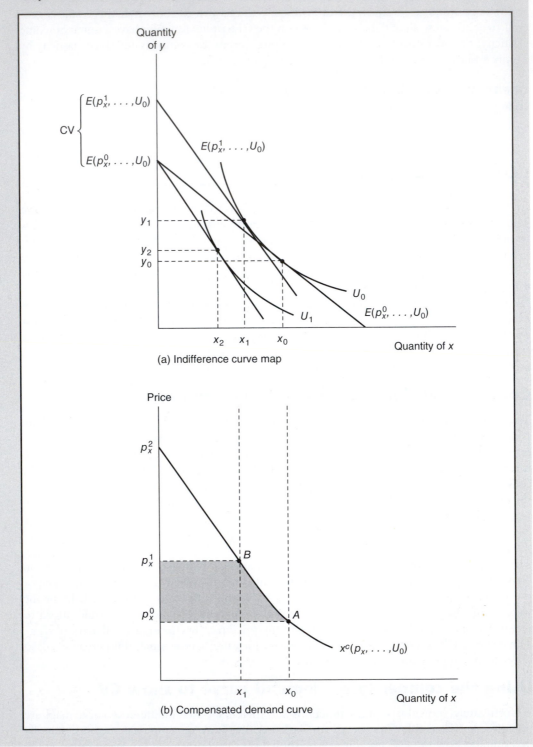

(a) Indifference curve map

(b) Compensated demand curve

bottom panel of Figure 5.8. Shephard's lemma shows that the compensated demand function for a good can be found directly from the expenditure function by differentiation:

$$x^c(p_x, p_y, U) = \frac{\partial E(p_x, p_y, U)}{\partial p_x}.$$ **(5.58)**

Hence, the compensation described in Equation 5.57 can be found by integrating across a sequence of small increments to price from p_x^0 to p_x^1:

$$\mathbf{CV} = \int_{p_x^0}^{p_x^1} dE = \int_{p_x^0}^{p_x^1} x^c(p_x, p_y, U_0)\, dp_x$$ **(5.59)**

while holding p_y and utility constant. The integral defined in Equation 5.59 has a geometric interpretation, which is shown in the lower panel of Figure 5.9: it is the shaded area to the left of the compensated demand curve and bounded by p_x^0 and p_x^1. So the welfare cost of this price increase can also be illustrated using changes in the area below the compensated demand curve.

The consumer surplus concept

There is another way to look at this issue. We can ask how much this person would be willing to pay for the right to consume all of this good that he or she wanted at the market price of p_x^0 rather than doing without the good completely. The compensated demand curve in the bottom panel of Figure 5.8 shows that if the price of x rose to p_x^2, this person's consumption would fall to zero and he or she would require an amount of compensation equal to area $p_x^2 A p_x^0$ in order to accept the change voluntarily. The right to consume x_0 at a price of p_x^0 is therefore worth this amount to this individual. It is the extra benefit that this person receives by being able to make market transactions at the prevailing market price. This value, given by the area below the compensated demand curve and above the market price, is termed *consumer surplus.* Looked at in this way, the welfare problem caused by a rise in the price of x can be described as a loss in consumer surplus. When the price rises from p_x^0 to p_x^1 the consumer surplus "triangle" decreases in size from $p_x^2 A p_x^0$ to $p_x^2 B p_x^1$. As the figure makes clear, that is simply another way of describing the welfare loss represented in Equation 5.59.

Welfare changes and the Marshallian demand curve

So far our analysis of the welfare effects of price changes has focused on the compensated demand curve. This is in some ways unfortunate because most empirical work on demand actually estimates ordinary (Marshallian) demand curves. In this section we will show that studying changes in the area below a Marshallian demand curve may in fact be quite a good way to measure welfare losses.

Consider the Marshallian demand curve $x(p_x, \ldots)$ illustrated in Figure 5.9. Initially this consumer faces the price p_x^0 and chooses to consume x_0. This consumption yields a utility level of U_0, and the initial compensated demand curve for x [that is, $x^c(p_x, p_y, U_0)$] also passes through the point x_0, p_x^0 (which we have labeled point A). When price rises to p_x^1, the Marshallian demand for good x falls to x_1 (point C on the demand curve) and this person's utility also falls to, say, U_1. There is another compensated demand curve associated with this lower level of utility, and it also is shown in Figure 5.9. Both the Marshallian demand curve and this new compensated demand curve pass through point C.

The presence of a second compensated demand curve in Figure 5.9 raises an intriguing conceptual question. Should we measure the welfare loss from the price rise as we did in Figure 5.8 using the compensating variation (CV) associated with the initial compensated demand curve (area $p_x^1 B A p_x^0$) or should we, perhaps, use this new compensated demand curve

FIGURE 5.9   Welfare Effects of Price Changes and the Marshallian Demand Curve

The usual Marshallian (nominal income constant) demand curve for good x is $x(p_x, \ldots)$. Further, $x^c(\ldots, U_0)$ and $x^c(\ldots, U_1)$ denote the compensated demand curves associated with the utility levels experienced when p_x^0 and p_x^1, respectively, prevail. The area to the left of $x(p_x, \ldots)$ between p_x^0 and p_x^1 is bounded by the similar areas to the left of the compensated demand curves. Hence, for small changes in price, the area to the left of the Marshallian demand curve is a good measure of welfare loss.

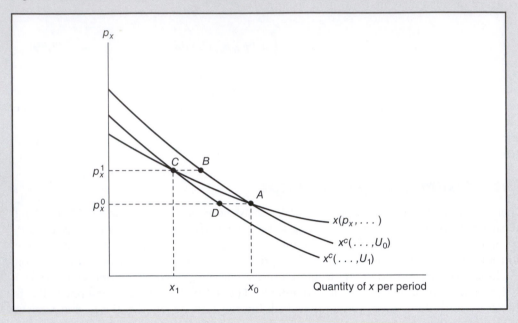

and measure the welfare loss as area $p_x^1 C D p_x^0$? A potential rationale for using the area under the second curve would be to focus on the individual's situation after the price rise (with utility level U_1). We might ask how much he or she would now be willing to pay to see the price return to its old, lower levels.[9] The answer to this would be given by area $p_x^1 C D p_x^0$. The choice between which compensated demand curve to use therefore boils down to choosing which level of utility one regards as the appropriate target for the analysis.

Luckily, the Marshallian demand curve provides a convenient compromise between these two measures. Because the size of the area between the two prices and below the Marshallian curve (area $p_x^1 C A p_x^0$) is smaller than that below the compensated demand curve based on U_0 but larger than that below the curve based on U_1, it does seem an attractive middle ground. Hence, this is the measure of welfare losses we will primarily use throughout this book.

DEFINITION

Consumer surplus. Consumer surplus is the area below the Marshallian demand curve and above market price. It shows what an individual would pay for the right to make voluntary transactions at this price. Changes in consumer surplus can be used to measure the welfare effects of price changes.

We should point out that some economists use either CV or EV to compute the welfare effects of price changes. Indeed, economists are often not very clear about which measure of welfare change they are using. Our discussion in the previous section shows that if income effects are small, it really does not make much difference in any case.

---

[9]This alternative measure of compensation is sometimes termed the "equivalent variation" (EV).

> **EXAMPLE 5.6** Welfare Loss from a Price Increase

These ideas can be illustrated numerically by returning to our old hamburger/soft drink example. Let's look at the welfare consequences of an unconscionable price rise for soft drinks (good x) from \$1 to \$4. In Example 5.3, we found that the compensated demand for good x was given by

$$x^c(p_x, p_y, V) = \frac{V p_y^{0.5}}{p_x^{0.5}}.$$ (5.60)

Hence, the welfare cost of the price increase is given by

$$\mathrm{CV} = \int_1^4 x^c(p_x, p_y, V)\, dp_x = \int_1^4 V p_y^{0.5} p_x^{-0.5}\, dp_x = 2 V p_y^{0.5} p_x^{0.5} \Big|_{p_x=1}^{p_x=4}.$$ (5.61)

If we use the values we have been assuming throughout this gastronomic feast ($V = 2$, $p_y = 4$), then

$$\mathrm{CV} = 2 \cdot 2 \cdot 2 \cdot (4)^{0.5} - 2 \cdot 2 \cdot 2 \cdot (1)^{0.5} = 8.$$ (5.62)

This figure would be cut in half (to 4) if we believed that the utility level after the price rise ($V = 1$) were the more appropriate utility target for measuring compensation. If instead we had used the Marshallian demand function

$$x(p_x, p_y, I) = 0.5 I p_x^{-1},$$

the loss would be calculated as

$$\mathrm{loss} = \int_1^4 x(p_x, p_y, I)\, dp_x = \int_1^4 0.5 I p_x^{-1}\, dp_x = 0.5 I \ln p_x \Big|_1^4.$$ (5.63)

So, with $I = 8$, this loss is

$$\mathrm{loss} = 4 \ln(4) - 4 \ln(1) = 4 \ln(4) = 4(1.39) = 5.55,$$ (5.64)

which seems a reasonable compromise between the two alternative measures based on the compensated demand functions.

QUERY: In this problem, none of the demand curves has a finite price at which demand goes to precisely zero. How does this affect the computation of total consumer surplus? Does this affect the types of welfare calculations made here?

REVEALED PREFERENCE AND THE SUBSTITUTION EFFECT

The principal unambiguous prediction that can be derived from the utility-maximation model is that the slope (or price elasticity) of the compensated demand curve is negative. The proof of this assertion relies on the assumption of a diminishing *MRS* and the related observation that, with a diminishing *MRS*, the necessary conditions for a utility maximum are also sufficient. To some economists, the reliance on a hypothesis about an unobservable utility function represented a weak foundation indeed on which to base a theory of demand. An alternative approach, which leads to the same result, was first proposed by Paul Samuelson in the late 1940s.[10] This approach, which Samuelson termed the *theory of revealed preference*, defines a principle of rationality that is based on observed behavior and

---

[10]Paul A. Samuelson, *Foundations of Economic Analysis* (Cambridge, MA: Harvard University Press, 1947).

then uses this principle to approximate an individual's utility function. In this sense, a person who follows Samuelson's principle of rationality behaves *as if* he or she were maximizing a proper utility function and exhibits a negative substitution effect. Because Samuelson's approach provides additional insights into our model of consumer choice, we will briefly examine it here.

Graphical approach

The principle of rationality in the theory of revealed preference is as follows: Consider two bundles of goods, A and B. If, at some prices and income level, the individual can afford both A and B but chooses A, we say that A has been "revealed preferred" to B. The principle of rationality states that under any different price-income arrangement, B can never be revealed preferred to A. If B is in fact chosen at another price-income configuration, it must be because the individual could not afford A. The principle is illustrated in Figure 5.10. Suppose that, when the budget constraint is given by I_1, point A is chosen even though B also could have been purchased. Then A has been revealed preferred to B. If, for some other budget constraint, B is in fact chosen, then it must be a case such as that represented by I_2, where A could not have been bought. If B were chosen when the budget constraint is I_3, this would be a violation of the principle of rationality because, with I_3, both A and B can be bought. With budget constraint I_3, it is likely that some point other than either A or B (say, C) will be bought. Notice how this principle uses observable reactions to alternative budget constraints to rank commodities rather than assuming the existence of a utility function itself. Also notice

FIGURE 5.10   Demonstration of the Principle of Rationality in the Theory of Revealed Preference

With income I_1 the individual can afford both points A and B. If A is selected then A is revealed preferred to B. It would be irrational for B to be revealed preferred to A in some other price-income configuration.

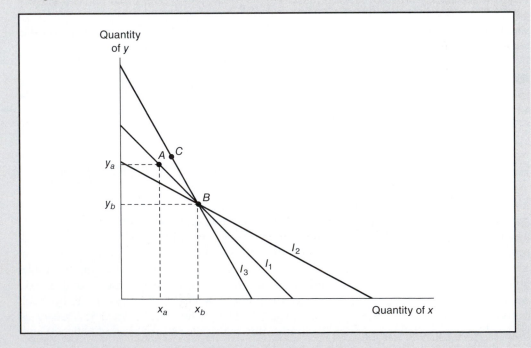

how the principle offers a glimpse of why indifference curves are convex. Now we turn to a formal proof.

Negativity of the substitution effect

Suppose that an individual is *indifferent* between two bundles, C (composed of x_C and y_C) and D (composed of x_D and y_D). Let p_x^C, p_y^C be the prices at which bundle C is chosen and p_x^D, p_y^D the prices at which bundle D is chosen.

Because the individual is indifferent between C and D, it must be the case that when C was chosen, D cost at least as much as C:

$$p_x^C x_C + p_y^C y_C \leq p_x^C x_D + p_y^C y_D. \tag{5.65}$$

A similar statement holds when D is chosen:

$$p_x^D x_D + p_y^D y_D \leq p_x^D x_C + p_y^D y_C. \tag{5.66}$$

Rewriting these equations gives

$$p_x^C (x_C - x_D) + p_y^C (y_C - y_D) \leq 0, \tag{5.67}$$

$$p_x^D (x_D - x_C) + p_y^D (y_D - y_C) \leq 0. \tag{5.68}$$

Adding these together yields

$$(p_x^C - p_x^D)(x_C - x_D) + (p_y^C - p_y^D)(y_C - y_D) \leq 0. \tag{5.69}$$

Now suppose that only the price of x changes; assume that $p_y^C = p_y^D$. Then

$$(p_x^C - p_x^D)(x_C - x_D) \leq 0. \tag{5.70}$$

But Equation 5.70 says that price and quantity move in the opposite direction when utility is held constant (remember, bundles C and D are equally attractive). This is precisely a statement about the nonpositive nature of the substitution effect:

$$\frac{\partial x^c(p_x, p_y, V)}{\partial p_x} = \frac{\partial x}{\partial p_x}\bigg|_{U=\text{constant}} \leq 0. \tag{5.71}$$

We have arrived at the result by an approach that requires neither the existence of a utility function nor the assumption of a diminishing *MRS*.

Mathematical generalization

Generalizing the revealed preference idea to n goods is straightforward. If at prices p_i^0, bundle x_i^0 is chosen instead of x_i^1 and if bundle x_i^1 is also affordable, then

$$\sum_{i=1}^{n} p_i^0 x_i^0 \geq \sum_{i=1}^{n} p_i^0 x_i^1; \tag{5.72}$$

that is, bundle 0 has been "revealed preferred" to bundle 1. Consequently, at the prices that prevail when bundle 1 is bought (say, p_i^1), it must be the case that x_i^0 is more expensive:

$$\sum_{i=1}^{n} p_i^1 x_i^0 > \sum_{i=1}^{n} p_i^1 x_i^1. \tag{5.73}$$

Although this initial definition of revealed preference focuses on the relationship between two bundles of goods, the most often used version of the basic principle requires a degree of transitivity for preferences among an arbitrarily large number of bundles. This is summarized by the following "strong" axiom.

DEFINITION

Strong axiom of revealed preference. The *strong axiom of revealed preference* states that if commodity bundle 0 is revealed preferred to bundle 1, and if bundle 1 is revealed preferred to bundle 2, and if bundle 2 is revealed preferred to bundle 3, ... , and if bundle $K - 1$ is revealed preferred to bundle K, *then* bundle K cannot be revealed preferred to bundle 0 (where K is any arbitrary number of commodity bundles).

Most other properties that we have developed using the concept of utility can be proved using this revealed preference axiom instead. For example, it is an easy matter to show that demand functions are homogeneous of degree 0 in all prices and income. It therefore is apparent that the revealed preference axiom and the existence of "well-behaved" utility functions are somehow equivalent conditions. That this is in fact the case was first shown by H. S. Houthakker in 1950. Houthakker showed that a set of indifference curves can always be derived for an individual who obeys the strong axiom of revealed preference.[11] Hence, this axiom provides a quite general and believable foundation for utility theory based on simple comparisons among alternative budget constraints. This approach is widely used in the construction of price indices and for a variety of other applied purposes.

SUMMARY

In this chapter, we used the utility-maximization model to study how the quantity of a good that an individual chooses responds to changes in income or to changes in that good's price. The final result of this examination is the derivation of the familiar downward-sloping demand curve. In arriving at that result, however, we have drawn a wide variety of insights from the general economic theory of choice.

- Proportional changes in all prices and income do not shift the individual's budget constraint and therefore do not change the quantities of goods chosen. In formal terms, demand functions are homogeneous of degree 0 in all prices and income.

- When purchasing power changes (that is, when income increases with prices remaining unchanged), budget constraints shift and individuals will choose new commodity bundles. For normal goods, an increase in purchasing power causes more to be chosen. In the case of inferior goods, however, an increase in purchasing power causes less to be purchased. Hence the sign of $\partial x_i / \partial I$ could be either positive or negative, although $\partial x_i / \partial I \geq 0$ is the most common case.

- A fall in the price of a good causes substitution and income effects that, for a normal good, cause more of the good to be purchased. For inferior goods, however, substitution and income effects work in opposite directions and no unambiguous prediction is possible.

- Similarly, a rise in price induces both substitution and income effects that, in the normal case, cause less to be demanded. For inferior goods the net result is again ambiguous.

- The Marshallian demand curve summarizes the total quantity of a good demanded at each possible price. Changes in price induce both substitution and income effects that prompt movements along the curve. For a normal good, $\partial x_i / \partial p_i \leq 0$ along this curve. If income, prices of other goods, or preferences change, then the curve may shift to a new location.

- Compensated demand curves illustrate movements along a given indifference curve for alternative prices. They are constructed by holding utility constant and exhibit only the substitution effects from a price change. Hence, their slope is unambiguously negative.

- Demand elasticities are often used in empirical work to summarize how individuals react to changes in prices and income. The most important such elasticity is the (own-) price elasticity of demand, e_{x, p_x}. This measures the proportionate change in quantity in response to a 1 percent change in price. A similar elasticity can be defined for movements along the compensated demand curve.

- There are many relationships among demand elasticities. Some of the more important ones are: (1) own-price

---

[11]H. S. Houthakker, "Revealed Preference and the Utility Function," *Economica* 17 (May 1950): 159–74.

elasticities determine how a price change affects total spending on a good; (2) substitution and income effects can be summarized by the Slutsky equation in elasticity form; and (3) various aggregation relations hold among elasticities—these show how the demands for different goods are related.

- Welfare effects of price changes can be measured by changing areas below either compensated or ordinary demand curves. Such changes affect the size of the consumer surplus that individuals receive from being able to make market transactions.

- The negativity of the substitution effect is the most basic conclusion from demand theory. This result can be shown using revealed preference theory and so does not require assuming the existence of a utility function.

PROBLEMS

5.1

Thirsty Ed drinks only pure spring water, but he can purchase it in two different-sized containers: 0.75 liter and 2 liter. Because the water itself is identical, he regards these two "goods" as perfect substitutes.

- a. Assuming Ed's utility depends only on the quantity of water consumed and that the containers themselves yield no utility, express this utility function in terms of quantities of 0.75L containers (x) and 2L containers (y).

- b. State Ed's demand function for x in terms of p_x, p_y, and I.

- c. Graph the demand curve for x, holding I and p_y constant.

- d. How do changes in I and p_y shift the demand curve for x?

- e. What would the compensated demand curve for x look like in this situation?

5.2

David N. gets $3 per week as an allowance to spend any way he pleases. Because he likes only peanut butter and jelly sandwiches, he spends the entire amount on peanut butter (at $0.05 per ounce) and jelly (at $0.10 per ounce). Bread is provided free of charge by a concerned neighbor. David is a particular eater and makes his sandwiches with exactly 1 ounce of jelly and 2 ounces of peanut butter. He is set in his ways and will never change these proportions.

- a. How much peanut butter and jelly will David buy with his $3 allowance in a week?

- b. Suppose the price of jelly were to rise to $0.15 an ounce. How much of each commodity would be bought?

- c. By how much should David's allowance be increased to compensate for the rise in the price of jelly in part (b)?

- d. Graph your results in parts (a) to (c).

- e. In what sense does this problem involve only a single commodity, peanut butter and jelly sandwiches? Graph the demand curve for this single commodity.

- f. Discuss the results of this problem in terms of the income and substitution effects involved in the demand for jelly.

5.3

As defined in Chapter 3, a utility function is homothetic if any straight line through the origin cuts all indifference curves at points of equal slope: The MRS depends on the ratio y/x.

- a. Prove that, in this case, $\partial x/\partial I$ is constant.

- b. Prove that if an individual's tastes can be represented by a homothetic indifference map then price and quantity must move in opposite directions; that is, prove that Giffen's paradox cannot occur.

5.4

As in Example 5.1, assume that utility is given by

$$\text{utility} = U(x, y) = x^{0.3}y^{0.7}.$$

a. Use the uncompensated demand functions given in Example 5.1 to compute the indirect utility function and the expenditure function for this case.

b. Use the expenditure function calculated in part (a) together with Shephard's lemma to compute the compensated demand function for good x.

c. Use the results from part (b) together with the uncompensated demand function for good x to show that the Slutsky equation holds for this case.

5.5

Suppose the utility function for goods x and y is given by

$$\text{utility} = U(x, y) = xy + y.$$

a. Calculate the uncompensated (Marshallian) demand functions for x and y and describe how the demand curves for x and y are shifted by changes in I or the price of the other good.

b. Calculate the expenditure function for x and y.

c. Use the expenditure function calculated in part (b) to compute the compensated demand functions for goods x and y. Describe how the compensated demand curves for x and y are shifted by changes in income or by changes in the price of the other good.

5.6

Over a three-year period, an individual exhibits the following consumption behavior:

	p_x	p_y	x	y
Year 1	3	3	7	4
Year 2	4	2	6	6
Year 3	5	1	7	3

Is this behavior consistent with the strong axiom of revealed preference?

5.7

Suppose that a person regards ham and cheese as pure complements—he or she will always use one slice of ham in combination with one slice of cheese to make a ham and cheese sandwich. Suppose also that ham and cheese are the only goods that this person buys and that bread is free.

a. If the price of ham is equal to the price of cheese, show that the own-price elasticity of demand for ham is -0.5 and that the cross-price elasticity of demand for ham with respect to the price of cheese is also -0.5.

b. Explain why the results from part (a) reflect only income effects, not substitution effects. What are the compensated price elasticities in this problem?

c. Use the results from part (b) to show how your answers to part (a) would change if a slice of ham cost twice the price of a slice of cheese.

d. Explain how this problem could be solved intuitively by assuming this person consumes only one good—a ham-and-cheese sandwich.

5.8

Show that the share of income spent on a good x is $s_x = \dfrac{d \ln E}{d \ln p_x}$, where E is total expenditure.

Analytical Problems

5.9 Share elasticities

In the Extensions to Chapter 4 we showed that most empirical work in demand theory focuses on income shares. For any good, x, the income share is defined as $s_x = p_x x / I$. In this problem we show that most demand elasticities can be derived from corresponding share elasticities.

a. Show that the elasticity of a good's budget share with respect to income ($e_{s_x, I} = \partial s_x / \partial I \cdot I / s_x$) is equal to $e_{x, I} - 1$. Interpret this conclusion with a few numerical examples.

b. Show that the elasticity of a good's budget share with respect to its own price ($e_{s_x, p_x} = \partial s_x / \partial p_x \cdot p_x / s_x$) is equal to $e_{x, p_x} + 1$. Again, interpret this finding with a few numerical examples.

c. Use your results from part (b) to show that the "expenditure elasticity" of good x with respect to its own price [$e_{x \cdot p_x, p_x} = \partial(p_x \cdot x) / \partial p_x \cdot 1/x$] is also equal to $e_{x, p_x} + 1$.

d. Show that the elasticity of a good's budget share with respect to a change in the price of some other good ($e_{s_x, p_y} = \partial s_x / \partial p_y \cdot p_y / s_x$) is equal to e_{x, p_y}.

e. In the Extensions to Chapter 4 we showed that with a CES utility function, the share of income devoted to good x is given by $s_x = 1/(1 + p_y^k p_x^{-k})$, where $k = \delta/(\delta - 1) = 1 - \sigma$. Use this share equation to prove Equation 5.56: $e_{x^c, p_x} = -(1 - s_x)\sigma$. *Hint:* This problem can be simplified by assuming $p_x = p_y$, in which case $s_x = 0.5$.

5.10 More on elasticities

Part (e) of Problem 5.9 has a number of useful applications because it shows how price responses depend ultimately on the underlying parameters of the utility function. Specifically, use that result together with the Slutsky equation in elasticity terms to show:

a. In the Cobb-Douglas case ($\sigma = 1$), the following relationship holds between the own-price elasticities of x and y: $e_{x, p_x} + e_{y, p_y} = -2$.

b. If $\sigma > 1$ then $e_{x, p_x} + e_{y, p_y} < -2$, and if $\sigma < 1$ then $e_{x, p_x} + e_{y, p_y} > -2$. Provide an intuitive explanation for this result.

c. How would you generalize this result to cases of more than two goods? Discuss whether such a generalization would be especially meaningful.

5.11 Aggregation of elasticities for many goods

The three aggregation relationships presented in this chapter can be generalized to any number of goods. This problem asks you to do so. We assume that there are n goods and that the share of income devoted to good i is denoted by s_i. We also define the following elasticities:

$$e_{i, I} = \frac{\partial x_i}{\partial I} \cdot \frac{I}{x_i},$$

$$e_{i, j} = \frac{\partial x_i}{\partial p_j} \cdot \frac{I}{x_i}.$$

Use this notation to show:

a. Homogeneity: $\sum_{j=1}^{n} e_{i, j} + e_{i, I} = 0$.

b. Engel aggregation: $\sum_{i=1}^{n} s_i e_{i, I} = 1$.

c. Cournot aggregation: $\sum_{i=1}^{n} s_i e_{i, j} = -s_j$.

5.12 Quasi-linear utility (revisited)

Consider a simple quasi-linear utility function of the form $U(x, y) = x + \ln y$.

a. Calculate the income effect for each good. Also calculate the income elasticity of demand for each good.

b. Calculate the substitution effect for each good. Also calculate the compensated own-price elasticity of demand for each good.

c. Show that the Slutsky equation applies to this function.

d. Show that the elasticity form of the Slutsky equation also applies to this function. Describe any special features you observe.

5.13 The almost ideal demand system

The general form of the almost ideal demand system (AIDS) is given by

$$\ln E(\vec{p}, U) = a_0 + \sum_{i=1}^{n} \alpha_i \ln p_i + \frac{1}{2} \sum_{i=1}^{n} \sum_{j=1}^{n} \gamma_{ij} \ln p_i \ln p_j + U\beta_0 \prod_{i=1}^{k} p_k^{\beta_k},$$

where $\vec{p}$ is the vector of prices, E is the expenditure function, and U is the level of utility required. For analytical ease, assume that the following restrictions apply:

$$\gamma_{ij} = \gamma_{ji}, \quad \sum_{i=1}^{n} \alpha_i = 1, \quad \text{and} \quad \sum_{j=1}^{n} \gamma_{ij} = \sum_{k=1}^{n} \beta_k = 0.$$

a. Derive the AIDS functional form for a two-goods case.

b. Given the previous restrictions, show that $E(\vec{p}, U)$ is homogeneous of degree 1 in all prices. This, along with the fact that this function resembles closely the actual data, makes it an "ideal" function.

c. Using the fact that $s_x = \dfrac{d \ln E}{d \ln p_x}$ (see Problem 5.8), calculate the income share of each of the two goods.

5.14 Price indifference curves

Price indifference curves are iso-utility curves with the prices of two goods on the x- and y-axes, respectively. Thus, they have the following general form: $(p_1, p_2) | v(p_1, p_2, I) = v_0$.

a. Derive the formula for the price indifference curves for the Cobb-Douglas case with $\alpha = \beta = 0.5$. Sketch one of them.

b. What does the slope of the curve show?

c. What is the direction of increasing utility in your graph?

SUGGESTIONS FOR FURTHER READING

Cook, P. J. "A 'One Line' Proof of the Slutsky Equation." *American Economic Review* 62 (March 1972): 139.

   Clever use of duality to derive the Slutsky equation; uses the same method as in Chapter 5 but with rather complex notation.

Fisher, F. M., and K. Shell. *The Economic Theory of Price Indices*. New York: Academic Press, 1972.

   Complete, technical discussion of the economic properties of various price indexes; describes "ideal" indexes based on utility-maximizing models in detail.

Mas-Colell, Andreu, Michael D. Whinston, and Jerry R. Green. *Microeconomic Theory*. New York: Oxford University Press, 1995.

   Chapter 3 covers much of the material in this chapter at a somewhat higher level. Section I on measurement of the welfare effects of price changes is especially recommended.

Samuelson, Paul A. *Foundations of Economic Analysis*. Cambridge, MA: Harvard University Press, 1947, Chap. 5.

   Provides a complete analysis of substitution and income effects. Also develops the revealed preference notion.

Silberberg, E., and W. Suen. *The Structure of Economics: A Mathematical Analysis*, 3rd ed. Boston: Irwin/McGraw-Hill, 2001.

Provides an extensive derivation of the Slutsky equation and a lengthy presentation of elasticity concepts.

Sydsaetter, K., A. Strom, and P. Berck. *Economist's Mathematical Manual.* Berlin: Springer-Verlag, 2003.

Provides a compact summary of elasticity concepts. The coverage of elasticity of substitution notions is especially complete.

Varian, H. *Microeconomic Analysis*, 3rd ed. New York: W. W. Norton, 1992.

Formal development of preference notions. Extensive use of expenditure functions and their relationship to the Slutsky equation. Also contains a nice proof of Roy's identity.

EXTENSIONS

Demand Concepts and the Evaluation of Price Indices

In Chapters 4 and 5 we introduced a number of related demand concepts, all of which were derived from the underlying model of utility maximization. Relationships among these various concepts are summarized in Figure E5.1. We have already looked at most of the links in the table formally. We have not yet discussed the mathematical relationship between indirect utility functions and Marshallian demand functions (Roy's identity), and we will do that below. All of the entries in the table make clear that there are many ways to learn something about the relationship between individuals' welfare and the prices they face. In this extension we will explore some of these approaches. Specifically, we will look at how the concepts can shed light on the accuracy of the consumer price index (CPI), the primary measure of inflation in the United States. We will also look at a few other price index concepts.

The CPI is a "market basket" index of the cost of living. Researchers measure the amounts that people consume of a set of goods in some base period (in the two-good case these base-period consumption levels might be denoted by x_0 and y_0) and then use current price data to compute the changing price of this market basket. Using this procedure, the cost of the market basket initially would be $I_0 = p_x^0 x_0 + p_y^0 y_0$ and the cost in period 1 would be $I_1 = p_x^1 x_0 + p_y^1 y_0$. The change in the cost of living between these two periods would then be measured by I_1/I_0. Although this procedure is an intuitively plausible way of measuring inflation and market basket price indices are widely used, such indices have many shortcomings.

E5.1 Expenditure functions and substitution bias

Market-basket price indices suffer from "substitution bias." Because the indices do not permit individuals to make substitutions in the market basket in response to changes in relative prices, they will tend to overstate

FIGURE E5.1   Relationships among Demand Concepts

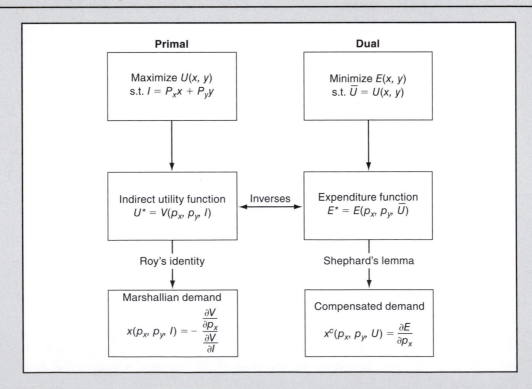

the welfare losses that people incur from rising prices. This exaggeration is illustrated in Figure E5.2. To achieve the utility level U_0 initially requires expenditures of E_0, resulting in a purchase of the basket x_0, y_0. If p_x/p_y falls, the initial utility level can now be obtained with expenditures of E_1 by altering the consumption bundle to x_1, y_1. Computing the expenditure level needed to continue consuming x_0, y_0 exaggerates how much extra purchasing power this person needs to restore his or her level of well-being. Economists have extensively studied the extent of this substitution bias. Aizcorbe and Jackman (1993), for example, find that this difficulty with a market basket index may exaggerate the level of inflation shown by the CPI by about 0.2 percent per year.

E5.2 Roy's identity and new goods bias

When new goods are introduced, it takes some time for them to be integrated into the CPI. For example, Hausman (1999, 2003) states that it took more than 15 years for cell phones to appear in the index. The problem with this delay is that market basket indices will fail to reflect the welfare gains that people experience from using new goods. To measure these costs, Hausman sought to measure a "virtual" price (p^*) at which the demand for, say, cell phones would be zero and then argued that the introduction of the good at its market price represented a change in consumer surplus that could be measured. Hence, the author

---

FIGURE E5.2   Substitution Bias in the CPI

Initially expenditures are given by E_0 and this individual buys x_0, y_0. If p_x/p_y falls, utility level U_0 can be reached most cheaply by consuming x_1, y_1 and spending E_1. Purchasing x_0, y_0 at the new prices would cost more than E_1. Hence, holding the consumption bundle constant imparts an upward bias to CPI-type computations.

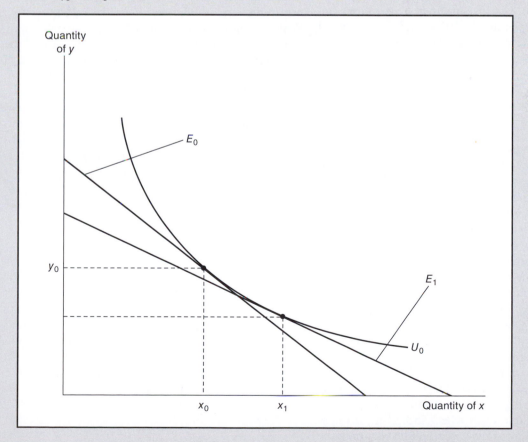

was faced with the problem of how to get from the Marshallian demand function for cell phones (which he estimated econometrically) to the expenditure function. To do so he used Roy's identity (see Roy, 1942). Remember that the consumer's utility-maximizing problem can be represented by the Lagrangian expression $\mathscr{L} = U(x, y) + \lambda(I - p_x x - p_y y)$. If we apply the envelope theorem to this expression, we know that

$$\frac{\partial U^*}{\partial p_x} = \frac{\partial \mathscr{L}}{\partial p_x} = -\lambda x(p_x, p_y, I),$$

$$\frac{\partial U^*}{\partial I} = \frac{\partial \mathscr{L}}{\partial I} = \lambda. \tag{i}$$

Hence the Marshallian demand function is given by

$$x(p_x, p_y, I) = \frac{-\partial U^*/\partial p_x}{\partial U^*/\partial I}. \tag{ii}$$

Using his estimates of the Marshallian demand function, Hausman integrated Equation ii to obtain the implied indirect utility function and then calculated its inverse, the expenditure function (check Figure E5.1 to see the logic of the process). Though this certainly is a roundabout scheme, it did yield large estimates for the gain in consumer welfare from cell phones—a present value in 1999 of more than $100 billion. Delays in the inclusion of such goods into the CPI can therefore result in a misleading measure of consumer welfare.

E5.3 Other complaints about the CPI

Researchers have found several other faults with the CPI as currently constructed. Most of these focus on the consequences of using incorrect prices to compute the index. For example, when the quality of a good improves, people are made better-off, though this may not show up in the good's price. Throughout the 1970s and 1980s the reliability of color television sets improved dramatically, but the price of a set did not change very much. A market basket that included "one color television set" would miss this source of improved welfare. Similarly, the opening of "big box" retailers such as Costco and Home Depot during the 1990s undoubtedly reduced the prices that consumers paid for various goods. But including these new retail outlets into the sample scheme for the CPI took several years, so the index misrepresented what people were actually paying. Assessing the magnitude of error introduced by these cases where incorrect prices are used in the CPI can also be accomplished by using the

various demand concepts in Figure E5.1. For a summary of this research, see Moulton (1996).

E5.4 Exact price indices

In principle, it is possible that some of the shortcomings of price indices such as the CPI might be ameliorated by more careful attention to demand theory. If the expenditure function for the representative consumer were known, for example, it would be possible to construct an "exact" index for changes in purchasing power that would take commodity substitution into account. To illustrate this, suppose there are only two goods and we wish to know how purchasing power has changed between period 1 and period 2. If the expenditure function is given by $E(p_x, p_y, U)$ then the ratio

$$I_{1,2} = \frac{E(p_x^2, p_y^2, \bar{U})}{E(p_x^1, p_y^1, \bar{U})} \tag{iii}$$

shows how the cost of attaining the target utility level $\bar{U}$ has changed between the two periods. If, for example, $I_{1,2} = 1.04$, then we would say that the cost of attaining the utility target had increased by 4 percent. Of course, this answer is only a conceptual one. Without knowing the representative person's utility function, we would not know the specific form of the expenditure function. But in some cases Equation iii may suggest how to proceed in index construction. Suppose, for example, that the typical person's preferences could be represented by the Cobb-Douglas utility function $U(x, y) = x^\alpha y^{1-\alpha}$. In this case it is easy to show that the expenditure function is a generalization of the one given in Example 4.4: $E(p_x, p_y, U) = p_x^\alpha p_y^{1-\alpha} U/\alpha^\alpha (1-\alpha)^{1-\alpha} = k p_x^\alpha p_y^{1-\alpha} U$. Inserting this function into Equation iii yields

$$I_{1,2} = \frac{k(p_x^2)^\alpha (p_y^2)^{1-\alpha} \bar{U}}{k(p_x^1)^\alpha (p_y^1)^{1-\alpha} \bar{U}} = \frac{(p_x^2)^\alpha (p_y^2)^{1-\alpha}}{(p_x^1)^\alpha (p_y^1)^{1-\alpha}}. \tag{iv}$$

So, in this case, the exact price index is a relatively simple function of the observed prices. The particularly useful feature of this example is that the utility target cancels out in the construction of the cost-of-living index (as it will anytime the expenditure function is homogeneous in utility). Notice also that the expenditure shares (α and $1 - \alpha$) play an important role in the index—the larger a good's share, the more important will changes be in that good's price in the final index.

E5.5 Development of exact price indices

The Cobb-Douglas utility function is, of course, a very simple one. Much recent research on price indices has focused on more general types of utility functions and on the discovery of the exact price indices they imply. For example, Feenstra and Reinsdorf (2000) show that the almost ideal demand system described in the Extensions to Chapter 4 implies an exact price index (I) that takes a "Divisia" form:

$$\ln(I) = \sum_{i=1}^{n} w_i \Delta \ln p_i \qquad \textbf{(v)}$$

(here the w_i are weights to be attached to the change in the logarithm of each good's price). Often the weights in Equation v are taken to be the budget shares of the goods. Interestingly, this is precisely the price index implied by the Cobb-Douglas utility function in Equation iv, since

$$
\begin{aligned}
\ln(I_{1,2}) &= \alpha \ln p_x^2 + (1 - \alpha) \ln p_y^2 \\
&\quad - \alpha \ln p_x^1 - (1 - \alpha) \ln p_y^1 \\
&= \alpha \Delta \ln p_x + (1 - \alpha) \Delta \ln p_y. \qquad \textbf{(vi)}
\end{aligned}
$$

In actual applications, the weights would change from period to period to reflect changing budget shares. Similarly, changes over several periods would be "chained" together from a number of single-period price change indices.

Changing demands for food in China. China has one of the fastest growing economies in the world: its GDP per capita is currently growing at a rate of about 8 percent per year. Chinese consumers also spend a large fraction of their incomes on food—approximately 38 percent of total expenditures in recent survey data. One implication of the rapid growth in Chinese incomes, however, is that patterns of food consumption are changing rapidly. Purchases of staples, such as rice or wheat, are declining in relative importance, whereas purchases of poultry, fish, and processed foods are growing rapidly. A recent paper by Gould and Villarreal (2006) studies these patterns in detail using the AIDS model. They identify a variety of substitution effects across specific food categories in response to changing relative prices. Such changing patterns imply that a fixed market basket price index (such as the U.S. Consumer Price Index) would be particularly inappropriate for measuring changes in the cost of living in China and that some alternative approaches should be examined.

References

Aizcorbe, Ana M., and Patrick C. Jackman. "The Commodity Substitution Effect in CPI Data, 1982–91." *Monthly Labor Review* (December 1993): 25–33.

Feenstra, Robert C., and Marshall B. Reinsdorf. "An Exact Price Index for the Almost Ideal Demand System." *Economics Letters* (February 2000): 159–62.

Gould, Brain W., and Hector J. Villarreal. "An Assessment of the Current Structure of Food Demand in Urban China." *Agricultural Economics* (January 2006): 1–16.

Hausman, Jerry. "Cellular Telephone, New Products, and the CPI." *Journal of Business and Economic Statistics* (April 1999): 188–94.

Hausman, Jerry. "Sources of Bias and Solutions to Bias in the Consumer Price Index." *Journal of Economic Perspectives* (Winter 2003): 23–44.

Moulton, Brent R. "Bias in the Consumer Price Index: What Is the Evidence?" *Journal of Economic Perspectives* (Fall 1996): 159–77.

Roy, R. *De l'utilité, contribution à la théorie des choix.* Paris: Hermann, 1942.

Demand Relationships among Goods

In Chapter 5 we examined how changes in the price of a particular good (say, good *x*) affect the quantity of that good chosen. Throughout the discussion, we held the prices of all other goods constant. It should be clear, however, that a change in one of these other prices could also affect the quantity of *x* chosen. For example, if *x* were taken to represent the quantity of automobile miles that an individual drives, this quantity might be expected to decline when the price of gasoline rises or increase when air and bus fares rise. In this chapter we will use the utility-maximization model to study such relationships.

THE TWO-GOOD CASE

We begin our study of the demand relationship among goods with the two-good case. Unfortunately, this case proves to be rather uninteresting because the types of relationships that can occur when there are only two goods are quite limited. Still, the two-good case is useful because it can be illustrated with two-dimensional graphs. Figure 6.1 starts our examination by showing two examples of how the quantity of *x* chosen might be affected by a change in the price of *y*. In both panels of the figure, p_y has fallen. This has the result of shifting the budget constraint outward from I_0 to I_1. In both cases, the quantity of good *y* chosen has also increased from y_0 to y_1 as a result of the decline in p_y, as would be expected if *y* is a normal good. For good *x*, however, the results shown in the two panels differ. In (a) the indifference curves are nearly L-shaped, implying a fairly small substitution effect. A decline in p_y does not induce a very large move along U_0 as *y* is substituted for *x*. That is, *x* drops relatively little as a result of the substitution. The income effect, however, reflects the greater purchasing power now available, and this causes the total quantity of *x* chosen to increase. Hence, $\partial x / \partial p_y$ is negative (*x* and p_y move in opposite directions).

In Figure 6.1b this situation is reversed: $\partial x / \partial p_y$ is positive. The relatively flat indifference curves in Figure 6.1b result in a large substitution effect from the fall in p_y. The quantity of *x* declines sharply as *y* is substituted for *x* along U_0. As in Figure 6.1a, the increased purchasing power from the decline in p_y causes more *x* to be bought, but now the substitution effect dominates and the quantity of *x* declines to x_1. In this case, then, *x* and p_y move in the same direction.

A mathematical treatment

The ambiguity in the effect of changes in p_y can be further illustrated by a Slutsky-type equation. By using procedures similar to those in Chapter 5, it is fairly simple to show that

$$\frac{\partial x(p_x, p_y, I)}{\partial p_y} = \text{substitution effect} + \text{income effect}$$

$$= \left. \frac{\partial x}{\partial p_y} \right|_{U=\text{constant}} - y \cdot \frac{\partial x}{\partial I}, \tag{6.1}$$

FIGURE 6.1   Differing Directions of Cross-Price Effects

In both panels, the price of y has fallen. In (a), substitution effects are small so the quantity of x consumed increases along with y. Because $\partial x/\partial p_y < 0$, x and y are *gross complements*. In (b), substitution effects are large so the quantity of x chosen falls. Because $\partial x/\partial p_y > 0$, x and y would be termed *gross substitutes*.

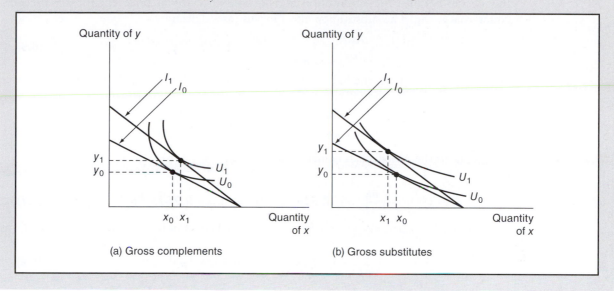

(a) Gross complements   (b) Gross substitutes

or, in elasticity terms,

$$e_{x,p_y} = e_{x^c,p_y} - s_y e_{x,I}.\tag{6.2}$$

Notice that the size of the income effect is determined by the share of good y in this person's purchases. The impact of a change in p_y on purchasing power is determined by how important y is to this person.

For the two-good case, the terms on the right side of Equations 6.1 and 6.2 have different signs. Assuming that indifference curves are convex, the substitution effect $\partial x/\partial p_y|_{U=\text{constant}}$ is positive. If we confine ourselves to moves along one indifference curve, increases in p_y increase x and decreases in p_y decrease the quantity of x chosen. But, assuming x is a normal good, the income effect $(-y\partial x/\partial I$ or $-s_y e_{x,I})$ is clearly negative. Hence, the combined effect is ambiguous; $\partial x/\partial p_y$ could be either positive or negative. Even in the two-good case, the demand relationship between x and p_y is rather complex.

EXAMPLE 6.1   Another Slutsky Decomposition for Cross-Price Effects

In Example 5.4 we examined the Slutsky decomposition for the effect of a change in the price of x. Now let's look at the cross-price effect of a change in y prices on x purchases. Remember that the uncompensated and compensated demand functions for x are given by

$$x(p_x, p_y, I) = \frac{0.5I}{p_x}\tag{6.3}$$

and

$$x^c(p_x, p_y, V) = V p_y^{0.5} p_x^{-0.5}.\tag{6.4}$$

(*continued*)

EXAMPLE 6.1   CONTINUED

As we have pointed out before, the Marshallian demand function in this case yields $\partial x/\partial p_y = 0$; that is, changes in the price of y do not affect x purchases. Now we show that this occurs because the substitution and income effects of a price change are precisely counterbalancing. The substitution effect in this case is given by

$$\frac{\partial x}{\partial p_y}\Big|_{U=\text{constant}} = \frac{\partial x^c}{\partial p_y} = 0.5\,V p_y^{-0.5} p_x^{-0.5}. \qquad (6.5)$$

Substituting for V from the indirect utility function ($V = 0.5\,I p_y^{-0.5} p_x^{-0.5}$) gives a final statement for the substitution effect:

$$\frac{\partial x}{\partial p_y}\Big|_{U=\text{constant}} = 0.25\,I p_y^{-1} p_x^{-1}. \qquad (6.6)$$

Returning to the Marshallian demand function for y ($y = 0.5\,I p_y^{-1}$) to calculate the income effect yields

$$-y\frac{\partial x}{\partial I} = -[0.5\,I p_y^{-1}] \cdot [0.5\,p_x^{-1}] = -0.25\,I p_y^{-1} p_x^{-1}, \qquad (6.7)$$

and combining Equations 6.6 and 6.7 gives the total effect of the change in the price of y as

$$\frac{\partial x}{\partial p_y} = 0.25\,I p_y^{-1} p_x^{-1} - 0.25\,I p_y^{-1} p_x^{-1} = 0. \qquad (6.8)$$

This makes clear that the reason that changes in the price of y have no effect on x purchases in the Cobb-Douglas case is that the substitution and income effects from such a change are precisely offsetting; neither of the effects alone, however, is zero.

Returning to our numerical example ($p_x = 1, p_y = 4, I = 8, V = 2$), suppose now that p_y falls to 2. This should have no effect on the Marshallian demand for good x. The compensated demand function in Equation 6.4 shows that the price change would cause the quantity of x demanded to decline from 4 to 2.83 ($= 2\sqrt{2}$) as y is substituted for x with utility unchanged. However, the increased purchasing power arising from the price decline precisely reverses this effect.

QUERY: Why would it be incorrect to argue that if $\partial_x/\partial p_y = 0$, then x and y have no substitution possibilities—that is, they must be consumed in fixed proportions? Is there any case in which such a conclusion could be drawn?

SUBSTITUTES AND COMPLEMENTS

With many goods, there is much more room for interesting relations among goods. It is relatively easy to generalize the Slutsky equation for any two goods x_i, x_j as

$$\frac{\partial x_i(p_1, \ldots, p_n, I)}{\partial p_j} = \frac{\partial x_i}{\partial p_j}\Big|_{U=\text{constant}} - x_j\frac{\partial x_i}{\partial I}, \qquad (6.9)$$

and again this can be readily translated into an elasticity relation:

$$e_{i,j} = e_{i,j}^c - s_j e_{i,I}. \qquad (6.10)$$

This says that the change in the price of any good (here, good j) induces income and substitution effects that may change the quantity of every good demanded. Equations 6.9 and 6.10 can be used to discuss the idea of substitutes and complements. Intuitively, these ideas are rather simple. Two goods are *substitutes* if one good may, as a result of changed conditions, replace the other in use. Some examples are tea and coffee, hamburgers and hot dogs, and butter and margarine. *Complements*, on the other hand, are goods that "go together," such as coffee and cream, fish and chips, or brandy and cigars. In some sense, "substitutes" substitute for one another in the utility function whereas "complements" complement each other.

There are two different ways to make these intuitive ideas precise. One of these focuses on the "gross" effects of price changes by including both income and substitution effects; the other looks at substitution effects alone. Because both definitions are used, we will examine each in detail.

Gross substitutes and complements

Whether two goods are substitutes or complements can be established by referring to observed price reactions as follows.

Gross substitutes and complements. Two goods, x_i and x_j, are said to be gross substitutes if

$$\frac{\partial x_i}{\partial p_j} > 0 \tag{6.11}$$

and gross complements if

$$\frac{\partial x_i}{\partial p_j} < 0. \tag{6.12}$$

DEFINITION

That is, two goods are gross substitutes if a rise in the price of one good causes *more* of the other good to be bought. The goods are gross complements if a rise in the price of one good causes *less* of the other good to be purchased. For example, if the price of coffee rises, the demand for tea might be expected to increase (they are substitutes), whereas the demand for cream might decrease (coffee and cream are complements). Equation 6.9 makes it clear that this definition is a "gross" definition in that it includes both income and substitution effects that arise from price changes. Because these effects are in fact combined in any real-world observation we can make, it might be reasonable always to speak only of "gross" substitutes and "gross" complements.

Asymmetry of the gross definitions

There are, however, several things that are undesirable about the gross definitions of substitutes and complements. The most important of these is that the definitions are not symmetric. It is possible, by the definitions, for x_1 to be a substitute for x_2 and at the same time for x_2 to be a complement of x_1. The presence of income effects can produce paradoxical results. Let's look at a specific example.

EXAMPLE 6.2 Asymmetry in Cross-Price Effects

Suppose the utility function for two goods (x and y) has the quasi-linear form

$$U(x, y) = \ln x + y. \tag{6.13}$$

Setting up the Lagrangian expression

$$\mathcal{L} = \ln x + y + \lambda(I - p_x x - p_y y) \tag{6.14}$$

(*continued*)

EXAMPLE 6.2   CONTINUED

yields the following first-order conditions:

$$\frac{\partial \mathcal{L}}{\partial x} = \frac{1}{x} - \lambda p_x = 0,$$

$$\frac{\partial \mathcal{L}}{\partial y} = 1 - \lambda p_y = 0, \tag{6.15}$$

$$\frac{\partial \mathcal{L}}{\partial \lambda} = I - p_x x - p_y y = 0.$$

Moving the terms in λ to the right and dividing the first equation by the second yields

$$\frac{1}{x} = \frac{p_x}{p_y}, \tag{6.16}$$

$$p_x x = p_y. \tag{6.17}$$

Substitution into the budget constraint now permits us to solve for the Marshallian demand function for y:

$$I = p_x x + p_y y = p_y + p_y y. \tag{6.18}$$

Hence,

$$y = \frac{I - p_y}{p_y}. \tag{6.19}$$

This equation shows that an increase in p_y must decrease spending on good y (that is, $p_y y$). Therefore, since p_x and I are unchanged, spending on x must rise. So

$$\frac{\partial x}{\partial p_y} > 0, \tag{6.20}$$

and we would term x and y gross substitutes. On the other hand, Equation 6.19 shows that spending on y is independent of p_x. Consequently,

$$\frac{\partial y}{\partial p_x} = 0 \tag{6.21}$$

and, looked at in this way, x and y would be said to be independent of each other; they are neither gross substitutes nor gross complements. Relying on gross responses to price changes to define the relationship between x and y would therefore run into ambiguity.

QUERY: In Example 3.4, we showed that a utility function of the form given by Equation 6.13 is not homothetic: the *MRS* does not depend only on the ratio of x to y. Can asymmetry arise in the homothetic case?

NET SUBSTITUTES AND COMPLEMENTS

Because of the possible asymmetries involved in the definition of gross substitutes and complements, an alternative definition that focuses only on substitution effects is often used.

DEFINITION

Net substitutes and complements. Goods x_i and x_j are said to be net substitutes if

$$\left.\frac{\partial x_i}{\partial p_j}\right|_{U=\text{constant}} > 0 \tag{6.22}$$

and net complements if

$$\left.\frac{\partial x_i}{\partial p_j}\right|_{U=\text{constant}} < 0. \qquad\qquad \textbf{(6.23)}$$

These definitions,[1] then, look only at the substitution terms to determine whether two goods are substitutes or complements. This definition is both intuitively appealing (because it looks only at the shape of an indifference curve) and theoretically desirable (because it is unambiguous). Once x_i and x_j have been discovered to be substitutes, they stay substitutes, no matter in which direction the definition is applied. As a matter of fact, the definitions are perfectly symmetric:

$$\left.\frac{\partial x_i}{\partial p_j}\right|_{U=\text{constant}} = \left.\frac{\partial x_j}{\partial p_i}\right|_{U=\text{constant}}. \qquad\qquad \textbf{(6.24)}$$

The substitution effect of a change in p_i on good x_j is identical to the substitution effect of a change in p_j on the quantity of x_i chosen. This symmetry is important in both theoretical and empirical work.[2]

   The differences between the two definitions of substitutes and complements are easily demonstrated in Figure 6.1a. In this figure, x and y are gross complements, but they are net substitutes. The derivative $\partial x/\partial p_y$ turns out to be negative (x and y are gross complements) because the (positive) substitution effect is outweighed by the (negative) income effect (a fall in the price of y causes real income to increase greatly, and, consequently, actual purchases of x increase). However, as the figure makes clear, if there are only two goods from which to choose, they must be net substitutes, although they may be either gross substitutes or gross complements. Because we have assumed a diminishing MRS, the own-price substitution effect must be negative and, consequently, the cross-price substitution effect must be positive.

SUBSTITUTABILITY WITH MANY GOODS

Once the utility-maximizing model is extended to many goods, a wide variety of demand patterns become possible. Whether a particular pair of goods are net substitutes or net complements is basically a question of a person's preferences, so one might observe all sorts of odd relationships. A major theoretical question that has concerned economists is whether substitutability or complementarity is more prevalent. In most discussions, we tend to regard goods as substitutes (a price rise in one market tends to increase demand in most other markets). It would be nice to know whether this intuition is justified.

---

[1]These are sometimes called "Hicksian" substitutes and complements, named after the British economist John Hicks, who originally developed the definitions.

[2]This symmetry is easily shown using Shephard's lemma. Compensated demand functions can be calculated from expenditure functions by differentiation:

$$x_i^c(p_1,\ldots,p_n,V) = \frac{\partial E(p_1,\ldots,p_n,V)}{\partial p_i}.$$

Hence, the substitution effect is given by

$$\left.\frac{\partial x_i}{\partial p_j}\right|_{U=\text{constant}} = \frac{\partial x_i^c}{\partial p_j} = \frac{\partial^2 E}{\partial p_j \partial p_i} = E_{ij}.$$

But now we can apply Young's theorem to the expenditure function:

$$E_{ij} = E_{ji} = \frac{\partial x_j^c}{\partial p_i} = \left.\frac{\partial x_j}{\partial p_i}\right|_{U=\text{constant}},$$

which proves the symmetry.

The British economist John Hicks studied this issue in some detail about 50 years ago and reached the conclusion that "most" goods must be substitutes. The result is summarized in what has come to be called "Hicks' second law of demand."[3] A modern proof starts with the compensated demand function for a particular good: $x_i^c(p_1, \ldots, p_n, V)$. This function is homogeneous of degree 0 in all prices (if utility is held constant and prices double, quantities demanded do not change because the utility-maximizing tangencies do not change). Applying Euler's theorem to the function yields

$$p_1 \cdot \frac{\partial x_i^c}{\partial p_1} + p_2 \cdot \frac{\partial x_i^c}{\partial p_2} + \cdots + p_n \cdot \frac{\partial x_i^c}{\partial p_n} = 0. \tag{6.25}$$

We can put this result into elasticity terms by dividing Equation 6.25 by x_i:

$$e_{i1}^c + e_{i2}^c + \cdots + e_{in}^c = 0. \tag{6.26}$$

But we know that $e_{ii}^c \leq 0$ because of the negativity of the own-substitution effect. Hence it must be the case that

$$\sum_{j \neq i} e_{ij}^c \geq 0. \tag{6.27}$$

In words, the sum of all the compensated cross-price elasticities for a particular good must be positive (or zero). This is the sense that "most" goods are substitutes. Empirical evidence seems generally consistent with this theoretical finding: instances of net complementarity between goods are encountered relatively infrequently in empirical studies of demand.

COMPOSITE COMMODITIES

Our discussion in the previous section showed that the demand relationships among goods can be quite complicated. In the most general case, an individual who consumes n goods will have demand functions that reflect $n(n + 1)/2$ different substitution effects.[4] When n is very large (as it surely is for all the specific goods that individuals actually consume), this general case can be unmanageable. It is often far more convenient to group goods into larger aggregates such as food, clothing, shelter, and so forth. At the most extreme level of aggregates, we might wish to examine one specific good (say, gasoline, which we might call x) and its relationship to "all other goods," which we might call y. This is the procedure we have been using in some of our two-dimensional graphs, and we will continue to do so at many other places in this book. In this section we show the conditions under which this procedure can be defended. In the Extensions to this chapter, we explore more general issues involved in aggregating goods into larger groupings.

Composite commodity theorem

Suppose consumers choose among n goods but that we are only interested specifically in one of them—say, x_1. In general, the demand for x_1 will depend on the individual prices of the other $n - 1$ commodities. But if all these prices move together, it may make sense to

---

[3]See John Hicks, *Value and Capital* (Oxford: Oxford University Press, 1939), mathematical appendices. There is some debate about whether this result should be called Hicks' "second" or "third" law. In fact, two other laws that we have already seen are listed by Hicks: (1) $\partial x_i^c / \partial p_i \leq 0$ (negativity of the own-substitution effect); and (2) $\partial x_i^c / \partial p_j = \partial x_j^c / \partial p_i$ (symmetry of cross-substitution effects). But he refers explicitly only to two "properties" in his written summary of his results.

[4]To see this, notice that all substitution effects, s_{ij}, could be recorded in an $n \times n$ matrix. However, symmetry of the effects ($s_{ij} = s_{ji}$) implies that only those terms on and below the principal diagonal of this matrix may be distinctly different from each other. This amounts to half the terms in the matrix ($n^2/2$) plus the remaining half of the terms on the main diagonal of the matrix ($n/2$).

lump them into a single "composite commodity," y. Formally, if we let $p_2^0, \ldots, p_n^0$ represent the initial prices of these goods, then we assume that these prices can only vary together. They might all double, or all decline by 50 percent, but the relative prices of $x_2, \ldots, x_n$ would not change. Now we define the composite commodity y to be total expenditures on $x_2, \ldots, x_n$, using the initial prices $p_2^0, \ldots, p_n^0$:

$$y = p_2^0 x_2 + p_3^0 x_3 + \cdots + p_n^0 x_n. \tag{6.28}$$

This person's initial budget constraint is given by

$$I = p_1 x_1 + p_2^0 x_2 + \cdots + p_n^0 x_n = p_1 x_1 + y. \tag{6.29}$$

By assumption, all of the prices $p_2, \ldots, p_n$ change in unison. Assume all of these prices change by a factor of t ($t > 0$). Now the budget constraint is

$$I = p_1 x_1 + t p_2^0 x_2 + \cdots + t p_n^0 x_n = p_1 x_1 + t y. \tag{6.30}$$

Consequently, the factor of proportionality, t, plays the same role in this person's budget constraint as did the price of $y (p_y)$ in our earlier two-good analysis. Changes in p_1 or t induce the same kinds of substitution effects we have been analyzing. So long as $p_2, \ldots, p_n$ move together, we can therefore confine our examination of demand to choices between buying x_1 or buying "everything else."[5] Simplified graphs that show these two goods on their axes can therefore be defended rigorously so long as the conditions of this "composite commodity theorem" (that all other prices move together) are satisfied. Notice, however, that the theorem makes no predictions about how choices of $x_2, \ldots, x_n$ behave; they need not move in unison. The theorem focuses only on total spending on $x_2, \ldots, x_n$, not on how that spending is allocated among specific items (although this allocation is assumed to be done in a utility-maximizing way).

Generalizations and limitations

The composite commodity theorem applies to any group of commodities whose relative prices all move together. It is possible to have more than one such commodity if there are several groupings that obey the theorem (i.e., expenditures on "food," "clothing," and so forth). Hence, we have developed the following definition.

Composite commodity. A composite commodity is a group of goods for which all prices move together. These goods can be treated as a single "commodity" in that the individual behaves as if he or she were choosing between other goods and total spending on the entire composite group.

DEFINITION

This definition and the related theorem are very powerful results. They help simplify many problems that would otherwise be intractable. Still, one must be rather careful in applying the theorem to the real world because its conditions are stringent. Finding a set of commodities whose prices move together is rare. Slight departures from strict proportionality may negate the composite commodity theorem if cross-substitution effects are large. In the Extensions to this chapter, we look at ways to simplify situations where prices move independently.

---

[5]The idea of a "composite commodity" was also introduced by J. R. Hicks in *Value and Capital*, 2nd ed. (Oxford: Oxford University Press, 1946), pp. 312–13. Proof of the theorem relies on the notion that to achieve maximum utility, the ratio of the marginal utilities for $x_2, \ldots, x_n$ must remain unchanged when $p_2, \ldots, p_n$ all move together. Hence, the n-good problem can be reduced to the two-dimensional problem of equating the ratio of the marginal utility from x to that from y to the "price ratio" p_1 / t.

EXAMPLE 6.3 Housing Costs as a Composite Commodity

Suppose that an individual receives utility from three goods: food (x), housing services (y) measured in hundreds of square feet, and household operations (z) as measured by electricity use.

If the individual's utility is given by the three-good CES function

$$\text{utility} = U(x, y, z) = -\frac{1}{x} - \frac{1}{y} - \frac{1}{z}, \tag{6.31}$$

then the Lagrangian technique can be used to calculate Marshallian demand functions for these goods as

$$x = \frac{I}{p_x + \sqrt{p_x p_y} + \sqrt{p_x p_z}},$$

$$y = \frac{I}{p_y + \sqrt{p_y p_x} + \sqrt{p_y p_z}}, \tag{6.32}$$

$$z = \frac{I}{p_z + \sqrt{p_z p_x} + \sqrt{p_z p_y}}.$$

If initially $I = 100$, $p_x = 1$, $p_y = 4$, and $p_z = 1$, then the demand functions predict

$$x^* = 25,$$
$$y^* = 12.5, \tag{6.33}$$
$$z^* = 25.$$

Hence, 25 is spent on food and a total of 75 is spent on housing-related needs. If we assume that housing service prices (p_y) and household operation prices (p_z) always move together, then we can use their initial prices to define the "composite commodity" housing (h) as

$$h = 4y + 1z. \tag{6.34}$$

Here, we also (arbitrarily) define the initial price of housing (p_h) to be 1. The initial quantity of housing is simply total dollars spent on h:

$$h = 4(12.5) + 1(25) = 75. \tag{6.35}$$

Furthermore, because p_y and p_z always move together, p_h will always be related to these prices by

$$p_h = p_z = 0.25 p_y. \tag{6.36}$$

Using this information, we can recalculate the demand function for x as a function of I, p_x, and p_h:

$$x = \frac{I}{p_x + \sqrt{4 p_x p_h} + \sqrt{p_x p_h}}$$

$$= \frac{I}{p_y + 3\sqrt{p_x p_h}}. \tag{6.37}$$

As before, initially $I = 100$, $p_x = 1$, and $p_h = 1$, so $x^* = 25$. Spending on housing can be most easily calculated from the budget constraint as $h^* = 75$, because spending on housing represents "everything" other than food.

An increase in housing costs. If the prices of y and z were to rise proportionally to $p_y = 16$, $p_z = 4$ (with p_x remaining at 1), then p_h would also rise to 4. Equation 6.37 now predicts that the demand for x would fall to

$$x^* = \frac{100}{1 + 3\sqrt{4}} = \frac{100}{7} \tag{6.38}$$

and that housing purchases would be given by

$$p_h b^* = 100 - \frac{100}{7} = \frac{600}{7}, \qquad (6.39)$$

or, because $p_h = 4$,

$$b^* = \frac{150}{7}. \qquad (6.40)$$

Notice that this is precisely the level of housing purchases predicted by the original demand functions for three goods in Equation 6.32. With $I = 100$, $p_x = 1$, $p_y = 16$, and $p_z = 4$, these equations can be solved as

$$x^* = \frac{100}{7},$$

$$y^* = \frac{100}{28}, \qquad (6.41)$$

$$z^* = \frac{100}{14},$$

and so the total amount of the composite good "housing" consumed (according to Equation 6.34) is given by

$$b^* = 4y^* + 1z^* = \frac{150}{7}. \qquad (6.42)$$

Hence, we obtained the same responses to price changes regardless of whether we chose to examine demands for the three goods x, y, and z or to look only at choices between x and the composite good h.

QUERY: How do we know that the demand function for x in Equation 6.37 continues to ensure utility maximization? Why is the Lagrangian constrained maximization problem unchanged by making the substitutions represented by Equation 6.36?

HOME PRODUCTION, ATTRIBUTES OF GOODS, AND IMPLICIT PRICES

So far in this chapter we have focused on what economists can learn about the relationships among goods by observing individuals' changing consumption of these goods in reaction to changes in market prices. In some ways this analysis skirts the central question of *why* coffee and cream go together or *why* fish and chicken may substitute for each other in a person's diet. To develop a deeper understanding of such questions, economists have sought to explore activities within individuals' households. That is, they have devised models of nonmarket types of activities such as parental child care, meal preparation, or do-it-yourself construction to understand how such activities ultimately result in demands for goods in the market. In this section we briefly review some of these models. Our primary goal is to illustrate some of the implications of this approach for the traditional theory of choice.

Household production model

The starting point for most models of household production is to assume that individuals do not receive utility directly from goods they purchase in the market (as we have been assuming so far). Instead, it is only when market goods are combined with time inputs by the individual that utility-providing outputs are produced. In this view, then, raw beef and uncooked potatoes yield no utility until they are cooked together to produce stew. Similarly, market purchases of beef and potatoes can be understood only by examining the individual's preferences for stew and the underlying technology through which it is produced.

In formal terms, assume as before that there are three goods that a person might purchase in the market: $x, y,$ and z. Purchasing these goods provides no direct utility, but the goods can be combined by the individual to produce either of two home-produced goods: a_1 or a_2. The technology of this household production can be represented by the production functions f_1 and f_2 (see Chapter 9 for a more complete discussion of the production function concept). Therefore,

$$a_1 = f_1(x, y, z),$$
$$a_2 = f_2(x, y, z), \tag{6.43}$$

and

$$\textbf{utility} = U(a_1, a_2). \tag{6.44}$$

The individual's goal is to choose x, y, z so as to maximize utility subject to the production constraints and to a financial budget constraint:[6]

$$p_x x + p_y y + p_z z = I. \tag{6.45}$$

Although we will not examine in detail the results that can be derived from this general model, two insights that can be drawn from it might be mentioned. First, the model may help clarify the nature of market relationships among goods. Because the production functions in Equations 6.43 are in principle measurable using detailed data on household operations, households can be treated as "multi-product" firms and studied using many of the techniques economists use to study production.

A second insight provided by the household production approach is the notion of the "implicit" or "shadow" prices associated with the home-produced goods a_1 and a_2. Because consuming more a_1, say, requires the use of more of the "ingredients" $x, y,$ and z, this activity obviously has an opportunity cost in terms of the quantity of a_2 that can be produced. To produce more bread, say, a person must not only divert some flour, milk, and eggs from using them to make cupcakes but may also have to alter the relative quantities of these goods purchased because he or she is bound by an overall budget constraint. Hence, bread will have an implicit price in terms of the number of cupcakes that must be forgone in order to be able to consume one more loaf. That implicit price will reflect not only the market prices of bread ingredients but also the available household production technology and, in more complex models, the relative time inputs required to produce the two goods. As a starting point, however, the notion of implicit prices can be best illustrated with a very simple model.

The linear attributes model

A particularly simple form of the household production model was first developed by K. J. Lancaster to examine the underlying "attributes" of goods.[7] In this model, it is the attributes of goods that provide utility to individuals, and each specific good contains a fixed set of attributes. If, for example, we focus only on the calories (a_1) and vitamins (a_2) that various foods provide, Lancaster's model assumes that utility is a function of these attributes and that individuals purchase various foods only for the purpose of obtaining the calories and vitamins they offer. In mathematical terms, the model assumes that the "production"

---

[6]Often household production theory also focuses on the individual's allocation of time to producing a_1 and a_2 or to working in the market. In Chapter 16 we look at a few simple models of this type.

[7]See K. J. Lancaster, "A New Approach to Consumer Theory," *Journal of Political Economy* 74 (April 1966): 132–57.

equations have the simple form

$$a_1 = a_x^1 x + a_y^1 y + a_z^1 z,$$
$$a_2 = a_x^2 x + a_y^2 y + a_z^2 z, \tag{6.46}$$

where a_x^1 represents the number of calories per unit of food x, a_x^2 represents the number of vitamins per unit of food x, and so forth. In this form of the model, then, there is no actual "production" in the home. Rather, the decision problem is how to choose a diet that provides the optimal mix of calories and vitamins given the available food budget.

Illustrating the budget constraints

To begin our examination of the theory of choice under the attributes model, we first illustrate the budget constraint. In Figure 6.2, the ray $0x$ records the various combinations of a_1 and a_2 available from successively larger amounts of good x. Because of the linear production technology assumed in the attributes model, these combinations of a_1 and a_2 lie along such a straight line, though in more complex models of home production that might not be the case. Similarly, rays of $0y$ and $0z$ show the quantities of the attributes a_1 and a_2 provided by various amounts of goods y and z that might be purchased.

If this person spends all of his or her income on good x, then the budget constraint (Equation 6.45) allows the purchase of

$$x^* = \frac{I}{p_x}, \tag{6.47}$$

and that will yield

$$a_1^* = a_x^1 x^* = \frac{a_x^1 I}{p_x},$$
$$a_2^* = a_x^2 x^* = \frac{a_x^2 I}{p_x}. \tag{6.48}$$

This point is recorded as point x^* on the $0x$ ray in Figure 6.2. Similarly, the points y^* and z^* represent the combinations of a_1 and a_2 that would be obtained if all income were spent on good y or good z, respectively.

Bundles of a_1 and a_2 that are obtainable by purchasing both x and y (with a fixed budget) are represented by the line joining x^* and y^* in Figure 6.2.[8] Similarly, the line x^*z^* represents the combinations of a_1 and a_2 available from x and z, and the line y^*z^* shows combinations available from mixing y and z. All possible combinations from mixing the three market goods are represented by the shaded triangular area $x^*y^*z^*$.

Corner solutions

One fact is immediately apparent from Figure 6.2: A utility-maximizing individual would never consume positive quantities of all three of these goods. Only the northeast perimeter of the $x^*y^*z^*$ triangle represents the maximal amounts of a_1 and a_2 available to this person given his or her income and the prices of the market goods. Individuals with a preference toward a_1 will have indifference curves similar to U_0 and will maximize utility by choosing a point such as E. The combination of a_1 and a_2 specified by that point can be obtained by

---

[8]Mathematically, suppose a fraction α of the budget is spent on x and $(1-\alpha)$ on y; then

$$a_1 = \alpha a_x^1 x^* + (1-\alpha)a_y^1 y^*,$$
$$a_2 = \alpha a_x^2 x^* + (1-\alpha)a_y^2 y^*.$$

The line x^*y^* is traced out by allowing α to vary between 0 and 1. The lines x^*z^* and y^*z^* are traced out in a similar way, as is the triangular area $x^*y^*z^*$.

FIGURE 6.2 Utility Maximization in the Attributes Model

The points x^*, y^*, and z^* show the amounts of attributes a_1 and a_2 that can be purchased by buying only x, y, or z, respectively. The shaded area shows all combinations that can be bought with mixed bundles. Some individuals may maximize utility at E, others at E'.

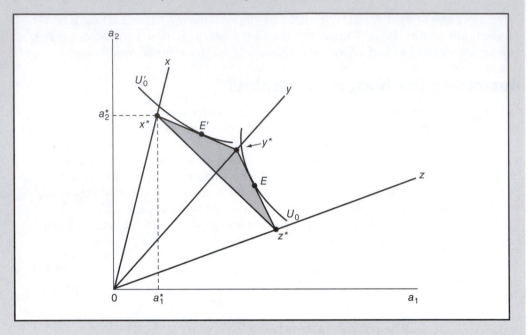

consuming only goods y and z. Similarly, a person with preferences represented by the indifference curve U'_0 will choose point E' and consume only goods x and y. The attributes model therefore predicts that corner solutions at which individuals consume zero amounts of some commodities will be relatively common, especially in cases where individuals attach value to fewer attributes (here, two) than there are market goods to choose from (three). If income, prices, or preferences change, then consumption patterns may also change abruptly. Goods that were previously consumed may cease to be bought and goods previously neglected may experience a significant increase in purchases. This is a direct result of the linear assumptions inherent in the production functions assumed here. In household production models with greater substitutability assumptions, such discontinuous reactions are less likely.

SUMMARY

In this chapter, we used the utility-maximizing model of choice to examine relationships among consumer goods. Although these relationships may be complex, the analysis presented here provided a number of ways of categorizing and simplifying them.

- When there are only two goods, the income and substitution effects from the change in the price of one good (say, p_y) on the demand for another good (x) usually work in opposite directions. The sign of $\partial x/\partial p_y$ is therefore ambiguous: its substitution effect is positive but its income effect is negative.

- In cases of more than two goods, demand relationships can be specified in two ways. Two goods (x_i and x_j) are "gross substitutes" if $\partial x_i/\partial p_j > 0$ and "gross complements" if $\partial x_i/\partial p_j < 0$. Unfortunately, because these price effects include income effects, they need not be symmetric. That is, $\partial x_i/\partial p_j$ does not necessarily equal $\partial x_j/\partial p_i$.

- Focusing only on the substitution effects from price changes eliminates this ambiguity because substitution effects are symmetric; that is, $\partial x_i^c/\partial p_j = \partial x_j^c/\partial p_i$. Now two goods are defined as net (or Hicksian) substitutes if $\partial x_i^c/\partial p_j > 0$ and net complements if $\partial x_i^c/\partial p_j < 0$. Hicks' "second law of demand" shows that net substitutes are more prevalent.

- If a group of goods has prices that always move in unison, then expenditures on these goods can be treated as a "composite commodity" whose "price" is given by the size of the proportional change in the composite goods' prices.

- An alternative way to develop the theory of choice among market goods is to focus on the ways in which market goods are used in household production to yield utility-providing attributes. This may provide additional insights into relationships among goods.

PROBLEMS

6.1

Heidi receives utility from two goods, goat's milk (m) and strudel (s), according to the utility function

$$U(m, s) = m \cdot s.$$

a. Show that increases in the price of goat's milk will not affect the quantity of strudel Heidi buys; that is, show that $\partial s / \partial p_m = 0$.

b. Show also that $\partial m / \partial p_s = 0$.

c. Use the Slutsky equation and the symmetry of net substitution effects to prove that the income effects involved with the derivatives in parts (a) and (b) are identical.

d. Prove part (c) explicitly using the Marshallian demand functions for m and s.

6.2

Hard Times Burt buys only rotgut whiskey and jelly donuts to sustain him. For Burt, rotgut whiskey is an inferior good that exhibits Giffen's paradox, although rotgut whiskey and jelly donuts are Hicksian substitutes in the customary sense. Develop an intuitive explanation to suggest why a rise in the price of rotgut must cause fewer jelly donuts to be bought. That is, the goods must also be gross complements.

6.3

Donald, a frugal graduate student, consumes only coffee (c) and buttered toast (bt). He buys these items at the university cafeteria and always uses two pats of butter for each piece of toast. Donald spends exactly half of his meager stipend on coffee and the other half on buttered toast.

a. In this problem, buttered toast can be treated as a composite commodity. What is its price in terms of the prices of butter (p_b) and toast (p_t)?

b. Explain why $\partial c / \partial p_{bt} = 0$.

c. Is it also true here that $\partial c / \partial p_b$ and $\partial c / \partial p_t$ are equal to 0?

6.4

Ms. Sarah Traveler does not own a car and travels only by bus, train, or plane. Her utility function is given by

$$\text{utility} = b \cdot t \cdot p,$$

where each letter stands for miles traveled by a specific mode. Suppose that the ratio of the price of train travel to that of bus travel (p_t / p_b) never changes.

a. How might one define a composite commodity for ground transportation?

b. Phrase Sarah's optimization problem as one of choosing between ground (g) and air (p) transportation.

c. What are Sarah's demand functions for g and p?

d. Once Sarah decides how much to spend on g, how will she allocate those expenditures between b and t?

6.5

Suppose that an individual consumes three goods, x_1, x_2, and x_3, and that x_2 and x_3 are similar commodities (i.e., cheap and expensive restaurant meals) with $p_2 = kp_3$, where $k < 1$—that is, the goods' prices have a constant relationship to one another.

a. Show that x_2 and x_3 can be treated as a composite commodity.

b. Suppose both x_2 and x_3 are subject to a transaction cost of t per unit (for some examples, see Problem 6.6). How will this transaction cost affect the price of x_2 relative to that of x_3? How will this effect vary with the value of t?

c. Can you predict how an income-compensated increase in t will affect expenditures on the composite commodity x_2 and x_3? Does the composite commodity theorem strictly apply to this case?

d. How will an income-compensated increase in t affect how total spending on the composite commodity is allocated between x_2 and x_3?

6.6

Apply the results of Problem 6.5 to explain the following observations:

a. It is difficult to find high-quality apples to buy in Washington State or good fresh oranges in Florida.

b. People with significant baby-sitting expenses are more likely to have meals out at expensive (rather than cheap) restaurants than are those without such expenses.

c. Individuals with a high value of time are more likely to fly the Concorde than those with a lower value of time.

d. Individuals are more likely to search for bargains for expensive items than for cheap ones. *Note:* Observations (b) and (d) form the bases for perhaps the only two murder mysteries in which an economist solves the crime; see Marshall Jevons, *Murder at the Margin* and *The Fatal Equilibrium*.

6.7

In general, uncompensated cross-price effects are not equal. That is,

$$\frac{\partial x_i}{\partial p_j} \neq \frac{\partial x_j}{\partial p_i}.$$

Use the Slutsky equation to show that these effects are equal if the individual spends a constant fraction of income on each good regardless of relative prices. (This is a generalization of Problem 6.1.)

6.8

Example 6.3 computes the demand functions implied by the three-good CES utility function

$$U(x, y, z) = -\frac{1}{x} - \frac{1}{y} - \frac{1}{z}.$$

a. Use the demand function for x in Equation 6.32 to determine whether x and y or x and z are gross substitutes or gross complements.

b. How would you determine whether x and y or x and z are net substitutes or net complements?

Analytical Problems

6.9 Consumer surplus with many goods

In Chapter 5, we showed how the welfare costs of changes in a single price can be measured using expenditure functions and compensated demand curves. This problem asks you to generalize this to price changes in two (or many) goods.

a. Suppose that an individual consumes n goods and that the prices of two of those goods (say, p_1 and p_2) rise. How would you use the expenditure function to measure the compensating variation (CV) for this person of such a price rise?

b. A way to show these welfare costs graphically would be to use the compensated demand curves for goods x_1 and x_2 by assuming that one price rose before the other. Illustrate this approach.

c. In your answer to part (b), would it matter in which order you considered the price changes? Explain.

d. In general, would you think that the CV for a price rise of these two goods would be greater if the goods were net substitutes or net complements? Or would the relationship between the goods have no bearing on the welfare costs?

6.10 Separable utility

A utility function is called *separable* if it can be written as

$$U(x,y) = U_1(x) + U_2(y),$$

where $U_i' > 0$, $U_i'' < 0$, and U_1, U_2 need not be the same function.

a. What does separability assume about the cross-partial derivative U_{xy}? Give an intuitive discussion of what word this condition means and in what situations it might be plausible.

b. Show that if utility is separable then neither good can be inferior.

c. Does the assumption of separability allow you to conclude definitively whether x and y are gross substitutes or gross complements? Explain.

d. Use the Cobb-Douglas utility function to show that separability is not invariant with respect to monotonic transformations. *Note:* Separable functions are examined in more detail in the Extensions to this chapter.

6.11 Graphing complements

Graphing complements is complicated because a complementary relationship between goods (under the Hicks definition) cannot occur with only two goods. Rather, complementarity necessarily involves the demand relationships among three (or more) goods. In his review of complementarity, Samuelson provides a way of illustrating the concept with a two-dimensional indifference curve diagram (see the Suggested Readings). To examine this construction, assume there are three goods that a consumer might choose. The quantities of these are denoted by x_1, x_2, x_3. Now proceed as follows.

a. Draw an indifference curve for x_2 and x_3, holding the quantity of x_1 constant at x_1^0. This indifference curve will have the customary convex shape.

b. Now draw a second (higher) indifference curve for x_2, x_3, holding x_1 constant at $x_1^0 - h$. For this new indifference curve, show the amount of extra x_2 that would compensate this person for the loss of x_1; call this amount j. Similarly, show that amount of extra x_3 that would compensate for the loss of x_1 and call this amount k.

c. Suppose now that an individual is given both amounts j and k, thereby permitting him or her to move to an even higher x_2/x_3 indifference curve. Show this move on your graph and draw this new indifference curve.

d. Samuelson now suggests the following definitions:

- If the new indifference curve corresponds to the indifference curve when $x_1 = x_1^0 - 2h$, goods 2 and 3 are independent.

- If the new indifference curve provides more utility than when $x_1 = x_1^0 - 2h$, goods 2 and 3 are complements.

- If the new indifference curve provides less utility than when $x_1 = x_1^0 - 2h$, goods 2 and 3 are substitutes.

Show that these graphical definitions are symmetric.

e. Discuss how these graphical definitions correspond to Hicks' more mathematical definitions given in the text.

f. Looking at your final graph, do you think that this approach fully explains the types of relationships that might exist between x_2 and x_3?

6.12 Shipping the good apples out

Details of the analysis suggested in Problems 6.5 and 6.6 were originally worked out by Borcherding and Silberberg (see the Suggested Readings) based on a supposition first proposed by Alchian and Allen. These authors look at how a transaction charge affects the relative demand for two closely substitutable items. Assume that goods x_2 and x_3 are close substitutes and are subject to a transaction charge of t per unit. Suppose also that good 2 is the more expensive of the two goods (i.e., "good apples" as opposed to "cooking apples"). Hence the transaction charge lowers the relative price of the more expensive good [that is, $(p_2 + t)/(p_3 + t)$ falls as t increases]. This will increase the relative demand for the expensive good if $\partial(x_2^c/x_3^c)/\partial t > 0$ (where we use compensated demand functions in order to eliminate pesky income effects). Borcherding and Silberberg show this result will probably hold using the following steps.

a. Use the derivative of a quotient rule to expand $\partial(x_2^c/x_3^c)/\partial t$.

b. Use your result from part (a) together with the fact that, in this problem, $\partial x_i^c/\partial t = \partial x_i^c/\partial p_2 + \partial x_i^c/\partial p_3$ for $i = 2, 3$, to show that the derivative we seek can be written as

$$\frac{\partial(x_2^c/x_3^c)}{\partial t} = \frac{x_2^c}{x_3^c}\left[\frac{s_{22}}{x_2} + \frac{s_{23}}{x_2} - \frac{s_{32}}{x_3} - \frac{s_{33}}{x_3}\right],$$

where $s_{ij} = \partial x_i^c/\partial p_j$.

c. Rewrite the result from part (b) in terms of compensated price elasticities:

$$e_{ij}^c = \frac{\partial x_i^c}{\partial p_j} \cdot \frac{p_j}{x_i^c}.$$

d. Use Hicks' third law (Equation 6.26) to show that the term in brackets in parts (b) and (c) can now be written as $[(e_{22} - e_{32})(1/p_2 - 1/p_3) + (e_{21} - e_{31})/p_3]$.

e. Develop an intuitive argument about why the expression in part (d) is likely to be positive under the conditions of this problem. *Hints:* Why is the first product in the brackets positive? Why is the second term in brackets likely to be small?

f. Return to Problem 6.6 and provide more complete explanations for these various findings.

SUGGESTIONS FOR FURTHER READING

Borcherding, T. E., and E. Silberberg. "Shipping the Good Apples Out—The Alchian-Allen Theorem Reconsidered," *Journal of Political Economy* (February 1978): 131–38.

> Good discussion of the relationships among three goods in demand theory. See also Problems 6.5 and 6.6.

Hicks, J. R. *Value and Capital,* 2nd ed. Oxford: Oxford University Press, 1946. See Chaps. I–III and related appendices.

> Proof of the composite commodity theorem. Also has one of the first treatments of net substitutes and complements.

Mas-Colell, A., M. D. Whinston, and J. R. Green. *Microeconomic Theory.* New York: Oxford University Press, 1995.

> Explores the consequences of the symmetry of compensated cross-price effects for various aspects of demand theory.

Rosen, S. "Hedonic Prices and Implicit Markets." *Journal of Political Economy* (January/February 1974): 34–55.

> Nice graphical and mathematical treatment of the attribute approach to consumer theory and of the concept of "markets" for attributes.

Samuelson, P. A. "Complementarity—An Essay on the 40th Anniversary of the Hicks-Allen Revolution in Demand Theory." *Journal of Economic Literature* (December 1977): 1255–89.

> Reviews a number of definitions of complementarity and shows the connections among them. Contains an intuitive, graphical discussion and a detailed mathematical appendix.

Silberberg, E., and W. Suen. *The Structure of Economics: A Mathematical Analysis,* 3rd ed. Boston: Irwin/McGraw-Hill, 2001.

> Good discussion of expenditure functions and the use of indirect utility functions to illustrate the composite commodity theorem and other results.

EXTENSIONS

Simplifying Demand and Two-Stage Budgeting

In Chapter 6 we saw that the theory of utility maximization in its full generality imposes rather few restrictions on what might happen. Other than the fact that net cross-substitution effects are symmetric, practically any type of relationship among goods is consistent with the underlying theory. This situation poses problems for economists who wish to study consumption behavior in the real world—theory just does not provide very much guidance when there are many thousands of goods potentially available for study.

There are two general ways in which simplifications are made. The first uses the composite commodity theorem from Chapter 6 to aggregate goods into categories within which relative prices move together. For situations where economists are specifically interested in changes in relative prices within a category of spending (such as changes in the relative prices of various forms of energy), this process will not do, however. An alternative is to assume that consumers engage in a two-stage process in their consumption decisions. First they allocate income to various broad groupings of goods (food, clothing, and so forth) and then, given these expenditure constraints, they maximize utility within each of the subcategories of goods using only information about those goods' relative prices. In that way, decisions can be studied in a simplified setting by looking only at one category at a time. This process is called "two-stage" budgeting. In these extensions, we first look at the general theory of two-stage budgeting and then turn to examine some empirical examples.

E6.1 Theory of two-stage budgeting

The issue that arises in two-stage budgeting can be stated succinctly: Does there exist a partition of goods into m nonoverlapping groups (denoted by $r = 1, m$) and a separate budget (I_r) devoted to each category such that the demand functions for the goods within any one category depend only on the prices of goods within the category and on the category's budget allocation? That is, can we partition goods so that demand is given by

$$x_i(p_1, \ldots, p_n, I) = x_{i \in r}(p_{i \in r}, I_r) \qquad \text{(i)}$$

for $r = 1, m, ?$ That it might be possible to do this is suggested by comparing the following two-stage maximization problem,

$$V^*(p_1, \ldots, p_n, I_1, \ldots, I_m)$$
$$= \max_{x_1, \ldots, x_n} \left[U(x_1, \ldots, x_n) \text{ s.t.} \sum_{i \in r} p_i x_i \le I_r, r = 1, m \right]$$

(ii)

and

$$\max_{I_1, \ldots, I_m} V^* \quad \text{s.t.} \quad \sum_{r=1}^{m} I_r = I,$$

to the utility-maximization problem we have been studying,

$$\max_{x_i} U(x_1, \ldots, x_n) \quad \text{s.t.} \quad \sum_{i=1}^{n} p_i x_i \le I. \qquad \text{(iii)}$$

Without any further restrictions, these two maximization processes will yield the same result; that is, Equation ii is just a more complicated way of stating Equation iii. So, some restrictions have to be placed on the utility function to ensure that the demand functions that result from solving the two-stage process will be of the form specified in Equation i. Intuitively, it seems that such a categorization of goods should work providing that changes in the price of a good in one category do not affect the allocation of spending for goods in any category other than its own. In Problem 6.9 we showed a case where this is true for an "additively separable" utility function. Unfortunately, this proves to be a very special case. The more general mathematical restrictions that must be placed on the utility function to justify two-stage budgeting have been derived (see Blackorby, Primont, and Russell, 1978), but these are not especially intuitive. Of course, economists who wish to study decentralized decisions by consumers (or, perhaps more importantly, by firms that operate many divisions) must do something to simplify matters. Now we look at a few applied examples.

E6.2 Relation to the composition commodity theorem

Unfortunately, neither of the two available theoretical approaches to demand simplification is completely satisfying. The composite commodity theorem requires that the relative prices for goods within one group remain constant over time, an assumption that has been rejected during many different historical periods.

On the other hand, the kind of separability and two-stage budgeting indicated by the utility function in Equation i also requires very strong assumptions about how changes in prices for a good in one group affect spending on goods in any other group. These assumptions appear to be rejected by the data (see Diewert and Wales, 1995).

Economists have tried to devise even more elaborate, hybrid methods of aggregation among goods. For example, Lewbel (1996) shows how the composite commodity theorem might be generalized to cases where within-group relative prices exhibit considerable variability. He uses this generalization for aggregating U.S. consumer expenditures into six large groups (food, clothing, household operation, medical care, transportation, and recreation). Using these aggregates, he concludes that his procedure is much more accurate than assuming two-stage budgeting among these expenditure categories.

E6.3 Homothetic functions and energy demand

One way to simplify the study of demand when there are many commodities is to assume that utility for certain subcategories of goods is homothetic and may be separated from the demand for other commodities. This procedure was followed by Jorgenson, Slesnick, and Stoker (1997) in their study of energy demand by U.S. consumers. By assuming that demand functions for specific types of energy are proportional to total spending on energy, the authors were able to concentrate their empirical study on the topic that is of most interest to them: estimating the price elasticities of demand for various types of energy. They conclude that most types of energy (that is, electricity, natural gas, gasoline, and so forth) have fairly elastic demand functions. Demand appears to be most responsive to price for electricity.

References

Blackorby, Charles, Daniel Primont, and R. Robert Russell. *Duality, Separability and Functional Structure: Theory and Economic Applications.* New York: North Holland, 1978.

Diewert, W. Erwin, and Terrence J. Wales. "Flexible Functional Forms and Tests of Homogeneous Separability." *Journal of Econometrics* (June 1995): 259–302.

Jorgenson, Dale W., Daniel T. Slesnick, and Thomas M. Stoker. "Two-Stage Budgeting and Consumer Demand for Energy." In Dale W. Jorgenson, Ed., *Welfare*, vol. 1: *Aggregate Consumer Behavior*, pp. 475–510. Cambridge, MA: MIT Press, 1997.

Lewbel, Arthur. "Aggregation without Separability: A Standardized Composite Commodity Theorem." *American Economic Review* (June 1996): 524–43.

Uncertainty and Information

In this chapter we will explore some of the basic elements of the theory of individual behavior in uncertain situations. Our general goal is to show why individuals do not like risk and how they may adopt strategies to reduce it. More generally, the chapter is intended to provide a brief introduction to issues raised by the possibility that information may be imperfect when individuals make utility-maximizing decisions. Some of the themes developed here will recur throughout the remainder of the book.

MATHEMATICAL STATISTICS

Many of the formal tools for modeling uncertainty in economic situations were originally developed in the field of mathematical statistics. Some of these tools were reviewed in Chapter 2 and in this chapter we will be making a great deal of use of the concepts introduced there. Specifically, four statistical ideas will recur throughout this chapter.

- *Random variable:* A random variable is a variable that records, in numerical form, the possible outcomes from some random event.[1]

- *Probability density function (PDF):* A function that shows the probabilities associated with the possible outcomes from a random variable.

- *Expected value of a random variable:* The outcome of a random variable that will occur "on average." The expected value is denoted by $E(x)$. If x is a discrete random variable with n outcomes then $E(x) = \sum_{i=1}^{n} x_i = f(x_i)$, where $f(x)$ is the PDF for the random variable x. If x is a continuous random variable, then $E(x) = \int_{-\infty}^{+\infty} x f(x)\, dx$.

- *Variance and standard deviation of a random variable:* These concepts measure the dispersion of a random variable about its expected value. In the discrete case, $\text{Var}(x) = \sigma_x^2 = \sum_{i=1}^{n} [x_i - E(x)]^2 f(x_i)$; in the continuous case, $\text{Var}(x) = \sigma_x^2 = \int_{-\infty}^{+\infty} [x - E(x)]^2 f(x)\, dx$. The standard deviation is the square root of the variance.

As we shall see, all of these concepts will come into play when we begin looking at the decision-making process of a person faced with a number of uncertain outcomes that can be conceptually represented by a random variable.

---

[1]When it is necessary to differentiate between random variables and nonrandom variables, we will use the notation $\tilde{x}$ to denote the fact that the variable x is random in that it takes on a number of potential randomly determined outcomes. Often, however, it will not be necessary to make the distinction because randomness will be clear from the context of the problem.

FAIR GAMES AND THE EXPECTED UTILITY HYPOTHESIS

A "fair game" is a random game with a specified set of prizes and associated probabilities that has an expected value of zero. For example, if you flip a coin with a friend for a dollar, the expected value of this game is zero because

$$E(x) = 0.5(+\$1) + 0.5(-\$1) = 0, \tag{7.1}$$

where wins are recorded with a plus sign and losses with a minus sign. Similarly, a game that promised to pay you $10 if a coin came up heads but would cost you only $1 if it came up tails would be "unfair" because

$$E(x) = 0.5(+\$10) + 0.5(-\$1) = \$4.50. \tag{7.2}$$

This game can easily be converted into a fair game, however, simply by charging you an entry fee of $4.50 for the right to play.[2]

It has long been recognized that most people would prefer not to play fair games. Although people may sometimes willingly flip a coin for a few dollars, they would generally balk at playing a similar game whose outcome was +$1 million or −$1 million. One of the first mathematicians to study the reasons for this unwillingness to engage in fair bets was Daniel Bernoulli in the eighteenth century.[3] His examination of the famous St. Petersburg paradox provided the starting point for virtually all studies of the behavior of individuals in uncertain situations.

St. Petersburg paradox

In the St. Petersburg paradox, the following game is proposed: A coin is flipped until a head appears. If a head first appears on the nth flip, the player is paid 2^n. This game has an infinite number of outcomes (a coin might be flipped from now until doomsday and never come up a head, although the likelihood of this is small), but the first few can easily be written down. If x_i represents the prize awarded when the first head appears on the ith trial, then

$$x_1 = \$2, \; x_2 = \$4, \; x_3 = \$8, \; ..., \; x_n = \$2^n. \tag{7.3}$$

The probability of getting a head for the first time on the ith trial is $\left(\frac{1}{2}\right)^i$; it is the probability of getting $(i-1)$ tails and then a head. Hence the probabilities of the prizes given in Equation 7.3 are

$$\pi_1 = \frac{1}{2}, \; \pi_2 = \frac{1}{4}, \; \pi_3 = \frac{1}{8}, \; ..., \; \pi_n = \frac{1}{2^n}. \tag{7.4}$$

The expected value of the St. Petersburg paradox game is therefore infinite:

$$E(x) = \sum_{i=1}^{\infty} \pi_i x_i = \sum_{i=1}^{\infty} 2^i (1/2^i)$$
$$= 1 + 1 + 1 + \cdots + 1 + \cdots = \infty. \tag{7.5}$$

Some introspection, however, should convince anyone that no player would pay very much (much less than infinity) to play this game. If I charged $1 billion to play the game, I would surely have no takers, despite the fact that $1 billion is still considerably less than the expected value of the game. This, then, is the paradox: Bernoulli's game is in some sense not worth its (infinite) expected dollar value.

---

[2]The games discussed here are assumed to yield no utility in their play other than the prizes; hence, the observation that many individuals gamble at "unfair" odds is not necessarily a refutation of this statement. Rather, such individuals can reasonably be assumed to be deriving some utility from the circumstances associated with the play of the game. It is therefore possible to differentiate the consumption aspect of gambling from the pure risk aspect.

[3]The original Bernoulli paper has been reprinted as D. Bernoulli, "Exposition of a New Theory on the Measurement of Risk," *Econometrica* 22 (January 1954): 23–36.

Expected utility

Bernoulli's solution to this paradox was to argue that individuals do not care directly about the dollar prizes of a game; rather, they respond to the utility these dollars provide. If we assume that the marginal utility of wealth declines as wealth increases, the St. Petersburg game may converge to a finite *expected utility* value that players would be willing to pay for the right to play. Bernoulli termed this expected utility value the *moral value* of the game because it represents how much the game is worth to the individual. Because utility may rise less rapidly than the dollar value of the prizes, it is possible that a game's moral value will fall short of its monetary expected value. Example 7.1 looks at some issues related to Bernoulli's solution.

EXAMPLE 7.1 Bernoulli's Solution to the Paradox and Its Shortcomings

Suppose, as did Bernoulli, that the utility of each prize in the St. Petersburg paradox is given by

$$U(x_i) = \ln(x_i). \tag{7.6}$$

This logarithmic utility function exhibits diminishing marginal utility (that is, $U' > 0$ but $U'' < 0$), and the expected utility value of this game converges to a finite number:

$$\textbf{expected utility} = \sum_{i=1}^{\infty} \pi_i U(x)_i$$

$$= \sum_{i=1}^{\infty} \frac{1}{2^i} \ln(2^i). \tag{7.7}$$

Some manipulation of this expression yields[4] the result that the expected utility value of this game is 1.39. An individual with this type of utility function might therefore be willing to invest resources that otherwise yield up to 1.39 units of utility (a certain wealth of about \$4 provides this utility) in purchasing the right to play this game. Assuming that the very large prizes promised by the St. Petersburg paradox encounter diminishing marginal utility therefore permitted Bernoulli to offer a solution to the paradox.

Unbounded utility. Bernoulli's solution to the St. Petersburg paradox, unfortunately, does not completely solve the problem. So long as there is no upper bound to the utility function, the paradox can be regenerated by redefining the game's prizes. For example, with the logarithmic utility function, prizes can be set as $x_i = e^{2^i}$, in which case

$$U(x_i) = \ln[e^{2^i}] = 2^i \tag{7.8}$$

and the expected utility value of the game would again be infinite. Of course, the prizes in this redefined game are very large. For example, if a head first appears on the fifth flip, a person would win $e^{2^5} = e^{32} = \$7.9 \cdot 10^{13}$, though the probability of winning this would be only $1/2^5 = 0.031$. The idea that people would pay a great deal (say, billions of dollars) to play games with small probabilities of such large prizes seems, to many observers, to be unlikely. Hence, in many respects the St. Petersburg game remains a paradox.

---

[4] *Proof:*

$$\textbf{expected utility} = \sum_{i=1}^{\infty} \frac{i}{2^i} \cdot \ln 2 = \ln 2 \sum_{i=1}^{\infty} \frac{i}{2^i}.$$

But the value of this final infinite series can be shown to be 2.0. Hence, expected utility $= 2 \ln 2 = 1.39$.

QUERY: Here are two alternative solutions to the St. Petersburg paradox. For each, calculate the expected value of the original game.

1. Suppose individuals assume that any probability less than 0.01 is in fact zero.

2. Suppose that the utility from the St. Petersburg prizes is given by

$$U(x_i) = \begin{cases} x_i & \text{if } x_i \leq 1,000,000, \\ 1,000,000 & \text{if } x_i > 1,000,000. \end{cases}$$

THE VON NEUMANN–MORGENSTERN THEOREM

In their book *The Theory of Games and Economic Behavior*, John von Neumann and Oscar Morgenstern developed mathematical models for examining the economic behavior of individuals under conditions of uncertainty.[5] To understand these interactions, it was necessary first to investigate the motives of the participants in such "games." Because the hypothesis that individuals make choices in uncertain situations based on expected utility seemed intuitively reasonable, the authors set out to show that this hypothesis could be derived from more basic axioms of "rational" behavior. The axioms represent an attempt by the authors to generalize the foundations of the theory of individual choice to cover uncertain situations. Although most of these axioms seem eminently reasonable at first glance, many important questions about their tenability have been raised. We will not pursue these questions here, however.[6]

The von Neumann–Morgenstern utility index

To begin, suppose that there are n possible prizes that an individual might win by participating in a lottery. Let these prizes be denoted by $x_1, x_2, \ldots, x_n$ and assume that these have been arranged in order of ascending desirability. Therefore, x_1 is the least preferred prize for the individual and x_n is the most preferred prize. Now assign arbitrary utility numbers to these two extreme prizes. For example, it is convenient to assign

$$\begin{aligned} U(x_1) &= 0, \\ U(x_n) &= 1, \end{aligned} \tag{7.9}$$

but any other pair of numbers would do equally well.[7] Using these two values of utility, the point of the von Neumann–Morgenstern theorem is to show that a reasonable way exists to assign specific utility numbers to the other prizes available. Suppose that we choose any other prize, say, x_i. Consider the following experiment. Ask the individual to state the probability, say, π_i, at which he or she would be indifferent between x_i with *certainty*, and a *gamble* offering prizes of x_n with probability π_i and x_1 with probability $(1 - \pi_i)$. It seems reasonable (although this is the most problematic assumption in the von Neumann–Morgenstern approach) that such a probability will exist: The individual will always be indifferent between a gamble and a sure thing, provided that a high enough probability of winning the best prize is offered. It also seems likely that π_i will be higher the more desirable x_i is; the better x_i is, the

---

[5]J. von Neumann and O. Morgenstern, *The Theory of Games and Economic Behavior* (Princeton, NJ: Princeton University Press, 1944). The axioms of rationality in uncertain situations are discussed in the book's appendix.

[6]For a discussion of some of the issues raised in the debate over the von Neumann–Morgenstern axioms, especially the assumption of independence, see C. Gollier, *The Economics of Risk and Time* (Cambridge, MA: MIT Press, 2001), chap. 1.

[7]Technically, a von Neumann–Morgenstern utility index is unique only up to a choice of scale and origin—that is, only up to a "linear transformation." This requirement is more stringent than the requirement that a utility function be unique up to a monotonic transformation.

better the chance of winning x_n must be to get the individual to gamble. The probability π_i therefore measures how desirable the prize x_i is. In fact, the von Neumann–Morgenstern technique is to define the utility of x_i as the expected utility of the gamble that the individual considers equally desirable to x_i:

$$U(x_i) = \pi_i \cdot U(x_n) + (1 - \pi_i) \cdot U(x_1). \tag{7.10}$$

Because of our choice of scale in Equation 7.9, we have

$$U(x_i) = \pi_i \cdot 1 + (1 - \pi_i) \cdot 0 = \pi_i. \tag{7.11}$$

By judiciously choosing the utility numbers to be assigned to the best and worst prizes, we have been able to devise a scale under which the utility number attached to any other prize is simply the probability of winning the top prize in a gamble the individual regards as equivalent to the prize in question. This choice of utility numbers is arbitrary. Any other two numbers could have been used to construct this utility scale, but our initial choice (Equation 7.9) is a particularly convenient one.

Expected utility maximization

In line with the choice of scale and origin represented by Equation 7.9, suppose that probability π_i has been assigned to represent the utility of every prize x_i. Notice in particular that $\pi_1 = 0, \pi_n = 1$, and that the other utility values range between these extremes. Using these utility numbers, we can show that a "rational" individual will choose among gambles based on their expected "utilities" (that is, based on the expected value of these von Neumann–Morgenstern utility index numbers).

As an example, consider two gambles. One gamble offers x_2, with probability q, and x_3, with probability $(1 - q)$. The other offers x_5, with probability t, and x_6, with probability $(1 - t)$. We want to show that this person will choose gamble 1 if and only if the expected utility of gamble 1 exceeds that of gamble 2. Now for the gambles:

$$\text{expected utility (1)} = q \cdot U(x_2) + (1 - q) \cdot U(x_3),$$
$$\text{expected utility (2)} = t \cdot U(x_5) + (1 - t) \cdot U(x_6). \tag{7.12}$$

Substituting the utility index numbers (that is, π_2 is the "utility" of x_2, and so forth) gives

$$\text{expected utility}(1) = q \cdot \pi_2 + (1 - q) \cdot \pi_3,$$
$$\text{expected utility}(2) = t \cdot \pi_5 + (1 - t) \cdot \pi_6. \tag{7.13}$$

We wish to show that the individual will prefer gamble 1 to gamble 2 if and only if

$$q \cdot \pi_2 + (1 - q) \cdot \pi_3 > t \cdot \pi_5 + (1 - t) \cdot \pi_6. \tag{7.14}$$

To show this, recall the definitions of the utility index. The individual is indifferent between x_2 and a gamble promising x_1 with probability $(1 - \pi_2)$ and x_n with probability π_2. We can use this fact to substitute gambles involving only x_1 and x_n for all utilities in Equation 7.13 (even though the individual is indifferent between these, the assumption that this substitution can be made implicitly assumes that people can see through complex lottery combinations). After a bit of messy algebra, we can conclude that gamble 1 is equivalent to a gamble promising x_n with probability $q\pi_2 + (1 - q)\pi_3$, and gamble 2 is equivalent to a gamble promising x_n with probability $t\pi_5 + (1 - t)\pi_6$. The individual will presumably prefer the gamble with the higher probability of winning the best prize. Consequently, he or she will choose gamble 1 if and only if

$$q\pi_2 + (1 - q)\pi_3 > t\pi_5 + (1 - t)\pi_6. \tag{7.15}$$

But this is precisely what we wanted to show. Consequently, we have proved that an individual will choose the gamble that provides the highest level of expected (von Neumann–Morgenstern) utility. We now make considerable use of this result, which can be summarized as follows.

Expected utility maximization. If individuals obey the von Neumann–Morgenstern axioms of behavior in uncertain situations, they will act as if they choose the option that maximizes the expected value of their von Neumann–Morgenstern utility index.

OPTIMIZATION PRINCIPLE

RISK AVERSION

Two lotteries may have the same expected monetary value but may differ in their riskiness. For example, flipping a coin for $1 and flipping a coin for $1,000 are both fair games, and both have the same expected value (0). However, the latter is in some sense more "risky" than the former, and fewer people would participate in the game where the prize was winning or losing $1,000. The purpose of this section is to discuss the meaning of the term *risky* and explain the widespread aversion to risk.

The term *risk* refers to the variability of the outcomes of some uncertain activity.[8] If variability is low, the activity may be approximately a sure thing. With no more precise notion of variability than this, it is possible to show why individuals, when faced with a choice between two gambles with the same expected value, will usually choose the one with a smaller variability of return. Intuitively, the reason behind this is that we usually assume that the marginal utility from extra dollars of prize money (that is, wealth) declines as the prizes get larger. A flip of a coin for $1,000 promises a relatively small gain of utility if you win but a large loss of utility if you lose. A bet of only $1 is "inconsequential," and the gain in utility from a win approximately counterbalances the decline in utility from a loss.[9]

Risk aversion and fair bets

This argument is illustrated in Figure 7.1. Here W^* represents an individual's current wealth and $U(W)$ is a von Neumann–Morgenstern utility index that reflects how he or she feels about various levels of wealth.[10] In the figure, $U(W)$ is drawn as a concave function of W to reflect the assumption of a diminishing marginal utility. It is assumed that obtaining an extra dollar adds less to enjoyment as total wealth increases. Now suppose this person is offered two fair gambles: a 50–50 chance of winning or losing h or a 50–50 chance of winning or losing $2h$. The utility of present wealth is $U(W^*)$. The expected utility if he or she participates in gamble 1 is given by $U^h(W^*)$:

$$U^h(W^*) = \frac{1}{2}U(W^* + h) + \frac{1}{2}U(W^* - h), \qquad (7.16)$$

and the expected utility of gamble 2 is given by $U^{2h}(W^*)$:

$$U^{2h}(W^*) = \frac{1}{2}U(W^* + 2h) + \frac{1}{2}U(W^* - 2h). \qquad (7.17)$$

It is geometrically clear from the figure that[11]

$$U(W^*) > U^h(W^*) > U^{2h}(W^*). \qquad (7.18)$$

---

[8]Often the statistical concepts of variance and standard deviation are used to measure risk. We will do so at several places later in this chapter.

[9]Technically, this result is a direct consequence of Jensen's inequality in mathematical statistics. The inequality states that if x is a random variable and $f(x)$ is a concave function of that variable, then $E[f(x)] \leq f[E(x)]$. In the utility context, this means that if utility is concave in a random variable measuring wealth (i.e., if $U'(W) > 0$ and $U''(W) < 0$), then the expected utility of wealth will be less than the utility associated with the expected value of W.

[10]Technically, $U(W)$ is an indirect utility function because it is the consumption allowed by wealth that provides direct utility. In Chapter 17 we will take up the relationship between consumption-based utility functions and their implied indirect utility of wealth functions.

[11]To see why the expected utilities for bet h and bet $2h$ are those shown, notice that these expected utilities are the average of the utilities from a favorable and an unfavorable outcome. Because W^* is halfway between $W^* + h$ and $W^* - h$, U^* is also halfway between $U(W^* + h)$ and $U(W^* - h)$.

FIGURE 7.1 Utility of Wealth from Two Fair Bets of Differing Variability

If the utility-of-wealth function is concave (i.e., exhibits a diminishing marginal utility of wealth), then this person will refuse fair bets. A 50–50 bet of winning or losing h dollars, for example, yields less utility $[U^h(W^*)]$ than does refusing the bet. The reason for this is that winning h dollars means less to this individual than does losing h dollars.

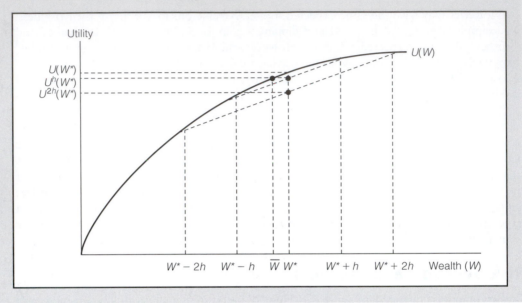

This person therefore will prefer his or her current wealth to that wealth combined with a fair gamble and will prefer a small gamble to a large one. The reason for this is that winning a fair bet adds to enjoyment less than losing hurts. Although in this case the prizes are equal, winning provides less than losing costs in utility terms.

Risk aversion and insurance

As a matter of fact, this person might be willing to pay some amount to avoid participating in any gamble at all. Notice that a certain wealth of $\overline{W}$ provides the same utility as does participating in gamble 1. This person would be willing to pay up to $W^* - \overline{W}$ in order to avoid participating in the gamble. This explains why people buy insurance. They are giving up a small, certain amount (the insurance premium) to avoid the risky outcome they are being insured against. The premium a person pays for automobile collision insurance, for example, provides a policy that agrees to repair his or her car should an accident occur. The widespread use of insurance would seem to imply that aversion to risk is quite prevalent. Hence, we introduce the following definition.

DEFINITION | **Risk aversion.** An individual who always refuses fair bets is said to be *risk averse*. If individuals exhibit a diminishing marginal utility of wealth, they will be risk averse. As a consequence, they will be willing to pay something to avoid taking fair bets.

EXAMPLE 7.2 Willingness to Pay for Insurance

To illustrate the connection between risk aversion and insurance, consider a person with a current wealth of $100,000 who faces the prospect of a 25 percent chance of losing his or her $20,000 automobile through theft during the next year. Suppose also that this person's von Neumann–Morgenstern utility index is logarithmic; that is, $U(W) = \ln(W)$.

If this person faces next year without insurance, expected utility will be

$$\textbf{expected utility} = 0.75\,U(100{,}000) + 0.25\,U(80{,}000)$$
$$= 0.75 \ln 100{,}000 + 0.25 \ln 80{,}000$$
$$= 11.45714. \qquad \textbf{(7.19)}$$

In this situation, a fair insurance premium would be $5,000 (25 percent of $20,000, assuming that the insurance company has only claim costs and that administrative costs are $0). Consequently, if this person completely insures the car, his or her wealth will be $95,000 regardless of whether the car is stolen. In this case, then,

$$\textbf{expected utility} = U(95{,}000)$$
$$= \ln(95{,}000)$$
$$= 11.46163. \qquad \textbf{(7.20)}$$

This person is made better-off by purchasing fair insurance. Indeed, we can determine the maximum amount that might be paid for this insurance protection (x) by setting

$$\textbf{expected utility} = U(100{,}000 - x)$$
$$= \ln(100{,}000 - x)$$
$$= 11.45714. \qquad \textbf{(7.21)}$$

Solving this equation for x yields

$$100{,}000 - x = e^{11.45714}. \qquad \textbf{(7.22)}$$

Therefore, the maximum premium is

$$x = 5{,}426. \qquad \textbf{(7.23)}$$

This person would be willing to pay up to $426 in administrative costs to an insurance company (in addition to the $5,000 premium to cover the expected value of the loss). Even when these costs are paid, this person is as well-off as he or she would be when facing the world uninsured.

QUERY: Suppose utility had been linear in wealth. Would this person be willing to pay anything more than the actuarially fair amount for insurance? How about the case where utility is a convex function of wealth?

MEASURING RISK AVERSION

In the study of economic choices in risky situations, it is sometimes convenient to have a quantitative measure of how averse to risk a person is. The most commonly used measure of risk aversion was initially developed by J. W. Pratt in the 1960s.[12] This risk aversion measure, $r(W)$, is defined as

$$r(W) = -\frac{U''(W)}{U'(W)}. \qquad \textbf{(7.24)}$$

Because the distinguishing feature of risk-averse individuals is a diminishing marginal utility of wealth $[U''(W) < 0]$, Pratt's measure is positive in such cases. The measure is invariant with respect to linear transformations of the utility function, and therefore not affected by which particular von Neumann–Morgenstern ordering is used.

---

[12]J. W. Pratt, "Risk Aversion in the Small and in the Large," *Econometrica* (January/April 1964): 122–36.

Risk aversion and insurance premiums

A useful feature of the Pratt measure of risk aversion is that it is proportional to the amount an individual will pay for insurance against taking a fair bet. Suppose the winnings from such a fair bet are denoted by the random variable h (this variable may be either positive or negative). Because the bet is fair, $E(h) = 0$. Now let p be the size of the insurance premium that would make the individual exactly indifferent between taking the fair bet h and paying p with certainty to avoid the gamble:

$$E[U(W + h)] = U(W - p), \tag{7.25}$$

where W is the individual's current wealth. We now expand both sides of Equation 7.25 using Taylor's series.[13] Because p is a fixed amount, a linear approximation to the right-hand side of the equation will suffice:

$$U(W - p) = U(W) - pU'(W) + \textbf{higher-order terms}. \tag{7.26}$$

For the left-hand side, we need a quadratic approximation to allow for the variability in the gamble, h:

$$E[U(W + h)] = E\left[U(W) + hU'(W) + \frac{h^2}{2}U''(W)\right.$$
$$\left. + \textbf{higher-order terms}\right] \tag{7.27}$$

$$= U(W) + E(h)U'(W) + \frac{E(h^2)}{2}U''(W)$$
$$+ \textbf{higher-order terms}. \tag{7.28}$$

If we recall that $E(h) = 0$ and then drop the higher-order terms and use the constant k to represent $E(h^2)/2$, we can equate Equations 7.26 and 7.28 as

$$U(W) - pU'(W) \cong U(W) + kU''(W) \tag{7.29}$$

or

$$p \cong -\frac{kU''(W)}{U'(W)} = kr(W). \tag{7.30}$$

That is, the amount that a risk-averse individual is willing to pay to avoid a fair bet is approximately proportional to Pratt's risk aversion measure.[14] Because insurance premiums paid are observable in the real world, these are often used to estimate individuals' risk aversion coefficients or to compare such coefficients among groups of individuals. It is therefore possible to use market information to learn quite a bit about attitudes toward risky situations.

Risk aversion and wealth

An important question is whether risk aversion increases or decreases with wealth. Intuitively, one might think that the willingness to pay to avoid a given fair bet would decline as wealth increases, because diminishing marginal utility would make potential losses less serious for high-wealth individuals. This intuitive answer is not necessarily correct, however, because diminishing marginal utility also makes the gains from winning gambles less attractive. So the

---

[13]Taylor's series provides a way of approximating any differentiable function around some point. If $f(x)$ has derivatives of all orders, it can be shown that

$$f(x + h) = f(x) + hf'(x) + (h^2/2)f''(x) + \textbf{higher-order terms}.$$

The point-slope formula in algebra is a simple example of Taylor's series.

[14]In this case, the factor of proportionality is also proportional to the variance of h because $\text{Var}(h) = E[h - E(h)]^2 = E(h^2)$. For an illustration where this equation fits exactly, see Example 7.3.

net result is indeterminate; it all depends on the precise shape of the utility function. Indeed, if utility is quadratic in wealth,

$$U(W) = a + bW + cW^2, \tag{7.31}$$

where $b > 0$ and $c < 0$, then Pratt's risk aversion measure is

$$r(W) = -\frac{U''(W)}{U'(W)} = \frac{-2c}{b + 2cW}, \tag{7.32}$$

which, contrary to intuition, increases as wealth increases.

On the other hand, if utility is logarithmic in wealth,

$$U(W) = \ln(W) \quad (W > 0), \tag{7.33}$$

then we have

$$r(W) = -\frac{U''(W)}{U'(W)} = \frac{1}{W}, \tag{7.34}$$

which does indeed decrease as wealth increases.

The exponential utility function

$$U(W) = -e^{-AW} = -\exp(-AW) \tag{7.35}$$

(where A is a positive constant) exhibits constant absolute risk aversion over all ranges of wealth, because now

$$r(W) = -\frac{U''(W)}{U'(W)} = \frac{A^2 e^{-AW}}{Ae^{-AW}} = A. \tag{7.36}$$

This feature of the exponential utility function[15] can be used to provide some numerical estimates of the willingness to pay to avoid gambles, as the next example shows.

EXAMPLE 7.3 Constant Risk Aversion

Suppose an individual whose initial wealth is W_0 and whose utility function exhibits constant absolute risk aversion is facing a 50–50 chance of winning or losing \$1,000. How much (f) would he or she pay to avoid the risk? To find this value, we set the utility of $W_0 - f$ equal to the expected utility from the gamble:

$$-\exp[-A(W_0 - f)] = -0.5\exp[-A(W_0 + 1{,}000)]$$
$$-0.5\exp[-A(W_0 - 1{,}000)]. \tag{7.37}$$

Because the factor $-\exp(-AW_0)$ is contained in all of the terms in Equation 7.37, this may be divided out, thereby showing that (for the exponential utility function) the willingness to pay to avoid a given gamble is independent of initial wealth. The remaining terms

$$\exp(Af) = 0.5\exp(-1{,}000A) + 0.5\exp(1{,}000A) \tag{7.38}$$

can now be used to solve for f for various values of A. If $A = 0.0001$, then $f = 49.9$; a person with this degree of risk aversion would pay about \$50 to avoid a fair bet of \$1,000. Alternatively, if $A = 0.0003$, this more risk-averse person would pay $f = 147.8$ to avoid the gamble. Because intuition suggests that these values are not unreasonable, values of the risk aversion parameter A in these ranges are sometimes used for empirical investigations.

(continued)

---

[15]Because the exponential utility function exhibits constant (absolute) risk aversion, it is sometimes abbreviated by the term *CARA utility*.

EXAMPLE 7.3 CONTINUED

A normally distributed risk. The constant risk aversion utility function can be combined with the assumption that a person faces a random threat to his or her wealth that follows a normal distribution (see Chapter 2) to arrive at a particularly simple result. Specifically, if a person's risky wealth follows a normal distribution with mean μ_W and variance σ_W^2, then the probability density function for wealth is given by $f(W) = (1/\sqrt{2\pi})e^{-z^2/2}$, where $z = [(W - \mu_W)/\sigma_W]$. If this person has a utility function for wealth given by $U(W) = -e^{-AW}$, then expected utility from his or her risky wealth is given by

$$E[U(W)] = \int_{-\infty}^{\infty} U(W)f(W)\,dW = \frac{1}{\sqrt{2\pi}}\int -e^{-AW}e^{-[(W-\mu_W)/\sigma_W]^2/2}\,dW. \qquad \textbf{(7.39)}$$

Perhaps surprisingly, this integration is not too difficult to accomplish, though it does take patience. Performing this integration and taking a variety of monotonic transformations of the resulting expression yields the final result that

$$E[U(W)] \cong \mu_W - \frac{A}{2}\cdot\sigma_W^2. \qquad \textbf{(7.40)}$$

Hence, expected utility is a linear function of the two parameters of the wealth probability density function, and the individual's risk aversion parameter (A) determines the size of the negative effect of variability on expected utility. For example, suppose a person has invested his or her funds so that wealth has an expected value of \$100,000 but a standard deviation (σ_W) of \$10,000. With the Normal distribution, he or she might therefore expect wealth to decline below \$83,500 about 5 percent of the time and rise above \$116,500 a similar fraction of the time. With these parameters, expected utility is given by $E[U(W)] = 100,000 - (A/2)(10,000)^2$. If $A = 0.0001 = 10^{-4}$, expected utility is given by $100,0000 - 0.5 \cdot 10^{-4} \cdot (10^4)^2 = 95,000$. Hence, this person receives the same utility from his or her risky wealth as would be obtained from a certain wealth of \$95,000. A more risk-averse person might have $A = 0.0003$ and in this case the "certainty equivalent" of his or her wealth would be \$85,000.

QUERY: Suppose this person had two ways to invest his or her wealth: Allocation 1, $\mu_W = 107,000$ and $\sigma_W = 10,000$; Allocation 2, $\mu_W = 102,000$ and $\sigma_W = 2,000$. How would this person's attitude toward risk affect his or her choice between these allocations?[16]

Relative risk aversion

It seems unlikely that the willingness to pay to avoid a given gamble is independent of a person's wealth. A more appealing assumption may be that such willingness to pay is inversely proportional to wealth and that the expression

$$rr(W) = Wr(W) = -W\frac{U''(W)}{U'(W)} \qquad \textbf{(7.41)}$$

might be approximately constant. Following the terminology proposed by J. W. Pratt,[17] the $rr(W)$ function defined in Equation 7.41 is a measure of *relative risk aversion*. The power utility function

---

[16]This numerical example (very roughly) approximates historical data on real returns of stocks and bonds, respectively, though the calculations are illustrative only.

[17]Pratt, "Risk Aversion."

$$U(W) = \frac{W^R}{R} \quad (R < 1, \; R \neq 0) \tag{7.42}$$

and

$$U(W) = \ln W \quad (R = 0)$$

exhibits diminishing absolute risk aversion,

$$r(W) = -\frac{U''(W)}{U'(W)} = -\frac{(R-1)W^{R-2}}{W^{R-1}} = -\frac{(R-1)}{W}, \tag{7.43}$$

but constant relative risk aversion:

$$rr(W) = Wr(W) = -(R-1) = 1 - R. \tag{7.44}$$

Empirical evidence[18] is generally consistent with values of R in the range of -3 to -1. Hence, individuals seem to be somewhat more risk averse than is implied by the logarithmic utility function, though in many applications that function provides a reasonable approximation. It is useful to note that the constant relative risk aversion utility function in Equation 7.42 has the same form as the general CES utility function we first described in Chapter 3. This provides some geometric intuition about the nature of risk aversion that we will explore later in this chapter.

EXAMPLE 7.4 Constant Relative Risk Aversion

An individual whose behavior is characterized by a constant relative risk aversion utility function will be concerned about proportional gains or loss of wealth. We can therefore ask what fraction of initial wealth (f) such a person would be willing to give up to avoid a fair gamble of, say, 10 percent of initial wealth. First, we assume $R = 0$, so the logarithmic utility function is appropriate. Setting the utility of this individual's certain remaining wealth equal to the expected utility of the 10 percent gamble yields

$$\ln[(1-f)W_0] = 0.5 \ln(1.1 W_0) + 0.5 \ln(0.9 W_0). \tag{7.45}$$

Because each term contains $\ln W_0$, initial wealth can be eliminated from this expression:

$$\ln(1-f) = 0.5[\ln(1.1) + \ln(0.9)] = \ln(0.99)^{0.5};$$

hence

$$(1-f) = (0.99)^{0.5} = 0.995$$

and

$$f = 0.005. \tag{7.46}$$

This person will thus sacrifice up to 0.5 percent of wealth to avoid the 10 percent gamble. A similar calculation can be used for the case $R = -2$ to yield

$$f = 0.015. \tag{7.47}$$

Hence this more risk-averse person would be willing to give up 1.5 percent of his or her initial wealth to avoid a 10 percent gamble.

QUERY: With the constant relative risk aversion function, how does this person's willingness to pay to avoid a given absolute gamble (say, of 1,000) depend on his or her initial wealth?

---

[18]Some authors write the utility function in Equation 7.42 as $U(W) = W^{1-a}/(1-a)$ and seek to measure $a = 1 - R$. In this case, a is the relative risk aversion measure. The constant relative risk aversion function is sometimes abbreviated as CRRA.

THE PORTFOLIO PROBLEM

One of the classic problems in the theory of behavior under uncertainty is the issue of how much of his or her wealth a risk-averse investor should invest in a risky asset. Intuitively, it seems that the fraction invested in risky assets should be smaller for more risk-averse investors, and one goal of our analysis will be to show that formally. To get started, assume that an investor has a certain amount of wealth, W_0, to invest in one of two assets. The first asset yields a certain return of r_f, whereas the second asset's return is a random variable, $\tilde{r}$. If we let the amount invested in the risky asset be denoted by k, then this person's wealth at the end of one period will be

$$W = (W_0 - k)(1 + r_f) + k(1 + \tilde{r}) = W_0(1 + r_f) + k(\tilde{r} - r_f). \qquad \textbf{(7.48)}$$

Notice three things about this end-of-period wealth. First, W is a random variable because its value depends on $\tilde{r}$. Second, k can be either positive or negative here depending on whether this person buys the risky asset or sells it short. As we shall see, however, in the usual case $E(\tilde{r} - r_f) > 0$ and this will imply $k \geq 0$. Finally, notice also that Equation 7.48 allows for a solution in which $k > W_0$. In this case, this investor would leverage his or her investment in the risky asset by borrowing at the risk-free rate r_f.

If we let $U(W)$ represent this investor's utility function, then the von Neumann–Morgenstern theorem states that he or she will choose k to maximize $E[U(W)]$. The first-order condition for such a maximum is[19]

$$\frac{\partial E[U(W)]}{\partial k} = \frac{\partial E[U(W_0(1 + r_f) + k(\tilde{r} - r_f))]}{\partial k} = E[U' \cdot (\tilde{r} - r_f)] = 0. \qquad \textbf{(7.49)}$$

Because this first-order condition lies at the heart of many problems in the theory of uncertainty, it may be worthwhile spending some time to understand it intuitively. Equation 7.49 is looking at the expected value of the product of marginal utility and the term $\tilde{r} - r_f$. Both of these terms are random. Whether $\tilde{r} - r_f$ is positive or negative will depend on how well the risky assets perform over the next period. But the return on this risky asset will also affect this investor's end-of-period wealth and thus will affect his or her marginal utility. If the investment does well, W will be large and marginal utility will be relatively low (because of diminishing marginal utility). If the investment does poorly, wealth will be relatively low and marginal utility will be relatively high. Hence, in the expected value calculation in Equation 7.49, negative outcomes for $\tilde{r} - r_f$ will be weighted more heavily than positive outcomes to take the utility consequences of these outcomes into account. If the expected value in Equation 7.49 were positive, a person could increase his or her expected utility by investing more in the risky asset. If the expected value were negative, he or she could increase expected utility by reducing the amount of the risky asset held. Only when the first-order condition holds will this person have an optimal portfolio.

Two other conclusions can be drawn from the optimality condition in Equation 7.49. First, so long as $E(\tilde{r} - r_f) > 0$, an investor will choose positive amounts of the risky asset. To see why, notice that meeting Equation 7.49 will require that fairly large values of U' be attached to situations where $\tilde{r} - r_f$ turns out to be negative. That can only happen if the investor owns positive amounts of the risky asset so that end-of-period wealth is low in such situations.

A second conclusion from the first-order condition in Equation 7.49 is that investors who are more risk averse will hold smaller amounts of the risky asset than will investors who are more tolerant of risk. Again, the reason relates to the shape of the U' function. For very risk-averse investors, marginal utility rises rapidly as wealth falls. Hence, they need relatively little exposure to potential negative outcomes from holding the risky asset to satisfy

---

[19]In calculating this first-order condition, we can differentiate through the expected value operator. See Chapter 2 for a discussion of differentiating integrals.

Equation 7.49. Investors who are more tolerant of risk will find that U' rises less rapidly when the risky asset performs poorly, so they will be willing to hold more of it.

In summary, then, a formal study of the portfolio problem confirms simple intuitions about how people choose to invest. To make further progress on the question requires that we make some specific assumptions about the investor's utility function. In Example 7.5, we look at a two examples.

EXAMPLE 7.5 The Portfolio Problem with Specific Utility Functions

In this problem we show the implications of assuming either CARA or CRRA utility for the solution to the portfolio allocation problem.

1. CARA Utility. If $U(W) = -\exp(-AW)$ then the marginal utility function is given by $U'(W) = A \exp(-AW)$; substituting for end-of-period wealth, we have

$$U'(W) = A \exp[-A(W_0(1 + r_f) + k(\tilde{r} - r_f))]$$
$$= A \exp[-AW_0(1 + r_f)] \exp[-Ak(\tilde{r} - r_f)]. \qquad \textbf{(7.50)}$$

That is, the marginal utility function can be separated into a random part and a nonrandom part (both initial wealth and the risk-free rate are nonrandom). Hence, the optimality condition from Equation 7.49 can be written as

$$E[U' \cdot (\tilde{r} - r_f)] = A \exp[-AW_0(1 + r_f)] E[\exp(-Ak(\tilde{r} - r_f)) \cdot (\tilde{r} - r_f)] = 0. \qquad \textbf{(7.51)}$$

Now we can divide by the exponential function of initial wealth, leaving an optimality condition that involves only terms in k, A, and $\tilde{r} - r_f$. Solving this condition for the optimal level of k can in general be quite difficult (but see Problem 7.14). Regardless of the specific solution, however, Equation 7.51 shows that this optimal investment amount will be a constant regardless of the level of initial wealth. Hence, the CARA function implies that the fraction of wealth that an investor holds in risky assets should decline as wealth increases—a conclusion that seems precisely contrary to empirical data, which tend to show the fraction of wealth held in risky assets rising with wealth.

2. CRRA Utility. If $U(W) = W^R / R$ then the marginal utility function is given by $U'(W) = W^{R-1}$. Substituting the expression for final wealth into this equation yields

$$U'(W) = [W_0(1 + r_f) + k(\tilde{r} - r_f)]^{R-1}$$
$$= [W_0(1 + r_f)]^{R-1} \left[1 + \frac{k}{W_0(1 + r_f)} \cdot (\tilde{r} - r_f)\right]. \qquad \textbf{(7.52)}$$

Inserting this expression into the optimality condition in Equation 7.49 shows that the term $[W_0(1 + r_f)]^{R-1}$ can be canceled out, implying that the optimal solution will not involve the absolute level of initial wealth but only the ratio $k/W_0(1 + r_f)$. In words, the CRRA utility function implies that all individuals with the same risk tolerance will hold the same fraction of wealth in risky assets, regardless of their absolute levels of wealth. Though this conclusion is slightly more in accord with the facts than is the conclusion from the CARA function, it still falls short of explaining why the fraction of wealth held in risky assets tends to rise with wealth.

QUERY: Can you suggest a reason why investors might increase the proportion of their portfolios invested in risky assets as wealth increases even though their preferences are characterized by the CRRA utility function?

THE STATE-PREFERENCE APPROACH TO CHOICE UNDER UNCERTAINTY

Although our analysis in this chapter has offered insights on a number of issues, it seems rather different from the approach we took in other chapters. The basic model of utility maximization subject to a budget constraint seems to have been lost. In order to make further progress in the study of behavior under uncertainty, we will therefore develop some new techniques that will permit us to bring the discussion of such behavior back into the standard choice-theoretic framework.

States of the world and contingent commodities

We start by assuming that the outcomes of any random event can be categorized into a number of *states of the world*. We cannot predict exactly what will happen, say, tomorrow, but we assume that it is possible to categorize all of the possible things that might happen into a fixed number of well-defined *states*. For example, we might make the very crude approximation of saying that the world will be in only one of two possible states tomorrow: It will be either "good times" or "bad times." One could make a much finer gradation of states of the world (involving even millions of possible states), but most of the essentials of the theory can be developed using only two states.

A conceptual idea that can be developed concurrently with the notion of states of the world is that of *contingent commodities*. These are goods delivered only if a particular state of the world occurs. As an example, "$1 in good times" is a contingent commodity that promises the individual $1 in good times but nothing should tomorrow turn out to be bad times. It is even possible, by stretching one's intuitive ability somewhat, to conceive of being able to purchase this commodity: I might be able to buy from someone the promise of $1 if tomorrow turns out to be good times. Because tomorrow could be bad, this good will probably sell for less than $1. If someone were also willing to sell me the contingent commodity "$1 in bad times," then I could assure myself of having $1 tomorrow by buying the two contingent commodities "$1 in good times" and "$1 in bad times."

Utility analysis

Examining utility-maximizing choices among contingent commodities proceeds formally in much the same way we analyzed choices previously. The principal difference is that, after the fact, a person will have obtained only one contingent good (depending on whether it turns out to be good or bad times). Before the uncertainty is resolved, however, the individual has two contingent goods from which to choose and will probably buy some of each because he or she does not know which state will occur. We denote these two contingent goods by W_g (wealth in good times) and W_b (wealth in bad times). Assuming that utility is independent of which state occurs[20] and that this individual believes that good times will occur with probability π, the expected utility associated with these two contingent goods is

$$V(W_g, W_b) = \pi U(W_g) + (1 - \pi) U(W_b). \tag{7.53}$$

This is the magnitude this individual seeks to maximize given his or her initial wealth, W.

---

[20]This assumption is untenable in circumstances where utility of wealth depends on the state of the world. For example, the utility provided by a given level of wealth may differ depending on whether an individual is "sick" or "healthy." We will not pursue such complications here, however. For most of our analysis, utility is assumed to be concave in wealth: $U'(W) > 0, U''(W) < 0$.

Prices of contingent commodities

Assuming that this person can purchase a dollar of wealth in good times for p_g and a dollar of wealth in bad times for p_b, his or her budget constraint is then

$$W = p_g W_g + p_b W_b. \tag{7.54}$$

The price ratio p_g/p_b shows how this person can trade dollars of wealth in good times for dollars in bad times. If, for example, $p_g = 0.80$ and $p_b = 0.20$, the sacrifice of \$1 of wealth in good times would permit this person to buy contingent claims yielding \$4 of wealth should times turn out to be bad. Whether such a trade would improve utility will, of course, depend on the specifics of the situation. But looking at problems involving uncertainty as situations in which various contingent claims are traded is the key insight offered by the state-preference model.

Fair markets for contingent goods

If markets for contingent wealth claims are well developed and there is general agreement about the likelihood of good times (π), then prices for these claims will be actuarially fair—that is, they will equal the underlying probabilities:

$$p_g = \pi,$$
$$p_b = (1 - \pi). \tag{7.55}$$

Hence, the price ratio p_g/p_b will simply reflect the odds in favor of good times:

$$\frac{p_g}{p_b} = \frac{\pi}{1 - \pi}. \tag{7.56}$$

In our previous example, if $p_g = \pi = 0.8$ and $p_b = (1 - \pi) = 0.2$ then $\pi/(1 - \pi) = 4$. In this case the odds in favor of good times would be stated as "4-to-1." Fair markets for contingent claims (such as insurance markets) will also reflect these odds. An analogy is provided by the "odds" quoted in horse races. These odds are "fair" when they reflect the true probabilities that various horses will win.

Risk aversion

We are now in a position to show how risk aversion is manifested in the state-preference model. Specifically, we can show that, if contingent claims markets are fair, then a utility-maximizing individual will opt for a situation in which $W_g = W_b$; that is, he or she will arrange matters so that the wealth ultimately obtained is the same no matter what state occurs.

As in previous chapters, maximization of utility subject to a budget constraint requires that this individual set the *MRS* of W_g for W_b equal to the ratio of these "goods" prices:

$$MRS = \frac{\partial V/\partial W_g}{\partial V/\partial W_b} = \frac{\pi U'(W_g)}{(1 - \pi) U'(W_b)} = \frac{p_g}{p_b}. \tag{7.57}$$

In view of the assumption that markets for contingent claims are fair (Equation 7.56), this first-order condition reduces to

$$\frac{U'(W_g)}{U'(W_b)} = 1$$

or[21]

$$W_g = W_b. \tag{7.58}$$

[21]This step requires that utility be state independent and that $U'(W) > 0$.

FIGURE 7.2 Risk Aversions in the State-Preference Model

The line I represents the individual's budget constraint for contingent wealth claims: $W = p_g W_g + p_b W_b$. If the market for contingent claims is actuarially fair $[p_g/p_b = \pi/(1 - \pi)]$, then utility maximization will occur on the certainty line where $W_g = W_b = W^*$. If prices are not actuarially fair, the budget constraint may resemble I' and utility maximization will occur at a point where $W_g > W_b$.

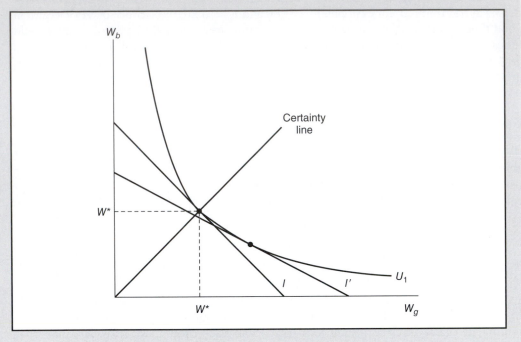

Hence this individual, when faced with fair markets in contingent claims on wealth, will be risk averse and will choose to ensure that he or she has the same level of wealth regardless of which state occurs.

A graphic analysis

Figure 7.2 illustrates risk aversion with a graph. This individual's budget constraint (I) is shown to be tangent to the U_1 indifference curve where $W_g = W_b$—a point on the "certainty line" where wealth (W^*) is independent of which state of the world occurs. At W^* the slope of the indifference curve $[\pi/(1 - \pi)]$ is precisely equal to the price ratio p_g/p_b.

If the market for contingent wealth claims were not fair, utility maximization might not occur on the certainty line. Suppose, for example, that $\pi/(1 - \pi) = 4$ but that $p_g/p_b = 2$ because ensuring wealth in bad times proves quite costly. In this case the budget constraint would resemble line I' in Figure 7.2 and utility maximization would occur below the certainty line.[22] In this case this individual would gamble a bit by opting for $W_g > W_b$, because claims on W_b are relatively costly. Example 7.6 shows the usefulness of this approach in evaluating some of the alternatives that might be available.

---

[22]Because (as Equation 7.58 shows) the *MRS* on the certainty line is always $\pi/(1 - \pi)$, tangencies with a flatter slope than this must occur below the line.

EXAMPLE 7.6 Insurance in the State-Preference Model

We can illustrate the state-preference approach by recasting the auto insurance illustration from Example 7.2 as a problem involving the two contingent commodities "wealth with no theft" (W_g) and "wealth with a theft" (W_b). If, as before, we assume logarithmic utility and that the probability of a theft (that is, $1 - \pi$) is 0.25, then

$$\text{expected utility} = 0.75\,U(W_g) + 0.25\,U(W_b)$$
$$= 0.75 \ln W_g + 0.25 \ln W_b. \tag{7.59}$$

If the individual takes no action then utility is determined by the initial wealth endowment, $W_g^* = 100{,}000$ and $W_b^* = 80{,}000$, so

$$\text{expected utility} = 0.75 \ln 100{,}000 + 0.25 \ln 80{,}000$$
$$= 11.45714. \tag{7.60}$$

To study trades away from these initial endowments, we write the budget constraint in terms of the prices of the contingent commodities, p_g and p_b:

$$p_g W_g^* + p_b W_b^* = p_g W_g + p_b W_b. \tag{7.61}$$

Assuming that these prices equal the probabilities of the two states ($p_g = 0.75, p_b = 0.25$), this constraint can be written

$$0.75(100{,}000) + 0.25(80{,}000) = 95{,}000 = 0.75\,W_g + 0.25\,W_b; \tag{7.62}$$

that is, the expected value of wealth is \$95,000, and this person can allocate this amount between W_g and W_b. Now maximization of utility with respect to this budget constraint yields $W_g = W_b = 95{,}000$. Consequently, the individual will move to the certainty line and receive an expected utility of

$$\text{expected utility} = \ln 95{,}000 = 11.46163, \tag{7.63}$$

a clear improvement over doing nothing. To obtain this improvement, this person must be able to transfer \$5,000 of wealth in good times (no theft) into \$15,000 of extra wealth in bad times (theft). A fair insurance contract would allow this because it would cost \$5,000 but return \$20,000 should a theft occur (but nothing should no theft occur). Notice here that the wealth changes promised by insurance—$dW_b/dW_g = 15{,}000/-5{,}000 = -3$—exactly equal the negative of the odds ratio $-\pi/(1 - \pi) = -0.75/0.25 = -3$.

A policy with a deductible provision. A number of other insurance contracts might be utility improving in this situation, though not all of them would lead to choices that lie on the certainty line. For example, a policy that cost \$5,200 and returned \$20,000 in case of a theft would permit this person to reach the certainty line with $W_g = W_b = 94{,}800$ and

$$\text{expected utility} = \ln 94{,}800 = 11.45953, \tag{7.64}$$

which also exceeds the utility obtainable from the initial endowment. A policy that costs \$4,900 and requires the individual to incur the first \$1,000 of a loss from theft would yield

$$W_g = 100{,}000 - 4{,}900 = 95{,}100,$$
$$W_b = 80{,}000 - 4{,}900 + 19{,}000 = 94{,}100; \tag{7.65}$$

then

$$\text{expected utility} = 0.75 \ln 95{,}100 + 0.25 \ln 94{,}100$$
$$= 11.46004. \tag{7.66}$$

Although this policy does not permit this person to reach the certainty line, it is utility improving. Insurance need not be complete in order to offer the promise of higher utility.

(*continued*)

EXAMPLE 7.6   CONTINUED

QUERY: What is the maximum amount an individual would be willing to pay for an insurance policy under which he or she had to absorb the first $1,000 of loss?

Risk aversion and risk premiums

The state-preference model is also especially useful for analyzing the relationship between risk aversion and individuals' willingness to pay for risk. Consider two people, each of whom starts with a certain wealth, W^*. Each person seeks to maximize an expected utility function of the form

$$V(W_g, W_b) = \pi \frac{W_g^R}{R} + (1 - \pi) \frac{W_b^R}{R}. \qquad (7.67)$$

Here the utility function exhibits constant relative risk aversion (see Example 7.4). Notice also that the function closely resembles the CES utility function we examined in Chapter 3 and elsewhere. The parameter R determines both the degree of risk aversion and the degree of curvature of indifference curves implied by the function. A very risk-averse individual will have a large negative value for R and have sharply curved indifference curves, such as U_1 shown in Figure 7.3. A person with more tolerance for risk will have a higher value of R and flatter indifference curves (such as U_2).[23]

---

[23]Tangency of U_1 and U_2 at W^* is ensured, because the MRS along the certainty line is given by $\pi/(1 - \pi)$ regardless of the value of R.

FIGURE 7.3   Risk Aversion and Risk Premiums

Indifference curve U_1 represents the preferences of a very risk-averse person, whereas the person with preferences represented by U_2 is willing to assume more risk. When faced with the risk of losing h in bad times, person 2 will require compensation of $W_2 - W^*$ in good times whereas person 1 will require a larger amount given by $W_1 - W^*$.

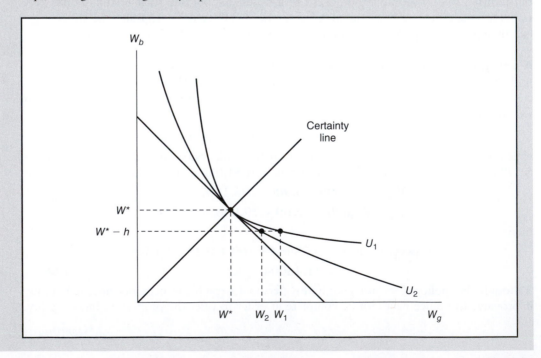

Suppose now these individuals are faced with the prospect of losing h dollars of wealth in bad times. Such a risk would be acceptable to individual 2 if wealth in good times were to increase from W^* to W_2. For the very risk-averse individual 1, however, wealth would have to increase to W_1 to make the risk acceptable. The difference between W_1 and W_2 therefore indicates the effect of risk aversion on willingness to assume risk. Some of the problems in this chapter make use of this graphic device for showing the connection between preferences (as reflected by the utility function in Equation 7.67) and behavior in risky situations.

THE ECONOMICS OF INFORMATION

Information is a valuable economic resource. People who know where to buy high-quality goods cheaply can make their budgets stretch further than those who don't; farmers with access to better weather forecasting may be able to avoid costly mistakes; and government environmental regulation can be more efficient if it is based on good scientific knowledge. Although these observations about the value of information have long been recognized, formal economic modeling of information acquisition and its implications for resource allocation are fairly recent.[24] Despite its late start, the study of information economics has become one of the major areas in current research. In this chapter we briefly survey some of the issues raised by this research. Far more detail on the economics of information is provided in Chapter 18.

PROPERTIES OF INFORMATION

One difficulty encountered by economists who wish to study the economics of information is that "information" itself is not easy to define. Unlike the economic goods we have been studying so far, the "quantity" of information obtainable from various actions is not well defined, and what information is obtained is not homogeneous among its users. The forms of economically useful information are simply too varied to permit the kinds of price-quantity characterizations we have been using for basic consumer goods. Instead, economists who wish to study information must take some care to specify what the informational environment is in a particular decision problem (this is sometimes called the *information set*) and how that environment might be changed through individual actions. As might be expected, this approach has resulted in a vast number of models of specific situations with little overall commonality among them.

A second complication involved in the study of information concerns some technical properties of information itself. Most information is durable and retains value after it has been used. Unlike a hot dog, which is consumed only once, knowledge of a special sale can be used not only by the person who discovers it but also by any friends with whom the information is shared. The friends then may gain from this information even though they don't have to spend anything to obtain it. Indeed, in a special case of this situation, information has the characteristic of a pure *public good* (see Chapter 19). That is, the information is both *nonrival* in that others may use it at zero cost and *nonexclusive* in that no individual can prevent others from using the information. The classic example of these properties is a new scientific discovery. When some prehistoric people invented the wheel, others could use it without detracting from the value of the discovery, and everyone who saw the wheel could copy it freely.

These technical properties of information imply that market mechanisms may often operate imperfectly in allocating resources to information provision and acquisition. Standard

---

[24]The formal modeling of information is sometimes dated from the path-breaking article by G. J. Stigler, "The Economics of Information," *Journal of Political Economy* (June 1961): 213–25.

models of supply and demand may therefore be of relatively limited use in understanding such activities. At a minimum, models have to be developed that accurately reflect the properties being assumed about the informational environment. Throughout the latter portions of this book, we will describe some of the situations in which such models are called for. Here, however, we will pay relatively little attention to supply-demand equilibria and will instead focus primarily on information issues that arise in the theory of individual choice.

THE VALUE OF INFORMATION

Developing models of information acquisition necessarily requires using tools from our study of uncertainty earlier in this chapter. Lack of information clearly represents a problem involving uncertainty for a decision maker. In the absence of perfect information, he or she may not be able to know exactly what the consequences of a particular action will be. Better information can reduce that uncertainty and therefore lead to better decisions that provide increased utility.

Information and subjective possibilities

This relationship between uncertainty and information acquisition can be illustrated using the state-preference model. Earlier we assumed that an individual forms subjective opinions about the probabilities of the two states of the world, "good times" and "bad times." In this model, information is valuable because it allows the individual to revise his or her estimates of these probabilities and to take advantage of these revisions. For example, information that foretold that tomorrow would definitely be "good times" would cause this person to revise his or her probabilities to $\pi_g = 1$, $\pi_b = 0$ and to change his or her purchases accordingly. When the information received is less definitive, the probabilities may be changed only slightly, but even small revisions may be quite valuable. If you ask some friends about their experiences with a few brands of DVD players you are thinking of buying, you may not want their opinions to dictate your choice. The prices of the players and other types of information (say, obtained from consulting *Consumer Reports*) will also affect your views. Ultimately, however, you must process all of these factors into a decision that reflects your assessment of the probabilities of various "states of the world" (in this case, the quality obtained from buying different brands).

A formal model

To illustrate why information has value, assume that an individual faces an uncertain situation involving "good" and "bad" times and that he or she can invest in a "message" that will yield some information about the probabilities of these outcomes. This message can take on two potential values, 1 or 2, with probabilities p and $(1 - p)$, respectively. If the message takes the value 1, then this person will believe that the probability of good times is given by π_g^1 [and the probability of bad times by $\pi_b^1 = (1 - \pi_g^1)$]. If the message takes the value 2, on the other hand, the probabilities are π_g^2 and $(1 - \pi_g^2)$. Once the message is received, this person has the opportunity to maximize expected utility on the basis of these probabilities. In general, it would be expected that he or she will make different decisions depending on what the message is. Let V_1 be the (indirect) maximal expected utility when the message takes the value 1 and V_2 be this maximal utility when the message takes the value 2. Hence, when this person is considering purchasing the message (that is, before it is actually received), expected utility is given by:

$$E_{\text{with } m} = pV_1 + (1 - p)V_2. \tag{7.68}$$

Now let's consider the situation of this person when he or she decides not to purchase the message. In this case, a single decision must be made that is based on the probabilities of good and bad times, π_g^0 and $(1 - \pi_g^0)$. Because the individual knows the various probabilities involved, consistency requires that $\pi_g^0 = p\pi_g^1 + (1-p)\pi_g^2$. Now let V_0 represent the maximal expected utility this person can obtain with these probabilities. Hence, we can write expected utility without the message as

$$E_{\text{without } m} = V_0 = pV_0 + (1 - p)V_0. \tag{7.69}$$

A comparison of Equations 7.68 and 7.69 shows that this person can always achieve $E_{\text{without } m}$ when he or she has the information provided by the message. That is, he or she can just choose to disregard what the message says. But if he or she chooses to make new, different decisions based on the information in the message, it must be the case that this information has value. That is:

$$E_{\text{with } m} \geq E_{\text{without } m}. \tag{7.70}$$

Presumably, then, this person will be willing to pay something for the message because of the better decision-making opportunities it provides.[25] Example 7.7 provides a simple illustration.

EXAMPLE 7.7 The Value of Information on Prices

To illustrate how new information may affect utility maximization, let's return to one of the first models we used in Chapter 4. There we showed that if an individual consumes two goods and utility is given by $U(x,y) = x^{0.5}y^{0.5}$, then the indirect utility function is

$$V(p_x, p_y, I) = \frac{I}{2p_x^{0.5}p_y^{0.5}}. \tag{7.71}$$

As a numerical example, we considered the case $p_x = 1, p_y = 4, I = 8$, and calculated that $V = I/2 \cdot 1 \cdot 2 = 2$. Now suppose that good y represents, say, a can of brand-name tennis balls, and this consumer knows that these can be bought at a price of either \$3 or \$5 from two stores but does not know which store charges which price. Because it is equally likely that either store has the lower price, the expected value of the price is \$4. But, because the indirect utility function is convex in price, this person receives an expected value of greater than $V = 2$ from shopping because he or she can buy more if the low-priced store is encountered. Before shopping, expected utility is

$$E[V(p_x, p_y, I)] = 0.5 \cdot V(1, 3, 8) + 0.5 \cdot V(1, 5, 8)$$
$$= 1.155 + 0.894 = 2.049. \tag{7.72}$$

If the consumer knew which store offered the lower price, utility would be even greater. If this person could buy at $p_y = 3$ with certainty, then indirect utility would be $V = 2.309$ and we can use this result to calculate what the value of this information is. That is, we can ask what level of income, I^*, would yield the same utility when $p_y = 3$, as is obtained when this person must choose which store to patronize by chance. Hence we need to solve the equation

$$V(p_x, p_y, I^*) = \frac{I^*}{2p_x^{0.5}p_y^{0.5}} = \frac{I^*}{2 \cdot 1 \cdot 3^{0.5}} = 2.049. \tag{7.73}$$

Solving this yields a value of $I^* = 7.098$. Hence, this person would be willing to pay up to $0.902 \, (= 8 - 7.098)$ for the information. Notice that availability of the price information

(continued)

---

[25]A more general way to state this result is to consider the properties of the individual's indirect expected utility function (V) as dependent on the probabilities in the problem. That is, $V(\pi_g) = \max[\pi_g U(W_g) + (1 - \pi_g)U(W_b)]$. Comparing Equations 7.68 and 7.69 amounts to comparing $pV(\pi_g^1) + (1-p)V(\pi_g^2)$ to $V(\pi_g^0) = V[p\pi_g^1 + (1-p)\pi_g^2]$. Because the V function is convex in π_g, the inequality in Equation 7.70 necessarily holds.

EXAMPLE 7.7 CONTINUED

helps this person in two ways: (1) it increases the probability he or she will patronize the low-price store from 0.5 to 1.0; and (2) it permits this person to take advantage of the lower price offered by buying more.

QUERY: It seems odd in this problem that expected utility with price uncertainty ($V = 2.049$) is greater than utility when price takes its expected value ($V = 2$). Does this violate the assumption of risk aversion?

FLEXIBILITY AND OPTION VALUE

The availability of new information allows individuals to make better decisions in situations involving uncertainty. It may therefore be beneficial to try to postpone making decisions until the information arrives. Of course, flexibility may sometimes involve costs of its own, so the decision-making process can become complex. For example, someone planning a trip to the Caribbean would obviously like to know whether he or she will have good weather. A vacationer who could wait until the last minute in deciding when to go could use the latest weather forecast to make that decision. But waiting may be costly (perhaps because last-minute airfares are much higher), so the choice can be a difficult one. Clearly the option to delay the decision is valuable, but whether this "option value" exceeds the costs involved in delay is the crucial question.

Modeling the importance of flexibility in decision making has become a major topic in the study of uncertainty and information. "Real option theory" has come to be an important component of financial and management theory. Other applications are beginning to emerge in such diverse fields as development economics, natural resource economics, and law and economics. Because this book focuses on general theory, however, we cannot pursue these interesting innovations here. Rather, our brief treatment will focus on how questions of flexibility might be incorporated into some of the models we have already examined, followed by a few concluding remarks.

Flexibility in the portfolio model

Some of the basic principles of real option theory can be illustrated by combining the portfolio choice model that we introduced earlier in this chapter with the idea of information messages introduced in the previous section. Suppose that an investor is considering putting some portion of his or her wealth (k) into a risky asset. The return on the asset is random and its characteristics will depend on whether there are "good times" or "bad times." The returns under these two situations are designated by $\tilde{r}_1$ and $\tilde{r}_2$, respectively. First, consider a situation where this person will get a message telling him or her whether it is good or bad times, but the message will arrive after the investment decision is made. The probability that the message will indicate good times is given by p. In this case, this person can be viewed as investing in a risky asset whose return is given by $\tilde{r}_0 = p\tilde{r}_1 + (1 - p)\tilde{r}_2$. Following the procedure outlined earlier, associated with this asset will be an optimal investment, k_0, and the expected utility associated with this portfolio will be U_0.

Suppose, alternatively, that this person has the flexibility to wait until after the message is received to decide on how his or her portfolio will be allocated. If the message reveals good times, then he or she will choose to invest k_1 in the risky asset and expected utility will be U_1.

On the other hand, if the message reveals bad times, then he or she will choose to invest k_2 in the risky asset and expected utility will be U_2. Hence, the expected utility provided by the option of waiting before choosing k will be

$$U^* = pU_1 + (1 - p)U_2. \qquad \textbf{(7.74)}$$

As before, it is clear that $U^* \geq U_0$. The investor could always choose to invest k_0 no matter what the message says, but if he or she chooses differing k's depending on the information in the message, it must be because that strategy provides more expected utility. When $U^* > U_0$, the option to wait has real value and this person will be willing to pay something (say, in forgone interest receipts) for that possibility.

Financial options

In some cases option values can be observed in actual markets. For example, financial options provide a buyer the right, but not the obligation, to conduct an economic transaction (typically buying or selling a stock) at specified terms at a certain date in the future. An option on Microsoft Corporation shares, for instance, might give the buyer the right (but not the obligation) to buy the stock in six months at a price of $30 per share. Or a foreign exchange option might provide the buyer with the right to buy euros at a price of $1.30 per euro in three months. All such options have value because they permit the owner to either make or decline the specified transaction depending on what new information becomes available over the option's duration. Such built-in flexibility is useful in a wide variety of investment strategies.

Options embedded in other transactions

Many other types of economic transactions have options embedded in them. For example, the purchase of a good that comes with a "money-back guarantee" gives the buyer an option to reverse the transaction should his or her experience with the good be unfavorable. Similarly, many mortgages provide the homeowner with the option to pay off the loan without penalty should conditions change. All such options are clearly valuable. A car buyer is not required to return his or her purchase if the car runs well and the homeowner need not pay off the mortgage if interest rates rise. Hence, embedding a buyer's option in a transaction can only increase the value of that transaction to the buyer. Contracts with such options would be expected to have higher prices. On the other hand, transactions with embedded seller options (for example, the right to repurchase a house at a stated price) will have lower prices. Examining price differences can therefore be one way to infer the value of some embedded options.

ASYMMETRY OF INFORMATION

One obvious implication of the study of information acquisition is that the level of information that an individual buys will depend on the per-unit price of information messages. Unlike the market price for most goods (which we usually assume to be the same for everyone), there are many reasons to believe that information costs may differ significantly among individuals. Some individuals may possess specific skills relevant to information acquisition (they may be trained mechanics, for example) whereas others may not possess such skills. Some individuals may have other types of experience that yield valuable information, whereas others may lack that experience. For example, the seller of a product will usually know more about its limitations than will a buyer, because the seller will know precisely how the good was made and where possible problems might arise. Similarly, large-scale repeat buyers of a good may have greater access to information about it than would first-time buyers. Finally, some individuals may have invested in some types of information services (for example, by having a computer link to a brokerage firm or by subscribing to *Consumer Reports*) that make the marginal cost of obtaining additional information lower than for someone without such an investment.

All of these factors suggest that the level of information will sometimes differ among the participants in market transactions. Of course, in many instances, information costs may be low and such differences may be minor. Most people can appraise the quality of fresh vegetables fairly well just by looking at them, for example. But when information costs are high and variable across individuals, we would expect them to find it advantageous to acquire different amounts of information. We will postpone a detailed study of such situations until Chapter 18.

SUMMARY

The goal of this chapter was to provide some basic material for the study of individual behavior in uncertain situations. The key concepts covered may be listed as follows.

- The most common way to model behavior under uncertainty is to assume that individuals seek to maximize the expected utility of their actions.

- Individuals who exhibit a diminishing marginal utility of wealth are risk averse. That is, they generally refuse fair bets.

- Risk-averse individuals will wish to insure themselves completely against uncertain events if insurance premiums are actuarially fair. They may be willing to pay more than actuarially fair premiums in order to avoid taking risks.

- Two utility functions have been extensively used in the study of behavior under uncertainty: the constant absolute risk aversion (CARA) function and the con-

stant relative risk aversion (CRRA) function. Neither is completely satisfactory on theoretical grounds.

- One of the most extensively studied issues in the economics of uncertainty is the "portfolio problem," which asks how an investor will split his or her wealth between risky and risk-free assets. In some cases it is possible to obtain precise solutions to this problem, depending on the nature of the risky assets that are available.

- The state-preference approach allows decision making under uncertainty to be approached in a familiar choice-theoretic framework. The approach is especially useful for looking at issues that arise in the economics of information.

- Information is valuable because it permits individuals to make better decisions in uncertain situations. Information can be most valuable when individuals have some flexibility in their decision making.

PROBLEMS

7.1

George is seen to place an even-money $100,000 bet on the Bulls to win the NBA Finals. If George has a logarithmic utility-of-wealth function and if his current wealth is $1,000,000, what must he believe is the minimum probability that the Bulls will win?

7.2

Show that if an individual's utility-of-wealth function is convex then he or she will prefer fair gambles to income certainty and may even be willing to accept somewhat unfair gambles. Do you believe this sort of risk-taking behavior is common? What factors might tend to limit its occurrence?

7.3

An individual purchases a dozen eggs and must take them home. Although making trips home is costless, there is a 50 percent chance that all of the eggs carried on any one trip will be broken during the trip. The individual considers two strategies: (1) take all 12 eggs in one trip; or (2) take two trips with 6 eggs in each trip.

a. List the possible outcomes of each strategy and the probabilities of these outcomes. Show that, on average, 6 eggs will remain unbroken after the trip home under either strategy.

b. Develop a graph to show the utility obtainable under each strategy. Which strategy will be preferable?

c. Could utility be improved further by taking more than two trips? How would this possibility be affected if additional trips were costly?

7.4

Suppose there is a 50–50 chance that a risk-averse individual with a current wealth of $20,000 will contract a debilitating disease and suffer a loss of $10,000.

a. Calculate the cost of actuarially fair insurance in this situation and use a utility-of-wealth graph (such as shown in Figure 7.1) to show that the individual will prefer fair insurance against this loss to accepting the gamble uninsured.

b. Suppose two types of insurance policies were available:

(1) a fair policy covering the complete loss; and

(2) a fair policy covering only half of any loss incurred.

Calculate the cost of the second type of policy and show that the individual will generally regard it as inferior to the first.

7.5

Ms. Fogg is planning an around-the-world trip on which she plans to spend $10,000. The utility from the trip is a function of how much she actually spends on it (Y), given by

$$U(Y) = \ln Y.$$

a. If there is a 25 percent probability that Ms. Fogg will lose $1,000 of her cash on the trip, what is the trip's expected utility?

b. Suppose that Ms. Fogg can buy insurance against losing the $1,000 (say, by purchasing traveler's checks) at an "actuarially fair" premium of $250. Show that her expected utility is higher if she purchases this insurance than if she faces the chance of losing the $1,000 without insurance.

c. What is the maximum amount that Ms. Fogg would be willing to pay to insure her $1,000?

7.6

In deciding to park in an illegal place, any individual knows that the probability of getting a ticket is p and that the fine for receiving the ticket is f. Suppose that all individuals are risk averse (that is, $U''(W) < 0$, where W is the individual's wealth).

  Will a proportional increase in the probability of being caught or a proportional increase in the fine be a more effective deterrent to illegal parking? *Hint:* Use the Taylor series approximation $U(W - f) = U(W) - f U'(W) + (f^2/2) U''(W)$.

7.7

A farmer believes there is a 50–50 chance that the next growing season will be abnormally rainy. His expected utility function has the form

$$\text{expected utility} = \frac{1}{2} \ln Y_{NR} + \frac{1}{2} \ln Y_R,$$

where Y_{NR} and Y_R represent the farmer's income in the states of "normal rain" and "rainy," respectively.

a. Suppose the farmer must choose between two crops that promise the following income prospects:

Crop	Y_{NR}	Y_R
Wheat	$28,000	$10,000
Corn	19,000	15,000

Which of the crops will he plant?

b. Suppose the farmer can plant half his field with each crop. Would he choose to do so? Explain your result.

c. What mix of wheat and corn would provide maximum expected utility to this farmer?

d. Would wheat crop insurance—which is available to farmers who grow only wheat and which costs $4,000 and pays off $8,000 in the event of a rainy growing season—cause this farmer to change what he plants?

7.8

In Equation 7.30 we showed that the amount an individual is willing to pay to avoid a fair gamble (h) is given by $p = 0.5 E(h^2) r(W)$, where $r(W)$ is the measure of absolute risk aversion at this person's initial level of wealth. In this problem we look at the size of this payment as a function of the size of the risk faced and this person's level of wealth.

a. Consider a fair gamble (v) of winning or losing $1. For this gamble, what is $E(v^2)$?

b. Now consider varying the gamble in part (a) by multiplying each prize by a positive constant k. Let $h = kv$. What is the value of $E(h^2)$?

c. Suppose this person has a logarithmic utility function $U(W) = \ln W$. What is a general expression for $r(W)$?

d. Compute the risk premium (p) for $k = 0.5, 1$, and 2 and for $W = 10$ and 100. What do you conclude by comparing the six values?

Analytical Problems

7.9 HARA Utility

The CARA and CRRA utility functions are both members of a more general class of utility functions called *harmonic absolute risk aversion* (HARA) functions. The general form for this function is $U(W) = \theta(\mu + W/\gamma)^{1-\gamma}$, where the various parameters obey the following restrictions:

- $\gamma \leq 1$,
- $\mu + W/\gamma > 0$,
- $\theta[(1 - \gamma)/\gamma] > 0$.

The reasons for the first two restrictions are obvious; the third is required so that $U' > 0$.

a. Calculate $r(W)$ for this function. Show that the reciprocal of this expression is linear in W. This is the origin of the term "harmonic" in the function's name.

b. Show that, when $\mu = 0$ and $\theta = [(1 - \gamma)/\gamma]^{\gamma - 1}$, this function reduces to the CRRA function given in Chapter 7 (see footnote 17).

c. Use your result from part (a) to show that if $\gamma \to \infty$ then $r(W)$ is a constant for this function.

d. Let the constant found in part (c) be represented by A. Show that the implied form for the utility function in this case is the CARA function given in Equation 7.35.

e. Finally, show that a quadratic utility function can be generated from the HARA function simply by setting $\gamma = -1$.

f. Despite the seeming generality of the HARA function, it still exhibits several limitations for the study of behavior in uncertain situations. Describe some of these shortcomings.

7.10 The resolution of uncertainty

In some cases individuals may care about the date at which the uncertainty they face is resolved. Suppose, for example, that an individual knows that his or her consumption will be 10 units today (c_1) but that tomorrow's consumption (c_2) will be either 10 or 2.5, depending on whether a coin comes up heads or tails. Suppose also that the individual's utility function has the simple Cobb-Douglas form

$$U(c_1, c_2) = \sqrt{c_1 c_2}.$$

a. If an individual cares only about the expected value of utility, will it matter whether the coin is flipped just before day 1 or just before day 2? Explain.

b. More generally, suppose that the individual's expected utility depends on the timing of the coin flip. Specifically, assume that

$$\text{expected utility} = E_1[\{E_2[U(c_1, c_2)]\}^\alpha],$$

where E_1 represents expectations taken at the start of day 1, E_2 represents expectations at the start of day 2, and α represents a parameter that indicates timing preferences. Show that if $\alpha = 1$, the individual is indifferent about when the coin is flipped.

c. Show that if $\alpha = 2$, the individual will prefer early resolution of the uncertainty—that is, flipping the coin at the start of day 1.

d. Show that if $\alpha = 0.5$, the individual will prefer later resolution of the uncertainty (flipping at the start of day 2).

e. Explain your results intuitively and indicate their relevance for information theory. *Note:* This problem is an illustration of "resolution seeking" and "resolution averse" behavior; see D. M. Kreps and E. L. Porteus, "Temporal Resolution of Uncertainty and Dynamic Choice Theory," *Econometrica* (January 1978): 185–200.

7.11 More on the CRRA function

For the constant relative risk aversion utility function (Equation 7.42), we showed that the degree of risk aversion is measured by $(1 - R)$. In Chapter 3 we showed that the elasticity of substitution for the same function is given by $1/(1 - R)$. Hence, the measures are reciprocals of each other. Using this result, discuss the following questions.

a. Why is risk aversion related to an individual's willingness to substitute wealth between states of the world? What phenomenon is being captured by both concepts?

b. How would you interpret the polar cases $R = 1$ and $R = -\infty$ in both the risk-aversion and substitution frameworks?

c. A rise in the price of contingent claims in "bad" times (P_b) will induce substitution and income effects into the demands for W_g and W_b. If the individual has a fixed budget to devote to these two goods, how will choices among them be affected? Why might W_g rise or fall depending on the degree of risk aversion exhibited by the individual?

d. Suppose that empirical data suggest an individual requires an average return of 0.5 percent before being tempted to invest in an investment that has a 50–50 chance of gaining or losing 5 percent. That is, this person gets the same utility from W_0 as from an even bet on $1.055 W_0$ and $0.955 W_0$.

   (1) What value of R is consistent with this behavior?

   (2) How much average return would this person require to accept a 50–50 chance of gaining or losing 10 percent?

   Note: This part requires solving nonlinear equations, so approximate solutions will suffice. The comparison of the risk-reward trade-off illustrates what is called the "equity premium puzzle" in that risky investments seem actually to earn much more than is consistent with the degree of risk aversion suggested by other data. See N. R. Kocherlakota, "The Equity Premium: It's Still a Puzzle," *Journal of Economic Literature* (March 1996): 42–71.

7.12 Graphing risky investments

Investment in risky assets can be examined in the state-preference framework by assuming that W^* dollars invested in an asset with a certain return r will yield $W^*(1 + r)$ in both states of the world, whereas investment in a risky asset will yield $W^*(1 + r_g)$ in good times and $W^*(1 + r_b)$ in bad times (where $r_g > r > r_b$).

    a. Graph the outcomes from the two investments.

    b. Show how a "mixed portfolio" containing both risk-free and risky assets could be illustrated in your graph. How would you show the fraction of wealth invested in the risky asset?

    c. Show how individuals' attitudes toward risk will determine the mix of risk-free and risky assets they will hold. In what case would a person hold no risky assets?

    d. If an individual's utility takes the constant relative risk aversion form (Equation 7.42), explain why this person will not change the fraction of risky assets held as his or her wealth increases.[26]

7.13 Taxing risks assets

Suppose the asset returns in Problem 7.12 are subject to taxation.

    a. Show, under the conditions of Problem 7.12, why a proportional tax on wealth will not affect the fraction of wealth allocated to risky assets.

    b. Suppose that only the returns from the safe asset were subject to a proportional income tax. How would this affect the fraction of wealth held in risky assets? Which investors would be most affected by such a tax?

    c. How would your answer to part (b) change if all asset returns were subject to a proportional income tax?

Note: This problem asks you to compute the *pre-tax* allocation of wealth that will result in *post-tax* utility maximization.

7.14 The portfolio problem with a Normally distributed risky asset

In Example 7.3 we showed that a person with a CARA utility function who faces a Normally distributed risk will have expected utility of the form $E[U(W)] = \mu_W - (A/2)\sigma_W^2$, where μ_W is the expected value of wealth and σ_W^2 is its variance. Use this fact to solve for the optimal portfolio allocation for a person with a CARA utility function who must invest k of his or her wealth in a Normally distributed risky asset whose expected return is μ_r and variance in return is σ_r^2 (your answer should depend on A). Explain your results intuitively.

---

[26]This problem and the next are taken from J. E. Stiglitz, "The Effects of Income, Wealth, and Capital Gains Taxation in Risk Taking," *Quarterly Journal of Economics* (May 1969): 263–83.

SUGGESTIONS FOR FURTHER READING

Arrow, K. J. "The Role of Securities in the Optimal Allocation of Risk Bearing." *Review of Economic Studies* 31 (1963): 91–96.

Introduces the state-preference concept and interprets securities as claims on contingent commodities.

———. "Uncertainty and the Welfare Economics of Medical Care." *American Economic Review* 53 (1963): 941–73.

Excellent discussion of the welfare implications of insurance. Has a clear, concise, mathematical appendix. Should be read in conjunction with Pauly's article on moral hazard (see Chapter 18).

Bernoulli, D. "Exposition of a New Theory on the Measurement of Risk." *Econometrica* 22 (1954): 23–36.

Reprint of the classic analysis of the St. Petersburg paradox.

Dixit, A. K., and R. S. Pindyck. *Investment under Uncertainty*. Princeton: Princeton University Press, 1994.

Focuses mainly on the investment decision by firms but has a good coverage of option concepts.

Friedman, M., and L. J. Savage. "The Utility Analysis of Choice." *Journal of Political Economy* 56 (1948): 279–304.

Analyzes why individuals may both gamble and buy insurance. Very readable.

Gollier, Christian. *The Economics of Risk and Time*. Cambridge, MA: MIT Press, 2001.

Contains a complete treatment of many of the issues discussed in this chapter. Especially good on the relationship between allocation under uncertainty and allocation over time.

Mas-Colell, Andreu, Michael D. Whinston, and Jerry R. Green. *Microeconomic Theory*. New York: Oxford University Press, 1995, chap. 6.

Provides a good summary of the foundations of expected utility theory. Also examines the "state independence" assumption in detail and shows that some notions of risk aversion carry over into cases of state dependence.

Pratt, J. W. "Risk Aversion in the Small and in the Large." *Econometrica* 32 (1964): 122–36.

Theoretical development of risk-aversion measures. Fairly technical treatment but readable.

Rothschild, M., and J. E. Stiglitz. "Increasing Risk: 1. A Definition." *Journal of Economic Theory* 2 (1970): 225–43.

Develops an economic definition of what it means for one gamble to be "riskier" than another. A sequel article in the Journal of Economic Theory *provides economic illustrations.*

Silberberg, E., and W. Suen. *The Structure of Economics: A Mathematical Analysis*, 3rd ed. Boston: Irwin/McGraw-Hill, 2001.

Chapter 13 provides a nice introduction to the relationship between statistical concepts and expected utility maximization. Also shows in detail the integration mentioned in Example 7.3.

EXTENSIONS

Portfolios of Many Risky Assets

The portfolio problem we studied in Chapter 7 looked at an investor's decision to invest a portion of his or her wealth in a single risky asset. In these Extensions we will see how this model can be generalized to consider portfolios with many such assets. Throughout our discussion we will assume that there are n risky assets. The return on each asset is a random variable denoted by r_i $(i = 1, n)$. The expected values and variances of these assets' returns are denoted by $E(r_i) = \mu_i$ and $\text{Var}(r_i) = \sigma_i^2$, respectively. An investor who invests a portion of his or her wealth in a portfolio of these assets will obtain a random return (r_P) given by

$$r_P = \sum_{i=1}^{n} \alpha_i r_i, \qquad \textbf{(i)}$$

where α_i (≥ 0) is the fraction of the risky portfolio held in asset i and where $\sum_{i=1}^{n} \alpha_i = 1$. In this situation, the expected return on this portfolio will be

$$E(r_P) = \mu_P = \sum_{i=1}^{n} \alpha_i \mu_i. \qquad \textbf{(ii)}$$

If the returns of each asset are independent, then the variance of the portfolio's return will be

$$\textbf{Var}(r_P) = \sigma_P^2 = \sum_{i=1}^{n} \alpha_i^2 \sigma_i^2. \qquad \textbf{(iii)}$$

If the returns are not independent, Equation iii would have to be modified to take covariances among the returns into account. Using this general notation, we now proceed to look at some aspects of this portfolio allocation problem.

E7.1 Diversification with two risky assets

Equation iii provides the basic rationale for holding many assets in a portfolio: so that diversification can reduce risk. Suppose, for example, that there are only two independent assets and that the expected returns and variances of those returns for each of the assets are identical. That is, assume $\mu_1 = \mu_2$ and $\sigma_1^2 = \sigma_2^2$. A person who invests his or her risky portfolio in only one of these seemingly identical assets will obtain $\mu_P = \mu_1 = \mu_2$ and $\sigma_P^2 = \sigma_1^2 = \sigma_2^2$. By mixing the assets, however, this investor can do better in the sense that he or she can get the same expected yield with lower variance. Notice that, no matter how this person

invests, the expected return on the portfolio will be the same:

$$\mu_P = \alpha_1 \mu_1 + (1 - \alpha_1)\mu_2 = \mu_1 = \mu_2. \quad \textbf{(iv)}$$

But the variance will depend on the allocation between the two assets:

$$\sigma_P^2 = \alpha_1^2 \sigma_1^2 + (1 - \alpha_1)^2 \sigma_2^2 = (1 - 2\alpha_1 + 2\alpha_1^2)\sigma_1^2.$$
$$\textbf{(v)}$$

Choosing α_1 to minimize this expression yields $\alpha_1 = 0.5$ and

$$\sigma_P^2 = 0.5\sigma_1^2. \qquad \textbf{(vi)}$$

Hence, holding half of one's portfolio in each asset yields the same expected return as holding only one asset, but it promises a variance of return that is only half as large. As we showed earlier in Chapter 7, this is the primary benefit of diversification.

E7.2 Efficient portfolios

With many assets, the optimal diversification problem is to choose asset weightings (the α's) so as to minimize the variance (or standard deviation) of the portfolio for each potential expected return. The solution to this problem yields an "efficiency frontier" for risky asset portfolios such as that represented by the line EE in Figure E7.1. Portfolios that lie below this frontier are inferior to those on the frontier because they offer lower expected returns for any degree of risk. Portfolio returns above the frontier are unattainable. Sharpe (1970) discusses the mathematics associated with constructing the EE frontier.

Mutual funds

The notion of portfolio efficiency has been widely applied to the study of mutual funds. In general, mutual funds are a good answer to small investors' diversification needs. Because such funds pool the funds of many individuals, they are able to achieve economies of scale in transactions and management costs. This permits fund owners to share in the fortunes of a much wider variety of equities than would be possible if each acted alone. But mutual fund managers have incentives of their own, so the portfolios they hold may not always be perfect representations of the risk attitudes of their clients. For example, Scharfstein and Stein (1990) develop a model that shows why mutual fund

FIGURE E7.1   Efficient Portfolios

The frontier *EE* represents optimal mixtures of risky assets that minimize the standard deviation of the portfolio, σ_P, for each expected return, μ_P. A risk-free asset with return μ_f offers investors the opportunity to hold mixed portfolios along *PP* that mix this risk-free asset with the market portfolio, *M*.

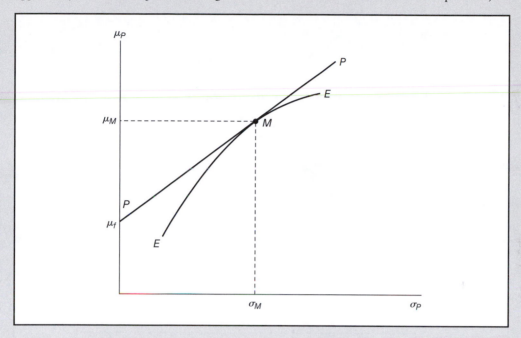

managers have incentives to "follow the herd" in their investment picks. Other studies, such as the classic investigation by Jensen (1968), find that mutual fund managers are seldom able to attain extra returns large enough to offset the expenses they charge investors. In recent years this has led many mutual fund buyers to favor "index" funds that seek simply to duplicate the market average (as represented, say, by the Standard and Poor's 500 stock index). Such funds have very low expenses and therefore permit investors to achieve diversification at minimal cost.

E7.3 Portfolio separation

If there exists a risk-free asset with expected return μ_f and $\sigma_f = 0$, then optimal portfolios will consist of mixtures of this asset with risky ones. All such portfolios will lie along the line *PP* in Figure 7.1, because this shows the maximum return attainable for each value of σ for various portfolio allocations. These allocations will contain only one specific set of risky assets: the set represented by point *M*. In equilibrium this will be the "market portfolio" consisting of all capital assets held in proportion to their market valuations. This market portfolio will provide an expected return of μ_M and a

standard deviation of that return of σ_M. The equation for the line *PP* that represents any mixed portfolio is given by the linear equation

$$\mu_P = \mu_f + \frac{\mu_M - \mu_f}{\sigma_M} \cdot \sigma_P. \qquad \textbf{(vii)}$$

This shows that the market line *PP* permits individual investors to "purchase" returns in excess of the risk-free return $(\mu_M - \mu_f)$ by taking on proportionally more risk (σ_P/σ_M). For choices on *PP* to the left of the market point *M*, $\sigma_P/\sigma_M < 1$ and $\mu_f < \mu_P < \mu_M$. High-risk points to the right of *M*—which can be obtained by borrowing to produce a leveraged portfolio—will have $\sigma_P/\sigma_M > 1$ and will promise an expected return in excess of what is provided by the market portfolio $(\mu_P > \mu_M)$. Tobin (1958) was one of the first economists to recognize the role that risk-free assets play in identifying the market portfolio and in setting the terms on which investors can obtain returns above risk-free levels.

E7.4 Individual choices

Figure E7.2 illustrates the portfolio choices of various investors facing the options offered by the line *PP*.

FIGURE E7.2   Investor Behavior and Risk Aversion

Given the market options PP, investors can choose how much risk they wish to assume. Very risk-averse investors (U_I) will hold mainly risk-free assets, whereas risk takers (U_{III}) will opt for leveraged portfolios.

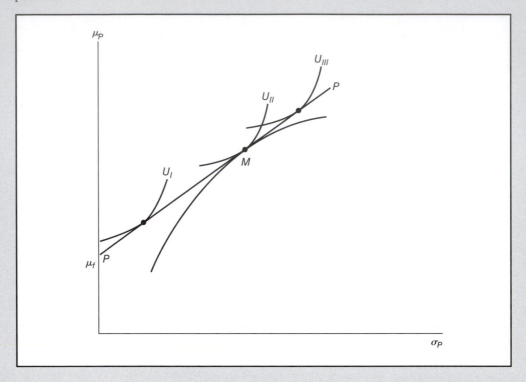

This figure illustrates the type of portfolio choice model previously described in this chapter. Individuals with low tolerance for risk (I) will opt for portfolios that are heavily weighted toward the risk-free asset. Investors willing to assume a modest degree of risk (II) will opt for portfolios close to the market portfolio. High-risk investors (III) may opt for leveraged portfolios. Notice that all investors face the same "price" of risk ($\mu_M - \mu_f$) with their expected returns being determined by how much relative risk (σ_P/σ_M) they are willing to incur. Notice also that the risk associated with an investor's portfolio depends only on the fraction of the portfolio invested in the market portfolio (α), since $\sigma_P^2 = \alpha^2\sigma_M^2 + (1-\alpha)^2 \cdot 0$. Hence, $\sigma_P/\sigma_M = \alpha$ and so the investor's choice of portfolio is equivalent to his or her choice of risk.

E7.5 Capital asset pricing model

Although the analysis of E7.4 shows how a portfolio that mixes a risk-free asset with the market portfolio will be priced, it does not describe the risk-return trade-off for a single asset. Because (assuming transactions are costless) an investor can always avoid risk unrelated to the overall market by choosing to diversify with a "market portfolio," such "unsystematic" risk will not warrant any excess return. An asset will, however, earn an excess return to the extent that it contributes to overall market risk. An asset that does not yield such extra returns would not be held in the market portfolio, so it would not be held at all. This is the fundamental insight of the capital asset pricing model (CAPM).

To examine these results formally, consider a portfolio that combines a small amount (α) of an asset with a random return of x with the market portfolio (which has a random return of M). The return on this portfolio (z) would be given by

$$z = \alpha x + (1 - \alpha)M. \qquad \text{(viii)}$$

The expected return is

$$\mu_z = \alpha\mu_x + (1 - \alpha)\mu_M \qquad \text{(ix)}$$

with variance

$$\sigma_z^2 = \alpha^2 \sigma_x^2 + (1-\alpha)^2 \sigma_M^2 + 2\alpha(1-\alpha)\sigma_{x,M}, \quad \textbf{(x)}$$

where $\sigma_{x,M}$ is the covariance between the return on x and the return on the market.

But our previous analysis shows

$$\mu_z = \mu_f + (\mu_M - \mu_f) \cdot \frac{\sigma_z}{\sigma_M}. \quad \textbf{(xi)}$$

Setting Equation ix equal to xi and differentiating with respect to α yields

$$\frac{\partial \mu_z}{\partial \alpha} = \mu_x - \mu_M = \frac{\mu_M - \mu_f}{\sigma_M} \frac{\partial \sigma_z}{\partial \alpha}. \quad \textbf{(xii)}$$

By calculating $\partial \sigma_z / \partial \alpha$ from Equation x and taking the limit as α approaches zero, we get

$$\mu_x - \mu_M = \frac{\mu_M - \mu_f}{\sigma_M} \left(\frac{\sigma_{x,M} - \sigma_M^2}{\sigma_M} \right), \quad \textbf{(xiii)}$$

or, rearranging terms,

$$\mu_x = \mu_f + (\mu_M - \mu_f) \cdot \frac{\sigma_{x,M}}{\sigma_M^2}. \quad \textbf{(xiv)}$$

Again, risk has a reward of $\mu_M - \mu_f$, but now the quantity of risk is measured by $\sigma_{x,M}/\sigma_M^2$. This ratio of the covariance between the return x and the market to the variance of the market return is referred to as the *beta* coefficient for the asset. Estimated beta coefficients for financial assets are reported in many publications.

Studies of the CAPM

This version of the capital asset pricing model carries strong implications about the determinants of any asset's expected rate of return. Because of this simplicity, the model has been subject to a large number of empirical tests. In general these find that the model's measure of systemic risk (beta) is indeed correlated with expected returns, while simpler measures of risk (for example, the standard deviation of past returns) are not. Perhaps the most influential early empirical test that reached such a conclusion was Fama and MacBeth (1973). But the CAPM itself explains only a small fraction of differences in the returns of various assets. And, contrary to the CAPM, a number of authors have found that many other economic factors significantly affect expected returns. Indeed, a prominent challenge to the CAPM comes from one of its original founders—see Fama and French (1992).

References

Fama, E. F., and K. R. French. "The Cross Section of Expected Stock Returns." *Journal of Finance* 47 (1992): 427–66.

Fama, E. F., and J. MacBeth. "Risk, Return, and Equilibrium." *Journal of Political Economy* 8 (1973): 607–36.

Jensen, M. "The Performance of Mutual Funds in the Period 1945–1964." *Journal of Finance* (May 1968): 386–416.

Scharfstein, D. S., and J. Stein. "Herd Behavior and Investment." *American Economic Review* (June 1990): 465–89.

Sharpe, W. F. *Portfolio Theory and Capital Markets.* New York: McGraw-Hill, 1970.

Tobin, J. "Liquidity Preference as Behavior Towards Risk." *Review of Economic Studies* (February 1958): 65–86.

Strategy and Game Theory

This chapter provides an introduction to noncooperative game theory, a tool used to understand the strategic interactions among two or more agents. The range of applications of game theory has been growing constantly, including all areas of economics (from labor economics to macroeconomics) and other fields such as political science and biology. Game theory is particularly useful in understanding the interaction between firms in an oligopoly, so the concepts learned here will be used extensively in Chapter 15. We begin with the central concept of Nash equilibrium and study its application in simple games. We then go on to study refinements of Nash equilibrium that are used in games with more complicated timing and information structures.

BASIC CONCEPTS

So far in Part II of this text, we have studied individual decisions made in isolation. In this chapter we study decision making in a more complicated, strategic setting. In a strategic setting, a person may no longer have an obvious choice that is best for him or her. What is best for one decision maker may depend on what the other is doing and vice versa.

For example, consider the strategic interaction between drivers and the police. Whether drivers prefer to speed may depend on whether the police set up speed traps. Whether the police find speed traps valuable depends on how much drivers speed. This confusing circularity would seem to make it difficult to make much headway in analyzing strategic behavior. In fact, the tools of game theory will allow us to push the analysis nearly as far, for example, as our analysis of consumer utility maximization in Chapter 4.

There are two major tasks involved when using game theory to analyze an economic situation. The first is to distill the situation into a simple game. Because the analysis involved in strategic settings quickly grows more complicated than in simple decision problems, it is important to simplify the setting as much as possible by retaining only a few essential elements. There is a certain art to distilling games from situations that is hard to teach. The examples in the text and problems in this chapter can serve as models that may help in approaching new situations.

The second task is to "solve" the given game, which results in a prediction about what will happen. To solve a game, one takes an equilibrium concept (Nash equilibrium, for example) and runs through the calculations required to apply it to the given game. Much of the chapter will be devoted to learning the most widely used equilibrium concepts (including Nash equilibrium) and to practicing the calculations necessary to apply them to particular games.

A *game* is an abstract model of a strategic situation. Even the most basic games have three essential elements: players, strategies, and payoffs. In complicated settings, it is sometimes also necessary to specify additional elements such as the sequence of moves and the information that players have when they move (who knows what when) to describe the game fully.

Players

Each decision maker in a game is called a *player*. These players may be individuals (as in poker games), firms (as in markets with few firms), or entire nations (as in military conflicts). A player is characterized as having the ability to choose from among a set of possible actions. Usually, the number of players is fixed throughout the "play" of the game. Games are sometimes characterized by the number of players involved (two-player, three-player, or n-player games). As does much of the economic literature, this chapter often focuses on two-player games because this is the simplest strategic setting.

We will label the players with numbers, so in a two-player game we will have players 1 and 2. In an n-player game we will have players $1, 2, ..., n$, with the generic player labeled i.

Strategies

Each course of action open to a player during the game is called a *strategy*. Depending on the game being examined, a strategy may be a simple action (drive over the speed limit or not) or a complex plan of action that may be contingent on earlier play in the game (say, speeding only if the driver has observed speed traps less than a quarter of the time in past drives). Many aspects of game theory can be illustrated in games in which players choose between just two possible actions.

Let S_1 denote the set of strategies open to player 1, S_2 the set open to player 2, and (more generally) S_i the set open to player i. Let $s_1 \in S_1$ be a particular strategy chosen by player 1 from the set of possibilities, $s_2 \in S_2$ the particular strategy chosen by player 2, and $s_i \in S_i$ for player i. A strategy *profile* will refer to a listing of particular strategies chosen by each of a group of players.

Payoffs

The final returns to the players at the conclusion of a game are called *payoffs*. Payoffs are measured in levels of utility obtained by the players. For simplicity, monetary payoffs (say, profits for firms) are often used. More generally, payoffs can incorporate nonmonetary outcomes such as prestige, emotion, risk preferences, and so forth. Players are assumed to prefer higher payoffs than lower payoffs.

In a two-player game, $u_1(s_1, s_2)$ denotes player 1's payoff given that he or she chooses s_1 and the other player chooses s_2 and similarly $u_2(s_2, s_1)$ denotes player 2's payoff. The fact player 1's payoff may depend on 2's strategy (and vice versa) is where the strategic interdependence shows up. In an n-player game, we can write the payoff of a generic player i as $u_i(s_i, s_{-i})$, which depends on player i's own strategy s_i and the profile $s_{-i} = (s_1, ..., s_{i-1}, s_{i+1}, ..., s_n)$ of the strategies of all players other than i.

PRISONERS' DILEMMA

The Prisoners' Dilemma, introduced by A. W. Tucker in the 1940s, is one of the most famous games studied in game theory and will serve here as a nice example to illustrate all the notation just introduced. The title stems from the following situation. Two suspects are arrested for a crime. The district attorney has little evidence in the case and is eager to extract a confession. She separates the suspects and tells each: "If you fink on your companion but your companion doesn't fink on you, I can promise you a reduced (one-year) sentence, whereas your companion will get four years. If you both fink on each other, you will each get a three-year sentence." Each suspect also knows that if neither of them finks then the lack of evidence will result in being tried for a lesser crime for which the punishment is a two-year sentence.

Boiled down to its essence, the Prisoners' Dilemma has two strategic players, the suspects, labeled 1 and 2. (There is also a district attorney, but since her actions have already been fully specified, there is no reason to complicate the game and include her in the specification.) Each player has two possible strategies open to him: fink or remain silent. We therefore write their strategy sets as $S_1 = S_2\{\text{fink}, \text{silent}\}$. To avoid negative numbers we will specify payoffs as the years of freedom over the next four years. For example, if suspect 1 finks and 2 does not, suspect 1 will enjoy three years of freedom and 2 none, that is, $u_1(\text{fink}, \text{silent}) = 3$ and $u_2(\text{silent}, \text{fink}) = 0$.

Extensive form

There are $2^2 = 4$ combinations of strategies and two payoffs to specify for each combination. So instead of listing all the payoffs, it will be clearer to organize them in a game tree or a matrix.

The game tree, also called the *extensive form*, is shown in Figure 8.1. The action proceeds from left to right. Each *node* (shown as a dot on the tree) represents a decision point for the player indicated there. The first move in this game belongs to player 1; he must choose whether to fink or be silent. Then player 2 makes his decision. The dotted oval drawn around the nodes at which player 2 moves indicates that the two nodes are in the same *information set*, that is, player 2 does not know what player 1 has chosen when 2 moves. We put the two nodes in the same information set because the district attorney approaches each suspect separately and does not reveal what the other has chosen. We will later look at games in which the second mover does have information about the first mover's choice and so the two nodes are in separate information sets. Payoffs are given at the end of the tree. The convention is for player 1's payoff to be listed first, then player 2's.

FIGURE 8.1   Extensive Form for the Prisoners' Dilemma

In this game, player 1 chooses to fink or be silent, and player 2 has the same choice. The oval surrounding 2's nodes indicates that they share the same (lack of) information: 2 does not know what strategy 1 has chosen because the district attorney approaches each player in secret. Payoffs are listed at the right.

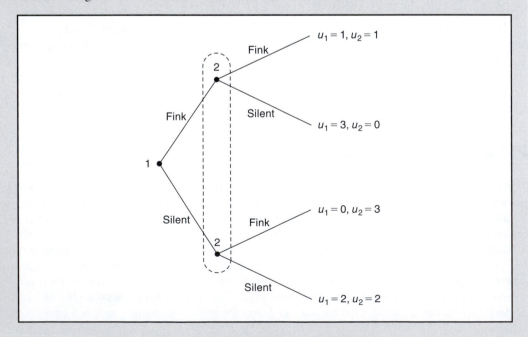

TABLE 8.1   Normal Form for the Prisoners' Dilemma

		Suspect 2	
		Fink	Silent
Suspect 1	Fink	$u_1 = 1, u_2 = 1$	$u_1 = 3, u_2 = 0$
	Silent	$u_1 = 0, u_2 = 3$	$u_1 = 2, u_2 = 2$

Normal form

Although the extensive form in Figure 8.1 offers a useful visual presentation of the complete structure of the game, sometimes it is more convenient to represent games in matrix form, called the *normal form* of the game; this is shown for the Prisoners' Dilemma in Table 8.1. Player 1 is the row player, and 2 is the column player. Each entry in the matrix lists the payoffs first for player 1 and then for 2.

Thinking strategically about the Prisoners' Dilemma

Although we have not discussed how to solve games yet, it is worth thinking about what we might predict will happen in the Prisoners' Dilemma. Studying Table 8.1, on first thought one might predict that both will be silent. This gives the most total years of freedom for both (four) compared to any other outcome. Thinking a bit deeper, this may not be the best prediction in the game. Imagine ourselves in player 1's position for a moment. We don't know what player 2 will do yet since we haven't solved out the game, so let's investigate each possibility. Suppose 2 chose to fink. By finking ourselves we would earn one year of freedom versus none if we remained silent, so finking is better for us. Suppose 2 chose to remain silent. Finking is still better for us than remaining silent since we get three rather than two years of freedom. Regardless of what the other player does, finking is better for us than being silent since it results in an extra year of freedom. Since players are symmetric, the same reasoning holds if we imagine ourselves in player 2's position. Therefore, the best prediction in the Prisoners' Dilemma is that both will fink. When we formally introduce the main solution concept—Nash equilibrium—we will indeed find that both finking is a Nash equilibrium.

The prediction has a paradoxical property: by both finking, the suspects only enjoy one year of freedom, but if they were both silent they would both do better, enjoying two years of freedom. The paradox should not be taken to imply that players are stupid or that our prediction is wrong. Rather, it reveals a central insight from game theory that pitting players against each other in strategic situations sometimes leads to outcomes that are inefficient for the players. (When we say the outcome is inefficient, we are focusing just on the suspects' utilities; if the focus were shifted to society at large, then both finking might be quite a good outcome for the criminal justice system—presumably the motivation behind the district attorney's offer.) The suspects might try to avoid the extra prison time by coming to an agreement beforehand to remain silent, perhaps reinforced by threats to retaliate afterwards if one or the other finks. Introducing agreements and threats leads to a game that differs from the basic Prisoners' Dilemma, a game that should be analyzed on its own terms using the tools we will develop shortly.

Solving the Prisoners' Dilemma was easy because there were only two players and two strategies and because the strategic calculations involved were fairly straightforward. It would be useful to have a systematic way of solving this as well as more complicated games. Nash equilibrium provides us with such a systematic solution.

NASH EQUILIBRIUM

In the economic theory of markets, the concept of equilibrium is developed to indicate a situation in which both suppliers and demanders are content with the market outcome. Given the equilibrium price and quantity, no market participant has an incentive to change his or her behavior. In the strategic setting of game theory, we will adopt a related notion of equilibrium, formalized by John Nash in the 1950s, called *Nash equilibrium*.[1] Nash equilibrium involves strategic choices that, once made, provide no incentives for the players to alter their behavior further. A Nash equilibrium is a strategy for each player that is the best choice for each player given the others' equilibrium strategies.

Nash equilibrium can be defined very simply in terms of *best responses*. In an n-player game, strategy s_i is a best response to rivals' strategies s_{-i} if player i cannot obtain a strictly higher payoff with any other possible strategy $s_i' \in S_i$ given that rivals are playing s_{-i}.

DEFINITION

Best response. s_i is a best response for player i to rivals' strategies s_{-i}, denoted $s_i \in BR_i(s_{-i})$, if

$$u_i(s_i, s_{-i}) \geq u_i(s_i', s_{-i}) \quad \text{for all} \quad s_i' \in S_i. \tag{8.1}$$

A technicality embedded in the definition is that there may be a set of best responses rather than a unique one; that is why we used the set inclusion notation $s_i \in BR_i(s_{-i})$. There may be a tie for the best response, in which case the set $BR_i(s_{-i})$ will contain more than one element. If there isn't a tie, then there will be a single best response s_i and we can simply write $s_i = BR_i(s_{-i})$.

We can now define a Nash equilibrium in an n-player game as follows.

DEFINITION

Nash equilibrium. A Nash equilibrium is a strategy profile $(s_1^*, s_2^*, ..., s_n^*)$ such that, for each player $i = 1, 2, ..., n$, s_i^* is a best response to the other players' equilibrium strategies s_{-i}^*. That is, $s_i^* \in BR_i(s_{-i}^*)$.

These definitions involve a lot of notation. The notation is a bit simpler in a two-player game. In a two-player game, (s_1^*, s_2^*) is a Nash equilibrium if s_1^* and s_2^* are mutual best responses against each other:

$$u_1(s_1^*, s_2^*) \geq u_1(s_1, s_2^*) \quad \text{for all} \quad s_1 \in S_1 \tag{8.2}$$

and

$$u_2(s_2^*, s_1^*) \geq u_2(s_2, s_1^*) \quad \text{for all} \quad s_2 \in S_2. \tag{8.3}$$

A Nash equilibrium is stable in that, even if all players revealed their strategies to each other, no player would have an incentive to deviate from his or her equilibrium strategy and choose something else. Nonequilibrium strategies are not stable in this way. If an outcome is not a Nash equilibrium, then at least one player must benefit from deviating. Hyperrational players could be expected to solve the inference problem and deduce that all would play a Nash equilibrium (especially if there is a unique Nash equilibrium). Even if players are not hyperrational, over the long run we can expect their play to converge to a Nash equilibrium as they abandon strategies that are not mutual best responses.

---

[1] John Nash, "Equilibrium Points in *n*-Person Games," *Proceedings of the National Academy of Sciences* 36 (1950): 48–49. Nash is the principal figure in the 2001 film *A Beautiful Mind* (see Problem 8.7 for a game-theory example from the film) and co-winner of the 1994 Nobel Prize in economics.

Besides this stability property, another reason Nash equilibrium is used so widely in economics is that it is guaranteed to exist for all games we will study (allowing for mixed strategies, to be defined below; Nash equilibria in pure strategies do not have to exist). Nash equilibrium has some drawbacks. There may be multiple Nash equilibria, making it hard to come up with a unique prediction. Also, the definition of Nash equilibrium leaves unclear how a player can choose a best-response strategy before knowing how rivals will play.

Nash equilibrium in the Prisoners' Dilemma

Let's apply the concepts of best response and Nash equilibrium to the example of the Prisoners' Dilemma. Our educated guess was that both players will end up finking. We will show that both finking is a Nash equilibrium of the game. To do this, we need to show that finking is a best response to the other players' finking. Refer to the payoff matrix in Table 8.1. If player 2 finks, we are in the first column of the matrix. If player 1 also finks, his payoff is 1; if he is silent, his payoff is 0. Since he earns the most from finking given player 2 finks, finking is player 1's best response to player 2's finking. Since players are symmetric, the same logic implies that player 2's finking is a best response to player 1's finking. Therefore, both finking is indeed a Nash equilibrium.

We can show more: that both finking is the only Nash equilibrium. To do so, we need to rule out the other three outcomes. Consider the outcome in which player 1 finks and 2 is silent, abbreviated (fink, silent), the upper right corner of the matrix. This is not a Nash equilibrium. Given that player 1 finks, as we have already said, player 2's best response is to fink, not to be silent. Symmetrically, the outcome in which player 1 is silent and 2 finks in the lower left corner of the matrix is not a Nash equilibrium. That leaves the outcome in which both are silent. Given that player 2 is silent, we focus our attention on the second column of the matrix: the two rows in that column show that player 1's payoff is 2 from being silent and 3 from finking. Therefore, silent is not a best response to fink and so both being silent cannot be a Nash equilibrium.

To rule out a Nash equilibrium, it is enough to find just one player who is not playing a best response and so would want to deviate to some other strategy. Considering the outcome (fink, silent), although player 1 would not deviate from this outcome (he earns 3, which is the most possible), player 2 would prefer to deviate from silent to fink. Symmetrically, considering the outcome (silent, fink), although player 2 does not want to deviate, player 1 prefers to deviate from silent to fink, so this is not a Nash equilibrium. Considering the outcome (silent, silent), both players prefer to deviate to another strategy. Having two players prefer to deviate is more than enough to rule out a Nash equilibrium.

Underlining best-response payoffs

A quick way to find the Nash equilibria of a game is to underline best-response payoffs in the matrix. The underlining procedure is demonstrated for the Prisoners' Dilemma in Table 8.2. The first step is to underline the payoffs corresponding to player 1's best responses. Player 1's

TABLE 8.2   Underlining Procedure in the Prisoners' Dilemma

		Suspect 2	
		Fink	Silent
Suspect 1	Fink	$u_1 = 1, u_2 = 1$	$u_1 = 3, u_2 = 0$
	Silent	$u_1 = 0, u_2 = 3$	$u_1 = 2, u_2 = 2$

best response is to fink if player 2 finks, so we underline $u_1 = 1$ in the upper left box, and to fink if player 2 is silent, so we underline $u_1 = 3$ in the upper left box. Next, we move to underlining the payoffs corresponding to player 2's best responses. Player 2's best response is to fink if player 1 finks, so we underline $u_2 = 1$ in the upper left box, and to fink if player 1 is silent, so we underline $u_2 = 3$ in the lower left box.

Now that the best-response payoffs have been underlined, we look for boxes in which every player's payoff is underlined. These boxes correspond to Nash equilibria. (There may be additional Nash equilibria involving mixed strategies, defined later in the chapter.) In Table 8.2, only in the upper left box are both payoffs underlined, verifying that (fink, fink)—and none of the other outcomes—is a Nash equilibrium.

Dominant Strategies

(Fink, fink) is a Nash equilibrium in the Prisoners' Dilemma because finking is a best response to the other player's finking. We can say more: finking is the best response to all of the other player's strategies, fink and silent. (This can be seen, among other ways, from the underlining procedure shown in Table 8.2: all player 1's payoffs are underlined in the row in which he plays fink, and all player 2's payoffs are underlined in the column in which he plays fink.)

A strategy that is a best response to any strategy the other players might choose is called a dominant strategy. Players do not always have dominant strategies, but when they do there is strong reason to believe they will play that way. Complicated strategic considerations do not matter when a player has a dominant strategy because what is best for that player is independent of what others are doing.

DEFINITION	**Dominant strategy.** A dominant strategy is a strategy s_i^* for player i that is a best response to all strategy profiles of other players. That is, $s_i^* \in BR_i(s_{-i})$ for all s_{-i}.

Note the difference between a Nash equilibrium strategy and a dominant strategy. A strategy that is part of a Nash equilibrium need only be a best response to one strategy profile of other players—namely, their equilibrium strategies. A dominant strategy must be a best response not just to the Nash equilibrium strategies of other players but to all the strategies of those players.

If all players in a game have a dominant strategy, then we say the game has a *dominant strategy equilibrium*. As well as being the Nash equilibrium of the Prisoners' Dilemma, (fink, fink) is a dominant strategy equilibrium. As is clear from the definitions, in any game with a dominant strategy equilibrium, the dominant strategy equilibrium is a Nash equilibrium. Problem 8.4 will show that when a dominant strategy exists, it is the unique Nash equilibrium.

Battle of the Sexes

The famous Battle of the Sexes game is another example that illustrates the concepts of best response and Nash equilibrium. The story goes that a wife (player 1) and husband (player 2) would like to meet each other for an evening out. They can go either to the ballet or to a boxing match. Both prefer to spend time together than apart. Conditional on being together, the wife prefers to go to the ballet and the husband to boxing. The extensive form of the game is presented in Figure 8.2 and the normal form in Table 8.3. For brevity we dispense with the u_1 and u_2 labels on the payoffs and simply re-emphasize the convention that the first payoff is player 1's and the second player 2's.

We will work with the normal form, examining each of the four boxes in Table 8.3 and determining which are Nash equilibria and which are not. Start with the outcome in which both players choose ballet, written (ballet, ballet), the upper left corner of the payoff matrix. Given that the husband plays ballet, the wife's best response is to play ballet (this gives her her

FIGURE 8.2   Extensive Form for the Battle of the Sexes

In this game, player 1 (wife) and player 2 (husband) choose to attend the ballet or a boxing match. They prefer to coordinate but disagree on which event to coordinate. Because they choose simultaneously, the husband does not know the wife's choice when he moves, so his decision nodes are connected in the same information set.

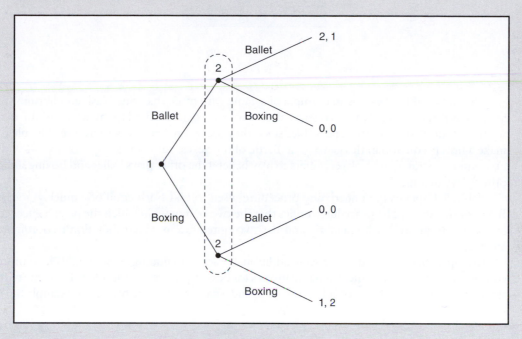

TABLE 8.3   Normal Form for the Battle of the Sexes

		Player 2 (Husband)	
		Ballet	Boxing
Player 1 (Wife)	Ballet	2, 1	0, 0
	Boxing	0, 0	1, 2

highest payoff in the matrix of 2). Using notation, ballet $= BR_1(\text{ballet})$. [We don't need the fancy set-inclusion symbol as in "ballet $\in BR_1(\text{ballet})$" because the husband has only one best response to the wife's choosing ballet.] Given that the wife plays ballet, the husband's best response is to play ballet. If he deviated to boxing then he would earn 0 rather than 1, since they would end up not coordinating. Using notation, ballet $= BR_2(\text{ballet})$. So (ballet, ballet) is indeed a Nash equilibrium. Symmetrically, (boxing, boxing) is a Nash equilibrium.

Consider the outcome (ballet, boxing) in the upper left corner of the matrix. Given the husband chooses boxing, the wife earns 0 from choosing ballet but 1 from choosing boxing, so ballet is not a best response for the wife to the husband's choosing boxing. In notation, ballet $\notin BR_1(\text{boxing})$. Hence (ballet, boxing) cannot be a Nash equilibrium. [The husband's strategy of boxing is not a best response to the wife's playing ballet either, so in fact both players would prefer to deviate from (ballet, boxing), although we only need to find one player who would want to deviate to rule out an outcome as a Nash equilibrium.] Symmetrically, (boxing, ballet) is not a Nash equilibrium, either.

TABLE 8.4   Underlining Procedure in the Battle of the Sexes

Player 2 (Husband)

		Ballet	Boxing
Player 1 (Wife)	Ballet	2, 1	0, 0
	Boxing	0, 0	1, 2

The Battle of the Sexes is an example of a game with more than one Nash equilibrium (in fact, it has three—a third in mixed strategies, as we will see). It is hard to say which of the two we have found so far is more plausible, since they are symmetric. It is therefore difficult to make a firm prediction in this game. The Battle of the Sexes is also an example of a game with no dominant strategies. A player prefers to play ballet if the other plays ballet and boxing if the other plays boxing.

Table 8.4 applies the underlining procedure, used to find Nash equilibria quickly, to the Battle of the Sexes. The procedure verifies that the two outcomes in which the players succeed in coordinating are Nash equilibria and the two outcomes in which they don't coordinate are not.

Examples 8.1, 8.2, and 8.3 provide additional practice in finding Nash equilibria in more complicated settings (a game that has many ties for best responses in Example 8.1, a game with three strategies for each player in Example 8.2, and a game with three players in Example 8.3).

EXAMPLE 8.1 The Prisoners' Dilemma Redux

In this variation on the Prisoners' Dilemma, a suspect is convicted and receives a sentence of four years if he is finked on and goes free if not. The district attorney does not reward finking. Table 8.5 presents the normal form for the game before and after applying the procedure for underlining best responses. Payoffs are again restated in terms of years of freedom.

Ties for best responses are rife. For example, given player 2 finks, player 1's payoff is 0 whether he finks or is silent. So there is a tie for 1's best response to 2's finking. This is an example of the set of best responses containing more than one element: $BR_1(\text{fink}) = \{\text{fink}, \text{silent}\}$.

TABLE 8.5   The Prisoners' Dilemma Redux

(a) Normal form

Suspect 2

		Fink	Silent
Suspect 1	Fink	0, 0	1, 0
	Silent	0, 1	1, 1

(b) Underlining procedure

Suspect 2

		Fink	Silent
Suspect 1	Fink	0, 0	1, 0
	Silent	0, 1	1, 1

The underlining procedure shows that there is a Nash equilibrium in each of the four boxes. Given that suspects receive no personal reward or penalty for finking, they are both indifferent between finking and being silent; thus any outcome can be a Nash equilibrium.

QUERY: Does any player have a dominant strategy? Can you draw the extensive form for the game?

EXAMPLE 8.2 Rock, Paper, Scissors

Rock, Paper, Scissors is a children's game in which the two players simultaneously display one of three hand symbols. Table 8.6 presents the normal form. The zero payoffs along the diagonal show that if players adopt the same strategy then no payments are made. In other cases, the payoffs indicate a $1 payment from loser to winner under the usual hierarchy (rock breaks scissors, scissors cut paper, paper covers rock).

TABLE 8.6   Rock, Paper, Scissors

(a) Normal form

		Player 2	
	Rock	Paper	Scissors
Rock	0, 0	−1, 1	1, −1
Paper	1, −1	0, 0	−1, 1
Scissors	−1, 1	1, −1	0, 0

(b) Underlying procedure

		Player 2	
	Rock	Paper	Scissors
Rock	0, 0	−1, 1	1, −1
Paper	1, −1	0, 0	−1, 1
Scissors	−1, 1	1, −1	0, 0

As anyone who has played this game knows, and as the underlining procedure reveals, none of the nine boxes represents a Nash equilibrium. Any strategy pair is unstable because it offers at least one of the players an incentive to deviate. For example, (scissors, scissors) provides an incentive for either player 1 or 2 to choose rock; (paper, rock) provides an incentive for 2 to choose scissors.

The game does have a Nash equilibrium—not any of the nine boxes in Table 8.6 but in mixed strategies, defined in the next section.

QUERY: Does any player have a dominant strategy? Why isn't (paper, scissors) a Nash equilibrium?

EXAMPLE 8.3 Three's Company

Three's Company is a three-player version of the Battle of the Sexes based on a 1970s sitcom of the same name about the misadventures of a man (Jack) and two women (Janet and Chrissy) who shared an apartment to save rent.

Modify the payoffs from the Battle of the Sexes as follows. Players get one "util" from attending their favorite event (Jack's is boxing and Janet and Chrissy's is ballet). Players get an additional util for each of the other players who shows up at the event with them. Table 8.7 presents the normal form. For each of player 3's strategies, there is a separate payoff matrix with all combinations of player 1 and 2's strategies. Each box lists the three players' payoffs in order.

TABLE 8.7   Three's Company

(a) Normal form

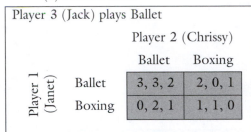

(b) Underlining Procedure

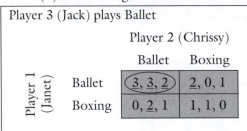

For players 1 and 2, the underlining procedure is the same as in a two-player game except that it must be repeated for the two payoff matrices. To underline player 3's best-response payoffs, compare the two boxes in the same position in the two different matrices. For example, given Janet and Chrissy both play ballet, we compare the third payoff in the upper-left box in both matrices: Jack's payoff is 2 in the first matrix (in which he plays ballet) and 1 in the second (in which he plays boxing). So we underline the 2.

As in the Battle of the Sexes, Three's Company has two Nash equilibria, one in which all go to ballet and one in which all go to boxing.

QUERY: What payoffs might make Three's Company even closer in spirit to the Battle of the Sexes? What would the normal form look like for Four's Company? (Four's Company is similar to Three's Company except with two men and two women.)

MIXED STRATEGIES

Players' strategies can be more complicated than simply choosing an action with certainty. In this section we study *mixed strategies*, which have the player randomly select from several possible actions. By contrast, the strategies considered in the examples so far have a player choose one action or another with certainty; these are called *pure strategies*. For example, in the Battle of the Sexes, we have considered the pure strategies of choosing either ballet or boxing for sure. A possible mixed strategy in this game would be to flip a coin and then attend the ballet if and only if the coin comes up heads, yielding a 50–50 chance of showing up at either event.

Although at first glance it may seem bizarre to have players flipping coins to determine how they will play, there are good reasons for studying mixed strategies. First, some games (such as Rock, Paper, Scissors) have no Nash equilibria in pure strategies. As we will see in the section on existence, such games will always have a Nash equilibrium in mixed strategies, so allowing for mixed strategies will enable us to make predictions in such games where it was impossible to do so otherwise. Second, strategies involving randomization are quite natural and familiar in certain settings. Students are familiar with the setting of class exams. Class time is usually too limited for the professor to examine students on every topic taught in class, but it may be sufficient to test students on a subset of topics to induce them to study all of the material. If students knew which topics were on the test then they might be inclined to study only those and not the others, so the professor must choose the topics at random in order to get the students to study everything. Random strategies are also familiar in sports (the same soccer player sometimes shoots to the right of the net and sometimes to the left on penalty kicks) and in card games (the poker player sometimes folds and sometimes bluffs with a similarly poor hand at different times). Third, it is possible to "purify" mixed strategies by specifying a more complicated game in which one or the other action is better for the player for privately known reasons and where that action is played with certainty.[2] For example, a history professor might decide to ask an exam question about World War I because, unbeknownst to the students, she recently read an interesting journal article about it.

To be more formal, suppose that player i has a set of M possible actions $A_i = \{a_i^1, \ldots, a_i^m, \ldots, a_i^M\}$, where the subscript refers to the player and the superscript to the different choices. A mixed strategy is a probability distribution over the M actions, $s_i = (\sigma_i^1, \ldots, \sigma_i^m, \ldots, \sigma_i^M)$, where σ_i^m is a number between 0 and 1 that indicates the probability of player i playing action a_i^m. The probabilities in s_i must sum to unity: $\sigma_i^1 + \cdots + \sigma_i^m + \cdots + \sigma_i^M = 1$.

In the Battle of the Sexes, for example, both players have the same two actions of ballet and boxing, so we can write $A_1 = A_2 = \{\text{ballet}, \text{boxing}\}$. We can write a mixed strategy as a pair of probabilities $(\sigma, 1 - \sigma)$, where σ is the probability that the player chooses ballet. The probabilities must sum to unity and so, with two actions, once the probability of one action is specified, the probability of the other is determined. Mixed strategy $(1/3, 2/3)$ means that the player plays ballet with probability $1/3$ and boxing with probability $2/3$; $(1/2, 1/2)$ means that the player is equally likely to play ballet or boxing; $(1, 0)$ means that the player chooses ballet with certainty; and $(0, 1)$ means that the player chooses boxing with certainty.

In our terminology, a mixed strategy is a general category that includes the special case of a pure strategy. A pure strategy is the special case in which only one action is played with

---

[2]John Harsanyi, "Games with Randomly Disturbed Payoffs: A New Rationale for Mixed-Strategy Equilibrium Points," *International Journal of Game Theory* 2 (1973): 1–23. Harsanyi was a co-winner (along with Nash) of the 1994 Nobel Prize in economics.

positive probability. Mixed strategies that involve two or more actions being played with positive probability are called *strictly mixed strategies*. Returning to the examples from the previous paragraph of mixed strategies in the Battle of the Sexes, all four strategies $(1/3, 2/3)$, $(1/2, 1/2)$, $(1, 0)$, and $(0, 1)$ are mixed strategies. The first two are strictly mixed and the second two are pure strategies.

With this notation for actions and mixed strategies behind us, we do not need new definitions for best response, Nash equilibrium, and dominant strategy. The definitions introduced when s_i was taken to be a pure strategy also apply to the case in which s_i is taken to be a mixed strategy. The only change is that the payoff function $u_i(s_i, s_{-i})$, rather than being a certain payoff, must be reinterpreted as the expected value of a random payoff, with probabilities given by the strategies s_i and s_{-i}. Example 8.4 provides some practice in computing expected payoffs in the Battle of the Sexes.

EXAMPLE 8.4 Expected Payoffs in the Battle of the Sexes

Let's compute players' expected payoffs if the wife chooses the mixed strategy $(1/9, 8/9)$ and the husband $(4/5, 1/5)$ in the Battle of the Sexes. The wife's expected payoff is

$$U_1\left(\left(\frac{1}{9}, \frac{8}{9}\right), \left(\frac{4}{5}, \frac{1}{5}\right)\right) = \left(\frac{1}{9}\right)\left(\frac{4}{5}\right)U_1(\text{ballet}, \text{ballet}) + \left(\frac{1}{9}\right)\left(\frac{1}{5}\right)U_1(\text{ballet}, \text{boxing})$$

$$+ \left(\frac{8}{9}\right)\left(\frac{4}{5}\right)U_1(\text{boxing}, \text{ballet}) + \left(\frac{8}{9}\right)\left(\frac{1}{5}\right)U_1(\text{boxing}, \text{boxing})$$

$$= \left(\frac{1}{9}\right)\left(\frac{4}{5}\right)(2) + \left(\frac{1}{9}\right)\left(\frac{1}{5}\right)(0) + \left(\frac{8}{9}\right)\left(\frac{4}{5}\right)(0) + \left(\frac{8}{9}\right)\left(\frac{1}{5}\right)(1)$$

$$= \frac{16}{45}. \tag{8.4}$$

To understand Equation 8.4, it is helpful to review the concept of expected value from Chapter 2. Equation (2.176) indicates that an expected value of a random variable equals the sum over all outcomes of the probability of the outcome multiplied by the value of the random variable in that outcome. In the Battle of the Sexes, there are four outcomes, corresponding to the four boxes in Table 8.3. Since players randomize independently, the probability of reaching a particular box equals the product of the probabilities that each player plays the strategy leading to that box. So, for example, the probability of (boxing, ballet)—that is, the wife plays boxing and the husband plays ballet—equals $(8/9) \times (4/5)$. The probabilities of the four outcomes are multiplied by the value of the relevant random variable (in this case, player 1's payoff) in each outcome.

Next we compute the wife's expected payoff if she plays the pure strategy of going to ballet [the same as the mixed strategy $(1, 0)$] and the husband continues to play the mixed strategy $(4/5, 1/5)$. Now there are only two relevant outcomes, given by the two boxes in the row in which the wife plays ballet. The probabilities of the two outcomes are given by the probabilities in the husband's mixed strategy. Therefore,

$$U_1\left(\text{ballet}, \left(\frac{4}{5}, \frac{1}{5}\right)\right) = \left(\frac{4}{5}\right)U_1(\text{ballet}, \text{ballet}) + \left(\frac{1}{5}\right)U_1(\text{ballet}, \text{boxing})$$

$$= \left(\frac{4}{5}\right)(2) + \left(\frac{1}{5}\right)(0) = \frac{8}{5}. \tag{8.5}$$

Finally, we will compute the general expression for the wife's expected payoff when she plays mixed strategy $(w, 1 - w)$ and the husband plays $(h, 1 - h)$: if the wife plays ballet with probability w and the husband with probability h, then

$$u_1((w, 1-w), (h, 1-h)) = (w)(h)U_1(\textbf{ballet, ballet}) + (w)(1-h)U_1(\textbf{ballet, boxing})$$
$$+ (1-w)(h)U_1(\textbf{boxing, ballet})$$
$$+ (1-w)(1-h)U_1(\textbf{boxing, boxing})$$
$$= (w)(h)(2) + (w)(1-h)(0) + (1-w)(h)(0)$$
$$+ (1-w)(1-h)(1)$$
$$= 1 - h - w + 3hw. \tag{8.6}$$

QUERY: What is the husband's expected payoff in each case? Show that his expected payoff is $2 - 2h - 2w + 3hw$ in the general case. Given the husband plays the mixed strategy $(4/5, 1/5)$, what strategy provides the wife with the highest payoff?

Computing Nash equilibrium of a game when strictly mixed strategies are involved is quite a bit more complicated than when pure strategies are involved. Before wading in, we can save a lot of work by asking whether the game even has a Nash equilibrium in strictly mixed strategies. If it does not then, having found all the pure-strategy Nash equilibria, one has finished analyzing the game. The key to guessing whether a game has a Nash equilibrium in strictly mixed strategies is the surprising result that almost all games have an odd number of Nash equilibria.[3]

Let's apply this insight to some of the examples considered so far. We found an odd number (one) of pure-strategy Nash equilibria in the Prisoners' Dilemma, suggesting we need not look further for one in strictly mixed strategies. In the Battle of the Sexes, we found an even number (two) of pure-strategy Nash equilibria, suggesting the existence of a third one in strictly mixed strategies. Example 8.2—Rock, Paper, Scissors—has no pure-strategy Nash equilibria. To arrive at an odd number of Nash equilibria, we would expect to find one Nash equilibrium in strictly mixed strategies.

EXAMPLE 8.5 Mixed-Strategy Nash Equilibrium in the Battle of the Sexes

A general mixed strategy for the wife in the Battle of the Sexes is $(w, 1-w)$ and for the husband is $(h, 1-h)$, where w and h are the probabilities of playing ballet for the wife and husband, respectively. We will compute values of w and h that make up Nash equilibria. Both players have a continuum of possible strategies between 0 and 1. Therefore, we cannot write these strategies in the rows and columns of a matrix and underline best-response payoffs to find the Nash equilibria. Instead, we will use graphical methods to solve for the Nash equilibria.

Given players' general mixed strategies, we saw in Example 8.4 that the wife's expected payoff is

$$u_1((w, 1-w), (h, 1-h)) = 1 - h - w + 3hw. \tag{8.7}$$

As Equation 8.7 shows, the wife's best response depends on h. If $h < 1/3$, she wants to set w as low as possible: $w = 0$. If $h > 1/3$, her best response is to set w as high as possible: $w = 1$. When $h = 1/3$, her expected payoff equals $2/3$ regardless of what w she chooses. In this case there is a tie for the best response, including any w from 0 to 1.

(continued)

[3]John Harsanyi, "Oddness of the Number of Equilibrium Points: A New Proof," *International Journal of Game Theory* 2 (1973): 235–50. Games in which there are ties between payoffs may have an even or infinite number of Nash equilibria. Example 8.1, the Prisoners' Dilemma Redux, has several payoff ties. The game has four pure-strategy Nash equilibria and an infinite number of different mixed strategy equilibria.

EXAMPLE 8.5 CONTINUED

FIGURE 8.3   Nash Equilibria in Mixed Strategies in the Battle of the Sexes

Ballet is chosen by the wife with probability w and by the husband with probability h. Players' best responses are graphed on the same set of axes. The three intersection points E_1, E_2, and E_3 are Nash equilibria. The Nash equilibrium in strictly mixed strategies, E_3, is $w^* = 2/3$ and $h^* = 1/3$.

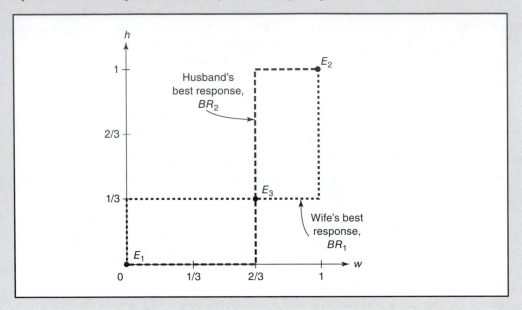

In Example 8.4, we stated that the husband's expected payoff is

$$U_2((h, 1 - h), (w, 1 - w)) = 2 - 2h - 2w + 3hw. \qquad (8.8)$$

When $w < 2/3$, his expected payoff is maximized by $h = 0$; when $w > 2/3$, his expected payoff is maximized by $h = 1$; and when $w = 2/3$, he is indifferent among all values of h, obtaining an expected payoff of $2/3$ regardless.

The best responses are graphed in Figure 8.3. The Nash equilibria are given by the intersection points between the best responses. At these intersection points, both players are best responding to each other, which is what is required for the outcome to be a Nash equilibrium. There are three Nash equilibria. The points E_1 and E_2 are the pure-strategy Nash equilibria we found before, with E_1 corresponding to the pure-strategy Nash equilibrium in which both play boxing and E_2 to that in which both play ballet. Point E_3 is the strictly mixed-strategy Nash equilibrium, which can can be spelled out as "the wife plays ballet with probability $2/3$ and boxing with probability $1/3$ and the husband plays ballet with probability $1/3$ and boxing with probability $2/3$." More succinctly, having defined w and h, we may write the equilibruim as "$w^* = 2/3$ and $h^* = 1/3$."

QUERY: What is a player's expected payoff in the Nash equilibrium in strictly mixed strategies? How does this payoff compare to those in the pure-strategy Nash equilibria? What arguments might be offered that one or another of the three Nash equilibria might be the best prediction in this game?

Example 8.5 runs through the lengthy calculations involved in finding all the Nash equilibria of the Battle of the Sexes, those in pure strategies and those in strictly mixed strategies. The steps involve finding players' expected payoffs as functions of general mixed strategies, using these to find players' best responses, and then graphing players' best responses to see where they intersect. A shortcut to finding the Nash equilibrium in strictly mixed strategies is based on the insight that a player will be willing to randomize between two actions in equilibrium only if he or she gets the same expected payoff from playing either action or, in other words, is indifferent between the two actions in equilibrium. Otherwise, one of the two actions would provide a higher expected payoff, and the player would prefer to play that action with certainty.

Suppose the husband is playing mixed strategy $(h, 1 - h)$, that is, playing ballet with probability h and boxing with probability $1 - h$. The wife's expected payoff from playing ballet is

$$U_1(\textbf{ballet}, (h, 1 - h)) = (h)(2) + (1 - h)(0) = 2h. \qquad \textbf{(8.9)}$$

Her expected payoff from playing boxing is

$$U_1(\textbf{boxing}, (h, 1 - h)) = (h)(0) + (1 - h)(1) = 1 - h. \qquad \textbf{(8.10)}$$

For the wife to be indifferent between ballet and boxing in equilibrium, Equations 8.9 and 8.10 must be equal: $2h = 1 - h$, implying $h^* = 1/3$. Similar calculations based on the husband's indifference between playing ballet and boxing in equilibrium show that the wife's probability of playing ballet in the strictly mixed strategy Nash equilibrium is $w^* = 2/3$. (Work through these calculations as an exercise.)

Notice that the wife's indifference condition does not "pin down" her equilibrium mixed strategy. The wife's indifference condition cannot pin down her own equilibrium mixed strategy because, given that she is indifferent between the two actions in equilibrium, her overall expected payoff is the same no matter what probability distribution she plays over the two actions. Rather, the wife's indifference condition pins down the other player's—the husband's—mixed strategy. There is a unique probability distribution he can use to play ballet and boxing that makes her indifferent between the two actions and thus makes her willing to randomize. Given any probability of his playing ballet and boxing other than $(1/3, 2/3)$, it would not be a stable outcome for her to randomize.

Thus, two principles should be kept in mind when seeking Nash equilibria in strictly mixed strategies. One is that a player randomizes over only those actions among which he or she is indifferent, given other players' equilibrium mixed strategies. The second is that one player's indifference condition pins down the *other* player's mixed strategy.

EXISTENCE

One of the reasons Nash equilibrium is so widely used is that a Nash equilibrium is guaranteed to exist in a wide class of games. This is not true for some other equilibrium concepts. Consider the dominant strategy equilibrium concept. The Prisoners' Dilemma has a dominant strategy equilibrium (both suspects fink), but most games do not. Indeed, there are many games—including, for example, the Battle of the Sexes—in which no player has a dominant strategy, let alone all the players. In such games, we can't make predictions using dominant strategy equilibrium but we can using Nash equilibrium.

The Extensions section at the end of this chapter will provide the technical details behind John Nash's proof of the existence of his equilibrium in all finite games (games with a finite number of players and a finite number of actions). The existence theorem does not guarantee the existence of a pure-strategy Nash equilibrium. We already saw an example: Rock, Paper,

Scissors in Example 8.2. However, if a finite game does not have a pure-strategy Nash equilibrium, the theorem guarantees that it will have a mixed-strategy Nash equilibrium. The proof of Nash's theorem is similar to the proof in Chapter 13 of the existence of prices leading to a general competitive equilibrium. The Extensions section includes an existence proof for games with a continuum of actions, as studied in the next section.

CONTINUUM OF ACTIONS

Most of the insight from economic situations can often be gained by distilling the situation down to a few or even two actions, as with all the games studied so far. Other times, additional insight can be gained by allowing a continuum of actions. To be clear, we have already encountered a continuum of *strategies*—in our discussion of mixed strategies—but still the probability distributions in mixed strategies were over a finite number of actions. In this section we focus on continuum of *actions*.

Some settings are more realistically modeled via a continuous range of actions. In Chapter 15, for example, we will study competition between strategic firms. In one model (Bertrand), firms set prices; in another (Cournot), firms set quantities. It is natural to allow firms to choose any nonnegative price or quantity rather than artificially restricting them to just two prices (say, $2 or $5) or two quantities (say, 100 or 1,000 units). Continuous actions have several other advantages. With continuous actions, the familiar methods from calculus can often be used to solve for Nash equilibria. It is also possible to analyze how the equilibrium actions vary with changes in underlying parameters. With the Cournot model, for example, we might want to know how equilibrium quantities change with a small increase in a firm's marginal costs or a demand parameter.

Tragedy of the Commons

Example 8.6 illustrates how to solve for the Nash equilibrium when the game (in this case, the Tragedy of the Commons) involves a continuum of actions. The first step is to write down the payoff for each player as a function of all players' actions. The next step is to compute the first-order condition associated with each player's payoff maximum. This will give an equation that can be rearranged into the best response of each player as a function of all other players' actions. There will be one equation for each player. With n players, the system of n equations for the n unknown equilibrium actions can be solved simultaneously by either algebraic or graphical methods.

EXAMPLE 8.6 Tragedy of the Commons

The term "Tragedy of the Commons" has come to signify environmental problems of overuse that arise when scarce resources are treated as common property.[4] A game-theoretic illustration of this issue can be developed by assuming that two herders decide how many sheep to graze on the village commons. The problem is that the commons is quite small and can rapidly succumb to overgrazing.

In order to add some mathematical structure to the problem, let q_i be the number of sheep that herder $i = 1, 2$ grazes on the commons, and suppose that the per-sheep value of grazing on the commons (in terms of wool and sheep-milk cheese) is

---

[4]This term was popularized by G. Hardin, "The Tragedy of the Commons," *Science* 162 (1968): 1243–48.

$$v(q_1, q_2) = 120 - (q_1 + q_2). \tag{8.11}$$

This function implies that the value of grazing a given number of sheep is lower the more sheep are around competing for grass. We cannot use a matrix to represent the normal form of this game of continuous actions. Instead, the normal form is simply a listing of the herders' payoff functions

$$u_1(q_1, q_2) = q_1 v(q_1, q_2) = q_1(120 - q_1 - q_2),$$
$$u_2(q_1, q_2) = q_2 v(q_1, q_2) = q_2(120 - q_1 - q_2). \tag{8.12}$$

To find the Nash equilibrium, we solve herder 1's value-maximization problem:

$$\max_{q_1}\{q_1(120 - q_1 - q_2)\}. \tag{8.13}$$

The first-order condition for a maximum is

$$120 - 2q_1 - q_2 = 0 \tag{8.14}$$

or, rearranging,

$$q_1 = 60 - \frac{q_2}{2} = BR_1(q_2). \tag{8.15}$$

Similar steps show that herder 2's best response is

$$q_2 = 60 - \frac{q_1}{2} = BR_2(q_1). \tag{8.16}$$

The Nash equilibrium is given by the pair (q_1^*, q_2^*) that satisfies Equations 8.15 and 8.16 simultaneously. Taking an algebraic approach to the simultaneous solution, Equation 8.16 can be substituted into Equation 8.15, which yields

$$q_1 = 60 - \frac{1}{2}\left(60 - \frac{q_1}{2}\right); \tag{8.17}$$

upon rearranging, this implies $q_1^* = 40$. Substituting $q_1^* = 40$ into Equation 8.17 implies $q_2^* = 40$ as well. Thus, each herder will graze 40 sheep on the common. Each earns a payoff of 1,600, as can be seen by substituting $q_1^* = q_2^* = 40$ into the payoff function in Equation 8.13.

Equations 8.15 and 8.16 can also be solved simultaneously using graphical methods. Figure 8.4 plots the two best responses on a graph with player 1's action on the horizontal axis and player 2's on the vertical axis. These best responses are simply lines and so are easy to graph in this example. (To be consistent with the axis labels, the inverse of Equation 8.15 is actually what is graphed.) The two best responses intersect at the Nash equilibrium E_1.

The graphical method is useful for showing how the Nash equilibrium shifts with changes in the parameters of the problem. Suppose the per-sheep value of grazing increases for the first herder while the second remains as in Equation 8.11, perhaps because the first herder starts raising merino sheep with more valuable wool. This change would shift the best response out for herder 1 while leaving 2's the same. The new intersection point (E_2 in Figure 8.4), which is the new Nash equilibrium, involves more sheep for 1 and fewer for 2.

The Nash equilibrium is not the best use of the commons. In the original problem, both herders' per-sheep value of grazing is given by Equation 8.11. If both grazed only 30 sheep then each would earn a payoff of 1,800, as can be seen by substituting $q_1 = q_2 = 30$ into Equation 8.13. Indeed, the "joint payoff maximization" problem

$$\max_{q_1}\{(q_1 + q_2)v(q_1, q_2)\} = \max_{q_1}\{(q_1 + q_2)(120 - q_1 - q_2)\} \tag{8.18}$$

is solved by $q_1 = q_2 = 30$ or, more generally, by any q_1 and q_2 that sum to 60.

(continued)

EXAMPLE 8.6 CONTINUED

FIGURE 8.4   Best-Response Diagram for the Tragedy of the Commons

The intersection, E_1, between the two herders' best responses is the Nash equilibrium. An increase in the per-sheep value of grazing in the Tragedy of the Commons shifts out herder 1's best response, resulting in a Nash equilibrium E_2 in which herder 1 grazes more sheep (and herder 2, fewer sheep) than in the original Nash equilibrium.

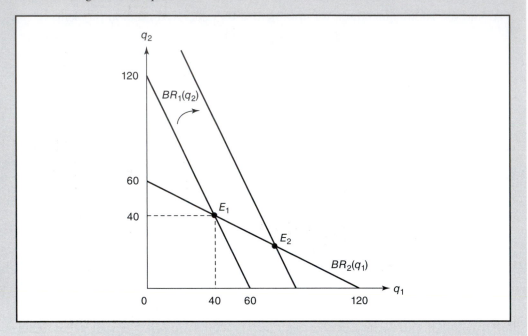

QUERY: How would the Nash equilibrium shift if both herders' benefits increased by the same amount? What about a decrease in (only) herder 2's benefit from grazing?

As Example 8.6 shows, graphical methods are particularly convenient for quickly determining how the equilibrium shifts with changes in the underlying parameters. The example shifted the benefit of grazing to one of herders. This exercise nicely illustrates the nature of strategic interaction. Herder 2's payoff function hasn't changed (only herder 1's has), yet his equilibrium action changes. The second herder observes the first's higher benefit, anticipates that the first will increase the number of sheep he grazes, and reduces his own grazing in response.

The Tragedy of the Commons shares with the Prisoners' Dilemma the feature that the Nash equilibrium is less efficient for all players than some other outcome. In the Prisoners' Dilemma, both fink in equilibrium when it would be more efficient for both to be silent. In the Tragedy of the Commons, the herders graze more sheep in equilibrium than is efficient. This insight may explain why ocean fishing grounds and other common resources can end up being overused even to the point of exhaustion if their use is left unregulated. More detail on such problems—involving what we will call negative externalities—is provided in Chapter 19.

SEQUENTIAL GAMES

In some games, the order of moves matters. For example, in a bicycle race with a staggered start, it may help to go last and thus know the time to beat. On the other hand, competition to establish a new high-definition video format may be won by the first firm to market its technology, thereby capturing an installed base of consumers.

Sequential games differ from the simultaneous games we have considered so far in that a player that moves later in the game can observe how others have played up to that moment. The player can use this information to form more sophisticated strategies than simply choosing an action; the player's strategy can be a contingent plan with the action played depending on what the other players have done.

To illustrate the new concepts raised by sequential games—and, in particular, to make a stark contrast between sequential and simultaneous games—we take a simultaneous game we have discussed already, the Battle of the Sexes, and turn it into a sequential game.

Sequential Battle of the Sexes

Consider the Battle of the Sexes game analyzed previously with all the same actions and payoffs, but now change the timing of moves. Rather than the wife and husband making a simultaneous choice, the wife moves first, choosing ballet or boxing; the husband observes this choice (say, the wife calls him from her chosen location) and then the husband makes his choice. The wife's possible strategies have not changed: she can choose the simple actions ballet or boxing (or perhaps a mixed strategy involving both actions, although this will not be a relevant consideration in the sequential game). The husband's set of possible strategies has expanded. For each of the wife's two actions, he can choose one of two actions, so he has four possible strategies, which are listed in Table 8.8. The vertical bar in the husband's strategies means "conditional on" and so, for example, "boxing | ballet" should be read as "the husband chooses boxing conditional on the wife's choosing ballet".

Given that the husband has four pure strategies rather than just two, the normal form (given in Table 8.9) must now be expanded to eight boxes. Roughly speaking, the normal form is twice as complicated as that for the simultaneous version of the game in Table 8.3. By contrast, the extensive form, given in Figure 8.5, is no more complicated than the extensive form for the simultaneous version of the game in Figure 8.2. The only difference between the

TABLE 8.8 Husband's Contingent Strategies

Contingent strategy	Written in conditional format
Always go to the ballet	(ballet | ballet, ballet | boxing)
Follow his wife	(ballet | ballet, boxing | boxing)
Do the opposite	(boxing | ballet, ballet | boxing)
Always go to boxing	(boxing | ballet, boxing | boxing)

TABLE 8.9 Normal Form for the Sequential Battle of the Sexes

		Husband			
		(Ballet | Ballet Ballet | Boxing)	(Ballet | Ballet Boxing | Boxing)	(Boxing | Ballet Ballet | Boxing)	(Boxing | Ballet Boxing | Boxing)
Wife	Ballet	2, 1	2, 1	0, 0	0, 0
	Boxing	0, 0	1, 2	0, 0	1, 2

FIGURE 8.5   Extensive Form for the Sequential Battle of the Sexes

In the sequential version of the Battle of the Sexes, the husband moves second after observing his wife's move. The husband's decision nodes are not gathered in the same information set.

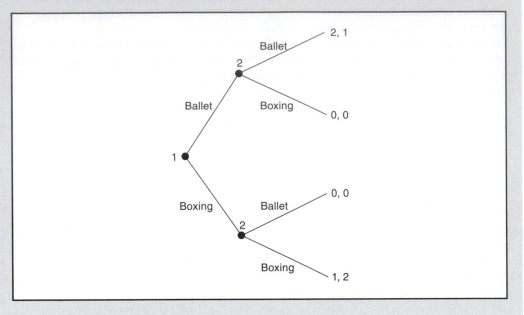

extensive forms is that the oval around the husband's decision nodes has been removed. In the sequential version of the game, the husband's decision nodes are not gathered together in the same information set because the husband observes his wife's action and so knows which node he is on before moving. We can begin to see why the extensive form becomes more useful than the normal form for sequential games, especially in games with many rounds of moves.

To solve for the Nash equilibria, consider the normal form in Table 8.9. Applying the method of underlining best-response payoffs—being careful to underline both payoffs in cases of ties for the best response—reveals three pure-strategy Nash equilibria:

1. wife plays ballet, husband plays (ballet | ballet, ballet | boxing);
2. wife plays ballet, husband plays (ballet | ballet, boxing | boxing);
3. wife plays boxing, husband plays (boxing | ballet, boxing | boxing).

As with the simultaneous version of the Battle of the Sexes, here again we have multiple equilibria. Yet now game theory offers a good way to select among the equilibria. Consider the third Nash equilibrium. The husband's strategy (boxing | ballet, boxing | boxing) involves the implicit threat that he will choose boxing even if his wife chooses ballet. This threat is sufficient to deter her from choosing ballet. Given that she chooses boxing in equilibrium, his strategy earns him 2, which is the best he can do in any outcome. So the outcome is a Nash equilibrium. But the husband's threat is not credible— that is, it is an empty threat. If the wife really were to choose ballet first, then he would be giving up a payoff of 1 by choosing boxing rather than ballet. It is clear why he would want to threaten to choose boxing, but it is not clear that such a threat should be believed. Similarly, the husband's strategy (ballet | ballet, ballet | boxing) in the first Nash equilibrium also involves an empty threat: that he will choose ballet if his wife chooses boxing. (This is an odd threat to make since he does not gain from making it, but it is an empty threat nonetheless.)

Another way to understand empty versus credible threats is by using the concept of the *equilibrium path*, the connected path through the game tree implied by equilibrium strategies.

FIGURE 8.6 Equilibrium Path

In the third of the Nash equilibria listed for the sequential Battle of the Sexes, the wife plays boxing and the husband plays (boxing | ballet, boxing | boxing), tracing out the branches indicated with thick lines (both solid and dashed). The dashed line is the equilibrium path; the rest of the tree is referred to as being "off the equilibrium path."

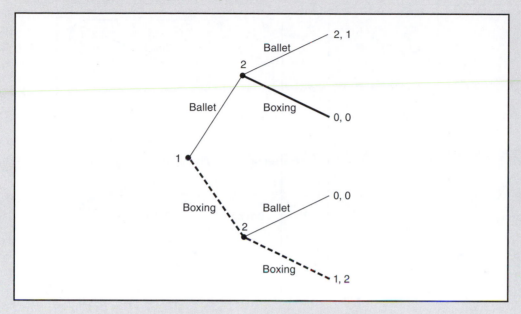

Figure 8.6 uses a dashed line to illustrate the equilibrium path for the third of the listed Nash equilibria in the sequential Battle of the Sexes. The third outcome is a Nash equilibrium because the strategies are rational along the equilibrium path. However, following the wife's choosing ballet—an event that is off the equilibrium path—the husband's strategy is irrational. The concept of subgame-perfect equilibrium in the next section will rule out irrational play both on and off the equilibrium path.

Subgame-perfect equilibrium

Game theory offers a formal way of selecting the reasonable Nash equilibria in sequential games using the concept of subgame-perfect equilibrium. Subgame-perfect equilibrium is a refinement that rules out empty threats by requiring strategies to be rational even for contingencies that do not arise in equilibrium.

Before defining subgame-perfect equilibrium formally, we need a few preliminary definitions. A *subgame* is a part of the extensive form beginning with a decision node and including everything that branches out to the right of it. A *proper subgame* is a subgame that starts at a decision node not connected to another in an information set. Conceptually, this means that the player who moves first in a proper subgame knows the actions played by others that have led up to that point. It is easier to see what a proper subgame is than to define it in words. Figure 8.7 shows the extensive forms from the simultaneous and sequential versions of the Battle of the Sexes with boxes drawn around the proper subgames in each. In the simultaneous Battle of the Sexes, there is only one decision node—the topmost mode—that is not connected to another in the same information set; hence there is only one proper subgame, the game itself. In the sequential Battle of the Sexes, there are three proper subgames: the game itself and two lower subgames starting with decision nodes where the husband gets to move.

FIGURE 8.7 Proper Subgames in the Battle of the Sexes

The simultaneous Battle of the Sexes in (a) has only one proper subgame: the whole game itself, labeled A. The sequential Battle of the Sexes in (b) has three proper subgames, labeled B, C, and D.

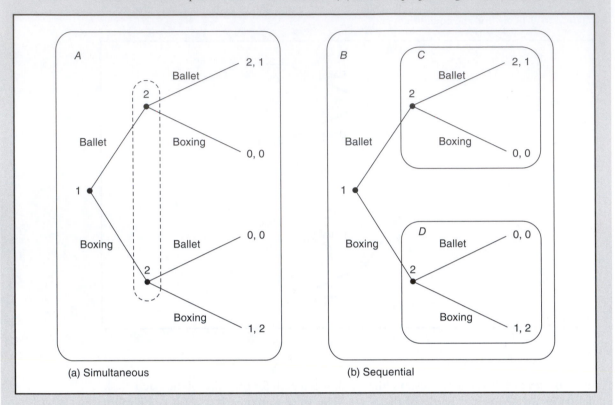

(a) Simultaneous   (b) Sequential

DEFINITION   **Subgame-perfect equilibrium.** A subgame-perfect equilibrium is a strategy profile $(s_1^*, s_2^*, \ldots, s_n^*)$ that constitutes a Nash equilibrium for every proper subgame.

A subgame-perfect equilibrium is always a Nash equilibrium. This is true because the whole game is a proper subgame of itself and so a subgame-perfect equilibrium must be a Nash equilibrium for the whole game. In the simultaneous version of the Battle of the Sexes, there is nothing more to say because there are no subgames other than the whole game itself.

In the sequential version of the Battle of the Sexes, subgame-perfect equilibrium has more bite. Strategies must not only form a Nash equilibrium on the whole game itself, they must also form Nash equilibria on the two proper subgames starting with the decision points at which the husband moves. These subgames are simple decision problems, so it is easy to compute the corresponding Nash equilibria. For subgame C, beginning with the husband's decision node following his wife's choosing ballet, he has a simple decision between ballet (which earns him a payoff of 1) and boxing (which earns him a payoff of 0). The Nash equilibrium in this simple decision subgame is for the husband to choose ballet. For the other subgame, D, he has a simple decision between ballet, which earns him 0, and boxing, which earns him 2. The Nash equilibrium in this simple decision subgame is for him to choose boxing. The husband therefore has only one strategy that can be part of a subgame-perfect equilibrium: (ballet | ballet, boxing | boxing). Any other strategy has him playing something that is not a Nash equilibrium for some proper subgame. Returning to the three enumerated Nash equilibria, only the second is subgame perfect; the first and the third are not. For example, the third equilibrium, in which the husband always goes to boxing, is ruled out as a subgame-perfect equilibrium because the

FIGURE 8.8   Applying Backward Induction

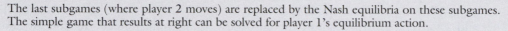

The last subgames (where player 2 moves) are replaced by the Nash equilibria on these subgames. The simple game that results at right can be solved for player 1's equilibrium action.

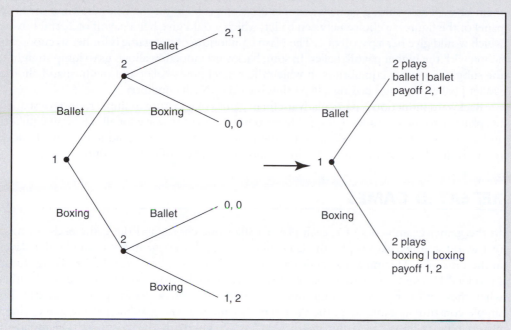

husband's strategy (boxing | boxing) is not a Nash equilibrium in proper subgame *C*. Subgame-perfect equilibrium thus rules out the empty threat (of always going to boxing) that we were uncomfortable with earlier.

More generally, subgame-perfect equilibrium rules out any sort of empty threat in a sequential game. In effect, Nash equilibrium requires behavior to be rational only on the equilibrium path. Players can choose potentially irrational actions on other parts of the game tree. In particular, one player can threaten to damage both in order to scare the other from choosing certain actions. Subgame-perfect equilibrium requires rational behavior both on and off the equilibrium path. Threats to play irrationally—that is, threats to choose something other than one's best response—are ruled out as being empty.

Subgame-perfect equilibrium is not a useful refinement for a simultaneous game. This is because a simultaneous game has no proper subgames besides the game itself and so subgame-perfect equilibrium would not reduce the set of Nash equilibria.

Backward induction

Our approach to solving for the equilibrium in the sequential Battle of the Sexes was to find all the Nash equilibria using the normal form and then to seek among those for the subgame-perfect equilibrium. A shortcut for finding the subgame-perfect equilibrium directly is to use *backward induction*, the process of solving for equilibrium by working backwards from the end of the game to the beginning. Backward induction works as follows. Identify all of the subgames at the bottom of the extensive form. Find the Nash equilibria on these subgames. Replace the (potentially complicated) subgames with the actions and payoffs resulting from Nash equilibrium play on these subgames. Then move up to the next level of subgames and repeat the procedure.

Figure 8.8 illustrates the use of backward induction to solve for the subgame-perfect equilibrium of the sequential Battle of the Sexes. First, we compute the Nash equilibria of the bottommost subgames at the husband's decision nodes. In the subgame following his wife's choosing ballet, he would choose ballet, giving payoffs 2 for her and 1 for him. In the subgame following his wife's choosing boxing, he would choose boxing, giving payoffs 1 for her and 2 for him. Next, substitute the husband's equilibrium strategies for the subgames themselves. The resulting game is a simple decision problem for the wife (drawn in the lower panel of the figure): a choice between ballet, which would give her a payoff of 2, and boxing, which would give her a payoff of 1. The Nash equilibrium of this game is for her to choose the action with the higher payoff, ballet. In sum, backward induction allows us to jump straight to the subgame-perfect equilibrium in which the wife chooses ballet and the husband chooses (ballet | ballet, boxing | boxing), bypassing the other Nash equilibria.

Backward induction is particularly useful in games that feature multiple rounds of sequential play. As rounds are added, it quickly becomes too hard to solve for all the Nash equilibria and then to sort through which are subgame-perfect. With backward induction, an additional round is simply accommodated by adding another iteration of the procedure.

REPEATED GAMES

In the games examined so far, each player makes one choice and the game ends. In many real-world settings, players play the same game over and over again. For example, the players in the Prisoners' Dilemma may anticipate committing future crimes and thus playing future Prisoners' Dilemmas together. Gasoline stations located across the street from each other, when they set their prices each morning, effectively play a new pricing game every day. The simple constituent game (e.g., the Prisoners' Dilemma or the gasoline-pricing game) that is played repeatedly is called the *stage game*. As we saw with the Prisoners' Dilemma, the equilibrium in one play of the stage game may be worse for all players than some other, more cooperative, outcome. Repeated play of the stage game opens up the possibility of cooperation in equilibrium. Players can adopt *trigger strategies*, whereby they continue to cooperate as long as all have cooperated up to that point but revert to playing the Nash equilibrium if anyone deviates from cooperation. We will investigate the conditions under which trigger strategies work to increase players' payoffs. As is standard in game theory, we will focus on subgame-perfect equilibria of the repeated games.

Finitely repeated games

For many stage games, repeating them a known, finite number of times does not increase the possibility for cooperation. To see this point concretely, suppose the Prisoners' Dilemma were repeated for T periods. Use backward induction to solve for the subgame-perfect equilibrium. The lowest subgame is the Prisoners' Dilemma stage game played in period T. Regardless of what happened before, the Nash equilibrium on this subgame is for both to fink. Folding the game back to period $T - 1$, trigger strategies that condition period-T play on what happens in period $T - 1$ are ruled out. Although a player might like to promise to play cooperatively in period T and so reward the other for playing cooperatively in period $T - 1$, we have just seen that nothing that happens in period $T - 1$ affects what happens subsequently because players both fink in period T regardless. It is as if period $T - 1$ were the last, and the Nash equilibrium of this subgame is again for both to fink. Working backward in this way, we see that players will fink each period; that is, players will simply repeat the Nash equilibrium of the stage game T times.

Reinhard Selten, winner of the Nobel Prize in economics for his contributions to game theory, showed that the same logic applies more generally to any stage game with a unique Nash equilibrium.[5] This result is called *Selten's theorem*:

> If the stage game has a unique Nash equilibrium, then the unique subgame-perfect equilibrium of the finitely repeated game is to play the Nash equilibrium every period.

If the stage game has multiple Nash equilibria, it may be possible to achieve some cooperation in a finitely repeated game. Players can use trigger strategies, sustaining cooperation in early periods on an outcome that is not an equilibrium of the stage game, by threatening to play in later periods the Nash equilibrium that yields a worse outcome for the player who deviates from cooperation. Example 8.7 illustrates how such trigger strategies work to sustain cooperation.

EXAMPLE 8.7 Cooperation in a Finitely Repeated Game

The stage game given in normal form in Table 8.10 has two pure-strategy Nash equilibria. In the "bad" pure-strategy equilibrium, each plays B and earns a payoff of 1; in the "good" equilibrium, each plays C and earns a payoff of 3. Players would earn still more (i.e., 4) if both played A, but this is not a Nash equilibrium. If one plays A, then the other would prefer to deviate to B and earn 5. There is a third, mixed-strategy Nash equilibrium in which each plays B with probability 3/4 and C with probability 1/4. The payoffs are graphed as solid circles in Figure 8.9.

TABLE 8.10 Stage Game for Example 8.7

		Player 2		
		A	B	C
Player 1	A	4, 4	0, 5	0, 0
	B	5, 0	1, 1	0, 0
	C	0, 0	0, 0	3, 3

If the stage game is repeated twice, a wealth of new possibilities arise in subgame-perfect equilibria. The same per-period payoffs (1 or 3) from the stage game can be obtained simply by repeating the pure-strategy Nash equilibria from the stage game twice. Per-period average payoffs of 2.5 can be obtained by alternating between the good and the bad stage-game equilibria.

A more cooperative outcome can be sustained with the following strategy: begin by playing A in the first period; if no one deviates from A, play C in the second period; if a player deviates from A, then play B in the second period. Backward induction can be used to show that these strategies form a subgame-perfect equilibrium. The strategies form a Nash equilibrium in second-period subgames by construction. It remains to check whether the strategies form a Nash equilibrium on the game as a whole. In equilibrium with these strategies, players earn $4 + 3 = 7$ in total across the two periods. By deviating to B in the first period, a player can increase his or her first-period payoff from 4 to 5, but this leads to both playing B in the second period, reducing the second-period payoff from 3 to 1. The total payoff across the two periods from this deviation is $5 + 1 = 6$, less than the 7 earned in the proposed equilibrium. The average per-period payoff in this subgame-perfect equilibrium is $7/2 = 3.5$ for each player.

Asymmetric equilibria are also possible. In one, player 1 begins by playing B and player 2 by playing A; if no one deviates then both play the good stage-game Nash equilibrium (both play C), and if someone deviates then both play the bad equilibrium (both play B). Player 2

(continued)

[5]R. Selten, "A Simple Model of Imperfect Competition, Where 4 Are Few and 6 Are Many," *International Journal of Game Theory* 2 (1973): 141–201.

EXAMPLE 8.7   CONTINUED

FIGURE 8.9   Per-Period Average Payoffs in Example 8.7

Solid circles indicate payoffs in Nash equilibria of the stage game. Squares (in addition to circles) indicate per-period average payoffs in subgame-perfect equilibria for $T = 2$ repetitions of the stage game. Triangles (in addition to circles and squares) indicate per-period average payoffs for $T = 3$.

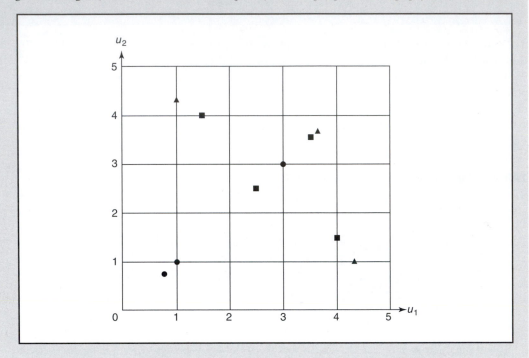

does not want to deviate to playing B in the first period because he or she earns 1 from this deviation in the first period and 1 in the second when they play the bad equilibrium for a total of $1 + 1 = 2$, whereas he or she earns more, $0 + 3 = 3$, in equilibrium. The average per-period payoff in this subgame-perfect equilibrium is $(5 + 3)/2 = 4$ for player 1 and $3/2 = 1.5$ for player 2. The reverse payoffs can be obtained by reversing the strategies. The average per-period payoffs from the additional subgame-perfect equilibria we computed for the twice-repeated game are graphed as squares in Figure 8.9.

If the game is repeated three times $(T = 3)$, then additional payoff combinations are possible in subgame-perfect equilibria. Players can cooperate on playing A for two periods and C in the last, a strategy that is sustained by the threat of immediately moving to the bad equilibrium (both play B) if anyone deviates in the first two periods. This subgame-perfect equilibrium gives each a per-period average payoff of $(4 + 4 + 3)/2 \approx 3.7$, more than the 3.5 that was the most both could earn in the $T = 2$ game. Asymmetric equilibria in the $T = 3$ game include the possibility that 1 plays B and 2 plays A for the first two periods and then both play C, with the threat of immediately moving to the bad equilibrium if anyone deviates. Player 1's per-period average payoff in this subgame-perfect equilibrium is $(5 + 5 + 3)/3 \approx 4.3$, and player 2's payoff is $(0 + 0 + 3)/3 = 1$. The reverse strategies and payoffs also constitute a possible subgame-perfect equilibrium. The payoffs from the additional subgame-perfect equilibria of the $T = 3$ game are graphed as triangles in Figure 8.9.

QUERY: There are many other subgame-perfect equilibrium payoffs for the repeated game than are shown in Figure 8.9. For the $T = 2$ game, can you find at least two other combinations of average per-period payoffs that can be attained in a subgame-perfect equilibrium?

For cooperation to be sustained in a subgame-perfect equilibrium, the stage game must be repeated often enough that the punishment for deviation (repeatedly playing the less-preferred Nash equilibrium) is severe enough to deter deviation. The more repetitions of the stage game T, the more severe the possible punishment and thus the greater the level of cooperation and the higher the payoffs that can be sustained in a subgame-perfect equilibrium. In Example 8.7, the most both players can earn in a subgame-perfect equilibrium increases from 3 to 3.5 to about 3.7 as T increases from 1 to 2 to 3.

Example 8.7 suggests that the range of sustainable payoffs in a subgame-perfect equilibrium expands as the number of repetitions T increases. In fact, the associated Figure 8.9 understates the expansion because it does not graph all subgame-perfect equilibrium payoffs for $T = 2$ and $T = 3$ (the Query in Example 8.7 asks you to find two more, for example). We are left to wonder how much the set of possibilities might expand for yet higher T. Jean Pierre Benoit and Vijay Krishna answer this question with their *folk theorem for finitely repeated games*:[6]

> Suppose that the stage game has multiple Nash equilibria and no player earns a constant payoff across all equilibria. Any feasible payoff in the stage game greater than the player's pure-strategy minmax value can be approached arbitrarily closely by the player's per-period average payoff in some subgame-perfect equilibrium of the finitely repeated game for large enough T.[7]

We will encounter other folk theorems in later sections of this chapter. Generally speaking, a folk theorem is a result that "anything is possible" in the limit with repeated games. Such results are called "folk" theorems because they were understood informally and thus were part of the "folk wisdom" of game theory well before anyone wrote down formal proofs.

To understand the folk theorem fully, we need to understand what feasible payoffs and minmax values are. A *feasible* payoff is one that can be achieved by some mixed-strategy profile in the stage game. Graphically, the feasible payoff set appears as the convex hull of the pure-strategy stage-game payoffs. The *convex hull* of a set of points is the border and interior of the largest polygon that can be formed by connecting the points with line segments. For example, Figure 8.10 graphs the feasible payoff set for the stage game from Example 8.7 as the upward-hatched region. To derive this set, one first graphs the pure-strategy payoffs from the stage game. Referring to the normal form in Table 8.10, the distinct pure-strategy payoffs are $(4, 4)$, $(0, 5), (0, 0), (5, 0), (1, 1)$, and $(3, 3)$. The convex hull is the polygon formed by line segments going from $(0, 0)$ to $(0, 5)$ to $(4, 4)$ to $(5, 0)$, and back to $(0, 0)$. Each point in the convex hull corresponds to the expected payoffs from some combination of mixed strategies for players 1 and 2 over actions A, B, and C. For example, the point $(3, 0)$ on the boundary of the convex hull corresponds to players' expected payoffs if 1 plays the mixed strategy $(0, 3/5, 2/5)$ and 2 plays A.

A *minmax* value is the least that player i can be forced to earn.

---

[6]J. P. Benoit and V. Krishna, "Finitely Repeated Games," *Econometrica* 53 (1985): 890–904.

[7]An additional, technical condition is that the dimension of the feasible set of payoffs must equal the number of players. In the two-player game in Example 8.7, this condition would require the feasible payoff set to be a region (which is the case, as shown in Figure 8.12) rather than a line or a point.

FIGURE 8.10   Folk Theorem for Finitely Repeated Games in Example 8.7

The feasible payoffs for the stage game in Example 8.7 are in the upward-hatched region; payoffs greater than each player's minmax values are in the downward-hatched region. Their intersection (the cross-hatched region) constitutes the per-period average payoffs that can be approached by some subgame-perfect equilibrium of the repeated game, according to the folk theorem for finitely repeated games. Regions are superimposed on the equilibrium payoffs from Figure 8.9.

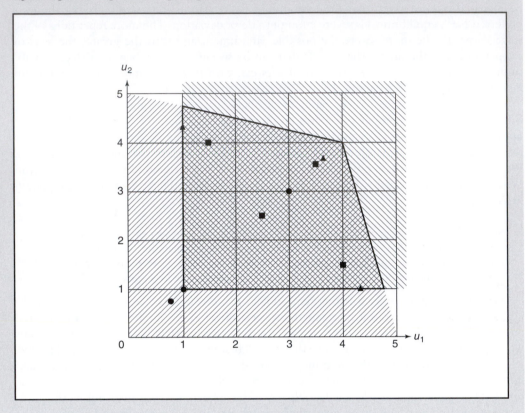

DEFINITION

Minmax value. The minmax value is the following payoff for player i:

$$\min_{s_{-i}} \left[\max_{s_i} \; u_i(s_i, s_{-i}) \right], \tag{8.19}$$

that is, the lowest payoff player i can be held to if all other players work against him or her but player i is allowed to choose a best response to them.

In Example 8.7, if 2 plays the mixed strategy $(0, 3/4, 1/4)$ then the most player 1 can earn in the stage game is $3/4$ (by playing any mixed strategy involving only actions B and C). A little work shows that $3/4$ is indeed player 1's minmax value: any other strategy for 2 besides $(0, 3/4, 1/4)$ would allow 1 to earn a higher payoff than $3/4$. The folk theorem for finitely repeated games involves the pure-strategy minmax value—that is, the minmax value when players are restricted to using only pure strategies. The pure-strategy minmax value is easier to compute than the general minmax value. The lowest that player 2 can hold 1 to in Example 8.7 is a payoff of 1; player 2 does this by playing B and then 1 responds by playing B. Figure 8.10 graphs the payoffs exceeding both players' pure-strategy minmax values as the downward-hatched region.

The folk theorem for finitely repeated games assures us that any payoffs in the cross-hatched region of Figure 8.10—payoffs that are feasible and above both players' pure strategy minmax values—can be approached as the per-period average payoffs in a subgame-perfect equilibrium if the stage game in Example 8.7 is repeated often enough. Payoffs $(4, 4)$ can be approached by having players cooperate on playing A for hundreds of periods and then playing C in the last period (threatening the bad equilibrium in which both play B if anyone deviates from cooperation). The average of hundreds of payoffs of 4 with one payoff of 3 comes arbitrarily close to 4. Therefore, a considerable amount of cooperation is possible if the game is repeated often enough.

Figure 8.10 also shows that many outcomes other than full cooperation are possible if the number of repetitions, T, is large. Although subgame-perfect equilibrium was selective in the sequential version of the Battle of the Sexes, allowing us to select one of three Nash equilibria, we see that subgame perfection may not be selective in repeated games. The folk theorem states that if the stage game has multiple Nash equilibria then almost anything can happen in the repeated game for T large enough.[8]

Infinitely repeated games

With finitely repeated games, the folk theorem applies only if the stage game has multiple equilibria. If, like the Prisoners' Dilemma, the stage game has only one Nash equilibrium, then Selten's theorem tells us that the finitely repeated game has only one subgame-perfect equilibrium: repeating the stage-game Nash equilibrium each period. Backward induction starting from the last period T unravels any other outcomes.

With infinitely repeated games, however, there is no definite ending period T from which to start backward induction. A folk theorem will apply to infinitely repeated games even if the underlying stage game has only one Nash equilibrium. Therefore, while both players fink every period in the unique subgame-perfect equilibrium of the finitely repeated Prisoners' Dilemma, players may end up cooperating (being silent) in the infinitely repeated version.

One difficulty with infinitely repeated games involves adding up payoffs across periods. With finitely repeated games, we could focus on average payoffs. With infinitely repeated games, the average is not well-defined because it involves an infinite sum of payoffs divided by an infinite number of periods. We will circumvent this problem with the aid of discounting. Let δ be the discount factor (discussed in the Chapter 17 Appendix) measuring how much a payoff unit is worth if received one period in the future rather than today. In Chapter 17 we show that δ is inversely related to the interest rate. If the interest rate is high then a person would much rather receive payment today than next period because investing today's payment would provide a return of principal plus a large interest payment next period. Besides the interest rate, δ can also incorporate uncertainty about whether the game continues in future periods. The higher the probability that the game ends after the current period, the lower the expected return from stage games that might not actually be played.

Factoring in a probability that the repeated game ends after each period makes the setting of an infinitely repeated game more believable. The crucial issue with an infinitely repeated game is not that it goes on forever but that its end is indeterminate. Interpreted in this way, there is a sense in which infinitely repeated games are more realistic than finitely repeated games with large T. Suppose we expect two neighboring gasoline stations to play a pricing game each day until electric cars replace gasoline-powered ones. It is unlikely the gasoline stations would know that electric cars were coming in exactly $T = 2,000$ days. More realistically, the gasoline stations will be uncertain about the end of gasoline-powered cars and so the end of their pricing game is indeterminate.

---

[8]The folk theorem for finitely repeated games does not necessarily capture all subgame-perfect equilibria. In Figure 8.12, the point $(3/4, 3/4)$ lies outside the cross-hatched region; nonetheless, it can be achieved in a subgame-perfect equilibrium in which, each period, both players play the Nash equilibrium of the stage game in strictly mixed strategies. Payoffs $(3/4, 3/4)$ are in a "gray area" between player's pure-strategy and mixed-strategy minmax values.

Players can sustain cooperation in infinitely repeated games by using *trigger strategies*: players continue cooperating unless someone has deviated from cooperation, and this deviation triggers some sort of punishment. In order for trigger strategies to form an equilibrium, the punishment must be severe enough to deter deviation.

Suppose both players use the following trigger strategy in the Prisoners' Dilemma: continue being silent if no one has deviated by playing fink; fink forever afterward if anyone has deviated to fink in the past. To show that this trigger strategy forms a subgame-perfect equilibrium, we need to check that a player cannot gain from deviating. Along the equilibrium path, both players are silent every period; this provides each with a payoff of 2 every period for a present discounted value of

$$V^{eq} = 2 + 2\delta + 2\delta^2 + 2\delta^3 + \cdots$$
$$+ 2(1 + \delta + \delta^2 + \delta^3 + \cdots)$$
$$= \frac{2}{1-\delta}. \tag{8.20}$$

A player who deviates by finking earns 3 in that period, but then both players fink every period from then on—each earning 1 per period for a total presented discounted payoff of

$$V^{dev} = 3 + (1)(\delta) + (1)(\delta^2) + (1)(\delta^3) + \cdots$$
$$+ 3 + \delta(1 + \delta + \delta^2 + \cdots)$$
$$= 3 + \frac{\delta}{1-\delta}. \tag{8.20}$$

The trigger strategies form a subgame-perfect equilibrium if $V^{eq} \geq V^{dev}$, implying that

$$\frac{2}{1-\delta} \geq 3 + \frac{\delta}{1-\delta}; \tag{8.22}$$

after multiplying through by $1 - \delta$ and rearranging, we obtain $\delta \geq 1/2$. In other words, players will find continued cooperative play desirable provided they do not discount future gains from such cooperation too highly. If $\delta < 1/2$, then no cooperation is possible in the infinitely repeated Prisoners' Dilemma; the only subgame-perfect equilibrium involves finking every period.

The trigger strategy we considered has players revert to the stage-game Nash equilibrium of finking each period forever. This strategy, which involves the harshest possible punishment for deviation, is called the *grim strategy*. Less harsh punishments include the so-called tit-for-tat strategy, which involves only one round of punishment for cheating. Since it involves the harshest punishment possible, the grim strategy elicits cooperation for the largest range of cases (the lowest value of δ) of any strategy. Harsh punishments work well because, if players succeed in cooperating, they never experience the losses from the punishment in equilibrium.[9]

The discount factor δ is crucial in determining whether trigger strategies can sustain cooperation in the Prisoners' Dilemma or, indeed, in any stage game. As δ approaches 1, grim-strategy punishments become infinitely harsh because they involve an unending stream of undiscounted losses. Infinite punishments can be used to sustain a wide range of possible outcomes. This is the logic behind the *folk theorem for infinitely repeated games*:[10]

---

[9]Nobel Prize–winning economist Gary Becker introduced a related point, the maximal punishment principle for crime. The principle says that even minor crimes should receive draconian punishments, which can deter crime with minimal expenditure on policing. The punishments are costless to society because no crimes are committed in equilibrium, so punishments never have to be carried out. See G. Becker, "Crime and Punishment: An Economic Approach," *Journal of Political Economy* 76 (1968): 169–217. Less harsh punishments may be suitable in settings involving uncertainty. For example, citizens may not be certain about the penal code; police may not be certain they have arrested the guilty party.

[10]This folk theorem is due to D. Fudenberg and E. Maskin, "The Folk Theorem in Repeated Games with Discounting or with Incomplete Information," *Econometrica* 54 (1986): 533–56.

FIGURE 8.11   Folk-Theorem Payoffs in the Infinitely Repeated Prisoners' Dilemma

Feasible payoffs are in the upward-hatched region; payoffs greater than each player's minmax values are in the downward-hatched region. Their intersection (the cross-hatched region) constitutes the achievable payoffs according to the folk theorem for infinitely repeated games.

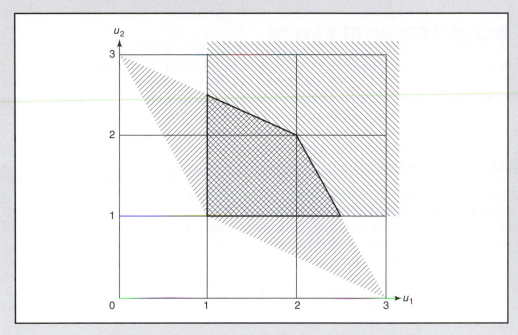

Any feasible payoff in the stage game greater than the player's minmax value can be obtained as the player's normalized payoff (normalized by multiplying by $1 - \delta$.) in some subgame-perfect equilibrium of the infinitely repeated game for δ close enough to 1.[11]

A few differences with the folk theorem for finitely repeated games are worth emphasizing. First, the limit involves increases in δ rather than in the number of periods T. The two limits are related. Interpreting δ as capturing the probability that the game continues into the next period, an increase in δ increases the expected number of periods the game is played in total—similar to an increase in T with the difference that now the end of the game is indefinite. Another difference between the two folk theorems is that the one for infinitely repeated games holds even if the stage game has just a single Nash equilibrium whereas the theorem for finitely repeated games requires the stage game to have multiple Nash equilibria.

A final technicality is that comparing stage-game payoffs with the present discounted value of a stream of payoffs from the infinitely repeated game is like comparing apples with oranges. To make the two comparable, we "normalize" the payoff from the infinitely repeated game via multiplying by $1 - \delta$. This normalization allows us to think of all payoffs in per-period terms for easy comparison.[12]

---

[11]As in footnote 9, an additional technical condition on the dimension of the feasible payoff set is also required.

[12]For example, suppose a player earns \$1 at the beginning of each period. The present discounted value of the stream of these \$1 payoffs for an infinite number of periods is

$$\$1 + \$1 \cdot \delta + \$1 \cdot \delta^2 + \$1 \cdot \delta^3 + \cdots = \frac{\$1}{1 - \delta}.$$

Multiplying through by $1 - \delta$ converts this stream of payments back into the per-period payoff of \$1. The Chapter 17 Appendix provides more detail on the calculation of present discounted values of annuity streams (though beware the

Figure 8.11 illustrates the folk theorem for infinitely repeated games in the case of the Prisoners' Dilemma. The figure shows the range of normalized payoffs that are possible in some subgame-perfect equilibrium of the infinitely repeated Prisoners' Dilemma. Again we see that subgame perfection may not be particularly selective in certain repeated games.

INCOMPLETE INFORMATION

In the games studied so far, players knew everything there was to know about the setup of the game, including each others' strategy sets and payoffs. Matters become more complicated, and potentially more interesting, if some players have information about the game that others do not. Poker would be quite different if all hands were played face up. The fun of playing poker comes from knowing what is in your hand but not others'. Incomplete information arises in many other real-world contexts besides parlor games. A sports team may try to hide the injury of a star player from future opponents to prevent them from exploiting this weakness. Firms' production technologies may be trade secrets, and thus firms may not know whether they face efficient or weak competitors. This section (and the next two) will introduce the tools needed to analyze games of incomplete information. The analysis integrates the material on game theory developed so far in this chapter with the material on uncertainty and information from the previous chapter.

Games of incomplete information can quickly become very complicated. Players that lack full information about the game will try to use what they do know to make inferences about what they do not. The inference process can be quite involved. In poker, for example, knowing what is in your hand can tell you something about what is in others'. A player that holds two aces knows that others are less likely to hold aces because two of the four aces are not available. Information on others' hands can also come from the size of their bets or from their facial expressions (of course, a big bet may be a bluff and a facial expression may be faked). Probability theory provides a formula, called Bayes' rule, for making inferences about hidden information. We will encounter Bayes' rule in a later section. The relevance of Bayes' rule in games of incomplete information has led them to be called *Bayesian games*.

To limit the complexity of the analysis, we will focus on the simplest possible setting throughout. We will focus on two-player games in which one of the players (player 1) has private information and the other (player 2) does not. The analysis of games of incomplete information is divided into two sections. The next section begins with the simple case in which the players move simultaneously. The subsequent section then analyzes games in which the informed player 1 moves first. Such games, called *signaling* games, are more complicated than simultaneous games because player 1's action may signal something about his private information to the uninformed player 2. We will introduce Bayes' rule at that point to help analyze player 2's inference about player 1's hidden information based on observations of player 1's action.

SIMULTANEOUS BAYESIAN GAMES

In this section we study a two-player, simultaneous-move game in which player 1 has private information but player 2 does not. (We will use "he" for player 1 and "she" for player 2 in order to facilitate the exposition.) We begin by studying how to model private information.

---

subtle difference that in Chapter 17 the annuity payments come at the end of each period rather than at the beginning as assumed here).

TABLE 8.11   Simple Game of Incomplete Information

		Player 2	
		L	*R*
U		$t, 2$	$0, 0$
D		$2, 0$	$2, 4$

Player 1 (on vertical axis, rows *U* and *D*); Player 2 (columns *L* and *R*)

Note: $t = 6$ with probability $1/2$ and $t = 0$ with probability $1/2$.

Player types and beliefs

John Harsanyi, who received the Nobel Prize in economics for his work on games with incomplete information, provided a simple way to model private information by introducing player characteristics or *types*.[13] Player 1 can be one of a number of possible such types, denoted t. Player 1 knows his own type. Player 2 is uncertain about t and must decide on her strategy based on beliefs about t.

Formally, the game begins at an initial node, called a *chance node*, at which a particular value t_k is randomly drawn for player 1's type t from a set of possible types $T = \{t_1, \ldots, t_k, \ldots, t_K\}$. Let $\Pr(t_k)$ be the probability of drawing the particular type t_k. Player 1 sees which type is drawn. Player 2 does not see the draw and only knows the probabilities, using them to form her beliefs about player 1's type. Thus the probability that player 2 places on player 1's being of type t_k is $\Pr(t_k)$.

Since player 1 observes his type t before moving, his strategy can be conditioned on t. Conditioning on this information may be a big benefit to a player. In poker, for example, the stronger a player's hand, the more likely the player is to win the pot and the more aggressively the player may want to bid. Let $s_1(t)$ be 1's strategy contingent on his type. Since player 2 does not observe t, her strategy is simply the unconditional one, s_2. As with games of complete information, players' payoffs depend on strategies. In Bayesian games, payoffs may also depend on types. We therefore write player 1's payoff as $u_1(s_1(t), s_2, t)$ and 2's as $u_2(s_2, s_1(t), t)$. Note that t appears in two places in 2's payoff function. Player 1's type may have a direct effect on 2's payoffs. Player 1's type also has an indirect effect through its effect on 1's strategy $s_1(t)$, which in turn affects 2's payoffs. Since 2's payoffs depend on t in these two ways, her beliefs about t will be crucial in the calculation of her optimal strategy.

Table 8.11 provides a simple example of a simultaneous Bayesian game. Each player chooses one of two actions. All payoffs are known except for 1's payoff when 1 chooses U and 2 chooses L. Player 1's payoff in outcome (U, L) is identified as his type, t. There are two possible values for player 1's type, $t = 6$ and $t = 0$, each occurring with equal probability. Player 1 knows his type before moving. Player 2's beliefs are that each type has probability $1/2$. The extensive form is drawn in Figure 8.12.

Bayesian-Nash equilibrium

Extending Nash equilibrium to Bayesian games requires two small matters of interpretation. First, recall that player 1 may play a different action for each of his types. Equilibrium requires that 1's strategy be a best response for each and every one of his types. Second, recall that player 2 is uncertain about player 1's type. Equilibrium requires that 2's strategy maximize an expected payoff, where the expectation is taken with respect to her beliefs about 1's type. We encountered expected payoffs in our discussion of mixed strategies. The calculations involved in computing the best response to the pure strategies of different types of rivals in a game of

---

[13]J. Harsanyi, "Games with Incomplete Information Played by Bayesian Players," *Management Science* 14 (1967/68): 159–82, 320–34, 486–502.

FIGURE 8.12   Extensive Form for Simple Game of Incomplete Information

This figure translates Table 8.11 into an extensive-form game. The initial chance node is indicated by an open circle. Player 2's decision nodes are in the same information set because she does not observe 1's type or action prior to moving.

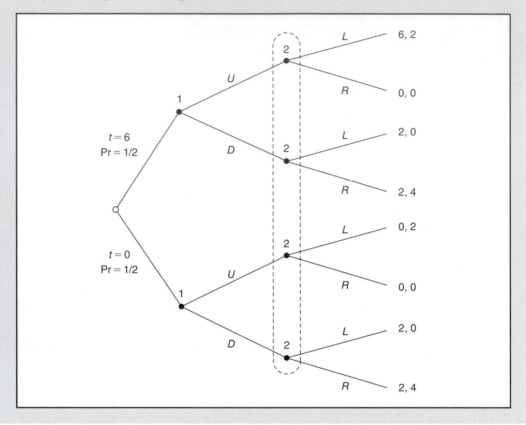

incomplete information are similar to the calculations involved in computing the best response to a rival's mixed strategy in a game of complete information.

Interpreted in this way, Nash equilibrium in the setting of a Bayesian game is called *Bayesian-Nash equilibrium*.

DEFINITION

Bayesian-Nash equilibrium. In a two-player, simultaneous-move game in which player 1 has private information, a Bayesian-Nash equilibrium is a strategy profile $(s_1^*(t), s_2^*)$ such that $s_1^*(t)$ is a best response to s_2^* for each type $t \in T$ of player 1,

$$U_1(s_1^*(t), s_2^*, t) \geq U_1(s_1', s_2^*, t) \quad \text{for all} \quad s_1' \in S_1, \tag{8.23}$$

and such that s_2^* is a best response to $s_1^*(t)$ given player 2's beliefs $\Pr(t_k)$ about player 1's types:

$$\sum_{t_k \in T} \Pr(t_k) U_2(s_2^*, s_1^*(t_k), t_k) \geq \sum_{t_k \in T} \Pr(t_k) U_2(s_2', s_1^*(t_k), t_k) \quad \text{for all} \quad s_2' \in S_2. \tag{8.24}$$

Since the difference between Nash equilibrium and Bayesian-Nash equilibrium is only a matter of interpretation, all our previous results for Nash equilibrium (including the existence proof) apply to Bayesian-Nash equilibrium as well.

EXAMPLE 8.8 Bayesian-Nash Equilibrium of Game in Figure 8.12

To solve for the Bayesian-Nash equilibrium of the game in Figure 8.12, first solve for the informed player's (player 1's) best responses for each of his types. If player 1 is of type $t = 0$ then he would choose D rather than U because he earns 0 by playing U and 2 by playing D regardless of what 2 does. If player 1 is of type $t = 6$, then his best response is U to 2's playing L and D to her playing R. This leaves only two possible candidates for an equilibrium in pure strategies:

1 plays $(U|t = 6, D|t = 0)$ and 2 plays L;

1 plays $(D|t = 6, D|t = 0)$ and 2 plays R.

The first candidate cannot be an equilibrium because, given that 1 plays $(U|t = 6, D|t = 0)$, 2 earns an expected payoff of 1 from playing L. Player 2 would gain by deviating to R, earning an expected payoff of 2.

The second candidate is a Bayesian-Nash equilibrium. Given that 2 plays R, 1's best response is to play D, providing a payoff of 2 rather than 0 regardless of his type. Given that both types of player 1 play D, player 2's best response is to play R, providing a payoff of 4 rather than 0.

QUERY: If the probability that player 1 is of type $t = 6$ is high enough, can the first candidate be a Bayesian-Nash equilibrium? If so, compute the threshold probability.

EXAMPLE 8.9 Tragedy of the Commons as a Bayesian Game

For an example of a Bayesian game with continuous actions, consider the Tragedy of the Commons in Example 8.6 but now suppose that herder 1 has private information regarding his value of grazing per sheep:

$$v_1(q_1, q_2, t) = t - (q_1 + q_2), \tag{8.25}$$

where 1's type is $t = 130$ (the "high" type) with probability $2/3$ and $t = 100$ (the "low" type) with probability $1/3$. Herder 2's value remains the same as in Equation 8.11.

To solve for the Bayesian-Nash equilibrium, we first solve for the informed player's (herder 1's) best responses for each of his types. For any type t and rival's strategy q_2, herder 1's value-maximization problem is

$$\max_{q_1}\{q_1 v_1(q_1, q_2, t)\} = \max_{q_1}\{q_1(t - q_1 - q_2)\}. \tag{8.26}$$

The first-order condition for a maximum is

$$t - 2q_1 - q_2 = 0. \tag{8.27}$$

Rearranging and then substituting the values $t = 130$ and $t = 100$, we obtain

$$q_{1H} = 65 - \frac{q_2}{2} \quad \text{and} \quad q_{1L} = 50 - \frac{q_2}{2}, \tag{8.28}$$

where q_{1H} is the quantity for the "high" type of herder 1 (that is, the $t = 130$ type) and q_{1L} for the "low" type (the $t = 130$ type).

Next we solve for 2's best response. Herder 2's expected payoff is

$$\frac{2}{3}[q_2(120 - q_{1H} - q_2)] + \frac{1}{3}[q_2(120 - q_{1L} - q_2)] = q_2(120 - \bar{q}_1 - q_2), \tag{8.29}$$

(*continued*)

EXAMPLE 8.9 CONTINUED

FIGURE 8.13 Equilibrium of the Bayesian Tragedy of the Commons

Best responses for herder 2 and both types of herder 1 are drawn as thick solid lines; the expected best response as perceived by 2 is drawn as the thick dashed line. The Bayesian-Nash equilibrium of the incomplete-information game is given by points A and C; Nash equilibria of the corresponding full-information games are given by points A' and C'.

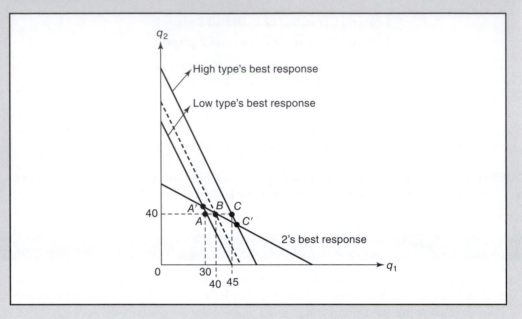

where

$$\bar{q}_1 = \frac{2}{3}q_{1H} + \frac{1}{3}q_{1L}. \tag{8.30}$$

Rearranging the first-order condition from the maximization of Equation 8.29 with respect to q_2 gives

$$q_2 = 60 - \frac{\bar{q}_1}{2}. \tag{8.31}$$

Substituting for q_{1H} and q_{1L} from Equation 8.28 into Equation 8.30 and then substituting the resulting expression for $\bar{q}_1$ into Equation 8.31 yields

$$q_2 = 30 + \frac{q_2}{4}, \tag{8.32}$$

implying that $q_2^* = 40$. Substituting $q_2^* = 40$ back into Equation 8.28 implies $q_{1H}^* = 45$ and $q_{1L}^* = 30$.

Figure 8.13 depicts the Bayesian-Nash equilibrium graphically. Herder 2 imagines playing against an average type of herder 1, whose average best response is given by the thick dashed line. The intersection of this best response and herder 2's at point B determines 2's equilibrium quantity, $q_2^* = 40$. The best response of the low (resp. high) type of herder 1 to $q_2^* = 40$ is given by point A (resp. point C). For comparison, the full-information Nash equilibria are drawn when herder 1 is known to be the low type (point A') or the high type (point C').

QUERY: Suppose herder 1 is the high type. How does the number of sheep each herder grazes change as the game moves from incomplete to full information (moving from point C'

to C)? What if herder 1 is the low type? Which type prefers full information and thus would like to signal its type? Which type prefers incomplete information and thus would like to hide its type? We will study the possibility player 1 can signal his type in the next section.

SIGNALING GAMES

In this section we move from simultaneous-move games of private information to sequential games in which the informed player, 1, takes an action that is observable to 2 before 2 moves. Player 1's action provides information, a signal, that 2 can use to update her beliefs about 1's type, perhaps altering the way 2 would play in the absence of such information. In poker, for instance, player 2 may take a big raise by player 1 as a signal that he has a good hand, perhaps leading 2 to fold. A firm considering whether to enter a market may take the incumbent firm's low price as a signal that the incumbent is a low-cost producer and thus a tough competitor, perhaps keeping the entrant out of the market. A prestigious college degree may signal that a job applicant is highly skilled.

The analysis of signaling games is more complicated than simultaneous games because we need to model how player 2 processes the information in 1's signal and then updates her beliefs about 1's type. To fix ideas, we will focus on a concrete application: a version of Michael Spence's model of job-market signaling, for which he won the 2001 Nobel Prize in economics.[14]

Job-market signaling

Player 1 is a worker who can be one of two types, high-skilled ($t = H$) or low-skilled ($t = L$). Player 2 is a firm that considers hiring the applicant. A low-skilled worker is completely unproductive and generates no revenue for the firm; a high-skilled worker generates revenue π. If the applicant is hired, the firm must pay the worker w (think of this wage as being fixed by government regulation). Assume $\pi > w > 0$. Therefore, the firm wishes to hire the applicant if and only if he or she is high-skilled. But the firm cannot observe the applicant's skill; it can observe only the applicant's prior education. Let c_H be the high type's cost of obtaining an education and c_L the low type's. Assume $c_H < c_L$, implying that education requires less effort for the high-skilled applicant than the low-skilled one. We make the extreme assumption that education does not increase the worker's productivity directly. The applicant may still decide to obtain an education because of its value as a signal of ability to future employers.

Figure 8.14 shows the extensive form. Player 1 observes his or her type at the start; player 2 observes only 1's action (education signal) before moving. Let $\Pr(H)$ and $\Pr(L)$ be 2's beliefs prior to observing 1's education signal that 1 is high- or low-skilled, respectively. These are called 1's *prior beliefs*. Observing 1's action will lead 2 to revise its beliefs to form what are called *posterior beliefs*. For example, the probability that the worker is high-skilled is, conditional on the worker's having obtained an education, $\Pr(H|E)$ and, conditional on no education, $\Pr(H|NE)$.

Player 2's posterior beliefs are used to compute its best response to 1's education decision. Suppose 2 sees 1 choose E. Then 2's expected payoff from playing J is

$$\Pr(H|E)(\pi - w) + \Pr(L|E)(-w) = \Pr(H|E)\pi - w, \qquad \textbf{(8.33)}$$

where the left-hand side of this equation follows from the fact that, since L and H are the only types, $\Pr(L|E) = 1 - \Pr(H|E)$. Player 2's payoff from playing NJ is 0. To determine its

---

[14]M. Spence, "Job-Market Signaling," *Quarterly Journal of Economics* 87 (1973): 355–74.

FIGURE 8.14 Job-Market Signaling

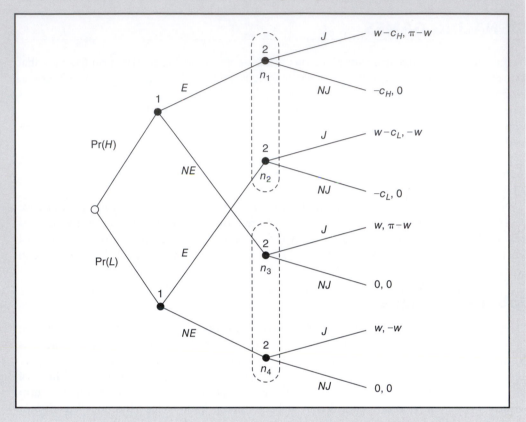

Player 1 (worker) observes his or her own type. Then 1 chooses to become educated (E) or not (NE). After observing 1's action, player 2 (firm) decides to make him or her a job offer (J) or not (NJ). The nodes in 2's information sets are labeled $n_1, ..., n_4$ for reference.

best response to E, player 2 compares the expected payoff in Equation 8.33 to 0. Player 2's best response is J if and only if $\Pr(H|E) \geq w/\pi$.

The question remains of how to compute posterior beliefs such as $\Pr(H|E)$. Rational players use a statistical formula, called *Bayes' rule*, to revise their prior beliefs to form posterior beliefs based on the observation of a signal.

Bayes' rule

Bayes' rule gives the following formula for computing player 2's posterior belief $\Pr(H|E)$:[15]

---

[15]Equation 8.34 can be derived from the definition of conditional probability in footnote 24 of Chapter 2. (Equation 8.35 can be derived similarly.) By definition,

$$\mathbf{Pr}(H|E) = \frac{\mathbf{Pr}(H \text{ and } E)}{\mathbf{Pr}(E)}.$$

Reversing the order of the two events in the conditional probability yields

$$\mathbf{Pr}(E|H) = \frac{\mathbf{Pr}(H \text{ and } E)}{\mathbf{Pr}(H)}$$

or, after rearranging,

$$\mathbf{Pr}(H \text{ and } E) = \mathbf{Pr}(E|H)\,\mathbf{Pr}(H).$$

Substituting the preceding equation into the first displayed equation of this footnote gives the numerator of Equation 8.34.

FIGURE 8.15   Bayes' Rule as a Black Box

Bayes' rule is a formula for computing player 2's posterior beliefs from other pieces of information in the game.

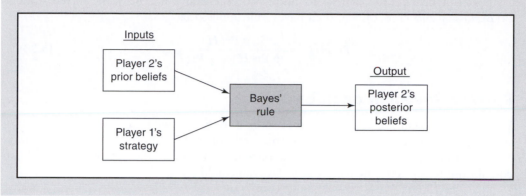

$$\mathbf{Pr}(H|E) = \frac{\mathbf{Pr}(E|H)\,\mathbf{Pr}(H)}{\mathbf{Pr}(E|H)\,\mathbf{Pr}(H) + \mathbf{Pr}(E|L)\,\mathbf{Pr}(L)}. \qquad (8.34)$$

Similarly, $\mathrm{Pr}(H|E)$ is given by

$$\mathbf{Pr}(H|NE) = \frac{\mathbf{Pr}(NE|H)\,\mathbf{Pr}(H)}{\mathbf{Pr}(NE|H)\,\mathbf{Pr}(H) + \mathbf{Pr}(NE|L)\,\mathbf{Pr}(L)}. \qquad (8.35)$$

Two sorts of probabilities appear on the left-hand side of Equations 8.34 and 8.35:

- the prior beliefs $\mathrm{Pr}(H)$ and $\mathrm{Pr}(L)$;
- the conditional probabilities $\mathrm{Pr}(E|H)$, $\mathrm{Pr}(NE|L)$, and so forth.

The prior beliefs are given in the specification of the game by the probabilities of the different branches from the initial chance node. The conditional probabilities $\mathrm{Pr}(E|H)$, $\mathrm{Pr}(NE|L)$, and so forth are given by player 1's equilibrium strategy. For example, $\mathrm{Pr}(E|H)$ is the probability that 1 plays E if he or she is of type H, $\mathrm{Pr}(NE|L)$ is the probability that 1 plays NE if he or she is of type L, and so forth. As the schematic diagram in Figure 8.15 summarizes, Bayes' rule can be thought of as a "black box" that takes prior beliefs and strategies as inputs and gives as outputs the beliefs we must know in order to solve for an equilibrium of the game: player 2's posterior beliefs.

When 1 plays a pure strategy, Bayes' rule often gives a simple result. Suppose, for example, that $\mathrm{Pr}(E|H) = 1$ and $\mathrm{Pr}(E|L) = 0$ or, in other words, that player 1 obtains an education if and only if he or she is high-skilled. Then Equation 8.34 implies

$$\mathbf{Pr}(H|E) = \frac{1 \cdot \mathbf{Pr}(H)}{1 \cdot \mathbf{Pr}(H) + 0 \cdot \mathbf{Pr}(L)} = 1. \qquad (8.36)$$

That is, player 2 believes that 1 must be high-skilled if it sees 1 choose E. On the other hand, suppose that $\mathrm{Pr}(E|H) = \mathrm{Pr}(E|L) = 1$—that is, suppose player 1 obtains an education regardless of his or her type. Then Equation 8.34 implies

---

The denominator follows because the events of player 1's being of type H or L are mutually exclusive and jointly exhaustive, so

$$\mathbf{Pr}(E) = \mathbf{Pr}(E \text{ and } H) + \mathbf{Pr}(E \text{ and } L)$$
$$= \mathbf{Pr}(E|H)\,\mathbf{Pr}(H) + \mathbf{Pr}(E|L)\,\mathbf{Pr}(L).$$

$$\Pr(H|E) = \frac{1 \cdot \Pr(H)}{1 \cdot \Pr(H) + 1 \cdot \Pr(L)} = \Pr(H), \qquad (8.37)$$

since $\Pr(H) + \Pr(L) = 1$. That is, seeing 1 play E provides no information about 1's type, so 2's posterior belief is the same as its prior. More generally, if 2 plays the mixed strategy $\Pr(E|H) = p$ and $\Pr(E|L) = q$, then Bayes' rule implies that

$$\Pr(H|E) = \frac{p \Pr(H)}{p \Pr(H) + q \Pr(L)}. \qquad (8.38)$$

Perfect Bayesian equilibrium

With games of complete information, we moved from Nash equilibrium to the refinement of subgame-perfect equilibrium in order to rule out noncredible threats in sequential games. For the same reason, with games of incomplete information we move from Bayesian-Nash equilibrium to the refinement of perfect Bayesian equilibrium.

DEFINITION

Perfect Bayesian equilibrium. A perfect Bayesian equilibrium consists of a strategy profile and a set of beliefs such that

- at each information set, the strategy of the player moving there maximizes his or her expected payoff, where the expectation is taken with respect to his or her beliefs; and
- at each information set, where possible, the beliefs of the player moving there are formed using Bayes' rule (based on prior beliefs and other players' strategies).

The requirement that players play rationally at each information set is similar to the requirement from subgame-perfect equilibrium that play on every subgame form a Nash equilibrium. The requirement that players use Bayes' rule to update beliefs ensures that players incorporate the information from observing others' play in a rational way.

The remaining wrinkle in the definition of perfect Bayesian equilibrium is that Bayes' rule need only be used "where possible." Bayes' rule is useless following a completely unexpected event—in the context of a signaling model, an action that is not played in equilibrium by any type of player 1. For example, if neither H nor L type chooses E in the job-market signaling game, then the denominators of Equations 8.34 and 8.35 equal zero and the fraction is undefined. If Bayes' rule gives an undefined answer, then perfect Bayesian equilibrium puts no restrictions on player 2's posterior beliefs and so we can assume any beliefs we like.

As we saw with games of complete information, signaling games may have multiple equilibria. The freedom to specify any beliefs when Bayes' rule gives an undefined answer may support additional perfect Bayesian equilibria. A systematic analysis of multiple equilibria starts by dividing the equilibria into three classes—separating, pooling, and hybrid. Then we look for perfect Bayesian equilibria within each class.

In a *separating equilibrium*, each type of player 1 chooses a different action. Therefore, player 2 learns 1's type with certainty after observing 1's action. The posterior beliefs that come from Bayes' rule are all zeros and ones. In a *pooling equilibrium*, different types of player 1 choose the same action. Observing 1's action provides 2 with no information about 1's type. Pooling equilibria arise when one of player 1's types chooses an action that would otherwise be suboptimal in order to hide his or her private information. In a *hybrid equilibrium*, one type of player 1 plays a strictly mixed strategy; it is called a hybrid equilibrium because the mixed strategy sometimes results in the types being separated and sometimes pooled. Player 2 learns a little about 1's type (Bayes' rule refines 2's beliefs a bit) but doesn't learn 1's type with certainty. Player 2 may respond to the uncertainty by playing a mixed strategy itself. The next three examples solve for the three different classes of equilibrium in the job-market signaling game.

EXAMPLE 8.10 Separating Equilibrium in the Job-Market Signaling Game

A good guess for a separating equilibrium is that the high-skilled worker signals his or her type by getting an education and the low-skilled worker does not. Given these strategies, player 2's beliefs must be $\Pr(H|E) = \Pr(L|NE) = 1$ and $\Pr(H|NE) = \Pr(L|E) = 0$ according to Bayes' rule. Conditional on these beliefs, if player 2 observes that player 1 obtains an education then 2 knows it must be at node n_1 rather than n_2 in Figure 8.14. Its best response is to offer a job (J), given the payoff of $\pi - w > 0$. If player 2 observes that player 1 does not obtain an education then 2 knows it must be at node n_4 rather than n_3, and its best response is not to offer a job (NJ) because $0 > -w$.

The last step is to go back and check that player 1 would not want to deviate from the separating strategy $(E|H, NE|L)$ given that 2 plays $(J|E, NJ|NE)$. Type H of player 1 earns $w - c_H$ by obtaining an education in equilibrium. If type H deviates and does not obtain an education, then he or she earns 0 because player 2 believes that 1 is type L and does not offer a job. For type H not to prefer to deviate, it must be that $w - c_H \geq 0$. Next turn to type L of player 1. Type L earns 0 by not obtaining an education in equilibrium. If type L deviates and obtains an education, then he or she earns $w - c_L$ because player 2 believes that 1 is type H and offers a job. For type L not to prefer to deviate, we must have $w - c_L \leq 0$. Putting these conditions together, there is separating equilibrium in which the worker obtains an education if and only if he or she is high-skilled and in which the firm offers a job only to applicants with an education if and only if $c_H \leq w \leq c_L$.

Another possible separating equilibrium is for player 1 to obtain an education if and only if he or she is low-skilled. This is a bizarre outcome—since we expect education to be a signal of high rather than low skill—and fortunately we can rule it out as a perfect Bayesian equilibrium. Player 2's best response would be to offer a job if and only if 1 did not obtain an education. Type L would earn $-c_L$ from playing E and w from playing NE, so it would deviate to NE.

QUERY: Why does the worker sometimes obtain an education even though it does not raise his or her skill level? Would the separating equilibrium exist if a low-skilled worker could obtain an education more easily than a high-skilled one?

EXAMPLE 8.11 Pooling Equilibria in the Job-Market Signaling Game

Let's investigate a possible pooling equilibrium in which both types of player 1 choose E. For player 1 not to deviate from choosing E, player 2's strategy must be to offer a job if and only if the worker is educated—that is, $(J|E, NJ|NE)$. If 2 doesn't offer jobs to educated workers, then 1 might as well save the cost of obtaining an education and choose NE. If 2 offers jobs to uneducated workers, then 1 will again choose NE because he or she saves the cost of obtaining an education and still earns the wage from the job offer.

Next, we investigate when $(J|E, NJ|NE)$ is a best response for 2. Player 2's posterior beliefs after seeing E are the same as its prior beliefs in this pooling equilibrium. Player 2's expected payoff from choosing J is

$$\mathbf{Pr}(H|E)(\pi - w) + \mathbf{Pr}(L|E)(-w) = \mathbf{Pr}(H)(\pi - w) + \mathbf{Pr}(L)(-w)$$
$$= \mathbf{Pr}(H)\pi - w. \tag{8.39}$$

For J to be a best response to E, Equation 8.39 must exceed 2's zero payoff from choosing NJ, which upon rearranging implies that $\Pr(H) \geq w/\pi$. Player 2's posterior beliefs at nodes n_3 and n_4 are not pinned down by Bayes' rule, because NE is never played in

(continued)

EXAMPLE 8.11   CONTINUED

equilibrium and so seeing 1 play *NE* is a completely unexpected event. Perfect Bayesian equilibrium allows us to specify any probability distribution we like for the posterior beliefs $\Pr(H|NE)$ at node n_3 and $\Pr(L|NE)$ at node n_4. Player 2's payoff from choosing *NJ* is 0. For *NJ* to be a best response to *NE*, 0 must exceed 2's expected payoff from playing *J*:

$$0 > \Pr(H|NE)(\pi - w) + \Pr(L|NE)(-w) = \Pr(H|NE)\pi - w, \qquad (8.40)$$

where the right-hand side follows because $\Pr(H|NE) + \Pr(L|NE) = 1$. Rearranging yields $\Pr(H|NE) \le w/\pi$.

In sum, in order for there to be a pooling equilibrium in which both types of player 1 obtain an education, we need $\Pr(H|NE) \le w/\pi \le \Pr(H)$. The firm has to be optimistic about the proportion of skilled workers in the population—$\Pr(H)$ must be sufficiently high—and pessimistic about the skill level of uneducated workers—$\Pr(H|NE)$ must be sufficiently low. In this equilibrium, type L pools with type H in order to prevent player 2 from learning anything about the worker's skill from the education signal.

The other possibility for a pooling equilibrium is for both types of player 1 to choose *NE*. There are a number of such equilibria depending on what is assumed about player 2's posterior beliefs out of equilibrium (that is, 2's beliefs after it observes 1 choosing *E*). Perfect Bayesian equilibrium does not place any restrictions on these posterior beliefs. Problem 8.12 asks you to search for various of these equilibria and introduces a further refinement of perfect Bayesian equilibrium (the *intuitive criterion*) that helps rule out unreasonable out-of-equilibrium beliefs and thus implausible equilibria.

QUERY: Return to the pooling outcome in which both types of player 1 obtain an education. Consider 2's posterior beliefs following the unexpected event that a worker shows up with no education. Perfect Bayesian equilibrium leaves us free to assume anything we want about these posterior beliefs. Suppose we assume that the firm obtains no information from the "no education" signal and so maintains its prior beliefs. Is the proposed pooling outcome an equilibrium? What if we assume that the firm takes "no education" as a bad signal of skill, believing that 1's type is L for certain?

EXAMPLE 8.12   Hybrid Equilibria in the Job-Market Signaling Game

One possible hybrid equilibrium is for type H always to obtain an education and for type L to randomize, sometimes pretending to be a high type by obtaining an education. Type L randomizes between playing E and NE with probabilities e and $1 - e$. Player 2's strategy is to offer a job to an educated applicant with probability j and not to offer a job to an uneducated applicant.

We need to solve for the equilibrium values of the mixed strategies e^* and j^* and the posterior beliefs $\Pr(H|E)$ and $\Pr(H|NE)$ that are consistent with perfect Bayesian equilibrium. The posterior beliefs are computed using Bayes' rule:

$$\Pr(H|E) = \frac{\Pr(H)}{\Pr(H) + e\Pr(L)} = \frac{\Pr(H)}{\Pr(H) + e[1 - \Pr(H)]} \qquad (8.41)$$

and $\Pr(H|NE) = 0$.

For type L of player 1 to be willing to play a strictly mixed strategy, he or she must get the same expected payoff from playing E—which equals $jw - c_L$, given 2's mixed strategy—as from playing NE—which equals 0 given that player 2 does not offer a job to uneducated applicants. Hence $jw - c_L = 0$ or, solving for j, $j^* = c_L/w$.

Player 2 will play a strictly mixed strategy (conditional on observing E) only if it gets the same expected payoff from playing J, which equals

$$\mathbf{Pr}(H|E)(\pi - w) + \mathbf{Pr}(L|E)(-w) = \mathbf{Pr}(H|E)\pi - w, \tag{8.42}$$

as from playing NJ, which equals 0. Setting Equation 8.42 equal to 0, substituting for $\mathrm{Pr}(H|E)$ from Equation 8.41, and then solving for e gives

$$e^* = \frac{(\pi - w)\mathbf{Pr}(H)}{w[1 - \mathbf{Pr}(H)]}. \tag{8.43}$$

QUERY: To complete our analysis: in this equilibrium, type H of player 1 cannot prefer to deviate from E. Is this true? If so, can you show it? How does the probability of type L trying to "pool" with the high type by obtaining an education vary with player 2's prior belief that player 1 is the high type?

Cheap Talk

Education is nothing more than a costly display in the job-market signaling game. The display must be costly—indeed, it must be more costly to the low-skilled worker—or else the skill levels could not be separated in equilibrium. While we do see some information communicated through costly displays in the real world, most information is communicated simply by having one party talk to another at low or no cost ("cheap talk"). Game theory can help explain why cheap talk is prevalent but also why cheap talk sometimes fails, forcing parties to resort to costly displays.

We will model cheap talk as a two-player signaling game in which player 1's strategy space consists of messages sent costlessly to player 2. The timing is otherwise the same as before: player 1 first learns his type ("state of the world" might be a better label than "type" here because player 1's private information will enter both players' payoff functions directly), player 1 communicates to 2, and 2 takes some action affecting both players' payoffs. The space of messages is potentially limitless: player 1 can use a more or less sophisticated vocabulary, can write a more or less detailed message, can speak in any of the thousands of languages in the world, and so forth. So the set of equilibria is even larger than would normally be the case in signaling games. We will analyze the range of possible equilibria from the least to the most informative perfect Bayesian equilibrium.

The maximum amount of information that can be contained in player 1's message will depend on how well-aligned the players' payoff functions are. Player 2 would like to know the state of the world because she might have different actions that are suitable in different situations. If player 1 has the same preferences as 2 over which of 2's actions are best in each state of the world, then 1 has every incentive to tell 2 precisely what the state of the world is, and 2 has every reason to believe 1's report. On the other hand, if their preferences diverge, then 1 would have an incentive to lie about the state of the world to induce 2 to take the action that 1 prefers. Of course, 2 would anticipate 1's lying and would refuse to believe the report. As preferences diverge, messages become less and less informative. In the limit, 1's messages are completely uninformative ("babble"); to communicate real information, player 1 would have to resort to costly displays. In the job-market signaling game, for example, the preferences of the worker and firm diverge when the worker is low-skilled. The worker would like to be hired and the firm would like not to hire the worker. The high-skilled worker must resort to the costly display (education) in order to signal his or her type.

The reason we see relatively more cheap talk than costly displays in the real world is probably because people try to associate with others with whom they share common interests and avoid those with whom they don't. Members of a family, players on a team, or co-workers within a firm tend to have the same goals and usually have little reason to lie to each other. Even in these examples, players' interests may not be completely aligned and so cheap talk may not be completely informative (think about teenagers talking to parents).

EXAMPLE 8.13 Simple Cheap Talk Game

Consider a game with three states of the world: A, B, and C. First player 1 privately observes the state, then 1 sends a message to player 2, and then 2 chooses an action, L or R. The interests of players 1 and 2 are aligned in states A and B: both agree that 2 should play L in state A and R in state B. Their interests diverge in state C: 1 prefers 2 to play L and 2 prefers to play R. Assume that states A and B are equally likely. Let d be the probability of state C. Here, d measures the divergence between players' preferences. Instead of the extensive form, which is complicated by having three states and an ill-defined message space for player 1, the game is represented schematically by the matrices in Table 8.12.

TABLE 8.12   Simple Cheap Talk Game

	Player 2		
	L	R	State A
Player 1	1, 1	0, 0	$\Pr(A) = (1 - d)/2$

	Player 2		
	L	R	State B
Player 1	0, 0	1, 1	$\Pr(B) = (1 - d)/2$

	Player 2		
	L	R	State C
Player 1	0, 1	1, 0	$\Pr(C) = d$

If $d = 0$ then players' incentives are completely aligned. The most informative equilibrium results in perfect communication: 1 announces the state truthfully; 2 plays L if 1 announces "A" and R if 1 announces "B".[16] For $d > 0$, there cannot be perfect communication. If communication were perfect, then whatever message 1 sends when the state is A perfectly reveals the state and so leads 2 to play L. But then 1 would have an incentive to lie when the true state is C and would thus send the same message as when the state is A. Player 1's messages can be no more refined than issuing one of the two messages "the state is either A or C" or "the state is B"; any attempt to distinguish between A and C would not be believed.

If there is not too much divergence between players' interests—in particular, if $d \leq 1/3$—then there is an equilibrium with imperfect but still informative communication. In this equilibrium, player 1 sends one of two truthful messages: "A or C" or "B." Then player 2 plays L conditional on the message "A or C" and R conditional on "B." Player 2's expected payoff from playing L following the message "A or C" equals

$$\Pr(A|\text{"}A\text{ or }C\text{"})(1) + \Pr(C|\text{"}A\text{ or }C\text{"})(0) = \Pr(A|\text{"}A\text{ or }C\text{"}). \qquad \textbf{(8.44)}$$

By Bayes' rule,

$$\Pr(A|\text{"}A\text{ or }C\text{"}) = \frac{\Pr(\text{"}A\text{ or }C\text{"}|A)\Pr(A)}{\Pr(\text{"}A\text{ or }C\text{"}|A)\Pr(A) + \Pr(\text{"}A\text{ or }C\text{"}|C)\Pr(C)} = \frac{1 - d}{1 + d}.$$

$$\textbf{(8.45)}$$

---

[16]At the other extreme, for $d = 0$ and indeed for all parameters, there is always an uninformative "babbling" equilibrium in which 1's messages contain no information and 2 pays no attention to what 1 says.

The second equality in Equation 8.45 holds upon substituting $\Pr(\text{``}A\text{ or }C\text{''}|A) = \Pr(\text{``}A\text{ or }C\text{''}|C) = 1$ (if the state is A or C, player 1's strategy is to announce "A or C" with certainty) and substituting the values of $\Pr(A)$ and $\Pr(C)$ in terms of d from Table 8.12. Player 2's expected payoff from deviating to U can be shown (using calculations similar to Equations 8.44 and 8.45) to equal

$$\Pr(C|\text{``}A\text{ or }C\text{''}) = \frac{2d}{1+d}. \tag{8.46}$$

In equilibrium, Equation 8.45 must exceed Equation 8.46, implying that $d \leq 1/3$.

   If players' interests are yet more divergent—in particular, if $d > 1/3$—then there are only uninformative "babbling" equilibria.

QUERY: Are players better-off in more informative equilibria? What difference would it make if player 1 announced "purple" instead of "A or C" and "yellow" instead of "B"? What features of a language would make it more or less efficient in a cheap-talk setting?

EXPERIMENTAL GAMES

Experimental economics is a recent branch of research that explores how well economic theory matches the behavior of experimental subjects in laboratory settings. The methods are similar to those used in experimental psychology—often conducted on campus using undergraduates as subjects—although experiments in economics tend to involve incentives in the form of explicit monetary payments paid to subjects. The importance of experimental economics was highlighted in 2002, when Vernon Smith received the Nobel Prize in economics for his pioneering work in the field. An important area in this field is the use of experimental methods to test game theory.

Experiments with the Prisoners' Dilemma

There have been hundreds of tests of whether players fink in the Prisoners' Dilemma as predicted by Nash equilibrium or whether they play the cooperative outcome of Silent. In one experiment, subjects played the game 20 times with each player being matched with a different, anonymous opponent to avoid repeated-game effects. Play converged to the Nash equilibrium as subjects gained experience with the game. Players played the cooperative action 43 percent of the time in the first five rounds, falling to only 20 percent of the time in the last five rounds.[17]

   As is typical with experiments, subjects' behavior tended to be noisy. Although 80 percent of the decisions were consistent with Nash-equilibrium play by the end of the experiment, still 20 percent of them were anomalous. Even when experimental play is roughly consistent with the predictions of theory, it is rarely entirely consistent.

Experiments with the Ultimatum Game

Experimental economics has also tested to see whether subgame-perfect equilibrium is a good predictor of behavior in sequential games. In one widely studied sequential game, the Ultimatum Game, the experimenter provides a pot of money to two players. The first mover (Proposer) proposes a split of this pot to the second mover. The second mover (Responder) then decides whether to accept the offer, in which case players are given the amount of money indicated, or reject the offer, in which case both players get nothing. In the subgame-perfect

---

[17]R. Cooper, D. V. DeJong, R. Forsythe, and T. W. Ross, "Cooperation Without Reputation: Experimental Evidence from Prisoner's Dilemma Games," *Games and Economic Behavior* (February 1996): 187–218.

equilibrium, the Proposer offers a minimal share of the pot and this is accepted by the Responder. One can see this by applying backward induction: the Responder should accept any positive division no matter how small; knowing this, the Proposer should offer the Responder only a minimal share.

In experiments, the division tends to be much more even than in the subgame-perfect equilibrium.[18] The most common offer is a 50–50 split. Responders tend to reject offers giving them less than 30 percent of the pot. This result is observed even when the pot is as high as $100, so that rejecting a 30 percent offer means turning down $30. Some economists have suggested that the money players receive may not be a true measure of their payoffs. They may care about other factors such as fairness and so obtain a benefit from a more equal division of the pot. Even if a Proposer does not care directly about fairness, the fear that the Responder may care about fairness and thus might reject an uneven offer out of spite may lead the Proposer to propose an even split.

The departure of experimental behavior from the predictions of game theory was too systematic in the Ultimatum Game to be attributed to noisy play, leading some game theorists to rethink the theory and add an explicit consideration for fairness.[19]

Experiments with the Dictator Game

To test whether players care directly about fairness or act out of fear of the other player's spite, researchers experimented with a related game, the Dictator Game. In the Dictator Game, the Proposer chooses a split of the pot, and this split is implemented without input from the Responder. Proposers tend to offer a less even split than in the Ultimatum Game but still offer the Responder some of the pot, suggesting that Responders have some residual concern for fairness. The details of the experimental design are crucial, however, as one ingenious experiment showed.[20] The experiment was designed so that the experimenter would never learn which Proposers had made which offers. With this element of anonymity, Proposers almost never gave an equal split to Responders and indeed took the whole pot for themselves two thirds of the time. Proposers seem to care more about appearing fair to the experimenter than truly being fair.

EVOLUTIONARY GAMES AND LEARNING

The frontier of game-theory research regards whether and how players come to play a Nash equilibrium. Hyperrational players may deduce each others' strategies and instantly settle upon the Nash equilibrium. How can they instantly coordinate on a single outcome when there are multiple Nash equilibria? What outcome would real-world players, for whom hyper-rational deductions may be too complex, settle on?

Game theorists have tried to model the dynamic process by which an equilibrium emerges over the long run from the play of a large population of agents who meet others at random and play a pairwise game. Game theorists analyze whether play converges to Nash equilibrium or some other outcome, which Nash equilibrium (if any) is converged to if there are multiple equilibria, and how long such convergence takes. Two models, which make varying assumptions about the level of players' rationality, have been most widely studied: an evolutionary model and a learning model.

---

[18]For a review of Ultimatum Game experiments and a textbook treatment of experimental economics more generally, see D. D. Davis and C. A. Holt, *Experimental Economics* (Princeton, NJ: Princeton University Press, 1993).

[19]See, for example, M. Rabin, "Incorporating Fairness into Game Theory and Economics," *American Economic Review* (December 1993): 1281–1302.

[20]E. Hoffman, K. McCabe, K. Shachat, and V. Smith, "Preferences, Property Rights, and Anonymity in Bargaining Games," *Games and Economic Behavior* (November 1994): 346–80.

In the evolutionary model, players do not make rational decisions; instead, they play the way they are genetically programmed. The more successful a player's strategy in the population, the more fit is the player and the more likely will the player survive to pass its genes on to future generations and so the more likely the strategy spreads in the population.

Evolutionary models were initially developed by John Maynard Smith and other biologists to explain the evolution of such animal behavior as how hard a lion fights to win a mate or an ant fights to defend its colony. While it may be more of a stretch to apply evolutionary models to humans, evolutionary models provide a convenient way of analyzing population dynamics and may have some direct bearing on how social conventions are passed down, perhaps through culture.

In a learning model, players are again matched at random with others from a large population. Players use their experiences of payoffs from past play to teach them how others are playing and how they themselves can best respond. Players usually are assumed to have a degree of rationality in that they can choose a static best response given their beliefs, may do some experimenting, and will update their beliefs according to some reasonable rule. Players are not fully rational in that they do not distort their strategies in order to affect others' learning and thus future play.

Game theorists have investigated whether more-or less-sophisticated learning strategies converge more or less quickly to a Nash equilibrium. Current research seeks to integrate theory with experimental study, trying to identify the specific algorithms that real-world subjects use when they learn to play games.

SUMMARY

This chapter provided a structured way to think about strategic situations. We focused on the most important solution concept used in game theory, Nash equilibrium. We then progressed to several more-refined solution concepts that are in standard use in game theory in more complicated settings (with sequential moves and incomplete information). Some of the principal results are as follows.

- All games have the same basic components: players, strategies, payoffs, and an information structure.

- Games can be written down in normal form (providing a payoff matrix or payoff functions) or extensive form (providing a game tree).

- Strategies can be simple actions, more complicated plans contingent on others' actions, or even probability distributions over simple actions (mixed strategies).

- A Nash equilibrium is a set of strategies, one for each player, that are mutual best responses. In other words, a player's strategy in a Nash equilibrium is optimal given that all others play their equilibrium strategies.

- A Nash equilibrium always exists in finite games (in mixed if not pure strategies).

- Subgame-perfect equilibrium is a refinement of Nash equilibrium that helps to rule out equilibria in sequential games involving noncredible threats.

- Repeating a stage game a large number of times introduces the possibility of using punishment strategies to attain higher payoffs than if the stage game is played once. If a finite game with multiple stages is repeated often enough or if players are sufficiently patient in an infinitely repeated game, then a folk theorem holds implying that essentially any payoffs are possible in the repeated game.

- In games of private information, one player knows more about his or her "type" than another. Players maximize their expected payoffs given knowledge of their own type and beliefs about the others'.

- In a perfect Bayesian equilibrium of a signaling game, the second mover uses Bayes' rule to update his or her beliefs about the first mover's type after observing the first mover's action.

- The frontier of game-theory research combines theory with experiments to determine whether players who may not be hyperrational come to play a Nash equilibrium, which particular equilibrium (if there are more than one), and what path leads to the equilibrium.

PROBLEMS

8.1

Consider the following game:

Player 2

	D	E	F
A	7, 6	5, 8	0, 0
B	5, 8	7, 6	1, 1
C	0, 0	1, 1	4, 4

Player 1

a. Find the pure-strategy Nash equilibria (if any).

b. Find the mixed-strategy Nash equilibrium in which each player randomizes over just the first two actions.

c. Compute players' expected payoffs in the equilibria found in parts (a) and (b).

d. Draw the extensive form for this game.

8.2

The mixed-strategy Nash equilibrium in the Battle of the Sexes in Table 8.3 may depend on the numerical values for the payoffs. To generalize this solution, assume that the payoff matrix for the game is given by

Player 2 (Husband)

	Ballet	Boxing
Ballet	$K, 1$	0, 0
Boxing	0, 0	1, K

Player 1 (Wife)

where $K \geq 1$. Show how the mixed-strategy Nash equilibrium depends on the value of K.

8.3

The game of Chicken is played by two macho teens who speed toward each other on a single-lane road. The first to veer off is branded the chicken, whereas the one who doesn't veer gains peer-group esteem. Of course, if neither veers, both die in the resulting crash. Payoffs to the Chicken game are provided in the following table.

Teen 2

	Veer	Don't veer
Veer	2, 2	1, 3
Don't veer	3, 1	0, 0

Teen 1

a. Draw the extensive form.

b. Find the pure-strategy Nash equilibrium or equilibria.

c. Compute the mixed-strategy Nash equilibrium. As part of your answer, draw the best-response function diagram for the mixed strategies.

d. Suppose the game is played sequentially, with teen A moving first and committing to this action by throwing away the steering wheel. What are teen B's contingent strategies? Write down the normal and extensive forms for the sequential version of the game.

e. Using the normal form for the sequential version of the game, solve for the Nash equilibria.

f. Identify the proper subgames in the extensive form for the sequential version of the game. Use backward induction to solve for the subgame-perfect equilibrium. Explain why the other Nash equilibria of the sequential game are "unreasonable."

8.4

Two neighboring homeowners, $i = 1, 2$, simultaneously choose how many hours l_i to spend maintaining a beautiful lawn. The average benefit per hour is

$$10 - l_i + \frac{l_j}{2},$$

and the (opportunity) cost per hour for each is 4. Homeowner i's average benefit is increasing in the hours neighbor j spends on his own lawn, since the appearance of one's property depends in part on the beauty of the surrounding neighborhood.

a. Compute the Nash equilibrium.

b. Graph the best-response functions and indicate the Nash equilibrium on the graph.

c. On the graph, show how the equilibrium would change if the intercept of one of the neighbor's average benefit functions fell from 6 to some smaller number.

8.5

The Academy Award–winning movie *A Beautiful Mind* about the life of John Nash dramatizes Nash's scholarly contribution in a single scene: his equilibrium concept dawns on him while in a bar bantering with his fellow male graduate students. They notice several women, one blond and the rest brunette, and agree that the blond is more desirable than the brunettes. The Nash character views the situation as a game among the male graduate students, along the following lines. Suppose there are n males who simultaneously approach either the blond or one of the brunettes. If male i alone approaches the blond, then he is successful in getting a date with her and earns payoff a. If one or more other males approach the blond along with i, the competition causes them all to lose her, and i (as well as the others who approached her) earns a payoff of zero. On the other hand, male i earns a payoff of $b > 0$ from approaching a brunette, since there are more brunettes than males, so i is certain to get a date with a brunette. The desirability of the blond implies $a > b$.

a. Argue that this game does not have a symmetric pure-strategy Nash equilibrium.

b. Solve for the symmetric mixed-strategy equilibrium. That is, letting p be the probability that a male approaches the blond, find p^*.

c. Show that the more males there are, the less likely it is in the equilibrium from part (b) that the blond is approached by at least one of them. *Note:* This paradoxical result was noted by S. Anderson and M. Engers in "Participation Games: Market Entry, Coordination, and the Beautiful Blond," *Journal of Economic Behavior & Organization* 63 (2007): 120–37.

8.6

Consider the following stage game.

Player 2

		A	B	C
Player 1	A	10, 10	−1, 15	−1, −12
	B	15, −1	0, 0	−1, −1
	C	−12, −1	−1, −1	8, 8

a. Compute a player's minmax value if the rival is restricted to pure strategies. Is this minmax value different than if the rival is allowed to use mixed strategies?

b. Suppose the stage game is played twice. Characterize the subgame-perfect equilibrium providing the highest total payoffs.

c. Draw a graph of the set of feasible per-period payoffs in the limit in a finitely repeated game according to the folk theorem.

8.7

Return to the game with two neighbors in Problem 8.5. Continue to suppose that player i's average benefit per hour of work on landscaping is

$$10 - l_i + \frac{l_j}{2}.$$

Continue to suppose that player 2's opportunity cost of an hour of landscaping work is 4. Suppose that 1's opportunity cost is either 3 or 5 with equal probability and that this cost is 1's private information.

a. Solve for the Bayesian-Nash equilibrium.

b. Indicate the Bayesian-Nash equilibrium on a best-response function diagram.

c. Which type of player 1 would like to send a truthful signal to 2 if it could? Which type would like to hide its private information?

8.8

In Blind Texan Poker, player 2 draws a card from a standard deck and places it against her forehead without looking at it but so player 1 can see it. Player 1 moves first, deciding whether to stay or fold. If player 1 folds, he must pay player 2 $50. If player 1 stays, the action goes to player 2. Player 2 can fold or call. If player 2 folds, she must pay player 1 $50. If 2 calls, the card is examined. If it is a low card (2 through 8), player 2 pays player 1 $100. If it is a high card (9, 10, jack, queen, king, or ace), player 1 pays player 2 $100.

a. Draw the extensive form for the game.

b. Solve for the hybrid equilibrium.

c. Compute the players' expected payoffs.

Analytical Problems

8.9 Dominant strategies

Prove that an equilibrium in dominant strategies is the unique Nash equilibrium.

8.10 Rotten Kid Theorem

In *A Treatise on the Family* (Cambridge, MA: Harvard University Press, 1981), Nobel laureate Gary Becker proposes his famous Rotten Kid Theorem as a sequential game between the potentially rotten child (player 1) and the child's parent (player 2). The child moves first, choosing an action r that affects his own income $Y_1(r)$ $[Y_1'(r) > 0]$ and the income of the parent $Y_2(r)$ $[Y_2'(r) < 0]$. Later, the parent moves, leaving a monetary bequest L to the child. The child cares only for his own utility, $U_1(Y_1 + L)$, but the parent maximizes $U_2(Y_2 - L) + \alpha U_1$, where $\alpha > 0$ reflects the parent's altruism toward the child. Prove that, in a subgame-perfect equilibrium, the child will opt for the value of r that maximizes $Y_1 + Y_2$ even though he has no altruistic intentions. *Hint:* Apply backward induction to the parent's problem first, which will give a first-order condition that implicitly determines L^*; although an explicit solution for L^* cannot be found, the derivative of L^* with respect to r—required in the child's first-stage optimization problem—can be found using the implicit function rule.

8.11 Alternatives to Grim Strategy

Suppose that the Prisoners' Dilemma stage game (see Table 8.1) is repeated for infinitely many periods.

a. Can players support the cooperative outcome by using *tit-for-tat* strategies, punishing deviation in a past period by reverting to the stage-game Nash equilibrium for just one period and then returning to cooperation? Are two periods of punishment enough?

b. Suppose players use strategies that punish deviation from cooperation by reverting to the stage-game Nash equilibrium for ten periods before returning to cooperation. Compute the threshold discount factor above which cooperation is possible on the outcome that maximizes the joint payoffs.

8.12 Refinements of perfect Bayesian equilibrium

Recall the job-market signaling game in Example 8.11.

a. Find the conditions under which there is a pooling equilibrium where both types of worker choose not to obtain an education (*NE*) and where the firm offers an uneducated worker a job. Be sure to specify beliefs as well as strategies.

b. Find the conditions under which there is a pooling equilibrium where both types of worker choose not to obtain an education (*NE*) and where the firm does not offer an uneducated worker a job. What is the lowest posterior belief that the worker is low-skilled conditional on obtaining an education consistent with this pooling equilibrium? Why is it more natural to think that a low-skilled worker would never deviate to *E* and so an educated worker must be high-skilled? Cho and Kreps's *intuitive criterion* is one of a series of complicated refinements of perfect Bayesian equilibrium that rule out equilibria based on unreasonable posterior beliefs as identified in this part; see I. K. Cho and D. M. Kreps, "Signalling Games and Stable Equilibria," *Quarterly Journal of Economics* 102 (1987): 179–221.

SUGGESTIONS FOR FURTHER READING

Fudenberg, D., and J. Tirole. *Game Theory*. Cambridge, MA: MIT Press, 1991.

   A comprehensive survey of game theory at the graduate-student level, though selected sections are accessible to advanced undergraduates.

Holt, C. A. *Markets, Games, & Strategic Behavior*. Boston: Pearson, 2007.

   An undergraduate text with emphasis on experimental games.

Rasmusen, E. *Games and Information,* 4th ed. Malden, MA: Blackwell, 2007.

   An advanced undergraduate text with many real-world applications.

Watson, Joel. *Strategy: An Introduction to Game Theory*. New York: Norton, 2002.

   An undergraduate text that balances rigor with simple examples (often 2 × 2 games). Emphasis on bargaining and contracting examples.

EXTENSIONS

Existence of Nash Equilibrium

This section will sketch John Nash's original proof that all finite games have at least one Nash equilibrium (in mixed if not in pure strategies). We will provide some of the details of the proof here; the original proof is in Nash (1950), and a clear textbook presentation of the full proof is provided in Fudenberg and Tirole (1991). The section concludes by mentioning a related existence theorem for games with continuous actions.

Nash's proof is similar to the proof of the existence of a general competitive equilibrium in Chapter 13. Both proofs rely on a fixed point theorem. The proof of the existence of Nash equilibrium requires a slightly more powerful theorem. Instead of Brouwer's fixed point theorem, which applies to functions, Nash's proof relies on Kakutani's fixed point theorem, which applies to correspondences—more general mappings than functions.

E8.1 Correspondences versus functions

A function maps each point in a first set to a single point in a second set. A correspondence maps a single point in the first set to possibly many points in the second set. Figure E8.1 illustrates the difference.

FIGURE E8.1   Comparision of Functions and Correspondences

The function graphed in (a) looks like a familiar curve. Each value of x is mapped into a single value of y. With the correspondence graphed in (b), each value of x may be mapped into many values of y. Correspondences can thus have bulges as shown by the gray regions in (b).

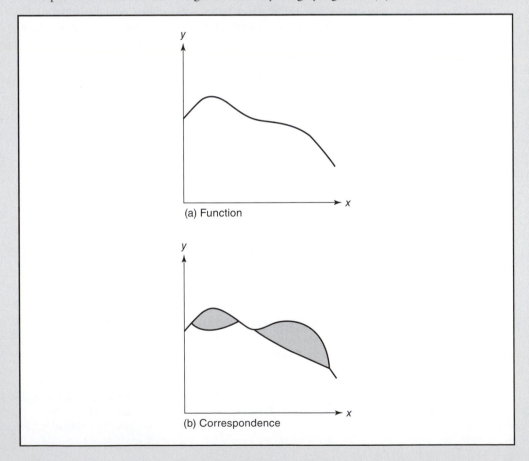

(a) Function

(b) Correspondence

An example of a correspondence that we have already seen is the best response, $BR_i(s_{-i})$. The best response need not map other players' strategies s_{-i} into a single strategy that is a best response for player i. There may be ties among several best responses. As shown in Figure 8.3, in the Battle of the Sexes, the husband's best response to the wife's playing the mixed strategy of going to ballet with probability $2/3$ and boxing with probability $1/3$ (or just $w = 2/3$ for short) is not just a single point but the whole interval of possible mixed strategies. Both the husband's and the wife's best responses in this figure are correspondences, not functions.

The reason Nash needed a fixed point theorem involving correspondences rather than just functions is precisely because his proof works with players' best responses to prove existence.

E8.2 Kakutani's fixed point theorem

Here is the statement of Kakutani's fixed point theorem:

Any convex, upper-semicontinuous corrrespondence $[f(x)]$ from a closed, bounded, convex set into itself has at least one fixed point (x^*) such that $x^* \in f(x^*)$.

Comparing the statement of Kakutani's fixed point theorem with Brouwer's in Chapter 13, they are similar except for the substitution of "correspondence" for "function" and for the conditions on the correspondence. Brouwer's theorem requires the function to be continuous; Kakutani's theorem requires the correspondence to be convex and upper semicontinuous.

These properties, which are related to continuity, are less familiar and worth spending a moment to understand. Figure E8.2 provides examples of correspondences violating (a) convexity and (b) upper semicontinuity. The figure shows why the two properties are needed to guarantee a fixed point. Without both properties, the correspondence can "jump" across the 45° line and so fail to have a fixed point—that is, a point for which $x = f(x)$.

E8.3 Nash's proof

We use $R(s)$ to denote the correspondence that underlies Nash's existence proof. This correspondence takes any profile of players' strategies $s = (s_1, s_2, \ldots, s_n)$ (possibly mixed) and maps it into another mixed strategy profile, the profile of best responses:

$$R(s) = (BR_1(s_{-1}), BR_2(s_{-2}), \ldots, BR_n(s_{-n})). \quad \textbf{(i)}$$

A fixed point of the correspondence is a strategy for which $s^* \in R(s^*)$; this is a Nash equilibrium because each player's strategy is a best response to others' strategies.

The proof checks that all the conditions involved in Kakutani's fixed point theorem are satisfied by the best-response correspondence $R(s)$. First, we need to show that the set of mixed-strategy profiles is closed, bounded, and convex. Since a strategy profile is just a list of individual strategies, the set of strategy profiles will be closed, bounded, and convex if each player's strategy set S_i has these properties individually. As Figure E8.3 shows for the case of two and three actions, the set of mixed strategies over actions has a simple shape.[1] The set is closed (contains its boundary), bounded (does not go off to infinity in any direction), and convex (the segment between any two points in the set is also in the set).

We then need to check that the best-response correspondence $R(s)$ is convex. Individual best responses cannot look like (a) in Figure E8.2, because if any two mixed strategies such as A and B are best responses to others' strategies then mixed strategies between them must also be best responses. For example, in the Battle of the Sexes, if $(1/3, 2/3)$ and $(2/3, 1/3)$ are best responses for the husband against his wife's playing $(2/3, 1/3)$ (where, in each pair, the first number is the probability of playing ballet and the second of playing boxing), then mixed strategies between the two such as $(1/2, 1/2)$ must also be best responses for him. Figure 8.3 showed that in fact all possible mixed strategies for the husband are best responses to the wife's playing $(2/3, 1/3)$.

Finally, we need to check that $R(s)$ is upper semicontinuous. Individual best responses cannot look like (b) in Figure E8.2. They cannot have holes like point D punched out of them because payoff functions $u_i(s_i, s_{-i})$ are continuous. Recall that payoffs, when written as functions of mixed strategies, are actually expected values with probabilities given by the strategies s_i and s_{-i}. As Equation 2.176 showed, expected values are linear functions of the underlying probabilities. Linear functions are of course continuous.

---

[1]Mathematicians study them so frequently that they have a special name for such a set: a *simplex*.

FIGURE E8.2   Kakutani's Conditions on Correspondences

The correspondence in (a) is not convex because the dashed vertical segment between A and B is not inside the correspondence. The correspondence in (b) is not upper semicontinuous because there is a path (C) inside the correspondence leading to a point (D) that, as indicated by the open circle, is not inside the correspondence. Both (a) and (b) fail to have fixed points.

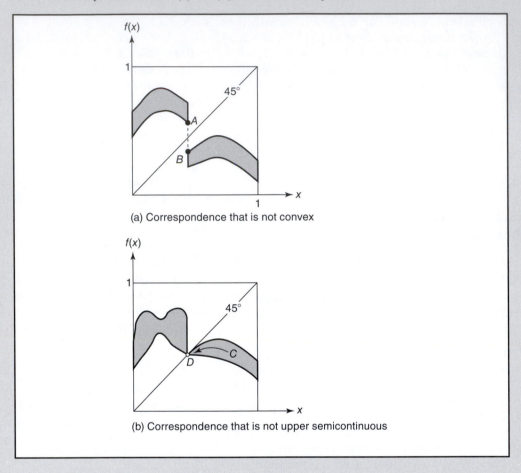

(a) Correspondence that is not convex

(b) Correspondence that is not upper semicontinuous

FIGURE E8.3   Set of Mixed Strategies for an Individual

Player 1's set of possible mixed strategies over two actions is given by the diagonal line segment in (a). The set for three actions is given by the shaded triangle on the three-dimensional graph in (b).

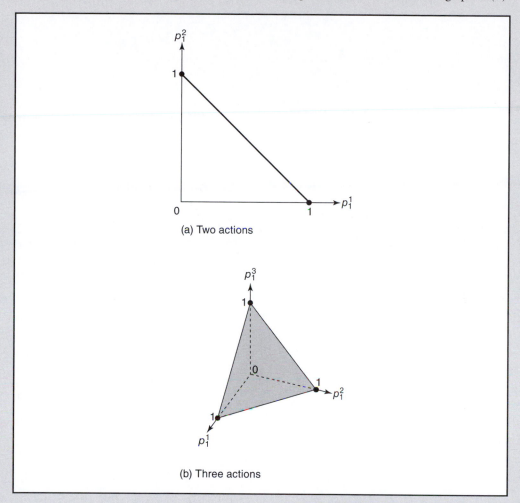

(a) Two actions

(b) Three actions

E8.4 Games with continuous actions

Nash's existence theorem applies to finite games—that is, games with a finite number of players and actions per player. Nash's theorem does not apply to games, such as the Tragedy of the Commons in Example 8.6, that feature continuous actions. Is a Nash equilibrium guaranteed to exist for these games, too? Glicksberg (1952) proved that the answer is "yes" as long as payoff functions are continuous.

References

Fudenberg, D., and J. Tirole. *Game Theory*. Cambridge, MA: MIT Press, 1991, sec. 1.3.

Glicksberg, I. L. "A Further Generalization of the Kakutani Fixed Point Theorem with Application to Nash Equilibrium Points." *Proceedings of the National Academy of Sciences* 38 (1952): 170–74.

Nash, John. "Equilibrium Points in *n*-Person Games." *Proceedings of the National Academy of Sciences* 36 (1950): 48–49.

Production and Supply

In this part we examine the production and supply of economic goods. Institutions that coordinate the transformation of inputs into outputs are called *firms*. They may be large institutions (such as Microsoft, Sony, or the U.S. Department of Defense) or small ones (such as "Mom and Pop" stores or self-employed individuals). Although they may pursue different goals (Microsoft may seek maximum profits, whereas an Israeli kibbutz may try to make members of the kibbutz as well off as possible), all firms must make certain basic choices in the production process. The purpose of Part 3 is to develop some tools for analyzing those choices.

In **Chapter 9** we examine ways of modeling the physical relationship between inputs and outputs. We introduce the concept of a *production function*, a useful abstraction from the complexities of real-world production processes. Two measurable aspects of the production function are stressed: its returns to scale (that is, how output expands when all inputs are increased) and its elasticity of substitution (that is, how easily one input may be replaced by another while maintaining the same level of output). We also briefly describe how technical improvements are reflected in production functions.

The production function concept is then used in **Chapter 10** to discuss costs of production. We assume that all firms seek to produce their output at the lowest possible cost, an assumption that permits the development of cost functions for the firm. Chapter 10 also focuses on how costs may differ between the short run and the long run.

In **Chapter 11** we investigate the firm's supply decision. To do so, we assume that the firm's manager will make input and output choices so as to maximize profits. The chapter concludes with the fundamental model of supply behavior by profit-maximizing firms that we will use in many subsequent chapters.

Production Functions

The principal activity of any firm is to turn inputs into outputs. Because economists are interested in the choices the firm makes in accomplishing this goal, but wish to avoid discussing many of the engineering intricacies involved, they have chosen to construct an abstract model of production. In this model the relationship between inputs and outputs is formalized by a *production function* of the form

$$q = f(k, l, m, \ldots), \tag{9.1}$$

where q represents the firm's output of a particular good during a period,[1] k represents the machine (that is, capital) usage during the period, l represents hours of labor input, m represents raw materials used,[2] and the notation indicates the possibility of other variables affecting the production process. Equation 9.1 is assumed to provide, for any conceivable set of inputs, the engineer's solution to the problem of how best to combine those inputs to get output.

MARGINAL PRODUCTIVITY

In this section we look at the change in output brought about by a change in one of the productive inputs. For the purposes of this examination (and indeed for most of the purposes of this book), it will be more convenient to use a simplified production function defined as follows.

Production function. The firm's *production function* for a particular good, q,

$$q = f(k, l), \tag{9.2}$$

shows the maximum amount of the good that can be produced using alternative combinations of capital (k) and labor (l).

DEFINITION

Of course, most of our analysis will hold for any two inputs to the production process we might wish to examine. The terms *capital* and *labor* are used only for convenience. Similarly, it would be a simple matter to generalize our discussion to cases involving more than two inputs; occasionally, we will do so. For the most part, however, limiting the discussion to two inputs will be quite helpful because we can show these inputs on two-dimensional graphs.

Marginal physical product

To study variation in a single input, we define marginal physical product as follows.

---

[1] Here we use a lowercase q to represent one firm's output. We reserve the uppercase Q to represent total output in a market. Generally, we assume that a firm produces only one output. Issues that arise in multiproduct firms are discussed in a few footnotes and problems.

[2] In empirical work raw material inputs often are disregarded and output, q, is measured in terms of "value added."

DEFINITION

Marginal physical product. The *marginal physical product* of an input is the additional output that can be produced by employing one more unit of that input while holding all other inputs constant. Mathematically,

$$\text{marginal physical product of capital} = MP_k = \frac{\partial q}{\partial k} = f_k,$$

$$\text{marginal physical product of labor} = MP_l = \frac{\partial q}{\partial l} = f_l. \tag{9.3}$$

Notice that the mathematical definitions of marginal product use partial derivatives, thereby properly reflecting the fact that all other input usage is held constant while the input of interest is being varied. For an example, consider a farmer hiring one more laborer to harvest the crop but holding all other inputs constant. The extra output this laborer produces is that farmhand's marginal physical product, measured in physical quantities, such as bushels of wheat, crates of oranges, or heads of lettuce. We might observe, for example, that 50 workers on a farm are able to produce 100 bushels of wheat per year, whereas 51 workers, with the same land and equipment, can produce 102 bushels. The marginal physical product of the 51st worker is then 2 bushels per year.

Diminishing marginal productivity

We might expect that the marginal physical product of an input depends on how much of that input is used. Labor, for example, cannot be added indefinitely to a given field (while keeping the amount of equipment, fertilizer, and so forth fixed) without eventually exhibiting some deterioration in its productivity. Mathematically, the assumption of diminishing marginal physical productivity is an assumption about the second-order partial derivatives of the production function:

$$\frac{\partial MP_k}{\partial k} = \frac{\partial^2 f}{\partial k^2} = f_{kk} = f_{11} < 0,$$

$$\frac{\partial MP_l}{\partial l} = \frac{\partial^2 f}{\partial l^2} = f_{ll} = f_{22} < 0. \tag{9.4}$$

The assumption of diminishing marginal productivity was originally proposed by the nineteenth-century economist Thomas Malthus, who worried that rapid increases in population would result in lower labor productivity. His gloomy predictions for the future of humanity led economics to be called the "dismal science." But the mathematics of the production function suggests that such gloom may be misplaced. Changes in the marginal productivity of labor over time depend not only on how labor input is growing, but also on changes in other inputs, such as capital. That is, we must also be concerned with $\partial MP_l / \partial k = f_{lk}$. In most cases, $f_{lk} > 0$, so declining labor productivity as *both l and k increase* is not a foregone conclusion. Indeed, it appears that labor productivity has risen significantly since Malthus' time, primarily because increases in capital inputs (along with technical improvements) have offset the impact of diminishing marginal productivity alone.

Average physical productivity

In common usage, the term *labor productivity* often means *average productivity*. When it is said that a certain industry has experienced productivity increases, this is taken to mean that output per unit of labor input has increased. Although the concept of average productivity is not nearly as important in theoretical economic discussions as marginal productivity is, it receives a great deal of attention in empirical discussions. Because average productivity is easily measured (say, as so many bushels of wheat per labor-hour input), it is often used as a measure of efficiency. We define the average product of labor (AP_l) to be

$$AP_l = \frac{\textbf{output}}{\textbf{labor input}} = \frac{q}{l} = \frac{f(k,l)}{l}. \qquad (9.5)$$

Notice that AP_l also depends on the level of capital employed. This observation will prove to be quite important when we examine the measurement of technical change at the end of this chapter.

EXAMPLE 9.1 A Two-Input Production Function

Suppose the production function for flyswatters during a particular period can be represented by

$$q = f(k,l) = 600k^2l^2 - k^3l^3. \qquad (9.6)$$

To construct the marginal and average productivity functions of labor (l) for this function, we must assume a particular value for the other input, capital (k). Suppose $k = 10$. Then the production function is given by

$$q = 60{,}000l^2 - 1{,}000l^3. \qquad (9.7)$$

Marginal product. The marginal productivity function (when $k = 10$) is given by

$$MP_l = \frac{\partial q}{\partial l} = 120{,}000l - 3{,}000l^2, \qquad (9.8)$$

which diminishes as l increases, eventually becoming negative. This implies that q reaches a maximum value. Setting MP_l equal to 0,

$$120{,}000l - 3{,}000l^2 = 0 \qquad (9.9)$$

yields

$$40l = l^2 \qquad (9.10)$$

or

$$l = 40 \qquad (9.11)$$

as the point at which q reaches its maximum value. Labor input beyond 40 units per period actually reduces total output. For example, when $l = 40$, Equation 9.7 shows that $q = 32$ million flyswatters, whereas when $l = 50$, production of flyswatters amounts to only 25 million.

Average product. To find the average productivity of labor in flyswatter production, we divide q by l, still holding $k = 10$:

$$AP_l = \frac{q}{l} = 60{,}000l - 1{,}000l^2. \qquad (9.12)$$

Again, this is an inverted parabola that reaches its maximum value when

$$\frac{\partial AP_l}{\partial l} = 60{,}000 - 2{,}000l = 0, \qquad (9.13)$$

which occurs when $l = 30$. At this value for labor input, Equation 9.12 shows that $AP_l = 900{,}000$, and Equation 9.8 shows that MP_l is also 900,000. When AP_l is at a maximum, average and marginal productivities of labor are equal.[3]

(*continued*)

---

[3]This result is quite general. Because

$$\frac{\partial AP_l}{\partial l} = \frac{l \cdot MP_l - q}{l^2},$$

at a maximum $l \cdot MP_l = q$ or $MP_l = AP_l$.

EXAMPLE 9.1 CONTINUED

Notice the relationship between total output and average productivity that is illustrated by this example. Even though total production of flyswatters is greater with 40 workers (32 million) than with 30 workers (27 million), output per worker is higher in the second case. With 40 workers, each worker produces 800,000 flyswatters per period, whereas with 30 workers each worker produces 900,000. Because capital input (flyswatter presses) is held constant in this definition of productivity, the diminishing marginal productivity of labor eventually results in a declining level of output per worker.

QUERY: How would an increase in k from 10 to 11 affect the MP_l and AP_l functions here? Explain your results intuitively.

ISOQUANT MAPS AND THE RATE OF TECHNICAL SUBSTITUTION

To illustrate possible substitution of one input for another in a production function, we use its *isoquant map*. Again, we study a production function of the form $q = f(k, l)$, with the understanding that "capital" and "labor" are simply convenient examples of any two inputs that might happen to be of interest. An isoquant (from *iso*, meaning "equal") records those combinations of k and l that are able to produce a given quantity of output. For example, all those combinations of k and l that fall on the curve labeled "$q = 10$" in Figure 9.1 are capable of producing 10 units of output per period. This isoquant then records the fact that there are many alternative ways of producing 10 units of output. One way might be represented by point A: We would use l_A and k_A to produce 10 units of output. Alternatively, we might prefer

FIGURE 9.1   An Isoquant Map

Isoquants record the alternative combinations of inputs that can be used to produce a given level of output. The slope of these curves shows the rate at which l can be substituted for k while keeping output constant. The negative of this slope is called the (marginal) *rate of technical substitution* (*RTS*). In the figure, the *RTS* is positive and diminishing for increasing inputs of labor.

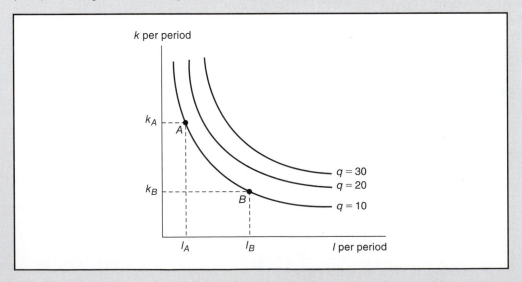

to use relatively less capital and more labor and therefore would choose a point such as *B*. Hence, we may define an isoquant as follows.

DEFINITION

Isoquant. An *isoquant* shows those combinations of *k* and *l* that can produce a given level of output (say, q_0). Mathematically, an isoquant records the set of *k* and *l* that satisfies

$$f(k, l) = q_0. \tag{9.14}$$

As was the case for indifference curves, there are infinitely many isoquants in the *k–l* plane. Each isoquant represents a different level of output. Isoquants record successively higher levels of output as we move in a northeasterly direction. Presumably, using more of each of the inputs will permit output to increase. Two other isoquants (for *q* = 20 and *q* = 30) are shown in Figure 9.1. You will notice the similarity between an isoquant map and the individual's indifference curve map discussed in Part 2. They are indeed similar concepts, because both represent "contour" maps of a particular function. For isoquants, however, the labeling of the curves is measurable—an output of 10 units per period has a quantifiable meaning. Economists are therefore more interested in studying the shape of production functions than in examining the exact shape of utility functions.

The marginal rate of technical substitution (*RTS*)

The slope of an isoquant shows how one input can be traded for another while holding output constant. Examining the slope provides information about the technical possibility of substituting labor for capital. A formal definition follows.

DEFINITION

Marginal rate of technical substitution. The *marginal rate of technical substitution* (*RTS*) shows the rate at which labor can be substituted for capital while holding output constant along an isoquant. In mathematical terms,

$$RTS \ (l \ \text{for} \ k) = \frac{-dk}{dl} \bigg|_{q=q_0}. \tag{9.15}$$

In this definition, the notation is intended as a reminder that output is to be held constant as *l* is substituted for *k*. The particular value of this trade-off rate will depend not only on the level of output but also on the quantities of capital and labor being used. Its value depends on the point on the isoquant map at which the slope is to be measured.

RTS and marginal productivities

To examine the shape of production function isoquants, it is useful to prove the following result: the *RTS* (of *l* for *k*) is equal to the ratio of the marginal physical productivity of labor (MP_l) to the marginal physical productivity of capital (MP_k). We begin by setting up the total differential of the production function:

$$dq = \frac{\partial f}{\partial l} \cdot dl + \frac{\partial f}{\partial k} \cdot dk = MP_l \cdot dl + MP_k \cdot dk, \tag{9.16}$$

which records how small changes in *l* and *k* affect output. Along an isoquant, $dq = 0$ (output is constant), so

$$MP_l \cdot dl = -MP_k \cdot dk. \tag{9.17}$$

This says that along an isoquant, the gain in output from increasing *l* slightly is exactly balanced by the loss in output from suitably decreasing *k*. Rearranging terms a bit gives

$$-\frac{dk}{dl} \bigg|_{q=q_0} = RTS \ (l \ \text{for} \ k) = \frac{MP_l}{MP_k}. \tag{9.18}$$

Hence the *RTS* is given by the ratio of the inputs' marginal productivities.

Equation 9.18 shows that those isoquants that we actually observe must be negatively sloped. Because both MP_l and MP_k will be nonnegative (no firm would choose to use a costly input that reduced output), the RTS also will be positive (or perhaps zero). Because the slope of an isoquant is the negative of the RTS, any firm we observe will not be operating on the positively sloped portion of an isoquant. Although it is mathematically possible to devise production functions whose isoquants have positive slopes at some points, it would not make economic sense for a firm to opt for such input choices.

Reasons for a diminishing *RTS*

The isoquants in Figure 9.1 are drawn not only with a negative slope (as they should be) but also as convex curves. Along any one of the curves, the RTS is *diminishing*. For high ratios of k to l, the RTS is a large positive number, indicating that a great deal of capital can be given up if one more unit of labor becomes available. On the other hand, when a lot of labor is already being used, the RTS is low, signifying that only a small amount of capital can be traded for an additional unit of labor if output is to be held constant. This assumption would seem to have some relationship to the assumption of diminishing marginal productivity. A hasty use of Equation 9.18 might lead one to conclude that a rise in l accompanied by a fall in k would result in a fall in MP_l, a rise in MP_k, and, therefore, a fall in the RTS. The problem with this quick "proof" is that the marginal productivity of an input depends on the level of *both* inputs—changes in l affect MP_k and vice versa. It is not possible to derive a diminishing RTS from the assumption of diminishing marginal productivity alone.

To see why this is so mathematically, assume that $q = f(k, l)$ and that f_k and f_l are positive (that is, the marginal productivities are positive). Assume also that $f_{kk} < 0$ and $f_{ll} < 0$ (that the marginal productivities are diminishing). To show that isoquants are convex, we would like to show that $d(RTS)/dl < 0$. Since $RTS = f_l/f_k$, we have

$$\frac{dRTS}{dl} = \frac{d(f_l/f_k)}{dl}.$$ (9.19)

Because f_l and f_k are functions of both k and l, we must be careful in taking the derivative of this expression:

$$\frac{dRTS}{dl} = \frac{f_k(f_{ll} + f_{lk} \cdot dk/dl) - f_l(f_{kl} + f_{kk} \cdot dk/dl)}{(f_k)^2}.$$ (9.20)

Using the fact that $dk/dl = -f_l/f_k$ along an isoquant and Young's theorem ($f_{kl} = f_{lk}$), we have

$$\frac{dRTS}{dl} = \frac{f_k^2 f_{ll} - 2f_k f_l f_{kl} + f_l^2 f_{kk}}{(f_k)^3}.$$ (9.21)

Because we have assumed $f_k > 0$, the denominator of this function is positive. Hence the whole fraction will be negative if the numerator is negative. Because f_{ll} and f_{kk} are both assumed to be negative, the numerator definitely will be negative if f_{kl} is positive. If we can assume this, we have shown that $dRTS/dl < 0$ (that the isoquants are convex)[4].

Importance of cross-productivity effects

Intuitively, it seems reasonable that the cross-partial derivative $f_{kl} = f_{lk}$ should be positive. If workers had more capital, they would have higher marginal productivities. But, although this is probably the most prevalent case, it does not necessarily have to be so. Some production functions have $f_{kl} < 0$, at least for a range of input values. When we assume a diminishing

[4]As we pointed out in Chapter 2, functions for which the numerator in Equation 9.21 is negative are called (strictly) *quasi-concave functions*.

RTS (as we will throughout most of our discussion), we are therefore making a stronger assumption than simply diminishing marginal productivities for each input—specifically, we are assuming that marginal productivities diminish "rapidly enough" to compensate for any possible negative cross-productivity effects. Of course, as we shall see later, with three or more inputs, things become even more complicated.

EXAMPLE 9.2 A Diminishing *RTS*

In Example 9.1, the production function for flyswatters was given by

$$q = f(k, l) = 600k^2l^2 - k^3l^3. \qquad (9.22)$$

General marginal productivity functions for this production function are

$$MP_l = f_l = \frac{\partial q}{\partial l} = 1,200k^2l - 3k^3l^2,$$

$$MP_k = f_k = \frac{\partial q}{\partial k} = 1,200kl^2 - 3k^2l^3. \qquad (9.23)$$

Notice that each of these depends on the values of both inputs. Simple factoring shows that these marginal productivities will be positive for values of k and l for which $kl < 400$.

Because

$$f_{ll} = 1,200k^2 - 6k^3l$$

and

$$f_{kk} = 1,200l^2 - 6kl^3, \qquad (9.24)$$

it is clear that this function exhibits diminishing marginal productivities for sufficiently large values of k and l. Indeed, again by factoring each expression, it is easy to show that $f_{ll}, f_{kk} < 0$ if $kl > 200$. However, even within the range $200 < kl < 400$ where the marginal productivity relations for this function behave "normally," this production function may not necessarily have a diminishing *RTS*. Cross-differentiation of either of the marginal productivity functions (Equation 9.23) yields

$$f_{kl} = f_{lk} = 2,400kl - 9k^2l^2, \qquad (9.25)$$

which is positive only for $kl < 266$.

The numerator of Equation 9.21 will therefore definitely be negative for $200 < kl < 266$, but for larger-scale flyswatter factories the case is not so clear, because f_{kl} is negative. When f_{kl} is negative, increases in labor input reduce the marginal productivity of capital. Hence, the intuitive argument that the assumption of diminishing marginal productivities yields an unambiguous prediction about what will happen to the *RTS* $(= f_l/f_k)$ as l increases and k falls is incorrect. It all depends on the relative effects on marginal productivities of diminishing marginal productivities (which tend to reduce f_l and increase f_k) and the contrary effects of cross-marginal productivities (which tend to increase f_l and reduce f_k). Still, for this flyswatter case, it is true that the *RTS* is diminishing throughout the range of k and l, where marginal productivities are positive. For cases where $266 < kl < 400$, the diminishing marginal productivities exhibited by the function are sufficient to overcome the influence of a negative value for f_{kl} on the convexity of isoquants.

QUERY: For cases where $k = l$, what can be said about the marginal productivities of this production function? How would this simplify the numerator for Equation 9.21? How does this permit you to more easily evaluate this expression for some larger values of k and l?

RETURNS TO SCALE

We now proceed to characterize production functions. A first question that might be asked about them is how output responds to increases in all inputs together. For example, suppose that all inputs were doubled: Would output double or would the relationship not be quite so simple? This is a question of the *returns to scale* exhibited by the production function that has been of interest to economists ever since Adam Smith intensively studied the production of pins. Smith identified two forces that came into operation when the conceptual experiment of doubling all inputs was performed. First, a doubling of scale permits a greater division of labor and specialization of function. Hence, there is some presumption that efficiency might increase—production might more than double. Second, doubling of the inputs also entails some loss in efficiency because managerial overseeing may become more difficult given the larger scale of the firm. Which of these two tendencies will have a greater effect is an important empirical question.

Presenting a technical definition of these concepts is misleadingly simple.

DEFINITION   **Returns to scale.** If the production function is given by $q = f(k, l)$ and if all inputs are multiplied by the same positive constant t (where $t > 1$), then we classify the *returns to scale* of the production function by

Effect on Output	Returns to Scale
I. $f(tk, tl) = tf(k, l) = tq$	Constant
II. $f(tk, tl) < tf(k, l) = tq$	Decreasing
III. $f(tk, tl) > tf(k, l) = tq$	Increasing

In intuitive terms, if a proportionate increase in inputs increases output by the same proportion, the production function exhibits constant returns to scale. If output increases less than proportionately, the function exhibits diminishing returns to scale. And if output increases more than proportionately, there are increasing returns to scale. As we shall see, it is theoretically possible for a function to exhibit constant returns to scale for some levels of input usage and increasing or decreasing returns for other levels.[5] Often, however, economists refer to the *degree* of returns to scale of a production function with the implicit notion that only a fairly narrow range of variation in input usage and the related level of output is being considered.

Constant returns to scale

There are economic reasons why a firm's production function might exhibit constant returns to scale. If the firm operates many identical plants, it may increase or decrease production simply by varying the number of them in current operation. That is, the firm can double output by doubling the number of plants it operates, and that will require it to employ precisely twice as many inputs. Alternatively, if one were modeling the behavior of an entire industry composed of many firms, the constant returns-to-scale assumption might

---

[5]A local measure of returns to scale is provided by the scale elasticity, defined as

$$e_{q,t} = \frac{\partial f(tk, tl)}{\partial t} \cdot \frac{t}{f(tk, tl)},$$

where this expression is to be evaluated at $t = 1$. This parameter can, in principle, take on different values depending on the level of input usage. For some examples using this concept, see Problem 9.9.

make sense because the industry can expand or contract by adding or dropping an arbitrary number of identical firms (see Chapter 12). Finally, studies of the entire U.S. economy have found that constant returns to scale is a reasonably good approximation to use for an "aggregate" production function. For all of these reasons, then, the constant returns-to-scale case seems worth examining in somewhat more detail.

When a production function exhibits constant returns to scale, it meets the definition of "homogeneity" that we introduced in Chapter 2. That is, the production is homogeneous of degree 1 in its inputs because

$$f(tk, tl) = t^1 f(k, l) = tq. \tag{9.26}$$

In Chapter 2 we showed that, if a function is homogeneous of degree k, its derivatives are homogeneous of degree $k - 1$. In this context this implies that the marginal productivity functions derived from a constant returns-to-scale production function are homogeneous of degree 0. That is,

$$MP_k = \frac{\partial f(k, l)}{\partial k} = \frac{\partial f(tk, tl)}{\partial k},$$
$$MP_l = \frac{\partial f(k, l)}{\partial l} = \frac{\partial f(tk, tl)}{\partial l} \tag{9.27}$$

for any $t > 0$. In particular, we can let $t = 1/l$ in Equations 9.27 and get

$$MP_k = \frac{\partial f(k/l, 1)}{\partial k},$$
$$MP_l = \frac{\partial f(k/l, 1)}{\partial l}. \tag{9.28}$$

That is, the marginal productivity of any input depends only on the ratio of capital to labor input, not on the absolute levels of these inputs. This fact is especially important, for example, in explaining differences in productivity among industries or across countries.

Homothetic production functions

One consequence of Equations 9.28 is that the $RTS (= MP_l / MP_k)$ for any constant returns-to-scale production function will depend only on the ratio of the inputs, not on their absolute levels. That is, such a function will be homothetic (see Chapter 2)—its isoquants will be radial expansions of one another. This situation is shown in Figure 9.2. Along any ray through the origin (where the ratio k/l does not change), the slopes of successively higher isoquants are identical. This property of the isoquant map will be very useful to us on several occasions.

A simple numerical example may provide some intuition about this result. Suppose a roof can be installed in one day by three workers with one hammer each or by two workers with two hammers each (these workers are ambidextrous). The RTS of hammers for workers is therefore one for one—one extra hammer can be substituted for one worker. If this production process exhibits constant returns to scale, two roofs can be installed in one day either by six workers with six hammers or by four workers with eight hammers. In the latter case, two hammers are substituted for two workers, so again the RTS is one for one. In constant returns-to-scale cases, expanding the level of production does not alter trade-offs among inputs, so production functions are homothetic.

A production function can have a homothetic indifference curve map even if it does not exhibit constant returns to scale. As we showed in Chapter 2, this property of homotheticity is retained by any monotonic transformation of a homogeneous function. Hence, increasing or decreasing returns to scale can be incorporated into a constant returns-to-scale function

FIGURE 9.2   Isoquant Map for a Constant Returns-to-Scale Production Function

For a constant returns-to-scale production function, the *RTS* depends only on the ratio of k to l, not on the scale of production. Consequently, each isoquant will be a radial blowup of the unit isoquant. Along any ray through the origin (a ray of constant k/l), the *RTS* will be the same on all isoquants.

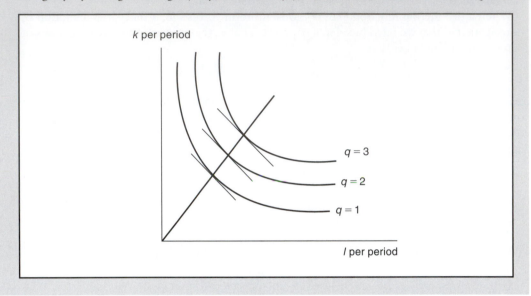

through an appropriate transformation. Perhaps the most common such transformation is exponential. So, if $f(k, l)$ is a constant returns-to-scale producton function, we can let

$$F(k, l) = [f(k, l)]^{\gamma}, \qquad (9.29)$$

where γ is any positive exponent. If $\gamma > 1$ then

$$F(tk, tl) = [f(tk, tl)]^{\gamma} = [tf(k, l)]^{\gamma} = t^{\gamma}[f(k, l)]^{\gamma} = t^{\gamma}F(k, l) > tF(k, l) \qquad (9.30)$$

for any $t > 1$. Hence, this transformed production function exhibits increasing returns to scale. An identical proof shows that the function F exhibits decreasing returns to scale for $\gamma < 1$. Because this function remains homothetic through all such transformations, we have shown that there are important cases where the issue of returns to scale can be separated from issues involving the shape of an isoquant. In the next section, we will look at how shapes of isoquants can be described.

The *n*-input case

The definition of returns to scale can be easily generalized to a production function with n inputs. If that production function is given by

$$q = f(x_1, x_2, ..., x_n) \qquad (9.31)$$

and if all inputs are multiplied by $t > 1$, we have

$$f(tx_1, tx_2, ..., tx_n) = t^k f(x_1, x_2, ..., x_n) = t^k q \qquad (9.32)$$

for some constant k. If $k = 1$, the production function exhibits constant returns to scale. Diminishing and increasing returns to scale correspond to the cases $k < 1$ and $k > 1$, respectively.

The crucial part of this mathematical definition is the requirement that all inputs be increased by the same proportion, t. In many real-world production processes, this provision may make little economic sense. For example, a firm may have only one "boss," and that number would not necessarily be doubled even if all other inputs were. Or the output of a farm may depend on the fertility of the soil. It may not be literally possible to double the acres planted while maintaining fertility, because the new land may not be as good as that already under cultivation. Hence, some inputs may have to be fixed (or at least imperfectly variable) for most practical purposes. In such cases, some degree of diminishing productivity (a result of increasing employment of variable inputs) seems likely, although this cannot properly be called "diminishing returns to scale" because of the presence of inputs that are held fixed.

THE ELASTICITY OF SUBSTITUTION

Another important characteristic of the production function is how "easy" it is to substitute one input for another. This is a question about the shape of a single isoquant rather than about the whole isoquant map. Along one isoquant, the rate of technical substitution will decrease as the capital-labor ratio decreases (that is, as k/l decreases); now we wish to define some parameter that measures this degree of responsiveness. If the RTS does not change at all for changes in k/l, we might say that substitution is easy because the ratio of the marginal productivities of the two inputs does not change as the input mix changes. Alternatively, if the RTS changes rapidly for small changes in k/l, we would say that substitution is difficult because minor variations in the input mix will have a substantial effect on the inputs' relative productivities. A scale-free measure of this responsiveness is provided by the *elasticity of substitution*, a concept we encountered in Part 2. Now we can provide a formal definition.

Elasticity of substitution. For the production function $q = f(k, l)$, the *elasticity of substitution* (σ) measures the proportionate change in k/l relative to the proportionate change in the RTS along an isoquant. That is,

DEFINITION

$$\sigma = \frac{\text{percent } \Delta(k/l)}{\text{percent } \Delta RTS} = \frac{d(k/l)}{dRTS} \cdot \frac{RTS}{k/l} = \frac{\partial \ln k/l}{\partial \ln RTS} = \frac{\partial \ln k/l}{\partial \ln f_l/f_k}. \tag{9.33}$$

Because along an isoquant, k/l and RTS move in the same direction, the value of σ is always positive. Graphically, this concept is illustrated in Figure 9.3 as a movement from point A to point B on an isoquant. In this movement, both the RTS and the ratio k/l will change; we are interested in the relative magnitude of these changes. If σ is high, then the RTS will not change much relative to k/l and the isoquant will be relatively flat. On the other hand, a low value of σ implies a rather sharply curved isoquant; the RTS will change by a substantial amount as k/l changes. In general, it is possible that the elasticity of substitution will vary as one moves along an isoquant and as the scale of production changes. Often, however, it is convenient to assume that σ is constant along an isoquant. If the production function is also homothetic, then—because all the isoquants are merely radial blowups—σ will be the same along all isoquants. We will encounter such functions later in this chapter and in many of its problems.[6]

The *n*-input case

Generalizing the elasticity of substitution to the many-input case raises several complications. One approach is to adopt a definition analogous to Equation 9.33; that is, to define the elasticity of substitution between two inputs to be the proportionate change in the ratio of

---

[6]The elasticity of substitution can be phrased directly in terms of the production function and its derivatives in the constant returns-to-scale case as

$$\sigma = \frac{f_k \cdot f_l}{f \cdot f_{k,l}}.$$

But this form is quite cumbersome. Hence usually the logarithmic definition in Equation 9.33 is easiest to apply. For a compact summary, see P. Berck and K. Sydsaeter, *Economist's Mathematical Manual* (Berlin: Springer-Verlag, 1999), chap. 5.

FIGURE 9.3 Graphic Description of the Elasticity of Substitution

In moving from point A to point B on the $q = q_0$ isoquant, both the capital-labor ratio (k/l) and the RTS will change. The elasticity of substitution (σ) is defined to be the ratio of these proportional changes; it is a measure of how curved the isoquant is.

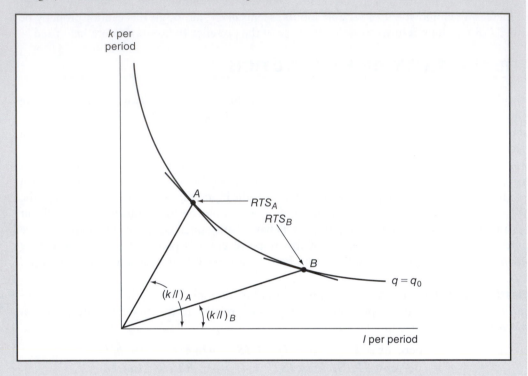

the two inputs to the proportionate change in the RTS between them while holding output constant.[7] To make this definition complete, it is necessary to require that all inputs other than the two being examined be held constant. However, this latter requirement (which is not relevant when there are only two inputs) restricts the value of this potential definition. In real-world production processes, it is likely that any change in the ratio of two inputs will also be accompanied by changes in the levels of other inputs. Some of these other inputs may be complementary with the ones being changed, whereas others may be substitutes, and to hold them constant creates a rather artificial restriction. For this reason, an alternative definition of the elasticity of substitution that permits such complementarity and substitutability in the firm's cost function is generally used in the n-good case. Because this concept is usually measured using cost functions, we will describe it in the next chapter.

FOUR SIMPLE PRODUCTION FUNCTIONS

In this section we illustrate four simple production functions, each characterized by a different elasticity of substitution. These are shown only for the case of two inputs, but generalization to many inputs is easily accomplished (see the Extensions for this chapter).

---

[7]That is, the elasticity of substitution between input i and input j might be defined as

$$\sigma_{ij} = \frac{\partial \ln(x_i/x_j)}{\partial \ln(f_j/f_i)}$$

for movements along $f(x_1, x_2, \ldots, x_n) = c$. Notice that the use of partial derivatives in this definition effectively requires that all inputs other than i and j be held constant when considering movements along the c isoquant.

Case 1: Linear ($\sigma = \infty$)

Suppose that the production function is given by

$$q = f(k, l) = ak + bl. \tag{9.34}$$

It is easy to show that this production function exhibits constant returns to scale: For any $t > 1$,

$$f(tk, tl) = atk + btl = t(ak + bl) = tf(k, l). \tag{9.35}$$

All isoquants for this production function are parallel straight lines with slope $-b/a$. Such an isoquant map is pictured in panel (a) of Figure 9.4. Because the RTS is constant along any straight-line isoquant, the denominator in the definition of σ (Equation 9.33) is equal to 0 and hence σ is infinite. Although this linear production function is a useful example, it is

FIGURE 9.4   Isoquant Maps for Simple Production Functions with Various Values for σ

Three possible values for the elasticity of substitution are illustrated in these figures. In (a), capital and labor are perfect substitutes. In this case, the RTS will not change as the capital-labor ratio changes. In (b), the fixed-proportions case, no substitution is possible. The capital-labor ratio is fixed at b/a. A case of limited substitutability is illustrated in (c).

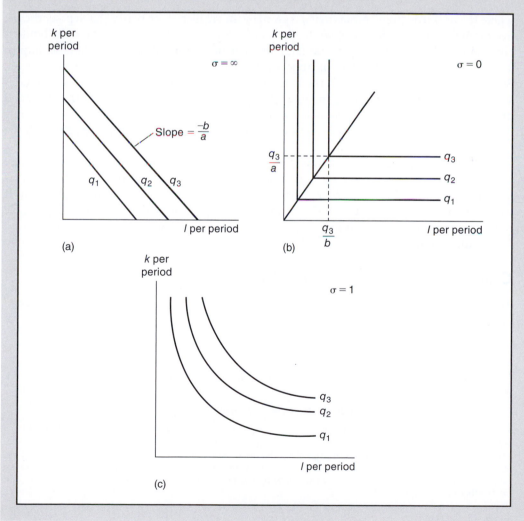

rarely encountered in practice because few production processes are characterized by such ease of substitution. Indeed, in this case, capital and labor can be thought of as perfect substitutes for each other. An industry characterized by such a production function could use *only* capital or *only* labor, depending on these inputs' prices. It is hard to envision such a production process: Every machine needs someone to press its buttons, and every laborer requires some capital equipment, however modest.

Case 2: Fixed proportions ($\sigma = 0$)

The production function characterized by $\sigma = 0$ is the important case of a *fixed-proportions production function*. Capital and labor must always be used in a fixed ratio. The isoquants for this production function are L-shaped and are pictured in panel (b) of Figure 9.4. A firm characterized by this production function will always operate along the ray where the ratio k/l is constant. To operate at some point other than at the vertex of the isoquants would be inefficient, because the same output could be produced with fewer inputs by moving along the isoquant toward the vertex. Because k/l is a constant, it is easy to see from the definition of the elasticity of substitution that σ must equal 0.

The mathematical form of the fixed-proportions production function is given by

$$q = \min(ak, bl), \quad a, b > 0, \tag{9.36}$$

where the operator "min" means that q is given by the smaller of the two values in parentheses. For example, suppose that $ak < bl$; then $q = ak$, and we would say that capital is the binding constraint in this production process. The employment of more labor would not raise output, and hence the marginal product of labor is zero; additional labor is superfluous in this case. Similarly, if $ak > bl$, then labor is the binding constraint on output and additional capital is superfluous. When $ak = bl$, both inputs are fully utilized. When this happens, $k/l = b/a$, and production takes place at a vertex on the isoquant map. If both inputs are costly, this is the only cost-minimizing place to operate. The locus of all such vertices is a straight line through the origin with a slope given by b/a.

The fixed-proportions production function has a wide range of applications.[8] Many machines, for example, require a certain number of people to run them, but any excess labor is superfluous. Consider combining capital (a lawn mower) and labor to mow a lawn. It will always take one person to run the mower, and either input without the other is not able to produce any output at all. It may be that many machines are of this type and require a fixed complement of workers per machine.[9]

Case 3: Cobb-Douglas ($\sigma = 1$)

The production function for which $\sigma = 1$, called a *Cobb-Douglas production function*,[10] provides a middle ground between the two polar cases previously discussed. Isoquants for

---

[8]With the form reflected by Equation 9.35, the fixed-proportions production function exhibits constant returns to scale because

$$f(tk, tl) = \min(atk, btl) = t \cdot \min(ak, bl) = tf(k, l)$$

for any $t > 1$. As before, increasing or decreasing returns can be easily incorporated into the functions by using a nonlinear transformation of this functional form—such as $[f(k, l)]^\gamma$, where γ may be greater than or less than 1.

[9]The lawn mower example points up another possibility, however. Presumably there is some leeway in choosing what size of lawn mower to buy. Hence, prior to the actual purchase, the capital-labor ratio in lawn mowing can be considered variable: Any device, from a pair of clippers to a gang mower, might be chosen. Once the mower is purchased, however, the capital-labor ratio becomes fixed.

[10]Named after C. W. Cobb and P. H. Douglas. See P. H. Douglas, *The Theory of Wages* (New York: Macmillan Co., 1934), pp. 132–f35.

the Cobb-Douglas case have the "normal" convex shape and are shown in panel (c) of Figure 9.4. The mathematical form of the Cobb-Douglas production function is given by

$$q = f(k, l) = Ak^a l^b, \tag{9.37}$$

where A, a, and b are all positive constants.

The Cobb-Douglas function can exhibit any degree of returns to scale, depending on the values of a and b. Suppose all inputs were increased by a factor of t. Then

$$f(tk, tl) = A(tk)^a (tl)^b = At^{a+b} k^a l^b$$
$$= t^{a+b} f(k, l). \tag{9.38}$$

Hence, if $a + b = 1$, the Cobb-Douglas function exhibits constant returns to scale because output also increases by a factor of t. If $a + b > 1$ then the function exhibits increasing returns to scale, whereas $a + b < 1$ corresponds to the decreasing returns-to-scale case. It is a simple matter to show that the elasticity of substitution is 1 for the Cobb-Douglas function.[11] This fact has led researchers to use the constant returns-to-scale version of the function for a general description of aggregate production relationships in many countries.

The Cobb-Douglas function has also proved to be quite useful in many applications because it is linear in logarithms:

$$\ln q = \ln A + a \ln k + b \ln l. \tag{9.39}$$

The constant a is then the elasticity of output with respect to capital input, and b is the elasticity of output with respect to labor input.[12] These constants can sometimes be estimated from actual data, and such estimates may be used to measure returns to scale (by examining the sum $a + b$) and for other purposes.

Case 4: CES production function

A functional form that incorporates all of the three previous cases and allows σ to take on other values as well is the constant elasticity of substitution (CES) production function first introduced by Arrow et al. in 1961.[13] This function is given by

$$q = f(k, l) = [k^\rho + l^\rho]^{\gamma/\rho} \tag{9.40}$$

for $\rho \leq 1$, $\rho \neq 0$, and $\gamma > 0$. This function closely resembles the CES utility function discussed in Chapter 3, though now we have added the exponent γ/ρ to permit explicit introduction of returns-to-scale factors. For $\gamma > 1$ the function exhibits increasing returns to scale, whereas for $\gamma < 1$ it exhibits diminishing returns.

---

[11]For the Cobb-Douglas function,

$$RTS = \frac{f_l}{f_k} = \frac{bAk^a l^{b-1}}{aAk^{a-1} l^b} = \frac{b}{a} \frac{k}{l}$$

or

$$\ln RTS = \ln(b/a) + \ln(k/l).$$

Hence

$$\sigma = \frac{\partial \ln k/l}{\partial \ln RTS} = 1.$$

[12]See Problem 9.5.

[13]K. J. Arrow, H. B. Chenery, B. S. Minhas, and R. M. Solow, "Capital-Labor Substitution and Economic Efficiency," *Review of Economics and Statistics* (August 1961): 225–50.

Direct application of the definition of σ to this function[14] gives the important result that

$$\sigma = \frac{1}{1 - \rho}. \tag{9.41}$$

Hence the linear, fixed-proportions, and Cobb-Douglas cases correspond to $\rho = 1$, $\rho = -\infty$, and $\rho = 0$, respectively. Proof of this result for the fixed proportions and Cobb-Douglas cases requires a limit argument.

Often the CES function is used with a distributional weight, β $(0 \leq \beta \leq 1)$, to indicate the relative significance of the inputs:

$$q = f(k, l) = [\beta k^\rho + (1 - \beta) l^\rho]^{\gamma/\rho}. \tag{9.42}$$

With constant returns to scale and $\rho = 0$, this function converges to the Cobb-Douglas form

$$q = f(k, l) = k^\beta l^{1-\beta}. \tag{9.43}$$

EXAMPLE 9.3 A Generalized Leontief Production Function

Suppose that the production function for a good is given by

$$q = f(k, l) = k + l + 2\sqrt{k \cdot l}. \tag{9.44}$$

This function is a special case of a class of functions named for the Russian-American economist Wassily Leontief.[15] The function clearly exhibits constant returns to scale because

$$f(tk, tl) = tk + tl + 2t\sqrt{kl} = tf(k, l). \tag{9.45}$$

Marginal productivities for the Leontief function are

$$
\begin{aligned}
f_k &= 1 + (k/l)^{-0.5}, \\
f_l &= 1 + (k/l)^{0.5}.
\end{aligned} \tag{9.46}
$$

Hence, marginal productivities are positive and diminishing. As would be expected (because this function exhibits constant returns to scale), the RTS here depends only on the ratio of the two inputs

$$RTS = \frac{f_l}{f_k} = \frac{1 + (k/l)^{0.5}}{1 + (k/l)^{-0.5}}. \tag{9.47}$$

This RTS diminishes as k/l falls, so the isoquants have the usual convex shape.

---

[14]For the CES function we have

$$RTS = \frac{f_l}{f_k} = \frac{(\gamma/\rho) \cdot q^{(\gamma-\rho)/\gamma} \cdot \rho l^{\rho-1}}{(\gamma/\rho) \cdot q^{(\gamma-\rho)/\gamma} \cdot \rho k^{\rho-1}} = \left(\frac{l}{k}\right)^{\rho-1} = \left(\frac{k}{l}\right)^{1-\rho}.$$

Applying the definition of the elasticity of substitution then yields

$$\sigma = \frac{\partial \ln(k/l)}{\partial \ln RTS} = \frac{1}{1 - \rho}.$$

Notice in this computation that the factor ρ cancels out of the marginal productivity functions, thereby ensuring that these marginal productivities are positive even when ρ is negative (as it is in many cases). This explains why ρ appears in two different places in the definition of the CES function.

[15]Lenotief was a pioneer in the development of input-output analysis. In input-output analysis, production is assumed to take place with a fixed-proportions technology. The Leontief production function generalizes the fixed-proportions case. For more details see the discussion of Leontief production functions in the Extensions to this chapter.

There are two ways you might calculate the elasticity of substitution for this production function. First, you might notice that in this special case the function can be factored as

$$q = k + l + 2\sqrt{kl} = (\sqrt{k} + \sqrt{l})^2 = (k^{0.5} + l^{0.5})^2, \qquad (9.48)$$

which makes clear that this function has a CES form with $\rho = 0.5$ and $\gamma = 1$. Hence the elasticity of substitution here is $\sigma = 1/(1 - \rho) = 2$.

Of course, in most cases it is not possible to do such a simple factorization. A more exhaustive approach is to apply the definition of the elasticity of substitution given in footnote 6 of this chapter:

$$\sigma = \frac{f_k f_l}{f \cdot f_{kl}} = \frac{[1 + (k/l)^{0.5}][1 + (k/l)^{-0.5}]}{q \cdot (0.5/\sqrt{kl})}$$

$$= \frac{2 + (k/l)^{0.5} + (k/l)^{-0.5}}{1 + 0.5(k/l)^{0.5} + 0.5(k/l)^{-0.5}} = 2. \qquad (9.49)$$

Notice that in this calculation the input ratio (k/l) drops out, leaving a very simple result. In other applications, one might doubt that such a fortuitous result would occur and hence doubt that the elasticity of substitution is constant along an isoquant (see Problem 9.7). But here the result that $\sigma = 2$ is intuitively reasonable, because that value represents a compromise between the elasticity of substitution for this production function's linear part $(q = k + l, \sigma = \infty)$ and its Cobb-Douglas part $(q = 2k^{0.5}l^{0.5}, \sigma = 1)$.

QUERY: What can you learn about this production function by graphing the $q = 4$ isoquant? Why does this function generalize the fixed proportions case?

TECHNICAL PROGRESS

Methods of production improve over time, and it is important to be able to capture these improvements with the production function concept. A simplified view of such progress is provided by Figure 9.5. Initially, isoquant q_0 records those combinations of capital and labor that can be used to produce an output level of q_0. Following the development of superior production techniques, this isoquant shifts to q_0'. Now the same level of output can be produced with fewer inputs. One way to measure this improvement is by noting that with a level of capital input of, say, k_1, it previously took l_2 units of labor to produce q_0, whereas now it takes only l_1. Output per worker has risen from q_0/l_2 to q_0/l_1. But one must be careful in this type of calculation. An increase in capital input to k_2 would also have permitted a reduction in labor input to l_1 along the original q_0 isoquant. In this case, output per worker would also rise, although there would have been no true technical progress. Use of the production function concept can help to differentiate between these two concepts and therefore allow economists to obtain an accurate estimate of the rate of technical change.

Measuring technical progress

The first observation to be made about technical progress is that historically the rate of growth of output over time has exceeded the growth rate that can be attributed to the growth in conventionally defined inputs. Suppose that we let

$$q = A(t)f(k, l) \qquad (9.50)$$

be the production function for some good (or perhaps for society's output as a whole). The term $A(t)$ in the function represents all the influences that go into determining q other than k (machine-hours) and l (labor-hours). Changes in A over time represent technical progress.

FIGURE 9.5   Technical Progress

Technical progress shifts the q_0 isoquant toward the origin. The new q_0 isoquant, q_0', shows that a given level of output can now be produced with less input. For example, with k_1 units of capital it now only takes l_1 units of labor to produce q_0, whereas before the technical advance it took l_2 units of labor.

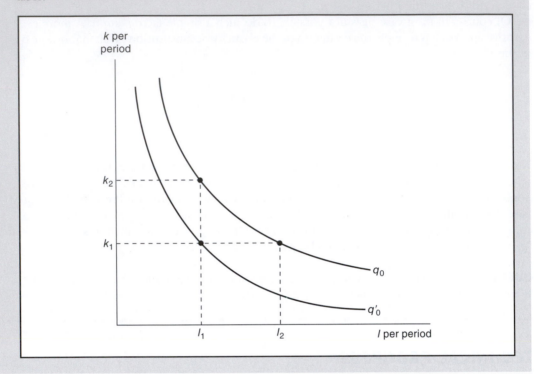

For this reason, A is shown as a function of time. Presumably $dA/dt > 0$; particular levels of input of labor and capital become more productive over time.

Differentiating Equation 9.50 with respect to time gives

$$\frac{dq}{dt} = \frac{dA}{dt} \cdot f(k, l) + A \cdot \frac{df(k, l)}{dt}$$

$$= \frac{dA}{dt} \cdot \frac{q}{A} + \frac{q}{f(k, l)} \left[\frac{\partial f}{\partial k} \cdot \frac{dk}{dt} + \frac{\partial f}{\partial l} \cdot \frac{dl}{dt} \right]. \tag{9.51}$$

Dividing by q gives

$$\frac{dq/dt}{q} = \frac{dA/dt}{A} + \frac{\partial f/\partial k}{f(k, l)} \cdot \frac{dk}{dt} + \frac{\partial f/\partial l}{f(k, l)} \cdot \frac{dl}{dt} \tag{9.52}$$

or

$$\frac{dq/dt}{q} = \frac{dA/dt}{A} + \frac{\partial f}{\partial k} \cdot \frac{k}{f(k, l)} \cdot \frac{dk/dt}{k} + \frac{\partial f}{\partial l} \cdot \frac{l}{f(k, l)} \cdot \frac{dl/dt}{l}. \tag{9.53}$$

Now, for any variable x, $(dx/dt)/x$ is the proportional rate of growth of x per unit of time. We shall denote this by G_x.[16] Hence, Equation 9.53 can be written in terms of growth rates as

---

[16]Two useful features of this definition are: (1) $G_{x \cdot y} = G_x + G_y$—that is, the growth rate of a product of two variables is the sum of each one's growth rate; and (2) $G_{x/y} = G_x - G_y$.

$$G_q = G_A + \frac{\partial f}{\partial k} \cdot \frac{k}{f(k,l)} \cdot G_k + \frac{\partial f}{\partial l} \cdot \frac{l}{f(k,l)} \cdot G_l, \tag{9.54}$$

but

$$\frac{\partial f}{\partial k} \cdot \frac{k}{f(k,l)} = \frac{\partial q}{\partial k} \cdot \frac{k}{q} = \text{elasticity of output with respect to capital input}$$
$$= e_{q,k}$$

and

$$\frac{\partial f}{\partial l} \cdot \frac{l}{f(k,l)} = \frac{\partial q}{\partial l} \cdot \frac{l}{q} = \text{elasticity of output with respect to labor input}$$
$$= e_{q,l}.$$

Growth accounting

Therefore, our growth equation finally becomes

$$G_q = G_A + e_{q,k}G_k + e_{q,l}G_l. \tag{9.55}$$

This shows that the rate of growth in output can be broken down into the sum of two components: growth attributed to changes in inputs (k and l) and other "residual" growth (that is, changes in A) that represents technical progress.

Equation 9.55 provides a way of estimating the relative importance of technical progress (G_A) in determining the growth of output. For example, in a pioneering study of the entire U.S. economy between the years 1909 and 1949, R. M. Solow recorded the following values for the terms in the equation:[17]

$$G_q = 2.75 \text{ percent per year,}$$
$$G_l = 1.00 \text{ percent per year,}$$
$$G_k = 1.75 \text{ percent per year,}$$
$$e_{q,l} = 0.65,$$
$$e_{q,k} = 0.35.$$

Consequently,

$$G_A = G_q - e_{q,l}G_l - e_{q,k}G_k$$
$$= 2.75 - 0.65(1.00) - 0.35(1.75)$$
$$= 2.75 - 0.65 - 0.60$$
$$= 1.50. \tag{9.56}$$

The conclusion Solow reached, then, was that technology advanced at a rate of 1.5 percent per year from 1909 to 1949. More than half of the growth in real output could be attributed to technical change rather than to growth in the physical quantities of the factors of production. More recent evidence has tended to confirm Solow's conclusions about the relative importance of technical change. Considerable uncertainty remains, however, about the precise causes of such change.

---

[17]R. M. Solow, "Technical Progress and the Aggregate Production Function," *Review of Economics and Statistics* 39 (August 1957): 312–f20.

EXAMPLE 9.4 Technical Progress in the Cobb-Douglas Production Function

The Cobb-Douglas production function provides an especially easy avenue for illustrating technical progress. Assuming constant returns to scale, such a production function with technical progress might be represented by

$$q = A(t)f(k, l) = A(t)k^\alpha l^{1-\alpha}. \tag{9.57}$$

If we also assume that technical progress occurs at a constant exponential (θ), then we can write $A(t) = Ae^{\theta t}$ and the production function becomes

$$q = Ae^{\theta t}k^\alpha l^{1-\alpha}. \tag{9.58}$$

A particularly easy way to study the properties of this type of function over time is to use "logarithmic differentiation":

$$\frac{\partial \ln q}{\partial t} = \frac{\partial \ln q}{\partial q} \cdot \frac{\partial q}{\partial t} = \frac{\partial q/\partial t}{q} = G_q = \frac{\partial[\ln A + \theta t + \alpha \ln k + (1 - \alpha) \ln l]}{\partial t}$$

$$= \theta + \alpha \cdot \frac{\partial \ln k}{\partial t} + (1 - \alpha) \cdot \frac{\partial \ln l}{\partial t} = \theta + \alpha G_k + (1-\alpha)G_l. \tag{9.59}$$

So this derivation just repeats Equation 9.55 for the Cobb-Douglas case. Here the technical change factor is explicitly modeled, and the output elasticities are given by the values of the exponents in the Cobb-Douglas.

The importance of technical progress can be illustrated numerically with this function. Suppose $A = 10, \theta = 0.03, \alpha = 0.5$ and that a firm uses an input mix of $k = l = 4$. Then, at $t = 0$, output is $40(= 10 \cdot 4^{0.5} \cdot 4^{0.5})$. After 20 years ($t = 20$), the production function becomes

$$q = 10e^{0.03 \cdot 20}k^{0.5}l^{0.5} = 10 \cdot (1.82)k^{0.5}l^{0.5} = 18.2k^{0.5}l^{0.5}. \tag{9.60}$$

In year 20 the original input mix now yields $q = 72.8$. Of course, one could also have produced $q = 72.8$ in year 0, but it would have taken a lot more inputs. For example, with $k = 13.25$ and $l = 4$, output is indeed 72.8 but much more capital is used. Output per unit of labor input would rise from 10 ($q/l = 40/4$) to 18.2 ($= 72.8/4$) in either circumstance, but only the first case would have been true technical progress.

Input-augmenting technical progress. It is tempting to attribute the increase in the average productivity of labor in this example to, say, improved worker skills, but that would be misleading in the Cobb-Douglas case. One might just as well have said that output per unit of capital rose from 10 to 18.2 over the 20 years and attribute this rise to improved machinery. A plausible approach to modeling improvements in labor and capital separately is to assume that the production function is

$$q = A(e^{\varphi t}k)^\alpha(e^{\varepsilon t}l)^{1-\alpha}, \tag{9.61}$$

where φ represents the annual rate of improvement in capital input and ε represents the annual rate of improvement in labor input. But, because of the exponential nature of the Cobb-Douglas function, this would be indistinguishable from our original example:

$$q = Ae^{[\alpha\varphi+(1-\alpha)\varepsilon]t}k^\alpha l^{1-\alpha} = Ae^{\theta t}k^\alpha l^{1-\alpha}, \tag{9.62}$$

where $\theta = \alpha\varphi + (1 - \alpha)\varepsilon$. Hence, to study technical progress in individual inputs, it is necessary either to adopt a more complex way of measuring inputs that allows for improving quality or (what amounts to the same thing) to use a multi-input production function.

QUERY: Actual studies of production using the Cobb-Douglas tend to find $\alpha \approx 0.3$. Use this finding together with Equation 9.62 to discuss the relative importance of improving capital and labor quality to the overall rate of technical progress.

SUMMARY

In this chapter we illustrated the ways in which economists conceptualize the production process of turning inputs into outputs. The fundamental tool is the production function, which—in its simplest form—assumes that output per period (q) is a simple function of capital and labor inputs during that period, $q = f(k, l)$. Using this starting point, we developed several basic results for the theory of production.

- If all but one of the inputs are held constant, a relationship between the single-variable input and output can be derived. From this relationship, one can derive the marginal physical productivity (MP) of the input as the change in output resulting from a one-unit increase in the use of the input. The marginal physical productivity of an input is assumed to decline as use of the input increases.

- The entire production function can be illustrated by its isoquant map. The (negative of the) slope of an isoquant is termed the *marginal rate of technical substitution* (RTS), because it shows how one input can be substituted for another while holding output constant. The RTS is the ratio of the marginal physical productivities of the two inputs.

- Isoquants are usually assumed to be convex—they obey the assumption of a diminishing RTS. This assumption cannot be derived exclusively from the assumption of diminishing marginal physical productivities. One must also be concerned with the effect of changes in one input on the marginal productivity of other inputs.

- The returns to scale exhibited by a production function record how output responds to proportionate increases in all inputs. If output increases proportionately with input use, there are constant returns to scale. If there are greater than proportionate increases in output, there are increasing returns to scale, whereas if there are less than proportionate increases in output, there are decreasing returns to scale.

- The elasticity of substitution (σ) provides a measure of how easy it is to substitute one input for another in production. A high σ implies nearly linear isoquants, whereas a low σ implies that isoquants are nearly L-shaped.

- Technical progress shifts the entire production function and its related isoquant map. Technical improvements may arise from the use of improved, more-productive inputs or from better methods of economic organization.

PROBLEMS

9.1

Power Goat Lawn Company uses two sizes of mowers to cut lawns. The smaller mowers have a 24-inch blade and are used on lawns with many trees and obstacles. The larger mowers are exactly twice as big as the smaller mowers and are used on open lawns where maneuverability is not so difficult. The two production functions available to Power Goat are:

	Output per Hour (square feet)	Capital Input (# of 24″ mowers)	Labor Input
Large mowers	8000	2	1
Small mowers	5000	1	1

a. Graph the $q = 40,000$ square feet isoquant for the first production function. How much k and l would be used if these factors were combined without waste?

b. Answer part (a) for the second function.

c. How much k and l would be used without waste if half of the 40,000-square-foot lawn were cut by the method of the first production function and half by the method of the second? How much k and l would be used if three fourths of the lawn were cut by the first method and one fourth by the second? What does it mean to speak of fractions of k and l?

d. On the basis of your observations in part (c), draw a $q = 40,000$ isoquant for the combined production functions.

9.2

Suppose the production function for widgets is given by

$$q = kl - 0.8k^2 - 0.2l^2,$$

where q represents the annual quantity of widgets produced, k represents annual capital input, and l represents annual labor input.

a. Suppose $k = 10$; graph the total and average productivity of labor curves. At what level of labor input does this average productivity reach a maximum? How many widgets are produced at that point?

b. Again assuming that $k = 10$, graph the MP_l curve. At what level of labor input does $MP_l = 0$?

c. Suppose capital inputs were increased to $k = 20$. How would your answers to parts (a) and (b) change?

d. Does the widget production function exhibit constant, increasing, or decreasing returns to scale?

9.3

Sam Malone is considering renovating the bar stools at Cheers. The production function for new bar stools is given by

$$q = 0.1k^{0.2}l^{0.8},$$

where q is the number of bar stools produced during the renovation week, k represents the number of hours of bar stool lathes used during the week, and l represents the number of worker hours employed during the period. Sam would like to provide 10 new bar stools, and he has allocated a budget of $10,000 for the project.

a. Sam reasons that because bar stool lathes and skilled bar stool workers both cost the same amount ($50 per hour), he might as well hire these two inputs in equal amounts. If Sam proceeds in this way, how much of each input will he hire and how much will the renovation project cost?

b. Norm (who knows something about bar stools) argues that once again Sam has forgotten his microeconomics. He asserts that Sam should choose quantities of inputs so that their marginal (not average) productivities are equal. If Sam opts for this plan instead, how much of each input will he hire and how much will the renovation project cost?

c. Upon hearing that Norm's plan will save money, Cliff argues that Sam should put the savings into more bar stools in order to provide seating to more of his USPS colleagues. How many more bar stools can Sam get for his budget if he follows Cliff's plan?

d. Carla worries that Cliff's suggestion will just mean more work for her in delivering food to bar patrons. How might she convince Sam to stick to his original 10–bar stool plan?

9.4

Suppose that the production of crayons (q) is conducted at two locations and uses only labor as an input. The production function in location 1 is given by $q_1 = 10l_1^{0.5}$ and in location 2 by $q_2 = 50l_2^{0.5}$.

a. If a single firm produces crayons in both locations, then it will obviously want to get as large an output as possible given the labor input it uses. How should it allocate labor between the locations in order to do so? Explain precisely the relationship between l_1 and l_2.

b. Assuming that the firm operates in the efficient manner described in part (a), how does total output (q) depend on the total amount of labor hired (l)?

9.5

As we have seen in many places, the general Cobb-Douglas production function for two inputs is given by

$$q = f(k, l) = Ak^\alpha l^\beta,$$

where $0 < \alpha < 1$ and $0 < \beta < 1$. For this production function:

a. Show that $f_k > 0, f_l > 0, f_{kk} < 0, f_{ll} < 0,$ and $f_{kl} = f_{lk} > 0$.

b. Show that $e_{q,k} = \alpha$ and $e_{e,l} = \beta$.

c. In footnote 5, we defined the scale elasticity as

$$e_{q,t} = \frac{\partial f(tk, tl)}{\partial t} \cdot \frac{t}{f(tk, tl)},$$

where the expression is to be evaluated at $t = 1$. Show that, for this Cobb-Douglas function, $e_{q,t} = \alpha + \beta$. Hence, in this case the scale elasticity and the returns to scale of the production function agree (for more on this concept see Problem 9.9).

d. Show that this function is quasi-concave.

e. Show that the function is concave for $\alpha + \beta \le 1$ but not concave for $\alpha + \beta > 1$.

9.6

Suppose we are given the constant returns-to-scale CES production function

$$q = [k^\rho + l^\rho]^{1/\rho}.$$

a. Show that $MP_k = (q/k)^{1-\rho}$ and $MP_l = (q/l)^{1-\rho}$.

b. Show that $RTS = (l/k)^{1-\rho}$; use this to show that $\sigma = 1/(1 - \rho)$.

c. Determine the output elasticities for k and l, and show that their sum equals 1.

d. Prove that

$$\frac{q}{l} = \left(\frac{\partial q}{\partial l}\right)^\sigma$$

and hence that

$$\ln\left(\frac{q}{l}\right) = \sigma \ln\left(\frac{\partial q}{\partial l}\right).$$

Note: The latter equality is useful in empirical work, because we may approximate $\partial q/\partial l$ by the competitively determined wage rate. Hence, σ can be estimated from a regression of $\ln(q/l)$ on $\ln w$.

9.7

Consider a generalization of the production function in Example 9.3:

$$q = \beta_0 + \beta_1 \sqrt{kl} + \beta_2 k + \beta_3 l,$$

where

$$0 \le \beta_i \le 1, \quad i = 0,\ldots,3.$$

a. If this function is to exhibit constant returns to scale, what restrictions should be placed on the parameters $\beta_0, \ldots, \beta_3$?

b. Show that, in the constant returns-to-scale case, this function exhibits diminishing marginal productivities and that the marginal productivity functions are homogeneous of degree 0.

c. Calculate σ in this case. Although σ is not in general constant, for what values of the β's does $\sigma = 0, 1,$ or ∞?

9.8

Show that Euler's theorem implies that, for a constant returns-to-scale production function $[q = f(k,l)]$,

$$q = f_k \cdot k + f_l \cdot l.$$

Use this result to show that, for such a production function, if $MP_l > AP_l$ then MP_k must be negative. What does this imply about where production must take place? Can a firm ever produce at a point where AP_l is increasing?

Analytical Problems

9.9 Local returns to scale

A local measure of the returns to scale incorporated in a production function is given by the scale elasticity $e_{q,t} = \partial f(tk, tl)/\partial t \cdot t/q$ evaluated at $t = l$.

a. Show that if the production function exhibits constant returns to scale then $e_{q,t} = 1$.

b. We can define the output elasticities of the inputs k and l as

$$e_{q,k} = \frac{\partial f(k,l)}{\partial k} \cdot \frac{k}{q},$$

$$e_{q,l} = \frac{\partial f(k,l)}{\partial l} \cdot \frac{l}{q}.$$

Show that $e_{q,t} = e_{q,k} + e_{q,l}$.

c. A function that exhibits variable scale elasticity is

$$q = (1 + k^{-1}l^{-1})^{-1}.$$

Show that, for this function, $e_{q,t} > 1$ for $q < 0.5$ and that $e_{q,t} < 1$ for $q > 0.5$.

d. Explain your results from part (c) intuitively. *Hint:* Does q have an upper bound for this production function?

9.10 Returns to scale and substitution

Although much of our discussion of measuring the elasticity of substitution for various production functions has assumed constant returns to scale, often that assumption is not necessary. This problem illustrates some of these cases.

a. In footnote 6 we showed that, in the constant returns-to-scale case, the elasticity of substitution for a two-input production function is given by

$$\sigma = \frac{f_k f_l}{f \cdot f_{kl}}.$$

Suppose now that we define the homothetic production function F as

$$F(k, l) = [f(k, l)]^\gamma,$$

where $f(k, l)$ is a constant returns-to-scale production function and γ is a positive exponent. Show that the elasticity of substitution for this production function is the same as the elasticity of substitution for the function f.

b. Show how this result can be applied to both the Cobb-Douglas and CES production functions.

9.11 More on Euler's theorem

Suppose that a production function $f(x_1, x_2, \ldots, x_n)$ is homogeneous of degree k. Euler's theorem shows that $\sum_i x_i f_i = kf$, and this fact can be used to show that the partial derivatives of f are homogeneous of degree $k - 1$.

a. Prove that $\sum_{i=1}^{n} \sum_{j=1}^{n} x_i x_j f_{ij} = k(k-1)f$.

b. In the case of $n = 2$ and $k = 1$, what kind of restrictions does the result of part (a) impose on the second-order partial derivative f_{12}? How do your conclusions change when $k > 1$ or $k < 1$?

c. How would the results of part (b) be generalized to a production function with any number of inputs?

d. What are the implications of this problem for the parameters of the multivariable Cobb-Douglas production function $f(x_1, x_2, \ldots, x_n) = \prod_{i=1}^{n} x_i^{\alpha_i}$ for $\alpha_i \geq 0$?

SUGGESTIONS FOR FURTHER READING

Clark, J. M. "Diminishing Returns." In *Encyclopaedia of the Social Sciences,* vol. 5. New York: Crowell-Collier and Macmillan, 1931, pp. 144–f46.

Lucid discussion of the historical development of the diminishing returns concept.

Douglas, P. H. "Are There Laws of Production?" *American Economic Review* 38 (March 1948): 1–f41.

A nice methodological analysis of the uses and misuses of production functions.

Ferguson, C. E. *The Neoclassical Theory of Production and Distribution.* New York: Cambridge University Press, 1969.

A thorough discussion of production function theory (as of 1970). Good use of three-dimensional graphs.

Fuss, M., and McFadden, D. *Production Economics: A Dual Approach to Theory and Application.* Amsterdam: North-Holland, 1980.

An approach with a heavy emphasis on the use of duality.

Mas-Collell, A., M. D. Whinston, and J. R. Green. *Microeconomic Theory.* New York: Oxford University Press, 1995.

Chapter 5 provides a sophisticated, if somewhat spare, review of production theory. The use of the profit function (see Chapter 11) is quite sophisticated and illuminating.

Shephard, R. W. *Theory of Cost and Production Functions.* Princeton, NJ: Princeton University Press, 1978.

Extended analysis of the dual relationship between production and cost functions.

Silberberg, E., and W. Suen. *The Structure of Economics: A Mathematical Analysis,* 3rd ed. Boston: Irwin/McGraw-Hill, 2001.

Thorough analysis of the duality between production functions and cost curves. Provides a proof that the elasticity of substitution can be derived as shown in footnote 6 of this chapter.

Stigler, G. J. "The Division of Labor Is Limited by the Extent of the Market." *Journal of Political Economy* 59 (June 1951): 185–f93.

Careful tracing of the evolution of Smith's ideas about economies of scale.

EXTENSIONS

Many-Input Production Functions

Most of the production functions illustrated in Chapter 9 can be easily generalized to many-input cases. Here we show this for the Cobb-Douglas and CES cases and then examine two quite flexible forms that such production functions might take. In all of these examples, the β's are nonnegative parameters and the n inputs are represented by $x_1, ..., x_n$.

E9.1 Cobb-Douglas

The many-input Cobb-Douglas production function is given by

$$q = \prod_{i=1}^{n} x_i^{\beta_i}. \tag{i}$$

a. This function exhibits constant returns to scale if

$$\sum_{i=1}^{n} \beta i = 1. \tag{ii}$$

b. In the constant-returns-to-scale Cobb-Douglas function, β_i is the elasticity of q with respect to input x_i. Because $0 \leq \beta < 1$, each input exhibits diminishing marginal productivity.

c. Any degree of increasing returns to scale can be incorporated into this function, depending on

$$\varepsilon = \sum_{i=1}^{n} \beta_i. \tag{iii}$$

d. The elasticity of substitution between any two inputs in this production function is 1. This can be shown by using the definition given in footnote 7 of this chapter:

$$\sigma_{ij} = \frac{\partial \ln(x_i/x_j)}{\partial \ln(f_j/f_i)}.$$

Here

$$\frac{f_j}{f_i} = \frac{\beta_j x_j^{\beta_j-1} \prod_{i\neq j} x_i^{\beta_i}}{\beta_i x_i^{\beta_i-1} \prod_{j\neq i} x_j^{\beta_j}} = \frac{\beta_j}{\beta_i} \cdot \frac{x_i}{x_j}.$$

Hence,

$$\ln\left(\frac{f_j}{f_i}\right) = \ln\left(\frac{\beta_j}{\beta_i}\right) + \ln\left(\frac{x_i}{x_j}\right)$$

and $\sigma_{ij} = 1$. Because this parameter is so constrained in the Cobb-Douglas function, the function is generally not used in econometric analyses of microeconomic data on firms. However, the function has a variety of general uses in macroeconomics, as the next example illustrates.

The Solow growth model

The many-input Cobb-Douglas production function is a primary feature of many models of economic growth. For example, Solow's (1956) pioneering model of equilibrium growth can be most easily derived using a two-input constant-returns-to-scale Cobb-Douglas function of the form

$$\Upsilon = AK^{\alpha}L^{1-\alpha}, \tag{iv}$$

where A is a technical change factor that can be represented by exponential growth of the form

$$A = e^{at}. \tag{v}$$

Dividing both sides of Equation iv by L yields

$$y = e^{at}k^{\alpha}, \tag{vi}$$

where

$$y = \Upsilon/L \text{ and } k = K/L.$$

Solow shows that economies will evolve toward an equilibrium value of k (the capital-labor ratio). Hence cross-country differences in growth rates can be accounted for only by differences in the technical change factor, a.

Two features of Equation vi argue for including more inputs in the Solow model. First, the equation as it stands is incapable of explaining the large differences in per capita output (y) that are observed around the world. Assuming $\alpha = 0.3$, say (a figure consistent with many empirical studies), it would take cross-country differences in K/L of as much as 4,000,000-to-1 to explain the 100-to-1 differences in per capita income observed—a clearly unreasonable magnitude. By introducing additional inputs, such as human capital, these differences become more explainable.

A second shortcoming of the simple Cobb-Douglas formulation of the Solow model is that it offers no explanation of the technical change parameter, a—its value is determined "exogenously." By adding additional factors, it becomes easier to understand how the parameter a may respond to economic incentives.

This is the key insight of literature on "endogenous" growth theory (for a summary, see Romer, 1996).

E9.2 CES

The many-input constant elasticity of substitution (CES) production function is given by

$$q = \left[\sum \beta_i x_i^\rho \right]^{\varepsilon/\rho}, \quad \rho \le 1. \qquad \text{(vii)}$$

a. By substituting mx_i for each output, it is easy to show that this function exhibits constant returns to scale for $\varepsilon = 1$. For $\varepsilon > 1$, the function exhibits increasing returns to scale.

b. The production function exhibits diminishing marginal productivities for each input because $\rho \le 1$.

c. As in the two-input case, the elasticity of substitution here is given by

$$\sigma = \frac{1}{1-\rho}, \qquad \text{(viii)}$$

and this elasticity applies to substitution between any two of the inputs.

Checking the Cobb-Douglas in the Soviet Union

One way in which the multi-input CES function is used is to determine whether the estimated substitution parameter (ρ) is consistent with the value implied by the Cobb-Douglas ($\rho = 0$, $\sigma = 1$). For example, in a study of five major industries in the former Soviet Union, E. Bairam (1991) finds that the Cobb-Douglas provides a relatively good explanation of changes in output in most major manufacturing sectors. Only for food processing does a lower value for σ seem appropriate.

The next three examples illustrate flexible-form production functions that may approximate any general function of n inputs. In the Chapter 10 extensions, we examine the cost function analogues to some of these functions, which are more widely used than the production functions themselves.

E9.3 Nested production functions

In some applications, Cobb-Douglas and CES production functions are combined into a "nested" single function. To accomplish this, the original n primary inputs are categorized into, say, m general classes of inputs. The specific inputs in each of these categories are then aggregated into a single composite input, and the final production function is a function of these m composites. For example, assume there are three primary inputs, x_1, x_2, x_3. Suppose, however, that x_1 and x_2 are relatively closely related in their use by firms (for example, capital and energy) whereas the third input (labor) is relatively distinct. Then one might want to use a CES aggregator function to construct a composite input for capital services of the form

$$x_4 = [\gamma x_1^\rho + (1 - \gamma) x_2^\rho]^{1/\rho}. \qquad \text{(ix)}$$

Then the final production function might take a Cobb-Douglas form:

$$q = x_3^\alpha x_4^\beta. \qquad \text{(x)}$$

This structure allows the elasticity of substitution between x_1 and x_2 to take on any value $[\sigma = 1/(1 - \rho)]$ but constrains the elasticity of substitution between x_3 and x_4 to be one. A variety of other options are available depending on how precisely the embedded functions are specified.

The dynamics of capital/energy substitutability

Nested production functions have been widely used in studies that seek to measure the precise nature of the substitutability between capital and energy inputs. For example, Atkeson and Kehoe (1999) use a model rather close to the one specified in Equations ix and x to try to reconcile two facts about the way in which energy prices affect the economy: (1) Over time, use of energy in production seems rather unresponsive to price (at least in the short-run); and (2) across countries, energy prices seem to have a large influence over how much energy is used. By using a capital service equation of the form given in Equation ix with a low degree of substitutability ($\rho = -2.3$)—along with a Cobb-Douglas production function that combines labor with capital services—they are able to replicate the facts about energy prices fairly well. They conclude, however, that this model implies a much more negative effect of higher energy prices on economic growth than seems actually to have been the case. Hence they ultimately opt for a more complex way of modeling production that stresses differences in energy use among capital investments made at different dates.

E9.4 Generalized Leontief

$$q = \sum_{i=1}^{n} \sum_{j=1}^{n} \beta_{ij} \sqrt{x_i x_j},$$

where $\beta_{ij} = \beta_{ji}$.

a.   The function considered in Problem 9.7 is a simple case of this function for the case $n = 2$. For $n = 3$, the function would have linear terms in the three inputs along with three radical terms representing all possible cross-products of the inputs.

b.   The function exhibits constant returns to scale, as can be shown by using mx_i. Increasing returns to scale can be incorporated into the function by using the transformation

$$q' = q^\varepsilon, \quad \varepsilon > 1.$$

c.   Because each input appears both linearly and under the radical, the function exhibits diminishing marginal productivities to all inputs.

d.   The restriction $\beta_{ij} = \beta_{ji}$ is used to ensure symmetry of the second-order partial derivatives.

E9.5 Translog

$$\ln q = \beta_0 + \sum_{i=1}^{n} \beta_i \ln x_i + 0.5 \sum_{i=1}^{n} \sum_{j=1}^{n} \beta_{ij} \ln x_i \ln x_j,$$
$$\beta_{ij} = \beta ji.$$

a.   Note that the Cobb-Douglas function is a special case of this function where $\beta_0 = \beta_{ij} = 0$ for all i, j.

b.   As for the Cobb-Douglas, this function may assume any degree of returns to scale. If

$$\sum_{i=1}^{n} \beta_i = 1 \quad \text{and} \quad \sum_{j=1}^{n} \beta_{ij} = 0$$

for all i, then this function exhibits constant returns to scale. The proof requires some care in dealing with the double summation.

c.   Again, the condition $\beta_{ij} = \beta_{ji}$ is required to ensure equality of the cross-partial derivatives.

Immigration

Because the translog production function incorporates a large number of substitution possibilities among various inputs, it has been widely used to study the ways in which newly arrived workers may substitute for existing workers. Of particular interest is the way in which the skill level of immigrants may lead to differing reactions in the demand for skilled and unskilled workers in the domestic economy. Studies of the United States and many other countries (Canada, Germany, France, and so forth) have suggested that the overall size of such effects is modest, especially given relatively small immigration flows. But there is some evidence that unskilled immigrant workers may act as substitutes for unskilled domestic workers but as complements to skilled domestic workers. Hence increased immigration flows may exacerbate trends toward rising wage differentials. For a summary, see Borjas (1994).

References

Atkeson, Andrew, and Patrick J. Kehoe. "Models of Energy Use: Putty-Putty versus Putty-Clay." *American Economic Review* (September 1999): 1028–43.

Bairam, Erkin. "Elasticity of Substitution, Technical Progress and Returns to Scale in Branches of Soviet Industry: A New CES Production Function Approach." *Journal of Applied Economics* (January–March 1991): 91–f96.

Borjas, G. J. "The Economics of Immigration." *Journal of Economic Literature* (December 1994): 1667–f1717.

Romer, David. *Advanced Macroeconomics.* New York: McGraw-Hill, 1996.

Solow, R. M. "A Contribution to the Theory of Economic Growth." *Quarterly Journal of Economics* (February 1956): 65–f94.

Cost Functions

In this chapter we illustrate the costs that a firm incurs when it produces output. In Chapter 11, we will pursue this topic further by showing how firms make profit-maximizing input and output decisions.

DEFINITIONS OF COSTS

Before we can discuss the theory of costs, some difficulties about the proper definition of "costs" must be cleared up. Specifically, we must differentiate between (1) accounting cost and (2) economic cost. The accountant's view of cost stresses out-of-pocket expenses, historical costs, depreciation, and other bookkeeping entries. The economist's definition of cost (which in obvious ways draws on the fundamental opportunity-cost notion) is that the cost of any input is given by the size of the payment necessary to keep the resource in its present employment. Alternatively, the economic cost of using an input is what that input would be paid in its next best use. One way to distinguish between these two views is to consider how the costs of various inputs (labor, capital, and entrepreneurial services) are defined under each system.

Labor costs

Economists and accountants regard labor costs in much the same way. To accountants, expenditures on labor are current expenses and hence costs of production. For economists, labor is an *explicit* cost. Labor services (labor-hours) are contracted at some hourly wage rate (w), and it is usually assumed that this is also what the labor services would earn in their best alternative employment. The hourly wage, of course, includes costs of fringe benefits provided to employees.

Capital costs

In the case of capital services (machine-hours), the two concepts of cost differ. In calculating capital costs, accountants use the historical price of the particular machine under investigation and apply some more-or-less arbitrary depreciation rule to determine how much of that machine's original price to charge to current costs. Economists regard the historical price of a machine as a "sunk cost," which is irrelevant to output decisions. They instead regard the *implicit* cost of the machine to be what someone else would be willing to pay for its use. Thus the cost of one machine-hour is the *rental rate* for that machine in its best alternative use. By continuing to use the machine itself, the firm is implicitly forgoing what someone else would be willing to pay to use it. This rental rate for one machine-hour will be denoted by v.[1]

---

[1] Sometimes the symbol r is chosen to represent the rental rate on capital. Because this variable is often confused with the related but distinct concept of the market interest rate, an alternative symbol was chosen here. The exact relationship between v and the interest rate is examined in Chapter 17.

Costs of entrepreneurial services

The owner of a firm is a residual claimant who is entitled to whatever extra revenues or losses are left after paying other input costs. To an accountant, these would be called *profits* (which might be either positive or negative). Economists, however, ask whether owners (or entrepreneurs) also encounter opportunity costs by working at a particular firm or devoting some of their funds to its operation. If so, these services should be considered an input, and some cost should be imputed to them. For example, suppose a highly skilled computer programmer starts a software firm with the idea of keeping any (accounting) profits that might be generated. The programmer's time is clearly an input to the firm, and a cost should be inputted for it. Perhaps the wage that the programmer might command if he or she worked for someone else could be used for that purpose. Hence some part of the accounting profits generated by the firm would be categorized as entrepreneurial costs by economists. Economic profits would be smaller than accounting profits and might be negative if the programmer's opportunity costs exceeded the accounting profits being earned by the business. Similar arguments apply to the capital that an entrepreneur provides to the firm.

Economic costs

In this book, not surprisingly, we use economists' definition of cost.

DEFINITION

Economic cost. The *economic cost* of any input is the payment required to keep that input in its present employment. Equivalently, the economic cost of an input is the remuneration the input would receive in its best alternative employment.

Use of this definition is not meant to imply that accountants' concepts are irrelevant to economic behavior. Indeed, accounting procedures are integrally important to any manager's decision-making process because they can greatly affect the rate of taxation to be applied against profits. Accounting data are also readily available, whereas data on economic costs must often be developed separately. Economists' definitions, however, do have the desirable features of being broadly applicable to all firms and of forming a conceptually consistent system. They therefore are best suited for a general theoretical analysis.

Two simplifying assumptions

As a start, we will make two simplifications about the inputs a firm uses. First, we assume that there are only two inputs: homogeneous labor (l, measured in labor-hours) and homogeneous capital (k, measured in machine-hours). Entrepreneurial costs are included in capital costs. That is, we assume that the primary opportunity costs faced by a firm's owner are those associated with the capital that the owner provides.

Second, we assume that inputs are hired in perfectly competitive markets. Firms can buy (or sell) all the labor or capital services they want at the prevailing rental rates (w and v). In graphic terms, the supply curve for these resources is horizontal at the prevailing factor prices. Both w and v are treated as "parameters" in the firm's decisions; there is nothing the firm can do to affect them. These conditions will be relaxed in later chapters (notably Chapter 16), but for the moment the price-taker assumption is a convenient and useful one to make.

Economic profits and cost minimization

Total costs for the firm during a period are therefore given by

$$\text{total costs} = C = wl + vk, \tag{10.1}$$

where, as before, l and k represent input usage during the period. Assuming the firm produces only one output, its total revenues are given by the price of its product (p) times its total output [$q = f(k, l)$, where $f(k, l)$ is the firm's production function]. Economic profits (π) are then the difference between total revenues and total economic costs.

Economic profits. *Economic profits* (π) are the difference between a firm's total revenues and its total costs:

$$\pi = \textbf{total revenue} - \textbf{total cost} = pq - wl - vk$$
$$= pf(k, l) - wl - vk. \tag{10.2}$$

Equation 10.2 shows that the economic profits obtained by a firm are a function of the amount of capital and labor employed. If, as we will assume in many places in this book, the firm seeks maximum profits, then we might study its behavior by examining how k and l are chosen so as to maximize Equation 10.2. This would, in turn, lead to a theory of supply and to a theory of the "derived demand" for capital and labor inputs. In the next chapter we will take up those subjects in detail. Here, however, we wish to develop a theory of costs that is somewhat more general and might apply to firms that are not necessarily profit maximizers. Hence, we begin the study of costs by finessing, for the moment, a discussion of output choice. That is, we assume that for some reason the firm has decided to produce a particular output level (say, q_0). The firm's revenues are therefore fixed at pq_0. Now we wish to examine how the firm can produce q_0 at minimal costs.

COST-MINIMIZING INPUT CHOICES

Mathematically, this is a constrained minimization problem. But before proceeding with a rigorous solution, it is useful to state the result to be derived with an intuitive argument. To minimize the cost of producing a given level of output, a firm should choose that point on the q_0 isoquant at which the rate of technical substitution of l for k is equal to the ratio w/v: It should equate the rate at which k can be traded for l in production to the rate at which they can be traded in the marketplace. Suppose that this were not true. In particular, suppose that the firm were producing output level q_0 using $k = 10$, $l = 10$, and assume that the RTS were 2 at this point. Assume also that $w = \$1$, $v = \$1$, and hence that $w/v = 1$ (which is unequal to 2). At this input combination, the cost of producing q_0 is $20. It is easy to show this is not the minimal input cost. For example, q_0 can also be produced using $k = 8$ and $l = 11$; we can give up two units of k and keep output constant at q_0 by adding one unit of l. But at this input combination, the cost of producing q_0 is $19 and hence the initial input combination was not optimal. A contradiction similar to this one can be demonstrated whenever the RTS and the ratio of the input costs differ.

Mathematical analysis

Mathematically, we seek to minimize total costs given $q = f(k, l) = q_0$. Setting up the Lagrangian expression

$$\mathcal{L} = wl + vk + \lambda[q_0 - f(k, l)], \tag{10.3}$$

the first-order conditions for a constrained minimum are

$$\frac{\partial \mathcal{L}}{\partial l} = w - \lambda \frac{\partial f}{\partial l} = 0,$$

$$\frac{\partial \mathcal{L}}{\partial k} = v - \lambda \frac{\partial f}{\partial k} = 0, \tag{10.4}$$

$$\frac{\partial \mathcal{L}}{\partial \lambda} = q_0 - f(k, l) = 0,$$

or, dividing the first two equations,

$$\frac{w}{v} = \frac{\partial f / \partial l}{\partial f / \partial k} = RTS \ (l \text{ for } k).$$ (10.5)

This says that the cost-minimizing firm should equate the RTS for the two inputs to the ratio of their prices.

Further interpretations

These first-order conditions for minimal costs can be manipulated in several different ways to yield interesting results. For example, cross-multiplying Equation 10.5 gives

$$\frac{f_k}{v} = \frac{f_l}{w}.$$ (10.6)

That is: for costs to be minimized, the marginal productivity per dollar spent should be the same for all inputs. If increasing one input promised to increase output by a greater amount per dollar spent than did another input, costs would not be minimal—the firm should hire more of the input that promises a bigger "bang per buck" and less of the more costly (in terms of productivity) input. Any input that cannot meet the common benefit-cost ratio defined in Equation 10.6 should not be hired at all.

Equation 10.6 can, of course, also be derived from Equation 10.4, but it is more instructive to derive its inverse:

$$\frac{w}{f_l} = \frac{v}{f_k} = \lambda.$$ (10.7)

This equation reports the extra cost of obtaining an extra unit of output by hiring either added labor or added capital input. Because of cost minimization, this marginal cost is the same no matter which input is hired. This common marginal cost is also measured by the Lagrangian multiplier from the cost-minimization problem. As is the case for all constrained optimization problems, here the Lagrangian multiplier shows how much in extra costs would be incurred by increasing the output constraint slightly. Because marginal cost plays an important role in a firm's supply decisions, we will return to this feature of cost minimization frequently.

Graphical analysis

Cost minimization is shown graphically in Figure 10.1. Given the output isoquant q_0, we wish to find the least costly point on the isoquant. Lines showing equal cost are parallel straight lines with slopes $-w/v$. Three lines of equal total cost are shown in Figure 10.1; $C_1 < C_2 < C_3$. It is clear from the figure that the minimum total cost for producing q_0 is given by C_1, where the total cost curve is just tangent to the isoquant. The cost-minimizing input combination is l^*, k^*. This combination will be a true minimum if the isoquant is convex (if the RTS diminishes for decreases in k/l). The mathematical and graphic analyses arrive at the same conclusion, as follows.

OPTIMIZATION PRINCIPLE | **Cost minimization.** In order to minimize the cost of any given level of input (q_0), the firm should produce at that point on the q_0 isoquant for which the RTS (of l for k) is equal to the ratio of the inputs' rental prices (w/v).

Contingent demand for inputs

Figure 10.1 exhibits the formal similarity between the firm's cost-minimization problem and the individual's expenditure-minimization problem studied in Chapter 4 (see Figure 4.6). In both problems, the economic actor seeks to achieve his or her target (output or utility) at minimal cost. In Chapter 5 we showed how this process is used to construct a theory of compensated demand for a good. In the present case, cost minimization leads to a demand for capital and labor input that is contingent on the level of output being produced. This is

FIGURE 10.1   Minimization of Costs Given $q = q_0$

A firm is assumed to choose k and l to minimize total costs. The condition for this minimization is that the rate at which k and l can be traded technically (while keeping $q = q_0$) should be equal to the rate at which these inputs can be traded in the market. In other words, the RTS (of l for k) should be set equal to the price ratio w/v. This tangency is shown in the figure; costs are minimized at C_1 by choosing inputs k^* and l^*.

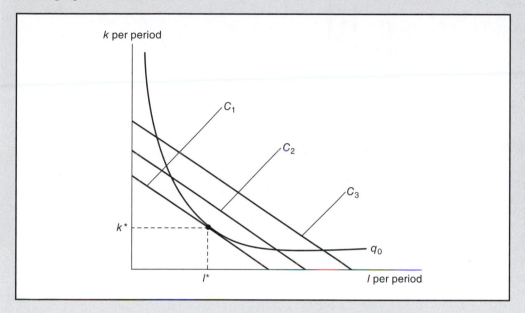

not, therefore, the complete story of a firm's demand for the inputs it uses because it does not address the issue of output choice. But studying the contingent demand for inputs provides an important building block for analyzing the firm's overall demand for inputs, and we will take up this topic in more detail later in this chapter.

The firm's expansion path

A firm can follow the cost-minimization process for each level of output: For each q, it finds the input choice that minimizes the cost of producing it. If input costs (w and v) remain constant for all amounts the firm may demand, we can easily trace this locus of cost-minimizing choices. This procedure is shown in Figure 10.2. The line $0E$ records the cost-minimizing tangencies for successively higher levels of output. For example, the minimum cost for producing output level q_1 is given by C_1, and inputs k_1 and l_1 are used. Other tangencies in the figure can be interpreted in a similar way. The locus of these tangencies is called the firm's *expansion path*, because it records how input expands as output expands while holding the prices of the inputs constant.

As Figure 10.2 shows, the expansion path need not be a straight line. The use of some inputs may increase faster than others as output expands. Which inputs expand more rapidly will depend on the shape of the production isoquants. Because cost minimization requires that the RTS always be set equal to the ratio w/v, and because the w/v ratio is assumed to be constant, the shape of the expansion path will be determined by where a particular RTS occurs on successively higher isoquants. If the production function exhibits constant returns to scale (or, more generally, if it is homothetic), then the expansion path will be a straight line because in that case the RTS depends only on the ratio of k to l. That ratio would be constant along such a linear expansion path.

FIGURE 10.2   The Firm's Expansion Path

The firm's expansion path is the locus of cost-minimizing tangencies. Assuming fixed input prices, the curve shows how inputs increase as output increases.

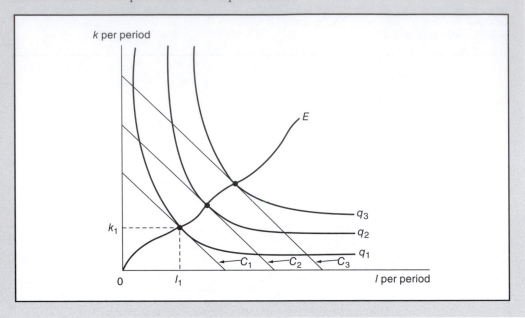

FIGURE 10.3   Input Inferiority

With this particular set of isoquants, labor is an inferior input, because less l is chosen as output expands beyond q_2.

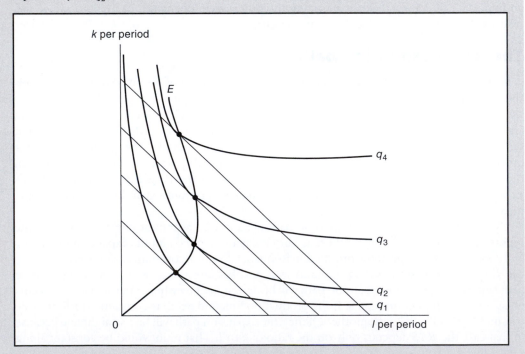

It would seem reasonable to assume that the expansion path will be positively sloped; that is, successively higher output levels will require more of both inputs. This need not be the case, however, as Figure 10.3 illustrates. Increases of output beyond q_2 actually cause the quantity of labor used to decrease. In this range, labor would be said to be an *inferior input*. The occurrence of inferior inputs is then a theoretical possibility that may happen, even when isoquants have their usual convex shape.

Much theoretical discussion has centered on the analysis of factor inferiority. Whether inferiority is likely to occur in real-world production functions is a difficult empirical question to answer. It seems unlikely that such comprehensive magnitudes as "capital" and "labor" could be inferior, but a finer classification of inputs may bring inferiority to light. For example, the use of shovels may decline as production of building foundations (and the use of backhoes) increases. In this book we shall not be particularly concerned with the analytical issues raised by this possibility, although complications raised by inferior inputs will be mentioned in a few places.

EXAMPLE 10.1 Cost Minimization

The cost-minimization process can be readily illustrated with two of the production functions we encountered in the last chapter.

1. Cobb-Douglas: $q = f(k, l) = k^\alpha l^\beta$. For this case the relevant Lagrangian expression for minimizing the cost of producing, say, q_0 is

$$\mathcal{L} = vk + wl + \lambda(q_0 - k^\alpha l^\beta), \tag{10.8}$$

and the first-order conditions for a minimum are

$$\frac{\partial \mathcal{L}}{\partial k} = v - \lambda \alpha k^{\alpha-1} l^\beta = 0,$$

$$\frac{\partial \mathcal{L}}{\partial l} = w - \lambda \beta k^\alpha l^{\beta-1} = 0, \tag{10.9}$$

$$\frac{\partial \mathcal{L}}{\partial \lambda} = q_0 - k^\alpha l^\beta = 0.$$

Dividing the second of these by the first yields

$$\frac{w}{v} = \frac{\beta k^\alpha l^{\beta-1}}{\alpha k^{\alpha-1} l^\beta} = \frac{\beta}{\alpha} \cdot \frac{k}{l}, \tag{10.10}$$

which again shows that costs are minimized when the ratio of the inputs' prices is equal to the *RTS*. Because the Cobb-Douglas function is homothetic, the *RTS* depends only on the ratio of the two inputs. If the ratio of input costs does not change, the firms will use the same input ratio no matter how much it produces—that is, the expansion path will be a straight line through the origin.

As a numerical example, suppose $\alpha = \beta = 0.5$, $w = 12$, $v = 3$, and that the firm wishes to produce $q_0 = 40$. The first-order condition for a minimum requires that $k = 4l$. Inserting that into the production function (the final requirement in Equation 10.9), we have $q_0 = 40 = k^{0.5} l^{0.5} = 2l$. So the cost-minimizing input combination is $l = 20$ and $k = 80$, and total costs are given by $vk + wl = 3(80) + 12(20) = 480$. That this is a true cost minimum is suggested by looking at a few other input combinations that also are capable of producing 40 units of output:

$$k = 40, l = 40, C = 600,$$

$$k = 10, l = 160, C = 2{,}220, \tag{10.11}$$

$$k = 160, l = 10, C = 600.$$

Any other input combination able to produce 40 units of output will also cost more than 480. Cost minimization is also suggested by considering marginal productivities. At the optimal point

(continued)

EXAMPLE 10.1   CONTINUED

$$MP_k = f_k = 0.5k^{-0.5}l^{0.5} = 0.5(20/80)^{0.5} = 0.25,$$
$$MP_l = f_l = 0.5k^{0.5}l^{-0.5} = 0.5(80/20)^{0.5} = 1.0;$$

(10.12)

hence, at the margin, labor is four times as productive as capital, and this extra productivity precisely compensates for the higher unit price of labor input.

2. CES: $q = f(k, l) = (k^\rho + l^\rho)^{\gamma/\rho}$. Again we set up the Lagrangian expression

$$\mathcal{L} = vk + wl + \lambda[q_0 - (k^\rho + l^\rho)^{\gamma/\rho}],$$

(10.13)

and the first-order conditions for a minimum are

$$\frac{\partial \mathcal{L}}{\partial k} = v - \lambda(\gamma/\rho)(k^\rho + l^\rho)^{(\gamma-\rho)/\rho}(\rho)k^{\rho-1} = 0,$$

$$\frac{\partial \mathcal{L}}{\partial l} = w - \lambda(\gamma/\rho)(k^\rho + l^\rho)^{(\gamma-\rho)/\rho}(\rho)l^{\rho-1} = 0,$$

(10.14)

$$\frac{\partial \mathcal{L}}{\partial \lambda} = q_0 - (k^\rho + l^\rho)^{(\gamma/\rho)} = 0.$$

Dividing the first two of these equations causes a lot of this mass of symbols to drop out, leaving

$$\frac{w}{v} = \left(\frac{l}{k}\right)^{\rho-1} = \left(\frac{k}{l}\right)^{1-\rho} = \left(\frac{k}{l}\right)^{1/\sigma}, \quad \text{or} \quad \frac{k}{l} = \left(\frac{w}{v}\right)^\sigma.$$

(10.15)

Because the CES function is also homothetic, the cost-minimizing input ratio is independent of the absolute level of production. The result in Equation 10.15 is a simple generalization of the Cobb-Douglas result (when $\sigma = 1$). With the Cobb-Douglas, the cost-minimizing capital-labor ratio changes directly in proportion to changes in the ratio of wages to capital rental rates. In cases with greater substitutability ($\sigma > 1$), changes in the ratio of wages to rental rates cause a greater than proportional increase in the cost-minimizing capital-labor ratio. With less substitutability ($\sigma < 1$), the response is proportionally smaller.

QUERY: In the Cobb-Douglas numerical example with $w/v = 4$, we found that the cost-minimizing input ratio for producing 40 units of output was $k/l = 80/20 = 4$. How would this value change for $\sigma = 2$ or $\sigma = 0.5$? What actual input combinations would be used? What would total costs be?

COST FUNCTIONS

We are now in a position to examine the firm's overall cost structure. To do so, it will be convenient to use the expansion path solutions to derive the total cost function.

DEFINITION

Total cost function. The *total cost function* shows that, for any set of input costs and for any output level, the minimum total cost incurred by the firm is

$$C = C(v, w, q).$$

(10.16)

Figure 10.2 makes clear that total costs increase as output, q, increases. We will begin by analyzing this relationship between total cost and output while holding input prices fixed. Then we will consider how a change in an input price shifts the expansion path and its related cost functions.

Average and marginal cost functions

Although the total cost function provides complete information about the output-cost relationship, it is often convenient to analyze costs on a per-unit-of-output basis because that approach corresponds more closely to the analysis of demand, which focused on the price per unit of a commodity. Two different unit cost measures are widely used in economics: (1) average cost, which is the cost per unit of output; and (2) marginal cost, which is the cost of one more unit of output. The relationship of these concepts to the total cost function is described in the following definitions.

Average and marginal cost functions. The *average cost function* (AC) is found by computing total costs per unit of output:

$$\text{average cost} = AC(v, w, q) = \frac{C(v, w, q)}{q}. \tag{10.17}$$

DEFINITION

The *marginal cost function* (MC) is found by computing the change in total costs for a change in output produced:

$$\text{marginal cost} = MC(v, w, q) = \frac{\partial C(v, w, q)}{\partial q}. \tag{10.18}$$

Notice that in these definitions, average and marginal costs depend both on the level of output being produced and on the prices of inputs. In many places throughout this book, we will graph simple two-dimensional relationships between costs and output. As the definitions make clear, all such graphs are drawn on the assumption that the prices of inputs remain constant and that technology does not change. If input prices change or if technology advances, cost curves generally will shift to new positions. Later in this chapter, we will explore the likely direction and size of such shifts when we study the entire cost function in detail.

Graphical analysis of total costs

Figures 10.4a and 10.5a illustrate two possible shapes for the relationship between total cost and the level of the firm's output. In Figure 10.4a, total cost is simply proportional to output. Such a situation would arise if the underlying production function exhibits constant returns to scale. In that case, suppose k_1 units of capital input and l_1 units of labor input are required to produce one unit of output. Then

$$C(q = 1) = vk_1 + wl_1. \tag{10.19}$$

To produce m units of output, then, requires mk_1 units of capital and ml_1 units of labor, because of the constant returns-to-scale assumption.[2] Hence

$$\begin{aligned}C(q = m) &= vmk_1 + wml_1 = m(vk_1 + wl_1) \\ &= m \cdot C(q = 1),\end{aligned} \tag{10.20}$$

and the proportionality between output and cost is established.

The situation in Figure 10.5a is more complicated. There it is assumed that initially the total cost curve is concave; although initially costs rise rapidly for increases in output, that rate of increase slows as output expands into the midrange of output. Beyond this middle range, however, the total cost curve becomes convex, and costs begin to rise progressively more rapidly. One possible reason for such a shape for the total cost curve is that there is some third factor of production (say, the services of an entrepreneur) that is fixed as capital and labor usage expands. In this case, the initial concave section of the curve might be explained by the

---

[2]The input combination ml_1, mk_1 minimizes the cost of producing m units of output because the ratio of the inputs is still k_1/l_1 and the RTS for a constant returns-to-scale production function depends only on that ratio.

FIGURE 10.4   Total, Average, and Marginal Cost Curves for the Constant Returns-to-Scale Case

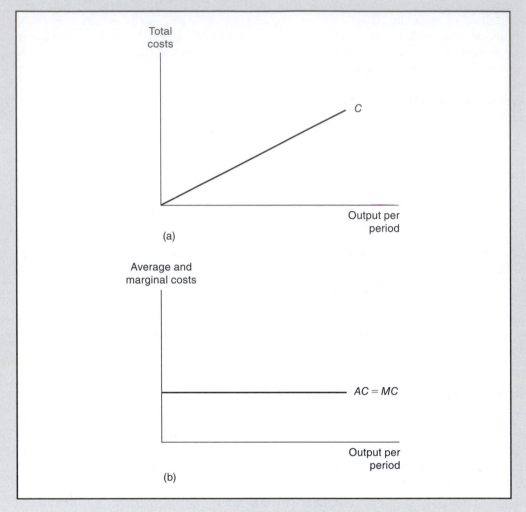

In (a) total costs are proportional to output level. Average and marginal costs, as shown in (b), are equal and constant for all output levels.

(a)

(b)

increasingly optimal usage of the entrepreneur's services—he or she needs a moderate level of production to utilize his or her skills fully. Beyond the point of inflection, however, the entrepreneur becomes overworked in attempting to coordinate production, and diminishing returns set in. Hence, total costs rise rapidly.

A variety of other explanations have been offered for the cubic-type total cost curve in Figure 10.5a, but we will not examine them here. Ultimately, the shape of the total cost curve is an empirical question that can be determined only by examining real-world data. In the Extensions to this chapter, we illustrate some of the literature on cost functions.

Graphical analysis of average and marginal costs

Information from the total cost curves can be used to construct the average and marginal cost curves shown in Figures 10.4b and 10.5b. For the constant returns-to-scale case (Figure 10.4), this is quite simple. Because total costs are proportional to output, average and marginal costs

FIGURE 10.5 Total, Average, and Marginal Cost Curves for the Cubic Total Cost Curve Case

If the total cost curve has the cubic shape shown in (a), average and marginal cost curves will be U-shaped. In (b) the marginal cost curve passes through the low point of the average cost curve at output level q^*.

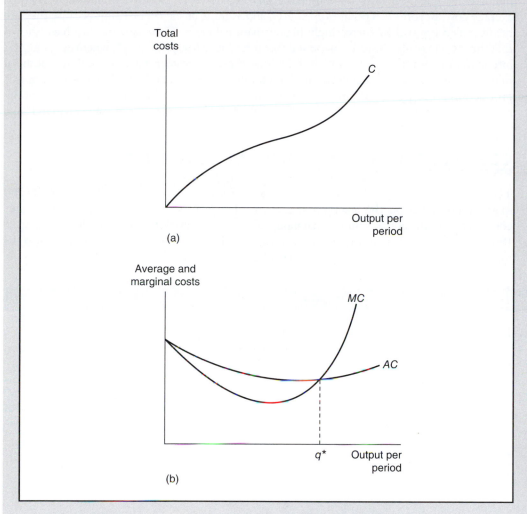

(a)

(b)

are constant and equal for all levels of output.[3] These costs are shown by the horizontal line $AC = MC$ in Figure 10.4b.

For the cubic total cost curve case (Figure 10.5), computation of the average and marginal cost curves requires some geometric intuition. As the definition in Equation 10.18 makes clear, marginal cost is simply the slope of the total cost curve. Hence, because of the assumed shape of the curve, the MC curve is U-shaped, with MC falling over the concave portion of the total cost curve and rising beyond the point of inflection. Because the slope is always positive, however, MC is always greater than 0. Average costs (AC) start out being equal to

---

[3]Mathematically, because $C = aq$ (where a is the cost of one unit of output),

$$AC = \frac{C}{q} = a = \frac{\partial C}{\partial q} = MC.$$

marginal cost for the "first" unit of output.[4] As output expands, however, AC exceeds MC, because AC reflects both the marginal cost of the last unit produced and the higher marginal costs of the previously produced units. So long as $AC > MC$, average costs must be falling. Because the lower costs of the newly produced units are below average cost, they continue to pull average costs downward. Marginal costs rise, however, and eventually (at q^*) equal average cost. Beyond this point, $MC > AC$, and average costs will be rising because they are being pulled upward by increasingly higher marginal costs. Consequently, we have shown that the AC curve also has a U-shape and that it reaches a low point at q^*, where AC and MC intersect.[5] In empirical studies of cost functions, there is considerable interest in this point of minimum average cost. It reflects the "minimum efficient scale" (MES) for the particular production process being examined. The point is also theoretically important because of the role it plays in perfectly competitive price determination in the long run (see Chapter 12).

COST FUNCTIONS AND SHIFTS IN COST CURVES

The cost curves illustrated in Figures 10.4 and 10.5 show the relationship between costs and quantity produced on the assumption that all other factors are held constant. Specifically, construction of the curves assumes that input prices and the level of technology do not change.[6] If these factors do change, the cost curves will shift. In this section, we delve further into the mathematics of cost functions as a way of studying these shifts. We begin with some examples.

EXAMPLE 10.2 Some Illustrative Cost Functions

In this example we calculate the cost functions associated with three different production functions. Later we will use these examples to illustrate some of the general properties of cost functions.

1. Fixed Proportions: $q = f(k, l) = \min(ak, bl)$. The calculation of cost functions from their underlying production functions is one of the more frustrating tasks for economics students.

---

[4]Technically, $AC = MC$ at $q = 0$. This can be shown by L'Hôpital's rule, which states that if $f(a) = g(a) = 0$ then

$$\lim_{x \to a} \frac{f(x)}{g(x)} = \lim_{x \to a} \frac{f'(x)}{g'(x)}.$$

In this case, $C = 0$ at $q = 0$, and so

$$\lim_{q \to 0} AC = \lim_{q \to 0} \frac{C}{q} = \lim_{q \to 0} \frac{\partial C/\partial q}{1} = \lim_{q \to 0} MC$$

or

$$AC = MC \text{ at } q = 0,$$

which was to be shown.

[5]Mathematically, we can find the minimum AC by setting its derivative equal to 0:

$$\frac{\partial AC}{\partial q} = \frac{\partial(C/q)}{\partial q} = \frac{q \cdot (\partial C/\partial q) - C \cdot 1}{q^2} = \frac{q \cdot MC - C}{q^2} = 0,$$

or

$$q \cdot MC - C = 0 \quad \text{or} \quad MC = C/q = AC.$$

[6]For multiproduct firms, an additional complication must be considered. For such firms it is possible that the costs associated with producing one output (say, q_1) are also affected by the amount of some other output being produced (q_2). In this case the firm is said to exhibit "economies of scope," and the total cost function will be of the form $C(q_1, q_2, w, v)$. Hence, q_2 must also be held constant in constructing the q_1 cost curves. Presumably increases in q_2 shift the q_1 cost curves downward.

So, let's start with a simple example. What we wish to do is show how total costs depend on input costs and on quantity produced. In the fixed-proportions case, we know that production will occur at a vertex of the L-shaped isoquants where $q = ak = bl$. Hence, total costs are

$$\textbf{total costs} = C(v, w, q) = vk + wl = v\left(\frac{q}{a}\right) + w\left(\frac{q}{b}\right) = q\left(\frac{v}{a} + \frac{w}{b}\right). \tag{10.21}$$

This is indeed the sort of function we want because it states total costs as a function of v, w, and q only together with some parameters of the underlying production function. Because of the constant returns-to-scale nature of this production function, it takes the special form

$$C(v, w, q) = qC(v, w, 1). \tag{10.22}$$

That is, total costs are given by output times the cost of producing one unit. Increases in input prices clearly increase total costs with this function, and technical improvements that take the form of increasing the parameters a and b reduce costs.

2. Cobb-Douglas: $q = f(k, l) = k^\alpha l^\beta$. This is our first example of burdensome computation, but we can clarify the process by recognizing that the final goal is to use the results of cost minimization to replace the inputs in the production function with costs. From Example 10.1 we know that cost minimization requires that

$$\frac{w}{v} = \frac{\beta}{\alpha} \cdot \frac{k}{l} \quad \text{and so} \quad k = \frac{\alpha}{\beta} \cdot \frac{w}{v} \cdot l.$$

Substitution into the production function permits a solution for labor input in terms of q, v, and w as

$$q = k^\alpha l^\beta = \left(\frac{\alpha}{\beta} \cdot \frac{w}{v}\right)^\alpha l^{\alpha+\beta} \quad \text{or} \quad l = q^{1/(\alpha+\beta)} \left(\frac{\beta}{\alpha}\right)^{\alpha/(\alpha+\beta)} w^{-\alpha/(\alpha+\beta)} v^{\alpha/(\alpha+\beta)}. \tag{10.23}$$

A similar set of manipulations gives

$$k = q^{1/(\alpha+\beta)} \left(\frac{\alpha}{\beta}\right)^{\beta/(\alpha+\beta)} w^{\beta/(\alpha+\beta)} v^{-\beta/(\alpha+\beta)}. \tag{10.24}$$

Now we are ready to derive total costs as

$$C(v, w, q) = vk + wl = q^{1/(\alpha+\beta)} B v^{\alpha/(\alpha+\beta)} w^{\beta/(\alpha+\beta)}, \tag{10.25}$$

where $B = (\alpha + \beta)\alpha^{-\alpha/(\alpha+\beta)}\beta^{-\beta/(\alpha+\beta)}$—a constant that involves only the parameters α and β. Although this derivation was a bit messy, several interesting aspects of this Cobb-Douglas cost function are readily apparent. First, whether the function is a convex, linear, or concave function of output depends on whether there are decreasing returns to scale ($\alpha + \beta < 1$), constant returns to scale ($\alpha + \beta = 1$), or increasing returns to scale ($\alpha + \beta > 1$). Second, an increase in any input price increases costs, with the extent of the increase being determined by the relative importance of the input as reflected by the size of its exponent in the production function. Finally, the cost function is homogeneous of degree 1 in the input prices—a general feature of all cost functions, as we shall show shortly.

3. CES: $q = f(k, l) = (k^\rho + l^\rho)^{\gamma/\rho}$. For this case, your author will mercifully spare you the algebra. To derive the total cost function, we use the cost-minimization condition specified in Equation 10.15, solve for each input individually, and eventually get

$$C(v, w, q) = vk + wl = q^{1/\gamma}(v^{\rho/(\rho-1)} + w^{\rho/(\rho-1)})^{(\rho-1)/\rho}$$
$$= q^{1/\gamma}(v^{1-\sigma} + w^{1-\sigma})^{1/(1-\sigma)}, \tag{10.26}$$

where the elasticity of substitution is given by $\sigma = 1/(1 - \rho)$. Once again the shape of the total cost is determined by the scale parameter (γ) for this production function, and the cost function is increasing in both of the input prices. The function is also homogeneous of degree 1 in those prices. One limiting feature of this form of the CES function is that the

(*continued*)

EXAMPLE 10.2   CONTINUED

inputs are given equal weights—hence their prices are equally important in the cost function. This feature of the CES is easily generalized, however (see Problem 10.7).

QUERY: How are the various substitution possibilities inherent in the CES function reflected in the CES cost function in Equation 10.26?

Properties of cost functions

These examples illustrate some properties of total cost functions that are quite general.

1. *Homogeneity.* The total cost functions in Example 10.3 are all homogeneous of degree 1 in the input prices. That is, a doubling of input prices will precisely double the cost of producing any given output level (you might check this out for yourself). This is a property of all proper cost functions. When all input prices double (or are increased by any uniform proportion), the ratio of any two input prices will not change. Because cost minimization requires that the ratio of input prices be set equal to the *RTS* along a given isoquant, the cost-minimizing input combination also will not change. Hence, the firm will buy exactly the same set of inputs and pay precisely twice as much for them. One implication of this result is that a pure, uniform inflation in all input costs will not change a firm's input decisions. Its cost curves will shift upward in precise correspondence to the rate of inflation.

2. *Total cost functions are nondecreasing in q, v, and w.* This property seems obvious, but it is worth dwelling on it a bit. Because cost functions are derived from a cost-minimization process, any decline in costs from an increase in one of the function's arguments would lead to a contradiction. For example, if an increase in output from q_1 to q_2 caused total costs to decline, it must be the case that the firm was not minimizing costs in the first place. It should have produced q_2 and thrown away an output of $q_2 - q_1$, thereby producing q_1 at a lower cost. Similarly, if an increase in the price of an input ever reduced total cost, the firm could not have been minimizing its costs in the first place. To see this, suppose the firm was using the input combination k_1, l_1 and that w increases. Clearly that will increase the cost of the initial input combination. But if changes in input choices actually caused total costs to decline, that must imply that there was a lower-cost input mix than k_1, l_1 initially. Hence we have a contradiction, and this property of cost functions is established.[7]

3. *Total cost functions are concave in input prices.* It is probably easiest to illustrate this property with a graph. Figure 10.6 shows total costs for various values of an input price, say, w, holding q and v constant. Suppose that initially a wage rate of w_1 prevails

---

[7]A formal proof could also be based on the envelope theorem as applied to constrained minimization problems. Consider the Lagrangian expression in Equation 10.3. As was pointed out in Chapter 2, we can calculate the change in the objective in such an expression (here, total cost) with respect to a change in a variable by differentiating the Lagrangian expression. Performing this differentiation yields

$$\frac{\partial C^*}{\partial q} = \frac{\partial \mathscr{L}}{\partial q} = \lambda\,(= MC) \geq 0,$$

$$\frac{\partial C^*}{\partial v} = \frac{\partial \mathscr{L}}{\partial v} = k \geq 0,$$

$$\frac{\partial C^*}{\partial w} = \frac{\partial \mathscr{L}}{\partial w} = l \geq 0.$$

Not only do these envelope results prove this property of cost functions, they also are quite useful in their own right, as we will show later in this chapter.

FIGURE 10.6 Cost Functions Are Concave in Input Prices

With a wage rate of w_1, total costs of producing q_1 are $C(v, w_1, q_1)$. If the firm does not change its input mix, costs of producing q_1 would follow the straight line C_{PSEUDO}. With input substitution, actual costs $C(v, w, q_1)$ will fall below this line, and hence the cost function is concave in w.

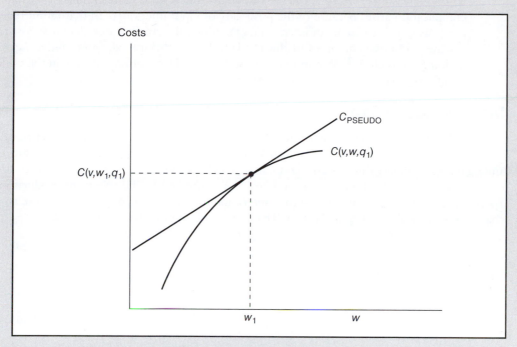

and that the total costs associated with producing q_1 are given by $C(v, w_1, q_1)$. If the firm did not change its input mix in response to changes in wages, then its total cost curve would be linear as reflected by the line $C_{\text{PSEUDO}}(\bar{v}, w, q_1) = \bar{v}\bar{k}_1 + w\bar{l}_1$ in the figure. But a cost-minimizing firm probably would change the input mix it uses to produce q_1 when wages change, and these actual costs $[C(v, w, q_1)]$ would fall below the "pseudo" costs. Hence, the total cost function must have the concave shape shown in Figure 10.6. One implication of this finding is that costs will be lower when a firm faces input prices that fluctuate around a given level than when they remain constant at that level. With fluctuating input prices, the firm can adapt its input mix to take advantage of such fluctuations by using a lot of, say, labor when its price is low and economizing on that input when its price is high.

4. *Average and marginal costs.* Some, but not all, of these properties of total cost functions carry over to their related average and marginal cost functions. Homogeneity is one property that carries over directly. Because $C(tv, tw, q) = tC(v, w, q)$, we have

$$AC(tv, tw, q) = \frac{C(tv, tw, q)}{q} = \frac{tC(v, w, q)}{q} = tAC(v, w, q) \qquad \textbf{(10.27)}$$

and[8]

$$MC(tv, tw, q) = \frac{\partial C(tv, tw, q)}{\partial q} = \frac{t\partial C(v, w, q)}{\partial q} = tMC(v, w, q). \qquad \textbf{(10.28)}$$

---

[8]This result does not violate the theorem that the derivative of a function that is homogeneous of degree k is homogeneous of degree $k - 1$, because we are differentiating with respect to q and total costs are homogeneous with respect to input prices only.

The effects of changes in q, v, and w on average and marginal costs are sometimes ambiguous, however. We have already shown that average and marginal cost curves may have negatively sloped segments, so neither AC nor MC is nondecreasing in q. Because total costs must not decrease when an input price rises, it is clear that average cost is increasing in w and v. But the case of marginal cost is more complex. The main complication arises because of the possibility of input inferiority. In that (admittedly rare) case, an increase in an inferior input's price will actually cause marginal cost to decline. Although the proof of this is relatively straightforward,[9] an intuitive explanation for it is elusive. Still, in most cases, it seems clear that the increase in the price of an input will increase marginal cost as well.

Input substitution

A change in the price of an input will cause the firm to alter its input mix. Hence, a full study of how cost curves shift when input prices change must also include an examination of substitution among inputs. To study this process, economists have developed a somewhat different measure of the elasticity of substitution than the one we encountered in the theory of production. Specifically, we wish to examine how the ratio of input usage (k/l) changes in response to a change in w/v, while holding q constant. That is, we wish to examine the derivative

$$\frac{\partial(k/l)}{\partial(w/v)} \tag{10.29}$$

along an isoquant.

Putting this in proportional terms as

$$s = \frac{\partial(k/l)}{\partial(w/v)} \cdot \frac{w/v}{k/l} = \frac{\partial \ln k/l}{\partial \ln w/v} \tag{10.30}$$

gives an alternative and more intuitive definition of the elasticity of substitution.[10] In the two-input case, s must be nonnegative; an increase in w/v will be met by an increase in k/l (or, in the limiting fixed-proportions case, k/l will stay constant). Large values of s indicate that firms change their input proportions significantly in response to changes in relative input prices, whereas low values indicate that changes in input prices have relatively little effect.

Substitution with many inputs

When there are only two inputs, the elasticity of substitution defined in Equation 10.30 is identical to the concept we defined in Chapter 9 (see Equation 9.32). This can be shown by remembering that cost minimization[11] requires that the firm equate its RTS (of l for k) to the input price ratio w/v. The major advantage of the definition of the elasticity of substitution in Equation 10.30 is that it is easier to generalize to many inputs than is the definition based on the production function. Specifically, suppose there are many inputs to the production process $(x_1, x_2, \ldots, x_n)$ that can be hired at competitive rental rates $(w_1, w_2, \ldots, w_n)$. Then the elasticity of substitution between any two inputs (s_{ij}) is defined as follows.

---

[9]The proof follows the envelope theorem results presented in footnote 7. Because the MC function can be derived by differentiation from the Lagrangian for cost minimization, we can use Young's theorem to show

$$\frac{\partial MC}{\partial v} = \frac{\partial(\partial \mathcal{L}/\partial q)}{\partial v} = \frac{\partial^2 \mathcal{L}}{\partial v \partial q} = \frac{\partial^2 \mathcal{L}}{\partial q \partial v} = \frac{\partial k}{\partial q}.$$

Hence, if capital is a normal input, an increase in v will raise MC whereas, if capital is inferior, an increase in v will actually reduce MC.

[10]This definition is usually attributed to R. G. D. Allen, who developed it in an alternative form in his *Mathematical Analysis for Economists* (New York: St. Martin's Press, 1938), pp. 504–9.

[11]In Example 10.1 we found that, for the CES production function, cost minimization requires that $k/l = (w/v)^\sigma$, so $\ln(k/l) = \sigma \ln(w/v)$ and therefore $s_{k,l} = \partial \ln(k/l)/\partial \ln(w/v) = \sigma$.

Elasticity of substitution. The elasticity of substitution[12] between inputs x_i and x_j is given by

DEFINITION

$$s_{i,j} = \frac{\partial(x_i/x_j)}{\partial(w_j/w_i)} \cdot \frac{w_j/w_i}{x_i/x_j} = \frac{\partial \ln(x_i/x_j)}{\partial \ln(w_j/w_i)}, \tag{10.31}$$

where output and all other input prices are held constant.

The major advantage of this definition in a multi-input context is that it provides the firm with the flexibility to adjust inputs other than x_i and x_j (while holding output constant) when input prices change. For example, a major topic in the theory of firms' input choices is to describe the relationship between capital and energy inputs. The definition in Equation 10.31 would permit a researcher to study how the ratio of energy to capital input changes when relative energy prices rise while permitting the firm to make any adjustments to labor input (whose price has not changed) that would be required for cost minimization. Hence this would give a realistic picture of how firms actually behave with regard to whether energy and capital are more like substitutes or complements. Later in this chapter we will look at this definition in a bit more detail, because it is widely used in empirical studies of production.

Quantitative size of shifts in cost curves

We have already shown that increases in an input price will raise total, average, and (except in the inferior input case) marginal costs. We are now in a position to judge the extent of such increases. First, and most obviously, the increase in costs will be influenced importantly by the relative significance of the input in the production process. If an input constitutes a large fraction of total costs, an increase in its price will raise costs significantly. A rise in the wage rate would sharply increase home-builders' costs, because labor is a major input in construction. On the other hand, a price rise for a relatively minor input will have a small cost impact. An increase in nail prices will not raise home costs very much.

A less obvious determinant of the extent of cost increases is input substitutability. If firms can easily substitute another input for the one that has risen in price, there may be little increase in costs. Increases in copper prices in the late 1960s, for example, had little impact on electric utilities' costs of distributing electricity, because they found they could easily substitute aluminum for copper cables. Alternatively, if the firm finds it difficult or impossible to substitute for the input that has become more costly, then costs may rise rapidly. The cost of gold jewelry, along with the price of gold, rose rapidly during the early 1970s, because there was simply no substitute for the raw input.

It is possible to give a precise mathematical statement of the quantitative sizes of all of these effects by using the elasticity of substitution. To do so, however, would risk further cluttering the book with symbols.[13] For our purposes, it is sufficient to rely on the previous intuitive discussion. This should serve as a reminder that changes in the price of an input will have the effect of shifting firms' cost curves, with the size of the shift depending on the relative importance of the input and on the substitution possibilities that are available.

Technical change

Technical improvements allow the firm to produce a given output with fewer inputs. Such improvements obviously shift total costs downward (if input prices stay constant). Although

---

[12]This definition is attributed to the Japanese economist M. Morishima, and these elasticities are sometimes referred to as "Morishima elasticities." In this version, the elasticity of substitution for substitute inputs is positive. Some authors reverse the order of subscripts in the denominator of Equation 10.31, and in this usage the elasticity of substitution for substitute inputs is negative.

[13]For a complete statement see Ferguson, *Neoclassical Theory of Production and Distribution* (Cambridge: Cambridge University Press, 1969), pp. 154–60.

the actual way in which technical change affects the mathematical form of the total cost curve can be complex, there are cases where one may draw simple conclusions. Suppose, for example, that the production function exhibits constant returns to scale and that technical change enters that function as described in Chapter 9 (that is, $q = A(t)f(k, l)$ where $A(0) = 1$). In this case, total costs in the initial period are given by

$$C_0 = C_0(v, w, q) = qC_0(v, w, 1). \tag{10.32}$$

Because the same inputs that produced one unit of output in period 0 will produce $A(t)$ units of output in period t, we know that

$$C_t(v, w, A(t)) = A(t)C_t(v, w, 1) = C_0(v, w, 1); \tag{10.33}$$

therefore, we can compute the total cost function in period t as

$$C_t(v, w, q) = qC_t(v, w, 1) = \frac{qC_0(v, w, 1)}{A(t)} = \frac{C_0(v, w, q)}{A(t)}. \tag{10.34}$$

Hence, total costs fall over time at the rate of technical change. Note that in this case technical change is "neutral" in that it does not affect the firm's input choices (so long as input prices stay constant). This neutrality result might not hold in cases where technical progress takes a more complex form or where there are variable returns to scale. Even in these more complex cases, however, technical improvements will cause total costs to fall.

EXAMPLE 10.3 Shifting the Cobb-Douglas Cost Function

In Example 10.2 we computed the Cobb-Douglas cost function as

$$C(v, w, q) = q^{1/(\alpha+\beta)} Bv^{\alpha/(\alpha+\beta)} w^{\beta/(\alpha+\beta)}, \tag{10.35}$$

where $B = (\alpha + \beta)\alpha^{-\alpha/(\alpha+\beta)}\beta^{-\beta/(\alpha+\beta)}$. As in the numerical illustration in Example 10.1, let's assume that $\alpha = \beta = 0.5$, in which case the total cost function is greatly simplified:

$$C(v, w, q) = 2qv^{0.5}w^{0.5}. \tag{10.36}$$

This function will yield a total cost curve relating total costs and output if we specify particular values for the input prices. If, as before, we assume $v = 3$ and $w = 12$, then the relationship is

$$C(3, 12, q) = 2q\sqrt{36} = 12q, \tag{10.37}$$

and, as in Example 10.1, it costs 480 to produce 40 units of output. Here average and marginal costs are easily computed as

$$AC = \frac{C}{q} = 12,$$
$$MC = \frac{\partial C}{\partial q} = 12. \tag{10.38}$$

As expected, average and marginal costs are constant and equal to each other for this constant returns-to-scale production function.

Changes in input prices. If either input price were to change, all of these costs would change also. For example, if wages were to increase to 27 (an easy number with which to work), costs would become

$$C(3, 27, q) = 2q\sqrt{81} = 18q,$$
$$AC = 18, \tag{10.39}$$
$$MC = 18.$$

Notice that an increase in wages of 125 percent raised costs by only 50 percent here, both because labor represents only 50 percent of all costs and because the change in input prices encouraged the firm to substitute capital for labor. The total cost function, because it is derived from the cost-minimization assumption, accomplishes this substitution "behind the scenes"—reporting only the final impact on total costs.

Technical progress.   Let's look now at the impact that technical progress can have on costs. Specifically, assume that the Cobb-Douglas production function is

$$q = A(t)k^{0.5}l^{0.5} = e^{.03t}k^{0.5}l^{0.5}. \tag{10.40}$$

That is, we assume that technical change takes an exponential form and that the rate of technical change is 3 percent per year. Using the results of the previous section (Equation 10.34) yields

$$C_t(v, w, q) = \frac{C_0(v, w, q)}{A(t)} = 2qv^{0.5}w^{0.5}e^{-.03t}. \tag{10.41}$$

So, if input prices remain the same then total costs fall at the rate of technical improvement— that is, at 3 percent per year. After, say, 20 years, costs will be (with $v = 3$, $w = 12$)

$$C_{20}(3, 12, q) = 2q\sqrt{36} \cdot e^{-.60} = 12q \cdot (0.55) = 6.6q,$$
$$AC_{20} = 6.6, \tag{10.42}$$
$$MC_{20} = 6.6.$$

Consequently, costs will have fallen by nearly 50 percent as a result of the technical change. This would, for example, more than have offset the wage rise illustrated previously.

QUERY: In this example, what are the elasticities of total costs with respect to changes in input costs? Is the size of these elasticities affected by technical change?

Contingent demand for inputs and Shephard's lemma

As we described earlier, the process of cost minimization creates an implicit demand for inputs. Because that process holds quantity produced constant, this demand for inputs will also be "contingent" on the quantity being produced. This relationship is fully reflected in the firm's total cost function and, perhaps surprisingly, contingent demand functions for all of the firm's inputs can be easily derived from that function. The process involves what has come to be called Shephard's lemma,[14] which states that the contingent demand function for any input is given by the partial derivative of the total cost function with respect to that input's price. Because Shephard's lemma is widely used in many areas of economic research, we will provide a relatively detailed examination of it.

The intuition behind Shephard's lemma is straightforward. Suppose that the price of labor (w) were to increase slightly. How would this affect total costs? If nothing else changed, it seems that costs would rise by approximately the amount of labor (l) that the firm was currently hiring. Roughly speaking, then, $\partial C/\partial w = l$, and that is what Shephard's lemma claims. Figure 10.6 makes roughly the same point graphically. Along the "pseudo" cost function all inputs are held constant, so an increase in the wage increases costs in direct proportion to the amount of labor used. Because the true cost function is tangent to the pseudo-function at the current wage, its slope (that is, its partial derivative) also will show the current amount of labor input demanded.

Technically, Shephard's lemma is one result of the envelope theorem that was first discussed in Chapter 2. There we showed that the change in the optimal value in a constrained optimization problem with respect to one of the parameters of the problem can be found by

---

[14]Named for R. W. Shephard, who highlighted the important relationship between cost functions and input demand functions in his *Cost and Production Functions* (Princeton, NJ: Princeton University Press, 1970).

differentiating the Lagrangian expression for that optimization problem with respect to this changing parameter. In the cost-minimization case, the Lagrangian expression is

$$\mathcal{L} = vk + wl + \lambda[\bar{q} - f(k,l)] \tag{10.43}$$

and the envelope theorem applied to either input is

$$\frac{\partial C(v,w,q)}{\partial v} = \frac{\partial \mathcal{L}(v,w,q,\lambda)}{\partial v} = k^c(v,w,q),$$
$$\frac{\partial C(v,w,q)}{\partial w} = \frac{\partial \mathcal{L}(v,w,q,\lambda)}{\partial w} = l^c(v,w,q), \tag{10.44}$$

where the notation is intended to make clear that the resulting demand functions for capital and labor input depend on v, w, and q. Because quantity produced enters these functions, input demand is indeed contingent on that variable. This feature of the demand functions is also reflected by the "c" in the notation.[15] Hence, the demand relations in Equation 10.44 do not represent a complete picture of input demand because they still depend on a variable that is under the firm's control. In the next chapter, we will complete the study of input demand by showing how the assumption of profit maximization allows us to effectively replace q in the input demand relationships with the market price of the firm's output, p.

EXAMPLE 10.4 Contingent Input Demand Functions

In this example, we will show how the total cost functions derived in Example 10.2 can be used to derive contingent demand functions for the inputs capital and labor.

1. Fixed Proportions: $C(v,w,q) = q(v/a + w/b)$. For this cost function, contingent demand functions are quite simple:

$$k^c(v,w,q) = \frac{\partial C(v,w,q)}{\partial v} = \frac{q}{a},$$
$$l^c(v,w,q) = \frac{\partial C(v,w,q)}{\partial w} = \frac{q}{b}. \tag{10.45}$$

In order to produce any particular output with a fixed proportions production function at minimal cost, the firm must produce at the vertex of its isoquants no matter what the inputs' prices are. Hence, the demand for inputs depends only on the level of output, and v and w do not enter the contingent input demand functions. Input prices may, however, affect total input demands in the fixed proportions case because they may affect how much the firm can sell.

2. Cobb-Douglas: $C(v,w,q) = q^{1/(\alpha+\beta)} B v^{\alpha/(\alpha+\beta)} w^{\beta/(\alpha+\beta)}$. In this case, the derivation is messier but also more instructive:

$$k^c(v,w,q) = \frac{\partial C}{\partial v} = \frac{\alpha}{\alpha+\beta} \cdot q^{1/(\alpha+\beta)} B v^{-\beta/(\alpha+\beta)} w^{\beta/(\alpha+\beta)}$$
$$= \frac{\alpha}{\alpha+\beta} \cdot q^{1/(\alpha+\beta)} B \left(\frac{w}{v}\right)^{\beta/(\alpha+\beta)},$$
$$l^c(v,w,q) = \frac{\partial C}{\partial w} = \frac{\beta}{\alpha+\beta} \cdot q^{1/(\alpha+\beta)} B v^{\alpha/(\alpha+\beta)} w^{-\alpha/(\alpha+\beta)}$$
$$= \frac{\beta}{\alpha+\beta} \cdot q^{1/(\alpha+\beta)} B \left(\frac{w}{v}\right)^{-\alpha/(\alpha+\beta)}. \tag{10.46}$$

---

[15]The notation mirrors that used for compensated demand curves in Chapter 5 (which were derived from the expenditure function). In that case, such demand functions were contingent on the utility target assumed.

Consequently, the contingent demands for inputs depend on both inputs' prices. If we assume $\alpha = \beta = 0.5$ (so $B = 2$), these reduce to

$$k^c(v, w, q) = 0.5 \cdot q \cdot 2 \cdot \left(\frac{w}{v}\right)^{0.5} = q\left(\frac{w}{v}\right)^{0.5},$$

$$l^c(v, w, q) = 0.5 \cdot q \cdot 2 \cdot \left(\frac{w}{v}\right)^{-0.5} = q\left(\frac{w}{v}\right)^{-0.5}. \tag{10.47}$$

With $v = 3$, $w = 12$, and $q = 40$, Equations 10.47 yield the result we obtained previously: that the firm should choose the input combination $k = 80$, $l = 20$ to minimize the cost of producing 40 units of output. If the wage were to rise to, say, 27, the firm would choose the input combination $k = 120$, $l = 40/3$ to produce 40 units of output. Total costs would rise from 480 to 520, but the ability of the firm to substitute capital for the now more expensive labor does save considerably. For example, the initial input combination would now cost 780.

3. CES: $C(v, w, q) = q^{1/\gamma}(v^{1-\sigma} + w^{1-\sigma})^{1/(1-\sigma)}$. The importance of input substitution is shown even more clearly with the contingent demand functions derived from the CES function. For that function,

$$k^c(v, w, q) = \frac{\partial C}{\partial v} = \frac{1}{1-\sigma} \cdot q^{1/\gamma}(v^{1-\sigma} + w^{1-\sigma})^{\sigma/(1-\sigma)}(1 - \sigma)v^{-\sigma}$$

$$= q^{1/\gamma}(v^{1-\sigma} + w^{1-\sigma})^{\sigma/(1-\sigma)}v^{-\sigma},$$

$$l^c(v, w, q) = \frac{\partial C}{\partial w} = \frac{1}{1-\sigma} \cdot q^{1/\gamma}(v^{1-\sigma} + w^{1-\sigma})^{\sigma/(1-\sigma)}(1 - \sigma)w^{-\sigma} \tag{10.48}$$

$$= q^{1/\gamma}(v^{1-\sigma} + w^{1-\sigma})^{\sigma/(1-\sigma)}w^{-\sigma}.$$

These functions collapse when $\sigma = 1$ (the Cobb-Douglas case), but we can study examples with either more ($\sigma = 2$) or less ($\sigma = 0.5$) substitutability and use Cobb-Douglas as the middle ground. If we assume constant returns to scale ($\gamma = 1$) and $v = 3$, $w = 12$, and $q = 40$, then contingent demands for the inputs when $\sigma = 2$ are

$$k^c(3, 12, 40) = 40(3^{-1} + 12^{-1})^{-2} \cdot 3^{-2} = 25.6,$$

$$l^c(3, 12, 40) = 40(3^{-1} + 12^{-1})^{-2} \cdot 12^{-2} = 1.6. \tag{10.49}$$

That is, the level of capital input is 16 times the amount of labor input. With less substitutability ($\sigma = 0.5$), contingent input demands are

$$k^c(3, 12, 40) = 40(3^{0.5} + 12^{0.5})^1 \cdot 3^{-0.5} = 120,$$

$$l^c(3, 12, 40) = 40(3^{0.5} + 12^{0.5})^1 \cdot 12^{-0.5} = 60. \tag{10.50}$$

So, in this case, capital input is only twice as large as labor input. Although these various cases cannot be compared directly because different values for σ scale output differently, we can, as an example, look at the consequence of a rise in w to 27 in the low-substitutability case. With $w = 27$, the firm will choose $k = 160$, $l = 53.3$. In this case, the cost savings from substitution can be calculated by comparing total costs when using the initial input combination ($= (3)120 + 27(60) = 1980$) to total costs with the optimal combination ($= (3)160 + 27(53.3) = 1919$). Hence, moving to the optimal input combination reduces total costs by only about 3 percent. In the Cobb-Douglas case, cost savings are over 20 percent.

QUERY: How would total costs change if w increased from 12 to 27 and the production function took the simple linear form $q = k + 4l$? What light does this result shed on the other cases in this example?

SHEPHARD'S LEMMA AND THE ELASTICITY OF SUBSTITUTION

One especially nice feature of Shephard's lemma is that it can be used to show how to derive information about input substitution directly from the total cost function through differentiation. Using the definition in Equation 10.31 yields

$$s_{i,j} = \frac{\partial \ln(x_i/x_j)}{\partial \ln(w_j/w_i)} = \frac{\partial \ln(C_i/C_j)}{\partial \ln(w_j/w_i)}, \tag{10.51}$$

where C_i and C_j are the partial derivatives of the total cost function with respect to the input prices. Once the total cost function is known (perhaps through econometric estimation), information about substitutability among inputs can thus be readily obtained from it. In the Extensions to this chapter, we describe some of the results that have been obtained in this way. Problems 10.11 and 10.12 provide some additional details about ways in which substitutability among inputs can be measured.

SHORT-RUN, LONG-RUN DISTINCTION

It is traditional in economics to make a distinction between the "short run" and the "long run." Although no very precise temporal definition can be provided for these terms, the general purpose of the distinction is to differentiate between a short period during which economic actors have only limited flexibility in their actions and a longer period that provides greater freedom. One area of study in which this distinction is quite important is in the theory of the firm and its costs, because economists are interested in examining supply reactions over differing time intervals. In the remainder of this chapter, we will examine the implications of such differential response.

To illustrate why short-run and long-run reactions might differ, assume that capital input is held fixed at a level of k_1 and that (in the short run) the firm is free to vary only its labor input.[16] Implicitly, we are assuming that alterations in the level of capital input are infinitely costly in the short run. As a result of this assumption, the short-run production function is

$$q = f(k_1, l), \tag{10.52}$$

where this notation explicitly shows that capital inputs may not vary. Of course, the level of output still may be changed if the firm alters its use of labor.

Short-run total costs

Total cost for the firm continues to be defined as

$$C = vk + wl \tag{10.53}$$

for our short-run analysis, but now capital input is fixed at k_1. To denote this fact, we will write

$$SC = vk_1 + wl, \tag{10.54}$$

where the S indicates that we are analyzing short-run costs with the level of capital input fixed. Throughout our analysis, we will use this method to indicate short-run costs, whereas long-run costs will be denoted by C, AC, and MC. Usually we will not denote the level of capital input explicitly, but it is understood that this input is fixed.

---

[16]Of course, this approach is for illustrative purposes only. In many actual situations, labor input may be less flexible in the short run than is capital input.

Fixed and variable costs

The two types of input costs in Equation 8.53 are given special names. The term vk_1 is referred to as (short-run) *fixed costs*; because k_1 is constant, these costs will not change in the short run. The term wl is referred to as (short-run) *variable costs*—labor input can indeed be varied in the short run. Hence we have the following definitions.

Short-run fixed and variable costs. *Short-run fixed costs* are costs associated with inputs that cannot be varied in the short run. *Short-run variable costs* are costs of those inputs that can be varied so as to change the firm's output level.

DEFINITION

The importance of this distinction is to differentiate between variable costs that the firm can avoid by producing nothing in the short run and costs that are fixed and must be paid regardless of the output level chosen (even zero).

Nonoptimality of short-run costs

It is important to understand that total short-run costs are not the minimal costs for producing the various output levels. Because we are holding capital fixed in the short run, the firm does not have the flexibility of input choice that we assumed when we discussed cost minimization earlier in this chapter. Rather, to vary its output level in the short run, the firm will be forced to use "nonoptimal" input combinations: The RTS will not be equal to the ratio of the input prices. This is shown in Figure 10.7. In the short run, the firm is constrained to use k_1 units of capital. To produce output level q_0, it therefore will use l_0 units of labor. Similarly, it will use l_1 units of labor to produce q_1 and l_2 units to produce q_2. The total costs of these input combinations are given by SC_0, SC_1, and SC_2, respectively. Only for the input combination k_1, l_1 is output being produced at minimal cost. Only at that point is the RTS equal to the ratio of the input prices. From Figure 10.7, it is clear that q_0 is being produced with "too much" capital in this short-run situation. Cost minimization should suggest a southeasterly movement along the q_0 isoquant, indicating a substitution of labor for capital in production. Similarly, q_2 is being produced with "too little" capital, and costs could be reduced by substituting capital for labor. Neither of these substitutions is possible in the short run. Over a longer period, however, the firm will be able to change its level of capital input and will adjust its input usage to the cost-minimizing combinations. We have already discussed this flexible case earlier in this chapter and shall return to it to illustrate the connection between long-run and short-run cost curves.

Short-run marginal and average costs

Frequently, it is more useful to analyze short-run costs on a per-unit-of-output basis rather than on a total basis. The two most important per-unit concepts that can be derived from the short-run total cost function are the *short-run average total cost function* (SAC) and the *short-run marginal cost function* (SMC). These concepts are defined as

$$SAC = \frac{\text{total costs}}{\text{total output}} = \frac{SC}{q},$$
$$SMC = \frac{\text{change in total costs}}{\text{change in output}} = \frac{\partial SC}{\partial q},$$

(10.55)

where again these are defined for a specified level of capital input. These definitions for average and marginal costs are identical to those developed previously for the long-run, fully flexible case, and the derivation of cost curves from the total cost function proceeds in exactly the same way. Because the short-run total cost curve has the same general type of cubic shape as did the total cost curve in Figure 10.5, these short-run average and marginal cost curves will also be U-shaped.

FIGURE 10.7   "Nonoptimal" Input Choices Must Be Made in the Short Run

Because capital input is fixed at k, in the short run the firm cannot bring its RTS into equality with the ratio of input prices. Given the input prices, q_0 should be produced with more labor and less capital than it will be in the short run, whereas q_2 should be produced with more capital and less labor than it will be.

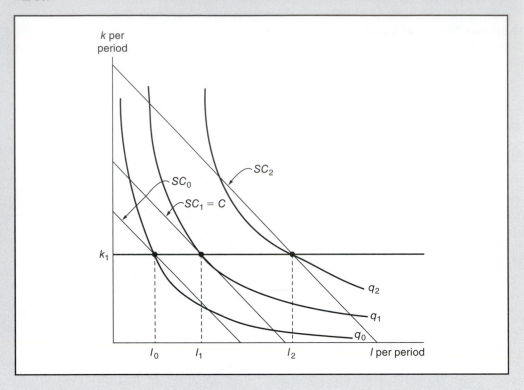

Relationship between short-run and long-run cost curves

It is easy to demonstrate the relationship between the short-run costs and the fully flexible long-run costs that were derived previously in this chapter. Figure 10.8 shows this relationship for both the constant returns-to-scale and cubic total cost curve cases. Short-run total costs for three levels of capital input are shown, although of course it would be possible to show many more such short-run curves. The figures show that long-run total costs (C) are always less than short-run total costs, except at that output level for which the assumed fixed capital input is appropriate to long-run cost minimization. For example, as in Figure 10.7, with capital input of k_1 the firm can obtain full cost minimization when q_1 is produced. Hence, short-run and long-run total costs are equal at this point. For output levels other than q_1, however, $SC > C$, as was the case in Figure 10.7.

Technically, the long-run total cost curves in Figure 10.8 are said to be an "envelope" of their respective short-run curves. These short-run total cost curves can be represented parametrically by

$$\text{short-run total cost} = SC(v, w, q, k), \tag{10.56}$$

and the family of short-run total cost curves is generated by allowing k to vary while holding v and w constant. The long-run total cost curve C must obey the short-run relationship in Equation 10.56 and the further condition that k be cost minimizing for any level of output. A first-order condition for this minimization is that

FIGURE 10.8 Two Possible Shapes for Long-Run Total Cost Curves

By considering all possible levels of capital input, the long-run total cost curve (C) can be traced. In (a), the underlying production function exhibits constant returns to scale: in the long run, though not in the short run, total costs are proportional to output. In (b), the long-run total cost curve has a cubic shape, as do the short-run curves. Diminishing returns set in more sharply for the short-run curves, however, because of the assumed fixed level of capital input.

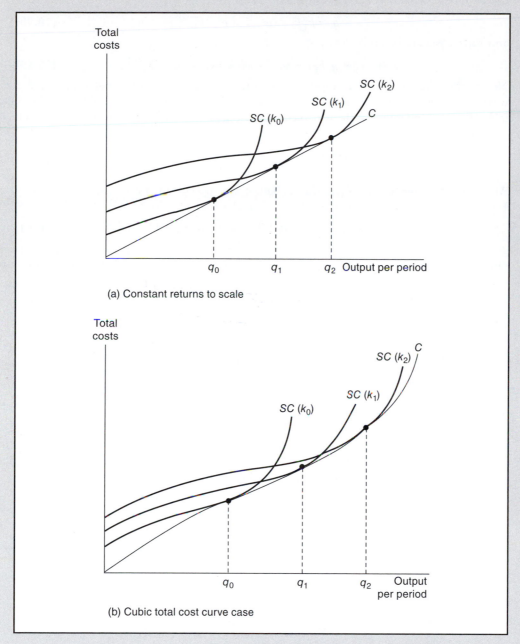

(a) Constant returns to scale

(b) Cubic total cost curve case

$$\frac{\partial SC(v, w, q, k)}{\partial k} = 0. \qquad (10.57)$$

Solving Equations 10.56 and 10.57 simultaneously then generates the long-run total cost function. Although this is a different approach to deriving the total cost function, it should give precisely the same results derived earlier in this chapter—as the next example illustrates.

EXAMPLE 10.5 Envelope Relations and Cobb-Douglas Cost Functions

Again we start with the Cobb-Douglas production function $q = k^\alpha l^\beta$, but now we hold capital input constant at k_1. So, in the short run,

$$q = k_1^\alpha l^\beta \quad \text{or} \quad l = q^{1/\beta} k_1^{-\alpha/\beta}, \tag{10.58}$$

and total costs are given by

$$SC(v, w, q, k_1) = vk_1 + wl = vk_1 + wq^{1/\beta} k_1^{-\alpha/\beta}. \tag{10.59}$$

Notice that the fixed level of capital enters into this short-run total cost function in two ways: (1) k_1 determines fixed costs; and (2) k_1 also in part determines variable costs because it determines how much of the variable input (labor) is required to produce various levels of output. To derive long-run costs, we require that k be chosen to minimize total costs:

$$\frac{\partial SC(v, w, q, k)}{\partial k} = v + \frac{-\alpha}{\beta} \cdot wq^{1/\beta} k^{-(\alpha+\beta)/\beta} = 0. \tag{10.60}$$

Although the algebra is messy, this equation can be solved for k and substituted into Equation 10.59 to return us to the Cobb-Douglas cost function:

$$C(v, w, q) = Bq^{1/(\alpha+\beta)} v^{\alpha/(\alpha+\beta)} w^{\beta/(\alpha+\beta)}. \tag{10.61}$$

Numerical example. If we again let $\alpha = \beta = 0.5$, $v = 3$, and $w = 12$, then the short-run cost function is

$$SC(3, 12, q, k) = 3k_1 + 12q^2 k_1^{-1}. \tag{10.62}$$

In Example 10.1 we found that the cost-minimizing level of capital input for $q = 40$ was $k = 80$. Equation 10.62 shows that short-run total costs for producing 40 units of output with $k = 80$ is

$$SC(3, 12, q, 80) = 3 \cdot 80 + 12 \cdot q^2 \cdot \frac{1}{80} = 240 + \frac{3q^2}{20}$$
$$= 240 + 240 = 480, \tag{10.63}$$

which is just what we found before. We can also use Equation 10.62 to show how costs differ in the short and long run. Table 10.1 shows that, for output levels other than $q = 40$, short-run costs are larger than long-run costs and that this difference is proportionally larger the farther one gets from the output level for which $k = 80$ is optimal.

TABLE 10.1 Difference between Short-Run and Long-Run Total Cost, $k = 80$

q	$C = 12q$	$SC = 240 + 3q^2/20$
10	120	255
20	240	300
30	360	375
40	480	480
50	600	615
60	720	780
70	840	975
80	960	1200

TABLE 10.2 Unit Costs in the Long Run and the Short Run, $k = 80$

q	AC	MC	SAC	SMC
10	12	12	25.5	3
20	12	12	15.0	6
30	12	12	12.5	9
40	12	12	12.0	12
50	12	12	12.3	15
60	12	12	13.0	18
70	12	12	13.9	21
80	12	12	15.0	24

It is also instructive to study differences between the long-run and short-run per-unit costs in this situation. Here $AC = MC = 12$. We can compute the short-run equivalents (when $k = 80$) as

$$SAC = \frac{SC}{q} = \frac{240}{q} + \frac{3q}{20},$$

$$SMC = \frac{\partial SC}{\partial q} = \frac{6q}{20}. \tag{10.64}$$

Both of these short-run unit costs are equal to 12 when $q = 40$. However, as Table 10.2 shows, short-run unit costs can differ significantly from this figure, depending on the output level that the firm produces. Notice in particular that short-run marginal cost increases rapidly as output expands beyond $q = 40$ because of diminishing returns to the variable input (labor). This conclusion plays an important role in the theory of short-run price determination.

QUERY: Explain why an increase in w will increase both short-run average cost and short-run marginal cost in this illustration, but an increase in v affects only short-run average cost.

Graphs of per-unit cost curves

The envelope total cost curve relationships exhibited in Figure 10.8 can be used to show geometric connections between short-run and long-run average and marginal cost curves. These are presented in Figure 10.9 for the cubic total cost curve case. In the figure, short-run and long-run average costs are equal at that output for which the (fixed) capital input is appropriate. At q_1, for example, $SAC(k_1) = AC$ because k_1 is used in producing q_1 at minimal costs. For movements away from q_1, short-run average costs exceed long-run average costs, thus reflecting the cost-minimizing nature of the long-run total cost curve.

Because the minimum point of the long-run average cost curve (AC) plays a major role in the theory of long-run price determination, it is important to note the various curves that pass through this point in Figure 10.9. First, as is always true for average and marginal cost curves, the MC curve passes through the low point of the AC curve. At q_1, long-run average and marginal costs are equal. Associated with q_1 is a certain level of capital input (say, k_1); the short-run average cost curve for this level of capital input is tangent to the AC curve at its minimum point. The SAC curve also reaches its minimum at output level q_1. For movements away from q_1, the AC curve is much flatter than the SAC curve, and this reflects the greater flexibility open to firms in the long run. Short-run costs rise rapidly because capital inputs are fixed. In the long run, such inputs are not fixed, and diminishing marginal productivities do

FIGURE 10.9   Average and Marginal Cost Curves for the Cubic Cost Curve Case

This set of curves is derived from the total cost curves shown in Figure 10.8. The *AC* and *MC* curves have the usual U-shapes, as do the short-run curves. At q_1, long-run average costs are minimized. The configuration of curves at this minimum point is quite important.

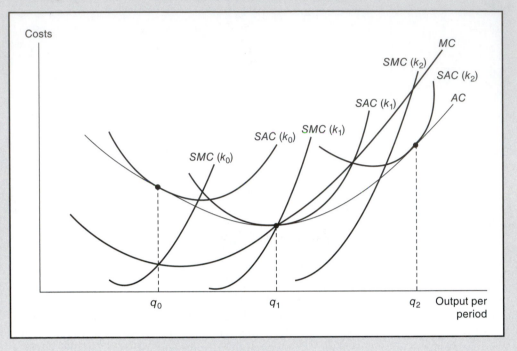

not occur so abruptly. Finally, because the *SAC* curve reaches its minimum at q_1, the short-run marginal cost curve (*SMC*) also passes through this point. The minimum point of the *AC* curve therefore brings together the four most important per-unit costs: at this point,

$$AC = MC = SAC = SMC. \tag{10.65}$$

For this reason, as we shall show in Chapter 12, the output level q_1 is an important equilibrium point for a competitive firm in the long run.

SUMMARY

In this chapter we examined the relationship between the level of output a firm produces and the input costs associated with that level of production. The resulting cost curves should generally be familiar to you because they are widely used in most courses in introductory economics. Here we have shown how such curves reflect the firm's underlying production function and the firm's desire to minimize costs. By developing cost curves from these basic foundations, we were able to illustrate a number of important findings.

- A firm that wishes to minimize the economic costs of producing a particular level of output should choose that input combination for which the rate of technical substitution (*RTS*) is equal to the ratio of the inputs' rental prices.

- Repeated application of this minimization procedure yields the firm's expansion path. Because the expansion path shows how input usage expands with the level of output, it also shows the relationship between output level and total cost. That relationship is summarized by the total cost function, $C(q, v, w)$, which shows production costs as a function of output levels and input prices.

- The firm's average cost ($AC = C/q$) and marginal cost ($MC = \partial C/\partial q$) functions can be derived directly from the total cost function. If the total cost curve has a general cubic shape then the *AC* and *MC* curves will be U-shaped.

- All cost curves are drawn on the assumption that the input prices are held constant. When input prices change, cost curves will shift to new positions. The extent of the shifts will be determined by the overall importance of the input whose price has changed and by the ease with which the firm may substitute one input for another. Technical progress will also shift cost curves.

- Input demand functions can be derived from the firm's total cost function through partial differentiation. These input demand functions will depend on the quantity of output that the firm chooses to produce and are therefore called "contingent" demand functions.

- In the short run, the firm may not be able to vary some inputs. It can then alter its level of production only by changing its employment of variable inputs. In so doing, it may have to use nonoptimal, higher-cost input combinations than it would choose if it were possible to vary all inputs.

PROBLEMS

10.1

In a famous article [J. Viner, "Cost Curves and Supply Curves," *Zeitschrift fur Nationalokonomie* 3 (September 1931): 23–46], Viner criticized his draftsman who could not draw a family of *SAC* curves whose points of tangency with the U-shaped *AC* curve were also the minimum points on each *SAC* curve. The draftsman protested that such a drawing was impossible to construct. Whom would you support in this debate?

10.2

Suppose that a firm produces two different outputs, the quantities of which are represented by q_1 and q_2. In general, the firm's total costs can be represented by $C(q_1, q_2)$. This function exhibits economies of scope if $C(q_1, 0) + C(0, q_2) > C(q_1, q_2)$ for all output levels of either good.

    a. Explain in words why this mathematical formulation implies that costs will be lower in this multiproduct firm than in two single-product firms producing each good separately.

    b. If the two outputs are actually the same good, we can define total output as $q = q_1 + q_2$. Suppose that in this case average cost $(= C/q)$ falls as q increases. Show that this firm also enjoys economies of scope under the definition provided here.

10.3

Professor Smith and Professor Jones are going to produce a new introductory textbook. As true scientists, they have laid out the production function for the book as

$$q = S^{1/2} J^{1/2},$$

where $q =$ the number of pages in the finished book, $S =$ the number of working hours spent by Smith, and $J =$ the number of hours spent working by Jones.

    Smith values his labor as \$3 per working hour. He has spent 900 hours preparing the first draft. Jones, whose labor is valued at \$12 per working hour, will revise Smith's draft to complete the book.

    a. How many hours will Jones have to spend to produce a finished book of 150 pages? Of 300 pages? Of 450 pages?

    b. What is the marginal cost of the 150th page of the finished book? Of the 300th page? Of the 450th page?

10.4

Suppose that a firm's fixed proportion production function is given by

$$q = \min(5k, 10l).$$

    a. Calculate the firm's long-run total, average, and marginal cost functions.

    b. Suppose that k is fixed at 10 in the short run. Calculate the firm's short-run total, average, and marginal cost functions.

c. Suppose $v = 1$ and $w = 3$. Calculate this firm's long-run and short-run average and marginal cost curves.

10.5

A firm producing hockey sticks has a production function given by

$$q = 2\sqrt{k \cdot l}.$$

In the short run, the firm's amount of capital equipment is fixed at $k = 100$. The rental rate for k is $v = \$1$, and the wage rate for l is $w = \$4$.

a. Calculate the firm's short-run total cost curve. Calculate the short-run average cost curve.

b. What is the firm's short-run marginal cost function? What are the SC, SAC, and SMC for the firm if it produces 25 hockey sticks? Fifty hockey sticks? One hundred hockey sticks? Two hundred hockey sticks?

c. Graph the SAC and the SMC curves for the firm. Indicate the points found in part (b).

d. Where does the SMC curve intersect the SAC curve? Explain why the SMC curve will always intersect the SAC curve at its lowest point.

Suppose now that capital used for producing hockey sticks is fixed at $\bar{k}$ in the short run.

e. Calculate the firm's total costs as a function of q, w, v, and $\bar{k}$.

f. Given q, w, and v, how should the capital stock be chosen to minimize total cost?

g. Use your results from part (f) to calculate the long-run total cost of hockey stick production.

h. For $w = \$4$, $v = \$1$, graph the long-run total cost curve for hockey stick production. Show that this is an envelope for the short-run curves computed in part (a) by examining values of $\bar{k}$ of 100, 200, and 400.

10.6

An enterprising entrepreneur purchases two firms to produce widgets. Each firm produces identical products, and each has a production function given by

$$q = \sqrt{k_i l_i}, \quad i = 1, 2.$$

The firms differ, however, in the amount of capital equipment each has. In particular, firm 1 has $k_1 = 25$ whereas firm 2 has $k_2 = 100$. Rental rates for k and l are given by $w = v = \$1$.

a. If the entrepreneur wishes to minimize short-run total costs of widget production, how should output be allocated between the two firms?

b. Given that output is optimally allocated between the two firms, calculate the short-run total, average, and marginal cost curves. What is the marginal cost of the 100th widget? The 125th widget? The 200th widget?

c. How should the entrepreneur allocate widget production between the two firms in the long run? Calculate the long-run total, average, and marginal cost curves for widget production.

d. How would your answer to part (c) change if both firms exhibited diminishing returns to scale?

10.7

Suppose the total-cost function for a firm is given by

$$C = q w^{2/3} v^{1/3}.$$

a. Use Shephard's lemma to compute the constant output demand functions for inputs l and k.

b. Use your results from part (a) to calculate the underlying production function for q.

10.8

Suppose the total-cost function for a firm is given by

$$C = q(v + 2\sqrt{vw} + w).$$

a. Use Shephard's lemma to compute the constant output demand function for each input, k and l.

b. Use the results from part (a) to compute the underlying production function for q.

c. You can check the result by using results from Example 10.2 to show that the CES cost function with $\sigma = 0.5$, $\rho = -1$ generates this total-cost function.

Analytical Problems

10.9 Generalizing the CES cost function

The CES production function can be generalized to permit weighting of the inputs. In the two-input case, this function is

$$q = f(k, l) = [(ak)^\rho + (bl)^\rho]^{\gamma/\rho}.$$

a. What is the total-cost function for a firm with this production function? *Hint:* You can, of course, work this out from scratch; easier perhaps is to use the results from Example 10.2 and reason that the price for a unit of capital input in this production function is v/a and for a unit of labor input is w/b.

b. If $\gamma = 1$ and $a + b = 1$, it can be shown that this production function converges to the Cobb-Douglas form $q = k^a l^b$ as $\rho \to 0$. What is the total cost function for this particular version of the CES function?

c. The relative labor cost share for a two-input production function is given by wl/vk. Show that this share is constant for the Cobb-Douglas function in part (b). How is the relative labor share affected by the parameters a and b?

d. Calculate the relative labor cost share for the general CES function introduced above. How is that share affected by changes in w/v? How is the direction of this effect determined by the elasticity of substitution, σ? How is it affected by the sizes of the parameters a and b?

10.10 Input demand elasticities

The own-price elasticities of contingent input demand for labor and capital are defined as

$$e_{l^c, w} = \frac{\partial l^c}{\partial w} \cdot \frac{w}{l^c}, \quad e_{k^c, v} = \frac{\partial k^c}{\partial v} \cdot \frac{v}{k^c}.$$

a. Calculate $e_{l^c, w}$ and $e_{k^c, v}$ for each of the cost functions shown in Example 10.2.

b. Show that, in general, $e_{l^c, w} + e_{l^c, v} = 0$.

c. Show that the cross-price derivatives of contingent demand functions are equal—that is, show that $\partial l^c/\partial v = \partial k^c/\partial w$. Use this fact to show that $s_l e_{l^c, v} = s_k e_{k^c, w}$ where s_l, s_k are, respectively, the share of labor in total cost (wl/C) and of capital in total cost (vk/C).

d. Use the results from parts (b) and (c) to show that $s_l e_{l^c, w} + s_k e_{k^c, w} = 0$.

e. Interpret these various elasticity relationships in words and discuss their overall relevance to a general theory of input demand.

10.11 The elasticity of substitution and input demand elasticities

The definition of the (Morishima) elasticity of substitution (Equation 10.51) can also be described in terms of input demand elasticities. This illustrates the basic asymmetry in the definition.

a. Show that if only w_j changes, $s_{i,j} = e_{x_i^c, w_j} - e_{x_j^c, w_j}$.

b. Show that if only w_i changes, $s_{j,i} = e_{x_j^c, w_i} - e_{x_i^c, w_i}$.

c. Show that if the production function takes the general CES form $q = [\sum_n x_i^\rho]^{1/\rho}$ for $\rho \neq 0$, then all of the Morishima elasticities are the same: $s_{i,j} = 1/(1 - \rho) = \sigma$. This is the only case in which the Morishima definition is symmetric.

10.12 The Allen elasticity of substitution

Many empirical studies of costs report an alternative definition of the elasticity of substitution between inputs. This alternative definition was first proposed by R. G. D. Allen in the 1930s and further clarified by H. Uzawa in the 1960s. This definition builds directly on the production function–based elasticity of substitution defined in footnote 6 of Chapter 9: $A_{i,j} = C_{ij}C/C_iC_j$, where the subscripts indicate partial differentiation with respect to various input prices. Clearly, the Allen definition is symmetric.

a. Show that $A_{i,j} = e_{x_i^c, w_j}/s_j$, where s_j is the share of input j in total cost.

b. Show that the elasticity of s_i with respect to the price of input j is related to the Allen elasticity by $e_{s_i, p_j} = s_j(A_{i,j} - 1)$.

c. Show that, with only two inputs, $A_{k,l} = 1$ for the Cobb-Douglas case and $A_{k,l} = \sigma$ for the CES case.

d. Read Blackorby and Russell (1989: "Will the Real Elasticity of Substitution Please Stand Up?") to see why the Morishima definition is preferred for most purposes.

SUGGESTIONS FOR FURTHER READING

Allen, R. G. D. *Mathematical Analysis for Economists*. New York: St. Martin's Press, 1938, various pages—see index.

> Complete (though dated) mathematical analysis of substitution possibilities and cost functions. Notation somewhat difficult.

Blackorby, C., and R. R. Russell. "Will the Real Elasticity of Substitution Please Stand Up? (A Comparison of the Allen/ Uzawa and Morishima Elasticities)." *American Economic Review* (September 1989): 882–88.

> A nice clarification of the proper way to measure substitutability among many inputs in production. Argues that the Allen/Uzawa definition is largely useless and that the Morishima definition is by far the best.

Ferguson, C. E. *The Neoclassical Theory of Production and Distribution*. Cambridge: Cambridge University Press, 1969, Chap. 6.

> Nice development of cost curves; especially strong on graphic analysis.

Fuss, M., and D. McFadden. *Production Economics: A Dual Approach to Theory and Applications*. Amsterdam: North-Holland, 1978.

> Difficult and quite complete treatment of the dual relationship between production and cost functions. Some discussion of empirical issues.

Knight, H. H. "Cost of Production and Price over Long and Short Periods." *Journal of Political Economics* 29 (April 1921): 304–35.

> Classic treatment of the short-run, long-run distinction.

Silberberg, E., and W. Suen. *The Structure of Economics: A Mathematical Analysis*, 3rd ed. Boston: Irwin/McGraw-Hill, 2001.

> Chapters 7–9 have a great deal of material on cost functions. Especially recommended are the authors' discussions of "reciprocity effects" and their treatment of the short-run–long-run distinction as an application of the Le Chatelier principle from physics.

Sydsaeter, K., A. Strom, and P. Berck. *Economists' Mathematical Manual*, 3rd ed. Berlin: Springer-Verlag, 2000.

> Chapter 25 provides a succinct summary of the mathematical concepts in this chapter. A nice summary of many input cost functions, but beware of typos.

EXTENSIONS

The Translog Cost Function

The two cost functions studied in Chapter 10 (the Cobb-Douglas and the CES) are very restrictive in the substitution possibilities they permit. The Cobb-Douglas implicitly assumes that $\sigma = 1$ between any two inputs. The CES permits σ to take any value, but it requires that the elasticity of substitution be the same between any two inputs. Because empirical economists would prefer to let the data show what the actual substitution possibilities among inputs are, they have tried to find more flexible functional forms. One especially popular such form is the translog cost function, first made popular by Fuss and McFadden (1978). In this extension we will look at this function.

E10.1 The translog with two inputs

In Example 10.2, we calculated the Cobb-Douglas cost function in the two-input case as $C(q, v, w) = Bq^{1/(\alpha+\beta)}v^{\alpha/(\alpha+\beta)}w^{\beta/(\alpha+\beta)}$. If we take the natural logarithm of this we have

$$\ln C(q, v, w) = \ln B + [1/(\alpha + \beta)]\ln q \\ + [\alpha/(\alpha + \beta)]\ln v \\ + [\beta/(\alpha + \beta)]\ln w. \quad \text{(i)}$$

That is, the log of total costs is linear in the logs of output and the input prices. The translog function generalizes this by permitting second-order terms in input prices:

$$\ln C(q, v, w) = \ln q + \beta_0 + \beta_1 \ln v + \beta_2 \ln w \\ + \beta_3(\ln v)^2 + \beta_4(\ln w)^2 \\ + \beta_5 \ln v \ln w, \quad \text{(ii)}$$

where this function implicitly assumes constant returns to scale (because the coefficient of $\ln q$ is 1.0)—although that need not be the case.

Some of the properties of this function are:

- For the function to be homogeneous of degree 1 in input prices, it must be the case that $\beta_1 + \beta_2 = 1$ and $\beta_3 + \beta_4 + \beta_5 = 0$.

- This function includes the Cobb-Douglas as the special case $\beta_3 = \beta_4 = \beta_5 = 0$. Hence, the function can be used to test statistically whether the Cobb-Douglas is appropriate.

- Input shares for the translog function are especially easy to compute using the result that $s_i = (\partial \ln C)/(\partial \ln w_i)$. In the two-input case, this yields

$$s_k = \frac{\partial \ln C}{\partial \ln v} = \beta_1 + 2\beta_3 \ln v + \beta_5 \ln w,$$

$$s_l = \frac{\partial \ln C}{\partial \ln w} = \beta_2 + 2\beta_4 \ln w + \beta_5 \ln v. \quad \text{(iii)}$$

In the Cobb-Douglas case ($\beta_3 = \beta_4 = \beta_5 = 0$) these shares are constant, but with the general translog function they are not.

- Calculating the elasticity of substitution in the translog case proceeds by using the result given in Problem 10.11 that $s_{k,l} = e_{k^c,w} - e_{l^c,w}$. Making this calculation is straightforward (provided one keeps track of how to use logarithms):

$$e_{k^c,w} = \frac{\partial \ln C_v}{\partial \ln w} = \frac{\partial \ln\left(\frac{C}{v} \cdot \frac{\partial \ln C}{\partial \ln v}\right)}{\partial \ln w}$$

$$= \frac{\partial\left[\ln C - \ln v + \ln\left(\frac{\partial \ln C}{\partial \ln v}\right)\right]}{\partial \ln w}$$

$$= s_l - 0 + \frac{\partial \ln s_k}{\partial s_k} \cdot \frac{\partial^2 \ln C}{\partial v \partial w} = s_l + \frac{\beta_5}{s_k}. \quad \text{(iv)}$$

Observe that, in the Cobb-Douglas case ($\beta_5 = 0$), the contingent price elasticity of demand for k with respect to the wage has a simple form: $e_{k^c,w} = s_l$. A similar set of manipulations yields $e_{l^c,w} = -s_k + 2\beta_4/s_l$ and, in the Cobb-Douglas case, $e_{l^c,w} = -s_k$. Bringing these two elasticities together yields

$$s_{k,l} = e_{k^c,w} - e_{l^c,w}$$

$$= s_l + s_k + \frac{\beta_5}{s_k} - \frac{2\beta_4}{s_l}$$

$$= 1 + \frac{s_l\beta_5 - 2s_k\beta_4}{s_k s_l}. \quad \text{(v)}$$

Again, in the Cobb-Douglas case we have $s_{k,l} = 1$, as should have been expected.

- The Allen elasticity of substitution (see Problem 10.12) for the translog function is $A_{k,l} = 1 + \beta_5/s_k s_l$. This function can also be used to calculate that the (contingent) cross-price elasticity of demand is $e_{k^c,w} = s_l A_{k,l} = s_l + \beta_5/s_k$, as was shown previously. Here again, $A_{k,l} = 1$ in the Cobb-Douglas case. In general, however, the Allen and Morishima definitions will differ even with just two inputs.

E10.2 The many-input translog cost function

Most empirical studies include more than two inputs. The translog cost function is especially easy to generalize to these situations. If we assume there are n inputs, each with a price of w_i $(i = 1, n)$, then this function is

$$C(q, w_1, \ldots, w_n) = \ln q + \beta_0 + \sum_{i=1}^{n} \beta_i \ln w_i$$
$$+ 0.5 \sum_{i=1}^{n} \sum_{j=1}^{n} \beta_{ij} \ln w_i \ln w_j,$$

$$\text{(vi)}$$

where we have once again assumed constant returns to scale. This function requires $\beta_{ij} = \beta_{ji}$, so each term for which $i \neq j$ appears twice in the final double sum (which explains the presence of the 0.5 in the expression). For this function to be homogeneous of degree 1 in the input prices, it must be the case that $\sum_{i=1}^{n} \beta_i = 1$ and $\sum_{i=1}^{n} \beta_{ij} = 0$. Two useful properties of this function are:

- Input shares take the linear form

$$s_i = \beta_i + \sum_{j=1}^{n} \beta_{ij} \ln w_j. \qquad \text{(vii)}$$

Again, this shows why the translog is usually estimated in a share form. Sometimes a term in $\ln q$ is also added to the share equations to allow for scale effects on the shares (see Sydsæter, Strøm, and Berck, 2000).

- The elasticity of substitution between any two inputs in the translog function is given by

$$s_{i,j} = 1 + \frac{s_j \beta_{ij} - s_i \beta_{jj}}{s_i s_j}. \qquad \text{(viii)}$$

Hence, substitutability can again be judged directly from the parameters estimated for the translog function.

E10.3 Some applications

The translog cost function has become the main choice for empirical studies of production. Two factors account for this popularity. First, the function allows a fairly complete characterization of substitution patterns among inputs—it does not require that the data fit any prespecified pattern. Second, the function's format incorporates input prices in a flexible way so that one can be reasonably sure that he or she has controlled for such prices in regression analysis. When such control is assured, measures of other aspects of the cost function (such as its returns to scale) will be more reliable.

One example of using the translog function to study input substitution is the study by Westbrook and Buckley (1990) of the responses that shippers made to changing relative prices of moving goods that resulted from deregulation of the railroad and trucking industries in the United States. The authors look specifically at the shipping of fruits and vegetables from the western states to Chicago and New York. They find relatively high substitution elasticities among shipping options and so conclude that deregulation had significant welfare benefits. Doucouliagos and Hone (2000) provide a similar analysis of deregulation of dairy prices in Australia. They show that changes in the price of raw milk caused dairy processing firms to undertake significant changes in input usage. They also show that the industry adopted significant new technologies in response to the price change.

An interesting study that uses the translog primarily to judge returns to scale is Latzko's (1999) analysis of the U.S. mutual fund industry. He finds that the elasticity of total costs with respect to the total assets managed by the fund is less than 1 for all but the largest funds (those with more than $4 billion in assets). Hence, the author concludes that money management exhibits substantial returns to scale. A number of other studies that use the translog to estimate economies of scale focus on municipal services. For example, Garcia and Thomas (2001) look at water supply systems in local French communities. They conclude that there are significant operating economies of scale in such systems and that some merging of systems would make sense. Yatchew (2000) reaches a similar conclusion about electricity distribution in small communities in Ontario, Canada. He finds that there are economies of scale for electricity distribution systems serving up to about 20,000 customers. Again, some efficiencies might be obtained from merging systems that are much smaller than this size.

References

Doucouliagos, H., and P. Hone. "Deregulation and Subequilibrium in the Australian Dairy Processing Industry." *Economic Record* (June 2000): 152–62.

Fuss, M., and D. McFadden, Eds. *Production Economics: A Dual Approach to Theory and Applications.* Amsterdam: North Holland, 1978.

Garcia, S., and A. Thomas. "The Structure of Municipal Water Supply Costs: Application to a Panel of French

Local Communities." *Journal of Productivity Analysis* (July 2001): 5–29.

Latzko, D. "Economies of Scale in Mutual Fund Administration." *Journal of Financial Research* (Fall 1999): 331–39.

Sydsæter, K., A. Strøm, and P. Berck. *Economists' Mathematical Manual*, 3rd ed. Berlin: Springer-Verlag, 2000.

Westbrook, M. D., and P. A. Buckley. "Flexible Functional Forms and Regularity: Assessing the Competitive Relationship between Truck and Rail Transportation." *Review of Economics and Statistics* (November 1990): 623–30.

Yatchew, A. "Scale Economies in Electricity Distribution: A Semiparametric Analysis." *Journal of Applied Econometrics* (March/April 2000): 187–210.

Profit Maximization

In Chapter 10 we examined the way in which firms minimize costs for any level of output they choose. In this chapter we focus on how the level of output is chosen by profit-maximizing firms. Before investigating that decision, however, it is appropriate to discuss briefly the nature of firms and the ways in which their choices should be analyzed.

THE NATURE AND BEHAVIOR OF FIRMS

As we pointed out at the beginning of our analysis of production, a firm is an association of individuals who have organized themselves for the purpose of turning inputs into outputs. Different individuals will provide different types of inputs, such as workers' skills and varieties of capital equipment, with the expectation of receiving some sort of reward for doing so.

Contractual relationships within firms

The nature of the contractual relationship between the providers of inputs to a firm may be quite complicated. Each provider agrees to devote his or her input to production activities under a set of understandings about how it is to be used and what benefit is to be expected from that use. In some cases these contracts are *explicit*. Workers often negotiate contracts that specify in considerable detail what hours are to be worked, what rules of work are to be followed, and what rate of pay is to be expected. Similarly, capital owners invest in a firm under a set of explicit legal principles about the ways in which that capital may be used, the compensation the owner can expect to receive, and whether the owner retains any profits or losses after all economic costs have been paid. Despite these formal arrangements, it is clear that many of the understandings between the providers of inputs to a firm are *implicit*; relationships between managers and workers follow certain procedures about who has the authority to do what in making production decisions. Among workers, numerous implicit understandings exist about how work tasks are to be shared; and capital owners may delegate much of their authority to managers and workers to make decisions on their behalf (General Motors' shareholders, for example, are never involved in how assembly-line equipment will be used, though technically they own it). All of these explicit and implicit relationships change in response to experiences and events external to the firm. Much as a basketball team will try out new plays and defensive strategies, so too firms will alter the nature of their internal organizations to achieve better long-term results.[1]

---

[1]The initial development of the theory of the firm from the notion of the contractual relationships involved can be found in R. H. Coase, "The Nature of the Firm," *Economica* (November 1937): 386–405.

Modeling firms' behavior

Although some economists have adopted a "behavioral" approach to studying firms' decisions, most have found that approach too cumbersome for general purposes. Rather, they have adopted a "holistic" approach that treats the firm as a single decision-making unit and sweeps away all the complicated behavioral issues about relationships among input providers. Under this approach, it is often convenient to assume that a firm's decisions are made by a single dictatorial manager who rationally pursues some goal, usually profit maximization. That is the approach we take here. In Chapter 18 we look at some of the informational issues that arise in intrafirm contracts.

PROFIT MAXIMIZATION

Most models of supply assume that the firm and its manager pursue the goal of achieving the largest economic profits possible. Hence we will use the following definition.

Profit-maximizing firm. A *profit-maximizing firm* chooses both its inputs and its outputs with the sole goal of achieving maximum economic profits. That is, the firm seeks to make the difference between its total revenues and its total economic costs as large as possible.

DEFINITION

This assumption—that firms seek maximum economic profits—has a long history in economic literature. It has much to recommend it. It is plausible because firm owners may indeed seek to make their asset as valuable as possible and because competitive markets may punish firms that do not maximize profits. The assumption also yields interesting theoretical results that can explain actual firms' decisions.

Profit maximization and marginalism

If firms are strict profit maximizers, they will make decisions in a "marginal" way. The entrepreneur will perform the conceptual experiment of adjusting those variables that can be controlled until it is impossible to increase profits further. This involves, say, looking at the incremental, or "marginal," profit obtainable from producing one more unit of output, or at the additional profit available from hiring one more laborer. As long as this incremental profit is positive, the extra output will be produced or the extra laborer will be hired. When the incremental profit of an activity becomes zero, the entrepreneur has pushed that activity far enough, and it would not be profitable to go further. In this chapter, we will explore the consequences of this assumption by using increasingly sophisticated mathematics.

Output choice

First we examine a topic that should be very familiar: what output level a firm will produce in order to obtain maximum profits. A firm sells some level of output, q, at a market price of p per unit. Total revenues (R) are given by

$$R(q) = p(q) \cdot q, \tag{11.1}$$

where we have allowed for the possibility that the selling price the firm receives might be affected by how much it sells. In the production of q, certain *economic* costs are incurred and, as in Chapter 10, we will denote these by $C(q)$.

The difference between revenues and costs is called *economic profits* (π). Because both revenues and costs depend on the quantity produced, economic profits will also. That is,

$$\pi(q) = p(q) \cdot q - C(q) = R(q) - C(q). \tag{11.2}$$

The necessary condition for choosing the value of q that maximizes profits is found by setting the derivative of Equation 11.2 with respect to q equal to 0:[2]

$$\frac{d\pi}{dq} = \pi'(q) = \frac{dR}{dq} - \frac{dC}{dq} = 0, \tag{11.3}$$

so the first-order condition for a maximum is that

$$\frac{dR}{dq} = \frac{dC}{dq}. \tag{11.4}$$

This is a mathematical statement of the "marginal revenue equals marginal cost" rule usually studied in introductory economics courses. Hence we have the following.

OPTIMIZATION PRINCIPLE

Profit maximization. To maximize economic profits, the firm should choose that output for which marginal revenue is equal to marginal cost. That is,

$$MR = \frac{dR}{dq} = \frac{dC}{dq} = MC. \tag{11.5}$$

Second-order conditions

Equation 11.4 or 11.5 is only a necessary condition for a profit maximum. For sufficiency, it is also required that

$$\frac{d^2\pi}{dq^2}\bigg|_{q=q^*} = \frac{d\pi'(q)}{dq}\bigg|_{q=q^*} < 0, \tag{11.6}$$

or that "marginal" profit must be decreasing at the optimal level of q. For q less than q^* (the optimal level of output), profit must be increasing [$\pi'(q) > 0$]; and for q greater than q^*, profit must be decreasing [$\pi'(q) < 0$]. Only if this condition holds has a true maximum been achieved. Clearly the condition holds if marginal revenue is decreasing (or constant) in q and marginal cost is increasing in q.

Graphical analysis

These relationships are illustrated in Figure 11.1, where the top panel depicts typical cost and revenue functions. For low levels of output, costs exceed revenues and so economic profits are negative. In the middle ranges of output, revenues exceed costs; this means that profits are positive. Finally, at high levels of output, costs rise sharply and again exceed revenues. The vertical distance between the revenue and cost curves (that is, profits) is shown in Figure 11.1b. Here profits reach a maximum at q^*. At this level of output it is also true that the slope of the revenue curve (marginal revenue) is equal to the slope of the cost curve (marginal cost). It is clear from the figure that the sufficient conditions for a maximum are also satisfied at this point, because profits are increasing to the left of q^* and decreasing to the right of q^*. Output level q^* is therefore a true profit maximum. This is not so for output level q^{**}. Although marginal revenue is equal to marginal cost at this output, profits are in fact at a minimum there.

---

[2]Notice that this is an unconstrained maximization problem; the constraints in the problem are implicit in the revenue and cost functions. Specifically, the demand curve facing the firm determines the revenue function, and the firm's production function (together with input prices) determines its costs.

FIGURE 11.1 Marginal Revenue Must Equal Marginal Cost for Profit Maximization

Because profits are defined to be revenues (R) minus costs (C), it is clear that profits reach a maximum when the slope of the revenue function (marginal revenue) is equal to the slope of the cost function (marginal cost). This equality is only a necessary condition for a maximum, as may be seen by comparing points q^* (a true *maximum*) and q^{**} (a true *minimum*), points at which marginal revenue equals marginal cost.

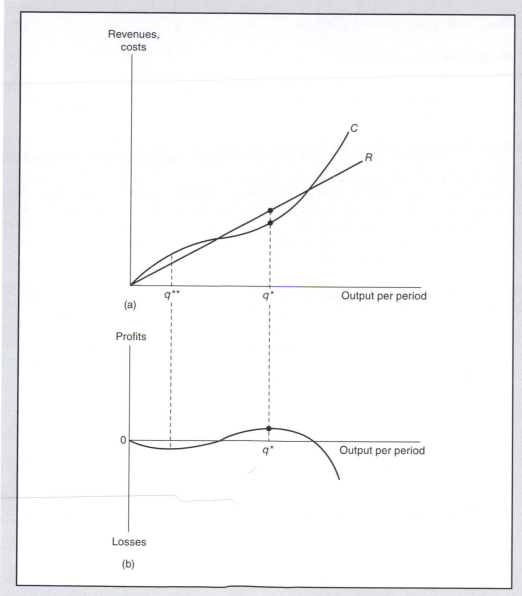

MARGINAL REVENUE

It is the revenue obtained from selling one more unit of output that is relevant to the profit-maximizing firm's output decision. If the firm can sell all it wishes without having any effect on market price, the market price will indeed be the extra revenue obtained from selling one more unit. Phrased in another way: if a firm's output decisions will not affect market price, then marginal revenue is equal to the price at which a unit sells.

A firm may not always be able to sell all it wants at the prevailing market price, however. If it faces a downward-sloping demand curve for its product, then more output can be sold only by reducing the good's price. In this case the revenue obtained from selling one more unit will be less than the price of that unit because, in order to get consumers to take the extra unit, the price of all other units must be lowered. This result can be easily demonstrated. As before, total revenue (R) is the product of the quantity sold (q) times the price at which it is sold (p), which may also depend on q. Marginal revenue (MR) is then defined to be the change in R resulting from a change in q.

DEFINITION

Marginal revenue. We define

$$\text{marginal revenue} = MR(q) = \frac{dR}{dq} = \frac{d[p(q) \cdot q]}{dq} = p + q \cdot \frac{dp}{dq}. \quad \textbf{(11.7)}$$

Notice that the marginal revenue is a function of output. In general, MR will be different for different levels of q. From Equation 11.7 it is easy to see that, if price does not change as quantity increases ($dp/dq = 0$), marginal revenue will be equal to price. In this case we say that the firm is a *price taker* because its output decisions do not influence the price it receives. On the other hand, if price falls as quantity increases ($dp/dq < 0$), marginal revenue will be less than price. A profit-maximizing manager must know how increases in output will affect the price received before making an optimal output decision. If increases in q cause market price to fall, this must be taken into account.

EXAMPLE 11.1 Marginal Revenue from a Linear Demand Function

Suppose a shop selling sub sandwichs (also called grinders, torpedoes, or, in Philadelphia, hoagies) faces a linear demand curve for its daily output over period (q) of the form

$$q = 100 - 10p. \quad \textbf{(11.8)}$$

Solving for the price the shop receives, we have

$$p = \frac{-q}{10} + 10, \quad \textbf{(11.9)}$$

and total revenues (as a function of q) are given by

$$R = pq = \frac{-q^2}{10} + 10q. \quad \textbf{(11.10)}$$

The sub firm's marginal revenue function is

$$MR = \frac{dR}{dq} = \frac{-q}{5} + 10, \quad \textbf{(11.11)}$$

and in this case $MR < p$ for all values of q. If, for example, the firm produces 40 subs per day, Equation 11.9 shows that it will receive a price of $6 per sandwich. But at this level of output Equation 11.11 shows that MR is only $2. If the firm produces 40 subs per day then total revenue will be $240 (= $6 × 40), whereas if it produced 39 subs then total revenue would be $238 (= $6.1 × 39) because price will rise slightly when less is produced. Hence the marginal revenue from the 40th sub sold is considerably less than its price. Indeed, for $q = 50$, marginal revenue is zero (total revenues are a maximum at $250 = $5 × 50), and any further expansion in daily sub output will actually result in a reduction in total revenue to the firm.

To determine the profit-maximizing level of sub output, we must know the firm's marginal costs. If subs can be produced at a constant average and marginal cost of $4, then Equation 11.11 shows that $MR = MC$ at a daily output of 30 subs. With this level of output, each sub will sell for $7 and profits are $90 [= ($7 − $4) · 30]. Although price exceeds average and marginal cost here by a substantial margin, it would not be in the firm's interest to expand output. With $q = 35$, for example, price will fall to $6.50 and profits will fall to $87.50 [= ($6.50 − $4.00) · 35]. Marginal revenue, not price, is the primary determinant of profit-maximizing behavior.

QUERY: How would an increase in the marginal cost of sub production to $5 affect the output decision of this firm? How would it affect the firm's profits?

Marginal revenue and elasticity

The concept of marginal revenue is directly related to the elasticity of the demand curve facing the firm. Remember that the elasticity of demand $(e_{q,p})$ is defined as the percentage change in quantity demanded that results from a 1 percent change in price:

$$e_{q,p} = \frac{dq/q}{dp/p} = \frac{dq}{dp} \cdot \frac{p}{q}.$$

Now, this definition can be combined with Equation 11.7 to give

$$MR = p + \frac{q\,dp}{dq} = p\left(1 + \frac{q}{p} \cdot \frac{dp}{dq}\right) = p\left(1 + \frac{1}{e_{q,p}}\right). \tag{11.12}$$

If the demand curve facing the firm is negatively sloped, then $e_{q,p} < 0$ and marginal revenue will be less than price, as we have already shown. If demand is elastic $(e_{q,p} < -1)$, then marginal revenue will be positive. If demand is elastic, the sale of one more unit will not affect price "very much" and hence more revenue will be yielded by the sale. In fact, if demand facing the firm is infinitely elastic $(e_{q,p} = -\infty)$, marginal revenue will equal price. The firm is, in this case, a price taker. However, if demand is inelastic $(e_{q,p} > -1)$, marginal revenue will be negative. Increases in q can be obtained only through "large" declines in market price, and these declines will actually cause total revenue to decrease.

The relationship between marginal revenue and elasticity is summarized by Table 11.1.

TABLE 11.1   Relationship between Elasticity and Marginal Revenue

$e_{q,p} < -1$	$MR > 0$
$e_{q,p} = -1$	$MR = 0$
$e_{q,p} > -1$	$MR < 0$

Price–marginal cost markup

If we assume the firm wishes to maximize profits, this analysis can be extended to illustrate the connection between price and marginal cost. Setting $MR = MC$ yields

$$MC = p\left(1 + \frac{1}{e_{q,p}}\right)$$

or

$$\frac{p}{MC} = \frac{e_{q,p}}{1 + e_{q,p}}. \tag{11.13}$$

That is, the "markup" of price over marginal cost depends in a very specific way on the elasticity of demand facing the firm. First, notice that this demand must be elastic $(e_{q,p} < -1)$.

If demand were inelastic, the ratio in Equation 11.13 would be negative and the equation would be nonsensical. This simply reflects that, when demand is inelastic, marginal revenue is negative and cannot be equated to a positive marginal cost. It is important to stress that it is the demand facing the firm that must be elastic. This may be consistent with an overall inelastic demand for the product in question if the firm faces competition from other firms producing the same good.

Equation 11.13 implies that the markup over marginal cost will be higher the closer $e_{q,p}$ is to -1. If the demand facing the firm is infinitely elastic (perhaps because there are many other firms producing the same good), then $e_{q,p} = -\infty$ and there is no markup ($p/MC = 1$). On the other hand, with an elasticity of demand of (say) $e_{q,p} = -2$, the markup over marginal cost will be 100 percent (i.e., $p/MC = 2$).

Marginal revenue curve

Any demand curve has a marginal revenue curve associated with it. If, as we sometimes assume, the firm must sell all its output at one price, it is convenient to think of the demand curve facing the firm as an *average revenue curve*. That is, the demand curve shows the revenue per unit (in other words, the price) yielded by alternative output choices. The marginal revenue curve, on the other hand, shows the extra revenue provided by the last unit sold. In the usual case of a downward-sloping demand curve, the marginal revenue curve will lie below the demand curve because, according to Equation 11.7, $MR < p$. In Figure 11.2 we have drawn such a curve together with the demand curve from which it was derived. Notice that for output levels greater than q_1, marginal revenue is negative. As output increases from 0 to q_1, total revenues ($p \cdot q$) increase. However, at q_1 total revenues ($p_1 \cdot q_1$) are as large as possible; beyond this output level, price falls proportionately faster than output rises.

FIGURE 11.2 Market Demand Curve and Associated Marginal Revenue Curve

Because the demand curve is negatively sloped, the marginal revenue curve will fall below the demand ("average revenue") curve. For output levels beyond q_1, MR is negative. At q_1, total revenues ($p_1 \times q_1$) are a maximum; beyond this point additional increases in q actually cause total revenues to fall because of the concomitant declines in price.

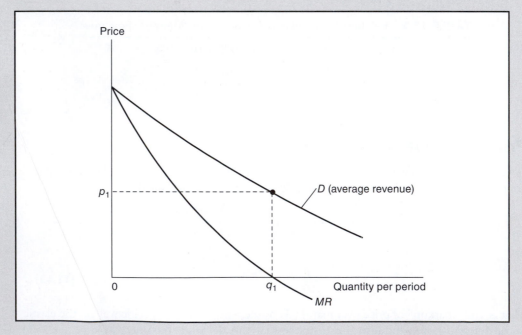

In Part 2 we talked in detail about the possibility of a demand curve's shifting because of changes in income, prices of other goods, or preferences. Whenever a demand curve does shift, its associated marginal revenue curve shifts with it. This should be obvious, because a marginal revenue curve cannot be calculated without referring to a specific demand curve.

EXAMPLE 11.2 The Constant Elasticity Case

In Chapter 5 we showed that a demand function of the form

$$q = ap^b \tag{11.14}$$

has a constant price elasticity of demand, and that this elasticity is given by the parameter b. To compute the marginal revenue function for this function, first solve for p:

$$p = \left(\frac{1}{a}\right)^{1/b} q^{1/b} = kq^{1/b}, \tag{11.15}$$

where $k = (1/a)^{1/b}$. Hence

$$R = pq = kq^{(1+b)/b}$$

and

$$MR = dR/dq = \frac{1+b}{b}kq^{1/b} = \frac{1+b}{b}p. \tag{11.16}$$

For this particular function, then, MR is proportional to price. If, for example, $e_{q,p} = b = -2$, then $MR = 0.5p$. For a more elastic case, suppose $b = -10$; then $MR = 0.9p$. The MR curve approaches the demand curve as demand becomes more elastic. Again, if $b = -\infty$; then $MR = p$; that is, in the case of infinitely elastic demand, the firm is a price taker. For inelastic demand, on the other hand, MR is negative (and profit maximization would be impossible).

QUERY: Suppose demand depended on other factors in addition to p. How would this change the analysis of this example? How would a change in one of these other factors shift the demand curve and its marginal revenue curve?

SHORT-RUN SUPPLY BY A PRICE-TAKING FIRM

We are now ready to study the supply decision of a profit-maximizing firm. In this chapter we will examine only the case in which the firm is a price taker. In Part 5 we will be looking at other cases in considerably more detail. Also, we will focus only on supply decisions in the short run here. Long-run questions concern entry and exit by firms and are the primary focus of the next chapter. The firm's set of short-run cost curves is therefore the appropriate model for our analysis.

Profit-maximizing decision

Figure 11.3 shows the firm's short-run decision. The market price[3] is given by P^*. The demand curve facing the firm is therefore a horizontal line through P^*. This line is labeled $P^* = MR$ as a reminder that an extra unit can always be sold by this price-taking firm without affecting the price it receives. Output level q^* provides maximum profits, because at q^* price is equal to short-run marginal cost. The fact that profits are positive can be seen by noting that

---

[3]We will usually use an uppercase italic P to denote market price for a single good here and in later chapters. When notation is complex, however, we will sometimes revert to using a lowercase p.

FIGURE 11.3 Short-Run Supply Curve for a Price-Taking Firm

In the short run, a price-taking firm will produce the level of output for which $SMC = P$. At P^*, for example, the firm will produce q^*. The SMC curve also shows what will be produced at other prices. For prices below $SAVC$, however, the firm will choose to produce no output. The heavy lines in the figure represent the firm's short-run supply curve.

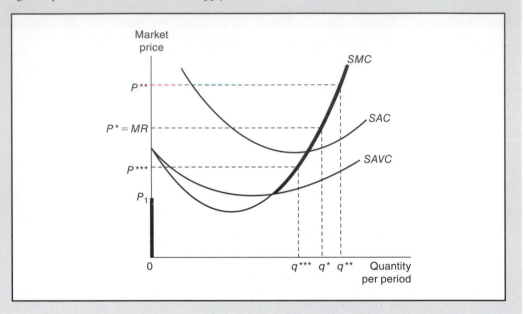

price at q^* exceeds average costs. The firm earns a profit on each unit sold. If price were below average cost (as is the case for P^{***}), the firm would have a loss on each unit sold. If price and average cost were equal, profits would be zero. Notice that at q^* the marginal cost curve has a positive slope. This is required if profits are to be a true maximum. If $P = MC$ on a negatively sloped section of the marginal cost curve then this would not be a point of maximum profits, because increasing output would yield more in revenues (price times the amount produced) than this production would cost (marginal cost would decline if the MC curve has a negative slope). Consequently, profit maximization requires both that $P = MC$ and that marginal cost be increasing at this point.[4]

The firm's short-run supply curve

The positively sloped portion of the short-run marginal cost curve is the short-run supply curve for this price-taking firm. That curve shows how much the firm will produce for every possible market price. For example, as Figure 11.3 shows, at a higher price of P^{**} the firm will produce q^{**} because it is in its interest to incur the higher marginal costs entailed by q^{**}. With a price of P^{***}, on the other hand, the firm opts to produce less (q^{***}) because only a

---

[4]Mathematically: because

$$\pi(q) = Pq - C(q),$$

profit maximization requires (the first-order condition)

$$\pi'(q) = P - MC(q) = 0$$

and (the second-order condition)

$$\pi''(q) - MC'(q) < 0.$$

Hence it is required that $MC'(q) > 0$; marginal cost must be increasing.

lower output level will result in lower marginal costs to meet this lower price. By considering all possible prices the firm might face, we can see by the marginal cost curve how much output the firm should supply at each price.

The shutdown decision. For very low prices we must be careful about this conclusion. Should market price fall below P_1, the profit-maximizing decision would be to produce nothing. As Figure 11.3 shows, prices less than P_1 do not cover average variable costs. There will be a loss on each unit produced in addition to the loss of all fixed costs. By shutting down production, the firm must still pay fixed costs but avoids the losses incurred on each unit produced. Because, in the short run, the firm cannot close down and avoid all costs, its best decision is to produce no output. On the other hand, a price only slightly above P_1 means the firm should produce some output. Although profits may be negative (which they will be if price falls below short-run average total costs, the case at P^{***}), the profit-maximizing decision is to continue production as long as variable costs are covered. Fixed costs must be paid in any case, and any price that covers variable costs will provide revenue as an offset to the fixed costs.[5] Hence we have a complete description of this firm's supply decisions in response to alternative prices for its output. These are summarized in the following definition.

Short-run supply curve. The firm's *short-run supply curve* shows how much it will produce at various possible output prices. For a profit-maximizing firm that takes the price of its output as given, this curve consists of the positively sloped segment of the firm's short-run marginal cost above the point of minimum average variable cost. For prices below this level, the firm's profit-maximizing decision is to shut down and produce no output.

DEFINITION

Of course, any factor that shifts the firm's short-run marginal cost curve (such as changes in input prices or changes in the level of fixed inputs employed) will also shift the short-run supply curve. In Chapter 12 we will make extensive use of this type of analysis to study the operations of perfectly competitive markets.

EXAMPLE 11.3 Short-Run Supply

In Example 10.5 we calculated the short-run total-cost function for the Cobb-Douglas production function as

$$SC(v, w, q, k) = vk_1 + wq^{1/\beta}k_1^{-\alpha/\beta},$$ **(11.17)**

(*continued*)

[5]Some algebra may clarify matters. We know that total costs equal the sum of fixed and variable costs,

$$SC = SFC + SVC,$$

and that profits are given by

$$\pi = R - SC = P \cdot q - SFC - SVC.$$

If $q = 0$, then variable costs and revenues are 0 and so

$$\pi = -SFC.$$

The firm will produce something only if $\pi > -SFC$. But that means that

$$P \cdot q > SVC \quad \text{or} \quad P > SVC/q.$$

EXAMPLE 11.3   CONTINUED

where k_1 is the level of capital input that is held constant in the short run.[6] Short-run marginal cost is easily computed as

$$SMC(v, w, q, k_1) = \frac{\partial SC}{\partial q} = \frac{w}{\beta} q^{(1-\beta)/\beta} k_1^{-\alpha/\beta}. \qquad (11.18)$$

Notice that short-run marginal cost is increasing in output for all values of q. Short-run profit maximization for a price-taking firm requires that output be chosen so that market price (P) is equal to short-run marginal cost:

$$SMC = \frac{w}{\beta} q^{(1-\beta)/\beta} k_1^{-\alpha/\beta} = P, \qquad (11.19)$$

and we can solve for quantity supplied as

$$q = \left(\frac{w}{\beta}\right)^{-\beta/(1-\beta)} k_1^{\alpha/(1-\beta)} P^{\beta/(1-\beta)}. \qquad (11.20)$$

This supply function provides a number of insights that should be familiar from earlier economics courses: (1) the supply curve is positively sloped—increases in P cause the firm to produce more because it is willing to incur a higher marginal cost;[7] (2) the supply curve is shifted to the left by increases in the wage rate, w—that is, for any given output price, less is supplied with a higher wage; (3) the supply curve is shifted outward by increases in capital input, k—with more capital in the short run, the firm incurs a given level of short-run marginal cost at a higher output level; and (4) the rental rate of capital, v, is irrelevant to short-run supply decisions because it is only a component of fixed costs.

Numerical example. We can pursue once more the numerical example from Example 10.5, where $\alpha = \beta = 0.5, v = 3, w = 12$, and $k_1 = 80$. For these specific parameters, the supply function is

$$q = \left(\frac{w}{0.5}\right)^{-1} \cdot (k_1)^1 \cdot P^1 = 40 \cdot \frac{P}{w} = \frac{40P}{12} = \frac{10P}{3}. \qquad (11.21)$$

That this computation is correct can be checked by comparing the quantity supplied at various prices with the computation of short-run marginal cost in Table 10.2. For example, if $P = 12$ then the supply function predicts that $q = 40$ will be supplied, and Table 10.2 shows that this will agree with the $P = SMC$ rule. If price were to double to $P = 24$, an output level of 80 would be supplied and, again, Table 10.2 shows that when $q = 80$, $SMC = 24$. A lower price (say $P = 6$) would cause less to be produced ($q = 20$).

Before adopting Equation 11.21 as *the* supply curve in this situation, we should also check the firm's shutdown decision. Is there a price where it would be more profitable to produce $q = 0$ than to follow the $P = SMC$ rule? From Equation 11.17 we know that short-run variable costs are given by

$$SVC = wq^{1/\beta} k_1^{-\alpha/\beta} \qquad (11.22)$$

and so

$$\frac{SVC}{q} = wq^{(1-\beta)/\beta} k_1^{-\alpha/\beta}. \qquad (11.23)$$

---

[6]Because capital input is held constant, the short-run cost function exhibits increasing marginal cost and will therefore yield a unique profit-maximizing output level. If we had used a constant returns-to-scale production function in the long run, there would have been no such unique output level. We discuss this point later in this chapter and in Chapter 12.

[7]In fact, the short-run elasticity of supply can be read directly from Equation 11.20 as $\beta/(1 - \beta)$.

A comparison of Equation 11.23 with Equation 11.18 shows that $SVC/q < SMC$ for all values of q provided that $\beta < 1$. So in this problem there is no price low enough such that, by following the $P = SMC$ rule, the firm would lose more than if it produced nothing.

In our numerical example, consider the case $P = 3$. With such a low price the firm would opt for $q = 10$. Total revenue would be $R = 30$, and total short-run costs would be $SC = 255$ (see Table 10.1). Hence, profits would be $\pi = R - SC = -225$. Although the situation is dismal for the firm, it is better than opting for $q = 0$. If it produces nothing it avoids all variable (labor) costs but still loses 240 in fixed costs of capital. By producing 10 units of output, its revenues cover variable costs ($R - SVC = 30 - 15 = 15$) and contribute 15 to offset slightly the loss of fixed costs.

QUERY: How would you graph the short-run supply curve in Equation 11.21? How would the curve be shifted if w rose to 15? How would it be shifted if capital input increased to $k_1 = 100$? How would the short-run supply curve be shifted if v fell to 2? Would any of these changes alter the firm's determination to avoid shutting down in the short run?

PROFIT FUNCTIONS

Additional insights into the profit-maximization process for a price-taking firm[8] can be obtained by looking at the profit function. This function shows the firm's (maximized) profits as depending only on the prices that the firm faces. To understand the logic of its construction, remember that economic profits are defined as

$$\pi = Pq - C = Pf(k, l) - vk - wl. \quad \textbf{(11.24)}$$

Only the variables k and l [and also $q = f(k, l)$] are under the firm's control in this expression. The firm chooses levels of these inputs in order to maximize profits, treating the three prices P, v, and w as fixed parameters in its decision. Looked at in this way, the firm's maximum profits ultimately depend only on these three exogenous prices (together with the form of the production function). We summarize this dependence by the *profit function*.

DEFINITION

Profit function. The firm's profit function shows its maximal profits as a function of the prices that the firm faces:

$$\Pi(P, v, w) \max_{k, l} \pi(k, l) = \max_{k, l}[Pf(k, l) - vk - wl]. \quad \textbf{(11.25)}$$

In this definition we use an upper case Π to indicate that the value given by the function is the maximum profits obtainable given the prices. This function implicitly incorporates the form of the firm's production function—a process we will illustrate in Example 11.4. The profit function can refer to either long-run or short-run profit maximization, but in the latter case we would need also to specify the levels of any inputs that are fixed in the short run.

Properties of the profit function

As for the other optimized functions we have already looked at, the profit function has a number of properties that are useful for economic analysis.

---

[8]Much of the analysis here would also apply to a firm that had some market power over the price it received for its product, but we will delay a discussion of that possibility until Part 5.

1. *Homogeneity.* A doubling of all of the prices in the profit function will precisely double profits—that is, the profit function is homogeneous of degree 1 in all prices. We have already shown that marginal costs are homogeneous of degree 1 in input prices, hence a doubling of input prices and a doubling of the market price of a firm's output will not change the profit-maximizing quantity it decides to produce. But, because both revenues and costs have doubled, profits will double. This shows that with pure inflation (where all prices rise together) firms will not change their production plans and the levels of their profits will just keep up with that inflation.

2. *Profit functions are nondecreasing in output price, P.* This result seems obvious—a firm could always respond to a rise in the price of its output by not changing its input or output plans. Given the definition of profits, they must rise. Hence, if the firm changes its plans, it must be doing so in order to make even more profits. If profits were to decline, the firm would not be maximizing profits.

3. *Profit functions are nonincreasing in input prices, v, and w.* Again, this feature of the profit function seems obvious. A proof is similar to that used above in our discussion of output prices.

4. *Profit functions are convex in output prices.* This important feature of profit functions says that the profits obtainable by averaging those available from two different output prices will be at least as large as those obtainable from the average[9] of the two prices. Mathematically,

$$\frac{\Pi(P_1, v, w) + \Pi(P_2, v, w)}{2} \geq \Pi\left[\frac{P_1 + P_2}{2}, v, w\right]. \tag{11.26}$$

The intuitive reason for this is that, when firms can freely adapt their decisions to two different prices, better results are possible than when they can make only one set of choices in response to the single average price. More formally, let $P_3 = (P_1 + P_2)/2$ and let q_i, k_i, l_i represent the profit-maximizing output and input choices for these various prices. Because of the profit-maximization assumption implicit in the function Π, we can write

$$\Pi(P_3, v, w) \equiv P_3 q_3 - v k_3 - w l_3 = \frac{P_1 q_3 - v k_3 - w l_3}{2} + \frac{P_2 q_3 - v k_3 - w l_3}{2}$$

$$\leq \frac{P_1 q_1 - v k_1 - w l_1}{2} + \frac{P_2 q_2 - v k_2 - w l_2}{2}$$

$$\equiv \frac{\Pi(P_1, v, w) + \Pi(P_2, v, w)}{2}, \tag{11.27}$$

which proves Equation 11.26. The convexity of the profit function has many applications to topics such as price stabilization. Some of these are discussed in the Extensions to this chapter.

Envelope results

Because the profit function reflects an underlying process of unconstrained maximization, we may also apply the envelope theorem to see how profits respond to changes in output and input prices. This application of the theorem yields a variety of useful results. Specifically,

---

[9]Although we only discuss a simple averaging of prices here, it is clear that with convexity a condition similar to Equation 11.26 holds for any weighted average price $\bar{P} = tP_1 + (1 - t)P_2$, where $0 \leq t \leq 1$.

using the definition of profits shows that

$$\frac{\partial \Pi(P, v, w)}{\partial P} = q(P, v, w),$$

$$\frac{\partial \Pi(P, v, w)}{\partial v} = -k(P, v, w), \qquad \text{(11.28)}$$

$$\frac{\partial \Pi(P, v, w)}{\partial w} = -l(P, v, w).$$

Again, these equations make intuitive sense: a small change in output price will increase profits in proportion to how much the firm is producing, whereas a small increase in the price of an input will reduce profits in proportion to the amount of that input being employed. The first of these equations says that the firm's supply function can be calculated from its profit function by partial differentiation with respect to the output price.[10] The second and third equations show that input demand functions[11] can also be derived from the profit functions. Because the profit function itself is homogeneous of degree 1, all of the functions described in Equations 11.28 are homogeneous of degree 0. That is, a doubling of both output and input prices will not change the input levels that the firm chooses; nor will this change the firm's profit-maximizing output level. All these findings also have short-run analogues, as will be shown later with a specific example.

Producer surplus in the short run

In Chapter 5 we discussed the concept of "consumer surplus" and showed how areas below the demand curve can be used to measure the welfare costs to consumers of price changes. We also showed how such changes in welfare could be captured in the individual's expenditure function. The process of measuring the welfare effects of price changes for firms is similar in short-run analysis, and this is the topic we pursue here. However, as we show in the next chapter, measuring the welfare impact of price changes for producers in the long run requires a very different approach because most such long-term effects are felt not by firms themselves but rather by their input suppliers. In general it is this long-run approach that will prove more useful for our subsequent study of the welfare impacts of price changes.

Because the profit function is nondecreasing in output prices, we know that if $P_2 > P_1$ then

$$\Pi(P_2, \dots) \geq \Pi(P_1, \dots),$$

and it would be natural to measure the welfare gain to the firm from the price change as

$$\textbf{welfare gain} = \Pi(P_2, \dots) - \Pi(P_1, \dots). \qquad \text{(11.29)}$$

Figure 11.4 shows how this value can be measured graphically as the area bounded by the two prices and above the short-run supply curve. Intuitively, the supply curve shows the minimum price that the firm will accept for producing its output. Hence, when market price rises from P_1 to P_2, the firm is able to sell its prior output level (q_1) at a higher price and also opts to sell additional output ($q_2 - q_1$) for which, at the margin, it likewise earns added profits on all but the final unit. Hence, the total gain in the firm's profits is given by area $P_2 A B P_1$. Mathematically, we can make use of the envelope results from the previous section to derive

---

[10] This relationship is sometimes referred to as "Hotelling's lemma"—after the economist Harold Hotelling, who discovered it in the 1930s.

[11] Unlike the input demand functions derived in Chapter 10, these input demand functions are not conditional on output levels. Rather, the firm's profit-maximizing output decision has already been taken into account in the functions. This demand concept is therefore more general than the one we introduced in Chapter 10, and we will have much more to say about it in the next section.

FIGURE 11.4   Changes in Short-Run Producer Surplus Measure Firm Profits

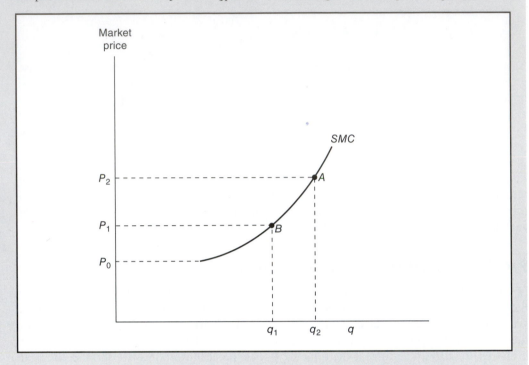

If price rises from P_1 to P_2 then the increase in the firm's profits is given by area P_2ABP_1. At a price of P_1, the firm earns short-run producer surplus given by area P_0BP_1. This measures the increase in short-run profits for the firm when it produces q_1 rather than shutting down when price is P_0 or below.

$$\text{welfare gain} = \int_{P_1}^{P_2} q(P) \, dP = \int_{P_1}^{P_2} \frac{\partial \Pi}{\partial P} \, dP = \Pi(P_2, \ldots) - \Pi(P_1, \ldots). \quad \textbf{(11.30)}$$

Thus, the geometric and mathematical measures of the welfare change agree.

Using this approach, we can also measure how much the firm values the right to produce at the prevailing market price relative to a situation where it would produce no output. If we denote the short-run shutdown price as P_0 (which may or may not be a price of zero), then the extra profits available from facing a price of P_1 are defined to be producer surplus:

$$\text{producer surplus} = \Pi(P_1, \ldots) - \Pi(P_0, \ldots) = \int_{P_0}^{P_1} q(P) \, dP. \quad \textbf{(11.31)}$$

This is shown as area P_1BP_0 in Figure 11.4. Hence we have the following formal definition.

DEFINITION   **Producer surplus.** Producer surplus is the extra return that producers earn by making transactions at the market price over and above what they would earn if nothing were produced. It is illustrated by the size of the area below the market price and above the supply curve.

In this definition we have made no distinction between the short run and the long run, though our development so far has involved only short-run analysis. In the next chapter we will see that the same definition can serve dual duty by describing producer surplus in the long run, so using this generic definition works for both concepts. Of course, as we will show, the meaning of long-run producer surplus is quite different from what we have studied here.

One more aspect of short-run producer surplus should be pointed out. Because the firm produces no output at its shutdown price, we know that $\Pi(P_0, \ldots) = -vk_1$; that is, profits at the shutdown price are solely made up of losses of all fixed costs. Therefore,

$$\textbf{producer surplus} = \Pi(P_1, \ldots) - \Pi(P_0, \ldots)$$
$$= \Pi(P_1, \ldots) - (-vk_1) = \Pi(P_1, \ldots) + vk_1. \quad \textbf{(11.32)}$$

That is, producer surplus is given by current profits being earned *plus* short-run fixed costs. Further manipulation shows that magnitude can also be expressed as

$$\textbf{producer surplus} = \Pi(P_1, \ldots) - \Pi(P_0, \ldots)$$
$$= P_1 q_1 - vk_1 - wl_1 + vk_1 = P_1 q_1 - wl_1. \quad \textbf{(11.33)}$$

In words, a firm's short-run producer surplus is given by the extent to which its revenues exceed its variable costs—this is, indeed, what the firm gains by producing in the short run rather than shutting down and producing nothing.

EXAMPLE 11.4 A Short-Run Profit Function

These various uses of the profit function can be illustrated with the Cobb-Douglas production function we have been using. Since $q = k^\alpha l^\beta$ and since we treat capital as fixed at k_1 in the short run, it follows that profits are

$$\pi = Pk_1^\alpha l^\beta - vk_1 - wl. \quad \textbf{(11.34)}$$

To find the profit function we use the first-order conditions for a maximum to eliminate l from this expression:

$$\frac{\partial \pi}{\partial l} = \beta Pk_1^\alpha l^{\beta-1} - w = 0 \quad \text{so} \quad l = \left(\frac{w}{\beta Pk_1^\alpha}\right)^{1/(\beta-1)}. \quad \textbf{(11.35)}$$

We can simplify the process of substituting this back into the profit equation by letting $A = (w/\beta Pk_1^\alpha)$. Making use of this shortcut, we have

$$\Pi(P, v, w, k_1) = Pk_1^\alpha A^{\beta/(\beta-1)} - vk_1 - wA^{1/(\beta-1)}$$
$$= wA^{1/(\beta-1)}\left(Pk_1^\alpha \frac{A}{w} - 1\right) - vk_1$$
$$= \frac{1-\beta}{\beta^{\beta/(\beta-1)}} w^{\beta/(\beta-1)} P^{1/(1-\beta)} k_1^{\alpha/(1-\beta)} - vk_1. \quad \textbf{(11.36)}$$

Though admittedly messy, this solution is what was promised—the firm's maximal profits are expressed as a function of only the prices it faces and its technology. Notice that the firm's fixed costs (vk_1) enter this expression in a simple linear way. The prices the firm faces determine the extent to which revenues exceed variable costs; then fixed costs are subtracted to obtain the final profit number.

Because it is always wise to check that one's algebra is correct, let's try out the numerical example we have been using. With $\alpha = \beta = 0.5$, $v = 3$, $w = 12$, and $k_1 = 80$, we know that at a price of $P = 12$ the firm will produce 40 units of output and use labor input of $l = 20$. Hence profits will be $\pi = R - C = 12 \cdot 40 - 3 \cdot 80 - 12 \cdot 20 = 0$. The firm will just break even at a price of $P = 12$. Using the profit function yields

$$\Pi(P, v, w, k_1) = \Pi(12, 3, 12, 80) = 0.25 \cdot 12^{-1} \cdot 12^2 \cdot 80 - 3 \cdot 80 = 0. \quad \textbf{(11.37)}$$

Thus, at a price of 12, the firm earns 240 in profits on its variable costs, and these are precisely offset by fixed costs in arriving at the final total. With a higher price for its output,

(continued)

EXAMPLE 11.4   CONTINUED

the firm earns positive profits. If the price falls below 12, however, the firm incurs short-run losses.[12]

Hotelling's lemma. We can use the profit function in Equation 11.36 together with the envelope theorem to derive this firm's short-run supply function:

$$q(P, v, w, k_1) = \frac{\partial \Pi}{\partial P} = \left(\frac{w}{\beta}\right)^{\beta/(\beta-1)} k_1^{\alpha/(1-\beta)} P^{\beta/(1-\beta)}, \qquad (11.38)$$

which is precisely the short-run supply function that we calculated in Example 11.3 (see Equation 11.20).

Producer surplus. We can also use the supply function to calculate the firm's short-run producer surplus. To do so, we again return to our numerical example: $\alpha = \beta = 0.5$, $v = 3$, $w = 12$, and $k_1 = 80$. With these parameters, the short-run supply relationship is $q = 10P/3$ and the shutdown price is zero. Hence, at a price of $P = 12$, producer surplus is

$$\text{producer surplus} = \int_0^{12} \frac{10P}{3} \, dP = \frac{10P^2}{6} \Bigg|_0^{12} = 240. \qquad (11.39)$$

This precisely equals short-run profits at a price of 12 ($\pi = 0$) plus short-run fixed costs ($= vk_1 = 3 \cdot 80 = 240$). If price were to rise to (say) 15 then producer surplus would increase to 375, which would still consist of 240 in fixed costs plus total profits at the higher price ($\Pi = 135$).

QUERY: How is the amount of short-run producer surplus here affected by changes in the rental rate for capital, v? How is it affected by changes in the wage, w?

PROFIT MAXIMIZATION AND INPUT DEMAND

Thus far, we have treated the firm's decision problem as one of choosing a profit-maximizing level of output. But our discussion throughout has made clear that the firm's output is, in fact, determined by the inputs it chooses to employ, a relationship that is summarized by the production function $q = f(k, l)$. Consequently, the firm's economic profits can also be expressed as a function of only the inputs it employs:

$$\pi(k, l) = Pq - C(q) = Pf(k, l) - (vk + wl). \qquad (11.40)$$

Viewed in this way, the profit-maximizing firm's decision problem becomes one of choosing the appropriate levels of capital and labor input.[13] The first-order conditions for a maximum are

$$\frac{\partial \pi}{\partial k} = P \frac{\partial f}{\partial k} - v = 0,$$

$$\frac{\partial \pi}{\partial l} = P \frac{\partial f}{\partial l} - w = 0. \qquad (11.41)$$

---

[12]In Table 10.2 we showed that if $q = 40$ then $SAC = 12$. Hence zero profits are also indicated by $P = 12 = SAC$.

[13]Throughout our discussion in this section, we assume that the firm is a price taker so the prices of its output and its inputs can be treated as fixed parameters. Results can be generalized fairly easily in the case where prices depend on quantity.

These conditions make the intuitively appealing point that a profit-maximizing firm should hire any input up to the point at which the input's marginal contribution to revenue is equal to the marginal cost of hiring the input. Because the firm is assumed to be a price taker in its hiring, the marginal cost of hiring any input is equal to its market price. The input's marginal contribution to revenue is given by the extra output it produces (the marginal product) times that good's market price. This demand concept is given a special name as follows.

Marginal revenue product. The marginal revenue product is the extra revenue a firm receives when it employs one more unit of an input. In the price-taking[14] case, $MRP_l = Pf_l$ and $MRP_k = Pf_k$.

DEFINITION

Hence, profit maximization requires that the firm hire each input up to the point at which its marginal revenue product is equal to its market price. Notice also that the profit-maximizing Equations 11.41 also imply cost minimization because $RTS = f_l/f_k = w/v$.

Second-order conditions

Because the profit function in Equation 11.40 depends on two variables, k and l, the second-order conditions for a profit maximum are somewhat more complex than in the single-variable case we examined earlier. In Chapter 2 we showed that, to ensure a true maximum, the profit function must be concave. That is,

$$\pi_{kk} = f_{kk} < 0, \qquad \pi_{ll} = f_{ll} < 0, \tag{11.42}$$

and

$$\pi_{kk}\pi_{ll} - \pi_{kl}^2 = f_{kk}f_{ll} - f_{kl}^2 > 0.$$

Therefore, concavity of the profit relationship amounts to requiring that the production function itself be concave. Notice that diminishing marginal productivity for each input is not sufficient to ensure increasing marginal costs. Expanding output usually requires the firm to use more capital *and* more labor. Thus we must also ensure that increases in capital input do not raise the marginal productivity of labor (and thereby reduce marginal cost) by a large enough amount to reverse the effect of diminishing marginal productivity of labor itself. The second part of Equation 11.42 therefore requires that such cross-productivity effects be relatively small—that they be dominated by diminishing marginal productivities of the inputs. If these conditions are satisfied, then marginal costs will be increasing at the profit-maximizing choices for k and l, and the first-order conditions will represent a local maximum.

Input demand functions

In principle, the first-order conditions for hiring inputs in a profit-maximizing way can be manipulated to yield input demand functions that show how hiring depends on the prices that the firm faces. We will denote these demand functions by

$$\begin{aligned} \text{capital demand} &= k(P, v, w), \\ \text{labor demand} &= l(P, v, w). \end{aligned} \tag{11.43}$$

Notice that, contrary to the input demand concepts discussed in Chapter 10, these demand functions are "unconditional"—that is, they implicitly permit the firm to adjust its output to changing prices. Hence, these demand functions provide a more complete picture of how prices affect input demand than did the contingent demand functions introduced in Chapter 10. We have already shown that these input demand functions can also be derived from the profit function through differentiation; in Example 11.5, we show that process

---

[14]If the firm is not a price taker in the output market, then this definition is generalized by using marginal revenue in place of price. That is, $MRP_l = \partial R/\partial l = \partial R/\partial q \cdot \partial q/\partial l = MR \cdot MP_l$. A similiar derivation holds for capital input.

explicitly. First, however, we will explore how changes in the price of an input might be expected to affect the demand for it. To simplify matters we look only at labor demand, but the analysis of the demand for any other input would be the same. In general, we conclude that the direction of this effect is unambiguous in all cases—that is, $\partial l / \partial w \leq 0$ no matter how many inputs there are. To develop some intuition for this result, we begin with some simple cases.

Single-input case

One reason for expecting $\partial l / \partial w$ to be negative is based on the presumption that the marginal physical product of labor declines as the quantity of labor employed increases. A decrease in w means that more labor must be hired to bring about the equality $w = P \cdot MP_l$: A fall in w must be met by a fall in MP_l (because P is fixed as required by the ceteris paribus assumption), and this can be brought about by increasing l. That this argument is strictly correct for the case of one input can be shown as follows. Write the total differential of the profit-maximizing Equation 11.41 as

$$dw = P \cdot \frac{\partial f_l}{\partial l} \cdot \frac{\partial l}{\partial w} \cdot dw$$

or

$$\frac{\partial l}{\partial w} = \frac{1}{P \cdot f_{ll}} \leq 0, \tag{11.44}$$

where the final inequality holds because the marginal productivity of labor is assumed to be diminishing ($f_{ll} \leq 0$). Hence we have shown that, at least in the single-input case, a ceteris paribus increase in the wage will cause less labor to be hired.

Two-input case

For the case of two (or more) inputs, the story is more complex. The assumption of a diminishing marginal physical product of labor can be misleading here. If w falls, there will not only be a change in l but also a change in k as a new cost-minimizing combination of inputs is chosen. When k changes, the entire f_l function changes (labor now has a different amount of capital to work with), and the simple argument used previously cannot be made. First we will use a graphic approach to suggest why, even in the two-input case, $\partial l / \partial w$ must be negative. A more precise, mathematical analysis is presented in the next section.

Substitution effect

In some ways, analyzing the two-input case is similar to the analysis of the individual's response to a change in the price of a good that was presented in Chapter 5. When w falls, we can decompose the total effect on the quantity of l hired into two components. The first of these components is called the *substitution effect*. If q is held constant at q_1, then there will be a tendency to substitute l for k in the production process. This effect is illustrated in Figure 11.5a. Because the condition for minimizing the cost of producing q_1 requires that $RTS = w/v$, a fall in w will necessitate a movement from input combination A to combination B. And because the isoquants exhibit a diminishing RTS, it is clear from the diagram that this substitution effect must be negative. A decrease in w will cause an increase in labor hired if output is held constant.

Output effect

It is not correct, however, to hold output constant. It is when we consider a change in q (the *output effect*) that the analogy to the individual's utility-maximization problem breaks down.

FIGURE 11.5 The Substitution and Output Effects of a Decrease in the Price of a Factor

When the price of labor falls, two analytically different effects come into play. One of these, the substitution effect, would cause more labor to be purchased if output were held constant. This is shown as a movement from point A to point B in (a). At point B, the cost-minimizing condition ($RTS = w/v$) is satisfied for the new, lower w. This change in w/v will also shift the firm's expansion path and its marginal cost curve. A normal situation might be for the MC curve to shift downward in response to a decrease in w as shown in (b). With this new curve (MC') a higher level of output (q_2) will be chosen. Consequently, the hiring of labor will increase (to l_2), also from this output effect.

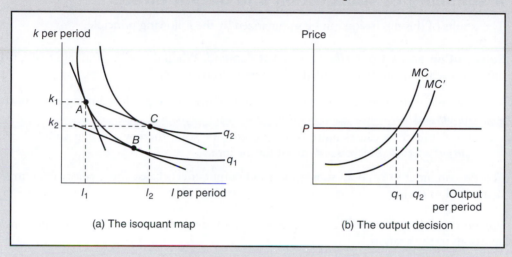

(a) The isoquant map   (b) The output decision

Consumers have budget constraints, but firms do not. Firms produce as much as the available demand allows. To investigate what happens to the quantity of output produced, we must investigate the firm's profit-maximizing output decision. A change in w, because it changes relative input costs, will shift the firm's expansion path. Consequently, all the firm's cost curves will be shifted, and probably some output level other than q_1 will be chosen. Figure 11.5b shows what might be considered the "normal" case. There the fall in w causes MC to shift downward to MC'. Consequently, the profit-maximizing level of output rises from q_1 to q_2. The profit-maximizing condition ($P = MC$) is now satisfied at a higher level of output. Returning to Figure 11.5a, this increase in output will cause even more l to be demanded as long as l is not an inferior input (see below). The result of both the substitution and output effects will be to move the input choice to point C on the firm's isoquant map. Both effects work to increase the quantity of labor hired in response to a decrease in the real wage.

The analysis provided in Figure 11.5 assumed that the market price (or marginal revenue, if this does not equal price) of the good being produced remained constant. This would be an appropriate assumption if only one firm in an industry experienced a fall in unit labor costs. However, if the decline were industrywide then a slightly different analysis would be required. In that case *all* firms' marginal cost curves would shift outward, and hence the industry supply curve would shift also. Assuming that output demand is downward sloping, this will lead to a decline in product price. Output for the industry and for the typical firm will still increase and (as before) more labor will be hired, but the precise cause of the output effect is different (see Problem 11.11).

Cross-price effects

We have shown that, at least in simple cases, $\partial l / \partial w$ is unambiguously negative; substitution *and* output effects cause more labor to be hired when the wage rate falls. From Figure 11.5 it should be clear that no definite statement can be made about how capital usage responds to the wage change. That is, the sign of $\partial k / \partial w$ is indeterminate. In the simple two-input case, a fall in the wage will cause a substitution away from capital; that is, less capital will be used to produce a given output level. However, the output effect will cause more capital to be demanded as part of the firm's increased production plan. Thus substitution and output effects in this case work in opposite directions, and no definite conclusion about the sign of $\partial k / \partial w$ is possible.

A summary of substitution and output effects

The results of this discussion can be summarized by the following principle.

OPTIMIZATION PRINCIPLE

Substitution and output effects in input demand. When the price of an input falls, two effects cause the quantity demanded of that input to rise:

1. the *substitution effect* causes any given output level to be produced using more of the input; and
2. the fall in costs causes more of the good to be sold, thereby creating an additional *output effect* that increases demand for the input.

For a rise in input price, both substitution and output effects cause the quantity of an input demanded to decline.

We now provide a more precise development of these concepts using a mathematical approach to the analysis.

A mathematical development

Our mathematical development of the substitution and output effects that arise from the change in an input price follows the method we used to study the effect of price changes in consumer theory. The final result is a Slutsky-style equation that resembles the one we derived in Chapter 5. However, the ambiguity stemming from Giffen's paradox in the theory of consumption demand does not occur here.

We start with a reminder that we have two concepts of demand for any input (say, labor): (1) the conditional demand for labor, denoted by $l^c(v, w, q)$; and (2) the unconditional demand for labor, which is denoted by $l(P, v, w)$. At the profit-maximizing choice for labor input, these two concepts agree about the amount of labor hired. The two concepts also agree on the level of output produced (which is a function of all the prices):

$$l(P, v, w) = l^c(v, w, q) = l^c(v, w, q(P, v, w)). \tag{11.45}$$

Differentiation of this expression with respect to the wage (and holding the other prices constant) yields

$$\frac{\partial l(P, v, w)}{\partial w} = \frac{\partial l^c(v, w, q)}{\partial w} + \frac{\partial l^c(v, w, q)}{\partial q} \cdot \frac{\partial q(P, v, w)}{\partial w}. \tag{11.46}$$

So, the effect of a change in the wage on the demand for labor is the sum of two components: a substitution effect in which output is held constant; and an output effect in which the wage change has its effect through changing the quantity of output that the firm opts to produce. The first of these effects is clearly negative—because the production function is quasi-concave (i.e., it has convex isoquants), the output-contingent demand for labor must be negatively sloped. Figure 11.5b provides an intuitive illustration of why the output effect in Equation 11.46 is negative, but it can hardly be called a proof. The particular complicating factor is the possibility that the input under consideration (here, labor) may be inferior. Perhaps oddly, inferior inputs also have negative output effects, but for rather arcane reasons that are best relegated to a footnote.[15] The bottom line, however, is that Giffen's paradox cannot occur in the theory of the firm's demand for inputs: input demand functions are unambiguously downward sloping. In this case the theory of profit maximization imposes more restrictions on what might happen than does the theory of utility maximization. In Example 11.5 we show how decomposing input demand into its substitution and output components can yield useful insights into how changes in input prices actually affect firms.

EXAMPLE 11.5 Decomposing Input Demand into Substitution and Output Components

To study input demand we need to start with a production function that has two features: (1) the function must permit capital-labor substitution (because substitution is an important part of the story); and (2) the production function must exhibit increasing marginal costs (so that the second-order conditions for profit maximization are satisfied). One function that satisfies these conditions is a three-input Cobb-Douglas function when one of the inputs is held fixed. So, let $q = f(k, l, g) = k^{0.25} l^{0.25} g^{0.5}$, where k and l are the familiar capital and labor inputs and g is a third input (size of the factory) that is held fixed at $g = 16$ (square meters?) for all of our analysis. The short-run production function is therefore $q = 4k^{0.25} l^{0.25}$. We assume that the factory can be rented at a cost of r per square meter per period. To study the demand for (say) labor input, we need both the total cost function and the profit function implied by this production function. Mercifully, your author has computed these functions for you as

$$C(v, w, r, q) = \frac{q^2 v^{0.5} w^{0.5}}{8} + 16r \qquad \textbf{(11.47)}$$

and

$$\Pi(P, v, w, r) = 2P^2 v^{-0.5} w^{-0.5} - 16r. \qquad \textbf{(11.48)}$$

As expected, the costs of the fixed input (g) enter as a constant in these equations, and these costs will play very little role in our analysis.

Envelope Results

Labor-demand relationships can be derived from both of these functions through differentiation:

$$l^c(v, w, r, q) = \frac{\partial C}{\partial w} = \frac{q^2 v^{0.5} w^{-0.5}}{16} \qquad \textbf{(11.49)}$$

and

$$l(P, v, w, r) = -\frac{\partial \Pi}{\partial w} = P^2 v^{-0.5} w^{-1.5}. \qquad \textbf{(11.50)}$$

These functions already suggest that a change in the wage has a larger effect on total labor demand than it does on contingent labor demand because the exponent of w is more negative in the total demand equation. That is, the output effect must also be playing a role here. To see that directly, we turn to some numbers.

(continued)

---

[15]In words, an increase in the price of an inferior reduces marginal cost and thereby increases output. But when output increases, less of the inferior input is hired. Hence the end result is a decrease in quantity demanded in response to an increase in price. A formal proof makes extensive use of envelope relationships:

$$\textbf{output effect} = \frac{\partial l^c}{\partial q} \cdot \frac{\partial q}{\partial w} = \frac{\partial l^c}{\partial q} \cdot \frac{-\partial l}{\partial P} = -\left(\frac{\partial l^c}{\partial q}\right)^2 \cdot \frac{\partial q}{\partial P}.$$

Because the second-order conditions for profit maximization require that $\partial q / \partial P > 0$, the output effect is clearly negative.

EXAMPLE 11.5   CONTINUED

Numerical example. Let's start again with the assumed values that we have been using in several previous examples: $v = 3$, $w = 12$, and $P = 60$. Let's first calculate what output the firm will choose in this situation. To do so, we need its supply function:

$$q(P, v, w, r) = \frac{\partial \Pi}{\partial P} = 4Pv^{-0.5}w^{-0.5}. \qquad (11.51)$$

With this function and the prices we have chosen, the firm's profit-maximizing output level is (surprise) $q = 40$. With these prices and an output level of 40, both of the demand functions predict that the firm will hire $l = 50$. Because the RTS here is given by k/l, we also know that $k/l = w/v$, so at these prices $k = 200$.

Suppose now that the wage rate rises to $w = 27$ but that the other prices remain unchanged. The firm's supply function (Equation 11.51) shows that it will now produce $q = 26.67$. The rise in the wage shifts the firm's marginal cost curve upward and, with a constant output price, this causes the firm to produce less. To produce this output, either of the labor-demand functions can be used to show that the firm will hire $l = 14.8$. Hiring of capital will also fall to $k = 133.3$ because of the large reduction in output.

We can decompose the fall in labor hiring from $l = 50$ to $l = 14.8$ into substitution and output effects by using the contingent demand function. If the firm had continued to produce $q = 40$ even though the wage rose, Equation 11.49 shows that it would have used $l = 33.33$. Capital input would have increased to $k = 300$. Because we are holding output constant at its initial level of $q = 40$, these changes represent the firm's substitution effects in response to the higher wage.

The decline in output needed to restore profit maximization causes the firm to cut back on its output. In doing so it substantially reduces its use of both inputs. Notice in particular that, in this example, the rise in the wage not only caused labor usage to decline sharply but also caused capital usage to fall because of the large output effect.

QUERY: How would the calculations in this problem be affected if all firms had experienced the rise in wages? Would the decline in labor (and capital) demand be greater or smaller than found here?

SUMMARY

In this chapter we studied the supply decision of a profit-maximizing firm. Our general goal was to show how such a firm responds to price signals from the marketplace. In addressing that question, we developed a number of analytical results.

- In order to maximize profits, the firm should choose to produce that output level for which marginal revenue (the revenue from selling one more unit) is equal to marginal cost (the cost of producing one more unit).

- If a firm is a price taker then its output decisions do not affect the price of its output, so marginal revenue is given by this price. If the firm faces a downward-sloping demand for its output, however, then it can sell more only at a lower price. In this case marginal revenue will be less than price and may even be negative.

- Marginal revenue and the price elasticity of demand are related by the formula

$$MR = P\left(1 + \frac{1}{e_{q,p}}\right),$$

where P is the market price of the firm's output and $e_{q,p}$ is the price elasticity of demand for its product.

- The supply curve for a price-taking, profit-maximizing firm is given by the positively sloped portion of its marginal cost curve above the point of minimum average variable cost (AVC). If price falls below minimum AVC, the firm's profit-maximizing choice is to shut down and produce nothing.

- The firm's reactions to changes in the various prices it faces can be studied through use of its profit function,

$\Pi(P, v, w)$. That function shows the maximum profits that the firm can achieve given the price for its output, the prices of its input, and its production technology. The profit function yields particularly useful envelope results. Differentiation with respect to market price yields the supply function while differentiation with respect to any input price yields (the negative of) the demand function for that input.

- Short-run changes in market price result in changes to the firm's short-run profitability. These can be measured graphically by changes in the size of producer surplus.

The profit function can also be used to calculate changes in producer surplus.

- Profit maximization provides a theory of the firm's derived demand for inputs. The firm will hire any input up to the point at which its marginal revenue product is just equal to its per-unit market price. Increases in the price of an input will induce substitution and output effects that cause the firm to reduce hiring of that input.

PROBLEMS

11.1

John's Lawn Moving Service is a small business that acts as a price taker (i.e., $MR = P$). The prevailing market price of lawn mowing is $20 per acre. John's costs are given by

$$\text{total cost} = 0.1q^2 + 10q + 50,$$

where q = the number of acres John chooses to cut a day.

a. How many acres should John choose to cut in order to maximize profit?

b. Calculate John's maximum daily profit.

c. Graph these results and label John's supply curve.

11.2

Would a lump-sum profits tax affect the profit-maximizing quantity of output? How about a proportional tax on profits? How about a tax assessed on each unit of output? How about a tax on labor input?

11.3

This problem concerns the relationship between demand and marginal revenue curves for a few functional forms.

a. Show that, for a linear demand curve, the marginal revenue curve bisects the distance between the vertical axis and the demand curve for any price.

b. Show that, for any linear demand curve, the vertical distance between the demand and marginal revenue curves is $-1/b \cdot q$, where $b \, (< 0)$ is the slope of the demand curve.

c. Show that, for a constant elasticity demand curve of the form $q = aP^b$, the vertical distance between the demand and marginal revenue curves is a constant ratio of the height of the demand curve, with this constant depending on the price elasticity of demand.

d. Show that, for any downward-sloping demand curve, the vertical distance between the demand and marginal revenue curves at any point can be found by using a linear approximation to the demand curve at that point and applying the procedure described in part (b).

e. Graph the results of parts (a)–(d) of this problem.

11.4

Universal Widget produces high-quality widgets at its plant in Gulch, Nevada, for sale throughout the world. The cost function for total widget production (q) is given by

$$\text{total cost} = 0.25q^2.$$

Widgets are demanded only in Australia (where the demand curve is given by $q = 100 - 2P$) and Lapland (where the demand curve is given by $q = 100 - 4P$). If Universal Widget can control the quantities supplied to each market, how many should it sell in each location in order to maximize total profits? What price will be charged in each location?

11.5

The production function for a firm in the business of calculator assembly is given by

$$q = 2\sqrt{l},$$

where q denotes finished calculator output and l denotes hours of labor input. The firm is a price taker both for calculators (which sell for P) and for workers (which can be hired at a wage rate of w per hour).

    a. What is the total cost function for this firm?

    b. What is the profit function for this firm?

    c. What is the supply function for assembled calculators $[q(P, w)]$?

    d. What is this firm's demand for labor function $[l(P, w)]$?

    e. Describe intuitively why these functions have the form they do.

11.6

The market for high-quality caviar is dependent on the weather. If the weather is good, there are many fancy parties and caviar sells for $30 per pound. In bad weather it sells for only $20 per pound. Caviar produced one week will not keep until the next week. A small caviar producer has a cost function given by

$$C = 0.5q^2 + 5q + 100,$$

where q is weekly caviar production. Production decisions must be made before the weather (and the price of caviar) is known, but it is known that good weather and bad weather each occur with a probability of 0.5.

    a. How much caviar should this firm produce if it wishes to maximize the expected value of its profits?

    b. Suppose the owner of this firm has a utility function of the form

$$\text{utility} = \sqrt{\pi},$$

       where π is weekly profits. What is the expected utility associated with the output strategy defined in part (a)?

    c. Can this firm owner obtain a higher utility of profits by producing some output other than that specified in parts (a) and (b)? Explain.

    d. Suppose this firm could predict next week's price but could not influence that price. What strategy would maximize expected profits in this case? What would expected profits be?

11.7

The Acme Heavy Equipment School teaches students how to drive construction machinery. The number of students that the school can educate per week is given by $q = 10 \min(k, l)^\gamma$, where k is the number of backhoes the firm rents per week, l is the number of instructors hired each week, and γ is a parameter indicating the returns to scale in this production function.

    a. Explain why development of a profit-maximizing model here requires $0 < \gamma < 1$.

    b. Suppposing $\gamma = 0.5$, calculate the firm's total cost function and profit function.

    c. If $v = 1000$, $w = 500$, and $P = 600$, how many students will Acme serve and what are its profits?

    d. If the price students are willing to pay rises to $P = 900$, how much will profits change?

    e. Graph Acme's supply curve for student slots, and show that the increase in profits calculated in part (d) can be plotted on that graph.

11.8

How would you expect an increase in output price, P, to affect the demand for capital and labor inputs?

    a. Explain graphically why, if neither input is inferior, it seems clear that a rise in P must not reduce the demand for either factor.

    b. Show that the graphical presumption from part (a) is demonstrated by the input demand functions that can be derived in the Cobb-Douglas case.

    c. Use the profit function to show how the presence of inferior inputs would lead to ambiguity in the effect of P on input demand.

Analytical Problems

11.9 A CES profit function

With a CES production function of the form $q = (k^\rho + l^\rho)^{\gamma/\rho}$ a whole lot of algebra is needed to compute the profit function as $\Pi(P, v, w) = KP^{1/(1-\gamma)}(v^{1-\sigma} + w^{1-\sigma})^{\gamma/(1-\sigma)(\gamma-1)}$, where $\sigma = 1/(1-\rho)$ and K is a constant.

    a. If you are a glutton for punishment (or if your instructor is), prove that the profit function takes this form. Perhaps the easiest way to do so is to start from the CES cost function in Example 10.2.

    b. Explain why this profit function provides a reasonable representation of a firm's behavior only for $0 < \gamma < 1$.

    c. Explain the role of the elasticity of substitution (σ) in this profit function.

    d. What is the supply function in this case? How does σ determine the extent to which that function shifts when input prices change?

    e. Derive the input demand functions in this case. How are these functions affected by the size of σ?

11.10 Some envelope results

Young's theorem can be used in combination with the envelope results in this chapter to derive some useful results.

    a. Show that $\partial l(P, v, w)/\partial v = \partial k(P, v, w)/\partial w$. Interpret this result using subtitution and output effects.

    b. Use the result from part (a) to show how a unit tax on labor would be expected to affect capital input.

    c. Show that $\partial q/\partial w = -\partial l/\partial P$. Interpret this result.

    d. Use the result from part (c) to discuss how a unit tax on labor input would affect quantity supplied.

11.11 More on the derived demand with two inputs

The demand for any input depends ultimately on the demand for the goods that input produces. This can be shown most explicitly by deriving an entire industry's demand for inputs. To do so, we assume that an industry produces a homogeneous good, Q, under constant returns to scale using only capital and labor. The demand function for Q is given by $Q = D(P)$, where P is the market price of the good being produced. Because of the constant returns-to-scale assumption, $P = MC = AC$. Throughout this problem let $C(v, w, 1)$ be the firm's unit cost function.

a. Explain why the total industry demands for capital and labor are given by $K = QC_v$ and $L = QC_w$.

b. Show that

$$\frac{\partial K}{\partial v} = QC_{vv} + D'C_v^2 \quad \text{and} \quad \frac{\partial L}{\partial w} = QC_{ww} + D'C_w^2.$$

c. Prove that

$$C_{vv} = \frac{-w}{v} C_{vw} \quad \text{and} \quad C_{ww} = \frac{-v}{w} C_{vw}.$$

d. Use the results from parts (b) and (c) together with the elasticity of substitution defined as $\sigma = CC_{vw}/C_v C_w$ to show that

$$\frac{\partial K}{\partial v} = \frac{wL}{Q} \cdot \frac{\sigma K}{vC} + \frac{D'K^2}{Q^2} \quad \text{and} \quad \frac{\partial L}{\partial w} = \frac{vK}{Q} \cdot \frac{\sigma L}{wC} + \frac{D'L^2}{Q^2}.$$

e. Convert the derivatives in part (d) into elasticities to show that

$$e_{K,v} = -s_L\sigma + s_K e_{Q,P} \quad \text{and} \quad e_{L,w} = -s_K\sigma + s_L e_{Q,P},$$

where $e_{Q,P}$ is the price elasticity of demand for the product being produced.

f. Discuss the importance of the results in part (e) using the notions of substitution and output effects from Chapter 11.

Note: The notion that the elasticity of the derived demand for an input depends on the price elasticity of demand for the output being produced was first suggested by Alfred Marshall. The proof given here follows that in D. Hamermesh, *Labor Demand* (Princeton, NJ: Princeton University Press, 1993).

11.12 Cross-price effects in input demand

With two inputs, cross-price effects on input demand can be easily calculated using the procedure outlined in Problem 11.11.

a. Use steps (b), (d), and (e) from Problem 11.11 to show that

$$e_{K,w} = s_L(\sigma + e_{Q,P}) \quad \text{and} \quad e_{L,v} = s_K(\sigma + e_{Q,P}).$$

b. Describe intuitively why input shares appear somewhat differently in the demand elasticities in part (e) of Problem 11.11 than they do in part (a) of this problem.

c. The expression computed in part (a) can be easily generalized to the many-input case as $e_{x_i, w_j} = s_j(A_{i,j} + e_{Q,P})$, where $A_{i,j}$ is the Allen elasticity of substitution defined in Problem 10.12. For reasons described in Problems 10.11 and 10.12, this approach to input demand in the multi-input case is generally inferior to using Morishima elasticities. One oddity might be mentioned, however. For the case $i = j$ this expression seems to say that $e_{L,w} = s_L(A_{L,L} + e_{Q,P})$, and if we jumped to the conclusion that $A_{L,L} = \sigma$ in the two-input case then this would contradict the result from Problem 11.11. You can resolve this paradox by using the definitions from Problem 10.12 to show that, with two inputs, $A_{L,L} = (-s_K/s_L) \cdot A_{K,L} = (-s_K/s_L) \cdot \sigma$ and so there is no disagreement.

SUGGESTIONS FOR FURTHER READING

Ferguson, C. E. *The Neoclassical Theory of Production and Distribution*. Cambridge, UK: Cambridge University Press, 1969.

Provides a complete analysis of the output effect in factor demand. Also shows how the degree of substitutability affects many of the results in this chapter.

Hicks, J. R. *Value and Capital*, 2nd ed. Oxford: Oxford University Press, 1947.

The Appendix looks in detail at the notion of factor complementarity.

Mas-Colell, A., M. D. Whinston, and J. R. Green. *Microeconomic Theory*. New York: Oxford University Press, 1995.

Provides an elegant introduction to the theory of production using vector and matrix notation. This allows for an arbitrary number of inputs and outputs.

Samuelson, P. A. *Foundations of Economic Analysis*. Cambridge, MA: Harvard University Press, 1947.

Early development of the profit function idea together with a nice discussion of the consequences of constant returns to scale for market equilibrium.

Sydsaeter, K., A. Strom, and P. Berck. *Economists' Mathematical Manual*, 3rd ed. Berlin: Springer-Verlag, 2000.

Chapter 25 offers formulas for a number of profit and factor demand functions.

Varian, H. R. *Microeconomic Analysis*, 3rd ed. New York: W. W. Norton, 1992.

Includes an entire chapter on the profit function. Varian offers a novel approach for comparing short- and long-run responses using the Le Chatelier principle.

EXTENSIONS

Applications of the Profit Function

In Chapter 11 we introduced the profit function. That function summarizes the firm's "bottom line" as it depends on the prices it faces for its outputs and inputs. In these extensions we show how some of the properties of the profit function have been used to assess important empirical and theoretical questions.

E11.1 Convexity and price stabilization

Convexity of the profit function implies that a firm will generally prefer a fluctuating output price to one that is stabilized (say, through government intervention) at its mean value. The result runs contrary to the direction of economic policy in many less developed countries, which tends to stress the desirability of stabilization of commodity prices. Several factors may account for this seeming paradox. First, many plans to "stabilize" commodity prices are in reality plans to raise the average level of these prices. Cartels of producers often have this as their primary goal, for example. Second, the convexity result applies for a single price-taking firm. From the perspective of the entire market, total revenues from stabilized or fluctuating prices will depend on the nature of the demand for the product.[1] A third complication that must be addressed in assessing price stabilization schemes is firms' expectations of future prices. When commodities can be stored, optimal production decisions in the presence of price stabilization schemes can be quite complex. Finally, the purpose of price stabilization schemes may in some situations be focused more on reducing risks for the consumers of basic commodities (such as food) than on the welfare of producers. Still, this fundamental property of the profit function suggests caution in devising price stabilization schemes that have desirable long-run effects on producers. For an extended theoretical analysis of these issues, see Newbury and Stiglitz (1981).

E11.2 Producer surplus and the short-run costs of disease

Disease episodes can severely disrupt markets, leading to short-run losses in producer and consumer surplus.

For firms, these losses can be computed as the short-run losses of profits from temporarily lower prices for their output or from the temporarily higher input prices they must pay. A particular extensive set of such calculations is provided by Harrington, Krupnick, and Spofford (1991) in their detailed study of a giardiasis outbreak in Pennsylvania in 1983. Although consumers suffered most of the losses associated with this outbreak, the authors also calculate substantial losses for restaurants and bars in the immediate area. Such losses arose both from reduced business for these firms and from the temporary need to use bottled water and other high-cost inputs in their operations. Quantitative calculations of these losses are based on profit functions described by the authors.

E11.3 Profit functions and productivity measurement

In Chapter 9 we showed that total factor productivity growth is usually measured as

$$G_A = G_q - s_k G_k - s_l G_l,$$

where

$$G_x = \frac{dx/dt}{x} = \frac{d \ln x}{dt}$$

and where s_k and s_l are the shares of capital and labor in total costs, respectively. One difficulty with making this calculation is that it requires measuring changes in input usage over time—a measurement that can be especially difficult for capital. The profit function provides an alternative way of measuring the same phenomenon without estimating input usage directly. To understand the logic of this approach, consider the production function we wish to examine, $q = f(k, l, t)$. We want to know how output would change over time if input levels were held constant. That is, we wish to measure $\partial(\ln q)/\partial t = f_t/f$. Notice the use of partial differentiation in this expression—in words, we want to know the proportionate change in f over time when other inputs are held constant. If the production function exhibits constant returns to scale and if the firm is a price taker for both inputs and its output, it is fairly easy[2] to show that this partial derivative is the measure of

---

[1]Specifically, for a constant elasticity demand function, total revenue will be a concave function of price if demand is inelastic but convex if demand is elastic. Hence, in the elastic case, producers will obtain higher total revenues from a fluctuating price than from a price stabilized at its mean value.

[2]The proof proceeds by differentiating the production function logarithmically with respect to time as $G_q = d(\ln q)/dt = e_{q,k} G_k + e_{q,l} G_l + f_t/f$ and then recognizing that, with constant returns to scale and price-taking behavior, $e_{q,k} = s_k$ and $e_{q,l} = s_l$.

changing total factor productivity we want—that is, $G_A = f_t/f$. Now consider the profit function, $\Pi(P, v, w, t)$. By definition, profits are given by

$$\pi = Pq - vk - wl = Pf - vk - wl,$$

so

$$\frac{\partial \ln \Pi}{\partial t} = \frac{Pf_t}{\Pi}$$

and thus

$$G_A = \frac{f_t}{f} = \frac{\Pi}{Pf} \cdot \frac{\partial \ln \Pi}{\partial t} = \frac{\Pi}{Pq} \cdot \frac{\partial \ln \Pi}{\partial t}. \qquad \textbf{(i)}$$

So, in this special case, changes in total factor productivity can be inferred from the share of profits in total revenue and the time derivative of the log of the profit function. But this conclusion can be readily generalized to cases of nonconstant returns to scale and even to firms that produce multiple outputs (see e.g. Kumbhakar, 2002). Hence, for situations where input and output prices are more readily available than input quantities, using the profit function is an attractive way to proceed.

Three examples of this use for the profit function might be mentioned. Karagiannis and Mergos (2000) reassess the major increases in total factor productivity that have been experienced by U.S. agriculture during the past 50 years using the profit function approach. They find results that are broadly consistent with those using more conventional measures. Huang (2000) adopts the same approach in a study of Taiwanese banking and finds significant increases in productivity that could not be detected using other methods. Finally, Coelli and Perelman (2000) use a modified profit function approach to measure the relative efficiency of European railroads. Perhaps not surprisingly, they find that Dutch railroads are the most efficient in Europe whereas those in Italy are the least efficient.

References

Coelli, T., and S. Perelman. "Technical Efficiency of European Railways: A Distance Function Approach." *Applied Economics* (December 2000): 1967–76.

Harrington, W. A., J. Krupnick, and W. O. Spofford. *Economics and Episodic Disease: The Benefits of Preventing a Giardiasis Outbreak.* Baltimore: Johns Hopkins University Press, 1991.

Huang, T. "Estimating X-Efficiency in Taiwanese Banking Using a Translog Shadow Profit Function." *Journal of Productivity Analysis* (November 2000): 225–45.

Karagiannis, G., and G. J. Mergos. "Total Factor Productivity Growth and Technical Change in a Profit Function Framework." *Journal of Productivity Analysis* (July 2000): 31–51.

Kumbhakar, S. "Productivity Measurement: A Profit Function Approach." *Applied Economics Letters* (April 2002): 331–34.

Newbury, D. M. G., and J. E. Stiglitz. *The Theory of Commodity Price Stabilization.* Oxford: Oxford University Press, 1981.

In Parts 2 and 3 we developed models to explain the demand for goods by utility-maximizing individuals and the supply of goods by profit-maximizing firms. In this part we will bring these two strands of analysis together to describe the process by which prices are determined. We will focus on only one specific model of price determination, the perfectly competitive model. That model assumes a large enough number of demanders and suppliers of each good so that each must be a price taker. In Part 5 we will illustrate some of the models that result from relaxing the strict price-taking assumptions of the competitive case, but in this part we assume price-taking behavior throughout.

Chapter 12 develops the familiar partial equilibrium model of price determination in competitive markets. The principal result is the Marshallian "cross" diagram of supply and demand that we first discussed in Chapter 1. This model illustrates a "partial" equilibrium view of price determination because it focuses on only a single market.

In the concluding sections of the chapter we show some of the ways in which such models are applied. A specific focus is on illustrating how the competitive model can be used to judge the welfare consequences for market participants of changes in market equilibria.

Although the partial equilibrium competitive model is useful for studying a single market in detail, it is inappropriate for examining relationships among markets. To capture such cross-market effects requires the development of "general" equilibrium models—a topic we take up in **Chapter 13**. There we show how an entire economy can be viewed as a system of interconnected competitive markets that determine all prices simultaneously. We also examine how welfare consequences of various economic questions can be studied in this model.

The Partial Equilibrium Competitive Model

In this chapter we describe the familiar model of price determination under perfect competition that was originally developed by Alfred Marshall in the late nineteenth century. That is, we provide a fairly complete analysis of the supply-demand mechanism as it applies to a single market. This is perhaps the most widely used model for the study of prices.

MARKET DEMAND

In Part 2 we showed how to construct individual demand functions that illustrate changes in the quantity of a good that a utility-maximizing individual chooses as the market price and other factors change. With only two goods (x and y) we concluded that an individual's (Marshallian) demand function can be summarized as

$$\textbf{quantity of } x \textbf{ demanded} = x(p_x, p_y, I). \tag{12.1}$$

Now we wish to show how these demand functions can be added up to reflect the demand of all individuals in a marketplace. Using a subscript i ($i = 1, n$) to represent each person's demand function for good x, we can define the total demand in the market as

$$\textbf{market demand for } X = \sum_{i=1}^{n} x_i(p_x, p_y, I_i). \tag{12.2}$$

Notice three things about this summation. First, we assume that everyone in this marketplace faces the same prices for both goods. That is, p_x and p_y enter Equation 12.2 without person-specific subscripts. On the other hand, each person's income enters into his or her own specific demand function. Market demand depends not only on the total income of all market participants but also on how that income is distributed among consumers. Finally, observe that we have used an uppercase X to refer to market demand—a notation we will soon modify.

The market demand curve

Equation 12.2 makes clear that the total quantity of a good demanded depends not only on its own price but also on the prices of other goods and on the income of each person. To construct the market demand curve for good X, we allow p_x to vary while holding p_y and the income of each person constant. Figure 12.1 shows this construction for the case where there are only two consumers in the market. For each potential price of x, the point on the market demand curve for X is found by adding up the quantities demanded by each person. For example, at a price of p_x^* person 1 demands x_1^* and person 2 demands x_2^*. The total quantity demanded in this two-person market is the sum of these two amounts ($X^* = x_1^* + x_2^*$). The point p_x^*, X^* is therefore one point on the market demand curve for X. Other points on the

FIGURE 12.1   Construction of a Market Demand Curve from Individual Demand Curves

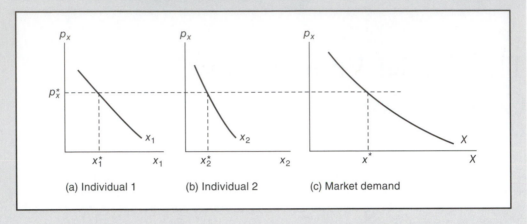

A market demand curve is the "horizontal sum" of each individual's demand curve. At each price the quantity demanded in the market is the sum of the amounts each individual demands. For example, at p_x^* the demand in the market is $x_1^* + x_2^* = x^*$.

(a) Individual 1   (b) Individual 2   (c) Market demand

curve are derived in a similar way. The market demand curve is thus a "horizontal sum" of each individual's demand curve.[1]

Shifts in the market demand curve

The market demand curve, then, summarizes the ceteris paribus relationship between X and p_x. It is important to keep in mind that the curve is in reality a two-dimensional representation of a many-variable function. Changes in p_x result in movements along this curve, but changes in any of the other determinants of the demand for X cause the curve to shift to a new position. A general rise in incomes would, for example, cause the demand curve to shift outward (assuming X is a normal good) because each individual would choose to buy more X at every price. Similarly, a rise in p_y would shift the demand curve to X outward if individuals regarded X and Y as substitutes, but it would shift the demand curve for X inward if the goods were regarded as complements. Accounting for all such shifts may sometimes require returning to examine the individual demand functions that constitute the market relationship, especially when examining situations in which the distribution of income changes and thereby raises some incomes while reducing others. To keep matters straight, economists usually reserve the term *change in quantity demanded* for a movement along a fixed demand curve in response to a change in p_x. Alternatively, any shift in the position of the demand curve is referred to as a *change in demand*.

EXAMPLE 12.1 Shifts in Market Demand

These ideas can be illustrated with a simple set of linear demand functions. Suppose individual 1's demand for oranges (x, measured in dozens per year) is given by[2]

$$x_1 = 10 - 2p_x + 0.1I_1 + 0.5p_y, \tag{12.3}$$

---

[1]Compensated market demand curves can be constructed in exactly the same way by summing each individual's compensated demand. Such a compensated market demand curve would hold each person's utility constant.

[2]This linear form is used to illustrate some issues in aggregation. It is difficult to defend this form theoretically, however. For example, it is not homogeneous of degree 0 in all prices and income.

where

p_x = price of oranges (dollars per dozen),
I_1 = individual 1's income (in thousands of dollars),
p_y = price of grapefruit (a gross substitute for oranges—dollars per dozen).

Individual 2's demand for oranges is given by

$$x_2 = 17 - p_x + 0.05I_2 + 0.5p_y. \tag{12.4}$$

Hence the market demand function is

$$X(p_x, p_y, I_1, I_2) = x_1 + x_2 = 27 - 3p_x + 0.1I_1 + 0.05I_2 + p_y. \tag{12.5}$$

Here the coefficient for the price of oranges represents the sum of the two individuals' coefficients, as does the coefficient for grapefruit prices. This reflects the assumption that orange and grapefruit markets are characterized by the law of one price. Because the individuals have differing coefficients for income, however, the demand function depends on each person's income.

To graph Equation 12.5 as a market demand curve, we must assume values for I_1, I_2, and p_y (because the demand curve reflects only the two-dimensional relationship between x and p_x). If $I_1 = 40$, $I_2 = 20$, and $p_y = 4$, then the market demand curve is given by

$$X = 27 - 3p_x + 4 + 1 + 4 = 36 - 3p_x, \tag{12.6}$$

which is a simple linear demand curve. If the price of grapefruit were to rise to $p_y = 6$ then the curve would, assuming incomes remain unchanged, shift outward to

$$X = 27 - 3p_x + 4 + 1 + 6 = 38 - 3p_x, \tag{12.7}$$

whereas an income tax that took 10 (thousand dollars) from individual 1 and transferred it to individual 2 would shift the demand curve inward to

$$X = 27 - 3p_x + 3 + 1.5 + 4 = 35.5 - 3p_x \tag{12.8}$$

because individual 1 has a larger marginal effect of income changes on orange purchases. All of these changes shift the demand curve in a parallel way because, in this linear case, none of them affects either individual's coefficient for p_x. In all cases, a rise in p_x of 0.10 (ten cents) would cause X to fall by 0.30 (dozen per year).

QUERY: For this linear case, when would it be possible to express market demand as a linear function of total income $(I_1 + I_2)$? Alternatively, suppose the individuals had differing coefficients for p_y. Would that change the analysis in any fundamental way?

Generalizations

Although our construction concerns only two goods and two individuals, it is easily generalized. Suppose there are n goods (denoted by $x_i, i = 1, n$) with prices $p_i, i = 1, n$. Assume also that there are m individuals in society. Then the jth individual's demand for the ith good will depend on all prices and on I_j, the income of this person. This can be denoted by

$$x_{i,j} = x_{i,j}(p_1, \dots, p_n, I_j), \tag{12.9}$$

where $i = 1, n$ and $j = 1, m$.

Using these individual demand functions, market demand concepts are provided by the following definition.

DEFINITION **Market demand.** The *market demand function* for a particular good (X_i) is the sum of each individual's demand for that good:

$$X_i = \sum_{j=1}^{m} x_{i,j}(p_1, \ldots, p_n, I_j). \tag{12.10}$$

The *market demand curve* for X_i is constructed from the demand function by varying p_i, while holding all other determinants of X_i constant. Assuming that each individual's demand curve is downward sloping, this market demand curve will also be downward sloping.

Of course, this definition is just a generalization of our prior discussion, but three features warrant repetition. First, the functional representation of Equation 12.10 makes clear that the demand for X_i depends not only on p_i but also on the prices of all other goods. A change in one of those other prices would therefore be expected to shift the demand curve to a new position. Second, the functional notation indicates that the demand for X_i depends on the entire distribution of individuals' incomes. Although in many economic discussions it is customary to refer to the effect of changes in aggregate total purchasing power on the demand for a good, this approach may be a misleading simplification because the actual effect of such a change on total demand will depend on precisely how the income changes are distributed among individuals. Finally, although they are obscured somewhat by the notation we have been using, the role of changes in preferences should be mentioned. We have constructed individuals' demand functions with the assumption that preferences (as represented by indifference curve maps) remain fixed. If preferences were to change, so would individual and market demand functions. Hence, market demand curves can clearly be shifted by changes in preferences. In many economic analyses, however, it is assumed that these changes occur so slowly that they may be implicitly held constant without misrepresenting the situation.

A simplified notation

Often in this book we shall be looking at only one market. In order to simplify the notation, in these cases we shall use Q_D to refer to the quantity of the particular good demanded in this market and P to denote its market price. As always, when we draw a demand curve in the Q–P plane, the ceteris paribus assumption is in effect. If any of the factors mentioned in the previous section (other prices, individuals' incomes, or preferences) should change, the Q–P demand curve will shift, and we should keep that possibility in mind. When we turn to consider relationships among two or more goods, however, we will return to the notation we have been using up until now (that is, denoting goods by x and y or by x_i).

Elasticity of market demand

When we use this notation for market demand, we will also use a compact notation for the price elasticity of the market demand function:

$$\text{price elasticity of market demand} = e_{Q,P} = \frac{\partial Q_D(P, P', I)}{\partial P} \cdot \frac{P}{Q_D}, \tag{12.11}$$

where the notation is intended as a reminder that the demand for Q depends on many factors other than its own price, such as the prices of other goods (P') and the incomes of all potential demanders (I). These other factors are held constant when computing the own-price elasticity of market demand. As in Chapter 5, this elasticity measures the proportionate response in quantity demanded to a 1 percent change in a good's price. Market demand is also characterized by whether demand is elastic ($e_{Q,P} < -1$) or inelastic ($0 > e_{Q,P} > -1$). Many of the other concepts examined in Chapter 5, such as the cross-price elasticity of demand or the income elasticity of demand, also carry over directly into the market context:[3]

$$\text{cross price elasticity of market demand} = \frac{\partial Q_D(P, P', I)}{\partial P'} \cdot \frac{P'}{Q_D};$$

$$\text{income elasticity of market demand} = \frac{\partial Q_D(P, P', I)}{\partial I} \cdot \frac{I}{Q_D}. \tag{12.12}$$

Given these conventions about market demand, we now turn to an extended examination of supply and market equilibrium in the perfectly competitive model.

TIMING OF THE SUPPLY RESPONSE

In the analysis of competitive pricing, it is important to decide the length of time to be allowed for a *supply response* to changing demand conditions. The establishment of equilibrium prices will be different if we are talking about a very short period of time during which most inputs are fixed than if we are envisioning a very long-run process in which it is possible for new firms to enter an industry. For this reason, it has been traditional in economics to discuss pricing in three different time periods: (1) very short run, (2) short run, and (3) long run. Although it is not possible to give these terms an exact chronological definition, the essential distinction being made concerns the nature of the supply response that is assumed to be possible. In the *very short run*, there is no supply response: quantity supplied is fixed and does not respond to changes in demand. In the *short run*, existing firms may change the quantity they are supplying, but no new firms can enter the industry. In the *long run*, new firms may enter an industry, thereby producing a very flexible supply response. In this chapter we will discuss each of these possibilities.

PRICING IN THE VERY SHORT RUN

In the very short run, or the *market period*, there is no supply response. The goods are already "in" the marketplace and must be sold for whatever the market will bear. In this situation, price acts only as a device for rationing demand. Price will adjust to clear the market of the quantity that must be sold during the period. Although the market price may act as a signal to producers in future periods, it does not perform such a function in the current period because current-period output is fixed. Figure 12.2 depicts this situation. Market demand is represented by the curve D. Supply is fixed at Q^*, and the price that clears the market is P_1. At P_1, individuals are willing to take all that is offered in the market. Sellers want to dispose of Q^* without regard to price (suppose that the good in question is perishable and will be worthless if it is not sold in the very short run). Hence P_1, Q^* is an equilibrium price-quantity combination. If demand should shift to D', then the equilibrium price would increase to P_2 but Q^* would stay fixed because no supply response is possible. The *supply curve* in this situation, then, is a vertical straight line at output Q^*.

The analysis of the very short run is not particularly useful for many markets. Such a theory may adequately represent some situations in which goods are perishable or must be

---

[3]In many applications, market demand is modeled in *per capita* terms and treated as referring to the "typical person." In such applications it is also common to use many of the relationships among elasticities discussed in Chapter 5. Whether such aggregation across individuals is appropriate is discussed briefly in the Extensions to this chapter.

FIGURE 12.2   Pricing in the Very Short Run

When quantity is fixed in the very short run, price acts only as a device to ration demand. With quantity fixed at Q^*, price P_1 will prevail in the marketplace if D is the market demand curve; at this price, individuals are willing to consume exactly that quantity available. If demand should shift upward to D', the equilibrium market price would rise to P_2.

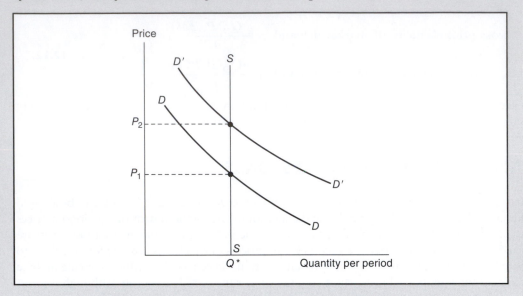

sold on a given day, as is the case in auctions. Indeed, the study of auctions provides a number of insights about the informational problems involved in arriving at equilibrium prices, which we take up in Chapter 18. But auctions are unusual in that supply is fixed. The far more usual case involves some degree of supply response to changing demand. It is presumed that a rise in price will bring additional quantity into the market. In the remainder of this chapter, we will examine this process.

Before beginning our analysis, we should note that increases in quantity supplied need not come only from increased production. In a world in which some goods are durable (that is, last longer than a single period), current owners of these goods may supply them in increasing amounts to the market as price rises. For example, even though the supply of Rembrandts is fixed, we would not want to draw the market supply curve for these paintings as a vertical line, such as that shown in Figure 12.2. As the price of Rembrandts rises, individuals and museums will become increasingly willing to part with them. From a market point of view, therefore, the supply curve for Rembrandts will have an upward slope, even though no new production takes place. A similar analysis would follow for many types of durable goods, such as antiques, used cars, vintage baseball cards, or corporate shares, all of which are in nominally "fixed" supply. Because we are more interested in examining how demand and production are related, we will not be especially concerned with such cases here. Chapter 14 does, however, contain a brief analysis of some issues related to durable goods.

SHORT-RUN PRICE DETERMINATION

In short-run analysis, the number of firms in an industry is fixed. These firms are able to adjust the quantity they are producing in response to changing conditions. They will do this by altering levels of usage for those inputs that can be varied in the short run, and we shall investigate this supply decision here. Before beginning the analysis, we should perhaps state explicitly the assumptions of this perfectly competitive model.

Perfect competition. A *perfectly competitive industry* is one that obeys the following assumptions.

DEFINITION

1. There are a large number of firms, each producing the same homogeneous product.
2. Each firm attempts to maximize profits.
3. Each firm is a price taker: It assumes that its actions have no effect on market price.
4. Prices are assumed to be known by all market participants—information is perfect.
5. Transactions are costless: Buyers and sellers incur no costs in making exchanges (for more on this and the previous assumption, see Chapter 18).

Now we will make use of these assumptions to study price determination in the short run.

Short-run market supply curve

In Chapter 11 we showed how to construct the short-run supply curve for a single profit-maximizing firm. To construct a market supply curve, we start by recognizing that the quantity of output supplied to the entire market in the short run is the sum of the quantities supplied by each firm. Because each firm uses the same market price to determine how much to produce, the total amount supplied to the market by all firms will obviously depend on price. This relationship between price and quantity supplied is called a *short-run market supply curve*. Figure 12.3 illustrates the construction of the curve. For simplicity assume there are only two firms, A and B. The short-run supply (that is, marginal cost) curves for firms A and B are shown in Figures 12.3a and 12.3b. The market supply curve shown in Figure 12.3c is the horizontal sum of these two curves. For example, at a price of P_1, firm A is willing to supply q_1^A and firm B is willing to supply q_1^B. Therefore, at this price the total supply in the market is given by Q_1, which is equal to $q_1^A + q_1^B$. The other points on the curve are constructed in an identical way. Because each firm's supply curve has a positive slope, the market supply curve

FIGURE 12.3 Short-Run Market Supply Curve

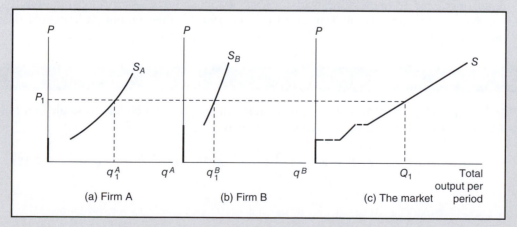

The supply (marginal cost) curves of two firms are shown in (a) and (b). The market supply curve (c) is the horizontal sum of these curves. For example, at P_1 firm A supplies q_1^A, firm B supplies q_1^B, and total market supply is given by $Q_1 = q_1^A + q_1^B$.

will also have a positive slope. The positive slope reflects the fact that short-run marginal costs increase as firms attempt to increase their outputs.

Short-run market supply

More generally, if we let $q_i(P, v, w)$ represent the short-run supply function for each of the n firms in the industry, we can define the short-run market supply function as follows.

DEFINITION

Short-run market supply function. The *short-run market supply function* shows total quantity supplied by each firm to a market:

$$Q_S(P, v, w) = \sum_{i=1}^{n} q_i(P, v, w). \tag{12.13}$$

Notice that the firms in the industry are assumed to face the same market price and the same prices for inputs.[4] The *short-run market supply curve* shows the two-dimensional relationship between Q and P, holding v and w (and each firm's underlying technology) constant. The notation makes clear that if v, w, or technology were to change, the supply curve would shift to a new location.

Short-run supply elasticity

One way of summarizing the responsiveness of the output of firms in an industry to higher prices is by the *short-run supply elasticity*. This measure shows how proportional changes in market price are met by changes in total output. Consistent with the elasticity concepts developed in Chapter 5, this is defined as follows.

DEFINITION

Short-run elasticity of supply ($e_{S,P}$).

$$e_{S,P} = \frac{\text{percentage change in } Q \text{ supplied}}{\text{percentage change in } P} = \frac{\partial Q_S}{\partial P} \cdot \frac{P}{Q_S}. \tag{12.14}$$

Because quantity supplied is an increasing function of price ($\partial Q_S / \partial P > 0$), the supply elasticity is positive. High values for $e_{S,P}$ imply that small increases in market price lead to a relatively large supply response by firms, because marginal costs do not rise steeply and input price interaction effects are small. Alternatively, a low value for $e_{S,P}$ implies that it takes relatively large changes in price to induce firms to change their output levels, because marginal costs rise rapidly. Notice that, as for all elasticity notions, computation of $e_{S,P}$ requires that input prices and technology be held constant. To make sense as a market response, the concept also requires that all firms face the same price for their output. If firms sold their output at different prices, we would need to define a supply elasticity for each firm.

EXAMPLE 12.2 A Short-Run Supply Function

In Example 11.3 we calculated the general short-run supply function for any single firm with a two-input Cobb-Douglas production function as

$$q_i(P, v, w) = \left(\frac{w}{\beta}\right)^{-\beta/(1-\beta)} k_1^{\alpha/(1-\beta)} P^{\beta/(1-\beta)}. \tag{12.15}$$

---

[4]Later in this chapter we show how this assumption can be relaxed.

If we let $\alpha = \beta = 0.5$, $v = 3$, $w = 12$, and $k_1 = 80$, then this yields the simple, single-firm supply function

$$q_i(P, v, w = 12) = \frac{10P}{3}. \tag{12.16}$$

Now assume that there are 100 identical such firms and that each firm faces the same market prices for both its output and its input hiring. Given these assumptions, the short-run market supply function is given by

$$Q_S(P, v, w = 12) = \sum_{i=1}^{100} q_i = \sum_{i=1}^{100} \frac{10P}{3} = \frac{1,000P}{3}. \tag{12.17}$$

So, at a price of (say) $P = 12$, total market supply will be 4,000, with each of the 100 firms supplying 40 units. We can compute the short-run elasticity of supply in this situation as

$$e_{S,P} = \frac{\partial Q_S(P, v, w)}{\partial P} \cdot \frac{P}{Q_S} = \frac{1,000}{3} \cdot \frac{P}{1,000P/3} = 1; \tag{12.18}$$

this might have been expected, given the unitary exponent of P in the supply function.

Effect of an increase in w. If all of the firms in this marketplace experienced an increase in the wage they must pay for their labor input, then the short-run supply curve would shift to a new position. To calculate the shift, we must return to the single firm's supply function (Equation 12.15) and now use a new wage, say, $w = 15$. If none of the other parameters of the problem have changed (the firm's production function and the level of capital input it has in the short run), the supply function becomes

$$q_i(P, v, w = 15) = \frac{8P}{3} \tag{12.19}$$

and the market supply function is

$$Q_S(P, v, w = 15) = \sum_{i=1}^{100} \frac{8P}{3} = \frac{800P}{3}. \tag{12.20}$$

So, at a price of $P = 12$, now this industry will supply only $Q_S = 3,200$, with each firm producing $q_i = 32$. In other words, the supply curve has shifted upward because of the increase in the wage. Notice, however, that the price elasticity of supply has not changed—it remains $e_{S,P} = 1$.

QUERY: How would the results of this example change by assuming different values for the weight of labor in the production function (that is, for α and β)?

Equilibrium price determination

We can now combine demand and supply curves to demonstrate the establishment of equilibrium prices in the market. Figure 12.4 shows this process. Looking first at Figure 12.4b, we see the market demand curve D (ignore D' for the moment) and the short-run supply curve S. The two curves intersect at a price of P_1 and a quantity of Q_1. This price-quantity combination represents an *equilibrium* between the demands of individuals and the costs of firms. The equilibrium price P_1 serves two important functions. First, this price acts as a signal to producers by providing them with information about how much should be produced: In order to maximize profits, firms will produce that output level for which marginal costs are equal to P_1. In the aggregate, then, production will be Q_1. A second function of the price is to ration demand. Given the market price P_1, utility-maximizing individuals will decide how much of their limited incomes to devote to buying the particular good. At a price of P_1, total quantity

FIGURE 12.4   Interactions of Many Individuals and Firms Determine Market Price in the Short Run

Market demand curves and market supply curves are each the horizontal sum of numerous components. These market curves are shown in (b). Once price is determined in the market, each firm and each individual treat this price as a fixed parameter in their decisions. Although individual firms and persons are important in determining price, their interaction as a whole is the sole determinant of price. This is illustrated by a shift in an individual's demand curve to d'. If only one individual reacts in this way, market price will not be affected. However, if everyone exhibits an increased demand, market demand will shift to D'; in the short run, price will rise to P_2.

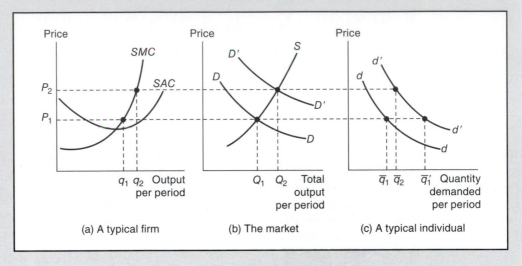

(a) A typical firm   (b) The market   (c) A typical individual

demanded will be Q_1, and this is precisely the amount that will be produced. Hence we define equilibrium price as follows.

DEFINITION

Equilibrium price. An *equilibrium price* is one at which quantity demanded is equal to quantity supplied. At such a price, neither demanders nor suppliers have an incentive to alter their economic decisions. Mathematically, an equilibrium price P^* solves the equation

$$Q_D(P^*, P', I) = Q_S(P^*, v, w) \tag{12.21}$$

or, more compactly,

$$Q_D(P^*) = Q_S(P^*). \tag{12.22}$$

The definition given in Equation 12.22 makes clear that an equilibrium price depends on the values of many exogenous factors, such as incomes or prices of other goods and of firms' inputs. As we will see in the next section, changes in any of these factors will likely result in a change in the equilibrium price required to equate quantity supplied to quantity demanded.

The implications of the equilibrium price (P_1) for a typical firm and a typical individual are shown in Figures 12.4a and 12.4c, respectively. For the typical firm the price P_1 will cause an output level of q_1 to be produced. The firm earns a small profit at this particular price because short-run average total costs are covered. The demand curve d (ignore d' for the moment) for a typical individual is shown in Figure 12.4c. At a price of P_1, this individual demands $\bar{q}_1$. By adding up the quantities that each individual demands at P_1 and the quantities that each firm supplies, we can see that the market is in equilibrium. The market supply and demand curves provide a convenient way of making such a summation.

Market reaction to a shift in demand

The three panels in Figure 12.4 can be used to show two important facts about short-run market equilibrium: the individual's "impotence" in the market and the nature of short-run supply response. First, suppose that a single individual's demand curve were to shift outward to d', as shown in Figure 12.4c. Because the competitive model assumes there are many demanders, this shift will have practically no effect on the market demand curve. Consequently, market price will be unaffected by the shift to d', that is, price will remain at P_1. Of course, at this price, the person for whom the demand curve has shifted will consume slightly more ($\bar{q}'_1$), as shown in Figure 12.4c. But this amount is a tiny part of the market.

If many individuals experience outward shifts in their demand curves, the entire market demand curve may shift. Figure 12.4b shows the new demand curve D'. The new equilibrium point will be at P_2, Q_2; at this point, supply-demand balance is reestablished. Price has increased from P_1 to P_2 in response to the demand shift. Notice also that the quantity traded in the market has increased from Q_1 to Q_2. The rise in price has served two functions. First, as in our previous analysis of the very short run, it has acted to ration demand. Whereas at P_1 a typical individual demanded $\bar{q}'_1$, at P_2 only $\bar{q}_2$ is demanded. The rise in price has also acted as a signal to the typical firm to increase production. In Figure 12.4a the firm's profit-maximizing output level has increased from q_1 to q_2 in response to the price rise. That is what we mean by a *short-run supply response*: An increase in market price acts as an inducement to increase production. Firms are willing to increase production (and to incur higher marginal costs) because the price has risen. If market price had not been permitted to rise (suppose that government price controls were in effect), then firms would not have increased their outputs. At P_1 there would now be an excess (unfilled) demand for the good in question. If market price is allowed to rise, a supply-demand equilibrium can be reestablished so that what firms produce is again equal to what individuals demand at the prevailing market price. Notice also that, at the new price P_2, the typical firm has increased its profits. This increasing profitability in the short run will be important to our discussion of long-run pricing later in this chapter.

SHIFTS IN SUPPLY AND DEMAND CURVES: A GRAPHICAL ANALYSIS

In previous chapters we established many reasons why either a demand curve or a supply curve might shift. These reasons are briefly summarized in Table 12.1. Although most of these merit little additional explanation, it is important to note that a change in the number of firms will shift the short-run market supply curve (because the sum in Equation 12.13 will be over a different number of firms). This observation allows us to tie together short-run and long-run analysis.

It seems likely that the types of changes described in Table 12.1 are constantly occurring in real-world markets. When either a supply curve or a demand curve does shift, equilibrium

TABLE 12.1   Reasons for Shifts in Demand or Supply Curves

Demand Curves Shift Because	Supply Curves Shift Because
• Incomes change	• Input prices change
• Prices of substitutes or complements change	• Technology changes
• Preferences change	• Number of producers changes

price and quantity will change. In this section we investigate graphically the relative magnitudes of such changes. In the next section we show the results mathematically.

Shifts in supply curves: importance of the shape of the demand curve

Consider first a shift inward in the short-run supply curve for a good. As in Example 12.2, such a shift might have resulted from an increase in the prices of inputs used by firms to produce the good. Whatever the cause of the shift, it is important to recognize that the effect of the shift on the equilibrium level of P and Q will depend on the shape of the demand curve for the product. Figure 12.5 illustrates two possible situations. The demand curve in Figure 12.5a is relatively price elastic; that is, a change in price substantially affects quantity demanded. For this case, a shift in the supply curve from S to S' will cause equilibrium price to rise only moderately (from P to P') while quantity declines sharply (from Q to Q'). Rather than being "passed on" in higher prices, the increase in the firms' input costs is met primarily by a decrease in quantity (a movement down each firm's marginal cost curve) and only a slight increase in price.

This situation is reversed when the market demand curve is inelastic. In Figure 12.5b a shift in the supply curve causes equilibrium price to rise substantially while quantity is little changed. The reason for this is that individuals do not reduce their demands very much if prices rise. Consequently, the shift upward in the supply curve is almost entirely passed on to demanders in the form of higher prices.

Shifts in demand curves: Importance of the shape of the supply curve

Similarly, a shift in a market demand curve will have different implications for P and Q, depending on the shape of the short-run supply curve. Two illustrations are shown in Figure 12.6.

FIGURE 12.5   Effect of a Shift in the Short-Run Supply Curve Depends on the Shape of the Demand Curve

In (a) the shift upward in the supply curve causes price to increase only slightly while quantity declines sharply. This results from the elastic shape of the demand curve. In (b) the demand curve is inelastic; price increases substantially, with only a slight decrease in quantity.

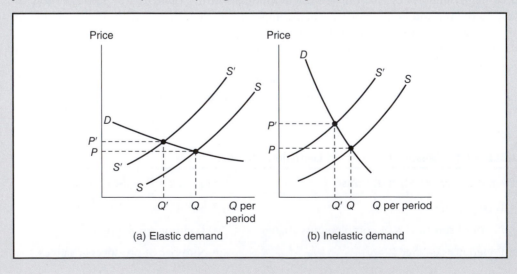

(a) Elastic demand

(b) Inelastic demand

FIGURE 12.6 Effect of a Shift in the Demand Curve Depends on the Shape of the Short-Run Supply Curve

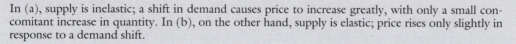

In (a), supply is inelastic; a shift in demand causes price to increase greatly, with only a small concomitant increase in quantity. In (b), on the other hand, supply is elastic; price rises only slightly in response to a demand shift.

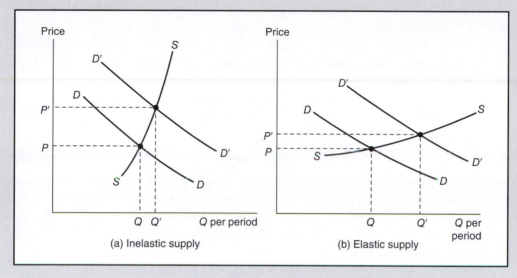

(a) Inelastic supply

(b) Elastic supply

In Figure 12.6a the supply curve for the good in question is inelastic. In this situation, a shift outward in the market demand curve will cause price to increase substantially. On the other hand, the quantity traded increases only slightly. Intuitively, what has happened is that the increase in demand (and in Q) has caused firms to move up their steeply sloped marginal cost curves. The concomitant large increase in price serves to ration demand.

Figure 12.6b shows a relatively elastic short-run supply curve. Such a curve would occur for an industry in which marginal costs do not rise steeply in response to output increases. For this case, an increase in demand produces a substantial increase in Q. However, because of the nature of the supply curve, this increase is not met by great cost increases. Consequently, price rises only moderately.

These examples again demonstrate Marshall's observation that demand and supply simultaneously determine price and quantity. Recall his analogy from Chapter 1: Just as it is impossible to say which blade of a scissors does the cutting, so too is it impossible to attribute price solely to demand or to supply characteristics. Rather, the effect of shifts in either a demand curve or a supply curve will depend on the shapes of both of the curves.

MATHEMATICAL MODEL OF MARKET EQUILIBRIUM

A general mathematical model of the supply-demand process can further illuminate the comparative statics of changing equilibrium prices and quantities. Suppose that the demand function is represented by

$$Q_D = D(P, \alpha), \tag{12.23}$$

where α is a parameter that allows us to shift the demand curve. It might represent consumer income, prices of other goods (this would permit the tying together of supply and demand in several related markets), or changing preferences. In general we expect that

$\partial D/\partial P = D_P < 0$, but $\partial D/\partial \alpha = D_\alpha$ may have any sign, depending precisely on what the parameter α means. Using this same procedure, we can write the supply relationship as

$$Q_S = S(P, \beta), \tag{12.24}$$

where β is a parameter that shifts the supply curve and might include such factors as input prices, technical changes, or (for a multiproduct firm) prices of other potential outputs. Here $\partial S/\partial P = S_P > 0$, but $\partial S/\partial \beta = S_\beta$ may have any sign. The model is closed by requiring that, in equilibrium,[5]

$$Q_D = Q_S. \tag{12.25}$$

To analyze the comparative statics of this model of equilibrium, we write the total differentials of the demand and supply functions as follows:

$$dQ_D = D_P dP + D_\alpha d\alpha;$$
$$dQ_S = S_P dP + S_\beta d\beta. \tag{12.26}$$

Because maintenance of equilibrium requires that

$$dQ_D = dQ_S, \tag{12.27}$$

we can solve these equations for the change in equilibrium price for any combination of shifts in demand (α) or supply (β). For example, suppose the demand parameter α were to change while β remains constant. Then, using the equilibrium condition, we have

$$D_P dP + D_\alpha d\alpha = S_P dP \tag{12.28}$$

or, manipulating terms a bit,

$$\frac{\partial P}{\partial \alpha} = \frac{D_\alpha}{S_P - D_P}. \tag{12.29}$$

Because the denominator of this expression is positive, the sign of $\partial P/\partial \alpha$ will be the same as the sign of D_α. If α represents consumer income (and if the good in question is normal), then D_α would be positive, and a rise in income would shift demand outward. This, as Equation 12.29 also indicates, would cause equilibrium price to rise—a result reflected graphically in Figure 12.6.

An elasticity interpretation

Further algebraic manipulation of Equation 12.29 yields a more useful comparative statics result. Multiplying both sides of that equation by α/P gives

$$e_{P,\alpha} = \frac{\partial P}{\partial \alpha} \cdot \frac{\alpha}{P} = \frac{D_\alpha}{S_P - D_P} \cdot \frac{\alpha}{P}$$
$$= \frac{D_\alpha(\alpha/Q)}{(S_P - D_P) \cdot P/Q} = \frac{e_{Q,\alpha}}{e_{S,P} - e_{Q,P}}. \tag{12.30}$$

Because all of the elasticities in this equation may be available from empirical studies, this equation can be a convenient way to make rough estimates of the effects of various events on equilibrium prices. As an example, suppose again that α represents consumer income and that there is interest in predicting how an increase in income affects the equilibrium price of, say, automobiles. Suppose empirical data suggest that $e_{Q,I} = e_{Q,\alpha} = 3.0$ and $e_{Q,P} = -1.2$

---

[5]The model could be further modified to show how the equilibrium quantity supplied is to be allocated among the firms in the industry. If, for example, the industry is composed of n identical firms, then the output of any one of them would be given by

$$q = \frac{Q}{n}.$$

In the short run, with n fixed, this would add little to our analysis. In the long run, however, n must also be determined by the model, as we show later in this chapter.

(these figures are from Table 12.3), and assume that $e_{S,P} = 1.0$. Substituting these figures into Equation 12.30 yields

$$e_{P,\alpha} = \frac{e_{Q,\alpha}}{e_{S,P} - e_{Q,P}} = \frac{3.0}{1.0 - (-1.2)}$$

$$= \frac{3.0}{2.2} = 1.36. \tag{12.31}$$

The empirical elasticity estimates therefore suggest that each 1 percent rise in consumer incomes results in a 1.36 percent rise in the equilibrium price of automobiles. Estimates of other kinds of shifts in supply or demand can be similarly modeled by manipulating Equations 12.26 and 12.27 and obtaining empirical estimates of the necessary parameters.

EXAMPLE 12.3 Equilibria with Constant Elasticity Functions

An even more complete analysis of supply-demand equilibrium can be provided if we use specific functional forms. Constant elasticity functions are especially useful for this purpose. Suppose the demand for automobiles is given by

$$Q_D(P, I) = 0.1 P^{-1.2} I^3; \tag{12.32}$$

here price (P) is measured in dollars, as is real family income (I). The supply function for automobiles is

$$Q_S(P, w) = 6,400 P w^{-0.5}, \tag{12.33}$$

where w is the hourly wage of automobile workers. Notice that the elasticities assumed here are those used previously in the text ($e_{Q,P} = -1.2$, $e_{Q,I} = 3.0$, and $e_{S,P} = 1$). If the values for the "exogenous" variables I and w are $20,000 and $25, respectively, then demand-supply equilibrium requires

$$Q_D = 0.1 P^{-1.2} I^3 = (8 \times 10^{11}) P^{-1.2}$$

$$= Q_S = 6,400 P w^{-0.5} = 1,280 P \tag{12.34}$$

or

$$P^{2.2} = (8 \times 10^{11})/1,280 = 6.25 \times 10^8$$

or

$$P^* = 9,957,$$
$$Q^* = 1,280 \cdot P^* = 12,745,000. \tag{12.35}$$

Hence, the initial equilibrium in the automobile market has a price of nearly $10,000 with about 13 million cars being sold.

A shift in demand. A 10 percent increase in real family income, all other factors remaining constant, would shift the demand function to

$$Q_D = (1.06 \times 10^{12}) P^{-1.2} \tag{12.36}$$

and, proceeding as before,

$$P^{2.2} = (1.06 \times 10^{12})/1,280 = 8.32 \times 10^8 \tag{12.37}$$

or

$$P^* = 11,339,$$
$$Q^* = 14,514,000. \tag{12.38}$$

(*continued*)

EXAMPLE 12.3 CONTINUED

As we predicted earlier, the 10 percent rise in real income made car prices rise by nearly 14 percent. In the process, quantity sold increased by about 1.77 million automobiles.

A shift in supply. An exogenous shift in automobile supply as a result, say, of changing auto workers' wages would also affect market equilibrium. If wages were to rise from $25 to $30 per hour, the supply function would shift to

$$Q_s(P, w) = 6,400P(30)^{-0.5} = 1,168P; \qquad (12.39)$$

returning to our original demand function (with $I = \$20,000$) then yields

$$P^{2.2} = (8 \times 10^{11})/1,168 = 6.85 \times 10^8 \qquad (12.40)$$

or

$$P^* = 10,381, \qquad (12.41)$$
$$Q^* = 12,125,000.$$

The 20 percent rise in wages, therefore, led to a 4.3 percent rise in auto prices and to a decline in sales of more than 600,000 units. Changing equilibria in many types of markets can be approximated by using this general approach together with empirical estimates of the relevant elasticities.

QUERY: Do the results of changing auto workers' wages agree with what might have been predicted using an equation similar to Equation 12.30?

LONG-RUN ANALYSIS

We saw in Chapter 10 that, in the long run, a firm may adapt all of its inputs to fit market conditions. For long-run analysis, then, we should use the firm's long-run cost curves. A profit-maximizing firm that is a price taker will produce the output level for which price is equal to long-run marginal cost (MC). However, we must consider a second and ultimately more important influence on price in the long run: the entry of entirely new firms into the industry or the exit of existing firms from that industry. In mathematical terms, we must allow the number of firms, n, to vary in response to economic incentives. The perfectly competitive model assumes that there are no special costs of entering or exiting from an industry. Consequently, new firms will be lured into any market in which (economic) profits are positive. Similarly, firms will leave any industry in which profits are negative. The entry of new firms will cause the short-run industry supply curve to shift outward, because there are now more firms producing than there were previously. Such a shift will cause market price (and industry profits) to fall. The process will continue until no firm contemplating entry would be able to earn a profit in the industry.[6] At that point, entry will cease and the industry will have an equilibrium number of firms. A similar argument can be made for the case in which some of the firms are suffering short-run losses. Some firms will choose to leave the industry, and this will cause the supply curve to shift to the left. Market price will rise, thus restoring profitability to those firms remaining in the industry.

---

[6]Remember that we are using the economists' definition of profits here. These profits represent a return to the owner of a business in excess of that which is strictly necessary to stay in the business.

Equilibrium conditions

For the purpose of this chapter, we shall initially assume that all the firms in an industry have identical cost curves; that is, no firm controls any special resources or technologies.[7] Because all firms are identical, the equilibrium long-run position requires that each firm earn exactly zero economic profits. In graphic terms, the long-run equilibrium price must settle at the low point of each firm's long-run average total cost curve. Only at this point do the two equilibrium conditions $P = MC$ (which is required for profit maximization) and $P = AC$ (which is required for zero profit) hold. It is important to emphasize, however, that these two equilibrium conditions have rather different origins. Profit maximization is a goal of firms. The $P = MC$ rule therefore derives from the behavioral assumptions we have made about firms and is similar to the output decision rule used in the short run. The zero-profit condition is not a goal for firms; firms obviously would prefer to have large, positive profits. The long-run operation of the market, however, forces all firms to accept a level of zero economic profits ($P = AC$) because of the willingness of firms to enter and to leave an industry in response to the possibility of making supranormal returns. Although the firms in a perfectly competitive industry may earn either positive or negative profits in the short run, in the long run only a level of zero profits will prevail. Hence, we can summarize this analysis by the following definition.

Long-run competitive equilibrium. A *perfectly competitive industry* is in *long-run equilibrium* if there are no incentives for profit-maximizing firms to enter or to leave the industry. This will occur when (a) the number of firms is such that $P = MC = AC$ and (b) each firm operates at the low point of its long-run average cost curve.

DEFINITION

LONG-RUN EQUILIBRIUM: CONSTANT COST CASE

To discuss long-run pricing in detail, we must make an assumption about how the entry of new firms into an industry affects the prices of firms' inputs. The simplest assumption we might make is that entry has no effect on the prices of those inputs—perhaps because the industry is a relatively small hirer in its various input markets. Under this assumption, no matter how many firms enter (or leave) an industry, each firm will retain the same set of cost curves with which it started. This assumption of constant input prices may not be tenable in many important cases, which we will look at in the next section. For the moment, however, we wish to examine the equilibrium conditions for a *constant cost industry*.

Initial equilibrium

Figure 12.7 demonstrates long-run equilibrium for an industry. For the market as a whole (Figure 12.7b), the demand curve is given by D and the short-run supply curve by SS. The short-run equilibrium price is therefore P_1. The typical firm (Figure 12.7a) will produce output level q_1 because, at this level of output, price is equal to short-run marginal cost (SMC). In addition, with a market price of P_1, output level q_1 is also a long-run equilibrium position for the firm. The firm is maximizing profits, because price is equal to long-run marginal costs (MC). Figure 12.7a also implies our second long-run equilibrium property: Price is equal to long-run average costs (AC). Consequently, economic profits are zero, and there is no incentive for firms either to enter or to leave the industry. The market depicted in Figure 12.7 is therefore in both short-run and long-run equilibrium. Firms are in equilibrium because

---

[7]If firms have different costs then very low-cost firms can earn positive long-run profits, and such extra profits will be reflected in the price of the resource that accounts for the firm's low costs. In this sense the assumption of identical costs is not very restrictive, because an active market for the firm's inputs will ensure that average costs (which include opportunity costs) are the same for all firms. See also the discussion of Ricardian rent later in this chapter.

FIGURE 12.7   Long-Run Equilibrium for a Perfectly Competitive Industry: Constant Cost Case

An increase in demand from D to D' will cause price to rise from P_1 to P_2 in the short run. This higher price will create profits in the industry, and new firms will be drawn into the market. If it is assumed that the entry of these new firms has no effect on the cost curves of the firms in the industry, then new firms will continue to enter until price is pushed back down to P_1. At this price, economic profits are zero. The long-run supply curve (LS) will therefore be a horizontal line at P_1. Along LS, output is increased by increasing the number of firms, each producing q_1.

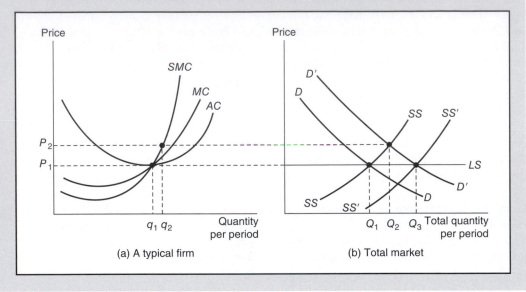

(a) A typical firm   (b) Total market

they are maximizing profits, and the number of firms is stable because economic profits are zero. This equilibrium will tend to persist until either supply or demand conditions change.

Responses to an increase in demand

Suppose now that the market demand curve in Figure 12.7b shifts outward to D'. If SS is the relevant short-run supply curve for the industry, then, in the short run, price will rise to P_2. The typical firm, in the short run, will choose to produce q_2 and will earn profits on this level of output. In the long run, these profits will attract new firms into the market. Because of the constant cost assumption, this entry of new firms will have no effect on input prices. New firms will continue to enter the market until price is forced down to the level at which there are again no pure economic profits. The entry of new firms will therefore shift the short-run supply curve to SS', where the equilibrium price (P_1) is reestablished. At this new long-run equilibrium, the price-quantity combination P_1, Q_3 will prevail in the market. The typical firm will again produce at output level q_1, although now there will be more firms than in the initial situation.

Infinitely elastic supply

We have shown that the *long-run supply curve* for the constant cost industry will be a horizontal straight line at price P_1. This curve is labeled LS in Figure 12.7b. No matter what happens to demand, the twin equilibrium conditions of zero long-run profits (because free entry is assumed) and profit maximization will ensure that no price other than P_1 can prevail in the long run.[8] For this reason, P_1 might be regarded as the "normal" price for this

---

[8]These equilibrium conditions also point out what seems to be, somewhat imprecisely, an "efficient" aspect of the long-run equilibrium in perfectly competitive markets: The good under investigation will be produced at minimum average cost. We will have much more to say about efficiency in the next chapter.

commodity. If the constant cost assumption is abandoned, however, the long-run supply curve need not have this infinitely elastic shape, as we show in the next section.

EXAMPLE 12.4 Infinitely Elastic Long-Run Supply

Handmade bicycle frames are produced by a number of identically sized firms. Total (long-run) monthly costs for a typical firm are given by

$$C(q) = q^3 - 20q^2 + 100q + 8,000, \tag{12.42}$$

where q is the number of frames produced per month. Demand for handmade bicycle frames is given by

$$Q_D = 2,500 - 3P, \tag{12.43}$$

where Q_D is the quantity demanded per month and P is the price per frame. To determine the long-run equilibrium in this market, we must find the low point of the typical firm's average cost curve. Since

$$AC = \frac{C(q)}{q} = q^2 - 20q + 100 + \frac{8,000}{q} \tag{12.44}$$

and

$$MC = \frac{\partial C(q)}{\partial q} = 3q^2 - 40q + 100 \tag{12.45}$$

and since we know this minimum occurs where $AC = MC$ we can solve for this output level:

$$q^2 - 20q + 100 + \frac{8,000}{q} = 3q^2 - 40q + 100$$

or

$$2q^2 - 20q = \frac{8,000}{q}, \tag{12.46}$$

which has a convenient solution of $q = 20$. With a monthly output of 20 frames, each producer has a long-run average and marginal cost of $500. This, then, is the long-run equilibrium price of bicycle frames (handmade frames cost a bundle, as any cyclist can attest). With $P = \$500$, Equation 12.43 shows $Q_D = 1,000$. The equilibrium number of firms is therefore 50. When each of these 50 firms produces 20 frames per month, supply will precisely balance what is demanded at a price of $500.

If demand in this problem were to increase to

$$Q_D = 3,000 - 3P, \tag{12.47}$$

then we would expect long-run output and the number of frames to increase. Assuming that entry into the frame market is free and that such entry does not alter costs for the typical bicycle maker, the long-run equilibrium price will remain at $500 and a total of 1,500 frames per month will be demanded. That will require 75 frame makers, so 25 new firms will enter the market in response to the increase in demand.

QUERY: Presumably, the entry of frame makers in the long run is motivated by the short-run profitability of the industry in response to the increase in demand. Suppose each firm's short-run costs were given by $SC = 50q^2 - 1,500q + 20,000$. Show that short-run profits are zero when the industry is in long-term equilibrium. What are the industry's short-run profits as a result of the increase in demand when the number of firms stays at 50?

SHAPE OF THE LONG-RUN SUPPLY CURVE

Contrary to the short-run situation, long-run analysis has very little to do with the shape of the (long-run) marginal cost curve. Rather, the zero-profit condition centers attention on the low point of the long-run average cost curve as the factor most relevant to long-run price determination. In the constant cost case, the position of this low point does not change as new firms enter the industry. Consequently, if input prices do not change then only one price can prevail in the long run regardless of how demand shifts—the long-run supply curve is horizontal at this price. Once the constant cost assumption is abandoned, this need not be the case. If the entry of new firms causes average costs to rise, the long-run supply curve will have an upward slope. On the other hand, if entry causes average costs to decline, it is even possible for the long-run supply curve to be negatively sloped. We shall now discuss these possibilities.

Increasing cost industry

The entry of new firms into an industry may cause the average costs of all firms to rise for several reasons. New and existing firms may compete for scarce inputs, thus driving up their prices. New firms may impose "external costs" on existing firms (and on themselves) in the form of air or water pollution. They may increase the demand for tax-financed services (police forces, sewage treatment plants, and so forth), and the required taxes may show up as increased costs for all firms. Figure 12.8 demonstrates two market equilibria in such an *increasing cost industry*. The initial equilibrium price is P_1. At this price the typical firm produces q_1, and total industry output is Q_1. Suppose now that the demand curve for the industry shifts outward to D'. In the short run, price will rise to P_2, since this is where D' and the industry's short-run supply curve (SS) intersect. At this price the typical firm will produce q_2 and will earn a substantial profit. This profit then attracts new entrants into the market and shifts the short-run supply curve outward.

FIGURE 12.8   An Increasing Cost Industry Has a Positively Sloped Long-Run Supply Curve

Initially, the market is in equilibrium at P_1, Q_1. An increase in demand (to D') causes price to rise to P_2 in the short run, and the typical firm produces q_2 at a profit. This profit attracts new firms into the industry. The entry of these new firms causes costs for a typical firm to rise to the levels shown in (b). With this new set of curves, equilibrium is reestablished in the market at P_3, Q_3. By considering many possible demand shifts and connecting all the resulting equilibrium points, the long-run supply curve (LS) is traced out.

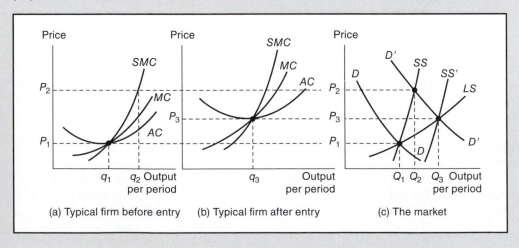

(a) Typical firm before entry   (b) Typical firm after entry   (c) The market

Suppose that this entry of new firms causes the cost curves of all firms to rise. The new firms may compete for scarce inputs, thereby driving up the prices of these inputs. A typical firm's new (higher) set of cost curves is shown in Figure 12.8b. The new long-run equilibrium price for the industry is P_3 (here $P_3 = MC = AC$), and at this price Q_3 is demanded. We now have two points (P_1, Q_1 and P_3, Q_3) on the long-run supply curve. All other points on the curve can be found in an analogous way by considering all possible shifts in the demand curve. These shifts will trace out the long-run supply curve LS. Here LS has a positive slope because of the increasing cost nature of the industry. Observe that the LS curve is flatter (more elastic) than the short-run supply curves. This indicates the greater flexibility in supply response that is possible in the long run. Still, the curve is upward sloping, so price rises with increasing demand. This situation is probably quite common; we will have more to say about it in later sections.

Decreasing cost industry

Not all industries exhibit constant or increasing costs. In some cases, the entry of new firms may reduce the costs of firms in an industry. For example, the entry of new firms may provide a larger pool of trained labor from which to draw than was previously available, thus reducing the costs associated with the hiring of new workers. Similarly, the entry of new firms may provide a "critical mass" of industrialization, which permits the development of more efficient transportation and communications networks. Whatever the exact reason for the cost reductions, the final result is illustrated in the three panels of Figure 12.9. The initial market equilibrium is shown by the price-quantity combination P_1, Q_1 in Figure 12.9c. At this price the typical firm produces q_1 and earns exactly zero in economic profits. Now suppose that market demand shifts outward to D'. In the short run, price will increase to P_2 and the typical firm will produce q_2. At this price level, positive profits are being earned. These profits cause new entrants to come into the market. If this entry causes costs to decline, a new set of cost curves for the typical firm might resemble those shown in Figure 12.9b. Now the new

FIGURE 12.9 A Decreasing Cost Industry Has a Negatively Sloped Long-Run Supply Curve

In (c), the market is in equilibrium at P_1, Q_1. An increase in demand to D' causes price to rise to P_2 in the short run, and the typical firm produces q_2 at a profit. This profit attracts new firms to the industry. If the entry of these new firms causes costs for the typical firm to fall, a set of new cost curves might look like those in (b). With this new set of curves, market equilibrium is reestablished at P_3, Q_3. By connecting such points of equilibrium, a negatively sloped long-run supply curve (LS) is traced out.

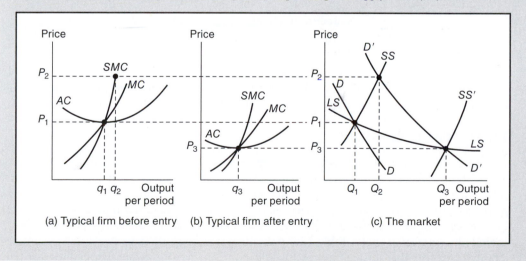

(a) Typical firm before entry   (b) Typical firm after entry   (c) The market

equilibrium price is P_3; at this price, Q_3 is demanded. By considering all possible shifts in demand, the long-run supply curve, LS, can be traced out. This curve has a negative slope because of the decreasing cost nature of the industry. Therefore, as output expands, price falls. This possibility has been used as the justification for protective tariffs to shield new industries from foreign competition. It is assumed (only occasionally correctly) that the protection of the "infant industry" will permit it to grow and ultimately to compete at lower world prices.

Classification of long-run supply curves

Thus we have shown that the long-run supply curve for a perfectly competitive industry may assume a variety of shapes. The principal determinant of the shape is the way in which the entry of firms into the industry affects all firms' costs. The following definitions cover the various possibilities.

DEFINITION | **Constant, increasing, and decreasing cost industries.** An industry supply curve exhibits one of three shapes.

Constant cost: Entry does not affect input costs; the long-run supply curve is horizontal at the long-run equilibrium price.

Increasing cost: Entry increases input costs; the long-run supply curve is positively sloped.

Decreasing cost: Entry reduces input costs; the long-run supply curve is negatively sloped.

Now we show how the shape of the long-run supply curve can be further quantified.

LONG-RUN ELASTICITY OF SUPPLY

The long-run supply curve for an industry incorporates information on internal firm adjustments to changing prices and changes in the number of firms and input costs in response to profit opportunities. All of these supply responses are summarized in the following elasticity concept.

DEFINITION | **Long-run elasticity of supply.** The *long-run elasticity of supply* $(e_{LS,\,P})$ records the proportionate change in long-run industry output in response to a proportionate change in product price. Mathematically,

$$e_{LS,\,P} = \frac{\text{percentage change in } Q}{\text{percentage change in } P} = \frac{\partial Q_{LS}}{\partial P} \cdot \frac{P}{Q_{LS}}. \qquad \textbf{(12.48)}$$

The value of this elasticity may be positive or negative, depending on whether the industry exhibits increasing or decreasing costs. As we have seen, $e_{LS,\,P}$ is infinite in the constant cost case, because industry expansions or contractions can occur without having any effect on product prices.

Empirical estimates

It is obviously important to have good empirical estimates of long-run supply elasticities. These indicate whether production can be expanded with only a slight increase in relative price (that is, supply is price elastic) or whether expansions in output can occur only if relative prices rise sharply (that is, supply is price inelastic). Such information can be used to assess the likely effect of shifts in demand on long-run prices and to evaluate alternative policy proposals intended to increase supply. Table 12.2 presents several long-run supply elasticity estimates. These relate primarily (though not exclusively) to natural resources because economists have

TABLE 12.2   Selected Estimates of Long-Run Supply Elasticities

Agricultural acreage	
Corn	0.18
Cotton	0.67
Wheat	0.93
Aluminum	Nearly infinite
Chromium	0–3.0
Coal (eastern reserves)	15.0–30.0
Natural gas (U.S. reserves)	0.20
Oil (U.S. reserves)	0.76
Urban housing	
Density	5.3
Quality	3.8

Sources: Agricultural acreage—M. Nerlove, "Estimates of the Elasticities of Supply of Selected Agricultural Commodities," *Journal of Farm Economics* 38 (May 1956): 496–509. Aluminum and chromium—estimated from U.S. Department of Interior, *Critical Materials Commodity Action Analysis* (Washington, DC: U.S. Government Printing Office, 1975). Coal—estimated from M. B. Zimmerman, "The Supply of Coal in the Long Run: The Case of Eastern Deep Coal," MIT Energy Laboratory Report No. MITEL 75–021 (September 1975). Natural gas—based on estimate for oil (see text) and J. D. Khazzoom, "The FPC Staff's Econometric Model of Natural Gas Supply in the United States," *The Bell Journal of Economics and Management Science* (Spring 1971): 103–17. Oil—E. W. Erickson, S. W. Millsaps, and R. M. Spann, "Oil Supply and Tax Incentives," *Brookings Papers on Economic Activity* 2 (1974): 449–78. Urban housing—B. A. Smith, "The Supply of Urban Housing," *Journal of Political Economy* 40 (August 1976): 389–405.

devoted considerable attention to the implications of increasing demand for the prices of such resources. As the table makes clear, these estimates vary widely depending on the spatial and geological properties of the particular resources involved. All of the estimates, however, suggest that supply does respond positively to price.

COMPARATIVE STATICS ANALYSIS OF LONG-RUN EQUILIBRIUM

Earlier in this chapter we showed how to develop a simple comparative statics analysis of changing short-run equilibria in competitive markets. By using estimates of the long-run elasticities of demand and supply, exactly the same sort of analysis can be conducted for the long run as well.

For example, the hypothetical auto market model in Example 12.3 might serve equally well for long-run analysis, though some differences in interpretation might be required. Indeed, in applied models of supply and demand it is often not clear whether the author intends his or her results to reflect the short run or the long run, and some care must be taken to understand how the issue of entry is being handled.

Industry structure

One aspect of the changing long-run equilibria in a perfectly competitive market that is obscured by using a simple supply-demand analysis is how the number of firms varies as market equilibria change. Because—as we will see in Part 5—the functioning of markets may in some cases be affected by the number of firms, and because there may be direct public policy interest in entry and exit from an industry, some additional analysis is required. In this section we will examine in detail determinants of the number of firms in the constant cost case. Brief reference will also be made to the increasing cost case, and some of the problems for this chapter examine that case in more detail.

Shifts in demand

Because the long-run supply curve for a constant cost industry is infinitely elastic, analyzing shifts in market demand is particularly easy. If the initial equilibrium industry output is Q_0 and if q^* represents the output level for which the typical firm's long-run average cost is minimized, then the initial equilibrium number of firms (n_0) is given by

$$n_0 = \frac{Q_0}{q^*}. \tag{12.49}$$

A shift in demand that changes equilibrium output to Q_1 will, in the long run, change the equilibrium number of firms to

$$n_1 = \frac{Q_1}{q^*}, \tag{12.50}$$

and the change in the number of firms is given by

$$n_1 - n_0 = \frac{Q_1 - Q_0}{q^*}. \tag{12.51}$$

That is, the change in the equilibrium number of firms is completely determined by the extent of the demand shift and by the optimal output level for the typical firm.

Changes in input costs

Even in the simple constant cost industry case, analyzing the effect of an increase in an input price (and hence an upward shift in the infinitely elastic long-run supply curve) is relatively complicated. First, in order to calculate the decline in industry output, it is necessary to know both the extent to which minimum average cost is increased by the input price rise and how such an increase in the long-run equilibrium price affects total quantity demanded. Knowledge of the typical firm's average cost function and of the price elasticity of demand permits such a calculation to be made in a straightforward way. But an increase in an input price may also change the minimum average cost output level for the typical firm. Such a possibility is illustrated in Figure 12.10. Both the average and marginal costs have been shifted upward by the input price increase, but because average cost has shifted up by a relatively greater extent than the marginal cost, the typical firm's optimal output level has increased from q_0^* to q_1^*. If the relative sizes of the shifts in cost curves were reversed, however, the typical firm's optimal output level would have fallen.[9] Taking account of this change in optimal scale, Equation 12.51 becomes

---

[9] A mathematical proof proceeds as follows. Optimal output q^* is defined such that

$$AC(v, w, q^*) = MC(v, w, q^*).$$

Differentiating both sides of this expression by (say) v yields

$$\frac{\partial AC}{\partial v} + \frac{\partial AC}{\partial q^*} \cdot \frac{\partial q^*}{\partial v} = \frac{\partial MC}{\partial v} + \frac{\partial MC}{\partial q^*} \cdot \frac{\partial q^*}{\partial v};$$

but $\partial AC / \partial q^* = 0$, because average costs are minimized. Manipulating terms, we obtain

$$\frac{\partial q^*}{\partial v} = \left(\frac{\partial MC}{\partial q^*} \right)^{-1} \cdot \left(\frac{\partial AC}{\partial v} - \frac{\partial MC}{\partial v} \right).$$

Since $\partial MC / \partial q > 0$ at the minimum AC, it follows that $\partial q^* / \partial v$ will be positive or negative depending on the sizes of the relative shifts in the AC and MC curves.

FIGURE 12.10   An Increase in an Input Price May Change Long-Run Equilibrium Output for the Typical Firm

An increase in the price of an input will shift average and marginal cost curves upward. The precise effect of these shifts on the typical firm's optimal output level (q^*) will depend on the relative magnitudes of the shifts.

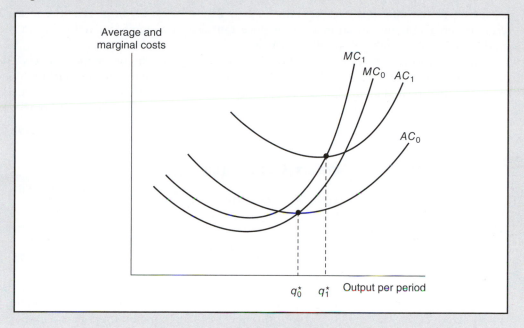

$$n_1 - n_0 = \frac{Q_1}{q_1^*} - \frac{Q_0}{q_0^*}, \qquad\qquad (12.52)$$

and a number of possibilities arise.

If $q_1^* \geq q_0^*$, the decline in quantity brought about by the rise in market price will definitely cause the number of firms to fall. However, if $q_1^* < q_0^*$ then the result will be indeterminate. Industry output will fall, but optimal firm size also will fall, so the ultimate effect on the number of firms depends on the relative magnitude of these changes. A decline in the number of firms still seems the most likely outcome when an input price increase causes industry output to fall, but an increase in n is at least a theoretical possibility.

EXAMPLE 12.5 Rising Input Costs and Industry Structure

A rise in costs for bicycle frame makers will alter the equilibrium described in Example 12.4, but the precise effect on market structure will depend on how costs increase. The effects of an increase in fixed costs are fairly clear: the long-run equilibrium price will rise and the size of the typical firm will also increase. This latter effect occurs because a rise in fixed costs raises AC but not MC. To ensure that the equilibrium condition for $AC = MC$ holds, output (and MC) must also rise. For example, if a rise in shop rents causes the typical frame maker's costs to increase to

$$C(q) = q^3 - 20q^2 + 100q + 11{,}616, \qquad\qquad (12.53)$$

it is an easy matter to show that $MC = AC$ when $q = 22$. The rise in rent has therefore increased the efficient scale of bicycle frame operations by 2 bicycle frames per month. At

(continued)

EXAMPLE 12.5 CONTINUED

$q = 22$, the long-run average cost and the marginal cost are both 672, and that will be the long-run equilibrium price for frames. At this price

$$Q_D = 2,500 - 3P = 484, \qquad (12.54)$$

so there will be room in the market now for only 22 ($= 484 \div 22$) firms. The rise in fixed costs resulted not only in an increase in price but also in a significant reduction in the number of frame makers (from 50 to 22).

Increases in other types of input costs may, however, have more complex effects. Although a complete analysis would require an examination of frame makers' production functions and their related input choices, we can provide a simple illustration by assuming that a rise in some variable input prices causes the typical firm's total cost function to become

$$C(q) = q^3 - 8q^2 + 100q + 4,950. \qquad (12.55)$$

Now

$$MC = 3q^2 - 16q + 100 \quad \text{and}$$
$$AC = q^2 - 8q + 100 + \frac{4,950}{q}. \qquad (12.56)$$

Setting $MC = AC$ yields

$$2q^2 - 8q = \frac{4,950}{q}, \qquad (12.57)$$

which has a solution of $q = 15$. This particular change in the total cost function has therefore significantly reduced the optimal size for frame shops. With $q = 15$, Equations 12.56 show $AC = MC = 535$, and with this new long-run equilibrium price we have

$$Q_D = 2,500 - 3P = 895. \qquad (12.58)$$

These 895 frames will, in equilibrium, be produced by about 60 firms ($895 \div 15 = 59.67$—problems don't always work out evenly!). Even though the increase in costs results in a higher price, the equilibrium number of frame makers expands from 50 to 60 because the optimal size of each shop is now smaller.

QUERY: How do the total, marginal, and average functions derived from Equation 12.55 differ from those in Example 12.4? Are costs always greater (for all levels of q) for the former cost curve? Why is long-run equilibrium price higher with the former curves? (See footnote 9 for a formal discussion.)

PRODUCER SURPLUS IN THE LONG RUN

In Chapter 11 we described the concept of short-run producer surplus, which represents the return to a firm's owners in excess of what would be earned if output were zero. We showed that this consisted of the sum of short-run profits plus short-run fixed costs. In long-run equilibrium, profits are zero and there are no fixed costs, so all such short-run surplus is eliminated. Owners of firms are indifferent about whether they are in a particular market, because they could earn identical returns on their investments elsewhere. Suppliers of firms' inputs may not be indifferent about the level of production in a particular industry, however. In the constant cost case, of course, input prices are assumed to be independent of the level of production on the presumption that inputs can earn the same amount in alternative occupations. But in the increasing cost case, entry will bid up some input prices and suppliers of these inputs will be made better off. Consideration of these price effects leads to the following alternative notion of producer surplus.

DEFINITION

Producer surplus. Producer surplus is the extra return that producers make by making transactions at the market price over and above what they would earn if nothing were produced. It is illustrated by the size of the area below the market price and above the supply curve.

Although this is the same definition we introduced in Chapter 11, the context is now different. Now the "extra returns that producers make" should be interpreted as meaning "the higher prices that productive inputs receive." For short-run producer surplus, the gainers from market transactions are firms that are able to cover fixed costs and possibly earn profits over their variable costs. For long-run producer surplus, we must penetrate back into the chain of production in order to identify who the ultimate gainers from market transactions are.

It is perhaps surprising that long-run producer surplus can be shown graphically in much the same way as short-run producer surplus. The former is given by the area above the *long-run* supply curve and below equilibrium market price. In the constant cost case, long-run supply is infinitely elastic and this area will be zero, showing that returns to inputs are independent of the level of production. With increasing costs, however, long-run supply will be positively sloped and input prices will be bid up as industry output expands. Because this notion of long-run producer surplus is widely used in applied analysis (as we show later in this chapter), we will provide a formal development.

Ricardian rent

Long-run producer surplus can be most easily illustrated with a situation first described by David Ricardo in the early part of the nineteenth century.[10] Assume there are many parcels of land on which a particular crop might be grown. These range from very fertile land (low costs of production) to very poor, dry land (high costs). The long-run supply curve for the crop is constructed as follows. At low prices only the best land is used. As output increases, higher-cost plots of land are brought into production because higher prices make it profitable to use this land. The long-run supply curve is positively sloped because of the increasing costs associated with using less fertile land.

Market equilibrium in this situation is illustrated in Figure 12.11. At an equilibrium price of P^*, owners of both the low-cost and the medium-cost firms earn (long-run) profits. The "marginal firm" earns exactly zero economic profits. Firms with even higher costs stay out of the market because they would incur losses at a price of P^*. Profits earned by the intramarginal firms can persist in the long run, however, because they reflect a return to a unique resource—low-cost land. Free entry cannot erode these profits even over the long term. The sum of these long-run profits constitutes long-run producer surplus, as given by area P^*EB in panel (d) of Figure 12.11. Equivalence of these areas can be shown by recognizing that each point in the supply curve in panel (d) represents minimum average cost for some firm. For each such firm, $P - AC$ represents profits per unit of output. Total long-run profits can then be computed by summing over all units of output.[11]

---

[10]See David Ricardo, *The Principles of Political Economy and Taxation* (1817; reprinted London: J. M. Dent and Son, 1965), chap. 2 and chap. 32.

[11]More formally, suppose that firms are indexed by i ($i = 1, \dots, n$) from lowest to highest cost and that each firm produces q^*. In the long-run equilibrium, $Q^* = n^* q^*$ (where n^* is the equilibrium number of firms and Q^* is total industry output). Suppose also the inverse of the supply function (competitive price as a function of quantity supplied) is given by $P = P(Q)$. Because of the indexing of firms, price is determined by the highest cost firm in the market: $P = P(iq^*) = AC_i$ and $P^* = P(Q^*) = P(n^* q^*)$. Now, in long-run equilibrium, profits for firm i are given by

$$\pi_i = (P^* - AC_i)q^*,$$

FIGURE 12.11   Ricardian Rent

Owners of low-cost and medium-cost land can earn long-run profits. Long-run producers' surplus represents the sum of all these rents—area $P^* EB$ in panel (d). Usually Ricardian rents will be capitalized into input prices.

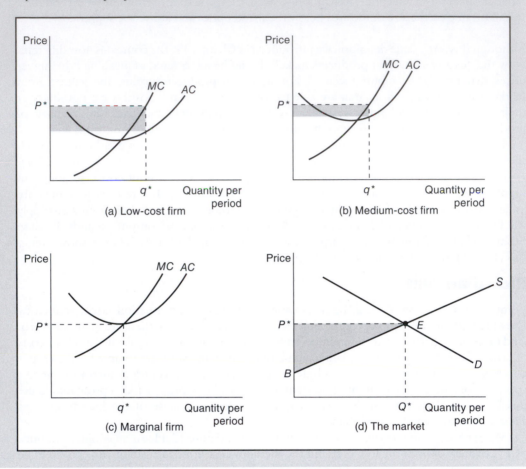

(a) Low-cost firm

(b) Medium-cost firm

(c) Marginal firm

(d) The market

Capitalization of rents

The long-run profits for the low-cost firms in Figure 12.11 will often be reflected in prices for the unique resources owned by those firms. In Ricardo's initial analysis, for example, one might expect fertile land to sell for more than an untillable rock pile. Because such prices will reflect the present value of all future profits, these profits are said to be "capitalized" into inputs' prices. Examples of capitalization include such disparate phenomena as the higher

---

and total profits are given by

$$
\begin{aligned}
\pi &= \int_0^{n^*} \pi_i \, di = \int_0^{n^*} (P^* - AC_i) q^* \, di \\
&= \int_0^{n^*} P^* q^* \, di - \int_0^{n^*} AC_i q^* \, di \\
&= P^* n^* q^* - \int_0^{n^*} P(iq^*) q^* \, di \\
&= P^* Q^* - \int_0^{Q^*} P(Q) \, dQ,
\end{aligned}
$$

which is the shaded area in panel (d) of Figure 12.11.

prices of nice houses with convenient access for commuters, the high value of rock and sport stars' contracts, and the lower value of land near toxic waste sites. Notice that in all of these cases it is market demand that determines rents—these rents are not traditional input costs that indicate forgone opportunities.

Input supply and long-run producer surplus

It is the scarcity of low-cost inputs that creates the possibility of Ricardian rent. If low-cost farmland were available at infinitely elastic supply, there would be no such rent. More generally, any input that is "scarce" (in the sense that it has a positively sloped supply curve to a particular industry) will obtain rents in the form of earning a higher return than would be obtained if industry output were zero. In such cases, increases in output not only raise firms' costs (and thereby the price for which the output will sell) but also generate factor rents for inputs. The sum of all such rents is again measured by the area above the long-run supply curve and below equilibrium price. Changes in the size of this area of long-run producer surplus indicate changing rents earned by inputs to the industry. Notice that, although long-run producer surplus is measured using the market supply curve, it is inputs to the industry that actually receive this surplus. Empirical measurements of changes in long-run producer surplus are widely used in applied welfare analysis to indicate how suppliers of various inputs fare as conditions change. The final sections of this chapter illustrate several such analyses.

ECONOMIC EFFICIENCY AND WELFARE ANALYSIS

Long-run competitive equilibria may have the desirable property of allocating resources "efficiently." Although we will have far more to say about this concept in a general equilibrium context in Chapter 13, here we can offer a partial equilibrium description of why the result might hold. Remember from Chapter 5 that the area below a demand curve and above market price represents consumer surplus—the extra utility consumers receive from choosing to purchase a good voluntarily rather than being forced to do without it. Similarly, as we saw in the previous section, producer surplus is measured as the area below market price and above the long-run supply curve, which represents the extra return that productive inputs receive rather than having no transactions in the good. Overall then, the area between the demand curve and the supply curve represents the sum of consumer and producer surplus: it measures the total additional value obtained by market participants by being able to make market transactions in this good. It seems clear that this total area is maximized at the competitive market equilibrium.

A graphic proof

Figure 12.12 shows a simplified proof. Given the demand curve (D) and the long-run supply curve (S), the sum of consumer and producer surplus is given by distance AB for the first unit produced. Total surplus continues to increase as additional output is produced—up to the competitive equilibrium level, Q^*. This level of production will be achieved when price is at the competitive level, P^*. Total consumer surplus is represented by the light shaded area in the figure, total producer surplus by the darker shaded area. Clearly, for output levels less than Q^* (say, Q_1), total surplus would be reduced. One sign of this misallocation is that, at Q_1, demanders would value an additional unit of output at P_1 whereas average and marginal costs would be given by P_2. Because $P_1 > P_2$, total welfare would clearly increase by producing one more unit of output. A transaction that involved trading this extra unit at any price between P_1 and P_2 would be mutually beneficial: both parties would gain.

The total welfare loss that occurs at output level Q_1 is given by area FEG. The distribution of surplus at output level Q_1 will depend on the precise (nonequilibrium) price that prevails in the market. At a price of P_1, consumer surplus would be reduced substantially to area

FIGURE 12.12   Competitive Equilibrium and Consumer/Producer Surplus

At the competitive equilibrium (Q^*), the sum of consumer surplus (shaded lighter gray) and producer surplus (shaded darker) is maximized. For an output level $Q_1 < Q^*$, there is a deadweight loss of consumer and producer surplus that is given by area *FEG*.

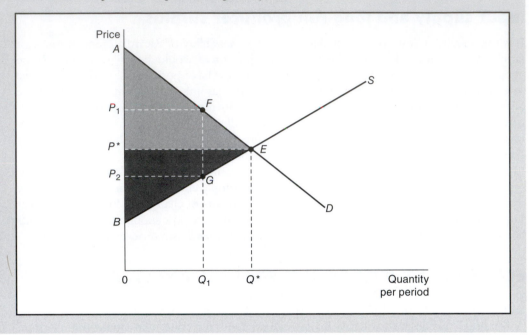

AFP_1, whereas producers might actually gain because producer surplus is now $P_1 FGB$. At a low price such as P_2 the situation would be reversed, with producers being much worse off than they were initially. Hence the distribution of the welfare losses from producing less than Q^* will depend on the price at which transactions are conducted. However, the size of the total loss is given by *FEG*, regardless of the price settled upon.[12]

A mathematical proof

Mathematically, we choose Q to maximize

$$\textbf{consumer surplus + producer surplus} = [U(Q) - PQ] + \left[PQ - \int_0^Q P(Q)\, dQ \right]$$

$$= U(Q) - \int_0^Q P(Q)\, dQ, \qquad \textbf{(12.59)}$$

where $U(Q)$ is the utility function of the representative consumer and $P(Q)$ is the long-run supply relation. In long-run equilibria along the long-run supply curve, $P(Q) = AC = MC$. Maximization of Equation 12.59 with respect to Q yields

$$U'(Q) = P(Q) = AC = MC, \qquad \textbf{(12.60)}$$

so maximization occurs where the marginal value of Q to the representative consumer is equal to market price. But this is precisely the competitive supply-demand equilibrium, because the demand curve represents consumers' marginal valuations whereas the supply curve reflects marginal (and, in long-term equilibrium, average) cost.

---

[12]Increases in output beyond Q^* also clearly reduce welfare.

Applied welfare analysis

The conclusion that the competitive equilibrium maximizes the sum of consumer and producer surplus mirrors a series of more general economic efficiency "theorems" we will examine in Chapter 13. Describing the major caveats that attach to these theorems is best delayed until that more extended discussion. Here we are more interested in showing how the competitive model is used to examine the consequences of changing economic conditions on the welfare of market participants. Usually such welfare changes are measured by looking at changes in consumer and producer surplus.

EXAMPLE 12.6 Welfare Loss Computations

Use of consumer and producer surplus notions makes possible the explicit calculation of welfare losses from restrictions on voluntary transactions. In the case of linear demand and supply curves, this computation is especially simple because the areas of loss are frequently triangular. For example, if demand is given by

$$Q_D = 10 - P \tag{12.61}$$

and supply by

$$Q_S = P - 2, \tag{12.62}$$

then market equilibrium occurs at the point $P^* = 6, Q^* = 4$. Restriction of output to $\bar{Q} = 3$ would create a gap between what demanders are willing to pay ($P_D = 10 - Q = 7$) and what suppliers require ($P_S = 2 + \bar{Q} = 5$). The welfare loss from restricting transactions is given by a triangle with a base of 2 ($= P_D - P_S = 7 - 5$) and a height of 1 (the difference between Q^* and $\bar{Q}$). Hence the welfare loss is one dollar if P is measured in dollars per unit and Q is measured in units. More generally, the loss will be measured in the units in which $P \cdot Q$ is measured.

Computations with constant elasticity curves. More realistic results can usually be obtained by using constant elasticity demand and supply curves based on econometric studies. In Example 12.3 we examined such a model of the U.S. automobile market. We can simplify that example a bit by assuming that P is measured in thousands of dollars and Q in millions of automobiles and that demand is given by

$$Q_D = 200P^{-1.2} \tag{12.63}$$

and supply by

$$Q_S = 1.3P. \tag{12.64}$$

Equilibrium in the market is given by $P^* = 9.87, Q^* = 12.8$. Suppose now that government policy restricts automobile sales to 11 (million) in order to control emissions of pollutants. An approximation to the direct welfare loss from such a policy can be found by the triangular method used earlier.

With $\bar{Q} = 11$, we have $P_D = (11/200)^{-0.83} = 11.1$ and $P_S = 11/1.3 = 8.46$. Hence, the welfare loss "triangle" is given by $0.5(P_D - P_S)(Q^* - \bar{Q}) = 0.5(11.1 - 8.46) \cdot (12.8 - 11) = 2.38$. Here the units are those of P times Q: billions of dollars. The approximate[13] value of the welfare loss is therefore \$2.4 billion, which might be weighed against the expected gain from emissions control.

(continued)

---

[13]A more precise estimate of the loss can be obtained by integrating $P_D - P_S$ over the range $Q = 11$ to $Q = 12.8$. With exponential demand and supply curves, this integration is often easy. In the present case, the technique yields an estimated welfare loss of 2.28, showing that the triangular approximation is not too bad even for relatively large price changes. Hence we will primarily use such approximations in later analysis.

EXAMPLE 12.6 CONTINUED

Distribution of loss. In the automobile case, the welfare loss is shared about equally by consumers and producers. An approximation for consumers' losses is given by $0.5(P_D - P^*) \cdot (Q^* - \bar{Q}) = 0.5(11.1 - 9.87)(12.8 - 11) = 1.11$ and for producers by $0.5(9.87 - 8.46) \cdot (12.8 - 11) = 1.27$. Because the price elasticity of demand is somewhat greater (in absolute value) than the price elasticity of supply, consumers incur less than half the loss and producers somewhat more than half. With a more price elastic demand curve, consumers would incur a smaller share of the loss.

QUERY: How does the size of the total welfare loss from a quantity restriction depend on the elasticities of supply and demand? What determines how the loss will be shared?

PRICE CONTROLS AND SHORTAGES

Sometimes governments may seek to control prices at below equilibrium levels. Although adoption of such policies may be based on noble motives, the controls deter long-run supply responses and create welfare losses for both consumers and producers. A simple analysis of this possibility is provided by Figure 12.13. Initially the market is in long-run equilibrium at P_1, Q_1 (point E). An increase in demand from D to D' would cause the price to rise to P_2 in the short run and encourage entry by new firms. Assuming this market is characterized by increasing costs (as reflected by the positively sloped long-run supply curve LS), price would fall somewhat as a result of this entry, ultimately settling at P_3. If these price changes were regarded as undesirable then the government could, in principle, prevent them by imposing a legally enforceable ceiling price of P_1. This would cause firms to continue to supply their previous output (Q_1); but, because at P_1 demanders now want to purchase Q_4, there will be a shortage given by $Q_4 - Q_1$.

Welfare evaluation

The welfare consequences of this price-control policy can be evaluated by comparing consumer and producer surplus measures prevailing under this policy to those that would have prevailed in the absence of controls. First, the buyers of Q_1 gain the consumer surplus given by area P_3CEP_1 because they can buy this good at a lower price than would exist in an uncontrolled market. This gain reflects a pure transfer from producers out of the amount of producer surplus that would exist without controls. What current consumers have gained from the lower price, producers have lost. Although this transfer does not represent a loss of overall welfare, it does clearly affect the relative well-being of the market participants.

Second, the area $AE'C$ represents the value of additional consumer surplus that would have been attained without controls. Similarly, the area $CE'E$ reflects additional producer surplus available in the uncontrolled situation. Together, these two areas (that is, area $AE'E$) represent the total value of mutually beneficial transactions that are prevented by the government policy of controlling price. This is, therefore, a measure of the pure welfare costs of that policy.

Disequilibrium behavior

The welfare analysis depicted in Figure 12.13 also suggests some of the types of behavior that might be expected as a result of the price-control policy. Assuming that observed market outcomes are generated by

$$Q(P_1) = \min[Q_D(P_1), Q_S(P_1)], \tag{12.65}$$

FIGURE 12.13   Price Controls and Shortages

A shift in demand from D to D' would raise price to P_2 in the short run. Entry over the long run would yield a final equilibrium of P_3, Q_3. Controlling the price at P_1 would prevent these actions and yield a shortage of $Q_4 - Q_1$. Relative to the uncontrolled situation, the price control yields a transfer from producers to consumers (area $P_3 CEP_1$) and a deadweight loss of forgone transactions given by the two areas $AE'C$ and $CE'E$.

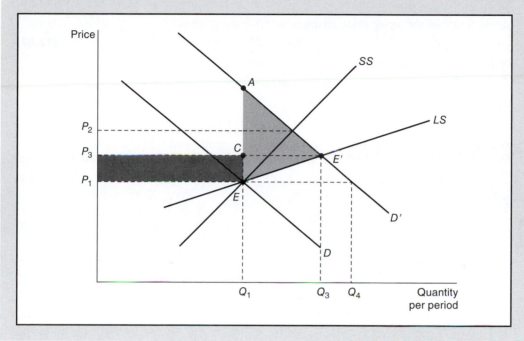

suppliers will be content with this outcome, but demanders will not because they will be forced to accept a situation of excess demand. They have an incentive to signal their dissatisfaction to suppliers through increasing price offers. Such offers may not only tempt existing suppliers to make illegal transactions at higher than allowed prices but may also encourage new entrants to make such transactions. It is this kind of activity that leads to the prevalence of black markets in most instances of price control. Modeling the resulting transactions is difficult for two reasons. First, these may involve non–price-taking behavior because the price of each transaction must be individually negotiated rather than set by "the market." Second, non-equilibrium transactions will often involve imperfect information. Any pair of market participants will usually not know what other transactors are doing, although such actions may affect their welfare by changing the options available. Some progress has been made in modeling such disequilibrium behavior using game theory techniques (see Chapter 18). However, other than the obvious prediction that transactions will occur at prices above the price ceiling, no general results have been obtained. The types of black-market transactions undertaken will depend on the specific institutional details of the situation.

TAX INCIDENCE ANALYSIS

The partial equilibrium model of competitive markets has also been widely used to study the impact of taxes. Although, as we will point out, these applications are necessarily limited by their inability to analyze tax effects that spread through many markets, they do provide important insights on a number of issues.

A mathematical model

The effect of a per-unit tax can be most easily studied using the mathematical model of supply and demand that was introduced previously. Now, however, we need to make a distinction between the price paid by demanders (P_D) and the price received by suppliers (P_S), because a per-unit tax (t) introduces a "wedge" between these two magnitudes:

$$P_D - P_S = t; \tag{12.66}$$

or, in terms of the small price changes we wish to examine,

$$dP_D - dP_S = dt. \tag{12.67}$$

Maintenance of equilibrium in the market requires

$$dQ_D = dQ_S$$

or

$$D_P dP_D = S_P dP_S, \tag{12.68}$$

where D_P and S_P are the price derivatives of the demand and supply functions, respectively. We can use Equations 12.67 and 12.68 to solve for the effect of the tax on P_D:

$$D_P dP_D = S_P dP_S = S_P(dP_D - dt). \tag{12.69}$$

Hence

$$\frac{dP_D}{dt} = \frac{S_P}{S_P - D_P} = \frac{e_S}{e_S - e_D}, \tag{12.70}$$

where e_S and e_D represent the price elasticities of supply and demand and where the final equation is derived by multiplying both numerator and denominator by P/Q. A similar set of manipulations for the change in supply price gives

$$\frac{dP_S}{dt} = \frac{e_D}{e_S - e_D}. \tag{12.71}$$

Because $e_D \leq 0$ and $e_S \geq 0$, these calculations provide the obvious results

$$\frac{dP_D}{dt} \geq 0,$$

$$\frac{dP_S}{dt} \leq 0. \tag{12.72}$$

If $e_D = 0$ (demand is perfectly inelastic), then $dP_D/dt = 1$ and the per-unit tax is completely paid by demanders. Alternatively, if $e_D = -\infty$, then $dP_S/dt = -1$ and the tax is wholly paid by producers. More generally, dividing Equation 12.71 by Equation 12.70 yields

$$-\frac{dP_S/dt}{dP_D/dt} = -\frac{e_D}{e_S}, \tag{12.73}$$

which shows that the actor with the less elastic responses (in absolute value) will experience most of the price change occasioned by the tax.

A welfare analysis

Figure 12.14 permits a simplified welfare analysis of the tax incidence issue. Imposition of the unit tax, t, creates a vertical wedge between the supply and demand curves, and the quantity traded declines to Q^{**}. Demanders incur a loss of consumer surplus given by area $P_D FEP^*$, of which $P_D FHP^*$ is transferred to the government as a portion of total tax revenues. The balance of total tax revenues ($P^* HGP_S$) is paid by producers, who incur a total loss of producer surplus given by area $P^* EGP_S$. Notice that the reduction in combined consumer and producer surplus exceeds total tax revenues collected by area FEG. This area represents a "deadweight" loss that arises because some mutually beneficial transactions are discouraged

FIGURE 12.14   Tax Incidence Analysis

Imposition of a specific tax of amount t per unit creates a "wedge" between the price consumers pay (P_D) and what suppliers receive (P_S). The extent to which consumers or producers pay the tax depends on the price elasticities of demand and supply.

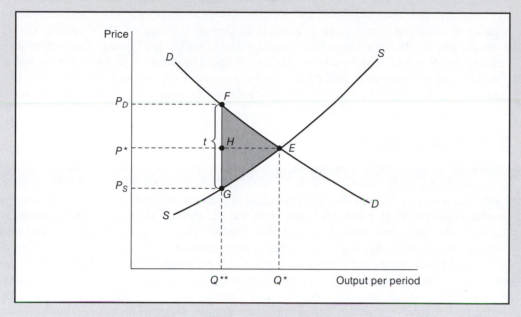

by the tax. In general, the sizes of all of the various areas illustrated in Figure 12.14 will be affected by the price elasticities involved. To determine the final incidence of the producers' share of the tax would require an explicit analysis of input markets—the burden of the tax would be reflected in reduced rents for those inputs characterized by relatively inelastic supply. More generally, a complete analysis of the incidence question requires a general equilibrium model that can treat many markets simultaneously. We discuss such models in the next chapter.

Deadweight loss and elasticity

All non–lump-sum taxes involve deadweight losses because they alter the behavior of economic actors. The size of such losses will depend in a rather complex way on the elasticities of demand and supply in the market. A linear approximation to the deadweight loss accompanying a small tax dt is given by

$$DW = -0.5(dt)(dQ). \tag{12.74}$$

But from the definition of elasticity, we know that

$$dQ = e_D dP_D \cdot \frac{Q_0}{P_0}, \tag{12.75}$$

where Q_0 and P_0 are the pretax values for quantity and price, respectively. Combining Equations 12.75 and 12.70 yields

$$dQ = e_D \frac{e_S}{e_S - e_D} \, dt \, \frac{Q_0}{P_0}, \tag{12.76}$$

and substitution into Equation 12.74 provides a final expression for the loss:

$$DW = -0.5\left(\frac{dt}{P_0}\right)^2 \frac{e_D e_S}{e_S - e_D} P_0 Q_0. \tag{12.77}$$

Clearly, deadweight losses are zero in cases in which either e_D or e_S is zero because then the tax does not alter the quantity of the good traded. More generally, deadweight losses are smaller in situations where e_D or e_S is small. In principle, Equation 12.77 can be used to evaluate the deadweight losses accompanying any complex tax system. This information might provide some insights on how a tax system could be designed to minimize the overall "excess burden" involved in collecting a needed amount of tax revenues (see Problems 12.9 and 12.10). Notice also that DW is proportional to the square of the tax rate—marginal excess burden increases with the tax rate.

Transaction costs

Although we have developed this discussion in terms of tax incidence theory, models incorporating a wedge between buyers' and sellers' prices have a number of other applications in economics. Perhaps the most important of these involve costs associated with making market transactions. In some cases these costs may be explicit. Most real estate transactions, for example, take place through a third-party broker, who charges a fee for the service of bringing buyer and seller together. Similar explicit transaction fees occur in the trading of stocks and bonds, boats and airplanes, and practically everything that is solid at auction. In all of these instances, buyers and sellers are willing to pay an explicit fee to an agent or broker who facilitates the transaction. In other cases, transaction costs may be largely implicit. Individuals trying to purchase a used car, for example, will spend considerable time and effort reading classified advertisements and examining vehicles, and these activities amount to an implicit cost of making the transaction.

EXAMPLE 12.7 The Excess Burden of a Tax

In Example 12.6 we examined the loss of consumer and producer surplus that would occur if automobile sales were cut from their equilibrium level of 12.8 (million) to 11 (million). An auto tax of $2,640 (i.e., 2.64 thousand dollars) would accomplish this reduction because it would introduce exactly the wedge between demand and supply price that was calculated previously. Since we have assumed $e_D = -1.2$ and $e_S = 1.0$ in Example 12.6 and since initial spending on automobiles is approximately $126 (billion), Equation 12.77 predicts that the excess burden from the auto tax would be

$$DW = 0.5\left(\frac{2.64}{9.87}\right)^2 \left(\frac{1.2}{2.2}\right)126 = 2.46. \tag{12.78}$$

This loss of 2.46 billion dollars is approximately the same as the loss from emissions control calculated in Example 12.6. It might be contrasted to total tax collections, which in this case amount to $29 billion ($2,640 per automobile times 11 million automobiles in the post-tax equilibrium). Here, the deadweight loss equals approximately 8 percent of total tax revenues collected.

Marginal burden. An incremental increase in the auto tax would be relatively more costly in terms of excess burden. Suppose the government decided to round the auto tax upward to a flat $3,000 per car. In this case, car sales would drop to approximately 10.7 (million). Tax collections would amount to $32.1 billion, an increase of $3.1 billion over what was computed previously. Equation 12.78 can be used to show that deadweight losses now amount to $3.17 billion—an increase of $0.71 billion above the losses experienced with the lower tax.

At the margin, then, additional deadweight losses amount to about 23 percent (0.72/3.1) of additional revenues collected. Hence marginal and average excess burden computations may differ significantly.

QUERY: Can you explain intuitively why the marginal burden of a tax exceeds its average burden? Under what conditions would the marginal excess burden of a tax exceed additional tax revenues collected?

To the extent that transaction costs are on a per-unit basis (as they are in the real estate, securities, and auction examples), our previous taxation example applies exactly. From the point of view of the buyers and sellers, it makes little difference whether t represents a per-unit tax or a per-unit transaction fee, because the analysis of the fee's effect on the market will be the same. That is, the fee will be shared between buyers and sellers depending on the specific elasticities involved. Trading volume will be lower than in the absence of such fees.[14] A somewhat different analysis would hold, however, if transaction costs were a lump-sum amount per transaction. In that case, individuals would seek to reduce the number of transactions made, but the existence of the charge would not affect the supply-demand equilibrium itself. For example, the cost of driving to the supermarket is mainly a lump-sum transaction cost on shopping for groceries. The existence of such a charge may not significantly affect the price of food items or the amount of food consumed (unless it tempts people to grow their own), but the charge will cause individuals to shop less frequently, to buy larger quantities on each trip, and to hold larger inventories of food in their homes than would be the case in the absence of such a cost.

Effects on the attributes of transactions

More generally, taxes or transaction costs may affect some attributes of transactions more than others. In our formal model, we assumed that such costs were based only on the physical quantity of goods sold. The desire of suppliers and demanders to minimize costs therefore led them to reduce quantity traded. When transactions involve several dimensions (such as quality, risk, or timing), taxes or transaction costs may affect some or all of these dimensions—depending on the precise basis on which the costs are assessed. For example, a tax on quantity may cause firms to upgrade product quality, or information-based transaction costs may encourage firms to produce less risky, standardized commodities. Similarly, a per-transaction cost (travel costs of getting to the store) may cause individuals to make fewer but larger transactions (and to hold larger inventories). The possibilities for these various substitutions will obviously depend on the particular circumstances of the transaction. We will examine several examples of cost-induced changes in attributes of transactions in later chapters.[15]

TRADE RESTRICTIONS

Restrictions on the flow of goods in international commerce have effects similar to those we just examined for taxes. Impediments to free trade may reduce mutually beneficial transactions and cause a variety of transfers among the various parties involved. Once again, the competitive model of supply and demand is frequently used to study these effects.

---

[14]This analysis does not consider possible benefits obtained from brokers. To the extent that these services are valuable to the parties in the transaction, demand and supply curves will shift outward to reflect this value. Hence trading volume may actually expand with the availability of services that facilitate transactions, although the costs of such services will continue to create a wedge between sellers' and buyers' prices.

[15]For the classic treatment of this topic, see Y. Barzel, "An Alternative Approach to the Analysis of Taxation," *Journal of Political Economy* (December 1976): 1177–97.

FIGURE 12.15 Opening of International Trade Increases Total Welfare

Opening of international trade lowers price from P^* to P_W, at which point domestic producers supply Q_2 and demanders buy Q_1. Imports amount to $Q_1 - Q_2$. The lower price results in a transfer from domestic producers to consumers (shaded lighter gray) and a net gain of consumer surplus (shaded darker gray).

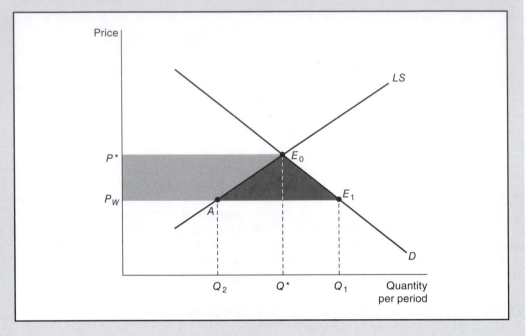

Gains from international trade

Figure 12.15 illustrates the domestic demand and supply curves for a particular good, say, shoes. In the absence of international trade, the domestic equilibrium price of shoes would be P^* and quantity would be Q^*. Although this equilibrium would exhaust all mutually beneficial transactions between domestic shoe producers and domestic demanders, opening of international trade presents a number of additional options. If world shoe prices, P_W, are less than the prevailing domestic price, P^*, then the opening of trade will cause prices to fall to this world level.[16] This drop in price will cause quantity demanded to increase to Q_1, whereas quantity supplied by domestic producers will fall to Q_2. Imported shoes will amount to $Q_1 - Q_2$. In short, what shoes domestic producers do not supply at the world price are instead provided by foreign sources.

The shift in the market equilibrium from E_0 to E_1 causes a large increase in consumer surplus, given by the area $P^* E_0 E_1 P_W$. Part of this gain reflects a transfer from domestic shoe producers (area $P^* E_0 A P_W$), and part represents an unambiguous welfare gain (area $E_0 E_1 A$). The source of consumer gains here is obvious: buyers get shoes at a lower price than was previously available in the domestic market. As in our analysis of taxation, losses of producer surplus are experienced by those inputs that give the long-run supply curve its upward slope. If, for example, the domestic shoe industry experiences increasing costs because shoemaker

---

[16]Throughout our analysis we will assume that this country is a price taker in the world market and can purchase all of the imports it wishes without affecting the price, P_W. For an analysis of an upward sloping supply curve for imports, see Problem 12.11.

wages are driven up as industry output expands, then the decline in output from Q^* to Q_2 as a result of trade will reverse this process, causing shoemaker wages to fall.

Tariff protection and the politics of trade

Shoemakers are unlikely to take wage losses arising from shoe imports lying down. Instead, they will press the government for protection from the flood of imported footwear. Because the loss of producer surplus is experienced by relatively few individuals whereas consumer gains from trade are spread across many shoe buyers, shoemakers may have considerably greater incentives to organize opposition to imports than consumers would have to organize to keep trade open. The result may be the adoption of protectionist measures.

Historically, the most important type of protection employed has been a tariff: a tax on the imported good. The effects of such a tax are shown in Figure 12.16. Now comparisons begin from the free-trade equilibrium, E_1. Imposition of a per-unit tariff on shoes for domestic buyers of amount t raises the effective price to $P_W + t = P_R$. This price rise causes quantity demanded to fall from Q_1 to Q_3, whereas domestic production expands from Q_2 to Q_4. The total quantity of shoe imports falls from $Q_1 - Q_2$ to $Q_3 - Q_4$. Because each imported pair of shoes is now subject to a tariff, total tariff revenues are given by the area BE_2DC, measured by $t(Q_3 - Q_4)$.

Imposition of the tariff on imported shoes creates a variety of welfare effects. Total consumer surplus is reduced by the area $P_R E_2 E_1 P_W$. Part of this, as we have seen, is transferred into tariff revenues and part is transferred into increased domestic producers' surplus (area $P_R BA P_W$). The two triangles, BCA and $E_2 E_1 D$, represent losses of consumer surplus that are not transferred to anyone; these are a deadweight loss from the tariff and are similar to the excess burden imposed

FIGURE 12.16   Effects of a Tariff

Imposition of a tariff of amount t raises price to $P_R = P_W + t$. This results in collection of tariff revenue (area BE_2DC), a transfer from consumers to producers (area $P_R BA P_W$), and two triangles measuring deadweight loss (shaded). A quota has similar effects, though in this case no revenues are collected.

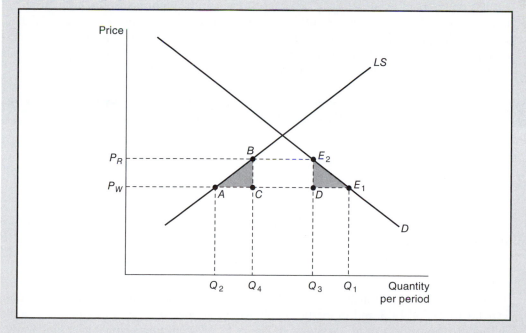

by any tax. All of these areas can be measured if good empirical estimates of the domestic supply and demand elasticities for imported goods are available, as we now show.

Quantitative estimates of deadweight losses

Estimates of the sizes of the welfare loss triangle in Figure 12.16 can be readily calculated. Because $P_R = (1 + t)P_W$, the proportional change in quantity demanded brought about by this price rise is given by

$$\frac{Q_3 - Q_1}{Q_1} = \frac{P_R - P_W}{P_W} \cdot e_D = te_D, \tag{12.79}$$

and the area of triangle $E_2 E_1 D$ is given by

$$DW_1 = 0.5(P_R - P_W)(Q_1 - Q_3) = -0.5t^2 e_D P_W Q_1. \tag{12.80}$$

Similarly, the loss in consumer surplus represented by area BCA is given by

$$DW_2 = 0.5(P_R - P_W)(Q_4 - Q_2) = 0.5t^2 e_S P_W Q_2. \tag{12.81}$$

Notice that the values of both DW_1 and DW_2 are convex functions of the tariff rate (t) and that each depends on the initial value of total revenues. When imports initially represent a large share of the domestic market and when e_D and e_S are of similar sizes (in absolute value), this suggests that DW_1 will generally be the larger of the two deadweight losses. These losses may be large relative to total transfers to producers (area $P_R BAP_W$), thereby leading to rather large estimates for the "costs" of some tariffs relative to the value of production benefits generated.

Other types of trade protection

Many other types of trade restrictions can be illustrated by adapting the tariff model we have already developed in Figure 12.16. A quota that limits imports to $Q_3 - Q_4$ would have effects that are very similar to those shown in the figure: market price would rise to P_R; a substantial transfer from consumers to domestic producers would occur (area $P_R BAP_W$); and there would be deadweight losses represented by the triangles BCA and $E_2 E_1 D$. With a quota, however, no revenues are collected by the government, so the loss of consumer surplus represented by area $BE_2 DC$ must go elsewhere. It might be captured by owners of import licenses or by foreign producers, depending on how quota rights are assigned. Nonquantitative restrictions such as inspection or testing requirements also impose cost and time delays that can be treated as an "implicit" tariff on imports. Figure 12.16 can easily be adapted to illustrate the effects of these impediments to trade.

EXAMPLE 12.8 Trade and Tariffs

These various aspects of trade policy can be illustrated with our simplified model of the automobile market. We have shown previously that, with a demand function given by

$$Q_D = 200P^{-1.2} \tag{12.82}$$

and supply by

$$Q_S = 1.3P, \tag{12.83}$$

the domestic market has a long-run equilibrium of

$$P^* = 9.87, \tag{12.84}$$
$$Q^* = 12.8.$$

If automobiles were available at a world price of 9 (thousand dollars), demand would expand to $Q_D = 14.3$ and domestic supply would shrink to $Q_S = 11.7$. Imports would amount to 2.6 (million) cars. As shown in Figure 12.15, consumers would gain significantly by the availability of imports (consumer surplus would expand by approximately 11.8 billion dollars), although a significant portion of this gain (10.7 billion) would represent a transfer from domestic producers to consumers.

Effects of a tariff. If pressure from domestic producers leads the government to adopt, say, a $500 tariff, then the world price of cars will rise to 9.5 (thousand dollars), quantity demanded will contract (to 13.4), and domestic supply will expand (to 12.4). Imports would contract to 1.0 (million) cars. The welfare effects of these changes can be calculated directly or can be approximated by the expressions in Equations 12.80 and 12.81. A direct calculation of DW_1 yields[17]

$$DW_1 = 0.5(0.5)(14.3 - 13.4) = 0.225, \qquad \textbf{(12.85)}$$

and for DW_2 we have

$$DW_2 = 0.5(0.5)(12.4 - 11.7) = 0.175. \qquad \textbf{(12.86)}$$

Hence the total deadweight loss from the tariff (0.4 billion) is approximately equal to total tariff revenue (0.5 billion).

Effects of a quota. An automobile import quota of 1 million cars would have identical effects to that of a $500 tariff. Equilibrium price would rise by $500, and there would be a large transfer from domestic consumers to domestic producers. Deadweight losses of $0.4 billion would also be the same as before. Now, however, there would be no tariff revenues. The $0.5 billion loss in consumer surplus will instead be transferred to whoever can appropriate the rights to import cars. Because the right to import a car is worth $500, it seems likely there will be active interest in acquiring such rights.

QUERY: What is the total transfer from consumers to producers as a result of the auto tariff or quota in this problem? Who would ultimately receive this transfer?

SUMMARY

In this chapter we developed a detailed model of how the equilibrium price is determined in a single competitive market. This model is basically the one first fully articulated by Alfred Marshall in the latter part of the nineteenth century. It remains the single most important component of all of microeconomics. Some of the properties of this model we examined may be listed as follows.

- Short-run equilibrium prices are determined by the interaction of what demanders are willing to pay (demand) and what existing firms are willing to produce (supply). Both demanders and suppliers act as price takers in making their respective decisions.

- In the long run, the number of firms may vary in response to profit opportunities. If free entry is assumed then firms will earn zero economic profits over the long run. Because firms also maximize profits, the long-run equilibrium condition is therefore $P = MC = AC$.

- The shape of the long-run supply curve depends on how the entry of new firms affects input prices. If entry has no impact on input prices, the long-run supply curve will be horizontal (infinitely elastic). If entry raises input prices, the long-run supply curve will have a positive slope.

- If shifts in long-run equilibrium affect input prices, this will also affect the welfare of input suppliers. Such welfare changes can be measured by changes in long-run producer surplus.

- The twin concepts of consumer and producer surplus provide useful ways of measuring the welfare impact on market participants of various economic changes. Changes in consumer surplus represent the monetary value of changes in consumer utility. Changes in producer surplus represent changes in the monetary returns that inputs receive.

- The competitive model can be used to study the impact of various economic policies. For example, it can be used

---

[17]Because the tariff here is approximately $t = .055$, Equation 12.80 yields an approximate DW_1 value of 0.234, whereas Equation 12.81 shows $DW_2 = 0.159$. The estimated total deadweight loss is approximately 0.4 billion.

to illustrate the transfers and welfare losses associated with price controls.

• The competitive model can also be applied to study taxation. The model illustrates both tax incidence (that is, who bears the actual burden of a tax) and the welfare losses associated with taxation (the excess burden). Similar conclusions can be derived by using the competitive model to study transactions costs.

• A final important application uses the competitive model to study international trading relationships. The model can help us identify those who win and those who lose from the opening of trade. It can also be used to examine the welfare impact of trade restrictions.

PROBLEMS

12.1

Suppose there are 100 identical firms in a perfectly competitive industry. Each firm has a short-run total cost function of the form

$$C(q) = \frac{1}{300}q^3 + 0.2q^2 + 4q + 10.$$

a. Calculate the firm's short-run supply curve with q as a function of market price (P).

b. On the assumption that there are no interaction effects among costs of the firms in the industry, calculate the short-run industry supply curve.

c. Suppose market demand is given by $Q = -200P + 8,000$. What will be the short-run equilibrium price-quantity combination?

12.2

Suppose there are 1,000 identical firms producing diamonds. Let the total cost function for each firm be given by

$$C(q, w) = q^2 + wq,$$

where q is the firm's output level and w is the wage rate of diamond cutters.

a. If $w = 10$, what will be the firm's (short-run) supply curve? What is the industry's supply curve? How many diamonds will be produced at a price of 20 each? How many more diamonds would be produced at a price of 21?

b. Suppose the wages of diamond cutters depend on the total quantity of diamonds produced and suppose the form of this relationship is given by

$$w = 0.002Q;$$

here Q represents total industry output, which is 1,000 times the output of the typical firm.

In this situation, show that the firm's marginal cost (and short-run supply) curve depends on Q. What is the industry supply curve? How much will be produced at a price of 20? How much more will be produced at a price of 21? What do you conclude about the shape of the short-run supply curve?

12.3

A perfectly competitive market has 1,000 firms. In the very short run, each of the firms has a fixed supply of 100 units. The market demand is given by

$$Q = 160,000 - 10,000P.$$

a. Calculate the equilibrium price in the very short run.

b. Calculate the demand schedule facing any one firm in this industry.

c. Calculate what the equilibrium price would be if one of the sellers decided to sell nothing or if one seller decided to sell 200 units.

d. At the original equilibrium point, calculate the elasticity of the industry demand curve and the elasticity of the demand curve facing any one seller.

Suppose now that, in the short run, each firm has a supply curve that shows the quantity the firm will supply (q_i) as a function of market price. The specific form of this supply curve is given by

$$q_i = -200 + 50P.$$

Using this short-run supply response, supply revised answers to (a)–(d).

12.4

A perfectly competitive industry has a large number of potential entrants. Each firm has an identical cost structure such that long-run average cost is minimized at an output of 20 units ($q_i = 20$). The minimum average cost is $10 per unit. Total market demand is given by

$$Q = 1,500 - 50P.$$

a. What is the industry's long-run supply schedule?

b. What is the long-run equilibrium price (P^*)? The total industry output (Q^*)? The output of each firm (q^*)? The number of firms? The profits of each firm?

c. The short-run total cost function associated with each firm's long-run equilibrium output is given by

$$C(q) = 0.5q^2 - 10q + 200.$$

Calculate the short-run average and marginal cost function. At what output level does short-run average cost reach a minimum?

d. Calculate the short-run supply function for each firm and the industry short-run supply function.

e. Suppose now that the market demand function shifts upward to $Q = 2,000 - 50P$. Using this new demand curve, answer part (b) for the very short run when firms cannot change their outputs.

f. In the short run, use the industry short-run supply function to recalculate the answers to (b).

g. What is the new long-run equilibrium for the industry?

12.5

Suppose that the demand for stilts is given by

$$Q = 1,500 - 50P$$

and that the long-run total operating costs of each stilt-making firm in a competitive industry are given by

$$C(q) = 0.5q^2 - 10q.$$

Entrepreneurial talent for stilt making is scarce. The supply curve for entrepreneurs is given by

$$Q_S = 0.25w,$$

where w is the annual wage paid.

Suppose also that each stilt-making firm requires one (and only one) entrepreneur (hence, the quantity of entrepreneurs hired is equal to the number of firms). Long-run total costs for each firm are then given by

$$C(q, w) = 0.5q^2 - 10q + w.$$

a. What is the long-run equilibrium quantity of stilts produced? How many stilts are produced by each firm? What is the long-run equilibrium price of stilts? How many firms will there be? How many entrepreneurs will be hired, and what is their wage?

b. Suppose that the demand for stilts shifts outward to

$$Q = 2,428 - 50P.$$

How would you now answer the questions posed in part (a)?

c. Because stilt-making entrepreneurs are the cause of the upward-sloping long-run supply curve in this problem, they will receive all rents generated as industry output expands. Calculate the increase in rents between parts (a) and (b). Show that this value is identical to the change in long-run producer surplus as measured along the stilt supply curve.

12.6

The handmade snuffbox industry is composed of 100 identical firms, each having short-run total costs given by

$$STC = 0.5q^2 + 10q + 5$$

and short-run marginal costs given by

$$SMC = q + 10,$$

where q is the output of snuffboxes per day.

a. What is the short-run supply curve for each snuffbox maker? What is the short-run supply curve for the market as a whole?

b. Suppose the demand for total snuffbox production is given by

$$Q = 1,100 - 50P.$$

What will be the equilibrium in this marketplace? What will each firm's total short-run profits be?

c. Graph the market equilibrium and compute total short-run producer surplus in this case.

d. Show that the total producer surplus you calculated in part (c) is equal to total industry profits plus industry short-run fixed costs.

e. Suppose the government imposed a $3 tax on snuffboxes. How would this tax change the market equilibrium?

f. How would the burden of this tax be shared between snuffbox buyers and sellers?

g. Calculate the total loss of producer surplus as a result of the taxation of snuffboxes. Show that this loss equals the change in total short-run profits in the snuffbox industry. Why don't fixed costs enter into this computation of the change in short-run producer surplus?

12.7

The perfectly competitive videotape copying industry is composed of many firms that can copy five tapes per day at an average cost of $10 per tape. Each firm must also pay a royalty to film studios, and the per-film royalty rate (r) is an increasing function of total industry output (Q):

$$r = 0.002Q.$$

Demand is given by

$$Q = 1,050 - 50P.$$

a. Assuming the industry is in long-run equilibrium, what will be the equilibrium price and quantity of copied tapes? How many tape firms will there be? What will the per-film royalty rate be?

b. Suppose that demand for copied tapes increases to

$$Q = 1,600 - 50P.$$

In this case, what is the long-run equilibrium price and quantity for copied tapes? How many tape firms are there? What is the per-film royalty rate?

c. Graph these long-run equilibria in the tape market and calculate the increase in producer surplus between the situations described in parts (a) and (b).

d. Show that the increase in producer surplus is precisely equal to the increase in royalties paid as Q expands incrementally from its level in part (b) to its level in part (c).

e. Suppose that the government institutes a $5.50 per-film tax on the film copying industry. Assuming that the demand for copied films is that given in part (a), how will this tax affect the market equilibrium?

f. How will the burden of this tax be allocated between consumers and producers? What will be the loss of consumer and producer surplus?

g. Show that the loss of producer surplus as a result of this tax is borne completely by the film studios. Explain your result intuitively.

12.8

The domestic demand for portable radios is given by

$$Q = 5,000 - 100P,$$

where price (P) is measured in dollars and quantity (Q) is measured in thousands of radios per year. The domestic supply curve for radios is given by

$$Q = 150P.$$

a. What is the domestic equilibrium in the portable radio market?

b. Suppose portable radios can be imported at a world price of $10 per radio. If trade were unencumbered, what would the new market equilibrium be? How many portable radios would be imported?

c. If domestic portable radio producers succeeded in having a $5 tariff implemented, how would this change the market equilibrium? How much would be collected in tariff revenues? How much consumer surplus would be transferred to domestic producers? What would the deadweight loss from the tariff be?

d. How would your results from part (c) be changed if the government reached an agreement with foreign suppliers to "voluntarily" limit the portable radios they export to 1,250,000 per year? Explain how this differs from the case of a tariff.

Analytical Problems

12.9 Ad valorem taxes

Throughout this chapter's analysis of taxes we have used per-unit taxes—that is, a tax of a fixed amount for each unit traded in the market. A similar analysis would hold for ad valorem taxes—that is, taxes on the value of the transaction (or, what amounts to the same thing, proportional taxes on price). Given an ad valorem tax rate of t ($t = 0.05$ for a 5 percent tax), the gap between the price demanders pay and what suppliers receive is given by $P_D = (1 + t)P_S$.

a. Show that, for an ad valorem tax,

$$\frac{d \ln P_D}{dt} = \frac{e_S}{e_S - e_D} \quad \text{and} \quad \frac{d \ln P_S}{dt} = \frac{e_D}{e_S - e_D}.$$

b. Show that the excess burden of a small tax is

$$DW = -0.5 \frac{e_D e_S}{e_S - e_D} t^2 P_0 Q_0.$$

c. Compare these results to those derived in this chapter for a unit tax.

12.10 The Ramsey formula for optimal taxation

The development of optimal tax policy has been a major topic in public finance for centuries.[18] Probably the most famous result in the theory of optimal taxation is due to the English economist Frank Ramsey, who conceptualized the problem as how to structure a tax system that would collect a given amount of revenues with the minimal deadweight loss.[19] Specifically, suppose there are n goods (x_i with prices p_i) to be taxed with a sequence of ad valorem taxes (see Problem 12.9) whose rates are given by t_i ($i = 1, n$). Total tax revenue is therefore given by $T = \sum_{i=1}^{n} t_i p_i x_i$. Ramsey's problem, then, is for a fixed T to choose tax rates that will minimize total deadweight loss $DW = \sum_{i=1}^{n} DW(t_i)$.

a. Use the Lagrangian multiplier method to show that the solution to Ramsey's problem requires $t_i = \lambda(1/e_S - 1/e_D)$, where λ is the Lagrangian multiplier for the tax constraint.

b. Interpret the Ramsey result intuitively.

c. Describe some shortcomings of the Ramsey approach to optimal taxation.

12.11 International trade by a large country

In our analysis of tariffs we assumed that the country in question faced a perfectly elastic supply curve for imports. Now assume that this country faces a positively sloped supply curve for imported goods.

a. Show graphically how the level of imports will be determined.

b. Use your graph from part (a) to demonstrate the effects of a tariff in this market.

c. Carefully identify the sources of the various changes in consumer and producer surplus that are brought about by the tariff in part (b).

d. Show how the deadweight losses brought about by the tariff in this case will depend on the elasticity of demand and the elasticities of supply of domestic and imported goods.

SUGGESTIONS FOR FURTHER READING

Arnott, R. "Time for Revision on Rent Control?" *Journal of Economic Perspectives* (Winter 1995): 99–120.

> *Provides an assessment of actual "soft" rent-control policies and provides a rationale for them.*

deMelo, J., and D. G. Tarr. "The Welfare Costs of U.S. Quotas in Textiles, Steel, and Autos." *Review of Economics and Statistics* (August 1990): 489–97.

> *A nice study of the quota question in a general equilibrium context. Finds that the quotas studied have the same quantitative effects as a tariff rate of about 20 percent.*

Knight, F. H. *Risk, Uncertainty and Profit.* Boston: Houghton Mifflin, 1921, chaps. 5 and 6.

> *Classic treatment of the role of economic events in motivating industry behavior in the long run.*

Marshall, A. *Principles of Economics*, 8th ed. New York: Crowell-Collier and Macmillan, 1920, book 5, chaps. 1, 2, and 3.

> *Classic development of the supply-demand mechanism.*

Mas-Colell, A., M. D. Whinston, and J. R. Green. *Microeconomic Theory.* New York: Oxford University Press, 1995, chap. 10.

> *Provides a compact analysis at a high level of theoretical precision. There is a good discussion of situations where competitive markets may not reach an equilibrium.*

Reynolds, L. G. "Cut-Throat Competition." *American Economic Review* 30 (December 1940): 736–47.

> *Critique of the notion that there can be "too much" competition in an industry.*

Robinson, J. "What Is Perfect Competition?" *Quarterly Journal of Economics* 49 (1934): 104–20.

> *Critical discussion of the perfectly competitive assumptions.*

Salanie, B. *The Economics of Taxation.* Cambridge, MA: MIT Press, 2003.

> *This provides a compact study of many issues in taxation. Describes a few simple models of incidence and develops some general equilibrium models of taxation.*

---

[18]The seventeenth-century French finance minister Jean-Baptiste Colbert captured the essence of the problem with his memorable statement that "the art of taxation consists in so plucking the goose as to obtain the largest possible amount of feathers with the smallest amount of hissing."

[19]See F. Ramsey, "A Contribution to the Theory of Taxation," *Economic Journal* (March 1927): 47–61.

Stigler, G. J. "Perfect Competition, Historically Contemplated." *Journal of Political Economy* 65 (1957): 1–17.

> *Fascinating discussion of the historical development of the competitive model.*

Varian, H. R. *Microeconomic Analysis,* 3rd ed. New York: W. W. Norton, 1992, chap. 13.

> *Terse but instructive coverage of many of the topics in this chapter. The importance of entry is stressed, though the precise nature of the long-run supply curve is a bit obscure.*

EXTENSIONS

Demand Aggregation and Estimation

In Chapters 4 through 6 we showed that the assumption of utility maximization implies several properties for individual demand functions:

- the functions are continuous;
- the functions are homogeneous of degree zero in all prices and income;
- income-compensated substitution effects are negative; and
- cross-price substitution effects are symmetric.

In this extension we will examine the extent to which these properties would be expected to hold for aggregated market demand functions and what, if any, restrictions should be placed on such functions. In addition, we illustrate some other issues that arise in estimating these aggregate functions and some results from such estimates.

E12.1 Continuity

The continuity of individual demand functions clearly implies the continuity of market demand functions. But there are situations in which market demand functions may be continuous while individual functions are not. Consider the case where goods—such as an automobile—must be bought in large, discrete units. Here individual demand is discontinuous, but the aggregated demands of many people are (nearly) continuous.

E12.2 Homogeneity and income aggregation

Because each individual's demand function is homogeneous of degree 0 in all prices and income, market demand functions are also homogeneous of degree 0 in all prices and *individual* incomes. However, market demand functions are not necessarily homogeneous of degree 0 in all prices and *total* income.

To see when demand might depend just on total income, suppose individual i's demand for X is given by

$$x_i = a_i(P) + b(P)y_i, \quad i = 1, n, \qquad \text{(i)}$$

where P is the vector of all market prices, $a_i(P)$ is a set of individual-specific price effects, and $b(P)$ is a marginal propensity-to-spend function that is the same across all individuals (although the value of this parameter may depend on market prices). In this case the market demand functions will depend on P and on total income:

$$\Upsilon = \sum_{i=1}^{n} y_i. \qquad \text{(ii)}$$

This shows that market demand reflects the behavior of a single "typical" consumer. Gorman (1959) shows that this is the most general form of demand function that can represent such a typical consumer.

E12.3 Cross-equation constraints

Suppose a typical individual buys k items and that expenditures on each are given by

$$p_j x_j = \sum_{i=1}^{k} a_{ij} p_i + b_j y, \quad j = 1, k. \qquad \text{(iii)}$$

If expenditures on these k items exhaust total income, that is,

$$\sum_{j=1}^{k} p_j x_j = y, \qquad \text{(iv)}$$

then summing over all goods shows that

$$\sum_{j=1}^{k} a_{ij} = 0 \quad \text{for all } i \qquad \text{(v)}$$

and that

$$\sum_{j=1}^{k} b_j = 1 \qquad \text{(vi)}$$

for each person. This implies that researchers are generally not able to estimate expenditure functions for k goods independently. Rather, some account must be taken of relationships between the expenditure functions for different goods.

E12.4 Econometric practice

The degree to which these theoretical concerns are reflected in the actual practices of econometricians varies widely. At the least sophisticated level, an equation similar to Equation iii might be estimated directly using ordinary least squares (OLS) with little attention to the ways in which the assumptions might be violated. Various elasticities could be calculated directly

TABLE 12.3 Representative Price and Income Elasticities of Demand

	Price Elasticity	Income Elasticity
Food	−0.21	+0.28
Medical services	−0.18	+0.22
Housing		
Rental	−0.18	+1.00
Owner occupied	−1.20	+1.20
Electricity	−1.14	+0.61
Automobiles	−1.20	+3.00
Gasoline	−0.55	+1.60
Beer	−0.26	+0.38
Wine	−0.88	+0.97
Marijuana	−1.50	0.00
Cigarettes	−0.35	+0.50
Abortions	−0.81	+0.79
Transatlantic air travel	−1.30	+1.40
Imports	−0.58	+2.73
Money	−0.40	+1.00

SOURCES: Food: H. Wold and L. Jureen, *Demand Analysis* (New York: John Wiley & Sons, 1953): 203. Medical services: income elasticity from R. Andersen and L. Benham, "Factors Affecting the Relationship between Family Income and Medical Care Consumption," in Herbert Klarman, Ed., *Empirical Studies in Health Economics* (Baltimore: Johns Hopkins University Press, 1970); price elasticity from W. C. Manning et al., "Health Insurance and the Demand for Medical Care: Evidence from a Randomized Experiment," *American Economic Review* (June 1987): 251–77. Housing: income elasticities from F. de Leeuw, "The Demand for Housing," *Review for Economics and Statistics* (February 1971); price elasticities from H. S. Houthakker and L. D. Taylor, *Consumer Demand in the United States* (Cambridge, MA: Harvard University Press, 1970): 166–67. Electricity: R. F. Halvorsen, "Residential Demand for Electricity," unpublished Ph.D. dissertation, Harvard University, December 1972. Automobiles: Gregory C. Chow, *Demand for Automobiles in the United States* (Amsterdam: North Holland, 1957). Gasoline: C. Dahl, "Gasoline Demand Survey," *Energy Journal* 7 (1986): 67–82. Beer and wine: J. A. Johnson, E. H. Oksanen, M. R. Veall, and D. Fritz, "Short-Run and Long-Run Elasticities for Canadian Consumption of Alcoholic Beverages," *Review of Economics and Statistics* (February 1992): 64–74. Marijuana: T. C. Misket and F. Vakil, "Some Estimate of Price and Expenditure Elasticities among UCLA Students," *Review of Economics and Statistics* (November 1972): 474–75. Cigarettes: F. Chalemaker, "Rational Addictive Behavior and Cigarette Smoking," *Journal of Political Economy* (August 1991): 722–42. Abortions: M. H. Medoff, "An Economic Analysis of the Demand for Abortions," *Economic Inquiry* (April 1988): 253–59. Transatlantic air travel: J. M. Cigliano, "Price and Income Elasticities for Airline Travel," *Business Economics* (September 1980): 17–21. Imports: M. D. Chinn, "Beware of Econometricians Bearing Estimates," *Journal of Policy Analysis and Management* (Fall 1991): 546–67. Money: D. L. Hoffman and R. H. Rasche, "Long-Run Income and Interest Elasticities of Money Demand in the United States," *Review of Economics and Statistics* (November 1991): 665–74.
NOTE: Price elasticity refers to interest rate elasticity.

from this equation—although, because of the linear form used, these would not be constant for changes in p_i or y. A constant elasticity formulation of Equation iii would be

$$\ln(p_j x_j) = \sum_{i=1}^{k} a_{ij} \ln(p_i) + b_j \ln y, \quad j = 1, k,$$

$$\text{(vii)}$$

where price and income elasticities would be given directly by

$$e_{x_j, p_j} = a_{j,j} - 1,$$
$$e_{x_j, p_i} = a_{i,j} \quad (i \neq j), \qquad \text{(viii)}$$
$$e_{x_j, y} = b_j.$$

Notice here, however, that no specific attention is paid to biases introduced by the use of aggregate income or by the disregard of possible cross-equation restrictions such as those in Equations v and vi. Further restrictions are also implied by the homogeneity of each of the demand functions $(\sum_{i=1}^{k} a_{ij} + b_j = -1)$, although this restriction too is often disregarded in the development of simple econometric estimates.

More sophisticated studies of aggregated demand equations seek to remedy these problems by explicitly considering potential income distribution effects and by estimating entire systems of demand equations. Theil (1971, 1975) provides a good introduction to some of the procedures used.

Econometric results

Table 12.3 reports a number of economic estimates of representative price and income elasticities drawn from a variety of sources. The original sources for these estimates should be consulted to determine the extent to which the authors have been attentive to the theoretical restrictions outlined previously. Overall, these estimates accord fairly well with intuition—the demand for transatlantic air travel is more price elastic than is the demand for medical care, for example. Perhaps somewhat surprising are the high price and income elasticities for owner-occupied housing, because "shelter" is often regarded in everyday discussion as a necessity. The very high estimated income elasticity of demand for automobiles probably conflates the measurement of both quantity and quality demanded. But it does suggest why the automobile industry is so sensitive to the business cycle.

References

Gorman, W. M. "Separable Utility and Aggregation." *Econometrica* (November 1959): 469–81.

Theil, H. *Principles of Econometrics.* New York: John Wiley & Sons, 1971, pp. 326–46.

———. *Theory and Measurement of Consumer Demand,* vol. 1. Amsterdam: North-Holland, 1975, chaps. 5 and 6.

General Equilibrium and Welfare

The partial equilibrium models of perfect competition that were introduced in Chapter 12 are clearly inadequate for describing all of the effects that occur when changes in one market have repercussions in other markets. They are therefore also inadequate for making general welfare statements about how well market economies perform. Instead, what is needed is an economic model that permits us to view many markets simultaneously. In this chapter we will develop a few simple versions of such models. The Extensions to the chapter show how general equilibrium models are applied to the real world.

PERFECTLY COMPETITIVE PRICE SYSTEM

The model we will develop in this chapter is primarily an elaboration of the supply-demand mechanism presented in Chapter 12. Here we will assume that all markets are of the type described in that chapter and refer to such a set of markets as a *perfectly competitive price system*. The assumption is that there is some large number of homogeneous goods in this simple economy. Included in this list of goods are not only consumption items but also factors of production. Each of these goods has an *equilibrium price*, established by the action of supply and demand.[1] At this set of prices, every market is cleared in the sense that suppliers are willing to supply the quantity that is demanded and consumers will demand the quantity that is supplied. We also assume that there are no transaction or transportation charges and that both individuals and firms have perfect knowledge of prevailing market prices.

The law of one price

Because we assume zero transactions cost and perfect information, each good obeys the law of one price: A homogeneous good trades at the same price no matter who buys it or which firm sells it. If one good traded at two different prices, demanders would rush to buy the good where it was cheaper, and firms would try to sell all their output where the good was more expensive. These actions in themselves would tend to equalize the price of the good. In the perfectly competitive market, then, each good must have only one price. This is why we may speak unambiguously of *the* price of a good.

Behavioral assumptions

The perfectly competitive model assumes that people and firms react to prices in specific ways.

---

[1]One aspect of this market interaction should be made clear from the outset. The perfectly competitive market determines only relative (not absolute) prices. In this chapter, we speak only of relative prices. It makes no difference whether the prices of apples and oranges are $.10 and $.20, respectively, or $10 and $20. The important point in either case is that two apples can be exchanged for one orange in the market.

1. There are assumed to be a large number of people buying any one good. Each person takes all prices as given and adjusts his or her behavior to *maximize utility*, given the prices and his or her budget constraint. People may also be suppliers of productive services (for example, labor), and in such decisions they also regard prices as given.[2]

2. There are assumed to be large number of firms producing each good, and each firm produces only a small share of the output of any one good. In making input and output choices, firms are assumed to operate to *maximize profits*. The firms treat all prices as given when making these profit-maximizing decisions.

These various assumptions should be familiar because we have been making them throughout this book. Our purpose here is to show how an entire economic system operates when all markets work in this way.

A SIMPLE GRAPHICAL MODEL OF GENERAL EQUILIBRIUM WITH TWO GOODS

We begin our analysis with a simple graphical model of general equilibrium involving only two goods, which we will call x and y. This model will prove very useful because it incorporates many of the features of far more complex general equilibrium representations of the economy.

General equilibrium demand

Ultimately, demand patterns in an economy are determined by individuals' preferences. For our simple model we will assume that all individuals have identical preferences, which can be represented by an indifference curve map[3] defined over quantities of the two goods, x and y. The benefit of this approach for our purposes is that this indifference curve map (which is identical to the ones used in Chapters 3–6) shows how individuals rank consumption bundles containing both goods. These rankings are precisely what we mean by "demand" in a general equilibrium context. Of course, we cannot actually illustrate which bundles of commodities will be chosen until we know the budget constraints that demanders face. Because incomes are generated as individuals supply labor, capital, and other resources to the production process, we must delay this illustration until we have examined the forces of production and supply in our model.

General equilibrium supply

Developing a notion of general equilibrium supply in this two-good model is a somewhat more complex process than describing the demand side of the market because we have not thus far illustrated production and supply of two goods simultaneously. Our approach is to use the familiar production possibility curve (see Chapter 1) for this purpose. By detailing the way in which this curve is constructed, we can also use this construction to examine the ways in which markets for outputs and inputs are related.

---

[2]Because one price represents the wage rate, the relevant budget constraint is in reality a time constraint. For a discussion, see Chapter 16.

[3]There are some technical problems in using a single indifference curve map to represent the preferences of an entire community of individuals. In this case the marginal rate of substitution (that is, the slope of the community indifference curve) will depend on how the available goods are distributed among individuals: The increase in total y required to compensate for a one-unit reduction in x will depend on which specific individual(s) the x is taken from. Although we will not discuss this issue in detail here, it has been widely examined in the international trade literature.

Edgeworth box diagram for production

Construction of the production possibility curve for two outputs (x and y) begins with the assumption that there are fixed amounts of capital and labor inputs that must be allocated to the production of the two goods. The possible allocations of these inputs can be illustrated with an Edgeworth box diagram with dimensions given by the total amounts of capital and labor available.

In Figure 13.1, the length of the box represents total labor-hours and the height of the box represents total capital-hours. The lower left-hand corner of the box represents the "origin" for measuring capital and labor devoted to production of good x. The upper right-hand corner of the box represents the origin for resources devoted to y. Using these conventions, any point in the box can be regarded as a fully employed allocation of the available resources between goods x and y. Point A, for example, represents an allocation in which the indicated number of labor hours are devoted to x production together with a specified number of hours of capital. Production of good y uses whatever labor and capital are "left over." Point A in Figure 13.1, for example, also shows the exact amount of labor and capital used in the production of good y. Any other point in the box has a similar interpretation. Thus, the Edgeworth box shows every possible way the existing capital and labor might be used to produce x and y.

Efficient allocations

Many of the allocations shown in Figure 13.1 are technically inefficient in that it is possible to produce both more x and more y by shifting capital and labor around a bit. In our model we

FIGURE 13.1 Construction of an Edgeworth Box Diagram for Production

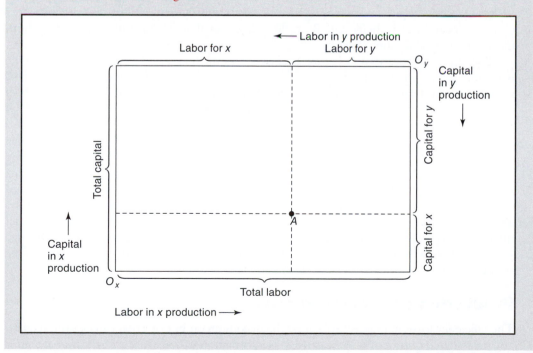

The dimensions of this diagram are given by the total quantities of labor and capital available. Quantities of these resources devoted to x production are measured from origin O_x; quantities devoted to y are measured from O_y. Any point in the box represents a fully employed allocation of the available resources to the two goods.

FIGURE 13.2   Edgeworth Box Diagram of Efficiency in Production

This diagram adds production isoquants for x and y to Figure 13.1. It then shows technically efficient ways to allocate the fixed amounts of k and l between the production of the two outputs. The line joining O_x and O_y is the locus of these efficient points. Along this line, the RTS (of l for k) in the production of good x is equal to the RTS in the production of y.

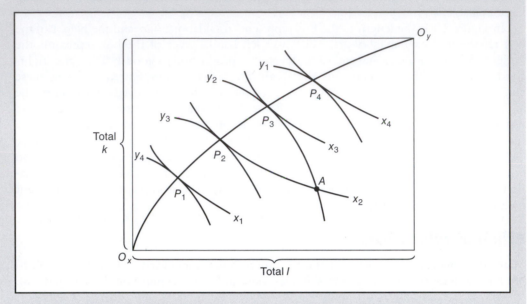

assume that competitive markets will not exhibit such inefficient input choices (for reasons we will explore in more detail later in the chapter). Hence we wish to discover the efficient allocations in Figure 13.1, because these illustrate the actual production outcomes in this model. To do so, we introduce isoquant maps for good x (using O_x as the origin) and good y (using O_y as the origin), as shown in Figure 13.2. In this figure it is clear that the arbitrarily chosen allocation A is inefficient. By reallocating capital and labor one can produce both more x than x_2 and more y than y_2.

The efficient allocations in Figure 13.2 are those such as P_1, P_2, P_3, and P_4, where the isoquants are tangent to one another. At any other points in the box diagram, the two goods' isoquants will intersect, and we can show inefficiency as we did for point A. At the points of tangency, however, this kind of unambiguous improvement cannot be made. In going from P_2 to P_3, for example, more x is being produced, but at the cost of less y being produced, so P_3 is not "more efficient" than P_2—both of the points are efficient. Tangency of the isoquants for good x and good y implies that their slopes are equal. That is, the RTS of capital for labor is equal in x and y production. Later we will show how competitive input markets will lead firms to make such efficient input choices.

The curve joining O_x and O_y that includes all of these points of tangency therefore shows all of the efficient allocations of capital and labor. Points off this curve are inefficient in that unambiguous increases in output can be obtained by reshuffling inputs between the two goods. Points on the curve $O_x O_y$ are all efficient allocations, however, because more x can be produced only by cutting back on y production and vice versa.

Production possibility frontier

The efficiency locus in Figure 13.2 shows the maximum output of y that can be produced for any preassigned output of x. We can use this information to construct a *production possibility*

FIGURE 13.3 Production Possibility Frontier

The production possibility frontier shows the alternative combinations of x and y that can be efficiently produced by a firm with fixed resources. The curve can be derived from Figure 13.2 by varying inputs between the production of x and y while maintaining the conditions for efficiency. The negative of the slope of the production possibility curve is called the rate of product transformation (RPT).

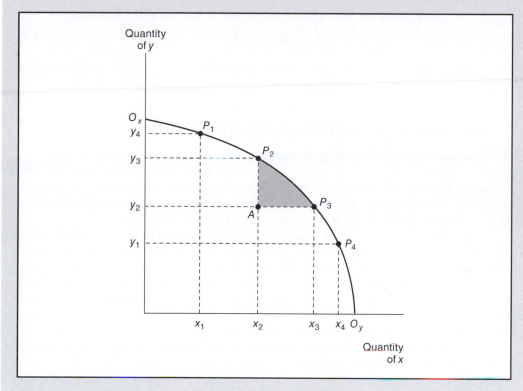

frontier, which shows the alternative outputs of x and y that can be produced with the fixed capital and labor inputs. In Figure 13.3 the $O_x O_y$ locus has been taken from Figure 13.2 and transferred onto a graph with x and y outputs on the axes. At O_x, for example, no resources are devoted to x production; consequently, y output is as large as is possible with the existing resources. Similarly, at O_y, the output of x is as large as possible. The other points on the production possibility frontier (say, P_1, P_2, P_3, and P_4) are derived from the efficiency locus in an identical way. Hence we have derived the following definition.

Production possibility frontier. The *production possibility frontier* shows the alternative combinations of two outputs that can be produced with fixed quantities of inputs if those inputs are employed efficiently.

DEFINITION

Rate of product transformation

The slope of the production possibility frontier shows how x output can be substituted for y output when total resources are held constant. For example, for points near O_x on the production possibility frontier, the slope is a small negative number—say, $-1/4$; this implies that, by reducing y output by 1 unit, x output could be increased by 4. Near O_y, on the other hand, the slope is a large negative number (say, -5), implying that y output must be reduced by 5 units in order to permit the production of one more x. The slope of the production possibility frontier, then, clearly shows the possibilities that exist for trading y for x in production. The negative of this slope is called the *rate of product transformation* (*RPT*).

DEFINITION

Rate of product transformation. The *rate of product transformation* (*RPT*) between two outputs is the negative of the slope of the production possibility frontier for those outputs. Mathematically,

$$RPT \text{ (of } x \text{ for } y) = -[\text{slope of production possibility frontier}]$$
$$= -\frac{dy}{dx} \text{ (along } O_x O_y). \tag{13.1}$$

The *RPT* records how x can be technically traded for y while continuing to keep the available productive inputs efficiently employed.

Shape of the production possibility frontier

The production possibility frontier illustrated in Figure 13.3 exhibits an increasing *RPT*. For output levels near O_x, relatively little y must be sacrificed to obtain one more x ($-dy/dx$ is small). Near O_y, on the other hand, additional x may be obtained only by substantial reductions in y output ($-dy/dx$ is large). In this section we will show why this concave shape might be expected to characterize most production situations.

A first step in that analysis is to recognize that *RPT* is equal to the ratio of the marginal cost of x (MC_x) to the marginal cost of y (MC_y). Intuitively, this result is obvious. Suppose, for example, that x and y are produced only with labor. If it takes two labor hours to produce one more x, we might say that MC_x is equal to 2. Similarly, if it takes only one labor hour to produce an extra y, then MC_y is equal to 1. But in this situation it is clear that the *RPT* is 2: two y must be forgone to provide enough labor so that x may be increased by one unit. Hence, the *RPT* is indeed equal to the ratio of the marginal costs of the two goods.

More formally, suppose that the costs (say, in terms of the "disutility" experienced by factor suppliers) of any output combination are denoted by $C(x, y)$. Along the production possibility frontier, $C(x, y)$ will be constant because the inputs are in fixed supply. Hence we can write the total differential of the cost function as

$$dC = \frac{\partial C}{\partial x} \cdot dx + \frac{\partial C}{\partial y} \cdot dy = 0 \tag{13.2}$$

for changes in x and y along the production possibility frontier. Manipulating Equation 13.2 yields

$$RPT = -\frac{dy}{dx} \text{ (along } O_x O_y) = \frac{\partial C/\partial x}{\partial C/\partial y} = \frac{MC_x}{MC_y}, \tag{13.3}$$

which was precisely what we wished to show: The *RPT* is a measure of the relative marginal costs of the two goods.

To demonstrate reasons why the *RPT* might be expected to rise for clockwise movements along the production possibility frontier, we can proceed by showing why the ratio of MC_x to MC_y should rise as x output expands and y output contracts. We first present two relatively simple arguments that apply only to special cases; then we turn to a more sophisticated general argument.

Diminishing returns

The most common rationale offered for the concave shape of the production possibility frontier is the assumption that both goods are produced under conditions of diminishing returns. Hence increasing the output of good x will raise its marginal cost, whereas decreasing the output of y will reduce its marginal cost. Equation 13.3 then shows that the RPT will increase for movements along the production possibility frontier from O_x to O_y. A problem with this explanation, of course, is that it applies only to cases in which both goods exhibit diminishing returns to scale, and that assumption is at variance with the theoretical reasons for preferring the assumption of constant or even increasing returns to scale as mentioned elsewhere in this book.

Specialized inputs

If some inputs were "more suited" for x production than for y production (and vice versa), the concave shape of the production frontier also could be explained. In that case, increases in x output would require drawing progressively less suitable inputs into the production of that good. Marginal costs of x would therefore rise. Marginal costs for y, on the other hand, would fall, since smaller output levels for y would permit the use of only those inputs most suited for y production. Such an argument might apply, for example, to a farmer with a variety of types of land under cultivation in different crops. In trying to increase the production of any one crop, the farmer would be forced to grow it on increasingly unsuitable parcels of land. Although this type of specialized input assumption has considerable importance in explaining a variety of real-world phenomena, it is nonetheless at variance with our general assumption of homogeneous factors of production. Hence it cannot serve as a fundamental explanation for concavity.

Differing factor intensities

Even if inputs are homogeneous and production functions exhibit constant returns to scale, the production possibility frontier will be concave if goods x and y use inputs in different proportions.[4] In the production box diagram of Figure 13.2, for example, good x is *capital intensive* relative to good y. That is, at every point along the $O_x O_y$ contract curve, the ratio of k to l in x production exceeds the ratio of k to l in y production: the bowed curve $O_x O_y$ is always above the main diagonal of the Edgeworth box. If, on the other hand, good y had been relatively capital intensive, the $O_x O_y$ contract curve would have been bowed downward below the diagonal. Although a formal proof that unequal factor intensities result in a concave production possibility frontier will not be presented here, it is possible to suggest intuitively why that occurs. Consider any two points on the frontier $O_x O_y$ in Figure 13.3— say, P_1 (with coordinates x_1, y_4) and P_3 (with coordinates x_3, y_2). One way of producing an output combination "between" P_1 and P_3 would be to produce the combination

$$\frac{x_1 + x_3}{2}, \frac{y_4 + y_2}{2}.$$

Because of the constant returns-to-scale assumption, that combination would be feasible and would fully utilize both factors of production. The combination would lie at the midpoint of a straight-line chord joining points P_1 and P_3. Although such a point is feasible, it is not efficient, as can be seen by examining points P_1 and P_3 in the box diagram of Figure 13.2. Because of the bowed nature of the contract curve, production at a point midway between P_1 and P_3 would be off the contract curve: producing at a point such as P_2 would provide more of both goods. The production possibility frontier in Figure 13.3 must therefore "bulge out" beyond the straight line $P_1 P_3$. Because such a proof could be constructed for any two points on $O_x O_y$, we have shown that the frontier is concave; that is, the RPT increases as the output of good X increases. When production is reallocated in a northeast direction along the $O_x O_y$ contract curve (in Figure 13.3), the capital-labor ratio decreases in the production of *both* x

---

[4]If, in addition to homogeneous factors and constant returns to scale, each good also used k and l in the same proportions under optimal allocations, then the production possibility frontier would be a straight line.

and y. Because good x is capital intensive, this change raises MC_x. On the other hand, because good y is labor intensive, MC_y falls. Hence the relative marginal cost of x (as represented by the RPT) rises.

Opportunity cost and supply

The production possibility curve demonstrates that there are many possible efficient combinations of the two goods and that producing more of one good necessitates cutting back on the production of some other good. This is precisely what economists mean by the term *opportunity cost*. The cost of producing more x can be most readily measured by the reduction in y output that this entails. The cost of one more unit of x is therefore best measured as the RPT (of x for y) at the prevailing point on the production possibility frontier. The fact that this cost increases as more x is produced represents the formulation of supply in a general equilibrium context.

EXAMPLE 13.1 Concavity of the Production Possibility Frontier

In this example we look at two characteristics of production functions that may cause the production possibility frontier to be concave.

Diminishing returns. Suppose that the production of both x and y depends only on labor input and that the production functions for these goods are

$$x = f(l_x) = l_x^{0.5},$$
$$y = f(l_y) = l_y^{0.5}. \tag{13.4}$$

Hence, production of each of these goods exhibits diminishing returns to scale. If total labor supply is limited by

$$l_x + l_y = 100, \tag{13.5}$$

then simple substitution shows that the production possibility frontier is given by

$$x^2 + y^2 = 100 \quad \text{for} \quad x, y \geq 0. \tag{13.6}$$

In this case, then, the frontier is a quarter-circle and is concave. The RPT can be calculated by taking the total differential of the production possibility frontier:

$$2x\,dx + 2y\,dy = 0 \quad \text{or} \quad RPT = \frac{-dy}{dx} = \frac{-(-2x)}{2y} = \frac{x}{y}, \tag{13.7}$$

and this slope increases as x output increases. A numerical illustration of concavity starts by noting that the points $(10, 0)$ and $(0, 10)$ both lie on the frontier. A straight line joining these two points would also include the point $(5, 5)$, but that point lies below the frontier. If equal amounts of labor are devoted to both goods then production is $x = y = \sqrt{50}$, which yields more of both goods than the midpoint.

Factor intensity. To show how differing factor intensities yield a concave production possibility frontier, suppose that the two goods are produced under constant returns to scale but with different Cobb-Douglas production functions:

$$x = f(k, l) = k_x^{0.5} l_x^{0.5},$$
$$y = g(k, l) = k_y^{0.25} l_y^{0.75}. \tag{13.8}$$

Suppose also that total capital and labor are constrained by

$$k_x + k_y = 100, \qquad l_x + l_y = 100. \tag{13.9}$$

It is easy to show that

$$RTS_x = \frac{k_x}{l_x} = \kappa_x, \qquad RTS_y = \frac{3k_y}{l_y} = 3\kappa_y, \qquad \textbf{(13.10)}$$

where $\kappa_i = k_i/l_i$. Being located on the production possibility frontier requires $RTS_x = RTS_y$ or $\kappa_x = 3\kappa_y$. That is, no matter how total resources are allocated to production, being on the production possibility frontier requires that x be the capital-intensive good (because, in some sense, capital is more productive in x production than in y production). The capital-labor ratios in the production of the two goods are also constrained by the available resources:

$$\frac{k_x + k_y}{l_x + l_y} = \frac{k_x}{l_x + l_y} + \frac{k_y}{l_x + l_y} = \alpha\kappa_x + (1 - \alpha)\kappa_y = \frac{100}{100} = 1, \qquad \textbf{(13.11)}$$

where $\alpha = l_x/(l_x + l_y)$—that is, α is the share of total labor devoted to x production. Using the condition that $\kappa_x = 3\kappa_y$, we can find the input ratios of the two goods in terms of the overall allocation of labor:

$$\kappa_y = \frac{1}{1 + 2\alpha}, \qquad \kappa_x = \frac{3}{1 + 2\alpha}. \qquad \textbf{(13.12)}$$

Now we are in a position to phrase the production possibility frontier in terms of the share of labor devoted to x production:

$$x = \kappa_x^{0.5} l_x = \kappa_x^{0.5}\alpha(100) = 100\alpha\left(\frac{3}{1 + 2\alpha}\right)^{0.5},$$

$$y = \kappa_y^{0.25} l_y = \kappa_y^{0.25}(1 - \alpha)(100) = 100(1 - \alpha)\left(\frac{1}{1 + 2\alpha}\right)^{0.25}. \qquad \textbf{(13.13)}$$

We could push this algebra even further to eliminate α from these two equations to get an explicit functional form for the production possibility frontier that involves only x and y, but we can show concavity with what we already have. First, notice that if $\alpha = 0$ (x production gets no labor or capital inputs) then $x = 0$, $y = 100$. With $\alpha = 1$, we have $x = 100$, $y = 0$. Hence, a linear production possibility frontier would include the point (50, 50). But if $\alpha = 0.39$, say, then

$$x = 100\alpha\left(\frac{3}{1 + 2\alpha}\right)^{0.5} = 39\left(\frac{3}{1.78}\right)^{0.5} = 50.6,$$

$$y = 100(1 - \alpha)\left(\frac{1}{1 + 2\alpha}\right)^{0.25} = 61\left(\frac{1}{1.78}\right)^{0.25} = 52.8, \qquad \textbf{(13.14)}$$

which shows that the actual frontier is bowed outward beyond a linear frontier. It is worth repeating that both of the goods in this example are produced under constant returns to scale and that the two inputs are fully homogeneous. It is only the differing input intensities involved in the production of the two goods that yields the concave production possibility frontier.

QUERY: How would an increase in the total amount of labor available shift the production possibility frontiers in these examples?

Determination of equilibrium prices

Given these notions of demand and supply in our simple two-good economy, we can now illustrate how equilibrium prices are determined. Figure 13.4 shows PP, the production possibility frontier for the economy, and the set of indifference curves represents individuals' preferences for these goods. First, consider the price ratio p_x/p_y. At this price ratio, firms will choose to produce the output combination x_1, y_1. Profit-maximizing firms will choose the

FIGURE 13.4   Determination of Equilibrium Prices

With a price ratio given by p_x/p_y, firms will produce x_1, y_1; society's budget constraint will be given by line C. With this budget constraint, individuals demand x_1' and y_1'; that is, there is an excess demand for good x and an excess supply of good y. The workings of the market will move these prices toward their equilibrium levels p_x^*, p_y^*. At those prices, society's budget constraint will be given by line C^*, and supply and demand will be in equilibrium. The combination x^*, y^* of goods will be chosen.

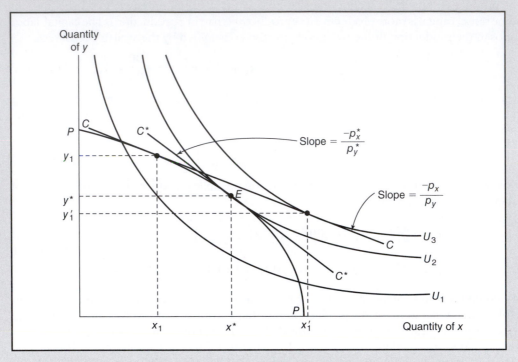

more profitable point on PP. At x_1, y_1 the ratio of the two goods' prices (p_x/p_y) is equal to the ratio of the goods' marginal costs (the RPT), so profits are maximized there. On the other hand, given this budget constraint (line C),[5] individuals will demand x_1', y_1'. Consequently, with these prices, there is an excess demand for good x (individuals demand more than is being produced) but an excess supply of good y. The workings of the marketplace will cause p_x to rise and p_y to fall. The price ratio p_x/p_y will rise; the price line will take on a steeper slope. Firms will respond to these price changes by moving clockwise along the production possibility frontier; that is, they will increase their production of good x and decrease their production of good y. Similarly, individuals will respond to the changing prices by substituting y for x in their consumption choices. These actions of both firms and individuals, then, serve to eliminate the excess demand for x and the excess supply of y as market prices change.

Equilibrium is reached at x^*, y^* with a price ratio of p_x^*/p_y^*. With this price ratio,[6] supply and demand are equilibrated for both good x and good y. Given p_x and p_y, firms will produce

---

[5]It is important to recognize why the budget constraint has this location. Because p_x and p_y are given, the value of total production is $p_x \cdot x_1 + p_y \cdot y_1$. This is the value of "GDP" in the simple economy pictured in Figure 13.4. It is also, therefore, the total income accruing to people in society. Society's budget constraint therefore passes through x_1, y_1 and has a slope of $-p_x/p_y$. This is precisely the budget constraint labeled C in the figure.

[6]Notice again that competitive markets determine only equilibrium relative prices. Determination of the absolute price level requires the introduction of money into this barter model.

x^* and y^* in maximizing their profits. Similarly, with a budget constraint given by C^*, individuals will demand x^* and y^*. The operation of the price system has cleared the markets for both x and y simultaneously. This figure therefore provides a "general equilibrium" view of the supply-demand process for two markets working together. For this reason we will make considerable use of this figure in our subsequent analysis.

COMPARATIVE STATICS ANALYSIS

As in our partial equilibrium analysis, the equilibrium price ratio p_x^*/p_y^* illustrated in Figure 13.4 will tend to persist until either preferences or production technologies change. This competitively determined price ratio reflects these two basic economic forces. If preferences were to shift, say, toward good x, then p_x/p_y would rise and a new equilibrium would be established by a clockwise move along the production possibility curve. More x and less y would be produced to meet these changed preferences. Similarly, technical progress in the production of good x would shift the production possibility curve outward, as illustrated in Figure 13.5. This would tend to lower the relative price of x and increase the quantity of x consumed (assuming x is a normal good). In the figure the quantity of y consumed also increases as a result of the income effect arising from the technical advance; but a slightly different drawing of the figure could have reversed that result if the substitution effect had been dominant. Example 13.2 looks at a few such effects.

FIGURE 13.5   Effects of Technical Progress in x Production

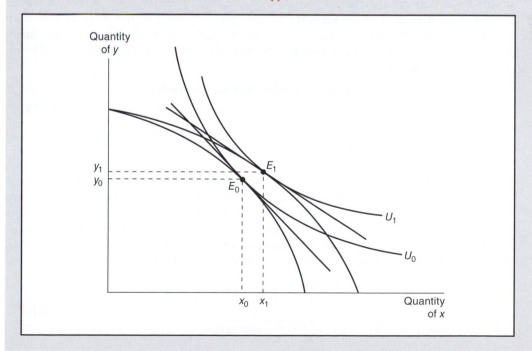

Technical advances that lower marginal costs of x production will shift the production possibility frontier. This will generally create income and substitution effects that cause the quantity of x produced to increase (assuming x is a normal good). Effects on the production of y are ambiguous because income and substitution effects work in opposite directions.

EXAMPLE 13.2 Comparative Statics in a General Equilibrium Model

To explore how general equilibrium models work, let's start with a simple example based on the production possibility frontier in Example 13.1. In that example we assumed that production of both goods was characterized by decreasing returns $x = l_x^{0.5}$ and $y = l_y^{0.5}$ and also that total labor available was given by $l_x + l_y = 100$. The resulting production possibility frontier was given by $x^2 + y^2 = 100$, and $RPT = x/y$. To complete this model we assume that the typical individual's utility function is given by $U(x, y) = x^{0.5}y^{0.5}$, so the demand functions for the two goods are

$$x = x(p_x, p_y, I) = \frac{0.5I}{p_x},$$

$$y = y(p_x, p_y, I) = \frac{0.5I}{p_y}. \tag{13.15}$$

Base-case equilibrium. Profit maximization by firms requires that $p_x/p_y = MC_x/MC_y = RPT = x/y$, and utility-maximizing demand requires that $p_x/p_y = y/x$. So equilibrium requires that $x/y = y/x$, or $x = y$. Inserting this result into the equation for the production possibility frontier shows that

$$x^* = y^* = \sqrt{50} = 7.07 \quad \text{and} \quad \frac{p_x}{p_y} = 1. \tag{13.16}$$

This is the equilibrium for our base case with this model.

The budget constraint. The budget constraint that faces individuals is not especially transparent in this illustration, so it may be useful to discuss it explicitly. In order to bring some degree of absolute pricing into the model, let's consider all prices in terms of the wage rate, w. Since total labor supply is 100, it follows that total labor income is $100w$. But, because of the diminishing returns assumed for production, each firm also earns profits. For firm x, say, the total cost function is $C(w, x) = wl_x = wx^2$, so $p_x = MC_x = 2wx = 2w\sqrt{50}$. The profits for firm x are therefore $\pi_x = (p_x - AC_x)x = (p_x - wx)x = wx^2 = 50w$. A similar computation shows that profits for firm y are also given by $50w$. Because general equilibrium models must obey the national income identity, we assume that consumers are also shareholders in the two firms and treat these profits also as part of their spendable incomes. Hence, total consumer income is

$$\textbf{total income = labor income + profits}$$

$$= 100w + 2(50w) = 200w. \tag{13.17}$$

This income will just permit consumers to spend $100w$ on each good by buying $\sqrt{50}$ units at a price of $2w\sqrt{50}$, so the model is internally consistent.

A shift in supply. There are only two ways in which this base-case equilibrium can be disturbed: (1) By changes in "supply"—that is, by changes in the underlying technology of this economy; or (2) by changes in "demand"—that is, by changes in preferences. Let's first consider changes in technology. Suppose that there is technical improvement in x production so that the production function is $x = 2l_x^{0.5}$. Now the production possibility frontier is given by $x^2/4 + y^2 = 100$, and $RPT = x/4y$. Proceeding as before to find the equilibrium in this model:

$$\frac{p_x}{p_y} = \frac{x}{4y} \quad \text{(supply)},$$

$$\frac{p_x}{p_y} = \frac{y}{x} \quad \text{(demand)}, \tag{13.18}$$

so $x^2 = 4y^2$ and the equilibrium is

$$x^* = 2\sqrt{50}, \quad y^* = \sqrt{50}, \quad \text{and} \quad \frac{p_x}{p_y} = \frac{1}{2}. \tag{13.19}$$

Technical improvements in x production have caused its relative price to fall and the consumption of this good to rise. As in many examples with Cobb-Douglas utility, the income and substitution effects of this price decline on y demand are precisely offsetting. Technical improvements clearly make consumers better off, however. Whereas utility was previously given by $U(x,y) = x^{0.5}y^{0.5} = \sqrt{50} = 7.07$, now it has increased to $U(x,y) = x^{0.5}y^{0.5} = (2\sqrt{50})^{0.5}(\sqrt{50})^{0.5} = \sqrt{2} \cdot \sqrt{50} = 10$. Technical change has increased consumer welfare substantially.

A shift in demand. If consumer preferences were to switch to favor good y as $U(x,y) = x^{0.1}y^{0.9}$, then demand functions would be given by $x = 0.1I/p_x$ and $y = 0.9I/p_y$, and demand equilibrium would require $p_x/p_y = y/9x$. Returning to the original production possibility frontier to arrive at an overall equilibrium, we have

$$\frac{p_x}{p_y} = \frac{x}{y} \quad (\text{supply}),$$

$$\frac{p_x}{p_y} = \frac{y}{9x} \quad (\text{demand}), \tag{13.20}$$

so $9x^2 = y^2$ and the equilibrium is given by

$$x^* = \sqrt{10}, \quad y^* = 3\sqrt{10}, \quad \text{and} \quad \frac{p_x}{p_y} = \frac{1}{3}. \tag{13.21}$$

Hence, the decline in demand for x has significantly reduced its relative price. Observe that in this case, however, we cannot make a welfare comparison to the previous cases because the utility function has changed.

QUERY: What are the budget constraints in these two alternative scenarios? How is income distributed between wages and profits in each case? Explain the differences intuitively.

GENERAL EQUILIBRIUM MODELING AND FACTOR PRICES

This very simple general equilibrium model therefore reinforces Marshall's observations about the importance of both supply and demand forces in the price determination process. By providing an explicit connection between the markets for all goods, the general equilibrium model makes it possible to examine more complex questions about market relationships than is possible by looking at only one market at a time. General equilibrium modeling also permits an examination of the connections between goods and factor markets; we can illustrate that with an important historical case.

The Corn Laws debate

High tariffs on grain imports were imposed by the British government following the Napoleonic wars. Debate over the effects of these Corn Laws dominated the analytical efforts of economists between the years 1829 and 1845. A principal focus of the debate concerned the effect that elimination of the tariffs would have on factor prices—a question that continues to have relevance today, as we will see.

FIGURE 13.6 Analysis of the Corn Laws Debate

Reduction of tariff barriers on grain would cause production to be reallocated from point E to point A; consumption would be reallocated from E to B. If grain production is relatively capital intensive, the relative price of capital would fall as a result of these reallocations.

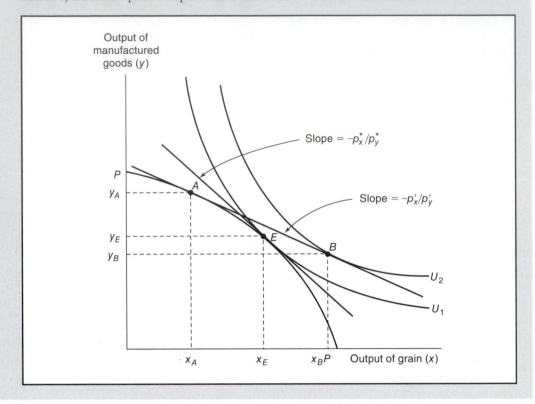

The production possibility frontier in Figure 13.6 shows those combinations of grain (x) and manufactured goods (y) that could be produced by British factors of production. Assuming (somewhat contrary to actuality) that the Corn Laws completely prevented trade, market equilibrium would be at E with the domestic price ratio given by p_x^*/p_y^*. Removal of the tariffs would reduce this price ratio to p_x'/p_y'. Given that new ratio, Britain would produce combination A and consume combination B. Grain imports would amount to $x_B - x_A$, and these would be financed by export of manufactured goods equal to $y_A - y_B$. Overall utility for the typical British consumer would be increased by the opening of trade. Use of the production possibility diagram therefore demonstrates the implications that relaxing the tariffs would have for the production of both goods.

Trade and factor prices

By referring to the Edgeworth production box diagram (Figure 13.2) that lies behind the production possibility frontier (Figure 13.3), it is also possible to analyze the effect of tariff reductions on factor prices. The movement from point E to point A in Figure 13.6 is similar to a movement from P_3 to P_1 in Figure 13.2, where production of x is decreased and production of y is increased.

This figure also records the reallocation of capital and labor made necessary by such a move. If we assume that grain production is relatively capital intensive, then the movement from P_3 to P_1 causes the ratio of k to l to rise in both industries.[7] This in turn will cause the relative price of capital to fall (and the relative price of labor to rise). Hence we conclude that repeal of the Corn Laws would be harmful to capital owners (that is, landlords) and helpful to laborers. It is not surprising that landed interests fought repeal of the laws.

Political support for trade policies

The possibility that trade policies may affect the relative incomes of various factors of production continues to exert a major influence on political debates about such policies. In the United States, for example, exports tend to be intensive in their use of skilled labor whereas imports tend to be intensive in unskilled labor input. By analogy to our discussion of the Corn Laws, it might thus be expected that further movements toward free trade policies would result in rising relative wages for skilled workers and in falling relative wages for unskilled workers. It is therefore not surprising that unions representing skilled workers (the machinists or aircraft workers) tend to favor free trade, whereas unions of unskilled workers (those in textiles, shoes, and related businesses) tend to oppose it.[8]

EXISTENCE OF GENERAL EQUILIBRIUM PRICES

So far we have more or less assumed that competitive markets can reach an equilibrium in which the forces of supply and demand are balanced in all markets simultaneously. But, given the assumptions we have made, such a simultaneous solution is by no means ensured. Beginning with the nineteenth-century investigations by Leon Walras, economists have used increasingly sophisticated tools to examine whether a set of prices that equilibrates all markets exists and, if so, how this set of prices can be found. In this section we will explore some aspects of this question.

A simple mathematical model

The essential aspects of the modern solution to the Walrasian problem can be demonstrated for the case where no production takes place. Suppose there are n goods (in absolutely fixed supply) in this economy and that they are distributed in some way among the individuals in society. Let S_i $(i = 1, ..., n)$ be the total supply of good i available, and let the price of good i be represented by p_i $(i = 1, ..., n)$. The total demand for good i depends on all the prices, and this function represents the sum of the individuals' demand functions for good i. This total demand function is denoted by

$$D_i(p_1, ..., p_n)$$

for $i = 1, ..., n$.

Because we are interested in the whole set of prices $p_1, ..., p_n$, it will be convenient to denote this whole set by P. Hence the demand functions can be written as

$$D_i(P).$$

Walras' problem then can be stated formally as: Does there exist an *equilibrium set of prices* (P^*) such that

$$D_i(P^*) = S_i \tag{13.22}$$

for all values of i? The question posed by Walras is whether a set of prices exists for which supply is equal to demand *in all markets simultaneously*.

---

[7]In the Corn Laws debate, attention actually centered on the factors of land and labor.

[8]The finding that the opening of trade will raise the relative price of the abundant factor is called the Stolper-Samuelson theorem after the economists who rigorously proved it in the 1950s.

Excess demand functions

In what follows it will be more convenient to work with excess demand functions for good i at any set of prices (P), which are defined to be[9]

$$ED_i(P) = D_i(P) - S_i, \quad i = 1, n. \tag{13.23}$$

Using this notation, the equilibrium conditions can be rewritten as

$$ED_i(P^*) = D_i(P^*) - S_i = 0, \quad i = 1, n. \tag{13.24}$$

This condition states that, at the equilibrium prices, excess demand must be zero in all markets.[10]

Walras himself noted several interesting features about the system of Equation 13.24. First, as we have already shown, the demand functions (and hence the excess demand functions) are *homogeneous of degree* 0. If all prices were to double (including the wages of labor), the quantity demanded of every good would remain unchanged. Hence we can only hope to establish equilibrium relative prices in a Walrasian-type model. A second assumption made by Walras was that the demand functions (and therefore the excess demand functions) are *continuous*: if prices were to change by only a small amount, quantities demanded would change by only a small amount. The assumptions of homogeneity and continuity are direct results of the theory of consumer behavior that we studied in Part 2.

Walras' law

A final observation that Walras made is that the n excess demand functions are not independent of one another. The equations are related by the formula

$$\sum_{i=1}^{n} p_i \cdot ED_i(P) = 0. \tag{13.25}$$

Equation 13.25 is usually called *Walras' law*. The equation states that the "total value" of excess demand is zero at *any* set of prices. There can be neither excess demand for all goods together nor excess supply. Proving Walras' law is a simple matter, although it is necessary to introduce some cumbersome notation. The proof rests on the fact that each individual in the economy is bound by a budget constraint. A simple example of the proof is given in the footnote;[11] the generalization of this proof is left to the reader.

---

[9]Although we will not do so, supply behavior can be introduced here by making S_i depend on P also.

[10]This equilibrium condition will be slightly amended later to allow for goods whose equilibrium price is zero.

[11]Suppose that there are two goods (A and B) and two individuals (Smith and Jones) in society. Let $D_A^S, D_B^S, S_A^S, S_B^S$ be Smith's demands and supplies of A and B, and use a similar notation for Jones's demands and supplies. Smith's budget constraint may be written as

$$p_A D_A^S + p_B D_B^S = p_A S_A^S + p_B S_B^S$$

or

$$p_A (D_A^S - S_A^S) + p_B (D_B^S - S_B^S) = 0$$

or

$$p_A ED_A^S + p_B ED_B^S = 0,$$

where ED_A^S and ED_B^S represent the excess demand of Smith for A and B, respectively.

A similar budget constraint holds for Jones:

$$p_A ED_A^J + p_B ED_B^J = 0;$$

hence, letting ED_A and ED_B represent total excess demands for A and B, it must be that

$$p_A \cdot (ED_A^S + ED_A^J) + p_B \cdot (ED_B^S + ED_B^J) = p_A \cdot ED_A + p_B \cdot ED_B = 0.$$

This is Walras' law exactly as it appears in Equation 13.25.

Walras' law, it should be stressed, holds for any set of prices—not just for equilibrium prices. The law can be seen to apply trivially to an equilibrium set of prices, because each of the excess demand functions will be equal to 0 at this set of prices. Walras' law shows that the equilibrium conditions in n markets are not independent. We do not have n independent equations in n unknowns (the n prices). Rather, Equation 13.24 represents only $(n - 1)$ independent equations, and hence we can hope to determine only $(n - 1)$ of the prices. But this was expected in view of the homogeneity property of the demand functions. We can hope to determine only equilibrium *relative prices*; nothing in this model permits the derivation of absolute prices.

Walras' proof of the existence of equilibrium prices

Having recognized these technical features of the system of excess demand equations, Walras turned to the question of the existence of a set of equilibrium (relative) prices. He tried to establish that the n equilibrium conditions of Equation 13.24 were sufficient, in this situation, to ensure that such a set of prices would in fact exist and thus that the exchange model had a consistent theoretical framework. A first indication that this existence of equilibrium prices might be ensured is provided by a simple counting of equations and unknowns. The market equilibrium conditions provide $(n - 1)$ *independent* equations in $(n - 1)$ unknown relative prices. Hence the elementary algebra of solving simultaneous linear equations suggests that an equilibrium solution might exist.

Unfortunately, as Walras recognized, the act of solving for equilibrium prices is not nearly as simple a matter as counting equations and unknowns. First, the equations are not necessarily linear. Hence the standard conditions for the existence of solutions to simultaneous linear equations do not apply in this case. Second, from consideration of the economics of the problem, it is clear that all the equilibrium prices must be nonnegative. A negative price has no meaning in the context of this problem. To attack these two difficulties, Walras developed a tedious proof that involved solving for equilibrium prices in a series of successive approximations. Without presenting Walras' proof in detail, it is instructive to see how he approached the problem.

Start with some initial, arbitrary set of prices. Holding the other $(n - 1)$ prices constant, find the equilibrium price in the market for good 1. Call this "provisional" equilibrium price p_1'. Now, holding p_1' and the other $(n - 2)$ prices constant, solve for the equilibrium price in the market for good 2. Call this price p_2'. Notice that in changing p_2 from its initial position to p_2', the price initially calculated for market 1 need no longer be an equilibrium price, because good 1 may be a substitute or a complement to good 2. This reflects that the system of equations is indeed simultaneous. Using the provisional prices p_1' and p_2', solve for a provisional p_3'. The proof proceeds in this way until a complete set of provisional relative prices has been calculated.

In the second iteration of Walras' proof, $p_2', \ldots, p_n'$ are held constant while a new equilibrium price is calculated for the first good. Call this new provisional price p_1''. Proceeding as outlined above, an entire new set of provisional relative prices $(p_1'', \ldots, p_n'')$ can be calculated. The proof continues to iterate in this way until a reasonable approximation to a set of equilibrium prices is achieved.

The importance of Walras' proof is its ability to demonstrate the simultaneous nature of the problem of finding equilibrium prices. It is, however, a cumbersome proof and is generally not used today. More recent work has used some relatively simple tools of advanced mathematics to demonstrate the existence of equilibrium prices in a formal and elegant way. To demonstrate such a proof, one advanced mathematical theorem must be described.

Brouwer's fixed point theorem

Because this section is purely mathematical, it is perhaps best to plunge right in by stating Brouwer's theorem:

FIGURE 13.7 A Graphical Illustration of Brouwer's Fixed Point Theorem

Because any continuous function must cross the 45° line somewhere in the unit square, this function must have a point for which $f(x^*) = x^*$. This point is called a "fixed point."

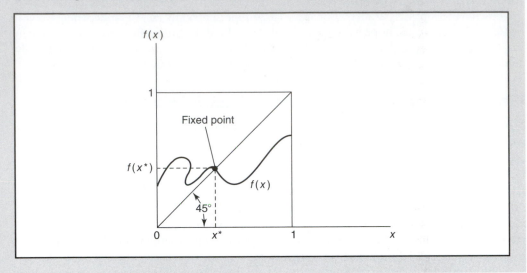

Any continuous mapping $[F(X)]$ of a closed, bounded, convex set into itself has at least one fixed point (X^*) such that $F(X^*) = X^*$.

Before analyzing this theorem on a word-by-word basis, perhaps an example will aid in understanding the terminology. Suppose that $f(x)$ is a continuous function defined on the interval $[0, 1]$ and that $f(x)$ takes on values also on the interval $[0, 1]$. This function then obeys the conditions of Brouwer's theorem; it must be the case that there exists some x^* such that $f(x^*) = x^*$. This fact is demonstrated in Figure 13.7. It is clear from this figure that any function, as long as it is continuous (as long as it has no "gaps"), must cross the 45° line somewhere. This point of crossing is a *fixed point*, because f maps this point (x^*) into itself.

To study the more general meaning of the theorem, we must define the terms *mapping*, *closed*, *bounded*, and *convex*. Definitions of these concepts will be presented in an extremely intuitive, nonrigorous way, because the costs of mathematical rigor greatly outweigh its possible benefits for the purposes of this book.

A *mapping* is a rule that associates the points in one set with points in another (or possibly the same) set. The most commonly encountered mappings are those that associate one point in n-dimensional space with some other point in n-dimensional space. Suppose that F is the mapping we wish to study. Then let X be a point for which the mapping is defined; the mapping associates X with some other point $Y = F(X)$. If a mapping is defined over a subset of an n-dimensional space (S) and if every point in S is associated (by the rule F) with some other point in S, then the mapping is said to map S *into* itself. In Figure 13.7 the function f maps the unit interval into itself. A mapping is *continuous* if points that are "close" to each other are mapped into other points that are "close" to each other.

The *Brouwer fixed point theorem* considers mappings defined on certain kinds of sets. These sets are required to be closed, bounded, and convex. Perhaps the simplest way to describe such sets is to say that they look like (n-dimensional analogies of) soap bubbles. They are *closed* in the sense that they contain their boundaries; the sets are *bounded* because none of their dimensions is infinitely large; and they are *convex* because they have no indentations in them. A technical description of the properties of such sets can be found in any elementary topology book.[12] For our purposes, however, it is only necessary to recognize that Brouwer's theorem is intended to apply to certain types of conveniently shaped sets. Therefore, in order to use the theorem to prove the existence of equilibrium prices, we must first describe a set of points that has these desirable properties.

Proof of the existence of equilibrium prices

The key to applying Brouwer's theorem to the exchange model just developed is to choose a suitable way for "normalizing" prices. Because only relative prices matter in the exchange model, it is convenient to assume that prices have been defined so that the sum of all prices is 1. Mathematically, for any arbitrary set of prices $(p_1, \ldots, p_n)$, we can instead deal with *normalized* prices of the form[13]

$$p'_i = \frac{p_i}{\sum_{i=1}^{n} p_i}. \tag{13.26}$$

These new prices will retain their original relative values ($p'_i / p'_j = p_i / p_j$) and will sum to 1:

$$\sum_{i=1}^{n} p'_i = 1. \tag{13.27}$$

Because of the degree-0 homogeneity of all the excess demand functions, this kind of normalization can always be made. Hence, for the remainder of this proof, we will assume that the feasible set of prices (call this set S) is composed of all possible combinations of n nonnegative numbers that sum to 1. To avoid complex notation, we drop the special symbols we have been using for such prices.

This set, S, is the one to which we can apply Brouwer's theorem. The set S is closed, bounded, and convex.[14] To apply Brouwer's theorem, we now will define a continuous mapping of S into itself. By a judicious choice of this mapping, we can show that the fixed point dictated by the theorem is in fact a set of equilibrium relative prices.

Free goods

Before demonstrating the details of the proof, we must redefine what is meant by an "equilibrium set of prices." We do not really require that excess demand be exactly equal to 0 in every market for an equilibrium. Rather, goods may exist for which the markets are in equilibrium but for which the available supply exceeds demand; there is negative excess demand. For this to be the case, however, it is necessary that the price of this particular good be zero. Hence, the equilibrium conditions of Equation 13.24 should be rewritten to take account of such *free goods*:

$$\begin{aligned} ED_i(P^*) &= 0 \quad \text{for } p_i^* > 0, \\ ED_i(P^*) &\leq 0 \quad \text{for } p_i^* = 0. \end{aligned} \tag{13.28}$$

Notice that such a set of equilibrium prices continues to obey Walras' law.

---

[12]For a development of the mathematics used in general equilibrium theory, see the references at the end of this chapter.

[13]One additional assumption must be made here: at least one of the prices is nonzero. In economic terms this means that at least one good is scarce. Without this assumption, a normalization of prices would not be possible—but studying economics in such a case would be unnecessary, because there would be no economic problem of scarcity.

[14]In two dimensions the set would simply be a straight line joining the coordinates $(0, 1)$ and $(1, 0)$. In three dimensions the set would be a triangular-shaped plane with vertices at $(0, 0, 1)$, $(0, 1, 0)$, and $(1, 0, 0)$. It is easy to see that each of these sets is closed, bounded, and convex.

Mapping the set of prices into itself

Using this definition of equilibrium and remembering that prices have been normalized to sum to 1, let's construct a continuous function that transforms one set of prices into another. The function builds on the Walrasian idea that, in order to achieve equilibrium, prices of goods in excess demand should be raised while those in excess supply should have their prices lowered. Hence, we define the mapping $F(P)$ for any (normalized) set of prices, P, such that the ith component of $F(P)$, denoted by $F^i(P)$, is given by

$$F^i(P) = p_i + ED_i(P) \qquad (13.29)$$

for all i. The mapping then performs the necessary task of appropriately raising and lowering prices. If, at p_i, good i is in excess demand [$ED_i(P) > 0$], then the price p_i is raised; if excess demand is negative, p_i is reduced. Because the excess demand functions are assumed to be continuous, this mapping will also be continuous. Two problems with the mapping of Equation 13.29 remain. First, nothing ensures that the new prices will be nonnegative. Hence, the mapping must be slightly redefined to be

$$F^i(P) = \max[p_i + ED_i(P), 0] \qquad (13.30)$$

for all i. The mapping of Equation 13.30 is also continuous.

A second problem with the mapping of Equation 13.30 is that the recalculated prices are not necessarily normalized; they will not sum to 1. It would be a simple matter, however, to normalize these new prices so they do sum to 1.[15] To avoid introducing additional notation, assume that this normalization has been done and hence that

$$\sum_{i=1}^{n} F^i(P) = 1. \qquad (13.31)$$

Application of Brouwer's theorem

With this normalization, then, F satisfies the conditions of the Brouwer fixed point theorem. It is a continuous mapping of the set S into itself. Hence there exists a point (P^*) that is mapped into itself. For this point,

$$p_i^* = \max[p_i^* + ED_i(P^*), 0] \qquad (13.32)$$

for all i.

But this says that P^* is an equilibrium set of prices: for $p_i^* > 0$,

$$p_i^* = p_i^* + ED_i(P^*)$$

---

[15]To accomplish this normalization, we first need to show that not all of the transformed prices will be zero: it is necessary to show that $p_i + ED_i(P) > 0$ for some i. This can be proved by contradiction. Assume that $p_i + ED_i(P) \leq 0$ for all i. Multiply this expression by p_i and sum over all values of i, giving

$$\sum_{i=1}^{n} p_i^2 + \sum_{i=1}^{n} p_i ED_i(P) \leq 0.$$

But

$$\sum_{i=1}^{n} p_i ED_i = 0$$

by Walras' law. Hence

$$\sum_{i=1}^{n} p_i^2 \leq 0,$$

and this implies that $p_i = 0$ for all i. However, we have already ruled out this situation (see footnote 13) and thus have proved that at least one of the transformed prices must be positive.

or

$$ED_i(P^*) = 0; \tag{13.33}$$

and for $p_i^* = 0$,

$$p_i^* + ED_i(P^*) \leq 0$$

or

$$ED_i(P^*) \leq 0. \tag{13.34}$$

We have therefore shown that the set of excess demand functions does in fact possess an equilibrium solution consisting of nonnegative prices. The simple exchange model developed here is consistent in that the market supply and demand functions necessarily have a solution. The homogeneity and continuity properties of the demand functions and the ability of Walras' law to tie together supply and demand are jointly responsible for this result.

Generalizations

Although this proof is a relatively old one in the field of general equilibrium theory, it does exhibit features of much of the more recent literature in this field. In particular, practically all modern proofs use Walras' law and rely on some type of fixed point theorem. More recent work has tended to focus on ways in which the proof of the existence of general equilibrium prices can be generalized to situations involving more complex supply assumptions and on how equilibrium prices can actually be computed. In later chapters of this book, we will examine some of these alternative supply assumptions, such as cases of imperfect competition and problems caused by "public goods" (which we define later in this chapter). In the next section we show how applied general equilibrium models based on fixed point theorems are constructed.

EXAMPLE 13.3 A General Equilibrium with Three Goods

The economy of Oz is composed only of three precious metals: (1) silver, (2) gold, and (3) platinum. There are 10 (thousand) ounces of each metal available. The demands for gold and platinum are given by

$$D_2 = -2\frac{p_2}{p_1} + \frac{p_3}{p_1} + 11 \quad \text{and}$$

$$D_3 = -\frac{p_2}{p_1} - 2\frac{p_3}{p_1} + 18, \tag{13.35}$$

respectively. Notice that the demands for gold and platinum depend on the relative prices of the two goods and that these demand functions are homogeneous of degree 0 in all three prices. Notice also that we have not written out the demand function for silver; but, as we will show, it can be derived from Walras' law.

Equilibrium in the gold and platinum markets requires that demand equal supply in both markets simultaneously:

$$-2\frac{p_2}{p_1} + \frac{p_3}{p_1} + 11 = 10,$$

$$-\frac{p_2}{p_1} - 2\frac{p_3}{p_1} + 18 = 10. \tag{13.36}$$

This system of simultaneous equations can be solved rather easily as

$$\frac{p_2}{p_1} = 2, \qquad \frac{p_3}{p_1} = 3. \tag{13.37}$$

(*continued*)

EXAMPLE 13.3 CONTINUED

In equilibrium, therefore, gold will have a price twice that of silver and platinum a price three times that of silver. The price of platinum will be 1.5 times that of gold.

Walras' law and the demand for silver. Because Walras' law must hold in this economy, we know that

$$p_1 ED_1 = -p_2 ED_2 - p_3 ED_3. \tag{13.38}$$

Solving Equations 13.36 for the excess demands (by moving the fixed supplies to the left-hand side) and substituting into Walras' law yields

$$p_1 ED_1 = 2\frac{p_2^2}{p_1} - \frac{p_2 p_3}{p_1} - p_2 + \frac{p_2 p_3}{p_1} + 2\frac{p_3^2}{p_1} - 8p_3 \tag{13.39}$$

or

$$ED_1 = 2\frac{p_2^2}{p_1^2} + 2\frac{p_3^2}{p_1^2} - \frac{p_2}{p_1} - 8\frac{p_3}{p_1}. \tag{13.40}$$

As expected, this function is homogeneous of degree 0 in the relative prices, and the market for silver is also in equilibrium ($ED_1 = 0$) at the relative prices computed previously. (Check this yourself!)

A change in supply. If gold supply decreases to 7 and platinum supply increases to 11, we would expect relative prices to change. It seems likely that the relative price of gold will rise. Similarly, because the rise in gold price will reduce the demand for platinum and platinum supply has increased, the relative price of platinum should fall. But that will reduce the demand for gold, so the end result is ambiguous—clearly, a simultaneous solution is called for. In fact, the solution to

$$-2\frac{p_2}{p_1} + \frac{p_3}{p_1} + 11 = 7 \quad \text{and}$$
$$-\frac{p_2}{p_1} - 2\frac{p_3}{p_1} + 18 = 11 \tag{13.41}$$

is

$$\frac{p_2}{p_1} = 3, \qquad \frac{p_3}{p_1} = 2. \tag{13.42}$$

So the price of gold rises relative to both silver and platinum, and the price of platinum falls relative to that of silver. All of these effects can be captured only in a simultaneous model.

QUERY: Is the silver market still in equilibrium given the new supplies of gold and platinum?

GENERAL EQUILIBRIUM MODELS

Two advances have resulted in the rapid development of general equilibrium modeling in recent years. First, the theory of economic equilibrium has been generalized to include many features of real-world economies such as imperfect competition, environmental externalities, and complex tax systems. Second, expanding computer capacity together with improvements in software (especially model "solvers") has made it possible to study models involving virtually any number of goods and households desired. In this section we will briefly explore some conceptual aspects of these models.[16] The Extensions to this chapter describe a few important applications.

Structure of general equilibrium models

Specification of any general equilibrium model begins by defining the number of goods to be included in the model. These "goods" include not only consumption goods but also intermediate goods that are used in the production of other goods (e.g., capital equipment), productive inputs such as labor or natural resources, and goods that are to be produced by the government (public goods). The goal of the model is then to solve for equilibrium prices for all of these goods and to study how these prices change when conditions change.

Some of the goods in a general equilibrium model are produced by firms. The technology of this production must be specified by production functions. The most common such specification is to use the types of CES production functions that we studied in Chapters 9 and 10, because these can yield some important insights about the ways in which inputs are substituted in the face of changing prices. In general, firms are assumed to maximize their profits given their production functions and given the input and output prices they face.

Demand is specified in general equilibrium models by defining utility functions for various types of households. Utility is treated as a function both of goods that are consumed and of inputs that are not supplied to the marketplace (for example, available labor that is not supplied to the market is consumed as leisure). Households are assumed to maximize utility. Their incomes are determined by the amounts of inputs they "sell" in the market and by the net result of any taxes they pay or transfers they receive.

Finally, a full general equilibrium model must specify how the government operates. If there are taxes in the model, how those taxes are to be spent on transfers or on public goods (which provide utility to consumers) must be modeled. If government borrowing is allowed, the bond market must be explicitly modeled. In short, the model must fully specify the flow of sources and uses of income that characterize the economy being modeled.

Solving general equilibrium models

Once technology (supply) and preferences (demand) have been specified, a general equilibrium model must be solved for equilibrium prices and quantities. The proof in the previous section shows that such a model will generally have such a solution, but actually finding that solution can sometimes be difficult—especially when the number of goods and households is large. General equilibrium models are usually solved on computers via modifications of an algorithm originally developed by Herbert Scarf in the 1970s.[17] This algorithm (or more modern versions of it) searches for market equilibria by mimicking the way markets work. That is, an initial solution is specified and then prices are raised in markets with excess demand and lowered in markets with excess supply until an equilibrium is found in which all excess demands are zero. Sometimes multiple equilibria will occur, but usually economic models have sufficient curvature in the underlying production and utility functions that the equilibrium found by the Scarf algorithm will be unique.

---

[16]This section is based on Walter Nicholson and Frank Westhoff, "General Equilibrium Models: Improving the Microeconomics Classroom," Working Paper, Department of Economics, Amherst College, 2007.

[17]Herbert Scarf with Terje Hansen, *On the Computation of Economic Equilibria* (New Haven, CT: Yale University Press, 1973).

Economic insights from general equilibrium models

General equilibrium models provide a number of insights about how economies operate that cannot be obtained from the types of partial equilibrium models studied in Chapter 12. Some of the most important of these are:

- All prices are endogenous in economic models. The exogenous elements of models are preferences and productive technologies.
- All firms and productive inputs are owned by households. All income ultimately accrues to households.
- Any model with a government sector is incomplete if it does not specify how tax receipts are used.
- The "bottom line" in any policy evaluation is the utility of households. Firms and governments are only intermediaries in getting to this final accounting.
- All taxes distort economic decisions along some dimension. The welfare costs of such distortions must always be weighed against the benefits of such taxes (in terms of public good production or equity-enhancing transfers).

Some of these insights are illustrated in the next two examples. In later chapters we will return to general equilibrium modeling whenever such a perspective seems necessary to gain a more complete understanding of the topic being covered.

EXAMPLE 13.4 A Simple General Equilibrium Model

Let's look at a simple general equilibrium model with only two households, two consumer goods (x and y), and two inputs (capital k and labor l). Each household has an "endowment" of capital and labor that it can choose to retain or sell in the market. These endowments are denoted by $\bar{k}_1, \bar{l}_1$ and $\bar{k}_2, \bar{l}_2$, respectively. Households obtain utility from the amounts of the consumer goods they purchase and from the amount of labor they do not sell into the market (that is, leisure $= \bar{l}_i - l_i$). The households have simple Cobb-Douglas utility functions:

$$U_1 = x_1^{0.5} y_1^{0.3} (\bar{l}_1 - l_1)^{0.2}, \qquad U_2 = x_2^{0.4} y_2^{0.4} (\bar{l}_2 - l_2)^{0.2}. \qquad \textbf{(13.43)}$$

Hence, household 1 has a relatively greater preference for good x than does household 2. Notice that capital does not enter into these utility functions directly. Consequently, each household will provide its entire endowment of capital to the marketplace. Households will retain some labor, however, because leisure provides utility directly.

Production of goods x and y is characterized by simple Cobb-Douglas technologies:

$$x = k_x^{0.2} l_x^{0.8}, \qquad y = k_y^{0.8} l_y^{0.2}. \qquad \textbf{(13.44)}$$

So, in this example, production of x is relatively labor intensive while production of y is relatively capital intensive.

To complete this model we must specify initial endowments of capital and labor. Here we assume that

$$\bar{k}_1 = 40, \ \bar{l}_1 = 24 \quad \text{and} \quad \bar{k}_2 = 10, \ \bar{l}_2 = 24. \qquad \textbf{(13.45)}$$

Although the households have equal labor endowments (i.e., 24 "hours"), household 1 has significantly more capital than does household 2.

Base-case simulation. Equations 13.43–13.45 specify our complete general equilibrium model in the absence of a government. A solution to this model will consist of four equilibrium prices (for x, y, k, and l) at which households maximize utility and firms maximize profits.[18] Because any general equilibrium model can compute only relative prices, we are free to impose a price normalization scheme. Here we assume that the prices will always sum to unity. That is,

$$p_x + p_y + p_k + p_l = 1. \tag{13.46}$$

Solving[19] for these prices yields

$$p_x = 0.363, \quad p_y = 0.253, \quad p_k = 0.136, \quad p_l = 0.248. \tag{13.47}$$

At these prices, total production of x is 23.7 and production of y is 25.1. The utility-maximizing choices for household 1 are

$$x_1 = 15.7, \quad y_1 = 8.1, \quad \bar{l}_1 - l_1 = 24 - 14.8 = 9.2, \quad U_1 = 13.5; \tag{13.48}$$

for household 2, these choices are

$$x_2 = 8.1, \quad y_2 = 11.6, \quad \bar{l}_2 - l_2 = 24 - 18.1 = 5.9, \quad U_2 = 8.75. \tag{13.49}$$

Observe that household 1 consumes quite a bit of good x but provides less in labor supply than does household 2. This reflects the greater capital endowment of household 1 in this base-case simulation. We will return to this base case in several later simulations.

QUERY: How would you show that each household obeys its budget constraint in this simulation? Does the budgetary allocation of each household exhibit the budget shares that are implied by the form of its utility function?

EXAMPLE 13.5 The Excess Burden of a Tax

In Chapter 12 we showed that taxation may impose an excess burden in addition to the tax revenues collected because of the incentive effects of the tax. With a general equilibrium model we can show much more about this effect. Specifically, assume that the government in the economy of Example 13.4 imposes an ad valorem tax of 0.4 on good x. This introduces a wedge between what demanders pay for this good x (p_x) and what suppliers receive for the good ($p'_x = (1 - t)p_x = 0.6p_x$). To complete the model we must specify what happens to the revenues generated by this tax. For simplicity we assume that these revenues are rebated to the households in a 50–50 split. In all other respects the economy remains as described in Example 13.4.

Solving for the new equilibrium prices in this model yields

$$p_x = 0.472, \quad p_y = 0.218, \quad p_k = 0.121, \quad p_l = 0.188. \tag{13.50}$$

At these prices, total production of x is 17.9 and total production of y is 28.8. Hence, the allocation of resources has shifted significantly toward y production. Even though the relative price of x experienced by consumers ($= p_x/p_y = 0.472/0.218 = 2.17$) has risen significantly from its value (of 1.43) in Example 13.4, the price ratio experienced by firms ($0.6p_x/p_y = 1.30$) has fallen somewhat from this prior value. One might therefore expect, on the basis of a partial equilibrium analysis, that consumers would demand less of good x and likewise that firms would similarly produce less of that good. Partial equilibrium analysis would not, however, allow us to predict the increased production of y (which comes about because the relative price of y has fallen for consumers but has risen for firms) nor the

(continued)

---

[18]Because firms' production functions are characterized by constant returns to scale, in equilibrium each earns zero profits so there is no need to specify firm ownership in this model.

[19]The computer program used to find these solutions is accessible at www.amherst.edu/~fwesthoff/compequ/FixedPointsCompEquApplet.html.

EXAMPLE 13.5 CONTINUED

reduction in relative input prices (because there is less being produced overall). A more complete picture of all of these effects can be obtained by looking at the final equilibrium positions of the two households. The post-tax allocation for household 1 is

$$x_1 = 11.6, \quad y_1 = 15.2, \quad \bar{l}_1 - l_1 = 11.8, \quad U_1 = 12.7; \qquad (13.51)$$

for household 2,

$$x_2 = 6.3, \quad y_2 = 13.6, \quad \bar{l}_2 - l_2 = 7.9, \quad U_2 = 8.96. \qquad (13.52)$$

Hence, imposition of the tax has made household 1 considerably worse-off: utility falls from 13.5 to 12.7. Household 2 is actually made slightly better-off by this tax, or transfer scheme, primarily because it receives a relatively large share of the tax proceeds that come mainly from household 1. Although total utility has declined (as predicted by the simple partial equilibrium analysis of excess burden), general equilibrium analysis gives a more complete picture of the distributional consequences of the tax. Notice also that the total amount of labor supplied falls as a result of the tax: total leisure rises from 15.1 (hours) to 19.7. Imposition of a tax on good x has therefore had a relatively substantial labor supply effect that is completely invisible in a partial equilibrium model.

QUERY: Would it be possible to make both households better-off (relative to Example 13.4) in this taxation scenario by changing how the tax revenues are redistributed?

WELFARE ECONOMICS

Although most people recognize the equilibrium properties of the competitive price system (after all, prices usually do not fluctuate widely from day to day), they see little overall pattern to the resulting allocation of resources. The relationships described by the competitive model are so complex it is hard to believe that any desirable outcome will emerge from the chaos. This view provides an open-ended rationale to tinker with the system—because the results of market forces are chaotic, surely human societies can do better through careful planning.

Smith's invisible hand hypothesis

It took the genius of Adam Smith to challenge this view, which was probably the prevalent one in the eighteenth century. To Smith, the competitive market system represented the polar opposite of chaos. Rather, it provided a powerful "invisible hand" that ensured resources would find their way to where they were most valued, thereby enhancing the "wealth" of the nation. In Smith's view, reliance on the economic self-interest of individuals and firms would result in a (perhaps surprisingly) desirable social outcome.

Smith's initial insights gave rise to modern welfare economics. Specifically, his widely quoted "invisible hand" image provided the impetus for what is now called the First Theorem of Welfare Economics—that there is a close correspondence between the efficient allocation of resources and the competitive pricing of these resources. Here we will investigate this correspondence in some detail. We begin by defining economic efficiency in input and output choices. Our definitions, which draw on the work of the nineteenth-century economist Vilfred Pareto, have already been described briefly in Chapter 12. Our goal here is to draw these discussions together and illustrate their underlying relationship to the competitive allocation of resources.

Pareto efficiency

We begin with Pareto's definition of economic efficiency.

Pareto efficient allocation. An allocation of resources is *Pareto efficient* if it is not possible (through further reallocations) to make one person better-off without making someone else worse-off.

DEFINITION

The Pareto definition thus identifies particular allocations as being "inefficient" if unambiguous improvements are possible. Notice that the definition does not require interperson comparisons of utility; "improvements" are defined by individuals themselves.

Efficiency in production

An economy is efficient in production if it is on its production possibility frontier. Formally, we can use Pareto's terminology to define productive efficiency as follows:

Productive efficiency. An allocation of resources is *efficient in production* (or "technically efficient") if no further reallocation would permit more of one good to be produced without necessarily reducing the output of some other good.

DEFINITION

As for Pareto efficiency itself, it is perhaps easiest to grasp this definition by studying its converse—an allocation would be inefficient if it were possible to move existing resources around a bit and get additional amounts of one good and no less of anything else. With technically efficient allocations, no such unambiguous improvements are possible. The trade-offs among outputs necessitated by movements along the production possibility frontier reflect the technically efficient nature of all of the allocations on the frontier.

Technical efficiency is an obvious precondition for overall Pareto efficiency. Suppose resources were allocated so that production was inefficient; that is, production was occurring at a point inside the production possibility frontier. It would then be possible to produce more of at least one good and no less of anything else. This increased output could be given to some lucky person, making him or her better-off (and no one else worse-off). Hence, inefficiency in production is also Pareto inefficiency. As we shall see in the next section, however, technical efficiency does not guarantee Pareto efficiency. An economy can be efficient at producing the wrong goods—devoting all available resources to producing left shoes would be a technically efficient use of those resources, but surely some Pareto improvement could be found in which everyone would be better-off.

Efficient allocation of resources among firms

In order to achieve technical efficiency, resources must be allocated correctly among firms. Intuitively, resources should be allocated to those firms where they can be most efficiently used. More precisely, the condition for efficient allocation is that the marginal physical product of any resource in the production of a particular good is the same no matter which firm produces that good.

A mathematical proof of this rule is straightforward. Suppose there are two firms producing the same good (x) and their production functions are given by $f_1(k_1, l_1)$ and $f_2(k_2, l_2)$. Assume also that total supplies of capital and labor are given by $\bar{k}$ and $\bar{l}$. The allocational problem is then to maximize

$$x = f_1(k_1, l_1) + f_2(k_2, l_2), \tag{13.53}$$

subject to the constraints

$$k_1 + k_2 = \bar{k},$$
$$l_1 + l_2 = \bar{l}. \tag{13.54}$$

Upon substituting the constraints into Equation 13.53, the maximization problem becomes

$$x = f_1(k_1, l_1) + f_2(\bar{k} - k_1, \bar{l} - l_1). \tag{13.55}$$

First-order conditions for a maximum are

$$\frac{\partial x}{\partial k_1} = \frac{\partial f_1}{\partial k_1} + \frac{\partial f_2}{\partial k_1} = \frac{\partial f_1}{\partial k_1} - \frac{\partial f_2}{\partial k_2} = 0 \quad \text{and}$$

$$\frac{\partial x}{\partial l_1} = \frac{\partial f_1}{\partial l_1} + \frac{\partial f_2}{\partial l_1} = \frac{\partial f_1}{\partial l_1} - \frac{\partial f_2}{\partial l_2} = 0 \tag{13.56}$$

or

$$\frac{\partial f_1}{\partial k_1} = \frac{\partial f_2}{\partial k_2} \quad \text{and} \quad \frac{\partial f_1}{\partial l_1} = \frac{\partial f_2}{\partial l_2}, \tag{13.57}$$

as was to be shown.

EXAMPLE 13.6 Gains from Efficiently Allocating Labor

To examine the quantitative gains in output from allocating resources efficiently, suppose two rice farms have production functions of the simple form

$$q = k^{1/4} l^{3/4} \tag{13.58}$$

but that one rice farm is more mechanized than the other. If capital for the first farm is given by $k_1 = 16$ and for the second farm by $k_2 = 625$, then

$$q_1 = 2l_1^{3/4},$$
$$q_2 = 5l_2^{3/4}. \tag{13.59}$$

If the total labor supply is 100, an equal allocation of labor to these two farms will provide total rice output of

$$Q = q_1 + q_2 = 2(50)^{3/4} + 5(50)^{3/4} = 131.6. \tag{13.60}$$

The efficient allocation is found by equalizing the marginal productivities:

$$\frac{\partial q_1}{\partial l_1} = \left(\frac{3}{2}\right) l_1^{-1/4} = \frac{\partial q_2}{\partial l_2} = \frac{15}{4} l_2^{-1/4}. \tag{13.61}$$

Hence, for efficiency, labor should be allocated such that

$$l_1 = \left(\frac{5}{2}\right)^{-4} l_2 = 0.0256 l_2. \tag{13.62}$$

Given the greater capitalization of farm 2, practically all of the available labor should be devoted to it. With 100 units of labor, 97.4 units should be allocated to farm 2 with only 2.6 units to farm 1. In this case total output will be

$$Q = q_1 + q_2 = 2(2.6)^{3/4} + 5(97.4)^{3/4} = 159.1. \tag{13.63}$$

This represents a gain of more than 20 percent over the rice output obtained under the equal allocation.

QUERY: Suppose capital were not fixed in this problem. How should capital *and* labor be allocated between the two farms?

Reaching the production possibility frontier

Although equality of marginal productivities will ensure the efficient allocation of resources among firms producing any one good, that condition is not enough to ensure that inputs are allocated efficiently among firms producing different goods. Earlier in this chapter (Figure 13.2) we saw that the condition for such efficiency is that the rates of technical substitution among inputs must be the same in the production of each good if production is to be on the production possibility frontier. Let's look at a more formal proof. Suppose there are only two goods being produced (x and y) using capital and labor as inputs. Because we have already discussed allocating resources among firms producing the same good, here we assume there is only a single firm producing each good. The production function for x is given by $x = f(k_x, l_x)$ and for good y by $y = g(k_y, l_y)$. Total availability of the inputs is constrained by $\bar{k} = k_x + k_y$ and $\bar{l} = l_x + l_y$. The problem of achieving technical efficiency is then to maximize the value of x for any specified value of y, say $\bar{y}$. Setting up the Lagrangian for this problem yields

$$\mathcal{L} = f(k_x, l_x) + \lambda[g(\bar{k} - k_x, \bar{l} - l_x) - \bar{y}], \qquad \textbf{(13.64)}$$

and the first-order conditions for a maximum are

$$\frac{\partial \mathcal{L}}{\partial k_x} = f_1 - \lambda g_1 = 0,$$

$$\frac{\partial \mathcal{L}}{\partial l_x} = f_2 - \lambda g_2 = 0, \qquad \textbf{(13.65)}$$

$$\frac{\partial \mathcal{L}}{\partial \lambda} = g(\bar{k} - k_x, \bar{l} - l_x) - \bar{y} = 0.$$

Dividing the first two of these equations yields the required result:

$$\frac{f_1}{f_2} = \frac{g_1}{g_2}. \qquad \textbf{(13.66)}$$

Therefore, in a situation with many firms and several outputs, the conditions specified in Equations 13.57 and 13.66 will ensure that production takes place on the production possibility frontier. That is, production will be technically efficient.

EFFICIENCY IN OUTPUT MIX

Technical efficiency will not necessarily ensure overall Pareto optimality, however. Demand must also be brought into the story. It does little good for an economy to be an efficient producer of yo-yos and xylophones if no one wants these goods. In order to ensure Pareto efficiency, we need some way to tie together individuals' preferences and the production possibilities. The condition necessary to ensure that the right goods are produced is that the *marginal rate of substitution* (*MRS*) for any two goods must equal the *rate of product transformation* (*RPT*) of the two goods. Simply phrased, the psychological rate of trade-off between the two goods in people's preferences must be equal to the rate at which they can be traded off in production.

A graphical proof

Figure 13.8 illustrates the requirement for efficiency in product mix for a very simple case, a single-person economy. It assumes that the one person in this economy (Robinson Crusoe?) produces only two goods (x and y). (This analysis could also apply to an economy of many individuals with identical preferences.) Those combinations of x and y that can be produced are given by the production possibility frontier PP. Any point on PP represents a point of technical efficiency. By superimposing the individual's indifference map on Figure 13.8,

FIGURE 13.8   Efficiency in Product Mix in a Robinson Crusoe Economy

In a single-person economy, the curve *PP* represents those combinations of *x* and *y* that can be produced. Every point on *PP* is efficient in a production sense. However, only the output combination at point *E* is a true utility maximum for the individual. At *E* the individual's *MRS* is equal to the rate at which *x* can technically be traded for *y* (*RPT*).

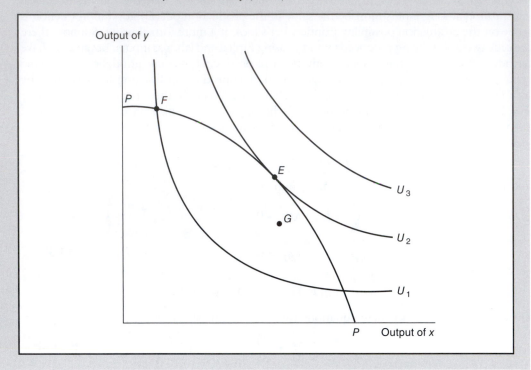

however, we see that only one point on *PP* provides maximum utility. This point of maximum utility is at *E*, where the curve *PP* is tangent to the individual's highest indifference curve, U_2. At this point of tangency, the individual's *MRS* (of *x* for *y*) is equal to the technical *RPT* (of *x* for *y*); hence, this is the required condition for overall efficiency. Notice that point *E* is preferred to every other point that is efficient in a productive sense. In fact, for any other point, such as *F*, on the curve *PP*, there exist points that are inefficient but are preferred to *F*. In Figure 13.8, the "inefficient" point *G* is preferred to the "efficient" point *F*. It would be preferable from the individual's point of view to produce inefficiently rather than be forced to produce the "wrong" combination of goods in an efficient way. Point *E* (which is efficiently produced) is superior to any such "second-best" solution.

A mathematical proof

To demonstrate this result mathematically, assume again there are only two goods (*x* and *y*) and one individual in society (again Robinson Crusoe), whose utility function is given by $U(x, y)$. Assume also that this society's production possibility frontier can be written in implicit form as $T(x, y) = 0$. Robinson's problem is to maximize utility subject to this production constraint. Setting up the Lagrangian expression for this problem yields

$$\mathcal{L} = U(x, y) + \lambda[T(x, y)], \tag{13.67}$$

and the first-order conditions for an interior maximum are

$$\frac{\partial \mathscr{L}}{\partial x} = \frac{\partial U}{\partial x} + \lambda \frac{\partial T}{\partial x} = 0,$$

$$\frac{\partial \mathscr{L}}{\partial y} = \frac{\partial U}{\partial y} + \lambda \frac{\partial T}{\partial y} = 0,$$

$$\frac{\partial \mathscr{L}}{\partial \lambda} = T(x, y) = 0.$$

(13.68)

Combining the first two of these equations yields

$$\frac{\partial U / \partial x}{\partial U / \partial y} = \frac{\partial T / \partial x}{\partial T / \partial y}$$

(13.69)

or

$$MRS \ (x \ \text{for} \ y) = -\frac{dy}{dx} \ (\text{along} \ T) = RPT \ (x \ \text{for} \ y),$$

(13.70)

as Figure 13.8 illustrated. We have shown that only if individuals' preferences are taken into account will resources be allocated in a Pareto efficient way. Without such an explicit reference to preferences, it would be possible—by reallocating production—to raise at least one person's utility without reducing anyone else's.

COMPETITIVE PRICES AND EFFICIENCY: THE FIRST THEOREM OF WELFARE ECONOMICS

The essence of the relationship between perfect competition and the efficient allocation of resources can be easily summarized. Attaining a Pareto efficient allocation of resources requires that (except when corner solutions occur) the rate of trade-off between any two goods, say x and y, should be the same for all economic agents. In a perfectly competitive economy, the ratio of the price of x to the price of y provides this common rate of trade-off to which all agents will adjust. Because prices are treated as fixed parameters both in individuals' utility-maximizing decisions and in firms' profit-maximizing decisions, all trade-off rates between x and y will be equalized to the rate at which x and y can be traded in the market (p_x/p_y). Because all agents face the same prices, all trade-off rates will be equalized and an efficient allocation will be achieved. This is the First Theorem of Welfare Economics.

Efficiency in production

To see how competitive markets achieve technical efficiency, consider first the requirement that every firm that produces a particular good (say, x) has identical marginal productivities of labor in the production of x. In Chapter 11 we showed that a profit-maximizing firm will hire additional units of any input (say, labor) up to the point at which its marginal contribution to revenues is equal to the marginal cost of hiring the input. If we let p_x represent the price of the good being sold and let f^1 and f^2 represent the production functions for two firms that produce x, then profit maximization requires that

$$p_x f_l^1 = w,$$

$$p_x f_l^2 = w.$$

(13.71)

Because both firms face both the same price for x and the same competitive wage rate, these equations imply

$$f_l^1 = f_l^2.$$

(13.72)

Consequently, every firm will have the same marginal productivity of labor in the production of x. The market has succeeded in bringing about an efficient allocation of each input among firms.

Competitive input markets will also ensure that inputs are employed efficiently across firms producing different goods. In Chapter 10 we saw that any firm will minimize costs by choosing an input combination for which the ratio of marginal products (that is, the rate of technical substitution) is equal to the inputs' prices. Hence, using our previous notation,

$$\frac{v}{w} = \frac{f_1}{f_2} \quad \text{and} \quad \frac{v}{w} = \frac{g_1}{g_2}. \tag{13.73}$$

Because competitive markets will ensure that inputs obey the law of one price, these cost-minimizing conditions will lead to the equality of rates of technical substitution required by Equation 13.66. Notice, as in the case for allocation of inputs among firms producing the same good, no firm needs to know anything about what the other firms are doing. Competitive input prices convey all the information necessary to achieve technical efficiency.

Efficiency in product mix

Proving that perfectly competitive markets lead to efficiency in the relationship between production and preferences is also straightforward. Because the price ratios quoted to consumers are the same ratios that the market presents to firms, the *MRS* shared by all individuals will be identical to the *RPT* shared by all firms. This will be true for any pair of goods. Consequently, an efficient mix of goods will be produced. Again, notice the two important functions that market prices perform. First, they ensure supply and demand will be equalized for all goods. If a good were produced in too great amounts, a market reaction would set in (its price would fall) that would cut back on production of the good and shift resources into other employment. The equilibrating of supply and demand in the market therefore ensures there will be neither excess demand nor excess supply. Second, equilibrium prices provide market trade-off rates for firms and individuals to use as parameters in their decisions. Because these trade-off rates are identical for firms and individuals, efficiency is ensured.

A graphical proof

Our discussion of general equilibrium modeling earlier in this chapter provides precisely the tools required to show this result graphically. Figure 13.9 repeats Figure 13.4, but now we are more interested in the efficiency properties of the general equilibrium solution illustrated. Given the production possibility frontier PP and preferences represented by the indifference curves, it is clear that x^*, y^* represents the efficient output mix (compare this figure to Figure 13.8). Possibly x^*, y^* could be decided upon in a centrally planned economy if the planning board had adequate information about production possibilities and individuals' preferences. Alternatively, reliance on competitive markets and the self-interest of firms and individuals will also lead to this allocation. Only with a price ratio of p_x^*/p_y^* will supply and demand be in equilibrium in this model, and that equilibrium will occur at the efficient product mix, E. Smith's invisible hand ensures not only that production is technically efficient (that output combinations lie on the production possibility frontier) but also that the forces of supply and demand lead to the Pareto efficient output combination. More complex models of competitive equilibrium price determination reach essentially the same conclusion.[20] This is the First Theorem of Welfare Economics.

---

[20]See, for example, K. J. Arrow and F. H. Hahn, *General Competitive Analysis* (San Francisco: Holden-Day, 1971), chaps. 4 and 5.

FIGURE 13.9   Competitive Equilibrium and Efficiency in Output Mix

Although all the output combinations on PP are technically efficient, only the combination x^*, y^* is Pareto optimal. A competitive equilibrium price ratio of p_x^*/p_y^* will lead this economy to this Pareto efficient solution.

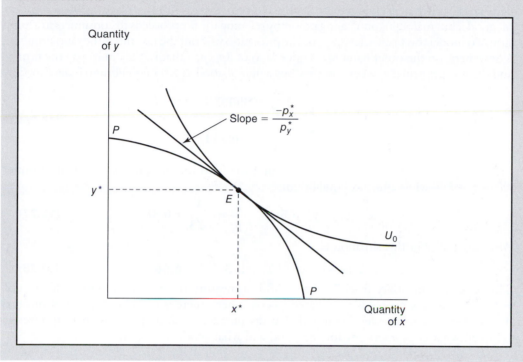

EXAMPLE 13.7   Efficiency and Inefficiency

The efficiency of competitive pricing can be shown with the simple general equilibrium models examined in Example 13.2. Each of the allocations found in that example are efficient given the preferences and productive technology that underlie them. That is, in each case utility is as large as possible given the production possibility frontier.

The base-case allocation $(x^* = y^* = \sqrt{50})$ is technically feasible in both of the other cases illustrated in Example 13.2, but it is not the best use of resources. For the situation where there is technical progress in the production of good x, the base-case allocation now lies inside the production possibility frontier. The allocation $(x^* = y^* = 10)$ clearly is Pareto superior to the base case. Another way to see this is by holding y^* constant at $\sqrt{50}$; then it is possible to produce $x^* = 2\sqrt{50}$ once the technical progress in good x is taken into account. Opting for the base-case allocation would forgo a substantial amount of x production (of course, only $x^* = y^* = 10$ is truly efficient given the new technology).

The base-case allocation would also be inefficient when preferences shift toward good y. With the new utility function, the base case would yield

$$U(x,y) = x^{0.1}y^{0.9} = (50)^{0.05}(50)^{0.45} = (50)^{0.5} = 7.07. \qquad \textbf{(13.74)}$$

Alternatively, the optimal allocation $[x^* = (10)^{0.5}, y^* = 3(10)^{0.5}]$ yields utility of

$$U(x,y) = x^{0.1}y^{0.9} = (10)^{0.05}(3)^{0.9}(10)^{0.45} = (3)^{0.9}(10)^{0.5} = 8.50. \qquad \textbf{(13.75)}$$

Clearly, efficiency requires that preferences and technology be tied together properly.

(continued)

EXAMPLE 13.7   CONTINUED

The excess burden of a tax, again. Consider again the modeling of taxation. Suppose that the government is unhappy with our base-case scenario because it believes people should not consume so much of good x. To address this concern, the government places a 200 percent tax on good x but maintains purchasing power by rebating the tax proceeds to consumers in a lump sum. To model this tax, we let p_x/p_y be the price ratio without the tax; this is the ratio firms see. Consumers, on the other hand, see a price ratio of $3p_x/p_y$—that is, they must pay the firm p_x and the government $2p_x$ whenever they buy a unit of good x. Now equilibrium is described by

$$\frac{p_x}{p_y} = \frac{x}{y} \quad \textbf{(supply)},$$

$$\frac{3p_x}{p_y} = \frac{y}{x} \quad \textbf{(demand)}.$$

(13.76)

Hence, $x/y = y/3x$ or $y^2 = 3x^2$. Substituting this into the production possibility frontier yields the following after-tax equilibrium:

$$x^* = 5, \quad y^* = 5\sqrt{3}, \quad \frac{p_x}{p_y} = \frac{1}{\sqrt{3}} = 0.58.$$

(13.77)

After-tax utility in this situation is

$$U(x, y) = x^{0.5}y^{0.5} = 5(3)^{0.25} = 6.58.$$

(13.78)

The reduction in utility from 7.07 to 6.58 is a measure of the excess burden of this tax. Here, because tax proceeds are rebated to consumers, there is no other burden of this tax. The welfare loss arises solely because the tax discourages x consumption by creating a wedge between what consumers pay for the good and what producers receive for it.

QUERY: Explain the various components of the consumer's budget constraint in the tax example studied here.

Laissez-faire policies

In its most dogmatic expression, the correspondence between competitive equilibrium and Pareto efficiency provides "scientific" support for the laissez-faire position taken by many economists. For example, there is some theoretical support for Smith's assertion that

> the natural effort of every individual to better his own condition, when suffered to exert itself with freedom and security, is so powerful a principle that it is alone, and without any assistance, not only capable of carrying on the society to wealth and prosperity, but of surmounting a hundred impertinent obstructions with which the folly of human laws too often encumbers its operations.[21]

Again, as Smith noted, it is not the "public spirit" of the baker that provides bread for individuals' consumption. Rather, bakers (and other producers) operate in their own self-interest when responding to market signals. Individuals also respond to these signals when deciding how to allocate their incomes. Government intervention in this smoothly functioning process may only result in a loss of Pareto efficiency.

Such a sweeping conclusion, of course, vastly overstates the general applicability of the simple models we have been using. No one should attempt to draw policy recommendations from a theoretical structure that pays so little attention to the institutional details of the real

---

[21]A. Smith, *The Wealth of Nations* (New York: Random House, Modern Library Edition, 1937), p. 508.

world. Still, the efficiency properties of the competitive system do provide a benchmark—a place to start when examining reasons why competitive markets may fail.

DEPARTING FROM THE COMPETITIVE ASSUMPTIONS

Factors that may distort the ability of competitive markets to achieve efficiency can be classed into four general groupings that include most of the interesting cases: (1) imperfect competition, (2) externalities, (3) public goods, and (4) imperfect information. Here we provide a brief summary of these groupings; we will return to them in later chapters.

Imperfect competition

"Imperfect competition" includes all those situations in which economic agents exert some market power in determining price. In this case, as we will see in Part 5, these agents will take such effects into account in their decisions. A firm that faces a downward-sloping demand curve for its product, for example, will recognize that the marginal revenue from selling one more unit is less than the market price of that unit. Because it is the marginal return to its decisions that motivates the profit-maximizing firm, marginal revenue rather than market price becomes the important magnitude. Market prices no longer carry the informational content required to achieve Pareto efficiency. Other cases of market power result in similar informational shortcomings.

Externalities

The competitive price system can also fail to allocate resources efficiently when there are interactions among firms and individuals that are not adequately reflected in market prices. Perhaps the prototype example is the case of a firm that pollutes the air with industrial smoke and other debris. Such a situation is termed an *externality*: an interaction between the firm's level of production and individuals' well-being that is not accounted for by the price system. A more complete discussion of the nature of externalities will be presented in Chapter 19, but here we can describe why the presence of such nonmarket interactions interferes with the ability of the price system to allocate resources efficiently. With externalities, market prices no longer reflect all of a good's costs of production. There is a divergence between *private* and *social* marginal cost, and these extra social costs (or possibly benefits) will not be reflected in market prices. Hence market prices will not carry the information about true costs that is necessary to establish an efficient allocation of resources. As we will show in Chapter 19, most of the study of environmental economics is concerned with potential ways to ameliorate the effects of such discrepancies.

Public goods

A similar problem in pricing occurs in the case of "public" goods. These are goods, such as national defense, which (usually) have two properties that make them unsuitable for production in markets. First, the goods are *nonrival* in that additional people can consume the benefits of them at zero cost. This property suggests that the "correct" price for such goods is zero—obviously a problem if they are going to be produced profitably. A second feature of many public goods is *nonexclusion*: extra individuals cannot be precluded from consuming the good. Hence, in a market context, most consumers will adopt a "free rider" stance—waiting for someone else to pay. Both of these technical features of public goods pose substantial problems for market economies. These problems are also examined in Chapter 19.

Imperfect information

Our discussion of the efficiency of perfectly competitive pricing has implicitly assumed that both suppliers and demanders know the equilibrium prices at which transactions occur. If economic actors are uncertain about prices or if markets cannot reach equilibrium, then there is no reason to expect that the efficiency property of competitive pricing will be retained. There are, of course, many ways in which imperfect information may affect market outcomes. And once it is admitted that information may be imperfect, it is important to construct models of how information is obtained and used by suppliers and demanders. To examine all of these issues here would take us too far away from our primary goals. In Chapter 18, however, we return to the topic of imperfect information by looking in detail at this rapidly expanding area of economic research.

These four impediments to efficiency suggest that one should be very careful in applying the First Theorem of Welfare Economics to actual policy choices. As we will discuss in later chapters, there may be good reason to interfere with market outcomes on efficiency grounds. There are also, of course, many bad reasons to interfere with markets—there are undoubtedly situations where the lessons of the First Theorem should be followed. The role of microeconomic analysis is to provide a systematic way of sorting through these cases.

DISTRIBUTION AND THE SECOND THEOREM OF WELFARE ECONOMICS

Although the First Theorem of Welfare Economics ensures that (under certain conditions) competitive markets will achieve efficient allocations, there is no guarantee that these allocations will achieve any sort of fair distribution of welfare among individuals. As A. K. Sen has pointed out, an allocation of resources may be Pareto efficient "even when some people are rolling in luxury and others are near starvation, as long as the starvers cannot be made better off without cutting into the pleasures of the rich…. In short, a society can be Pareto optimal and still be perfectly disgusting."[22] Although a formal treatment of social welfare economics is beyond the scope of this book, here we will look briefly at the nature of the distributional issue.

An exchange economy

To study distribution in its simplest setting, assume there are only two people in society, Smith and Jones. Assume also that the total quantities of two goods (x and y) to be distributed among these people are in fixed supply. Now we can use the Edgeworth box diagram introduced earlier in this chapter to illustrate all possible allocations of these goods between Smith and Jones. In Figure 13.10, the dimensions of the Edgeworth box are given by the total quantities of the goods available. Smith's indifference curves are drawn with origin O_S, and Jones's indifference curves are drawn with origin O_J. Any point within the box represents a possible allocation of the goods to these two people, and we can use the indifference curves to evaluate the utility derived by each person from such allocations.

Mutually beneficial transactions

Any point within the Edgeworth box at which the *MRS* for Smith is unequal to that for Jones offers an opportunity for Pareto improvements. Consider the potential allocation A in Figure 13.10. This point lies on the point of intersection of Smith's indifference curve U_S^1 and Jones's indifference curve U_J^3. Obviously, the marginal rates of substitution (the slopes of the indifference curves) are not equal at A. Any allocation in the oval-shape shaded area represents a mutually beneficial trade for these two people—they can both move to a higher level

---

[22]A. K. Sen, *Collective Choice and Social Welfare* (San Francisco: Holden-Day, 1970), p. 22.

FIGURE 13.10 Edgeworth Box Diagram of Pareto Efficiency in Exchange

The points on the curve O_S, O_J are efficient in the sense that, at these allocations, Smith cannot be made better-off without making Jones worse-off (and vice versa). An allocation such as A, on the other hand, is inefficient because both Smith and Jones can be made better-off by choosing to move into the shaded area. Notice that, along O_S, O_J, the MRS for Smith is equal to that for Jones. The line O_S, O_J is called the *contract curve*.

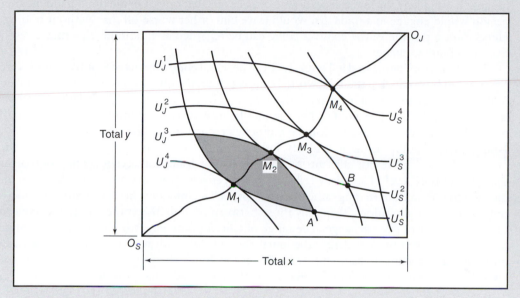

of utility by adopting a trade that moves them into this area. When the marginal rates of substitution of Smith and Jones are equal, however, such mutually beneficial trades are not available. The points M_1, M_2, M_3, and M_4 in Figure 13.10 indicate tangencies of these individuals' indifference curves, and movement away from such points must make at least one of the people worse-off. A move from M_2 to A, for example, reduces Smith's utility from U_S^2 to U_S^1 even though Jones is made no worse-off by the move. Alternatively, a move from M_2 to B makes Jones worse-off but keeps the utility level of Smith constant. In general, then, these points of tangency do not offer the promise of additional mutually beneficial trading and so are Pareto efficient.

Contract curve

The set of all Pareto efficient allocations in an Edgeworth box diagram is called the *contract curve*. In Figure 13.10, this set of points is represented by the line running from O_S to O_J and includes the tangencies M_1, M_2, M_3, and M_4 (and many other such tangencies). Points off the contract curve (such as A or B) are inefficient, so mutually beneficial trades are possible. But, as its name implies, the contract curve represents the exhaustion of all such trading opportunities. Even a move along the contract curve (say, from M_1 to M_2) cannot represent a mutually beneficial trade because there will always be a winner (Smith) and a loser (Jones). These observations may be summarized as follows.

Contract curve. In an exchange economy, all efficient allocations of existing goods lie along a (multidimensional) *contract curve*. Points off that curve are necessarily inefficient, because individuals can be made unambiguously better-off by moving to the curve. Along the contract curve, however, individuals' preferences are rivals in the sense that one individual's situation may be improved only if someone else is made worse-off.

DEFINITION

Exchange with initial endowments

In our previous discussion we assumed that fixed quantities of the two goods could be allocated in any way conceivable. A somewhat different analysis would hold if the individuals participating in the exchange possessed specific quantities of the goods at the start. There would still be the definite possibility that each person could benefit from voluntary trade, because it is unlikely the initial allocations would be efficient ones. On the other hand, neither person would engage in a trade that would leave him or her worse-off than without trading. Hence only a portion of the contract curve can be regarded as allocations that might result from voluntary exchange.

These ideas are illustrated in Figure 13.11. The initial endowments of Smith and Jones are represented by point A in the Edgeworth box. As before, the dimensions of the box are taken to be the total quantities of the two goods available. The contract curve of efficient allocations is represented by the line O_S, O_J. Let the indifference curve of Smith that passes through point A be called U_S^A, and let Jones's indifference curve through A be denoted by U_J^A. Notice that, at point A, the individuals' indifference curves are not tangent and hence the initial endowments are not efficient. Neither Smith nor Jones will accept trading outcomes that give a utility level of less than U_S^A or U_J^A, respectively. It would be preferable for an individual to refrain from trading rather than accept such an inferior outcome. Thus, if we focus only on efficient allocations, then only those between M_1 and M_2 on the contract curve can occur as a result of free exchange. The range of efficient outcomes from voluntary exchange has been narrowed by considering the initial endowments with which the individuals enter into trading. If the initial distribution of goods favors Jones, then any final allocation will also favor Jones because it is in Jones's interest to refuse any trade that provides less utility.

FIGURE 13.11   Exchange with Initial Endowments

If individuals start with initial endowments (such as those represented by point A), then neither would be willing to accept an allocation that promised a lower level of utility than point A does: Smith would not accept any allocation below U_S, and Jones would not accept any allocation below U_J^A. Therefore, not every point on the contract curve can result from free exchange. Only the efficient allocations between M_1 and M_2 are eligible if each individual is free to refrain from trading and we require that the final allocation be efficient.

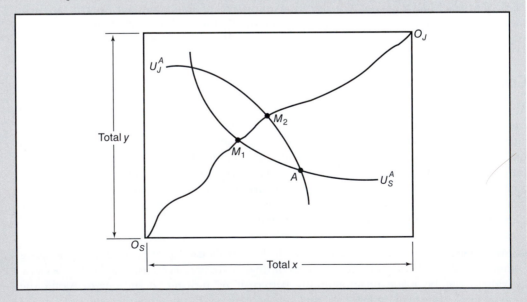

The distributional dilemma and the Second Theorem of Welfare Economics

This, then, is the distributional dilemma in its most abstract setting. If initial endowments are skewed in favor of some economic actors, the Pareto efficient allocations promised by the competitive price system will also tend to favor those actors. Voluntary transactions cannot overcome large differences in initial endowments, and some sort of transfers (possibly lump sum) will be needed to attain more equal results.

These thoughts lead to what is sometimes called the "Second Theorem of Welfare Economics." In general terms, the theorem states that any desired distribution of welfare among the individuals in an economy can be achieved in an efficient manner through competitive pricing if initial endowments are adjusted appropriately. It is this theorem that allows economists to make a sharp distinction between the *efficiency* issues that arise in a particular economic problem and the *equity* issues that arise in that problem. Put simply, economists frequently argue for using the efficiency properties of competitive prices to "make the pie as big as possible" and then for adjusting the resulting distribution to be "fair" through the use of lump-sum transfers. Unfortunately, implementing the required lump-sum transfers is easier said than done—virtually all tax/transfer systems have real efficiency costs. Hence, the First and Second Theorems of Welfare Economics are not cure-alls for every economic policy question. Still, there are many cases where both efficiency and equity concerns suggest reliance on competitive pricing, so the wisdom of interference in market transactions to achieve distributional goals is not always a forgone conclusion. Rather, the correct application of applied welfare economics to any issue requires an independent assessment of both allocational and distributional issues.

EXAMPLE 13.8 A Two-Person Exchange Economy

To fix these ideas, consider an exchange economy in which there are exactly 1,000 soft drinks (x) and 1,000 hamburgers (y). If we let Smith's utility be represented by

$$U_S(x_S, y_S) = x_S^{2/3} y_S^{1/3} \qquad (13.79)$$

and Jones's utility by

$$U_J(x_J, y_J) = x_J^{1/3} y_J^{2/3}, \qquad (13.80)$$

then we can compute the efficient ways of allocating soft drinks and hamburgers. Notice at the start that Smith has a relative preference for soft drinks whereas Jones tends to prefer hamburgers, as reflected by the differing exponents in the utility functions of the two individuals. We might therefore expect that efficient allocations would give relatively more soft drinks to Smith and relatively more hamburgers to Jones.

To find the efficient points in this situation, suppose we let Smith start at any preassigned utility level, U_S. Our problem now is to choose x_S, y_S, x_J, and y_J to make Jones's utility as large as possible given Smith's utility constraint. Setting up the Lagrangian for this problem yields

$$\begin{aligned}\mathcal{L} &= U_J(x_J, y_J) + \lambda[U_S(x_S, y_S) - \bar{U}_S] \\ &= x_J^{1/3} y_J^{2/3} + \lambda(x_S^{2/3} y_S^{1/3} - \bar{U}_S).\end{aligned} \qquad (13.81)$$

Remember that Jones simply gets what Smith doesn't, and vice versa. Hence

$$\begin{aligned}x_J &= 1,000 - x_S \quad \text{and} \\ y_J &= 1,000 - y_S.\end{aligned} \qquad (13.82)$$

(continued)

EXAMPLE 13.8   CONTINUED

Our Lagrangian is therefore a function of the two variables x_S and y_S:

$$\mathcal{L} = (1{,}000 - x_S)^{1/3}(1{,}000 - y_s)^{2/3} + \lambda(x_S^{2/3}y_S^{1/3} - \bar{U}). \qquad \textbf{(13.83)}$$

The first-order conditions for a maximum are

$$\frac{\partial \mathcal{L}}{\partial x_S} = -\frac{1}{3}\left(\frac{1{,}000 - y_S}{1{,}000 - x_S}\right)^{2/3} + \frac{2\lambda}{3}\left(\frac{y_S}{x_S}\right)^{1/3} = 0,$$

$$\frac{\partial \mathcal{L}}{\partial y_S} = -\frac{2}{3}\left(\frac{1{,}000 - x_S}{1{,}000 - y_S}\right)^{1/3} + \frac{\lambda}{3}\left(\frac{x_S}{y_S}\right)^{2/3} = 0. \qquad \textbf{(13.84)}$$

Moving the terms in λ to the right side of these equations and dividing the top equation by the bottom gives[23]

$$\frac{1}{2}\left(\frac{1{,}000 - y_S}{1{,}000 - x_S}\right) = 2\left(\frac{y_S}{x_S}\right) \qquad \textbf{(13.85)}$$

or

$$\frac{x_S}{1{,}000 - x_S} = \frac{4y_S}{1{,}000 - y_S}, \qquad \textbf{(13.86)}$$

which is our required condition for efficiency. We can now use Equation 13.86 to calculate any number of Pareto efficient allocations. In Table 13.1 we have done so for a few values of x_S ranging from 0 to 1,000 (that is, for situations in which Smith gets nothing to situations where he or she gets everything).

Pareto efficiency. To illustrate why points off this contract curve are inefficient, consider an initial allocation in which Smith and Jones share x and y equally. With 500 units of each item, both Smith and Jones receive a utility of 500 (assuming that such utility measurement is meaningful). But, by using your basic scientific calculator, it is a relatively simple matter to show that there are many allocations on the contract curve that offer more utility to both people. Table 13.1 shows that this is nearly true for the allocations where Smith gets 600 or 700 soft drinks, and the precise boundaries of such mutually beneficial trades can be easily calculated. For example, consider $x_S = 660$, $y_S = 327$, $x_J = 340$, and $y_J = 673$. For this allocation, Smith's utility is 522 and Jones's is 536. Both are clearly better off than at the initial allocation, and one might expect some sort of trading to take place that moves them toward the contract curve.

Effects of initial endowments. To see how initial endowments may restrict the range of Pareto efficient solutions in this economy, suppose Smith starts in a very favorable position with $x_S = 800$, $y_S = 800$. Then Jones gets $x_J = 200$, $y_J = 200$, and the initial utility levels are $U_S = 800$, $U_J = 200$. There are Pareto improvements that might be made from these initial endowments, but none of them will improve Jones's situation very much. For example, if we hold Smith's utility at 800, the efficient allocation $x_S = 884$, $y_S = 657$, $x_J = 116$, $y_J = 343$ will increase Jones's utility from 200 to 239. But that is the best that Jones can do given the constraint that Smith cannot be made worse-off. The efficiency gains to Jones, while significant, do very little to move the overall allocation toward more equal outcomes.

---

[23]Notice that Equation 13.85 is a restatement of the condition that the individuals' marginal rates of substitution must be equal for an efficient allocation. That is, Smith's $MRS = (\partial U_S/\partial x)/(\partial U_S/\partial y) = 2(y/x)$ and Jones's $MRS = (\partial U_J/\partial x)/(\partial U_J/\partial y) = 1/2(y/x)$.

TABLE 13.1   Pareto Efficient Allocations of 1,000 Soft Drinks and 1,000 Hamburgers to Smith and Jones

x_S	y_S	$U_S = x_S^{2/3} y_S^{1/3}$	$x_J = 1{,}000 - x_S$	$y_J = 1{,}000 - y_S$	$U_J = x_J^{1/3} y_J^{2/3}$
0	0	0	1,000	1,000	1,000
100	27	65	900	973	948
200	59	133	800	941	891
300	97	206	700	903	830
400	143	284	600	857	761
500	200	368	500	800	684
600	273	461	400	727	596
700	368	565	300	632	493
800	500	684	200	500	368
900	692	825	100	308	212
1,000	1,000	1,000	0	0	0

QUERY: Would different preferences for the two people in this example offer greater scope for equalizing outcomes from voluntary transactions? Are there any preferences for Smith and Jones for which voluntary transactions would lead to equality even from very unequal initial allocations?

SUMMARY

This chapter has provided a general exploration of Adam Smith's conjectures about the efficiency properties of competitive markets. We began with a description of how to model many competitive markets simultaneously and then used that model to make a few statements about welfare. Some highlights of this chapter are listed here.

- Preferences and production technologies provide the building blocks upon which all general equilibrium models are based. One particularly simple version of such a model uses individual preferences for two goods together with a concave production possibility frontier for those two goods.

- Competitive markets can establish equilibrium prices by making marginal adjustments in prices in response to information about the demand and supply for individual goods. Walras' law ties markets together so that such a solution is assured (in most cases).

- General equilibrium models can usually be solved by using computer algorithms. The resulting solutions yield many insights about the economy that are not obtainable from partial equilibrium analysis of single markets.

- Competitive prices will result in a Pareto-efficient allocation of resources. This is the First Theorem of Welfare Economics.

- Factors that interfere with competitive markets' abilities to achieve efficiency include (1) market power, (2) externalities, (3) existence of public goods, and (4) imperfect information.

- Competitive markets need not yield equitable distributions of resources, especially when initial endowments are highly Skewed. In theory, any desired distribution can be attained through competitive markets accompanied by appropriate transfers of initial endowments (the Second Theorem of Welfare Economics). But there are many practical problems in implementing such transfers.

PROBLEMS

13.1

Suppose the production possibility frontier for guns (x) and butter (y) is given by

$$x^2 + 2y^2 = 900.$$

a. Graph this frontier

b. If individuals always prefer consumption bundles in which $y = 2x$, how much x and y will be produced?

c. At the point described in part (b), what will be the RPT and hence what price ratio will cause production to take place at that point? (This slope should be approximated by considering small changes in x and y around the optimal point.)

d. Show your solution on the figure from part (a).

13.2

Suppose two individuals (Smith and Jones) each have 10 hours of labor to devote to producing either ice cream (x) or chicken soup (y). Smith's utility function is given by

$$U_S = x^{0.3}y^{0.7},$$

whereas Jones's is given by

$$U_J = x^{0.5}y^{0.5}.$$

The individuals do not care whether they produce x or y, and the production function for each good is given by

$$x = 2l \quad \text{and} \quad y = 3l,$$

where l is the total labor devoted to production of each good.

a. What must the price ratio, p_x/p_y, be?

b. Given this price ratio, how much x and y will Smith and Jones demand? *Hint:* Set the wage equal to 1 here.

c. How should labor be allocated between x and y to satisfy the demand calculated in part (b)?

13.3

Consider an economy with just one technique available for the production of each good.

Good	Food	Cloth
Labor per unit output	1	1
Land per unit output	2	1

a. Suppose land is unlimited but labor equals 100. Write and sketch the production possibility frontier.

b. Suppose labor is unlimited but land equals 150. Write and sketch the production possibility frontier.

c. Suppose labor equals 100 and land equals 150. Write and sketch the production possibility frontier. *Hint:* What are the intercepts of the production possibility frontier? When is land fully employed? Labor? Both?

d. Explain why the production possibility frontier of part (c) is concave.

e. Sketch the relative price of food as a function of its output in part (c).

f. If consumers insist on trading 4 units of food for 5 units of cloth, what is the relative price of food? Why?

g. Explain why production is exactly the same at a price ratio of $p_F/p_C = 1.1$ as at $p_F/p_C = 1.9$.

h. Suppose that capital is also required for producing food and clothing and that capital requirements per unit of food and per unit of clothing are 0.8 and 0.9, respectively. There are 100 units of capital available. What is the production possibility curve in this case? Answer part (e) for this case.

13.4

Suppose that Robinson Crusoe produces and consumes fish (F) and coconuts (C). Assume that, during a certain period, he has decided to work 200 hours and is indifferent as to whether he spends this time fishing or gathering coconuts. Robinson's production for fish is given by

$$F = \sqrt{l_F}$$

and for coconuts by

$$C = \sqrt{l_C},$$

where l_F and l_C are the number of hours spent fishing or gathering coconuts. Consequently,

$$l_C + l_F = 200.$$

Robinson Crusoe's utility for fish and coconuts is given by

$$\text{utility} = \sqrt{F \cdot C}.$$

a. If Robinson cannot trade with the rest of the world, how will he choose to allocate his labor? What will the optimal levels of F and C be? What will his utility be? What will be the RPT (of fish for coconuts)?

b. Suppose now that trade is opened and Robinson can trade fish and coconuts at a price ratio of $p_F/p_C = 2/1$. If Robinson continues to produce the quantities of F and C from part (a), what will he choose to consume once given the opportunity to trade? What will his new level of utility be?

c. How would your answer to part (b) change if Robinson adjusts his production to take advantage of the world prices?

d. Graph your results for parts (a), (b), and (c).

13.5

Smith and Jones are stranded on a desert island. Each has in his possession some slices of ham (H) and cheese (C). Smith is a very choosy eater and will eat ham and cheese only in the fixed proportions of 2 slices of cheese to 1 slice of ham. His utility function is given by $U_S = \min(H, C/2)$.

Jones is more flexible in his dietary tastes and has a utility function given by $U_J = 4H + 3C$. Total endowments are 100 slices of ham and 200 slices of cheese.

a. Draw the Edgeworth box diagram that represents the possibilities for exchange in this situation. What is the only exchange ratio that can prevail in any equilibrium?

b. Suppose Smith initially had $40H$ and $80C$. What would the equilibrium position be?

c. Suppose Smith initially had $60H$ and $80C$. What would the equilibrium position be?

d. Suppose Smith (much the stronger of the two) decides not to play by the rules of the game. Then what could the final equilibrium position be?

13.6

In the country of Ruritania there are two regions, A and B. Two goods (x and y) are produced in both regions. Production functions for region A are given by

$$x_A = \sqrt{l_x},$$
$$y_A = \sqrt{l_y};$$

here l_x and l_y are the quantities of labor devoted to x and y production, respectively. Total labor available in region A is 100 units; that is,

$$l_x + l_y = 100.$$

Using a similar notation for region B, production functions are given by

$$x_B = \frac{1}{2}\sqrt{l_x},$$

$$y_B = \frac{1}{2}\sqrt{l_y}.$$

There are also 100 units of labor available in region B:

$$l_x + l_y = 100.$$

a. Calculate the production possibility curves for regions A and B.

b. What condition must hold if production in Ruritania is to be allocated efficiently between regions A and B (assuming labor cannot move from one region to the other)?

c. Calculate the production possibility curve for Ruritania (again assuming labor is immobile between regions). How much total y can Ruritania produce if total x output is 12? *Hint:* A graphical analysis may be of some help here.

13.7

Use the computer algorithm discussed in footnote 19 to examine the consequences of the following changes to the model in Example 13.4. For each change, describe the final results of the modeling and offer some intuition about why the results worked as they did.

a. Change the preferences of household 1 to $U_1 = x_1^{0.6} y_1^{0.2} (\bar{l}_1 - l_1)^{0.2}$.

b. Reverse the production functions in Equation 13.44 so that x becomes the capital-intensive good.

c. Increase the importance of leisure in each household's utility function.

Analytical Problems

13.8 Tax equivalence theorem

Use the computer algorithm discussed in footnote 19 to show that a uniform ad valorem tax of both goods yields the same equilibrium as does a uniform tax on both inputs that collects the same revenue. *Note:* This tax equivalence theorem from the theory of public finance shows that taxation may be done on either the output or input sides of the economy with identical results.

13.9 Returns to scale and the production possibility frontier

The purpose of this problem is to examine the relationships among returns to scale, factor intensity, and the shape of the production possibility frontier.

Suppose there are fixed supplies of capital and labor to be allocated between the production of good x and good y. The production functions for x and y are given (respectively) by

$$x = k^\alpha l^\beta \quad \text{and} \quad y = k^\gamma l^\delta,$$

where the parameters $\alpha, \beta, \gamma, \delta$ will take on different values throughout this problem.

Using either intuition, a computer, or a formal mathematical approach, derive the production possibility frontier for x and y in the following cases.

a. $\alpha = \beta = \gamma = \delta = 1/2$.

b. $\alpha = \beta = 1/2, \gamma = 1/3, \delta = 2/3$.

c. $\alpha = \beta = 1/2, \gamma = \delta = 2/3$.

d. $\alpha = \beta = \gamma = \delta = 2/3$.

e. $\alpha = \beta = 0.6, \gamma = 0.2, \delta = 1.0$.

f. $\alpha = \beta = 0.7, \gamma = 0.6, \delta = 0.8$.

Do increasing returns to scale always lead to a convex production possibility frontier? Explain.

13.10 The Rybczynski theorem

The country of Podunk produces only wheat and cloth, using as inputs land and labor. Both are produced by constant returns-to-scale production functions. Wheat is the relatively land-intensive commodity.

a. Explain, in words or with diagrams, how the price of wheat relative to cloth (p) determines the land-labor ratio in each of the two industries.

b. Suppose that p is given by external forces (this would be the case if Podunk were a "small" country trading freely with a "large" world). Show, using the Edgeworth box, that if the supply of labor increases in Podunk then the output of cloth will rise and the output of wheat will fall. *Note:* This result was discovered by the Polish economist Tadeusz Rybczynski. It is a fundamental result in the theory of international trade.

13.11 Walras' law

Suppose there are only three goods (x_1, x_2, x_3) in an economy and that the excess demand functions for x_2 and x_3 are given by

$$ED_2 = -\frac{3p_2}{p_1} + \frac{2p_3}{p_1} - 1,$$

$$ED_3 = \frac{4p_2}{p_1} - \frac{2p_3}{p_1} - 2.$$

a. Show that these functions are homogeneous of degree 0 in p_1, p_2, and p_3.

b. Use Walras' law to show that, if $ED_2 = ED_3 = 0$, then ED_1 must also be 0. Can you also use Walras' law to calculate ED_1?

c. Solve this system of equations for the equilibrium relative prices p_2/p_1 and p_3/p_1. What is the equilibrium value for p_3/p_2?

13.12 Initial endowments and prices

In Example 13.8, each individual has an initial endowment of 500 units of each good.

a. Express the demand for Smith and Jones for goods x and y as functions of p_x and p_y and their initial endowments.

b. Use the demand functions from part (a), together with the observation that total demand for each good must be 1,000, to calculate the equilibrium price ratio p_x/p_y in this situation. What are the equilibrium consumption levels of each good by each person?

c. How would the answers to this problem change for the following initial endowments?

	Smith's Endowment		Jones's Endowment	
	x	y	x	y
i	0	1,000	1,000	0
ii	600	600	400	400
iii	400	400	600	600
iv	1,000	1,000	0	0

Explain these varying results.

SUGGESTIONS FOR FURTHER READING

Arrow, K. J., and F. H. Hahn. *General Competitive Analysis*. Amsterdam: North-Holland, 1978, chaps. 1, 2, and 4.

Sophisticated mathematical treatment of general equilibrium analysis. Each chapter has a good literary introduction.

Debreu, G. *Theory of Value*. New York: John Wiley & Sons, 1959.

Basic reference; difficult mathematics. Does have a good introductory chapter on the mathematical tools used.

Debreu, G. "Existence of Competitive Equilibrium." In K. J. Arrow and M. D. Intriligator, Eds., *Handbook of Mathematical Economics*, vol. 2. Amsterdam: North-Holland, 1982, pp. 697–743.

Fairly difficult survey of existence proofs based on fixed point theorems. Contains a comprehensive set of references.

Ginsburgh, V., and M. Keyzer. *The Structure of Applied General Equilibrium Models*. Cambridge, MA: MIT Press, 1997.

Detailed discussions of the problems in implementing computable general equilibrium models. Some useful references to the empirical literature.

Harberger, A. "The Incidence of the Corporate Income Tax." *Journal of Political Economy* (January/February 1962): 215–40.

Nice use of a two-sector general equilibrium model to examine the final burden of a tax on capital.

Mas-Colell, A., M. D. Whinston, and J. R. Green. *Microeconomic Theory*. Oxford: Oxford University Press, 1995.

Part Four is devoted to general equilibrium analysis. Chapters 17 (existence) and 18 (connections to game theory) are especially useful. Chapters 19 and 20 pursue several of the topics in the Extensions to this chapter.

Salanie, B. *Microeconomic Models of Market Failure*. Cambridge, MA: MIT Press, 2000.

Nice summary of the theorems of welfare economics along with detailed analyses of externalities, public goods, and imperfect competition.

Sen, A. K. *Collective Choice and Social Welfare*. San Francisco: Holden-Day, 1970, chaps. 1 and 2.

Basic reference on social choice theory. Early chapters have a good discussion of the meaning and limitations of the Pareto efficiency concept.

EXTENSIONS

Computable General Equilibrium Models

As discussed briefly in Chapter 13, recent improvements in computer technology have made it feasible to develop computable general equilibrium (CGE) models of considerable detail. These may involve literally hundreds of industries and individuals, each with somewhat different technologies or preferences. The general methodology employed with these models is to assume various forms for production and utility functions, then choose particular parameters of those functions based on empirical evidence. Numerical general equilibrium solutions are then generated by the models and compared to real-world data. After "calibrating" the models to reflect reality, various policy elements in the models are varied as a way of providing general equilibrium estimates of the overall impact of those policy changes. In this extension we briefly review a few of these types of applications.

E13.1 Trade models

One of the first uses for applied general equilibrium models was to the study of the impact of trade barriers. Because much of the debate over the effects of such barriers (or of their reduction) focuses on impacts on real wages, such general equilibrium models are especially appropriate for the task.

Two unusual features tend to characterize such models. First, because the models often have an explicit focus on domestic versus foreign production of specific goods, it is necessary to introduce a large degree of product differentiation into individuals' utility functions. That is, "U.S. textiles" are treated as being different from "Mexican textiles" even though, in most trade theories, textiles might be treated as homogeneous goods. Modelers have found they must allow for only limited substitutability among such goods if their models are to replicate actual trade patterns.

A second feature of CGE models of trade is the interest in incorporating increasing returns-to-scale technologies into their production sectors. This permits the models to capture one of the primary advantages of trade for smaller economies. Unfortunately, introduction of the increasing returns-to-scale assumption also requires that the models depart from perfectly competitive, price-taking assumptions. Often some type of markup pricing, together with Cournot-type imperfect competition (see Chapter 15), is used for this purpose.

North American free trade

Some of the most extensive CGE modeling efforts have been devoted to analyzing the impact of the North American Free Trade Agreement (NAFTA). Virtually all of these models find that the agreement offered welfare gains to all of the countries involved. Gains for Mexico accrued primarily because of reduced U.S. trade barriers on Mexican textiles and steel. Gains to Canada came primarily from an increased ability to benefit from economies of scale in certain key industries. Brown (1992) surveys a number of CGE models of North American free trade and concludes that gains on the order of 2–3 percent of GDP might be experienced by both of these countries. For the United States, gains from NAFTA might be considerably smaller; but even in this case, significant welfare gains were found to be associated with the increased competitiveness of domestic markets.

E13.2 Tax and transfer models

A second major use of CGE models is to evaluate potential changes in a nation's tax and transfer policies. For these applications, considerable care must be taken in modeling the factor supply side of the models. For example, at the margin, the effects of rates of income taxation (either positive or negative) can have important labor supply effects that only a general equilibrium approach can model properly. Similarly, tax/transfer policy can also affect savings and investment decisions, and for these too it may be necessary to adopt more detailed modeling procedures (for example, differentiating individuals by age so as to examine effects of retirement programs).

The Dutch MIMIC model

Probably the most elaborate tax/transfer CGE model is that developed by the Dutch Central Planning Bureau—the Micro Macro Model to Analyze the Institutional Context (MIMIC). This model puts emphasis on social welfare programs and on some of the problems they seek to ameliorate (most notably unemployment, which is missing from many other CGE models).

Gelauff and Graaflund (1994) summarize the main features of the MIMIC model. They also use it to analyze such policy proposals as the 1990s tax reform in the Netherlands and potential changes to the generous unemployment and disability benefits in that country.

E13.3 Environmental models

CGE models are also appropriate for understanding the ways in which environmental policies may affect the economy. In such applications, the production of pollutants is considered as a major side effect of the other economic activities in the model. By specifying environmental goals in terms of a given reduction in these pollutants, it is possible to use these models to study the economic costs of various strategies for achieving these goals. One advantage of the CGE approach is to provide some evidence on the impact of environmental policies on income distribution—a topic largely omitted from more narrow, industry-based modeling efforts.

Assessing CO_2 reduction strategies

Concern over the possibility that CO_2 emissions in various energy-using activities may be contributing to global warming has led to a number of plans for reducing these emissions. Because the repercussions of such reductions may be widespread and varied, CGE modeling is one of the preferred assessment methods. Perhaps the most elaborate such model is that developed by the OECD—the General Equilibrium Environmental (GREEN) model. The basic structure of this model is described by Burniaux, Nicoletti, and Oliviera-Martins (1992). The model has been used to simulate various policy options that might be adopted by European nations to reduce CO_2 emissions, such as institution of a carbon tax or increasingly stringent emissions regulations for automobiles and power plants. In general, these simulations suggest that economic costs of these policies would be relatively modest given the level of restrictions currently anticipated. But most of the policies would have adverse distributional effects that may require further attention through government transfer policy.

E13.4 Regional and urban models

A final way in which CGE models can be used is to examine economic issues that have important spatial dimensions. Construction of such models requires careful attention to issues of transportation costs for goods and moving costs associated with labor mobility, because particular interest is focused on where transactions occur. Incorporation of these costs into CGE models is in many ways equivalent to adding extra levels of product differentiation, because these affect the relative prices of otherwise homogeneous goods. Calculation of equilibria in regional markets can be especially sensitive to how transport costs are specified.

Changing government procurement

CGE regional models have been widely used to examine the local impact of major changes in government spending policies. For example, Hoffmann, Robinson, and Subramanian (1996) use a CGE model to evaluate the regional impact of reduced defense expenditures on the California economy. They find that the size of the effects depends importantly on the assumed costs of migration for skilled workers. A similar finding is reported by Bernat and Hanson (1995), who examine possible reductions in U.S. price-support payments to farms. Although such reductions would offer overall efficiency gains to the economy, they could have significant negative impacts on rural areas.

References

Bernat, G. A., and K. Hanson. "Regional Impacts of Farm Programs: A Top-Down CGE Analysis." *Review of Regional Studies* (Winter 1995): 331–50.

Brown, D. K. "The Impact of North American Free Trade Area: Applied General Equilibrium Models." In N. Lustig, B. P. Bosworth, and R. Z. Lawrence, Eds., *North American Free Trade: Assessing the Impact*. Washington, DC: Brookings Institution, 1992, pp. 26–68.

Burniaux, J. M., G. Nicoletti, and J. Oliviera-Martins. "GREEN: A Global Model for Quantifying the Costs of Policies to Curb CO_2 Emissions." OECD *Economic Studies* (Winter 1992): 49–92.

Gelauff, G. M. M., and J. J. Graaflund. *Modeling Welfare State Reform*. Amsterdam: North Holland, 1994.

Hoffmann, S., S. Robinson, and S. Subramanian. "The Role of Defense Cuts in the California Recession: Computable General Equilibrium Models and Interstate Fair Mobility." *Journal of Regional Science* (November 1996): 571–95.

Market Power

In this part we examine the consequences of relaxing the assumption that firms are price takers. When firms have some power to set prices, they will no longer treat them as fixed parameters in their decisions but will instead treat price setting as one part of the profit-maximization process. Usually this will mean prices no longer accurately reflect marginal costs and the efficiency theorems that apply to competitive markets no longer hold.

Chapter 14 looks at the relatively simple case where there is only a single monopoly supplier of a good. This supplier can choose to operate at any point on the demand curve for its product that it finds most profitable. Its activities are constrained only by this demand curve, not by the behavior of rival producers. As we shall see, this offers the firm a number of avenues for increasing profits, such as employing novel pricing schemes or adapting the characteristics of its product. Although such decisions will indeed provide more profits for the monopoly, in general they will also result in welfare losses for consumers (relative to perfect competition).

In **Chapter 15** we consider markets with few producers. Models of such markets are considerably more complicated than are markets of monopoly (or of perfect competition, for that matter) because the demand curve faced by any one firm will depend in an important way on what its rivals choose to do. Studying the possibilities will usually require game-theoretic ideas to capture accurately the strategic possibilities involved. Hence you should review the basic game theory material in Chapter 8 before plunging into Chapter 15, whose general conclusion is that outcomes in markets with few firms will depend crucially on the details of how the "game" is played. In many cases the same sort of inefficiencies that occur in monopoly markets appear in imperfectly competitive markets as well.

Monopoly

A *monopoly* is a single firm that serves an entire market. This single firm faces the market demand curve for its output. Using its knowledge of this demand curve, the monopoly makes a decision on how much to produce. Unlike the perfectly competitive firm's output decision (which has no effect on market price), the monopoly's output decision will, in fact, determine the good's price. In this sense, monopoly markets and markets characterized by perfect competition are polar opposite cases.

At times it is more convenient to treat monopolies as having the power to set prices. Technically, a monopoly can choose that point on the market demand curve at which it prefers to operate. It may choose either market price or quantity, but not both. In this chapter we will usually assume that monopolies choose the quantity of output that maximizes profits and then settle for the market price that the chosen output level yields. It would be a simple matter to rephrase the discussion in terms of price setting, and in some places we shall do so.

BARRIERS TO ENTRY

Given these conventions, we have the following definition.

Monopoly. A *monopoly* is a single supplier to a market. This firm may choose to produce at any point on the market demand curve.

DEFINITION

The reason a monopoly exists is that other firms find it unprofitable or impossible to enter the market. *Barriers to entry* are therefore the source of all monopoly power. If other firms could enter a market then the firm would, by definition, no longer be a monopoly. There are two general types of barriers to entry: technical barriers and legal barriers.

Technical barriers to entry

A primary technical barrier is that the production of the good in question may exhibit decreasing marginal (and average) costs over a wide range of output levels. The technology of production is such that relatively large-scale firms are low-cost producers. In this situation (which is sometimes referred to as *natural monopoly*), one firm may find it profitable to drive others out of the industry by cutting prices. Similarly, once a monopoly has been established, entry will be difficult because any new firm must produce at relatively low levels of output and therefore at relatively high average costs. It is important to stress that the range of declining costs need only be "large" relative to the market in question. Declining costs on some absolute scale are not necessary. For example, the production and delivery of concrete does not exhibit declining marginal costs over a broad range of output when compared to the total U.S. market. However, in any particular small town, declining marginal costs may permit a monopoly to be established. The high costs of transportation in this industry tend to isolate one market from another.

Another technical basis of monopoly is special knowledge of a low-cost productive technique. But the problem for the monopoly that fears entry is keeping this technique uniquely to itself. When matters of technology are involved, this may be extremely difficult, unless the technology can be protected by a patent (see next paragraph). Ownership of unique resources—such as mineral deposits or land locations, or the possession of unique managerial talents—may also be a lasting basis for maintaining a monopoly.

Legal barriers to entry

Many pure monopolies are created as a matter of law rather than as a matter of economic conditions. One important example of a government-granted monopoly position is in the legal protection of a product by a patent or copyright. Prescription drugs, computer chips, and Disney animated movies are examples of profitable products that are shielded (for a time) from direct competition by potential imitators. Because the basic technology for these products is uniquely assigned to one firm, a monopoly position is established. The defense made of such a governmentally granted monopoly is that the patent and copyright system makes innovation more profitable and therefore acts as an incentive. Whether the benefits of such innovative behavior exceed the costs of having monopolies is an open question that has been much debated by economists.

A second example of a legally created monopoly is the awarding of an exclusive franchise to serve a market. These franchises are awarded in cases of public utility (gas and electric) service, communications services, the post office, some television and radio station markets, and a variety of other situations. The argument usually put forward in favor of creating these franchised monopolies is that the industry in question is a natural monopoly: Average cost is diminishing over a broad range of output levels, and minimum average cost can be achieved only by organizing the industry as a monopoly. The public utility and communications industries are often considered good examples. Certainly, that does appear to be the case for local electricity and telephone service where a given network probably exhibits declining average cost up to the point of universal coverage. But recent deregulation in telephone services and electricity generation show that, even for these industries, the natural monopoly rationale may not be all-inclusive. In other cases, franchises may be based largely on political rationales. This seems to be true for the postal service in the United States and for a number of nationalized industries (airlines, radio and television, banking) in other countries.

Creation of barriers to entry

Although some barriers to entry may be independent of the monopolist's own activities, other barriers may result directly from those activities. For example, firms may develop unique products or technologies and take extraordinary steps to keep these from being copied by competitors. Or firms may buy up unique resources to prevent potential entry. The De Beers cartel, for example, controls a large fraction of the world's diamond mines. Finally, a would-be monopolist may enlist government aid in devising barriers to entry. It may lobby for legislation that restricts new entrants so as to "maintain an orderly market" or for health and safety regulations that raise potential entrants' costs. Because the monopolist has both special knowledge of its business and significant incentives to pursue these goals, it may have considerable success in creating such barriers to entry.

The attempt by a monopolist to erect barriers to entry may involve real resource costs. Maintaining secrecy, buying unique resources, and engaging in political lobbying are all costly activities. A full analysis of monopoly should involve not only questions of cost minimization and output choice (as under perfect competition) but also an analysis of profit-maximizing creation of entry barriers. However, we will not provide a detailed investigation of such questions here.[1] Instead, we will generally assume that the monopolist can do nothing to affect barriers to entry and that the firm's costs are therefore similar to what a competitive firm's costs would be.

PROFIT MAXIMIZATION AND OUTPUT CHOICE

To maximize profits, a monopoly will choose to produce that output level for which marginal revenue is equal to marginal cost. Because the monopoly, in contrast to a perfectly competitive firm, faces a negatively sloped market demand curve, marginal revenue will be less than the market price. To sell an additional unit, the monopoly must lower its price on all units to be sold if it is to generate the extra demand necessary to absorb this marginal unit. The profit-maximizing output level for a firm is then the level Q^* in Figure 14.1. At that level, marginal revenue is equal to marginal costs, and profits are maximized.

Given the monopoly's decision to produce Q^*, the demand curve D indicates that a market price of P^* will prevail. This is the price that demanders as a group are willing to pay for the output of the monopoly. In the market, an equilibrium price-quantity combination of P^*, Q^* will be observed. Assuming $P^* > AC$, this output level will be profitable, and the monopolist will have no incentive to alter output levels unless demand or cost conditions change. Hence we have the following principle.

---

[1] For a simple treatment, see R. A. Posner, "The Social Costs of Monopoly and Regulation," *Journal of Political Economy* 83 (August 1975): 807–27.

FIGURE 14.1 Profit Maximization and Price Determination for a Monopoly

A profit-maximizing monopolist produces that quantity for which marginal revenue is equal to marginal cost. In the diagram this quantity is given by Q^*, which will yield a price of P^* in the market. Monopoly profits can be read as the rectangle of P^*EAC.

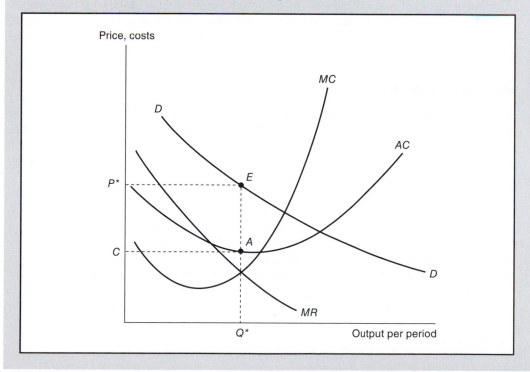

Monopolist's output. A monopolist will choose to produce that output for which marginal revenue equals marginal cost. Because the monopolist faces a downward-sloping demand curve, market price will exceed marginal revenue and the firm's marginal cost at this output level.

The inverse elasticity rule, again

In Chapter 11 we showed that the assumption of profit maximization implies that the gap between a price of a firm's output and its marginal cost is inversely related to the price elasticity of the demand curve faced by the firm. Applying Equation 11.13 to the case of monopoly yields

$$\frac{P - MC}{P} = -\frac{1}{e_{Q,P}}, \tag{14.1}$$

where now we use the elasticity of demand for the entire market ($e_{Q,P}$) because the monopoly is the sole supplier of the good in question. This observation leads to two general conclusions about monopoly pricing. First, a monopoly will choose to operate only in regions in which the *market* demand curve is elastic ($e_{Q,P} < -1$). If demand were inelastic, then marginal revenue would be negative and thus could not be equated to marginal cost (which presumably is positive). Equation 14.1 also shows that $e_{Q,P} > -1$ implies an (implausible) negative marginal cost.

A second implication of Equation 14.1 is that the firm's "markup" over marginal cost (measured as a fraction of price) depends inversely on the elasticity of market demand. For example, if $e_{Q,P} = -2$ then Equation 14.1 shows that $P = 2MC$, whereas if $e_{Q,P} = -10$ then $P = 1.11MC$. Notice also that if the elasticity of demand were constant along the entire demand curve, the proportional markup over marginal cost would remain unchanged in response to changes in input costs. Market price, therefore, moves proportionally to marginal cost: increases in marginal cost will prompt the monopoly to increase its price proportionally, and decreases in marginal cost will cause the monopoly to reduce its price proportionally. Even if elasticity is not constant along the demand curve, it seems clear from Figure 14.1 that increases in marginal cost will increase price (though not necessarily in the same proportion). So long as the demand curve facing the monopoly is downward sloping, upward shifts in MC will prompt the monopoly to reduce output and thereby obtain a higher price.[2] We will examine all these relationships mathematically in Examples 14.1 and 14.2.

Monopoly profits

Total profits earned by the monopolist can be read directly from Figure 14.1. These are shown by the rectangle P^*EAC and again represent the profit per unit (price minus average cost) times the number of units sold. These profits will be positive if market price exceeds average total cost. If $P^* < AC$, however, then the monopolist can operate only at a long-term loss and will decline to serve the market.

Because (by assumption) no entry is possible into a monopoly market, the monopolist's positive profits can exist even in the long run. For this reason, some authors refer to the profits that a monopoly earns in the long run as *monopoly rents*. These profits can be regarded as a return to that factor that forms the basis of the monopoly (a patent, a favorable location, or a dynamic entrepreneur, for example); hence another possible owner might be willing to pay that amount in rent for the right to the monopoly. The potential for profits is the reason why some firms pay other firms for the right to use a patent and why concessioners at sporting events (and on some highways) are willing to pay for the right to the concession. To the

---

[2]The comparative statics of a shift in the demand curve facing the monopolist are not so clear, however, and no unequivocal prediction about price can be made. For an analysis of this issue, see the discussion that follows and Problem 14.4.

FIGURE 14.2 Monopoly Profits Depend on the Relationship between the Demand and Average Cost Curves

Both of the monopolies in this figure are equally "strong" if by this we mean they produce similar divergences between market price and marginal cost. However, because of the location of the demand and average cost curves, it turns out that the monopoly in (a) earns high profits whereas that in (b) earns no profits. Consequently, the size of profits is not a measure of the strength of a monopoly.

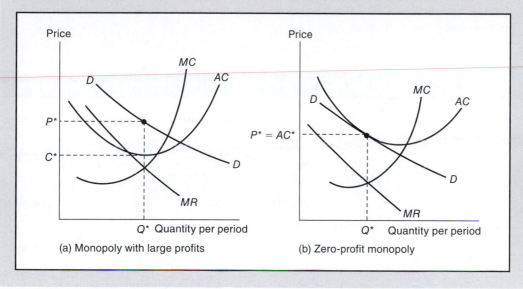

(a) Monopoly with large profits (b) Zero-profit monopoly

extent that monopoly rights are given away at less than their true market value (as in radio and television licensing), the wealth of the recipients of those rights is increased.

Although a monopoly may earn positive profits in the long run,[3] the size of such profits will depend on the relationship between the monopolist's average costs and the demand for its product. Figure 14.2 illustrates two situations in which the demand, marginal revenue, and marginal cost curves are rather similar. As Equation 14.1 suggests, the price–marginal cost markup is about the same in these two cases. But average costs in Figure 14.2a are considerably lower than in Figure 14.2b. Although the profit-maximizing decisions are similar in the two cases, the level of profits ends up being quite different. In Figure 14.2a the monopolist's price (P^*) exceeds the average cost of producing Q^* (labeled AC^*) by a large extent, and significant profits are obtained. In Figure 14.2b, however, $P^* = AC^*$ and the monopoly earns zero economic profits, the largest amount possible in this case. Hence, large profits from a monopoly are not inevitable, and the actual extent of economic profits may not always be a good guide to the significance of monopolistic influences in a market.

There is no monopoly supply curve

In the theory of perfectly competitive markets presented in Part 4, it was possible to speak of an industry supply curve. We constructed the long-run supply curve by allowing the market demand curve to shift and observing the supply curve that was traced out by the series of equilibrium price-quantity combinations. This type of construction is not possible for

---

[3]As in the competitive case, the profit-maximizing monopolist would be willing to produce at a loss in the short run as long as market price exceeds average variable cost.

monopolistic markets. With a fixed market demand curve, the supply "curve" for a monopoly will be only one point—namely, that price-quantity combination for which $MR = MC$. If the demand curve should shift then the marginal revenue curve would also shift, and a new profit-maximizing output would be chosen. However, connecting the resulting series of equilibrium points on the market demand curves would have little meaning. This locus might have a very strange shape, depending on how the market demand curve's elasticity (and its associated MR curve) changes as the curve is shifted. In this sense the monopoly firm has no well-defined "supply curve." Each demand curve is a unique profit-maximizing opportunity for a monopolist.

EXAMPLE 14.1 Calculating Monopoly Output

Suppose the market for Olympic-quality Frisbees (Q, measured in Frisbees bought per year) has a linear demand curve of the form

$$Q = 2{,}000 - 20P \qquad (14.2)$$

or

$$P = 100 - Q/20, \qquad (14.3)$$

and let the costs of a monopoly Frisbee producer be given by

$$C(Q) = 0.05Q^2 + 10{,}000. \qquad (14.4)$$

To maximize profits, this producer chooses that output level for which $MR = MC$. In order to solve this problem we must phrase both MR and MC as functions of Q alone. Toward this end, write total revenue as

$$P \cdot Q = 100Q - \frac{Q^2}{20}. \qquad (14.5)$$

Consequently,

$$MR = 100 - \frac{Q}{10} = MC = 0.1Q \qquad (14.6)$$

and

$$Q^* = 500, \qquad P^* = 75. \qquad (14.7)$$

At the monopoly's preferred output level,

$$C(Q) = 0.05(500)^2 + 10{,}000 = 22{,}500,$$
$$AC = \frac{22{,}500}{500} = 45. \qquad (14.8)$$

Using this information, we can calculate profits as

$$\pi = (P^* - AC) \cdot Q^* = (75 - 45) \cdot 500 = 15{,}000. \qquad (14.9)$$

Observe that at this equilibrium there is a large markup between price (75) and marginal cost ($MC = 0.1Q = 50$). Yet as long as entry barriers prevent a new firm from producing Olympic-quality Frisbees, this gap and positive economic profits can persist indefinitely.

QUERY: How would an increase in fixed costs from 10,000 to 12,500 affect the monopoly's output plans? How would profits be affected? Suppose total costs shifted to $C(Q) = 0.075Q^2 + 10{,}000$. How would the equilibrium change?

EXAMPLE 14.2 Monopoly with Simple Demand Curves

We can derive a few simple facts about monopoly pricing in cases where the demand curve facing the monopoly takes a simple algebraic form and the firm has constant marginal costs (that is, $C(Q) = cQ$ and $MC = c$).

Linear demand. Suppose that the inverse demand function facing the monopoly is of the linear form $P = a - bQ$. In this case, $PQ = aQ - bQ^2$ and $MR = dPQ/dQ = a - 2bQ$. Hence profit maximization requires that

$$MR = a - 2bQ = MC = c \quad \text{or} \quad Q = \frac{a-c}{2b}. \qquad (14.10)$$

Inserting this solution for the profit-maximizing output level back into the inverse demand function yields a direct relationship between price and marginal cost:

$$P = a - bQ = a - \frac{a-c}{2} = \frac{a+c}{2}. \qquad (14.11)$$

An interesting implication is that, in this linear case, $dP/dc = 1/2$. That is, only half of the amount of any increase in marginal cost will show up in the market price of the monopoly product.[4]

Constant elasticity demand. If the demand curve facing the monopoly takes the constant elasticity form $Q = aP^e$ (where e is the price elasticity of demand), then we know $MR = P(1 + 1/e)$ and so profit maximization requires

$$P\left(1 + \frac{1}{e}\right) = c \quad \text{or} \quad P = c\left(\frac{e}{1+e}\right). \qquad (14.12)$$

Because it must be the case that $e < -1$ for profit maximization, price will clearly exceed marginal cost and this gap will be larger the closer e is to -1. Notice also that $dP/dc = e/(1+e)$ and so any given increase in marginal cost will increase price by more than this amount. Of course, as we have already pointed out, the proportional increase in marginal cost and price will be the same. That is, $e_{P,c} = dP/dc \cdot c/P = 1$.

QUERY: The demand function in both of these cases is shifted by the parameter a. Discuss the effects of such a shift for both linear and constant elasticity demand. Explain your results intuitively.

MONOPOLY AND RESOURCE ALLOCATION

In Chapter 13 we briefly mentioned why the presence of monopoly distorts the allocation of resources. Because the monopoly produces a level of output for which $MC = MR < P$, the market price of its good no longer conveys accurate information about production costs. Hence, consumers' decisions will no longer reflect true opportunity costs of production, and resources will be misallocated. In this section we explore this misallocation in some detail in a partial equilibrium context.

[4]Notice that when $c = 0$ we have $P = a/2$. That is, price should be halfway between zero and the price intercept of the demand curve.

Basis of comparison

To evaluate the allocational effect of a monopoly, we need a precisely defined basis of comparison. A particularly useful comparison is provided by the perfectly competitive, constant cost industry. In this case, as we showed in Chapter 12, the industry's long-run supply curve will be infinitely elastic with price equal to both marginal and average cost. It is convenient to think of a monopoly as arising from the "capture" of such a competitive industry and to treat the individual firms that constituted the competitive industry as now being single plants in the monopolist's empire. A prototype case would be John D. Rockefeller's purchase of most of the U.S. petroleum refineries in the late nineteenth century and his decision to operate them as part of the Standard Oil trust. We can then compare the performance of this monopoly to the performance of the previously competitive industry to arrive at a statement about the welfare consequences of monopoly.

A graphical analysis

Figure 14.3 shows a simple linear demand curve for a product produced by a constant cost industry. If this market were competitive, output would be Q^*—that is, production would occur where price is equal to long-run average and marginal cost. Under a simple single-price monopoly, output would be Q^{**} because this is the level of production for which marginal revenue is equal to marginal cost. The restriction in output from Q^* to Q^{**} represents the

FIGURE 14.3   Allocational and Distributional Effects of Monopoly

Monopolization of this previously competitive market would cause output to be reduced from Q^* to Q^{**}. Consumer expenditures and productive inputs worth AEQ^*Q^{**} are reallocated to the production of other goods. Consumer surplus equal to $P^{**}BAP^*$ is transferred into monopoly profits. There is a deadweight loss given by BEA.

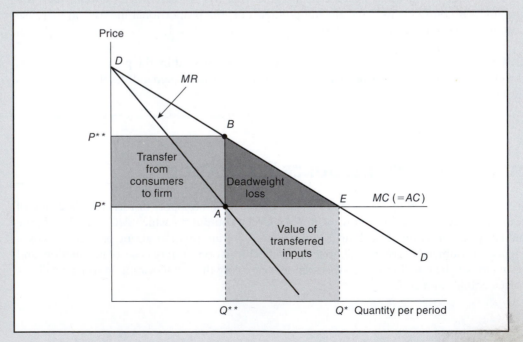

misallocation brought about through monopolization. The total value of resources released by this output restriction is shown in Figure 14.3 as area AEQ^*Q^{**}. Essentially, the monopoly closes down some of the plants that were operating in the competitive case. These transferred inputs can be productively employed elsewhere, so area AEQ^*Q^{**} is not a social loss.

The restriction in output from Q^* to Q^{**} involves a total loss in consumer surplus of $P^{**}BEP^*$. Part of this loss is captured by the monopoly as profits. These profits are measured by $P^{**}BAP^*$, and they reflect a transfer of income from consumers to the firm. As with any transfer, difficult issues of equity arise in attempting to assess whether or not such a transfer is "equitable." However, there is no ambiguity about the loss in consumers' surplus given by area BEA, because this loss is not transferred to anyone. It is a pure "deadweight" loss and represents the principal measure of the allocational harm of the monopoly.[5]

To illustrate the nature of this deadweight loss, consider Example 14.1, in which we calculated an equilibrium price of $75 and a marginal cost of $50. This gap between price and marginal cost is an indication of the efficiency-improving trades that are forgone through monopolization. Undoubtedly, there is a would-be buyer who is willing to pay, say, $60 for an Olympic Frisbee but not $75. A price of $60 would more than cover all of the resource costs involved in Frisbee production, but the presence of the monopoly prevents such a mutually beneficial transaction between Frisbee users and the providers of Frisbee-making resources. For this reason, the monopoly equilibrium is not Pareto optimal—an alternative allocation of resources would make all parties better off. Economists have made many attempts to estimate the overall cost of these deadweight losses in actual monopoly situations. Most of these estimates are rather small when viewed in the context of the whole economy.[6] Allocational losses are larger, however, for some narrowly defined industries.

EXAMPLE 14.3 Welfare Losses and Elasticity

The allocational effects of monopoly can be characterized fairly completely in the case of constant marginal costs and a constant price elasticity demand curve. To do so, assume again that constant marginal (and average) costs for a monopolist are given by c and that the demand curve has a constant elasticity form of

$$Q = P^e, \tag{14.13}$$

where e is the price elasticity of demand ($e < -1$). We know the competitive price in this market will be

$$P_c = c \tag{14.14}$$

and the monopoly price is given by

$$P_m = \frac{c}{1 + 1/e}. \tag{14.15}$$

(*continued*)

---

[5]If the monopolized industry has a positively sloped long-run supply curve, then some of the deadweight losses will also be reflected in reduced rents for inputs.

[6]The classic study is A. Harberger, "Monopoly and Resource Allocation," *American Economic Review* (May 1954): 77–87. Harberger estimates that such losses constitute about 0.1 percent of gross national product.

EXAMPLE 14.3   CONTINUED

The consumer surplus associated with any price (P_0) can be computed as

$$CS = \int_{P_0}^{\infty} Q(P) \, dP$$

$$= \int_{P_0}^{\infty} P^e \, dP$$

$$= \left. \frac{P^{e+1}}{e+1} \right|_{P_0}^{\infty}$$

$$= -\frac{P_0^{e+1}}{e+1}. \tag{14.16}$$

Hence, under perfect competition we have

$$CS_c = -\frac{c^{e+1}}{e+1} \tag{14.17}$$

and, under monopoly,

$$CS_m = -\frac{\left(\dfrac{c}{1+1/e}\right)^{e+1}}{e+1}. \tag{14.18}$$

Taking the ratio of these two surplus measures yields

$$\frac{CS_m}{CS_c} = \left(\frac{1}{1+1/e}\right)^{e+1}. \tag{14.19}$$

If $e = -2$, for example, then this ratio is $\frac{1}{2}$: consumer surplus under monopoly is half what it is under perfect competition. For more elastic cases this figure falls a bit (because output restrictions under monopoly are more significant). For elasticities closer to -1, the ratio increases.

Profits. The transfer from consumer surplus into monopoly profits can also be computed fairly easily in this case. Monopoly profits are given by

$$\pi_m = P_m Q_m - cQ_m = \left(\frac{c}{1+1/e} - c\right) Q_m$$

$$= \left(\frac{-c/e}{1+1/e}\right) \cdot \left(\frac{c}{1+1/e}\right)^e = -\left(\frac{c}{1+1/e}\right)^{e+1} \cdot \frac{1}{e}. \tag{14.20}$$

Dividing this expression by Equation 14.17 yields

$$\frac{\pi_m}{CS_c} = \left(\frac{e+1}{e}\right)\left(\frac{1}{1+1/e}\right)^{e+1} = \left(\frac{e}{1+e}\right)^e. \tag{14.21}$$

For $e = -2$ this ratio is $\frac{1}{4}$. Hence, one fourth of the consumer surplus enjoyed under perfect competition is transferred into monopoly profits. The deadweight loss from monopoly in this case is therefore also a fourth of the level of consumer surplus under perfect competition.

QUERY: Suppose $e = -1.5$. What fraction of consumer surplus is lost through monopolization? How much is transferred into monopoly profits? Why do these results differ from the case $e = -2$?

MONOPOLY, PRODUCT QUALITY, AND DURABILITY

The market power enjoyed by a monopoly may be exercised along dimensions other than the market price of its product. If the monopoly has some leeway in the type, quality, or diversity of the goods it produces, then it would not be surprising for the firm's decisions to differ from those that might prevail under a competitive organization of the market. Whether a monopoly will produce higher-quality or lower-quality goods than would be produced under competition is unclear, however. It all depends on the firm's costs and the nature of consumer demand.

A formal treatment of quality

Suppose consumers' willingness to pay for quality (X) is given by the inverse demand function $P(Q, X)$, where

$$\frac{\partial P}{\partial Q} < 0 \quad \text{and} \quad \frac{\partial P}{\partial X} > 0.$$

If the costs of producing Q and X are given by $C(Q, X)$, the monopoly will choose Q and X to maximize

$$\pi = P(Q, X)Q - C(Q, X). \tag{14.22}$$

The first-order conditions for a maximum are

$$\frac{\partial \pi}{\partial Q} = P(Q, X) + Q\frac{\partial P}{\partial Q} - C_Q = 0, \tag{14.23}$$

$$\frac{\partial \pi}{\partial X} = Q\frac{\partial P}{\partial X} - C_X = 0. \tag{14.24}$$

The first of these equations repeats the usual rule that marginal revenue equals marginal cost for output decisions. The second equation states that, when Q is appropriately set, the monopoly should choose that level of quality for which the marginal revenue attainable from increasing the quality of its output by one unit is equal to the marginal cost of making such an increase. As might have been expected, the assumption of profit maximization requires the monopolist to proceed to the margin of profitability along all of the dimensions it can. Notice, in particular, that the marginal demander's valuation of quality per unit is multiplied by the monopolist's output level when determining the profit-maximizing choice.

The level of product quality chosen under competitive conditions will also be the one that maximizes net social welfare:

$$SW = \int_0^{Q^*} P(Q, X)\, dQ - C(Q, X), \tag{14.25}$$

where Q^* is the output level determined through the competitive process of marginal cost pricing, given X. Differentiation of Equation 14.25 with respect to X yields the first-order condition for a maximum:

$$\frac{\partial SW}{\partial X} = \int_0^{Q^*} P_X(Q, X)\, dQ - C_X = 0. \tag{14.26}$$

The difference between the quality choice specified in Equation 14.24 and Equation 14.26 is that the former looks at the marginal valuation of one more unit of quality assuming Q is at its profit-maximizing level, whereas the latter looks at the marginal value of quality averaged across all output levels.[7] Therefore, even if a monopoly and a perfectly competitive industry choose the same output level, they might opt for differing quality levels because each is concerned with a different margin in its decision making. Only by knowing the specifics of the problem is it possible to predict the direction of these differences. For an example, see Problem 14.9; more detail on the theory of product quality and monopoly is provided in Problem 14.11.

The durability of durable goods

Much of the research on the effect of monopolization on quality has focused on durable goods. These are goods such as automobiles, houses, or refrigerators that provide services to their owners over several periods rather than being completely consumed soon after they are bought. The element of time that enters into the theory of durable goods leads to many interesting problems and paradoxes. Initial interest in the topic started with the question of whether monopolies would produce goods that lasted as long as would similar goods produced under perfect competition. The intuitive notion that monopolies would "under-produce" durability (just as they choose an output below the competitive level) was soon shown to be incorrect by the Australian economist Peter Swan[8] in the early 1970s.

Swan's insight was to view the demand for durable goods as the demand for a flow of services (i.e., automobile transportation) over several periods. He argued that both a monopoly and a competitive market would seek to minimize the cost of providing this flow to consumers. The monopoly would, of course, choose an output level that restricted the flow of services so as to maximize profits, but—assuming constant returns to scale in production—there is no reason that durability per se would be affected by market structure. This result is sometimes referred to as "Swan's independence assumption." Output decisions can be treated independently from decisions about product durability.

Subsequent research on the Swan result has focused on showing how it can be undermined by different assumptions about the nature of a particular durable good or by relaxing the implicit assumption that all demanders are the same. For example, the result depends critically on how durable goods deteriorate. The simplest type of deterioration is illustrated by a durable good, such as a light bulb, that provides a constant stream of services until it becomes worthless. With this type of good, Equations 14.24 and 14.26 are identical, so Swan's independence result holds. Even when goods deteriorate smoothly, the independence result continues to hold if a constant flow of services can be maintained by simply replacing what has been used—this requires that new goods and old goods be perfect substitutes and infinitely divisible. Outdoor house paint may, more or less, meet this requirement. On the other hand, most goods clearly do not. It is just not possible to replace a run-down refrigerator with, say, half of a new one. Once such more complex forms of deterioration are considered, Swan's result may not hold because we can no longer fall back upon the notion of providing a given flow of services at minimal cost over time. In these more complex cases, however, it is not always the case that a monopoly will produce less durability than will a competitive market—it all depends on the nature of the demand for durability.

---

[7]The average marginal valuation (AV) of product quality is given by

$$AV = \int_0^{Q^*} P_X(Q, X) \, dQ/Q.$$

Hence $Q \cdot AV = C_x$ is the quality rule adopted to maximize net welfare under perfect competition. Compare this to Equation 14.24.

[8]P. L. Swan, "Durability of Consumption Goods," *American Economic Review* (December 1970): 884–94.

Time inconsistency and heterogeneous demand

Focusing on the service flow from durable goods provides important insights on durability, but it does leave an important question unanswered—when should the monopoly produce the actual durable goods needed to provide the desired service flow? Suppose, for example, that a light-bulb monopoly decides that its profit-maximizing output decision is to supply the services provided by 1 million 60-watt bulbs. If the firm decides to produce 1 million bulbs in the first period, what is it to do in the second period (say, before any of the original bulbs burn out)? Because the monopoly chooses a point on the service demand curve where $P > MC$, it has a clear incentive to produce more bulbs in the second period by cutting price a bit. But consumers can anticipate this, so they may reduce their first-period demand, waiting for a bargain. Hence, the monopoly's profit-maximizing plan will unravel. Ronald Coase was the first economist to note this "time inconsistency" that arises when a monopoly produces a durable good.[9] Coase argued that its presence would severely undercut potential monopoly power—in the limit, competitive pricing is the only outcome that can prevail in the durable goods case. Only if the monopoly can succeed in making a credible commitment not to produce more in the second period can it succeed in its plan to achieve monopoly profits on the service flow from durable goods.

Recent modeling of the durable goods question has examined how a monopolist's choices are affected in situations where there are different types of demanders.[10] In such cases, questions about the optimal choice of durability and about credible commitments become even more complicated. The monopolist must not only settle on an optimal scheme for each category of buyers, it must also ensure that the scheme intended for, (say) type-1 demanders is not also attractive to type-2 demanders. Studying these sorts of models would take us too far afield, but some illustrations of how such "incentive compatible constraints" work are provided in the Extensions to this chapter and in Chapter 18.

PRICE DISCRIMINATION

In some circumstances a monopoly may be able to increase profits by departing from a single-price policy for its output. The possibility of selling identical goods at different prices is called price discrimination.[11]

Price discrimination. A monopoly engages in *price discrimination* if it is able to sell otherwise identical units of output at different prices.

DEFINITION

Whether a price discrimination strategy is feasible depends crucially on the inability of buyers of the good to practice arbitrage. In the absence of transactions or information costs, the "law of one price" implies that a homogeneous good must sell everywhere for the same price. Consequently, price discrimination schemes are doomed to failure because demanders who can buy from the monopoly at lower prices will be more attractive sources of the good—for those who must pay high prices—than is the monopoly itself. Profit-seeking middlemen will

---

[9]R. Coase, "Durability and Monopoly," *Journal of Law and Economics* (April 1972): 143–49.

[10]For a summary, see M. Waldman, "Durable Goods Theory for Real World Markets," *Journal of Economic Perspectives* (Winter 2003): 131–54.

[11]A monopoly may also be able to sell differentiated products at differential price-cost margins. Here, however, we treat price discrimination only for a monopoly that produces a single homogeneous product.

destroy any discriminatory pricing scheme. However, when resale is costly or can be prevented entirely, then price discrimination becomes possible.

First-degree or perfect price discrimination

If each buyer can be separately identified by a monopolist, then it may be possible to charge
each the maximum price he or she would willingly pay for the good. This strategy of *perfect*
(or *first-degree*) price discrimination would then extract all available consumer surplus,
leaving demanders as a group indifferent between buying the monopolist's good or doing
without it. The strategy is illustrated in Figure 14.4. The figure assumes that buyers are
arranged in descending order of willingness to pay. The first buyer is willing to pay up to P_1
for Q_1 units of output, so the monopolist charges P_1 and obtains total revenues of $P_1 Q_1$, as
indicated by the lightly shaded rectangle. A second buyer is willing to pay up to P_2 for
$Q_2 - Q_1$ units of output, so the monopolist obtains total revenue of $P_2(Q_2 - Q_1)$ from this
buyer. Notice that this strategy cannot succeed unless the second buyer is unable to resell the
output he or she buys at P_2 to the first buyer (who pays $P_1 > P_2$).

The monopolist will proceed in this way up to the point at which the marginal buyer is no
longer willing to pay the good's marginal cost (labeled *MC* in Figure 14.4). Hence total
quantity produced will be Q^*. Total revenues collected will be given by the area DEQ^*0. All
consumer surplus has been extracted by the monopolist and there is no deadweight loss in
this situation. (Compare Figures 14.3 and 14.4.) The allocation of resources under perfect
price discrimination is therefore efficient, though it does entail a large transfer from consumer
surplus into monopoly profits.

FIGURE 14.4   Perfect Price Discrimination

Under perfect price discrimination, the monopoly charges a different price to each buyer. It sells Q_1
units at P_1, $Q_2 - Q_1$ units at P_2, and so forth. In this case the firm will produce Q^*, and total
revenues will be DEQ^*0.

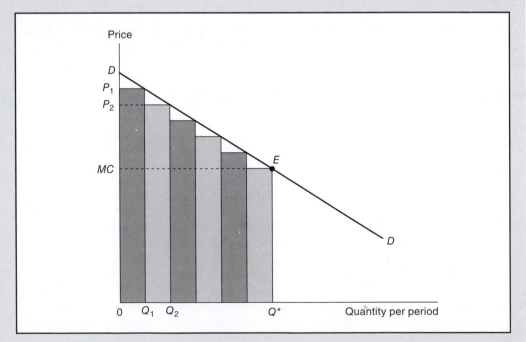

EXAMPLE 14.4 First-Degree Price Discrimination

Consider again the Frisbee monopolist in Example 14.1. Because there are relatively few high-quality Frisbees sold, the monopolist may find it possible to discriminate perfectly among a few world-class flippers. In this case it will choose to produce that quantity for which the marginal buyer pays exactly the marginal cost of a Frisbee:

$$P = 100 - \frac{Q}{20} = MC = 0.1Q. \qquad \text{(14.27)}$$

Hence

$$Q^* = 666$$

and, at the margin, price and marginal cost are given by

$$P = MC = 66.6. \qquad \text{(14.28)}$$

Now we can compute total revenues by integration:

$$R = \int_0^{Q^*} P(Q)\, dQ = 100Q - \left.\frac{Q^2}{40}\right|_0^{666}$$
$$= 55{,}511. \qquad \text{(14.29)}$$

Total costs are

$$C(Q) = 0.05Q^2 + 10{,}000 = 32{,}178; \qquad \text{(14.30)}$$

total profits are given by

$$\pi = R - C = 23{,}333, \qquad \text{(14.31)}$$

which represents a substantial increase over the single-price policy examined in Example 14.1 (which yielded 15,000).

QUERY: What is the maximum price any Frisbee buyer pays in this case? Use this to obtain a geometric definition of profits.

Third-degree price discrimination through market separation

First-degree price discrimination poses a considerable information burden for the monopoly—it must know the demand function for each potential buyer. A less stringent requirement would be to assume the monopoly can separate its buyers into relatively few identifiable markets (such as "rural-urban," "domestic-foreign," or "prime-time–off-prime") and pursue a separate monopoly pricing policy in each market. Knowledge of the price elasticities of demand in these markets is sufficient to pursue such a policy. The monopoly then sets a price in each market according to the inverse elasticity rule. Assuming that marginal cost is the same in all markets, the result is a pricing policy in which

$$P_i\left(1 + \frac{1}{e_i}\right) = P_j\left(1 + \frac{1}{e_j}\right) \qquad \text{(14.32)}$$

or

$$\frac{P_i}{P_j} = \frac{(1 + 1/e_j)}{(1 + 1/e_i)},\qquad\text{(14.33)}$$

where P_i and P_j are the prices charged in markets i and j, which have price elasticities of demand given by e_i and e_j. An immediate consequence of this pricing policy is that the profit-maximizing price will be higher in markets in which demand is less elastic. If, for example, $e_i = -2$ and $e_j = -3$, then Equation 14.33 shows that $P_i/P_j = 4/3$—prices will be one third higher in market i, the less elastic market.

Figure 14.5 illustrates this result for two markets that the monopoly can serve at constant marginal cost (MC). Demand is less elastic in market 1 than in market 2, so the gap between price and marginal revenue is larger in the former market. Profit maximization requires that the firm produce Q_1^* in market 1 and Q_2^* in market 2, resulting in a higher price in the less elastic market. So long as arbitrage between the two markets can be prevented, this price difference can persist. The two-price discriminatory policy is clearly more profitable for the monopoly than a single-price policy would be, because the firm can always opt for the latter policy should market conditions warrant.

The welfare consequences of third-degree price discrimination are, in principle, ambiguous. Relative to a single-price policy, the discriminating policy requires raising the price in the less elastic market and reducing it in the more elastic one. Hence, the changes have an

FIGURE 14.5   Separated Markets Raise the Possibility of Third-Degree Price Discrimination

If two markets are separate, then a monopolist can maximize profits by selling its product at different prices in the two markets. This would entail choosing that output for which $MC = MR$ in each of the markets. The diagram shows that the market with a less elastic demand curve will be charged the higher price by the price discriminator.

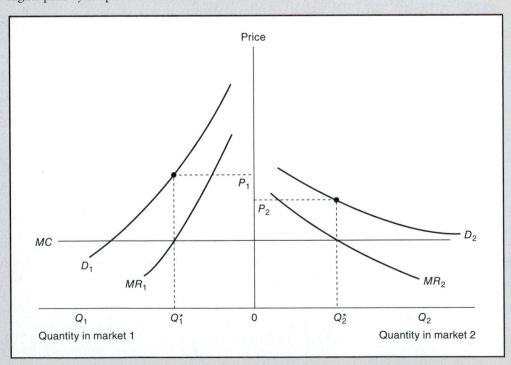

offsetting effect on total allocational losses. A more complete analysis suggests the intuitively plausible conclusion that the multiple-price policy will be allocationally superior to a single-price policy only in situations in which total output is increased through discrimination. Example 14.5 illustrates a simple case of linear demand curves in which a single-price policy does result in greater allocational losses.[12]

EXAMPLE 14.5 Third-Degree Price Discrimination

Suppose that a monopoly producer of widgets has a constant marginal cost of $c = 6$ and sells its products in two separated markets whose inverse demand functions are

$$P_1 = 24 - Q_1 \quad \text{and} \quad P_2 = 12 - 0.5Q_2. \tag{14.34}$$

Notice that consumers in market 1 are more eager to buy than are consumers in market 2 in the sense that the former are willing to pay more for any given quantity. Using the results for linear demand curves from Example 14.2 shows that the profit-maximizing price-quantity combinations in these two markets are:

$$P_1^* = \frac{24+6}{2} = 15, \quad Q_1^* = 9, \quad P_2^* = \frac{12+6}{2} = 9, \quad Q_2^* = 6. \tag{14.35}$$

With this pricing strategy, profits are $\pi = (15 - 6) \cdot 9 + (9 - 6) \cdot 6 = 81 + 18 = 99$. We can compute the deadweight losses in the two markets by recognizing that the competitive output (with $P = MC = 6$) in market 1 is 18 and in market 2 is 12:

$$\begin{aligned} DW &= DW_1 + DW_2 \\ &= 0.5(P_1^* - 6)(18 - 9) + 0.5(P_2^* - 6)(12 - 6) \\ &= 40.5 + 9 = 49.5. \end{aligned} \tag{14.36}$$

A single-price policy. In this case, constraining the monopoly to charge a single price would reduce welfare. Under a single-price policy the monopoly would simply cease serving market 2, since it can maximize profits by charging a price of 15 and at that price no widgets will be bought in market 2 (because the maximum willingness to pay is 12). Total deadweight loss in this situation is therefore increased from its level in Equation 14.36 because total potential consumer surplus in market 2 is now lost:

$$DW = DW_1 + DW_2 = 40.5 + 0.5(12 - 6)(12 - 0) = 40.5 + 36 = 76.5. \tag{14.37}$$

This illustrates a situation where third-degree price discrimination is welfare improving over a single price policy—when the discriminatory policy permits "smaller" markets to be served. Whether such a situation is common is an important policy question (consider, for example, the case of U.S. pharmaceutical manufacturers charging higher prices at home than abroad).

QUERY: Suppose these markets were no longer separated. How would you construct the market demand in this situation? Would the monopolist's profit-maximizing single price still be 15?

---

[12]For a detailed discussion, see R. Schmalensee, "Output and Welfare Implications of Monopolistic Third-Degree Price Discrimination," *American Economic Review* (March 1981): 242–47. See also Problem 14.13.

SECOND-DEGREE PRICE DISCRIMINATION THROUGH PRICE SCHEDULES

The examples of price discrimination examined in the previous section require the monopoly to separate demanders into a number of categories and then choose a profit-maximizing price for each such category. An alternative approach would be for the monopoly to choose a (possibly rather complex) price schedule that provides incentives for demanders to separate themselves depending on how much they wish to buy. Such schemes include quantity discounts, minimum purchase requirements or "cover" charges, and tie-in sales. These plans would be adopted by a monopoly if they yielded greater profits than would a single-price policy, after accounting for any possible costs of implementing the price schedule. Because the schedules will result in demanders paying different prices for identical goods, this form of (second-degree) price discrimination is feasible only when there are no arbitrage possibilities. Here we look at one simple case. The Extensions to this chapter and portions of Chapters 15 and 18 look at other aspects of second-degree price discrimination.

Two-part tariffs

One form of pricing schedule that has been extensively studied is a linear two-part tariff, under which demanders must pay a fixed fee for the right to consume a good and a uniform price for each unit consumed. The prototype case, first studied by Walter Oi, is an amusement park (perhaps Disneyland) that sets a basic entry fee coupled with a stated marginal price for each amusement used.[13] Mathematically, this scheme can be represented by the tariff any demander must pay to purchase q units of a good:

$$T(q) = a + pq, \tag{14.38}$$

where a is the fixed fee and p is the marginal price to be paid. The monopolist's goal then is to choose a and p to maximize profits, given the demand for this product. Because the average price paid by any demander is given by

$$\bar{p} = \frac{T}{q} = \frac{a}{q} + p, \tag{14.39}$$

this tariff is feasible only when those who pay low average prices (those for whom q is large) cannot resell the good to those who must pay high average prices (those for whom q is small).

One approach described by Oi for establishing the parameters of this linear tariff would be for the firm to set the marginal price, p, equal to MC and then set a so as to extract the maximum consumer surplus from a given set of buyers. One might imagine buyers being arrayed according to willingness to pay. The choice of $p = MC$ would then maximize consumer surplus for this group, and a could be set equal to the surplus enjoyed by the least eager buyer. He or she would then be indifferent about buying the good, but all other buyers would experience net gains from the purchase.

This feasible tariff might not be the most profitable, however. Consider the effects on profits of a small increase in p above MC. This would result in no net change in the profits earned from the least willing buyer. Quantity demanded would drop slightly at the margin where $p = MC$, and some of what had previously been consumer surplus (and therefore part of the fixed fee, a) would be converted into variable profits because now $p > MC$. For all other demanders, profits would be increased by the price rise. Although each will pay a bit less

---

[13]W. Y. Oi, "A Disneyland Dilemma: Two-Part Tariffs for a Mickey Mouse Monopoly," *Quarterly Journal of Economics* (February 1971): 77–90. Interestingly, the Disney empire once used a two-part tariff but abandoned it because the costs of administering the payment schemes for individual rides became too high. Like other amusement parks, Disney moved to a single-admissions price policy (which still provided them with ample opportunities for price discrimination, especially with the multiple parks at Disney World).

in fixed charges, profits per unit bought will rise to a greater extent.[14] In some cases it is possible to make an explicit calculation of the optimal two-part tariff. Example 14.6 provides an illustration. More generally, however, optimal schedules will depend on a variety of contingencies. Some of the possibilities are examined in the Extensions to this chapter.

EXAMPLE 14.6 Two-Part Tariffs

In order to illustrate the mathematics of two-part tariffs, let's return to the demand equations introduced in Example 14.5 but now assume that they apply to two specific demanders:

$$q_1 = 24 - p_1,$$
$$q_2 = 24 - 2p_2, \tag{14.40}$$

where now the p's refer to the marginal prices faced by these two buyers.[15]

An Oi tariff. Implementing the two-part tariff suggested by Oi would require the monopolist to set $p_1 = p_2 = MC = 6$. Hence, in this case, $q_1 = 18$ and $q_2 = 12$. With this marginal price, demander 2 (the less eager of the two) obtains consumer surplus of $36 [= 0.5 \cdot (12 - 6) \cdot 12]$. That is the maximal entry fee that might be charged without causing this person to leave the market. Consequently, the two-part tariff in this case would be $T(q) = 36 + 6q$. If the monopolist opted for this pricing scheme, its profits would be

$$\pi = R - C = T(q_1) + T(q_2) - AC(q_1 + q_2)$$
$$= 72 + 6 \cdot 30 - 6 \cdot 30 = 72. \tag{14.41}$$

These fall short of those obtained in Example 14.5.

The optimal tariff. The optimal two-part tariff in this situation can be computed by noting that total profits with such a tariff are $\pi = 2a + (p - MC)(q_1 + q_2)$. Here the entry fee, a, must equal the consumer surplus obtained by person 2. Inserting the specific parameters of this problem yields

$$\pi = 0.5 \cdot 2q_2(12 - p) + (p - 6)(q_1 + q_2)$$
$$= (24 - 2p)(12 - p) + (p - 6)(48 - 3p)$$
$$= 18p - p^2. \tag{14.42}$$

Hence, maximum profits are obtained when $p = 9$ and $a = 0.5(24 - 2p)(12 - p) = 9$. Therefore the optimal tariff is $T(q) = 9 + 9q$. With this tariff, $q_1 = 15$ and $q_2 = 6$, and the monopolist's profits are $81 [= 2(9) + (9 - 6) \cdot (15 + 6)]$. The monopolist might opt for this pricing scheme if it were under political pressure to have a uniform pricing policy and to agree not to price demander 2 "out of the market." The two-part tariff permits a degree of differential pricing ($\bar{p}_1 = 9.60$, $\bar{p}_2 = 9.75$) but appears "fair" because all buyers face the same schedule.

QUERY: Suppose a monopolist could choose a different entry fee for each demander. What pricing policy would be followed?

---

[14]This follows because $q_i(mc) > q_1(mc)$, where $q_i(mc)$ is the quantity demanded when $p = MC$ for all except the least willing buyer (person 1). Hence the gain in profits from an increase in price above MC, $\Delta pq_i(mc)$, exceeds the loss in profits from a smaller fixed fee, $\Delta pq_1(mc)$.

[15]The theory of utility maximization that underlies these demand curves is that the quantity demanded is determined by the marginal price paid, whereas the entry fee a determines whether $q = 0$ might instead be optimal.

REGULATION OF MONOPOLY

The regulation of natural monopolies is an important subject in applied economic analysis. The utility, communications, and transportation industries are highly regulated in most countries, and devising regulatory procedures that induce these industries to operate in a desirable way is an important practical problem. Here we will examine a few aspects of the regulation of monopolies that relate to pricing policies.

Marginal cost pricing and the natural monopoly dilemma

Many economists believe it is important for the prices charged by regulated monopolies to reflect marginal costs of production accurately. In this way the deadweight loss may be minimized. The principal problem raised by an enforced policy of marginal cost pricing is that it will require natural monopolies to operate at a loss. Natural monopolies, by definition, exhibit decreasing average costs over a broad range of output levels. The cost curves for such a firm might look like those shown in Figure 14.6. In the absence of regulation the monopoly would produce output level Q_A and receive a price of P_A for its product. Profits in this situation are given by the rectangle $P_A ABC$. A regulatory agency might instead set a price of P_R for the monopoly. At this price, Q_R is demanded, and the marginal cost of producing this output level is also P_R. Consequently, marginal cost pricing has been achieved. Unfortunately, because of the negative slope of the firm's average cost curve, the price P_R (= marginal cost) falls below average costs. With this regulated price, the monopoly must operate at a loss

FIGURE 14.6   Price Regulation for a Decreasing Cost Monopoly

Because natural monopolies exhibit decreasing average costs, marginal costs fall below average costs. Consequently, enforcing a policy of marginal cost pricing will entail operating at a loss. A price of P_R, for example, will achieve the goal of marginal cost pricing but will necessitate an operating loss of $GFEP_R$.

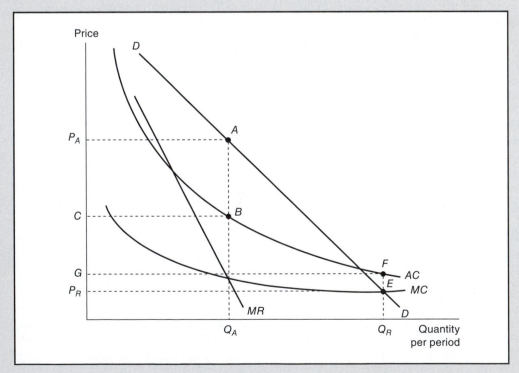

of $GFEP_R$. Because no firm can operate indefinitely at a loss, this poses a dilemma for the regulatory agency: Either it must abandon its goal of marginal cost pricing, or the government must subsidize the monopoly forever.

Two-tier pricing systems

One way out of the marginal cost pricing dilemma is the implementation of a multiprice system. Under such a system the monopoly is permitted to charge some users a high price while maintaining a low price for marginal users. In this way the demanders paying the high price in effect subsidize the losses of the low-price customers. Such a pricing scheme is shown in Figure 14.7. Here the regulatory commission has decided that some users will pay a relatively high price, P_1. At this price, Q_1 is demanded. Other users (presumably those who would not buy the good at the P_1 price) are offered a lower price, P_2. This lower price generates additional demand of $Q_2 - Q_1$. Consequently, a total output of Q_2 is produced at an average cost of A. With this pricing system, the profits on the sales to high-price demanders (given by the rectangle P_1DBA) balance the losses incurred on the low-priced sales ($BFEC$). Furthermore, for the "marginal user," the marginal cost pricing rule is being followed: it is the "intramarginal" user who subsidizes the firm so it does not operate at a loss. Although in practice it may not be so simple to establish pricing schemes that maintain marginal cost pricing and cover operating costs, many regulatory commissions do use price schedules that intentionally discriminate against some users (for example, businesses) to the advantage of others (consumers).

FIGURE 14.7 Two-Tier Pricing Schedule

By charging a high price (P_1) to some users and a low price (P_2) to others, it may be possible for a regulatory commission to (1) enforce marginal cost pricing and (2) create a situation where the profits from one class of user (P_1DBA) subsidize the losses of the other class ($BFEC$).

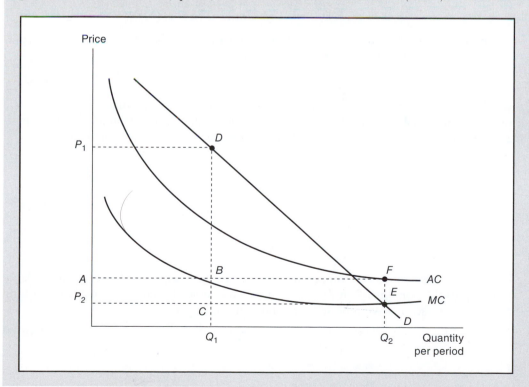

Rate of return regulation

Another approach followed in many regulatory situations is to permit the monopoly to charge a price above marginal cost that is sufficient to earn a "fair" rate of return on investment. Much analytical effort is then devoted to defining the "fair" rate concept and to developing ways in which it might be measured. From an economic point of view, some of the most interesting questions about this procedure concern how the regulatory activity affects the firm's input choices. If, for example, the rate of return allowed to firms exceeds what owners might obtain on investment under competitive circumstances, there will be an incentive to use relatively more capital input than would truly minimize costs. And if regulators delay in making rate decisions, this may give firms cost-minimizing incentives that would not otherwise exist. We will now briefly examine a formal model of such possibilities.[16]

A formal model

Suppose a regulated utility has a production function of the form

$$q = f(k, l).$$

(14.43)

This firm's actual rate of return on capital is then defined as

$$s = \frac{pf(k, l) - wl}{k},$$

(14.44)

where p is the price of the firm's output (which depends on q) and w is the wage rate for labor input. If s is constrained by regulation to be equal to (say) $\bar{s}$, then the firm's problem is to maximize profits

$$\pi = pf(k, l) - wl - vk$$

(14.45)

subject to this regulatory constraint. Setting up the Lagrangian expression for this problem yields

$$\mathscr{L} = pf(k, l) - wl - vk + \lambda[wl + \bar{s}k - pf(k, l)].$$

(14.46)

Notice that if $\lambda = 0$, regulation is ineffective and the monopoly behaves like any profit-maximizing firm. If $\lambda = 1$, Equation 14.46 reduces to

$$\mathscr{L} = (\bar{s} - v)k,$$

(14.47)

which, assuming $\bar{s} > v$ (which it must be if the firm is not to earn less than the prevailing rate of return on capital elsewhere), means this monopoly will hire infinite amounts of capital—an implausible result. Hence, $0 < \lambda < 1$. The first-order conditions for a maximum are

$$\frac{\partial \mathscr{L}}{\partial l} = pf_l - w + \lambda(w - pf_1) = 0,$$

$$\frac{\partial \mathscr{L}}{\partial k} = pf_k - v + \lambda(\bar{s} - pf_k) = 0,$$

(14.48)

$$\frac{\partial \mathscr{L}}{\partial \lambda} = wl + \bar{s}k - pf(k, l) = 0.$$

The first of these conditions implies that the regulated monopoly will hire additional labor input up to the point at which $pf_l = w$—a result that holds for any profit-maximizing firm. For capital input, however, the second condition implies that

$$(1 - \lambda)pf_k = v - \lambda\bar{s}$$

(14.49)

[16]This model is based on H. Averch and L. L. Johnson, "Behavior of the Firm under Regulatory Constraint," *American Economic Review* (December 1962): 1052–69.

or

$$pf_k = \frac{v - \lambda \bar{s}}{1 - \lambda} = v - \frac{\lambda(\bar{s} - v)}{1 - \lambda}. \tag{14.50}$$

Because $\bar{s} > v$ and $\lambda < 1$, Equation 14.50 implies

$$pf_k < v. \tag{14.51}$$

The firm will hire more capital (and achieve a lower marginal productivity of capital) than it would under unregulated conditions. "Overcapitalization" may therefore be a regulatory-induced misallocation of resources for some utilities. Although we shall not do so here, it is possible to examine other regulatory questions using this general analytical framework.

DYNAMIC VIEWS OF MONOPOLY

The static view that monopolistic practices distort the allocation of resources provides the principal economic rationale for favoring antimonopoly policies. Not all economists believe that the static analysis should be definitive, however. Some authors, most notably J. A. Schumpeter, have stressed the beneficial role that monopoly profits can play in the process of economic development.[17] These authors place considerable emphasis on innovation and the ability of particular types of firms to achieve technical advances. In this context the profits that monopolistic firms earn provide funds that can be invested in research and development. Whereas perfectly competitive firms must be content with a normal return on invested capital, monopolies have "surplus" funds with which to undertake the risky process of research. More important, perhaps, the possibility of attaining a monopolistic position—or the desire to maintain such a position—provides an important incentive to keep one step ahead of potential competitors. Innovations in new products and cost-saving production techniques may be integrally related to the possibility of monopolization. Without such a monopolistic position, the full benefits of innovation could not be obtained by the innovating firm.

Schumpeter stresses the point that the monopolization of a market may make it less costly for a firm to plan its activities. Being the only source of supply for a product eliminates many of the contingencies that a firm in a competitive market must face. For example, a monopoly may not have to spend as much on selling expenses (advertising, brand identification, and visiting retailers, for example) as would be the case in a more competitive industry. Similarly, a monopoly may know more about the specific demand curve for its product and may more readily adapt to changing demand conditions. Of course, whether any of these purported benefits of monopolies outweigh their allocational and distributional disadvantages is an empirical question. Issues of innovation and cost savings cannot be answered by recourse to a priori arguments; detailed investigation of real-world markets is a necessity.

SUMMARY

In this chapter we have examined models of markets in which there is only a single monopoly supplier. Unlike the competitive case investigated in Part 4, monopoly firms do not exhibit price-taking behavior. Instead, the monopolist can choose the price-quantity combination on the market demand curve that is most profitable. A number of consequences then follow from this market power.

- The most profitable level of output for the monopolist is the one for which marginal revenue is equal to marginal cost. At this output level, price will exceed marginal cost. The profitability of the monopolist will depend on the relationship between price and average cost.

- Relative to perfect competition, monopoly involves a loss of consumer surplus for demanders. Some of this is

---

[17]See, for example, J. A. Schumpeter, *Capitalism, Socialism and Democracy*, 3rd ed. (New York: Harper & Row, 1950), especially chap. 8.

transferred into monopoly profits, whereas some of the loss in consumer supply represents a deadweight loss of overall economic welfare—a sign of Pareto inefficiency.

- Monopolists may opt for different levels of quality than would perfectly competitive firms. Durable goods monopolists may be constrained by markets for used goods.

- A monopoly may be able to increase its profits further through price discrimination—that is, charging different prices to different categories of buyers. The ability of the monopoly to practice price discrimination depends on its ability to prevent arbitrage among buyers.

- Governments often choose to regulate natural monopolies (firms with diminishing average costs over a broad range of output levels). The type of regulatory mechanisms adopted can affect the behavior of the regulated firm.

PROBLEMS

14.1

A monopolist can produce at constant average and marginal costs of $AC = MC = 5$. The firm faces a market demand curve given by $Q = 53 - P$.

a. Calculate the profit-maximizing price-quantity combination for the monopolist. Also calculate the monopolist's profits.

b. What output level would be produced by this industry under perfect competition (where price = marginal cost)?

c. Calculate the consumer surplus obtained by consumers in case (b). Show that this exceeds the sum of the monopolist's profits and the consumer surplus received in case (a). What is the value of the "deadweight loss" from monopolization?

14.2

A monopolist faces a market demand curve given by

$$Q = 70 - p.$$

a. If the monopolist can produce at constant average and marginal costs of $AC = MC = 6$, what output level will the monopolist choose in order to maximize profits? What is the price at this output level? What are the monopolist's profits?

b. Assume instead that the monopolist has a cost structure where total costs are described by

$$C(Q) = 0.25Q^2 - 5Q + 300.$$

With the monopolist facing the same market demand and marginal revenue, what price-quantity combination will be chosen now to maximize profits? What will profits be?

c. Assume now that a third cost structure explains the monopolist's position, with total costs given by

$$C(Q) = 0.0133Q^3 - 5Q + 250.$$

Again, calculate the monopolist's price-quantity combination that maximizes profits. What will profit be? *Hint:* Set $MC = MR$ as usual and use the quadratic formula to solve the second-order equation for Q.

d. Graph the market demand curve, the MR curve, and the three marginal cost curves from parts (a), (b), and (c). Notice that the monopolist's profit-making ability is constrained by (1) the market demand curve (along with its associated MR curve) and (2) the cost structure underlying production.

14.3

A single firm monopolizes the entire market for widgets and can produce at constant average and marginal costs of

$$AC = MC = 10.$$

Originally, the firm faces a market demand curve given by

$$Q = 60 - P.$$

a. Calculate the profit-maximizing price-quantity combination for the firm. What are the firm's profits?

b. Now assume that the market demand curve shifts outward (becoming steeper) and is given by

$$Q = 45 - 0.5P.$$

What is the firm's profit-maximizing price-quantity combination now? What are the firm's profits?

c. Instead of the assumptions of part (b), assume that the market demand curve shifts outward (becoming flatter) and is given by

$$Q = 100 - 2P.$$

What is the firm's profit-maximizing price-quantity combination now? What are the firm's profits?

d. Graph the three different situations of parts (a), (b), and (c). Using your results, explain why there is no real supply curve for a monopoly.

14.4

Suppose the market for Hula Hoops is monopolized by a single firm.

a. Draw the initial equilibrium for such a market.

b. Now suppose the demand for Hula Hoops shifts outward slightly. Show that, in general (contrary to the competitive case), it will not be possible to predict the effect of this shift in demand on the market price of Hula Hoops.

c. Consider three possible ways in which the price elasticity of demand might change as the demand curve shifts: it might increase, it might decrease, or it might stay the same. Consider also that marginal costs for the monopolist might be rising, falling, or constant in the range where $MR = MC$. Consequently, there are nine different combinations of types of demand shifts and marginal cost slope configurations. Analyze each of these to determine for which it is possible to make a definite prediction about the effect of the shift in demand on the price of Hula Hoops.

14.5

Suppose a monopoly market has a demand function in which quantity demanded depends not only on market price (P) but also on the amount of advertising the firm does (A, measured in dollars). The specific form of this function is

$$Q = (20 - P)(1 + 0.1A - 0.01A^2).$$

The monopolistic firm's cost function is given by

$$C = 10Q + 15 + A.$$

a. Suppose there is no advertising ($A = 0$). What output will the profit-maximizing firm choose? What market price will this yield? What will be the monopoly's profits?

b. Now let the firm also choose its optimal level of advertising expenditure. In this situation, what output level will be chosen? What price will this yield? What will the level of advertising be? What are the firm's profits in this case? *Hint:* This can be worked out most easily by assuming the monopoly chooses the profit-maximizing price rather than quantity.

14.6

Suppose a monopoly can produce any level of output it wishes at a constant marginal (and average) cost of $5 per unit. Assume the monopoly sells its goods in two different markets separated by some distance. The demand curve in the first market is given by

$$Q_1 = 55 - P_1,$$

and the demand curve in the second market is given by

$$Q_2 = 70 - 2P_2.$$

a. If the monopolist can maintain the separation between the two markets, what level of output should be produced in each market, and what price will prevail in each market? What are total profits in this situation?

b. How would your answer change if it costs demanders only $5 to transport goods between the two markets? What would be the monopolist's new profit level in this situation?

c. How would your answer change if transportation costs were zero and then the firm was forced to follow a single-price policy?

d. Suppose the firm could adopt a linear two-part tariff under which marginal prices must be equal in the two markets but lump-sum entry fees might vary. What pricing policy should the firm follow?

14.7

Suppose a perfectly competitive industry can produce widgets at a constant marginal cost of $10 per unit. Monopolized marginal costs rise to $12 per unit because $2 per unit must be paid to lobbyists to retain the widget producers' favored position. Suppose the market demand for widgets is given by

$$Q_D = 1,000 - 50P.$$

a. Calculate the perfectly competitive and monopoly outputs and prices.

b. Calculate the total loss of consumer surplus from monopolization of widget production.

c. Graph your results and explain how they differ from the usual analysis.

14.8

Suppose the government wishes to combat the undesirable allocational effects of a monopoly through the use of a subsidy.

a. Why would a lump-sum subsidy not achieve the government's goal?

b. Use a graphical proof to show how a per-unit-of-output subsidy might achieve the government's goal.

c. Suppose the government wants its subsidy to maximize the difference between the total value of the good to consumers and the good's total cost. Show that, in order to achieve this goal, the government should set

$$\frac{t}{P} = -\frac{1}{e_{Q,P}},$$

where t is the per-unit subsidy and P is the competitive price. Explain your result intuitively.

14.9

Suppose a monopolist produces alkaline batteries that may have various useful lifetimes (X). Suppose also that consumers' (inverse) demand depends on batteries' lifetimes and quantity (Q) purchased according to the function

$$P(Q, X) = g(X \cdot Q),$$

where $g' < 0$. That is, consumers care only about the product of quantity times lifetime: They are willing to pay equally for many short-lived batteries or few long-lived ones. Assume also that battery costs are given by

$$C(Q, X) = C(X)Q,$$

where $C'(X) > 0$. Show that, in this case, the monopoly will opt for the same level of X as does a competitive industry even though levels of output and prices may differ. Explain your result. *Hint:* Treat XQ as a composite commodity.

Analytical Problems

14.10 Taxation of a monopoly good

The taxation of monopoly can sometimes produce results different from those that arise in the competitive case. This problem looks at some of those cases. Most of these can be analyzed by using the inverse elasticity rule (Equation 14.1).

a. Consider first an ad valorem tax on the price of a monopoly's good. This tax reduces the net price received by the monopoly from P to $P(1 - t)$—where t is the proportional tax rate. Show that, with a linear demand curve and constant marginal cost, the imposition of such a tax causes price to rise by less than the full extent of the tax.

b. Suppose that the demand curve in part (a) were a constant elasticity curve. Show that the price would now increase by precisely the full extent of the tax. Explain the difference between these two cases.

c. Describe a case where the imposition of an ad valorem tax on a monopoly would cause the price to rise by more than the tax.

d. A specific tax is a fixed amount per unit of output. If the tax rate is τ per unit, total tax collections are τQ. Show that the imposition of a specific tax on a monopoly will reduce output more (and increase price more) than will the imposition of an ad valorem tax that collects the same tax revenue.

14.11 More on the welfare analysis of quality choice

An alternative way to study the welfare properties of a monopolist's choices is to assume the existence of a utility function for the customers of the monopoly of the form utility $= U(Q, X)$, where Q is quantity consumed and X is the quality associated with that quantity. A social planner's problem then would be to choose Q and X to maximize social welfare as represented by $SW = U(Q, X) - C(Q, X)$.

a. What are the first-order conditions for a welfare maximum?

b. The monopolist's goal is to choose the Q and X that maximize $\pi = P(Q, X) \cdot Q - C(Q, X)$. What are the first-order conditions for this maximization?

c. Use your results from parts (a) and (b) to show that, at the monopolist's preferred choices, $\partial SW / \partial Q > 0$. That is, as we have already shown, prove that social welfare would be improved if more were produced. *Hint:* Assume that $\partial U / \partial Q = P$.

d. Show that, at the monopolist's preferred choices, the sign of $\partial SW / \partial X$ is ambiguous—that is, it cannot be determined (on the sole basis of the general theory of monopoly) whether the monopolist produces either too much or too little quality.

14.12 The welfare effects of third-degree price discrimination

In an important 1985 paper,[18] Hal Varian shows how to assess third-degree price discrimination using only properties of the indirect utility function (see Chapter 3). This problem provides a simplified version of his approach. Suppose that a single good is sold in two separated markets. Quantities in the

---

[18]H. R. Varian, "Price Discrimination and Social Welfare," *American Economic Review* (September 1985): 870–75.

two markets are designated by q_1, q_2 with prices p_1, p_2. Consumers of the good are assumed to be characterized by an indirect utility function that takes a quasi-linear form: $V(p_1, p_2, I) = v(p_1, p_2) + I$. Income is assumed to have an exogenous component $(\bar{I})$, and the monopoly earns profits of $\pi = p_1 q_1 + p_2 q_2 - c(q_1 + q_2)$, where c is marginal and average cost (which is assumed to be constant).

a. Given this setup, let's first show some facts about this kind of indirect utility function.

(1) Use Roy's identity (see the Extensions to Chapter 5) to show that the Marshallian demand functions for the two goods in this problem are given by $q_i(p_1, p_2, I) = -\partial v/\partial p_i$.

(2) Show that the function $v(p_1, p_2)$ is convex in the prices.

(3) Because social welfare (SW) can be measured by the indirect utility function of the consumers, show that the welfare impact of any change in prices is given by $\Delta SW = \Delta v + \Delta \pi$. How does this expression compare to the notion (introduced in Chapter 12) that any change in welfare is the sum of changes in consumer and producer surplus?

b. Suppose now that we wish to compare the welfare associated with a single-price policy for these two markets, $p_1 = p_2 = \bar{p}$, to the welfare associated with different prices in the two markets, $p_1 = p_1^*$ and $p_2 = p_2^*$. Show that an upper bound to the change in social welfare from adopting a two-price policy is given by $\Delta SW \leq (\bar{p} - c)(q_1^* + q_2^* - \bar{q}_1 - \bar{q}_2)$. *Hint:* Use a first-order Taylor expansion for the function v around p_1^*, p_2^* together with Roy's identity and the fact that v is convex.

c. Show why the results of part (b) imply that, for social welfare to increase from the adoption of the two-price policy, total quantity demanded must increase.

d. Use an approach similar to that taken in part (b) to show that a lower bound to the change in social welfare from adopting a two-price policy is given by $\Delta SW \geq (p_1^* - c)(q_1^* - \bar{q}_1) + (p_2^* - c)(q_2^* - \bar{q}_2)$. Can you interpret this lower bound condition?

e. Notice that the approach taken here never uses the fact that the price-quantity combinations studied are profit maximizing for the monopolist. Can you think of situations (other than third-degree price discrimination) where the analysis here might apply? *Note:* Varian shows that the bounds for welfare changes can be tightened a bit in the price discrimination case by using profit maximization.

SUGGESTIONS FOR FURTHER READING

Posner, R. A. "The Social Costs of Monopoly and Regulation." *Journal of Political Economy* 83 (1975): 807–27.

> *An analysis of the probability that monopolies will spend resources on the creation of barriers to entry and thus have higher costs than perfectly competitive firms.*

Schumpeter, J. A. *Capitalism, Socialism and Democracy*, 3rd ed. New York: Harper & Row, 1950.

> *Classic defense of the role of the entrepreneur and economic profits in the economic growth process.*

Spence, M. "Monopoly, Quality, and Regulation." *Bell Journal of Economics* (April 1975): 417–29.

> *Develops the approach to product quality used in this text and provides a detailed analysis of the effects of monopoly.*

Stigler, G. J. "The Theory of Economic Regulation." *Bell Journal of Economics and Management Science* 2 (Spring 1971): 3.

> *Early development of the "capture" hypothesis of regulatory behavior—that the industry captures the agency supposed to regulate it and uses that agency to enforce entry barriers and further enhance profits.*

Tirole, J. *The Theory of Industrial Organization.* Cambridge, MA: MIT Press, 1989, chaps. 1–3.

> *A complete analysis of the theory of monopoly pricing and product choice.*

Varian, H. R. *Microeconomic Analysis*, 3rd ed. New York: W. W. Norton, 1992, chap. 14.

> *Provides a succinct analysis of the role of incentive compatibility constraints in second-degree price discrimination.*

EXTENSIONS

Optimal Linear Two-part Tariffs

In Chapter 14 we examined a simple illustration of ways in which a monopoly may increase profits by practicing second-degree price discrimination—that is, by establishing price (or "outlay") schedules that prompt buyers to separate themselves into distinct market segments. Here we pursue the topic of linear tariff schedules a bit further. Nonlinear pricing schedules are discussed in Chapter 18.

E14.1 Structure of the problem

To examine issues related to price schedules in a simple context for each demander, we define the "valuation function" as

$$v_i(q) = p_i(q) \cdot q + s_i, \qquad \text{(i)}$$

where $p_i(q)$ is the inverse demand function for individual i and s_i is consumer surplus. Hence v_i represents the total value to individual i of undertaking transactions of amount q, which includes total spending on the good plus the value of consumer surplus obtained. Here we will assume (a) there are only two demanders[1] (or homogeneous groups of demanders) and (b) person 1 has stronger preferences for this good than person 2 in the sense that

$$v_1(q) > v_2(q) \qquad \text{(ii)}$$

for all values of q. The monopolist is assumed to have constant marginal costs (denoted by c) and chooses a tariff (revenue) schedule, $T(q)$, that maximizes profits given by

$$\pi = T(q_1) + T(q_2) - c(q_1 + q_2), \qquad \text{(iii)}$$

where q_i represents the quantity chosen by person i. In selecting a price schedule that successfully differentiates among consumers, the monopolist faces two constraints. To ensure that the low-demand person (2) is actually served, it is necessary that

$$v_2(q_2) - T(q_2) \geq 0. \qquad \text{(iv)}$$

That is, person 2 must derive a net benefit from her optimal choice, q_2. Person 1, the high-demand individual, must also obtain a net gain from his chosen consumption level (q_1) and must prefer this choice to

the output choice made by person 2:

$$v_1(q_1) - T(q_1) \geq v_1(q_2) - T(q_2). \qquad \text{(v)}$$

If the monopolist does not recognize this "incentive compatibility" constraint, it may find that person 1 opts for the portion of the price schedule intended for person 2, thereby destroying the goal of obtaining self-selected market separation. Given this general structure, we can proceed to illustrate a number of interesting features of the monopolist's problem.

E14.2 Pareto superiority

Permitting the monopolist to depart from a simple single-price scheme offers the possibility of adopting "Pareto superior" tariff schedules under which all parties to the transaction are made better-off. For example, suppose the monopolist's profit-maximizing price is p_M. At this price, person 2 consumes q_2^M and receives a net value from this consumption of

$$v_2(q_2^M) - p_M q_2^M. \qquad \text{(vi)}$$

A tariff schedule for which

$$T(q) = \begin{cases} p_M q & \text{for } q \leq q_2^M, \\ a + \bar{p}q & \text{for } q > q_2^M, \end{cases} \qquad \text{(vii)}$$

where $a > 0$ and $c < \bar{p} < p_M$, may yield increased profits for the monopolist as well as increased welfare for person 1. Specifically, consider values of a and $\bar{p}$ such that

$$a + \bar{p}q_1^M = p_M q_1^M$$

or

$$a = (p_M - \bar{p})q_1^M, \qquad \text{(viii)}$$

where q_1^M represents consumption of person 1 under a single-price policy. In this case, then, a and $\bar{p}$ are set so that person 1 can still afford to buy q_1^M under the new price schedule. Because $\bar{p} < p_M$, however, he will opt for $q_1^* > q_1^M$. Because person 1 could have bought q_1^M but chose q_1^* instead, he must be better-off under the new schedule. The monopoly's profits are now given by

$$\pi = a + \bar{p}q_1 + p_M q_2^M - c(q_1 + q_2^M) \qquad \text{(ix)}$$

and

$$\pi - \pi_M = a + \bar{p}q_1 + p_M q_1^M - c(q_1 - q_1^M), \qquad \text{(x)}$$

---

[1] Generalizations to many demanders are nontrivial. For a discussion, see Wilson (1993, chaps. 2–5).

where π_M is the monopoly's single-price profits $[= (p_M - c)(q_1^M + q_2^M)]$. Substitution for a from Equation viii shows

$$\pi - \pi_M = (\bar{p} - c)(q_1 - q_1^M) > 0. \quad \text{(xi)}$$

Hence, this new price schedule also provides more profits to the monopoly, some of which might be shared with person 2. The price schedule is Pareto superior to a single monopoly price. The notion that multipart schedules may be Pareto superior has been used not only in the study of price discrimination but also in the design of optimal tax schemes and auction mechanisms (see Willig, 1978).

Pricing a farmland reserve

The potential Pareto superiority of complex tariff schedules is used by R. B. W. Smith (1995) to estimate a least-cost method for the U.S. government to finance a conservation reserve program for farmland. The specific plan the author studies would maintain a 34-million-acre reserve out of production in any given year. He calculates that use of carefully constructed (nonlinear) tariff schedules for such a program might cost only $1 billion annually.

E14.3 Tied sales

Sometimes a monopoly will market two goods together. This situation poses a number of possibilities for discriminatory pricing schemes. Consider, for example, laser printers that are sold with toner cartridges or electronic game players sold with patented additional games. Here the pricing situation is similar to that examined in Chapter 14—usually consumers buy only one unit of the basic product (the printer or camera) and thereby pay the "entry" fee. Then they consume a variable number of tied products (toner and film). Because our analysis in Chapter 14 suggests that the monopoly will choose a price for its tied product that exceeds marginal cost, there will be a welfare loss relative to a situation in which the tied good is produced competitively. Perhaps for this reason, tied sales are prohibited by law in some cases. Prohibition may not necessarily increase welfare, however, if the monopoly declines to serve low-demand consumers in the absence of such a practice (Oi, 1971).

Automobiles and wine

One way in which tied sales can be accomplished is through creation of a multiplicity of quality variants that appeal to different classes of buyers. Automobile companies have been especially ingenious at devising quality variants of their basic models (for example, the Honda Accord comes in DX, LX, EX, and SX configurations) that act as tied goods in separating buyers into various market niches. A 1992 study by J. E. Kwoka examines one specific U.S. manufacturer (Chrysler) and shows how market segmentation is achieved through quality variation. The author calculates that significant transfer from consumer surplus to firms occurs as a result of such segmentation.

Generally, this sort of price discrimination in a tied good will be infeasible if that good is also produced under competitive conditions. In such a case the tied good will sell for marginal cost, and the only possibility for discriminatory behavior open to the monopolist is in the pricing of its basic good (that is, by varying "entry fees" among demanders). In some special cases, however, choosing to pay the entry fee will confer monopoly power in the tied good on the monopolist even though it is otherwise reduced under competitive conditions. For example, Locay and Rodriguez (1992) examine the case of restaurants' pricing of wine. Here group decisions to patronize a particular restaurant may confer monopoly power to the restaurant owner in the ability to practice wine price discrimination among buyers with strong grape preferences. Since the owner is constrained by the need to attract groups of customers to the restaurant, the power to price discriminate is less than under the pure monopoly scenario.

References

Kwoka, J. E. "Market Segmentation by Price-Quality Schedules: Some Evidence from Automobiles." *Journal of Business* (October 1992): 615–28.

Locay, L., and A. Rodriguez. "Price Discrimination in Competitive Markets." *Journal of Political Economy* (October 1992): 954–68.

Oi, W. Y. "A Disneyland Dilemma: Two-Part Tariffs on a Mickey Mouse Monopoly." *Quarterly Journal of Economics* (February 1971): 77–90.

Smith, R. B. W. "The Conservation Reserve Program as a Least Cost Land Retirement Mechanism." *American Journal of Agricultural Economics* (February 1995): 93–105.

Willig, R. "Pareto Superior Non-Linear Outlay Schedules." *Bell Journal of Economics* (January 1978): 56–69.

Wilson, W. *Nonlinear Pricing.* Oxford: Oxford University Press, 1993.

Imperfect Competition

This chapter discusses oligopolies, markets with relatively few firms (but more than one) that fall between the extremes of perfect competition and monopoly. Oligopolies raise the possibility of strategic interaction among firms. To analyze this strategic interaction rigorously, we will apply the concepts from game theory that were introduced in Chapter 8. Our game-theoretic analysis will show that small changes in details concerning the variables firms choose, the timing of their moves, or their information about market conditions or rival actions can have a dramatic effect on market outcomes. The first half of the chapter deals with short-term decisions such as pricing and output and the second half with longer-term decisions such as investment, advertising, and entry.

SHORT-RUN DECISIONS: PRICING AND OUTPUT

The first half of this chapter will analyze firms' short-run (pricing and/or output) decisions in an *oligopoly*, a market with relatively few firms but more than one. It is difficult to predict exactly the possible outcomes for price and output when there are few firms; prices depend on how aggressively firms compete, which in turn depends on which strategic variables firms choose, how much information firms have about rivals, and how often firms interact with each other in the market.

For example, consider the Bertrand game studied in the next section. The game involves two identical firms choosing prices simultaneously for their identical products in their one meeting in the market. The Bertrand game has a Nash equilibrium at point *C* in Figure 15.1. Even though there may be only two firms in the market, in this equilibrium they behave as if they were perfectly competitive, setting price equal to marginal cost and earning zero profit. We will discuss whether the Bertrand game is a realistic depiction of actual firm behavior, but an analysis of the model shows that it is possible to think up rigorous game-theoretic models in which one extreme—the competitive outcome—can emerge in very concentrated markets with few firms.

At the other extreme, as indicated by point *M* in Figure 15.1, firms as a group may act as a cartel, recognizing that they can affect price and coordinate their decisions. Indeed, they may be able to act as a perfect cartel and achieve the highest possible profits—namely, the profit a monopoly would earn in the market. One way to maintain a cartel is to bind firms with explicit pricing rules. Such explicit pricing rules are often prohibited by antitrust law. But firms need not resort to explicit pricing rules if they interact on the market repeatedly; they can collude tacitly. High collusive prices can be maintained with the tacit threat of a price war if any firm undercuts. We will analyze this game formally and discuss the difficulty of maintaining collusion.

The Bertrand and cartel models determine the outer limits between which actual prices in an imperfectly competitive market are set (one such intermediate price is represented by

FIGURE 15.1   Pricing and Output under Imperfect Competition

Market equilibrium under imperfect competition can occur at many points on the demand curve. In this figure, which assumes that marginal costs are constant over all output ranges, the equilibrium of the Bertrand game occurs at point C, also corresponding to the perfectly competitive outcome. The perfect cartel outcome occurs at point M, also corresponding to the monopoly outcome. Many solutions may occur between points M and C, depending on the specific assumptions made about how firms compete. For example, the equilibrium of the Cournot game might occur at a point such as A. The deadweight loss given by the shaded triangle is increasing as one moves from point C to M.

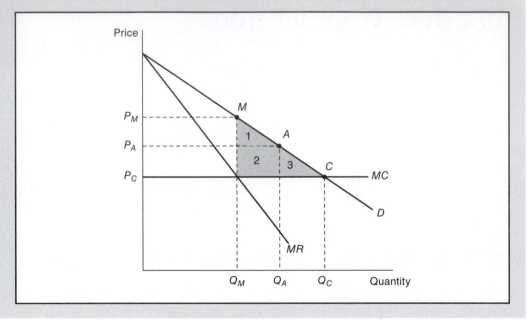

point A in Figure 15.1). This band of outcomes may be very wide, and given the plethora of available models there may be a model for nearly every point within the band. For example, in a later section we will show how the Cournot model, in which firms set quantities rather than prices as in the Bertrand model, leads to an outcome (such as point A) somewhere between C and M in Figure 15.1.

It is important to know where the industry is on the line between points C and M because total welfare (as measured by the sum of consumer surplus and firms' profits; see Chapter 12) depends on the location of this point. At point C, total welfare is as high as possible; at point A, total welfare is lower by the area of the shaded triangle 3. In Chapter 12, this shortfall in total welfare relative to the highest possible level was called *deadweight loss*. At point M, deadweight loss is even greater and is given by the area of shaded regions 1, 2, and 3. The closer the imperfectly competitive outcome to C and the farther from M, the higher is total welfare and the better-off society will be.[1]

---

[1]Since this section deals with short-run decision variables (price and quantity), the discussion of total welfare in this paragraph focuses on short-run considerations. As discussed in a later section, an imperfectly competitive market may produce considerably more deadweight loss than a perfectly competitive one in the short run yet provide more innovation incentives, leading to lower production costs and new products and perhaps higher total welfare in the long run. The patent system intentionally impairs competition by granting a monopoly right in order to improve innovation incentives.

BERTRAND MODEL

The Bertrand model is named after the economist who first proposed it.[2] The model is a game involving two identical firms, labeled 1 and 2, producing identical products at a constant marginal cost (and constant average cost) c. The firms choose prices p_1 and p_2 simultaneously in a single period of competition. Since firms' products are perfect substitutes, all sales go to the firm with the lowest price. Sales are split evenly if $p_1 = p_2$. Let $D(p)$ be market demand.

We will look for the Nash equilibrium. The game has a continuum of actions, as does Example 8.6 (the Tragedy of the Commons) in Chapter 8. Unlike Example 8.6, we cannot use calculus to derive best-response functions because the profit functions are not differentiable here. Starting from equal prices, if one firm lowers its price by the smallest amount then its sales and profit would essentially double. We will proceed by first guessing what the Nash equilibrium is and then spending some time to verify that our guess was in fact correct.

Nash equilibrium of the Bertrand game

The only pure-strategy Nash equilibrium of the Bertrand game is $p_1^* = p_2^* = c$. That is, the Nash equilibrium involves both firms charging marginal cost. In saying that this is the only Nash equilibrium, we are making two statements that need to be verified: this outcome is a Nash equilibrium; and there is no other Nash equilibrium.

To verify that this outcome is a Nash equilibrium, we need to show that both firms are playing a best response to each other—or, in other words, that neither firm has an incentive to deviate to some other strategy. In equilibrium, firms charge a price equal to marginal cost, which in turn is equal to average cost. But a price equal to average cost means firms earn zero profit in equilibrium. Can a firm earn more than the zero it earns in equilibrium by deviating to some other price? No. If it deviates to a higher price then it will make no sales and therefore no profit, not strictly more than in equilibrium. If it deviates to a lower price, then it will make sales but will be earning a negative margin on each unit sold, since price would be below marginal cost. So the firm would earn negative profit, less than in equilibrium. Because there is no possible profitable deviation for the firm, we have succeeded in verifying that both firms' charging marginal cost is a Nash equilibrium.

It is clear that marginal cost pricing is the only pure-strategy Nash equilibrium. If prices exceeded marginal cost, the high-price firm would gain by undercutting the other slightly and capturing all of market demand. More formally, to verify that $p_1^* = p_2^* = c$ is the only Nash equilibrium, we will go one by one through an exhaustive list of cases for various values of p_1, p_2, and c, verifying that none besides $p_1 = p_2 = c$ is a Nash equilibrium. To reduce the number of cases, assume firm 1 is the low-price firm—that is, $p_1 \le p_2$. The same conclusions would be reached taking 2 to be the low-price firm.

There are three exhaustive cases: (i) $c > p_1$, (ii) $c < p_1$, and (iii) $c = p_1$. Case (i) cannot be a Nash equilibrium. Firm 1 earns a negative margin $p_1 - c$ on every unit it sells and, since it makes positive sales, it must earn negative profit. It could earn higher profit by deviating to a higher price. For example, firm 1 could guarantee itself zero profit by deviating to $p_1 = c$.

Case (ii) cannot be a Nash equilibrium, either. At best firm 2 gets only half of market demand (if $p_1 = p_2$) and at worst gets no demand (if $p_1 < p_2$). Firm 2 could capture all of market demand by undercutting firm 1's price by a tiny amount ε. This ε could be chosen small enough that market price and total market profit are hardly affected. If $p_1 = p_2$ prior to the deviation, the deviation would essentially double firm 2's profit. If $p_1 < p_2$ prior to the deviation, the deviation would result in firm 2 moving from zero to positive profit. In either case, firm 2's deviation would be profitable.

---

[2]J. Bertrand, "Théorie Mathematique de la Richesse Sociale," *Journal de Savants* (1883): 499–508.

Case (iii) includes the subcase of $p_1 = p_2 = c$, which we saw is a Nash equilibrium. The only remaining subcase in which $p_1 \leq p_2$ is $c = p_1 < p_2$. This subcase cannot be a Nash equilibrium: firm 1 earns zero profit here but could earn positive profit by deviating to a price slightly above c but still below p_2.

Though the analysis focused on the game with two firms, it is clear that the same outcome would arise for any number of firms $n \geq 2$. The Nash equilibrium of the n-firm Bertrand game is $p_1^* = p_2^* = \cdots = p_n^* = c$.

Bertrand paradox

The Nash equilibrium of the Bertrand model is the same as the perfectly competitive outcome. Price is set to marginal cost, and firms earn zero profit. This result—that the Nash equilibrium in the Bertrand model is the same as in perfect competition even though there may be only two firms in the market—is called the Bertrand paradox. It is paradoxical that competition between as few as two firms would be so tough. The Bertrand paradox is a general result in the sense that we did not specify the marginal cost c or the demand curve, so the result holds for any c and any downward-sloping demand curve.

In another sense, the Bertrand paradox is not very general; it can be undone by changing various of the model's other assumptions. Each of the next several sections will present a different model generated by changing a different one of the Bertrand assumptions. In the next section, for example, we will assume that firms choose quantity rather than price, leading to what is called the Cournot game. We will see that firms do not end up charging marginal cost and earning zero profit in the Cournot game. In subsequent sections, we will show that the Bertrand Paradox can also be avoided if still other assumptions are changed: if firms face capacity constraints rather than being able to produce an unlimited amount at cost c, if products are slightly differentiated rather than being perfect substitutes, or if firms engage in repeated interaction rather than one round of competition.

COURNOT MODEL

The Cournot model, named after the economist who proposed it,[3] is similar to the Bertrand except that firms are assumed to simultaneously choose quantities rather than prices. As we will see, this simple change in strategic variable will lead to a big change in implications. Price will be above marginal cost and firms will earn positive profit in the Nash equilibrium of the Cournot game. It is somewhat surprising (but nonetheless an important point to keep in mind) that this simple change in choice variable matters in the strategic setting of an oligopoly when it did not matter with a monopoly: the monopolist obtained the same profit-maximizing outcome whether it chose prices or quantities.

We will start with a general version of the Cournot game with n firms indexed by $i = 1, \ldots, n$. Each firm chooses its output q_i of an identical product simultaneously. The outputs are combined into a total industry output $Q = q_1 + q_2 + \cdots + q_n$, resulting in market price $P(Q)$. Observe that $P(Q)$ is the inverse demand curve corresponding to the market demand curve $Q = D(P)$. Assume market demand is downward sloping and so

---

[3]A. Cournot, *Researches into the Mathematical Principles of the Theory of Wealth*, trans. N. T. Bacon (New York: Macmillan, 1897). Although the Cournot model appears after Bertrand's in this chapter, Cournot's work, originally published in 1838, predates Bertrand's. Cournot's work is one of the first formal analyses of strategic behavior in oligopolies, and his solution concept anticipated Nash equilibrium.

inverse demand is, too; that is, $P'(Q) < 0$. Firm i's profit equals its total revenue, $P(Q)q_i$, minus its total cost, $C_i(q_i)$:

$$\pi_i = P(Q)q_i - C_i(q_i). \tag{15.1}$$

Nash equilibrium of the Cournot game

Unlike the Bertrand game, the profit function (15.1) in the Cournot game is differentiable; hence we can proceed to solve for the Nash equilibrium of this game just as we did in Example 8.6, the Tragedy of the Commons. That is, we find each firm i's best response by taking the first-order condition of the objective function (15.1) with respect to q_i:

$$\frac{\partial \pi_i}{\partial q_i} = \underbrace{P(Q) + P'(Q)q_i}_{MR} - \underbrace{C_i'(q_i)}_{MC} = 0. \tag{15.2}$$

Equation 15.2 must hold for all $i = 1, \ldots, n$ in the Nash equilibrium.

According to Equation 15.2, the familiar condition for profit maximization from Chapter 11—marginal revenue (MR) equals marginal cost (MC)—holds for the Cournot firm. As we will see from an analysis of the particular form that the marginal revenue term takes for the Cournot firm, price is above the perfectly competitive level (above marginal cost) but below the level in a perfect cartel that maximizes firms' joint profits.

In order for Equation 15.2 to equal 0, price must exceed marginal cost by the magnitude of the "wedge" term $P'(Q)q_i$. If the Cournot firm produces another unit on top of its existing production of q_i units then, since demand is downward sloping, the additional unit causes market price to fall by $P'(Q)$, leading to a loss of revenue of $P'(Q)q_i$ (the wedge term) from firm i's existing production.

To compare the Cournot outcome with the perfect cartel outcome, note that the objective for the cartel is to maximize joint profit:

$$\sum_{j=1}^{n} \pi_j = P(Q) \sum_{j=1}^{n} q_j - \sum_{j=1}^{n} C_j(q_j). \tag{15.3}$$

Taking the first-order condition of Equation 15.3 with respect to q_i gives

$$\frac{\partial}{\partial q_i} \left(\sum_{j=1}^{n} \pi_j \right) = \underbrace{P(Q) + P'(Q) \sum_{j=1}^{n} q_j}_{MR} - \underbrace{C_i'(q_i)}_{MC} = 0. \tag{15.4}$$

This first-order condition is similar to Equation 15.2 except that the wedge term,

$$P'(Q) \sum_{j=1}^{n} q_j = P'(Q)Q, \tag{15.5}$$

is larger in magnitude with a perfect cartel than with Cournot firms. In maximizing joint profits, the cartel accounts for the fact that an additional unit of firm i's output, by reducing market price, reduces the revenue earned on *all* firms' existing output. Hence $P'(Q)$ is multiplied by total cartel output Q in Equation 15.5. The Cournot firm accounts for the reduction in revenue only from its own existing output q_i. Hence, Cournot firms will end up overproducing relative to the joint profit–maximizing outcome. That is, the extra production in the Cournot outcome relative to a perfect cartel will end up in lower joint profit for the firms. What firms would regard as overproduction is good for society because it means that the Cournot outcome (point A, referring back to Figure 15.1) will involve more total welfare than the perfect cartel outcome (point M in Figure 15.1).

EXAMPLE 15.1 Natural-Spring Duopoly

As a numerical example of some of these ideas, we will consider a case with just two firms and simple demand and cost functions. Following Cournot's nineteenth-century example of two natural springs, we assume that each spring owner has a large supply of (possibly healthful) water and faces the problem of how much to provide the market. A firm's cost of pumping and bottling q_i liters is $C_i(q_i) = cq_i$, implying that marginal costs are a constant c per liter. Inverse demand for spring water is

$$P(Q) = a - Q, \tag{15.6}$$

where a is the demand intercept (measuring the strength of spring-water demand) and $Q = q_1 + q_2$ is total spring-water output. We will now examine various models of how this market might operate.

Bertrand model. In the Nash equilibrium of the Bertrand game, the two firms set price equal to marginal cost. Hence market price is $P^* = c$, total output is $Q^* = a - c$, firm profit is $\pi_i^* = 0$, and total profit for all firms is $\Pi^* = 0$. For the Bertrand quantity to be positive we must have $a > c$, which we will assume throughout the problem.

Cournot model. The solution for the Nash equilibrium follows Example 8.6 quite closely. Profits for the two Cournot firms are

$$\pi_1 = P(Q)q_1 - cq_1 = (a - q_1 - q_2 - c)q_1,$$
$$\pi_2 = P(Q)q_2 - cq_2 = (a - q_1 - q_2 - c)q_2. \tag{15.7}$$

Using the first-order conditions to solve for the best-response functions, we obtain

$$q_1 = \frac{a - q_2 - c}{2}, \qquad q_2 = \frac{a - q_1 - c}{2}. \tag{15.8}$$

Solving Equations 15.8 simultaneously yields the Nash equilibrium

$$q_1^* = q_2^* = \frac{a - c}{3}. \tag{15.9}$$

Total output is thus $Q^* = (2/3)(a - c)$. Substituting total output into the inverse demand curve implies an equilibrium price of $P^* = (a + 2c)/3$. Substituting price and outputs into the profit functions (Equations 15.7) implies $\pi_1^* = \pi_2^* = (1/9)(a - c)^2$, so total market profit equals $\Pi^* = \pi_1^* + \pi_2^* = (2/9)(a - c)^2$.

Perfect cartel. The objective function for a perfect cartel involves joint profits

$$\pi_1 + \pi_2 = (a - q_1 - q_2 - c)q_1 + (a - q_1 - q_2 - c)q_2. \tag{15.10}$$

The two first-order conditions for maximizing Equation 15.10 with respect to q_1 and q_2 are the same:

$$\frac{\partial}{\partial q_1}(\pi_1 + \pi_2) = \frac{\partial}{\partial q_2}(\pi_1 + \pi_2) = a - 2q_1 - 2q_2 - c = 0. \tag{15.11}$$

The first-order conditions do not pin down market shares for firms in a perfect cartel because they produce identical products at constant marginal cost. But Equation 15.11 does pin down total output: $q_1^* + q_2^* = Q^* = (1/2)(a - c)$. Substituting total output into inverse demand implies that the cartel price is $P^* = (1/2)(a + c)$. Substituting price and quantities into Equation 15.10 implies a total cartel profit of $\Pi^* = (1/4)(a - c)^2$.

Comparison. Moving from the Bertrand model to the Cournot model to a perfect cartel, since $a > c$ we can show that quantity Q^* falls from $a - c$ to $(2/3)(a - c)$ to $(1/2)(a - c)$. It can also be shown that price P^* and industry profit Π^* rise. For example, if $a = 120$ and $c = 0$ (implying that inverse demand is $P(Q) = 120 - Q$ and that production is costless), then market quantity is 120 with Bertrand competition, 80 with Cournot competition, and 60 with a perfect cartel. Price rises from 0 to 40 to 60 across the cases and industry profit rises from 0 to 3,200 to 3,600.

QUERY: In a perfect cartel, do firms play a best response to each other's quantities? If not, in which direction would they like to change their outputs? What does this say about the stability of cartels?

EXAMPLE 15.2 Cournot Best-Response Diagrams

Continuing with the natural-spring duopoly from Example 15.1, it is instructive to solve for the Nash equilibrium using graphical methods. We will graph the best-response functions given in Equation 15.8; the intersection between the best responses is the Nash equilibrium. As background, you may want to review a similar diagram (Figure 8.4) for the Tragedy of the Commons.

The linear best-response functions are most easily graphed by plotting their intercepts, as shown in Figure 15.2. The best-response functions intersect at the point $q_1^* = q_2^* = (a - c)/3$, which was the Nash equilibrium of the Cournot game computed using algebraic methods in Example 15.1.

FIGURE 15.2   Best-Response Diagram for Cournot Duopoly

Firms' best responses are drawn as thick lines; their intersection (E) is the Nash equilibrium of the Cournot game. Isoprofit curves for firm 1 increase until point M is reached, which is the monopoly outcome for firm 1.

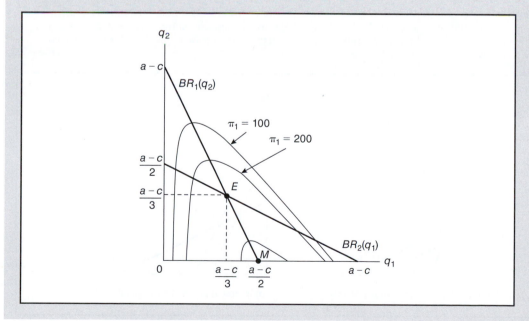

(continued)

EXAMPLE 15.2 CONTINUED

Figure 15.2 displays firms' isoprofit curves. An *isoprofit curve* for firm 1 is the locus of quantity pairs providing it with the same profit level. To compute the isoprofit curve associated with a profit level of (say) 100, we start by setting Equation 15.7 equal to 100:

$$\pi_1 = (a - q_1 - q_2 - c)q_1 = 100. \tag{15.12}$$

Then we solve for q_2 to facilitate graphing the isoprofit:

$$q_2 = a - c - q_1 - \frac{100}{q_1}. \tag{15.13}$$

Several example isoprofits for firm 1 are shown in the figure. As profit increases from 100 to 200 to yet higher levels, the associated isoprofits shrink down to the monopoly point, which is the highest isoprofit on the diagram. To understand why the individual isoprofits are shaped like frowns, refer back to Equation 15.13. As q_1 approaches 0, the last term $(-K/q_1)$ dominates, causing the left side of the frown to turn down. As q_1 increases, the $-q_1$ term in Equation 15.13 begins to dominate, causing the right side of the frown to turn down.

Figure 15.3 shows how to use best-response diagrams to quickly tell how changes in such underlying parameters as the demand intercept a or marginal cost c would affect the equilibrium. Panel (a) depicts an increase in both firms' marginal cost c. The best responses shift inward, resulting in a new equilibrium that involves lower output for both. Although firms have the same marginal cost in this example, one can imagine a model in which firms have different marginal cost parameters and so can be varied independently. Panel (b) depicts an increase in just firm 1's marginal cost; only firm 1's best response shifts. The new equilibrium involves lower output for firm 1 and higher output for firm 2. Though firm 2's best response does not shift, it still increases its output as it anticipates a reduction in firm 1's output and best-responds to this anticipated output reduction.

FIGURE 15.3 Shifting Cournot Best Responses

Firms' initial best responses are drawn as solid lines, resulting in a Nash equilibrium at point E'. Panel (a) depicts an increase in both firms' marginal costs, shifting their best responses—now given by the dashed lines—inward. The new intersection point, and thus the new equilibrium, is point E''. Panel (b) depicts an increase in just firm 1's marginal cost.

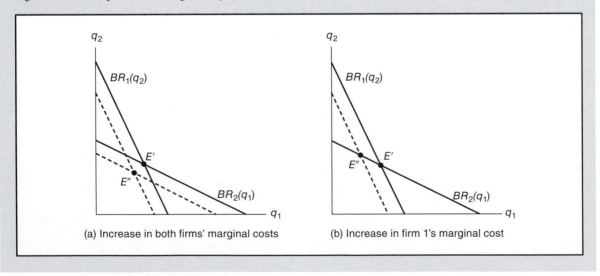

(a) Increase in both firms' marginal costs

(b) Increase in firm 1's marginal cost

QUERY: Explain why firm 1's individual isoprofits reach a peak on its best-response function in Figure 15.2. What would firm 2's isoprofits look like in Figure 15.2? How would you represent an increase in demand intercept a in Figure 15.3?

Varying the number of Cournot firms

The Cournot model is particularly useful for policy analysis because it can represent the whole range of outcomes from perfect competition to perfect cartel/monopoly (i.e., the whole range of points between C and M in Figure 15.1) by varying the number of firms n from $n = \infty$ to $n = 1$. For simplicity, consider the case of identical firms, which here means the n firms sharing the same cost function $C(q_i)$. In equilibrium, firms will produce the same share of total output: $q_i = Q/n$. Substituting $q_i = Q/n$ into Equation 15.2, the wedge term becomes $P'(Q)Q/n$. The wedge term disappears as n grows large; firms become infinitesimally small. An infinitesimally small firm effectively becomes a price taker because it produces so little that any fall in market price from an increase in output hardly affects its revenue. Price approaches marginal cost and the market outcome approaches the perfectly competitive one. As n falls to 1, the wedge term approaches that in Equation 15.5, implying the Cournot outcome approaches that of a perfect cartel. As the Cournot firm's market share grows, it internalizes the revenue loss from a fall in market price to a greater extent.

EXAMPLE 15.3 Natural-Spring Oligopoly

Return to the natural springs in Example 15.1, but now consider a variable number n of firms rather than just two. The profit of one of them, firm i, is

$$\pi_i = P(Q)q_i - cq_i = (a - Q - c)q_i = (a - q_i - Q_{-i} - c)q_i. \qquad \textbf{(15.14)}$$

It is convenient to express total output as $Q = q_i + Q_{-i}$, where $Q_{-i} = Q - q_i$ is the output of all firms except for i. Taking the first-order condition of Equation 15.20 with respect to q_i, we recognize that firm i takes Q_{-i} as a given and so treats it as a constant in the differentiation,

$$\frac{\partial \pi_i}{\partial q_i} = a - 2q_i - Q_{-i} - c = 0, \qquad \textbf{(15.15)}$$

which holds for all $i = 1, 2, \ldots, n$.

The key to solving the system of n equations for the n equilibrium quantities is to recognize that the Nash equilibrium involves equal quantities because firms are symmetric. Symmetry implies that

$$Q^*_{-i} = Q^* - q^*_i = nq^*_i - q^*_i = (n - 1)q^*_i. \qquad \textbf{(15.16)}$$

Substituting Equation 15.16 into 15.15 yields

$$a - 2q^*_i - (n - 1)q^*_i - c = 0, \qquad \textbf{(15.17)}$$

or $q^*_i = (a - c)/(n + 1)$.

Total market output is

$$Q^* = nq^*_i = \left(\frac{n}{n + 1}\right)(a - c), \qquad \textbf{(15.18)}$$

(continued)

EXAMPLE 15.3   CONTINUED

and market price is

$$P^* = a - Q^* = \left(\frac{1}{n+1}\right)a + \left(\frac{n}{n+1}\right)c. \tag{15.19}$$

Substituting for q_i^*, Q^*, and P^* into the firm's profit Equation 15.14, we have that total profit for all firms is

$$\Pi^* = n\pi_i^* = n\left(\frac{a-c}{n+1}\right)^2. \tag{15.20}$$

Setting $n = 1$ in Equations 15.18–15.20 gives the monopoly outcome, which gives the same price, total output, and profit as in the perfect cartel case computed in Example 15.1. Letting n grow without bound in Equations 15.18–15.20 gives the perfectly competitive outcome, the same outcome computed in Example 15.1 for the Bertrand case.

QUERY: We used the trick of imposing symmetry after taking the first-order condition for firm i's quantity choice. It might seem simpler to impose symmetry *before* taking the first-order condition. Why would this be a mistake? How would the incorrect expressions for quantity, price, and profit compare to the correct ones here?

Prices or quantities?

Moving from price competition in the Bertrand model to quantity competition in the Cournot model changes the market outcome dramatically. This change is surprising on first thought. After all, the monopoly outcome from Chapter 14 is the same whether we assume the monopolist sets price or quantity. Further thought suggests why price and quantity are such different strategic variables. Starting from equal prices, a small reduction in one firm's price allows it to steal all of market demand from its competitors. This sharp benefit from undercutting makes price competition extremely "tough." Quantity competition is "softer." Starting from equal quantities, a small increase in one firm's quantity has only a marginal effect on the revenue that other firms receive from their existing output. Firms have less of an incentive to outproduce each other with quantity competition than to undercut each other with price competition.

An advantage of the Cournot model is its realistic implication that the industry grows more competitive as the number n of firms entering the market increases from monopoly to perfect competition. In the Bertrand model there is a discontinuous jump from monopoly to perfect competition if just two firms enter, and additional entry beyond two has no additional effect on the market outcome.

An apparent disadvantage of the Cournot model is that firms in real-world markets tend to set prices rather than quantities, contrary to the Cournot assumption that firms choose quantities. For example, grocers advertise prices for orange juice, say $2.50 a container, in newpaper circulars rather than the number of containers it stocks. As we will see in the next section, the Cournot model applies even to the orange juice market if we reinterpret quantity to be the firm's *capacity*, defined as the most the firm can sell given the capital it has in place and other available inputs in the short run.

CAPACITY CONSTRAINTS

For the Bertrand model to generate the Bertrand paradox (the result that two firms essentially behave as perfect competitors), firms must have unlimited capacities. Starting from equal prices, if a firm lowers its price the slightest amount then its demand essentially doubles. The firm can satisfy this increased demand because it has no capacity constraints, giving firms a big incentive to undercut. If the undercutting firm could not serve all the demand at its lower price because of capacity constraints, that would leave some residual demand for the higher-priced firm and would decrease the incentive to undercut.

More realistically, firms may not have an unlimited ability to meet all demand. Consider a two-stage game in which firms build capacity in the first stage and firms choose prices p_1 and p_2 in the second stage.[4] Firms cannot sell more in the second stage than the capacity built in the first stage. If the cost of building capacity is sufficiently high, it turns out that the subgame-perfect equilibrium of this sequential game leads to the same outcome as the Nash equilibrium of the Cournot model.

To see this result, we will analyze the game using backward induction. Consider the second-stage pricing game supposing the firms have already built capacities $\overline{q}_1$ and $\overline{q}_2$ in the first stage. Let $\overline{p}$ be the price that would prevail when production is at capacity for both firms. A situation in which

$$p_1 = p_2 < \overline{p} \tag{15.21}$$

is not a Nash equilibrium. At this price, total quantity demanded exceeds total capacity, so firm 1 could increase its profits by raising price slightly and continuing to sell $\overline{q}_1$. Similarly,

$$p_1 = p_2 > \overline{p} \tag{15.22}$$

is not a Nash equilibrium because now total sales fall short of capacity. At least one firm (say, firm 1) is selling less than its capacity. By cutting price slightly, firm 1 can increase its profits by selling up to its capacity, $\overline{q}_1$. Hence, the Nash equilibrium of this second-stage game is for firms to choose the price at which quantity demanded exactly equals the total capacity built in the first stage:[5]

$$p_1 = p_2 = \overline{p}. \tag{15.23}$$

Anticipating that the price will be set such that firms sell all their capacity, the first-stage capacity choice game is essentially the same as the Cournot game. The equilibrium quantities, price, and profits will thus be the same as in the Cournot game. Thus, even in markets (such as orange juice sold in grocery stores) where it looks like firms are setting prices, the Cournot model may prove more realistic than it first seems.

PRODUCT DIFFERENTIATION

Another way to avoid the Bertrand paradox is to replace the assumption that the firms' products are identical with the assumption that firms produce differentiated products. Many (if not most) real-world markets exhibit product differentiation. For example, toothpaste brands vary somewhat from supplier to supplier—differing in flavor, fluoride content, whitening agents, endorsement from the American Dental Association, and so forth. Even if

---

[4]The model is due to D. Kreps and J. Scheinkman, "Quantity Precommitment and Bertrand Competition Yield Cournot Outcomes," *Bell Journal of Economics* (Autumn 1983): 326–37.

[5]For completeness, it should be noted that there is no pure-strategy Nash equilibrium of the second-stage game with unequal prices ($p_1 \neq p_2$). The low-price firm would have an incentive to raise its price and/or the high-price firm would have an incentive to lower its price. For large capacities, there may be a complicated mixed-strategy Nash equilibrium, but this can be ruled out by supposing the cost of building capacity is sufficiently high.

suppliers' product attributes are similar, suppliers may still be differentiated in another dimension: physical location. Because demanders will be closer to some suppliers than to others, they may prefer nearby sellers because buying from them involves less travel time.

Meaning of "the market"

The possibility of product differentiation introduces some fuzziness into what we mean by the market for a good. With identical products, demanders were assumed to be indifferent about which firm's output they bought; hence they shop at the lowest-price firm, leading to the law of one price. The law of one price no longer holds if demanders strictly prefer one supplier to another at equal prices. Are green-gel and white-paste toothpastes in the same market or in two different ones? Is a pizza parlor at the outskirts of town in the same market as one in the middle of town?

With differentiated products, we will take *the market* to be a group of closely related products that are more substitutable among each other (as measured by cross-price elasticities) than with goods outside the group. We will be somewhat loose with this definition, avoiding precise thresholds for how high the cross-price elasticity must be between goods within the group (and how low with outside goods). Arguments about which goods should be included in a product group often dominate antitrust proceedings, and we will try to avoid this contention here.

Bertrand competition with differentiated products

Return to the Bertrand model but now suppose there are n firms that simultaneously choose prices p_i $(i = 1, \ldots, n)$ for their differentiated products. Product i has its own specific attributes a_i, possibly reflecting special options, quality, brand advertising, or location. A product may be endowed with the attribute (orange juice is by definition made from oranges and cranberry juice from cranberries) or the attribute may be the result of the firm's choice and spending level (the orange juice supplier can spend more and make its juice from fresh oranges rather than from frozen concentrate). The various attributes serve to differentiate the products. Firm i's demand is

$$q_i(p_i, P_{-i}, a_i, A_{-i}), \tag{15.24}$$

where P_{-i} is a list of all other firms' prices besides i's and A_{-i} is a list of all other firms' attributes besides i's. Firm i's total cost is

$$C_i(q_i, a_i) \tag{15.25}$$

and profit is thus

$$\pi_i = p_i q_i - C_i(q_i, a_i). \tag{15.26}$$

With differentiated products, the profit function (Equation 15.26) is differentiable, so we do not need to solve for the Nash equilibrium on a case-by-case basis as we did in the Bertrand model with identical products. We can solve for the Nash equilibrium as in the Cournot model, solving for best-response functions by taking each firm's first-order condition (here with respect to price rather than quantity). The first-order condition from Equation 15.26 with respect to p_i is

$$\frac{\partial \pi_i}{\partial p_i} = \underbrace{q_i + p_i \frac{\partial q_i}{\partial p_i}}_{A} - \underbrace{\frac{\partial C_i}{\partial q_i} \cdot \frac{\partial q_i}{\partial p_i}}_{B} = 0. \tag{15.27}$$

The first two terms (labeled A) on the right-hand side of Equation 15.27 are a sort of marginal revenue—not the usual marginal revenue from an increase in quantity, but rather the marginal revenue from an increase in price. The increase in price increases revenue on existing sales of q_i units, but we must also consider the negative effect of the reduction in sales ($\partial q_i / \partial p_i$ multiplied by the price p_i) that would have been earned on these sales. The last term, labeled B, is the cost savings associated with the reduced sales that accompany an increased price.

The Nash equilibrium can be found by simultaneously solving the system of first-order conditions in Equation 15.27 for all $i = 1, \ldots, n$. If the attributes a_i are also choice variables (rather than just endowments), there will be another set of first-order conditions to consider. For firm i, the first-order condition with respect to a_i has the form

$$\frac{\partial \pi_i}{\partial a_i} = p_i \frac{\partial q_i}{\partial a_i} - \frac{\partial C_i}{\partial a_i} - \frac{\partial C_i}{\partial q_i} \cdot \frac{\partial q_i}{\partial a_i} = 0. \tag{15.28}$$

The simultaneous solution of these first-order conditions can be quite complex, and they yield few definitive conclusions about the nature of market equilibrium. Some insights from particular cases will be developed in the next two examples.

EXAMPLE 15.4 Toothpaste as a Differentiated Product

Suppose two firms produce toothpaste, one a green gel and the other a white paste. Suppose for simplicity that production is costless. Demand for product i is

$$q_i = a_i - p_i + \frac{p_j}{2}. \tag{15.29}$$

The positive coefficient on p_j, the other good's price, indicates that the goods are gross substitutes. Firm i's demand is increasing in the attribute a_i, which we will take to be demanders' inherent preference for the variety in question; we will suppose that this is an endowment rather than a choice variable for the firm (and so will abstract from the role of advertising to promote preferences for a variety).

Algebraic solution. Firm i's profit is

$$\pi_i = p_i q_i - C_i(q_i) = p_i \left(a_i - p_i + \frac{p_j}{2} \right), \tag{15.30}$$

where $C_i(q_i) = 0$ because i's production is costless. The first-order condition for profit maximization with respect to p_i is

$$\frac{\partial \pi_i}{\partial p_i} = a_i - 2p_i + \frac{p_j}{2} = 0. \tag{15.31}$$

Solving for p_i gives the following best-response functions for $i = 1, 2$:

$$p_1 = \frac{1}{2} \left(a_1 + \frac{p_2}{2} \right), \qquad p_2 = \frac{1}{2} \left(a_2 + \frac{p_1}{2} \right). \tag{15.32}$$

Solving Equations 15.32 simultaneously gives the Nash equilibrium prices

$$p_i^* = \frac{8}{15} a_i + \frac{2}{15} a_j. \tag{15.33}$$

The associated profits are

$$\pi_i^* = \left(\frac{8}{15} a_i + \frac{2}{15} a_j \right)^2. \tag{15.34}$$

(*continued*)

EXAMPLE 15.4 CONTINUED

FIGURE 15.4 Best Responses for Bertrand Model with Differentiated Products

Firm' best responses drawn as thick lines; their intersection (E) is the Nash equilibrium. Isoprofit curves for firm 1 increase moving out along firm 1's best-response function.

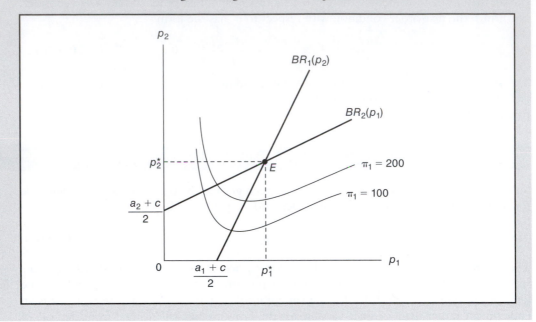

Firm i's equilibrium price is not only increasing in its own attribute, a_i, but also in the other product's attribute, a_j. An increase in a_j causes firm j to increase its price, which increases firm i's demand and thus the price i charges.

Graphical solution. We could also have solved for equilibrium prices graphically, as in Figure 15.4. The best responses in Equation 15.32 are upward sloping. They intersect at the Nash equilibrium, point E. The isoprofit curves for firm 1 are smile-shaped. To see this, take the expression for firm 1's profit in Equation 15.30, set it equal to a certain profit level (say, 100), and solve for p_2 to facilitate graphing it on the best-response diagram. We have

$$p_2 = \frac{100}{p_1} + p_1 - a_1. \qquad \textbf{(15.35)}$$

The smile turns up as p_1 approaches 0 because the denominator of $100/p_1$ approaches 0. The smile turns up as p_1 grows large because then the second term on the right-hand side of Equation 15.35 grows large. Isoprofit curves for firm 1 increase as one moves away from the origin along its best-response function.

QUERY: How would a change in the demand intercepts be represented on the diagram?

EXAMPLE 15.5 Hotelling's Beach

A simple model in which identical products are differentiated because of the location of their suppliers (spatial differentiation) was provided by H. Hotelling in the 1920s.[6] As shown in Figure 15.5, two ice cream stands, labeled A and B, are located along a beach of length L. The stands make identical ice cream cones, which for simplicity are assumed to be costless to produce. Let a and b represent the firms' locations on the beach. (We will take the locations of the ice cream stands as given; in a later example we will revisit firms' equilibrium location choices.) Assume that demanders are located uniformly along the beach, one at each unit of length. Carrying ice cream a distance d back to one's beach umbrella costs td^2, since ice cream melts more the higher the temperature t and the further one must walk.[7] Consistent with the Bertrand assumption, firms choose prices p_A and p_B simultaneously.

FIGURE 15.5   Hotelling's Beach

Ice cream stands A and B are located at points a and b along a beach of length L. The consumer who is indifferent between buying from the two stands is located at x. Consumers to the left of x buy from A and to the right buy from B.

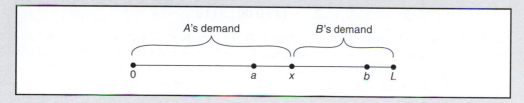

Determining demands. Let x be the location of the consumer who is indifferent between buying from the two ice cream stands. The following condition must be satisfied by x:

$$p_A + t(x - a)^2 = p_B + t(b - x)^2. \tag{15.36}$$

The left-hand side of Equation 15.36 is the generalized cost of buying from A (including the price paid and the cost of transporting the ice cream the distance $x - a$). Similarly, the right-hand side is the generalized cost of buying from B. Solving Equation 15.36 for x yields

$$x = \frac{b + a}{2} + \frac{p_B - p_A}{2t(b - a)}. \tag{15.37}$$

If prices are equal, the indifferent consumer is located midway between a and b. If A's price is less than B's, then x shifts toward A. (This is the case shown in Figure 15.5.)

Since all demanders between 0 and x buy from A and since there is one consumer per unit distance, it follows that A's demand equals x:

$$q_A(p_A, p_B, a, b) = x = \frac{b + a}{2} + \frac{p_B - p_A}{2t(b - a)}. \tag{15.38}$$

The remaining $L - x$ consumers constitute B's demand:

$$q_B(p_B, p_A, b, a) = L - x = L - \frac{b + a}{2} + \frac{p_A - p_B}{2t(b - a)}. \tag{15.39}$$

(*continued*)

---

[6]H. Hotelling, "Stability in Competition," *Economic Journal* 39 (1929): 41–57.

[7]The assumption of quadratic "transportation costs" turns out to simplify later work, when we compute firms' equilibrium locations in the model.

EXAMPLE 15.5 CONTINUED

Solving for Nash equilibrium. The Nash equilibrium is found in the same way as in Example 15.4 except that, for demands, we use Equations 15.38 and 15.39 in place of Equation 15.29. Skipping the details of the calculations, the Nash equilibrium prices are

$$p_A^* = \frac{t}{3}(b - a)(2L + a + b),$$
$$p_B^* = \frac{t}{3}(b - a)(4L - a - b). \tag{15.40}$$

These prices will depend on the precise location of the two stands and will differ from each other. For example, if we assume that the beach is $L = 100$ yards long, $a = 40$ yards, $b = 70$ yards, and $t = \$0.001$ (one tenth of a penny), then $p_A^* = \$3.10$ and $p_B^* = \$2.90$. These price differences arise only from the locational aspects of this problem—the cones themselves are identical and costless to produce. Because A is somewhat more favorably located than B, it can charge a higher price for its cones without losing too much business to B. Using Equation 15.38 shows that

$$x = \frac{110}{2} + \frac{3.10 - 2.90}{(2)(0.001)(110)} \approx 52, \tag{15.41}$$

so stand A sells 52 cones whereas B sells only 48 despite its lower price. At point x, the consumer is indifferent between walking the 12 yards to A and paying \$3.10 or walking 18 yards to B and paying \$2.90. The equilibrium is inefficient in that a consumer slightly to the right of x would incur a shorter walk by patronizing A but still chooses B because of A's power to set higher prices.

Equilibrium profits are

$$\pi_A^* = \frac{t}{18}(b - a)(2L + a + b)^2,$$
$$\pi_B^* = \frac{t}{18}(b - a)(4L - a - b)^2. \tag{15.42}$$

Somewhat surprisingly, the ice cream stands benefit from faster melting, as measured here by the transportation cost t. For example, if we take $L = 100$, $a = 40$, $b = 70$, and $t = \$0.001$ as in the previous paragraph, then $\pi_A^* = \$160$ and $\pi_B^* = \$140$ (rounding to the nearest dollar). If transportation costs doubled to $t = \$0.002$, then profits would double to $\pi_A^* = \$320$ and $\pi_B^* = \$280$.

The transportation/melting cost is the only source of differentiation in the model. If $t = 0$, then we can see from Equation 15.40 that prices equal 0 (which is marginal cost given that production is costless) and from Equation 15.42 that profits equal 0—in other words, the Bertrand paradox results.

QUERY: What happens to prices and profits if ice cream stands locate in the same spot? If they locate at the opposite ends of the beach?

Consumer search and price dispersion

Hotelling's model analyzed in Example 15.5 suggests the possibility that competitors may have some ability to charge prices above marginal cost and earn positive profits even if the physical characteristics of the goods they sell are identical. Firms' various locations—closer to some demanders and farther from others—may lead to spatial differentiation. The Internet makes the physical location of stores less relevant to consumers, especially if shipping charges are independent of distance (or are not assessed). Even in this setting, firms can avoid the Bertrand paradox if we drop the assumption that demanders know every firm's price in the market. Instead we will assume that demanders face a small cost s, called a *search cost*, to visit the store (or click to its website) to find its price.

In P. Diamond's search model, demanders search by picking one of the n stores at random and learning its price.[8] Demanders know the equilibrium distribution of prices but not which store is charging which price. Demanders get their first price search for free but then must pay s for additional searches. They need at most one unit of the good, and they all have the same gross surplus v for the one unit.

Not only do stores manage to avoid the Bertrand paradox in this model, they obtain the polar opposite outcome: all charge the monopoly price v, which extracts all consumer surplus! This outcome holds no matter how small the search cost s is—as long as s is positive (say, a penny). It is easy to see that all stores charging v is an equilibrium. If all charge the same price v then demanders may as well buy from the first store they search, since additional searches are costly and do not end up revealing a lower price. It can also be seen that this is the only equilibrium. Consider any outcome in which at least one store charges less than v, and consider the lowest-price store (label it i) in this outcome. Store i could raise its price p_i by as much as s and still make all the sales it did before. The lowest price a demander could expect to pay elsewhere is no less than p_i, and the demander would have to pay the cost s to find this other price.

Less extreme equilibria are found in models where consumers have different search costs.[9] For example, suppose one group of consumers can search for free and another group has to pay s per search. In equilibrium, there will be some price dispersion across stores. One set of stores serves the low–search-cost demanders (and the lucky high–search-cost consumers who happen to stumble upon a bargain). These bargain stores sell at marginal cost. The other stores serve the high–search-cost demanders at a price that makes these demanders indifferent between buying immediately and taking a chance that the next price search will uncover a bargain store.

TACIT COLLUSION

In Chapter 8, we showed that players may be able to earn higher payoffs in the subgame-perfect equilibrium of an infinitely repeated game than from simply repeating the Nash equilibrium from the single-period game indefinitely. For example, we saw that, if players are patient enough, they can cooperate on playing silent in the infinitely repeated version of the Prisoners' Dilemma rather than finking on each other each period. From the perspective of oligopoly theory, the issue is whether firms must endure the Bertrand paradox (marginal cost pricing and zero profits) in each period of a repeated game or whether they might instead achieve more profitable outcomes through tacit collusion.

A distinction should be drawn between tacit collusion and the formation of an explicit cartel. An explicit cartel involves legal agreements enforced with external sanctions if the agreements (for example, to sustain high prices or low outputs) are violated. Tacit collusion can only be enforced through punishments internal to the market—that is, only those that can be generated within a subgame-perfect equilibrium of a repeated game. Antitrust laws generally forbid the formation of explicit cartels, so tacit collusion is usually the only way for firms to raise prices above the static level.

---

[8]P. Diamond, "A Model of Price Adjustment," *Journal of Economic Theory* 3 (1971): 156–68.

[9]The following model is due to S. Salop and J. Stiglitz, "Bargains and Ripoffs: A Model of Monopolistically Competitive Price Dispersion," *Review of Economic Studies* 44 (1977): 493–510.

Finitely repeated game

Taking the Bertrand game to be the stage game, Selten's theorem from Chapter 8 tells us that repeating the stage game any finite number of times T does not change the outcome. The only subgame-perfect equilibrium of the finitely repeated Bertrand game is to repeat the stage-game Nash equilibrium—marginal cost pricing—in each of the T periods. The game unravels through backward induction. In any subgame starting in period T, the unique Nash equilibrium will be played regardless of what happened before. Since the outcome in period $T - 1$ does not affect the outcome in the next period, it is as if period $T - 1$ is the last period, and the unique Nash equilibrium must be played then, too. Applying backward induction, the game unravels in this manner all the way back to the first period.

Infinitely repeated game

If the stage game is repeated infinitely many periods, however, the folk theorem applies. The folk theorem indicates that any feasible and individually rational payoff can be sustained each period in an infinitely repeated game as long as the discount factor, δ, is close enough to unity. Recall that the discount factor is the value in the present period of one dollar earned one period in the future—a measure, roughly speaking, of how patient players are. Since the monopoly outcome (with profits divided among the firms) is a feasible and individually rational outcome, the folk theorem implies that the monopoly outcome must be sustainable in a subgame-perfect equilibrium for δ close enough to 1. Let us investigate the threshold value of δ needed.

First suppose there are two firms competing in a Bertrand game each period. Let Π_M denote the monopoly profit and P_M the monopoly price in the stage game. The firms may collude tacitly to sustain the monopoly price—with each firm earning an equal share of the monopoly profit—by using the grim trigger strategy of continuing to collude as long as no firm has undercut P_M in the past but reverting to the stage-game Nash equilibrium of marginal cost pricing every period from then on if any firm deviates by undercutting. Successful tacit collusion provides the profit stream

$$
\begin{aligned}
V^{\text{collude}} &= \frac{\Pi_M}{2} + \delta \cdot \frac{\Pi_M}{2} + \delta^2 \cdot \frac{\Pi_M}{2} + \cdots \\
&= \frac{\Pi_M}{2}(1 + \delta + \delta^2 + \cdots) \\
&= \left(\frac{\Pi_M}{2}\right)\left(\frac{1}{1 - \delta}\right).
\end{aligned} \tag{15.43}
$$

Refer to Chapter 8 for a discussion of adding up a series of discount factors $1 + \delta + \delta^2 + \cdots$. We need to check that a firm has no incentive to deviate. By undercutting the collusive price P_M slightly, a firm can obtain essentially all of the monopoly profit for itself in the current period. This deviation would trigger the grim strategy punishment of marginal cost pricing in the second and all future periods, so all firms would earn zero profit from there on. Hence, the stream of profits from deviating is $V^{\text{deviate}} = \Pi_M$.

For this deviation not to be profitable we must have $V^{\text{collude}} \geq V^{\text{deviate}}$ or, upon substituting,

$$
\left(\frac{\Pi_M}{2}\right)\left(\frac{1}{1 - \delta}\right) \geq \Pi_M. \tag{15.44}
$$

Rearranging Equation 15.44, the condition reduces to $\delta \geq 1/2$. To prevent deviation, firms must value the future enough that the threat of losing profits by reverting to the one-period Nash equilibrium outweighs the benefit of undercutting and taking the whole monopoly profit in the present period.

EXAMPLE 15.6 Tacit Collusion in a Bertrand Model

Bertrand duopoly. Suppose only two firms produce a certain medical device used in surgery. The medical device is produced at constant average and marginal cost of $10, and the demand for the device is given by

$$Q = 5{,}000 - 100P. \tag{15.45}$$

If the Bertrand game is played in a single period, then each firm will charge $10 and a total of 4,000 devices will be sold. Because the monopoly price in this market is $30, firms have a clear incentive to consider collusive strategies. At the monopoly price, total profits each period are $40,000 and each firm's share of total profits is $20,000. According to Equation 15.44, collusion at the monopoly price is sustainable if

$$20{,}000\left(\frac{1}{1-\delta}\right) \geq 40{,}000 \tag{15.46}$$

or if $\delta \geq 1/2$, as we saw.

Is the condition $\delta \geq 1/2$ likely to be met in this market? That depends on what factors we consider in computing δ, including the interest rate and possible uncertainty about whether the game will continue. Leave aside uncertainty for a moment and consider only the interest rate. If the period length is one year, then it might be reasonable to assume an annual interest rate of $r = 10\%$. As shown in the Appendix to Chapter 17, $\delta = 1/(1 + r)$, so if $r = 10\%$ then $\delta = 0.91$. This value of δ clearly exceeds the threshold of $1/2$ needed to sustain collusion. For δ to be less than the $1/2$ threshold for collusion, we must incorporate uncertainty into the discount factor. There must be a significant chance that the market will not continue into the next period—perhaps because a new surgical procedure is developed that renders the medical device obsolete.

We focused on the best possible collusive outcome: the monopoly price of $30. Would collusion be easier to sustain at a lower price, say $20? No. At a price of $20, total profits each period are $30,000 and each firm's share is $15,000. Substituting into Equation 15.44, collusion can be sustained if

$$15{,}000\left(\frac{1}{1-\delta}\right) \geq 30{,}000, \tag{15.47}$$

again implying $\delta \geq 1/2$. Whatever collusive profit the firms try to sustain will cancel out from both sides of Equation 15.44, leaving the condition $\delta \geq 1/2$. We therefore get a discrete jump in firms' ability to collude as they become more patient—that is, as δ increases from 0 to 1.[10] For δ below $1/2$, no collusion is possible. For δ above $1/2$, any price between marginal cost and the monopoly price can be sustained as a collusive outcome. In the face of this multiplicity of subgame-perfect equilibria, economists often focus on the one that is most profitable for the firms, but the formal theory as to why firms would play one or another of the equilibria is still unsettled.

Bertrand oligopoly. Now suppose n firms produce the medical device. The monopoly profit continues to be $40,000, but each firm's share is now only $40{,}000/n$. By undercutting the monopoly price slightly, a firm can still obtain the whole monopoly profit for itself regardless of how many other firms there are. Replacing the collusive profit of $20,000 in

(continued)

---

[10]The discrete jump in firms' ability to collude is a feature of the Bertrand model; the ability to collude increases continuously with δ in the Cournot model of Example 15.7.

EXAMPLE 15.6 CONTINUED

Equation 15.46 with $\$40,000/n$, we have that the n firms can successfully collude on the monopoly price if

$$\frac{40,000}{n}\left(\frac{1}{1-\delta}\right) \geq 40,000, \qquad (15.48)$$

or

$$\delta \geq 1 - \frac{1}{n}. \qquad (15.49)$$

Taking the "reasonable" discount factor of $\delta = 0.91$ used previously, collusion is possible when 11 or fewer firms are in the market and impossible with 12 or more. With 12 or more firms, the only subgame-perfect equilibrium involves marginal cost pricing and zero profits.

Equation 15.49 shows that tacit collusion is easier the more patient are firms (as we saw before) and the fewer of them there are. One rationale used by antitrust authorities to challenge certain mergers is that a merger may reduce n to a level such that Equation 15.49 begins to be satisfied and collusion becomes possible, resulting in higher prices and lower total welfare.

QUERY: A period can be interpreted as the length of time it takes for firms to recognize and respond to undercutting by a rival. What would be the relevant period for competing gasoline stations in a small town? In what industries would a year be a reasonable period?

EXAMPLE 15.7 Tacit Collusion in a Cournot Model

Suppose that there are again two firms producing medical devices but that each period they now engage in quantity (Cournot) rather than price (Bertrand) competition. We will again investigate the conditions under which firms can collude on the monopoly outcome. To generate the monopoly outcome in a period, firms need to produce 1,000 each; this leads to a price of $30, total profits of $40,000, and firm profits of $20,000. The present discounted value of the stream of these collusive profits is

$$V^{\text{collude}} = 20,000\left(\frac{1}{1-\delta}\right). \qquad (15.50)$$

Computing the present discounted value of the stream of profits from deviating is somewhat complicated. The optimal deviation is not as simple as producing the whole monopoly output oneself and having the other firm produce nothing. The other firm's 1,000 units would be provided to the market. The optimal deviation (by firm 1, say) would be to best-respond to firm 2's output of 1,000. To compute this best response, first note that if demand is given by Equation 15.45 then inverse demand is given by

$$P = 50 - \frac{Q}{100}. \qquad (15.51)$$

Firm 1's profit is

$$\pi_1 = Pq_1 - cq_1 = q_1\left(40 - \frac{q_1 + q_2}{100}\right). \qquad (15.52)$$

Taking the first-order condition with respect to q_1 and solving for q_1 yields the best-response function

$$q_1 = 2,000 - \frac{q_2}{2}. \qquad (15.53)$$

Firm 1's optimal deviation when firm 2 produces 1,000 units is to increase its output from 1,000 to 1,500. Substituting these quantities into Equation 15.52 implies that firm 1 earns $22,500 in the period in which it deviates.

How much firm 1 earns in the second and later periods following a deviation depends on the trigger strategies firms use to punish deviation. Assume that firms use the grim strategy of reverting to the Nash equilibrium of the stage game—in this case, the Nash equilibrium of the Cournot game—every period from then on. In the Nash equilibrium of the Cournot game, each firm best-responds to the other in accordance with the best-response function in Equation 15.53 (switching subscripts in the case of firm 2). Solving these best-response equations simultaneously implies that the Nash equilibrium outputs are $q_1^* = q_2^* = 4{,}000/3$ and that profits are $\pi_1^* = \pi_2^* = \$17{,}778$. Firm 1's present discounted value of the stream of profits from deviation is

$$V^{\text{deviate}} = 22{,}500 + 17{,}778\delta + 17{,}778\delta^2 + 17{,}778\delta^3 + \cdots$$

$$= 22{,}500 + (17{,}778 \cdot \delta)(1 + \delta + \delta^2 + \cdots)$$

$$= \$22{,}500 + \$17{,}778\left(\frac{\delta}{1-\delta}\right). \tag{15.54}$$

We have $V^{\text{collude}} \geq V^{\text{deviate}}$ if

$$\$20{,}000\left(\frac{1}{1-\delta}\right) \geq \$22{,}500 + \$17{,}778\left(\frac{\delta}{1-\delta}\right) \tag{15.55}$$

or, after some algebra, if $\delta \geq 0.53$.

Unlike with the Bertrand stage game, with the Cournot stage game there is a possibility of some collusion for discount factors below 0.53. However, the outcome would have to involve higher outputs and lower profits than monopoly.

QUERY: The benefit to deviating is lower with the Cournot stage game than with the Bertrand stage game because the Cournot firm cannot steal all the monopoly profit with a small deviation. Why then is a more stringent condition ($\delta \geq 0.53$ rather than $\delta \geq 0.5$) needed to collude on the monopoly outcome in the Cournot duopoly compared to the Bertrand duopoly?

LONGER-RUN DECISIONS: INVESTMENT, ENTRY, AND EXIT

The chapter has so far focused on the most basic short-run decisions regarding what price or quantity to set. The scope for strategic interaction expands when we introduce longer-run decisions. Take the case of the market for cars. Longer-run decisions include whether to update the basic design of the car, a process that might take up to two years to complete. Longer-run decisions may also include investing in robotics to lower production costs, moving manufacturing plants to locate closer to consumers and cheap inputs, engaging in a new advertising campaign, and entering or exiting certain product lines (say, ceasing the production of station wagons or starting production of hybrid cars). In making such decisions, an oligopolist must consider how rivals will respond to it. Will competition with existing rivals become tougher or milder? Will the decision lead to the exit of current rivals or encourage new ones to enter? Is it better to be the first to make such a decision or to wait until after rivals move?

Flexibility versus commitment

Crucial to our analysis of longer-run decisions such as investment, entry, and exit is how easy it is to reverse a decision once it has been made. On first thought, it might seem that it is better for a firm to be able to easily reverse decisions, since this would give the firm more flexibility in responding to changing circumstances. For instance, a car manufacturer might be more willing to invest in developing a hybrid-electric car if it could easily change the design back to a standard gasoline-powered one should the price of gasoline (and the demand for hybrid cars along with it) fall unexpectedly. Absent strategic considerations—and so for the case of a monopolist—a firm would always value flexibility and reversibility. The "option value" provided by flexibility is discussed in further detail in Chapter 7.

Surprisingly, the strategic considerations that arise in an oligopoly setting may lead a firm to prefer its decision be irreversible. What the firm loses in terms of flexibility may be offset by the value of being able to commit to the decision. We will see a number of instances of the value of commitment in the next several sections. If a firm can commit to an action before others move, the firm may gain a first-mover advantage. A firm may use its first-mover advantage to stake out a claim to a market by making a commitment to serve it and in the process limit the kinds of actions its rivals find profitable. Commitment is essential for a first-mover advantage. If the first mover could secretly reverse its decision, then its rival would anticipate the reversal and the firms would be back in the game with no first-mover advantage.

We already encountered a simple example of the value of commitment in the Battle of the Sexes game from Chapter 8. In the simultaneous version of the model, there were three Nash equilibria. In one pure-strategy equilibrium, the wife obtains her highest payoff by attending her favorite event with her husband, but she obtains lower payoffs in the other two equilibria (a pure-strategy equilibrium in which she attends her less favored event and a mixed-strategy equilibrium giving her the lowest payoff of all three). In the sequential version of the game, if a player were given the choice between being the first mover and having the ability to commit to attending an event or being the second mover and having the flexibility to be able to meet up with the first wherever he or she showed up, a player would always choose the ability to commit. The first mover can guarantee his or her preferred outcome as the unique subgame-perfect equilibrium by committing to attend his or her favorite event.

Sunk costs

Expenditures on irreversible investments are called *sunk costs*.

DEFINITION

> **Sunk cost.** A sunk cost is an expenditure on an investment that cannot be reversed and has no resale value.

Sunk costs include expenditures on unique types of equipment (for example, a newsprint-making machine) or job-specific training for workers (developing the skills to use the newsprint machine). There is sometimes confusion between sunk costs and what we have called *fixed costs*. They are similar in that they do not vary with the firm's output level in a production period and are incurred even if no output is produced in that period. But instead of being incurred periodically, as are many fixed costs (heat for the factory, salaries for secretaries and other administrators), sunk costs are incurred only once in connection with a single investment.[11] Some fixed costs may be avoided over a sufficiently long run—say, by

---

[11]Mathematically, the notion of sunk costs can be integrated into the per-period total cost function as

$$C_t(q_t) = S + F_t + cq_t,$$

where S is the per-period amortization of sunk costs (for example, the interest paid for funds used to finance capital investments), F_t is the per-period fixed costs, c is marginal cost, and q_t is per-period output. If $q_t = 0$ then $C_t = S + F_t$, but if the production period is long enough then some or all of F_t may also be avoidable. No portion of S is avoidable, however.

reselling the plant and equipment involved—but sunk costs can never be recovered because the investments involved cannot be moved to a different use. When the firm makes a sunk investment it has committed itself to that investment, and this may have important consequences for its strategic behavior.

First-mover advantage in the Stackelberg model

The simplest setting to illustrate the first-mover advantage is in the Stackelberg model, named after the economist who first analyzed it.[12] The model is similar to a duopoly version of the Cournot model except that—rather than simultaneously choosing the quantities of their identical outputs—firms move sequentially, with firm 1 (the leader) choosing its output first and then firm 2 (the follower) choosing after observing firm 1's output.

We use backward induction to solve for the subgame-perfect equilibrium of this sequential game. Begin with the follower's output choice. Firm 2 chooses the output q_2 that maximizes its own profit, taking firm 1's output q_1 as given. In other words, firm 2 best-responds to firm 1's output. This results in the same best-response function for firm 2 as we computed in the Cournot game from the first-order condition (Equation 15.2). Label this best-response function $BR_2(q_1)$.

Turn then to the leader's output choice. Firm 1 recognizes that it can influence the follower's action because the follower best-responds to 1's observed output. Substituting $BR_2(q_1)$ into the profit function for firm 1 given by Equation 15.1, we have

$$\pi_1 = P(q_1 + BR_2(q_1))q_1 - C_1(q_1). \tag{15.56}$$

The first-order condition with respect to q_1 is

$$\frac{\partial \pi_1}{\partial q_1} = P(Q) + P'(Q)q_1 + \underbrace{P'(Q)BR_2'(q_1)q_1}_{S} - C_i'(q_i) = 0. \tag{15.57}$$

This is the same first-order condition computed in the Cournot model (see Equation 15.2) except for the addition of the term S, which accounts for the strategic effect of firm 1's output on firm 2's. The strategic effect S will lead firm 1 to produce more than it would have in a Cournot model. By overproducing, firm 1 leads firm 2 to reduce q_2 by the amount $BR_2'(q_1)$; the fall in 2's output increases market price, thus increasing the revenue that 1 earns on its existing sales. We know that q_2 falls with an increase in q_1 because best-response functions under quantity competition are generally downward sloping; see Figure 15.2 for an illustration.

The strategic effect would be absent if the leader's output choice were unobservable to the follower or if the leader could reverse its output choice in secret. The leader must be able to commit to an observable output choice or else firms are back in the Cournot game. It is easy to see that the leader prefers the Stackelberg game to the Cournot game. The leader could always reproduce the outcome from the Cournot game by choosing its Cournot output in the Stackelberg game. The leader can do even better by producing more than its Cournot output, thereby taking advantage of the strategic effect S.

---

[12]H. von Stackelberg, *The Theory of the Market Economy*, trans. A. T. Peacock (New York: Oxford University Press, 1952).

EXAMPLE 15.8 Stackelberg Springs

Recall the two natural-spring owners from Example 15.1. Now, rather than having them choose outputs simultaneously as in the Cournot game, assume that they choose outputs sequentially as in the Stackelberg game, with firm 1 being the leader and firm 2 the follower.

Firm 2's output. We will solve for the subgame-perfect equilibrium using backward induction, starting with firm 2's output choice. We already found firm 2's best-response function in Equation 15.8, repeated here:

$$q_2 = \frac{a - q_1 - c}{2}. \tag{15.58}$$

Firm 1's output. Now fold the game back to solve for firm 1's output choice. Substituting 2's best response from Equation 15.58 into 1's profit function from Equation 15.56 yields

$$\pi_1 = \left[a - q_1 - \left(\frac{a - q_1 - c}{2} \right) - c \right] q_1 = \frac{1}{2} (a - q_1 - c) q_1. \tag{15.59}$$

Taking the first-order condition,

$$\frac{\partial \pi_1}{\partial q_1} = \frac{1}{2} (a - 2q_1 - c) = 0, \tag{15.60}$$

and solving gives $q_1^* = (a - c)/2$. Substituting q_1^* back into firm 2's best-response function gives $q_2^* = (a - c)/4$. Profits are $\pi_1^* = (1/8)(a - c)^2$ and $\pi_2^* = (1/16)(a - c)^2$.

To provide a numerical example, suppose $a = 120$ and $c = 0$. Then $q_1^* = 60$, $q_2^* = 30$, $\pi_1^* = \$1,800$, and $\pi_2^* = \$900$. Firm 1 produces twice as much and earns twice as much as firm 2. Recall from the simultaneous Cournot game in Example 15.1 that, for these numerical values, total market output was 80 and total industry profit was 3,200, implying that each of the two firms produced $80/2 = 40$ units and earned $\$3,200/2 = \$1,600$. Therefore, when firm 1 is the first mover in a sequential game, it produces $(60 - 40)/40 = 33.3\%$ more and earns $(1,800 - 1,600)/1,600 = 12.5\%$ more than in the simultaneous game.

Graphing the Stackelberg outcome. Figure 15.6 illustrates the Stackelberg equilibrium on a best-response function diagram. The leader realizes that the follower will always best-respond, so the resulting outcome will always be on the follower's best-response function. The leader effectively picks the point on the follower's best-response function that maximizes the leader's profit. The highest isoprofit (highest in terms of profit level, but recall from Figure 15.2 that higher profit levels are reached as one moves down toward the horizontal axis) is reached at the point S of tangency between firm 1's isoprofit and firm 2's best-response function. This is the Stackelberg equilibrium. Compared to the Cournot equilibrium at point C, the Stackelberg equilibrium involves higher output and profit for firm 1. Firm 1's profit is higher because, by committing to the high output level, firm 2 is forced to respond by reducing its output.

Commitment is required for the outcome to stray from firm 1's best-response function, as happens at point S. If firm 1 could secretly reduce q_1 (perhaps because q_1 is actually capacity that can be secretly reduced by reselling capital equipment for close to its purchase price to a manufacturer of another product that uses similar capital equipment), then it would move back to its best response, firm 2 would best-respond to this lower quantity, and so on, following the dotted arrows from S back to C.

FIGURE 15.6 Stackelberg Game

Best-response functions from the Cournot game are drawn as thick lines. Frown-shaped curves are firm 1's isoprofits. Point C is the Nash equilibrium of the Cournot game (involving simultaneous output choices). The Stackelberg equilibrium is point S, the point at which the highest isoprofit for firm 1 is reached on 2's best-response function. At S, 1's isoprofit is tangent to 2's best-response function. If firm 1 cannot commit to its output then the outcome unravels, following the dotted line from S back to C.

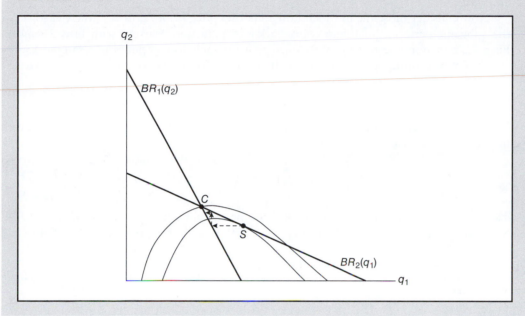

QUERY: What would be the outcome if the identity of the first mover were not given and instead firms had to compete to be the first? How would firms vie for this position? Do these considerations help explain overinvestment in Internet firms and telecommunications during the "dot-com bubble"?

Contrast with price leadership

In the Stackelberg game, the leader uses what has been called a "top dog" strategy,[13] aggressively overproducing to force the follower to scale back its production. The leader earns more than in the associated simultaneous game (Cournot), while the follower earns less. While it is generally true that the leader prefers the sequential game to the simultaneous game (the leader can do at least as well, and generally better, by playing its Nash equilibrium strategy from the simultaneous game), it is not generally true that the leader harms the follower by behaving as a "top dog." Sometimes the leader benefits by behaving as a "puppy dog," as illustrated in Example 15.9.

---

[13]"Top dog," "puppy dog," and other colorful labels for strategies are due to D. Fudenberg and J. Tirole, "The Fat Cat Effect, the Puppy Dog Ploy and the Lean and Hungry Look," *American Economic Review, Papers and Proceedings* 74 (1984): 361–68.

EXAMPLE 15.9 Price-Leadership Game

Return to Example 15.4, in which two firms chose price for differentiated toothpaste brands simultaneously. So that the following calculations do not become too tedious, we make the simplifying assumptions that $a_1 = a_2 = 1$ and $c = 0$. Substituting these parameters back into Example 15.4 shows that equilibrium prices are $2/3 \approx 0.667$ and profits are $4/9 \approx 0.444$ for each firm.

Now consider the game in which firm 1 chooses price before firm 2.[14] We will solve for the subgame-perfect equilibrium using backward induction, starting with firm 2's move. Firm 2's best response to its rival's choice p_1 is the same as computed in Example 15.4—which, upon substituting $a_2 = 1$ and $c = 0$ into Equation 15.32, is

$$p_2 = \frac{1}{2} + \frac{p_1}{4}. \tag{15.61}$$

Fold the game back to firm 1's move. Substituting firm 2's best response into firm 1's profit function from Equation 15.30 gives

$$\pi_1 = p_1 \left[1 - p_1 + \frac{1}{2} \left(\frac{1}{2} + \frac{p_1}{4} \right) \right] = \frac{p_1}{8} (10 - 7p_1). \tag{15.62}$$

Taking the first-order condition and solving for the equilibrium price, we obtain $p_1^* \approx 0.714$. Substituting into Equation 15.61 gives $p_2^* \approx 0.679$. Equilibrium profits are $\pi_1^* \approx 0.446$ and

---

[14]Sometimes this game is called the Stackelberg price game, although technically the original Stackelberg game involved quantity competition.

FIGURE 15.7 Price-Leadership Game

Thick lines are best-response functions from the game in which firms choose prices for differentiated products. U-shaped curves are firm 1's isoprofits. Point B is the Nash equilibrium of the simultaneous game, and L is the subgame-perfect equilibrium of the sequential game in which firm 1 moves first. At L, 1's isoprofit is tangent to 2's best response.

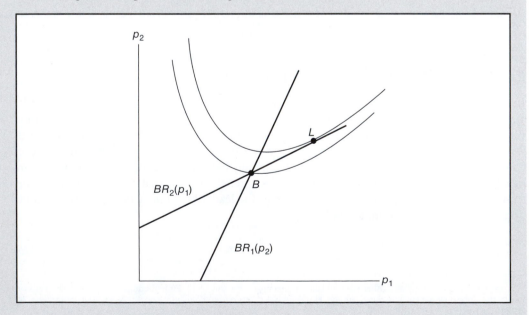

$\pi_2^* \approx 0.460$. Both firms' prices and profits are higher in this sequential game than in the simultaneous one, but now the follower earns even more than the leader.

As illustrated in the best-response function diagram in Figure 15.7, firm 1 commits to a high price in order to induce firm 2 to raise its price also, essentially "softening" the competition between them. The leader needs a moderate price increase (from 0.667 to 0.714) in order to induce the follower to raise its price slightly (from 0.667 to 0.679), so the leader's profits do not increase as much as the follower's.

QUERY: What choice variable realistically is easier to commit to, prices or quantities? What business strategies do firms use to increase their commitment to their list prices?

We say that the first mover is playing a "puppy dog" strategy in Example 15.9 because it increases its price relative to the simultaneous-move game; when translated into outputs, this means that the first mover ends up producing less than in the simultaneous-move game. It is as if the first mover strikes a less aggressive posture in the market and so leads its rival to compete less aggressively.

A comparison of Figures 15.6 and 15.7 suggests the crucial difference between the games that leads the first mover to play a "top dog" strategy in the quantity game and a "puppy dog" strategy in the price game: the best-response functions have different slopes. The goal is to induce the follower to compete less aggressively. The slopes of the best-response functions determine whether the leader can best do that by playing aggressively itself or by softening its strategy. The first mover plays a "top dog" strategy in the sequential quantity game or, indeed, any game in which best responses slope down. When best responses slope down, playing more aggressively induces a rival to respond by competing less aggressively. Conversely, the first mover plays a "puppy dog" strategy in the price game or any game in which best responses slope up. When best responses slope up, playing less aggressively induces a rival to respond by competing less aggressively.

Knowing the slope of firms' best responses therefore provides considerable insight into the sort of strategies firms will choose if they have commitment power. The Extensions at the end of this chapter provide further technical details, including shortcuts for determining the slope of a firm's best-response function just by looking at its profit function.

STRATEGIC ENTRY DETERRENCE

We saw that, by committing to an action, a first mover may be able to manipulate the second mover into being a less aggressive competitor. In this section we will see that the first mover may be able to prevent the entry of the second mover entirely, leaving the first mover as the sole firm in the market. In this case, the firm may not behave as an unconstrained monopolist because it may have distorted its actions in order to fend off the rival's entry.

In deciding whether to deter the second mover's entry, the first mover must weigh the costs and benefits relative to accommodating entry—that is, allowing entry to happen. Accommodating entry does not mean behaving nonstrategically. The first mover would move off its best-response function to manipulate the second mover into being less competitive, as described in the previous section. The cost of deterring entry is that the first mover would have to move off its best-response function even further than it would if it accommodates entry. The benefit is that it operates alone in the market and has market demand to itself. Deterring entry is relatively easy for the first mover if the second mover must pay a substantial sunk cost to enter the market.

EXAMPLE 15.10 Deterring Entry of a Natural Spring

Recall Example 15.8, where two natural-spring owners choose outputs sequentially. We now add an entry stage: in particular, after observing firm 1's initial quantity choice, firm 2 decides whether or not to enter the market. Entry requires the expenditure of sunk cost K_2, after which firm 2 can choose output. Market demand and cost are as in Example 15.8. To simplify the calculations, we will take the specific numerical values $a = 120$ and $c = 0$ [implying that inverse demand is $P(Q) = 120 - Q$ and that production is costless]. To further simplify, we will abstract from firm 1's entry decision and assume that it has already sunk any cost needed to enter before the start of the game. We will look for conditions under which firm 1 prefers to deter rather than accommodate firm 2's entry.

Accommodating entry. Start by computing firm 1's profit if it accommodates firm 2's entry, denoted π_1^{acc}. This has already been done in Example 15.8, in which there was no issue of deterring 2's entry. There we found firm 1's equilibrium output to be $(a - c)/2 = q_1^{acc}$ and its profit to be $(a - c)^2/8 = \pi_1^{acc}$. Substituting the specific numerical values $a = 120$ and $c = 0$, we have $q_1^{acc} = 60$ and $\pi_1^{acc} = (120 - 0)^2/8 = 1{,}800$.

Deterring entry. Next, compute firm 1's profit if it deters firm 2's entry, denoted π_1^{det}. To deter entry, firm 1 needs to produce an amount q_1^{det} high enough that, even if firm 2 best-responds to q_1^{det}, it cannot earn enough profit to cover its sunk cost K_2. We know from Equation 15.58 that firm 2's best-response function is

$$q_2 = \frac{120 - q_1}{2}. \tag{15.63}$$

Substituting for q_2 in firm 2's profit function (Equation 15.7) and simplifying gives

$$\pi_2 = \left(\frac{120 - q_1^{det}}{2} \right)^2 - K_2. \tag{15.64}$$

Setting firm 2's profit in Equation 15.64 equal to 0 and solving yields

$$q_1^{det} = 120 - 2\sqrt{K_2}; \tag{15.65}$$

q_1^{det} is the firm-1 output needed to keep firm 2 out of the market. At this output level, firm 1's profit is

$$\pi_1^{det} = 2\sqrt{K_2}(120 - 2\sqrt{K_2}), \tag{15.66}$$

which we found by substituting q_1^{det}, $a = 120$, and $c = 0$ into firm 1's profit function from Equation 15.7. We also set $q_2 = 0$ because, if firm 1 is successful in deterring entry, it operates alone in the market.

Comparison. The final step is to juxtapose π_1^{acc} and π_1^{det} to find the condition under which firm 1 prefers deterring to accommodating entry. To simplify the algebra, let $x = 2\sqrt{K_2}$. Then $\pi_1^{det} = \pi_1^{acc}$ if

$$x^2 - 120x + 1{,}800 = 0. \tag{15.67}$$

Applying the quadratic formula yields

$$x = \frac{120 \pm \sqrt{7200}}{2}. \tag{15.68}$$

Taking the smaller root (since we will be looking for a minimum threshold), we have $x = 17.6$ (rounding to the nearest decimal). Substituting $x = 17.6$ into $x = 2\sqrt{K_2}$ and solving for K_2 yields

$$K_2 = \left(\frac{x}{2}\right)^2 = \left(\frac{17.6}{2}\right)^2 \approx 77. \tag{15.69}$$

If $K_2 = 77$, then entry is so cheap for firm 2 that firm 1 would have to increase its output all the way to $q_1^{det} = 102$ in order to deter entry. This is a significant distortion above what it would produce when accommodating entry: $q_1^{acc} = 60$. If $K_2 < 77$ then the output distortion needed to deter entry wastes so much profit that firm 1 prefers to accommodate entry. If $K_2 > 77$, output need not be distorted as much to deter entry, so firm 1 prefers to deter entry.

QUERY: Suppose the first mover must pay the same entry cost as the second, $K_1 = K_2 = K$. Suppose further that K is high enough that the first mover prefers to deter rather than accommodate the second mover's entry. Wouldn't this sunk cost be high enough to keep the first mover out of the market, too? Why or why not?

A real-world example of overproduction (or overcapacity) to deter entry is provided by the 1945 antitrust case against Alcoa, a U.S. aluminum manufacturer. A U.S. Federal Court ruled that Alcoa maintained much higher capacity than was needed to serve the market as a strategy to deter rivals' entry, and it held that Alcoa was in violation of antitrust laws.

To recap what we have learned in the last two sections: with quantity competition, the first mover plays a "top dog" strategy regardless of whether it deters or accommodates the second mover's entry. True, the entry-deterring strategy is more aggressive than the entry-accommodating one, but this difference is one of degree rather than kind. However, with price competition (as in Example 15.9), the first mover's entry-deterring strategy would differ in kind from its entry-accommodating strategy. It would play a "puppy dog" strategy if it wished to accommodate entry, because this is how it manipulates the second mover into playing less aggressively. It plays a "top dog" strategy of lowering its price relative to the simultaneous game if it wants to deter entry. Two general principles emerge.

- Entry deterrence is always accomplished by a "top dog" strategy whether competition is in quantities or prices, or (more generally) whether best-response functions slope down or up. The first mover simply wants to create an inhospitable environment for the second mover.

- If firm 1 wants to accommodate entry, whether it should play a "puppy dog" or "top dog" strategy depends on the nature of competition—in particular, on the slope of the best-response functions.

These principles apply more generally beyond the commitments to a fixed quantity or price that we have studied so far. Example 15.11 shows that a first mover might choose the placement of its product strategically to put it in the best competitive position. The placement of the product is literally the firm's physical location in the example, but location could also be interpreted as some other attribute of the product, such as sweetness or whitening additives in toothpaste.

EXAMPLE 15.11 Product Placement on Hotelling's Beach

We will return to Hotelling's beach in Example 15.5 and investigate where the ice cream stands would choose to locate under alternative scenarios. To model the location decisions formally, we will suppose that, prior to the price competition in Example 15.5, there is an

(continued)

EXAMPLE 15.11 CONTINUED

initial entry/location stage. Firm A moves first and chooses its location a on the unit interval. Firm B observes a and decides whether to enter and, if it enters, its location b. Let K_B be the sunk cost that B must pay to enter the market (abstract from A's entry cost for simplicity). We will solve for the subgame-perfect equilibrium of this sequential game using backward induction.

Firm B's location. We have already solved for the Nash equilibrium of the pricing subgame given that both stands enter and locate at arbitrary points a and b on the line. Equation 15.42 lists the stands' payoffs. Fold the game back to consider firm B's location, supposing it has entered. To find B's optimal location, take the derivative of B's payoff in Equation 15.42 with respect to b:

$$\frac{t}{18}(4L - a - b)(4L + a - 3b). \tag{15.70}$$

This derivative is positive for all values of a and b between 0 and L. We have a "corner" solution: B wants to locate as far as possible to the right of the beach, that is, $b = L$. Substituting $b = L$ into the stands' payoffs, we have

$$\pi_A = \frac{t}{18}(L - a)(3L + a)^2,$$

$$\pi_B = \frac{t}{18}(L - a)(3L - a)^2 - K_B. \tag{15.71}$$

Note that we have subtracted B's sunk entry cost in the expression for its profit.

Next, fold the game one step back to solve for A's location. A's optimal location depends on whether it wants to deter or accept B's entry. We analyze both possibilities in turn.

Entry deterrence. To deter B's entry, A wants to choose a location that reduces B's payoff to zero or below. A technical point before proceeding is that we will restrict A's location to the left half of the beach: $a \leq L/2$. If A were to locate in the right half, B would respond by leapfrogging A and locating in the left half. The outcome would be the mirror image of the one derived here, so we need not analyze that case separately.

A glance at Equation 15.71 shows that B's payoff falls the closer A locates to the right. Among locations $a \leq L/2$, the greatest harm A can inflict on B is to locate right in the middle of the interval: $a = L/2$. Substituting $a = L/2$ into Equation 15.71, we see that B's profit can be reduced to $t(5/12)^2 L^3 - K_B$, which is negative if

$$K_B > 0.174tL^3. \tag{15.72}$$

For example, if the beach is $L = 100$ yards long and transport costs are $t = \$0.01$ per yard, then B's entry can be deterred if it involves a sunk cost greater than \$1,740. If it is at all possible for A to deter B's entry, then A will certainly want to do so. If A deters B's entry, then A ends up alone in the middle of the market, which happens to be the best location for a monopolist. (Locating in the middle minimizes transportation costs for the monopolist's consumers and allows the monopolist to charge a higher price.) Luckily for A in this game, A's monopoly strategy is the same as the most aggressive "top dog" strategy it can use to deter entry.

Entry accommodation. If the condition in Equation 15.72 does not hold, then it is impossible for A to deter B's entry and so A has no choice but to accommodate entry. What is A's optimal location then? We know that B will locate at $b = L$ and that A's profit is given by Equation 15.71. Taking the first derivative of Equation 15.71 with respect to a gives

$$-\frac{t}{18}(3L + a)(L + 3a),\qquad(15.73)$$

which is negative. We have a "corner" solution: A wants to locate as far as possible to the left, that is, $a = 0$.

If A cannot deter B's entry, it pursues a "puppy dog" strategy of locating as far from B as possible. Why does A shy away from the middle of the interval? After all, holding prices constant, moving closer to the middle would increase A's market share. The reason is that prices are not held constant. Moving closer to the middle would increase the aggressiveness of the price competition between A and B, and the resulting reduction in prices would offset the benefit of increased market share.

QUERY: Suppose the national park service that operates the beach regulates the price that ice cream stands can charge. Would A's entry-deterring strategy change? Would A's entry-accommodating strategy change? Why or why not?

SIGNALING

The preceding sections have shown that the first mover's ability to commit may afford it a big strategic advantage. In this section we will analyze another possible first-mover advantage: the ability to signal. If the second mover has incomplete information about market conditions (costs, demand, and so forth), then it may try to learn about these conditions by observing how the first mover behaves. The first mover may try to distort its actions in order to manipulate what the second learns. The analysis in this section is closely tied to the material on signaling games in Chapter 8, and the reader may want to review that material before proceeding with this section.

The ability to signal may be a plausible benefit of being a first mover in some settings in which the benefit we studied earlier—commitment—is implausible. For example, in industries where the capital equipment is readily adapted to manufacture other products, costs are not very "sunk" and so capacity commitments may not be especially credible. The first mover can reduce its capacity with little loss. For another example, the price-leadership game involved a commitment to price. It is hard to see what sunk costs are involved in setting a price and thus what commitment value it has.[15] Yet even in the absence of commitment value, prices may have strategic, signaling value.

Entry-deterrence model

Consider the incomplete-information game in Figure 15.8. The game involves a first mover (firm 1) and a second mover (firm 2) that choose prices for their differentiated products. Firm 1 has private information about its marginal cost, which can take on one of two values: high with probability $\Pr(H)$ or low with probability $\Pr(L) = 1 - \Pr(H)$. In period 1, firm 1 serves the market alone. At the end of the period, firm 2 observes firm 1's price and decides

---

[15]The Query in Example 15.9 asks you to consider reasons why a firm may be able to commit to a price. The firm may gain commitment power by using contracts (e.g., long-term supply contracts with customers or a most-favored customer clause, which ensures that if the firm lowers price in the future to other customers then the favored customer gets a rebate on the price difference). The firm may advertise a price through an expensive national advertising campaign. The firm may have established a valuable reputation as charging "everyday low prices."

FIGURE 15.8   Signaling for Entry Deterrence

Firm 1 signals its private information about its cost (high H or low L) through the price it sets in the first period. Firm 2 observes 1's price and then decides whether or not to enter. If 2 enters, the firms compete as duopolists; otherwise, 1 operates alone on the market again in the second period. Firm 2 earns positive profit if and only if it enters against a high-cost rival.

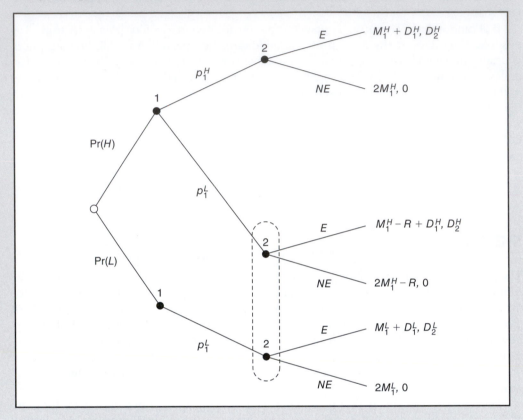

whether or not to enter the market. If it enters, it sinks an entry cost K_2 and learns the true level of firm 1's costs; then firms compete as duopolists in the second period, choosing prices for differentiated products as in Example 15.4 or 15.5. (We do not need to be specific about the exact form of demands.) If firm 2 does not enter, it obtains a payoff of zero and firm 1 again operates alone in the market. Assume there is no discounting between periods.

Firm 2 draws inferences about firm 1's cost from the price that 1 charges in the first period. Firm 2 earns more if it competes against the high-cost type because the high-cost type's price will be higher, and as we saw in Examples 15.4 and 15.5, the higher the rival's price for a differentiated product, the higher the firms own demand and profit. Let D_i^t be the duopoly profit (not including entry costs) for firm $i \in \{1, 2\}$ if firm 1 is of type $t \in \{L, H\}$. To make the model interesting, we will suppose $D_2^L < K_2 < D_2^H$, so that firm 2 earns more than its entry cost if it faces the high-cost type but not if it faces the low-cost type. Otherwise, the information in firm 1's signal would be useless because firm 2 would always enter or always stay out regardless of 1's type.

To simplify the model, we will suppose that the low-cost type only has one relevant action in the first period—namely, setting its monopoly price p_1^L. The high-cost type can choose one of two prices: it can set the monopoly price associated with its type, p_1^H, or it can choose the same price as the low type, p_1^L. Presumably, the optimal monopoly price is increasing in marginal cost, so $p_1^L < p_1^H$. Let M_1^t be firm 1's monopoly profit if it is of type $t \in \{L, H\}$ (the profit if it is alone and charges its optimal monopoly price p_1^H if it is the high type and p_1^L if it is the low type). Let R be the high type's loss relative to the optimal monopoly profit in the first period if it charges p_1^L rather than its optimal monopoly price p_1^H. Thus, if the high type charges p_1^H in the first period then it earns M_1^H in that period, but if it charges p_1^L it earns $M_1^H - R$.

Separating equilibrium

We will look for two kinds of perfect Bayesian equilibria: separating and pooling. In a separating equilibrium, the different types of the first mover must choose different actions. Here, there is only one such possibility for firm 1: the low-cost type chooses p_1^L and the high-cost type chooses p_1^H. Firm 2 learns firm 1's type from these actions perfectly and stays out upon seeing p_1^L and enters upon seeing p_1^H. It remains to check whether the high-cost type would prefer to deviate to p_1^L. In equilibrium, the high type earns a total profit of $M_1^H + D_1^H$: M_1^H in the first period because it charges its optimal monopoly price, and D_1^H in the second because firm 2 enters and the firms compete as duopolists. If the high type were to deviate to p_1^L then it would earn $M_1^H - R$ in the first period, the loss R coming from charging a price other than its first-period optimum, but firm 2 would think it is the low type and would not enter. Hence firm 1 would earn M_1^H in the second period, for a total of $2M_1^H - R$ across periods. For deviation to be unprofitable we must have

$$M_1^H + D_1^H \geq 2M_1^H - R \tag{15.74}$$

or (upon rearranging)

$$R \geq M_1^H - D_1^H. \tag{15.75}$$

That is, the high-type's loss from distorting its price from its monopoly optimum in the first period exceeds its gain from deterring firm 2's entry in the second period.

If the condition in Equation 15.75 does not hold, there still may be a separating equilibrium in an expanded game in which the low type can charge other prices beside p_1^L. The high type could distort its price downward below p_1^L, increasing the first-period loss the high type would suffer from pooling with the low type to such an extent that the high type would rather charge p_1^H even if this results in firm 2's entry.

Pooling equilibrium

If the condition in Equation 15.75 does not hold, then the high type would prefer to pool with the low type if pooling deters entry. Pooling deters entry if firm 2's prior belief that firm 1 is the high type, $\Pr(H)$—which is equal to its posterior belief in a pooling equilibrium—is low enough that firm 2's expected payoff from entering,

$$\mathbf{Pr}(H)D_2^H + [1 - \mathbf{Pr}(H)]D_2^L - K_2 \tag{15.76}$$

is less than its payoff of zero from staying out of the market.

Predatory pricing

The incomplete-information model of entry deterrence has been used to explain why a rational firm might want to engage in *predatory pricing*, the practice of charging an artificially low price to prevent potential rivals from entering or to force existing rivals to exit. The predatory firm sacrifices profits in the short run to gain a monopoly position in future periods.

Predatory pricing is prohibited by antitrust laws. In the most famous antitrust case, dating back to 1911, John D. Rockefeller—owner of the Standard Oil company that controlled a substantial majority of refined oil in the United States—was accused of attempting to monopolize the oil market by cutting prices dramatically to drive rivals out and then raising prices after rivals had exited the market or sold out to Standard Oil. Predatory pricing remains a controversial antitrust issue because of the difficulty in distinguishing between predatory conduct, which authorities would like to prevent, and competitive conduct, which authorities would like to promote. In addition, economists initially had trouble developing game-theoretic models in which predatory pricing is rational and credible.

Suitably interpreted, predatory pricing may emerge as a rational strategy in the incomplete-information model of entry deterrence. Predatory pricing can show up in a separating equilibrium—in particular, in the expanded model where the low-cost type can separate only by reducing price below its monopoly optimum. Total welfare is actually higher in this separating equilibrium than it would be in its full-information counterpart. Firm 2's entry decision is the same in both outcomes, but the low-cost type's price may be lower (to signal its type) in the predatory outcome.

Predatory pricing can also show up in a pooling equilibrium. In this case it is the high-cost type that charges an artificially low price, pricing below its first-period optimum in order to keep firm 2 out of the market. Whether social welfare is lower in the pooling equilibrium than in a full-information setting is unclear. In the first period, price is lower (and total welfare presumably higher) in the pooling equilibrium than in a full-information setting. On the other hand, deterring firm 2's entry results in higher second-period prices and lower welfare. Weighing the first-period gain against the second-period loss would require detailed knowledge of demand curves, discount factors, and so forth.

The incomplete-information model of entry deterrence is not the only model of preda-tory pricing that economists have developed. Another model involves frictions in the market for financial capital that stem perhaps from informational problems (between borrowers and lenders) of the sort we will discuss in Chapter 18. With limits on borrowing, firms may only have limited resources to "make a go" in a market. A larger firm may force financially strapped rivals to endure losses until their resources are exhausted and they are forced to exit the market.

HOW MANY FIRMS ENTER?

To this point, we have taken the number of firms in the market as given, often assuming that there are at most two firms (as in Examples 15.1, 15.3, and 15.10). We did allow for a general number of firms, n, in some of our analysis (as in Examples 15.3 and 15.7) but were silent about how this number n was determined. In this section, we provide a game-theoretic analysis of the number of firms by introducing a first stage in which a large number of potential entrants can each choose whether or not to enter. We will abstract from first-mover advantages, entry deterrence, and other strategic considerations by assuming that firms make their entry decisions simultaneously. Strategic considerations are interesting and important, but we have already developed some insights into strategic considerations from the previous sections and—by abstracting from them—we can simplify the analysis here.

Barriers to entry

In order for the market to be oligopolistic with a finite number of firms rather than perfectly competitive with an infinite number of infinitesimal firms, some factors, called *barriers to entry*, must eventually make entry unattractive or impossible. We discussed many of these factors at length in the previous chapter on monopoly. If a sunk cost is required to enter the market, then—even if firms can freely choose whether or not to enter—only a limited number of firms will choose to enter in equilibrium, because competition among more than that number would drive profits below the level needed to recoup the sunk entry cost.

Government intervention in the form of patents or licensing requirements may prevent firms from entering even if it would be profitable for them to do so.

Some of the new concepts discussed in this chapter may introduce additional barriers to entry. Search costs may prevent consumers from finding new entrants with lower prices and/or higher quality than existing firms. Product differentiation may raise entry barriers because of strong brand loyalty. Existing firms may bolster brand loyalty through expensive advertising campaigns, and softening this brand loyalty may require entrants to conduct similarly expensive advertising campaigns. Existing firms may take other strategic measures to deter entry, such as committing to a high capacity or output level, engaging in predatory pricing, or other measures discussed in previous sections.

Long-run equilibrium

Consider the following game-theoretic model of entry in the long run. A large number of symmetric firms are potential entrants into a market. Firms make their entry decisions simultaneously. Entry requires the expenditure of sunk cost K. Let n be the number of firms that decide to enter. In the next stage, the n firms engage in some form of competition over a sequence of periods during which they earn the present discounted value of some constant profit stream. To simplify, we will usually collapse the sequence of periods of competition into a single period. Let $g(n)$ be the profit earned by an individual firm in this competition subgame [not including the sunk cost, so $g(n)$ is a gross profit]. Presumably, the more firms in the market, the more competitive the market is and the less an individual firm earns, so $g'(n) < 0$.

We will look for a subgame-perfect equilibrium in pure strategies.[16] This will be the number of firms, n^*, satisfying two conditions. First, the n^* entering firms earn enough to cover their entry cost: $g(n^*) \geq K$. Otherwise at least one of them would have preferred to have deviated to not entering. Second, an additional firm cannot earn enough to cover its entry cost: $g(n^* + 1) \leq K$. Otherwise a firm that remained out of the market could have profitably deviated by entering. Given that $g'(n) < 0$, we can put these two conditions together and say that n^* is the greatest integer satisfying $g(n^*) \geq K$.

This condition is reminiscent of the zero-profit condition for long-run equilibrium under perfect competition. The slight nuance here is that active firms are allowed to earn positive profits. Especially if K is large relative to the size of the market, there may only be a few long-run entrants (so the market looks like a canonical oligopoly) earning well above what they need to cover their sunk costs, yet an additional firm does not enter because its entry would depress individual profit enough that the entrant could not cover its large sunk cost.

Is the long-run equilibrium efficient? Does the oligopoly involve too few or too many firms relative to what a benevolent social planner would choose for the market? Suppose the social planner can choose the number of firms (restricting entry through licenses and promoting entry through subsidizing the entry cost) but cannot regulate prices or other competitive conduct of the firms once in the market. The social planner would choose n to maximize

$$CS(n) + ng(n) - nK, \tag{15.77}$$

where $CS(n)$ is equilibrium consumer surplus in an oligopoly with n firms, $ng(n)$ is total equilibrium profit (gross of sunk entry costs) across all firms, and nK is the total expenditure on sunk entry costs. Let n^{**} be the social planner's optimum.

---

[16]A symmetric mixed-strategy equilibrium also exists in which sometimes more and sometimes fewer firms enter than can cover their sunk costs. There are multiple pure-strategy equilibria depending on the identity of the n^* entrants, but n^* is uniquely identified.

In general, the long-run equilibrium number of firms, n^*, may be greater or less than the social optimum, n^{**}, depending on two offsetting effects: the *appropriability effect* and the *business-stealing effect*.

- The social planner takes account of the benefit of increased consumer surplus from lower prices, but firms do not appropriate consumer surplus and so do not take into account this benefit. This appropriability effect would lead a social planner to choose more entry than in the long-run equilibrium: $n^{**} > n^*$.

- Working in the opposite direction is that entry causes the profits of existing firms to fall, as indicated by the derivative $g'(n) < 0$. Entry increases the competitiveness of the market, destroying some of firms' profits. In addition, the entrant "steals" some market share from existing firms—hence the name business-stealing effect. The marginal firm does not take other firms' loss in profits when making its entry decision, whereas the social planner would. The business-stealing effect biases long-run equilibrium toward more entry than a social planner would choose: $n^{**} < n^*$.

Depending on the functional forms for demand and costs, the appropriability effect dominates in some cases and there is less entry in long-run equilibrium than is efficient. In other cases, the business-stealing effect dominates and there is more entry in long-run equilibrium than is efficient, as in Example 15.12.

EXAMPLE 15.12 Cournot in the Long Run

Long-run equilibrium. Return to Example 15.3 of a Cournot oligopoly. We will determine the long-run equilibrium number of firms in the market. Let K be the sunk cost a firm must pay to enter the market in an initial entry stage. Suppose there is one period of Cournot competition after entry. To further simplify the calculations, assume that $a = 1$ and $c = 0$. Substituting these values back into Example 15.3, we have that an individual firm's gross profit is

$$g(n) = \left(\frac{1}{n+1}\right)^2. \tag{15.78}$$

The long-run equilibrium number of firms is the greatest integer n^* satisfying $g(n^*) \geq K$. Ignoring integer problems, n^* satisfies

$$n^* = \frac{1}{\sqrt{K}} - 1. \tag{15.79}$$

Social planner's problem. We first compute the individual terms in the social planner's objective function (Equation 15.77). Consumer surplus equals the area of the shaded triangle in Figure 15.9, which, using the formula for the area of a triangle, is

$$CS(n) = \frac{1}{2}Q(n)[a - P(n)] = \frac{n^2}{2(n+1)^2}; \tag{15.80}$$

here the last equality comes from substituting for price and quantity from Equations 15.18 and 15.19. Total profits for all firms (gross of sunk costs) equal the area of the shaded rectangle:

$$ng(n) = Q(n)P(n) = \frac{n}{(n+1)^2}. \tag{15.81}$$

FIGURE 15.9 Profit and Consumer Surplus in Example 15.12

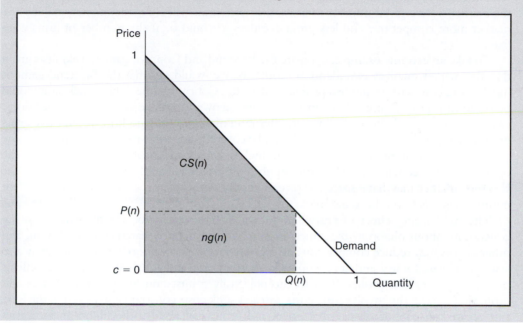

Equilibrium for n firms drawn for the demand and cost assumptions in Example 15.12. Consumer surplus, $CS(n)$, is the area of the shaded triangle. Total profits $ng(n)$ for all firms (gross of sunk costs) is the area of the shaded rectangle.

Substituting from Equations 15.80 and 15.81 into the social planner's objective function (Equation 15.77) gives

$$\frac{n^2}{2(n+1)^2} + \frac{n}{(n+1)^2} - nK. \qquad (15.82)$$

After removing positive constants, the first-order condition with respect to n is

$$1 - K(n+1)^3 = 0, \qquad (15.83)$$

implying that

$$n^{**} = \frac{1}{K^{1/3}} - 1. \qquad (15.84)$$

Ignoring integer problems, this is the optimal number of firms for a social planner.

Comparison. If $K < 1$ (a condition required for there to be any entry), then $n^{**} < n^*$ and so there is more entry in long-run equilibrium than a social planner would choose. To take a particular numerical example, let $K = 0.1$. Then $n^* = 2.16$ and $n^{**} = 1.15$, implying that the market would be a duopoly in long-run equilibrium, but a social planner would have preferred a monopoly.

QUERY: If the social planner could set both the number of firms and the price in this example, what choices would he or she make? How would these compare to long-run equilibrium?

Feedback effect

We found that certain factors decreased the stringency of competition and increased firms' profits (e.g., quantity rather than price competition, product differentiation, search costs, discount factors sufficient to sustain collusion). A feedback effect is that the more profitable the market is for a given number of firms, the more firms will enter the market, making the market more competitive and less profitable than it would be if the number of firms were fixed.

To take an extreme example, compare the Bertrand and Cournot games. Taking as given that the market involves two identical producers, we would say that the Bertrand game is much more competitive and less profitable than the Cournot game. This conclusion would be reversed if firms facing a sunk entry cost were allowed to make rational entry decisions. Only one firm would choose to enter the Bertrand market. A second firm would drive gross profit to zero, and so its entry cost would not be covered. The long-run equilibrium outcome would involve a monopolist and thus the highest prices and profits possible, exactly the opposite of our conclusions when the number of firms was fixed! On the other hand, the Cournot market may have space for several entrants driving prices and profits below their monopoly levels in the Bertrand market.

The moderating effect of entry should lead economists to be careful when drawing conclusions about oligopoly outcomes. Product differentiation, search costs, collusion, and other factors may reduce competition and increase profits in the short run, but they may also lead to increased entry and competition in the long run and thus have ambiguous effects overall on prices and profits. Perhaps the only truly robust conclusions about prices and profits in the long run involve sunk costs. Greater sunk costs constrain entry even in the long run, so we can confidently say that prices and profits will tend to be higher in industries requiring higher sunk costs (as a percentage of sales) to enter.[17]

INNOVATION

At the end of the previous chapter, we asked which market structure—monopoly or perfect competition—leads to more innovation in new products and cost-reducing processes. If monopoly is more innovative, will the long-run benefits of innovation offset the short-run deadweight loss of monopoly? The same questions can be asked in the context of oligopoly. Do concentrated market structures, with few firms perhaps charging high prices, provide better incentives for innovation? Which is more innovative, a large or a small firm? An established firm or an entrant? Answers to these questions can help inform policy toward mergers, entry regulation, and small-firm subsidies.

As we will see with the aid of some simple models, there is no definite answer as to what level of concentration is best for long-run total welfare. We will derive some general trade-offs, but quantifying these trade-offs to determine whether a particular market would be more innovative if it were concentrated or unconcentrated will depend on the nature of competition for innovation, the nature of competition for consumers, and the specification of demand and cost functions. The same can be said for determining what firm size or age is most innovative.

The models we introduce here are of *product* innovations, the invention of a product (e.g., plasma televisions) that did not exist before. Another class of innovations is that of *process* innovations, which reduce the cost of producing existing products—for example, the use of robot technology in automobile manufacture.

---

[17]For more on robust conclusions regarding industry structure and competitiveness, see J. Sutton, *Sunk Costs and Market Structure* (Cambridge, MA: MIT Press, 1991).

Monopoly on innovation

Begin by supposing that only a single firm, call it firm 1, has the capacity to innovate. For example, a pharmaceutical manufacturer may have an idea for a malaria vaccine that no other firm is aware of. How much would the firm be willing to complete research and development for the vaccine and to test it with large-scale clinical trials? How does this willingness to spend (which we will take as a measure of the innovativeness of the firm) depend on concentration of firms in the market?

Suppose first that there is currently no other vaccine available for malaria. If firm 1 successfully develops the vaccine, then it will be a monopolist. Letting Π_M be the monopoly profit, firm 1 would be willing to spend as much as Π_M to develop the vaccine. Next, to examine the case of a less concentrated market, suppose that another firm (firm 2) already has a vaccine on the market for which firm 1's would be a therapeutic substitute. If firm 1 also develops its vaccine, the firms compete as duopolists. Let π_D be the duopoly profit. In a Bertrand model with identical products, $\pi_D = 0$, but $\pi_D > 0$ in other models—for example, models involving quantity competition or collusion. Firm 1 would be willing to spend as much as π_D to develop the vaccine in this case. Comparing the two cases, since $\Pi_M > \pi_D$, it follows that firm 1 would be willing to spend more (and, by this measure, would be more innovative) in a more concentrated market. The general principle here can be labeled a *dissipation effect*: competition dissipates some of the profit from innovation and thus reduces incentives to innovate. The dissipation effect is part of the rationale behind the patent system. A patent grants monopoly rights to an inventor, intentionally restricting competition in order to ensure higher profits and greater innovation incentives.

Another comparison that can be made is to see which firm, 1 or 2, has more of an incentive to innovate given that it has a monopoly on the initial idea. Firm 1 is initially out of the market and must develop the new vaccine to enter. Firm 2 is already in the malaria market with its first vaccine but can consider developing a second one as well, which we will continue to assume is a perfect substitute. As shown in the previous paragraph, firm 1 would be willing to pay up to π_D for the innovation. Firm 2 would not be willing to pay anything, since it is currently a monopolist in the malaria vaccine market and would continue as a monopolist whether or not it developed the second medicine. (Crucial to this conclusion is that the firm with the initial idea can fail to develop it but still not worry that the other firm will take the idea; we will change this assumption in the next subsection.) Therefore, the potential competitor (firm 1) is more innovative by our measure than the existing monopolist (firm 2). The general principle here has been labeled a *replacement effect*: firms gain less incremental profit, and thus have less incentive to innovate, if the new product replaces an existing product already making profit than if the firm is a new entrant in the market. The replacement effect can explain turnover in certain industries where old firms become increasingly conservative and are eventually displaced by innovative and quickly growing startups, as Microsoft displaced IBM as the dominant company in the computer industry.

Competition for innovation

New firms are not always more innovative than existing firms. The dissipation effect may counteract the replacement effect, leading old firms to be more innovative. To see this trade-off requires yet another variant of the model. Suppose now that more than one firm has an initial idea for a possible innovation and that they compete to see which can develop the idea into a viable product. For example, the idea for a new malaria vaccine may have occurred to scientists in two firms' laboratories at about the same time, and the firms may engage in a race to see who can produce a viable vaccine from this initial idea. Continue to assume that firm 2 already has a malaria vaccine on the market and that this new vaccine would be a perfect substitute for it.

The difference between the models in this and the previous section is that, if firm 2 does not win the race to develop the idea, then the idea does not simply fall by the wayside but rather is developed by the competitor, firm 1. Firm 2 has an incentive to win the innovation competition to prevent firm 1 from becoming a competitor. Formally, if firm 1 wins the innovation competition then it enters the market and is a competitor with firm 2, earning duopoly profit π_D. As we have repeatedly seen, this is the maximum that firm 1 would pay for the innovation. Firm 2's profit is Π_M if it wins the competition for the innovation but π_D if it loses and firm 1 wins. Firm 2 would pay up to the difference, $\Pi_M - \pi_D$, for the innovation. If $\Pi_M > 2\pi_D$—that is, if industry profit under a monopoly is greater than under a duopoly, which it is when some of the monopoly profit is dissipated by duopoly competition—then $\Pi_M - \pi_D > \pi_D$, and firm 2 will have more incentive to innovate than firm 1.

This model explains the puzzling phenomenon of dominant firms filing for "sleeping patents": patents that are never implemented. Dominant firms have a substantial incentive—as we have seen, possibly greater than entrants'—to file for patents to prevent entry and preserve their dominant position. While the replacement effect may lead to turnover in the market and innovation by new firms, the dissipation effect may help preserve the position of dominant firms and retard the pace of innovation.

SUMMARY

Many markets fall between the polar extremes of perfect competition and monopoly. In such imperfectly competitive markets, determining market price and quantity is complicated because equilibrium involves strategic interaction among the firms. In this chapter, we used the tools of game theory developed in Chapter 8 to study strategic interaction in oligopoly markets. We first analyzed oligopoly firms' short-run choices such as prices and quantities and then went on to analyze firms' longer-run decisions such as product location, innovation, entry, and the deterrence of entry. We found that seemingly small changes in modeling assumptions may lead to big changes in equilibrium outcomes. Predicting behavior in oligopoly markets may therefore be difficult based on theory alone and may require knowledge of particular industries and careful empirical analysis. Still, some general principles did emerge from our theoretical analysis that aid in understanding oligopoly markets.

- One of the most basic oligopoly models, the Bertand model involves two identical firms that set prices simultaneously. The equilibrium resulted in the Bertrand paradox: even though the oligopoly is the most concentrated possible, firms behave as perfect competitors, pricing at marginal cost and earning zero profit.

- The Bertrand paradox is not the inevitable outcome in an oligopoly but can be escaped by changing assumptions underlying the Bertrand model—for example, allowing for quantity competition, differentiated products, search costs, capacity constraints, or repeated play leading to collusion.

- As in the Prisoners' Dilemma, firms could profit by coordinating on a less competitive outcome, but this outcome will be unstable unless firms can explicitly collude by forming a legal cartel or tacitly collude in a repeated game.

- For tacit collusion to sustain super-competitive profits, firms must be patient enough that the loss from a price war in future periods to punish undercutting exceeds the benefit from undercutting in the current period.

- Whereas a nonstrategic monopolist prefers flexibility to respond to changing market conditions, a strategic oligopolist may prefer to commit to a single choice. The firm can commit to the choice if it involves a sunk cost that cannot be recovered if the choice is later reversed.

- A first mover can gain an advantage by committing to a different action from what it would choose in the Nash equilibrium of the simultaneous game. To deter entry, the first mover should commit to reducing the entrant's profits using an aggressive "top dog" strategy (high output or low price). If it does not deter entry, the first mover should commit to a strategy leading its rival to compete less aggressively. This is sometimes a "top dog" and sometimes a "puppy dog" strategy, depending on the slope of firms' best responses.

- Holding the number of firms in an oligopoly constant in the short run, the introduction of a factor that softens competition (product differentiation, search costs, collusion, and so forth) will raise firms' profit, but an offsetting effect in the long run is that entry—which tends to reduce oligopoly profit—will be more attractive.

- Innovation may be even more important than low prices for total welfare in the long run. Determining which oligopoly structure is the most innovative is difficult because offsetting effects (dissipation and replacement) are involved.

PROBLEMS

15.1

Assume for simplicity that a monopolist has no costs of production and faces a demand curve given by $Q = 150 - P$.

a. Calculate the profit-maximizing price-quantity combination for this monopolist. Also calculate the monopolist's profit.

b. Suppose instead that there are two firms in the market facing the demand and cost conditions just described for their identical products. Firms choose quantities simultaneously as in the Cournot model. Compute the outputs in the Nash equilibrium. Also compute market output, price, and firm profits.

c. Suppose the two firms choose prices simultaneously as in the Bertrand model. Compute the prices in the Nash equilibrium. Also compute firm output and profit as well as market output.

d. Graph the demand curve and indicate where the market price-quantity combinations from parts (a)–(c) appear on the curve.

15.2

Suppose that firms' marginal and average costs are constant and equal to c and that inverse market demand is given by $P = a - bQ$, where $a, b > 0$.

a. Calculate the profit-maximizing price-quantity combination for a monopolist. Also calculate the monopolist's profit.

b. Calculate the Nash equilibrium quantities for Cournot duopolists, which choose quantities for their identical products simultaneously. Also compute market output, market price, and firm and industry profits.

c. Calculate the Nash equilibrium prices for Bertrand duopolists, which choose prices for their identical products simultaneously. Also compute firm and market output as well as firm and industry profits.

d. Suppose now that there are n identical firms in a Cournot model. Compute the Nash equilibrium quantities as functions of n. Also compute market output, market price, and firm and industry profits.

e. Show that the monopoly outcome from part (a) can be reproduced in part (d) by setting $n = 1$, that the Cournot duopoly outcome from part (b) can be reproduced in part (d) by setting $n = 2$ in part (d), and that letting n approach infinity yields the same market price, output, and industry profit as in part (c).

15.3

Let c_i be the constant marginal and average cost for firm i (so that firms may have different marginal costs). Suppose demand is given by $P = 1 - Q$.

a. Calculate the Nash equilibrium quantities assuming there are two firms in a Cournot market. Also compute market output, market price, firm profits, industry profits, consumer surplus, and total welfare.

b. Represent the Nash equilibrium on a best-response function diagram. Show how a reduction in firm 1's cost would change the equilibrium. Draw a representative isoprofit for firm 1.

15.4

Suppose that firms 1 and 2 operate under conditions of constant average and marginal cost but that firm 1's marginal cost is $c_1 = 10$ and firm 2's is $c_2 = 8$. Market demand is $Q = 500 - 20P$.

a. Suppose firms practice Bertrand competition, that is, setting prices for their identical products simultaneously. Compute the Nash equilibrium prices. (To avoid technical problems in this question, assume that if firms charge equal prices then the low-cost firm makes all the sales.)

b. Compute firm output, firm profit, and market output.

c. Is total welfare maximized in the Nash equilibrium? If not, suggest an outcome that would maximize total welfare, and compute the deadweight loss in the Nash equilibrium compared to your outcome.

15.5

Consider the following Bertrand game involving two firms producing differentiated products. Firms have no costs of production. Firm 1's demand is

$$q_1 = 1 - p_1 + bp_2,$$

where $b > 0$. A symmetric equation holds for firm 2's demand.

a. Solve for the Nash equilibrium of the simultaneous price-choice game.

b. Compute the firms' outputs and profits.

c. Represent the equilibrium on a best-response function diagram. Show how an increase in b would change the equilibrium. Draw a representative isoprofit curve for firm 1.

15.6

Recall Example 15.6, which covers tacit collusion. Suppose (as in the example) that a medical device is produced at constant average and marginal cost of $10 and that the demand for the device is given by

$$Q = 5,000 - 100P.$$

The market meets each period for an infinite number of periods. The discount factor is δ.

a. Suppose that n firms engage in Bertrand competition each period. Suppose it takes two periods to discover a deviation because it takes two periods to observe rivals' prices. Compute the discount factor needed to sustain collusion in a subgame-perfect equilibrium using grim strategies.

b. Now restore the assumption that, as in Example 15.7, deviations are detected after just one period. Next, assume that n is not given but rather is determined by the number of firms that choose to enter the market in an initial stage in which entrants must sink a one-time cost K to participate in the market. Find an upper bound on n. *Hint:* Two conditions are involved.

15.7

Assume as in Problem 15.1 that two firms with no production costs, facing demand $Q = 150 - P$, choose quantities q_1 and q_2.

a. Compute the subgame-perfect equilibrium of the Stackelberg version of the game in which firm 1 chooses q_1 first and then firm 2 chooses q_2.

b. Now add an entry stage after firm 1 chooses q_1. In this stage, firm 2 decides whether or not to enter. If it enters then it must sink cost K_2, after which it is allowed to choose q_2. Compute the threshold value of K_2 above which firm 1 prefers to deter firm 2's entry.

c. Represent the Cournot, Stackelberg, and entry-deterrence outcomes on a best-response function diagram.

15.8

Recall the Hotelling model of competition on a linear beach from Example 15.5. Suppose for simplicity that ice cream stands can locate only at the two ends of the line segment (zoning prohibits commercial development in the middle of the beach). This question asks you to analyze an entry-deterring strategy involving product proliferation.

a. Consider the subgame in which firm A has two ice cream stands, one at each end of the beach, and B locates along with A at the right endpoint. What is the Nash equilibrium of this subgame? *Hint:* Bertrand competition ensues at the right endpoint.

b. If B must sink an entry cost K_B, would it choose to enter given that firm A is in both ends of the market and remains there after entry?

c. Is A's product proliferation strategy credible? Or would A exit the right end of the market after B enters? To answer these questions, compare A's profits for the case in which it has a stand on the left side and both it and B have stands on the right to the case in which A has one stand on the left end and B has one stand on the right end (so B's entry has driven A out of the right side of the market).

Analytical Problems

15.9 Herfindahl index of market concentration

One way of measuring market concentration is through the use of the Herfindahl index, which is defined as

$$H = \sum_{i=1}^{n} s_i^2,$$

where $s_i = q_i/Q$ is firm i's market share. The higher is H, the more concentrated the industry is said to be. Intuitively, more concentrated markets are thought to be less competitive because dominant firms in concentrated markets face little competitive pressure. We will assess the validity of this intuition using several models.

a. If you have not already done so, answer Problem 15.2(d) by computing the Nash equilibrium of this n-firm Cournot game. Also compute market output, market price, consumer surplus, industry profit, and total welfare. Compute the Herfindahl index for this equilibrium.

b. Suppose two of the n firms merge, leaving the market with $n - 1$ firms. Recalculate the Nash equilibrium and the rest of the items requested in part (a). How does the merger affect price, output, profit, consumer surplus, total welfare, and the Herfindahl index?

c. Put the model used in parts (a) and (b) aside and turn to a different setup: that of Problem 15.3, where Cournot duopolists face different marginal costs. Use your answer to Problem 15.3(a) to compute equilibrium firm outputs, market output, price, consumer surplus, industry profit, and total welfare, substituting the particular cost parameters $c_1 = c_2 = 1/4$. Also compute the Herfindahl index.

d. Repeat your calculations in part (c) while assuming that firm 1's marginal cost c_1 falls to 0 but c_2 stays at 1/4. How does the merger affect price, output, profit, consumer surplus, total welfare, and the Herfindahl index?

e. Given your results from parts (a)–(d), can we draw any general conclusions about the relationship between market concentration on the one hand and price, profit, or total welfare on the other?

15.10 Inverse elasticity rule

Use the first-order condition (Equation 15.2) for a Cournot firm to show that the usual inverse elasticity rule from Chapter 11 holds under Cournot competition (where the elasticity is associated with an individual firm's residual demand, the demand left after all rivals sell their output on the market). Manipulate Equation 15.2 in a different way to obtain an equivalent version of the inverse elasticity rule:

$$\frac{P - MC}{P} = -\frac{s_i}{e_{Q,P}},$$

where $s_i = Q/q_i$ is firm i's market share and $e_{Q,P}$ is the elasticity of market demand. Compare this version of the inverse elasticity rule to that for a monopolist from the previous chapter.

15.11 Competition on a circle

Hotelling's model of competition on a linear beach is used widely in many applications, but one application that is difficult to study in the model is free entry. Free entry is easiest to study in a model with symmetric firms, but more than two firms on a line cannot be symmetric, because those located nearest the endpoints will have only one neighboring rival while those located nearer the middle will have two.

To avoid this problem, Steven Salop introduced competition on a circle.[18] As in the Hotelling model, demanders are located at each point and each demands one unit of the good. A consumer's surplus equals v (the value of consuming the good) minus the price paid for the good as well as the cost of having to travel to buy from the firm. Let this travel cost be td, where t is a parameter measuring how burdensome travel is and d is the distance traveled (note that we are here assuming a linear rather than a quadratic travel-cost function, in contrast to Example 15.5).

Initially, we take as given that there are n firms in the market and that each has the same cost function $C_i = K + cq_i$, where K is the sunk cost required to enter the market [this will come into play in part (e) of the question, where we consider free entry] and c is the constant marginal cost of production. For simplicity, assume that the circumference of the circle equals 1 and that the n firms are located evenly around the circle at intervals of $1/n$. The n firms choose prices p_i simultaneously.

a. Each firm i is free to choose its own price (p_i) but is constrained by the price charged by its nearest neighbor to either side. Let p^* be the price these firms set in a symmetric equilibrium. Explain why the extent of any firm's market on either side (x) is given by the equation

$$p + tx = p^* + t[(1/n) - x].$$

b. Given the pricing decision analyzed in part (a), firm i sells $q_i = 2x$ because it has a market on both sides. Calculate the profit-maximizing price for this firm as a function of p^*, c, t, and n.

c. Noting that in a symmetric equilibrium all firms' prices will be equal to p^*, show that $p_i = p^* = c + t/n$. Explain this result intuitively.

d. Show that a firm's profits are $t/n^2 - K$ in equilibrium.

e. What will the number of firms n^* be in long-run equilibrium in which firms can freely choose to enter?

f. Calculate the socially optimal level of differentiation in this model, defined as the number of firms (and products) that minimizes the sum of production costs plus demander travel costs. Show that this number is precisely half the number calculated in part (e). Hence, this model illustrates the possibility of overdifferentiation.

15.12 Signaling with entry accommodation

This question will explore signaling when entry deterrence is impossible, so the signaling firm accommodates its rival's entry. Assume deterrence is impossible because the two firms do not pay a sunk cost

---

[18]See S. Salop, "Monopolistic Competition with Outside Goods," *Bell Journal of Economics* (Spring 1979): 141–56.

to enter or remain in the market. The setup of the model will follow Example 15.4, so the calculations there will aid the solution of this problem. In particular, firm i's demand is given by

$$q_i = a_i - p_i + \frac{p_j}{2},$$

where a_i is product i's attribute (say, quality). Production is costless. Firm 1's attribute can be one of two values: either $a_1 = 1$, in which case we say firm 1 is the low type, or $a_1 = 2$, in which case we say it is the high type. Assume there is no discounting across periods for simplicity.

a. Compute the Nash equilibrium of the game of complete information in which firm 1 is the high type and firm 2 knows that firm 1 is the high type.

b. Compute the Nash equilibrium of the game in which firm 1 is the low type and firm 2 knows that firm 1 is the low type.

c. Solve for the Bayesian-Nash equilibrium of the game of incomplete information in which firm 1 can be either type with equal probability. Firm 1 knows its type, but firm 2 only knows the probabilities. Since we did not spend time in this chapter on Bayesian games, you may want to consult Chapter 8 (especially Example 8.9).

d. Which of firm 1's types gains from incomplete information? Which type would prefer complete information (and thus would have an incentive to signal its type if possible)? Does firm 2 earn more profit on average under complete information or under incomplete information?

e. Consider a signaling variant of the model that has two periods. Firms 1 and 2 choose prices in the first period, when 2 has incomplete information about 1's type. Firm 2 observes firm 1's price in this period and uses the information to update its beliefs about 1's type. Then firms engage in another period of price competition. Show that there is a separating equilibrium in which each type of firm 1 charges the same prices as computed in part (d). You may assume that, if firm 1 chooses an out-of-equilibrium price in the first period, then firm 2 believes that firm 1 is the low type with probability 1. *Hint:* To prove the existence of a separating equilibrium, show that the loss to the low type from trying to pool in the first period exceeds the second-period gain from having convinced firm 2 that it is the high type. Use your answers from parts (a)–(d) where possible to aid in your solution.

SUGGESTIONS FOR FURTHER READING

Carlton, D. W., and J. M. Perloff. *Modern Industrial Organization*, 4th ed. Boston: Addison-Wesley, 2005.

> Classic undergraduate text on industrial organization that covers theoretical and empirical issues.

Kwoka, J. E., Jr., and L. J. White. *The Antitrust Revolution*, 4th ed. New York: Oxford University Press, 2004.

> Summarizes economic arguments on both sides of a score of important recent antitrust cases. Demonstrates the policy relevance of the theory developed in this chapter.

Pepall, L., D. J. Richards, and G. Norman. *Industrial Organization: Contemporary Theory and Practice*, 2nd ed. Cincinnati: Thomson South-Western, 2002.

> An undergraduate textbook providing a simple but thorough treatment of oligopoly theory. Uses the Hotelling model in a variety of additional applications including advertising.

Sutton, J. *Sunk Costs and Market Structure* (Cambridge, MA: MIT Press, 1991).

> Argues that the robust predictions of oligopoly theory regard the size and nature of sunk costs. Second half provides detailed case studies of competition in various manufacturing industries.

Tirole, J. *The Theory of Industrial Organization*. Cambridge, MA: MIT Press, 1988.

> A comprehensive survey of the topics discussed in this chapter and a host of others. Standard text used in graduate courses, but selected sections are accessible to advanced undergraduates.

EXTENSIONS

Strategic Substitutes and Complements

We saw in the chapter that one can often understand the nature of strategic interaction in a market simply from the slope of firms' best-response functions. For example, we argued that a first mover that wished to accept rather than deter entry should commit to a strategy that leads its rival to behave less aggressively. What sort of strategy this is depends on the slope of firms' best responses. If best responses slope downward, as in a Cournot model, then the first mover should play a "top dog" strategy and produce a large quantity, leading its rival to reduce its production. If best responses slope upward, as in a Bertrand model with price competition for differentiated products, then the first mover should play a "puppy dog" strategy and charge a high price, leading its rival to increase its price as well.

More generally, we have seen repeatedly that best-response function diagrams are often quite helpful in understanding the nature of Nash equilibrium, how the Nash equilibrium changes with parameters of the model, how incomplete information might affect the game, and so forth. Simply knowing the slope of the best-response function is often all one needs to draw a usable best-response function diagram.

By analogy to similar definitions from consumer and producer theory, game theorists define firms' actions to be *strategic substitutes* if an increase in the level of the action (e.g., output, price, investment) by one firm is met by a decrease in that action by its rival. On the other hand, actions are *strategic complements* if an increase in an action by one firm is met by an increase in that action by its rival.

E15.1 Nash equilibrium

To make these ideas precise, suppose that firm 1's profit, $\pi^1(a_1, a_2)$, is a function of its action a_1 and its rival's (firm 2's) action a_2. (Here we have moved from subscripts to superscripts for indicating the firm to which the profits belong in order to make room for subscripts that will denote partial derivatives.) Firm 2's profit function is denoted similarly. A Nash equilibrium is a profile of actions for each firm, (a_1^*, a_2^*), such that each firm's equilibrium action is a best response to the other's. Let $BR_1(a_2)$ be firm 1's best-response function and let $BR_2(a_1)$ be firm 2's; then a Nash equilibrium is given by $a_1^* = BR_1(a_2^*)$ and $a_2^* = BR_2(a_1^*)$.

E15.2 Best-response functions in more detail

The first-order condition for firm 1's action choice is

$$\pi_1^1(a_1, a_2) = 0, \tag{i}$$

where subscripts for π represent partial derivatives with respect to its various arguments. A unique maximum, and thus a unique best response, is guaranteed if we assume that the profit function is concave:

$$\pi_{11}^1(a_1, a_2) < 0. \tag{ii}$$

Given a rival's action a_2, the solution to Equation i for a maximum is firm 1's best-response function:

$$a_1 = BR_1(a_2). \tag{iii}$$

Since the best response is unique, $BR_1(a_2)$ is indeed a function rather than a correspondence (see Chapter 8 for more on correspondences).

The strategic relationship between actions is determined by the slope of the best-response functions. If best responses are downward sloping [i.e., if $BR_1'(a_2) < 0$ and $BR_2'(a_1) < 0$] then a_1 and a_2 are strategic substitutes. If best responses are upward sloping [i.e., if $BR_1'(a_2) > 0$ and $BR_2'(a_1) > 0$] then a_1 and a_2 are strategic complements.

E15.3 Inferences from the profit function

We just saw that a direct route for determining whether actions are strategic substitutes or complements is first to solve explicitly for best-response functions and then to differentiate them. In some applications, however, it is difficult or impossible to find an explicit solution to Equation i. We can still determine whether actions are strategic substitutes or complements by drawing inferences directly from the profit function.

Substituting Equation iii into the first-order condition of Equation i gives

$$\pi_1^1(BR_1(a_2), a_2) = 0. \tag{iv}$$

Totally differentiating Equation iv with respect to a_2 yields, after dropping the arguments of the functions for brevity,

$$\pi_{11}^1 BR_1' + \pi_{12}^1 = 0. \tag{v}$$

Rearranging Equation v gives the derivative of the best-response function:

$$BR_1' = -\frac{\pi_{12}^1}{\pi_{11}^1}. \qquad \textbf{(vi)}$$

In view of the second-order condition (Equation ii), the denominator of Equation vi is negative. Thus the sign of BR_1' is the same as the sign of the numerator, π_{12}^1. That is, $\pi_{12}^1 > 0$ implies $BR_1' > 0$ and $\pi_{12}^1 < 0$ implies $BR_1' < 0$. The strategic relationship between the actions can be inferred directly from the cross-partial derivative of the profit function.

E15.4 Cournot model

In the Cournot model, profits are given as a function of the two firms' quantities:

$$\pi^1(q_1, q_2) = q_1 P(q_1, q_2) - C(q_1). \qquad \textbf{(vii)}$$

The first-order condition is

$$\pi_1^1 = q_1 P'(q_1 + q_2) + P(q_1 + q_2) - C'(q_1), \qquad \textbf{(viii)}$$

as we have already seen (Equation 15.2). The derivative of Equation viii with respect to q_2 is, after dropping functions' arguments for brevity,

$$\pi_{12}^1 = q_1 P'' + P'. \qquad \textbf{(ix)}$$

Because $P' < 0$, the sign of π_{12}^1 will depend on the sign of P''—that is, the curvature of demand. With linear demand, $P'' = 0$ and so π_{12}^1 is clearly negative. Quantities are strategic substitutes in the Cournot model with linear demand. Figure 15.2 illustrates this general principle. This figure is drawn for an example involving linear demand, and indeed the best responses are downward sloping.

More generally, quantities are strategic substitutes in the Cournot model unless the demand curve is "very" convex (i.e., unless P'' is positive and large enough to offset the last term in Equation ix). For a more detailed discussion see Bulow, Geanakoplous, and Klemperer (1985).

E15.5 Bertrand model with differentiated products

In the Bertrand model with differentiated products, demand can be written as

$$q_1 = D^1(p_1, p_2). \qquad \textbf{(x)}$$

See Equation 15.24 for a related expression. Using this notation, profit can be written as

$$\begin{aligned} \pi^1 &= p_1 q_1 - C(q_1) \\ &= p_1 D^1(p_1, p_2) - C(D^1(p_1, p_2)). \end{aligned} \qquad \textbf{(xi)}$$

The first-order condition with respect to p_1 is

$$\begin{aligned} \pi_1^1 &= p_1 D_1^1(p_1, p_2) + D^1(p_1, p_2) \\ &\quad - C'(D^1(p_1, p_2)) D_1^1(p_1, p_2). \end{aligned} \qquad \textbf{(xii)}$$

The cross-partial derivative is, after dropping functions' arguments for brevity,

$$\pi_{12}^1 = p_1 D_{12}^1 + D_2^1 - C' D_{12}^1 - C'' D_2^1 D_1^1. \qquad \textbf{(xiii)}$$

Interpreting this mass of symbols is no easy task. In the special case of constant marginal cost ($C'' = 0$) and linear demand ($D_{12}^1 = 0$), the sign of π_{12}^1 is given by the sign of D_2^1 (i.e., how a firm's demand is affected by changes in the rival's price). In the usual case when the two goods are themselves substitutes, we have $D_2^1 > 0$ and so $\pi_{12}^1 > 0$. That is, prices are strategic complements. The terminology here can seem contradictory, so the result bears repeating: If the goods that the firms sell are substitutes, then the variables the firms choose—prices—are strategic complements. Firms in such a duopoly would either raise or lower prices together (see Tirole, 1988). We saw an example of this in Figure 15.4. The figure was drawn for the case of linear demand and constant marginal cost, and we saw that best responses are upward sloping.

E15.6 Entry accommodation in a sequential game

Consider a sequential game in which firm 1 chooses a_1 and then firm 2 chooses a_2. Suppose firm 1 finds it more profitable to accommodate than to deter firm 2's entry. Since firm 2 moves after firm 1, we can substitute 2's best response into 1's profit function to obtain

$$\pi^1(a_1, BR_2(a_1)). \qquad \textbf{(xiv)}$$

Firm 1's first-order condition is

$$\pi_1^1 + \underbrace{\pi_2^1 BR_2'}_{S} = 0. \qquad \textbf{(xv)}$$

By contrast, the first-order condition from the simultaneous game (see Equation i) is simply $\pi_1^1 = 0$. The first-order conditions from the sequential and simultaneous games differ in the term S. This term captures the strategic effect of moving first—that is, whether the first mover would choose a higher or lower action in the sequential game than in the simultaneous game.

The sign of S is determined by the signs of the two factors in S. We will argue in the next paragraph that these two factors will typically have the same sign (both positive or both negative), implying that $S > 0$ and hence that the first mover will typically distort its action upward in the sequential game compared to the simultaneous game. This result confirms the findings from several of the examples in the text. In Figure 15.6, we see that the Stackelberg quantity is higher than the Cournot quantity. In Figure 15.7, we see that the price leader distorts its price upward in the sequential game compared to the simultaneous one.

Section E15.3 showed that the sign of BR_2' is the same as the sign of π_{12}^2. If there is some symmetry to the market, then the sign of π_{12}^2 will be the same as the sign of π_{12}^1. Typically, π_2^1 and π_{12}^1 will have the same sign. For example, consider the case of Cournot competition. By Equation 15.1, firm 1's profit is

$$\pi_1 = P(q_1 + q_2)q_1 - C(q_1). \qquad \textbf{(xvi)}$$

Therefore,

$$\pi_2^1 = P'(q_1 + q_2)q_1. \qquad \textbf{(xvii)}$$

Since demand is downward sloping, it follows that $\pi_2^1 < 0$. Differentiating Equation xvii with respect to q_1 yields

$$\pi_{12}^1 = P' + q_1 P''. \qquad \textbf{(xviii)}$$

This expression is also negative if demand is linear (so $P'' = 0$) or if demand is not too convex (so the last term in Equation xviii does not swamp the term P').

E15.7 Extension to general investments

The model from the previous section can be extended to general investments—that is, beyond a mere commitment to a quantity or price. Let K_1 be this general investment—(say) advertising, investment in lower-cost manufacturing, or product positioning—sunk at the outset of the game. The two firms then choose their product-market actions a_1 and a_2 (representing prices or quantities) simultaneously in the second period. Firms' profits in this extended model are, respectively,

$$\pi^1(a_1, a_2, K_1) \quad \text{and} \quad \pi^2(a_1, a_2). \qquad \textbf{(xix)}$$

The analysis is simplified by assuming that firm 2's profit is not directly a function of K_1, although firm 2's profit will indirectly depend on K_1 in equilibrium because equilibrium actions will depend on K_1. Let

$a_1^*(K_1)$ and $a_2^*(K_1)$ be firms' actions in a subgame-perfect equilibrium:

$$a_1^*(K_1) = BR_1(a_2^*(K_1), K_1),$$
$$a_2^*(K_1) = BR_2(a_1^*(K_1)). \qquad \textbf{(xx)}$$

Since firm 2's profit function does not depend directly on K_1 in Equation xix, neither does its best response in Equation xx.

The analysis here draws on Fudenberg and Tirole (1984) and Tirole (1988). Substituting from Equation xx into Equation xix, the firms' Nash equilibrium profits in the subgame following firm 1's choice of K_1 are

$$\pi^{1*}(K_1) = \pi^1(a_1^*(K_1), a_2^*(K_1), K_1),$$
$$\pi^{2*}(K_1) = \pi^2(a_1^*(K_1), a_2^*(K_1)). \qquad \textbf{(xxi)}$$

Fold the game back to firm 1's first-period choice of K_1. Because firm 1 wants to accommodate entry, it chooses K_1 to maximize $\pi^{1*}(K_1)$. Totally differentiating $\pi^{1*}(K_1)$, the first-order condition is

$$\frac{d\pi^{1*}}{dK_1} = \pi_1^1 \frac{da_1^*}{dK_1} + \pi_2^1 \frac{da_2^*}{dK_1} + \frac{\partial \pi^1}{\partial K_1}$$

$$= \underbrace{\pi_2^1 \frac{da_2^*}{dK_1}}_{S} + \frac{\partial \pi^1}{\partial K_1}. \qquad \textbf{(xxii)}$$

The second equality in Equation xxii holds by the envelope theorem. (The envelope theorem just says that $\pi_1^1 \cdot da_1^*/dK_1$ disappears because a_1 is chosen optimally in the second period, so $\pi_1^1 = 0$ by the first-order condition for a_1.) The first of the remaining two terms in Equation xxii, S, is the strategic effect of an increase in K_1 on firm 1's profit through firm 2's action. If firm 1 cannot make an observable commitment to K_1, then S disappears from Equation xxii and only the last term, the direct effect of K_1 on firm 1's profit, will be present.

The sign of S determines whether firm 1 strategically over- or underinvests in K_1 when it can make a strategic commitment. We have the following steps:

$$\text{sign}(S) = \text{sign}\left(\pi_1^2 \frac{da_2^*}{dK_1}\right)$$

$$= \text{sign}\left(\pi_1^2 BR_2' \frac{da_1^*}{dK_1}\right)$$

$$= \text{sign}\left(\frac{d\pi^{2*}}{dK_1} BR_2'\right). \qquad \textbf{(xxiii)}$$

The first line of Equation xxiii holds if there is some symmetry to the market, so that the sign of π_2^1 equals the sign of π_1^2. The second line follows from differentiating $a_2^*(K_1)$ in Equation xx. The third line follows by totally differentiating π^{2*} in Equation xxi:

$$\frac{d\pi^{2*}}{dK_1} = \pi_1^2 \frac{da_1^*}{dK_1} + \pi_2^2 \frac{da_2^*}{dK_1}$$

$$= \pi_1^2 \frac{da_1^*}{dK_1}, \qquad \textbf{(xxiv)}$$

where the second equality again follows from the envelope theorem.

By Equation xxiii, the sign of the strategic effect S is determined by the sign of two factors. The first factor, $d\pi^{2*}/dK_1$, indicates the effect of K_1 on firm 2's equilibrium profit in the subgame. If $d\pi^{2*}/dK_1 < 0$, then an increase in K_1 harms firm 2 and we say that investment makes firm 1 "tough." If $d\pi^{2*}/dK_1 > 0$, then an increase in K_1 benefits firm 2 and we say that investment makes firm 1 "soft." The second factor, BR_2', is the slope of firm 2's best response, which depends on whether actions a_1 and a_2 are strategic substitutes or complements. Each of the two terms in S can have one of two signs for a total of four possible combinations, displayed in Table 15.1. If investment makes firm 1 "tough", then the strategic effect S leads firm 1 to reduce K_1 if actions are strategic complements or to increase K_1 if actions are strategic substitutes. The opposite is true if investment makes firm 1 "soft."

For example, actions could be prices in a Bertrand model with differentiated products and thus would be strategic complements. Investment K_1 could be advertising that steals market share from firm 2. Table 15.1 indicates that, when K_1 is observable, firm 1 should strategically underinvest in order to induce less aggressive price competition from firm 2.

E15.8 Most-favored customer program

The preceding analysis applies even if K_1 is not a continuous investment variable but instead a 0–1 choice. For example, consider the decision by firm 1 of whether to start a most-favored-customer program (studied in Cooper, 1986). A most-favored customer program rebates the price difference (sometimes in addition to a premium) to past customers if the firm lowers its price in the future. Such a program makes firm 1 "soft" by reducing its incentive to cut price. If firms compete in strategic complements (say, in a Bertrand model with differentiated products), then Table 15.1 says that firm 1 should "overinvest" in the most-favored customer program, meaning that it should be more willing to implement the program if doing so is observable to its rival. The strategic effect leads to less aggressive price competition and thus to higher prices and profits.

One's first thought might have been that such a most-favored customer program should be beneficial to consumers and lead to lower prices, since the clause promises payments back to them. As we can see from this example, strategic considerations sometimes prove one's initial intuition wrong, suggesting that caution is warranted when examining strategic situations.

E15.9 Trade policy

The analysis in Section E15.7 applies even if K_1 is not a choice by firm 1 itself. For example, researchers in international trade sometimes take K_1 to be a government's policy choice on behalf of its domestic firms. Brander and Spencer (1985) studied a model of international trade in which exporting firms from country 1 engage in Cournot competition with domestic firms

TABLE 15.1 Strategic Effect When Accommodating Entry

		Firm 1's Investment	
		"Tough" ($d\pi^{2*}/dK_1 < 0$)	"Soft" ($d\pi^{2*}/dK_1 > 0$)
Actions	Strategic Complements ($BR' > 0$)	Underinvest ($-$)	Overinvest ($+$)
	Strategic Substitutes ($BR' < 0$)	Overinvest ($+$)	Underinvest ($-$)

in country 2. The actions (quantities) are strategic substitutes. The authors ask whether the government of country 1 would want to implement an export subsidy program, a decision that plays the role of K_1 in their model. An export subsidy makes exporting firms "tough" because it effectively lowers their marginal costs, increasing their exports to country 2 and reducing market price there. According to Table 15.1, the government of country 1 should overinvest in the subsidy policy, adopting the policy if it is observable to domestic firms in country 2 but not otherwise. The model explains why countries unilaterally adopt export subsidies and other trade interventions when free trade would be globally efficient (at least in this simple model).

Our analysis can be used to show that Brander and Spencer's rationalization of export subsidies may not hold up under alternative assumptions about competition. If exporting firms and domestic firms were to compete in strategic complements (say, Bertrand competition in differentiated products rather than Cournot competition), then an export subsidy would be a bad idea according to Table 15.1. Country 1 should then underinvest in the export subsidy (that is, not adopt it) to avoid overly aggressive price competition.

E15.10 Entry deterrence

Continue with the model from Section E15.7, but now suppose that firm 1 prefers to deter rather than accommodate entry. Firm 1's objective is then to choose K_1 to reduce 2's profit π^{2*} to zero. Whether firm 1 should distort K_1 upward or downward to accomplish this depends only on the sign of $d\pi^{2*}/dK_1$—that is, on whether investment makes firm 1 "tough" or "soft"— and not on whether actions are strategic substitutes or complements. If investment makes firm 1 "tough," it should overinvest to deter entry relative to the case in which it cannot observably commit to investment. On the other hand, if investment makes firm 1 "soft," it should underinvest to deter entry.

For example, if K_1 is an investment in marginal cost reduction, this likely makes firm 1 "tough" and so it should overinvest to deter entry. If K_1 is an advertisement that increases demand for the whole product category more than its own brand (advertisements for a particular battery brand involving an unstoppable, battery-powered bunny may increase sales of all battery brands if consumers have difficulty remembering exactly which battery was in the bunny), then this will likely make firm 1 "soft," so it should underinvest to deter entry.

References

Brander, J. A., and B. J. Spencer. "Export Subsidies and International Market Share Rivalry." *Journal of International Economics* 18 (February 1985): 83–100.

Bulow, J., G. Geanakoplous, and P. Klemperer. "Multimarket Oligopoly: Strategic Substitutes and Complements." *Journal of Political Economy* (June 1985): 488–511.

Cooper, T. "Most-Favored-Customer Pricing and Tacit Collusion." *Rand Journal of Economics* 17 (Autumn 1986): 377–88.

Fudenberg, D., and J. Tirole. "The Fat Cat Effect, the Puppy Dog Ploy and the Lean and Hungry Look." *American Economic Review, Papers and Proceedings* 74 (May 1984): 361–68.

Tirole, J. *The Theory of Industrial Organization*. Cambridge, MA: MIT Press, 1988, chap. 8.

Pricing in Input Markets

Our study of input demand in Chapter 11 was quite general in that it can be applied to any factor of production. In Chapters 16 and 17 we take up several issues specifically related to pricing in the labor and capital markets. **Chapter 16** focuses mainly on labor supply. Most of our analysis deals with labor supply decisions of single individuals. Labor supply by unions is also considered, as is the possibility that a labor market may be noncompetitive on the demand side.

In **Chapter 17** we examine the market for capital. The central purpose of the chapter is to emphasize the connection between capital and the allocation of resources over time. Some care is also taken to integrate the theory of capital into the models of firms' behavior we developed in Part 3. A brief appendix to Chapter 17 presents some useful mathematical results about interest rates.

In *The Principles of Political Economy and Taxation*, Ricardo wrote:

> The produce of the earth . . . is divided among three classes of the community, namely, the proprietor of the land, the owner of the stock of capital necessary for its cultivation, and the laborers by whose industry it is cultivated. To determine the laws which regulate this distribution is the principal problem in Political Economy.*

The purpose of Part 6 is to illustrate how the study of these "laws" has advanced since Ricardo's time.

---

*D. Ricardo, *The Principles of Political Economy and Taxation* (1817; reprinted, London: J. M. Dent and Son, 1965), p. 1.

Labor Markets

In this chapter we examine some aspects of input pricing that are related particularly to the labor market. Because we have already discussed questions about the demand for labor (or any other input) in some detail in Chapter 11, here we will be concerned primarily with analyzing the supply of labor.

ALLOCATION OF TIME

In Part 2 we studied the way in which an individual chooses to allocate a fixed amount of income among a variety of available goods. Individuals must make similar choices in deciding how they will spend their time. The number of hours in a day (or in a year) is absolutely fixed, and time must be used as it "passes by." Given this fixed amount of time, any individual must decide how many hours to work; how many hours to spend consuming a wide variety of goods, ranging from cars and television sets to operas; how many hours to devote to self-maintenance; and how many hours to sleep. By examining how individuals choose to divide their time among these activities, economists are able to understand the labor supply decision.

Simple two-good model

For simplicity we start by assuming there are only two uses to which an individual may devote his or her time—either engaging in market work at a real wage rate of w per hour or not working. We shall refer to nonwork time as "leisure," but this word is not meant to carry any connotation of idleness. Time not spent in market work can be devoted to work in the home, to self-improvement, or to consumption (it takes time to use a television set or a bowling ball).[1] All of those activities contribute to an individual's well-being, and time will be allocated to them in what might be assumed to be a utility-maximizing way.

More specifically, assume that an individual's utility during a typical day depends on consumption during that period (c) and on hours of leisure enjoyed (h):

$$\text{utility} = U(c, h). \tag{16.1}$$

Notice that in writing this utility function we have used two "composite" goods, consumption and leisure. Of course, utility is actually derived by devoting real income and time to the consumption of a wide variety of goods and services.[2] In seeking to maximize utility,

---

[1]Perhaps the first formal theoretical treatment of the allocation of time was given by G. S. Becker in "A Theory of the Allocation of Time," *Economic Journal* 75 (September 1965): 493–517.

[2]This observation leads to the consideration of how such activities are produced in the home. For an influential survey, see R. Gronau, "Home Production: A Survey," in O. C. Ashenfelter and R. Layard, Eds., *Handbook of Labor Economics* (Amsterdam: North-Holland, 1986), vol. 1, pp. 273–304.

an individual is bound by two constraints. The first of these concerns is available time. If we let l represent hours of work, then

$$l + h = 24. \tag{16.2}$$

That is, the day's time must be allocated either to work or to leisure (nonwork). A second constraint records the fact that an individual can purchase consumption items only by working (later in this chapter we will allow for the availability of nonlabor income). If the real hourly market wage rate the individual can earn is given by w, then the income constraint is given by

$$c = wl. \tag{16.3}$$

Combining the two constraints, we have

$$c = w(24 - h) \tag{16.4}$$

or

$$c + wh = 24w. \tag{16.5}$$

This combined constraint has an important interpretation. Any person has a "full income" given by $24w$. That is, an individual who worked all the time would have this much command over real consumption goods each day. Individuals may spend their full income either by working (for real income and consumption) or by not working and thereby enjoying leisure. Equation 16.5 shows that the opportunity cost of consuming leisure is w per hour; it is equal to earnings forgone by not working.

Utility maximization

The individual's problem, then, is to maximize utility subject to the full income constraint. Given the Lagrangian expression

$$\mathcal{L} = U(c, h) + \lambda(24w - c - wh), \tag{16.6}$$

the first-order conditions for a maximum are

$$\frac{\partial \mathcal{L}}{\partial c} = \frac{\partial U}{\partial c} - \lambda = 0,$$
$$\frac{\partial \mathcal{L}}{\partial h} = \frac{\partial U}{\partial h} - w\lambda = 0. \tag{16.7}$$

Dividing the two lines in Equation 16.7, we obtain

$$\frac{\partial U / \partial h}{\partial U / \partial c} = w = MRS \ (h \text{ for } c). \tag{16.8}$$

Hence we have derived the following principle.

OPTIMIZATION PRINCIPLE | **Utility-maximizing labor supply decision.** To maximize utility given the real wage w, the individual should choose to work that number of hours for which the marginal rate of substitution of leisure for consumption is equal to w.

Of course, the result derived in Equation 16.8 is only a necessary condition for a maximum. As in Chapter 4, this tangency will be a true maximum provided the MRS of leisure for consumption is diminishing.

Income and substitution effects of a change in *w*

A change in the real wage rate (w) can be analyzed in a manner identical to that used in Chapter 5. When w rises, the "price" of leisure becomes higher: a person must give up more in lost wages for each hour of leisure consumed. As a result, the substitution effect of an increase in w on the hours of leisure will be negative. As leisure becomes more expensive, there is reason to consume less of it. However, the income effect will be positive—because leisure is a normal good, the higher income resulting from a higher w will increase the demand for leisure. Thus, the income and substitution effects work in opposite directions. It is impossible to predict on a priori grounds whether an increase in w will increase or decrease the demand for leisure time. Because leisure and work are mutually exclusive ways to spend one's time, it is also impossible to predict what will happen to the number of hours worked. The substitution effect tends to increase hours worked when w increases, whereas the income effect—because it increases the demand for leisure time—tends to decrease the number of hours worked. Which of these two effects is the stronger is an important empirical question.[3]

A graphical analysis

The two possible reactions to a change in w are illustrated in Figure 16.1. In both graphs, the initial wage is w_0 and the initial optimal choices of c and h are given by the point c_0, h_0. When the wage rate increases to w_1, the optimal combination moves to point c_1, h_1. This movement

---

[3]If the family is taken to be the relevant decision unit, then even more complex questions arise about the income and substitution effects that changes in the wages of one family member will have on the labor force behavior of other family members.

FIGURE 16.1   Income and Substitution Effects of a Change in the Real Wage Rate *w*

Because the individual is a supplier of labor, the income and substitution effects of an increase in the real wage rate (w) work in opposite directions in their effects on the hours of leisure demanded (or on hours of work). In (a) the substitution effect (movement to point S) outweighs the income effect, and a higher wage causes hours of leisure to decline to h_1. Hours of work therefore increase. In (b) the income effect is stronger than the substitution effect, and h increases to h_1. In this case, hours of work decline.

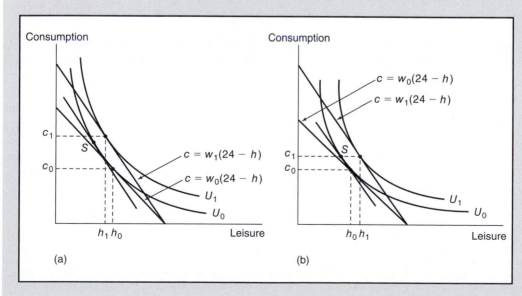

can be considered the result of two effects. The substitution effect is represented by the movement of the optimal point from c_0, h_0 to S and the income effect by the movement from S to c_1, h_1. In the two panels of Figure 16.1, these two effects combine to produce different results. In panel (a) the substitution effect of an increase in w outweighs the income effect, and the individual demands less leisure ($h_1 < h_0$). Another way of saying this is that the individual will work longer hours when w rises.

In panel (b) of Figure 16.1 the situation is reversed. The income effect of an increase in w more than offsets the substitution effect, and the demand for leisure increases ($h_1 > h_0$). The individual works shorter hours when w rises. In the cases examined in Chapter 5 this would have been considered an unusual result—when the "price" of leisure rises, the individual demands more of it. For the case of normal consumption goods, the income and substitution effects work in the same direction. Only for "inferior" goods do they differ in sign. In the case of leisure and labor, however, the income and substitution effects always work in opposite directions. An increase in w makes an individual better-off because he or she is a *supplier* of labor. In the case of a consumption good, individuals are made worse-off when a price rises because they are *consumers* of that good. We can summarize this analysis as follows.

<table>
<tr><td>OPTIMIZATION
PRINCIPLE</td><td>**Income and substitution effects of a change in the real wage.** When the real wage rate increases, a utility-maximizing individual may increase or decrease hours worked. The substitution effect will tend to increase hours worked as the individual substitutes earnings for leisure, which is now relatively more costly. On the other hand, the income effect will tend to reduce hours worked as the individual uses his or her increased purchasing power to buy more leisure hours.</td></tr>
</table>

We now turn to examine a mathematical development of these responses that provides additional insights into the labor supply decision.

A MATHEMATICAL ANALYSIS OF LABOR SUPPLY

To derive a mathematical statement of labor supply decisions, it is helpful first to amend the budget constraint slightly to allow for the presence of nonlabor income. To do so, we rewrite Equation 16.3 as

$$c = wl + n, \tag{16.9}$$

where n is real nonlabor income and may include such items as dividend and interest income, receipt of government transfer benefits, or simply gifts from other persons. Indeed, n could stand for lump-sum taxes paid by this individual, in which case its value would be negative.

Maximization of utility subject to this new budget constraint would yield results virtually identical to those we have already derived. That is, the necessary condition for a maximum described in Equation 16.8 would continue to hold as long as the value of n is unaffected by the labor-leisure choices being made; that is, so long as n is a lump-sum receipt or loss of income,[4] the only effect of introducing nonlabor income into the analysis is to shift the budget constraints in Figure 16.1 outward or inward in a parallel manner without affecting the trade-off rate between earnings and leisure.

---

[4]In many situations, however, n itself may depend on labor supply decisions. For example, the value of welfare or unemployment benefits a person can receive depends on his or her earnings, as does the amount of income taxes paid. In such cases the slope of the individual's budget constraint will no longer be reflected by the real wage but must instead reflect the *net* return to additional work after taking increased taxes and reductions in transfer payments into account. For some examples, see the problems at the end of this chapter.

This discussion suggests that we can write the individual's labor supply function as $l(w, n)$ to indicate that the number of hours worked will depend both on the real wage rate and on the amount of real nonlabor income received. On the assumption that leisure is a normal good, $\partial l/\partial n$ will be negative; that is, an increase in n will raise the demand for leisure and (because there are only 24 hours in the day) reduce l. Before studying wage effects on labor supply $(\partial l/\partial w)$, we will find it helpful to consider the dual problem to the individual's primary utility-maximization problem.

Dual statement of the problem

As we showed in Chapter 5, related to the individual's primary problem of utility maximization given a budget constraint is the dual problem of minimizing the expenditures necessary to attain a given utility level. In the present context, this problem can be phrased as choosing values for consumption (c) and leisure time $(h = 24 - l)$ such that the amount of spending,

$$E = c - wl - n, \tag{16.10}$$

required to attain a given utility level [say, $U_0 = U(c, h)$] is as small as possible. As in Chapter 5, solving this minimization problem will yield exactly the same solution as solving the utility-maximization problem.

Now we can apply the envelope theorem to the minimum value for these extra expenditures calculated in the dual problem. Specifically, a small change in the real wage will change the minimum expenditures required by

$$\frac{\partial E}{\partial w} = -l. \tag{16.11}$$

Intuitively, each \$1 increase in w reduces the required value of E by \$$l$, because that is the extent to which labor earnings are increased by the wage change. This result is similar to Shephard's lemma in the theory of production (see Chapter 11); here the result shows that a labor supply function can be calculated from the expenditure function by partial differentiation. Because utility is held constant in the dual expenditure minimization approach, this function should be interpreted as a "compensated" (constant utility) labor supply function, which we will denote by $l^c(w, U)$ to avoid confusing it with the uncompensated labor supply function $l(w, n)$ introduced earlier.

Slutsky equation of labor supply

Now we can use these concepts to derive a Slutsky-type equation that reflects the substitution and income effects that result from changes in the real wage. We begin by recognizing that the expenditures being minimized in the dual problem of Equation 16.11 play the role of nonlabor income in the primal utility-maximization problem. Hence, by definition, for the utility-maximizing choice we have

$$l^c(w, U) = l[w, E(w, U)] = l(w, n). \tag{16.12}$$

Partial differentiation of both sides of Equation 16.12 with respect to w yields

$$\frac{\partial l^c}{\partial w} = \frac{\partial l}{\partial w} + \frac{\partial l}{\partial E} \cdot \frac{\partial E}{\partial w}, \tag{16.13}$$

and by using the envelope relation from Equation 16.11 for $\partial E/\partial w$ we obtain

$$\frac{\partial l^c}{\partial w} = \frac{\partial l}{\partial w} - l\frac{\partial l}{\partial E} = \frac{\partial l}{\partial w} - l\frac{\partial l}{\partial n}. \tag{16.14}$$

Introducing a slightly different notation for the compensated labor supply function,

$$\frac{\partial l^c}{\partial w} = \frac{\partial l}{\partial w}\bigg|_{U=U_0}, \tag{16.15}$$

and then rearranging terms gives the final Slutsky equation for labor supply:

$$\frac{\partial l}{\partial w} = \frac{\partial l}{\partial w}\bigg|_{U=U_0} + l\frac{\partial l}{\partial n}. \tag{16.16}$$

In words (as we have previously shown), the change in labor supplied in response to a change in the real wage can be disaggregated into the sum of a substitution effect in which utility is held constant and an income effect that is analytically equivalent to an appropriate change in nonlabor income. Because the substitution effect is positive (a higher wage increases the amount of work chosen when utility is held constant) and the term $\partial l/\partial n$ is negative, this derivation shows that the substitution and income effects work in opposite directions. The mathematical development supports the earlier conclusions from our graphical analysis and suggest at least the theoretical possibility that labor supply might respond negatively to increases in the real wage. The mathematical development also suggests that the importance of negative income effects may be greater the greater is the amount of labor itself being supplied.

EXAMPLE 16.1 Labor Supply Functions

Individual labor supply functions can be constructed from underlying utility functions in much the same way that we constructed demand functions in Part 2. Here we will begin with a fairly extended treatment of a simple Cobb-Douglas case and then provide a shorter summary of labor supply with CES utility.

1. Cobb-Douglas utility. Suppose that an individual's utility function for consumption, c, and leisure, h, is given by

$$U(c,h) = c^\alpha h^\beta, \tag{16.17}$$

and assume for simplicity that $\alpha + \beta = 1$. This person is constrained by two equations: (1) an income constraint that shows how consumption can be financed,

$$c = wl + n, \tag{16.18}$$

where n is nonlabor income; and (2) a total time constraint

$$l + h = 1, \tag{16.19}$$

where we have arbitrarily set the available time to be 1. By combining the financial and time constraints into a "full income" constraint, we can arrive at the following Lagrangian expression for this utility-maximization problem:

$$\mathscr{L} = U(c,h) + \lambda(w + n - wh - c) = c^\alpha h^\beta + \lambda(w + n - wh - c). \tag{16.20}$$

First-order conditions for a maximum are

$$\frac{\partial \mathscr{L}}{\partial c} = \alpha c^{-\beta} h^\beta - \lambda = 0,$$

$$\frac{\partial \mathscr{L}}{\partial h} = \beta c^\alpha h^{-\alpha} - \lambda w = 0, \tag{16.21}$$

$$\frac{\partial \mathscr{L}}{\partial \lambda} = w + n - wh - c = 0.$$

Dividing the first of these by the second yields

$$\frac{\alpha h}{\beta c} = \frac{\alpha h}{(1-\alpha)c} = \frac{1}{w} \quad \text{or} \quad wh = \frac{1-\alpha}{\alpha} \cdot c. \tag{16.22}$$

Substitution into the full income constraint then yields the familiar results

$$c = \alpha(w + n),$$

$$h = \frac{\beta(w + n)}{w}. \tag{16.23}$$

In words, this person spends a fixed fraction, α, of his or her full income $(w + n)$ on consumption and the complementary fraction, $\beta = 1 - \alpha$, on leisure (which costs w per unit). The labor supply function for this person is then given by

$$l(w, n) = 1 - h = (1 - \beta) - \frac{\beta n}{w}. \tag{16.24}$$

2. Properties of the Cobb-Douglas labor supply function. This labor supply function shares many of the properties exhibited by consumer demand functions derived from Cobb-Douglas utility. For example, if $n = 0$ then $\partial l / \partial w = 0$—this person always devotes $1 - \beta$ proportion of his or her time to working, no matter what the wage rate. Income and substitution effects of a change in w are precisely offsetting in this case, just as they are with cross-price effects in Cobb-Douglas demand functions.

On the other hand, if $n > 0$ then $\partial l / \partial w > 0$. When there is positive nonlabor income, this person spends βn of it on leisure. But leisure "costs" w per hour, so an increase in the wage means that fewer hours of leisure can be bought. Hence, a rise in w increases labor supply.

Finally, observe that $\partial l / \partial n < 0$. An increase in nonlabor income allows this person to buy more leisure, so labor supply decreases. One interpretation of this result is that transfer programs (such as welfare benefits or unemployment compensation) reduce labor supply. Another interpretation is that lump-sum taxation increases labor supply. But actual tax and transfer programs are seldom lump sum—usually they affect net wage rates as well. Hence, any precise prediction requires a detailed look at how such programs affect the budget constraint.

3. CES labor supply. In the Extensions to Chapter 4 we derived the general form for demand functions generated from a CES (constant elasticity of substitution) utility function. We can apply that derivation directly here to study CES labor demand. Specifically, if utility is given by

$$U(c, h) = \frac{c^\delta}{\delta} + \frac{h^\delta}{\delta}, \tag{16.25}$$

then budget share equations are given by

$$s_c = \frac{c}{w + n} = \frac{1}{1 + w^\kappa},$$

$$s_h = \frac{wh}{w + n} = \frac{1}{1 + w^{-\kappa}}, \tag{16.26}$$

where $\kappa = \delta / (\delta - 1)$. Solving explicitly for leisure demand gives

$$h = \frac{w + n}{w + w^{1-\kappa}} \tag{16.27}$$

(continued)

EXAMPLE 16.1   CONTINUED

and

$$l(w, n) = 1 - h = \frac{w^{1-\kappa} - n}{w + w^{1-\kappa}}. \tag{16.28}$$

It is perhaps easiest to explore the properties of this function by taking some examples. If $\delta = 0.5$ and $\kappa = -1$, the labor supply function is

$$l(m, n) = \frac{w^2 - n}{w + w^2} = \frac{1 - n/w^2}{1 + 1/w}. \tag{16.29}$$

If $n = 0$ then clearly $\partial l/\partial w > 0$; because of the relatively high degree of substitutability between consumption and leisure in this utility function, the substitution effect of a higher wage outweighs the income effect. On the other hand, if $\delta = -1$ and $\kappa = 0.5$ then the labor supply function is

$$l(w, n) = \frac{w^{0.5} - n}{w + w^{0.5}} = \frac{1 - n/w^{0.5}}{1 + w^{0.5}}. \tag{16.30}$$

Now (when $n = 0$) $\partial l/\partial w < 0$; because there is a smaller degree of substitutability in the utility function, the income effect outweighs the substitution effect in labor supply.[5]

QUERY: Why does the effect of nonlabor income in the CES case depend on the consumption/leisure substitutability in the utility function?

MARKET SUPPLY CURVE FOR LABOR

We can plot a curve for market supply of labor based on individual labor supply decisions. At each possible wage rate we add together the quantity of labor offered by each individual to arrive at a market total. One particularly interesting aspect of this procedure is that, as the wage rate rises, more individuals may be induced to enter the labor force. Figure 16.2 illustrates this possibility for the simple case of two people. For a real wage below w_1, neither individual chooses to work. Consequently, the market supply curve of labor (Figure 16.2c) shows that no labor is supplied at real wages below w_1. A wage in excess of w_1 causes individual 1 to enter the labor market. However, as long as wages fall short of w_2, individual 2 will not work. Only at a wage-rate above w_2 will both individuals participate in the labor market. In general, the possibility of the entry of new workers makes the market supply of labor somewhat more responsive to wage-rate increases than would be the case if the number of workers were assumed to be fixed.

The most important example of higher real wage rates inducing increased labor force participation is the labor force behavior of married women in the United States in the post–World War II period. Since 1950 the percentage of working married women has increased from 32 percent to over 65 percent; economists attribute this, at least in part, to the increasing wages that women are able to earn.

---

[5]In the Cobb-Douglas case ($\delta = 0, \kappa = 0$), the constant-share result (for $n = 0$) is given by $l(w, n) = (w - n)/2w = 0.5 - n/2w$.

FIGURE 16.2   Construction of the Market Supply Curve for Labor

As the real wage rises, there are two reasons why the supply of labor may increase. First, higher real wages may cause each person in the market to work more hours. Second, higher wages may induce more individuals (for example, individual 2) to enter the labor market.

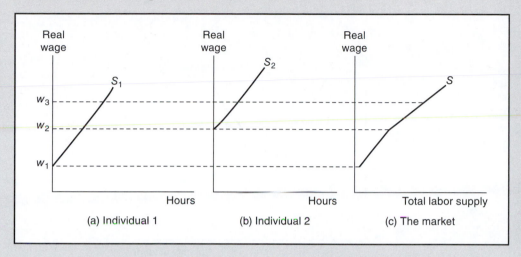

(a) Individual 1   (b) Individual 2   (c) The market

LABOR MARKET EQUILIBRIUM

Equilibrium in the labor market is established through the interaction of individuals' labor supply decisions with firms' decisions about how much labor to hire. That process is illustrated by the familiar supply-demand diagram in Figure 16.3. At a real wage rate of w^*, the quantity of labor demanded by firms is precisely matched by the quantity supplied by individuals. A real wage higher than w^* would create a disequilibrium in which the quantity of labor supplied is greater than the quantity demanded. There would be some involuntary unemployment at such a wage, and this may create pressure for the real wage to fall. Similarly, a real wage lower than w^* would result in disequilibrium behavior because firms would want to hire more workers than are available. In the scramble to hire workers, firms may bid up real wages to restore equilibrium.

Possible reasons for disequilibria in the labor market are a major topic in macroeconomics, especially in relationship to the business cycle. Perceived failures of the market to adjust to changing equilibria have been blamed on "sticky" real wages, inaccurate expectations by workers or firms about the price level, the impact of government unemployment insurance programs, labor market regulations and minimum wages, and intertemporal work decisions by workers. Microeconomic modeling of all of these possibilities has played a major role in recent advances in macroeconomics, though we will not pursue these topics here because that would take us away from the primary purposes of this book.

Equilibrium models of the labor market can also be used to study a number of questions about taxation and regulatory policy. For example, the tax incidence modeling illustrated in Chapter 12 can be readily adapted to the study of employment taxation. One interesting possibility that arises in the study of labor markets is that a given policy intervention may shift both demand and supply functions—a possibility we examine in Example 16.2.

FIGURE 16.3   Equilibrium in the Labor Market

A real wage of w^* creates an equilibrium in the labor market with an employment level of l^*.

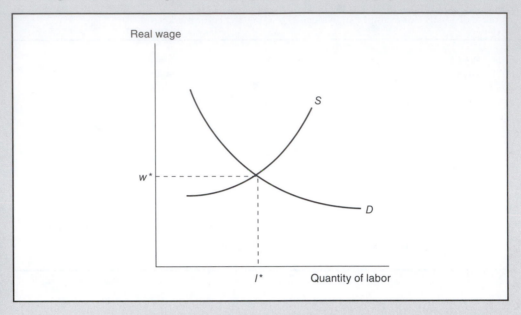

EXAMPLE 16.2 Mandated Benefits

A number of recent laws have mandated that employers provide special benefits to their workers such as health insurance, paid time off, or minimum severance packages. The effect of such mandates on equilibrium in the labor market depends importantly on how the benefits are valued by workers. Suppose that, prior to implementation of a mandate, the supply and demand for labor are given by

$$l_S = a + bw,$$
$$l_D = c - dw. \tag{16.31}$$

Setting $l_S = l_D$ yields an equilibrium wage of

$$w^* = \frac{c - a}{b + d}. \tag{16.32}$$

Now suppose that the government mandates that all firms provide a particular benefit to their workers and that this benefit costs t per unit of labor hired. Unit labor costs therefore increase to $w + t$. Suppose also that the new benefit has a monetary value to workers of k per unit of labor supplied—hence the net return from employment rises to $w + k$. Equilibrium in the labor market then requires that

$$a + b(w + k) = c - d(w + t). \tag{16.33}$$

A bit of manipulation of this expression shows that the net wage is given by

$$w^{**} = \frac{c - a}{b + d} - \frac{bk + dt}{b + d} = w^* - \frac{bk + dt}{b + d}. \tag{16.34}$$

If workers derive no value from the mandated benefit ($k = 0$), then the mandate is just like a tax on employment: employees pay a share of the tax given by the ratio $d/(b + d)$ and the equilibrium quantity of labor hired falls. Qualitatively similar results will occur so long as

$k < t$. On the other hand, if workers value the benefit at precisely its cost $(k = t)$, then the new wage falls precisely by the amount of this cost $(w^{**} = w^* - t)$ and the equilibrium level of employment does not change. Finally, if workers value the benefit at more than it costs the firm to provide it $(k > t$—a situation where one might wonder why the benefit was not already provided), then the equilibrium wage will fall by more than the benefit costs and equilibrium employment will increase.

QUERY: How would you graph this analysis? Would its conclusions depend on using linear supply and demand functions?

Wage variation

One topic that should be mentioned in connection with the supply-demand diagram in Figure 16.3 concerns how differences in workers and jobs can lead to differences in observed wages. Such wage variation has increased significantly in many economies in recent years, and examining the nature of supply and demand in the labor market can go a long way toward explaining it. Here we look briefly at two factors that are important in competitive labor markets before turning to a more extended discussion of imperfect competition in the labor market.

Human capital. Because the firm's demand for labor depends on the worker's marginal productivity, differences in productivity among workers should lead to different wages. Perhaps the most important source of such productivity differences is the human capital embodied in workers. Such capital is accumulated during a worker's lifetime through formal education, other formal methods of acquiring skills (such as a job training course), on-the-job training, and general life experiences. This process has much in common with the process of investing in physical capital—a topic we take up in the next chapter. Workers invest both money and their own time in acquiring skills in the hope that those skills will pay off in the labor market. Presumably, in making decisions about undertaking these activities, workers look at the rate of return that might be expected from their investments. Only those investments in skills that promise a return higher than can be made elsewhere will be undertaken. Of course, investing in human capital is different from investing in physical capital, primarily because human capital, once acquired, cannot be divested. This makes human capital investments somewhat more risky than are more liquid investments, and consequently rates of return may be higher.[6] Because human capital is both costly and raises worker productivity, it would be expected to have an unambiguously positive effect on real wages.

Compensating differentials. People obviously prefer some jobs to others. Factors such as pleasant working conditions, flexible hours, or easy commuting may make an individual willing to accept a job that pays less than others offer. This supply effect would be manifested in lower wages for such jobs. Alternatively, jobs that are unpleasant or involve significant risks will require higher wages if they are to be attractive to workers (see Problem 16.3). Such supply-induced differences in wages are termed "compensating wage differentials" because they compensate for job characteristics that workers value. The variation in such characteristics therefore explains some portion of the variation in wages.

---

[6]Pioneering work in the theory of human capital can be found in Gary Becker, *Human Capital: A Theoretical and Empirical Analysis with Special Reference to Education* (New York: National Bureau of Economic Research, 1964).

MONOPSONY IN THE LABOR MARKET

In many situations firms are not price takers for the inputs they buy. That is, the supply curve for, say, labor faced by the firm is not infinitely elastic at the prevailing wage rate. It often may be necessary for the firm to offer a wage above that currently prevailing if it is to attract more employees. In order to study such situations, it is most convenient to examine the polar case of *monopsony* (a single buyer) in the labor market. If there is only one buyer in the labor market, then this firm faces the entire market supply curve. To increase its hiring of labor by one more unit, it must move to a higher point on this supply curve. This will involve paying not only a higher wage to the "marginal worker" but also additional wages to those workers already employed. The marginal expense associated with hiring the extra unit of labor (ME_l) therefore exceeds its wage rate. We can show this result mathematically as follows. The total cost of labor to the firm is wl. Hence the change in those costs brought about by hiring an additional worker is

$$ME_l = \frac{\partial wl}{\partial l} = w + l \frac{\partial w}{\partial l}. \qquad (16.35)$$

In the competitive case, $\partial w / \partial l = 0$ and the marginal expense of hiring one more worker is simply the market wage, w. However, if the firm faces a positively sloped labor supply curve, then $\partial w / \partial l > 0$ and the marginal expense exceeds the wage. These ideas are summarized in the following definition.

DEFINITION

Marginal input expense. The *marginal expense* (*ME*) associated with any input is the increase in total costs of the input that results from hiring one more unit. If the firm faces an upward-sloping supply curve for the input, the marginal expense will exceed the market price of the input.

A profit-maximizing firm will hire any input up to the point at which its marginal revenue product is just equal to its marginal expense. This result is a generalization of our previous discussion of marginalist choices to cover the case of monopsony power in the labor market. As before, any departure from such choices will result in lower profits for the firm. If, for example, $MRP_l > ME_l$, then the firm should hire more workers because such an action would increase revenues more than costs. Alternatively, if $MRP_l < ME_l$, employment should be reduced because that would lower costs more rapidly than revenues.

Graphical analysis

The monopsonist's choice of labor input is illustrated in Figure 16.4. The firm's demand curve for labor (D) is drawn negatively sloped, as we have shown it must be.[7] Here also the ME_l curve associated with the labor supply curve (S) is constructed in much the same way that the marginal revenue curve associated with a demand curve can be constructed. Because S is positively sloped, the ME_l curve lies everywhere above S. The profit-maximizing level of labor input for the monopsonist is given by l_1, for at this level of input the profit-maximizing condition holds. At l_1 the wage rate in the market is given by w_1. Notice that the quantity of labor demanded falls short of that which would be hired in a perfectly competitive labor market (l^*). The firm has restricted input demand by virtue of its monopsonistic position in

---

[7]Figure 16.4 is intended only as a pedagogic device and cannot be rigorously defended. In particular, the curve labeled D, although it is supposed to represent the "demand" (or marginal revenue product) curve for labor, has no precise meaning for the monopsonist buyer of labor, because we cannot construct this curve by confronting the firm with a fixed wage rate. Instead, the firm views the entire supply curve, S, and uses the auxiliary curve ME_l to choose the most favorable point on S. In a strict sense, there is no such thing as the monopsonist's demand curve. This is analogous to the case of a monopoly, for which we could not speak of a monopolist's "supply curve."

FIGURE 16.4 Pricing in a Monopsonistic Labor Market

If a firm faces a positively sloped supply curve for labor (S), it will base its decisions on the marginal expense of additional hiring (ME_l). Because S is positively sloped, the ME_l curve lies above S. The curve S can be thought of as an "average cost of labor curve," and the ME_l curve is marginal to S. At l_1 the equilibrium condition $ME_l = MRP_l$ holds, and this quantity will be hired at a market wage rate w_1. Notice that the monopsonist buys less labor than would be bought if the labor market were perfectly competitive (l^*).

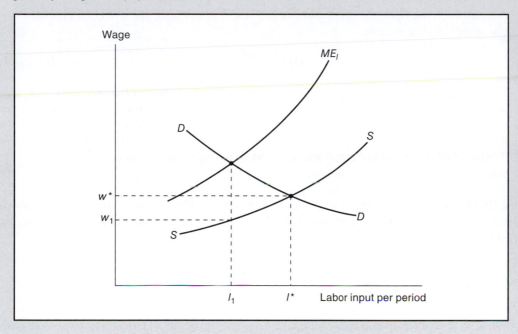

the market. The formal similarities between this analysis and that of monopoly presented in Chapter 14 should be clear. In particular, the "demand curve" for a monopsonist consists of a single point given by l_1, w_1. The monopsonist has chosen this point as the most desirable of all points on the supply curve, S. A different point will not be chosen unless some external change (such as a shift in the demand for the firm's output or a change in technology) affects labor's marginal revenue product.[8]

EXAMPLE 16.3 Monopsonistic Hiring

To illustrate these concepts in a simple context, suppose a coal mine's workers can dig two tons of coal per hour and coal sells for $10 per ton. The marginal revenue product of a coal miner is therefore $20 per hour. If the coal mine is the only hirer of miners in a local area and faces a labor supply curve of the form

$$l = 50w, \qquad\qquad \textbf{(16.36)}$$

(*continued*)

---

[8]A monopsony may also practice price discrimination in all of the ways described for a monopoly in Chapter 14. For a detailed discussion of the comparative statics analysis of factor demand in the monopoly and monopsony cases, see W. E. Diewert, "Duality Approaches to Microeconomic Theory," in K. J. Arrow and M. D. Intriligator, Eds., *Handbook of Mathematical Economics* (Amsterdam: North-Holland, 1982), vol. 2, pp. 584–90.

EXAMPLE 16.3   CONTINUED

then this firm must recognize that its hiring decisions affect wages. Expressing the total wage bill as a function of l,

$$wl = \frac{l^2}{50}, \tag{16.37}$$

permits the mine operator (perhaps only implicitly) to calculate the marginal expense associated with hiring miners:

$$ME_l = \frac{\partial wl}{\partial l} = \frac{l}{25}. \tag{16.38}$$

Equating this to miners' marginal revenue product of $20 implies that the mine operator should hire 500 workers per hour. At this level of employment the wage will be $10 per hour—only half the value of the workers' marginal revenue product. If the mine operator had been forced by market competition to pay $20 per hour regardless of the number of miners hired, then market equilibrium would have been established with $l = 1{,}000$ rather than the 500 hired under monopsonistic conditions.

QUERY: Suppose the price of coal rises to $15 per ton. How would this affect the monopsonist's hiring and the wages of coal miners? Would the miners benefit fully from the increase in their MRP?

LABOR UNIONS

Workers may at times find it advantageous to join together in a labor union to pursue goals that can more effectively be accomplished by a group. If association with a union were wholly voluntary, we could assume that every union member derives a positive benefit from belonging. Compulsory membership (the "closed shop"), however, is often used to maintain the viability of the union organization. If all workers were left on their own to decide on membership, their rational decision might be not to join the union, thereby avoiding dues and other restrictions. However, they would benefit from the higher wages and better working conditions that have been won by the union. What appears to be rational from each individual worker's point of view may prove to be irrational from a group's point of view, because the union is undermined by "free riders." Compulsory membership therefore may be a necessary means of maintaining the union as an effective bargaining agent.

Unions' goals

A good starting place for our analysis of union behavior is to describe union goals. A first assumption we might make is that the goals of a union are in some sense an adequate representation of the goals of its members. This assumption avoids the problem of union leadership and disregards the personal aspirations of those leaders, which may be in conflict with rank-and-file goals. Union leaders therefore are assumed to be conduits for expressing the desires of the membership.[9]

In some respects, unions can be analyzed in the same way as monopoly firms. The union faces a demand curve for labor; because it is the sole source of supply, it can choose at

---

[9]Much recent analysis, however, revolves around whether "potential" union members have some voice in setting union goals and how union goals may affect the desires of workers with differing amounts of seniority on the job.

FIGURE 16.5   Three Possible Points on the Labor Demand Curve
That a Monopolistic Union Might Choose

A union has a monopoly in the supply of labor, so it may choose it most preferred point on the demand curve for labor. Three such points are shown in the figure. At point E_1, total labor payments $(w \cdot l)$ are maximized; at E_2, the economic rent that workers receive is maximized; and at E_3, the total amount of labor services supplied is maximized.

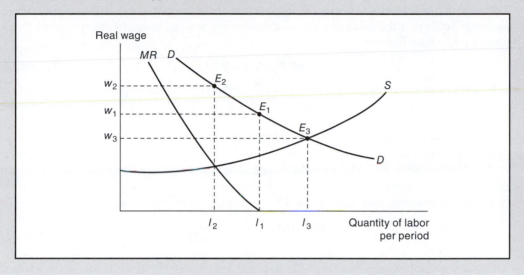

which point on this curve it will operate. The point actually chosen by the union will obviously depend on what particular goals it has decided to pursue. Three possible choices are illustrated in Figure 16.5. For example, the union may choose to offer that quantity of labor that maximizes the total wage bill $(w \cdot l)$. If this is the case, it will offer that quantity for which the "marginal revenue" from labor demand is equal to 0. This quantity is given by l_1 in Figure 16.5, and the wage rate associated with this quantity is w_1. The point E_1 is therefore the preferred wage-quantity combination. Notice that at wage rate w_1 there may be an excess supply of labor, and the union must somehow allocate available jobs to those workers who want them.

Another possible goal the union may pursue would be to choose the quantity of labor that would maximize the total economic rent (that is, wages less opportunity costs) obtained by those members who are employed. This would necessitate choosing that quantity of labor for which the additional total wages obtained by having one more employed union member (the marginal revenue) are equal to the extra cost of luring that member into the market. The union should therefore choose that quantity, l_2, at which the marginal revenue curve crosses the supply curve.[10] The wage rate associated with this quantity is w_2, and the desired wage-quantity combination is labeled E_2 in the diagram. With the wage w_2, many individuals who desire to work at the prevailing wage are left unemployed. Perhaps the union may "tax" the large economic rent earned by those who do work to transfer income to those who don't.

A third possibility would be for the union to aim for maximum employment of its members. This would involve choosing the point w_3, l_3, which is precisely the point that would result if the market were organized in a perfectly competitive way. No employment greater than l_3 could be achieved, because the quantity of labor that union members supply would be reduced for wages less than w_3.

---

[10]Mathematically, the union's goal is to choose l so as to maximize $wl -$ (area under S), where S is the compensated supply curve for labor and reflects workers' opportunity costs in terms of forgone leisure.

EXAMPLE 16.4 Modeling a Union

In Example 16.3 we examined a monopsonistic hirer of coal miners who faced a supply curve given by

$$l = 50w. \qquad (16.39)$$

To study the possibilities for unionization to combat this monopsonist, assume (contrary to Example 16.3) that the monopsonist has a downward-sloping marginal revenue product for labor curve of the form

$$MRP = 70 - 0.1l. \qquad (16.40)$$

It is easy to show that, in the absence of an effective union, the monopsonist in this situation will choose the same wage-hiring combination it did in Example 16.3: 500 workers will be hired at a wage of $10.

If the union can establish control over labor supply to the mine owner, then several other options become possible. The union could press for the competitive solution, for example. A contract of $l = 583$, $w = 11.66$ would equate supply and demand. Alternatively, the union could act as a monopolist facing the demand curve given by Equation 16.40. It could calculate the marginal increment yielded by supplying additional workers as

$$\frac{d(l \cdot MRP)}{dl} = 70 - 0.2l. \qquad (16.41)$$

The intersection between this "marginal revenue" curve and the labor supply curve (which indicates the "marginal opportunity cost" of workers' labor supply decisions) yields maximum rent to the unions' workers:

$$\frac{l}{50} = 70 - 0.2l \qquad (16.42)$$

or

$$3,500 = 11l. \qquad (16.43)$$

Such a calculation would therefore suggest a contract of $l = 318$ and a wage (MRP) of $38.20. The fact that both the competitive and union monopoly supply contracts differ significantly from the monopsonist's preferred contract indicates that the ultimate outcome here is likely to be determined through bilateral bargaining. Notice also that the wage differs significantly depending on which side has market power.

QUERY: Which, if any, of the three wage contracts described in this example might represent a Nash equilibrium?

EXAMPLE 16.5 A Union Bargaining Model

Game theory can be used to gain insights into the economics of unions. As a simple illustration, suppose a union and a firm engage in a two-stage game. In the first stage, the union sets the wage rate its workers will accept. Given this wage, the firm then chooses its employment level. This two-stage game can be solved by backward induction. Given the wage w specified by the union, the firm's second-stage problem is to maximize

$$\pi = R(l) - wl \qquad (16.44)$$

where R is the total revenue function of the firm expressed as a function of employment. The first-order condition for a maximum here (assuming that the wage is fixed) is the familiar

$$R'(l) = w. \tag{16.45}$$

Assuming l^* solves Equation 16.45, the union's goal is to choose w to maximize utility

$$U(w, l) = U[w, l^*(w)], \tag{16.46}$$

and the first-order condition for a maximum is

$$U_1 + U_2 l' = 0 \tag{16.47}$$

or

$$U_1 / U_2 = -l'. \tag{16.48}$$

In words, the union should choose w so that its MRS is equal to the absolute value of the slope of the firm's labor demand function. The w^*, l^* combination resulting from this game is clearly a Nash equilibrium.

Efficiency of the labor contract. The labor contract w^*, l^* is Pareto inefficient. To see this, notice that Equation 16.48 implies that small movements along the firm's labor demand curve (l) leave the union equally well-off. But the envelope theorem implies that a decline in w must increase profits to the firm. Hence there must exist a contract w^p, l^p (where $w^p < w^*$ and $l^p > l^*$) with which both the firm and union are better-off.

The inefficiency of the labor contract in this two-stage game is similar to the inefficiency of some of the repeated Nash equilibria we studied in Chapter 15. This suggests that, with repeated rounds of contract negotiations, trigger strategies might be developed that form a subgame-perfect equilibrium and maintain Pareto-superior outcomes. For a simple example, see Problem 16.10.

QUERY: Suppose the firm's total revenue function differed depending on whether the economy was in an expansion or a recession. What kinds of labor contracts might be Pareto optimal?

SUMMARY

In this chapter we examined some models that focus on pricing in the labor market. Because labor demand was already treated as being derived from the profit-maximization hypothesis in Chapter 11, most of the new material here focused on labor supply. Our primary findings were as follows.

- A utility-maximizing individual will choose to supply an amount of labor at which his or her marginal rate of substitution of leisure for consumption is equal to the real wage rate.

- An increase in the real wage creates substitution and income effects that work in opposite directions in affecting the quantity of labor supplied. This result can be summarized by a Slutsky-type equation much like the one already derived in consumer theory.

- A competitive labor market will establish an equilibrium real wage at which the quantity of labor supplied by individuals is equal to the quantity demanded by firms.

- Monopsony power by firms on the demand side of the labor market will reduce both the quantity of labor hired and the real wage. As in the monopoly case, there will also be a welfare loss.

- Labor unions can be treated analytically as monopoly suppliers of labor. The nature of labor market equilibrium in the presence of unions will depend importantly on the goals the union chooses to pursue.

PROBLEMS

16.1

Suppose there are 8,000 hours in a year (actually there are 8,760) and that an individual has a potential market wage of $5 per hour.

a. What is the individual's full income? If he or she chooses to devote 75 percent of this income to leisure, how many hours will be worked?

b. Suppose a rich uncle dies and leaves the individual an annual income of $4,000 per year. If he or she continues to devote 75 percent of full income to leisure, how many hours will be worked?

c. How would your answer to part (b) change if the market wage were $10 per hour instead of $5 per hour?

d. Graph the individual's supply of labor curve implied by parts (b) and (c).

16.2

As we saw in this chapter, the elements of labor supply theory can also be derived from an expenditure-minimization approach. Suppose a person's utility function for consumption and leisure takes the Cobb-Douglas form $U(c, h) = c^\alpha h^{1-\alpha}$. Then the expenditure-minimization problem is

$$\text{minimize } c - w(24 - h) \text{ s.t. } U(c, h) = c^\alpha h^{1-\alpha} = \bar{U}.$$

a. Use this approach to derive the expenditure function for this problem.

b. Use the envelope theorem to derive the compensated demand functions for consumption and leisure.

c. Derive the compensated labor supply function. Show that $\partial l^c / \partial w > 0$.

d. Compare the compensated labor supply function from part (c) to the uncompensated labor supply function in Example 16.1 (with $n = 0$). Use the Slutsky equation to show why income and substitution effects of a change in the real wage are precisely offsetting in the uncompensated Cobb-Douglas labor supply function.

16.3

A welfare program for low-income people offers a family a basic grant of $6,000 per year. This grant is reduced by $0.75 for each $1 of other income the family has.

a. How much in welfare benefits does the family receive if it has no other income? If the head of the family earns $2,000 per year? How about $4,000 per year?

b. At what level of earnings does the welfare grant become zero?

c. Assume the head of this family can earn $4 per hour and that the family has no other income. What is the annual budget constraint for this family if it does not participate in the welfare program? That is, how are consumption (c) and hours of leisure (h) related?

d. What is the budget constraint if the family opts to participate in the welfare program? (Remember, the welfare grant can only be positive.)

e. Graph your results from parts (c) and (d).

f. Suppose the government changes the rules of the welfare program to permit families to keep 50 percent of what they earn. How would this change your answers to parts (d) and (e)?

g. Using your results from part (f), can you predict whether the head of this family will work more or less under the new rules described in part (f)?

16.4

Suppose demand for labor is given by

$$l = -50w + 450$$

and supply is given by

$$l = 100w,$$

where l represents the number of people employed and w is the real wage rate per hour.

a. What will be the equilibrium levels for w and l in this market?

b. Suppose the government wishes to raise the equilibrium wage to $4 per hour by offering a subsidy to employers for each person hired. How much will this subsidy have to be? What will the new equilibrium level of employment be? How much total subsidy will be paid?

c. Suppose instead that the government declared a minimum wage of $4 per hour. How much labor would be demanded at this price? How much unemployment would there be?

d. Graph your results.

16.5

Carl the clothier owns a large garment factory on an isolated island. Carl's factory is the only source of employment for most of the islanders, and thus Carl acts as a monopsonist. The supply curve for garment workers is given by

$$l = 80w,$$

where l is the number of workers hired and w is their hourly wage. Assume also that Carl's labor demand (marginal revenue product) curve is given by

$$l = 400 - 40MRP_l.$$

a. How many workers will Carl hire to maximize his profits, and what wage will he pay?

b. Assume now that the government implements a minimum wage law covering all garment workers. How many workers will Carl now hire, and how much unemployment will there be if the minimum wage is set at $4 per hour?

c. Graph your results.

d. How does a minimum wage imposed under monopsony differ in results as compared with a minimum wage imposed under perfect competition? (Assume the minimum wage is above the market-determined wage.)

16.6

The Ajax Coal Company is the only hirer of labor in its area. It can hire any number of female workers or male workers it wishes. The supply curve for women is given by

$$l_f = 100w_f$$

and for men by

$$l_m = 9w_m^2,$$

where w_f and w_m are the hourly wage rates paid to female and male workers, respectively. Assume that Ajax sells its coal in a perfectly competitive market at $5 per ton and that each worker hired (both men and women) can mine 2 tons per hour. If the firm wishes to maximize profits, how many female and male workers should be hired, and what will the wage rates be for these two groups? How much will Ajax earn in profits per hour on its mine machinery? How will that result compare to one in which Ajax was constrained (say, by market forces) to pay all workers the same wage based on the value of their marginal products?

16.7

Universal Fur is located in Clyde, Baffin Island, and sells high-quality fur bow ties throughout the world at a price of $5 each. The production function for fur bow ties (q) is given by

$$q = 240x - 2x^2,$$

where x is the quantity of pelts used each week. Pelts are supplied only by Dan's Trading Post, which obtains them by hiring Eskimo trappers at a rate of $10 per day. Dan's weekly production function for pelts is given by

$$x = \sqrt{l},$$

where l represents the number of days of Eskimo time used each week.

   a. For a quasi-competitive case in which both Universal Fur and Dan's Trading Post act as price takers for pelts, what will be the equilibrium price (p_x) and how many pelts will be traded?

   b. Suppose Dan acts as a monopolist, while Universal Fur continues to be a price taker. What equilibrium will emerge in the pelt market?

   c. Suppose Universal Fur acts as a monopsonist but Dan acts as a price taker. What will the equilibrium be?

   d. Graph your results, and discuss the type of equilibrium that is likely to emerge in the bilateral monopoly bargaining between Universal Fur and Dan.

16.8

Following in the spirit of the labor market game described in Example 16.5, suppose the firm's total revenue function is given by

$$R = 10l - l^2$$

and the union's utility is simply a function of the total wage bill:

$$U(w, l) = wl.$$

   a. What is the Nash equilibrium wage contract in the two-stage game described in Example 16.5?

   b. Show that the alternative wage contract $w' = l' = 4$ is Pareto superior to the contract identified in part (a).

   c. Under what conditions would the contract described in part (b) be sustainable as a subgame-perfect equilibrium?

Analytical Problems

16.9 Compensating wage differentials for risk

An individual receives utility from daily income (y), given by

$$U(y) = 100y - \frac{1}{2}y^2.$$

The only source of income is earnings. Hence $y = wl$, where w is the hourly wage and l is hours worked per day. The individual knows of a job that pays $5 per hour for a certain 8-hour day. What wage must be offered for a construction job where hours of work are random—with a mean of 8 hours and a standard deviation of 6 hours—to get the individual to accept this more "risky" job? *Hint:* This problem makes use of the statistical identity

$$E(x^2) = \text{Var } x + E(x^2).$$

16.10 Family labor supply

A family with two adult members seeks to maximize a utility function of the form

$$U(c, h_1, h_2),$$

where c is family consumption and h_1 and h_2 are hours of leisure of each family member. Choices are constrained by

$$c = w_1(24 - h_1) + w_2(24 - h_2) + n,$$

where w_1 and w_2 are the wages of each family member and n is nonlabor income.

a. Without attempting a mathematical presentation, use the notions of substitution and income effects to discuss the likely signs of the cross-substitution effects $\partial h_1/\partial w_2$ and $\partial h_2/\partial w_1$.

b. Suppose that one family member (say, individual 1) can work in the home, thereby converting leisure hours into consumption according to the function

$$c_1 = f(h_1),$$

where $f' > 0$ and $f'' < 0$. How might this additional option affect the optimal division of work among family members?

16.11 A few results from demand theory

The theory developed in this chapter treats labor supply as the mirror image of the demand for leisure. Hence, the entire body of demand theory developed in Part 2 of the text becomes relevant to the study of labor supply as well. Here are three examples.

a. *Roy's identity.* In the Extensions to Chapter 5 we showed how demand functions can be derived from indirect utility functions by using Roy's identity. Use a similar approach to show that the labor supply function associated with the utility maximization problem described in Equation 16.20 can be derived from the indirect utility function by

$$l(w, n) = \frac{\partial V(w, n)/\partial w}{\partial V(w, n)/\partial n}.$$

Illustrate this result for the Cobb-Douglas case described in Example 16.1.

b. *Substitutes and complements.* A change in the real wage will affect not only labor supply, it may also affect the demand for specific items in the preferred consumption bundle. Develop a Slutsky-type equation for the cross-price effect of a change in w on a particular consumption item and then use it to discuss whether leisure and the item are (net or gross) substitutes or complements. Provide an example of each type of relationship.

c. *Labor supply and marginal expense.* Use a derivation similar to that used to calculate marginal revenue for a given demand curve to show that $ME_l = w\left(1 + 1/e_{l,w}\right)$.

16.12 Optimal wage taxation

The study of an optimal income tax structure is one of the most important topics in public economics. In this problem we investigate some aspects of this problem by assuming that individuals receive income only from the labor market. Hence income is given by $I = wl$, and we are interested in the properties of the tax function $T(I)$. The most customary way to describe the tax function is by the structure of marginal tax rates implied by the function—that is, by the function $T'(I)$. Two factors generate the distribution of incomes: (1) the distribution of wages (which are assumed to reflect individuals' skills and are unaffected by taxation); and (2) individual labor supply choices (which may be affected by taxation). To simplify matters we will assume that the distribution of wages is uniform over the interval $[0, 1]$. Hence, the distribution is characterized by a density function in which $f(w) = 1$ and by a cumulative distribution function for which $F(w) = w$.

a. Assume first that labor supply is unaffected by taxation because leisure does not enter into the utility function. In this case then the distribution of income is unaffected by what tax function is chosen. Show that, if individuals' utility of income functions are identical and logarithmic, then a proportional tax function $[T(I) = kI]$ will equilibrate the utility tax burden $[U(I) - U(I - T(I))]$ across taxpayers.

b. Describe how the conclusions about burden sharing from part (a) would be modified for utility functions that depart from the logarithmic form.

c. An alternative approach to defining optimality focuses on an explicit social welfare function that assigns social values to individual utility of the form $\psi[U(I - T(I))]$, where $\psi' > 0$ and $\psi'' < 0$. Total social welfare is therefore given by $SW = \int \psi \, dw$. Show that, if there is no labor supply response to taxation, then the optimal tax scheme for any given revenue target is one that equalizes after-tax incomes.

d. Characterizing the optimal tax structure for more general social welfare functions is difficult. For an extended discussion see B. Salanie, *The Economics of Taxation* (Cambridge, MA: MIT Press, 2003), chap. 4. For the simple case in which changes in marginal tax rates influence labor supply choices only over a narrow range of wages (say, in the neighborhood of w_0), wages are distributed as we have assumed, and the social welfare function seeks to maximize revenues from those who pay taxes, Salanie shows that the optimal marginal tax function is characterized by

$$\frac{T'(I)}{1 - T'(I)} = \left(1 + \frac{1}{e_{l,w}}\right)\left(\frac{1 - w_0}{w_0}\right).$$

Try to prove this yourself by assuming that, for a tax schedule to be optimal, any small increase in the marginal rate must not increase revenues.

e. Discuss the role that the elasticity of labor supply plays in determining the optimal marginal tax rate in part (d).

f. How does the optimal marginal tax rate calculated in part (d) depend on wages? Explain this result intuitively.

SUGGESTIONS FOR FURTHER READING

Ashenfelter, O. C., and D. Card. *Handbook of Labor Economics*, vol. 3. Amsterdam: North Holland, 1999.

Contains a variety of high-level essays on many labor market topics. Survey articles on labor supply and demand in volumes 1 and 2 (1986) are also highly recommended.

Becker, G. "A Theory of the Allocation of Time." *Economic Journal* (September 1965): 493–517.

One of the most influential papers in microeconomics. Becker's observations on both labor supply and consumption decisions were revolutionary.

Binger, B. R., and E. Hoffman. *Microeconomics with Calculus*, 2nd ed. Reading, MA: Addison-Wesley, 1998.

Chapter 17 has a thorough discussion of the labor supply model, including some applications to household labor supply.

Hamermesh, D. S. *Labor Demand*. Princeton, NJ: Princeton University Press, 1993.

The author offers a complete coverage of both theoretical and empirical issues. The book also has nice coverage of dynamic issues in labor demand theory.

Silberberg, E., and W. Suen. *The Structure of Economics: A Mathematical Analysis*, 3rd ed. Boston: Irwin/McGraw-Hill, 2001.

Provides a nice discussion of the dual approach to labor supply theory.

Capital and Time

In this chapter we provide an introduction to the theory of capital. In many ways that theory resembles our previous analysis of input pricing in general—the principles of profit-maximizing input choice do not change. But capital theory adds an important time dimension to economic decision making; our goal here is to explore that extra dimension. We begin with a broad characterization of the capital accumulation process and the notion of the rate of return. Then we turn to more specific models of economic behavior over time.

CAPITAL AND THE RATE OF RETURN

When we speak of the capital stock of an economy, we mean the sum total of machines, buildings, and other reproducible resources in existence at some point in time. These assets represent some part of an economy's past output that was not consumed but was instead set aside to be used for production in the future. All societies, from the most primitive to the most complex, engage in capital accumulation. Hunters in a primitive society taking time off from hunting to make arrows, individuals in a modern society using part of their incomes to buy houses, or governments taxing citizens in order to purchase dams and post office buildings are all engaging in essentially the same sort of activity: some portion of current output is being set aside for use in producing output in future periods. Present "sacrifice" for future gain is the essential aspect of capital accumulation.

Rate of return

The process of capital accumulation is pictured schematically in Figure 17.1. In both panels of the figure, society is initially consuming level c_0 and has been doing so for some time. At time t_1 a decision is made to withhold some output (amount s) from current consumption for one period. Starting in period t_2, this withheld consumption is in some way put to use producing future consumption. An important concept connected with this process is the *rate of return*, which is earned on that consumption that is put aside. In panel (a), for example, all of the withheld consumption is used to produce additional output only in period t_2. Consumption is increased by amount x in period t_2 and then returns to the long-run level c_0. Society has saved in one year in order to splurge in the next year. The (one-period) rate of return from this activity is defined as follows.

Single-period rate of return. The *single-period rate of return* (r_1) on an investment is the extra consumption provided in period 2 as a fraction of the consumption forgone in period 1. That is,

DEFINITION

$$r_1 = \frac{x - s}{s} = \frac{x}{s} - 1. \qquad (17.1)$$

FIGURE 17.1   Two Views of Capital Accumulation

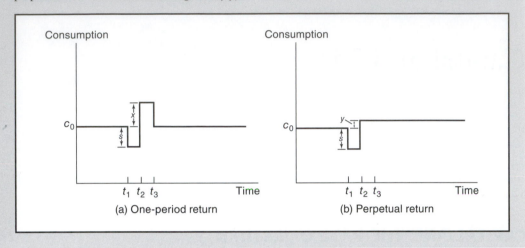

In (a), society withdraws some current consumption (s) to gorge itself (with x extra consumption) in the next period. The one-period rate of return would be measured by $x/s - 1$. The society in (b) takes a more long-term view and uses s to increase its consumption perpetually by y. The perpetual rate of return would be given by y/s.

If $x > s$ (if more consumption comes out of this process than went into it), we would say that the one-period rate of return to capital accumulation is positive. For example, if withholding 100 units from current consumption permitted society to consume an extra 110 units next year, then the one-period rate of return would be

$$\frac{110}{100} - 1 = 0.10$$

or 10 percent.

In panel (b) of Figure 17.1, society takes a more long-term view in its capital accumulation. Again, an amount s is set aside at time t_1. Now, however, this set-aside consumption is used to raise the consumption level for all periods in the future. If the permanent level of consumption is raised to $c_0 + y$, we define the perpetual rate of return as follows.

DEFINITION   **Perpetual rate of return.** The *perpetual rate of return* (r_∞) is the permanent increment to future consumption expressed as a fraction of the initial consumption forgone. That is,

$$r_\infty = \frac{y}{s}. \tag{17.2}$$

If capital accumulation succeeds in raising c_0 permanently, then r_∞ will be positive. For example, suppose that society set aside 100 units of output in period t_1 to be devoted to capital accumulation. If this capital would permit output to be raised by 10 units for every period in the future (starting at time period t_2), the perpetual rate of return would be 10 percent.

When economists speak of the rate of return to capital accumulation, they have in mind something between these two extremes. Somewhat loosely we shall speak of the rate of return as being a measure of the terms at which consumption today may be turned into consumption tomorrow (this will be made more explicit soon). A natural question to ask is how the economy's rate of return is determined. Again, the equilibrium arises from the supply and demand for present and future goods. In the next section we present a simple two-period model in which this supply-demand interaction is demonstrated.

DETERMINING THE RATE OF RETURN

In this section we will describe how operation of supply and demand in the market for "future" goods establishes an equilibrium rate of return. We begin by analyzing the connection between the rate of return and the "price" of future goods. Then we show how individuals and firms are likely to react to this price. Finally, these actions are brought together (as we have done for the analysis of other markets) to demonstrate the determination of an equilibrium price of future goods and to examine some of the characteristics of that solution.

Rate of return and price of future goods

For most of the analysis in this chapter, we assume there are only two periods to be considered: the current period (denoted by the subscript 0) and the next period (subscript 1). We will use r to denote the (one-period) rate of return between these two periods. Hence, as defined in the previous section,

$$r = \frac{\Delta c_1}{\Delta c_0} - 1, \tag{17.3}$$

where the Δ notation indicates the change in consumption during the two periods. Rewriting Equation 17.3 yields

$$\frac{\Delta c_1}{\Delta c_0} = 1 + r \tag{17.4}$$

or

$$\frac{\Delta c_0}{\Delta c_1} = \frac{1}{1+r}. \tag{17.5}$$

The term on the left of Equation 17.5 records how much c_0 must be forgone if c_1 is to be increased by 1 unit; that is, the expression represents the relative "price" of 1 unit of c_1 in terms of c_0. So we have defined the price of future goods.[1]

Price of future goods. The relative *price of future goods* (p_1) is the quantity of present goods that must be forgone to increase future consumption by 1 unit. That is,

$$p_1 = \frac{\Delta c_0}{\Delta c_1} = \frac{1}{1+r}. \tag{17.6}$$

DEFINITION

We now proceed to develop a demand-supply analysis of the determination of p_1. By so doing we also will have developed a theory of the determination of r, the rate of return in this simple model.

Demand for future goods

The theory of the demand for future goods is one further application of the utility-maximization model developed in Part 2 of this book. Here the individual's utility depends on present and future consumption [that is, utility $= U(c_0, c_1)$], and he or she must decide how much current wealth (W) to allocate to these two goods.[2] Wealth not spent on current consumption can be invested at the rate of return r to obtain consumption next period.

[1]This price is identical to the discount factor introduced in connection with repeated games in Chapter 8.
[2]For an analysis of the case where the individual has income in both periods, see Problem 17.1.

FIGURE 17.2   Individual's Intertemporal Utility Maximization

When faced with the intertemporal budget constraint $W = c_0 + p_1 c_1$, the individual will maximize utility by choosing to consume c_0^* currently and c_1^* in the next period. A fall in p_1 (an increase in the rate of return, r) will cause c_1 to rise, but the effect on c_0 is indeterminate because substitution and income effects operate in opposite directions (assuming that both c_0 and c_1 are normal goods).

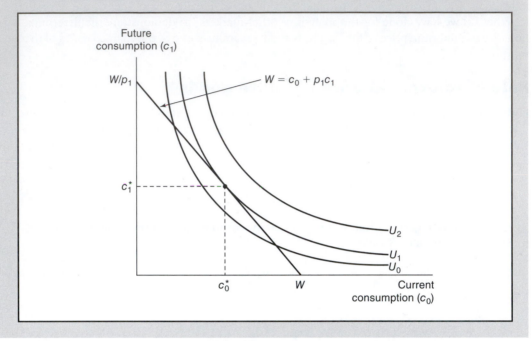

As before, p_1 reflects the present cost of future consumption, and the individual's budget constraint is given by

$$W = c_0 + p_1 c_1. \tag{17.7}$$

This constraint is illustrated in Figure 17.2. If the individual chooses to spend all of his or her wealth on c_0, then total current consumption will be W with no consumption occurring in period 2. Alternatively, if $c_0 = 0$, then c_1 will be given by $W/p_1 = W(1 + r)$. That is, if all wealth is invested at the rate of return r, current wealth will grow to $W(1 + r)$ in period 2.[3]

Utility maximization

Imposing the individual's indifference curve map for c_0 and c_1 onto the budget constraint in Figure 17.2 illustrates utility maximization. Here utility is maximized at the point c_0^*, c_1^*. The individual consumes c_0^* currently and chooses to save $W - c_0^*$ to consume next period. This future consumption can be found from the budget constraint as

$$p_1 c_1^* = W - c_0^* \tag{17.8}$$

---

[3]This observation yields an alternative interpretation of the intertemporal budget constraint, which can be written in terms of the rate of return as

$$W = c_0 + \frac{c_1}{1 + r}.$$

This illustrates that it is the "present value" of c_1 that enters into the individual's current budget constraint. The concept of present value is discussed in more detail later in this chapter.

or

$$c_1^* = \frac{(W - c_0^*)}{p_1} \qquad (17.9)$$

$$= (W - c_0^*)(1 + r). \qquad (17.10)$$

In words, wealth that is not currently consumed $(W - c_0^*)$ is invested at the rate of return, r, and will grow to yield c_1^* in the next period.

EXAMPLE 17.1 Intertemporal Impatience

Individuals' utility-maximizing choices over time will obviously depend on how they feel about the relative merits of consuming currently or waiting to consume in the future. One way of reflecting the possibility that people exhibit some impatience in their choices is to assume that the utility from future consumption is implicity discounted in the individual's mind. For example, we might assume that the utility function for consumption, $U(c)$, is the same in both periods (with $U' > 0$, $U'' < 0$) but that period 1's utility is discounted in the individual's mind by a "rate of time preference" of $1/(1 + \delta)$ (where $\delta > 0$). If the intertemporal utility function is also separable (for more discussion of this concept, see the Extensions to Chapter 6), we can write

$$U(c_0, c_1) = U(c_0) + \frac{1}{1 + \delta} U(c_1). \qquad (17.11)$$

Maximization of this function subject to the intertemporal budget constraint

$$W = c_0 + \frac{c_1}{1 + r} \qquad (17.12)$$

yields the following Lagrangian expression:

$$\mathcal{L} = U(c_0, c_1) + \lambda \left[W - c_0 - \frac{c_1}{1 + r} \right], \qquad (17.13)$$

and the first-order conditions for a maximum are

$$\frac{\partial \mathcal{L}}{\partial c_0} = U'(c_0) - \lambda = 0,$$

$$\frac{\partial \mathcal{L}}{\partial c_1} = \frac{1}{1 + \delta} U'(c_1) - \frac{\lambda}{1 + r} = 0, \qquad (17.14)$$

$$\frac{\partial \mathcal{L}}{\partial \lambda} = W - c_0 - \frac{c_1}{1 + r} = 0.$$

Dividing the first and second of these and rearranging terms gives[4]

$$U'(c_0) = \frac{1 + r}{1 + \delta} U'(c_1). \qquad (17.15)$$

Because the utility function for consumption is assumed to be the same in two periods, we can conclude that $c_0 = c_1$ if $r = \delta$, that $c_0 > c_1$ if $\delta > r$ [to obtain $U'(c_0) < U'(c_1)$ requires $c_0 > c_1$], and that $c_0 < c_1$ for $r > \delta$. Whether this individual's consumption increases or

(continued)

---

[4]Equation 17.15 is sometimes called the "Euler equation" for intertemporal utility maximization. As we show, once a specific utility function is defined, the equation indicates how consumption changes over time.

EXAMPLE 17.1 CONTINUED

decreases from period 0 to period 1 will therefore depend on exactly how impatient he or she is. Although a consumer may have a preference for present goods ($\delta > 0$), he or she may still consume more in the future than in the present if the rate of return received on savings is high enough.

Consumption smoothing. Because utility functions exhibit diminishing marginal utility of consumption, individuals will seek to equalize their consumption across periods. The extent of such smoothing will depend on the curvature of the utility function. Suppose, for example, that an individual's utility function takes the CES form

$$U(c) = \begin{cases} c^R/R & \text{if } R \neq 0 \text{ and } R \leq 1, \\ \ln(c) & \text{if } R = 0. \end{cases} \tag{17.16}$$

Suppose also that this person's rate of time preference is $\delta = 0$. In this case Equation 17.15 can be written as

$$c_0^{R-1} = (1+r)c_1^{R-1} \quad \text{or} \quad \frac{c_1}{c_0} = (1+r)^{1/(1-R)}. \tag{17.17}$$

If $r = 0$, this person will equalize consumption no matter what his or her utility function is. But a positive interest rate will encourage unequal consumption because in that case future goods are relatively cheaper. The degree to which a positive interest rate will encourage consumption inequality is determined by the value of R (which is sometimes referred to as the "coefficient of fluctuation aversion" in this context). For example, if $R = 0$ then $c_1/c_0 = 1 + r$ and so, with a 5 percent interest rate, consumption in period 1 will be 5 percent higher than in period 0. On the other hand, if this person is more averse to consumption fluctuations then R might take a value such as -3. In this case (with a 5 percent interest rate),

$$\frac{c_1}{c_0} = (1+r)^{0.25} = (1.05)^{0.25} = 1.012. \tag{17.18}$$

That is, consumption in period 1 will be only about 1 percent higher than in period 0. The real interest rate has a substantially smaller effect in encouraging this person to depart from an equalized consumption pattern when he or she is averse to fluctuations.

QUERY: Empirical data show that per capita consumption has increased at an annual rate of approximately 2 percent in the U.S. economy over the past 50 years. What real interest rate would be needed to make this increase utility maximizing (again assuming that $\delta = 0$)? *Note:* We will return to the relationship between consumption smoothing and the real interest rate in Example 17.2. Problem 17.12 shows how intertemporal discount rates that follow a hyperbolic pattern can be used to explain why people may sometimes make decisions that seem "shortsighted."

Effects of changes in *r*

A comparative statics analysis of the equilibrium illustrated in Figure 17.2 is straightforward. If p_1 falls (that is, if r rises), then both income and substitution effects will cause more c_1 to be demanded—except in the unlikely event that c_1 is an inferior good. Hence, the demand curve for c_1 will be downward sloping. An increase in r effectively lowers the price of c_1, and consumption of that good thereby increases. This demand curve is labeled D in Figure 17.3.

FIGURE 17.3   Determination of the Equilibrium Price of Future Goods

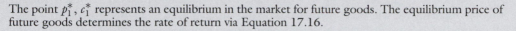

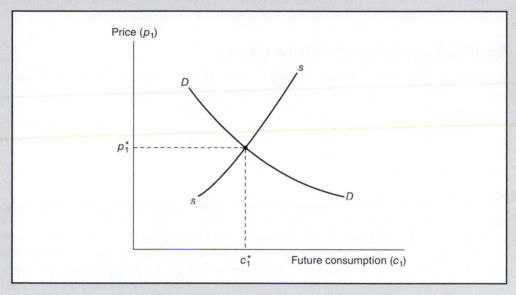

The point p_1^*, c_1^* represents an equilibrium in the market for future goods. The equilibrium price of future goods determines the rate of return via Equation 17.16.

Before leaving our discussion of individuals' intertemporal decisions, we should point out that the analysis does not permit an unambiguous statement to be made about the sign of $\partial c_0/\partial p_1$. In Figure 17.2, substitution and income effects work in opposite directions and so no definite prediction is possible. A fall in p_1 will cause the individual to substitute c_1 for c_0 in his or her consumption plans. But the fall in p_1 raises the real value of wealth, and this income effect causes both c_0 and c_1 to increase. Phrased somewhat differently, the model illustrated in Figure 17.2 does not permit a definite prediction about how changes in the rate of return affect current-period wealth accumulation (saving). A higher r produces substitution effects that favor more saving and income effects that favor less. Ultimately, then, the direction of the effect is an empirical question.

Supply of future goods

In one sense the analysis of the supply of future goods is quite simple. We can argue that an increase in the relative price of future goods (p_1) will induce firms to produce more of them, because the yield from doing so is now greater. This reaction is reflected in the positively sloped supply curve S in Figure 17.3. It might be expected that, as in our previous perfectly competitive analysis, this supply curve reflects the increasing marginal costs (or diminishing returns) firms experience when attempting to turn present goods into future ones through capital accumulation.

Unfortunately, delving deeper into the nature of capital accumulation runs into complications that have occupied economists for hundreds of years.[5] Basically, all of these derive from problems in developing a tractable model of the capital accumulation process. For our model of individual behavior this problem did not arise, because we could assume that the "market" quoted a rate of return to individuals so they could adapt their behavior to it. We shall also follow this route when describing firms' investment decisions later in the chapter. But to

---

[5]For a discussion of some of this debate, see M. Blaug, *Economic Theory in Retrospect*, rev. ed. (Homewood, IL: Richard D. Irwin, 1978), chap. 12.

develop an adequate model of capital accumulation by firms, we must describe precisely how c_0 is "turned into" c_1, and doing so would take us too far afield into the intricacies of capital theory. Instead, we will be content to draw the supply curve in Figure 17.3 with a positive slope on the presumption that such a shape is intuitively reasonable. Much of the subsequent analysis in this chapter may serve to convince you that this is indeed the case.

Equilibrium price of future goods

Equilibrium in the market shown in Figure 17.3 is at p_1^*, c_1^*. At that point, individuals' supply and demand for future goods are in balance, and the required amount of current goods will be put into capital accumulation to produce c_1^* in the future.[6]

There are a number of reasons to expect that p_1 will be less than 1; that is, it will cost less than the sacrifice of one current good to "buy" one good in the future. As we showed in Example 17.1, it might be argued that individuals require some reward for waiting. Everyday adages ("a bird in the hand is worth two in the bush," "live for today") and more substantial realities (the uncertainty of the future and the finiteness of life) suggest that individuals are generally impatient in their consumption decisions. Hence, capital accumulation such as that shown in Figure 17.3 will take place only if the current sacrifice is in some way worthwhile.

There are also supply reasons for believing p_1 will be less than 1. All of these involve the idea that capital accumulation is "productive": Sacrificing one good today will yield more than one good in the future. Some simple examples of the productivity of capital investment are provided by such pastoral activities as the growing of trees or the aging of wine and cheese. Tree nursery owners and vineyard and dairy operators "abstain" from selling their wares in the belief that time will make them more valuable in the future. Although it is obvious that capital accumulation in a modern industrial society is more complex than growing trees (consider building a steel mill or an electric power system), economists believe the two processes have certain similarities. In both cases, investing current goods makes the production process longer and more complex, thereby increasing the contribution of other resources used in production.

The equilibrium rate of return

We can now define the relationship of the rate of return (r) to what we have called the price of future goods:

$$p_1^* = \frac{1}{1+r}.$$ (17.19)

Because we believe that p_1^* will be less than 1, the rate of return (r) will be positive. For example, if $p_1^* = 0.9$ then r will equal approximately 0.11, and we would say that the rate of return to capital accumulation is "11 percent." By withholding 1 unit of current consumption, the consumption of future goods can be increased by 1.11. The rate of return and p_1 are equivalent ways of measuring the terms on which present goods can be turned into future goods.

Rate of return, real interest rates, and nominal interest rates

The concept of the rate of return that we have been analyzing here is sometimes used synonymously with the related concept of the "real" interest rate. In this context, both are taken to refer to the real return that is available from capital accumulation. This concept must

---

[6]This is a much simplified form of an analysis orginally presented by I. Fisher, *The Rate of Interest* (New York: Macmillan, 1907).

be differentiated from the nominal interest rate actually available in financial markets. Specifically, if overall prices are expected to increase by $\dot{p}_e$ between two periods (that is, $\dot{p}_e = 0.10$ for a 10 percent inflation rate), then we would expect the nominal interest rate (i) to be given by the equation

$$1 + i = (1 + r)(1 + \dot{p}_e), \qquad (17.20)$$

because a would-be lender would expect to be compensated for both the opportunity cost of not investing in real capital (r) and for the general rise in prices ($\dot{p}_e$). Expansion of Equation 17.17 yields

$$1 + i = 1 + r + \dot{p}_e + r\dot{p}_e; \qquad (17.21)$$

and assuming $r \cdot \dot{p}_e$ is small, we have the simpler approximation

$$i = r + \dot{p}_e. \qquad (17.22)$$

If the real rate of return is 4 percent (0.04) and the expected rate of inflation is 10 percent (0.10), then the nominal interest rate would be approximately 14 percent (0.14). Therefore, the difference between observed nominal interest rates and real interest rates may be substantial in inflationary environments.

EXAMPLE 17.2 Determination of the Real Interest Rate

A simple model of real interest rate determination can be developed by assuming that consumption grows at some exogenous rate, g. For example, suppose that the only consumption good is perishable fruit and that this fruit comes from trees that are growing at the rate g. More realistically, g might be determined by macroeconomic forces, such as the rate of technical change in the Solow growth model (see the Extensions to Chapter 9). No matter how the growth rate is determined, the real interest rate must adjust so that consumers are willing to accept this rate of growth in consumption.

Optimal consumption. The typical consumer wants his or her consumption pattern to maximize the utility received from this consumption over time. That is, the goal is to maximize

$$\text{utility} = \int_0^\infty e^{-\delta t} U(c(t)) \, dt, \qquad (17.23)$$

where δ is the rate of pure time preference. At each instant of time, this person earns a wage w and earns interest r on his or her capital stock k. Hence, this person's capital evolves according to the equation

$$\frac{dk}{dt} = w + rk - c \qquad (17.24)$$

and is bound by the endpoint constraints $k(0) = 0$ and $k(\infty) = 0$. Setting up the augmented Hamiltonian for this dynamic optimization problem (see Chapter 2) yields

$$H = e^{-\delta t} U(c) + \lambda(w + rk - c) + k\frac{d\lambda}{dt}. \qquad (17.25)$$

The "maximum principle" therefore requires:

$$H_c = e^{-\delta t} U'(c) - \lambda = 0;$$

$$H_k = r\lambda + \frac{d\lambda}{dt} = 0 \quad \text{or} \quad r\lambda = -\frac{d\lambda}{dt}. \qquad (17.26)$$

(continued)

EXAMPLE 17.2 CONTINUED

Solving the differential equation implied by the second of these conditions yields the conclusion that $\lambda = e^{-rt}$, and substituting this into the first of the conditions shows that

$$U'(c) = e^{(\delta - r)t}. \tag{17.27}$$

Hence, consistent with our results in Example 17.1, marginal utility should rise or fall over time depending on the relationship between the rate of time preference and the real rate of interest. When utility takes the CES form of $U(c) = c^R/R$ and $U'(c) = c^{R-1}$, Equation 17.27 gives the explicit solution:

$$c(t) = \exp\left\{ \frac{r - \delta}{1 - R} t \right\}, \tag{17.28}$$

where $\exp\{x\} = e^x$. So, if $r > \delta$ then consumption should rise over time, but the extent of this increase should be affected by how willing this person is to tolerate unequal consumption.

Real interest rate determination. The only "price" in this simple economy is the real interest rate. This rate must adjust so that consumers will accept the rate of growth of consumption that is being determined exogenously. Hence it must be the case that

$$g = \frac{r - \delta}{1 - R} \quad \text{or} \quad r = \delta + (1 - R)g. \tag{17.29}$$

If $g = 0$, then the real rate of interest will equal the rate of time preference. With a positive growth rate of consumption, the real interest rate must exceed the rate of time preference to encourage people to accept consumption growth.

Real interest rate paradox. Equation 17.29 provides the basis for what is sometimes termed the "real interest rate paradox." Over time, real consumption grows at about 1.6 percent per year in the U.S. economy, and other evidence suggests that R is around -2 or -3. Hence, even when the rate of time preference is zero, the real interest rate should be at least $r = 0 + (1 + 2) \cdot 0.016 = 0.048$ (that is, about 5 percent). But empirical evidence shows that the real, risk-free rate in the United States over the past 75 years has been only about 2 percent—far lower than it should be. Either there is something wrong with this model, or people are more flexible in their consumption decisions than is believed.

QUERY: How should the results of this example be augmented to allow for the possibility that g may be subject to random fluctuations? (See also Problem 17.9.)

THE FIRM'S DEMAND FOR CAPITAL

Firms rent machines in accordance with the same principles of profit maximization we derived in Chapter 11. Specifically, in a perfectly competitive market, the firm will choose to hire that number of machines for which the marginal revenue product is precisely equal to their market rental rate. In this section we first investigate the determinants of this market rental rate, and we assume that all machines are rented. Later in the section, because most firms buy machines and hold them until they deteriorate rather than rent them, we shall examine the particular problems raised by such ownership.

Determinants of market rental rates

Consider a firm in the business of renting machines to other firms. Suppose the firm owns a machine (say, a car or a backhoe) that has a current market price of p. How much will the firm charge its clients for the use of the machine? The owner of the machine faces two kinds of costs: depreciation on the machine and the *opportunity cost* of having its funds tied up in a machine rather than in an investment earning the current available rate of return. If it is assumed that depreciation costs per period are a constant percentage (d) of the machine's market price and that the real interest rate is given by r, then the total costs to the machine owner for one period are given by

$$pd + pr = p(r + d). \tag{17.30}$$

If we assume that the machine rental market is perfectly competitive, then no long-run profits can be earned by renting machines. The workings of the market will ensure that the rental rate per period for the machine (v) is exactly equal to the costs of the machine owner. Hence we have the basic result that

$$v = p(r + d). \tag{17.31}$$

The competitive rental rate is the sum of forgone interest and depreciation costs the machine's owner must pay. For example, suppose the real interest rate is 5 percent (that is, 0.05) and the physical depreciation rate is 15 percent (0.15). Suppose also that the current market price of the machine is \$10,000. Then, in this simple model, the machine would have an annual rental rate of \$2,000 [$= \$10,000 \times (0.05 + 0.15)$] per year; \$500 of this would represent the opportunity cost of the funds invested in the machine, and the remaining \$1,500 would reflect the physical costs of deterioration.

Nondepreciating machines

In the hypothetical case of a machine that does not depreciate ($d = 0$), Equation 17.31 can be written as

$$\frac{v}{P} = r. \tag{17.32}$$

In equilibrium an infinitely long-lived (nondepreciating) machine is equivalent to a perpetual bond (see the Appendix to this chapter) and hence must "yield" the market rate of return. The rental rate as a percentage of the machine's price must be equal to r. If $v/p > r$ then everyone would rush out to buy machines, because renting out machines would yield more than rates of return elsewhere. Similarly, if $v/p < r$ then no one would be in the business of renting out machines, because more could be made on alternative investments.

Ownership of machines

Our analysis so far has assumed that firms rent all of the machines they use. Although such rental does take place in the real world (for example, many firms are in the business of leasing airplanes, trucks, freight cars, and computers to other firms), it is more common for firms to own the machines they use. A firm will buy a machine and use it in combination with the labor it hires to produce output. The ownership of machines makes the analysis of the demand for capital somewhat more complex than that of the demand for labor. However, by recognizing the important distinction between a *stock* and a *flow*, we can show that these two demands are quite similar.

A firm uses *capital services* to produce output. These services are a *flow* magnitude. It is the number of machine-hours that is relevant to the productive process (just as it is labor-hours), not the number of machines per se. Often, however, the assumption is made that the flow of capital services is proportional to the *stock* of machines (100 machines, if fully employed for 1 hour, can deliver 100 machine hours of service); therefore, these two different concepts are often used synonymously. If during a period a firm desires a certain number of machine hours, this is usually taken to mean that the firm desires a certain number of machines. The firm's demand for capital services is also a demand for capital.[7]

A profit-maximizing firm in perfect competition will choose its level of inputs so that the marginal revenue product from an extra unit of any input is equal to its cost. This result also holds for the demand for machine hours. The cost of capital services is given by the rental rate (v) in Equation 17.31. This cost is borne by the firm whether it rents the machine in the open market or owns the machine itself. In the former case it is an explicit cost, whereas in the latter case the firm is essentially in two businesses: (1) producing output; and (2) owning machines and renting them to itself. In this second role the firms' decisions would be the same as any other machine rental firm because it incurs the same costs. The fact of ownership, to a first approximation, is irrelevant to the determination of cost. Hence our prior analysis of capital demand applies to the owners by case as well.

DEFINITION	**Demand for capital.** A profit-maximizing firm that faces a perfectly competitive rental market for capital will hire additional capital input up to the point at which its marginal revenue product (MRP_k) is equal to the market rental rate, v. Under perfect competition, the rental rate will reflect both depreciation costs and opportunity costs of alternative investments. Thus we have

$$MRP_k = v = p(r + d). \tag{17.33}$$

Theory of investment

If a firm obeys the profit-maximizing rule of Equation 17.33 and finds that it desires more capital services than can be provided by its currently existing stock of machinery, then it has two choices. First, it may hire the additional machines that it needs in the rental market. This would be formally identical to its decision to hire additional labor. Second, the firm can buy new machinery to meet its needs. This second alternative is the one most often chosen; we call the purchase of new equipment by the firm *investment*.

Investment demand is an important component of "aggregate demand" in macroeconomic theory. It is often assumed this demand for plant and equipment (that is, machines) is inversely related to the real rate of interest, or what we have called the "rate of return." Using the analysis developed in this part of the text, we can demonstrate the links in this argument. A fall in the real interest rate (r) will, ceteris paribus, decrease the rental rate on capital (Equation 17.31). Because forgone interest represents an implicit cost for the owner of a machine, a decrease in r in effect reduces the price (that is, the rental rate) of capital inputs. This fall in v implies that capital has become a relatively less expensive input; this will prompt firms to increase their capital usage.

PRESENT DISCOUNTED VALUE APPROACH TO INVESTMENT DECISIONS

When a firm buys a machine, it is in effect buying a stream of net revenues in future periods. To decide whether to purchase the machine, the firm must compute the present discounted value of this stream.[8] Only by doing so will the firm have taken adequate account of the effects of forgone interest. This provides an alternative approach to explaining the investment decision.

---

[7]Firms' decisions on how intensively to use a given capital stock during a period are often analyzed as part of the study of business cycles.

[8]See the Appendix to this chapter for an extended discussion of present discounted value.

Consider a firm in the process of deciding whether to buy a particular machine. The machine is expected to last n years and will give its owner a stream of monetary returns (that is, marginal revenue products) in each of the n years. Let the return in year i be represented by R_i. If r is the present real interest rate and if this rate is expected to prevail for the next n years, then the present discounted value (PDV) of the net revenue flow from the machine to its owner is given by

$$PDV = \frac{R_1}{1+r} + \frac{R_2}{(1+r)^2} + \cdots + \frac{R_n}{(1+r)^n}. \qquad \textbf{(17.34)}$$

This present discounted value represents the total value of the stream of payments provided by the machine—once adequate account is taken of the fact that these payments occur in different years. If the PDV of this stream of payments exceeds the price (p) of the machine then the firm, and other similar firms, should make the purchase. Even when the effects of the interest payments the firm could have earned on its funds had it not purchased the machine are taken into account, the machine promises to return more than its prevailing price. On the other hand, if $p > PDV$, the firm would be better off to invest its funds in some alternative that promises a rate of return of r. When account is taken of forgone interest, the machine does not pay for itself. Thus, in a competitive market, the only equilibrium that can prevail is that in which the price of a machine is equal to the present discounted value of the net revenues from the machine. Only in this situation will there be neither an excess demand for machines nor an excess supply of machines. Hence, market equilibrium requires that

$$p = PDV = \frac{R_1}{1+r} + \frac{R_2}{(1+r)^2} + \cdots + \frac{R_n}{(1+r)^n}. \qquad \textbf{(17.35)}$$

We shall now use this condition to show two situations in which the present discounted value criterion of investment yields the same equilibrium conditions described earlier in the chapter.

Simple case

Assume first that machines are infinitely long lived and that the marginal revenue product (R_i) is the same in every year. This uniform return also will equal the rental rate for machines (v), because that is what another firm would pay for the machine's use during any period. With these simplifying assumptions, we may write the present discounted value from machine ownership as

$$PDV = \frac{v}{(1+r)} + \frac{v}{(1+r)^2} + \cdots + \frac{v}{(1+r)^n} + \cdots$$

$$= v \cdot \left(\frac{1}{(1+r)} + \frac{1}{(1+r)^2} + \cdots + \frac{1}{(1+r)^n} + \cdots \right)$$

$$= v \cdot \left(\frac{1}{1 - 1/(1+r)} - 1 \right)$$

$$= v \cdot \left(\frac{1+r}{r} - 1 \right)$$

$$= v \cdot \frac{1}{r}. \qquad \textbf{(17.36)}$$

But in equilibrium $p = PDV$, so

$$p = v \cdot \frac{1}{r} \tag{17.37}$$

or

$$\frac{v}{p} = r, \tag{17.38}$$

as was already shown in Equation 17.32. For this case, the present discounted value criterion gives results identical to those outlined in the previous section.

General case

Equation 17.31 can also be derived for the more general case in which the rental rate on machines is not constant over time and in which there is some depreciation. This analysis is most easily carried out by using continuous time. Suppose that the rental rate for a *new* machine at any time s is given by $v(s)$. Assume also that the machine depreciates exponentially at the rate of d.[9] The net rental rate (and the marginal revenue product) of a machine therefore declines over time as the machine gets older. In year s, the net rental rate on an *old* machine bought in a previous year (t) would be

$$v(s)e^{-d(s-t)}, \tag{17.39}$$

because $s - t$ is the number of years over which the machine has been decaying. For example, suppose that a machine is bought new in 2000. Its net rental rate in 2005 then would be the rental rate earned by new machines in 2005 [$v(2005)$] discounted by the e^{-5d} to account for the amount of depreciation that has taken place over the five years of the machine's life.

If the firm is considering buying the machine when it is new in year t, it should discount all of these net rental amounts back to that date. The present value of the net rental in year s discounted back to year t is therefore (if r is the interest rate)

$$e^{-r(s-t)}v(s)e^{-d(s-t)} = e^{(r+d)}v(s)e^{-(r+d)s} \tag{17.40}$$

because, again, $(s - t)$ years elapse from when the machine is bought until the net rental is received. The present discounted value of a machine bought in year t is therefore the sum (integral) of these present values. This sum should be taken from year t (when the machine is bought) over all years into the future:

$$PDV(t) = \int_t^{\infty} e^{(r+d)t}v(s)e^{-(r+d)s} \, ds. \tag{17.41}$$

Since in equilibrium the price of the machine at year t [$p(t)$] will be equal to this present value, we have the following fundamental equation:

$$p(t) = \int_t^{\infty} e^{(r+d)t}v(s)e^{-(r+d)s} \, ds. \tag{17.42}$$

---

[9]In this view of depreciation, machines are assumed to "evaporate" at a fixed rate per unit of time. This model of decay is in many ways identical to the assumptions of radioactive decay made in physics. There are other possible forms that physical depreciation might take; this is just one that is mathematically tractable.

It is important to keep the concept of physical depreciation (depreciation that affects a machine's productivity) distinct from accounting depreciation. The latter concept is important only in that the method of accounting depreciation chosen may affect the rate of taxation on the profits from a machine. From an economic point of view, however, the cost of a machine is a sunk cost: any choice on how to "write off" this cost is to some extent arbitrary.

This rather formidable equation is simply a more complex version of Equation 17.35 and can be used to derive Equation 17.31. First rewrite the equation as

$$p(t) = e^{(r+d)t} \int_t^\infty v(s)e^{-(r+d)s}\, ds. \qquad (17.43)$$

Now differentiate with respect to t, using the rule for taking the derivative of a product:

$$\frac{dp(t)}{dt} = (r+d)e^{(r+d)t} \int_t^\infty v(s)e^{-(r+d)s}\, ds - e^{(r+d)t}v(t)e^{-(r+d)t}$$

$$= (r+d)p(t) - v(t). \qquad (17.44)$$

Hence

$$v(t) = (r+d)p(t) - \frac{dp(t)}{dt}. \qquad (17.45)$$

This is precisely the result shown earlier in Equation 17.31 except that the term $-dp(t)/dt$ has been added. The economic explanation for the presence of this added term is that it represents the capital gains accruing to the owner of the machine. If the machine's price can be expected to rise, for example, the owner may accept somewhat less than $(r+d)p$ for its rental.[10] On the other hand, if the price of the machine is expected to fall $[dp(t)/dt < 0]$, the owner will require more in rent than is specified in Equation 17.31. If the price of the machine is expected to remain constant over time, then $dp(t)/dt = 0$ and the equations are identical. This analysis shows there is a definite relationship between the price of a machine at any time, the stream of future profits the machine promises, and the current rental rate for the machine.

EXAMPLE 17.3 Cutting Down a Tree

As an example of the *PDV* criterion, consider the case of a forester who must decide when to cut down a growing tree. Suppose the value of the tree at any time, t, is given by $f(t)$ (where $f'(t) > 0$, $f''(t) < 0$) and that l dollars were invested initially as payments to workers who planted the tree. Assume also that the (continuous) market interest rate is given by r. When the tree is planted, the present discounted value of the tree owner's profits is given by

$$PDV(t) = e^{-rt}f(t) - l, \qquad (17.46)$$

which is simply the difference between (the present value of) revenues and present costs. The forester's decision, then, consists of choosing the harvest date t to maximize this value. As always, this value may be found by differentiation:

$$\frac{dPDV(t)}{dt} = e^{-rt}f'(t) - re^{-rt}f(t) = 0 \qquad (17.47)$$

or, dividing both sides by e^{-rt},

$$f'(t) - rf(t) = 0. \qquad (17.48)$$

Therefore,

$$r = \frac{f'(t)}{f(t)} \qquad (17.49)$$

(continued)

---

[10] For example, rental houses in suburbs with rapidly appreciating house prices will usually rent for less than the landlord's actual costs because the landlord also gains from price appreciation.

EXAMPLE 17.3 CONTINUED

Two features of this optimal condition are worth noting. First, observe that the cost of the initial labor input drops out upon differentiation. This cost is (even in a literal sense) a "sunk" cost that is irrelevant to the profit-maximizing decision. Second, Equation 17.49 can be interpreted as saying the tree should be harvested when the rate of interest is equal to the proportional rate of growth of the tree. This result makes intuitive sense. If the tree is growing more rapidly than the prevailing interest rate then its owner should leave his or her funds invested in the tree, because the tree provides the best return available. On the other hand, if the tree is growing less rapidly than the prevailing interest rate, then the tree should be cut and the funds obtained from its sale should be invested elsewhere at the rate r.

Equation 17.49 is only a necessary condition for a maximum. By differentiating Equation 17.48 again it is easy to see that it is also required that, at the chosen value of t,

$$f''(t) - rf'(t) < 0 \tag{17.50}$$

if the first-order conditions are to represent a true maximum. Because we assumed $f'(t) > 0$ (the tree is always growing) and $f''(t) < 0$ (the growth slows over time), it is clear that this condition holds.

A numerical illustration. Suppose trees grow according to the equation

$$f(t) = \exp\{0.4\sqrt{t}\}. \tag{17.51}$$

This equation always exhibits a positive growth rate $[f'(t) > 0]$ and, because

$$\frac{f'(t)}{f(t)} = \frac{0.2}{\sqrt{t}}, \tag{17.52}$$

the tree's proportional growth rate diminishes over time. If the real interest rate were, say, 0.04, then we could solve for the optimal harvesting age as

$$r = 0.04 = \frac{f'(t)}{f(t)} = \frac{0.2}{\sqrt{t}} \tag{17.53}$$

or

$$\sqrt{t} = \frac{0.2}{0.4} = 5,$$

so

$$t^* = 25. \tag{17.54}$$

Up to 25 years of age, the volume of wood in the tree is increasing at a rate in excess of 4 percent per year, so the optimal decision is to permit the tree to stand. But for $t > 25$, the annual growth rate falls below 4 percent and so the forester can find better investments—perhaps planting new trees.

A change in the interest rate. If the real interest rate rises to 5 percent, then Equation 17.53 becomes

$$r = 0.05 = \frac{0.2}{\sqrt{t}}, \tag{17.55}$$

and the optimal harvest age would be

$$t^* = \left(\frac{0.2}{0.05}\right)^2 = 16. \tag{17.56}$$

The higher real interest rate discourages investment in trees by prompting the forester to choose an earlier harvest date.[11]

QUERY: Suppose all prices (including those of trees) were rising at 10 percent per year. How would this change the optimal harvesting results in this problem?

NATURAL RESOURCE PRICING

Pricing of natural resources has been a concern of economists at least since the time of Thomas Malthus. A primary issue has been whether the market system can achieve a desirable allocation of such resources given their ultimately finite and exhaustible nature. In this section we look at a simple model of resource pricing to illustrate some of the insights that economic analysis can provide.

Profit-maximizing pricing and output

Suppose that a firm owns a finite stock of a particular resource. Let the stock of the resource at any time be denoted by $x(t)$ and current production from this stock by $q(t)$. Hence, the stock of this resource evolves according to the differential equation

$$\frac{dx(t)}{dt} = \dot{x}(t) = -q(t), \tag{17.57}$$

where we use the dot notation to denote a time derivative. The stock of this resource is constrained by $x(0) = \bar{x}$ and $x(\infty) = 0$. Extraction of this resource exhibits constant average and marginal cost for changes in output levels, but this cost may change over time. Hence the firm's total costs at any point in time are $C(t) = c(t)q(t)$. The firm's goal then is to maximize the present discounted value of profits subject to the constraint given in Equation 17.57. If we let $p(t)$ be the price of the resource at time t, then profits are given by

$$\pi = \int_0^\infty [p(t)q(t) - c(t)q(t)]e^{-rt}\, dt, \tag{17.58}$$

where r is the real interest rate (assumed to be constant throughout our analysis). Setting up the augmented Hamiltonian for this dynamic optimization problem yields

$$H = [p(t)q(t) - c(t)q(t)]e^{-rt} + \lambda[-q(t)] + x(t)\frac{d\lambda}{dt}. \tag{17.59}$$

The maximum principle applied to this dynamic problem has two first-order conditions for a maximum:

$$H_q = [p(t) - c(t)]e^{-rt} - \lambda = 0,$$

$$H_x = \frac{d\lambda}{dt} = 0. \tag{17.60}$$

The second of these conditions implies that the "shadow price" of the resource stock should remain constant over time. Because producing a unit of the resource reduces the stock by

---

[11]For further tree-related economics, see Problems 17.4 and 17.11.

precisely 1 unit no matter when it is produced, any time path along which this shadow price changed would be nonoptimal. Substituting this result into the first condition yields

$$\frac{d\lambda}{dt} = \dot{\lambda}(\dot{p} - \dot{c})e^{-rt} - r(p - c)e^{-rt} = 0. \tag{17.61}$$

Dividing by e^{-rt} and rearranging terms provides an equation that explains how the price of the resource must change over time:

$$\dot{p} = r(p - c) + \dot{c}. \tag{17.62}$$

Notice that the price change has two components. The second component shows that price changes must follow any changes in marginal extraction costs. The first shows that, even if extraction costs do not change, there will be an upward trend in prices that reflects the scarcity value of the resource. The firm will have an incentive to delay some resource production only if so refraining will yield a return equivalent to the real interest rate. Otherwise it is better for the firm to sell all its resource assets and invest the funds elsewhere. This result, first noted[12] by Harold Hotelling in the early 1930s, can be further simplified by assuming that marginal extraction costs are always zero. In this case, Equation 17.62 reduces to the simple differential equation

$$\dot{p} = rp, \tag{17.63}$$

whose solution is

$$p = p_0 e^{rt}. \tag{17.64}$$

That is, prices rise exponentially at the real rate of interest. More generally, suppose that marginal costs also follow an exponential trend given by

$$c(t) = c_0 e^{\gamma t}, \tag{17.65}$$

where γ may be either positive or negative. In this case, the solution to the differential Equation 17.62 is

$$p(t) = (p_0 - c_0)e^{rt} + c_0 e^{\gamma t}. \tag{17.66}$$

This makes it even clearer that the resource price is influenced by two trends: an increasing scarcity rent that reflects the asset value of the resource, and the trend in marginal extraction costs.

EXAMPLE 17.4 Can Resource Prices Decrease?

Although Hotelling's original observation suggests that natural resource prices should rise at the real rate of interest, Equation 17.66 makes clear that this conclusion is not unambiguous. If marginal extraction costs fall because of technical advances (that is, if γ is negative), then it is possible that the resource price will fall. The conditions that would lead to falling resource prices can be made more explicit by calculating the first and second time derivatives of price in Equation 17.66:

$$\frac{dp}{dt} = r(p_0 - c_0)e^{rt} + \gamma c_0 e^{\gamma t},$$
$$\frac{d^2 p}{dt^2} = r^2(p_0 - c_0)e^{rt} + \gamma^2 c_0 e^{\gamma t} > 0. \tag{17.67}$$

---

[12]H. Hotelling, "The Economics of Exhaustible Resources," *Journal of Political Economy* (April 1931): 137–75.

Because the second derivative is always positive, we need only examine the sign of the first derivative at $t = 0$ to conclude when prices decline. At this initial date,

$$\frac{dp}{dt} = r(p_0 - c_0) + \gamma c_0. \tag{17.68}$$

Hence, prices will decline (at least initially), providing

$$\frac{-\gamma}{r} > \frac{p_0 - c_0}{c_0}. \tag{17.69}$$

Clearly this condition cannot be met if marginal extraction costs are increasing over time ($\gamma > 0$). But if costs are falling, a period of declining real price is possible. For example, if $r = 0.05$ and $\gamma = -0.02$, then prices would fall provided initial scarcity rents were less than 40 percent of extraction costs. Although prices must eventually turn up, a fairly abundant resource that experienced significant declines in extraction costs could have a relatively long period of falling prices. This seems to have been the case for crude oil, for example.

QUERY: Is the firm studied in this section a price taker? How would the analysis differ if the firm were a monopolist? (See also Problem 17.10.)

Generalizing the model

The description of natural resource pricing given here provides only a brief glimpse of this important topic.[13] Some additional issues that have been considered by economists include social optimality, substitution, and renewable resources.

Social Optimality. Are the price trends described in Equation 17.66 economically efficient? That is, do they maximize consumer surplus in addition to maximizing the firm's profits? Our previous discussion of optimal consumption over time suggests that the marginal utility of consumption should change in certain prescribed ways if the consumer is to remain on his or her optimal path. Because individuals will consume any resource up to the point at which its price is proportional to marginal utility, it seems plausible that the price trends calculated here might be consistent with optimal consumption. But a more complete analysis would need to introduce the consumer's rate of time preference and his or her willingness to substitute for an increasingly high-priced resource, so there is no clear-cut answer. Rather, the optimality of the path indicated by Equation 17.66 will depend on the specifics of the situation.

Substitution. A related issue is how substitute resources should be integrated into this analysis. A relatively simple answer is provided by considering how the initial price (p_0) should be chosen in Equation 17.66. If that price is such that the initial price-quantity combination is a market equilibrium, then—assuming all other finite resource prices follow a similar time trend—relative resource prices will not change and (with certain utility functions) the price-quantity time paths for all of them may constitute an equilibrium. An alternative approach would be to assume that a perfect substitute for the resource will be developed at some date in the future. If this new resource is available in perfectly elastic supply, then its availability would put a cap on the price or the original resource; this also would have implications for p_0 (see Problem 17.7). But all of these solutions to modeling

---

[13]For a sampling of dynamic optimization models applied to natural resource issues, see J. M. Conrad and C. W. Clark, *Natural Resource Economics: Notes and Problems* (Cambridge: Cambridge University Press, 2004).

substitutability are special cases. To model the situation more generally requires a dynamic general equilibrium model capable of capturing interactions in many markets.

Renewable Resources. A final complication that might be added to the model of resource pricing presented here is the possibility that the resource in question is not finite: it can be renewed through natural or economic actions. This would be the case for timber or fishing grounds, where various types of renewal activities are possible. The formal consideration of renewable resources requires a modification of the differential equation defining changes in the resource stock, which no longer takes the simple form given in Equation 17.57. Specification of profit-maximizing price trajectories in such cases can become quite complicated.

SUMMARY

In this chapter we examined several aspects of the theory of capital, with particular emphasis on integrating it with the theory of resource allocation over time. Some of the results were as follows.

- Capital accumulation represents the sacrifice of present for future consumption. The rate of return measures the terms at which this trade can be accomplished.

- The rate of return is established through mechanisms much like those that establish any equilibrium price. The equilibrium rate of return will be positive, reflecting not only individuals' relative preferences for present over future goods but also the positive physical productivity of capital accumulation.

- The rate of return (or real interest rate) is an important element in the overall costs associated with capital ownership. It is an important determinant of the market rental rate on capital, v.

- Future returns on capital investments must be discounted at the prevailing real interest rate. Use of such present value notions provides an alternative way to approach studying the firm's investment decisions.

- Individual wealth accumulation, natural resource pricing, and other dynamic problems can be studied using the techniques of optimal control theory. Often such models will yield competitive-type results.

PROBLEMS

17.1

An individual has a fixed wealth (W) to allocate between consumption in two periods (c_1 and c_2). The individual's utility function is given by

$$U(c_1, c_2),$$

and the budget constraint is

$$W = c_1 + \frac{c_2}{1+r},$$

where r is the one-period interest rate.

a. Show that, in order to maximize utility given this budget constraint, the individual should choose c_1 and c_2 such that the MRS (of c_1 for c_2) is equal to $1+r$.

b. Show that $\partial c_2 / \partial r \geq 0$ but that the sign of $\partial c_1 / \partial r$ is ambiguous. If $\partial c_1 / \partial r$ is negative, what can you conclude about the price elasticity of demand for c_2?

c. How would your conclusions from part (b) be amended if the individual received income in each period (y_1 and y_2) such that the budget constraint is given by

$$y_1 - c_1 + \frac{y_2 - c_2}{1+r} = 0?$$

17.2

Assume that an individual expects to work for 40 years and then retire with a life expectancy of an additional 20 years. Suppose also that the individual's earnings rise at a rate of 3 percent per year and that the interest rate is also 3 percent (the overall price level is constant in this problem). What (constant) fraction of income must the individual save in each working year to be able to finance a level of retirement income equal to 60 percent of earnings in the year just prior to retirement?

17.3

As scotch whiskey ages, its value increases. One dollar of scotch at year 0 is worth $V(t) = \exp\{2\sqrt{t} - 0.15t\}$ dollars at time t. If the interest rate is 5 percent, after how many years should a person sell scotch in order to maximize the *PDV* of this sale?

17.4

As in Example 17.3, suppose trees are produced by applying 1 unit of labor at time 0. The value of the wood contained in a tree is given at any time t by $f(t)$. If the market wage rate is w and the real interest rate is r, what is the *PDV* of this production process, and how should t be chosen to maximize this *PDV*?

a. If the optimal value of t is denoted by t^*, show that the "no pure profit" condition of perfect competition will necessitate that

$$w = e^{-rt}f(t^*).$$

Can you explain the meaning of this expression?

b. A tree sold before t^* will not be cut down immediately. Rather, it still will make sense for the new owner to let the tree continue to mature until t^*. Show that the price of a u-year-old tree will be we^{ru} and that this price will exceed the value of the wood in the tree $[f(u)]$ for every value of u except $u = t^*$ (when these two values are equal).

c. Suppose a landowner has a "balanced" woodlot with one tree of "each" age from 0 to t^*. What is the value of this woodlot? *Hint:* It is the sum of the values of all trees in the lot.

d. If the value of the woodlot is V, show that the instantaneous interest on V (that is, $r \cdot V$) is equal to the "profits" earned at each instant by the landowner, where by profits we mean the difference between the revenue obtained from selling a fully matured tree $[f(t^*)]$ and the cost of planting a new one (w). This result shows there is no pure profit in borrowing to buy a woodlot, because one would have to pay in interest at each instant exactly what would be earned from cutting a fully matured tree.

17.5

This problem focuses on the interaction of the corporate profits tax with firms' investment decisions.

a. Suppose (contrary to fact) that profits were defined for tax purposes as what we have called pure economic profits. How would a tax on such profits affect investment decisions?

b. In fact, profits are defined for tax purposes as

$$\pi' = pq - wl - \text{depreciation},$$

where depreciation is determined by governmental and industry guidelines that seek to allocate a machine's costs over its "useful" lifetime. If depreciation were equal to actual physical deterioration and if a firm were in long-run competitive equilibrium, how would a tax on π' affect the firm's choice of capital inputs?

c. Given the conditions of part (b), describe how capital usage would be affected by adoption of "accelerated depreciation" policies, which specify depreciation rates in excess of physical deterioration early in a machine's life but much lower depreciation rates as the machine ages.

d. Under the conditions of part (c), how might a decrease in the corporate profits tax affect capital usage?

17.6

A high-pressure life insurance salesman was heard to make the following argument: "At your age a $100,000 whole life policy is a much better buy than a similar term policy. Under a whole life policy you'll have to pay $2,000 per year for the first four years but nothing more for the rest of your life. A term policy will cost you $400 per year, essentially forever. If you live 35 years, you'll pay only $8,000 for the whole life policy, but $14,000 (= $400 \cdot 35$) for the term policy. Surely, the whole life is a better deal."

Assuming the salesman's life expectancy assumption is correct, how would you evaluate this argument? Specifically, calculate the present discounted value of the premium costs of the two policies assuming the interest rate is 10 percent.

17.7

Suppose that a perfect substitute for crude oil will be discovered in 15 years and that the price of this substitute will be the equivalent of an oil price of $125 per barrel. Suppose the current marginal extraction cost for oil is $7 per barrel. Assume also that the real interest rate is 5 percent and that real extraction costs fall at a rate of 2 percent annually. If crude oil prices follow the path described in Equation 17.66, what should the current price of crude oil be? Does your answer shed any light on actual pricing in the crude oil market?

Analytical Problems

17.8 Capital gains taxation

Suppose an individual has W dollars to allocate between consumption this period (c_0) and consumption next period (c_1) and that the interest rate is given by r.

a. Graph the individual's initial equilibrium and indicate the total value of current-period savings ($W - c_0$).

b. Suppose that, after the individual makes his or her savings decision (by purchasing one-period bonds), the interest rate falls to r'. How will this alter the individual's budget constraint? Show the new utility-maximizing position. Discuss how the individual's improved position can be interpreted as resulting from a "capital gain" on his or her initial bond purchases.

c. Suppose the tax authorities wish to impose an "income" tax based on the value of capital gains. If all such gains are valued in terms of c_0 as they are "accrued," show how those gains should be measured. Call this value G_1.

d. Suppose instead that capital gains are measured as they are "realized"—that is, capital gains are defined to include only that portion of bonds that is cashed in to buy additional c_0. Show how these realized gains can be measured. Call this amount G_2.

e. Develop a measure of the true increase in utility that results from the fall in r, measured in terms of c_0. Call this "true" capital gain G_3. Show that $G_3 < G_2 < G_1$. What do you conclude about a tax policy that taxes only realized gains?

Note: This problem is adapted from J. Whalley, "Capital Gains Taxation and Interest Rate Changes," *National Tax Journal* (March 1979): 87–91.

17.9 Precautionary saving and prudence

The Query to Example 17.2 asks how uncertainty about the future might affect a person's savings decisions. In this problem we explore this question more fully. All of our analysis is based on the simple two-period model in Example 17.1.

a. To simplify matters, assume that $r = \delta$ in Equation 17.15. If consumption is certain, this implies that $U'(c_0) = U'(c_1)$ or $c_0 = c_1$. But suppose that consumption in period 1 will be subject to a zero-mean random shock, so that $c_1 = c_1^p + x$, where c_1^p is planned period-1 consumption and x is a random variable with an expected value of 0. Describe why, in this context, utility maximization requires $U'(c_0) = E[U'(c_1)]$.

b. Use Jensen's inequality (see Chapters 2 and 7) to show that this person will opt for $c_1^p > c_0$ if and only if U' is convex—that is, if and only if $U''' > 0$.

c. Kimball[14] suggests using the term "prudence" to describe a person whose utility function is characterized by $U''' > 0$. Describe why the results from part (b) show that such a definition is consistent with everyday usage.

d. In Example 17.2 we showed that real interest rates in the U.S. economy seem too low to reconcile actual consumption growth rates with evidence on individuals' willingness to experience consumption fluctuations. If consumption growth rates were uncertain, would this explain or exacerbate the paradox?

17.10 Monopoly and natural resource prices

Suppose that a firm is the sole owner of a stock of a natural resource.

a. How should the analysis of the maximization of the discounted profits from selling this resource (Equation 17.58) be modified to take this fact into account?

b. Suppose that the demand for the resource in question had a constant elasticity form $q(t) = a[p(t)]^b$. How would this change the price dynamics shown in Equation 17.62?

c. How would the answer to Problem 17.7 be changed if the entire crude oil supply were owned by a single firm?

17.11 Renewable timber economics

The calculations in Problem 17.4 assume there is no difference between the decisions to cut a single tree and to manage a woodlot. But managing a woodlot also involves replanting, which should be explicitly modeled. To do so, assume a lot owner is considering planting a single tree at a cost w, harvesting the tree at t^*, planting another, and so forth forever. The discounted stream of profits from this activity is then

$$V = -w + e^{-rt}[f(t) - w] + e^{-r2t}[f(t) - w] + \cdots + e^{-rnt}[f(t) - w] + \cdots.$$

a. Show that the total value of this planned harvesting activity is given by

$$V = \frac{f(t) - w}{e^{-rt} - 1} - w.$$

b. Find the value of t that maximizes V. Show that this value solves the equation

$$f'(t^*) = rf(t^*) + rV(t^*).$$

c. Interpret the results of part (b): How do they reflect optimal usage of the "input" time? Why is the value of t^* specified in part (b) different from that in Example 17.2?

d. Suppose tree growth (measured in constant dollars) follows the logistic function

$$f(t) = 50/(1 + e^{10-0.1t}).$$

What is the maximum value of the timber available from this tree?

e. If tree growth is characterized by the equation given in part (d), what is the optimal rotation period if $r = 0.05$ and $w = 0$? Does this period produce a "maximum sustainable" yield?

f. How would the optimal period change if r fell to 0.04?

Note: The equation derived in part (b) is known in forestry economics as Faustmann's equation.

---

[14]M. S. Kimball, "Precautionary Savings in the Small and in the Large," *Econometrica* (January 1990): 53–73.

17.12 Hyperbolic discounting

The notion that people might be "shortsighted" was formalized by David Laibson in "Golden Eggs and Hyperbolic Discounting" (*Quarterly Journal of Economics*, May 1997, pp. 443–477). In this paper the author hypothesizes that individuals maximize an intertemporal utility function of the form

$$\text{utility} = U(c_t) + \beta \sum_{\tau=1}^{\tau=T} \delta^\tau U(c_{t+\tau}),$$

where $0 < \beta < 1$ and $0 < \delta < 1$. The particular time pattern of these discount factors leads to the possibility of shortsightedness.

    a. Laibson suggests hypothetical values of $\beta = 0.6$ and $\delta = 0.99$. Show that, for these values, the factors by which future consumption is discounted follow a general hyperbolic pattern. That is, show that the factors drop significantly for period $t + 1$ and then follow a steady geometric rate of decline for subsequent periods.

    b. Describe intuitively why this pattern of discount rates might lead to shortsighted behavior.

    c. More formally, calculate the *MRS* between c_{t+1} and c_{t+2} at time t. Compare this to the *MRS* between c_{t+1} and c_{t+2} at time $t + 1$. Explain why, with a constant real interest rate, this would imply "dynamically inconsistent" choices over time. Specifically, how would the relationship between optimal c_{t+1} and c_{t+2} differ from these two perspectives?

    d. Laibson explains that the pattern described in part (c) will lead "early selves" to find ways to constrain "future selves" and so achieve full utility maximization. Explain why such constraints are necessary.

    e. Describe a few of the ways in which people seek to constrain their future choices in the real world.

SUGGESTIONS FOR FURTHER READING

Blaug, M. *Economic Theory in Retrospect*, rev. ed. Homewood, IL: Richard D. Irwin, 1978, chap. 12.

Good review of Austrian capital theory and of attempts to conceptualize the capital accumulation process.

Conrad, J. M., and C. W. Clark. *Natural Resource Economics: Notes and Problems*. Cambridge: Cambridge University Press, 2004.

Provides several illustrations of how optimal control theory can be applied to problems in natural resource pricing.

Dixit, A. K. *Optimization in Economic Theory*, 2nd ed. New York: Oxford University Press, 1990.

Extended treatment of optimal control theory in a fairly easy-to-follow format.

Dorfman, R. "An Economic Interpretation of Optimal Control Theory." *American Economic Review* 59 (December 1969): 817–31.

Uses the approach of this chapter to examine optimal capital accumulation. Excellent intuitive introduction.

Hotelling, H. "The Economics of Exhaustible Resources." *Journal of Political Economy* 39 (April 1931): 137–75.

Fundamental work on allocation of natural resources. Analyzes both competitive and monopoly cases.

Mas-Colell, A., M. D. Whinston, and J. R. Green. *Microeconomic Theory*. New York: Oxford University Press, 1995.

Chapter 20 offers extensive coverage of issues in defining equilibrium over time. The discussion of "overlapping generations" models is especially useful.

Ramsey, F. P. "A Mathematical Theory of Saving." *Economic Journal* 38 (December 1928): 542–59.

One of the first uses of the calculus of variations to solve economic problems.

Solow, R. M. *Capital Theory and the Rate of Return*. Amsterdam: North-Holland, 1964.

Lectures on the nature of capital. Very readable.

Sydsaeter, K., A. Strom, and P. Berck. *Economists' Mathematical Manual*, 3rd ed. Berlin: Springer-Verlag, 2000.

Chapter 27 provides a variety of formulas that are valuable for finance and growth theory.

The Mathematics of Compound Interest

The purpose of this appendix is to gather some simple results concerning the mathematics of compound interest. These results have applications in a wide variety of economic problems that range from macroeconomic policy to the optimal way of raising Christmas trees.

We assume there is a current prevailing market interest rate of i per period—say, of one year. This interest rate is assumed to be both certain and constant over all future periods.[1] If $1 is invested at this rate i and if the interest is then compounded (that is, future interest is paid on post interest earned), then: at the end of one period, $1 will be

$$\$1 \times (1 + i);$$

at the end of two periods, $1 will be

$$\$1 \times (1 + i) \times (1 + i) = \$1 \times (1 + i)^2;$$

and at the end of n periods, $1 will be

$$\$1 \times (1 + i)^n.$$

Similarly, N grows like

$$\$N \times (1 + i)^n.$$

PRESENT DISCOUNTED VALUE

The *present value* of $1 payable one period from now is

$$\frac{\$1}{1 + i}.$$

---

[1]The assumption of a constant i is obviously unrealistic. Because problems introduced by considering an interest rate that varies from period to period greatly complicate the notation without adding a commensurate degree of conceptual knowledge, such an analysis is not undertaken here. In many cases the generalization to a varying interest rate is merely a trivial application of the notion that any multiperiod interest rate can be regarded as resulting from compounding several single-period rates. If we let r_{ij} be the interest rate prevailing between periods i and j (where $i < j$), then

$$1 + r_{ij} = (1 + r_{i,i+1}) + (1 + r_{i+1,i+2}) + \cdots + (1 + r_{j-1,j}).$$

This is simply the amount an individual would be willing to pay now for the promise of $1 at the end of one period. Similarly, the present value of $1 payable n periods from now is

$$\frac{\$1}{(1+i)^n},$$

and the present value of $\$N$ payable n periods from now is

$$\frac{\$N}{(1+i)^n}.$$

The *present discounted value* of a stream of payments $N_0, N_1, N_2, ..., N_n$ (where the subscripts indicate the period in which the payment is to be made) is

$$PDV = N_0 + \frac{N_1}{(1+i)} + \frac{N_2}{(1+i)^2} + \cdots + \frac{N_n}{(1+i)^n}. \tag{17A.1}$$

The *PDV* is the amount an individual would be willing to pay in return for a promise to receive the stream $N_0, N_1, N_2, ..., N_n$. It represents the amount that would have to be invested now if one wished to duplicate the payment stream.

Annuities and perpetuities

An *annuity* is a promise to pay $\$N$ in each period for n periods, starting next period. The *PDV* of such a contract is

$$PDV = \frac{N}{1+i} + \frac{N}{(1+i)^2} + \cdots + \frac{N}{(1+i)^n}. \tag{17A.2}$$

Let $\delta = 1/(1+i)$; then,

$$PDV = N(\delta + \delta^2 + \cdots + \delta^n)$$
$$= N\delta(1 + \delta + \delta^2 + \cdots + \delta^{n-1})$$
$$= N\delta\left(\frac{1-\delta^n}{1-\delta}\right). \tag{17A.3}$$

Observe that

$$\lim_{n\to\infty} \delta^n = 0.$$

Therefore, for an annuity of infinite duration,

$$PDV \text{ of infinite annuity} = \lim_{n\to\infty} PDV = N\delta\left(\frac{1}{1-\delta}\right); \tag{17A.4}$$

by the definition of δ,

$$N\delta\left(\frac{1}{1-\delta}\right) = N\left(\frac{1}{1+i}\right)\left(\frac{1}{1-1/(1+i)}\right)$$
$$= N\left(\frac{1}{1+i}\right)\left(\frac{1+i}{i}\right) = \frac{N}{i}. \tag{17A.5}$$

This case of an infinite-period annuity is sometimes called a *perpetuity* or a *consol*. The formula simply says that the amount that must be invested if one is to obtain $\$N$ per period forever is simply $\$N/i$, because this amount of money would earn $\$N$ in interest each period $(i \cdot \$N/i = \$N)$.

The special case of a bond

An n-period *bond* is a promise to pay $\$N$ each period, starting next period, for n periods. It also promises to return the principal (face) value of the bond at the end of n periods. If the principal value of the bond is $\$P$ (usually $\$1,000$ in the U.S. bond market), then the present discounted value of such a promise is

$$PDV = \frac{N}{1+i} + \frac{N}{(1+i)^2} + \cdots + \frac{N}{(1+i)^n} + \frac{P}{(1+i)^n}. \qquad \text{(17A.6)}$$

Again, let $\delta = 1/(1+i)$; then,

$$PDV = N\delta + N\delta^2 + \cdots + (N+P)\delta^n. \qquad \text{(17A.7)}$$

Equation 17A.7 can be looked at in another way. Suppose we knew the price (say, B) at which the bond is currently trading. Then we could ask what value of i gives the bond a PDV equal to B. To find this i we set

$$B = PDV = N\delta + N\delta^2 + \cdots + (N+P)\delta^n. \qquad \text{(17A.8)}$$

Because B, N, and P are known, we can solve this equation for δ and hence for i.[2] The i that solves the equation is called the *yield* on the bond and is the best measure of the return actually available from the bond. The yield of a bond represents the return available both from direct interest payments and from any price differential between the initial price (B) and the maturity price (P).

Notice that, as i increases, PDV decreases. This is a precise way of formulating the well-known concept that bond prices (PDVs) and interest rates (yields) are inversely correlated.

CONTINUOUS TIME

Thus far our approach has dealt with discrete time—the analysis has been divided into periods. Often it is more convenient to deal with continuous time. In such a case the interest on an investment is compounded "instantaneously" and growth over time is "smooth." This facilitates the analysis of maximization problems because exponential functions are more easily differentiated. Many financial intermediaries (for example, savings banks) have adopted (nearly) continuous interest formulas in recent years.

Suppose that i is given as the (nominal) interest rate per year but that half this nominal rate is compounded every six months. Then, at the end of one year, the investment of $\$1$ would have grown to

$$\$1 \times \left(1 + \frac{i}{2}\right)^2. \qquad \text{(17A.9)}$$

Observe that this is superior to investing for one year at the simple rate i, because interest has been paid on interest; that is,

$$\left(1 + \frac{i}{2}\right)^2 > (1+i). \qquad \text{(17A.10)}$$

---

[2]Because this equation is an nth-degree polynomial, there are in reality n solutions (roots). Only one of these solutions is the relevant one reported in bond tables or on calculators. The other solutions are either imaginary or unreasonable. In the present example there is only one real solution.

TABLE 17A.1   Effective Annual Interest Rates for Selected Continuously Compounded Rates

Continuously Compounded Rate	Effective Annual Rate
3.0%	3.05%
4.0	4.08
5.0	5.13
5.5	5.65
6.0	6.18
6.5	6.72
7.0	7.25
8.0	8.33
9.0	9.42
10.0	10.52

Consider the limit of this process: for the nominal rate of i per period, consider the amount that would be realized if i were in fact "compounded n times during the period." Letting $n \to \infty$, we have

$$\lim_{n \to \infty} \left(1 + \frac{i}{n} \right)^n. \qquad \text{(17A.11)}$$

This limit exists and is simply e^i, where e is the base of natural logarithms (the value of e is approximately 2.72). It is important to note that $e^i > (1 + i)$—it is much better to have continuous compounding over the period than to have simple interest.

We can ask what continuous rate r yields the same amount at the end of one period as the simple rate i. We are looking for the value of r that solves the equation

$$e^r = (1 + i). \qquad \text{(17A.12)}$$

Hence,

$$r = \ln(1 + i). \qquad \text{(17A.13)}$$

Using this formula, it is a simple matter to translate from discrete interest rates into continuous ones. If i is measured as a decimal yearly rate, then r is a yearly continuous rate. Table 17A.1 shows the effective annual interest rate (i) associated with selected interest rates (r) that are continuously compounded.[3] Tables similar to 17A.1 often appear in the windows of savings banks advertising the "true" yields on their accounts.

Continuous growth

One dollar invested at a continuous interest rate of r will become

$$V = \$1 \cdot e^{rT} \qquad \text{(17A.14)}$$

---

[3]To compute the figures in Table 17A.1, interest rates are used in decimal rather than percent form (that is, a 5 percent interest rate is recorded as 0.05 for use in Equation 17A.12).

after T years. This growth formula is a convenient one to work with. For example, it is easy to show that the instantaneous relative rate of change in V is, as would be expected, simply given by r:

$$\textbf{relative rate of change} = \frac{dV/dt}{V} = \frac{re^{rt}}{e^{rt}} = r. \qquad \textbf{(17A.15)}$$

Continuous interest rates also are convenient for calculating present discounted values. Suppose we wished to calculate the PDV of \$1 to be paid T years from now. This would be given by[4]

$$\frac{\$1}{e^{rT}} = \$1 \times e^{-rT}. \qquad \textbf{(17A.16)}$$

The logic of this calculation is exactly the same as that used in the discrete time analysis of this appendix: future dollars are worth less than present dollars.

Payment streams

One interesting application of continuous discounting occurs in calculating the PDV of \$1 per period paid in small installments at each instant of time from today (time 0) until time T. Because there would be an infinite number of payments, the mathematical tool of integration must be used to compute this result:

$$PDV = \int_0^T e^{-rt}\, dt. \qquad \textbf{(17A.17)}$$

What this expression means is that we are adding all the discounted dollars over the time period 0 to T.

The value of this definite integral is given by

$$PDV = \frac{-e^{-rt}}{r}\bigg|_0^T$$

$$= \frac{-e^{-rT}}{r} + \frac{1}{r}. \qquad \textbf{(17A.18)}$$

As T aproaches infinity, this value becomes

$$PDV = \frac{1}{r}, \qquad \textbf{(17A.19)}$$

as was the case for the infinitely long annuity considered in the discrete case.

Continuous discounting is particularly convenient for calculating the PDV of an arbitrary stream of payments over time. Suppose that $f(t)$ records the number of dollars to be paid during period t. Then the PDV of the payment at time t is

$$e^{-rt}f(t), \qquad \textbf{(17A.20)}$$

and the PDV of the entire stream from the present time (year 0) until year T is given by

$$\int_0^T f(t)e^{-rt}\, dt. \qquad \textbf{(17A.21)}$$

---

[4]In physics this formula occurs as an example of "radioactive decay." If 1 unit of a substance decays continuously at the rate δ then, after T periods, $e^{-\delta T}$ units will remain. This amount never exactly reaches zero no matter how large T is. Depreciation can be treated the same way in capital theory.

Often, economic agents may seek to maximize an expression such as that given in Equation 17A.21. Use of continuous time makes the analysis of such choices straightforward because standard calculus methods of maximization can be used.

Duration

The use of continuous time can also clarify a number of otherwise rather difficult financial concepts. For example, suppose we wished to know how long, on average, it takes for an individual to receive a payment from a given payment stream, $f(t)$. The present value of the stream is given by

$$V = \int_0^T f(t)e^{-rt}\, dt. \tag{17A.22}$$

Differentiation of this value by the discount factor, e^{-r}, yields

$$\frac{\partial V}{\partial e^{-r}} = \int_0^T tf(t)e^{-r(t-1)}\, dt, \tag{17A.23}$$

and the elasticity of this change is given by

$$e = \frac{\partial V}{\partial e^{-r}} \cdot \frac{e^{-r}}{V} = \frac{\int_0^T tf(t)e^{-rt}\,dt}{V}. \tag{17A.24}$$

Hence the elasticity of the present value of this payment stream with respect to the annual discount factor (which is similar to, say, the elasticity of bond prices with respect to changes in interest rates) is given by the ratio of the present value of a time-weighted stream of payments to an unweighted stream. Conceptually, then, this elasticity represents the average time an individual must wait to receive the typical payment. In the financial press this concept is termed the *duration* of the payment stream. This is an important measure of the volatility of the present value of such a stream with respect to interest rate changes.[5]

---

[5]As an example, a duration of 8 years would mean that the mean length of time that the individual must wait for the typical payment is 8 years. It also means that the elasticity of the value of this stream with respect to the discount factor is 8.0. Because the elasticity of the discount factor itself with respect to the interest rate is simply $-r$, the elasticity of the value of the stream with respect to this interest rate is $-8r$. If $r = 0.05$, for example, then the elasticity of the present value of this stream with respect to r is -0.40.

Market Failure

In this part we look more closely at some of the reasons why markets may perform poorly in allocating resources. We will also examine some of the ways in which such market failures might be mitigated.

Chapter 18 focuses on situations where some market participants are better informed than others. In such cases of *asymmetric information*, establishing efficient contracts between these parties can be quite complicated and may involve a variety of strategic choices. We will see that in many situations the first-best, fully informed solution is not attainable. Therefore, second-best solutions that may involve some efficiency losses must be considered.

Externalities are the principal topic of **Chapter 19**. The first part of the chapter is concerned with situations in which the actions of one economic actor directly affect the well-being of another actor. We show that, unless these costs or benefits can be internalized into the decision process, resources will be misallocated. In the second part of the chapter we turn to a particular type of externality, that posed by "public goods": goods that are both nonexclusive and nonrival. We show that markets will often under-allocate resources to such goods, so other ways of financing (such as compulsary taxation) should be considered. Chapter 19 concludes with an examination of how voting may affect this process.

Asymmetric Information

Markets may not be fully efficient when one side has information that the other side does not (asymmetric information). Contracts with more complex terms than simple per-unit prices may be used to help solve problems raised by such asymmetric information. The two important classes of asymmetric information problems studied in this chapter include adverse selection problems, in which a party obtains asymmetric information about market conditions before signing the contract, and moral hazard problems, in which one party's actions during the term of the contract are unobservable to the other. Carefully designed contracts may reduce such problems by providing incentives to reveal one's information and take appropriate actions. But these contracts seldom eliminate the inefficiencies entirely. Surprisingly, unbridled competition may worsen private information problems, although a carefully designed auction can harness competitive forces to the auctioneer's advantage.

COMPLEX CONTRACTS AS A RESPONSE TO ASYMMETRIC INFORMATION

So far, the transactions we have studied have involved simple contracts. We assumed that firms bought inputs from suppliers at constant per-unit prices and likewise sold output to consumers at constant per-unit prices. Many real-world transactions involve much more complicated contracts. Rather than an hourly wage, a corporate executive's compensation usually involves complex features such as the granting of stock, stock options, and bonuses. Expensive durable goods such as appliances and cars often carry warranties that can be extended for an extra fee. Insurance policies may cap the insurer's liability and may require the customer to bear costs in the form of deductibles and copayments. Rather than being sold at a posted price, some goods are sold at auction with reserve prices and other complicated features. In this chapter, we will show that such complex contracts and sales methods may arise as a way for transacting parties to deal with the problem of asymmetric information.

Asymmetric information

Transactions can involve a considerable amount of uncertainty. The value of a snow shovel will depend on how much snow falls during the winter season. The value of a hybrid car will depend on how much gasoline prices rise in the future. By itself, uncertainty need not introduce inefficiencies. Buyers and sellers can handle uncertainty by exchanging contingent commodities (introduced in Chapter 7). For example, rather than buying a snow shovel outright, a consumer could buy the services of the shovel during the month of January conditional on snowfall of 10 inches or more. With markets for such commodities covering every possible future contingency, the same results that ensured the efficiency of perfect competition under perfect certainty would also hold under uncertainty.

Uncertainty need not lead to inefficiency when both sides of a transaction have the same limited knowledge concerning the future, but it can lead to inefficiency when one side has better information. The side with better information is said to have *private information* or, equivalently, *asymmetric information*. There are several sources of asymmetric information. Parties will often have "inside information" concerning themselves that the other side does not have. Consider the case of health insurance. A customer seeking insurance will often have private information about his or her own health status and family medical history that the insurance company does not. Consumers in good health may not bother to purchase health insurance at the prevailing rates. A consumer in poor health would have higher demand for insurance, wishing to shift the burden of large anticipated medical expenses to the insurer. A medical examination may help the insurer learn about a customer's health status, but examinations are costly and may not reveal all of the customer's private health information. The customer will be reluctant to report family medical history and genetic disease honestly if the insurer might use this information to deny coverage or raise premiums. The customer also has better information about lifestyle choices that may affect health and thus medical expenses—for example, eating a healthy diet and not smoking. The insurer might like to condition coverage on the maintenance of a healthy lifestyle, but it may be prohibitively expensive for the insurer to monitor such behaviors day in and day out (and the customer again cannot be expected to reveal information about his or her behavior if this could be used to reduce coverage or increase premiums).

Other sources of asymmetric information arise when what is being bought is an agent's service. The buyer may not always be able to monitor how hard and well the agent is working. The agent may have better information about the requirements of the project because of his or her expertise, which is the reason the agent was hired in the first place. For example, a repairer called to fix a kitchen appliance will know more about the true severity of the appliance's mechanical problems than does the homeowner.

Asymmetric information can lead to inefficiencies. Insurance companies may offer less insurance and charge higher premiums than if they could observe the health of potential clients and could require customers to obey strict health regimens. The whole market may unravel as consumers who expect their health expenditures to be lower than the average insured consumer's withdraw from the market in successive stages, leaving only the few worst health risks as consumers. With appliance repair, the repairer may pad his or her bill by replacing parts that still function and may take longer than needed—a waste of resources.

The value of contracts

Contractual provisions can be added in order to circumvent some of these inefficiencies. An insurance company can offer lower health insurance premiums to customers who submit to medical exams or who are willing to bear the cost of some fraction of their own medical services. Lower-risk consumers may be more willing than high-risk consumers to submit to medical exams and to bear a fraction of their medical expenses. A homeowner may buy a service contract that stipulates a fixed fee for keeping the appliance running rather than a payment for each service call and part needed in the event the appliance breaks down.

Although contracts may help reduce the inefficiencies associated with asymmetric information, rarely do they eliminate the inefficiencies altogether. In the health insurance example, having some consumers undertake a medical exam requires the expenditure of real resources. Requiring low-risk consumers to bear some of their own medical expenditures means that they are not fully insured, which is a social loss to the extent that a risk-neutral insurance company would be a more efficient risk bearer than a risk-averse consumer. A fixed-fee contract to maintain an appliance may lead the homeowner to be careless when handling the appliance because any subsequent malfunction is the repairman's problem, not the home-owner's. It may also lead the repairer to supply too little effort, overlooking potential problems in the hope that nothing breaks until after the service contract expires (and so then the problems become the homeowner's).

PRINCIPAL-AGENT MODEL

Models of asymmetric information can quickly become quite complicated and so, before considering a full-blown market model with many suppliers and demanders, we will devote much of our analysis to a simpler model—called a principal-agent model—in which there is only one party on each side of the market. The party who proposes the contract is called the *principal*. The party who decides whether or not to accept the contract and then performs under the terms of the contract (if accepted) is called the *agent*. The agent is typically the party with the asymmetric information. We will use "she" for the principal and "he" for the agent to facilitate the exposition.

Two leading models

Two models of asymmetric information are studied most often. In a first model, the agent's actions taken during the term of the contract affect the principal, but the principal does not observe these actions directly. The principal may observe outcomes that are correlated with the agent's actions but not the actions themselves. This first model is called a hidden-action model. For historical reasons stemming from the insurance context, the hidden-action model is also called a *moral hazard model*.

In a second model, the agent has private information about the state of the world before signing the contract with the principal. The agent's private information is called his *type*, consistent with our terminology from games of private information studied in Chapter 8. The second model is thus called a hidden-type model. For historical reasons stemming from its application in the insurance context, which we discuss later, the hidden-type model is also called an *adverse selection model*.

As indicated by Table 18.1, the hidden-type and hidden-action models cover a wide variety of applications. Note that the same party might be a principal in one setting and an agent in another. For example, a company's CEO is the principal in dealings with the company's employees but is the agent of the firm's shareholders. We will study several of the applications from Table 18.1 in detail throughout the remainder of this chapter.

TABLE 18.1 Applications of the Principal-Agent Model

		Agent's private information	
Principal	Agent	Hidden type	Hidden action
Shareholders	Manager	Managerial skill	Effort, executive decisions
Manager	Employee	Job skill	Effort
Homeowner	Appliance repairer	Skill, severity of appliance malfunction	Effort, unnecessary repairs
Student	Tutor	Subject knowledge	Preparation, patience
Monopoly	Customer	Value for good	Care to avoid breakage
Health insurer	Insurance purchaser	Preexisting condition	Risky activity
Parent	Child	Moral fiber	Delinquency

First, second, and third best

In a full-information environment, the principal could propose a contract to the agent that maximizes their joint surplus and captures all of this surplus for herself, leaving the agent with just enough surplus to make him indifferent between signing the contract or not. This outcome is called the *first best*, and the contract implementing this outcome is called the *first-best contract*. The first best is a theoretical benchmark that is unlikely to be achieved in practice because the principal is rarely fully informed. The outcome that maximizes the principal's surplus subject to the constraint that the principal is less well informed than the agent is called the *second best*, and the contract that implements this outcome is called the *second-best contract*. Adding further constraints to the principal's problem besides the informational constraint—for example, restricting contracts to some simple form such as constant per-unit prices—leads to the third best, the fourth best, and so on, depending on how many constraints are added.

Since this chapter is in the part of the book that examines market failures, we will be interested in determining how important a market failure is asymmetric information. Comparing the first to the second best will allow us to quantify the reduction in total welfare due to asymmetric information.

Also illuminating is a comparison of the second and third best. This comparison will indicate how surpluses are affected when moving from simple contracts in the third best to potentially quite sophisticated contracts in the second best. Of course, the principal's surplus cannot decrease when she has access to a wider range of contracts with which to maximize her surplus. However, total welfare—the sum of the principal's and agent's surplus in a principal-agent model—may decrease. Figure 18.1 suggests why. In the example in panel (a) of the figure, the complex contract increases the total welfare "pie" that is divided between the principal and the agent. The principal likes the complex contract because it allows her to obtain a roughly constant share of a bigger pie. In panel (b), the principal likes the complex contract even though the total welfare pie is smaller with it than with the simple contract. The complex contract allows her to appropriate a larger slice at the expense of reducing the pie's total size. The different cases in panels (a) and (b) will come up in the applications analyzed in subsequent sections.

HIDDEN ACTIONS

The first of the two important models of asymmetric information is the hidden-action model, also sometimes called the moral hazard model in insurance and other contexts. The principal would like the agent to take an action that maximizes their joint surplus (and given that the principal makes the contract offer, she would like to appropriate most of the surplus for herself). In the application to the owner-manager relationship that we will study, the owner would like the manager whom she hires to show up during business hours and work diligently. In the application to the accident insurance, the insurance company would like the insured individual to avoid accidents. The agent's actions may be unobservable to the principal. Observing the action may require the principal to monitor the agent at all times, and such monitoring may be prohibitively expensive. If the agent's action is unobservable then he will prefer to shirk, choosing an action to suit himself rather than the principal. In the owner-manager application, shirking might mean showing up late for work and slacking off while on the job; in the insurance example, shirking might mean taking more risk than the insurance company would like.

Although contracts cannot prevent shirking directly by tying the agent's compensation to his action—because his action is unobservable—contracts can mitigate shirking by tying compensation to observable outcomes. In the owner-manager application, the relevant observable outcome might be the firm's profit. The owner may be able to induce the manager to work hard by tying the manager's pay to the firm's profit, which depends on

FIGURE 18.1   The Contracting "Pie"

The total welfare is the area of the circle ("pie"); the principal's surplus is the area of the shaded region. In panel (a), the complex contract increases total welfare and the principal's surplus along with it because she obtains a constant share. In panel (b), the principal offers the complex contract—even though this reduces total welfare—because the complex contract allows her to appropriate a larger share.

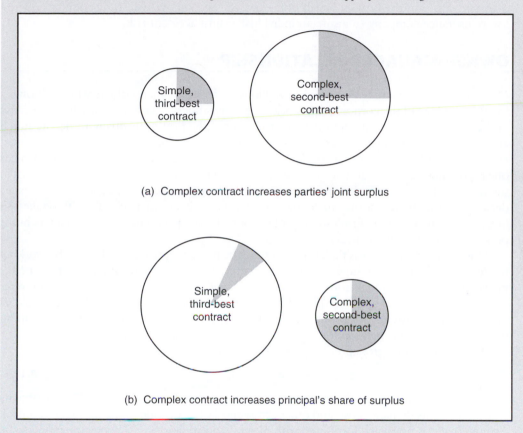

(a) Complex contract increases parties' joint surplus

(b) Complex contract increases principal's share of surplus

the manager's effort. The insurance company may be able to induce the individual to take care by having him bear some of the cost of any accident.

Often, the principal is more concerned with the observable outcome than with the agent's unobservable action anyway, so it seems the principal should do just as well by conditioning the contract on outcomes as on actions. The problem is that the outcome may depend in part on random factors outside of the agent's control. In the owner-manager application, the firm's profit may depend on consumer demand, which may depend on unpredictable economic conditions. In the insurance application, whether an accident occurs depends in part on the care taken by the individual but also on a host of other factors, including other people's actions and acts of nature. Tying the agent's compensation to partially random outcomes exposes him to risk. If the agent is risk averse, then this exposure causes disutility and requires the payment of a risk premium before he will accept the contract (see Chapter 7). In many applications, the principal is less risk averse and thus is a more efficient risk bearer than the agent. In the owner-manager application, the owner might be one of many shareholders who each hold only a small share of the firm in a diversified portfolio. In the insurance application, the company may insure a large number of agents, whose accidents are uncorrelated, and thus face little aggregate risk. If there were no issue of incentives then the agent's compensation should be independent of risky outcomes, completely insuring him against risk and shifting the risk to the efficient bearer: the principal. The second-best contract strikes the optimal balance between incentives and insurance, but it does not provide as strong incentives or as full insurance as the first-best contract.

In the following sections, we will study two specific applications of the hidden-action model. First, we will study employment contracts signed between a firm's owners and a manager who runs the firm on behalf of the owners. Second, we will study contracts offered by an insurance company to insure an individual against accident risk.

OWNER-MANAGER RELATIONSHIP

Modern corporations may be owned by millions of dispersed shareholders who each own a small percentage of the corporation's stock. The shareholders—who may have little expertise in the line of business and who may own too little of the firm individually to devote much attention to it—delegate the operation of the firm to a managerial team consisting of the chief executive (CEO) and other officers. We will simplify the setting and suppose that the firm has one representative owner and one manager. The owner, who plays the role of the principal in the model, offers a contract to the manager, who plays the role of the agent. The manager decides whether to accept the employment contract and, if so, what action $e \geq 0$ to take. An increase in e increases the firm's gross profit (not including payments to the manager) but is personally costly to the manager.

One interpretation of e is the effort and time the manager puts in on the job. By working harder, the manager can supervise workers better, make more informed and thus better managerial decisions, and so forth. To fix ideas, we will often interpret e in this way and refer to it as effort, but it can be interpreted in other ways. For example, e can be intepreted as making such distasteful but profitable decisions as firing unproductive workers, trimming perks, and avoiding expansion for the mere sake of enlarging his "empire."

Assume the firm's gross profit π_g takes the following simple form:

$$\pi_g = e + \varepsilon. \tag{18.1}$$

Gross profit is increasing in the manager's effort e and also depends on a random variable ε, which represents demand, cost, and other economic factors outside of the manager's control. Assume that ε is normally distributed with mean 0 and variance σ^2. The manager's personal disutility (or cost) of undertaking effort $c(e)$ is increasing $[c'(e) > 0]$ and convex $[c''(e) > 0]$.

Let s be the salary—which may depend on effort and/or gross profit, depending on what the owner can observe—offered as part of the contract between the owner and manager. Because the owner represents individual shareholders who each own a small share of the firm as part of a diversified portfolio, we will assume that she is risk neutral. Letting net profit π_n equal gross profit minus payments to the manager,

$$\pi_n = \pi_g - s, \tag{18.2}$$

the risk-neutral owner wants to maximize the expected value of her net profit:

$$E(\pi_n) = E(e + \varepsilon - s) = e - E(s). \tag{18.3}$$

To introduce a trade-off between incentives and risk, we will assume the manager is risk averse; in particular, we assume the manager has a utility function with respect to salary whose constant absolute risk aversion parameter is $A > 0$. We can use the results from Example 7.3 to show that his expected utility is

$$E(U) = E(s) - \frac{A}{2} \mathbf{Var}(s) - c(e). \tag{18.4}$$

We will examine the optimal salary contract that induces the manager to take appropriate effort e under different informational assumptions. We will study the first-best contract, when the owner can observe e perfectly, and then the second-best contract when there is asymmetric information about e.

First best (full-information case)

With full information, it is relatively easy to design an optimal salary contract. The owner can pay the manager a fixed salary s^* if he exerts the first-best level of effort e^* (which we will compute shortly) and nothing otherwise. The manager's expected utility from the contract can be found by substituting the expected value $[E(s^*) = s^*]$ and variance $[\text{Var}(s^*) = 0]$ of the fixed salary as well as the effort e^* into Equation 18.4. For the manager to accept the contract, this expected utility must exceed what he would obtain from his next-best job offer:

$$E(U) = s^* - c(e^*) \geq 0, \tag{18.5}$$

where we have assumed for simplicity that he obtains 0 from his next-best job offer. In principal-agent models, a condition like Equation 18.5 is called a *participation constraint*, ensuring the agent's participation in the contract.

The owner optimally pays the lowest salary satisfying Equation 18.5: $s^* = c(e^*)$. The owner's net profit then is

$$E(\pi_n) = e^* - E(s^*) = e^* - c(e^*), \tag{18.6}$$

which is maximized for e^* satisfying the first-order condition

$$c'(e^*) = 1. \tag{18.7}$$

At an optimum, the marginal cost of effort, $c'(e^*)$, equals the marginal benefit, 1.

Second best (hidden-action case)

If the owner can observe the manager's effort, then she can implement the first best by simply ordering the manager to exert the first-best effort level. If she cannot observe effort, the contract cannot be conditioned on e. However, she can still induce the manager to exert some effort if the manager's salary depends on the firm's gross profit. The manager is given performance pay: the more the firm earns, the more the manager is paid.

Notice that a constant salary independent of the firm's gross profit would not induce the manager to exert any effort. With a constant salary s, the manager's expected utility from Equation 18.4 would equal $s - c(e)$, which is maximized by choosing the lowest level of effort possible: $e = 0$.

Instead of a constant salary, suppose the owner offers the manager one that is linear in gross profit:

$$s(\pi_g) = a + b\pi_g, \tag{18.8}$$

where a is the fixed component of salary and b measures the slope, sometimes called the *power*, of the incentive scheme. If $b = 0$ then the salary is constant and, as we saw, provides no effort incentives. As b increases toward 1, the incentive scheme provides increasingly powerful incentives. The fixed component a can be thought of as the manager's base salary and b as the incentive pay in the form of stocks, stock options, and performance bonuses.

The owner-manager relationship can be viewed as a three-stage game. In the first stage, the owner sets the salary, which amounts to choosing a and b. In the second stage, the manager decides whether or not to accept the contract. In the third stage, the manager decides how much effort to exert conditional on accepting the contract. We will solve for the subgame-perfect equilibrium of this game by using backward induction, starting with the manager's choice of e in the last stage and taking as given that the manager was offered salary scheme $a + b\pi_g$ and accepted it. Substituting from Equation 18.8 into Equation 18.4, the manager's expected utility from the linear salary is

$$E(a + b\pi_g) - \frac{A}{2}\operatorname{Var}(a + b\pi_g) - c(e). \tag{18.9}$$

Reviewing a few facts about expectations and variances of a random variable will help us simplify Equation 18.9. First note that

$$E(a + b\pi_g) = E(a + be + b\varepsilon) = a + be + bE(\varepsilon) = a + be, \tag{18.10}$$

because the expected value of a linear function of the random variable ε is a linear function of the expected value of ε.[1] Furthermore,

$$\operatorname{Var}(a + b\pi_g) = \operatorname{Var}(a + be + b\varepsilon) = b\operatorname{Var}(\varepsilon) = b^2\sigma^2, \tag{18.11}$$

which follows from the formula for the variance of a linear function of a random variable (see Problem 2.14). Therefore, Equation 18.9 reduces to

$$\text{manager's expected utility} = a + be - \frac{Ab^2\sigma^2}{2} - c(e). \tag{18.12}$$

The first-order condition for the choice of e that maximizes the manager's expected utility in Equation 18.12 yields

$$c'(e) = b. \tag{18.13}$$

Because $c(e)$ is convex, the marginal cost of effort $c'(e)$ is increasing in e. Hence, as shown in Figure 18.2, the higher is the power b of the incentive scheme, the more effort e the manager exerts. The manager's effort depends only on the slope, b, and not on the fixed part, a, of his incentive scheme.

Now fold the game back to the manager's second-stage choice of whether to accept the contract. The manager accepts the contract if his expected utility in Equation 18.12 is nonnegative or, upon rearranging, if

$$a \geq c(e) + \frac{Ab^2\sigma^2}{2} - be. \tag{18.14}$$

Equation 18.14 indicates that the fixed part of the salary, a, must be high enough for the manager to accept the contract.

Next, fold the game back to the owner's first-stage choice of the parameters a and b of the salary scheme. The owner's objective is to maximize her expected surplus, which (upon substituting from Equation 18.10 into 18.3) is

$$\text{owner's surplus} = e(1 - b) - a, \tag{18.15}$$

subject to two constraints. The first constraint (Equation 18.14) is that the manager must accept the contract in the second stage. As mentioned in the previous section, this is called a participation constraint. Although Equation 18.14 is written as an inequality, it is clear that the owner will keep lowering a until the condition holds with equality, since a does not affect the manager's effort and since the owner does not want to pay the manager any more than necessary to induce him to accept the contract. The second constraint (Equation 18.13) is that the manager will choose e to suit himself rather than the owner, who cannot observe e. This is called the *incentive compatibility constraint*. Substituting the constraints into Equation 18.15 allows us to express the owner's surplus as a function only of the manager's effort:

---

[1]This point is established in Problem 2.13, where it is shown that $E[g(X)] \leq g[E(X)]$ if g is concave and $E[g(X)] \geq g[E(X)]$ if g is convex. If g is linear (and thus simultaneously concave and convex) then both inequalities must hold, implying $E[g(X)] = g[E(X)]$.

FIGURE 18.2 Manager's Effort Responds to Increased Incentives

Because the manager's marginal cost of effort, $c'(e)$, slopes upward, an increase in the power of the incentive scheme from b_1 to b_2 induces the manager to increase his effort from e_1 to e_2.

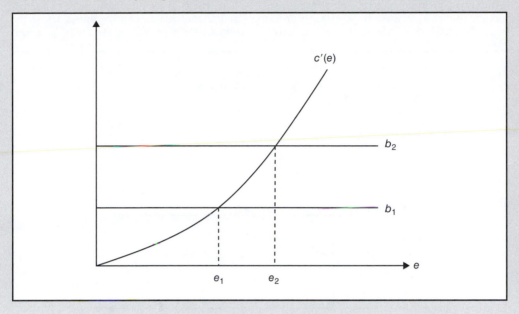

$$e - c(e) - \frac{A\sigma^2 c'(e)^2}{2}. \tag{18.16}$$

The second-best effort e^{**} satisfies the first-order condition

$$c'(e^{**}) = \frac{1}{1 + A\sigma^2 c''(e^{**})}. \tag{18.17}$$

The right-hand side of Equation 18.17 is also equal to the power b^{**} of the incentive scheme in the second best, since $c'(e^{**}) = b^{**}$ by Equation 18.13.

The second-best effort is less than 1 and thus is less than the first-best effort $e^* = 1$. The presence of asymmetric information leads to lower equilibrium effort. If the owner cannot specify e in a contract, then she can induce effort only by tying the manager's pay to firm profit; however, doing so introduces variation into his pay for which the risk-averse manager must be paid a risk premium. This risk premium (the third term in Equation 18.16) adds to the owner's cost of inducing effort. As shown in Figure 18.3, an increase in the marginal cost of inducing effort leads to a lower level of effort in the second than in the first best.

If effort incentives were not an issue, then the risk-neutral owner would be better-off bearing all risk herself and insuring the risk-averse manager against any fluctuations in profit by offering a constant salary, as we saw in the first-best problem. Yet if effort is unobservable then a constant salary will not provide any incentive to exert effort. The second-best contract trades off the owner's desire to induce high effort (which would come from setting b close to 1) against her desire to insure the risk-averse manager against variations in his salary (which would come from setting b close to 0). Hence the resulting value of b^{**} falls somewhere between 0 and 1.

In short, the fundamental trade-off in the owner-manager relationship is between incentives and insurance. The more risk averse is the manager (i.e., the higher is A), the more important is insurance relative to incentives. The owner insures the manager by reducing the

FIGURE 18.3   First- versus Second-Best Effort

The owner's marginal cost of inducing effort (MC) is effectively higher in the second best (when effort is unobservable) than in the first best (when effort is observable) because the manager requires a higher risk premium to accept a higher-powered incentive scheme that exposes him more to fluctuations in profit. An increase in the manager's risk aversion or in the variance of profit causes MC in the second best to shift as indicated by the bold arrow, resulting in a further reduction in equilibrium effort.

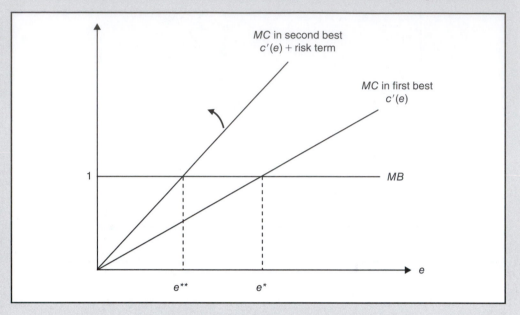

dependence of his salary on fluctuating profit, reducing b^{**} and therefore e^{**}. For the same reason, the more that profit varies owing to factors outside of the manager's control (i.e., the higher is σ^2), the lower is b^{**} and e^{**}.[2]

EXAMPLE 18.1 Owner-Manager Relationship

As a numerical example of some of these ideas, suppose the manager's cost of effort has the simple form $c(e) = e^2/2$ and suppose $\sigma^2 = 1$.

First best. The first-best level of effort satisfies $c'(e^*) = e^* = 1$. A first-best contract specifies that the manager exerts first-best effort $e^* = 1$ in return for a fixed salary of $1/2$, which leaves the manager indifferent between accepting the contract and pursuing his next-best available job (which we have assumed provides him with utility 0). The owner's net profit equals $1/2$.

Second best. The second-best contract depends on the degree of the manager's risk measured by A. Suppose first that $A = 1$.[3] Then, by Equation 18.17, the second-best level of effort is $e^{**} = 1/2$, and $b^{**} = 1/2$ as well. To compute the fixed part a^{**} of the manager's salary, recall that Equation 18.14 holds as an equality in the second best and substitute the

---

[2]A study has confirmed that CEOs and other top executives receive more powerful incentives if they work for firms with less volatile stock prices. See R. Aggarwal and A. Samwick, "The Other Side of the Trade-off: The Impact of Risk on Executive Compensation," *Journal of Political Economy* 107 (1999): 65–105.

[3]To make the calculations easier, we have scaled A up from its more realistic values in Chapter 7 and have rescaled several other parameters as well.

variables computed so far, yielding $a^{**} = 0$. The manager receives no fixed pay but does receive incentive pay equal to 50 cents for every dollar of gross profit. Substituting the variables computed so far into Equation 18.15, we see that the owner's expected net profit is $1/4$.

Now suppose $A = 2$, so that the manager is more risk averse. The second-best effort falls to $e^{**} = 1/3$, and b^{**} falls to $1/3$ as well. The fixed part of the manager's salary rises to $a^{**} = 1/18$. The owner's expected net profit falls to $1/6$.

Empirical evidence. In an influential study of performance pay, Jensen and Murphy estimated that $b = 0.003$ for top executives in a sample of large U.S. firms, which is orders of magnitude smaller than the values of b^{**} we just computed.[4] The fact that real-world incentive schemes are less sensitive to performance than theory would indicate is a puzzle for future research to unravel.

QUERY: How would the analysis change if the owners did not perfectly observe gross profit but instead depended on the manager for a self-report? Could this explain the puzzle that top executives' incentives are unexpectedly low-powered? Relate your discussion to the wave of accounting scandals at Enron and other firms.

Comparison to standard model of the firm

It is natural to ask how the results with hidden information about the manager's action compare to the standard model of a perfectly competitive market with no asymmetric information. First, the presence of hidden information raises a possibility of shirking and inefficiency that is completely absent in the standard model. The manager does not exert as much effort as he would if effort were observable. Even if the owner does as well as she can in the presence of asymmetric information to provide incentives for effort, she must balance the benefits of incentives against the cost of exposing the manager to too much risk.

Second, although the manager can be regarded as an input like any other (capital, labor, materials, and so forth) in the standard model, he becomes a unique sort of input when his actions are hidden information. It is not enough to pay a fixed unit price for this input as a firm would the rental rate for capital or the market price for materials. How productive the manager is depends on how his compensation is structured. The same can be said for any sort of labor input: workers may shirk on the job unless monitored or given incentives not to shirk.

MORAL HAZARD IN INSURANCE

Another important context in which hidden actions lead to inefficiencies is the market for insurance. Individuals can take a variety of actions that influence the probability that a risky event will occur. Homeowners contemplating possible losses from fire, for example, can install sprinkler systems or keep fire extinguishers at convenient locations. Similarly, people may buy antitheft devices for cars or eat healthy food in an attempt to reduce the likelihood of illness. In these activities, utility-maximizing individuals will pursue risk reduction up to the point at which marginal gains from additional precautions are equal to the marginal cost of these precautions.

In the presence of insurance coverage, however, this calculation may change. If a person is fully insured against losses then he or she will have a reduced incentive to undertake costly precautions, which may increase the likelihood of a loss occurring. In the automobile

---

[4] M. Jensen and K. Murphy, "Performance Pay and Top-Management Incentives," *Journal of Political Economy* 98 (1990): 225–64.

insurance case, for example, a person who has a policy that covers theft may park in less safe areas or refrain from installing antitheft devices. This behavioral response to insurance coverage is termed *moral hazard*.

DEFINITION

> **Moral hazard.** The effect of insurance coverage on an individual's precautions, which may change the likelihood or size of losses.

The use of the term "moral" to describe this response is perhaps unfortunate. There is nothing particularly "immoral" about the behavior being described, since individuals are simply responding to the incentives they face. In some applications, this response might even be desirable. For example, people with medical insurance may be encouraged to seek early treatment because the insurance reduces their out-of-pocket cost of medical care. But, because insurance providers may find it costly to measure and evaluate such responses, moral hazard may have important implications for the allocation of resources. To examine these, we need a model of utility-maximizing behavior by insured individuals.

Mathematical model

Suppose a risk-averse individual faces the possibility of incurring a loss (l) that will reduce his initial wealth (W_0). The probability of loss is π. An individual can reduce the probability of loss by spending more on preventive measures (e).[5] Let $U(W)$ be the individual's utility given wealth W.

An insurance company (here playing the role of principal) offers an insurance contract involving a payment x to the individual if a loss occurs. The premium for this coverage is p. If the individual takes the coverage, then his wealth in state 1 (no loss) and state 2 (loss) are

$$W_1 = W_0 - e - p \quad \text{and}$$
$$W_2 = W_0 - e - p - l + x, \tag{18.18}$$

and his expected utility is

$$(1 - \pi)U(W_1) + \pi U(W_2). \tag{18.19}$$

The risk-neutral insurance company's objective is to maximize expected profit:

$$\textbf{expected insurance profit} = p - \pi x. \tag{18.20}$$

First-best insurance contract

In the first-best case, the insurance company can perfectly monitor the agent's precautionary effort e. It sets e and the other terms of the insurance contract (x and p) to maximize its expected profit subject to the participation constraint that the individual accepts the contract:

$$(1 - \pi)U(W_1) + \pi U(W_2) \geq \bar{U}, \tag{18.21}$$

where $\bar{U}$ is the highest utility the individual can attain in the absence of insurance. It is clear that the insurance company will increase the premium until the participation constraint holds with equality. Thus, the first-best insurance contract is the solution to a maximization problem subject to an equality constraint, which we can use Lagrangian methods to solve. The associated Lagrangian is

$$\mathcal{L} = p - \pi x + \lambda[(1 - \pi)U(W_1) + \pi U(W_2) - \bar{U}]. \tag{18.22}$$

---

[5]For consistency, we use the same variable e as we did for managerial effort. In this context, since e is subtracted from the individual's wealth, e should be thought of as either a direct expenditure or the monetary equivalent of the disutility of effort.

The first-order conditions are

$$0 = \frac{\partial \mathcal{L}}{\partial p} = 1 - \lambda[(1 - \pi)U'(W_0 - e - p) + \pi U'(W_0 - e - p - l + x)], \tag{18.23}$$

$$0 = \frac{\partial \mathcal{L}}{\partial x} = -\pi + \lambda \pi U'(W_0 - e - p - l + x), \tag{18.24}$$

$$0 = \frac{\partial \mathcal{L}}{\partial e} = -\frac{\partial \pi}{\partial e}x - \lambda\left\{(1 - \pi)U'(W_0 - e - p) + \pi U'(W_0 - e - p - l + x)\right.$$

$$\left. - \frac{\partial \pi}{\partial e}[U(W_0 - e - p) + U(W_0 - e - p - l + x)]\right\}. \tag{18.25}$$

These conditions may seem complicated, but they quickly reduce down to provide simple results. Equations 18.23 and 18.24 together imply

$$\frac{1}{\lambda} = (1 - \pi)U'(W_0 - e - p) + \pi U'(W_0 - e - p - l + x)$$

$$= U'(W_0 - e - p - l + x), \tag{18.26}$$

which in turn implies $x = l$. This is the familiar result that the first best involves full insurance. Take Equation 18.25 and substitute for λ from Equation 18.26; then, with $x = l$, we have

$$\frac{\partial \pi}{\partial e}l = 1. \tag{18.27}$$

At an optimum, the marginal social benefit of precaution (the reduction in the probability of a loss multiplied by the amount of the loss) equals the marginal social cost of precaution (which here is just 1). In sum, the first-best insurance contract provides the individual with full insurance but requires him to choose the socially efficient level of precaution.

Second-best insurance contract

To obtain the first best, the insurance company would need to monitor the insured individual to ensure that the person was constantly taking the first-best level of precaution, e^*. In the case of insurance for automobile accidents, the company would have to make sure that the driver never exceeds a certain speed, always keeps alert, and never drives while talking on his cell phone, for example. Even if a black-box recorder could be installed to constantly track the car's speed, it would still be impossible to monitor the driver's alertness. Similarly, for health insurance, it would be impossible to watch everything the insured party eats to make sure he doesn't eat anything unhealthy.

Assume for simplicity that the insurance company cannot monitor precaution e at all, so that e cannot be specified by the contract directly. This second-best problem is similar to the first-best except that a new constraint must to be added: an incentive compatibility constraint specifying that the agent is free to choose the level of precaution that suits him and maximizes his expected utility,

$$(1 - \pi)U(W_1) + \pi U(W_2). \tag{18.28}$$

Unlike the first best, the second-best contract will typically not involve full insurance. Under full insurance, $x = l$ and (as Equation 18.18 shows) $W_1 = W_2$. But then the insured party's expected utility from Equation 18.28 is

$$U(W_1) = U(W_0 - e - p), \tag{18.29}$$

which is maximized by choosing the lowest level of precaution possible, $e = 0$.

To induce the agent to take precaution, the company should provide him only partial insurance. Exposing the individual to some risk induces him to take at least some precaution. The company will seek to offer just the right level of partial insurance: not too much insurance (else the agent's precaution drops too low) and not too little insurance (else the agent would not be willing to pay much in premiums). The principal faces the same trade-off in this insurance example as in the owner-manager relationship studied previously: incentives versus insurance.

The solution for the optimal second-best contract is quite complicated, given the general functional forms for utility that we are using.[6] Example 18.2 provides some further practice on the moral hazard problem with specific functional forms.

EXAMPLE 18.2 Insurance and Precaution against Car Theft

In Example 7.2 we examined an individual's decision to purchase insurance against the theft of a $20,000 car. Here we reexamine the market for theft insurance when he can also take the precaution of installing a car alarm that costs $1,750 and that reduces the probability of theft from 0.25 to 0.15.

No insurance. In the absence of insurance, the individual can decide either not to install the alarm, in which case (as we saw from Example 7.2) his expected utility is 11.4571, or to install the alarm, in which case his expected utility is

$$0.85 \ln(100,000 - 1,750) + 0.25 \ln(100,000 - 1,750 - 20,000) = 11.4590. \quad (18.30)$$

He prefers to install the device.

First best. The first-best contract maximizes the insurance company's profit given that it requires the individual to install an alarm and can costlessly verify whether the individual has complied. The first-best contract provides full insurance, paying the full $20,000 if the car is stolen. The highest premium p that the company can charge leaves the individual indifferent between accepting the full-insurance contract and going without insurance:

$$\ln(100,000 - 1,750 - p) = 11.4590. \quad (18.31)$$

Solving for p yields

$$98,250 - p = e^{11.4590}, \quad (18.32)$$

implying that $p = 3,298$. (Note that the e in Equation 18.32 is the number 2.7818..., not the individual's precaution.) The company's profit equals the premium minus the expected payout: $3,298 - (0.15 \times 20,000) = \$298$.

Second best. If the company cannot monitor whether the individual has installed an alarm, then it has two choices. It can induce him to install the alarm by offering only partial insurance, or it can disregard the alarm and provide him with full insurance.

If the company offers full insurance, then the individual will certainly save the $1,750 by not installing the alarm. The highest premium that the company can charge him solves

$$\ln(100,000 - p) = 11.4590, \quad (18.33)$$

implying that $p = 5,048$. The company's profit is then $5,048 - (0.25 \times 20,000) = \$48$.

On the other hand, the company can induce the individual to install the alarm if it reduces the payment after theft from the full $20,000 down to $3,374 and lowers the premium

---

[6]For more analysis see S. Shavell, "On Moral Hazard and Insurance," *Quarterly Journal of Economics* (November 1979): 541–62.

to $602. (These contractual terms are within a decimal place of the second best as computed by the authors using numerical methods; we will forgo the complicated computations and just take these terms as given.) Let's check that the individual would indeed want to install the alarm. His expected utility if he accepts the contract and installs the alarm is

$$0.15 \ln(100{,}000 - 1{,}750 - 602)$$

$$+ 0.85 \ln(100{,}000 - 1{,}750 - 602 - 20{,}000 + 3{,}374) = 11.4611, \qquad \textbf{(18.34)}$$

the same as if he accepts the contract and does not install the alarm:

$$0.25 \ln(100{,}000 - 602)$$

$$+ 0.75 \ln(100{,}000 - 602 - 20{,}000 + 3{,}374) = 11.4611. \qquad \textbf{(18.35)}$$

His expected utility in either event is slightly higher than the 11.4590 obtained if he does not accept the contract. The insurance company's profit is $602 - (0.15 \times 3{,}374) = \$96$. Thus, partial insurance is more profitable than full insurance when the company cannot observe precaution.

QUERY: What is the most that the insurance company would be willing to spend in order to monitor whether the individual has installed an alarm?

Competitive insurance market

So far in this chapter we have studied insurance using the same principal-agent framework as we used to study the owner-manager relationship. In particular, we have assumed that a monopoly insurance company (principal) makes a take-it-or-leave-it offer to the individual (agent). This is a different perspective than in Chapter 7, where we implicitly assumed that insurance is offered at fair rates—that is, at a premium that just covers the insurer's expected payouts for losses. Fair insurance would arise in a perfectly competitive insurance market.

With competitive insurers, the first best maximizes the insurance customer's expected utility given that the contract can specify his precaution level. The second best maximizes the customer's expected utility under the constraint that his precaution level must be induced by having the contract offer only partial insurance.

Our conclusions about the moral hazard problem remain essentially unchanged when moving from a monopoly insurer to perfect competition. The first best still involves full insurance and a precaution level satisfying Equation 18.27. The second best still involves partial insurance and a moderate level of precaution. The main difference is in the distribution of surplus: insurance companies no longer earn positive profits, since the extra surplus now accrues to the individual.

EXAMPLE 18.3 Competitive Theft Insurance

Return to Example 18.2, but now assume that car theft insurance is sold by perfectly competitive companies rather than by a monopolist.

First best. If companies can costlessly verify whether or not the individual has installed an alarm, then the first-best contract requires him to install the alarm and fully insures him for a premium of 3,000. This is a fair insurance premium because it equals the expected payout for a loss: $3{,}000 = 0.15 \times 20{,}000$. Firms earn zero profit at this fair premium. The individual's expected utility rises to 11.4643 from the 11.4590 of Example 18.2.

(continued)

EXAMPLE 18.3 CONTINUED

Second best. Suppose now that insurance companies cannot observe whether the individual has installed an alarm. The second-best contract is similar to that computed in Example 18.2 except that the $96 earned by the monopoly insurer is essentially converted to a reduced premium charged by competing insurers. The equilibrium premium is $p = 506$ and the payment for loss is $x = 3,374$.

QUERY: Which case—monopoly or perfect competition—best describes the typical insurance market? Which types of insurance (car, health, life, disability) and which countries do you think have more competitive markets?

HIDDEN TYPES

Next we turn to the other leading variant of principal-agent model: the model of hidden types. Whereas in the hidden-action model the agent has private information about a choice he has made, in the hidden-type model he has private information about an innate characteristic he cannot choose. For example, a student's type may be his innate intelligence as opposed to an action such as the effort he expends in studying for an exam.

At first glance, it is not clear why there should be a fundamental economic difference between hidden types and hidden actions that requires us to construct a whole new model (and devote a whole new section to it). The fundamental economic difference is this: In a hidden-type model, the agent has private information *before* signing a contract with the principal; in a hidden-action model, the agent obtains private information afterwards.

Having private information before signing the contract changes the game between the principal and the agent. In the hidden-action model, the principal shares symmetric information with the agent at the contracting stage and so can design a contract that extracts all of the agent's surplus. In the hidden-type model, the agent's private information at the time of contracting puts him in a better position. There is no way for the principal to extract all the surplus from all types of agents. A contract that extracts all the surplus from the "high" types (those who benefit more from a given contract) would provide the "low" types with negative surplus, and they would refuse to sign it. The principal will try to extract as much surplus as possible from agents through clever contract design. She will even be willing to shrink the size of the contracting pie, sacrificing some joint surplus in order to obtain a larger share for herself [as in panel (b) of Figure 18.1].

To extract as much surplus as possible from each type while ensuring that low types are not "scared off," the principal will offer a contract in the form of a cleverly designed menu that include options targeted to each agent type. The menu of options will be more profitable for the principal than a contract with a single option, but the principal will still not be able to extract all the surplus from all agent types. Since the agent's type is hidden, he cannot be forced to select the option targeted at his type but is free to select any of the options, and this ability will ensure that the high types always end up with positive surplus.

To make these ideas more concrete, we will study two applications of the hidden-type model that are important in economics. First we will study the optimal nonlinear pricing problem, and then we will study private information in insurance.

NONLINEAR PRICING

In the first application of the hidden-type model, we consider a monopolist (the principal) who sells to a consumer (the agent) with private information about his own valuation for the good. Rather than allowing the consumer to purchase any amount he wants at a constant price per unit, the monopolist offers the consumer a nonlinear price schedule. The nonlinear price schedule is a menu of different-sized bundles at different prices, from which the consumer makes his selection. In such schedules, the larger bundle generally sells for a higher total price but a lower per-unit price than a smaller bundle.

Our approach builds on the analysis of second-degree price discrimination in Chapter 14. Here we analyze general nonlinear pricing schedules, the most general form of second-degree price discrimination. (In the earlier chapter, we limited our attention to a simpler form of second-degree price discrimination involving two-part tariffs.) The linear, two-part, and general nonlinear pricing schedules are plotted in Figure 18.4. The figure graphs the total tariff—the total cost to the consumer of buying q units—for the three different schedules. Basic and intermediate economics courses focus on the case of a constant per-unit price, which is called a linear pricing schedule. The linear pricing schedule is graphed as a straight line that intersects the origin (because nothing needs to be paid if no units are purchased). The two-part tariff is also a straight line, but its intercept—reflecting the fixed fee—is above the origin. The darkest curve is a general nonlinear pricing schedule.

Examples of nonlinear pricing schedules include a coffee shop's selling three different sizes—say, a small (8-ounce) cup for $1.50, a medium (12-ounce) cup for $1.80, and a large (16-ounce) cup for $2.00. Although larger cups cost more in total, they cost less per ounce (18.75 cents per ounce for the small, 15 for the medium, and 12.5 for the large). The consumer does not have the choice of buying as much coffee as he wants at a given per-ounce price; instead he must pick one of these three menu options, each specifying a particular bundled quantity. In other examples, the "q" that is bundled in a menu item is the *quality* of a single unit of the product rather than the *quantity* or number of units. For example, an airline ticket involves a single unit (i.e., a single flight) whose quality varies depending on the class of the

FIGURE 18.4   Shapes of Various Pricing Schedules

The graph shows the shape of three different pricing schedules. Darker curves are more complicated pricing schedules and so represent more sophisticated forms of second-degree price discrimination.

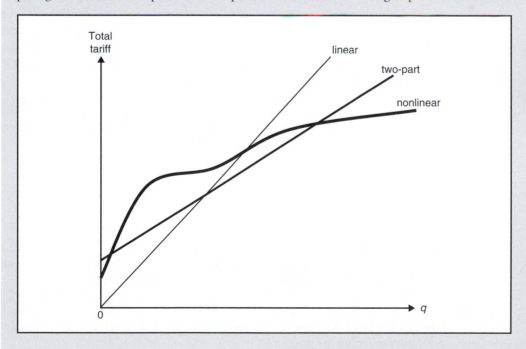

ticket, which ranges from first class, with fancy drinks and meals and plush seats offering plenty of leg room, to coach class, with peanuts for meals and small seats having little leg room.

Mathematical model

To understand the economic principles involved in nonlinear pricing, consider a formal model in which a single consumer obtains surplus

$$U = \theta v(q) - T \tag{18.36}$$

from consuming a bundle of q units of a good for which he pays a total tariff of T. The first term in the consumer's utility function, $\theta v(q)$, reflects the consumer's benefit from consumption. Assume $v'(q) > 0$ and $v''(q) < 0$, implying that the consumer prefers more of the good to less but that the marginal benefit of more units is declining. The consumer's type is given by θ, which can be high (θ_H) with probability β and low (θ_L) with probability $1 - \beta$. The high type enjoys consuming the good more than the low type: $0 < \theta_L < \theta_H$. The total tariff T paid by the consumer for the bundle is subtracted from his benefit to compute his net surplus.

For simplicity, we are assuming that there is a single consumer in the market. The analysis would likewise apply to markets with many consumers, a proportion β of which are high types and $1 - \beta$ of which are low types. The only complication in extending the model to many consumers is that we would need to assume that consumers cannot divide bundles into smaller packages for resale among themselves. (Of course, such repackaging would be impossible for a single unit of the good involving a bundle of quality; and reselling may be impossible even for quantity bundles if the costs of reselling are prohibitive.)

Suppose the monopolist has a constant marginal and average cost c of producing a unit of the good. Then the monopolist's profit from selling a bundle of q units for a total tariff of T is

$$\Pi = T - cq. \tag{18.37}$$

First-best nonlinear pricing

In the first-best case, the monopolist can observe the consumer's type θ before offering him a contract. The monopolist chooses the contract terms q and T to maximize her profit subject to Equation 18.37 and subject to a participation constraint that the consumer accepts the contract. Setting the consumer's utility to 0 if he rejects the contract, the participation constraint may be written as

$$\theta v(q) - T \geq 0. \tag{18.38}$$

The monopolist will choose the highest value of T satisfying the participation constraint: $T = \theta v(q)$. Substituting this value of T into the monopolist's profit function yields

$$\theta v(q) - cq. \tag{18.39}$$

Taking the first-order condition and rearranging provides a condition for the first-best quantity:

$$\theta v'(q) = c. \tag{18.40}$$

This equation is easily interpreted. In the first best, the marginal social benefit of increased quantity on the left-hand side [the consumer's marginal private benefit, $\theta v'(q)$] equals the marginal social cost on the right-hand side [the monopolist's marginal cost, c].

The first-best quantity offered to the high type (q_H^*) satisfies Equation 18.40 for $\theta = \theta_H$, and that offered to the low type (q_L^*) satisfies the equation for $\theta = \theta_L$. The tariffs are set so as to extract all the type's surplus. The first best for the monopolist is identical to what we termed first-degree price discrimination in Chapter 14.

It is instructive to derive the monopolist's first best in a different way, using methods similar to those used to solve the consumer's utility maximization problem in Chapter 4. The contract (q, T) can be thought of as a bundle of two different "goods" over which the monopolist has preferences. The monopolist regards T as a good (more money is better than less) and q as a bad (higher quantity requires higher production costs). Her indifference curve (actually an isoprofit curve) over (q, T) combinations is a straight line with slope c. To see this, note that the slope of the monopolist's indifference curve is her marginal rate of substitution:

$$MRS = -\frac{\partial \Pi / \partial q}{\partial \Pi / \partial T} = -\frac{(-c)}{1} = c. \tag{18.41}$$

The monopolist's indifference curves are drawn as dashed lines in Figure 18.5. Because q is a bad for the monopolist, her indifference curves are higher as one moves toward the upper left.

Figure 18.5 also draws indifference curves for the two consumer types: the high type's (labeled U_H^0) and the low type's (labeled U_L^0). Because T is a bad for consumers, higher indifference curves for both types of consumer are reached as one moves toward the lower right. The U_H^0 indifference curve for the high type is special because it intersects the origin, implying that the high type gets the same surplus as if he didn't sign the contract at all. The first-best contract offered by the monopolist to the high type is point A, at which the highest indifference curve for the monopolist still intersects the high type's U_H^0 indifference curve and thus still provides the high type with nonnegative surplus. This is a point of tangency between the contracting parties' indifference curves—that is, a point at which the indifference curves have the same slope. The monopolist's indifference curves have slope c everywhere, as

FIGURE 18.5 First-Best Nonlinear Pricing

The consumer's indifference curves over the bundle of contractual terms are drawn as solid lines (the darker one for the high type and lighter for the low type); the monopolist's isoprofits are drawn as dashed lines. Point A is the first-best contract option offered to the high type, and point B is that offered to the low type.

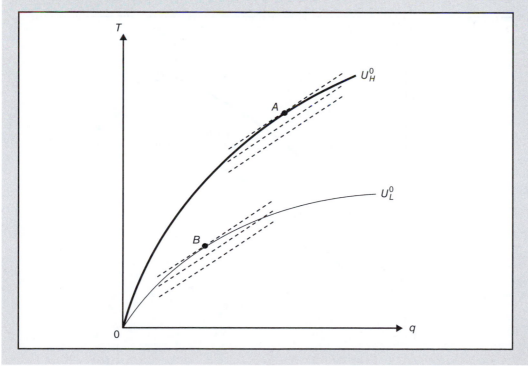

we saw in Equation 18.41. The slope of type θ's indifference curve is the marginal rate of substitution:

$$MRS = -\frac{\partial U/\partial q}{\partial U/\partial T} = -\frac{\theta v'(q)}{-1} = \theta v'(q).$$ (18.42)

Equating the slopes gives the same condition for the first best as we found in Equation 18.40 (marginal social benefit equals marginal social cost of an additional unit). The same arguments imply that point B is the first-best contract offered to the low type, and we can again verify that Equation 18.40 is satisfied there.

To summarize, the first-best contract offered to each type specifies a quantity (q_H^* or q_L^*, respectively) that maximizes social surplus given the type of consumer and a tariff (T_H^* or T_L^*, respectively) that allows the monopolist to extract all of the type's surplus.

Second-best nonlinear pricing

Now suppose that the monopolist does not observe the consumer's type when offering him a contract but knows only the distribution ($\theta = \theta_H$ with probability β and $\theta = \theta_L$ with probability $1 - \beta$). As Figure 18.6 shows, the first-best contract would no longer "work" because the high type obtains more utility (moving from the indifference curve labeled U_H^0 to the one labeled U_H^2) by choosing the bundle targeted to the low type (B) rather than the bundle targeted to him (A). In other words, choosing A is no longer incentive compatible for

FIGURE 18.6   First Best Not Incentive Compatible

The first-best contract, involving points A and B, is not incentive compatible if the consumer has private information about his type. The high type can reach a higher indifference curve by choosing the bundle (B) that is targeted at the low type. To keep him from choosing B, the monopolist must reduce the high type's tariff by replacing bundle A with C.

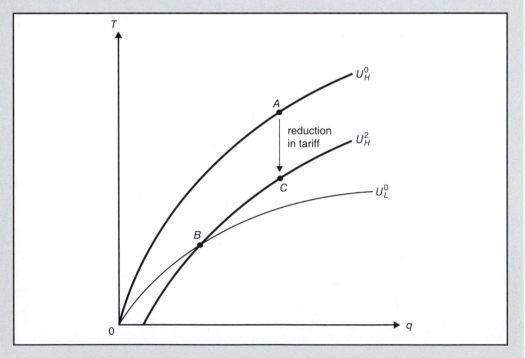

FIGURE 18.7   Second-Best Nonlinear Pricing

The second-best contract is indicated by the circled points D and E. Relative to the incentive-compatible contract found in Figure 18.6 (points B and C), the second-best contract distorts the low type's quantity (indicated by the move from B to D) in order to make the low type's bundle less attractive to the high type. This allows the principal to charge tariff to the high type (indicated by the move from C to E).

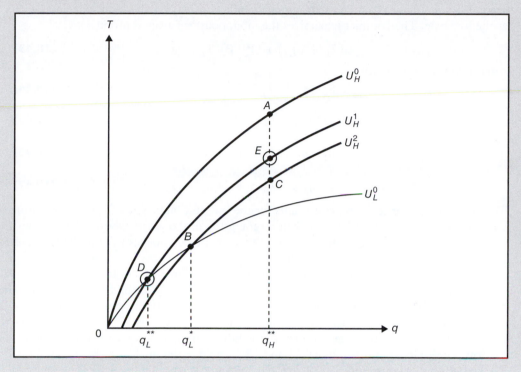

the high type. In order to keep the high type from choosing B, the monopolist must reduce the high type's tariff, offering C instead of A.

The substantial reduction in the high type's tariff (indicated by the downward-pointing arrow) puts a big dent in the monopolist's expected profit. The monopolist can do better than offering the menu of contracts (B, C): she can distort the low type's bundle in order to make it less attractive to the high type. Then the high type's tariff need not be reduced as much to keep him from choosing the wrong bundle. Figure 18.7 shows how this new contract would work. The monopolist reduces the quantity in the low type's bundle (while reducing the tariff so that the low type stays on his U_L^0 indifference curve and thus continues to accept the contract), offering bundle D rather than B. The high type obtains less utility from D than B, as D reaches only his U_H^1 indifference curve and is short of his U_H^2 indifference curve. To keep the high type from choosing D, the monopolist needs only lower the high type's tariff by the amount given by the vertical distance between A and E rather than all the way down to C.

Relative to (B, C), the second-best menu of contracts (D, E) trades off a distortion in the low type's quantity (moving from the first-best quantity in B to the lower quantity in D and destroying some social surplus in the process) against an increase in the tariff that can be extracted from the high type in moving from C to E. An attentive student might wonder why the monopolist would want to make this trade-off. After all, the monopolist must reduce the low type's tariff in moving from B to D or else the low type would refuse to accept the contract. How can we be sure that this reduction in the low type's tariff doesn't more than offset any increase in the high type's tariff? The reason is that a reduction in quantity harms the high type more than it does the low type. As Equation 18.42 shows, the consumer's marginal rate of substitution between contractual terms (quantity and tariff) depends on his type θ and is higher for the high type. Since the high type values quantity more than does the low type, the high type would pay more to avoid the decrease in quantity in moving from B to D than would the low type.

Further insight can be gained from an algebraic characterization of the second best. The second-best contract is a menu that targets bundle (q_H, T_H) at the high type and (q_L, T_L) at the low type. The contract maximizes the monopolist's expected profit,

$$\beta(T_H - cq_H) + (1 - \beta)(T_L - cq_L), \tag{18.43}$$

subject to four constraints:

$$\theta_L v(q_L) - T_L \geq 0, \tag{18.44}$$

$$\theta_H v(q_H) - T_H \geq 0, \tag{18.45}$$

$$\theta_L v(q_L) - T_L \geq \theta_L v(q_H) - T_H, \tag{18.46}$$

$$\theta_H v(q_H) - T_H \geq \theta_H v(q_L) - T_L. \tag{18.47}$$

The first two are participation constraints for the low and high type of consumer, ensuring that they accept the contract rather than forgoing the monopolist's good. The last two are incentive compatibility constraints, ensuring that each type chooses the bundle targeted to him rather than the other type's bundle.

As suggested by the graphical analysis in Figure 18.7, only two of these constraints play a role in the solution. The most important constraint was to keep the high type from choosing the low type's bundle; this is Equation 18.47 (incentive compatibility constraint for the high type). The other relevant constraint was to keep the low type on his U_L^0 indifference curve to prevent him from rejecting the contract; this is Equation 18.44 (participation constraint for the low type). Hence, Equations 18.44 and 18.47 hold with equality in the second best.

The other two constraints can be ignored, as can be seen in Figure 18.7. The high type's second-best bundle E puts him on a higher indifference curve (U_H^1) than if he rejects the contract (U_H^0), so the high type's participation constraint (Equation 18.45) can be safely ignored. The low type would be on a lower indifference curve if he chose the high type's bundle (E) rather than his own (D), so the low type's incentive compatibility constraint (Equation 18.46) can also be safely ignored.

Treating Equations 18.44 and 18.47 as equalities and using them to solve for T_L and T_H yields

$$T_L = \theta_L v(q_L) \tag{18.48}$$

and

$$\begin{aligned} T_H &= \theta_H[v(q_H) - v(q_L)] + T_L \\ &= \theta_H[v(q_H) - v(q_L)] + \theta_L v(q_L). \end{aligned} \tag{18.49}$$

By substituting these expressions for T_L and T_H into the monopolist's objective function (Equation 18.39), we convert a complicated maximization problem with four inequality constraints into the simpler unconstrained problem of choosing q_L and q_H to maximize

$$\beta\{\theta_H[v(q_H) - v(q_L)] + \theta_L v(q_L) - cq_H\} + (1 - \beta)[\theta_L v(q_L) - cq_L]. \tag{18.50}$$

The low type's quantity satisfies the first-order condition with respect to q_L, which (upon considerable rearranging) yields

$$\theta_L v'(q_L^{**}) = c + \frac{\beta(\theta_H - \theta_L)v'(q_L^{**})}{1 - \beta}. \tag{18.51}$$

The last term is clearly positive and so the equation implies that $\theta_L v'(q_L^{**}) > c$, whereas $\theta_L v'(q_L^*) = c$ in the first best. Since $v(q)$ is concave, we see that the second-best quantity is lower than the first best, verifying the insight from our graphical analysis that the low type's quantity is distorted downward in the second best to extract surplus from the high type.

The high type's quantity satisfies the first-order condition from the maximization of Equation 18.43 with respect to q_H; upon rearranging, this yields

$$\theta_H v'(q_H^{**}) = c. \tag{18.52}$$

This condition is identical to the first best, implying that there is no distortion of the high type's quantity in the second best. There is no reason to distort the high type's quantity because there is no higher type from whom to extract surplus. The result that the highest type is offered an efficient contract is often referred to as "no distortion at the top."

Returning to the low type's quantity, how much the monopolist distorts this quantity downward depends on the probabilities of the two consumer types or—equivalently, in a model with many consumers—on the relative proportions of the two types. If there are many low types (β is low) then the monopolist would not be willing to distort the low type's quantity very much, because the loss from this distortion would be substantial and there would be few high types from whom additional surplus could be extracted. The more high types (the higher is β), the more the monopolist is willing to distort the low type's quantity downward. Indeed, if there are enough high types, the monopolist may decide not to serve the low types at all and just offer one bundle that would be purchased by the high types. This would allow the monopolist to squeeze all the surplus from the high types because they would have no other option.

EXAMPLE 18.4 Monopoly Coffee Shop

The college has a single coffee shop whose marginal cost is 5 cents per ounce of coffee. The representative customer is equally likely to be a coffee hound (high type with $\theta_H = 20$) or a regular Joe (low type with $\theta_L = 15$). Assume $v(q) = 2\sqrt{q}$.

First best. Substituting the functional form $v(q) = 2\sqrt{q}$ into the condition for first-best quantities [$\theta v'(q) = c$] and rearranging, we have $q = (\theta/c)^2$. Therefore, $q_L^* = 9$ and $q_H^* = 16$. The tariff extracts all of each type's surplus [$T = \theta v(q)$], here implying that $T_L^* = 90$ and $T_H^* = 160$. The shop's expected profit is

$$\frac{1}{2}(T_H^* - cq_H^*) + \frac{1}{2}(T_L^* - cq_L^*) = 62.5 \tag{18.53}$$

cents per customer. The first best can be implemented by having the owner sell a 9-ounce cup for 90 cents to the low type and a 16-ounce cup for $1.60 to the high type. (Somehow the barista can discern the customer's type just by looking at him as he walks in the door.)

Incentive compatibility when types are hidden. The first best is not incentive compatible if the barista cannot observe the customer's type. The high type obtains no surplus from the 16-ounce cup sold at $1.60. If he instead paid 90 cents for the 9-ounce cup, he would obtain a surplus of $\theta_H v(9) - 90 = 30$ cents. Keeping the same cup sizes as in the first best, the price for the large cup would have to be reduced by 30 cents (to $1.30) in order to keep the high type from buying the small cup. The shop's expected profit from this incentive compatible menu is

$$\frac{1}{2}[130 - (5)(16)] + \frac{1}{2}[90 - (5)(9)] = 47.5. \tag{18.54}$$

(*continued*)

EXAMPLE 18.4   CONTINUED

Second best. The shop can do even better by reducing the size of the small cup to make it less attractive to high demanders. The size of the small cup in the second best satisfies Equation 18.51, which, for the functional forms in this example, implies that

$$\theta_L q_L^{-1/2} = c + (\theta_H - \theta_L) q_L^{-1/2} \qquad (18.55)$$

or, rearranging,

$$q_L^{**} = \left[\frac{2\theta_L - \theta_H}{c} \right]^2 = \left[\frac{(2)(15) - 20}{5} \right]^2 = 4. \qquad (18.56)$$

The highest price that can be charged without losing the low-type customers is

$$T_L^{**} = \theta_L v(q_L^{**}) = (15)(2\sqrt{4}) = 60. \qquad (18.57)$$

The large cup is the same size as in the first best: 16 ounces. It can be sold for no more than $1.40 or else the coffee hound would buy the 4-ounce cup instead. Although the total tariff for the large cup is higher at $1.40 than for the small cup at 60 cents, the unit price is lower (8.75 cents versus 15 cents per ounce). Hence the large cup sells at a quantity discount.

The shop's expected profit is

$$\frac{1}{2}[140 - (5)(16)] + \frac{1}{2}[60 - (5)(4)] = 50 \qquad (18.58)$$

cents per consumer. Reducing the size of the small cup from 9 to 4 ounces allows the shop to recapture some of the profit lost when the customer's type cannot be observed.

QUERY: Investigate the menu of your favorite local coffee shop. Looking at just the largest and smallest cup sizes on the menu, determine whether these sizes and prices are consistent with reasonable values of the parameters c, θ_H, and θ_L and of the proportion of high and low types (β and $1 - \beta$) [still assuming that $v(q) = 2\sqrt{q}$ as in this example].

ADVERSE SELECTION IN INSURANCE

For the second application of the hidden-type model, we will return to the insurance market in which an individual with state-independent preferences and initial income W_0 faces the prospect of loss l. Assume the individual can be one of two types: a high-risk type with probability of loss π_H or a low-risk type with probability π_L, where $\pi_H > \pi_L$. We will first assume the insurance company is a monopolist; later we will study the case of competitive insurers. The presence of hidden risk types in an insurance market is said to lead to *adverse selection*. Insurance tends to attract more risky than safe consumers (the "selection" in adverse selection) because it is more valuable to risky types, yet risky types are more expensive to serve (the "adverse" in adverse selection).

DEFINITION

Adverse selection. The problem facing insurers that risky types are both more likely to accept an insurance policy and more expensive to serve.

As we will see, if the insurance company is clever then it can mitigate the adverse selection problem by offering a menu of contracts. The policy targeted to the safe type offers only partial insurance so that it is less attractive to the high-risk type.

FIGURE 18.8   First Best for a Monopoly Insurer

In the first best, the monopoly insurer offers policy A to the high-risk type and B to the low-risk type. Both types are fully insured. The premiums are sufficiently high to keep each type on his indifference curve through the no-insurance point (E).

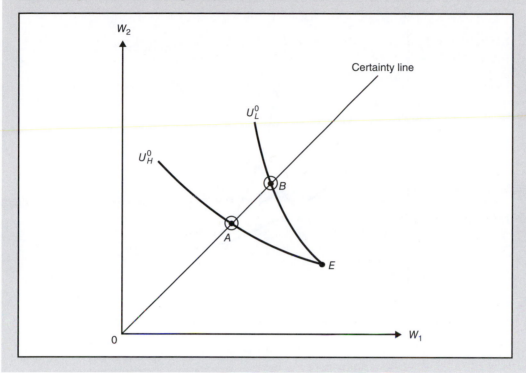

First best

In the first best, the insurer can observe the individual's risk type and offer a different policy to each. Our previous analysis of insurance makes it clear that the first best involves full insurance for each type, so the insurance payment x in case of a loss equals the full amount of the loss l. Different premiums are charged to each type and are set to extract all of the surplus that each type obtains from the insurance.

The solution is shown in Figure 18.8 (the construction of this figure is discussed further in Chapter 7). Without insurance, each type finds himself at point E. Point A (resp., B) is the first-best policy offered to the high-risk (resp., low-risk) type. Points A and B lie on the certainty line because both are fully insured. Since the premiums extract each type's surplus from insurance, both types are on their indifference curves through the no-insurance point E. The high type's premium is higher, so A is further down the certainty line toward the origin than is B.[7]

---

[7]Mathematically, A appears further down the certainty line than B in Figure 18.8 because the high type's indifference curve through E is flatter than the low type's. To see this, note that expected utility equals $(1 - \pi) U(W_1) + \pi U(W_2)$ and so the *MRS* is given by

$$-\frac{dW_1}{dW_2} = \frac{(1 - \pi) U'(W_1)}{\pi U'(W_2)}.$$

At a given (W_1, W_2) combination on the graph, the marginal rates of substitution differ only because the underlying probabilities of loss differ. Since

FIGURE 18.9 Second Best for a Monopoly Insurer

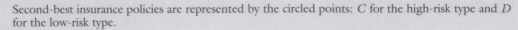

Second-best insurance policies are represented by the circled points: C for the high-risk type and D for the low-risk type.

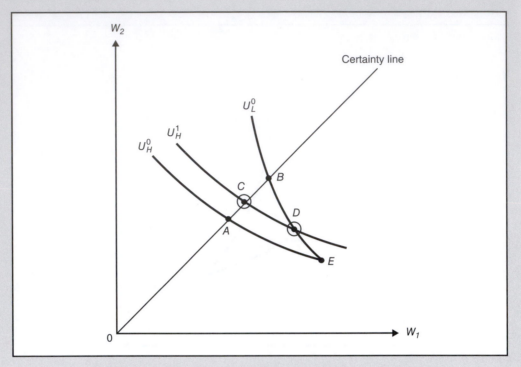

Second best

If the monopoly insurer cannot observe the agent's type, then the first-best contracts will not be incentive compatible: the high-risk type would claim to be low risk and take full insurance coverage at the lower premium. As in the nonlinear pricing problem, the second best will involve a menu of contracts. Other principles from the nonlinear pricing problem also carry over here. The high type continues to receive the first-best quantity (here, full insurance)—there is no distortion at the top. The low type's quantity is distorted downward from the first best, so he receives only partial insurance. Again we see that, with hidden types, the principal is willing to sacrifice some social surplus in order to extract some of the surplus the agent would otherwise derive from his private information.

Figure 18.9 depicts the second best. If the insurer tried to offer a menu containing the first-best contracts A and B, then the high-risk type would choose B rather than A. To maintain incentive compatibility, the insurer distorts the low type's policy from B along its indifference curve u_L^0 down to D. The low type is only partially insured, and this allows the insurer to extract more surplus from the high type. The high type continues to be fully insured, but the increase in his premium shifts his policy down the certainty line to C.

$$\frac{1 - \pi_H}{\pi_H} < \frac{1 - \pi_L}{\pi_L},$$

it follows that the high-risk type's indifference curve will be flatter. This proof follows the analysis presented in M. Rothschild and J. Stiglitz, "Equilibrium in Competitive Insurance Markets: An Essay on the Economics of Imperfect Information," *Quarterly Journal of Economics* (November 1976): 629–50.

EXAMPLE 18.5 Insuring the Little Red Corvette

The analysis of automobile insurance in Example 18.2 (which is based on Example 7.2) can be recast as an adverse selection problem. Suppose that the probability of theft depends not on the act of installing an antitheft device but rather on the color of the car. Because thieves prefer red to gray cars, the probability of theft is higher for red cars ($\pi_H = 0.25$) than for gray cars ($\pi_L = 0.15$).

First best. The monopoly insurer can observe the car color and offer different policies for different colors. Both colors are fully insured for the $20,000 loss of the car. The premium is the maximum amount that each type would be willing to pay in lieu of going without insurance; as computed in Example 7.2, this amount is $5,426 for the high type (red cars). Similar calculations show that a gray-car owner's expected utility if he is not insured is 11.4795, and the maximum premium he would be willing to pay for full insurance is $3,287. Although the insurer pays more claims for red cars, the higher associated premium more than compensates and so the expected profit from a policy sold for a red car is $5,426 - (0.25)(20,000) = \$426$ versus $3,287 - (0.15)(20,000) = \$287$ for a gray car.

Second best. Suppose the insurer does not observe the color of the customer's car and knows only that 10 percent of all cars are red and the rest are gray. The second-best menu of insurance policies—consisting of a premium/insurance coverage bundle (p_H, x_H) targeted for high-risk, red cars and (p_L, x_L) for low-risk, gray cars—is indicated by the circled points in Figure 18.9. Red cars are fully insured: $x_H = 20,000$. To solve for the rest of the contractual parameters, observe that x_H, p_H, and p_L can be found as the solution to the maximization of expected insurer profit

$$0.1\left[p_H - (0.25)(20,000)\right] + 0.9\left[p_L - (0.15)(x_L)\right] \quad \textbf{(18.59)}$$

subject to a participation constraint for the low type,

$$0.85\ln(100,000 - p_L) + 0.15\ln(100,000 - p_L - 20,000 + x_L) \geq 11.4795, \quad \textbf{(18.60)}$$

and to an incentive compatibility constraint for the high type,

$$\ln(100,000 - p_H) \geq 0.75\ln(100,000 - p_L) + 0.25\ln(100,000 - p_L - 20,000 + x_L). \quad \textbf{(18.61)}$$

Participation and incentive compatibility constraints for the other types can be ignored, just as in the nonlinear pricing problem. This maximization problem is too difficult to solve by hand, but it can be solved numerically using popular spreadsheet programs or other mathematical software. The second-best values that result are $x_H^{**} = 20,000$, $p_H^{**} = 4,154$, $x_L^{**} = 11,556$, and $p_L^{**} = 1,971$.

QUERY: Look at the spreadsheet associated with this example on the website for this textbook. Play around with different probabilities of the two car colors. What happens when red cars become sufficiently common? (Even if you cannot access the spreadsheet, you should be able to guess the answer.)

Competitive insurance market

Assume now that insurance is provided not by a monopoly but rather by a perfectly competitive market, resulting in fair insurance. Figure 18.10 depicts the equilibrium in which insurers can observe each individual's risk type. Lines EF and EG are drawn with

FIGURE 18.10   Competitive Insurance Equilibrium with Perfect Information

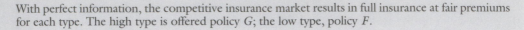

> With perfect information, the competitive insurance market results in full insurance at fair premiums for each type. The high type is offered policy G; the low type, policy F.

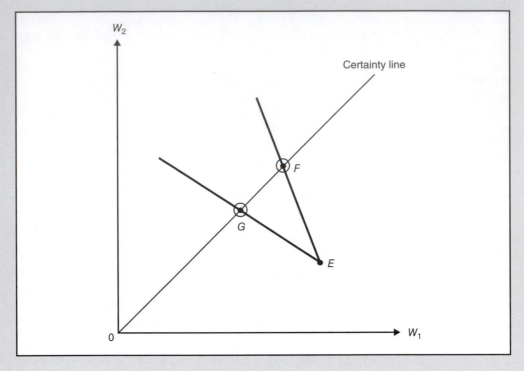

slopes $-(1 - \pi_L)/\pi_L$ and $-(1 - \pi_H)/\pi_H$, respectively, and show the market opportunities for each person to trade W_1 for W_2 by purchasing fair insurance.[8] The low-risk type is sold policy F, and the high-risk type is sold policy G. Each type receives full insurance at a fair premium.

However, the outcome in Figure 18.10 is unstable if insurers cannot observe risk types. The high type would claim to be low risk and take contract F. But then insurers that offered F would earn negative expected profit: at F, insurers break even serving only the low-risk types, so adding individuals with a higher probability of loss would push the company below the break-even point.

The competitive equilibrium with unobservable types is shown in Figure 18.11. The equilibrium is similar to the second best for a monopoly insurer. A set of policies are offered that separates the types. The high-risk type is fully insured at point G, the same policy as he was offered in the first best. The low-risk type is offered policy J, which features partial insurance. The low type would be willing to pay more for fuller insurance, preferring a policy

---

[8]To derive these slopes, called *odds ratios*, note that fair insurance requires the premium to satisfy $p = \pi x$. Substituting into W_1 and W_2 yields

$$W_1 = W_0 - p = W_0 - \pi x \quad \text{and}$$
$$W_2 = W_0 - p - l + x = W_0 - l + (1 - \pi)x.$$

Hence, a \$1 increase in the insurance payment (x) reduces W_1 by π and increases W_2 by $1 - \pi$.

FIGURE 18.11   Competitive Insurance Equilibrium with Hidden Types

With hidden types, the high-risk type continues to be offered first-best policy G but the low-risk type is rationed, receiving only partial insurance at J in order to keep the high-risk type from pooling.

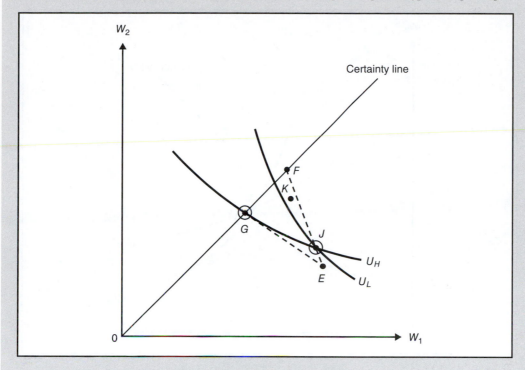

such as K. Because K is below line EF, an insurer would earn positive profit from selling such a policy to low-risk types only. The problem is that K would also attract high-risk types, leading to insurer losses. Hence insurance is rationed to the low-risk type.

With hidden types, the competitive equilibrium must involve a set of separating contracts; it cannot involve a single policy that pools both types. This can be shown with the aid of Figure 18.12. To be accepted by both types and allow the insurer to at least break even, the pooling contract would have to be a point (such as M) within triangle EFG. But M cannot be a final equilibrium because at M there exist further trading opportunities. To see this, note that—as indicated in the figure and discussed earlier in the chapter—the indifference curve for the high type (U_H) is flatter than that for the low type (U_H). Consequently, there are insurance policies such as N that are unattractive to high-risk types, attractive to low-risk types, and profitable to insurers (because such policies lie below EF).

Assuming that no barriers prevent insurers from offering new contracts, policies such as N will be offered and will "skim the cream" of low-risk individuals from any pooling equilibrium. Insurers that continue to offer M are left with the "adversely selected" individuals, whose risk is so high that insurers cannot expect to earn any profit by serving them.

FIGURE 18.12   Impossibility of a Competitive Pooling Equilibrium

Pooling contract M cannot be an equilibrium because there exist insurance policies such as N that are profitable to insurers and are attractive to low-risk types but not to high-risk types.

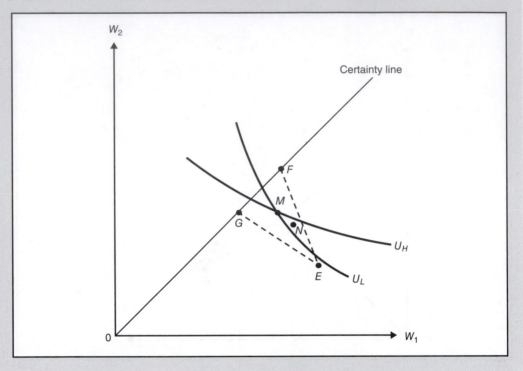

EXAMPLE 18.6 Competitive Insurance for the Little Red Corvette

Recall the automobile insurance analysis in Example 18.5, but now assume that insurance is provided by a competitive market rather than a monopolist. Under full information, the competitive equilibrium involves full insurance for both types at a fair premium of $(0.25)(20{,}000) = \$5{,}000$ for high-risk, red cars and $(0.15)(20{,}000) = \$3{,}000$ for low-risk, gray cars.

If insurers cannot observe car colors, then in equilibrium the coverage for the two types will still be separated into two policies. The policy targeted for red cars is the same as under full information. The policy targeted for gray cars involves a fair premium $p_L = 0.15 x_L$ and an insurance level that does not give red-car owners an incentive to deviate by pooling on the gray-car policy:

$$0.75 \ln(100{,}000 - p_L) + 0.25 \ln(100{,}000 - p_L - 20{,}000 + x_L) = \ln(95{,}000).$$

(18.62)

Figure 18.13 provides a graphical solution for p_L. The figure graphs the left-hand side of Equation 18.62 (after substituting the condition for fair insurance, $x_L = p_L/0.15$) versus the right-hand side. With a precise enough graph, one can see that the intersection is at $p_L = 453$. The associated insurance level is $x_L = 3{,}020$.

QUERY: How much more would gray-car owners be willing to pay for full insurance? Would an insurer profit from selling full insurance at this higher premium if it sold only to owners of gray cars? Why then do the companies ration insurance to gray cars by insuring them partially?

FIGURE 18.13 Graphical Solution to Equation 18.62

The two sides of Equation 18.62 are equal when $p_L = 453$.

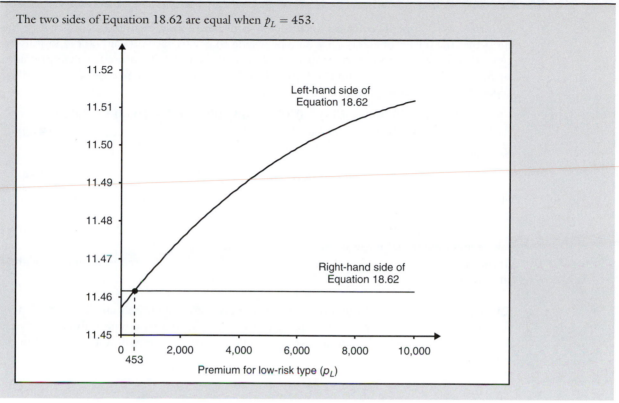

MARKET SIGNALING

In all the models studied so far, the uninformed principal moved first—making a contract offer to the agent, who had private information. If the information structure is reversed and the informed player moves first, then the analysis becomes much more complicated, putting us in the world of signaling games studied in Chapter 8. When the signaler is a principal who is offering a contract to an agent, the signaling games becomes complicated because the strategy space of contractual terms is virtually limitless. Compare the simpler strategy space of Spence's education signaling game in Chapter 8, where the worker chose one of just two actions: to obtain an education or not. We do not have space to delve too deeply into complex signaling games here nor to repeat Chapter 8's discussion of simpler signaling games. We will be content to gain some insights from a few simple applications.

Signaling in competitive insurance markets

In a competitive insurance market with adverse selection (i.e., hidden risk types), we saw that the low-risk type receives only partial insurance in equilibrium. He would benefit from report of his type, perhaps hiring an independent auditor to certify that type so the report would be credible. The low-risk type would be willing to pay the difference between his equilibrium and his first-best surplus in order to issue such a credible signal.

It is important that there be some trustworthy auditor or other way to verify the authenticity of such reports, because a high-risk individual would now have an even greater incentive to make false reports. The high-risk type may even be willing to pay a large bribe to the auditor for a false report.

EXAMPLE 18.7 Certifying Car Color

Return to the competitive market for automobile insurance from Example 18.6. Let R be the most that the owner of a gray car would be willing to pay to have his car color (and thus his type) certified and reported to the market. He would then be fully insured at a fair premium of $3,000, earning surplus $\ln(100,000 - 3,000 - R)$. In the absence of such a certified report, his expected surplus is

$$0.85 \ln(100,000 - 453) + 0.15 \ln(100,000 - 453 - 20,000 + 3,020)$$
$$= 11.4803. \tag{18.63}$$

Solving for R in the equation

$$\ln(100,000 - 453 - R) = 11.4803 \tag{18.64}$$

yields $R = 207$. Thus the low-risk type would be willing to pay up to $207 to have a credible report of his type issued to the market.

The owner of the red car would pay a bribe as high as $2,000—the difference between his fair premium with full information ($5,000) and the fair premium charged to an individual known to be of low risk ($3,000). Therefore, the authenticity of the report is a matter of great importance.

QUERY: How would the equilibrium change if reports are not entirely credible (i.e., if there is some chance the high-risk individual can successfully send a false report about his type)? What incentives would an auditor have to maintain his or her reputation for making honest reports?

Market for lemons

Markets for used goods raise an interesting possibility for signaling. Cars are a leading example: having driven the car over a long period of time, the seller has much better information about its reliability and performance than a buyer, who can take only a short test drive. Yet even the mere act of offering the car for sale can be taken as a signal of car quality by the market. The signal is not positive: the quality of the good must be below the threshold that would have induced the seller to keep it. As George Akerlof showed in the article for which he won the Nobel Prize in economics, the market may unravel in equilibrium so that only the lowest-quality goods, the "lemons," are sold.[9]

To gain more insight into this result, consider the used-car market. Suppose there is a continuum of qualities from low-quality lemons to high-quality gems and that only the owner of a car knows its type. Because buyers cannot differentiate between lemons and gems, all used cars will sell for the same price, which is a function of the average car quality. A car's owner will choose to keep it if the car is at the upper end of the quality spectrum (since a good car is worth more than the prevailing market price) but will sell the car if it is at the low end (since these are worth less than the market price). This reduction in average quality of cars offered for sale will reduce market price, leading would-be sellers of the highest-quality remaining cars to withdraw from the market. The market continues to unravel until only the worst-quality lemons are offered for sale.

The lemons problem leads the market for used cars to be much less efficient than it would be under the standard competitive model in which quality is known. (Indeed, in the standard

---

[9]G. A. Akerlof, "The Market for 'Lemons': Quality Uncertainty and the Market Mechanism," *Quarterly Journal of Economics* (August 1970): 488–500.

model the issue of quality does not arise, because all goods are typically assumed to be of the same quality.) Whole segments of the market disappear—along with the gains from trade in these segments—because higher-quality items are no longer traded. In the extreme, the market can simply break down with nothing (or perhaps just a few of the worst items) being sold. The lemons problem can be mitigated by trustworthy used-car dealers, by development of car-buying expertise by the general public, by sellers providing proof that their cars are trouble-free, and by sellers offering money-back guarantees. But anyone who has ever shopped for a used car knows that the problem of potential lemons is a real one.

EXAMPLE 18.8   Used-Car Market

Suppose the quality q of used cars is uniformly distributed between 0 and 20,000. Sellers value their cars at q. Buyers (equal in number to the sellers) place a higher value on cars, $q + b$, so there are gains to be made from trade in the used-car market. Under full information about quality, all used cars would be sold. But this does not occur when sellers have private information about quality and buyers know only the distribution. Let p be the market price. Sellers offer their cars for sale if and only if $q \leq p$. The quality of a car offered for sale is thus uniformly distributed between 0 and p, implying that expected quality is

$$\int_0^p q \left(\frac{1}{p} \right) dq = \frac{p}{2} \tag{18.65}$$

(see Chapter 2 for background on the uniform distribution). Hence, a buyer's expected net surplus is

$$\frac{p}{2} + b - p = b - \frac{p}{2}. \tag{18.66}$$

There may be multiple equilibria, but the one with the most sales involves the highest value of p for which Equation 18.66 is nonnegative: $b - p/2 = 0$, implying that $p^* = 2b$. Only a fraction $2b/20{,}000$ of the cars are sold. As b falls, the market for used cars dries up.

QUERY: What would the equilibrium look like in the full-information case?

AUCTIONS

The monopolist has difficulty extracting surplus from the agent in the nonlinear pricing problem because high-demand consumers could guarantee themselves a certain surplus by choosing the low demanders' bundle. A seller can often do better if several consumers compete against each other for her scarce supplies in an auction. Competition among consumers in an auction can help the seller solve the hidden-type problem, because high-value consumers are then pushed to bid high so they don't lose the good to another bidder. In the setting of an auction, the principal's "offer" is no longer a simple contract or menu of contracts as in the nonlinear pricing problem; instead, her offer is the format of the auction itself. Different formats might lead to substantially different outcomes and more or less revenue for the seller, so there is good reason for sellers to think carefully about how to design the auction. There is also good reason for buyers to think carefully about what bidding strategies to use.

Auctions have received a great deal of attention in the economics literature ever since William Vickery's seminal work, for which he won the Nobel Prize in economics.[10] Auctions

---

[10] W. Vickery, "Counterspeculation, Auctions, and Competitive Sealed Tenders," *Journal of Finance* (March 1961): 8–37.

continue to grow in significance as a market mechanism and are used for selling such goods as airwave spectrum, Treasury bills, foreclosed houses, and collectibles on the Internet auction site eBay.

There are a host of different auction formats. Auctions can involve sealed bids or open outcries. Sealed-bid auctions can be first price (the highest bidder wins the object and must pay the amount bid) or second price (the highest bidder still wins but need only pay the next-highest bid). Open-outcry auctions can be either ascending, as in the so-called English auction where buyers yell out successively higher bids until no one is willing to top the last, or descending, as in the so-called Dutch auction where the auctioneer starts with a high price and progressively lowers it until one of the participants stops the auction by accepting the price at that point. The seller can decide whether or not to set a "reserve clause," which requires bids to be over a certain threshold else the object will not be sold. Even more exotic auction formats are possible. In an "all-pay" auction, for example, bidders pay their bids even if they lose.

A powerful and somewhat surprising result due to Vickery is that, in simple settings (risk-neutral bidders who each know their valuation for the good perfectly, no collusion, etc.), many of the different auction formats listed here (and more besides) provide the monopolist with the same expected revenue in equilibrium. To see why this result is surprising, we will analyze two auction formats in turn—a first-price and a second-price sealed-bid auction—supposing that a single object is to be sold.

In the first-price sealed-bid auction, all bidders simultaneously submit secret bids. The auctioneer unseals the bids and awards the object to the highest bidder, who pays his or her bid. In equilibrium, it is a weakly dominated strategy to submit a bid b greater than or equal to the buyer's valuation v.

DEFINITION   **Weakly dominated strategy.** A strategy is *weakly dominated* if there is another strategy that does at least as well against all rivals' strategies and strictly better against at least one.

A buyer receives no surplus if he bids $b = v$ no matter what his rivals bid: if the buyer loses, he gets no surplus; if he wins, he must pay his entire surplus back to the seller and again gets no surplus. By bidding less than his valuation, there is a chance that others' valuations (and consequent bids) are low enough that the bidder wins the object and derives a positive surplus. Bidding more than his valuation is even worse than just bidding his valuation. There is good reason to think that players avoid weakly dominated strategies, meaning here that bids will be below buyers' valuations.

In a second-price sealed-bid auction, the highest bidder pays the next-highest bid rather than his own. This auction format has a special property in equilibrium. All bidding strategies are weakly dominated by the strategy of bidding exactly one's valuation. Vickery's analysis of second-price auctions and of the property that they induce bidders to reveal their valuations has led them to be called *Vickery auctions* or *Vickery mechanisms*.

We will prove that, in this kind of auction, bidding something other than one's true valuation is weakly dominated by bidding one's valuation. Let v be a buyer's valuation and b his bid. If the two variables are not equal then there are two cases to consider: either $b < v$ or $b > v$. Consider the first case ($b < v$). Let $\tilde{b}$ be the highest rival bid. If $\tilde{b} > v$, then the buyer loses whether his bid is b or v, so there is a tie between the strategies. If $\tilde{b} < b$, then the buyer wins the object whether his bid is b or v and his payment is the same (the second-highest bid, $\tilde{b}$) in either case, so again we have a tie. We no longer have a tie if $\tilde{b}$ lies between b and v. If the buyer bids b then he loses the object and obtains no surplus. If he bids v then he wins the object and obtains a net surplus of $v - \tilde{b} > 0$, so bidding v is strictly better than bidding $b < v$ in this case. Similar logic shows that bidding v weakly dominates bidding $b > v$.

The reason that bidding one's valuation is weakly dominant is that the winner's bid does not affect the amount he has to pay, for that depends on someone else's (the second-highest bidder's) bid. But bidding one's valuation ensures the buyer wins the object when he should.

With an understanding of equilibrium bidding in second-price auctions, we can compare first- and second-price sealed-bid auctions. Each format has plusses and minuses with regard to the revenue the seller earns. On the one hand, bidders shade their bids below their valuations in the first-price auction but not in the second-price auction, a "plus" for second-price auctions. On the other hand, the winning bidder pays the highest bid in the first-price auction but only the second-highest bid in the second-price auction, a "minus" for second-price auctions. The surprising result proved by Vickery is that these plusses and minuses balance perfectly, so that both auction types provide the seller with the same expected revenue. Rather than working through a general proof of this *revenue equivalence* result, we will show in Example 18.9 that it holds in a particular case.

EXAMPLE 18.9 Art Auction

Suppose two buyers (1 and 2) bid for a painting in a first-price sealed-bid auction. Buyer i's valuation, v_i, is a random variable that is uniformly distributed between 0 and 1 and is independent of the other buyer's valuation. Buyers' valuations are private information. We will look for a symmetric equilibrium in which buyers bid a constant fraction of their valuations, $b_i = kv_i$. The remaining step is to solve for the equilibrium value of k.

Symmetric equilibrium. Given that buyer 1 knows his own type v_1 and knows buyer 2's equilibrium strategy $b_2 = kv_2$, buyer 1 best responds by choosing the bid b_1 maximizing his expected surplus

$$\Pr(1 \text{ wins auction})(v_1 - b_1) + \Pr(1 \text{ loses auction})(0)$$
$$= \Pr(b_1 > b_2)(v_1 - b_1)$$
$$= \Pr(b_1 > kv_2)(v_1 - b_1)$$
$$= \Pr(v_2 < b_1/k)(v_1 - b_1)$$
$$= \frac{b_1}{k}(v_1 - b_1). \tag{18.67}$$

We have ignored the possibility of equal bids, because they would only occur in equilibrium if buyers had equal valuations yet the probability is zero that two independent and continuous random variables equal each other.

The only tricky step in Example 18.67 is the last one. The discussion of cumulative distribution functions in Chapter 2 shows that the probability $\Pr(v_2 < x)$ can be written as

$$\Pr(v_2 < x) = \int_{-\infty}^{x} f(v_2) \, dv_2, \tag{18.68}$$

where f is the probability density function. But for a random variable uniformly distributed between 0 and 1 we have

$$\int_{0}^{x} f(v_2) \, dv_2 = \int_{0}^{x} (1) \, dv_2 = x, \tag{18.69}$$

so $\Pr(v_2 < x) = b_1/k$.

Taking the first-order condition of Equation 18.67 with respect to b_1 and rearranging yields $b_1 = v_1/2$. Hence $k^* = 1/2$, implying that buyers shade their valuations down by half in forming their bids.

(continued)

EXAMPLE 18.9   CONTINUED

Order statistics. Before computing the seller's expected revenue from the auction, we will introduce the notion of an order statistic. If n independent draws are made from the same distribution and if they are arranged from smallest to largest, then the kth lowest draw is called the kth-*order statistic*, denoted $X_{(k)}$. For example: with n random variables, the nth-order statistic $X_{(n)}$ is the largest of the n draws; the $(n-1)$th-order statistic $X_{(n-1)}$ is the second largest; and so on. Order statistics are so useful that statisticians have done a lot of work to characterize their properties. For instance, statisticians have computed that if n draws are taken from a uniform distribution between 0 and 1, then the expected value of the kth-order statistic is

$$E(X_{(k)}) = \frac{k}{n+1}. \tag{18.70}$$

This formula may be found in many standard statistical references.

Expected revenue. The expected revenue from the first-price auction equals

$$E(\max(b_1, b_2)) = \frac{1}{2}E(\max(v_1, v_2)). \tag{18.71}$$

But $\max(v_1, v_2)$ is the largest-order statistic from two draws of a uniform random variable between 0 and 1, the expected value of which is $2/3$ (according to Equation 18.70). Therefore, the expected revenue from the auction equals $(1/2)(2/3) = 1/3$.

Second-price auction. Suppose that the seller decides to use a second-price auction to sell the painting. In equilibrium, buyers bid their true valuations: $b_i = v_i$. The seller's expected revenue is $E(\min(b_1, b_2))$ because the winning bidder pays an amount equal to the loser's bid. But $\min(b_1, b_2) = \min(v_1, v_2)$, and the latter is the first-order statistic for two draws from a random variable uniformly distributed between 0 and 1 whose expected value is $1/3$ (according to Equation 18.70). This is the same expected revenue generated by the first-price auction.

QUERY: In the first-price auction, could the seller try to boost bids up toward buyers' valuations by specifying a reservation price r such that no sale is made if the maximal bid falls below r? What are the trade-offs involved for the seller from such a reservation price? Would a reservation price help boost revenue in a second-price auction?

In more complicated economic environments, the long list of different auction formats do not necessarily yield the same revenue. One complication that is frequently considered is supposing that the good has the same value to all bidders but that they do not know exactly what that value is: each bidder has only an imprecise estimate of what his or her valuation might be. For example, bidders for oil tracts may have each conducted their own surveys of the likelihood that there is oil below the surface. All bidders' surveys taken together may give a clear picture of the likelihood of oil, but each one separately may give only a rough idea. For another example, the value of a work of art depends in part on its resale value (unless the bidder plans on keeping it in the family forever), which in turn depends on others' valuations; each bidder knows his or her own valuation but perhaps not others'. An auction conducted in such an economic environment is called a *common values* auction.

The most interesting issue that arises in a common values setting is the so-called winner's curse. The winning bidder realizes that every other bidder probably thought the good was worth less, meaning that he or she probably overestimated the value of the good. The winner's curse sometimes leads inexperienced bidders to regret having won the auction.

Sophisticated bidders take account of the winner's curse by shading down their bids below their (imprecise) estimates of the value of the good, so they never regret having won the auction in equilibrium.

Analysis of the common values setting is rather complicated, and the different auction formats previously listed no longer yield equivalent revenue. Roughly speaking, auctions that incorporate other bidders' information in the price paid tend to provide the seller with more revenue. For example, a second-price auction tends to be better than a first-price auction because the price paid in a second-price auction depends on what other bidders think the object is worth. If other bidders thought the object was not worth much then the second-highest bid will be low and the price paid by the winning bidder will be low, precluding the winner's curse.

SUMMARY

In this chapter we have provided a survey of some issues that arise in modeling markets with asymmetric information. Asymmetric information can lead to market inefficiencies relative to the first-best benchmark, which assumes perfect information. Cleverly designed contracts can often recover some of this lost surplus. We examined some of the following specific issues.

- Asymmetric information is often studied using a principal-agent model in which a principal offers a contract to an agent who has private information. The two main variants of the principal-agent model are the models of hidden actions and of hidden types.

- In a hidden-action model (called a moral hazard model in an insurance context), the principal tries to induce the agent to take appropriate actions by tying the agent's payments to observable outcomes. Doing so exposes the agent to random fluctuations in these outcomes, which is costly for a risk-averse agent.

- In a hidden-type model (called an adverse selection model in an insurance context), the principal cannot extract all the surplus from high types because they can always gain positive surplus by pretending to be a low type. In an effort to extract the most surplus possible, the principal offers a menu of contracts from which

different types of agent can select. The principal distorts the quantity in the contract targeted to low types in order to make this contract less attractive to high types, thus extracting more surplus in the contract targeted to the high types.

- Most of the insights gained from the basic form of the principal-agent model, in which the principal is a monopolist, carry over to the case of competing principals. The main change is that agents obtain more surplus.

- The lemons problem arises when sellers have private information about the quality of their goods. Sellers whose goods are higher than average quality may refrain from selling at the market price, which reflects the average quality of goods sold on the market. The market may collapse, with goods of only the lowest quality being offered for sale.

- The principal can extract more surplus from agents if several of them are pitted against each other in an auction setting. In a simple economic environment, a variety of common auction formats generate the same revenue for the seller. Differences in auction format may generate different level of revenue in more complicated settings.

PROBLEMS

18.1

A personal-injury lawyer works as an agent for his injured plaintiff. The expected award from the trial (taking into account the plaintiff's probability of prevailing and the damage award if she prevails) is l, where l is the lawyer's effort. Effort costs the lawyer $l^2/2$.

a. What is the lawyer's effort, his surplus, and the plaintiff's surplus in equilibrium when the lawyer obtains the customary $1/3$ contingency fee (that is, the lawyer gets $1/3$ of the award if the plaintiff prevails)?

b. Repeat part (a) for a general contingency fee of c.

c. What is the optimal contingency fee from the plaintiff's perspective? Compute the associated surpluses for the lawyer and plaintiff.

d. What would be the optimal contingency fee from the plaintiff's perspective if she could "sell" the case to her lawyer [that is, if she could ask him for an up-front payment in return for a specified contingency fee, possibly higher than in part (c)]? Compute the up-front payment (assuming that the plaintiff makes the offer to the lawyer) and the associated surpluses for the lawyer and plaintiff. Do they do better in this part than in part (c)? Why do you think selling cases in this way is outlawed in many countries?

18.2

Solve for the optimal linear price per ounce of coffee that the coffee shop would charge in Example 18.4. How does the shop's profit compare to when it uses nonlinear prices? *Hint:* Your first step should be to compute each type's demand at a linear price p.

18.3

Return to the nonlinear pricing problem facing the monopoly coffee shop in Example 18.4, but now suppose the proportion of high demanders increases to $2/3$ and the proportion of low demanders falls to $1/3$. What is the optimal menu in the second-best situation? How does the menu compare to the one in Example 18.4?

18.4

Suppose there is a 50–50 chance that an individual with logarithmic utility from wealth and with a current wealth of $20,000 will suffer a loss of $10,000 from a car accident. Insurance is competitively provided at actuarily fair rates.

a. Compute the outcome if the individual buys full insurance.

b. Compute the outcome if the individual buys only partial insurance covering half the loss. Show that the outcome in part (a) is preferred.

c. Now suppose that individuals who buy the partial rather than the full insurance policy take more care when driving, reducing the damage from loss from $10,000 to $7,000. What would be the actuarily fair price of the partial policy? Does the individual now prefer the full or the partial policy?

18.5

Suppose that left-handed people are more prone to injury than right-handed people. Lefties have an 80 percent chance of suffering an injury leading to a $1,000 loss (in terms of medical expenses and the monetary equivalent of pain and suffering) but righties have only a 20 percent chance of suffering such an injury. The population contains equal numbers of lefties and righties. Individuals all have logarithmic utility-of-wealth functions and initial wealth of $10,000. Insurance is provided by a monopoly company.

a. Compute the first best for the monopoly insurer (i.e., supposing it can observe the individual's dominant hand).

b. Take as given that, in the second best, the monopolist prefers not to serve righties at all and targets only lefties. Knowing this, compute the second-best menu of policies for the monopoly insurer.

c. Use a spreadsheet program (such as the one on the website associated with Example 18.5) or other mathematical software to solve numerically the constrained optimization problem for the second best. Make sure to add constraints bounding the insurance payments for righties: $0 \leq x_R \leq 1,000$. Establish that the constraint $0 \leq x_R$ is binding and so righties are not served in the second best.

18.6

Consider the same setup as in Problem 18.5, but assume that insurance is offered by competitive insurers.

    a. Assume insurance companies cannot distinguish lefties from righties and so offer a single contract. If both types are equally likely to buy insurance, what would be the actuarially fair premium for full insurance?

    b. Which types will buy insurance at the premium calculated in (a)?

    c. Given your results from part (b), will the insurance premiums be correctly computed?

18.7

Suppose 100 cars will be offered on the used-car market. Let 50 of them be good cars, each worth $10,000 to a buyer, and let 50 be lemons, each worth only $2,000.

    a. Compute a buyer's maximum willingness to pay for a car if he or she cannot observe the car's quality.

    b. Suppose that there are enough buyers relative to sellers that competition among them leads cars to be sold at their maximum willingness to pay. What would the market equilibrium be if sellers value good cars at $8,000? At $6,000?

18.8

Consider the following simple model of a common values auction. Two buyers each obtain a private signal about the value of an object. The signal can be either high (H) or low (L) with equal probability. If both obtain signal H, the object is worth 1; otherwise, it is worth 0.

    a. What is the expected value of the object to a buyer who sees signal L? To a buyer who sees signal H?

    b. Suppose buyers bid their expected value computed in part (a). Show that they earn negative profit conditional on observing signal H—an example of the winner's curse.

Analytical Problems

18.9 Doctor-patient relationship

Consider the principal-agent relationship between a patient and doctor. Suppose that the patient's utility function is given by $U_P(m, x)$, where m denotes medical care (whose quantity is determined by the doctor) and x denotes other consumption goods. The patient faces budget constraint $I_c = p_m m + x$, where p_m is the relative price of medical care. The doctor's utility function is given by $U_d(I_d) + U_p$—that is, the doctor derives utility from income but, being altruistic, also derives utility from the patient's well-being. Moreover, the additive specification implies that the doctor is a perfect altruist in the sense that his or her utility increases one-for-one with the patient's. The doctor's income comes from the patient's medical expenditures: $I_d = p_m m$. Show that, in this situation, the doctor will generally choose a level of m that is higher than a fully informed patient would choose.

18.10 Diagrams with three types

Suppose the agent can be one of three types rather than just two as in the chapter.

    a. Return to the monopolist's problem of computing the optimal nonlinear price. Represent the first best in a schematic diagram by modifying Figure 18.5. Do the same for the second best by modifying Figure 18.7.

    b. Return to the monopolist's problem of designing optimal insurance policies. Represent the first best in a schematic diagram by modifying Figure 18.8. Do the same for the second best by modifying Figure 18.9.

18.11 Increasing competition in an auction

A painting is auctioned to n bidders, each with a private value for the painting that is uniformly distributed between 0 and 1.

a. Compute the equilibrium bidding strategy in a first-price sealed-bid auction. Compute the seller's expected revenue in this auction. *Hint:* Use the formula for the expected value of the kth-order statistic for uniform distributions in Equation 18.70.

b. Compute the equilibrium bidding strategy in a second-price sealed-bid auction. Compute the seller's expected revenue in this auction using the hint from part (a).

c. Do the two auction formats exhibit revenue equivalence?

d. For each auction format, how do bidders' strategies and the seller's revenue change with an increase in the number of bidders?

18.12 Team effort

Increasing the size of a team that creates a joint product may dull incentives, as this problem will illustrate.[11] Suppose n partners together produce a revenue of $R = e_1 + \cdots + e_n$; here e_i is partner i's effort, which costs him $c(e_i) = e_i^2/2$ to exert.

a. Compute the equilibrium effort and surplus (revenue minus effort cost) if each partner receives an equal share of the revenue.

b. Compute the equilibrium effort and average surplus if only one partner gets a share. Is it better to concentrate the share or to disperse it?

c. Return to part (a) and take the derivative of surplus per partner with respect to n. Is surplus per partner increasing or decreasing in n? What is the limit as n increases?

d. Some commentators say that ESOPs (employee stock ownership plans, whereby part of the firm's shares are distributed among all its workers) are beneficial because they provide incentives for employees to work hard. What does your answer to part (c) say about the incentive properties of ESOPs for modern corporations, which may have thousands of workers?

SUGGESTIONS FOR FURTHER READING

Bolton, P., and M. Dewatripont. *Contract Theory*. Cambridge, MA: MIT Press, 2005.

> Comprehensive graduate textbook treating all topics in this chapter and many other topics in contract theory.

Krishna, V. *Auction Theory*. San Diego: Academic Press, 2002.

> Advanced text on auction theory.

Lucking-Reiley, D. "Using Field Experiments to Test Equivalence between Auction Formats: Magic on the Internet." *American Economic Review* (December 1999): 1063–80.

> Tests the revenue equivalence theorem by selling Magic playing cards over the Internet using various auction formats.

Milgrom, P. "Auctions and Bidding: A Primer." *Journal of Economic Perspectives* (Summer 1989): 3–22.

> Intuitive discussion of methods used and research questions explored in the field of auction theory.

Rothschild, M., and J. Stiglitz. "Equilibrium in Competitive Insurance Markets: An Essay on the Economics of Imperfect Information." *Quarterly Journal of Economics* (November 1976): 629–50.

> Presents a nice graphic treatment of the adverse selection problem. Contains ingenious illustrations of various possibilities for separating equilibria.

Salanié, B. *The Economics of Contracts: A Primer*. Cambridge, MA: MIT Press, 1997.

> A concise treatment of contract theory at a deeper level than this chapter.

Shavell, S. *Economic Analysis of Accident Law*. Cambridge, MA: Harvard University Press, 1987.

> Classic reference analyzing the effect of different laws on the level of precaution undertaken by victims and injurers. Discusses how the availability of insurance affects parties' behavior.

---

[11]The classic reference on the hidden-action problem with multiple agents is B. Holmström, "Moral Hazard in Teams," *Bell Journal of Economics* (Autumn 1982): 324–40.

EXTENSIONS

Nonlinear Pricing with a Continuum of Types

In this extension, we will expand the analysis of nonlinear pricing to allow for a continuum of consumer types rather than just two. The extension will be especially valuable for students who are interested in seeing new applications of optimal control techniques introduced in Chapter 2 to applications beyond dynamic choice problems. Be warned that the mathematics used here is some of the most complicated in the book. For those not interested in practicing optimal control, the main point to take away from this extension is "reassurance": we can rest assured that the conclusions we have drawn from the simple two-type model in this chapter indeed hold in more general settings. Besides drawing on Chapter 2, the extension draws on Section 2.3.3 of Bolton and Dewatripont (2005).

E18.1 Remaining questions about hidden-type models

We analyzed the simplest possible hidden-type model in Chapter 18. The agent's type could be one of only two possible values. In the nonlinear pricing application, for example, the agent was a consumer who could have high or low demand. In the application to adverse selection in insurance, the agent was an individual who could have a high or low probability of an accident. We derived a number of insights from the analysis, including that the low type's contract was distorted downward relative to the first best although the high type's contract was not. The latter insight was summarized as "no distortion at the top."

The analysis left a number of open questions. How general are the first-order conditions characterizing the second-best contract? Does "no distortion at the top" mean that only the highest type's contract is efficient, or that all but the very lowest type's are, or something in between? Does the monopolist want to serve all types, or will the lowest types be left off the menu? We cannot tell by analyzing a two-type model, but we can answer these questions by extending the analysis to a continuous distribution of types. As mentioned previously, the other motivation for this extension is to show the power of the optimal control methods introduced in Chapter 2 for solving problems beyond dynamic choice problems.

E18.2 Nonlinear pricing model

For concreteness, we will focus our analysis on the nonlinear pricing problem for a monopolist. The monopolist offers a menu of bundles, one for each type θ, where a bundle is a specification of a quantity $q(\theta)$ and a total tariff for this quantity $T(\theta)$. The consumer has private information about his type, but the monopolist knows only the distribution from which θ is drawn. Let $\varphi(\theta)$ be the associated probability density function and $\Phi(\theta)$ the cumulative distribution function. Suppose all types fall in the interval between θ_L at the low end and θ_H at the high end. (Review the section on probability and statistics from Chapter 2 for these and other concepts used in this extension.)

As before, the consumer's utility function is $U(\theta) = \theta v(q(\theta)) - T(\theta)$. The monopolist's profit from serving type θ is $\Pi(\theta) = T(\theta) - cq(\theta)$, where c is the constant marginal and average cost of production.

E18.3 First best

The first best is easy to solve for. Each type is offered the socially optimal quantity, which satisfies the condition $\theta v'(q) = c$. Each type is charged the tariff that extracts all of his surplus $T(\theta) = \theta v(q(\theta))$. The monopolist earns profit $\theta v(q(\theta)) - cq(\theta)$, which is clearly all of the social surplus.

E18.4 Second best

The monopolist's second-best pricing scheme is the menu of bundles $q(\theta)$ and $T(\theta)$ that maximizes its expected profit,

$$\int_{\theta_L}^{\theta_H} \Pi(\theta)\varphi(\theta)\, d\theta = \int_{\theta_L}^{\theta_H} [T(\theta) - cq(\theta)]\varphi(\theta)\, d\theta, \quad \textbf{(i)}$$

subject to participation and incentive compatibility constraints for the consumer. As we have seen, the participation constraint is a concern only for the lowest type that the monopolist serves. Then all types will participate as long as θ_L does. The relevant participation constraint is thus

$$\theta_L v(q(\theta_L)) - T(\theta_L) \geq 0. \quad \textbf{(ii)}$$

That all types participate in the contract does not require the monopolist to serve them with a positive quantity. The monopolist may choose to offer the null contract (zero quantity and tariff) to a range of types. By reducing some types down to the null contract, the monopolist can extract even more surplus from higher types.

Incentive compatibility requires additional discussion. Incentive compatibility requires that type θ prefer its bundle to any other type's, say, $q(\tilde{\theta})$ and $T(\tilde{\theta})$. In other words, $\theta v(q(\tilde{\theta})) - T(\tilde{\theta})$ is maximized at $\tilde{\theta} = \theta$. Taking the first-order condition with respect to $\tilde{\theta}$ yields

$$\theta v'(q(\tilde{\theta}))q'(\tilde{\theta}) - T'(\tilde{\theta}) = 0 \quad \text{for} \quad \tilde{\theta} = \theta; \quad \textbf{(iii)}$$

that is,

$$\theta v'(q(\theta))q'(\theta) - T'(\theta) = 0. \quad \textbf{(iv)}$$

Equation iv is both necessary and sufficient for incentive compatibility under a set of conditions that hold in many examples but are a bit too technical to discuss here.

E18.5 Rewriting the problem

There are too many derivatives in Equation iv for us to apply the optimal control methods from Chapter 2. The analogous equation in Chapter 2 (Equation 2.148) has only one derivative. To obtain a workable incentive compatibility constraint, observe that

$$\begin{aligned} U'(\theta) &= v(q(\theta)) + \theta v'(q(\theta))q'(\theta) - T'(\theta) \\ &= v(q(\theta)), \end{aligned} \quad \textbf{(v)}$$

where the second line follows from Equation iv. Now we have expressed the incentive compatibility constraint in a form with only one derivative, as required. Since the differential equation $U'(\theta) = v(q(\theta))$ involves the derivative of $U(\theta)$ rather than of $T(\theta)$, we can make the substitution $T(\theta) = \theta v(q(\theta)) - U(\theta)$ everywhere in the maximization problem to put it in terms of $q(\theta)$ and $U(\theta)$ rather than $q(\theta)$ and $T(\theta)$.

The reformulated problem is to maximize

$$\int_{\theta_L}^{\theta_H} [\theta v(q(\theta)) - U(\theta) - cq(\theta)]\varphi(\theta)\, d\theta \quad \textbf{(vi)}$$

subject to the participation constraint (inequality ii) and the incentive compatibility constraint $U'(\theta) = v(q(\theta))$. By Equation 2.150, the Hamiltonian associated with the optimal control problem is

$$\begin{aligned} H = &[\theta v(q(\theta)) - U(\theta) - cq(\theta)]\varphi(\theta) \\ &+ \lambda(\theta)v(q(\theta)) + U(\theta)\lambda'(\theta). \end{aligned} \quad \textbf{(vii)}$$

To see how this Hamiltonian is constructed, θ is here playing the role played by t in Chapter 2, $q(\theta)$ is playing the role of control variable $c(t)$, $U(\theta)$ is playing the role of the state variable $x(t)$,

$$[\theta v(q(\theta)) - U(\theta) - cq(\theta)]\varphi(\theta) \quad \textbf{(viii)}$$

is playing the role of f, and $U'(\theta) = v(q(\theta))$ is playing the role of differential equation

$$\frac{dx(t)}{dt} = g(x(t), c(t), t). \quad \textbf{(ix)}$$

E18.6 Optimal control solution

Analogous to the conditions $\partial H/\partial c = 0$ and $\partial H/\partial x = 0$ from Equation 2.151, here the conditions for the optimal control solution are

$$\frac{\partial H}{\partial q} = [\theta v'(q(\theta)) - c]\varphi(\theta) + \lambda(\theta)v'(\theta) = 0, \quad \textbf{(x)}$$

$$\frac{\partial H}{\partial U} = -\varphi(\theta) + \lambda'(\theta) = 0. \quad \textbf{(xi)}$$

To cast these conditions in a more useful form, we shall eliminate the Lagrange multiplier. The second equation implies $\lambda'(\theta) = \varphi(\theta)$. By the fundamental theorem of calculus (discussed in Chapter 2),

$$\begin{aligned} \lambda(\theta_H) - \lambda(\theta) &= \int_{\theta}^{\theta_H} \lambda'(s)\, ds \\ &= \int_{\theta}^{\theta_H} \varphi(s)\, ds \\ &= \Phi(\theta_H) - \Phi(\theta) \\ &= 1 - \Phi(\theta), \end{aligned} \quad \textbf{(xii)}$$

where $\Phi(\theta_H) = 1$ because Φ is a cumulative distribution function, which equals 1 when evaluated at the greatest possible value of the random variable. Therefore,

$$\begin{aligned} \lambda(\theta) &= \lambda(\theta_H) + \Phi(\theta) - 1 \\ &= \Phi(\theta) - 1, \end{aligned} \quad \textbf{(xiii)}$$

since $\lambda(\theta_H) = 0$ [there are no types above θ_H from whom to extract surplus, so the value from distorting type θ_H's contract as measured by $\lambda(\theta_H)$ is 0]. Substituting into Equation x and rearranging yields

$$\theta v'(q(\theta)) = c + \frac{1 - \Phi(\theta)}{\varphi(\theta)}v'(q(\theta)). \quad \textbf{(xiv)}$$

FIGURE E18.1   Nonlinear Pricing Schedule for Continuum of Types

The graph is based on calculations for uniformly distributed types. Larger bundles receive per-unit price discount.

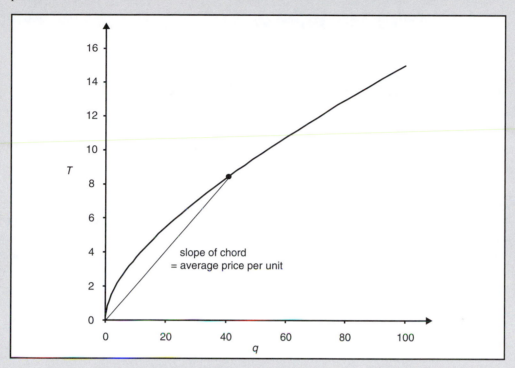

This equation tells us a lot about the second best. Because $\Phi(\theta_H) = 1$, for the highest type the equation reduces to $\theta_H v'(q(\theta_H)) = c$, the first-best condition. We again have "no distortion at the top" for the high type, but all other types face some downward distortion in $q(\theta)$. To see this, note that $\theta v'(q(\theta)) > c$ for these other types, implying that $q(\theta)$ is less than the first best for all $\theta < \theta_H$.

E18.7 Uniform example

Suppose θ is uniformly distributed between 0 and 1 and that $v(q) = 2\sqrt{q}$. Then $\varphi(\theta) = 1$ and $\Phi(\theta) = \theta$. Equation xiv implies that

$$q(\theta) = \left(\frac{2\theta - 1}{c}\right)^2. \tag{xv}$$

It is apparent from Equation xv that only types above 1/2 are served. By leaving types below 1/2 unserved, the monopolist can extract more surplus from the higher-value consumers whom it does serve. To compute the tariff, observe that

$$
\begin{aligned}
T(\theta) &= \int_{1/2}^{\theta} T'(s)\, ds \\
&= \int_{1/2}^{\theta} sv'(q(s))q'(s)\, ds \\
&= \frac{4\theta^2 - 1}{2c},
\end{aligned}
\tag{xvi}
$$

where the first equality holds by the fundamental theorem of calculus, the second by Equation iv, and the third by Equation xv.

Figure E18.1 graphs the resulting nonlinear pricing schedule. Each point on the schedule is a bundle targeted at a particular type. The implied per-unit price can be found by looking at the slope of the chord from the origin to the graph. It is clear that this chord is declining as q increases, implying that the per-unit price is falling, which in turn implies that the schedule involves quantity discounts for large purchases.

Reference

Bolton, P., and M. Dewatripont. *Contract Theory.* Cambridge, MA: MIT Press, 2005.

Externalities and Public Goods

In Chapter 13 we looked briefly at a few problems that may interfere with the allocational efficiency of perfectly competitive markets. Here we will examine two of those problems—externalities and public goods—in more detail. This examination has two purposes. First, we wish to show clearly why the existence of externalities and public goods may distort the allocation of resources. In so doing it will be possible to illustrate some additional features of the type of information provided by competitive prices and some of the circumstances that may diminish the usefulness of that information. Our second reason for looking more closely at externalities and public goods is to suggest ways in which the allocational problems they pose might be mitigated. We will see that, at least in some cases, the efficiency of competitive market outcomes may be more robust than might have been anticipated.

DEFINING EXTERNALITIES

Externalities occur because economic actors have effects on third parties that are not reflected in market transactions. Chemical makers spewing toxic fumes on their neighbors, jet planes waking up people, and motorists littering the highway are, from an economic point of view, all engaging in the same sort of activity: they are having a direct effect on the well-being of others that is outside market channels. Such activities might be contrasted to the direct effects of markets. When I choose to purchase a loaf of bread, for example, I (perhaps imperceptibly) raise the price of bread generally, and that may affect the well-being of other bread buyers. But such effects, because they are reflected in market prices, are not externalities and do not affect the market's ability to allocate resources efficiently.[1] Rather, the rise in the price of bread that results from my increased purchase is an accurate reflection of societal preferences, and the price rise helps ensure that the right mix of products is produced. That is not the case for toxic chemical discharges, jet noise, or litter. In these cases, market prices (of chemicals, air travel, or disposable containers) may not accurately reflect actual social costs because they may take no account of the damage being done to third parties. Information being conveyed by market prices is fundamentally inaccurate, leading to a misallocation of resources.

As a summary, then, we have developed the following definition.

DEFINITION

Externality. An *externality* occurs whenever the activities of one economic actor affect the activities of another in ways that are not reflected in market transactions.

---

[1]Sometimes effects of one economic agent on another that take place through the market system are termed *pecuniary* externalities to differentiate such effects from the *technological* externalities we are discussing. Here the use of the term *externalities* will refer only to the latter type, because these are the only type with consequences for the efficiency of resource allocation by competitive markets.

Before analyzing in detail why failing to take externalities into account can lead to a misallocation of resources, we will examine a few examples that should clarify the nature of the problem.

Interfirm externalities

To illustrate the externality issue in its simplest form, we consider two firms: one producing good x and the other producing good y. The production of good x is said to have an external effect on the production of y if the output of y depends not only on the inputs chosen by the y-entrepreneur but also on the level at which the production of x is carried on. Notationally, the production function for good y can be written as

$$y = f(k, l; x), \tag{19.1}$$

where x appears to the right of the semicolon to show that it is an effect on production over which the y-entrepreneur has no control.[2] As an example, suppose the two firms are located on a river, with firm y being downstream from x. Suppose firm x pollutes the river in its productive process. Then the output of firm y may depend not only on the level of inputs it uses itself but also on the amount of pollutants flowing past its factory. The level of pollutants, in turn, is determined by the output of firm x. In the production function shown by Equation 19.1, the output of firm x would have a negative marginal physical productivity $\partial y / \partial x < 0$. Increases in x output would cause less y to be produced. In the next section we return to analyze this case more fully, since it is representative of most simple types of externalities.

Beneficial externalities

The relationship between two firms may be beneficial. Most examples of such positive externalities are rather bucolic in nature. Perhaps the most famous, proposed by J. Meade, involves two firms, one producing honey (raising bees) and the other producing apples.[3] Because the bees feed on apple blossoms, an increase in apple production will improve productivity in the honey industry. The beneficial effects of having well-fed bees is a positive externality to the beekeeper. In the notation of Equation 19.1, $\partial y / \partial x$ would now be positive. In the usual perfectly competitive case, the productive activities of one firm have no direct effect on those of other firms: $\partial y / \partial x = 0$.

Externalities in utility

Externalities also can occur if the activities of an economic actor directly affect an individual's utility. Most common examples of environmental externalities are of this type. From an economic perspective it makes little difference whether such effects are created by firms (in the form, say, of toxic chemicals or jet noise) or by other individuals (litter or, perhaps, the noise from a loud radio). In all such cases the amount of such activities would enter directly into the individual's utility function in much the same way as firm x's output entered into firm y's production function in Equation 19.1. As in the case of firms, such externalities may sometimes be beneficial (you may actually like the song being played on your neighbor's radio). So, again, a situation of zero externalities can be regarded as the middle ground in which other agents' activities have no direct effect on individuals' utilities.

One special type of utility externality that is relevant to the analysis of social choices arises when one individual's utility depends directly on the utility of someone else. If, for example, Smith cares about Jones's welfare, then we could write his or her utility function (U_S) as

$$\text{utility} = U_S(x_1, \ldots, x_n; U_J), \tag{19.2}$$

---

[2]We will find it necessary to redefine the assumption of "no control" considerably as the analysis of this chapter proceeds.

[3]J. Meade, "External Economies and Diseconomies in a Competitive Situation," *Economic Journal* 62 (March 1952): 54–67.

where $x_1, \ldots, x_n$ are the goods that Smith consumes and U_J is Jones's utility. If Smith is altruistic and wants Jones to be well-off (as might happen if Jones were a close relative), $\partial U_S / \partial U_J$ would be positive. If, on the other hand, Smith were envious of Jones, then it might be the case that $\partial U_S / \partial U_J$ would be negative; that is, improvements in Jones's utility make Smith worse-off. The middle ground between altruism and envy would occur if Smith were indifferent to Jones's welfare ($\partial U_S / \partial U_J = 0$), and that is what we have usually assumed throughout this book (for a brief discussion, see the Extensions to Chapter 3).

Public goods externalities

Goods that are "public" or "collective" in nature will be the focus of our analysis in the second half of this chapter. The defining characteristic of these goods is nonexclusion; that is, once the goods are produced (either by the government or by some private entity), they provide benefits to an entire group—perhaps to everyone. It is technically impossible to restrict these benefits to the specific group of individuals who pay for them, so the benefits are available to all. As we mentioned in Chapter 13, national defense provides the traditional example. Once a defense system is established, all individuals in society are protected by it whether they wish to be or not and whether they pay for it or not. Choosing the right level of output for such a good can be a tricky process, because market signals will be inaccurate.

EXTERNALITIES AND ALLOCATIVE INEFFICIENCY

Externalities lead to inefficient allocations of resources because market prices do not accurately reflect the additional costs imposed on or benefits provided to third parties. To illustrate these inefficiencies requires a general equilibrium model, because inefficient allocations in one market throw into doubt the efficiency of market-determined outcomes everywhere. Here we choose a very simple and, in some ways, rather odd general equilibrium model that allows us to make these points in a compact way. Specifically, we assume there is only one person in our simple economy and that his or her utility depends on the quantities of x and y consumed. Consumption levels of these two goods are denoted by x_c and y_c, so

$$\text{utility} = U(x_c, y_c). \tag{19.3}$$

This person has initial stocks of x and y (denoted by x^* and y^*) and can either consume these directly or use them as intermediary goods in production. To simplify matters, we assume that good x is produced using only good y, according to the production function

$$x_o = f(y_i), \tag{19.4}$$

where subscript o refers to outputs and i to inputs. To illustrate externalities, we assume that the output of good y depends not only on how much x is used as an input in the production process but also on the x production level itself. Hence this would model a situation, say, where y is downriver from firm x and must cope with the pollution created by production of x output. The production function for y is given by

$$y_o = g(x_i, x_o), \tag{19.5}$$

where $g_1 > 0$ (more x input produces more y output), but $g_2 < 0$ (additional x output reduces y output because of the externality involved).

The quantities of each good in this economy are constrained by the initial stocks available and by the additional production that takes place:

$$x_c + x_i = x_o + x^*, \tag{19.6}$$

$$y_c + y_i = y_o + y^*. \tag{19.7}$$

Finding the efficient allocation

The economic problem for this society, then, is to maximize utility subject to the four constraints represented by Equations 19.4–19.7. To solve this problem we must introduce four Lagrangian multipliers. The Lagrangian expression for this maximization problem is

$$\mathcal{L} = U(x_c, y_c) + \lambda_1[f(y_i) - x_o] + \lambda_2[g(x_i, x_0) - y_o]$$
$$+ \lambda_3(x_c + x_i - x_o - x^*) + \lambda_4(y_c + y_i - y_o - y^*), \qquad \textbf{(19.8)}$$

and the six first-order conditions for a maximum are

$$\partial \mathcal{L}/\partial x_c = U_1 + \lambda_3 = 0, \qquad \text{[i]}$$
$$\partial \mathcal{L}/\partial y_c = U_2 + \lambda_4 = 0, \qquad \text{[ii]}$$
$$\partial \mathcal{L}/\partial x_i = \lambda_2 g_1 + \lambda_3 = 0, \qquad \text{[iii]}$$
$$\partial \mathcal{L}/\partial y_i = \lambda_1 f_y + \lambda_4 = 0, \qquad \text{[iv]} \qquad \textbf{(19.9)}$$
$$\partial \mathcal{L}/\partial x_o = -\lambda_1 + \lambda_2 g_2 - \lambda_3 = 0, \qquad \text{[v]}$$
$$\partial \mathcal{L}/\partial y_o = -\lambda_2 - \lambda_4 = 0. \qquad \text{[vi]}$$

Eliminating the λs from these equations is a straightforward process. Taking the ratio of Equations i and ii yields the familiar result

$$MRS = \frac{U_1}{U_2} = \frac{\lambda_3}{\lambda_4}. \qquad \textbf{(19.10)}$$

But Equations iii and vi also imply

$$MRS = \frac{\lambda_3}{\lambda_4} = \frac{\lambda_2 g_1}{\lambda_2} = g_1. \qquad \textbf{(19.11)}$$

Hence optimality in y production requires that the individual's MRS in consumption equal the marginal productivity of x in the production of y. This conclusion repeats the result from Chapter 13, where we showed that efficient output choice requires that dy/dx in consumption be equal to dy/dx in production.

To achieve efficiency in x production, we must also consider the externality that this production poses to y. Combining Equations iv–vi gives

$$MRS = \frac{\lambda_3}{\lambda_4} = \frac{-\lambda_1 + \lambda_2 g_2}{\lambda_4} = \frac{-\lambda_1}{\lambda_4} + \frac{\lambda_2 g_2}{\lambda_4}$$
$$= \frac{1}{f_y} - g_2. \qquad \textbf{(19.12)}$$

Intuitively, this equation requires that the individual's MRS must also equal dy/dx obtained through x production. The first term in the expression, $1/f_y$, represents the reciprocal of the marginal productivity of y in x production—this is the first component of dy/dx as it relates to x production. The second term, g_2, represents the negative impact that added x production has on y output—this is the second component of dy/dx as it relates to x production. This final term occurs because of the need to consider the externality from x production. If g_2 were zero, then Equations 19.11 and 19.12 would represent essentially the same condition for efficient production, which would apply to both x and y. With the externality, however, determining an efficient level of x production is more complex.

Inefficiency of the competitive allocation

Reliance on competitive pricing in this simple model will result in an inefficient allocation of resources. With equilibrium prices p_x and p_y, a utility-maximizing individual would opt for

$$MRS = p_x/p_y \tag{19.13}$$

and the profit-maximizing producer of good y would choose x input according to

$$p_x = p_y g_1. \tag{19.14}$$

Hence the efficiency condition (Equation 19.11) would be satisfied. But the producer of good x would choose y input so that

$$p_y = p_x f_y \quad \text{or} \quad \frac{p_x}{p_y} = \frac{1}{f_y}. \tag{19.15}$$

That is, the producer of x would disregard the externality that its production poses for y and so the other efficiency condition (Equation 19.12) would not be met. This failure results in an overproduction of x relative to the efficient level. To see this, note that the marginal product of y in producing x (f_y) is smaller under the market allocation represented by Equation 19.15 than under the optimal allocation represented by Equation 19.12. More y is used to produce x in the market allocation (and hence more x is produced) than is optimal. Example 19.1 provides a quantitative example of this nonoptimality in a partial equilibrium context.

EXAMPLE 19.1 Production Externalities

As a partial equilibrium illustration of the losses from failure to consider production externalities, suppose two newsprint producers are located along a river. The upstream firm (x) has a production function of the form

$$x = 2{,}000 l_x^{1/2}, \tag{19.16}$$

where l_x is the number of workers hired per day and x is newsprint output in feet. The downstream firm (y) has a similar production function, but its output may be affected by the chemicals firm x pours into the river:

$$y = \begin{cases} 2{,}000 l_y^{1/2}(x - x_0)^a & \text{for } x > x_0, \\ 2{,}000 l_y^{1/2} & \text{for } x \le x_0, \end{cases} \tag{19.17}$$

where x_0 represents the river's natural capacity for neutralizing pollutants. If $\alpha = 0$ then x's production process has no effect on firm y, but if $\alpha < 0$, an increase in x above x_0 causes y's output to decline.

Assuming newsprint sells for \$1 per foot and workers earn \$50 per day, firm x will maximize profits by setting this wage equal to labor's marginal revenue product:

$$50 = p \cdot \frac{\partial x}{\partial l_x} = 1{,}000 l_x^{-1/2}. \tag{19.18}$$

The solution then is $l_x = 400$. If $\alpha = 0$ (there are no externalities), firm y will also hire 400 workers. Each firm will produce 40,000 feet of newsprint.

Effects of an externality. When firm x does have a negative externality ($\alpha < 0$), its profit-maximizing hiring decision is not affected—it will still hire $l_x = 400$ and produce $x = 40{,}000$. But for firm y, labor's marginal product will be lower because of this externality. If $\alpha = -0.1$ and $x_0 = 38{,}000$, for example, then profit maximization will require

$$50 = p \cdot \frac{\partial y}{\partial l_y} = 1{,}000 l_y^{-1/2}(x - 38{,}000)^{-0.1}$$

$$= 1{,}000 l_y^{-1/2}(2{,}000)^{-0.1}$$

$$= 468 l_y^{-1/2}. \tag{19.19}$$

Solving this equation for l_y shows that firm y now hires only 87 workers because of this lowered productivity. Output of firm y will now be

$$y = 2,000(87)^{1/2}(2,000)^{-0.1} = 8,723. \qquad \textbf{(19.20)}$$

Because of the externality ($\alpha = -0.1$), newsprint output will be lower than without the externality ($\alpha = 0$).

Inefficiency. We can demonstrate that decentralized profit maximization is inefficient in this situation by imagining that firms x and y merge and that the manager must decide how to allocate the combined workforce. If one worker is transferred from firm x to firm y, then x output becomes

$$x = 2,000(399)^{1/2}$$
$$= 39,950; \qquad \textbf{(19.21)}$$

for firm y,

$$y = 2,000(88)^{1/2}(1,950)^{-0.1}$$
$$= 8,796. \qquad \textbf{(19.22)}$$

Total output has increased by 23 feet of newsprint with no change in total labor input. The market-based allocation was inefficient because firm x did not take into account the negative effect of its hiring decisions on firm y.

Marginal productivity. This can be illustrated in another way by computing the true social marginal productivity of labor input to firm x. If that firm were to hire one more worker, its own output would rise to

$$x = 2,000(401)^{1/2} = 40,050. \qquad \textbf{(19.23)}$$

As profit maximization requires, the (private) marginal value product of the 401st worker is equal to the wage. But increasing x's output now also has an effect on firm y—its output declines by about 21 units. Hence, the social marginal revenue product of labor to firm x actually amounts to only \$29 (\$50 − \$21). That is why the manager of a merged firm would find it profitable to shift some workers from firm x to firm y.

QUERY: Suppose $\alpha = +0.1$. What would that imply about the relationship between the firms? How would such an externality affect the allocation of labor?

SOLUTIONS TO THE EXTERNALITY PROBLEM

Incentive-based solutions to the allocational harm of externalities start from the basic observation that output of the externality-producing activity is too high under a market-determined equilibrium. Perhaps the first economist to provide a complete analysis of this distortion was A. C. Pigou, who in the 1920s suggested that the most direct solution would simply be to tax the externality-creating entity.[4] All incentive-based[5] solutions to the externality problem stem from this basic insight.

---

[4]A. C. Pigou, *The Economics of Welfare* (London: MacMillan, 1920). Pigou also recognized the importance of subsidizing goods that yield positive externalities.

[5]We do not discuss purely regulatory solutions here, although the study of such solutions forms an important part of most courses in environmental economics. See W. J. Baumol and W. E. Oates, *The Theory of Environmental Policy*, 2nd ed. (Cambridge: Cambridge University Press, 2005) and the Extensions to this chapter.

A graphic analysis

Figure 19.1 provides the traditional illustration of an externality together with Pigou's taxation solution. The competitive supply curve for good x also represents that good's private marginal costs of production (MC). When the demand for x is given by DD, the market equilibrium will occur at x_1. The external costs involved in x production create a divergence between private marginal costs (MC) and overall social marginal costs (MC')—the vertical distance between the two curves represents the costs that x production poses for third parties (in our examples, only on firm y). Notice that the per-unit costs of these externalities need not be constant, independent of x-output. In the figure, for example, the size of these external costs rises as x output expands (that is, MC' and MC become further apart). At the market-determined output level x_1, the comprehensive social marginal cost exceeds the market price p_1, thereby indicating that the production of x has been pushed "too far." It is clear from the figure that the optimal output level is x_2, at which the market price p_2 paid for the good now reflects all costs.

As is the case for any tax, imposition of a Pigovian tax would create a vertical wedge between the demand and supply curves for good x. In Figure 19.1 this optimal tax is shown as t. Imposition of this tax serves to reduce output to x_2, the social optimum. Tax collections equal the precise amount of external harm that x production causes. These collections might be used to compensate firm y for these costs, but this is not crucial to the analysis. Notice here that the tax must be set at the level of harm prevailing at the optimum (that is, at x_2), not at the level of harm at the original market equilibrium (x_1). This point is also made in the next example and more completely in the next section by returning to our simple general equilibrium model.

FIGURE 19.1   Graphic Analysis of an Externality

The demand curve for good x is given by DD. The supply curve for x represents the private marginal costs (MC) involved in x production. If x production imposes external costs on third parties, social marginal costs (MC') will exceed MC by the extent of these costs. Market equilibrium occurs at x_1 and, at this output level, social marginal costs exceed what consumers pay for good x. A tax of amount t that reflects the costs of the externalities would achieve the efficient output of x—given by output level x_2.

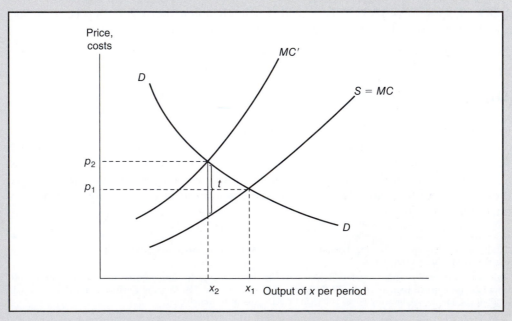

EXAMPLE 19.2 A Pigovian Tax on Newsprint

The inefficiency in Example 19.1 arises because the upstream newsprint producer (firm x) takes no account of the effect that its production has on firm y. A suitably chosen tax on firm x can cause it to reduce its hiring to a level at which the externality vanishes. Because the river can absorb the pollutants generated with an output of $x = 38{,}000$, we might consider imposing a tax (t) on the firm's output that encourages it to reduce output to this level. Because output will be 38,000 if $l_x = 361$, we can calculate t from the labor demand condition:

$$(1 - t)MP_L = (1 - t)1{,}000(361)^{-0.5} = 50, \tag{19.24}$$

or

$$t = 0.05. \tag{19.25}$$

Such a 5 percent tax would effectively reduce the price firm x receives for its newsprint to $0.95 and provide it with an incentive to reduce its hiring by 39 workers. Now, because the river can handle all the pollutants that x produces, there is no externality in the production function of firm y. It will hire 400 workers and produce 40,000 feet of newsprint per day. Observe that total newsprint output is now 78,000, a significantly higher figure than would be produced in the untaxed situation. The taxation solution provides a considerable improvement in the efficiency of resource allocation.

QUERY: The tax rate proposed here (0.05) seems rather small given the significant output gains obtained relative to the situation in Example 19.1. Can you explain why? Would a merged firm opt for $x = 38{,}000$ even without a tax?

Taxation in the general equilibrium model

The optimal Pigovian tax in our general equilibrium model is to set $t = -p_y g_2$. That is, the per-unit tax on good x should reflect the marginal harm that x does in reducing y output, valued at the market price of good y. Notice again that this tax must be based on the value of this externality at the optimal solution; because g_2 will generally be a function of the level of x output, a tax based on some other output level would be inappropriate. With the optimal tax, firm x now faces a net price for its output of $p_x - t$ and will choose y input according to

$$p_y = (p_x - t)f_y. \tag{19.26}$$

Hence the resulting allocation of resources will achieve

$$MRS = \frac{p_x}{p_y} = \frac{1}{f_y} + \frac{t}{p_y} = \frac{1}{f_y} - g_2, \tag{19.27}$$

which is precisely what is required for optimality (compare to the efficiency condition, Equation 19.12). The Pigovian taxation solution can be generalized in a variety of ways that provide insights about the conduct of policy toward externalities. For example, in an economy with many x-producers, the tax would convey information about the marginal impact that output from any one of these would have on y output. Hence the tax scheme mitigates the need for regulatory attention to the specifics of any particular firm. It does require that regulators have enough information to set taxes appropriately—that is, they must know firm y's production function.

Pollution rights

An innovation that would mitigate the informational requirements involved with Pigovian taxation is the creation of a market for "pollution rights." Suppose, for example, that firm x must purchase from firm y rights to pollute the river they share. In this case, x's decision to purchase these rights is identical to its decision to choose its output level, because it cannot produce without them. The net revenue x receives per unit is given by $p_x - r$, where r is the payment the firm must make for each unit it produces. Firm y must decide how many rights to sell to firm x. Because it will be paid r for each right, it must "choose" x output to maximize its profits:

$$\pi_y = p_y g(x_i, x_0) + rx_0; \tag{19.28}$$

the first-order condition for a maximum is

$$\frac{\partial \pi_y}{\partial x_0} = p_y g_2 + r = 0 \quad \text{or} \quad r = -p_y g_2. \tag{19.29}$$

Equation 19.29 makes clear that the equilibrium solution to pricing in the pollution rights market will be identical to the Pigovian tax equilibrium. From the point of view of firm x it makes no difference whether a tax of amount t is paid to the government or a royalty r of the same amount is paid to firm y. So long as $t = r$ (a condition ensured by Equation 19.29), the same efficient equilibrium will result.

The Coase theorem

In a famous 1960 paper, Ronald Coase showed that the key feature of the pollution rights equilibrium is that these rights be well defined and tradable with zero transaction costs.[6] The initial assignment of rights is irrelevant because subsequent trading will always yield the same efficient equilibrium. In our example we initially assigned the rights to firm y, allowing that firm to trade them away to firm x for a per-unit fee r. If the rights had been assigned to firm x instead, that firm still would have to impute some cost to using these rights themselves rather than selling them to firm y. This calculation, in combination with firm y's decision about how many such rights to buy, will again yield an efficient result.

To illustrate the Coase result, assume that firm x is given x^T rights to produce (and to pollute). It can choose to use some of these to support its own production (x_0), or it may sell some to firm y (an amount given by $x^T - x_0$). Gross profits for x are given by

$$\pi_x = p_x x_0 + r(x^T - x_0) = (p_x - r)x_0 + rx^T = (p_x - r)f(y_i) + rx^T \tag{19.30}$$

and for y by

$$\pi_y = p_y g(x_i, x_0) - r(x^T - x_0). \tag{19.31}$$

Clearly, profit maximization in this situation will lead to precisely the same solution as in the case where firm y was assigned the rights. Because the overall total number of rights (x^T) is a constant, the first-order conditions for a maximum will be exactly the same in the two cases. This independence of initial rights assignment is usually referred to as the *Coase theorem*.

Although the results of the Coase theorem may seem counterintuitive (how can the level of pollution be independent of who initially owns the rights?), it is in reality nothing more than the assertion that, in the absence of impediments to making bargains, all mutually beneficial transactions will be completed. When transaction costs are high or when information is asymmetric, initial rights assignments *will* matter because the sorts of trading implied by the Coase theorem may not occur. It is therefore the limitations of the Coase theorem that provide the most interesting opportunities for further analysis. This analysis has been especially far reaching in the field of law and economics,[7] where the theorem has been

---

[6]R. Coase, "The Problem of Social Cost," *Journal of Law and Economics* 3 (October 1960): 1–44.

[7]The classic text is R. A. Posner, *Economic Analysis of Law*, 4th ed. (Boston: Little, Brown, 1992). A more mathematical approach is T. J. Miceli, *Economics of the Law* (New York: Oxford University Press, 1997).

applied to such topics as tort liability laws, contract law, and product safety legislation (see Problem 19.4).

ATTRIBUTES OF PUBLIC GOODS

We now turn our attention to a related set of problems about the relationship between competitive markets and the allocation of resources: those raised by the existence of public goods. We begin by providing a precise definition of this concept and then examine why such goods pose allocational problems. We then briefly discuss theoretical ways in which such problems might be mitigated before turning to examine how actual decisions on public goods are made through voting.

The most common definitions of public goods stress two attributes of such goods: nonexclusivity and nonrivalness. We now describe these attributes in detail.

Nonexclusivity

The first property that distinguishes public goods concerns whether individuals may be excluded from the benefits of consuming the good. For most private goods such exclusion is indeed possible: I can easily be excluded from consuming a hamburger if I don't pay for it. In some cases, however, such exclusion is either very costly or impossible. National defense is the standard example. Once a defense system is established, everyone in a country benefits from it whether they pay for it or not. Similar comments apply, on a more local level, to goods such as mosquito control or a program to inoculate against disease. In these cases, once the programs are implemented, no one in the community can be excluded from those benefits whether he or she pays for them or not. Hence, we can divide goods into two categories according to the following definition.

Exclusive goods. A good is *exclusive* if it is relatively easy to exclude individuals from benefiting from the good once it is produced. A good is *nonexclusive* if it is impossible (or costly) to exclude individuals from benefiting from the good.

DEFINITION

Nonrivalry

A second property that characterizes public goods is nonrivalry. A nonrival good is one for which additional units can be consumed at zero social marginal cost. For most goods, of course, consumption of additional amounts involves some marginal costs of production. Consumption of one more hot dog requires that various resources be devoted to its production. However, for certain goods this is not the case. Consider, for example, having one more automobile cross a highway bridge during an off-peak period. Because the bridge is already in place, having one more vehicle cross requires no additional resource use and does not reduce consumption elsewhere. Similarly, having one more viewer tune in to a television channel involves no additional cost, even though this action would result in additional consumption taking place. Therefore, we have developed the following definition.

Nonrival goods. A good is *nonrival* if consumption of additional units of the good involves zero social marginal costs of production.

DEFINITION

Typology of public goods

The concepts of nonexclusion and nonrivalry are in some ways related. Many nonexclusive goods are also nonrival. National defense and mosquito control are two examples of goods for which exclusion is not possible and additional consumption takes place at zero marginal cost. Many other instances might be suggested. The concepts, however, are not identical: some goods may possess

TABLE 19.1 Examples Showing the Typology of Public and Private Goods

		Exclusive	
		Yes	No
Rival	Yes	Hot dogs, automobiles, houses	Fishing grounds, public grazing land, clean air
	No	Bridges, swimming pools, satellite television transmission (scrambled)	National defense, mosquito control, justice

one property but not the other. For example, it is impossible (or at least very costly) to exclude some fishing boats from ocean fisheries, yet the arrival of another boat clearly imposes social costs in the form of a reduced catch for all concerned. Similarly, use of a bridge during off-peak hours may be nonrival, but it is possible to exclude potential users by erecting toll booths. Table 19.1 presents a cross-classification of goods by their possibilities for exclusion and their rivalry. Several examples of goods that fit into each of the categories are provided. Many of the examples, other than those in the upper left corner of the table (exclusive and rival private goods), are often produced by governments. That is especially the case for nonexclusive goods because, as we shall see, it is difficult to develop ways of paying for such goods other than through compulsory taxation. Nonrival goods often are privately produced (there are, after all, private bridges, swimming pools, and highways that consumers must pay to use) as long as nonpayers can be excluded from consuming them.[8] Still, we will use the following stringent definition, which requires both conditions.

DEFINITION | **Public good.** A good is a (pure) *public good* if, once produced, no one can be excluded from benefiting from its availability and if the good is nonrival—the marginal cost of an additional consumer is zero.

PUBLIC GOODS AND RESOURCE ALLOCATION

To illustrate the allocational problems created by public goods, we again employ a simple general equilibrium model. In this model there are only two individuals—a single-person economy would not experience problems from public goods because he or she would incorporate all of the goods' benefits into consumption decisions. We denote these two individuals by A and B. There are also only two goods in this economy. Good y is an ordinary private good, and each person begins with an allocation of this good given by y^{A*} and y^{B*}, respectively. Each person may choose to consume some of his or her y directly or to devote some portion of it to the production of a single public good, x. The amounts contributed are given by y_s^A and y_s^B, and the public good is produced according to the production function

$$x = f(y_s^A + y_s^B). \tag{19.32}$$

Resulting utilities for these two people in this society are given by

$$U^A[(x, (y^{A*} - y_s^A)] \tag{19.33}$$

---

[8]Nonrival goods that permit imposition of an exclusion mechanism are sometimes referred to as *club goods*, because provision of such goods might be organized along the lines of private clubs. Such clubs might then charge a "membership" fee and permit unlimited use by members. The optimal size of a club is determined by the economies of scale present in the production process for the club good. For an analysis, see R. Cornes and T. Sandler, *The Theory of Externalities, Public Goods, and Club Goods* (Cambridge: Cambridge University Press, 1986).

and

$$U^B[(x, (y^{B*} - y_s^B)].$$ (19.34)

Notice here that the level of public good production, x, enters identically into each person's utility function. This is the way in which the nonexclusivity and nonrivalry characteristics of such goods are captured mathematically. Nonexclusivity is reflected by the fact that each person's consumption of x is the same and independent of what he or she contributes individually to its production. Nonrivalry is shown by the fact that the consumption of x by each person is identical to the total amount of x produced. Consumption of x benefits by A does not diminish what B can consume. These two characteristics of good x constitute the barriers to efficient production under most decentralized decision schemes, including competitive markets.

The necessary conditions for efficient resource allocation in this problem consist of choosing the levels of public goods subscriptions (y_s^A and y_s^B) that maximize, say, A's utility for any given level of B's utility. The Lagrangian expression for this problem is

$$\mathcal{L} = U^A(x, y^{A*} - y_s^A) + \lambda[U^B(x, y^{B*} - y_s^B) - K],$$ (19.35)

where K is a constant level of B's utility. The first-order conditions for a maximum are

$$\frac{\partial \mathcal{L}}{\partial y_s^A} = U_1^A f' - U_2^A + \lambda U_1^B f' = 0,$$ (19.36)

$$\frac{\partial \mathcal{L}}{\partial y_s^B} = U_1^A f' - \lambda U_2^B + \lambda U_1^B f' = 0.$$ (19.37)

A comparison of these two equations yields the immediate result that

$$\lambda U_2^B = U_2^A.$$ (19.38)

As might have been expected here, optimality requires that the marginal utility of y consumption for A and B be equal except for the constant of proportionality, λ. This equation may now be combined with either Equation 19.36 or 19.37 to derive the optimality condition for producing the public good x. Using Equation 19.36, for example, gives

$$\frac{U_1^A}{U_2^A} + \frac{\lambda U_1^B}{\lambda U_2^B} = \frac{1}{f'}$$ (19.39)

or, more simply,

$$MRS^A + MRS^B = \frac{1}{f'}.$$ (19.40)

The intuition behind this condition, which was first articulated by P. A. Samuelson,[9] is that it is an adaptation of the efficiency conditions described in Chapter 13 to the case of public goods. For such goods, the MRS in consumption must reflect the amount of y that *all* consumers would be willing to give up to get one more x, because everyone will obtain the benefits of the extra x output. Hence it is the sum of each individual's MRS that should be equated to dy/dx in production (here given by $1/f'$).

Failure of a competitive market

Production of goods x and y in competitive markets will fail to achieve this allocational goal. With perfectly competitive prices p_x and p_y, each individual will equate his or her MRS to the price ratio p_x/p_y. A producer of good x would also set $1/f'$ to be equal to p_x/p_y, as would be

---

[9]P. A. Samuelson, "The Pure Theory of Public Expenditure," *Review of Economics and Statistics* (November 1954): 387–89.

FIGURE 19.2 Derivation of the Demand for a Public Good

For a public good, the price individuals are willing to pay for one more unit (their "marginal valuations") is equal to the sum of what each individual would pay. Hence, for public goods, the demand curve must be derived by a vertical summation rather than the horizontal summation used in the case of private goods.

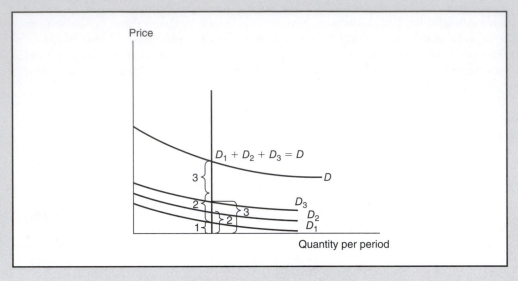

required for profit maximization. This behavior would not achieve the optimality condition expressed in Equation 19.40. The price ratio p_x/p_y would be "too low" in that it would provide too little incentive to produce good x. In the private market, a consumer takes no account of how his or her spending on the public good benefits others, so that consumer will devote too few resources to such production.

The allocational failure in this situation can be ascribed to the way in which private markets sum individual demands. For any given quantity, the market demand curve reports the marginal valuation of a good. If one more unit were produced, it could then be consumed by someone who would value it at this market price. For public goods, the value of producing one more unit is in fact the sum of each consumer's valuation of that extra output, because all consumers will benefit from it. In this case, then, individual demand curves should be added vertically (as shown in Figure 19.2) rather then horizontally (as they are in competitive markets). The resulting price on such a public good demand curve will then reflect, for any level of output, how much an extra unit of output would be valued by all consumers. But the usual market demand curve will not properly reflect this full marginal valuation.

Inefficiency of a Nash equilibrium

An alternative approach to the production of public goods in competitive markets might rely on individuals' voluntary contributions. Unfortunately, this also will yield inefficient results. Consider the situation of person A, who is thinking about contributing s_A of his or her initial y endowment to public goods production. The utility maximization problem for A is then

$$\text{choose } s_A \text{ to maximize } U^A[f(s_A + s_B), y^{A*} - s_A]. \qquad (19.41)$$

The first-order condition for a maximum is

$$U_1^A f' - U_2^A = 0 \quad \text{or} \quad \frac{U_1^A}{U_2^A} = MRS^A = \frac{1}{f'}. \tag{19.42}$$

Because a similar logic will apply to person B, efficiency condition 19.40 will once more fail to be satisfied. Again the problem is that each person considers only his or her benefit from investing in the public good, taking no account of the benefits provided to others. With many consumers, this direct benefit may be very small indeed. (For example, how much do one person's taxes contribute to national defense in the United States?) In this case, any one person may opt for $s_A = 0$ and become a pure "free rider," hoping to benefit from the expenditures of others. If every person adopts this strategy, then no resources will be subscribed to public goods. Example 19.3 illustrates the free-rider problem in a situation that may be all too familiar.

EXAMPLE 19.3 Purchasing a Public Good: The Roommates' Dilemma

To illustrate the nature of the public goods problem numerically, suppose two Bohemian roommates with identical preferences derive utility from the number of paintings hung on their hovel's walls (x) and on the number of granola bars (y) they eat. The specific form of the utility function is given by

$$U_i(x, y_i) = x^{1/3} y_i^{2/3} \quad \text{for } i = 1, 2. \tag{19.43}$$

Observe that utility for each person depends on the total number of paintings hung and on the number of granola bars each person consumes individually. Hence, in this problem the enjoyment of paintings constitutes a public good.

If we assume that each roommate has $300 to spend and that $p_x = \$100$ and $p_y = \$0.20$, then we can explore the consequences of various expenditure allocations. We know from previous Cobb-Douglas examples that, if each person lived alone, each would spend $\frac{1}{3}$ of his or her income on paintings ($x = 1$) and $\frac{2}{3}$ on granola bars ($y = 1,000$).

Public goods provision and strategy. When the roommates live together, however, each must think about what the other will do. Each could, for example, assume that the other will buy the paintings. In this case $x = 0$ and both people end up with a zero utility level. Alternatively, person 1 might assume that person 2 will buy no paintings. If that proves to be the case, then person 1 would choose to purchase a painting and receive a utility of

$$U_1(x, y_1) = 1^{1/3}(1,000)^{2/3} = 100; \tag{19.44}$$

person 2's utility would then be

$$U_2(X, Y_2) = 1^{1/3}(1,500)^{2/3} = 131. \tag{19.45}$$

Clearly, person 2 has gained from his or her free-rider position. Person 1's purchases provide an externality to person 2. Of course, person 2's purchases of paintings—should he or she choose to be socially conscious—would also provide an externality to person 1.

Inefficiency of allocation. That the solution obtained in Equations 19.44 and 19.45 (along with many other possibilities) is inefficient can be shown by calculating each person's marginal rate of substitution:

$$MRS_i = \frac{\partial U_i/\partial x}{\partial U_i/\partial y_i} = \frac{y_i}{2x}. \tag{19.46}$$

(continued)

EXAMPLE 19.3   CONTINUED

Hence, at the allocations described,

$$MRS_1 = \frac{1,000}{2} = 500,$$

$$MRS_2 = \frac{1,500}{2} = 750.$$

(19.47)

The roommates in total would be willing to sacrifice 1,250 granola bars for one more painting—a sacrifice that would actually cost them only 500 bars combined. Relying on decentralized decision making in this case is inefficient—too few paintings are bought.

An efficient allocation. To calculate the efficient level of painting purchases, we must set the sum of each person's MRS equal to the goods' price ratio, because such a sum correctly reflects the trade-offs the roommates living together would make:

$$MRS_1 + MRS_2 = \frac{y_1}{2x} + \frac{y_2}{2x} = \frac{y_1 + y_2}{2x} = \frac{p_x}{p_y} = \frac{100}{0.20}.$$

(19.48)

Consequently,

$$y_1 + y_2 = 1,000x,$$

(19.49)

which can be substituted into the combined budget constraint

$$0.20(y_1 + y_2) + 100x = 600$$

(19.50)

to obtain

$$x = 2,$$
$$y_1 + y_2 = 2,000.$$

(19.51)

Allocating the cost of paintings. Assuming the roommates split the cost of the two paintings and use their remaining funds to buy granola bars, each will finally receive a utility of

$$U_i = 2^{1/3}1,000^{2/3} = 126.$$

(19.52)

Although person 1 may not be able to coerce person 2 into such a joint sharing of cost, a 75–25 split provides a utility of

$$U_1 = 2^{1/3}750^{2/3} = 104,$$
$$U_2 = 2^{1/3}1,250^{2/3} = 146,$$

(19.53)

which is Pareto superior to the solution obtained when person 1 acts alone. Many other financing schemes would also yield allocations that are Pareto superior to those discussed previously. Which of these, if any, might be chosen depends on how well each roommate plays the strategic financing game.

QUERY: Show that, in this example, an efficient solution would be obtained if two people living separately decided to live together and pool their paintings. Would you expect that result to hold generally?

LINDAHL PRICING OF PUBLIC GOODS

An important conceptual solution to the public goods problem was first suggested by the Swedish economist Erik Lindahl[10] in the 1920s. Lindahl's basic insight was that individuals

---

[10]Excerpts from Lindahl's writings are contained in R. A. Musgrave and A. T. Peacock, Eds., *Classics in the Theory of Public Finance* (London: Macmillan, 1958).

might voluntarily consent to be taxed for beneficial public goods if they knew that others were also being taxed. Specifically, Lindahl assumed that each individual would be presented by the government with the proportion of a public good's cost he or she would be expected to pay and then reply (honestly) with the level of public good output he or she would prefer. In the notation of our simple general equilibrium model, individual A would be quoted a specific percentage (α^A) and then asked the level of public goods that he or she would want given the knowledge that this fraction of total cost would have to be paid. To answer that question (truthfully), this person would choose that overall level of public goods output, x, that maximizes

$$\text{utility} = U^A[x, y^{A*} - \alpha^A f^{-1}(x)]. \tag{19.54}$$

The first-order condition for this utility-maximizing choice of x is given by

$$U_1^A - \alpha U_2^B\left(\frac{1}{f'}\right) = 0 \quad \text{or} \quad MRS^A = \frac{\alpha^A}{f'}. \tag{19.55}$$

Individual B, presented with a similar choice, would opt for a level of public goods satisfying

$$MRS^B = \frac{\alpha^B}{f'}. \tag{19.56}$$

An equilibrium would then occur where $\alpha^A + \alpha^B = 1$—that is, where the level of public goods expenditure favored by the two individuals precisely generates enough in tax contributions to pay for it. For in that case

$$MRS^A + MRS^B = \frac{\alpha^A + \alpha^B}{f'} = \frac{1}{f'}, \tag{19.57}$$

and this equilibrium would be efficient (see Equation 19.40). Hence, at least on a conceptual level, the Lindahl approach solves the public good problem. Presenting each person with the equilibrium tax share "price" will lead him or her to opt for the efficient level of public goods production.

EXAMPLE 19.4 A Lindahl Solution for the Roommates

Lindahl pricing provides a conceptual solution to the roommates' problem of buying paintings in Example 19.3. If "the government" (or perhaps social convention) suggests that each roommate will pay half of painting purchases, then each would face an effective price of paintings of $50. Since the utility functions for the roommates imply that a third of each person's total income of $300 will be spent on paintings, it follows that each will be willing to spend $100 on such art and will, if each is honest, report that he or she would like to have two paintings. Hence the solution will be $x = 2$ and $y_1 = y_2 = 1,000$. This is indeed the efficient solution calculated in Example 19.3. The problem with this solution, of course, is that neither roommate has an incentive to truthfully report what his or her demand is for public goods given the Lindahl price. Rather, each will know that he or she would be better off by following one of the free-rider scenarios laid out in Example 19.3. As in the Prisoners' Dilemma studied in Chapter 8, the Lindahl solution—though Pareto optimal—is not a stable equilibrium.

QUERY: Although the 50–50 sharing in this example might arise from social custom, in fact the optimality of such a split is a special feature of this problem. What is it about this problem that leads to such a Lindahl outcome? Under what conditions would Lindahl prices result in other than a 50–50 sharing?

Shortcomings of the Lindahl solution

Unfortunately, Lindahl's solution is only a conceptual one. We have already seen in our examination of the Nash equilibrium for public goods production and in our roommates' example that the incentive to be a free rider in the public goods case is very strong. This fact makes it difficult to envision how the information necessary to compute equilibrium Lindahl shares might be obtained. Because individuals know their tax shares will be based on their reported demands for public goods, they have a clear incentive to understate their true preferences—in so doing they hope that the "other guy" will pay. Hence, simply asking people about their demands for public goods should not be expected to reveal their true demands. It also appears to be difficult to design truth-revealing voting mechanisms—for reasons we will examine in the next chapter. In general, then, Lindahl's solution remains a tantalizing but not readily achievable target.

Local public goods

Some economists believe that demand revelation for public goods may be more tractable at the local level.[11] Because there are many communities in which individuals might reside, they can indicate their preferences for public goods (that is, for their willingness to pay Lindahl tax shares) by choosing where to live. If a particular tax burden is not utility maximizing then people can, in principle, "vote with their feet" and move to a community that does provide optimality. Hence, with perfect information, zero costs of mobility, and enough communities, the Lindahl solution may be implemented at the local level. Similar arguments apply to other types of organizations (such as private clubs) that provide public goods to their members; given a sufficiently wide spectrum of club offerings, an efficient equilibrium might result. Of course, the assumptions that underlie the purported efficiency of such choices by individuals are quite strict. Even minor relaxation of these assumptions may yield inefficient results owing to the fragile nature of the way in which the demand for public goods is revealed.

EXAMPLE 19.5 The Relationship between Environmental Externalities and Public Goods Production

In recent years, economists have begun to study the relationship between the two issues we have been discussing in this chapter: externalities and public goods. The basic insight from this examination is that one must take a general equilibrium view of these problems in order to identify solutions that are efficient overall. Here we illustrate this point by returning to the computable general equilibrium model firms described in Chapter 13 (see Example 13.4). To simplify matters we will now assume that this economy includes only a single representative person whose utility function is given by

$$\text{utility} = U(x, y, l, g, c) = x^{0.5} y^{0.3} l^{0.2} g^{0.1} c^{0.2}, \qquad \textbf{(19.58)}$$

where we have added terms for the utility provided by public goods (g), which are initially financed by a tax on labor, and by clean air (c). Production of the public good requires capital and labor input according to the production function $g = k^{0.5} l^{0.5}$; there is an externality in the production of good y, so that the quantity of clean air is given by $c = 10 - 0.2y$. The production functions for goods x and y remain as described in Example 13.4, as do the endowments of k and l. Hence, our goal is to allocate resources in such a way that utility is maximized.

Base case: Optimal public goods production with no Pigovian tax. If no attempt is made to control the externality in this problem, then the optimal level of public goods production

---

[11]The classic reference is C. M. Tiebout, "A Pure Theory of Local Expenditures," *Journal of Political Economy* (October 1956): 416–24.

requires $g = 2.93$ and this is financed by a tax rate of 0.25 on labor. Output of good y in this case is 29.7, and the quantity of clean air is given by $c = 10 - 5.94 = 4.06$. Overall utility in this situation is $U = 19.34$. This is the highest utility that can be obtained in this situation without regulating the externality.

A Pigovian tax. As suggested by Figure 19.1, a unit tax on the production of good y may improve matters in this situation. With a tax rate of 0.1, for example, output of good y is reduced to $y = 27.4$ ($c = 10 - 5.48 = 4.52$), and the revenue generated is used to expand public goods production to $g = 3.77$. Utility is raised to $U = 19.38$. By carefully specifying how the revenue generated by the Pigovian tax is used, a general equilibrium model permits a more complete statement of welfare effects.

The "double dividend" of environmental taxes. The solution just described is not optimal, however. Production of public goods is actually too high in this case, since the revenues from environmental taxes are also used to pay for public goods. In fact, simulations show that optimality can be achieved by reducing the labor tax to 0.20 and public goods production to $g = 3.31$. With these changes, utility expands even further to $U = 19.43$. This result is sometimes referred to as the "double dividend" of environmental taxation: not only do these taxes reduce externalities relative to the untaxed situation (now $c = 10 - 5.60 = 4.40$), but also the extra governmental revenue made available thereby may permit the reduction of other distorting taxes.

QUERY: Why does the quantity of clean air decline slightly when the labor tax is reduced relative to the situation where it is maintained at 0.25? More generally, describe whether environmental taxes would be expected always to generate a double dividend.

VOTING AND RESOURCE ALLOCATION

Voting is used as a social decision process in many institutions. In some instances, individuals vote directly on policy questions. That is the case in some New England town meetings, many statewide referenda (for example, California's Proposition 13 in 1977), and for many of the national policies adopted in Switzerland. Direct voting also characterizes the social decision procedure used for many smaller groups and clubs such as farmers' cooperatives, university faculties, or the local Rotary Club. In other cases, however, societies have found it more convenient to use a representative form of government, in which individuals vote directly only for political representatives, who are then charged with making decisions on policy questions. For our study of public choice theory, we will begin with an analysis of direct voting. This is an important subject not only because such a procedure applies to many cases but also because elected representatives often engage in direct voting (in Congress, for example), and the theory we will illustrate applies to those instances as well.

Majority rule

Because so many elections are conducted on a majority rule basis, we often tend to regard that procedure as a natural and, perhaps, optimal one for making social choices. But even a cursory examination indicates that there is nothing particularly sacred about a rule requiring that a policy obtain 50 percent of the vote to be adopted. In the U.S. Constitution, for example, two thirds of the states must adopt an amendment before it becomes law. And 60 percent of the U.S. Senate must vote to limit debate on controversial issues. Indeed, in some institutions (Quaker meetings, for example), unanimity may be required for social decisions. Our discussion of the Lindahl equilibrium concept suggests there may exist a distribution of tax shares

TABLE 19.2   Preferences That Produce the Paradox of Voting

Preferences	Choices: A—Low Spending B—Medium Spending C—High Spending		
	Smith	Jones	Fudd
	A	B	C
	B	C	A
	C	A	B

that would obtain unanimous support in voting for public goods. But arriving at such unanimous agreements is usually thwarted by emergence of the free-rider problem. Examining in detail the forces that lead societies to move away from unanimity and to choose some other determining fraction would take us too far afield here. We instead will assume throughout our discussion of voting that decisions will be made by majority rule. Readers may wish to ponder for themselves what kinds of situations might call for a decisive proportion of other than 50 percent.

The paradox of voting

In the 1780s, the French social theorist M. de Condorcet observed an important peculiarity of majority rule voting systems—they may not arrive at an equilibrium but instead may cycle among alternative options. Condorcet's paradox is illustrated for a simple case in Table 19.2. Suppose there are three voters (Smith, Jones, and Fudd) choosing among three policy options. For our subsequent analysis we will assume the policy options represent three levels of spending (A low, B medium, or C high) on a particular public good, but Condorcet's paradox would arise even if the options being considered did not have this type of ordering associated with them. Preferences of Smith, Jones, and Fudd among the three policy options are indicated in Table 19.2. These preferences give rise to Condorcet's paradox.

Consider a vote between options A and B. Here option A would win, because it is favored by Smith and Fudd and opposed only by Jones. In a vote between options A and C, option C would win, again by 2 votes to 1. But in a vote of C versus B, B would win and we would be back where we started. Social choices would endlessly cycle among the three alternatives. In subsequent votes, any choice initially decided upon could be defeated by an alternative, and no equilibrium would ever be reached. In this situation, the option finally chosen will depend on such seemingly nongermane issues as when the balloting stops or how items are ordered on an agenda—rather than being derived in some rational way from the preferences of voters.

Single-peaked preferences and the median voter theorem

Condorcet's voting paradox arises because there is a degree of irreconcilability in the preferences of voters. One might therefore ask whether restrictions on the types of preferences allowed could yield situations where equilibrium voting outcomes are more likely. A fundamental result about this probability was discovered by Duncan Black in 1948.[12] Black showed that equilibrium

---

[12]D. Black, "On the Rationale of Group Decision Making," *Journal of Political Economy* (February 1948): 23–34.

FIGURE 19.3 Single-Peaked Preferences and the Median Voter Theorem

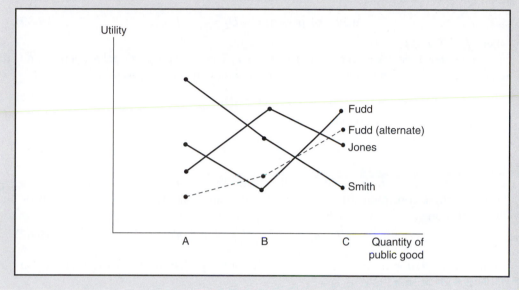

This figure illustrates the preferences in Table 19.2. Smith's and Jones's preferences are single peaked, but Fudd's have two local peaks and these yield the voting paradox. If Fudd's preferences had instead been single peaked (the dashed line), then option B would have been chosen as the preferred choice of the median voter (Jones).

voting outcomes always occur in cases where the issue being voted upon is one-dimensional (such as how much to spend on a public good) and where voters' preferences are "single peaked." To understand what the notion of single peaked means, consider again Condorcet's paradox. In Figure 19.3 we illustrate the preferences that gave rise to the paradox by assigning hypothetical utility levels to options A, B, and C that are consistent with the preferences recorded in Table 19.2. For Smith and Jones, preferences are single peaked: as levels of public goods expenditures rise, there is only one local utility-maximizing choice (A for Smith, B for Jones). Fudd's preferences, on the other hand, have two local maxima (A and C). It is these preferences that produced the cyclical voting pattern. If instead Fudd had the preferences represented by the dashed line in Figure 19.3 (where now C is the only local utility maximum), then there would be no paradox. In this case, option B would be chosen because that option would defeat both A and C by votes of 2 to 1. Here B is the preferred choice of the "median" voter (Jones), whose preferences are "between" the preferences of Smith and the revised preferences of Fudd.

Black's result is quite general and applies to any number of voters. If choices are unidimensional[13] and if preferences are single peaked, then majority rule will result in the selection of the project that is most favored by the median voter. Hence, that voter's preferences will determine what public choices are made. This result is a key starting point for many models of the political process. In such models, the median voter's preferences dictate policy choices—either because that voter determines which policy gets a majority of votes in a direct election or because the median voter will dictate choices in competitive elections in which candidates must adopt policies that appeal to this voter.

---

[13]The result can be generalized a bit to deal with multidimensional policies if individuals can be characterized in their support for such policies along a single dimension.

A SIMPLE POLITICAL MODEL

To illustrate how the median voter theorem is applied in political models, suppose a community is characterized by a large number (n) of voters each with an income given by y_i. The utility of each voter depends on his or her consumption of a private good (c_i) and of a public good (g) according to the additive utility function

$$\text{utility of person } i = U_i = c_i + f(g), \tag{19.59}$$

where $f_g > 0$ and $f_{gc} < 0$.

Each voter must pay income taxes to finance g. Taxes are proportional to income and are imposed at a rate t. Therefore, each person's budget constraint is given by

$$c_i = (1 - t)y_i. \tag{19.60}$$

The government is also bound by a budget constraint:

$$g = \sum_1^n ty_i = tny^A, \tag{19.61}$$

where y^A denotes average income for all voters.

Given these constraints, the utility of person i can be written as a function of his or her choice of g only:

$$U_i(g) = \left(y^A - \frac{g}{n}\right)\frac{y_i}{y^A} + f(g). \tag{19.62}$$

Utility maximization for person i shows that his or her preferred level of expenditures on the public good satisfies

$$\frac{dU_i}{dg} = -\frac{y_i}{ny^A} + f_g(g) = 0 \quad \text{or} \quad g = f_g^{-1}\left(\frac{y_i}{ny^A}\right). \tag{19.63}$$

This shows that desired spending on g is inversely related to income. Because (in this model) the benefits of g are independent of income but taxes increase with income, high-income voters can expect to have smaller net gains (or even losses) from public spending than can low-income voters.

The median voter equilibrium

If g is determined here through majority rule, its level will be chosen to be that level favored by the "mean voter." In this case, voters' preferences align exactly with incomes, so g will be set at that level preferred by the voter with median income (y^m). Any other level for g would not get 50 percent of the vote. Hence, equilibrium g is given by

$$g^* = f_g^{-1}\left(\frac{y^m}{ny^A}\right) = f_g^{-1}\left[\left(\frac{1}{n}\right)\left(\frac{y^m}{y^A}\right)\right]. \tag{19.64}$$

In general, the distribution of income is skewed to the right in practically every political jurisdiction in the world. With such an income distribution, $y^m < y^A$, and the difference between the two measures becomes larger the more skewed is the income distribution. Hence Equation 19.64 suggests that, ceteris paribus, the more unequal is the income distribution in a democracy, the higher will be tax rates and the greater will be spending on public goods. Similarly, laws that extend the vote to increasingly poor segments of the population can also be expected to increase such spending.

Optimality of the median voter result

Although the median voter theorem permits a number of interesting positive predictions about the outcome of voting, the normative significance of these results is more difficult to pinpoint. In this example, it is clear that the result does not replicate the Lindahl voluntary equilibrium—high-income voters would not voluntarily agree to the taxes imposed.[14] The result also does not necessarily correspond to any simple criterion for social welfare. For example, under a "utilitarian" social welfare criterion, g would be chosen so as to maximize the sum of utilities:

$$SW = \sum_1^n U_i = \sum\left[\left(y^A - \frac{g}{n}\right)\frac{y_i}{y^A} + f(g)\right] = ny^A - g + nf(g). \quad \text{(19.65)}$$

The optimal choice for g is then found by differentiation:

$$\frac{dSW}{dg} = -1 + nf_g = 0,$$

or

$$g^* = f_g^{-1}\left(\frac{1}{n}\right) = f_g^{-1}\left[\left(\frac{1}{n}\right)\left(\frac{y^A}{y^A}\right)\right], \quad \text{(19.66)}$$

which shows that a utilitarian choice would opt for the level of g favored by the voter with *average* income. That output of g would be smaller than that favored by the median voter because $y^m < y^A$. In Example 19.6 we take this analysis a bit further by showing how it might apply to governmental transfer policy.

EXAMPLE 19.6 Voting for Redistributive Taxation

Suppose voters were considering adoption of a lump-sum transfer to be paid to every person and financed through proportional taxation. If we denote the per-person transfer by b, then each individual's utility is now given by

$$U_i = c_i + b \quad \text{(19.67)}$$

and the government budget constraint is

$$nb = tny^A \quad \text{or} \quad b = ty^A. \quad \text{(19.68)}$$

For a voter whose income is greater than average, utility would be maximized by choosing $b = 0$, because such a voter would pay more in taxes than he or she would receive from the transfer. Any voter with less than average income will gain from the transfer no matter what the tax rate is. Hence such voters (including the decisive median voter) will opt for $t = 1$ and $b = y^A$. That is, they would vote to fully equalize incomes through the tax system. Of course, such a tax scheme is unrealistic—primarily because a 100 percent tax rate would undoubtedly create negative work incentives that reduce average income.

To capture such incentive effects, assume[15] that each person's income has two components, one responsive to tax rates $[y_i(t)]$ and one not responsive (n_i). Assume also that the average value of n_i is 0 but that its distribution is skewed to the right, so $n_m < 0$. Now utility is given by

$$U_i = (1 - t)[y_i(t) + n_i] + b. \quad \text{(19.69)}$$

Assuming that each person first optimizes over those variables (such as labor supply) that affect $y_i(t)$, the first-order condition[16] for a maximum in his or her political decisions about

(continued)

---

[14]Although they might if the benefits of g were also proportional to income.

[15]What follows represents a much simplified version of a model first developed by T. Romer in "Individual Welfare, Majority Voting, and the Properties of a Linear Income Tax," *Journal of Public Economics* (December 1978): 163–68.

[16]Equation 19.70 can be derived from 19.69 through differentiation and by recognizing that $dy_i/dt = 0$ because of the assumption of individual optimization.

EXAMPLE 19.6   CONTINUED

t and b then become (using the government budget constraint in Equation 19.68)

$$\frac{dU_i}{dt} = -n_i + t\,\frac{dy^A}{dt} = 0. \tag{19.70}$$

Hence for voter i the optimal redistributive tax rate is given by

$$t_i = \frac{n_i}{dy^A/dt}. \tag{19.71}$$

Assuming political competition under majority-rule voting will opt for that policy favored by the median voter, the equilibrium rate of taxation will be

$$t^* = \frac{n_m}{dy^A/dt}. \tag{19.72}$$

Because both n_m and dy^A/dt are negative, this rate of taxation will be positive. The optimal tax will be greater the farther n_m is from its average value (that is, the more unequally income is distributed). Similarly, the larger are distortionary effects from the tax, the smaller the optimal tax. This model then poses some rather strong testable hypotheses about redistribution in the real world.

QUERY: Would progressive taxation be more likely to raise or lower t^* in this model?

VOTING MECHANISMS

The problems involved in majority rule voting arise in part because such voting is simply not informative enough to provide accurate appraisals of how people value public goods. This situation is in some ways similar to some of the models of asymmetric information examined in the previous chapter. Here voters are more informed than is the government about the value they place on various tax-spending packages. Resource allocation would be improved if mechanisms could be developed that encourage people to be more accurate in what they reveal about these values. In this section we examine two such mechanisms. Both are based on the basic insight from Vickrey second-price auctions (see Chapter 18) that incorporating information about other bidders' valuations into decision makers' calculations can yield a greater likelihood of revealing truthful valuations.

The Groves mechanism

In a 1973 paper, T. Groves proposed a way to incorporate the Vickrey insight into a method for encouraging people to reveal their demands for a public good.[17] To illustrate this mechanism, suppose that there are n individuals in a group and each has a private (and unobservable) net valuation u_i for a proposed taxation–expenditure project. In seeking information about these valuations, the government states that, should the project be undertaken, each person will receive a transfer given by

$$t_i = \sum_{-i} v_i, \tag{19.73}$$

where v_i represents the valuation reported by person i and the notation "$-i$" is used to indicate that the summation is to be made over all individuals other than person i. If the project is not undertaken, then no transfers are made.

---

[17]T. Groves, "Incentives in Teams," *Econometrica* (July 1973): 617–31.

Given this setup, the problem for voter i is to choose his or her reported net valuation so as to maximize utility, which is given by

$$\text{utility} = u_i + t_i = u_i + \sum_{-i} v_i. \qquad (19.74)$$

Since the project will be undertaken only if $\sum_n v_i > 0$ and since each person will wish the project to be undertaken only if it raises utility (that is, $u_i + \sum_{-i} v_i > 0$), it follows that a utility-maximizing strategy is to set $v_i = u_i$. Hence, the Groves mechanism encourages each person to be truthful in his or her reporting of valuations for the project.

The Clarke mechanism

A similar mechanism was proposed by E. Clarke, also in the early 1970s.[18] This mechanism also envisions asking individuals about their net valuations for some public project, but it focuses mainly on "pivotal voters"—those whose reported valuations can change the overall evaluation from negative to positive or vice versa. For all other voters, there are no special transfers, on the presumption that (barring strategic behavior among voters) reporting a nonpivotal valuation will not change the decision, so he or she might as well report truthfully. For voters reporting pivotal valuations, however, the Clarke mechanism incorporates a Pigovian-like tax (or transfer) to encourage truth telling. To see how this works, suppose that the net valuations reported by all other voters are negative ($\sum_{-i} v_i < 0$), but that a truthful statement of the valuation by person i would make the project acceptable ($u_i + \sum_{-i} v_i > 0$). Here, as for the Groves mechanism, a transfer of $t_i = \sum_{-i} v_i$ (which in this case would be negative—that is, a tax) would encourage this pivotal voter to report $v_i = u_i$. Similarly, if all other individuals reported valuations favorable to a project ($\sum_{-i} v_i > 0$) but inclusion of person i's evaluation of the project would make it unfavorable, then a transfer of $t_i = \sum_{-i} v_i$ (which in this case is positive) would encourage this pivotal voter to choose $v_i = u_i$ also. Overall, then, the Clarke mechanism is also truth revealing. Notice that in this case the transfers play much the same role that Pigovian taxes did in our examination of externalities. If other voters view a project as unfavorable, then voter i must compensate them for accepting it. On the other hand, if other voters find the project acceptable, then voter i must be sufficiently against the project that he or she cannot be "bribed" by other voters into accepting it.

Generalizations

The voter mechanisms we have been describing are sometimes called *VCG mechanisms* after the three pioneering economists in this area of research (Vickrey, Clarke, and Groves). These mechanisms can be generalized to include multiple governmental projects, alternative concepts of voter equilibrium, or an infinite number of voters. One assumption behind the mechanisms that does not seem amenable to generalization is the quasi-linear utility functions that we have been using throughout. Whether this assumption provides a good approximation for modeling political decision making remains an open question, however.

---

[18]E. Clarke, "Multipart Pricing for Public Goods," *Public Choice* (Fall 1971): 19–33.

SUMMARY

In this chapter we have examined market failures that arise from externality (or spillover) effects involved in the consumption or production of certain types of goods. In some cases it may be possible to design mechanisms to cope with these externalities in a market setting, but important limits are involved in such solutions. Some specific issues we examined were as follows.

- Externalities may cause a misallocation of resources because of a divergence between private and social marginal cost. Traditional solutions to this divergence include mergers among the affected parties and adoption of suitable (Pigovian) taxes or subsidies.

- If transactions costs are small, then private bargaining among the parties affected by an externality may bring social and private costs into line. The proof that resources will be efficiently allocated under such circumstances is sometimes called the *Coase theorem*.

- Public goods provide benefits to individuals on a nonexclusive basis—no one can be prevented from consuming such goods. Such goods are also usually nonrival in that the marginal cost of serving another user is zero.

- Private markets will tend to underallocate resources to public goods because no single buyer can appropriate all of the benefits that such goods provide.

- A Lindahl optimal tax-sharing scheme can result in an efficient allocation of resources to the production of public goods. However, computing these tax shares requires substantial information that individuals have incentives to hide.

- Majority rule voting does not necessarily lead to an efficient allocation of resources to public goods. The median voter theorem provides a useful way of modeling the actual outcomes from majority rule in certain situations.

- Several truth-revealing voting mechanisms have been developed. Whether these are robust to the special assumptions made or capable of practical application remain unresolved questions.

PROBLEMS

19.1

A firm in a perfectly competitive industry has patented a new process for making widgets. The new process lowers the firm's average cost, meaning that this firm alone (although still a price taker) can earn real economic profits in the long run.

    a. If the market price is $20 per widget and the firm's marginal cost is given by $MC = 0.4q$, where q is the daily widget production for the firm, how many widgets will the firm produce?

    b. Suppose a government study has found that the firm's new process is polluting the air and estimates the social marginal cost of widget production by this firm to be $SMC = 0.5q$. If the market price is still $20, what is the socially optimal level of production for the firm? What should be the rate of a government-imposed excise tax to bring about this optimal level of production?

    c. Graph your results.

19.2

On the island of Pago Pago there are 2 lakes and 20 anglers. Each angler can fish on either lake and keep the average catch on his particular lake. On Lake x, the total number of fish caught is given by

$$F^x = 10l_x - \frac{1}{2}l_x^2,$$

where l_x is the number of people fishing on the lake. For Lake y, the relationship is

$$F^y = 5l_y.$$

    a. Under this organization of society, what will be the total number of fish caught?

    b. The chief of Pago Pago, having once read an economics book, believes it is possible to raise the total number of fish caught by restricting the number of people allowed to fish on Lake x.

What number should be allowed to fish on Lake x in order to maximize the total catch of fish? What is the number of fish caught in this situation?

c. Being opposed to coercion, the chief decides to require a fishing license for Lake x. If the licensing procedure is to bring about the optimal allocation of labor, what should the cost of a license be (in terms of fish)?

d. Explain how this example sheds light on the connection between property rights and externalities.

19.3

Suppose the oil industry in Utopia is perfectly competitive and that all firms draw oil from a single (and practically inexhaustible) pool. Assume that each competitor believes that it can sell all the oil it can produce at a stable world price of $10 per barrel and that the cost of operating a well for one year is $1,000.

Total output per year (Q) of the oil field is a function of the number of wells (n) operating in the field. In particular,

$$Q = 500n - n^2,$$

and the amount of oil produced by each well (q) is given by

$$q = \frac{Q}{n} = 500 - n. \tag{19.75}$$

a. Describe the equilibrium output and the equilibrium number of wells in this perfectly competitive case. Is there a divergence between private and social marginal cost in the industry?

b. Suppose now that the government nationalizes the oil field. How many oil wells should it operate? What will total output be? What will the output per well be?

c. As an alternative to nationalization, the Utopian government is considering an annual license fee per well to discourage overdrilling. How large should this license fee be if it is to prompt the industry to drill the optimal number of wells?

19.4

There is considerable legal controversy about product safety. Two extreme positions might be termed *caveat emptor* (let the buyer beware) and *caveat vendor* (let the seller beware). Under the former scheme producers would have no responsibility for the safety of their products: buyers would absorb all losses. Under the latter scheme this liability assignment would be reversed: firms would be completely responsible under law for losses incurred from unsafe products. Using simple supply and demand analysis, discuss how the assignment of such liability might affect the allocation of resources. Would safer products be produced if firms were strictly liable under law? How do possible information asymmetries affect your results?

19.5

Suppose a monopoly produces a harmful externality. Use the concept of consumer surplus in a partial equilibrium diagram to analyze whether an optimal tax on the polluter would necessarily be a welfare improvement.

19.6

Suppose there are only two individuals in society. Person A's demand curve for mosquito control is given by

$$q_n = 100 - p;$$

for person B, the demand curve for mosquito control is given by

$$q_b = 200 - p.$$

a. Suppose mosquito control is a pure public good; that is, once it is produced, everyone benefits from it. What would be the optimal level of this activity if it could be produced at a constant marginal cost of $120 per unit?

b. If mosquito control were left to the private market, how much might be produced? Does your answer depend on what each person assumes the other will do?

c. If the government were to produce the optimal amount of mosquito control, how much will this cost? How should the tax bill for this amount be allocated between the individuals if they are to share it in proportion to benefits received from mosquito control?

19.7

Suppose the production possibility frontier for an economy that produces one public good (y) and one private good (x) is given by

$$x^2 + 100y^2 = 5,000.$$

This economy is populated by 100 identical individuals, each with a utility function of the form

$$\text{utility} = \sqrt{x_i y},$$

where x_i is the individual's share of private good production ($= x/100$). Notice that the public good is nonexclusive and that everyone benefits equally from its level of production.

a. If the market for x and y were perfectly competitive, what levels of those goods would be produced? What would the typical individual's utility be in this situation?

b. What are the optimal production levels for x and y? What would the typical individual's utility level be? How should consumption of good x be taxed to achieve this result? *Hint:* The numbers in this problem do not come out evenly, and some approximations should suffice.

Analytical Problems

19.8 More on Lindahl equilibrium

The analysis of public goods in Chapter 19 exclusively used a model with only two individuals. The results are readily generalized to n persons—a generalization pursued in this problem.

a. With n persons in an economy, what is the condition for efficient production of a public good? Explain how the characteristics of the public good are reflected in these conditions.

b. What is the Nash equilibrium in the provision of this public good to n persons? Explain why this equilibrium is inefficient. Also explain why the underprovision of this public good is more severe than in the two-person cases studied in the chapter.

c. How is the Lindahl solution generalized to n persons? Is the existence of a Lindahl equilibrium guaranteed in this more complex model?

19.9 Taxing pollution

Suppose that there are n firms each producing the same good but with differing production functions. Output for each of these firms depends only on labor input, so the functions take the form $q_i = f_i(l_i)$. In its production activities each firm also produces some pollution, the amount of which is determined by a firm-specific function of labor input of the form $g_i(l_i)$.

a. Suppose that the government wishes to place a cap of amount K on total pollution. What is the efficient allocation of labor among firms?

b. Will a uniform Pigovian tax on the output of each firm achieve the efficient allocation described in part (a)?

c. Suppose that, instead of taxing output, the Pigovian tax is applied to each unit of pollution. How should this tax be set? Will the tax yield the efficient allocation described in part (a)?

d. What are the implications of the problem for adopting pollution control strategies? (For more on this topic see the Extensions to this chapter.)

19.10 Vote trading

Suppose there are three individuals in society trying to rank three social states (A, B, and C). For each of the methods of social choice indicated, develop an example to show how the resulting social ranking of A, B, and C will be intransitive (as in the Paradox of voting) or indeterminate.

a. Majority rule without vote trading.

b. Majority rule with vote trading.

c. Point voting where each voter can give 1, 2, or 3 points to each alternative and the alternative with the highest point total is selected.

19.11 Public choice of unemployment benefits

Suppose individuals face a probability of u that they will be unemployed next year. If they are unemployed they will receive unemployment benefits of b, whereas if they are employed they receive $w(1 - t)$, where t is the tax used to finance unemployment benefits. Unemployment benefits are constrained by the government budget constraint $ub = tw(1 - u)$.

a. Suppose the individual's utility function is given by

$$U = (y_i)^\delta / \delta,$$

where $1 - \delta$ is the degree of constant relative risk aversion. What would be the utility-maximizing choices for b and t?

b. How would the utility-maximizing choices for b and t respond to changes in the probability of unemployment, u?

c. How would b and t change in response to changes in the risk aversion parameter δ?

19.12 Probabilistic voting

Probabilistic voting is a way of modeling the voting process that introduces continuity into individuals' voting decisions. In this way, calculus-type derivations become possible. To take an especially simple form of this approach, suppose there are n voters and two candidates (labeled A and B) for elective office. Each candidate proposes a platform that promises a net gain or loss to each voter. These platforms are denoted by θ_i^A and θ_i^B, where $i = 1, \ldots, n$. The probability that a given voter will vote for candidate A is given by $\pi_i^A = f[U_i(\theta_i^A) - U_i(\theta_i^B)]$, where $f' > 0 > f''$. The probability that the voter will vote for candidate B is $\pi_i^B = 1 - \pi_i^A$.

a. How should each candidate chose his or her platform so as to maximize the probability of winning the election subject to the constraint $\sum_n \theta_i^A = \sum_n \theta_i^B = 0$? (Do these constraints seem to apply to actual political candidates?)

b. Will there exist a Nash equilibrium in platform strategies for the two candidates?

c. Will the platform adopted by the candidates be socially optimal in the sense of maximizing a utilitarian social welfare? [Social welfare is given by $SW = \sum_n U_i(\theta_i)$.]

SUGGESTIONS FOR FURTHER READING

Alchian, A., and H. Demsetz. "Production, Information Costs, and Economic Organization." *American Economic Review* 62 (December 1972): 777–95.

> *Uses externality arguments to develop a theory of economic organizations.*

Barzel, Y. *Economic Analysis of Property Rights*. Cambridge: Cambridge University Press, 1989.

> *Provides a graphical analysis of several economic questions that are illuminated through use of the property rights paradigm.*

Black, D. "On the Rationale of Group Decision Making." *Journal of Political Economy* (February 1948): 23–34. Reprinted in K. J. Arrow and T. Scitovsky, Eds., *Readings in Welfare Economics*. Homewood, IL: Richard D. Irwin, 1969.

> *Early development of the median voter theorem.*

Buchanan, J. M., and G. Tullock. *The Calculus of Consent*. Ann Arbor: University of Michigan Press, 1962.

> *Classic analysis of the properties of various voting schemes.*

Cheung, S. N. S. "The Fable of the Bees: An Economic Investigation." *Journal of Law and Economics* 16 (April 1973): 11–33.

> *Empirical study of how the famous bee–orchard owner externality is handled by private markets in the state of Washington.*

Coase, R. H. "The Market for Goods and the Market for Ideas." *American Economic Review* 64 (May 1974): 384–91.

> *Speculative article about notions of externalities and regulation in the "marketplace of ideas."*

———. "The Problem of Social Cost." *Journal of Law and Economics* 3 (October 1960): 1–44.

> *Classic article on externalities. Many fascinating historical legal cases.*

Cornes, R., and T. Sandler. *The Theory of Externalities, Public Goods, and Club Goods*. Cambridge: Cambridge University Press, 1986.

> *Good theoretical analysis of many of the issues raised in this chapter. Good discussions of the connections between returns to scale, excludability, and club goods.*

Demsetz, H. "Toward a Theory of Property Rights." *American Economic Review, Papers and Proceedings* 57 (May 1967): 347–59.

> *Brief development of a plausible theory of how societies come to define property rights.*

Mas-Colell, A., M. D. Whinston, and J. R. Green. *Microeconomic Theory*. New York: Oxford University Press, 1995.

> *Chapter 11 covers much of the same ground as this chapter does, though at a somewhat more abstract level.*

Olson, M. *The Logic of Collective Action*. Cambridge, MA: Harvard University Press, 1965.

> *Analyzes the effects of individual incentives on the willingness to undertake collective action. Many fascinating examples.*

Persson, T., and G. Tabellini. *Political Economics: Explaining Economic Policy*. Cambridge, MA: MIT Press, 2000.

> *A complete summary of recent models of political choices. Covers voting models and issues of institutional frameworks.*

Posner, R. A. *Economic Analysis of Law*, 5th ed. Boston: Little, Brown, 1998.

> *In many respects the "bible" of the law and economics movement. Posner's arguments are not always economically correct but are unfailingly interesting and provocative.*

Samuelson, P. A. "The Pure Theory of Public Expenditures." *Review of Economics and Statistics* 36 (November 1954): 387–89.

> *Classic statement of the efficiency conditions for public goods production.*

EXTENSIONS

Pollution Abatement

Although our discussion of externalities focused on how Pigovian taxes can make goods' markets operate more efficiently, similar results also apply to the study of the technology of pollution abatement. In these Extensions we briefly review this alternative approach. We assume there are only two firms, A and B, and that their output levels (q_A and q_B, respectively) are fixed throughout our discussion. It is an inescapable scientific principle that production of physical goods (as opposed to services) must obey the conservation of matter. Hence production of q_A and q_B is certain to involve some emission by-products, e_A and e_B. The physical amounts of these emissions (or at least their harmful components) can be abated using inputs z_A and z_B (which cost p per unit). The resulting levels of emissions are given by

$$f^A(q_A, z_A) = e_A \quad \text{and} \quad f^B(q_B, z_B) = e_B, \quad \textbf{(i)}$$

where, for each firm's abatement function, $f_1 > 0$ and $f_2 < 0$.

E19.1 Optimal abatement

If a regulatory agency has decided that e^* represents the maximum allowable level of emissions from these firms, then this level would be achieved at minimal cost by solving the Lagrangian expression

$$\mathcal{L} = pz_A + pz_B + \lambda(f^A + f^B - e^*). \quad \textbf{(ii)}$$

First-order conditions for a minimum are

$$p + \lambda f_2^A = 0 \quad \text{and} \quad p + \lambda f_2^B = 0. \quad \textbf{(iii)}$$

Hence we have

$$\lambda = -p/f_2^A = -p/f_2^B. \quad \textbf{(iv)}$$

This equation makes the rather obvious point that cost-minimizing abatement is achieved when the marginal cost of abatement (universally referred to as MAC in the environmental literature) is the same for each firm. A uniform standard that required equal emissions from each firm would not be likely to achieve that efficient result—considerable cost savings might be attainable under equalization of MACs as compared to such uniform regulation.

E19.2 Emission taxes

The optimal solution described in Equation iv can be achieved by imposing an emission tax (t) equal to λ on each firm (presumably this tax would be set at a level that reflects the marginal harm that a unit of emissions causes). With this tax, each firm seeks to minimize $pz_i + tf^i(q_i, z_i)$, which does indeed yield the efficient solution

$$t = -p/f_2^A = -p/f_2^B. \quad \textbf{(v)}$$

Notice that, as in the analysis of Chapter 19, one benefit of the taxation solution is that the regulatory authority need not know the details of the firms' abatement functions. Rather, the firms themselves make use of their own private information in determining abatement strategies. If these functions differ significantly among firms then it would be expected that emissions reductions would also differ.

Emission taxes in the United Kingdom

Hanley, Shogren, and White (1997) review a variety of emission taxation schemes that have been implemented in the United Kingdom. They show that marginal costs of pollution abatement vary significantly (perhaps as much as thirtyfold) among firms. Hence, relative to uniform regulation, the cost savings from taxation schemes can be quite large. For example, the authors review a series of studies of the Tees estuary that report annual cost savings in the range of £10 million (1976 pounds). The authors also discuss some of the complications that arise in setting efficient effluent taxes when emission streams do not have a uniform mix of pollutants or when pollutants may accumulate to dangerous levels over time.

E19.3 Tradable permits

As we illustrated in Chapter 19, many of the results achievable through Pigovian taxation can also be achieved through a tradable permit system. In this case, the regulatory agency would set the number of permits (s^*) equal to e^* and allocate these permits in some way among firms ($s_A + s_B = s^*$). Each firm may then buy or sell any number of permits desired but must also ensure that its emissions are equal to the number of permits it holds. If the market price of permits is given by p_s, then each firm's problem is again to minimize

$$pz_i + p_s(e_i - s_i), \quad \textbf{(vi)}$$

which yields an identical solution to that derived in Equations iv and v with $p_s = t = \lambda$. Hence the tradable permit solution would be expected to yield the same sort of cost savings as do taxation schemes.

SO$_2$ trading

The U.S. Clean Air Act of 1990 established the first large-scale program of tradable emission permits. These focused on sulfur dioxide emissions with the goal of reducing acid rain arising from power-plant burning of coal. Schmalensee et al. (1998) review early experiences under this program. They conclude that it is indeed possible to establish large and well-functioning markets in emission permits. More than five million (one-ton) emission permits changed hands in the most recent year examined—at prices that averaged about $150 per permit. The authors also show that firms using the permit system employed a wide variety of compliance strategies. This suggests that the flexibility inherent in the permit system led to considerable cost savings. One interesting aspect of this review of SO$_2$ permit trading is the authors' speculations about why the permit prices were only about half what had been expected. They attribute a large part of the explanation to an initial "overinvestment" in emission cleaning technology by power companies in the mistaken belief that permit prices, once the system was implemented, would be in the $300–$400 range. With such large fixed-cost investments, the marginal cost of removing a ton of SO$_2$ may have been as low as $65/ton, thereby exerting a significant downward force on permit prices.

E19.4 Innovation

Although taxes and tradable permits appear to be mathematically equivalent in the models we have been describing, this equivalence may vanish once the dynamics of innovation in pollution abatement technology is considered. Of course, both procedures offer incentives to adopt new technologies: if a new process can achieve a given emission reduction at a lower MAC, it will be adopted under either scheme. Yet in a detailed analysis of dynamics under the two approaches, Milliman and Prince (1989) argue that taxation is better. Their reasoning is that the taxation approach encourages a more rapid diffusion of new abatement technology because incremental profits attainable from adoption are greater than with permits. Such rapid diffusion may also encourage environmental agencies to adopt more stringent emission targets because these targets will now more readily meet cost-benefit tests.

References

Hanley, N., J. F. Shogren, and B. White. *Environmental Economics in Theory and Practice.* New York: Oxford University Press, 1997.

Millman, S. R., and R. Prince. "Firm Incentive to Promote Technological Change in Pollution Control." *Journal of Environmental Economics and Management* (November 1989): 247–65.

Schmalensee, R., P. L. Joskow, A. D. Ellerman, J. P. Montero, and E. M. Bailey. "An Interim Evaluation of the Sulfur Dioxide Trading Program." *Journal of Economic Perspectives* (Summer 1998): 53–68.

Brief Answers to Queries

The following brief answers to the queries that accompany each example in the text may help students test their understanding of the concepts being presented.

CHAPTER 1

1.1

If price depends on quantity, differentiation of $p(q) \cdot q$ would be more complicated. This would lead to the concept of marginal revenue—a topic we encounter in many places in this book.

1.2

The reduced form in Equation 1.16 shows that $\partial p^*/\partial a = 1/225$. So, if a increases by 450, p^* should increase by 2—which is what a direct solution shows.

1.3

If all labor is devoted to x production, then $x = \sqrt{200} = 14.1$ with full employment and $x = \sqrt{180} = 13.4$ with unemployment. Hence the efficiency cost of unemployment is 0.7 units of x. Similar calculations show that the efficiency cost in terms of good y is about 1.5 units of that good. With reductions in both goods, one would need to know the relative price of x in terms of y in order to aggregate the losses.

CHAPTER 2

2.1

The first-order condition for a maximum is $\partial \pi/\partial l = 50/\sqrt{l} - 10 = 0, l^* = 25, \pi^* = 250$.

2.2

No, only the exponential function (or a function that approximates it over a range) has constant elasticity.

2.3

These would be concentric circles centered at $x_1 = 1$, $x_2 = 2$. For $y = 10$, the "circle" is a single point.

2.4

For different constants, each production possibility frontier is a successively larger quarter ellipse centered at the origin.

2.5

$\partial y^*/\partial b = 0$ because x_1 would always be set at b for optimality, and the term $(x_1 - b)$ would vanish.

2.6

With $x_1 + x_2 = 2$, $x_1 = 0.5$, $x_2 = 1.5$. Now $y^* = 9.5$. For $x_1 + x_2 \geq 3$, the unconstrained optimum is attainable.

2.7

A circular field encloses maximal area for minimum perimeter. Proof requires a limit argument.

2.8

The local maximum is also a global maximum here. The constancy of the second derivative implies the slope of the function decreases at a constant rate.

2.9

This function resembles an inverted cone that has only one highest point.

2.10

A linear constraint would be represented by a plane in these three-dimensional figures. Such a plane would have a unique tangency to the surfaces in both Figures 2.4(a) and 2.4(c). For an unconstrained maximum, however, the plane would be horizontal, so only Figure 2.4(a) would have a maximum.

2.11

Such a transformation would not preserve homogeneity. However it would not affect the trade-off between the x's: for any constant k, $-f_1/f_2 = -x_2/x_1$.

2.12

Total variable costs of this expansion would be

$$\int_{100}^{110} 0.2q \, dq = 0.1q^2 \Big|_{100}^{110} = 1{,}210 - 1{,}000 = 210.$$

This could also be calculated by subtracting total costs when $q = 100 (1{,}500)$ from total costs when $q = 110 (1{,}710)$. Fixed costs would cancel out in this subtraction.

2.13

As we show in Chapter 17, a higher value for δ will cause wine to be consumed earlier. A lower value for γ will make the consumer less willing to experience consumption fluctuations.

2.14

If $g(x)$ is concave, then values of this function will increase less rapidly than does x itself. Hence $E[g(x)] < g[E(x)]$. In Chapter 7 this is used to explain why a person with a diminishing marginal utility of wealth will be risk averse.

2.15

Using the results from Examples 2.14 and 2.15 for the uniform distribution gives $\mu_x = (b - a)/2 = 6$, $\sigma_x^2 = (b - a)^2/12 = 12$, and $\sigma_x = 12^{0.5} = 3.464$. In this case, 57.7 percent ($= 2 \cdot 3.464/12$) of the distribution is within one standard deviation of the mean. This is less than the comparable figure for the Normal distribution because the uniform distribution is not bunched around the mean. However, unlike the Normal, the entire uniform distribution is within two standard deviations of the mean because that distribution does not have long tails.

CHAPTER 3

3.1

The derivation here holds utility constant to create an implicit relationship between y and x. Changes in x also implicitly change y because of this relationship (Equation 3.11).

3.2

The MRS is not changed by such a doubling in Examples 1 and 3. In Example 2 the MRS would be changed because $(1 + x)/(1 + y) \neq (1 + 2x)/(1 + 2y)$.

3.3

For homothetic functions, the MRS is the same for every point along a positively sloped ray through the origin.

3.4

The indifference curves here are "horizontally parallel." That is, for any given level of y, the MRS is the same no matter what the value of x is. One implication of this (as we shall see in Chapter 4) is that the effect of additional income on purchases of good y is zero—after a point all extra income is channeled into the good with constant marginal utility (good x).

CHAPTER 4

4.1

Constant shares imply $\partial x/\partial p_y = 0$ and $\partial y/\partial p_x = 0$. Notice p_y does not enter into Equation 4.23; p_x does not enter into 4.24.

4.2

Budget shares are not affected by income, but they may be affected by changes in relative prices. This is the case for all homothetic functions.

4.3

Since a doubling of all prices and nominal income does not change the budget constraint, it will not change utility-maximizing choices. Indirect utility is homogeneous of degree zero in all prices and nominal income.

4.4

In the Cobb-Douglas case, with $p_y = 3$, $E(1,3,2) = 2 \cdot 1 \cdot 3^{0.5} \cdot 2 = 6.93$, so this person should have his or her income reduced by a lump-sum 1.07 to compensate for the fall in prices. In the fixed proportions case, the original consumption bundle now costs 7, so the compensation is -1.0. Notice that with fixed proportions the consumption bundle does not change, but with the Cobb-Douglas, the new choice is $x = 3.46$, $y = 1.15$ because this person takes advantage of the reduction in the price of y.

CHAPTER 5

5.1

The shares equations computed from Equations 5.5 or 5.7 show that this individual always spends all of his or her income regardless of p_x, p_y, and I. That is, the shares sum to one.

5.2

If $x = 0.5I/p_x$ then $I = 100$ and $p_x = 1$ imply that $x = 50$. In Equation 5.11, $x = 0.5(100/1) = 50$ also. If p_x rises to 2.0, the Cobb-Douglas predicts $x = 25$. The CES implies $x = 100/6 = 16.67$. The CES is more responsive to price.

5.3

Since proportional changes in p_x and p_y do not induce substitution effects, holding V constant implies that x and y will not change. That should be true for all compensated demand functions.

5.4

A larger exponent for, say, x in the Cobb-Douglas function will increase the share of income devoted to that good and increase the relative importance of the income effect in the Slutsky decomposition. This is easiest to see using the Slutsky equation in elasticity form (Example 5.5).

5.5

Consider the Cobb-Douglas case for which $e_{x,p_x} = -1$ regardless of budget shares. The Slutsky equation in elasticity terms shows that, because the income effect here is $-s_x e_{x,I} = -s_x(1) = -s_x$, the compensated price elasticity is $e^c_{x,p_x} = e_{x,p_x} + s_x = -(1 - s_x)$. This occurs because proportional changes in x demand will be larger when the share devoted to that good is smaller because they are starting from a smaller base.

5.6

Typically it is assumed that demand goes to zero at some finite price when calculating total consumer surplus. The specific assumption made does not affect calculations of changes in consumer surplus.

CHAPTER 6

6.1

Since $\partial x/\partial p_y$ includes both income and substitution effects, this derivative could be 0 if the effects offset each other. The conclusion that $\partial x/\partial p_y = 0$ implies the goods must be used in fixed proportions would hold only if the income effect of this price change were 0.

6.2

Asymmetry can occur with homothetic preferences since, although substitution effects are symmetric, income effects may differ in size.

6.3

Since the relationships between p_y, p_z, and p_h never change, the maximization problem will always be solved the same way.

CHAPTER 7

7.1

In case 1, the probability of seven heads is less than 0.01. Hence the value of the original game is $6. In case 2, the prize for obtaining the first head on the twentieth flip is over $1 million. The value of the game in this case is $19 + 1,000,000/2^{19} = \$20.91$.

7.2

With linear utility, the individual would care only about expected dollar values and would be indifferent about buying actuarially fair insurance. When utility U is a convex function of wealth ($U > 0$, $U'' > 0$), the individual prefers to gamble and will buy insurance only if it costs less than is actuarially justified.

7.3

If $A = 10^{-4}$:

$$CE(\#1) = 107,000 - 0.5 \cdot 10^{-4} \cdot (10^4)^2$$
$$= 102,000,$$
$$CE(\#2) = 102,000 - 0.5 \cdot 10^{-4} \cdot 4 \cdot 10^6$$
$$= 101,800.$$

So the riskier allocation is preferred. On the other hand, if $A = 3 \cdot 10^{-4}$ then the less risky allocation is preferred.

7.4

Willingness to pay is a declining function of wealth (Equation 7.43). With $R = 0$ the person will pay 50 to avoid a 1,000 bet if $W_0 = 10,000$ but only 5 if $W_0 = 100,000$. With $R = 2$ he or she will pay 149 to avoid a 1,000 bet if $W_0 = 10,000$ but only 15 if $W_0 = 100,000$.

7.5

One possible reason is that any investor in risky assets incurs transactions costs. If there are economies of scale to these costs, then individuals with greater wealth will face lower transactions costs and will increase the share of their portfolios invested in risky assets.

7.6

The actuarially fair price for such a policy is $0.25 \cdot 19{,}000 = 4{,}750$. The maximum amount the individual would pay (X) solves the equation

$$11.45714 = 0.75 \ln(100{,}000 - x) \\ + 0.25 \ln(99{,}000 - x).$$

Solving this yields an approximate value of $x = \$5{,}120$. This person would be willing to pay up to $370 in administrative costs for the deductible policy.

7.7

Although price is uncertain, the model here allows the individual to buy more y when he or she encounters a low price and less when a high price is encountered. Because V is a convex function of p_y, the mean of V for two different values of p_y exceeds the value of V at the mean of p_y. This has no relationship to risk aversion, which concerns choices among options with the same expected value.

CHAPTER 8

8.1

Best responses are not unique, so the game has no dominant strategies. The extensive form looks like Figure 8.1 with different payoffs.

8.2

No dominant strategies. (Paper, scissors) isn't a Nash equilibrium because player 1 would deviate to rock.

8.3

It might be closer to the Battle of the Sexes to specify a payoff of 0 rather than 1 if a player plays favorite action when no other player does. The normal form for Four's Company could be represented with four matrices, one for each strategy profile for players 3 and 4.

8.4

If the wife plays mixed strategy $(1/9, 8/9)$ and the husband plays $(4/5, 1/5)$, then his expected payoff is $4/9$. If she plays $(1, 0)$ and he plays $(4/5, 1/5)$, his expected payoff is $4/5$. If he plays $(4/5, 1/5)$, her best response is to play ballet.

8.5

Players earn $2/3$ in the mixed-strategy Nash equilibrium. This is less than the payoff even in the less desirable of the two pure-strategy Nash equilibria. Symmetry might favor the mixed-strategy Nash equilibrium.

8.6

The Nash equilibrium would involve higher quantities for both if their benefits increased. If herder 2's benefit decreased, his or her quantity would fall and the other's would rise.

8.7

There are a number of possible answers. One is to play the mixed-strategy Nash equilibrium first and then the "good" stage-game Nash equilibrium, for an average payoff of $15/8$. Another would be to play the mixed-strategy Nash equilibrium first and then the "bad" stage-game Nash equilibrium, for an average payoff of $7/8$.

8.8

Yes. Letting p be the probability that player 1 is type $t = 6$, player 2's expected payoff from choosing L is $2p$. This is at least as high as 2's expected payoff of $4(1 - p)$ from choosing R if $p \geq 2/3$.

8.9

Moving from incomplete to full information increases herder 1's output and decreases the rival's if 1 is the high type. The opposite is true if 1 is the low type. The high type prefers full information and would like to somehow signal its type; the low type prefers incomplete information and would like to conceal its type.

8.10

Obtaining an education informs the firm about the worker's ability and thus may increase the high-skill worker's salary. The separating equilibrium would not exist if the low-skill worker could get an education more cheaply than the high-skill one.

8.11

The proposed pooling outcome cannot be an equilibrium if the firm's posterior beliefs equal its priors after unexpectedly seeing an uneducated worker. Then its beliefs would be the same whether or not it encountered an educated worker, it would have the same best response, and workers would deviate from E. If the firm has pessimistic posteriors following NE, then the outcome is an equilibrium because the firm's best response to NE would be NJ, inducing both types of worker to pool on E.

8.12

In equilibrium, type H obtains an expected payoff of $j^*w - c_H = c_L - c_H$. This exceeds the payoff of 0 from deviating to NE. Type L pools with type H on E with probability e^*. But $de^*/d\Pr(H) = (\pi - w)/\pi$. Since this expression is positive, type L must increase its probability of playing E to offset an increase in $\Pr(H)$ and still keep player 2 indifferent between J and NJ.

8.13

Players earn more in more informative equilibria. Suppose $0 < d < 1/3$. In a babbling equilibrium, player 1 earns expected payoff $(1-d)/2$ and player 2 earns $(1+d)/2$. In the most informative equilibrium, player 1 earns 1 and player 2 earns $1-d$, lower payoffs than in the babbling equilibrium if $d < 1/3$. In theory, there is no difference between announcing "A or C" and announcing the agreed-upon synonym "purple." In practice, it might be difficult for players to coordinate on the meaning of a nonsense word. Languages are more efficient the more precise they are and the more widespread agreement there is about meanings, but there may be trade-offs between these two features.

CHAPTER 9

9.1

Now, with $k = 11$:

$$q = 72{,}600l^2 - 1{,}331l^3,$$
$$MP_l = 145{,}200l - 3{,}993l^2,$$
$$AP_l = 72{,}600l - 1{,}331l^2.$$

In this case, AP_l reaches its maximal value at $l = 27.3$ rather than at $l = 30$.

9.2

Since k and l enter f symmetrically, if $k = l$ then $f_k = f_l$ and $f_{kk} = f_{ll}$. Hence, the numerator of Equation 9.21 will be negative if $f_{kl} > f_{ll}$. Combining Equations 9.24 and 9.25 (and remembering $k = l$) shows this holds for $k = l < 20$.

9.3

The $q = 4$ isoquant contains the points $k = 4$, $l = 0$; $k = 1$, $l = 1$; and $k = 0$, $l = 4$. It is therefore fairly sharply convex. It seems possible that an L-shaped isoquant might be approximated for particular coefficients of the linear and radical terms.

9.4

Because the composite technical change factor is $\theta = \alpha\varphi + (1 - \alpha)\varepsilon$, a value of $\alpha = 0.3$ implies that technical improvements in labor will be weighted more highly in determining the overall result.

CHAPTER 10

10.1

If $\sigma = 2$, $\rho = 0.5$, $k/l = 16$, $l = 8/5$, $k = 128/5$, $C = 96$.

If $\sigma = 0.5$, $\rho = -1$, $k/l = 2$, $l = 60$, $k = 120$, $C = 1080$.

Notice that changes in σ also change the scale of the production function, so the total cost figures cannot be compared directly.

10.2

The expression for unit costs is $(v^{1-\sigma} + w^{1-\sigma})^{1/(1-\sigma)}$. If $\sigma = 0$ then this function is linear in $w + v$. For $\sigma > 0$ the function is increasingly convex, showing that large increases in w can be offset by small decreases in v.

10.3

The elasticities are given by the exponents in the cost functions and are unaffected by technical change as modeled here.

10.4

In this case $\sigma = \infty$. With $w = 4v$, cost minimization could use the inputs in any combination (for q constant) without changing costs. A rise in w would cause the firm to switch to using only capital and would not affect total costs. This shows that the impact on costs of an increase in the price of a single input depends importantly on the degree of substitution.

10.5

Because capital costs are fixed in the short run, they do not affect short-run marginal costs (in mathematical terms, the derivative of a constant is zero). Capital costs do, however, affect short-run average costs. In Figure 10.9 an increase in v would shift MC, AC, and all of the $SATC$ curves upward, but would leave the SMC curves unaffected.

CHAPTER 11

11.1

If $MC = 5$, profit maximization requires $q = 25$. Now $P = 7.50$, $R = 187.50$, $C = 125$, and $\pi = 62.50$.

11.2

Factors other than p can be incorporated into the constant term a. These would shift D and MR but would not affect the elasticity calculations.

11.3

When w rises to 15, supply shifts inward to $q = 8P/5$. When k increases to 100, supply shifts outward to $q = 25P/6$. A change in v would not affect short-run marginal cost or the shutdown decision.

11.4

A change in v has no effect on SMC but it does affect fixed costs. A change in w would affect SMC and short-run supply.

11.5

A rise in wages for all firms would shift the market supply curve upward, raising the product price. Because total output must fall given a negatively sloped demand curve, each firm must produce less. Again, both substitution and output effects would then be negative.

CHAPTER 12

12.1

The ability to sum incomes in this linear case would require that each person have the same coefficient for income. Because each person faces the same price, aggregation requires only adding the price coefficients.

12.2

A value for β other than 0.5 would mean that the exponent of price would not be 1.0. The higher is β the more price elastic is short-run supply.

12.3

Following steps similar to those used to derive Equation 10.36 yields

$$e_{P,\beta} = \frac{-e_{Q,\beta}}{e_{S,P} - e_{Q,P}}$$

Here $e_{Q,\beta} = e_{Q,w} = -0.5$, so $e_{P,\beta} = -(-0.5)/2.2 = 0.227$. Multiplication by 0.20 (since wages rose 20

percent) predicts a price rise of 4.5 percent, very close to the number in the example.

12.4

The short-run supply curve is given by $Q_s = 0.5P + 750$, and the short-term equilibrium price is 643. Each firm earns approximately $2,960 in profits in the short run.

12.5

Total and average costs for Equation 12.55 exceed those for Equation 12.42 for $q > 15.9$. Marginal costs for Equation 12.55 always exceed those for Equation 12.42. Optimal output is lower with Equation 12.55 than with Equation 12.42 because marginal costs increase more than average costs.

12.6

Losses from a given restriction in quantity will be greater when supply and/or demand is less elastic. The actor with the least elastic response will bear the greater share of the loss.

12.7

An increase in t unambiguously increases deadweight loss. Because increases in t reduce quantity, however, total tax revenues are subject to countervailing effects. Indeed, if $t/(P + t) \geq -1/e_{Q,P}$ then $dtQ/dt < 0$.

12.8

Total transfer to domestic producers is (in billions) $0.5 \cdot (11.7) + 0.5(0.5)(0.7) = 6.03$. This would be gained as rents to those inputs that give the auto supply curve its positive slope. With a quota, domestic producers may also be able to gain some portion of what would have been tariff revenue.

CHAPTER 13

13.1

An increase in labor input will shift the first frontier out uniformly. In the second case, such an increase will shift the y-intercept out farther than the x-intercept because good y uses labor intensively.

13.2

In all three scenarios the total value of output is $200w$, composed half of wages and half of profits. With the shift in supply, consumers still devote $100w$ to each good. Purchases of x are twice those of y because y costs twice as much. With the shift in demand, the consumer spends $20w$ on good x and $180w$ on good y. But good y now costs three times what x costs, so consumers buy only three times as much y as they do x.

13.3

Walras' law ensures that the silver market is in equilibrium. Recalculating Equation 16.40 gives

$$ED_1 = 2(p_2/p_1)^2 + 2(p_3/p_1)^2 - 4p_2/p_1 - 7p_3/p_1$$

or, at the new relative prices,

$$= 2(3)^2 + 2(2)^2 - 4(3) - 7(2) = 0.$$

13.4

The consumers here also spend some of their total income on leisure. For person 1, say, total income with the equilibrium prices is $40 \cdot 0.136 + 24 \cdot 0.248 = 11.4$. The Cobb-Douglas exponents imply that this person will spend half of this on good x. Hence, total spending on that good will be 5.7, which is also equal to the quantity of x bought (15.7) multiplied by this good's equilibrium price (0.363).

13.5

No—such redistribution could not make both better-off owing to the excess burden of the tax.

13.6

Because each production function exhibits constant returns to scale, any allocation of capital will be efficient if labor is allocated appropriately.

13.7

Total post-transfer consumer income is $300w$, which is allocated equally to each good. Firms producing good y get this as total revenue ($150w$). Firms producing good x receive only $50w$ in revenues because $100w$ goes to the government in taxes. For these firms, total (after-tax) revenue is $p_x \cdot x = 50w$. Consumer spending on good x, however, is $3p_x \cdot x = 150w$. In this case, GDP is still $200w$: $50w$ in x production and $150w$ in y production. There is $100w$ in taxes and transfers, but this figure is not part of GDP.

13.8

The indifference curves are relatively flat here, implying that these individuals are quite willing to substitute one good for another. This flexibility implies a relatively narrow range of mutually beneficial trading opportunities at point A. With less flexible preferences, the number of opportunities is increased because the individuals may start trading from widely differing marginal rates of substitution.

CHAPTER 14

14.1

The increase in fixed costs would not alter the output decisions because it would not affect marginal costs. It would, however, raise AC by 5 and reduce profits to 12,500. With the new C function, MC would rise to $0.15Q$. In this case, $Q^* = 400$, $P^* = 80$, $C = 22,000$, and $\pi = 10,000$.

14.2

For the linear case, an increase in a would increase price by $a/2$. A shift in the price intercept has an effect similar to an increase in marginal cost in this case. In the constant elasticity case, the term a does not enter into the calculation of price. For a given elasticity of demand, the gap between price and marginal cost is the same no matter what a is.

14.3

With $e = -1.5$, the ratio of monopoly to competitive consumer surplus is 0.58 (Equation 14.19). Profits represent 19 percent of competitive consumer surplus (Equation 14.21).

14.4

If $Q = 0$, $P = 100$. Total profits are given by the triangular area between the demand curve and the MC curve, less fixed costs. This area is $0.5(100)(666) = 33,333$. So $\pi = 33,333 - 10,000 = 23,333$.

14.5

One must be careful when summing the demand functions. For $P > 12$, there is no demand in market 2, so the monopoly solution in that case yields profits of 81. For $P < 12$, market demand is $Q = 48 - 3P$ or $P = 16 - Q/3$. In this case the monopoly price would be 11. Profits would be $(11 - 6) \cdot 15 = 75$, so it is still not worthwhile to serve market 2. Profits are maximized when $P = 15$.

CHAPTER 15

15.1

Members of a perfect cartel produce less than their best responses, so cartels may be unstable.

15.2

A point on firm 1's best response must involve a tangency between 1's isoprofit and a horizontal line of height q_2. This isoprofit reaches a peak at this point. Firm 2's isoprofits look something like right parentheses that peak on 2's best-response curve. An increase in demand intercept would shift out both best responses, resulting in higher quantities in equilibrium.

15.3

The first-order condition is the mathematical representation of the optimal choice. Imposing symmetry before taking a first-order condition is like allowing firm i to choose the others' outputs as well as its own. Making this mistake would lead to the monopoly rather than the Cournot outcome in this example.

15.4

An increase in the demand intercepts would shift out both best responses, leading to an increase in equilibrium prices.

15.5

Locating in the same spot leads to marginal cost pricing as in the Bertrand model with homogeneous products. Locating at opposite ends of the beach results in the softest price competition and the highest prices.

15.6

It is reasonable to suppose that competing gas stations monitor each other's prices and could respond to a price change within the day, so one day would be a reasonable period length. A year would be a reasonable period for producers of small cartons of milk for school lunches, because the contracts might be renegotiated each new school year.

15.7

Reverting to the stage-game Nash equilibrium is a less harsh punishment in a Cournot model (firms earn positive profit) than a Bertrand model (firms earn zero profit).

15.8

Firms might race to be the first to market, investing in research and development and capacity before sufficient demand has materialized. In this way, they may compete away all the profits from being first, a possible explanation for the puncturing of the dot-com bubble. Investors may even have overestimated the advantages of being first in the affected industries.

15.9

In most industries, price can be changed quickly—perhaps instantly—whereas quantity may be more difficult to adjust, requiring the installation of more capacity. Thus, price is more difficult to commit to. Among other ways, firms can commit to prices by mentioning price in their national advertising campaigns, by offering price guarantees, and by maintaining a long-run reputation for not discounting list price.

15.10

Entry reduces market shares and lower prices from tougher competition, so one firm may earn enough profit to cover its fixed cost where two firms would not.

15.11

A's entry-deterring strategy would still be to locate in the middle, since this leaves the smallest niche for B to enter and is worst for B's profits. A's accommodating strategy would change from the unregulated price case. A would locate in the middle, since this captures the biggest market share for A. It does not have to worry about the strategic effect of depressing price, since price is regulated.

15.12

The social planner would have one firm charge marginal cost prices. This would eliminate any deadweight loss from pricing and also economize on fixed costs.

CHAPTER 16

16.1

Nonlabor income permits the individual to "buy" leisure but the amount of such purchases depends on labor-leisure substitutability.

16.2

The conclusion does not depend on linearity. So long as the demand and supply curves are conventionally shaped, the curves will be shifted vertically by the parameters t and k.

16.3

Now $MRP = \$30$ per hour. In this case, the monopsony will hire 750 workers, and wages will be \$15 per hour. As before, the wage remains at only half the MRP.

16.4

The monopsonist wants to be on its demand for labor curve; the union (presumably) wants to be on the labor supply curve of its members. Only the supply-demand equilibrium ($l = 583$, $w = 11.67$) satisfies both these curves. Whether this is indeed a Nash equilibrium depends, among other things, on whether the union defines its payoffs as being accurately reflected by the labor supply curve.

16.5

If the firm is risk neutral, workers risk averse, optimal contracts might have lower wages in exchange for more-stable income.

CHAPTER 17

17.1

Using Equation 17.17 yields $c_1/c_0 = 1.02 = (1 + r)^{1/(1-R)}$. Hence $1 + r = (1.02)^{1-R}$. If $R = 0$ then $r = 0.02$; if $R = -3$ then $r = 0.082$.

17.2

If g is uncertain, the future marginal utility of consumption will be a random variable. If $U'(c)$ is convex, its expected value with uncertain growth will be greater than its value when growth is at its expected value. The effect is similar to what would occur with a lower growth rate. Equation 17.29 shows that the risk-free interest rate must fall to accommodate such a lower g.

17.3

With an inflation rate of 10 percent, the nominal value of the tree would rise at an additional 10 percent per year. But such revenues would have to be discounted by an identical amount to calculate real profits so the optimal harvesting age would not change.

17.4

For a monopolist, an equation similar to Equation 17.62 would hold with marginal revenue replacing price. With a constant elasticity demand curve, price would have the same growth rate under monopoly as under perfect competition.

CHAPTER 18

18.1

The manager would have an incentive to overstate gross profits unless some discipline were imposed by an audit. If audits are costly, the efficient arrangement might involve few audits with harsh punishments for false reports. If harsh punishments are impossible, the power of the manager's incentives might have to be reduced. Enron's managers did overstate profits. Auditors did not catch or were complicit in the overstatement. The harsh punishments meted out may deter future corporate crimes even if audits continue to be not especially effective.

18.2

The insurer would be willing to pay the difference between its first- and second-best profits, $298 - 96 = \$202$.

18.3

Insurance markets are generally thought to be fairly competitive, except where regulation has limited entry. It is hard to say which segment is most competitive. The fact that the individuals purchase car insurance whereas firms purchase health insurance on behalf of their employees "in bulk" may affect the nature of competition.

18.4

The corner coffee shop in Hanover charges \$1.25 for an 8-ounce cup and \$1.55 for a 16-ounce cup. This menu is not consistent with reasonable values of θ_H and θ_L. Substituting the quantity and tariff for the small cup into the equation $\theta_L v(q_L) - T_L$ yields $\theta_L = 22.1$, which is greater than the $\theta_H = 12.8$ that results from substituting the menu terms into $\theta_H v(q_H) - T_H = \theta_H v(q_L) - T_L$. Perhaps actual utility functions are different from those assumed here.

18.5

The insurance company decides to offer just one policy targeted to red cars and ignores gray cars.

18.6

Gray-car owners obtain utility of 11.48033 in the competitive equilibrium under asymmetric information. They would obtain the same utility under full insurance with a premium of \$3,207. The difference between this and the equilibrium premium (\$453) is \$2,754. Any premium between \$3,000 and \$3,207 would allow an insurance company to break even from its sales just for gray cars. The problem is that red-car owners would deviate to the policy, causing the company to make negative profit.

18.7

If the reports are fairly credible, then gray cars may still be able to get as full insurance with reporting as without, but not as full as with 100 percent credibility. Auditors have short-run incentives to take bribes to issue "gray" reports. In the long run, dishonesty will reduce the fees the auditor can charge. He or she would like to maintain high fees by establishing a reputation for honest reporting (which would be ruined if ever discovered to be dishonest).

18.8

If there are fewer sellers than buyers, then all the cars will sell. A car of quality q will sell at a price of $q + b$. If there are fewer buyers than sellers, then all buyers will purchase a car but some cars will be left unsold (a random selection of them). The equilibrium price will equal the car's quality: q.

18.9

Yes, reservation prices can often help. The trade-offs involved in increasing the reservation price are, on the one hand, that buyers are encouraged to increase their bids, but, on the other hand, that the probability the object goes unsold increases. In a second-price auction, buyers bid their valuations without a reservation price, and a reservation price would not induce them to bid above their valuations.

CHAPTER 19

19.1

Production of x would have a beneficial impact on y so labor would be underallocated to x by competitive markets.

19.2

The tax is relatively small because of the nature of the externality that vanishes with only a relatively minor reduction in x output. A merged firm would also find $x = 38,000$ to be a profit-maximizing choice.

19.3

The roommates' separate allocations are $x = 1$, $y = 1,000$, so they would achieve the efficient allocation if they moved in together. This results from the simple additive nature of the MRS values in the Cobb-Douglas case and would not be expected to hold generally.

19.4

The roommates have identical preferences here and therefore identical marginal rates of substitution. If each pays half the price of the public good then the sum of their MRSs will be precisely the ratio of the price of the public good to the price of the private good, as required in Equation 19.40. With differing MRSs, the sharing might depart from 50–50 to ensure efficiency

19.5

Reduction of the labor tax increases after-tax income and the demand for good y. With a fixed Pigovian tax, pollution rises. More generally, the likelihood of a double dividend depends on the precise demand relationship in people's utility functions between clean air and the other items being taxed (here, labor).

19.6

Progressive taxation should raise t^* because the median voter can gain more revenue from high-income tax payers without incurring high tax costs.

Solutions to Odd-Numbered Problems

Only very brief solutions to most of the odd-numbered problems in the text are given here. Complete solutions to all of the problems are contained in the *Solutions Manual*, which is available to instructors upon request.

CHAPTER 2

2.1

a. $8x$, $6y$
b. 8, 12
c. $8xdx + 6ydy$
d. $dy/dx = -4x/3y$.
e. $x = 1$, $U = (4)(1) + (3)(4) = 16$.
f. $dy/dx = -2/3$.
g. $U = 16$ contour line is an ellipse.

2.3

Both approaches yield $x = y = 0.5$.

2.5

a. The first-order condition for a maximum is $-gt + 40 = 0$, so $t^* = 40/g$.
b. Substitution yields $f(t^*) = -0.5g(40/g)^2 + 40(40/g) = 800/g$. So $\partial f(t^*)/\partial g = -800/g^2$.
c. This follows because $\partial f/\partial g = -0.5(t^*)^2$.
d. $\partial f/\partial g = -0.5(40/g)^2 = -0.8$, so each 0.1 increase in g reduces maximum height by 0.08.

2.7

a. First-order conditions require $f_1 = f_2 = 1$. Hence, $x_2 = 5$. With $k = 10$, $x_1 = 5$.
b. With $k = 4$, $x_1 = -1$.
c. $x_1 = 0$, $x_2 = -4$.
d. With $k = 20$, $x_1 = 15$, $x_2 = 5$. Because marginal value of x_1 is constant, every addition to k beyond 5 adds only to that variable.

2.9

Since $f_{ii} < 0$, the condition for concavity implies that the matrix of second-order partials is negative definite. Hence the quadratic form involving $[f_1, f_2]$ will be

negative as required for quasi-concavity. The converse is not true, as shown by the Cobb-Douglas function with $\alpha + \beta > 1$.

2.11

a. $f'' = \delta(\delta - 1)x^{\delta-2} < 0$.
b. Since $f_{11}, f_{22} < 0$ and $f_{12}, f_{21} = 0$, Equation 2.98 obviously holds.
c. This preserves quasi-concavity but not concavity.

2.13

a. $g[E(x)] = E(c + dx) = c + dE(x) \geq E[g(x)]$.
b. Just reverse the inequality.
c. Let $u = 1 - F(x)$, $du = -f(x)$, $x = v$, and $dv = dx$. Apply Equation 2.136.
d. Use the hint and the fact that $\int_t^\infty xf(x)\,dx \geq \int_t^\infty tf(x)\,dx$.
e. (1) $\int_1^\infty 2x^{-3}\,dx = -x^{-2}\big|_1^\infty = 1$.
   (2) $F(x) = 1 - x^{-2}$.
   (3) $E(x) = 1$.
   (4) $\Pr(x \geq t) = 1 - F(t) = t^{-2} \leq 1/t$.
f. (1) $\int_{-1}^2 x^2/3\,dx = x^3/9\big|_{-1}^2 = 1$.
   (2) $E(x) = 5/4$.
   (3) $\Pr(-1 \leq x \leq 0) = 1/9$.
   (4) $f(x|A) = 9f(x)/8 = 3x^2/8$.
   (5) $E(x|A) = 1.5$.
   (6) The expected value is increased by looking only at positive values for x.

CHAPTER 3

3.1

a. No
b. Yes
c. Yes
d. No
e. Yes

3.3

The shape of the marginal utility function is not necessarily an indicator of convexity of indifference curves.

3.5

a. $U(h, b, m, r) = \min(h, 2b, m, 0.5r)$.
b. A fully condimented hot dog
c. $1.60
d. $2.10—an increase of 31 percent.
e. Price would increase only to $1.725—an increase of 7.8 percent.
f. Raise prices so that a fully condimented hot dog rises in price to $2.60. This would be equivalent to a lump-sum reduction in purchasing power.

3.7

a. Indifference curve is linear—$MRS = 1/3$.
b. $\alpha = 2$, $\beta = 1$.
c. Just knowing the MRS at a known point can identify the ratio of the Cobb-Douglas exponents.

3.9

a.–c. See detailed solutions.

3.11

It follows, since $MRS = MU_x/MU_y \cdot MU_x$ doesn't depend on y or vice versa. 3.1(b) is a counterexample.

3.13

a. $MRS = f_x/f_y = y$.
b. $f_{xx} = f_{xy} = 0$, so the condition for quasi-concavity reduces to $-1/y^2 < 0$.
c. An indifference curve is given by $y = \exp(k - x)$.
d. Marginal utility of x is constant, marginal utility of y diminishes. As income rises, consumers will eventually choose only added x.
e. y could be a particular good, whereas x could be "everything else."

CHAPTER 4

4.1

a. $t = 5$ and $s = 2$.
b. $t = 5/2$ and $s = 4$. Costs $2 so needs extra $1.

4.3

a. $c = 10$, $b = 3$, and $U = 127$.
b. $c = 4$, $b = 1$, and $U = 79$.

4.5

a. $g = I/(p_g + p_v/2)$; $v = I/(2p_g + p_v)$.
b. Utility $= m = v = I/(2p_g + p_v)$.
c. $E = m(2p_g + p_v)$.

4.7

a. See detailed solutions.
b. Requires expenditure of 12.

c. Subsidy is 5/9 per unit. Total cost of subsidy is 5.
d. Expenditures to reach $U = 2$ are 9.71. To reach $U = 3$ requires 4.86 more. A subsidy on good x must be 0.74 per unit and costs 8.29.
e. With fixed proportions the lump sum and single good subsidy would cost the same.

4.9

If $p_x/p_y < a/b$ then $E = p_x U/a$. If $p_x/p_y > a/b$ then $E = p_y U/b$. If $p_x/p_y = a/b$ then $E = p_x U/a = p_y U/b$.

4.11

a. Set $MRS = p_x/p_y$.
b. Set $\delta = 0$.
c. Use $p_x x/p_y y = (p_x/p_y)^{\delta/(\delta-1)}$.

4.13

a. See detailed solutions.
b. Multiplying prices and income by 2 does not change V.
c. Obviously $\partial V/\partial I > 0$.
d. $\partial V/\partial p_x, \partial V/\partial p_y < 0$.
e. Just exchange I and V.
f. Multiplying the prices by 2 doubles E.
g. Just take partials.
h. Show $\partial E/\partial p_x > 0, \partial^2 E/\partial p_x^2 < 0$.

CHAPTER 5

5.1

a. $U = x + \frac{3}{8}y$.
b. $x = I/p_x$ if $p_x \le \frac{3}{8}p_y$.

   $x = 0$ if $p_x > \frac{3}{8}p_y$.
d. Changes in p_y don't affect demand until they reverse the inequality.
e. Just two points (or vertical lines).

5.3

a. It is obvious since p_x/p_y doesn't change.
b. No good is inferior.

5.5

a. $x = \dfrac{I - p_x}{2p_x}$, $y = \dfrac{I + p_x}{2p_y}$.

   Hence, changes in p_y do not affect x, but changes in p_x do affect y.

b. $V = \dfrac{(I + p_x)^2}{4p_x p_y}$ and so $E = \sqrt{4p_x p_y V} - p_x$.

c. The compensated demand function for x depends on p_y, whereas the uncompensated function did not.

5.7

a. Use the Slutsky equation in elasticity form. Because there are no substitution effects, $e_{h,p_h} = 0 - s_h e_{h,I} = 0 - 0.5 = -0.5$.

b. Compensated price elasticity is zero for both goods, which are consumed in fixed proportions.

c. Now $s_h = 2/3$ so $e_{h,p_h} = -2/3$.

d. For a ham and cheese sandwich (sw), $e_{sw,psw} = -1$, $e_{sw,p_h} = e_{sw,p_{sw}} \cdot e_{p_{sw},p_h} = (-1) \cdot 0.5 = -0.5$.

5.9

a. $\dfrac{\partial s_x}{\partial I} = \dfrac{p_x I \, \partial x/\partial I - p_x x}{I^2}$. Multiplication by $\dfrac{I}{s_x} = \dfrac{I^2}{p_x x}$

gives the result.

b.–d. All of these proceed as in part (a).

e. Use Slutsky equation—see detailed solutions.

5.11

a. Just follow the approaches used in the two-good cases in the text (see detailed solutions).

5.13

a. $\ln E(p_x, p_y, U) =$
$a_0 + \alpha_1 \ln p_x + \alpha_2 \log p_y + \frac{1}{2}\gamma_{11}(\ln p_x)^2$
$+ \frac{1}{2}\gamma_{22}(\ln p_y)^2 + \gamma_{12}\ln p_x \ln p_y + U\beta_0 p_x^{\beta_1} p_y^{\beta_2}$.

b. Doubling all prices adds log 2 to the log of the expenditure function, thereby doubling it (with U held constant).

c. $s_x = \alpha_1 + \gamma_{11}\ln p_x + \gamma_{12}\ln p_y + U\beta_0\beta_1 p_x^{\beta_1-1} p_y^{\beta_2}$.

CHAPTER 6

6.1

a. Convert this to a Cobb-Douglas with $\alpha = \beta = 0.5$. Result follows from prior examples.

b. Also follows from Cobb-Douglas

c. Set $\partial m/\partial p_s = \partial s/\partial p_m$ and cancel the symmetric substitution effects.

d. Use the Cobb-Douglas representation.

6.3

a. $p_{bt} = 2p_b + p_t$.

b. Since p_c and I are constant, $c = I/2p_c$ is also constant.

c. Yes—since changes in p_b or p_t affect only p_{bt}.

6.5

a. $p_2 x_2 + p_3 x_3 = p_3(kx_2 + x_3)$.

b. Relative price $= (p_2 + t)/(p_3 + t)$.
Approaches $p_2/p_3 < 1$ as $t \to 0$.
Approaches 1 as $t \to \infty$.
So, an increase in t raises the relative price of x_2.

c. Does not strictly apply since changes in t change relative prices.

d. May reduce spending on x_2—the effect on x_3 is uncertain.

6.7

Show $x_i \cdot \partial x_j/\partial I = x_j \cdot \partial x_i/\partial I$ and use symmetry of net substitution effects.

6.9

a. $CV = E(p'_1, p'_2, \bar{p}_3, \ldots, \bar{p}_n, \bar{U}) - E(p_1, p_2, \bar{p}_3, \ldots, \bar{p}_n, \bar{U})$.

b. See graphs in detailed solutions—note that change in one price shifts compensated demand curve in the other market.

c. Symmetry of cross-price effects implies that order is irrelevant.

d. Smaller for complements than for substitutes.

6.11

See graphs in detailed solutions or in Samuelson reference.

CHAPTER 7

7.1

$P = 0.525$.

7.3

a. One trip: expected value $= 0.5 \cdot 0 + 0.5 \cdot 12 = 6$.
Two trip: expected value $= 0.25 \cdot 0 + 0.5 \cdot 6 + 0.25 \cdot 12 = 6$.

b. Two-trip strategy is preferred because of smaller variance.

c. Adding trips reduces variance, but at a diminishing rate. So desirability depends on the trips' cost.

7.5

a. $E(U) = 0.75 \ln(10,000) + 0.25 \ln(9,000) = 9.1840$.

b. $E(U) = \ln(9,750) = 9.1850$—insurance is preferable.

c. $260

7.7

a. Plant corn.

b. Yes, a mixed crop should be chosen. Diversification increases variance, but takes advantage of wheat's high yield.

c. 44 percent wheat, 56 percent corn

d. The farmer would only plant wheat.

7.9

a. $r(W) = (\mu + W/\gamma)^{-1}$.

b. If $\mu = 0, \theta = [(1-\gamma)/\gamma]^{\gamma-1}, U(W) = W^{1-\gamma}/(1-\gamma)^{1-\gamma}, rr(W) = \gamma$.

c. $r(W) \to 1/\mu$.

d. Let $A = 1/\mu$.

e. $U(W) = \theta(W^2 - 2\mu W + \mu^2)$.

f. For example, function may be unbounded and so St. Petersburg paradox can be regenerated.

7.11

a. Risk aversion is an unwillingness to substitute between states.

b. $R = 1$ implies perfect substitution, $R = -\infty$ implies zero substitution.

c. Depends on whether goods are gross substitutes or gross complements.

d. *i.* $R \approx -3$.

   ii. A 2 percent premium roughly compensates for a 10 percent gamble with $R = -3$.

7.13

a. If utility of wealth is homothetic, then uniform tax will not affect allocation.

b. Increases incentives to hold risky assets, especially for those less risk averse.

c. Tax on asset returns will increase allocation to risky assets—see graph in detailed solutions.

CHAPTER 8

8.1

a. (C, F)

b. Each player randomizes over the two actions with equal probability.

c. Players each earn 4 in the pure-strategy equilibrium. Players 1 and 2 earn 6 and 7, respectively, in the mixed-strategy equilibrium.

d. The extensive form is similar to Figures 18.1 and 18.2 but has three branches from each node rather than two.

8.3

a. The extensive form is similar to Figures 8.1 and 8.2.

b. (Don't veer, veer) and (veer, don't veer)

c. Players randomize with equal probabilities over the two actions.

d. Teen 2 has four contingent strategies: always veer, never veer, do the same as Teen 1, and do the opposite of Teen 1.

e. The first is (don't veer, always veer), the second is (don't veer, do the opposite), and the third is (veer, never veer).

f. (Don't veer, do the opposite) is a subgame-perfect equilibrium.

8.5

a. If all play blond, then one would prefer to deviate to brunette to obtain a positive payoff. If all play brunette, then one would prefer to deviate to blond for payoff a rather than b.

b. Playing brunette provides a certain payoff of b and blond provides a payoff of a with probability $(1 - p)^{n-1}$ (the probability no other player approaches the blond). Equating the two payoffs yields $p^* = 1 - (b/a)^{1/(n-1)}$.

c. The probability the blond is approached by at least one male equals 1 minus the probability no males approach her: $1 - (1 - p^*)^n = 1 - (b/a)^{n/(n-1)}$. This expression is decreasing in n because $n/(n-1)$ is decreasing in n and b/a is a fraction.

8.7

a. The best-response function is $l_{LC} = 3.5 + l_2/4$ for the low-cost type of player 1, $l_{HC} = 2.5 + l_2/4$ for the high-cost type, and $l_2 = 3 + \bar{l}_1/4$ for player 2, where $\bar{l}_1$ is the average for player 1. Solving these equations yields $l_{LC}^* = 4.5$, $l_{HC}^* = 3.5$, and $l_2^* = 4$.

c. The low-cost type of player 1 earns 20.25 in the Bayesian-Nash equilibrium and 20.55 in the full-information game, so it would prefer to signal its type if it could. Similar calculations show that the high-cost player would like to hide its type.

8.9

For any strategy profile besides the dominant-strategy equilibrium, each player would have an incentive to deviate to its dominant strategy, ruling out the profile as a Nash equilibrium.

8.11

a. The condition for cooperation to be sustainable with one period of punishment is $\delta \geq 1$, so one period of punishment is not enough. Two periods of punishment are enough as long as $\delta^2 + \delta - 1 \geq 0$, or $\delta \geq 0.62$.

b. The required condition is that the present discounted value of the payoffs from cooperating, $2/(1 - \delta)$, exceed that from deviating, $3 + \delta(1 - \delta^{10})/(1 - \delta) + 2\delta^{11}/(1 - \delta)$. Simplifying, $2\delta - \delta^{11} - 1 \geq 0$. Using numerical or graphical methods, this condition can be shown to be $\delta \geq 0.50025$, not much stricter than the condition for cooperation with infinitely many periods of punishment ($\delta \geq 1/2$).

CHAPTER 9

9.1

a. $k = 10$ and $l = 5$.

b. $k = 8$ and $l = 8$.

c. $k = 9$, $l = 6.5$, $k = 9.5$, and $l = 5.75$ (fractions of hours).

d. The isoquant is linear between solutions (a) and (b).

9.3

a. $q = 10$, $k = 100$, $l = 100$, $C = 10{,}000$.
b. $q = 10$, $k = 33$, $l = 132$, $C = 8{,}250$.
c. $q = 12.13$, $k = 40$, $l = 160$, $C = 10{,}000$.
d. Carla's ability to influence the decision depends on whether she can impose any costs on the bar if she is unhappy serving the additional tables. Such ability depends on whether Carla is a draw for Cheers' customers.

9.5

Let $A = 1$ for simplicity.

a. $f_k = \alpha k^{\alpha-1} l^\beta > 0$, $f_l = \beta k^\alpha l^{\beta-1} > 0$,
    $f_{kk} = \alpha(\alpha - 1)k^{\alpha-2}l^\beta < 0$,
    $f_{ll} = \beta(\beta - 1)k^\alpha l^{\beta-2} < 0$,
    $f_{kl} = f_{lk} = \alpha\beta k^{\alpha-1}l^{\beta-1} > 0$.
b. $e_{q,k} = f_k \cdot k/q = \alpha$, $e_{q,l} = f_l \cdot l/q = \beta$.
c. $f(tk, tl) = t^{\alpha+\beta}f(k, l)$;
    $\partial f(tk, tl)/\partial t \cdot t/f(k, l) = (\alpha + \beta)t^{\alpha+\beta}$.
    At $t = 1$ this is just $\alpha + \beta$.
d., e. Apply the definitions using the derivatives from part (a).

9.7

a. $\beta_0 = 0$.
b. $MP_k = \beta_2 + \frac{1}{2}\beta_1\sqrt{l/k}$; $MP_L = \beta_3 + \frac{1}{2}\beta_1\sqrt{k/l}$.
c. In general, σ is not constant. If $\beta_2 = \beta_3 = 0, \sigma = 1$. If $\beta_1 = 0, \sigma = \infty$.

9.9

a. If $f(tk, tl) = tf(k, l)$ then $e_{q,t} = \partial f(tk, tl)/\partial t \cdot t/f(tk, tl)$. If $t \to 1$ then $f(k, l)/f(k, l) = 1$.
b. Apply Euler's theorem and use part (a): $f(k, l) = f_k k + f_l l$.
c. $e_{q,t} = 2(1 - q)$. Hence $q < 0.5$ implies $e_{q,t} > 1$ and $q > 0.5$ implies $e_{q,t} < 1$.
d. The production function has an upper bound of $q = 1$.

9.11

a. Apply Euler's theorem to each f_i.
b. With $n = 2$, $k^2 f_{kk} + 2kl f_{kl} + l^2 f_{ll} = k(k - 1)f(k, l)$. If $k = 1$, this implies $f_{kl} > 0$. If $k > 1$, it is even clearer that f_{kl} must be positive. For $k < 1$, the case is not so clear.
c. Implies that $f_{ij} > 0$ is more common for $k = 1$.
d. $\left(\sum \alpha_i\right)^2 - \sum \alpha_i = k(k - 1)$.

CHAPTER 10

10.1

a. The draftsman is right because the minimum of SAC curves occurs where the slope is zero. In the constant-returns-to-scale case, both are correct.

10.3

a., b. $q = 150, J = 25, MC = 4$;
    $q = 300, J = 100, MC = 8$;
    $q = 450, J = 225, MC = 12$.

10.5

a. $q = 2\sqrt{k \cdot l}$; $k = 100$, $q = 20\sqrt{l}$, $l = q^2/400$.
    $SC = vk + wl = 100 + q^2/100$,
    $SAC = SC/q = 100/q + q/100$.
b. $SMC = q/50$.

q	SC	SAC	SMC
25	106.25	4.25	0.50
50	125	2.5	1
100	200	2	2
200	500	2.5	4

c., d. As long as the marginal cost of producing one more unit is below the average-cost curve, average costs will be falling. Similarly, if the marginal cost of producing one more unit is higher than the average cost, then average costs will be rising. Therefore, the SMC curve must intersect the SAC curve at its lowest point.
e. $C = v\bar{k} + wq^2/4\bar{k}$.
f. $\bar{k} = (q/2)w^{1/2}v^{1/2}$.
g. $C = qw^{1/2}v^{1/2}$.
h. Yields an envelope relationship.

10.7

a. $l = \partial C/\partial w = \frac{2}{3}q(v/w)^{1/3}$.
    $k = \frac{1}{3}q(w/v)^{2/3}$.
b. $q = Bl^{2/3}k^{1/3}$ where B is a constant.

10.9

a. $C = q^{1/\gamma}[(v/a)^{1-\sigma} + (w/b)^{1-\sigma}]^{1/(1-\sigma)}$.
b. $C = qa^{-a}b^{-b}v^a w^b$.
c. $wl/vk = b/a$.
d. $l/k = [(v/a)/(w/b)]^\sigma$ so $wl/vk = (v/w)^{\sigma-1}(b/a)^\sigma$. Labor's relative share is an increasing function of b/a. If $\sigma > 1$, labor's share moves in the same direction as v/w. If $\sigma < 1$, labor's relative share moves in the opposite direction to v/w. This accords with intuition on how substitutability should affect shares.

10.11

a. $s_{i,j} = \partial \ln C_i/\partial \ln w_j - \partial \ln C_j/\partial \ln w_j = e_{x_i^c, w_j} - e_{x_j^c, w_j}$.
b. $s_{i,j} = \partial \ln C_j/\partial \ln w_i - \partial \ln C_i/\partial \ln w_i = e_{x_j^c, w_i} - e_{x_i^c, w_i}$.
c. See detailed solutions.

CHAPTER 11

11.1
a. $q = 50$.
b. $\pi = 200$.
c. $q = 5P - 50$.

11.3
a., b. $q = a + bP$, $P = q/b - a/b$, $R = P_q = (q^2 - aq)/b$, $mr = 2q/b - a/b$, and the mr curve has double the slope of the demand curve, so $d - mr = -q/b$.
c. $mr = P(1 + 1/e) = P(1 + 1/b)$.
d. It follows since $e = \partial q/\partial P \cdot P/q$.

11.5
a. $C = wq^2/4$.
b. $\pi(P, w) = P^2/w$.
c. $q = 2P/w$.
d. $l(P, w) = P^2/w^2$.

11.7
a. Diminishing returns is needed to ensure that a profit-maximizing output choice exists.
b. $C(q, v, w) = (w + v)q^2/100, \Pi(P, v, w) = 25P^2/(w + v)$.
c. $q = \partial\Pi/\partial P = 50P/(w + v) = 20, \Pi = 6,000$.
d. $q = 30, \Pi = 13,500$.

11.9
b. Diminishing returns is needed to ensure increasing marginal cost.
c. σ determines how firms adapt to disparate input prices.
d. $q = \partial\Pi/\partial P$
   $= 1/(1 - \gamma)KP^{\gamma/(\gamma-1)}(v^{1-\sigma} + w^{1-\sigma})^{\gamma/(1-\sigma)(\gamma-1)} \cdot$
   The size of σ does not affect the supply elasticity, but greater substitutability implies that increases in one input price will shift the supply curve less.
e. See detailed solutions.

11.11
a. Shephard's lemma shows C_v, C_w are the demands for inputs when $Q = 1$. The result follows from the assumption of constant returns to scale.
b. Differentiate results from part (a).
c. Follows because C is homogeneous of degree 1 in the input prices.
d. Substitution
e. Substitution of elasticity definitions.
f. The substitution effect is similar to that for a single firm. The output effect is derived from moving along the demand curve for the product.

CHAPTER 12

12.1
a. $q = 10\sqrt{P} - 20$.
b. $Q = 1,000\sqrt{P} - 2,000$.
c. $P = 25; Q = 3,000$.

12.3
a. $P = 6$.
b. $q = 60,100 - 10,000P$.
c. $P = 6.01, P = 5.99$.
d. $e_{q,p} = -600$.
   a' $P = 6$.
   b' $Q = 359,800 - 59,950P$.
   c' $P = 6.002; P = 5.998$.
   d' $e_{q,p} = -0.6; e_{q,p} = -3,597$.

12.5
a. $n = 50, Q = 1,000, q = 20, P = 10$, and $w = 200$.
b. $n = 72, Q = 1,728, q = 24, P = 14$, and $w = 288$.
c. The increase for the makers = \$5,368. The linear approximation for the supply curve yields approximately the same result.

12.7
a. $P = 11, Q = 500$, and $r = 1$.
b. $P = 12, Q = 1,000$, and $r = 2$.
c. $\Delta PS = 750$.
d. Δ rents $= 750$.

12.9
a. Use exponential demand and supply: $Q_D = aP^b$, $Q_S = cP^d$. If P is supplier price, then demand is $Q_D = a(1 + t)^b P^b$ and equilibrium requires $a(1 + t)^b/c = P^{d-b}$. Taking logs of this expression, using the approximation that $\ln(1 + t) \approx t$, and differentiating with respect to t yields $d \ln P/dt = b/(d - b)$. A similar expression holds for demand price.
b. $DW \approx 0.5\Delta P\Delta Q \approx 0.5tP_0\Delta \ln Q \cdot Q_0 = 0.5td \cdot \Delta \ln P \cdot P_0 Q_0 = 0.5t^2[db/(d - b)]P_0 Q_0$.
c. These results are almost identical to those in the chapter, and may often be easier to use.

12.11
a. Foreign supply curve augments domestic one (see graph in detailed solutions).
b. Tariff shifts foreign portion of supply curve (see graph).
c. Loss of consumer surplus is similar to perfectly elastic case. Tariff also causes a loss of some foreign producer surplus in this case.

CHAPTER 13

13.1

b. If $y = 2x$, $x^2 + 2(2x)^2 = 900$; $9x^2 = 900$; $x = 10$, $y = 20$.

c. If $x = 9$ on the production possibility frontier, $y = \sqrt{819/2} = 20.24$.
   If $x = 11$ on the frontier, $y = \sqrt{779/2} = 19.74$.
   Hence, RPT is approximately $-\Delta y/\Delta x = -(-0.50)/2 = 0.25$.

13.3

Let F = Food, C = Cloth.

a. Labor constraint: $F + C = 100$.
b. Land constraint: $2F + C = 150$.
c. Outer frontier satisfies both constraints.
d. Frontier is concave because it must satisfy both constraints. Since the $RPT = 1$ for the labor constraint and 2 for the land constraint, the production possibility frontier of part (c) exhibits an increasing RPT; hence it is concave.
e. Constraints intersect at $F = 50$, $C = 50$. For $F < 50$, $dC/dF = -1$ so $P_F/P_C = 1$. For $F > 50$, $dC/dF = -2$ so $P_F/P_C = 2$.
f. If for consumers $dC/dF = -\frac{5}{4}$ then $P_F/P_C = \frac{5}{4}$.
g. If $P_F/P_C = 1.9$ or $P_F/P_C = 1.1$, will still choose $F = 50$, $C = 50$ since both price lines are "tangent" to production possibility frontier at its kink.
h. $0.8F + 0.9C = 100$. Capital constraint: $C = 0, F = 125, F = 0, C = 111.1$. This results in the same PPF since capital constraint is nowhere binding.

13.5

a. The contract curve is a straight line. Only equilibrium price ratio is $P_H/P_C = 4/3$.
b. Initial equilibrium on the contract curve
c. Not on the contract curve—equilibrium is between $40H$, $80C$ and $48H$, $96C$.
d. Smith takes everything; Jones starves.

13.7

a. $p_x = 0.374, p_y = 0.238, p_k = 0.124, p_l = 0.264$, $x = 26.2, y = 22.3$.
b. $p_x = 0.284, p_y = 0.338, p_k = 0.162, p_l = 0.217$, $x = 30.2, y = 18.5$.
c. Raises price of labor and relative price of x.

13.9

Computer simulations show that increasing returns to scale is still compatible with a concave production possibility frontier provided the input intensities of the two goods are suitably different.

13.11

a. Doubling prices leaves excess demands unchanged.
b. Since, by Walras' law, $p_1 ED_1 = 0$ and $ED_1 = 0$. The excess demand in market 1 can be calculated explicitly as: $ED_1 = (3p_2^2 - 6p_2 p_3 + 2p_3^2 + p_1 p_2 + 2p_1 p_3)/p_1^2$. This is also homogeneous of degree 0 in the prices.
c. $p_2/p_1 = 3$, $p_3/p_1 = 5$.

CHAPTER 14

14.1

a. $Q = 24$, $P = 29$, and $\pi = 576$.
b. $MC = P = 5$ and $Q = 48$.
c. Consumers' surplus = 1,152. Under monopoly, consumer surplus = 288, profits = 576, deadweight loss = 288.

14.3

a. $Q = 25$, $P = 35$, and $\pi = 625$.
b. $Q = 20$, $P = 50$, and $\pi = 800$.
c. $Q = 40$, $P = 30$, and $\pi = 800$.

14.5

a. $P = 15$, $Q = 5$, $C = 65$, and $\pi = 10$.
b. $A = 3$, $P = 15$, $Q = 6.05$, and $\pi = 12.25$.

14.7

a. Under competition: $P = 10$, $Q = 500, CS = 2,500$. Under monopoly: $P = 16$, $Q = 200$, $CS = 400$.
b. See graph in detailed solutions.
c. Loss of 2,100, of which 800 is transferred to monopoly profits, 400 is a loss from increased costs (not relevant in usual analysis), and 900 is a deadweight loss.

14.9

First-order conditions for a maximum imply $X = C(X)/C'(X)$—that is, X is chosen independently of Q.

14.11

a. $\partial U/\partial Q - \partial C/\partial Q = 0$, $\partial U/\partial X - \partial C/\partial X = 0$.
b. $P + Q[\partial P/\partial Q] - \partial C/\partial Q = 0$, $\partial P/\partial X \cdot Q - \partial C/\partial X = 0$.
c. Using the hint, parts (a) and (b) imply $\partial SW/\partial Q = -Q[\partial P/\partial Q] > 0$.
d. $\partial SW/\partial X = \partial U/\partial X - \partial P/\partial X \cdot Q$, where the derivatives are calculated at the monopolist's profit-maximizing choices. It is generally not possible to sign this expression.

CHAPTER 15

15.1

a. $P^m = Q^m = 75$, $\Pi^m = 5,625$.
b. $P^c = q_i^c = 50$, $\pi_i^c = 2,500$.
c. $P^b = 0$, $Q^b = 150$, $\pi_i^b = 0$.

15.3

a. The best-response function for firm 1 is $q_1 = (1 - q_2 - c_1)/2$ and similarly for firm 2. The equilibrium quantities are $q_i^c = (1 - 2c_i + c_j)/3$. Further, $Q^c = (2 - c_1 - c_2)/3$, $P^c = (1 + c_1 + c_2)/3$, $\pi_i^c = (1 - 2c_1 + c_2)^2/9$, $\Pi^c = \pi_1^c + \pi_2^c$, $CS^c = (2 - c_1 - c_2)^2/18$, and $W^c = \Pi^c + CS^c$.
b. The diagram looks like Figure 15.2. A reduction in firm 1's cost would shift its best response out, increasing its equilibrium output and reducing 2's.

15.5

a. Firm i's best response is $p_i = (1 + bp_j)/2$. The Nash equilibrium is $p_i^* = 1/(2 - b)$.
b. $q_i^* = (1 - 2b)/(2 - b)$; $\pi_i^* = 1/(2 - b)^2$.
c. The diagram would look like Figure 15.4. An increase in b would shift out both best responses and result in higher equilibrium prices for both.

15.7

a. Firm 2's best response is $q_2 = (150 - q_1)/2$. Substituting this into firm 1's profit function and taking the first-order condition yields $150 - 2q_1 = 0$, implying $q_1^* = 75$ and $q_2^* = 75/2$.
b. If firm 1 accommodates 2's entry, the outcome in part (a) arises, and 1 earns 2,812.5. To deter 2's entry, 1 needs to produce $\bar{q}_1$ sufficiently high that even if 2 best-responds to $\bar{q}_1$, generating profit $(150 - \bar{q}_1)^2/4 - K_2$, this profit is less than or equal to 0. The threshold value of $\bar{q}_1$ is $\bar{q}_1 = 150 - 2\sqrt{K_2}$. Firm 1's profit from operating alone in the market and producing this output is $(150 - 2\sqrt{K_2})(2\sqrt{K_2})$, which exceeds 2,812.5 if (as can be shown by graphing both sides of the inequality) $K_2 \geq 120.6$.

15.9

a. Firm i's profit is $q_i(a - bq_i - bQ_{-i} - c)$ with associated first-order condition $a - 2b - bQ_{-i} - c = 0$. Imposing symmetry $[Q_{-i}^* = (n - 1)q_i^*]$ and solving, $q_i^* = (a - c)/(n + 1)b$. Further, $Q^* = n(a - c)/(n + 1)b$, $P^* = (a + nc)/(n + 1)$, $\Pi^* = n\pi_i^* = (n/b)[(a - c)/(n + 1)]2$, $CS^* = (n^2/b) \cdot [(a - c)/(n + 1)]^2$, and $W^* = [n/(n + 1)] \cdot [(a - c)^2/b]$. Because firms are symmetric, $s_i = 1/n$, implying $H = n(1/n)^2 = 1/n$.
b. We can obtain a rough idea of the effect of merger by seeing how the variables in part (a) change with

a reduction in n. Per-firm output, price, industry profit, and the Herfindahl index increase. Total output, consumer surplus, and welfare decrease.
c. Substituting $c_1 = c_2 = 1/4$ into the answers for 15.3, we have $q_i^* = 1/4$, $Q^* = 1/2$, $P^* = 1/2$, $\Pi^* = 1/8$, $CS^* = 1/8$, and $W^* = 1/4$. Also, $H = 1/2$.
d. Substituting $c_1 = 0$ and $c_2 = 1/4$ into the answers for 15.3, we have $q_1^* = 5/12$, $q_1^* = 2/12$, $Q^* = 7/12$, $P^* = 5/12$, $\Pi^* = 29/144$, $CS^* = 49/288$, and $W^* = 107/288$. Also, $H = 29/49$.
e. Comparing part (a) with (b) suggests that increases in the Herfindahl index are associated with lower welfare. The opposite is evidenced in the comparison of part (c) to (d): welfare and the Herfindahl increase together. General conclusions are thus hard to reach.

15.11

a. This is the indifference condition for a consumer located distance x from firm i.
b. The profit-maximizing price is $p = (p^* + c + t/n)/2$.
c. Setting $p = p^*$ and solving for p^* gives the specified answer. Equilibrium price is increasing in cost and the degree of differentiation, given by the transportation cost and the spacing between firms (depending on their numbers).
d. Substituting $p = p^* = c + t/n$ into the profit function gives the specified answer.
e. Setting $t/n^2 - K = 0$ and solving for n yields $n^* = \sqrt{t/K}$.
f. Total transportation costs equal the number of half-segments between firms, $2n$, times the transportation costs of consumers on the half segment, $\int_0^{1/2n} tx \, dx = t/8n^2$. Total fixed cost equal nF. The number of firms minimizing the sum of the two is $n^{**} = (1/2)\sqrt{t/K}$.

CHAPTER 16

16.1

a. Full income $= 40,000$; $l = 2,000$ hours.
b. $l = 1,400$ hours.
c. $l = 1,700$ hours.
d. Supply is asymptotic to 2,000 hours as w rises.

16.3

a. Grant $= 6,000 - 0.75(I)$.
   If $I = 0$ Grant $= 6,000$.
   $I = 2,000$ Grant $= 4,500$.
   $I = 4,000$ Grant $= 3,000$.
b. Grant $= 0$ when $6,000 - 0.75I = 0$, $I = 6,000/0.75 = 8,000$.
c. Assume there are 8,000 hours in the year. Full Income $= 4 \times 8,000 = 32,000 = c + 4h$.

d. Full Income

$= 32,000 + \text{grant}$

$= 32,000 + 6,000 - 0.75 \cdot 4(8,000 - h)$

$= 38,000 - 24,000 + 3h = c + 4h$

or $14,000 = c + h$ for $I < 8,000$. That is: for $h < 6,000$ hours, welfare grant creates a kink in the budget constraint at 6,000 hours of leisure.

16.5

a. For $ME_l = MRP_l$, $l/40 = 10 - l/40$ so $2l/40 = 10$ and $l = 200$. Get w from supply curve: $w = l/80 = 200/80 = \$2.50$.

b. For Carl, the marginal expense of labor now equals the minimum wage—$w_m = \$4.00$. Setting this equal to the MRP yields $l = 240$.

c. Under perfect competition, a minimum wage means higher wages but fewer workers employed. Under monopsony, a minimum wage may result in higher wages *and* more workers employed.

16.7

a. Since $q = 240x - 2x^2$, total revenue is $5q = 1,200x - 10x^2$. $MRP = \partial TR/\partial x = 1,200 - 20x$. Production of pelts $x = \sqrt{l}$. Total cost $= wl = 10x^2$. Marginal cost $= \partial C/\partial x = 20x$. Under competition, price of pelts $= MC = 20x$, $MRP = p_x = MC = 20x$; $x = 30$, $p_x = 600$.

b. From Dan's perspective, demand for pelts $= MRP = 1,200 - 20x$, $R = p_x \cdot x = 1,200x - 20x^2$. Marginal revenue: $\partial R/\partial x = 1,200 - 40x$ set equal to marginal cost $= 20x$. Yields $x = 20$, $p_x = 800$.

c. From UF's perspective, supply of pelts $= MC = 20x = p_x$, total cost $p_x x = 20x^2$ and $ME_x = \partial C/\partial x = 40x$. So $ME_x = 40x = MRP_x = 1,200 - 20x$ with a solution of $x = 20$, $p_x = 400$.

16.9

$E[U(y_{\text{job}_1})] = 100 \cdot 40 - 0.5 \cdot 1,600 = 3,200$.

$E[U(y_{\text{job}_2})] = E[U(wh)] = E[100wh - 0.5(wh)^2] = 800w - 0.5 \cdot [36w^2 + 64w^2] = 800w - 50w^2$.

16.11

a. $\partial V/\partial w = \lambda(1 - h) = \lambda l(w, n)$, $\partial V/\partial n = \lambda$, $l(w, n) = (\partial V/\partial w)/(\partial V/\partial n)$.

b. $\partial x_i/\partial w = \partial x_i/\partial w|_{U=\text{constant}} + l[\partial x_i/\partial n]$.

c. $ME_l = \partial wl/\partial l = w + l\partial w/\partial l = w[1 + 1/(e_{l,w})]$.

CHAPTER 17

17.1

b. Income and substitution effects work in opposite directions. If $\partial c_1/\partial r < 0$, then c_2 is price elastic.

c. Budget constraint passes through y_1, y_2, and rotates through this point as r changes. Income effect depends on whether $y_1 > c_1$ or $y_1 < c_1$ initially.

17.3

25 years

17.5

a. Not at all

b. Tax would be on opportunity cost of capital.

c. Taxes are paid later, so cost of capital is reduced.

d. If tax rates decline, the benefit of accelerated depreciation is reduced.

17.9

a. Maximizes expected utility.

b. If marginal utility is convex, applying Jensen's inequality to that function implies $E[U'(c_1)] > U'[E(c_1)] = U'(c_0)$. So must increase next period's consumption to yield equality.

c. Part (b) shows that this person will save more when next period's consumption is random.

d. Prompting added precautionary savings would require an even higher r, exacerbating the paradox.

17.11

a. Use $x/(1 - x) = x + x^2 + \cdots$ for $x < 1$.

b. See detailed solutions for derivative.

c. The increased output from a higher t must be balanced against (1) the delay in getting the first yield and (2) the opportunity cost of a delay in all future rotations.

d. $f(t)$ is asymptotic to 50 as $t \to \infty$.

e. $t^* = 100$.

f. $t^* = 104.1$.

CHAPTER 18

18.1

a. The lawyer maximizes $(1/3)l - l^2/2$, yielding equilibrium effort $l^* = 1/3$. His surplus is $1/18$ and the plaintiff's is $(2/3)l^* = 2/9$.

b. The lawyer maximizes $cl - l^2/2$, yielding equilibrium effort $l^* = c$. His surplus is $c^2/2$ and the plaintiff's is $c(1 - c)$.

c. The optimal contingency fee for the plaintiff is $c^* = 1/2$, maximizing her surplus $c(1 - c)$. Her surplus is $1/4$ and the lawyer's is $1/8$.

d. With a 100% contingency fee, the lawyer chooses $l^* = 1$ and earns a surplus of $1/2$, which the plaintiff can extract initially by selling the case to him.

18.3

a. The low type's second-best quantity satisfies Equation 18.51 at the new parameter values: $q_L^{**} = 1$. The tariff is $T_L^{**} = \theta_L v(1) = 30$. The high type's quantity is the same as in the first best: $q_H^{**} = 16$. The tariff just satisfies incentive compatibility: $T_H^{**} = 150$.

18.5

a. With no insurance, a lefty's expected utility is 9.1261 and a righty's is 9.1893. The monopolist fully insures both at a premium that reduces each to his no-insurance utility: $p_L = 808$ and $p_H = 208$.
b. Lefties receive the same policy as in part (a).
c. Lefties are fully insured. The second-best values of the other policy terms (p_L, p_R, and x_R) maximize the insurer's expected profit
$[p_L - (0.8)(1,000)]/2 + [p_R - 0.2x_R]/2$ subject to the righty's participation and lefty's incentive compatibility constraints. A spreadsheet calculation shows that the solution is approximately $p_L^{**} = 808$, $p_R^{**} = 0$, and $x_R^{**} = 0$.

18.7

a. $(1/2)(10,000) + (1/2)(2,000) = \$6,000$.
b. If sellers value cars at 8,000, only lemons will be sold at a market price of \$2,000. If sellers value cars at 6,000, all cars will be sold at a market price of \$6,000.

18.9

The optimum of the fully informed patient satisfies $(\partial U_p/\partial m)/(\partial U_p/\partial x) = p_m$ or $MRS = p_m$, where MRS is the patient's marginal rate of substitution. The doctor's optimum satisfies $p_m U_d' + \partial U_p/\partial m - p_m \partial U_p/\partial x = 0$. Rearranging, this implies $MRS < p_m$, in turn implying that the doctor chooses more medical care (a diagram of the patient's indifference curves helps to show this).

18.11

a. Bidder 1 maximizes $\Pr(b_1 > \max(b_2, \ldots, b_n))(v_1 - b_1)$, which equals $(v_1 - b_1)\Pi_{i=2}^n \Pr(v_i < b_1/k)$ assuming rivals use linear bidding strategies, which in turn equals $(v_1 - b_1)(b_1/k)^{n-1}$. Maximizing with respect to b_1 yields $b_1 = v_1(n-1)/n$. Expected revenue is $E(v_{(n)})(n-1)/n$. This equals $(n-1)/(n+1)$, using the formula for the expected value of the maximum order statistic $v_{(n)}$.
b. Buyers bid $b_i = v_i$. Expected revenue is $E(v_{(n-1)}) = (n-1)/(n+1)$.
c. Yes.
d. Bids converge to valuations in the first-price auction but don't change in the second-price auction. Expected revenue approaches 1.

CHAPTER 19

19.1

a. $P = 20$ and $q = 50$.
b. $P = 20$, $q = 40$, $MC = 16$, and tax $= 4$.

19.3

a. $n = 400$. The externality arises because one well's drilling affects all wells' output.
b. $n = 200$.
c. Fee $= 2,000$/well.

19.5

The tax will improve matters only if the output restriction required by the externality exceeds the output restriction brought about by the monopoly.

19.7

a. If each person is a free rider, utility will be 0.
b. $y = 5$, $x = 50$, $x/100 = 0.5$, and utility $= \sqrt{2.5}$.

19.9

a. Want g_i' to be the same for all firms.
b. A uniform tax will not achieve the result in part (a).
c. In general optimal pollution tax is $t = (p - w/f') \cdot 1/g'$, which will vary from firm to firm. However, if firms have simple linear production functions given by $q_i = al_i$, then a uniform tax can achieve efficiency even if g_i differs among firms. In this case the optimal tax is $t = \lambda(a - w)/a$, where λ is the value of the Lagrangian in the social optimum described in part (a).
d. It is more efficient to tax pollution than to tax output.

19.11

a. Choose b and t so that y is the same in each state. Requires $t = U$.
b. b always $= (1 - t)w$ and $t = U$.
c. No. Because this person is risk averse, he or she will always opt for equal income in each state.

Glossary of Frequently Used Terms

Some of the terms that are used frequently in this book are defined below. The reader may wish to use the index to find those sections of the text that give more complete descriptions of these concepts.

Adverse Selection The problem facing insurers that risky types are both more likely to accept an insurance policy and more expensive to serve.

Asymmetric Information A situation in which an agent on one side of a transaction has information that the agent on the other side does not have.

Bayesian-Nash Equilibrium A strategy profile in a two-player simultaneous-move game in which player 1 has private information. This generalizes the Nash equilibrium concept to allow for player 2's beliefs about player 1's type.

Bertrand Paradox The Nash equilibrium in a simultaneous-move pricing game is competitive pricing even when there are only two firms.

Best Response s_i is a best response for player i to rivals' strategies, s_{-i}, denoted by $s_i \in BR_i(s_{-i})$, if $U_i(s_i, s_{-i}) \geq U_i(s_i', s_{-i})$ for all $s_i' \in S_i$.

Ceteris Paribus Assumption The assumption that all other relevant factors are held constant when examining the influence of one particular variable in an economic model. Reflected in mathematical terms by the use of partial differentiation.

Coase Theorem Result attributable to R. Coase: if bargaining costs are zero, an efficient allocation of resources can be attained in the presence of externalities through reliance on bargaining among the parties involved.

Compensated Demand Function Function showing relationship between the price of a good and the quantity consumed while holding real income (or utility) constant. Denoted by $x^c(p_x, p_y, U)$.

Compensating Variation (CV) The compensation required to restore a person's original utility level when prices change.

Compensating Wage Differentials Differences in real wages that arise when the characteristics of occupations cause workers in their supply decisions to prefer one job over another.

Complements (Gross) Two goods such that if the price of one rises, the quantity consumed of the other will fall. Goods x and y are gross complements if $\partial x / \partial p_y < 0$. *See also* Substitutes (Gross).

Complements (Net) Two goods such that if the price of one rises, the quantity consumed of the other will fall, holding real income (utility) constant. Goods x and y are net complements if

$$\partial x / \partial p_y \big|_{U=\bar{U}} < 0.$$

Such compensated cross-price effects are symmetric, that is,

$$\partial x / \partial p_y \big|_{U=\bar{U}} = \partial y / \partial p_x \big|_{U=\bar{U}}.$$

See also Substitutes (Net). Also called Hicksian substitutes and complements.

Composite Commodity A group of goods whose prices all move together—the relative prices of goods in the group do not change. Such goods can be treated as a single commodity in many applications.

Concave Function A function that lies everywhere below its tangent plane.

Constant Cost Industry An industry in which expansion of output and entry by new firms has no effect on the cost curves of individual firms.

Constant Returns to Scale *See* Returns to Scale.

Consumer Surplus The area below the Marshallian demand curve and above market price. Shows what an individual would pay for the right to make voluntary transactions at this price. Changes in consumer surplus can be used to measure the welfare effects of price changes.

Contingent Input Demand *See* Input Demand Functions.

Contour Line The set of points along which a function has a constant value. Useful for graphing three-dimensional functions in two dimensions. Individuals' indifference curve maps and firms' production isoquant maps are examples.

Contract Curve The set of all the efficient allocations of goods among those individuals in an exchange economy. Each of these allocations has the property that no one individual can be made better off without making someone else worse off.

Cost Function *See* Total Cost Function.

Cournot Equilibrium Equilibrium in duopoly quantity-setting game. A similar concept applies to an n-person game.

Deadweight Loss A loss of mutually beneficial transactions. Losses in consumer and producer surplus that are not transferred to another economic agent.

Decreasing Cost Industry An industry in which expansion of output generates cost-reducing externalities that cause the cost curves of those firms in the industry to shift downward.

Decreasing Returns to Scale *See* Returns to Scale.

Demand Curve A graph showing the ceteris paribus relationship between the price of a good and the quantity of that good purchased. A two-dimensional representation of the demand function $x = x(p_x, p_y, I)$. This is referred to as "Marshallian" demand to differentiate it from the compensated (Hicksian) demand concept.

Diminishing Marginal Productivity *See* Marginal Physical Product.

Diminishing Marginal Rate of Substitution *See* Marginal Rate of Substitution.

Discount Factor The degree to which a payoff next period is discounted in making this period's decisions; denoted by δ in the text. If r is the single-period interest rate, then usually $\delta = 1/(1 + r)$.

Discrimination, Price Occurs whenever a buyer or seller is able to use its market power effectively to separate markets and to follow a different price policy in each market. *See also* Price Discrimination.

Dominant Strategy A strategy, s_i^*, for player i that is a best response to the all-strategy profile of other players.

Duality The relationship between any constrained maximization problem and its related "dual" constrained minimization problem.

Economic Efficiency Exists when resources are allocated so that no activity can be increased without cutting back on some other activity. *See also* Pareto-Efficient Allocation.

Edgeworth Box Diagram A graphic device used to demonstrate economic efficiency. Most frequently used to illustrate the contract curve in an exchange economy, but also useful in the theory of production.

Elasticity A unit-free measure of the proportional effect of one variable on another. If $y = f(x)$, then $e_{y,x} = \partial y/\partial x \cdot x/y$.

Entry Conditions Characteristics of an industry that determine the ease with which a new firm may begin production. Under perfect competition, entry is assumed to be costless, whereas in a monopolistic industry there are significant barriers to entry.

Envelope Theorem A mathematical result: the change in the maximum value of a function brought about by a change in a parameter of the function can be found by partially differentiating the function with respect to the parameter (when all other variables take on their optimal values).

Equilibrium A situation in which no actors have an incentive to change their behavior. At an equilibrium price, the quantity demanded by individuals is exactly equal to that which is supplied by all firms.

Euler's Theorem A mathematical theorem: if $f(x_1, ..., x_n)$ is homogeneous of degree k, then

$$f_1 x_1 + f_2 x_2 + \cdots + f_n x_n = kf(x_1, ..., x_n).$$

Exchange Economy An economy in which the supply of goods is fixed (that is, no production takes place). The available goods, however, may be reallocated among individuals in the economy.

Expansion Path The locus of those cost-minimizing input combinations that a firm will choose to produce various levels of output (when the prices of inputs are held constant).

Expected Utility The average utility expected from a risky situation. If there are n outcomes, $x_1, ..., x_n$ with probabilities $p_1, ..., p_n$ ($\sum p_i = 1$), then the expected utility is given by

$$E(U) = p_1 U(x_1) + p_2 U(x_2) + \cdots + p_n U(x_n).$$

Expenditure Function A function derived from the individual's dual expenditure minimization problem. Shows the minimum expenditure necessary to achieve a given utility level:

$$\text{expenditures} = E(p_x, p_y, U).$$

Externality An effect of one economic agent on another that is not taken into account by normal market behavior.

First-Mover Advantage The advantage that may be gained by the player who moves first in a game.

First-Order Conditions Mathematical conditions that must necessarily hold if a function is to take on its maximum or minimum value. Usually show that any activity should be increased to the point at which marginal benefits equal marginal costs.

Fixed Costs Costs that do not change as the level of output changes in the short run. Fixed costs are in many respects irrelevant to the theory of short-run price determination. *See also* Variable Costs.

General Equilibrium Model A model of an economy that portrays the operation of many markets simultaneously.

Giffen's Paradox A situation in which the increase in a good's price leads individuals to consume more of the good. Arises because the good in question is inferior and because the income effect induced by the price change is stronger than the substitution effect.

Hidden Action An action taken by one party to a contract that cannot be directly observed by the other party.

Hidden Type A characteristic of one party to a contract that cannot be observed by the other party prior to agreeing to the contract.

Homogeneous Function A function, $f(x_1, x_2, ..., x_n)$, is homogeneous of degree k if

$$f(mx_1, mx_2, ..., mx_n) = m^k f(x_1, x_2, ..., x_n).$$

Homothetic Function A function that can be represented as a monotonic transformation of a homogeneous function. The slopes of the contour lines for such a function depend only on the ratios of the variables that enter the function, not on their absolute levels.

Income and Substitution Effects Two analytically different effects that come into play when an individual is faced with a changed price for some good. Income effects arise because a change in the price of a good will affect an individual's purchasing power. Even if purchasing power is held constant, however, substitution effects will cause individuals to reallocate their expectations. Substitution effects are reflected in movements along an indifference curve, whereas income effects entail a movement to a different indifference curve. *See also* Slutsky Equation.

Increasing Cost Industry An industry in which the expansion of output creates cost-increasing externalities, which cause the cost curves of those firms in the industry to shift upward.

Increasing Returns to Scale *See* Returns to Scale.

Indifference Curve Map A contour map of an individual's utility function showing those alternative bundles of goods from which the individual derives equal levels of welfare.

Indirect Utility Function A representative of utility as a function of all prices and income.

Individual Demand Curve The ceteris paribus relationship between the quantity of a good an individual chooses to consume and the good's price. A two-dimensional representation of $x = x(p_x, p_y, I)$ for one person.

Inferior Good A good that is bought in smaller quantities as an individual's income rises.

Inferior Input A factor of production that is used in smaller amounts as a firm's output expands.

Input Demand Functions These functions show how input demand for a profit-maximizing firm is based on input prices and on the demand for output. The input demand function for labor, for example, can be written as $l = l(P, v, w)$, where P is the market price of the firm's output. *Contingent* input demand functions $[l^c(v, w, q)]$ are derived from cost minimization and do not necessarily reflect profit-maximizing output choices.

Isoquant Map A contour map of the firm's production function. The contours show the alternative combinations of productive inputs that can be used to produce a given level of output.

Kuhn-Tucker Conditions First-order conditions for an optimization problem in which inequality constraints are present. These are generalizations of the first-order conditions for optimization with equality constraints.

Limit Pricing Choice of low-price strategies to deter entry.

Lindahl Equilibrium A hypothetical solution to the public goods problem: the tax share that each individual pays plays the same role as an equilibrium market price in a competitive allocation.

Long Run *See* Short Run–Long Run Distinction.

Lump Sum Principle The demonstration that general purchasing power taxes or transfers are more efficient than taxes or subsidies on individual goods.

Marginal Cost (MC) The additional cost incurred by producing one more unit of output: $MC = \partial C / \partial q$.

Marginal Physical Product (MP) The additional output that can be produced by one more unit of a particular input while holding all other inputs constant. It is usually assumed that an input's marginal productivity diminishes as additional units of the input are put into use while holding other inputs fixed. If $q = f(k, l)$, $MP_l = \partial q / \partial l$.

Marginal Rate of Substitution (MRS) The rate at which an individual is willing to trade one good for another while remaining equally well off. The MRS is the absolute value of the slope of an indifference curve. $MRS = -dy/dx|_{U = \bar{U}}$.

Marginal Revenue (MR) The additional revenue obtained by a firm when it is able to sell one more unit of output. $MR = \partial p \cdot q / \partial q = p(1 + 1/e_{q, p})$.

Marginal Revenue Product (MRP) The extra revenue that accrues to a firm when it sells the output that is produced by one more unit of some input. In the case of labor, for example, $MRP_l = MR \cdot MP_l$.

Marginal Utility (MU) The extra utility that an individual receives by consuming one more unit of a particular good.

Market Demand The sum of the quantities of a good demanded by all individuals in a market. Will depend on the price of the good, prices of other goods, each consumer's preferences, and on each consumer's income.

Market Period A very short period over which quantity supplied is fixed and not responsive to changes in market price.

Mixed Strategy A strategy in which a player chooses which pure strategy to play probabilistically.

Monopoly An industry in which there is only a single seller of the good in question.

Monopsony An industry in which there is only a single buyer of the good in question.

Moral Hazard The effect of insurance coverage on individuals' decisions to undertake activities that may change the likelihood or sizes of losses.

Nash Equilibrium A strategy profile $(s_1^*, s_2^*, \ldots, s_n^*)$ such that, for each player i, s_i is a best response to the other players' equilibrium strategies s_{-i}^*.

Normal Good A good for which quantity demanded increases (or stays constant) as an individual's income increases.

Normative Analysis Economic analysis that takes a position on how economic actors or markets should operate.

Oligopoly An industry in which there are only a few sellers of the good in question.

Opportunity Cost Doctrine The simple, though far-reaching, observation that the true cost of any action can be measured by the value of the best alternative that must be forgone when the action is taken.

Output and Substitution Effects Come into play when a change in the price of an input that a firm uses causes the firm to change the quantities of inputs it will demand. The substitution effect would occur even if output were held constant, and it is reflected by movements along an isoquant. Output effects, on the other hand, occur when output levels change and the firm moves to a new isoquant.

Paradox of Voting Illustrates the possibility that majority rule voting may not yield a determinate outcome but may instead cycle among alternatives.

Pareto Efficient Allocation An allocation of resources in which no one individual can be made better off without making someone else worse off.

Partial Equilibrium Model A model of a single market that ignores repercussions in other markets.

Perfect Competition The most widely used economic model: there are assumed to be a large number of buyers and sellers for any good, and each agent is a price taker. *See also* Price Taker.

Positive Analysis Economic analysis that seeks to explain and predict actual economic events.

Present Discounted Value (*PDV*) The current value of a sum of money that is payable sometime in the future. Takes into account the effect of interest payments.

Price Discrimination Selling identical goods at different prices. Requires sellers to have the ability to prevent resale. There are three types: first degree—selling each unit at a different price to the individual willing to pay the most for it ("perfect price discrimination"); second degree—adopting price schedules that give buyers an incentive to separate themselves into differing price categories; third degree—charging different prices in separated markets.

Price Elasticity Most important application of the elasticity concept, this reflects the proportional change in quantity demanded in response to a proportional change in price: If $q = f(p, \ldots)$, $e_{q,p} = \partial q / \partial p \cdot p / q$.

Price Taker An economic agent that makes decisions on the assumption that these decisions will have no effect on prevailing market prices.

Principal-Agent Relationship The hiring of one person (the agent) by another person (the principal) to make economic decisions.

Prisoners' Dilemma Originally studied in the theory of games but has widespread applicability. The crux of the dilemma is that each individual, faced with the uncertainty of how others will behave, may be led to adopt a course of action that proves to be detrimental for all those individuals making the same decision. A strong coalition might have led to a solution preferred by everyone in the group.

Producer Surplus The extra return that producers make by making transactions at the market price over and above what they would earn if nothing were produced. It is illustrated by the size of the area below the market price and above the supply curve.

Production Function A conceptual mathematical function that records the relationship between a firm's inputs and its outputs. If output is a function of capital and labor only, this would be denoted by $q = f(k, l)$.

Production Possibility Frontier The locus of all the alternative quantities of several outputs that can be produced with fixed amounts of productive inputs.

Profit Function The relationship between a firm's maximum profits (Π^*) and the output and input prices it faces:
$$\Pi^* = \Pi^*(P, v, w).$$

Profits The difference between the total revenue a firm receives and its total economic costs of production. Economic profits equal zero under perfect competition in the long run. Monopoly profits may be positive, however.

Property Rights Legal specification of ownership and the rights of owners.

Public Good A good that once produced is available to all on a nonexclusive basis. Many public goods are also nonrival—additional individuals may benefit from the good at zero marginal costs.

Quasi-concave Function A function for which the set of all points for which $f(X) > k$ is convex.

Rate of Product Transformation (*RPT*) The rate at which one output can be traded for another in the productive process while holding the total quantities of inputs constant. The *RPT* is the absolute value of the slope of the production possibility frontier.

Rate of Return The rate at which present goods can be transformed into future goods. For example, a one-period rate of return of 10 percent implies that forgoing 1 unit of output this period will yield 1.10 units of output next period.

Rate of Technical Substitution (*RTS*) The rate at which one input may be traded off against another in the productive process while holding output constant. The *RTS* is the absolute value of the slope of an isoquant.
$$RTS = -\left. \frac{dk}{dl} \right|_{q=q_0}.$$

Rent Payments to a factor of production that are in excess of that amount necessary to keep it in its current employment.

Rent-Seeking Activities Economic agents engage in rent-seeking activities when they utilize the political process to generate economic rents that would not ordinarily occur in market transactions.

Rental Rate The cost of hiring one machine for one hour. Denoted by v in the text.

Returns to Scale A way of classifying production functions that records how output responds to proportional increases in all inputs. If a proportional increase in all inputs causes output to increase by a smaller proportion, the production function is said to exhibit decreasing returns to scale. If output increases by a greater proportion than the inputs, the production function exhibits increasing returns. Constant returns to scale is the middle ground where both inputs and outputs increase by the same proportions. Mathematically, if $f(mk, ml) = m^k f(k, l)$, $k > 1$ implies increasing returns, $k = 1$ constant returns, and $k < 1$ decreasing returns.

Risk Aversion Unwillingness to accept fair bets. Arises when an individual's utility of wealth function is concave [that is, $U'(W) > 0$, $U''(W) < 0$]. Absolute risk aversion is measured by $r(W) = -U''(W)/U'(W)$. Relative risk aversion is measured by

$$rr(W) = \frac{-WU''(W)}{U'(W)}.$$

Second-Order Conditions Mathematical conditions required to ensure that points for which first-order conditions are satisfied are indeed true maximum or true minimum points. These conditions are satisfied by functions that obey certain convexity assumptions.

Shephard's Lemma Application of the envelope theorem, which shows that a consumer's compensated demand functions and a firm's (constant output) input demand functions can be derived from partial differentiation of expenditure functions or total cost functions, respectively.

Shifting of a Tax Market response to the imposition of a tax that causes the incidence of the tax to be on some economic agent other than the one who actually pays the tax.

Short Run, Long Run Distinction A conceptual distinction made in the theory of production that differentiates between a period of time over which some inputs are regarded as being fixed and a longer period in which all inputs can be varied by the producer.

Signaling Actions taken by individuals in markets characterized by hidden types in an effort to identify their true type.

Slutsky Equation A mathematical representation of the substitution and income effects of a price change on utility-maximizing choices:

$$\partial x/\partial p_x = \partial x/\partial p_x \big|_{U=\bar{U}} - X(\partial x/\partial I).$$

Social Welfare Function A hypothetical device that records societal views about equity among individuals.

Subgame-Perfect Equilibrium A strategy profile $(s_1^*, s_2^*, ..., s_n^*)$ that constitutes a Nash equilibrium for every proper subgame.

Substitutes (Gross) Two goods such that if the price of one increases, more of the other good will be demanded. That is x and y are gross substitutes if $\partial x/\partial p_y > 0$. *See also* Complements; Slutsky Equation.

Substitutes (Net) Two goods such that if the price of one increases, more of the other good will be demanded if utility is held constant. That is, x and y are net substitutes if

$$\partial x/\partial p_y \big|_{U=\bar{U}} > 0.$$

Net substitutability is symmetric in that

$$\partial x/\partial p_y \big|_{U=\bar{U}} = \partial y/\partial p_x \big|_{U=\bar{U}}.$$

See also Complements; Slutsky Equation.

Substitution Effects *See* Income and Substitution Effects; Output and Substitution Effects; Slutsky Equation.

Sunk Cost An expenditure on an investment that cannot be reversed and has no resale value.

Supply Function For a profit-maximizing firm, a function that shows quantity supplied (q) as a function of output price (P) and input prices (v, w):

$$q = q(P, v, w).$$

Supply Response Increases in production prompted by changing demand conditions and market prices. Usually a distinction is made between short-run and long-run supply responses.

Tacit Collusion Choice of cooperative (monopoly) strategies without explicit collusion.

Total Cost Function The relationship between (minimized) total costs, output, and input prices

$$C = C(v, w, q).$$

Utility Function A mathematical conceptualization of the way in which individuals rank alternative bundles of commodities. If there are only two goods, x and y, utility is denoted by

$$\text{utility} = U(x, y).$$

Variable Costs Costs that change in response to changes in the level of output being produced by a firm. This is in contrast to fixed costs, which do not change.

von Neumann–Morgenstern Utility A ranking of outcomes in uncertain situations such that individuals choose among these outcomes on the basis of their expected utility values.

Wage The cost of hiring one worker for one hour. Denoted by w in the text.

Walrasian Price Adjustment The assumption that markets are cleared through price adjustments in response to excess demand or supply.

Zero-Sum Game A game in which winnings for one player are losses for the other player.

Index

Author names are in italics; glossary terms are in boldface.

A

Addiction, 111
Adverse selection, 629, 650–57
   competitive insurance market and, 653–57
   first-best contract, 651–52
   second-best contract, 652–53
Agents
   asymmetric information and, 628
   principal-agent model, 629–30
   type, 629
Aizcorbe, Ana M., 179
Akerlof, George, 658
Alcoa, entry deterrence by, 549
Aleskerov, Fuad, 110
Allocative inefficiency, 672–75
Almost ideal demand system (AIDS), 139, 181
Altruism
   behaviors, altruistic, 111
   utility maximization and, 113–14
Anderson, S., 285
Annuities, compound interest and, 620
Anti-derivatives, 56–57
   calculation of, 56–57
   fundamental theorem of calculus and, 58–59
Antitrust laws
   Alcoa, action against, 549
   exclusive cartels and, 537
Appropriability effect, 556
Aquinas, St. Thomas, 8
Arguments of utility functions, 89–90
Assumptions
   optimization assumptions, 6–7
   positive-normative distinction, 7
   testing, 4
   See also Ceteris paribus assumption
Asymmetric equilibria, 261–63
Asymmetric information, 225–26, 627–29
   auctions, 659–63
   hidden-action model, 630–32
   hidden-types model, 642
   owner-manager relationship, 632–36

principal-agent model, 629–30
   See also Adverse selection; Insurance; Nonlinear pricing; Signaling
Atkeson, Andrew, 321
Attributes model
   corner solutions and, 193–94
   and home production model, 192
Auctions, 659–63
   common values auctions, 662–63
   equilibrium in, 660–63
   weakly dominated strategy, 660–61
   winner's curse, 662–63
Automobiles
   signaling in used-car market, 658–59
   tariffs, 520
Average cost function (AC), 331
   graphical analysis of, 332–34
   properties of, 337–38
   short-run average total cost function (SAC), 345
   short-run marginal cost function (SMC), 345
Average productivity, 296–97
Average revenue curve, 364
Axioms of rational choice, 87–88

B

Backward induction, 259–60
Bairam, Erkin, 321
Balance in consumption, 94–97
Barriers to entry, 491–93
   creation of, 492–93
   legal barriers, 492
   and oligopolies, 554–55
   technical barriers, 491–92
Battle of the Sexes, 242–46
   backward induction in, 259–60
   expected payoffs in, 248–49
   extensive form for, 243
   mixed strategies in, 247–51
   Nash equilibrium in, 242–51
   proper subgames in, 258
   as sequential game, 255–57
Bayesian games, 268–78
   Tragedy of the Commons as, 271–73
Bayesian-Nash equilibrium, 269–73
   for Tragedy of the Commons, 272–73
Bayes' rule, 268
   as black box, 275

perfect Bayesian equilibrium, 276–79
   signaling and, 553
   in signaling games, 274–76
Becker, Gary, 111
Behrman, Jere R., 137
Beliefs
   players' beliefs, 269
   posterior beliefs, 273–74
   prior beliefs, 273–74
Benefit-cost ratio, 38–39
Benefits, mandated, 582–83
Benoit, Jean Pierre, 263
Bentham, Jeremy, 88
Berck, P., 356
Bergstrom, Theodore C., 111
Bernat, G. A., 488
Berndt, Ernst R., 111
Bernoulli, Daniel, 204–5
Bernoulli's game, 203
Bertrand game, 521, 523–24
   best responses with differentiated products, 534
   capacity constraints, 531
   continuum of action in, 252
   feedback effect in, 558
   Nash equilibrium of, 521–24
   natural-spring duopoly in, 526–27
   product differentiation and, 531–37
   strategic substitutes/complements in, 567
   tacit collusion in, 538–40
Bertrand paradox, 524
   capacity constraints and, 531
   product differentiation and, 531–37
   and search cost, 537
Best response, 291, 566
   in Battle of the Sexes game, 242–46
   payoffs in, 241–42
   strategic substitutes/complements and, 566
Beta coefficients for asset, 235
Binomial distribution, 66
   expected values of, 69
   variances and standard deviations for, 71
Biology and utility, 111
Black, Duncan, 688–89
Blackorby, Charles, 200
Bolton, P., 667
Bonds, compound interest on, 621

727

S